OXFORD PAPERBACK REFERENCE

The Concise Oxford Dictionary of
Phrase and
Fable

Elizabeth Knowles has been Managing Editor of Oxford Quotations Dictionaries since 1993 and is a historical lexicographer, having previously worked for ten years on the *New Shorter Oxford English Dictionary*.

Oxford
Paperback
Reference

The most authoritative and up-to-date reference
books for both students and the general reader.

*forthcoming

The Concise
Oxford Dictionary of

Phrase and
Fable

Edited by
ELIZABETH KNOWLES

OXFORD
UNIVERSITY PRESS

OXFORD
UNIVERSITY PRESS

Great Clarendon Street, Oxford OX2 6DP

Oxford University Press is a department of the University of Oxford.
It furthers the University's objective of excellence in research, scholarship,
and education by publishing worldwide in

Oxford New York

Auckland Bangkok Buenos Aires Cape Town Chennai
Dar es Salaam Delhi Hong Kong Istanbul Karachi Kolkata
Kuala Lumpur Madrid Melbourne Mexico City Mumbai Nairobi
São Paulo Shanghai Singapore Taipei Tokyo Toronto

Oxford is a registered trade mark of Oxford University Press
in the UK and in certain other countries

Published in the United States
by Oxford University Press Inc., New York

British Library Cataloguing in Publication Data
Data available

Library of Congress Cataloging in Publication Data
Data available

ISBN 019-2801252

3

Typeset in Photina and Quay Sans
by Interactive Sciences Ltd, Gloucester
Printed in Great Britain by
Clays Ltd, St Ives plc

INTRODUCTION

The *Concise Oxford Dictionary of Phrase and Fable* is drawn from the *Oxford Dictionary of Phrase and Fable*, published in 2000, and the selection of entries is designed to reflect the richness and diversity of the parent text.

Concise Phrase and Fable brings together words, phrases, and names with cultural resonance: items from history and religion, mythology, biography, folk customs and superstitions, science and technology, philosophy, and popular culture. Entries have been chosen for their figurative or allusive connotations, or for their centrality to the development of a civilization or culture.

Many entries are found to link the ancient and modern worlds. **Gaia**, in Greek mythology the Earth personified as a goddess, is also the name in James Lovelock's **Gaia hypothesis** for the earth viewed as a vast self-regulating organism. The name of the biblical **Eve** is found in the modern-day **African Eve hypothesis**. The electronic digital computer used at Bletchley Park in the Second World War was **Colossus**—a name reaching back to antiquity and the **Colossus of Rhodes**.

Allusions range from figures of classical mythology and history (**Bellerophon**, **Cassandra**, **Chiron**, **Messalina**) and the Bible (**Absalom, Job**) to popular culture (**Indiana Jones**, **the Simpsons**, **the Slayer**). Many events, particularly tragic ones, have acquired a particular resonance, such as the loss of the **Titanic** and the **Challenger Disaster**. There are a range of entries from the history of ideas and cultural and scientific development, such as **cold fusion**, the **Delian problem**, and the **Red Queen hypothesis**.

Phrases (although not transparent idioms) form a key part of the book, especially where there is background information to give: **cruel and unusual punishment**, **just war**, **poor little rich girl**, and **spoil the Egyptians**, are some examples here. The stories behind the phrases may come from a variety of sources: **Chicken Little** derives from a nursery story, but **bunny boiler** and **up to eleven** come from films of the 1980s.

A number of phrases are derived from popular proverbs: **move mountains** from the saying 'Faith will move mountains', and **birds of a feather** from the saying 'Birds of a feather flock together.' Entries in the *Dictionary* range from short definitions for quick access to more detailed accounts of a significant word, name, or phrase. The book is organized alphabetically, in a word by word system of keywords (which are distinguished by heavier type). Cross-references to related entries (the target keyword being indicated by small type and an arrow) are given where it is felt that explicit direction to that entry will be helpful. Where a word appears in a number of phrases, the individual items are likely to be subsumed under a main heading: for example, **golden calf** and **golden hour** will both be found at the entry for **golden**, while **silver bullet** is at the entry for **silver**.

The *Concise Dictionary* has drawn on its parent volume and on Oxford's online resources. Susan Ratcliffe, Associate Editor for Quotations Dictionaries, has again made an essential contribution to the work, and John McNeill has once more commented knowledgeably and helpfully on earlier versions of the text. Proofreading was carried out by Kim Allen and Carolyn Garwes. I am most grateful to those named (and many unnamed) for their assistance in completing this book. It has been a great pleasure to revisit the area of figurative and allusive usage in the language today; it is hoped that the result will be useful and enjoyable to our readers.

ELIZABETH KNOWLES
Oxford 2002

A The first letter of the modern English alphabet and of the ancient Roman one, corresponding to Greek *alpha* and Hebrew *aleph*.

A1 means excellent, first-rate; in Lloyd's Register of Shipping, it is used of ships in first-class condition as to hull (A) and stores (1).

See also ➤ EXHIBIT *A*.

Aaron in the Bible, the brother of ➤ MOSES and traditional founder of the Jewish priesthood, the first anointed high priest. He was persuaded by the people to make an image of God in the form of a ➤ GOLDEN *calf*, thereby earning Moses' displeasure.

abacus an oblong frame with rows of wires or grooves along which beads are slid, used for calculating; possibly a development of the classical counting board, it was widely used in Europe in the Middle Ages and is still used in some countries.

The word in this sense dates from the late 17th century; it is recorded in late Middle English, denoting a board strewn with sand on which to draw figures, and comes via Latin from Greek *abax, abak-* 'slab, drawing board', of Semitic origin, and probably related to Hebrew *'ābāq* 'dust'.

Abaddon a name for the Devil (Revelation 9:11) or for hell. Recorded from late Middle English, *Abaddon* comes via Greek from Hebrew *'ăbaddōn* 'destruction'. Its use for 'hell' derives from Milton's *Paradise Regained* (1671).

abandon ship take to the lifeboats and leave a ship in imminent danger of sinking (often as a formal order to crew); in extended usage, desert what is seen as a failing organization.

Abba in the New Testament, God as father; in the Syrian Orthodox and Coptic Churches, a title given to bishops and patriarchs. The word comes via Greek from Aramaic *abbā* 'father'.

Abbasid a member of a dynasty of caliphs who ruled in Baghdad from 750 to 1258, named after *Abbas* (566–652), the prophet ➤ MUHAMMAD's uncle and founder of the dynasty.

Abdera a Greek city in Thrace whose inhabitants were proverbial for their stupidity, although it was also the birthplace of the philosopher ➤ DEMOCRITUS.

Abdication Crisis the constitutional crisis, resulting from the king of England's determination to marry a divorced woman, Wallis Simpson, which culminated in the abdication of Edward VIII in 1936.

Abednego in Daniel 1:7, the name, meaning 'servant of Nego' (a form of 'Nebo') given by King Nebuchadnezzaar to Azariah, one of those cast into the ➤ BURNING *fiery furnace*.

Abel in the Bible, the younger son of Adam and Eve, murdered by his jealous brother ➤ CAIN, after Abel's offering to God of a lamb was accepted by God, while Cain's sheaves were rejected.

Abelard and Héloïse a type of doomed lovers. Peter *Abelard* (1079–1142), a French scholar, theologian, and philosopher, was noted for an independence of mind which led to his being twice condemned for heresy. A lecturer in Paris, his academic career was cut short in 1118 by his tragic love affair with his pupil Héloïse. Abelard was castrated at her uncle's instigation; he entered a monastery, and Héloïse became a nun. Abelard and Héloïse are buried together in Paris.

Aberfan a village in South Wales where, in 1966, a slag heap collapsed, overwhelming houses and a school and killing 28 adults and 116 children.

abigail archaic term for a lady's maid. The term comes from the name of the 'waiting gentlewoman' in Beaumont and Fletcher's popular play of *The Scornful Lady*; so named possibly in biblical allusion to the expression 'thine handmaid' frequently applied to herself by Abigail, future wife of King David (1 Samuel 25:24–31).

abiogenesis a technical term for ➤ SPONTANEOUS *generation*, which was introduced by the English biologist Thomas Henry Huxley

(1825–95) in an address to the British Association for the Advancement of Science at Liverpool in September 1870.

Oath of Abjuration an oath disclaiming allegiance to James Francis Edward Stuart (1688–1766, known as the ➤ OLD *Pretender*), son of James II, or his descendants as claimants to the British throne. The Abjuration Act of 1701 made it compulsory for candidates for military or religious office to take the oath. It was finally abolished in 1858 and replaced by a version of the *Oath of Allegiance*.

ablaut alternation in the vowels of related word forms, especially in Germanic strong verbs (e.g. in *sing, sang, sung*).

Abolitionists in the 19th century, supporters of the abolition of the slave-trade; the term is recorded from the early 19th century.

Abominable Snowman a popular name for the ➤ YETI, recorded from the early 1920s.

abracadabra a word said by conjurors when performing a magic trick. The term is recorded from the late 17th century, as a mystical word engraved and used as a charm against illness; it comes from Latin (from a Greek base), and is first recorded in a 2nd-century poem.

Abraham in the Bible, the Hebrew patriarch from whom all Jews trace their descent (Genesis 11:27–25:10), and who is directed by God to leave his own country for another land. In Genesis 22 he is ordered by God to sacrifice his son ➤ ISAAC as a test of faith, a command later revoked.

Abraham's bosom is where the righteous dead are said to lie at peace; the term comes from Luke 66:22. In 16th- and 17th-century England, the name **Abraham man** was applied to former or occasional inmates of the Hospital of St. Mary of Bethlehem in London, licensed to beg on his discharge, or a similarly licensed beggar discharged from a charitable institution (perhaps in allusion to the biblical story of the beggar Lazarus in Luke 16).

Absalom the third and favourite son of ➤ DAVID, who rebelled against his father and was killed; he is taken as the type of a rebellious son who is loved and mourned despite his rebellion.

According to the biblical account, Absalom was killed when he rode beneath an oak tree and the branches caught in his long hair, trapping him, so that he could be dispatched by David's commander ➤ JOAB.

Absalom and Achitophel is an allegorical poem (1681) by John Dryden, dealing with the succession crisis centring on the ➤ EXCLUSION *Bill* of 1680; in the poem, *Absalom* stands for the ➤ *Duke of* MONMOUTH, Charles II's illegitimate son, and his counsellor *Achitophel* is his supporter the Earl of Shaftesbury.

absolute pitch the ability to recognize the pitch of a note or produce any given note; also called perfect pitch.

Abu Simbel the site of two huge rock-cut temples in southern Egypt, built during the reign of Ramses II in the 13th century BC and commemorating him and his first wife Nefertari. Following the building of the High Dam at Aswan, the monument was rebuilt higher up the hillside.

Abyla former name (now Jebel Musa) for one of the two rocks forming the ➤ PILLARS *of Hercules.*

St Acacius reputed martyr, of no known date, said to have been put to death with 10,000 companions by a pagan army; he is reputed to have prayed before his death that those venerating their memory would be granted health and strength, and from this he is traditionally counted as one of the ➤ FOURTEEN *Holy Helpers*. His feast day is 22 June.

Académie française a French literary academy with a constant membership of forty, responsible for the standard form of the French language and for compiling and revising a definitive dictionary of the French language. Its tendency is to defend traditional literary and linguistic rules and to discourage innovation. It was founded by Cardinal Richelieu in 1635.

Academy the philosophical school of Plato; *Akadēmeia* was the name of the garden where Plato originally taught, named after the hero *Akadēmos.*

Academy award any of a series of awards of the Academy of Motion Picture Arts and Sciences (Hollywood, US) given annually since 1928 for achievement in the film industry in various categories; an ➤ OSCAR.

Acadia a former French colony established in 1604 in the territory now forming Nova Scotia in Canada, ceded to Britain in 1763.

acanthus a conventionalized representation of the leaf of this plant is used especially as a decoration for Corinthian column capitals. The term in this sense dates from the mid 18th century; the name of the plant comes via Latin from Greek *akanthos*, from *akantha* 'thorn', from *akē* 'sharp point'.

the acceptable face of— the tolerable or acceptable aspect of something regarded as hostile or alarming. Often ironic, and deriving from Edward Heath's comment made in 1973 about the activities of the Lonrho company as showing 'the unpleasant and unacceptable face of capitalism'.

an accident waiting to happen a potentially disastrous situation, especially one brought about by negligent or faulty procedures; a person certain to cause trouble.

accidents will happen however careful you try to be, it is inevitable that some unfortunate or unforeseen events will occur; from the early 19th-century proverb, *accidents will happen in the best regulated families*.

accidie spiritual or mental sloth; apathy. Recorded from Middle English (figuring in lists of the ➤ SEVEN *deadly sins*), the word comes via Latin from Greek *akēdia* 'listlessness', from *a-* 'without' + *kēdos* 'care'.

there's no accounting for tastes it is impossible to explain why different people like different things (often used about something considered unappealing by the speaker). Of proverbial origin, and since the late 18th century the usual English form of the Latin tag *de gustibus non est disputandum* 'there is no disputing about tastes.'

have an ace up one's sleeve have an effective resource or piece of information held in reserve. The *ace*, the card marked with a single pip, is the highest card in many card games, and so represents the greatest advantage a dishonest player could gain over an opponent.

Aceldama in the New Testament, a field near Jerusalem purchased with the blood money given to Judas for his betrayal of Jesus, the ➤ POTTER's *field*.

Achaean of or relating to *Achaea* in ancient Greece; (especially in Homeric contexts) Greek. The Achaeans were among the earliest Greek-speaking inhabitants of Greece, being established there well before the 12th century BC. Some scholars identify them with the Mycenaeans of the 14th–13th centuries BC. The Greek protagonists in the Trojan War are regularly called Achaeans in the *Iliad*, though this may have referred only to the leaders.

Achaemenid a member of the dynasty ruling in Persia from Cyrus I to Darius III (553–330 BC); the name comes from Greek *Akhaimenēs* 'Achaemenes', the reputed ancestor of the dynasty.

fidus Achates Latin phrase ('faithful Achates') meaning a faithful friend and follower. Achates was a companion of ➤ AENEAS, whose loyalty to his friend was so exemplary as to become proverbial.

Acheron in Greek mythology, one of the rivers of ➤ HADES.

Achilles in Greek mythology, a hero of the ➤ TROJAN *War*, son of Peleus and ➤ THETIS. During his infancy his mother plunged him in the Styx, thus making his body invulnerable except for the heel by which she held him: this was where in the end he was to be mortally wounded. The term **Achilles' heel**, for a person's only vulnerable spot, comes from this story, as does the name **Achilles tendon** for the tendon attaching the calf to the heel muscle.

When the expedition to Troy was mounted, Thetis tried to protect her son by putting him in the charge of the centaur ➤ CHIRON on the island of Scyros. Odysseus, visiting the island in search of him, found only what appeared to be a group of women, but when a battle-cry was heard one of the girls, the disguised Achilles, revealed himself by seizing sword and shield.

During the Trojan War Achilles withdrew from fighting following a bitter quarrel with ➤ AGAMEMNON. After his friend Patroclus was killed by Hector, Achilles re-entered the battle and killed ➤ HECTOR but was later wounded in the heel by an arrow shot by Paris and died. His armour was seen as an emblem of valour; when it was awarded to ➤ ODYSSEUS, ➤ AJAX committed suicide.

acid test a conclusive test for the success or value of something; the reference is to the testing for gold by means of nitric acid.

Acis in Greek mythology, a young shepherd, lover of the sea nymph ➤ GALATEA, who was killed out of jealousy by his rival ➤ POLYPHEMUS; as he died, Galatea turned him into a river.

acolyte a person assisting a priest in a religious service or procession; until 1 January 1973, the office of *acolyte* was one of the four Minor Orders of the Roman Catholic Church.

Recorded from Middle English, the word comes via Old French or ecclesiastical Latin, from Greek *akolouthos* 'follower'.

acorn the fruit of the oak; recorded in Old English in the form *æcern*, the word is of Germanic origin and is related to *acre*; later however it was associated by popular etymology with *oak* and *corn*.

In the UK, an oak-leaf sprig with two acorns is the emblem of the National Trust.

acre a unit of land area equal to 4,840 square yards (0.405 hectare). In Old English, *æcer* denoted the amount of land a yoke of oxen could plough in a day; it is a word of Germanic origin, ultimately from an Indo-European root shared by Sanskrit *ajra*, Latin *ager*, and Greek *agros*, 'field'.

acropolis a citadel or fortified part of an ancient Greek city, typically one built on a hill; **the Acropolis** is the name given to the ancient citadel at Athens, containing the Parthenon and other notable buildings, mostly dating from the 5th century BC. The word comes (in the early 17th century) from Greek *akropolis*, from *akron* 'summit' + *polis* 'city'.

acrostic a poem, word puzzle, or other composition in which certain letters in each line form a word or words. The word is recorded from the late 16th century, and comes via French from Greek *akrostikhis*, from *akron* 'end' + *stikhos* 'row, line of verse'.

act and deed part of a formula used in concluding a legal transaction by signing a document.

Actaeon in Greek mythology, a hunter who, because he accidentally saw ➤ ARTEMIS bathing, was changed by her into a stag and killed by his own hounds.

Actes and Monuments title of the martyrology by John Foxe (1516–87); the book, less formally known as *Foxe's Martyrs*, was enormously popular, going through nine editions, each with additional material, between 1563 and 1684. Intended as a history of the Christian Church through the suffering of its martyrs, it focuses in particular on the Protestant martyrs of the 16th and 17th centuries.

action this day annotation as used by Winston Churchill at the Admiralty in 1940.

Battle of Actium a naval battle which took place in 31 BC off the promontory of Actium in western Greece, in the course of which Octavian defeated ➤ MARK *Antony*. This cleared

the way for Octavian to become sole ruler of Rome as the emperor ➤ AUGUSTUS.

Actors' Studio an acting workshop in New York City, founded in 1947 by Elia Kazan and others, and a leading centre of method acting.

Acts of the Apostles a New Testament book immediately following the Gospels and relating the history of the early Church, and in particular the missionary journeys of St Paul and others.

Adam (in the biblical and Koranic traditions) the name of the first man. According to the Book of Genesis, Adam was created by God as the progenitor of the human race and lived with Eve in the garden of Eden.

In the Bible the Book of Genesis describes how Adam was formed from the dust of the ground and God's breath; Eve, the first woman, was created from one of Adam's ribs as his companion. They lived together in the Garden of Eden until the serpent tempted Eve to eat an apple from the forbidden tree; she persuaded Adam to do the same. As a result of this original sin of disobedience they were both expelled from the garden.

The expression **the old Adam** means the unregenerate condition or character, and depends on the identification of Adam as the figure referred to by St Paul in Romans 6:6. (See also *second Adam* at ➤ SECOND.)

The projection formed in the neck by the thyroid cartilage was named the **Adam's apple** from the notion that a piece of the forbidden fruit became lodged in Adam's throat. **Adam's rib** was the rib from which ➤ EVE was formed, as in Genesis 2:22.

Adam comes from Hebrew *'āḏām* 'man', later taken to be a name.

Addams Family in the cartoons of Charles Addams (1912–88), a family of ghouls including ➤ MORTICIA and her husband Gomez, living in a gothic house on Cemetery Ridge.

Adelphi the name of a group of buildings in London between the Strand and the Thames, laid out by the four brothers, James, John, Robert, and William Adam, and thus called *Adelphi* (from the Greek word for 'brothers'); the name of the theatre in the vicinity of these buildings, at which a certain type of melodrama was prevalent *c.* 1882–1900.

Adi Granth the principal sacred scripture of Sikhism. Originally compiled under the direction of Arjan Dev (1563–1606), the fifth

Sikh guru, it contains hymns and religious poetry as well as the teachings of the first five gurus. Successive gurus added to the text: the tenth and last guru, Gobind Singh (1666–1708), declared that henceforth there would be no more gurus, the *Adi Granth* taking their place.

The name comes from Sanskrit *ādigrantha*, literally 'first book', based on *grantha* 'literary composition', from *granth* 'to tie'.

Aditi in Hindu belief, a primeval goddess who is the mother of many gods.

admirable Crichton see ➤ CRICHTON.

Adonai a Hebrew name for God.

Adonais the name given by Shelley to Keats in the pastoral elegy *Adonais* (1821), written on the death of Keats, and likening him to the Greek god of beauty and fertility; the origin of the name *Adonais* is unclear, but it may represent the name ➤ ADONIS, or the Hebrew ➤ ADONAI.

Adonis in classical mythology, a beautiful youth loved by both Aphrodite and Persephone. He was killed by a boar, but Zeus decreed that he should spend the winter of each year in the underworld with Persephone and the summer months with Aphrodite. According to the legend, the rose sprang from the earth where his blood was shed.

In extended usage, an *Adonis* is an extremely handsome young man.

cave of Adullam in the Bible, the cave in the hills of Judah in which ➤ DAVID hid from Saul (1 Samuel 22:10), and where his supporters gathered to him. The name **Adullamites** was given to a group of Liberal rebels in the House of Commons in 1866 who were opposed to the Reform Bill; the term comes from a speech by the Liberal politician John Bright (1811–89), saying that their leader Robert Lowe had 'retired into what may be called his political Cave of Adullam.'

Advent the first season of the Church year, leading up to Christmas and including the four preceding Sundays. The name is recorded from Old English, and comes from Latin *adventus* 'arrival', in Christian writings applied particularly to the coming of the Saviour. The season's progress may be marked on an **Advent calendar**, made of card containing small numbered flaps, one of which is opened on each day of Advent to reveal a picture appropriate to the season. An **Advent candle** is a candle lit during Advent; especially each candle in a ring of four, lit on successive Sundays in Advent to symbolize the coming of light into the world at Christmas (when a fifth central candle completes the group).

Advent Sunday is the first Sunday in Advent; in the Western Church the Sunday closest to St Andrew's Day (30 November); in the Orthodox Church *Advent Sunday* falls in the middle of November.

the Adversary Satan, the Devil, as in 1 Peter 5:8, 'Your adversary the devil'.

Advocates' Library in Edinburgh, founded by Sir George Mackenzie (1636–91) in 1689 as the library of the Faculty of Advocates, and from 1925 the National Library of Scotland.

advowson in ecclesiastical law, the right to recommend a member of the Anglican clergy for a vacant benefice, or to make such an appointment. The word is recorded from Middle English, in the sense 'patronage of a religious house or benefice' with the obligation to defend it and speak for it, and comes ultimately from Latin *advocare* 'summon'.

aedile either of two (later four) Roman magistrates responsible for public buildings and originally also for the public games and the supply of corn to the city. The word comes (in the mid 16th century) from Latin *aedilis* 'concerned with buildings'.

Aegeus in Greek mythology, king of Athens and father of ➤ THESEUS, who threw himself into the sea in the (mistaken) belief that his son had been killed by the ➤ MINOTAUR; according to some, this was the origin of the name of the *Aegean Sea*.

Aegir in Scandinavian mythology, the god of the sea.

aegis in classical art and mythology, an attribute of Zeus and Athena (or their Roman counterparts Jupiter and Minerva) usually represented as a goatskin shield. The word (denoting armour or a shield, especially that of a god) is recorded from the early 17th century and comes ultimately from Greek *aigis* 'shield of Zeus'.

Aegisthus in Greek mythology, the lover of his cousin's wife Clytemnestra, who killed her husband ➤ AGAMEMNON; Aegisthus and Clytemnestra were in turn killed by her son ➤ ORESTES.

Aelia Capitolina the new city which the Emperor Hadrian built *c.*130 AD on the site of Jerusalem (destroyed by ➤ TITUS in 70 AD).

Aeneas in classical mythology, a Trojan leader, son of Anchises and Aphrodite, and legendary ancestor of the Romans. When Troy fell to the Greeks he escaped and after wandering many years eventually reached Italy. The story of his voyage is recounted in Virgil's *Aeneid*.

Aeolian mode in music, the mode represented by the natural diatonic scale A–A (containing a minor 3rd, 6th, and 7th). The term is recorded from the late 18th century, and comes from Latin *Aeolius* 'from Aeolis' (an ancient coastal district of Asia Minor).

Aeolus in Greek mythology, the god of the winds; in Homer's *Odyssey*, a mortal to whom Zeus had given command of the winds, and who in Virgil's *Aeneid* is shown as keeping them imprisoned in a cave. His name has given rise to the name of the **Aeolian harp**, a stringed instrument producing musical sounds on exposure to a current of air.

Aesculapius in Roman mythology, the god of medicine; equivalent of the Greek ➤ AS-CLEPIUS.

Aesir the Norse gods and goddesses collectively, including Odin, Thor, and Balder.

Aesop (6th century BC), Greek storyteller. The moral animal fables associated with him were probably collected from many sources, and initially communicated orally; they were later popularized by the Roman poet Phaedrus, who translated some of them into Latin. Aesop is said to have lived as a slave on the island of Samos.

Aesthetic Movement a literary and artistic movement which flourished in England in the 1880s, devoted to 'art for art's sake' and rejecting the notion that art should have a social or moral purpose. Its chief exponents included Oscar Wilde, Max Beerbohm, Aubrey Beardsley, and others associated with the journal the *Yellow Book*.

The word is recorded from the late 18th century, in the sense 'relating to perception by the senses', and comes ultimately from Greek *aisthesthai* 'perceive'. The sense 'concerned with beauty' was coined in German in the mid 18th century and adopted into English in the early 19th century, but its use was controversial until much later in the century.

affluent society a society in which material wealth is widely distributed; often with allusion to the book of that title (1958) by the American economist John Kenneth Galbraith.

afreet in Arabian and Muslim mythology, a powerful jinn or demon; the word is recorded in English from the late 18th century, and comes from Arabic *'ifrīt*.

always something new out of Africa mid 16th-century saying, encapsulating a traditional view of Africa as a mysterious continent; from the *Historia Naturalis* of the Roman writer Pliny the Elder (AD 23–79), '*Semper aliquid novi Africam adferre* [Africa always brings [us] something new,' referring to Africa as a traditional source of hybrid animals.

African Eve hypothesis the hypothesis (based on study of mitochondrial DNA) that modern humans have a common female ancestor who lived in Africa around 200,000 years ago.

Aga Khan the spiritual leader of the Khoja branch of Ismalian Muslims. The first Aga Khan was given his title in 1818 by the shah of Persia and subsequently moved with the majority of the Nizaris to the Indian subcontinent.

Aga saga a type of popular novel set in a semi-rural location and concerning the domestic and emotional lives of articulate, middle-class characters; their comfortable background is typified by possession of a kitchen with an *Aga* stove, notionally an emblem of affluent middle-class rural life.

Agamemnon in Greek mythology, king of Mycenae and brother of Menelaus, commander-in-chief of the Greek forces in the ➤ TROJAN *War*. On his return home from Troy he was murdered by his wife Clytemnestra and her lover ➤ AEGISTHUS; his murder was avenged by his son ➤ ORESTES and daughter Electra.

The early 19th-century saying **brave men lived before Agamemnon**, meaning that to be remembered the exploits of a hero must be recorded, derives ultimately from the *Odes* of the Roman poet Horace (65–8 BC).

Aganippe in Greek mythology, a fountain at the foot of Mount Helicon, dedicated to the Muses, a source of poetic inspiration.

agape in Christian theology, Christian love, especially as distinct from erotic love or simple affection; a communal meal in token of

Christian fellowship, as held by early Christians in commemoration of the ➤ LAST *Supper*. The word is recorded from the early 17th century, and comes from Greek *agapē* 'brotherly love'.

St Agatha a virgin martyr, said to have died at Catania in Sicily. According to later legend, when a pagan consul invoked edicts against Christianity in order to seduce her, she was imprisoned in a brothel and tortured, her breasts being cut off; she died in prison.

She is invoked against fire (especially the eruptions of Mount Etna) and diseases of the breast; she is also patroness of bell-founders. Her emblem in art is a dish with her breasts on it, sometimes mistaken for a dish with two loaves. Her feast day is 5 February.

Agave in classical mythology, the daughter of ➤ CADMUS and Harmonia and mother of Pentheus. In Euripides' *The Bacchae*, she refuses to acknowledge the divinity of ➤ DIONYSUS, and as punishment is driven mad as a ➤ BACCHANT; in their frenzy, she and her companions tear Pentheus apart.

The name *Agave* comes from the Greek word *agauos* 'illustrious'.

Agent Orange a defoliant chemical used by the US in the Vietnam War.

Battle of Agincourt a battle in northern France in 1415 during the Hundred Years War, in which the English under Henry V defeated a large French army. The victory, achieved largely by use of the longbow, allowed Henry to occupy Normandy and consolidate his claim to the French throne.

Aglaia in Greek mythology, one of the ➤ THREE *Graces*.

St Agnes (died *c*.304), Roman martyr, said to have been a Christian virgin who refused to marry, she was martyred during the reign of Diocletian. She is the patron saint of virgins and her emblem is a lamb (Latin *agnus*). Her feast day is 21 January.

agnostic a person holding the view that nothing can be known of the existence of God or anything beyond material phenomena. The word is recorded from the mid 19th century, and comes from *a*- 'not' + *gnostic* 'of or relating to knowledge'; it was coined by the English biologist Thomas Henry Huxley (1825–95) to describe his own beliefs.

Agnus Dei Latin phrase meaning 'Lamb of God', in the Christian Church a name for

Christ, recorded from late Middle English; *Agnus Dei* is used both for an invocation beginning with the words 'Lamb of God' forming a set part of the Mass, and a figure of a lamb bearing a cross or flag, as an emblem of Christ.

agony extreme mental suffering; the **Agony in the Garden** was the anguish of Christ in the ➤ *Garden of* GETHSEMANE, as in Luke 22:44; *agony* in this passage is used in Wyclif's translation.

An **agony column** was originally (in the mid 19th century) the column of a newspaper containing special advertisements, particularly those for missing relatives or friends, and thus containing evidence of great distress. Later (the current meaning), it became a column in a newspaper or magazine offering advice on personal problems to readers who write in; an **agony aunt** is the female author of a newspaper column providing such advice.

agora in ancient Greece, a public open space used for assemblies and markets; the term **agoraphobia** for extreme or irrational fear of open or public places, leading to panic attacks and reclusive behaviour, derives from this.

Agra a city on the River Jumna in northern India. Founded in 1566, Agra was the capital of the Mogul empire until 1658.

Agrarian Revolution the transformation of British agriculture during the 18th century, characterized by the enclosure of common land and the introduction of technological innovations such as the seed drill and the rotation of crops.

Ahab a king of ancient Israel who persecuted the prophets, husband of ➤ JEZEBEL, who allowed her persecution and arranged killing of ➤ NABOTH; Ahab was warned by the prophet ➤ ELIJAH that his sin would bring disaster on his dynasty.

Captain Ahab in Herman Melville's novel *Moby Dick* (1851), the whaling captain whose leg has been bitten off by the white whale, ➤ MOBY *Dick*, and who is monomaniacally determined on revenge; his obsession leads, after a three-day pursuit, to the destruction of his ship, the *Pequod*, and the deaths of all but one (see ➤ ISHMAEL) of her crew.

Ahasuerus name given in the Hebrew scriptures to the Emperor Xerxes, husband of ➤ ESTHER. *Ahasuerus* is also the name of a king in the Book of Daniel, and is traditionally the name of the ➤ WANDERING *Jew*.

ahimsa in the Hindu, Buddhist, and Jainist tradition, respect for all living things and avoidance of violence towards others. The word comes from Sanskrit, from *a* 'non-, without' + *hiṃsā* 'violence'.

Ahitophel the treacherous counsellor of King David who deserted to ➤ ABSALOM, and hanged himself when Absalom ignored his advice (2 Samuel 17:23).

Aholah and Aholibah in the Bible (Ezekiel ch. 23), two sisters who personify prostitution, and will be destroyed for their sins; in the prophecy of Ezekiel, Aholah is said to stand for Samaria and Aholibah for Jerusalem.

Ahriman the evil spirit in the doctrine of ➤ ZOROASTRIANISM, the opponent of ➤ AHURA *Mazda*.

Ahura Mazda the creator god of Zoroastrianism, the force for good and the opponent of ➤ AHRIMAN; also called ➤ ORMAZD. The name is Avestan, and means literally 'wise deity'.

aid and abet help and encourage someone, perhaps in a dubious or nefarious enterprise. *Abet*, which is also used in formal legal contexts, is related to an Old French term meaning 'encourage (a hound) to bite'.

St Aidan (d. AD 651), Irish missionary. While a monk in the monastery at Iona he set out to Christianize Northumbria, founding a church and monastery at Lindisfarne in 635 and becoming its first bishop. His feast day is 31 August.

Aintree a suburb of Liverpool, site of a racecourse over which the Grand National is run.

air regarded as one of the four ➤ ELEMENTS in ancient and medieval philosophy and in astrology (it is considered essential to the nature of the signs of Gemini, Aquarius, and Libra).

have them rolling in the aisles be very amusing; originally with the literal meaning of making an audience laugh uncontrollably.

Ajanta Caves a series of caves in the state of Maharashtra, south central India, containing Buddhist frescoes and sculptures dating from the 1st century BC to the 7th century AD.

Ajax in Greek mythology, a hero of the Trojan war, the son of Telamon, king of Salamis;

he was proverbial for his size and strength. After the death of ➤ ACHILLES, he quarrelled with Odysseus as to which of them should have Achilles' armour; when it was awarded to Odysseus, Ajax committed suicide.

He is sometimes referred to as **the Greater Ajax** to distinguish him from **the Lesser Ajax**, son of Oileus, leader of the Locrian forces who fought on the Greek side at Troy.

Akela name of the leader of the wolf pack in Kipling's *Jungle Books* (1894–5); he is known as the *Lone Wolf*, and his name comes from Hindi *akelā* 'single, solitary'.

The name is used informally for the adult leader of a group of Cub Scouts (formerly Wolf Cubs).

Akhenaten (14th century BC), Egyptian pharaoh of the 18th dynasty, reigned 1379–1362 BC, who came to the throne as Amenhotep IV. The husband of ➤ NEFERTITI, he introduced the monotheistic solar cult of ➤ ATEN and moved the capital from Thebes to the newly built city of Akhetaten. He was succeeded by his son-in-law, ➤ TUTANKHAMEN, who abandoned the new religion early in his reign.

Akhetaten an ancient Egyptian capital built by Akhenaten in *c*.1375 BC when he established the new worship of the sun disc Aten. It was abandoned four years after his death, when the court returned to the former capital, Thebes.

Akkad the capital city which gave its name to an ancient kingdom traditionally founded by Sargon in north central Mesopotamia. Its site is lost.

Akkadian is the extinct language of Akkad, written in cuneiform, with two dialects, Assyrian and Babylonian, widely used from about 3500 BC. It is the oldest Semitic language for which records exist.

Alabama claims made by the US against Britain for losses caused in the Civil War by British-built Confederate ships, particularly the cruiser *Alabama*, which captured or destroyed 66 ships before being itself sunk in June 1864. The case helped establish international rulings for the limitations on a neutral government in wartime, and in 1872 the tribunal decided that Britain was legally liable for losses caused by the *Alabama* and other ships.

Aladdin in the Arabian Nights, the name of a poor boy in China who becomes master of a magic lamp and ring; he has a palace built for him by the ➤ SLAVE *of the Lamp*, and marries the Sultan's daughter.

The story first became a pantomime in England in 1788; in 1861 H. J. Byron's dramatization established what are now some of the main pantomime features. Aladdin's mother was named *Widow Twankay* (see ➤ WIDOW *Twankey*), and the magician who tries to steal the lamp was named *Abanazar*.

Aladdin's cave is a cave full of treasures revealed to him by a magician; shut inside by the magician, he escapes with the aid of a magic ring (which summons the *Slave of the Ring*) and returns to his mother with the lamp which he has found in the cave. They find that rubbing **Aladdin's lamp** summons a powerful genie, the ➤ SLAVE *of the Lamp*, who has the power to grant any request.

Alamo the Franciscan mission which was the site of a desperate and ultimately unsuccessful defence against Santa Ana in the Texan War of Independence; on 6 March 1836, it was captured by Mexican troops, and all the defenders (including Davy Crockett) were killed.

In the battle of San Jacinto, 21 April 1836, where the Texans defeated the Mexican forces and captured Santa Ana, troops used the battle-cry (attributed to Colonel Sidney Sherman) 'Remember the Alamo!'

alarums and excursions confused noise and bustle; from a stage direction occurring in slightly varying forms in a number of Shakespeare's history plays, as 3 *Henry VI* and *Richard III*.

St Alban (3rd century), the first British Christian martyr, a native of Verulamium (now St Albans). Alban was converted and baptized by a fugitive priest whom he sheltered. When soldiers searched his house, he put on the priest's cloak and was arrested and condemned to death. His feast day is 22 June.

Albany an ancient name for the northern part of Scotland, which from the Middle Ages was a royal title.

In London, *Albany* is the name of an exclusive block of flats in Piccadilly. Built in 1770 on the site of an earlier property by the architect William Chambers (1726–96), in 1791 it was purchased by George III's son Frederick, Duke of York and Albany, after whom it was named York House. In 1802 it was converted into 'residential chambers for bachelor gentlemen', being renamed **Albany House** in 1803.

albatross the *albatross* is traditionally believed to bring bad luck, and the word is used for a source of frustration or guilt or an encumbrance, in allusion to Coleridge's poem about the ➤ ANCIENT *Mariner* and his shooting of the bird.

Alberich in German legend, the king of the elves, equivalent of French ➤ OBERON; in the ➤ NIBELUNGENLIED he is the guardian of the Nibelung treasure who is defeated by ➤ SIEGFRIED. In Wagner's ➤ RING *Cycle*, Alberich is a dwarf who steals the Rhinemaidens' gold.

Albert Memorial a Victorian Gothic memorial (1863–72) to Prince Albert in Kensington Gardens, London, designed by George Gilbert Scott, and often held as typifying the grand Victorian style; after being boarded up for a number of years, it was substantially restored in the 1990s.

St Albertus Magnus (*c.*1200–80), Dominican theologian, philosopher, and scientist; known as *Doctor Universalis*. A teacher of St Thomas Aquinas, he was a pioneer in the study of Aristotle and contributed significantly to the comparison of Christian theology and pagan philosophy. His feast day is 15 November.

Albigenses the members of a heretic sect in southern France in the 12th–13th centuries, identified with the Cathars. Their teaching was a form of Manichaean dualism, with an extremely strict moral and social code including the condemnation of both marriage and procreation. The heresy spread rapidly until ruthlessly crushed by the elder Simon de Montfort's crusade (1209–31) and by an Inquisition.

The name is from medieval Latin, from *Albiga*, the Latin name of *Albi*, the town in southern France where the *Albigenses* originated.

Albion a poetic or literary term for Britain or England (often used in referring to ancient or historical times). Recorded in Old English, the word comes from Latin and is probably of Celtic origin; ultimately related to Latin *albus* 'white', in allusion to the white cliffs of Dover.

Alcatraz a rocky island in San Francisco Bay, California. It was, between 1934 and 1963, the site of a top-security federal prison.

Alcestis in Greek mythology, wife of Admetus, king of Pherae in Thessaly, whose life she saved by consenting to die on his behalf. She was brought back from Hades by Hercules.

alchemy the medieval forerunner of chemistry, based on the supposed transformation of matter. It was concerned particularly with attempts to convert base metals into gold or find a universal elixir.

Alchemy was based on the possible transmutation of all matter, and was far wider in scope than the attempt to turn base metals into gold. The rise of mechanical philosophy in the 17th century gradually undermined alchemy and it became an aspect of the occult.

The term comes (in late Middle English) via Old French and medieval Latin from Arabic *alkīmiyā'*, from *al* 'the' + *kīmiyā'* (from Greek *khēmia*, *khēmeia* 'art of transmuting metals').

Alcibiades (*c*.450–404 BC), Athenian general and statesman. He led the unsuccessful Athenian expeditions against Sparta and Sicily during the Peloponnesian War but fled to Sparta after being charged with sacrilege. He later held commands for Athens against Sparta and Persia before being exiled and later assassinated in Phrygia.

Alcmene in Greek mythology, the mother by ➤ ZEUS of Hercules.

Aldermaston a village near Reading in southern England, site of the Atomic Weapons Research Establishment. From 1958 to 1963 a march between Aldermaston and London took place each year in protest against the development and production of nuclear weapons.

Alecto in Greek mythology, one of the ➤ FURIES.

Aleppo an ancient city in northern Syria, which was formerly an important commercial centre on the trade route between the Mediterranean and the countries of the East.

Alexander¹ (356–323 BC), king of Macedon 336–323, son of Philip II; known as **Alexander the Great**. He conquered Persia, Egypt, Syria, Mesopotamia, Bactria, and the Punjab; in Egypt he founded the city of Alexandria. According to Plutarch, Alexander wept when he was told that there were an infinite number of worlds, saying, 'Is it not worthy of tears that, when the number of worlds is infinite, we have not yet become lords of a single one?'

After his death from a fever at Babylon his empire quickly fell apart, but he became a model for subsequent imperialist conquerors and the subject of fantastic legends.

Alexander² in Greek mythology, the name given to Paris of Troy (see ➤ PARIS¹), by the shepherds who brought him up in exile.

Alexander technique a system designed to promote well-being by retraining one's awareness and habits of posture to ensure minimum effort and strain. It is named after Frederick Matthias *Alexander* (1869–1955), the Australian-born actor and elocutionist who developed it.

Alexandra Rose Day a day in June when rose emblems are sold for charity; it was originally established by Queen *Alexandra* (1844–1925) to raise money for British hospitals.

alexandrine an iambic line of twelve syllables or six feet. The term comes (in the late 16th century) from French, from *Alexandre* (see ➤ ALEXANDER¹), the subject of an Old French poem in this metre.

Alhambra a fortified Moorish palace, the last stronghold of the Muslim kings of Granada, built between 1248 and 1354 near Granada in Spain. It is an outstanding piece of Moorish architecture with its marble courts and fountains, delicate columns and archways, and wall decorations of carved and painted stucco.

Ali Baba the hero of a story supposed to be from the *Arabian Nights* (but actually first added to the text in a French translation of the early 18th century), who discovered the magic formula (➤ OPEN *sesame*) which opened a cave where forty thieves kept their treasure.

Planning to recover what they had lost, the thieves concealed themselves in Ali Baba's courtyard in forty tall oil jars, but Ali Baba's slave *Morgiana*, discovering their presence, poured boiling oil into the jars and killed them, saving her master.

Alice the heroine of two books by Lewis Carroll, *Alice's Adventures in Wonderland* (1865) and *Through the Looking Glass* (1872); as depicted by the illustrator Tenniel, Alice is a child with long straight fair hair held back with a band of ribbon (in a style now known as an **Alice band**), who meets a bewildering variety of playing-card, chess-board, and other characters in the worlds she finds down a rabbit hole and on the other side of a mirror. The stories were originally told by Carroll (pseudonym of Charles Lutwidge Dodgson, 1832–98) to Alice Liddell, 10-year-old daughter of the Dean of Christ Church, Oxford.

alkahest the hypothetical universal solvent sought by alchemists. Recorded from the mid 17th century, the word is sham Arabic, and was probably invented by Paracelsus.

All Blacks the New Zealand Rugby team, named from the colour of the players' strip; the name was first applied to the team by British journalists at the beginning of the 1905 tour of Britain.

all-singing all-dancing with every possible attribute, able to perform any necessary function; a phrase applied particularly in the area of computer technology, but originally coming from descriptions of show business acts. The term may derive ultimately from a series of posters produced in 1929 to promote the new sound cinema such as that advertising the Hollywood musical *Broadway Melody*, which proclaimed the words *All talking All singing All dancing.*

All Souls' Day a Catholic festival with prayers for the souls of the dead in Purgatory, held on 2 November.

be all things to all men be able or try to please everybody, often with an implication of duplicity; originally probably in allusion to 1 Corinthians 9:22.

Allah the name of God among Muslims (and Arab Christians). The name comes from Arabic *'allāh*, contraction of *al-'ilāh* 'the god'.

Allahabad a city in the state of Uttar Pradesh, north central India, which is situated at the confluence of the sacred Jumna and Ganges Rivers, and is a place of Hindu pilgrimage.

allegory a story, poem, or picture which can be interpreted to reveal a hidden meaning, typically a moral or political one. The word comes (in late Middle English) via Old French and Latin from Greek *allēgoria*, from *allos* 'other' + *-agoria* 'speaking'.

alliteration the rhetorical device of commencing adjacent or closely connected words with the same sound or syllable. The

term comes from Latin *ad-* (expressing addition) + *littera* 'letter'.

Ally Pally an informal name for *Alexandra Palace* in Muswell Hill, North London, the original headquarters of BBC television.

Ally Sloper name of a character in a series of humorous publications, as *Some Playful Episodes in the Career of Ally Sloper* (1873), having a prominent nose and receding forehead and noted for his dishonest and bungling practices.

alma mater the university, school, or college that one once attended. The phrase is recorded from the mid 17th century, in the general sense 'someone or something providing nourishment'; in Latin, literally 'bounteous mother', a title given to various Roman goddesses, notably Ceres and Cybele.

Almagest an Arabic version of Ptolemy's astronomical treatise; in the Middle Ages (also with lower-case initial) any celebrated treatise on astrology and alchemy. The word comes from Old French, based on Arabic, from *al* 'the' + Greek *megistē* 'greatest (composition)'.

almanac an annual calendar containing important dates and statistical information such as astronomical data and tide tables. Recorded from late Middle English, the word comes via medieval Latin from Greek, but ultimately is of unknown origin.

Almanach de Gotha an annual publication giving information about European royalty, nobility, and diplomats, published in *Gotha* 1763–1944 and revived in 1968; the presence of a family in the book was considered to establish aristocratic credentials.

almighty dollar a phrase expressing the power of money; originally with allusion to the American writer Washington Irving (1783–1859) in 1836.

Almohad a member of a Berber Muslim movement and dynasty that conquered the Spanish and North African empire of the ➤ ALMORAVIDS in the 12th century, taking the capital Marrakesh in 1147. They were driven out of Spain in 1212 but held on to Marrakesh until 1269.

Almoravid a member of a federation of Muslim Berber peoples that established an empire in Morocco, Algeria, and Spain in the second half of the 11th century. They were in turn driven out by the ➤ ALMOHADS, losing their capital Marrakesh in 1147.

alms money or food given to poor people. Recorded from Old English (in the form *ælmysse, ælmesse*), the word comes via Christian Latin from Greek *eleēmosunē* 'compassion', and ultimately from *eleos* 'mercy'.

Alnaschar a beggar in the ➤ ARABIAN *Nights* who destroys his livelihood by indulging in visions of riches and grandeur.

aloha a Hawaiian word used in greeting or parting from someone. The **Aloha State** is an informal name for Hawaii.

Alph the sacred river in Xanadu referred to in Coleridge's 'Kubla Khan'.

alpha the first letter of the Greek alphabet (A, α), transliterated as 'a'. The phrase **alpha and omega** 'the beginning and the end' (*omega* is the last letter of the Greek alphabet, as *alpha* is the first) is especially used by Christians as a title for Jesus.

alphabet a set of letters or symbols in a fixed order used to represent the basic set of speech sounds of a language, especially the set of letters from A to Z.

The origin of the alphabet goes back to the Phoenician system of the 2nd millennium BC, from which the modern Hebrew and Arabic systems are ultimately derived. The Greek alphabet, which emerged in 1000–900 BC, developed two branches, Cyrillic (which became the script of Russian) and Etruscan (from which derives the Roman alphabet used in the West).

Recorded from the early 16th century, the word comes via late Latin from Greek *alpha, bēta*, the first two letters of the Greek alphabet.

Alpheus in Greek mythology, a river-god who fell in love with the nymph ➤ ARETHUSA. Having fled to Ortygia to escape him, she was turned into a fountain; according to the legend, Alpheus then flowed under the sea to reach the fountain, and this gave rise to the ancient belief that the water of the river Alpheus flowed through the sea without mixing with it.

Alphonsine tables astronomical tables invented in 1252 by Alfonso X 'the Wise' (1221–84), King of Castile.

Altamira the site of a cave with Palaeolithic rock paintings, south of Santander in northern Spain, discovered in 1879. The paintings are realistic depictions of deer, wild boar, and especially bison; they are dated to the Upper Magdalenian period.

altar the table in a Christian church at which the bread and wine are consecrated in communion services; a table or flat-topped block used as the focus for a religious ritual, especially for making sacrifices or offerings to a deity. The word comes ultimately from Latin *altus* 'high'.

alto-relievo a sculpture or carving in high relief; the term comes (in the mid 17th century) from Italian *alto-rilievo*.

Amalthea in Greek mythology, the she-goat who suckled the infant ➤ ZEUS when he was hidden to protect him from his father ➤ CRONUS; **Amalthea's horn** is another name for the ➤ CORNUCOPIA or horn of plenty.

amaranth in poetic and literary usage, an imaginary flower that never fades, and is thus taken as a type of immortality; the name comes ultimately from Greek *amarantos* 'unfading'.

Tell el-Amarna the site of the ruins of the ancient Egyptian capital Akhetaten, on the east bank of the Nile. A series of cuneiform tablets known as the **Amarna Letters** was discovered on the site in 1887, providing valuable insight into Near Eastern diplomacy of the 14th century BC.

Amaryllis name of a shepherdess in the pastoral poetry of Virgil and Ovid, used by Milton in 'Lycidas' (1638).

Amaterasu the principal deity of the Japanese Shinto religion, the sun goddess and ancestor of Jimmu, founder of the imperial dynasty.

Amati a family of Italian violin-makers from Cremona. In the 16th and 17th centuries three generations of the *Amatis* (Andrea, *c.*1520–*c.*80 and his sons and grandson Nicolò, 1596–1684) developed the basic proportions of the violin, viola, and cello, refining the body outlines, soundholes, purfling, and scroll. Antonio Stradivari worked in Nicolò's workshop.

Amazon a member of a legendary race of female warriors believed by the ancient Greeks to exist in Scythia or elsewhere on the edge of the known world; in extended usage, a very tall and strong or athletic woman.

The Amazons, who appear in many Greek legends, were allies of the Trojans in the ➤ TROJAN *War*, and their queen, Penthesilea, was killed by Achilles. One of the labours of Hercules was to obtain the girdle of Hippolyta, queen of the Amazons.

The name comes (in late Middle English, via Latin) from Greek *Amazōn*, explained by the Greeks as 'breastless' (as if from *a-* 'without' + *mazos* 'breast'), referring to the fable that the Amazons cut off the right breast so as not to interfere with the use of a bow, but probably a folk etymology of an unknown foreign word.

The Amazon river in South America, which initially bore various names after its discovery in 1500, was finally called *Amazon* after a legendary race of female warriors believed to live on its banks.

amber a piece of amber was traditionally used as an amulet to attract lovers.

Amber often contains the bodies of trapped insects (the plot of Michael Crichton's thriller *Jurassic Park* and the 1993 Spielberg film based on it turned on the hypothesis that dinosaur DNA from the blood on which such insects had fed could be recovered from the insect bodies).

The word is recorded from late Middle English (also in sense ➤ AMBERGRIS), and comes via Old French from Arabic *'anbar* 'ambergris', later 'amber'.

ambergris a wax-like substance that originates as a secretion in the intestines of the sperm whale, found floating in tropical seas. It is soft, black, and unpleasant-smelling when fresh, slowly becoming harder, paler, and sweeter-smelling, and used in perfume manufacture.

The word comes (in late Middle English) from Old French *ambre gris* 'grey amber', as distinct from *ambre jaune* 'yellow amber' (the resin).

ambo a raised platform in a church from which scriptures and litanies were read. Originally single, by the 6th century they were organized in pairs, one for the Epistles on the south side of the church, and one for the Gospels on the north side.

St Ambrose (*c*.339–97), Doctor of the Church and bishop of Milan. A champion of orthodoxy, he also encouraged developments in church music. He was partly responsible for the conversion of St Augustine

of Hippo, and forced the emperor Theodosius to do public penance for a massacre carried out on his orders at Thessalonica; for this Ambrose is sometimes shown with a scourge.

According to legend, when he was a child a swarm of bees settled on his mouth, symbolizing his future eloquence. His emblems are a beehive and a scourge, and his feast day is 7 December.

ambrosia in Greek and Roman mythology, the food of the gods, associated with their immortality. The word comes (in the mid 16th century) via Latin from Greek, 'elixir of life', from *ambrotos* 'immortal'.

Ambrosius Aurelianus in the account of ➤ GILDAS, a 5th-century leader of Romano-British resistance to the Saxons; in the later chronicle of Geoffrey of Monmouth, he is said to have been the elder brother of ➤ UTHER *Pendragon* and to have preceded him as king after defeating and killing ➤ VORTIGERN.

amen an exclamation, meaning 'so be it', uttered at the end of a prayer or hymn. Recorded from Old English, the word comes via ecclesiastical Latin from Greek *amēn*, from Hebrew 'truth, certainty', used adverbially as expression of agreement, and adopted in the Septuagint as a solemn expression of belief or affirmation.

Amenhotep the name of four Egyptian pharaohs, the fourth of whom adopted the worship of ➤ ATEN and changed his name to ➤ AKHENATEN.

America the name was apparently coined in M. Waldseemüller *Cosmographiae Introductio* (1507) and coming from *Americus*, modern Latin form of the name of the Italian explorer *Amerigo* Vespucci (1451–1512), who navigated the coast of South America in 1501.

America's Cup an international yachting race held every three to four years, named after the yacht *America*, which won it in 1851. The *America*'s owners gave the trophy to the New York Yacht Club as a perpetual international challenge trophy, and it remained in the club's possession for 132 years. An Australian crew won it in 1983, but the Americans won it back in 1987, and held it until 1995, when New Zealand were successful.

American Civil War the war between the northern US states (usually known as the

Union) and the Confederate states of the South, 1861–5.

The war was fought over the issues of slavery and states' rights. The pro-slavery Southern states seceded from the Federal Union following the election of Abraham Lincoln on an anti-slavery platform, but were defeated by the North after failing to gain foreign recognition.

American dream the traditional social ideals of the United States, such as equality, democracy, and material prosperity; the term is recorded from the 1930s.

War of American Independence the war of 1775–83 in which the American colonists won independence from British rule. The war was triggered by resentment of the economic policies of Britain, particularly the right of Parliament to tax the colonies. Following disturbances such as the Boston Tea Party of 1773, fighting broke out in 1775; a year later the Declaration of Independence was signed. The British army surrendered at Yorktown in 1781.

amethyst traditionally supposed to prevent drunkenness. Recorded from Middle English, the word comes via Old French and Latin *amethustos* 'not drunken'.

Amidah a prayer, part of the Jewish liturgy, consisting of a varying number of blessings recited while the worshippers stand. The word is recorded from the late 19th century and comes from Hebrew, literally 'standing'.

Amish the members of a strict Mennonite sect noted for maintaining their traditional culture. The sect was founded by a Swiss preacher, Jakob Amman (or Amen) (*c.*1645–*c.*1730), in the 1690s, and beginning in *c.*1720, the Amish migrated to North America and established major settlements in Pennsylvania, Ohio, and elsewhere.

Ammon Greek and Roman form of the name of the Egyptian god ➤ AMUN. **Ammon's son** is an epithet of ➤ ALEXANDER *the Great*, from the story in Plutarch of Alexander's visit to the temple of Ammon in Egypt, where he was greeted by the high priest as the son of the god.

Amnesty International an independent international organization in support of human rights, especially for prisoners of conscience, founded in London in 1961. The organization was awarded the Nobel Peace Prize in 1977.

amok in the phrase **run amok**, behave uncontrollably and disruptively. The word comes (in the mid 17th century) from Portuguese *amouco*, from Malay *amok* 'rushing in a frenzy'. Early use was as a noun denoting a Malay in a homicidal frenzy; the adverb use dates from the late 17th century.

Amos a Hebrew minor prophet (*c.*760 BC), a shepherd of Tekoa, near Jerusalem; also, a book of the Bible containing his prophecies.

Amos and Andy the hardworking *Amos* and his lazy friend *Andy* are characters in an American radio series set in Harlem, New York, from the 1920s to the 1940s, and later transferred to television (1951–66).

ampersand the sign &, standing for *and*, as in *Smith & Co*, or Latin *et*, as in *&c.*. The word is recorded from the mid 19th century, and is an alteration of *and per se and* '& by itself is *and*', chanted as an aid to learning the sign.

amphisbaena a fabled snake with a head at each end, able to move in either direction. The name comes (in late Middle English) via Latin from Greek *amphisbaina*, from *amphis* 'both ways' + *bainein* 'go'.

Amphitrite in Greek mythology, a sea goddess, wife of ➤ POSEIDON and mother of ➤ TRITON.

ampulla a flask for sacred uses such as holding the oil for anointing the sovereign at a coronation. Recorded in this sense from late Middle English, the word is Latin, originally denoting a roughly spherical Roman flask with two handles, and is a diminutive of *amphora*.

amrit a syrup considered divine by Sikhs and taken by them at baptism and in religious observances. The word comes from Sanskrit *amṛta* 'immortal'.

Amritsar a city in the state of Punjab in NW India, founded in 1577 by Ram Das (1534–81), fourth guru of the Sikhs. It became the centre of the Sikh faith and the site of its holiest temple, the ➤ GOLDEN *Temple*. It was the scene of a riot in 1919, in which 400 people were killed by British troops.

Amu Darya a river of central Asia, rising in the Pamirs and flowing into the Aral Sea, which in classical times was known as the ➤ OXUS.

amulet an ornament or small piece of jewellery thought to give protection against evil, danger, or disease. The word is recorded from the late 16th century; it comes from Latin, but is of unknown origin.

Amun a supreme god of the ancient Egyptians, identified with the sun god Ra, and in Greek and Roman times with Zeus. As a national god of Egypt he was associated in a triad with Mut and Khonsu. A variant form of the name is ➤ AMMON.

Amurath the name of several Turkish sultans. Amurath in 1574 murdered his brothers on succeeding to the throne, and his successor in 1596 did the same.

Anabaptists the doctrine that baptism should only be administered to believing adults, held by a radical Protestant sect which emerged during the 1520s and 1530s, following the ideas of reformers such as Zwingli. *Anabaptists* also advocated complete separation of Church and state and many of their beliefs are today carried on by the ➤ MENNONITES.

Recorded from the mid 16th century, the name comes via ecclesiastical Latin from Greek *anabaptismos*, from *ana-* 'over again' + *baptismos* 'baptism'.

Anacharsis said by Herodotus to have been a Scythian prince of the 6th century BC, who having travelled widely (and according to one account found that in Greece the Spartans were the only people with whom it was possible to hold a sensible conversation), returned to Scythia, and was killed by his own people, perhaps for trying to introduce the worship of the ➤ MAGNA *mater*.

Anacreon (*c.*570–478 BC), Greek lyric poet. The surviving fragments of his work include iambic invectives and elegiac epitaphs, but he is most famous for his poetry written in celebration of love and wine.

Anadyomene in Pliny's *Natural History*, an epithet of Aphrodite in a picture by Apelles, shown emerging from the sea; the word is Greek, and means 'rising from the sea'.

anagram a word, phrase, or name formed by rearranging the letters of another, such as *spar*, formed from *rasp*. Recorded from the late 16th century, the word comes via French or modern Latin from Greek *ana-* 'back, anew' + *gramma* 'letter'.

sons of Anak in the Bible (Numbers ch. 13), a race of giants living in the land of Canaan.

in the last analysis when everything has been considered; used to suggest that an associated statement expresses the basic truth about a complicated situation.

Anancy the name (from Twi *ananse* 'spider') of a trickster spider character found in many folktales (or ➤ NANCY *stories*) of West Africa and the West Indies.

Ananias in the Bible, the husband of ➤ SAPPHIRA, who with his wife was struck dead for attempting to cheat St Peter; his name is used allusively to denote a liar.

Anastasia the youngest daughter (1901–?18) of the last tsar of Russia, now thought to have died with the rest of her family at ➤ YEKATERINBURG; for many years there were rumours that one or more of the family had escaped the massacre, and a number of claimants appeared.

St Anastasia martyr and married virgin, said to have died at Sirmium. By the 5th century she was venerated in Rome as a Roman martyr, perhaps because her cult became conflated with the titulus Anastasiae, an ancient church by the Circus Maximus. Her name is of interest, deriving from the Greek, *Anastasis*, or Resurrection, although the ➤ GOLDEN *Legend* explains it as referring to her standing on high, raised from vices to virtues. Her feast day is 25 December.

anathema a person or thing accursed or consigned to damnation; the formal act or formula of cursing. The word comes (in the early 16th century) from ecclesiastical Latin 'excommunicated person, excommunication', from Greek *anathema* 'thing devoted to evil, accursed thing', from *anatithenai* 'to set up'.

The words **anathema maranatha** occur together in 1 Corinthians 16:22, and were formerly thought to represent an intensification of *anathema*, but according to modern criticism, they do not belong together, and ➤ MARANATHA represents a distinct sentence.

Anchises in Greek legend, the ruler of Dardanus and father of ➤ AENEAS; according to the *Aeneid*, when Troy fell he was carried out of the burning ruins on his son's shoulders.

anchor figuratively, a source of security and confidence. An *anchor* in Christian tradition is a symbol of hope, from a passage in Hebrews 6:19; it is also the emblem of ➤ *St*

CLEMENT, who was martyred by being thrown into the sea with an anchor round his neck.

anchorite a religious recluse; the name comes (in Middle English via Latin) from ecclesiastical Greek, from *anakhōrein* 'retire'.

Ancien Régime the political and social system in France (the 'old rule') before the Revolution of 1789.

ancient demesne land recorded in Domesday Book as belonging to the Crown.

ancient lights the right of access to light of a property, established by custom and used to prevent the construction of buildings on adjacent property which would obstruct such access. Recorded from the mid 18th century, from *lights* meaning 'light from the sky'.

Ancient Mariner eponymous hero of Coleridge's poem, sole survivor of a disastrous voyage in which the ship after a storm is drawn to the South Pole, who stops one of three wedding guests and forces him to listen to his story.

The mariner had shot an ➤ ALBATROSS and brought down a curse on his ship; the dead albatross was hung round the mariner's neck as a penance. The rest of the crew died, but the mariner lived on, and was finally released from the burden. Afterward he was compelled constantly to travel and tell his story as an exemplum of divine grace, and the term *Ancient Mariner* is sometimes used allusively to denote someone's unwanted presence.

Ancient of Days a name for God, from the scriptural title in Daniel 7:9, 'the Ancient of Days did sit, whose garments were white as snow'.

Andersonville a village in Sumter county, Georgia, which during the American Civil War was the site of a Confederate military prison for Union soldiers; its high death rate was notorious.

Andorra a small autonomous principality in the southern Pyrenees, between France and Spain, whose independence dates from the late 8th century, when ➤ CHARLEMAGNE is said to have granted the Andorrans self-government for their help in defeating the Moors. Andorra retained a feudal system, and was governed jointly by the French head of state and the Spanish bishop of Urgel,

until 1993, when a revised constitution was adopted.

St Andrew an Apostle, the brother of St Peter, and like him a fisherman. The X-shaped cross (the ➤ SALTIRE) became associated with his name during the Middle Ages because he is said to have died by crucifixion on such a cross. St Andrew is the patron saint of Scotland (his relics were supposedly brought to Scotland by ➤ *St* RULE) and Russia. He is often shown in art with a fishing-net. His feast day is 30 November.

Androcles a runaway slave (in a story by Aulus Gellius, 2nd century AD) who extracted a thorn from the paw of a lion, which later recognized him and refrained from attacking him when he faced it in the arena.

android an automaton resembling a human being; in science fiction, a synthetic human being. The term comes (in the early 18th century, in the modern Latin form) from modern Latin *androides*, from Greek *anēr, andr-* 'man' + the suffix *-oid* denoting form or resemblance.

Andromache in Greek mythology, the wife of ➤ HECTOR. She became the slave of ➤ NEOPTOLEMUS (son of Achilles) after the fall of Troy.

Andromeda in Greek mythology, an Ethiopian princess whose mother ➤ CASSIOPEIA boasted that she herself (or, in some stories, her daughter) was more beautiful than the nereids. In revenge Poseidon sent a sea monster to ravage the country; to placate him Andromeda was fastened to a rock and exposed to the monster, from which she was rescued by ➤ PERSEUS.

Andromeda is also the name of a large northern constellation between Perseus and Pegasus, with few bright stars. It is chiefly notable for the **Andromeda Galaxy** (or **Great Nebula of Andromeda**), a conspicuous spiral galaxy probably twice as massive as our own and located 2 million light years away.

An **Andromeda strain**, after the title of a book by Michael Crichton, is a hypothetical, novel type of micro-organism, especially one created by genetic engineering, whose release into the environment could cause widespread destruction of life.

Andy Pandy a clown puppet who was one of the central characters of the television series for young children, *Watch with Mother*, from 1950.

Aneirin Welsh poet of the 6th century, to whom the poem *Y Gododdin*, commemorating a British defeat at Catraeth (Catterick) is attributed.

angel a spiritual being more powerful and intelligent than a human being, especially in Jewish, Christian, Muslim, and other theologies, one acting as a messenger, agent, or attendant of God (see also ➤ ANGELS). The term is also used for a person regarded as a messenger of God, especially (in biblical translations, as at Revelation 2:1, 'the angel of the church of Ephesus') in the early Church.

An *angel* was also the name given to a former English coin minted between the reigns of Edward IV and Charles I and bearing the figure of the archangel Michael killing a dragon.

An *angel* is the symbol of ➤ St MATTHEW and ➤ St CECILIA.

An **angel in the house** is a woman who is completely devoted to her husband and family, from the title of a poem (1854–62) by Coventry Patmore. The term is often used pejoratively.

The **Angel of the North** is a steel sculpture of a winged figure, over 20 metres tall and with a wingspan of 54 metres, created by the British sculptor Antony Gormley (1950–) and assembled on site near the A1 in Gateshead in February 1998; it is positioned to mark the southern entry to Tyneside.

To **entertain an angel unawares** is not to realize the status of one's guest; the allusion is biblical, to Hebrews 13:2, 'Be not forgetful to entertain strangers: for thereby some have entertained angels unawares.'

Recorded in Old English in the form *engel*, the word comes ultimately via ecclesiastical Latin from Greek *angelos* 'messenger'; it was superseded in Middle English by forms from Old French *angele*.

Angel Falls a waterfall in the Guiana Highlands of SE Venezuela which is the highest waterfall in the world, with an uninterrupted descent of 978 m (3,210 ft). The falls were discovered in 1935 by the American aviator and prospector James *Angel* (*c*.1899–1956).

the Angelic Doctor another name for ➤ St THOMAS *Aquinas*.

the angelic salutation another name for the ➤ SALUTATION.

Fra Angelico the Italian painter Giovanni da Fiesole (*c*.1400–55). His work was intended chiefly for contemplation and instruction, and his simple and direct style shows an understanding of contemporary developments in Renaissance painting, especially perspective.

angels in Christian angelology, *angels* form the ninth and lowest order of the ninefold ➤ CELESTIAL *hierarchy*, ranking directly below the archangels.

The **Angels of Mons** are protective spirits supposedly seen over the First World War battlefield; the origin was in fact a short story, 'The Angel of Mons' (1915) by Arthur Machen (1843–1947), which circulated widely by word of mouth as a factual account.

The question **how many angels can dance on the head of a pin?** was regarded satirically as a characteristic speculation of scholastic philosophy, particularly as exemplified by 'Doctor Scholasticus' (Anselm of Laon, d. 1117) and as used in medieval comedies.

On the side of the angels means on the side of what is right. The phrase was used notably by Benjamin Disraeli in a speech of 1864 to allude to the controversy over the origins of humankind set alight by the publication of Charles Darwin's *The Origin of Species* (1859), 'Is man an ape or an angel? Now I am on the side of the angels.'

See also *not Angles but angels* at ➤ ANGLE.

Angelus a Roman Catholic devotion commemorating the Incarnation of Jesus and including the Hail Mary, said at morning, noon, and sunset; a ringing of church bells announcing this. The word is recorded from the mid 17th century, and comes from the Latin phrase *Angelus domini* 'the angel of the Lord', the opening words of the devotion.

Angevin any of the Plantagenet kings of England, especially those who were also counts of ➤ ANJOU (Henry II, Richard I, and John), descended from Geoffrey, Count of Anjou. The name comes via French from medieval Latin *Andegavinus*, from *Andegavum* 'Angers', the town in western France which is the former capital of Anjou.

Angkor the capital of the ancient kingdom of Khmer in NW Cambodia, noted for its temples, especially the **Angkor Wat** (mid 12th century); the site was rediscovered in 1860.

Angle a member of a Germanic people, originally inhabitants of what is now Schleswig-Holstein, who came to England in the 5th century AD. The Angles founded kingdoms in Mercia, Northumbria, and East Anglia and gave their name to England and the English.

The name comes from Latin *Angli* 'the people of Angul', a district of Schleswig (now in northern Germany), so named because of its angular shape.

The comment **not Angles but Angels** is attributed to ➤ GREGORY *the Great* (AD c.540–604), on seeing fair-haired English slaves in Rome; the story is oral tradition, based on Bede's *Historia Ecclesiastica.*

Anglesey an island of North Wales, which in the 1st century AD was a centre of Druid power and resistance to Roman invasion; in AD 61 it was attacked by Suetonius Paulinus, who killed Druid priests and cut down sacred groves.

Anglican of, relating to, or denoting the Church of England or any Church in communion with it. The name comes (in the early 17th century) from medieval Latin *Anglicanus* (its adoption suggested by *Anglicana ecclesia* 'the English Church' in the Magna Carta), ultimately from the base of ➤ ANGLE.

Anglo-Catholicism a tradition within the Anglican Church which is close to Catholicism in its doctrine and worship and is broadly identified with High Church Anglicanism. As a movement, Anglo-Catholicism grew out of the ➤ OXFORD *Movement* of the 1830s and 1840s.

Anglo-Irish of English descent but born or resident in Ireland, or a member of such a family, and associated particularly with the ➤ PROTESTANT *Ascendancy.*

Anglo-Saxon relating to or denoting the Germanic inhabitants of England from their arrival in the 5th century up to the Norman Conquest. The **Anglo-Saxon Chronicle** is an early record in English of events in England, from the beginning of the Christian period to 1154.

angry white male a right-wing or anti-liberal white man, especially a working-class one; the term is first recorded in the US in the early 1990s.

angry young man a young man dissatisfied with and outspoken against existing social and political structures, originally, a member of a group of socially conscious writers in the 1950s, including particularly the playwright John Osborne. The phrase, the title of a book (1951) by Leslie Paul, was used of Osborne in the publicity material for his play *Look Back in Anger* (1956), in which the characteristic views were articulated by the anti-hero Jimmy Porter.

anima mundi a power supposed to organize the whole universe and coordinate its parts; the term is recorded in English from the late 16th century, and comes from medieval Latin (as used by Peter Abelard) meaning literally 'soul of the world', apparently formed to render Greek *psukhē tou kosmou.*

Animal Farm a fable (1945) by George Orwell which consists of a satire on Russian Communism as it developed under Stalin. The animals of the farm, led by the pigs, revolt against the cruel farmer, and achieve an apparent life of freedom, but as power corrupts their rulers, they are led to a world in which the slogan is 'All animals are equal but some animals are more equal than others.'

animal, vegetable, and mineral the three traditional divisions into which natural objects have been classified; the classification (earlier in Latin) is first recorded in English in the early 18th century. From the mid 19th century, **animal, vegetable, (or) mineral** became the name of a parlour game in which players had to guess the identity of an object, having been told to which of the three groups it belongs; they are traditionally allowed up to twenty questions, to be answered by 'yes' or 'no'.

Anjou a former province of western France, on the Loire. It was an English possession from 1154, when it was inherited by Henry II as count of Anjou, until 1204, when it was lost to France by King John; it is the origin of the name ➤ ANGEVIN for the dynasty of Plantagenet kings.

ankh an object resembling a cross, but with a loop in place of the upper limb, used in ancient Egyptian art as a symbol of life. Recorded in English from the late 19th century, the word comes from Egyptian, and means literally 'life, soul'.

Annals of the Four Masters a 17th century compilation of earlier Irish chronicles, such as the *Annals of Connacht* and the *Annals of Ulster*; its Irish name is *Annála Ríoghachta Éireann* 'Annals of the Kingdom of Ireland'. It was produced in the 1630s by the Franciscan Michael O'Clery and three collaborators.

Annapurna a ridge of the Himalayas, in north central Nepal, the highest peak of which rises to 8,078 m (26,503 ft); it is named for an aspect of the goddess ➤ PARVATI, and may be referred to as the type of an almost unconquerable height.

St Anne traditionally the mother of the Virgin Mary, first mentioned by name in the apocryphal gospel of James (2nd century). The extreme veneration of St Anne in the late Middle Ages was attacked by Luther and other reformers. She is the patron saint of Brittany and the province of Quebec in Canada. Her feast day is 26 July.

anno domini system of dating from the birth of Christ (see ➤ DIONYSIUS²); the Latin words (abbreviated as AD) mean 'in the year of our Lord'. The term is recorded in English from the late 16th century; from the late 19th century, it has also been used humorously to designate advanced or advancing age.

Annunciation the announcement of the Incarnation, made by Gabriel to Mary; the **Feast of the Annunciation** is celebrated on 25 March, otherwise called *Lady Day*. In art, representations often show Mary sitting with a book on her lap, her pose either shrinking or accepting; Gabriel often holds a lily.

annus horribilis a dreadful year; the Latin phrase, modelled on ➤ ANNUS *mirabilis*, was used notably by Queen Elizabeth II in 1992 when looking back on a year which had seen severe marital difficulties for her children and a fire at Windsor Castle.

annus mirabilis a remarkable or auspicious year, from modern Latin ('wonderful year') in *Annus Mirabilis: the year of wonders, 1666*, the title of a poem (1667) by Dryden; its subjects were the Dutch War and the Fire of London.

Annwn in Celtic mythology, the underworld, ruled over by ➤ ARAWN.

anorak a socially inept and studious or obsessive person with unfashionable and largely solitary interests. The meaning dates from the 1980s and derives from the anoraks worn by ➤ TRAINSPOTTERS, regarded as typifying this kind of person.

the Anschluss the annexation of Austria by Germany in 1938.

St Anselm (*c.*1033–1109), Italian-born philosopher and theologian, Archbishop of Canterbury 1093–1109. He worked to free the Church from secular control and believed that the best way to defend the faith was by intellectual reasoning. His writings include *Cur Deus Homo?* a mystical study on the Atonement, and *Proslogion*, an ontological

'proof' of the existence of God. His feast day is 21 April.

ant the *ant* is proverbial for its industry, often with biblical reference to Proverbs 6:6.

Antaeus in Greek mythology, a giant, the son of Poseidon and Earth, who compelled all comers to wrestle with him; he gained renewed strength with the ground, and overcame and killed all opponents until he was defeated by Hercules.

up the ante increase what is at stake or under discussion, especially in a conflict or dispute. Ante here comes from the Latin word for 'before', and as an English term it was originally (in the early 19th century) a term in poker and similar gambling games, meaning 'a stake put up by a player before drawing cards'.

antebellum occurring or existing before a particular war, especially the American Civil War.

antediluvian of or belonging to a time before the biblical Flood; utterly out of date, very antiquated.

anthem a musical setting of a religious text to be sung by a choir during a church service, especially in Anglican or Protestant Churches. Recorded from Old English in the form *antefn, antifne* (denoting a composition sung antiphonally), from late Latin *antiphona* 'antiphon, a short sentence sung or recited before or after a psalm or canticle'.

anthemion an ornamental design of alternating motifs resembling clusters of narrow leaves or honeysuckle petals.

anthology a published collection of poems or other pieces of writing; a similar collection of songs or musical compositions issued in one album. The word comes, in the mid 17th century, via French or medieval Latin from Greek *anthologia*, from *anthos* 'flower' + *-logia* 'collection'; in Greek, the word originally denoted a collection of the 'flowers' of verse, i.e. small choice poems or epigrams, by various authors.

St Anthony of Egypt (*c.*251–356), Egyptian hermit, the founder of monasticism. During his seclusion in the Egyptian desert he attracted a number of followers whom he organized into a community; his hermit life is also noted for the temptations he underwent, especially from demons in the guise of beautiful women. He is said to have visited, and arranged the burial of, St Paul, the first Christian hermit (see ➤ St PAUL[2]).

In the Middle Ages the belief arose that praying to St Anthony would effect a cure for ergotism, and the Order of Hospitallers of St Anthony (founded at La Motte *c*.1100, with members of the Order wearing black robes marked by a blue tau cross) became a pilgrimage centre. The little bells rung by Hospitallers asking for alms were afterwards hung round the necks of animals as a protection against disease, and pigs which belonged to the Order were allowed to roam about the streets (see ➤ TANTONY *pig*). His traditional emblems are pigs and bells, and he is the patron saint of basket-makers and swineherds. His feast day is 17 January.

St Anthony's cross is another name for the ➤ TAU cross, worn by the Order of Hospitallers of St Anthony of Egypt. **St Anthony's fire**, a name for inflammation of the skin due to ergot poisoning, reflects the belief that St Anthony could cure the illness.

St Anthony of Padua (1195–1231), Portuguese Franciscan friar, whose charismatic preaching in the south of France and Italy made many converts. He is sometimes shown preaching to fishes (as St Francis is shown with birds), and in one popular legend a mule kneels before him, rejecting a bundle of hay in favour of the consecrated hosts. His devotion to the poor is commemorated by alms known as **St Anthony's bread**; he is also invoked to find lost articles.

He is often shown with a book and a lily, in the company of the Christ Child; he may also be represented in a nut-tree in honour of his preference for solitude. His feast day is 13 June.

anthropophagi cannibals, especially in legends or fables. Recorded from the mid 16th century, the word comes via Latin from Greek *anthrōpophagos* 'man-eating'.

antic hay an absurd dance; the phrase comes originally from Christopher Marlowe's *Edward II* (1593).

Antichrist a great personal opponent of Christ, expected by the early Church to appear before the end of the world. The name is recorded from Old English and comes via Old French or ecclesiastical Latin from Greek *antíkhristos* 'against Christ'.

Antigone in Greek mythology, daughter of Oedipus and Jocasta, the subject of a tragedy by Sophocles. She was sentenced to death for defying her uncle Creon, king of Thebes, by burying the ritually unburied body of her brother ➤ POLYNICES, but she took her own life before the sentence could be carried out, and Creon's son Haemon, who was engaged to her, killed himself.

antinomian of or relating to the view that Christians are released by grace from the obligation of observing the moral law. Attributed to St Paul by his opponents, this doctrine was held by many Gnostic sects, and also by some radical Protestant groups at the Reformation.

The word is recorded from the mid 17th century, and comes ultimately from Greek *anti-* 'opposite, against' + *nomos* 'law'.

Antioch a city in southern Turkey which was the ancient capital of Syria under the Seleucid kings, who founded it *c*.300 BC.

the Antipodes Australia and New Zealand (used by inhabitants of the northern hemisphere). The name comes (in late Middle English, via French and late Latin) from Greek *antipodes* 'having the feet opposite', from *anti-* 'against' + *pous, pod-* 'foot'. The term originally denoted the inhabitants of opposite sides of the earth.

antipope a person set up as Pope in opposition to one canonically chosen, and applied particularly to those who resided at ➤ AVIGNON during the ➤ GREAT *Schism*. Recorded from late Middle English (in form *antipape*) the name comes from medieval Latin *antipapa*, on the pattern of ➤ ANTICHRIST.

Anton Piller order in English law, a court order which requires the defendant in proceedings to permit the plaintiff or his or her legal representatives to enter the defendant's premises in order to obtain evidence essential to the plaintiff's case. It was named (in the 1970s) after *Anton Piller*, German manufacturers of electric motors, who were involved in legal proceedings (1975) in which such an order was granted.

Antonine Wall a defensive fortification running across the narrowest part of southern Scotland between the Firth of Forth and the Firth of Clyde, built *c*.140 AD, in the reign of the Roman emperor *Antoninus* Pius (86–161).

Mark Antony (*c*.83–30 BC), Roman general and triumvir. A supporter of ➤ JULIUS *Caesar*, in 43 he was appointed one of the triumvirate after Caesar's murder. Following the battle of Philippi he took charge of the Eastern Empire, where he established his association with ➤ CLEOPATRA. Quarrels with Octavian (see ➤ AUGUSTUS) led finally to his defeat at the battle of Actium and to his suicide.

antonym a word opposite in meaning to another (e.g. *bad* and *good*).

Anubis in ancient Egyptian theology, the god of mummification, protector of tombs, usually represented as having a jackal's head.

Anzac a member of the Australian and New Zealand Army Corps; the acronym is recorded from 1915, in accounts of ➤ GALLIPOLI. **Anzac Day**, 25 April, commemorates the landings of the corps in the ➤ GALLIPOLI Peninsula on 25 April, 1915.

Aonia a region of Boeotia in ancient Greece containing Mount Helicon, sacred to the Muses.

Aotearoa Maori name for New Zealand, literally 'land of the long white cloud'.

apartheid the former South African policy of racial segregation of other groups from the white inhabitants. Adopted by the successful Afrikaner National Party as a slogan in the 1948 election, apartheid extended and institutionalized existing racial segregation.
    The word is recorded from the 1940s, and comes from Afrikaans, meaning literally 'separateness'.

ape before the introduction of ➤ MONKEY, the word for a monkey, and afterwards still sometimes so used, especially in poetic and literary sources, and when the animal is taken as typifying the ability to imitate human behaviour, especially in an absurd or unthinking way.

appeal from Philip drunk to Philip sober proverbial saying, implying that an opinion or decision reflects only a passing mood. The original allusion is to Philip, King of Macedon, father of Alexander the Great, who is said to have been the subject of such an appeal.

appeal to Caesar appeal to the highest possible authority, originally with reference to the claim made by the apostle Paul to have his case heard in Rome, which was his right as a Roman citizen, 'I appeal unto Caesar' (Acts 25:11).

Apelles (4th century BC), Greek painter. He is now known only from written sources, as by Pliny's account of his ➤ VENUS *Anadyomene*, but was highly acclaimed throughout the ancient world.

aphorism a concise statement of a scientific principle, typically by a classical author; a pithy observation which contains a general truth. The word comes from the 'Aphorisms of Hippocrates', and was transferred to other sententious statements to the principles of physical science, and then to statements of principles generally.

Aphrodite in Greek mythology, the goddess of beauty, fertility, and sexual love. She is variously described as the daughter of Zeus and Dione, or as being born from the sea. Her cult was of Eastern origin, hence her identification with Astarte and Ishtar. Her Roman equivalent is ➤ VENUS.
    The name is Greek, and means literally 'foam-born', from *aphros* 'foam'.

Apis in Egyptian mythology, a god depicted as a bull, symbolizing fertility and strength in war.

Apocalypse the complete final destruction of the world, especially as described in the biblical book of Revelation. The word is recorded from Old English, and comes ultimately, via Old French and ecclesiastical Latin, from Greek *apokaluptein* 'uncover, reveal'.

apocatastasis the Christian doctrine which holds that ultimately all free moral creatures, including devils, will share in the grace of salvation. The doctrine has never enjoyed wide acceptance. Recorded from the late 17th century, the word comes via Latin from the Greek term for 're-establishment'.

Apocrypha biblical or related writings not forming part of the accepted canon of Scripture. The Old Testament Apocrypha include writings (dating from around 300 BC to AD 100) which appeared in the Septuagint and Vulgate versions but not in the Hebrew Bible; most are accepted by the Roman Catholic and Orthodox Churches as the 'deutero-canonical' books. The New Testament Apocrypha include texts attributed to Apostles and other biblical figures but not regarded as authentic by the Councils of the Church.
    Recorded from late Middle English, the word comes from ecclesiastical Latin *apocrypha (scripta)* 'hidden (writings)', ultimately from Greek *apokruptein* 'hide away'. The adjective **apocryphal**, meaning of doubtful authenticity, mythical, fictional, is recorded from the late 16th century.

Apollo in Greek mythology, a god, son of Zeus and Leto and brother of ➤ ARTEMIS. He is associated with music, poetic inspiration, archery, prophecy, medicine, pastoral life, and the sun; the sanctuary at ➤ DELPHI was dedicated to him.

Apollo is also the name for the American space programme for landing astronauts on the moon. *Apollo 8* was the first mission to orbit the moon (1968), *Apollo 11* was the first to land astronauts (1969), and five further landings took place up to 1972.

The **Apollo Belvedere** is an ancient statue of Apollo, now in the Belvedere Gallery of the Vatican Museum.

Apollyon a name for the Devil, in Revelation 9:11.'

In Bunyan's *Pilgrim's Progress*, Christian has to fight to get past the 'foul fiend' *Apollyon*, who blocks his path

Recorded from late Middle English (in Wyclif's translation of the Bible) the name comes (via late Latin, in the Vulgate) from Greek *Apolluōn* (translating ➤ ABADDON), and ultimately from *apo-* 'quite' + *ollunai* 'destroy'.

apologia a formal written defence of one's opinions or conduct; the word is Latin, and is recorded from the late 18th century, but its currency is largely due to John Henry Newman's *Apologia pro Vita Sua* (1864), the history of his religious life up to the time of his reception into the Roman Catholic Church in 1845.

apopthegm a concise saying or maxim; an aphorism. The word is recorded from the mid 16th century, and comes ultimately (via French or modern Latin) from Greek *apophthengesthai* 'speak out'.

apostate a person who renounces a religious or political belief or principle. Recorded from Middle English, the word comes via ecclesiastical Latin from Greek *apostatēs* 'apostate, runaway slave'.

Apostle[1] each of the twelve chief disciples of Jesus Christ. The twelve Apostles were Peter, Andrew, James, John, Philip, Bartholomew, Thomas, Matthew, James (the Less), Judas (or Thaddaeus), Simon, and Judas Iscariot. After the suicide of Judas Iscariot his place was taken by Matthias.

The term is also applied to any important early Christian teacher, especially St Paul, and to the first successful Christian missionary in a country or to a people.

An **Apostle spoon** is a teaspoon with the figure of an Apostle or saint on the handle.

The **Apostles' Creed** is a statement of Christian belief used in the Western Church, dating from the 4th century and traditionally ascribed to the twelve Apostles.

Recorded from Old English (in form *apostol*) the word comes via ecclesiastical Latin from Greek *apostolos* 'messenger', from *apostellein* 'send forth'.

Apostle[2] a member of an exclusive society in the University of Cambridge (officially 'The Cambridge Conversazione Society') formed in Cambridge in 1820, for the purpose of friendship and formal discussion. Members are elected for life.

Apostolic Fathers the Christian leaders of the early Church immediately succeeding the Apostles.

apostolic succession (in Christian thought) the uninterrupted transmission of spiritual authority from the Apostles through successive popes and bishops, taught by the Roman Catholic Church but denied by most Protestants.

apothecary a person who prepared and sold medicines and drugs. Recorded from late Middle English, the word comes via Old French and late Latin from Greek *apothēkē* 'storehouse'.

apotheosis originally (in the late 16th century) this denotes the elevation of someone to divine status, or deification; in later use, the meaning develops of the highest point in the development of something; a culmination or climax. The word comes via ecclesiastical Latin from Greek, from *apotheoun* 'make a god of', from *apo* 'from' + *theos* 'god'.

Appalachian Mountains a North American mountain system, stretching from Quebec and Maine in the North to Georgia and Alabama in the South. For some 200 years it served as a barrier to westward expansion by early European settlers.

The **Appalachian Trail** is a 3,200-km (about 2,000-mile) footpath through the Appalachian Mountains from Mount Katahdin in Maine to Springer Mountain in Georgia.

Appian Way the principal road southward from Rome in classical times, named after the censor Appius Claudius Caecus, who in 312 BC built the section to Capua; it was later extended to Brindisi.

apple traditionally the fruit with which ➤ EVE was tempted by the serpent. *Apples* are also an emblem of ➤ St DOROTHY.

In Greek mythology, the **apple of discord** was the golden apple inscribed 'For the fairest,' said to have been thrown by Eris, the personification of discord, into the assembly of the gods, and contended for by Hera, Athene, and Aphrodite. Paris of Troy (see ➤ PARIS¹), chosen by the gods to adjudicate, awarded the apple to Aphrodite; the result was to be the ➤ TROJAN *War*.

In Australia, **Apple Island** is an informal name for Tasmania, because of its popular identification as an apple-growing region.

The apple never falls far from the tree, meaning that salient family characteristics are usually inherited, is a mid 19th-century proverbial saying

The **apple of one's eye** is a person of whom one is extremely fond and proud, originally denoting the pupil of the eye, considered to be a globular solid body, extended as a symbol of something cherished.

A **rotten apple** is a bad person in a group, typically one whose behaviour is likely to have a corrupting influence on the rest; with allusion to the fact that a rotten apple causes other fruit with which it is in contact to rot.

To **upset the apple cart** is to spoil a plan or disturb the status quo; *apple cart* as a metaphor for a satisfactory but possibly precarious state of affairs is recorded in various expressions from the late 18th century onwards.

See also ➤ BIG *Apple*, ➤ BOB *for apples*, ➤ GOLDEN *apple*.

Johnny Appleseed byname for the American nurseryman John Chapman (1774–1845), who sold or gave apple seedlings to pioneers to establish apple trees throughout the midwest; according to legend, *Johnny Appleseed* is a figure who constantly travels planting apple seedlings for others to enjoy.

by appointment indicating that a particular manufacturer holds a Royal Warrant for the supply of goods to the sovereign or a particular member of the royal family.

Appomattox the court house at *Appomattox*, Virginia, was the site on 9 April 1865 of the end of the American Civil War, with the formal surrender of the Confederate forces.

seal of approval an official statement or indication that something is accepted or regarded favourably; **stamp of approval** is also used. The term comes from the practice of putting a stamp (formerly a seal) on official documents.

April the fourth month of the year, in the northern hemisphere usually considered the second month of spring, often referred to allusively as characterized by changeable weather, with sudden showers and sunshine.

April Fool's Day is 1 April, in many Western countries traditionally an occasion for playing tricks. This custom has been observed for hundreds of years, but its origin is unknown. It is also called *All Fools' Day*.

tied to one's mother's apron strings traditional phrase, meaning that a person who should be grown up is still subject to their mother's dominance; from the mid 16th century, an *apron string* as the fastening of an apron has been used to symbolize the role of the mistress of a household.

apse a large semicircular or polygonal recess in a church, arched or with a domed roof and typically at the church's eastern end. Recorded from the early 19th century, the word comes (in the sense 'either of two points on the orbit of a planet or satellite that are nearest to or furthest from the body round which it moves' from *apsis* (denoting in the early 17th century the orbit of a planet), from Greek *apsis, hapsis* 'arch, vault', perhaps from *haptein* 'fasten, join').

Apuleius (born *c*.123 AD), Roman writer, born in Africa. His writings are characterized by an exuberant and bizarre use of language and he is best known for the *Metamorphoses* (*The Golden Ass*), a picaresque novel which recounts the adventures of a man who is transformed into an ass.

Aquarian a member of an early Christian sect using water instead of wine in the Eucharist.

Aquarius in astrology, the eleventh sign of the ➤ ZODIAC, which the sun enters about 21 January. The name is from Latin 'of water', used as a noun to mean 'water carrier'.

The **Age of Aquarius** is an astrological age which is about to begin, marked by the precession of the vernal equinox into Aquarius, believed by some to herald worldwide peace and harmony.

Aquitaine a region and former province of SW France, on the Bay of Biscay, centred on Bordeaux. A province of the Roman Empire and a medieval duchy, it became an English possession by the marriage of Eleanor of Aquitaine to Henry II, and remained so until 1453.

arabesque an ornamental design consisting of intertwined flowing lines, originally meaning 'in the Arab style'.

Arabia a peninsula of SW Asia, largely desert, lying between the Red Sea and the Persian Gulf and bounded on the north by Jordan and Iraq, which is the original homeland of the Arabs and the historic centre of Islam; in literary use, it may be referred to as a rich and distant eastern land (**Araby** is an archaic variant of the name).

An **Arabian bird** is a phoenix, a unique specimen; the phrase comes originally from Shakespeare's *Antony and Cleopatra* (1606–7).

The **Arabian Nights** are a collection of stories and romances written in Arabic. The king of Samarkand has killed all his wives after one night's marriage until he marries ➤ SCHEHERAZADE, who saves her life by entertaining him with stories. The stories include the tales of ➤ ALADDIN and ➤ SINBAD *the Sailor*. The collection is also known as *The Thousand and One Nights*.

Arabic numerals any of the numerals 0, 1, 2, 3, 4, 5, 6, 7, 8, and 9. Arabic numerals reached western Europe (replacing Roman numerals) through Arabia by about AD 1200 but probably originated in India.

Arachne a woman of Colophon in Lydia, a skilful weaver who challenged ➤ ATHENE to a contest. Athene destroyed Arachne's work and Arachne tried to hang herself, but Athene changed her into a spider. The name comes from Greek *arakhnē* 'spider'.

Aragon an autonomous region of NE Spain, bounded on the north by the Pyrenees and on the east by Catalonia and Valencia; capital, Saragossa. Formerly an independent kingdom, which was conquered in the 5th century by the Visigoths and then in the 8th century by the Moors, it was united with Catalonia in 1137 and with Castile in 1479.

Aramaic a branch of the Semitic family of languages, especially the language of Syria used as a lingua franca in the Near East from the 6th century BC, later dividing into varieties one of which included Syriac and Mandaean. It replaced Hebrew locally as the language of the Jews, and though displaced by Arabic in the 7th century AD, it still has about 200,000 speakers in scattered communities.

Aramis name of one of the ➤ THREE *Musketeers* who befriend ➤ D'ARTAGNAN in Dumas' novel.

Aran Islands a group of three islands, Inishmore, Inishmaan, and Inisheer, off the west coast of the Republic of Ireland, traditionally a stronghold of the Gaelic-speaking culture.

Aranyaka each of a set of Hindu sacred treatises based on the Brahmanas, composed in Sanskrit *c*.700 BC. Intended only for initiates, the Aranyakas contain mystical and philosophical material and explications of esoteric rites.

Mount Ararat a pair of volcanic peaks in eastern Turkey, near the borders with Armenia and Iran. The higher peak, which rises to 5,165 m (16,946 ft), is the traditional site of the resting place of Noah's ark after the Flood (Genesis 8:4).

Arawn in Welsh mythology, the king of ➤ ANNWN, the underworld, who was said to have made a friend of ➤ PWYLL, prince of Dyfed, and to have exchanged kingdoms with him for a year.

arbiter elegantiarum a judge of artistic taste and etiquette, a Latin term meaning 'judge of elegance', used by Tacitus to describe ➤ PETRONIUS, arbiter of taste at Nero's court.

Arbor Day a day set apart annually in the US, Australia, New Zealand, and elswhere for the planting of trees.

Arc de Triomphe a ceremonial arch standing at the top of the Champs Élysées in Paris, commissioned by Napoleon to commemorate his victories in 1805–6. Inspired by the Arch of Constantine in Rome, it was completed in 1836. The Unknown Soldier was buried under the centre of the arch on Armistice Day 1920.

Arcadia a mountainous district in the Peloponnese of southern Greece. In poetic fantasy it represents a pastoral paradise the home of song-loving shepherds, and in Greek mythology it is the home of Pan.

Et in Arcadia ego is a Latin phrase, meaning literally 'And I too in Arcadia'; a tomb inscription, of disputed interpretation, often depicted in classical paintings, notably by Poussin in 1655.

arcanum a great secret or mystery; one of the supposed great secrets of nature which alchemists tried to discover. Recorded from the late 16th century, the word represents the use as a noun of the neuter of the Latin adjective *arcanus* 'mysterious, secret', from *arcere* 'to shut up', from *arca* 'chest'.

archangel an angel of greater than ordinary rank; (in traditional Christian angelology) a being of the eighth-highest order of the ninefold celestial hierarchy. The name is recorded from Middle English, and comes via Anglo-Norman French and ecclesiastical Latin, from ecclesiastical Greek *arkhangelos*, from *arkhi-* 'chief' + *angelos* 'messenger, angel'.

the Archers a farming soap opera, which has been broadcasting its 'everyday story of country folk' since 1950, and which was originally conceived as a vehicle by which the Ministry of Agriculture could disseminate information. The story has now covered several generations of the *Archer* family and their neighbours.

archetype an original which has been imitated; (in Jungian theory) a primitive mental image inherited from the earliest human ancestors, and supposed to be present in the collective unconscious.

archeus the immaterial principle supposed by the Paracelsians to govern animal and vegetable life; a vital force. It was believed that the chief *archeus* was situated in the stomach, and that subordinate *archei* regulated the action of other organs.

Archie Bunker a man of similar background and prejudices to *Archie Bunker*, a character in a US television comedy series, *All in the Family*, representing a poorly educated white blue-collar worker with strong racist and sexist prejudices.

Archimedes (*c.*287–212 BC), Greek mathematician and inventor of Syracuse. He is famous for his discovery of **Archimedes' principle**, a law stating that a body totally or partially immersed in a fluid is subject to an upward force equal in magnitude to the weight of fluid it displaces. (See also ➤ EUREKA.)

archon the chief magistrate, or, after the time of ➤ SOLON, each of the nine chief magistrates, of ancient Athens. Recorded from the late 16th century, the word comes from Greek *arkhōn* 'ruler'.

the Forest of Arden the home of the banished Duke in Shakespeare's *As You Like It*; it is often understood as representing the actual forest in Warwickshire called Arden and

referred to in romance literature, but is actually based on the forest of the Ardennes in the Low Countries (now Belgium).

are you now or have you ever been a member of the Communist Party? formal question put to those appearing before the Committee on UnAmerican Activities during the McCarthy campaign of 1950–4 against alleged Communists in the US government and other institutions; the allusive form *are you now or have you ever been?* derives from this.

are you sitting comfortably? Then we'll begin introduction to stories on *Listen with Mother*, BBC radio programme for small children, 1950–82.

Areopagus (in ancient Athens) a hill on which was sited the highest governmental council and later a judicial court. The name comes from Greek *Areios pagos* 'hill of Ares'; the name for the site came to denote the court itself.
   Areopagitica, the title of Milton's pamphlet on the freedom of the press published in 1644, derives from this name. The publication was partly inspired by attempts by Parliament to suppress Milton's own pamphlet on divorce.

Ares in Greek mythology, the war god, son of Zeus and Hera; his Roman equivalent is ➤ MARS.

Arethusa the nymph with whom ➤ ALPHEUS fell in love, and who was turned into a fountain in her attempt to escape him.

argent silver as a heraldic tincture. Recorded from late Middle English (denoting silver coins), the word comes via Old French from Latin *argentum* 'silver'.

Argo in Greek mythology, the ship in which Jason and his companions, the **Argonauts**, sailed in the quest for the Golden Fleece. Their story is one of the oldest Greek sagas, known to Homer, and may reflect early explorations in the Black Sea.

Argos a city in the NE Peloponnese of Greece. One of the oldest cities of ancient Greece, it dominated the Peloponnese and the western Aegean in the 7th century BC. **Argive**, a citizen of Argos, is used especially by Homer to mean Greek.

argosy in poetic and literary use, a large merchant ship, originally one from ➤ RAGUSA or Venice. Recorded from the late 16th century, the word apparently comes from Italian *Ragusea (nave)* '(vessel of) Ragusa'.

argument from design in Christian theology, the argument that God's existence is demonstrable from the evidence of design in the universe.

Argus in Greek mythology, a vigilant watchman with a hundred eyes, who was set by Hera to watch ➤ Io, and who was killed by Hermes. After his death, his eyes were said to have been transferred by Hera to the eyelike markings on the tail of a peacock. The term **Argus-eyed** is used to mean extremely vigilant, sharp-sighted.

Ariadne in Greek mythology, the daughter of King Minos of Crete and Pasiphaë. She helped ➤ THESEUS to escape from the Minotaur's labyrinth by giving him a ball of thread, which he unravelled as he went in and used to trace his way out again after killing the Minotaur. They fled together but he deserted her on the island of Naxos.

Arianism in Christian theology, the main heresy denying the divinity of Christ, originating with the Alexandrian priest *Arius* (*c*.250–*c*.336). Arianism maintained that the son of God was created by the Father and was therefore neither coeternal nor consubstantial with the Father. It retained a foothold among Germanic peoples until the conversion of the Franks to Catholicism (496).

Ariel the name of a fairy in Shakespeare's *The Tempest*, who has been rescued from the enchantment of the witch Sycorax by ➤ PROSPERO and who must serve his new master until he is released; Ariel is the airy spirit who contrasts with the gross and animal ➤ CALIBAN.

The name was given to a satellite of Uranus discovered in 1851, the twelfth closest to the planet and the fourth largest (diameter 1,160 km), and subsequently to a series of six American and British satellites devoted to studies of the ionosphere and X-ray astronomy (1962–79).

Aries a small constellation (the Ram), said to represent the ram whose Golden Fleece was sought by Jason and the Argonauts; in astrology, the first sign of the zodiac, which the sun enters at the vernal equinox (about 20 March).

Arimasp any of a mythical race of one-eyed men in northern Europe who tried to take gold guarded by griffins; the name comes via

Latin from Greek, and is said to mean in Scythian 'one-eyed'.

Ludovico Ariosto (1474–1533), Italian poet. His *Orlando Furioso* (final version 1532), about the exploits of Roland (Orlando) and other knights of Charlemagne, was the greatest of the Italian romantic epics; Spenser used its narrative form as a model for his *Faerie Queene*.

In *Childe Harold*, **Ariosto of the North** is Byron's name for Scott.

Aristides an Athenian statesman and general of the 5th century BC, known as **Aristides the Just**. He commanded the Athenian army at the battle of Plataea, but came into conflict with ➤ THEMISTOCLES and was ostracized.

Aristophanes (*c*.450–*c*.385 BC), Greek comic dramatist. His surviving plays are characterized by exuberant language and the satirization of leading contemporary figures.

Aristotelian logic the traditional system of logic expounded by Aristotle and developed in the Middle Ages, concerned chiefly with deductive reasoning as expressed in syllogisms.

Aristotle (384–322 BC), Greek philosopher and scientist. A pupil of Plato and tutor to Alexander the Great, he founded a school (the Lyceum) outside Athens. He is one of the most influential thinkers in the history of Western thought and his work was central to Arabic and medieval philosophy. His surviving works cover a vast range of subjects, including logic, ethics, metaphysics, politics, natural science, and physics.

Aristotle's lantern is a conical structure of calcareous plates and muscles supporting the rasping teeth of a sea urchin. The term derives from Aristotle's *Historia Animalium*, where the body of the echinus is said to be shaped like the frame of a lantern.

arithmetic the branch of mathematics dealing with the properties and manipulation of numbers. The term comes (in Middle English, via Old French and Latin) from Greek *arithmētikē (tekhnē)* '(art) of counting', from *arithmos* 'number'. Early forms such as *arsmetrike* were influenced by Latin *ars metrica* 'measuring art'.

In the Middle Ages, arithmetic was counted as one of the ➤ SEVEN *liberal arts*, and was one of the subjects of the ➤ QUADRIVIUM.

Arjuna a Kshatriya prince in the Mahabharata, one of the two main characters in the

Bhagavadgita, the charioteer to whom Krishna gives counsel during the battle.

ark a chest or coffer, especially (more fully the **Ark of the Covenant**) the wooden chest which contained the tablets of the laws of the ancient Israelites. Carried by the Israelites on their wanderings in the wilderness, it was cherished by them in the Promised Land; its temporary loss to the Philistines (1 Samuel 4) caused Eli's daughter-in-law to name her son ➤ Ichabod. The Ark was later placed by Solomon in the Temple at Jerusalem, but was lost when Nebuchadnezzar's forces destroyed the Temple in 586 BC. The phrases **lay hands on the ark**, **touch the ark**, mean treat irreverently what is held to be sacred.

In the Bible, the **ark** is the floating covered vessel built by Noah to save his family and two of every kind of animal from the Flood; ➤ Noah's ark. The informal phrase **have come out of the ark** means be very antiquated.

Arlington National Cemetery the American national burial ground in Arlington County, Virginia, which is the resting place of important soldiers and statesman.

the Armada a Spanish naval invasion force sent against England in 1588 by Philip II of Spain. It was defeated by the English fleet and almost completely destroyed by storms off the Hebrides. The word *armada* comes (in the mid 16th century, meaning 'a fleet of warships') via Spanish and ultimately from Latin *armare* 'to arm'.

Armageddon (in the New Testament) the last battle between good and evil before the Day of Judgement; the place where this will be fought. In extended usage, *Armageddon* means a dramatic and catastrophic conflict, especially one seen as likely to destroy the world or the human race.

The name is Greek, and comes from Hebrew *har mĕgiddōn* 'hill of Megiddo'.

armchair critic one whose views are based on theorizing rather than first-hand experience; *armchair* in this sense is recorded from the 19th century.

armed at all points prepared in every particular; the expression is recorded from late Middle English, but often refers directly to a First Folio variant reading of Shakespeare's *Hamlet*.

Armenian Church an independent Christian Church established in Armenia since

c.300 and influenced by Roman and Byzantine as well as Syrian traditions. A small Armenian Catholic Church also exists (see ➤ Uniate).

Arminian an adherent of the doctrines of Jacobus Arminius (Latinized name of Jakob Hermandszoon, 1560–1609), a Dutch Protestant theologian who rejected the Calvinist doctrine of predestination. His teachings had a considerable influence on Methodism.

Armistice Day the anniversary of the armistice of 11 November 1918, now replaced by Remembrance Sunday in the UK and Veterans Day in the US.

Armorica an ancient region of NW France between the Seine and the Loire, equating to modern Brittany.

an army marches on its stomach proverbial saying, mid 19th century, asserting the importance of proper provisioning for troops; variously attributed to Frederick the Great and Napoleon.

Arnhem a town in the eastern Netherlands, situated on the River Rhine. During the Second World War, in September 1944, Allied airborne troops made a landing nearby but were overwhelmed by German forces (see also ➤ a bridge too far).

arrows *arrows* are the emblem of ➤ St Edmund the Martyr and of ➤ St Sebastian.

be art and part in be an accessory or participant in (by *art* in contriving or *part* in executing).

art deco the predominant decorative art style of the 1920s and 1930s, characterized by precise and boldly delineated geometric shapes and strong colours.

art for art's sake the idea that a work has no purpose beyond itself; the slogan of aestheticians holding that the chief or only aim of a work of art is the self-expression of the individual artist who creates it.

art is long, life is short there is so much knowledge to acquire that a lifetime is not sufficient; proverbial saying, late 14th century; originally from the Greek physician Hippocrates (c.460–357 BC).

art nouveau a style of decorative art, architecture, and design prominent in western Europe and the US from about 1890 until the

First World War and characterized by intricate linear designs and flowing curves based on natural forms.

Artemis in Greek mythology, a goddess, daughter of Zeus and sister of ➤ APOLLO. She was a huntress and is typically depicted with a bow and arrows, and was also identified with Selene, goddess of the moon; her Roman equivalent is ➤ DIANA.

the Artesian State an informal name for South Dakota.

the Artful Dodger nickname of Jack Dawkins, a leading member of Fagin's gang of child pickpockets in Dickens's *Oliver Twist*.

Arthur a legendary king of Britain, historically perhaps a 5th or 6th century Romano-British chieftain or general. Stories of his life, his court at Camelot, the exploits of his knights such as Lancelot and the quest for the Holy Grail, were developed by Malory, Chrétien de Troyes, and other medieval writers.

According to the traditional stories Arthur, son of Uther Pendragon, was brought up in ignorance of his birth, but proved his identity as the king's son when he pulled the sword (➤ EXCALIBUR) from the stone. Guided by ➤ MERLIN, he ruled Britain wisely, but in the end his leadership was fatally weakened by the adulterous love of his wife Guinevere and friend Lancelot, and Arthur himself was forced to fight a last battle against his nephew ➤ MORDRED and his supporters. Fatally wounded, he was taken by barge to ➤ AVALON, so that his body was never found; he is thus one of the legendary heroes who may return to his kingdom should the need arise.

Arthur's Seat is a hill overlooking Edinburgh from the east, traditionally associated with Arthur.

an article of faith a firmly held belief; *article* here used in the sense of 'a statement or item in a summary of religious belief'.

the Articles of War regulations made for the government of the military and naval forces of Great Britain and the United States; the term is recorded from the early 18th century.

artificial intelligence the theory and development of computer systems able to perform tasks normally requiring human intelligence, such as visual perception, speech recognition, decision-making, and translation between languages.

Arts and Crafts Movement an English decorative arts movement of the second half of the 19th century which sought to revive the ideal of craftsmanship in an age of increasing mechanization and mass production. William Morris was its most prominent member.

Aryan relating to or denoting a people speaking an Indo-European language who invaded northern India in the 2nd millennium BC; (in Nazi ideology) relating to or denoting people of Caucasian race not of Jewish descent. The idea that there was an 'Aryan' race corresponding to the parent Indo-European language was proposed by certain 19th-century writers, and was taken up by Hitler and other proponents of racist ideology, but it has been generally rejected by scholars.

Ascalon the ancient Greek name for *Ashqelon*, an ancient Mediterranean city, situated to the south of modern Tel Aviv, in Israel. A Philistine city state from the 12th to the 8th century BC, it was conquered by Alexander the Great in 332 BC.

Ascension in Christian belief, the ascent of Christ into heaven on the fortieth day after the Resurrection. **Ascension Day** is the Thursday 40 days after Easter, on which Christ's Ascension is celebrated in the Christian Church. **Ascensiontide** is the ten-day period between Ascension Day and the eve of Pentecost.

asceticism the practice of severe self-discipline and abstention from all forms of indulgence, typically for religious reasons. The term comes (in the mid 17th century, via medieval Latin or Greek) from Greek *askētēs* 'monk', from *askein* 'to exercise'.

Asclepius in Greek mythology, a hero and god of healing, son of Apollo, often represented bearing a staff with a serpent coiled round it. He sometimes bears a scroll or tablet, probably representing medical learning.

Ascot a town in southern England, southwest of Windsor. Its racecourse is the site of an annual race meeting (**Ascot week**) founded by Queen Anne in 1711 (see also ➤ ROYAL *Ascot*).

Asgard in Scandinavian mythology, a region in the centre of the universe, inhabited by the gods.

ash a tree, from whose wood spear-shafts were traditionally made, which has given its name to an Old English runic letter, ᚠ, so named from the word of which it was the first letter.

Ash Wednesday the first day of Lent in the Western Christian Church, marked by services of penitence, and so named from the custom of marking the foreheads of penitents with ➤ ASHES on that day.

Asher (in the Bible) a Hebrew patriarch, son of Jacob and Zilpah (Genesis 30:12, 13); the tribe of Israel traditionally descended from him.

Asherah a Canaanitish goddess; a tree-trunk or wooden post symbolizing this goddess, found in high places devoted to the worship of ➤ BAAL.

ashes often taken as a symbol of mourning or penitence (as in ➤ SACKCLOTH *and ashes*).
   The Ashes is a trophy for the winner of a series of test matches in a cricket season between England and Australia. The name comes from a mock obituary notice published in the *Sporting Times* (2 September 1882), with reference to the symbolical remains of English cricket being taken to Australia after a sensational victory by the Australians at the Oval.
   Ashes to ashes, dust to dust is a phrase from the burial service in the *Book of Common Prayer*, 'we therefore commit his body to the ground, earth to earth, ashes to ashes, dust to dust; in sure and certain hope of the Resurrection to eternal life.'
   To **turn to ashes in one's mouth** is to become a bitter disappointment; the allusion is to ➤ DEAD SEA *fruit*.
   See also ➤ DUST *and ashes*, ➤ RISE *from the ashes*.

Ashkenazi a Jew of central or eastern European descent. The Ashkenazim became established in the Frankish and other Germanic-speaking kingdoms in the early Middle Ages; subsequently large groups migrated from France and Germany to the Slavic countries from the 12th century onwards.

Ashmolean Museum a museum of art and antiquities in Oxford, founded by the English antiquary Elias *Ashmole* (1617–92), who presented his collection of rarities to Oxford University in 1677 as the nucleus of the museum. It opened in 1683 and was the first public institution of its kind in England.

ashrama in Hinduism, any of the four stages of an ideal life, ascending from the status of pupil to the total renunciation of the world.

Ashtaroth biblical name for the Canaanite goddess ➤ ASTARTE.

Ashura the tenth of Muharram, celebrated as a holy day by Sunni Muslims and as a day of mourning (the anniversary of the death of Husain) by Shiite Muslims.

Aslan name of the lion who is the central character of C. S. Lewis's ➤ NARNIA chronicles, and whose death and resurrection in the first book reflects the Christian theme of the series.

Asmodeus a demon in the apocryphal book of ➤ TOBIT, who has killed the former husbands of Sara on their wedding-nights.

Asoka emperor of India *c.*269–232 BC, who was converted to Buddhism and established it as the state religion.
   The **Asoka pillar** is a pillar with four lions on the capital, built by the Emperor *Asoka* at Sarnath in Uttar Pradesh to mark the spot where the Buddha publicly preached his doctrine, and adopted as a symbol by the government of India.

asp another name for the Egyptian cobra; it is particularly associated with ➤ CLEOPATRA, who is said to have committed suicide by allowing herself to be bitten by an asp, and has become a type of venomous poison.

Aspasia a Greek courtesan, lover of ➤ PERICLES and noted for her intellect and supposed political influence.

aspen a poplar tree with leaves that tremble in the breeze, supposedly from shame because the Cross was made from its wood.

asperges the rite of sprinkling holy water at the beginning of the Mass, still used occasionally in Catholic churches. The term comes (in the late 16th century) from the first word of the Latin text of Psalms 50(51):9 (literally 'thou shalt purge'), recited before mass during the sprinkling of holy water.

asphodel an everlasting flower said to grow in the ➤ ELYSIAN *fields*. The name is recorded from late Middle English and comes via Latin from the Greek base of ➤ DAFFODIL.

aspidistra as a house plant taken as typifying middle-class gentility and conventionality, particularly with reference to the title of

George Orwell's novel *Keep the Aspidistra Flying* (1936).

ass a donkey, proverbially taken as a type of patience and stupidity.

The epithet **ass-eared** was applied to ➤ MIDAS after he had unwisely given judgement against Apollo in a contest of flute-playing.

An **ass in a lion's skin** is a foolish or cowardly person who adopts a heroic pose or appearance; the allusion is to a fable in which a donkey dresses up in the skin of a lion to appear terrible.

Assassins the Nizari branch of Ismaili Muslims at the time of the Crusades, renowned as militant fanatics and popularly supposed to use hashish before going on murder missions. The name comes (in the mid 16th century, from French or medieval Latin) from Arabic *ḥašīšī* 'hashish-eater'.

assault and battery in law, the action of threatening a person together with the action of making physical contact with them.

assay the testing of a metal or ore to determine its ingredients and quality. The word is recorded from Middle English, in the general sense 'testing, or a test of, the merit of someone or something', and comes ultimately from Old French *essai* 'trial'.

In the UK, the **assay office** is an institution authorized to award hallmarks to articles made from precious metals. There are currently four in Britain, at London, Birmingham, Sheffield, and Edinburgh.

Assisi a town in the province of Umbria in central Italy, famous as the birthplace of ➤ St FRANCIS, whose tomb is located there.

Assumption the reception of the Virgin Mary bodily into heaven, formally declared a doctrine of the Roman Catholic Church in 1950. The **Feast of the Assumption** is celebrated in the Roman Catholic Church on 15 August.

Assyria an ancient country in what is now northern Iraq, and which from the early part of the 2nd millennium BC was the centre of a succession of empires; it was at its peak in the 8th and late 7th centuries BC, when its rule stretched from the Persian Gulf to Egypt. It fell in 612 BC to a coalition of Medes and Babylonians.

Astarte a Phoenician goddess of fertility and sexual love who corresponds to the Babylonian and Assyrian goddess Ishtar and who became identified with the Egyptian Isis, the Greek Aphrodite, and others. In the Bible she is referred to as *Ashtaroth* or Ashtoreth and her worship is linked with that of Baal.

asterisk a symbol (*) used to mark printed or written text, typically as a reference to an annotation or to stand for omitted matter. The word comes (in late Middle English) via late Latin from Greek *asteriskos* 'small star'.

Astérix hero of a French comic cartoon, created by the French writer René Goscinny (1924–77) with the illustrator Albert Uderzo, set in Gaul at the time of the Gallic wars; Astérix and his friend Obélix belong to the only tribe unconquered by the Romans.

Astley's Amphitheatre a theatrical entertainment, regarded as the first modern circus, founded in London in 1770 by the English theatrical manager and former soldier Philip Astley (1742–1814), who as an equestrian performer was initially the only performer; by 1798 he was allowed to name his now fashionable establishment Astley's Royal Amphitheatre.

Astolat in the Arthurian Romances, the site of ➤ LANCELOT's meeting with ➤ ELAINE; according to Malory's *Morte D'Arthur*, it is to be identified with Guildford in Surrey.

Astraea a Roman goddess associated with justice, said to have been the last deity to leave the earth, who having lived among humankind during the Golden Age and in retreat in the mountains during the Silver Age, finally left the world for heaven during the evils of the Bronze Age. Her name, which means 'starry maiden', was later used as an epithet of Elizabeth I.

astral of or relating to a supposed non-physical realm of existence to which various psychic and paranormal phenomena are ascribed, and in which the physical human body is said to have a counterpart. The word comes (in the early 17th century) from Latin *astralis*, from *astrum* 'star'.

astrolabe an instrument used to make astronomical measurements, typically of the altitudes of celestial bodies, and in navigation for calculating latitude, before the development of the sextant. In its basic form (known from classical times) it consists of a disc with the edge marked in degrees and a pivoted pointer. Recorded from late Middle English, the word comes ultimately (via Old

French and medieval Latin) from Greek *astrolabos* 'star-taking'.

astrology the study of movements and relative positions of celestial bodies interpreted as having an influence on human affairs and the natural world. Ancient observers of the heavens developed elaborate systems of explanation based on the movements of the sun, moon, and planets through the constellations of the zodiac, for predicting events and for casting horoscopes. By 1700 astrology had lost intellectual credibility in the West, but continued to have popular appeal. Modern astrology is based on that of the Greeks, but other systems are extant, e.g. that of China.

The term (in full **natural astrology**) originally denoted the practical uses of astronomy, applied in the measurement of time and the prediction of natural phenomena. The commonest sense today (in full **judicial astrology**, relating to human affairs) dates from the mid 16th century.

The word is recorded from late Middle English, and comes ultimately (via Old French and Latin) from Greek *astron* 'star'.

Astrophel name adopted by Philip Sidney in his sonnet sequence *Astrophel and Stella*; the name means 'star-lover', and the poems give the course of his unhappy love for Stella (the 'star', modelled on Penelope Rich).

Astur in Macaulay's *Lays of Ancient Rome*, one of the chieftains who joins ➤ Lars PORSENA and Sextus in their attack on Rome; although fighting for a discredited cause, he is seen as a figure of martial valour and dignity.

asymmetrical warfare involving subversive attack by small, highly-organized groups on a nation with highly developed forms of technological defence; in 2001, the term was used in discussions of the terrorist destruction of the World Trade Center in New York.

Atahualpa (*c.*1502–33), last Inca ruler, put to death by the Spanish conquistador Francisco Pizarro.

Atalanta in Greek mythology, a huntress who would marry only someone who could beat her in a foot race. She was beaten when a suitor threw down three golden apples which she stopped to pick up.

Atargatis in Assyrian mythology, a fertility goddess, resembling ➤ ASTARTE, and shown as half-fish, half-woman.

Ate infatuation, rashness; personified by the Greeks as a destructive goddess.

Aten in Egyptian mythology, the sun or solar disc, the deity of a strong monotheistic cult, particularly during the reign of ➤ AKHENATEN.

St Athanasius (*c.*296–373), Greek theologian and upholder of Christian orthodoxy against ➤ ARIANISM. He aided the ascetic movement in Egypt and introduced knowledge of monasticism to the West. His feast day is 2 May.

The **Athanasian Creed** is a summary of Christian doctrine formerly attributed to St Athanasius, but probably dating from the 5th century. It is included in the *Book of Common Prayer* for use at morning prayer on certain occasions.

Atharva Veda a collection of hymns and ritual utterances in early Sanskrit, added at a later stage to the existing Veda material. The name comes from Sanskrit *Atharvan* (the name of Brahma's eldest son, said to be the author of the collection) + *veda* '(sacred) knowledge'.

atheism the theory or belief that God does not exist. The word comes (in the late 16th century, via French) from Greek *atheos*, from *a-* 'without' + *theos* 'god'.

atheling a prince or lord in Anglo-Saxon England. Recorded from Old English (in the form *ætheling*) the word is of West Germanic origin, from a base meaning 'race, family'.

Athelstan (895–939), king of England 925–39. Athelstan came to the thrones of Wessex and Mercia in 924 before effectively becoming the first king of all England. He successfully invaded both Scotland and Wales and inflicted a heavy defeat on an invading Danish army.

Athene in Greek mythology, the patron goddess of Athens, typically allegorized into a personification of wisdom. Her statues show her as female but fully armed, and in classical times the owl is regularly associated with her. The principal story concerning her is that she sprang, fully armed and uttering her war cry, from the head of Zeus. She is also called ➤ PALLAS. Her Roman equivalent is ➤ MINERVA.

The **Athenaeum** was originally the temple of the goddess Athene in ancient Athens, which was used for teaching; the term is used in the names of libraries or institutions for literary or scientific study, especially in *the Athenaeum*, a London club founded in 1824, originally for men of distinction in literature, art, and learning.

Athens the capital of Greece, originally a flourishing city state of ancient Greece, which was an important cultural centre in the 5th century BC.

The **Athens of America** is a name for Boston, and the **Athens of the North** a name for Edinburgh.

Athos name of the eldest and most serious of the ► THREE *Musketeers* who befriend ►D'ARTAGNAN in Dumas' novel; it is revealed that the murderous agent of Cardinal Richelieu whom they eventually defeat is his estranged and treacherous wife.

Mount Athos a narrow, mountainous peninsula in NE Greece, projecting into the Aegean Sea. It is inhabited by monks of the Orthodox Church, who forbid women and even female animals to set foot on the peninsula.

Atlanta the state capital of Georgia, which during the Civil War was a Confederate stronghold. Its loss in 1864 to the Union forces under Sherman after a long siege was a turning point in the Civil War.

atlantes stone carvings of male figures, used as columns to support the entablature of a Greek or Greek-style building; the word is the plural form of Greek *atlas* (see ►ATLAS).

Atlantic The name of the ocean comes (in late Middle English) via Latin from Greek, from *Atlas, Atlant-*. It originally referred to Mount *Atlas* in Libya, hence to the sea near the west African coast, later extended to the whole ocean. The **Battle of the Atlantic** was a succession of sea operations during the Second World War in which Axis naval and air forces attempted to destroy ships carrying supplies from North America to the UK.

The **Atlantic Charter** is a declaration of eight common principles in international relations drawn up by Churchill and Roosevelt in August 1941. The charter, which stipulated freely chosen governments, free trade, freedom of the seas, and disarmament of current aggressor states, and condemned territorial changes made against the wishes of local populations, provided the ideological basis for the United Nations organization.

Atlantis a legendary island, beautiful and prosperous, which was overwhelmed by the sea. As described by Plato, Atlantis was west of the Pillars of Hercules and ruled part of Europe and Africa.

Atlas in Greek mythology, a Titan who was punished for his part in the revolt against Zeus by being made to support the heavens (a popular explanation of why the sky does not fall). He became identified with the Atlas Mountains. According to a later story Perseus, with the aid of Medusa's head, turned Atlas into a mountain.

The word *atlas* to designate a collection of maps in a volume, is said to be derived from a representation of Atlas supporting the heavens placed as a frontispiece to early works of this kind, and to have been first used by the Flemish cartographer Gerard Mercator in the 16th century.

Charles Atlas (1893–1972), American bodybuilder, creator of a highly successful mail-order bodybuilding course.

Atli in Norse legend, the king of the Huns, who marries the Niblung princess Gudrun; she allows him to kill her brothers, Gunnar and Hogni, in revenge for their murder of her husband ► SIGURD, but finally kills Atli herself. Atli represents the historical ► ATTILA; his Germanic equivalent in the *Nibelungenlied* is *Etzel*.

atman in Hindu philosophy, the spiritual life principle of the universe, especially when regarded as immanent in the real self of the individual. Various strands in Hindu thought differ in the way they regard the relationship (or identity) of the individual atman or 'self' and the universal Atman.

The word comes from Sanskrit *ātman*, literally 'essence, breath'.

atomic theory the theory that all matter is made up of tiny indivisible particles or atoms, which in ancient times was taught notably by Democritus and Epicurus. According to the modern version, the atoms of each element are effectively identical, but differ from those of other elements, and unite to form compounds in fixed proportions.

atonement reparation, in Christian belief the reconciliation of God and mankind through Jesus Christ. The word comes (in the early 16th century, denoting unity or reconciliation, especially between God and man), from *at one* + the suffix *-ment*, influenced by medieval Latin *adunamentum* 'unity', and earlier *onement* from an obsolete verb *one* 'to unite'.

The **Day of Atonement** is another term for
➤ Yom *Kippur*.

Atreus in Greek legend, the son of ➤ Pelops
and father of ➤ Agamemnon and Menelaus.
He quarrelled with his brother Thyestes and
invited him to a banquet at which he served
up the flesh of Thyestes' own children; the
resultant curse on the house of Atreus would
in time bring about the murder of his own
son.

Atropos in Greek mythology, one of the
three ➤ Fates; her name means literally 'inflexible', and her role was to cut the thread of
life spun and measured by her sisters.

Attalid a member of a Hellenistic dynasty
named after *Attalus I* (reigned 241–197 BC),
which flourished in the 3rd and 2nd centuries BC. The Attalid kings established their
capital, Pergamum, as a leading cultural centre of the Greek world.

Attic the dialect of Greek used by the ancient Athenians, which was the chief literary
form of classical Greek. The word is late 16th
century, and comes from Greek *Attikos*.
    Attic salt is refined, delicate, poignant wit;
recorded from the mid 18th century, the
phrase is a translation of Latin *sal Atticum*.

Atticus name given to the Roman writer
and businessman Titus Pomponius (110–32
BC), friend and correspondent of ➤ Cicero;
the name *Atticus* reflected his long residence
in Athens.

Attila (406–53), king of the Huns 434–53. He
ravaged vast areas between the Rhine and
the Caspian Sea, inflicting great devastation
on the eastern Roman Empire, before being
defeated by the joint forces of the Roman
army and the Visigoths at Châlons in 451. He
was called the *Scourge of God* (translating
Latin *flagellum Dei*) by medieval chroniclers.
    The **Attila Line** is the boundary separating
Greek and Turkish-occupied Cyprus, named
after the **Attila Plan**, a secret Turkish plan of
1964 to partition the country.

Attis in Anatolian mythology, the youthful
consort of ➤ Cybele. His death (after castrat-
ing himself) and resurrection were associated with the spring festival and with a
sacrifice for the crops; his symbol was the
pine tree.

John Aubrey (1626–97), English antiquarian and author, chiefly remembered for *Brief
Lives*, a collection of biographies of eminent

people (a bowdlerized edition was first published in 1813).

Sweet Auburn the ideal village, recalled
in Goldsmith's *The Deserted Village* (1770), de-
populated as a result of the growth of trade
and the decline of the countryside.

Augean stables in Greek mythology, vast
stables (belonging to King *Augeas*) which had
never been cleaned; this was achieved (as the
sixth of his Labours) by ➤ Hercules, who
cleaned them in a day by diverting the River
Alpheus to flow through them. The term is
often used figuratively to refer to corruption
or waste developed over a long period.

Augsburg Confession a statement of the
Lutheran position, drawn up mainly by
Melancthon and approved by Luther before
being presented to the Emperor Charles V at
Augsburg on 25 June 1530.

augur in ancient Rome a religious official
who observed natural signs, especially the
behaviour of birds, interpreting these as an
indication of divine approval or disapproval.
    Recorded from late Middle English, the
word comes from Latin, meaning 'diviner'.

August the eighth month of the year. Recorded from Old English, the name comes
from Latin *augustus* 'consecrated, venerable';
named after ➤ Augustus Caesar, the first
Roman emperor.

Augustan connected with or occurring
during the reign of the Roman emperor Augustus; especially, relating to or denoting
Latin literature of this period, including the
works of Virgil, Horace, Ovid, and Livy.
    Augustan in a literary sense also means re-
lating to or denoting 17th- and 18th-century
English literature of a style considered refined and classical, including the works of
Pope, Addison, and Swift.

St Augustine of Canterbury (d. *c.*604),
Italian churchman. Sent from Rome by Pope
Gregory the Great to refound the Church in
England in 597, he was favourably received
by King Ethelbert, who was afterwards converted, founded a monastery at Canterbury
and became its first bishop, but failed to
reach agreement with the existing Celtic
Church over questions of discipline and practice. His feast day is 26 May.

St Augustine of Hippo (354–430), Doctor
of the Church; his early life was marked by a
series of spiritual crises, and he is known for
a famous prayer in his *Confessions*, 'Give me

chastity and continency—but not yet.' Augustine was baptized by St Ambrose in 386 and henceforth lived a monastic life. He became bishop of Hippo in North Africa in 396. His writings, such as *Confessions* and the *City of God*, dominated subsequent Western theology. His feast day is 28 August.

The **Augustinians** are a religious order observing a rule derived from the writings of St Augustine.

Augustus (63 BC–AD 14), the first Roman emperor; also called (until 27 BC) *Octavian*. He was adopted by the will of his great-uncle ➤ JULIUS *Caesar* and gained supreme power by his defeat of ➤ MARK *Antony* in 31 BC. In 27 BC he was given the title *Augustus* ('venerable') and became in effect the first Roman emperor.

auld the Scottish form of *old*.

The **Auld Alliance** is an informal term for the political relationship of France and Scotland between the 14th and the 16th century.

Auld lang syne is a Scottish phrase meaning times long past. The phrase was popularized as the title and refrain of a song by Robert Burns (1788), now traditionally sung on New Year's Eve.

Auld Reekie is an informal name for Edinburgh, recorded from the early 19th century and meaning literally 'Old Smoky'.

Aulis the port in Boeotia where Agamemnon offered his daughter ➤ IPHIGENIA as a sacrifice to Artemis when the Greek fleet was becalmed on the way to Troy.

Aunt Edna Terence Rattigan's name for a typical female theatregoer of conventional tastes, 'a nice respectable, middle-class, middle-aged, maiden lady, with time on her hands and the money to help her pass it.'

Aunt Sally a game in which players throw sticks or balls at a wooden dummy; in figurative usage, a person or thing subjected to much criticism, especially one set up as an easy target for it.

Auntie an informal term for the BBC regarded as a conservative institution.

Aurangzeb (1618–1707), Mogul emperor of Hindustan 1658–1707, who increased the Mogul empire to its greatest extent, and who assumed the title *Alamgir* ('Conqueror of the World'). His reign was a period of great wealth and splendour, but rebellions and wars weakened the empire and it declined sharply after his death.

Marcus Aurelius (121–80), Roman emperor 161–80. The adopted successor of Antoninus Pius, he was occupied for much of his reign with wars against invading Germanic tribes. His *Meditations*, a collection of aphorisms and reflections, are evidence of his philosophical nature.

aureole a circle of light or brightness depicted in art around the head or body of a person represented as holy.

aurochs a large wild Eurasian ox that was the ancestor of domestic cattle. It was probably exterminated in Britain in the Bronze Age, and the last one was killed in Poland in 1627.

Aurora in Roman mythology, the goddess of the dawn, equivalent of the Greek ➤ EOS. Most of the stories about her tell of handsome men being kidnapped to live with her.

From the early 18th century, *aurora* has been used to designate a natural electrical phenomenon characterized by the appearance of streamers of reddish or greenish light in the sky, especially near the northern or southern magnetic pole. The effect is caused by the interaction of charged particles from the sun with atoms in the upper atmosphere. In northern and southern regions it is respectively called **aurora borealis** or **northern lights** and aurora australis or **southern lights**.

Auschwitz a Nazi concentration camp in the Second World War, near the town of Oświęcim (Auschwitz) in Poland. It may be referred to as a symbol of the Holocaust.

auspices originally, the observation of bird-flight in divination; later, a divine or prophetic token. In ancient Rome, an *auspex* (from Latin *avis* 'bird' + *-specere* 'to look') observed the flight of birds to take omens for the guidance of affairs; a flight of birds was the omen which established ➤ ROMULUS rather than his brother Remus as king.

Auster in Latin writing, the south wind.

Battle of Austerlitz a battle in 1805 near the town of Austerlitz (now in the Czech Republic), in which Napoleon defeated the Austrians and Russians.

Australia Day a national public holiday in Australia, commemorating the founding on 26 January 1788 of the colony of New South Wales.

War of the Austrian Succession a group of several related conflicts (1740–8), involving most of the states of Europe, that were triggered by the death of the Emperor Charles VI and the accession of his daughter ➤ MARIA *Theresa* in 1740 to the Austrian throne.

Authorized Version an English translation of the Bible made in 1611 at the order of James I and still widely used, though never formally 'authorized'. Also called the *King James Bible.*

auto-da-fé the burning of a heretic by the Spanish Inquisition; the phrase is recorded in English from the early 18th century, and comes from Portuguese, literally 'act of faith'.

Autolycus in Greek mythology, a notable thief who was a son of Hermes, and who stole his neighbours' flocks and concealed them among his own animals.
    In Shakespeare's *The Winter's Tale*, the pedlar and petty thief *Autolycus* describes himself as a 'snapper up of unconsidered trifles'.

autumn the season after summer and before winter, when crops and fruits are gathered and leaves fall, in the northern hemisphere from September to November and in the southern hemisphere from March to May. The name is recorded from late Middle English, and comes ultimately (perhaps via Old French) from Latin *autumnus.*

Avalon in Arthurian legend, the place to which Arthur was conveyed after death; in Welsh mythology, the kingdom of the dead.

Avar a member of a nomadic equestrian people from central Asia who built up a large kingdom in SE Europe from the 6th century but were conquered by Charlemagne (791–9).

avatar in Hindu belief, a manifestation of a deity or released soul in bodily form on earth; an incarnate divine teacher. The word comes from Sanskrit *avatāra* 'descent'.

ave Latin greeting, meaning 'hail, be well'. According to Suetonius' *Lives of the Caesars*, gladiators in the arena saluted the Roman emperor with the words, '*Ave Caesar, morituri te salutant* [Hail Caesar, those who are about to die salute you].'
    Ave atque vale is Latin for 'hail and farewell!'
    Ave Maria is a Latin prayer to the Virgin Mary used in Catholic worship. The first line is adapted from Luke 1:28; the second was added in the Middle Ages. The name comes from the opening words, literally 'hail, Mary!'

Avebury a village in Wiltshire, site of one of Britain's major henge monuments of the late Neolithic period. The monument consists of a bank and ditch containing the largest known stone circle, with two smaller circles and other stone settings within it. It is the centre of a complex ritual landscape that also contains a stone avenue, chambered tombs, ➤ SILBURY *Hill*, and various other monuments.

Avernus a lake near Naples in Italy, which fills the crater of an extinct volcano, described by Virgil and other Latin writers as the entrance to the underworld; *Avernus* may also be used for the underworld itself. The name was said to come from Greek and mean 'birdless (lake)', because the poisons rising from it were believed to kill birds flying over it.

Averroës (*c.*1126–98), Spanish-born Islamic philosopher, judge, and physician. His extensive body of work includes writings on jurisprudence, science, philosophy, and religion. His highly influential commentaries on Aristotle sought to reconcile Aristotle with Plato and the Greek philosophical tradition with the Arabic.

Avesta the sacred writings of Zoroastrianism, compiled in the 4th century, and written in an ancient Iranian language closely related to Vedic Sanskrit.

Avicenna (980–1037), Persian-born Islamic philosopher and physician; Arabic name ibn-Sina. His philosophical system, drawing on Aristotle but in many ways closer to Neoplatonism, was the major influence on the development of scholasticism. His *Canon of Medicine*, which combined his own knowledge with Roman and Arabic medicine, was a standard medieval medical text.

Avignon a city on the Rhône in SE France, which from 1309 until 1377 the residence of the popes during their exile from Rome and was papal property until the French Revolution.

awkward squad composed of recruits and soldiers who need further training; first recorded in Robert Burns's 'Don't let the awkward squad fire over me', shortly before his death in 1796.

have an axe to grind have a private, and sometimes malign, motive for doing or being involved in something (to *grind* an axe is to sharpen its blade).

the Axis the alliance of Germany and Italy formed before and during the Second World War, later extended to include Japan and other countries.

Ayers Rock a red rock mass in Northern Territory, Australia, south-west of Alice Springs, the largest monolith in the world.

In 1980 it was the site of a famous mystery, the disappearance of a nine-week-old girl said to have been carried off by a dingo; the child's body was never found, and although her mother was tried and convicted of her murder in 1982, the verdict was later quashed. In 1995 an inquest concluded that an open verdict was the only possible finding.

Ayers Rock is named after Sir Henry Ayers, Premier of South Australia in 1872–3; its Aboriginal name is *Uluru*.

Ayesha[1] name of the youngest wife of Muhammad, who nursed him in his last illness, and who is traditionally depicted as a model of piety.

Ayesha[2] name of the central character of Rider Haggard's *She* (1887), the mysterious and long-lived queen who is otherwise known as She-who-must-be-obeyed.

Ayurveda the traditional Hindu system of medicine, which is based on the idea of balance in bodily systems and uses diet, herbal treatment, and yogic breathing.

azoth the alchemists' name for mercury, as the essential first principle of all metals. Also, the universal remedy of Paracelsus.

Azrael in Jewish and Muslim mythology, the angel who severs the soul from the body.

Aztec a member of the American Indian people dominant in Mexico before the Spanish conquest of the 16th century. The Aztecs arrived in the central valley of Mexico after the collapse of the Toltec civilization in the 12th century. Their rich and elaborate civilization centred on the city of Tenochtitlán, which boasted vast pyramids, temples, and palaces with fountains. Aztec rulers (the last and most famous of whom was Montezuma) tended to be despotic, and captives taken in war were offered as sacrifices to the gods.

The name comes via French or Spanish from Nahuatl *aztecatl* 'person of Aztlan', their legendary place of origin.

azure the heraldic term for blue. Recorded from Middle English (denoting a blue dye) the word comes via Old French and medieval Latin from Arabic *al* 'the' + *lāzaward* (from Persian *lāžward* 'lapis lazuli').

B the second letter of the modern English alphabet and of the ancient Roman one, corresponding to Greek *beta*, Hebrew *beth*, used symbolically to denote the second of two or more hypothetical persons or things.

See also ➤ *not know a B from a* BATTLEDORE.

ba in ancient Egyptian belief, the soul of a person or god, which survived after death but which had to be sustained with offerings of food. It was typically represented as a human-headed bird. See also ➤ KA.

Baader-Meinhof Group another name for ➤ RED *Army Faction*.

Baal a male fertility god whose cult was widespread in ancient Phoenician and Canaanite lands and was strongly resisted by the Hebrew prophets. The name comes from Hebrew *ba'al* 'lord'.

Baalbek a town in eastern Lebanon, site of the ancient city of Heliopolis. Its principal monuments date from the Roman period.

Baba Yaga a celebrated witch of Russian folklore, the 'Bony-legged One', who lives in a house on chicken-legs and flies about in a mortar, using a pestle as oar and a broom to sweep away her tracks.

Babar the elephant hero of a series of picture-books, written and drawn by Jean de Brunhoff (1899–1937) and then by his son Laurent (1925–); *Babar* as a young elephant has lived with people, but has returned to the jungle to become king of the elephants with his cousin and wife Celeste.

Babbitt a term for a materialistic, complacent, and conformist businessman, from the name of the protagonist of the novel *Babbitt* by Sinclair Lewis.

Tower of Babel in the Bible, a tower built in an attempt to reach heaven, which God frustrated by confusing the languages of its builders so that they could not understand one another (Genesis 11:1–9). The story was probably inspired by the Babylonian ziggurat, and may be an attempt to explain the existence of different languages.

babes in the wood inexperienced people in a situation calling for experience; the reference is to the two children in a 16th-century ballad, the *Children in the Wood*, whose wicked uncle wishes to steal their inheritance. Abandoned in a forest, the children die of starvation and the robins cover their bodies with leaves; the uncle and his accomplice are subsequently brought to justice.

Babi Yar the name of a deep ravine to the north of Kiev in the Ukraine, site of the mass-killing of Jews by SS squads between 1941 and 1943. *Babi Yar* has become a symbol of the Holocaust.

Babieca the name of ➤ El CID's horse, said to have carried his master's dead body on its last journey from Valencia to Burgos. The name means informally 'stupid', and reflects the story that El Cid as a boy chose what appeared to be a clumsy and awkward colt, which grew into his famous horse.

Babism a religion founded in 1844 by the Persian Mirza Ali Muhammad of Shiraz (1819–50, popularly known as 'The Bab'), who taught that a new prophet would follow Muhammad. Babism developed into Baha'i when Baha'ullah claimed to be this prophet.

Babrius a Greek writer of fables who lived probably in the second century AD but about whom nothing is known. The fables, which exist today in two books (of which the second is incomplete), are based on the fables of Aesop with some apparently original additions.

Babur (1483–1530), first Mogul emperor of India *c.*1525–30, descendant of Tamerlane. He invaded India *c.*1525 and conquered the territory from the Oxus to Patna. A Muslim, he instigated the policy of religious toleration towards his non-Muslim subjects which was continued by later Mogul emperors.

baby a very young child. In figurative use, **one's baby** is one's particular responsibility or concern. To be **left holding the baby** is to be left with sole (and unwelcome) responsibility for something.

A **baby boomer** is a person born during the temporary marked increase in the birth rate following the Second World War.

To **throw the baby out with the bathwater** is to discard something valuable along with other things that are inessential or undesirable. Based on a German saying recorded from the early 16th century, but not recorded in English until the mid 19th century by Thomas Carlyle.

Babylon an ancient city in Mesopotamia, the capital of Babylonia in the 2nd millennium BC under Hammurabi. The city (of which only ruins now remain) lay on the Euphrates and was noted by Classical writers for its luxury, its fortifications, and its legendary Hanging Gardens. The name is also given in Revelation to the mystical city of the Apocalypse, and it is taken as the type of a great and decadent city. *Babylon* is also used (chiefly among Rastafarians) as a contemptuous or dismissive term for aspects of white culture seen as degenerate or oppressive, especially the police.

The **Babylonian Captivity** is the captivity of the Israelites in Babylon, lasting from their deportation by Nebuchadnezzar in 586 BC until their release by Cyrus the Great in 539 BC. It is taken as a type of grieving exile.

baccalaureate a university bachelor's degree. The word comes (in the mid 17th century) from French *baccalauréat* or medieval Latin *baccalaureatus*, from *baccalaureus* 'bachelor'. The earlier form *baccalarius* was altered by wordplay to conform with *bacca lauri* 'laurel berry', because of the laurels awarded to scholars.

Bacchae in ancient Greece, priestesses or female devotees of the Greek god Bacchus; ➤ BACCHANTS.

Bacchanalia the Roman festival of Bacchus, typified by scenes of drunken revelry and celebration.

bacchants priestesses or female devotees of the god Bacchus. They are depicted wearing the skins of fawns or panthers and wreaths of ivy, oak, or fir, each carrying a thyrsus.

Bacchus in Greek mythology, another name for ➤ DIONYSUS.

Bach flower remedies preparations of the flowers of various plants used in a system of complementary medicine intended to relieve ill health by influencing underlying emotional states, named after Edward *Bach* (1886–1936), British physician.

a back number a person whose methods or ideas are regarded as out of date, and who is no long seen as important. In literal use, this was originally the issue of a periodical before the current one.

back of beyond a term (first recorded in Sir Walter Scott's *The Antiquary*, 1816, as a humorous phrase for some very out of the way place), used in Australia for the far inland regions remote from large towns or closely settled districts, the backblocks.

back of Bourke the remote and sparsely populated inland of Australia; *Bourke* is a town in New South Wales.

a back-seat driver someone who lectures or criticizes the person who is actually in control, from the idea of a passenger in the back of a car giving the driver unwanted advice.

back slang slang in which words are spoken as though they were spelled backwards (e.g. *redraw* for *warder*).

back the wrong horse in figurative use, make a wrong or inappropriate choice.

back to basics a political catchphrase of the early 1990s, embodying a conscious return to what are seen as fundamental principles of self-respect, decency, and honesty. The use of the phrase derived from a speech made by John Major, then Prime Minister, to the Conservative Party Conference in 1993.

put someone's back up make someone annoyed or angry, in allusion to the idea of a cat's arching its back in anger.

backroom boys people who provide vital scientific and technical support for those in the field who become public figures; the expression derives from a reference by Lord Beaverbrook in 1941 to, 'the boys in the back rooms…they are the men who do the work.'

the Backs in Cambridge, the college gardens which back on to the River Cam; the name is recorded from the late 19th century.

Francis Bacon (1561–1626), English statesman and philosopher, described by Izaak Walton as 'the great Secretary of Nature and all learning, Sir Francis Bacon'. As a scientist he advocated the inductive method; his views were instrumental in the founding of the Royal Society in 1660.

Baconian philosophy is the inductive method of reasoning associated with Francis Bacon, whose radical philosophical beliefs proved very influential in the century following his death.

The **Baconian theory** is the theory, first promulgated in the late nineteenth century, that Francis Bacon (as the head of a group including Raleigh and Spenser) was the true author of the plays attributed to Shakespeare, and that a great system of thought was concealed in them by ciphers. The American writer Delia Salter Bacon (1811–59) was one of the earliest and most enthusiastic proponents of the theory.

Roger Bacon (*c.*1214–94), English philosopher, scientist, and Franciscan friar. Most notable for his work in the field of optics, he emphasized the need for an empirical approach to scientific study. He eventually fell foul of his own order, which imprisoned him for 'suspect novelties'.

bring home the bacon achieve success. The phrase probably derives from bacon in much earlier *save one's bacon*, recorded from the mid 17th century, and may in turn go back to idea that pig's meat was an essential and common article of food.

Bacon's Rebellion a rebellion led by a Virginia planter, Nathaniel *Bacon* (1647–76), against the arbitrary rule of the crown authorities.

Bactria an ancient country in central Asia, corresponding to the northern part of modern Afghanistan. Traditionally the home of Zoroaster, it was the seat of a powerful Indo-Greek kingdom in the 3rd and 2nd centuries BC.

bad hair day a day on which everything seems to go wrong, characterized as a day on which one's hair is particularly unmanageable; an expression which became current in the 1990s.

Badger State an informal name for Wisconsin.

Badlands a barren plateau region of the western US, mainly in North and South Dakota and Nebraska.

Battle of Badon Hill an ancient British battle (the location of which is uncertain), in AD 516, in which the forces of King Arthur successfully defended themselves against the Saxons. Another source implies that the battle was fought *c.*500, but does not connect it with Arthur.

Karl Baedeker (1801–59), German publisher, who in 1827 started his own publishing firm in Koblenz. He is remembered chiefly for the series of guidebooks to which he gave his name and which are still published today.

In the Second World War, the name **Baedeker raids** was given to raids carried out by the Luftwaffe in April and May 1942 on places of cultural and historical importance in Britain.

William Baffin (*c.*1584–1622), English navigator and explorer, the pilot of several expeditions in search of the North-West Passage 1612–16. He discovered the largest island of the Canadian Arctic in 1616; this and the strait between it and Greenland are named after him.

bag and baggage with all one's belongings, completely. Originally, this was a military phrase denoting all the property of an army collectively, and of the soldiers individually, and to march out **with bag and baggage** indicated that an army or a commander was making an honourable retreat, without surrender of any possessions.

bag lady a homeless woman who carries her possessions around in shopping bags; the phrase was first recorded in the US in the 1970s.

Baggins the family name of the ➤ HOBBITS, Bilbo and Frodo, who in Tolkien's *The Hobbit* and *Lord of the Rings* come into possession of the One Ring of power.

Baghdad the capital of modern-day Iraq, on the River Tigris, which was a thriving city under the Abbasid caliphs, notably ➤ HARUN ar-Rashid, in the 8th and 9th centuries.

Baha'i a monotheistic religion founded in the 19th century as a development of ➤ BABISM, emphasizing the essential oneness of humankind and of all religions and seeking world peace.

bailey the outer wall of a castle and a court enclosed by it. Recorded from Middle English, the word probably comes from Old French *baile* 'palisade, enclosure'.

Bairam either of two annual Muslim festivals, the *Greater Bairam*, held at the end of the

Islamic year, and the *Lesser Bairam*, held at the end of *Ramadan*.

fish or cut bait in North American usage, stop vacillating and act on or disengage from something.

Bajazet ruler of the Ottomans (1389–1402), who overran the provinces of the eastern Empire and besieged Constantinople, but was defeated and taken prisoner by Timor (➤ TAMERLANE).

Baker Street Irregulars the gang of street urchins who appear in three of the ➤ *Sherlock* HOLMES stories, and who are used by Holmes for carrying messages and maintaining surveillance on suspected persons; Holmes lived at 221b Baker Street.

baker's dozen a group of thirteen; the expression comes (in the late 16th century) from the former bakers' custom of adding an extra loaf to a dozen sold to a retailer, this representing the latter's profit.

Balaam a non-Israelite prophet whose story is related in the biblical book of *Numbers*. In allusive use he is often taken as an example of an evil diviner who would sell his prophetic powers to the highest bidder, although his powers are questionable: although supposedly a seer, he is repeatedly unable to see the divine messenger that is visible even to his donkey. The animal is finally granted the power of speech by God to address her master, and it has been suggested that this is the origin of the (archaic) journalist's slang usage *Balaam* to mean 'superfluous or trivial material used to fill up a column'. (The term **Balaam basket** was used for an editor's container for unwanted material.)

Battle of Balaclava a battle of the Crimean War, fought between Russia and an alliance of British, French, and Turkish forces in and around the port of Balaclava (now Balaklava) in the southern Crimea in 1854. The battle ended inconclusively; it is chiefly remembered as the scene of the ➤ CHARGE *of the Light Brigade*.

balance of nature a state of equilibrium produced by the interaction of living organisms, ecological balance; the phrase is recorded from the early 20th century.

balance of power a situation in which states of the world have roughly equal power. The phrase in this sense is recorded from the early 18th century.

Vasco Núñez de Balboa (1475–1519), Spanish explorer. In 1511 Balboa joined an expedition to Darien (in Panama) as a stowaway, but rose to command it after a mutiny. In 1513 he reached the western coast of the isthmus of Darien (Panama), thereby becoming the first European to see the Pacific Ocean.

baldachin a ceremonial canopy of stone, metal, or fabric over an altar, throne, or doorway. Recorded from the late 16th century (denoting a rich brocade of silk and gold thread) the word comes ultimately from Italian *Baldacco* 'Baghdad', place of origin of the original brocade.

Balder in Scandinavian mythology, a son of Odin and god of the summer sun. He was invulnerable to all things except mistletoe, with which the god Loki, by a trick, induced the blind god Hödur to kill him.

Balfour surname of the Conservative statesman Arthur James *Balfour* (1848–1930).
  The **Balfour Declaration** was a declaration in favour of a Jewish national home in Palestine, issued in 1917 by Balfour as Foreign Secretary.
  Mr Balfour's poodle is the House of Lords; from the title of a book (1954) by Roy Jenkins, and ultimately in allusion to a speech by Lloyd George of 1907, in which he described the House of Lords as the 'poodle' of Balfour as Prime Minister.

the Balkans the countries occupying the part of SE Europe lying south of the Danube and Sava Rivers, forming a peninsula bounded by the Adriatic and Ionian Seas in the west, the Aegean and Black Seas in the east, and the Mediterranean in the south. The peninsula was taken from the Byzantine Empire by the Ottoman Turks in the 14th and 15th centuries, and parts remained under Turkish control until 1912–13. After the First World War the peninsula was divided between Greece, Albania, Bulgaria, and Yugoslavia (which broke up in 1991–3), with Turkey retaining only a small area including Constantinople (Istanbul).
  The term **Balkanize** meaning 'divide (a region or body) into smaller mutually hostile states or groups' is recorded from the 1920s.
  The **Balkan Wars** were two wars of 1912–13 that were fought over the last European territories of the Ottoman Empire. In 1912 Bulgaria, Serbia, Greece, and Montenegro forced Turkey to give up Albania and Macedonia,

leaving the area around Constantinople (Istanbul) as the only Ottoman territory in Europe. The following year Bulgaria disputed with Serbia, Greece, and Romania for possession of Macedonia, which was partitioned between Greece and Serbia.

Balkis the name of the queen of Sheba in Arabic literature.

ball-flower an architectural ornament resembling a ball within the petals of a flower.

a whole new ball game a completely new set of circumstances. Originally North American, referring to a game of baseball.

the ball is in someone's court it is that particular person's turn to act next. The metaphor comes from tennis or a similar ball game where different players use particular areas of a marked court.

a ball of fire a person who is full of energy and enthusiasm. Recorded in this sense from the mid 20th century, although earlier in literal use. In the 19th century, *ball of fire* was also a slang term for a glass of brandy.

ballad a poem or song narrating a story in short stanzas. Traditional ballads are typically of unknown authorship, having been passed on orally from one generation to the next as part of the folk culture. Recorded from the late 15th century (denoting a light, simple song), the word comes via Old French from Provençal *balada* 'to dance', from late Latin. The sense 'narrative poem' dates from the mid 18th century, and was used by Johnson in the *Rambler*.

Ballarat a mining and sheep-farming centre in Victoria, Australia, which is the site of the discovery in 1851 of the largest gold reserves in Australia.

when the balloon goes up when the action or trouble starts, probably with allusion to the release of a balloon to mark the start of an event.

ballot a procedure by which people vote secretly on a particular issue. The word is recorded from the mid 16th century, and originally denoted a small coloured ball placed in a container to register a vote; it comes from Italian *ballotta*, diminutive of *balla* 'ball'.

in the ballpark in a particular area or range; in the US, a *ballpark* is a baseball ground.

balm in Gilead comfort in distress, succour; originally with reference to Jeremiah 8:22.

Balmoral Castle a holiday residence of the British royal family, on the River Dee in Scotland. The estate was bought in 1847 by Prince Albert, who rebuilt and refurbished the castle.

baloney foolish or deceptive talk, nonsense. The word is said to be a corruption of *Bologna*, from *Bologna sausage*, but the connection remains conjectural.

Balthasar the traditional name of one of the ➤ MAGI.

Balthazar a very large wine bottle, equivalent in capacity to sixteen regular bottles. The name comes, in the 1930s, from the king of Babylon (otherwise ➤ BELSHAZZAR), who 'made a great feast … and drank wine before a thousand' (Daniel 5:1).

Baltic Exchange an association of companies, based in London, whose members are engaged in numerous international trading activities, especially the chartering of vessels to carry cargo. The name comes from *Virginia and Baltic*, one of many coffee houses where shipowners and merchants met in London in the 18th century, the coffee house being so named by association with areas of much of the trade. In April 1992, the Baltic Exchange building in London was seriously damaged by an IRA bomb.

Bambi eponymous name of the young deer in Felix Salten's story for children (1923); filmed by Disney in 1942, the story became widely known, and *Bambi* is used to refer to the wide-eyed and consciously appealing look and manner of a young and timid animal.

bamboo curtain a political and economic barrier between China and non-Communist countries, on the model of ➤ IRON *curtain*.

Bamian a city in central Afghanistan, near which were the remains of two colossal statues of Buddha. These were destroyed in 2001 by the ruling Taliban regime.

ban the bomb US anti-nuclear slogan, adopted from 1953 onwards by the Campaign for Nuclear Disarmament.

second banana the second most important person in an organization or activity. Originally (mid 20th century), US theatrical slang meaning the supporting comedian in a show. The expression *top banana*, meaning the most important person in an organization or activity, is of similar origin.

banana republic a small state dependent on foreign capital, typically as a result of the domination of the economy by a single trade, and hence politically unstable; the name was particularly used of Central American states which were heavily dependent on their fruit-exporting trade.

Banbury an Oxfordshire town formerly noted for the number and fervour of its Puritan inhabitants, as for its cakes and cheese.

A **Banbury cake** is a flat pastry with a spicy currant filling, originally made in Banbury. The expression **thin as Banbury cheese** means very thin; in Shakespeare's *The Merry Wives of Windsor* (1597), Slender is addressed as 'You Banbury cheese'.

Banbury Cross was a market cross in Banbury, referred to in the nursery rhyme, 'Ride a cock-horse to Banbury Cross, To see a fine lady upon a white horse.' The original Cross was in fact destroyed at the end of the 16th century.

Band of Hope a name given (from about 1847) to associations of young people who pledged themselves to temperance; the name is first recorded in a temperance song of 1847 by J. Tunnicliff.

Bandar-log in Kipling's *Jungle Books*, the monkey people, who talk constantly of their abilities and their plans but who achieve nothing, taken as the type of irresponsible chattering people.

bandersnatch a fierce mythical creature immune to bribery and capable of moving very fast. The name was coined by Lewis Carroll in *Through the Looking Glass* (1871).

bands a collar with two hanging strips, worn by certain lawyers, clerics, and academics as part of their formal dress.

bank holiday a day on which banks are officially closed, kept as a public holiday; traditionally, bills payable on these days are paid on the following day. *Bank holidays* originated as certain Saints' days and anniversaries, to the number in all of about 33 days per annum, were kept as Holidays at the Bank of England.

Battle of Bannockburn a battle which took place near Stirling in central Scotland in 1314, in which the English army of Edward II, advancing to break the siege of Stirling

Castle, was defeated by the Scots under Robert the Bruce, who subsequently re-established Scotland as a separate kingdom.

banns a notice read out on three successive Sundays in a parish church, announcing an intended marriage and giving the opportunity for objections. Recorded from Middle English, the word represents the plural of *ban* 'proclamation'.

Banqueting House a hall in Whitehall Palace designed (1622) by Inigo Jones; it was from a window in the *Banqueting House* that Charles I stepped onto the scaffold for his execution.

Banquo a character in Shakespeare's *Macbeth* who is murdered on Macbeth's orders, and whose ghost subsequently appears at Macbeth's banqueting table, invisible to all except Macbeth himself; he embodies both a reminder of Macbeth's guilt, and the warning that his usurpation of power will ultimately fail.

banshee in Irish legend, a female spirit whose wailing warns of a death in the house. Recorded from the late 17th century, the term comes from Irish *bean sidhe*, from Old Irish *ben side* 'woman of the fairies'.

bantam the *bantam* cock is noted for its aggression. It is apparently named after the province of *Bantam* in Java, although the fowl is not native there.

Bantamweight is a weight in boxing and other sports intermediate between flyweight and featherweight. In the amateur boxing scale it ranges from 51 to 54 kg.

banyan an Indian fig tree, the branches of which produce aerial roots which later become accessory trunks, so that a mature tree may cover several hectares in this manner.

Recorded from the late 16th century, the word comes via Portuguese from Gujarati *vāniyo* 'man of the trading caste', from Sanskrit. Originally denoting a Hindu merchant, the term was applied, by Europeans in the mid 17th century, to a particular tree under which such traders had built a pagoda.

In naval slang, **banyan day** (recorded from the mid 18th century) means a day on which no meat is served, originally with reference to the vegetarianism of *banyans*, or Hindus of the trading caste.

banzai a Japanese battle cry; a form of greeting used to the Japanese emperor. In

Japanese, the word means literally 'ten thousand years (of life to you)'.

From the 1980s, the word has been used to designate extremely fast driving, especially in motor racing; a **banzai lap** is a lap of a course taken particularly rapidly.

baptism in the Christian Church, the religious rite of sprinkling water on a person's head or of immersing them in water, symbolizing purification or regeneration and admission to the Christian Church. Recorded from Middle English, the word comes via Old French and ecclesiastical Latin from ecclesiastical Greek *baptismos* 'ceremonial washing', from *baptizein* 'immerse, baptize'.

A **baptism of blood** is the death by violence of unbaptized martyrs, regarded as a form of baptism. A **baptism of fire** is a difficult or painful new undertaking or experience, from the original sense of 'a soldier's first battle'.

baptist a person who practises baptism; **The Baptist** is the epithet of St ▶ JOHN *the Baptist*.

A *Baptist* is a member of a Protestant Christian denomination advocating baptism only of adult believers by total immersion.

bar¹ in heraldry, a charge in the form of a narrow horizontal stripe across the shield.

bar² in a court of law, the barrier or rail at which a prisoner stands. In the Inns of Court, formerly, a barrier or partition separating the seats of the benchers from the rest of the hall, to which students, after they had reached a certain standing, were 'called' (long popularly understood to refer to that in a court of justice, beyond which the King's or Queen's Counsel (and Serjeants-at-Law) have place, but not ordinary barristers).

The *bar* denotes the profession of barrister; in British usage, barristers collectively.

bar³ in horse racing, except the horses indicated (used when stating the odds); the expression is recorded from the mid 19th century.

bar mitzvah the religious initiation ceremony of a Jewish boy who has reached the age of 13 and is regarded as ready to observe religious precepts and eligible to take part in public worship. The term comes from Hebrew *bar miṣwāh*, literally 'son of the commandment'. (See also ▶ BAT *mitzvah*.)

Barabbas the prisoner released by ▶ PILATE to the crowd instead of Jesus. In allusive terms Barabbas's name is used to convey the sense of evil being chosen over good.

barb a small horse of a hardy breed originally from North Africa. Recorded from the mid 17th century, the name comes via French from Italian *barbero* 'of ▶ BARBARY'.

St Barbara a supposed virgin-martyr, whose cult became very popular in the later Middle Ages. According to the *Golden Legend* she was shut up in a tower by her father, and while he was away became a Christian; she ordered a third window to be made in the building in honour of the Holy Trinity. At her father's instigation she was tried and condemned to death for her Christianity; by some accounts, her father was her executioner. On her death, he was struck by lightning and died.

The usual emblem for Barbara is a tower, although she may also be shown with a sword as the instrument of her execution. She is the patron of those in danger of sudden death. She is also taken as one of the ▶ FOURTEEN *Holy Helpers*. Her feast day (suppressed in the Roman calendar of 1969) was formerly 4 December.

Barbarossa nickname ('Redbeard') of Frederick I (*c*.1123–90), king of Germany and Holy Roman emperor.

Barbarossa was the code name for the military operation in which Hitler's armies launched their invasion of the Soviet Union in 1941.

Barbary a former name (also **Barbary States**) for the [Saracen] countries of North and NW Africa, together with Moorish Spain. The area was noted between the 16th and 18th centuries as a haunt of pirates.

The **Barbary Coast** was a nickname for a district of San Francisco (the ▶ TENDERLOIN) regarded as the main centre for vice and corruption. The original *Barbary Coast* was the Mediterranean coast of North Africa from Morocco to Egypt, taken as the home of the corsairs and a source of violence and danger.

Barbican the complex of high-rise buildings around the **Barbican Centre** in the City of London. A *barbican* is the outer defence of a city or castle, especially a double tower above a gate or drawbridge; it is recorded from the 17th century as being retained as the name of a street in London. Recorded from Middle English, the word probably comes ultimately from Arabic.

Barbie doll trademark name for a doll representing a conventionally attractive and fashionably dressed young woman, used allusively for a woman who is attractive in a glossily artificial way, but who is considered to lack sense and character.

Barchester the fictional cathedral city of the county of ➤ BARSETSHIRE, featuring in the novels of the Anglican Church by Anthony Trollope and (in the 20th century) Angela Thirkell; M. R. James also used it as the setting for one of his ghost stories, 'The Stalls of Barchester Cathedral'.

bard a poet, traditionally one reciting epics and associated with a particular oral tradition. Recorded from Middle English, the word is of Celtic origin (*bàrd* in Scottish Gaelic, *bard* in Irish and Welsh). In Scotland in the 16th century it was a derogatory term for an itinerant musician, but was later romanticized by Sir Walter Scott.
  The **Bard of Avon** is a name for Shakespeare, recorded from the late 19th century.
  Bardolatry, excessive admiration of Shakespeare, is first recorded in 1901 in George Bernard Shaw's Preface to *Three Plays for Puritans*.

Bardolph in Shakspeare's *Henry IV* parts 1 and 2, Falstaff's red-nosed companion (see ➤ BUBUKLE); he is said in *Henry V* to have been hanged for robbing a French church shortly before Agincourt, but in *The Merry Wives of Windsor* he becomes tapster at the Garter Inn.

Barebones Parliament the nickname of Cromwell's Parliament of 1653, from one of its members, Praise-God *Barbon*, an Anabaptist leather seller of Fleet Street. It replaced the ➤ RUMP *Parliament*, but was itself dissolved within a few months.

Willem Barents (d. 1597), Dutch explorer. The leader of several expeditions in search of the North-East Passage to Asia, Barents discovered Spitsbergen and reached Novaya Zemlya, off the coast of which he died; the **Barents Sea** is named after him.

would not touch with a bargepole would not have anything to do with someone or something. A *bargepole* is a long pole used to propel a barge and fend off obstacles.

barghest a demonic spirit, said to appear in the form of a large dog, and to guard the graves of those who have died by violence.

Barisal guns booming sounds of unknown origin heard in *Barisal*, a town in Bangladesh

and certain other regions, especially on the water.

bark up the wrong tree pursue a misguided course of action; originally US (mid 19th century), referring to a dog which has mistaken the tree in which a quarry has taken refuge.

Barkis in Dickens's *David Copperfield*, the carrier who is the suitor of David's nurse Peggotty, to whom he sends the message 'Barkis is willin' '.

barleycorn a grain of barley, formerly constituting a unit of measurement. **John Barleycorn** (recorded from the 17th century) is the personification of barley, especially as the grain from which malt liquor is made.

Barmecide illusory or imaginary, and therefore disappointing. The word comes from Arabic *Barmakī*, the name of a prince in the ➤ ARABIAN *Nights*, who gave a beggar a feast consisting of ornate but empty dishes.

St Barnabas one of the earliest Christian disciples at Jerusalem; an Apostle, but not one of the original twelve (see ➤ APOSTLE[1]). A Jewish Cypriot and a Levite, he was originally called Joseph; the name Barnabas means 'son of consolation'. He introduced Paul to the other apostles, and with him undertook the first missionary journey, which began in Cyprus. Later Paul and Barnabas quarrelled and separated; Barnabas returned to Cyprus and evangelized there. According to legend, he was martyred at Salamis in 61 AD. His feast day is 11 June.

Barnaby Rudge eponymous hero of the novel by Dickens set at the time of the ➤ GORDON *Riots*. Barnaby, a simple-minded boy, has a pet raven ('Grip') for his constant companion.

barnacle goose an arctic goose which, because its breeding grounds were long unknown, was believed to hatch from the shell of the crustacean to which it gave its name, or, according to another story, from the fruit of a particular tree growing by the seashore, from which the birds were said to hatch as the fruit dropped into water.

Barnard's Inn one of the ➤ INNS *of Chancery*, belonging to ➤ GRAY's *Inn* and existing from *c*.1454; it was originally named for and owned by the *Mackworth* family, and the name *Barnard* was derived from a later tenant called Lionel Barnard.

Thomas John Barnardo (1845–1905), Irish-born doctor and philanthropist. He founded the East End Mission for destitute children in 1867, the first of many such homes. Now known as Dr Barnardo's Homes, they cater chiefly for those with physical and mental disabilities.

barnstorm (chiefly in North America), tour rural districts giving theatrical performances, originally often in barns; in extended usage, make a rapid tour of (an area), typically as part of a political campaign.

Phineas Taylor Barnum (1810–91), American showman. He billed his circus, opened in 1871, as 'The Greatest Show on Earth'; ten years later he founded the Barnum and Bailey circus with his former rival Anthony Bailey (1847–1906).

In psychology, the **Barnum effect** is the tendency to accept as true types of information such as character assessments or horoscopes, even when the information is so vague as to be worthless. The term comes from Barnum's name; *Barnum* was in use from the mid 19th century as a noun in the sense 'nonsense, humbug'.

baron a member of the lowest order of the British nobility. Baron is not used as a form of address, barons usually being referred to as 'Lord'. Also, a similar member of a foreign nobility.

A **baron of beef** is a joint of beef consisting of two sirloins joined at the backbone. The term is first recorded in Samuel Johnson's *Dictionary* (1755).

A **baron of the Cinque Ports** in historical usage is a freeman of the ➤ CINQUE PORTS, who had feudal service of bearing the canopy over the head of the sovereign on the day of coronation; also, until the Reform Bill of 1832, a burgess returned by these ports to Parliament.

The **Barons' War** was the English civil war of 1264–7 between forces led by Henry III and Simon de Montfort respectively.

Recorded from Middle English, *baron* comes via Old French from medieval Latin *baro*, *baron-* 'warrior', and is probably of Germanic origin.

baronet a member of the lowest hereditary titled British order, with the status of a commoner but able to use the prefix 'Sir'. The term originally denoted a gentleman, not a

nobleman, summoned by the king to attend parliament; the current order was instituted in the early 17th century.

baroque relating to or denoting a style of European architecture, music, and art of the 17th and 18th centuries that followed mannerism and is characterized by ornate detail. In architecture the period is exemplified by the palace of Versailles and by the work of Wren in England. Major composers include Vivaldi, Bach, and Handel; Caravaggio and Rubens are important baroque artists.

The word comes (in the mid 18th century) from French, originally denoting a pearl of irregular shape.

barrack-room lawyer a person who likes to give authoritative-sounding opinions on subjects in which they are not qualified, especially legal matters. The term comes originally from military slang.

over a barrel in a helpless position, at someone's mercy. Perhaps referring to the condition of a person who has been rescued from drowning and is placed over a barrel to clear the lungs of water.

barrel of salt a barrel of salt is the emblem of St Rupert, 8th-century bishop of Worms and Salzburg, who encouraged the development of salt-mines near Salzburg.

barrelhouse a cheap or disreputable bar; an unrestrained and unsophisticated style of jazz. The name comes (in the late 19th century) from the rows of barrels along the walls of such a bar.

Day of the Barricades during the ➤ FRENCH *Wars of Religion*, 12 May 1588, the day on which the people of Paris rose in support of Guise and the Catholic League against Henri III, and blockaded the streets with casks filled with earth and paving stones. The word, in the earlier form *barricado*, is recorded from the late 16th century, and comes ultimately from Spanish *barrica*, related to *barrel*, since barrels were (as on this occasion) often used in their construction.

barrister a person called to the *bar* and entitled to practise as an advocate, particularly in the higher courts; the word is recorded from late Middle English, and may be formed on the pattern of *minister*.

Barsetshire a fictional county, created by Anthony Trollope for a series of novels and also used by Angela Thirkell; its cathedral city is ➤ BARCHESTER. *Barsetshire* may now be used allusively for an idealized rural county. See also ➤ BORSETSHIRE.

St Bartholomew an apostle of the 1st century AD, whose apostolate is said to have included India and Armenia. He was martyred by being flayed alive, and his traditional emblem is a flaying-knife. He is the patron saint of tanners, and his feast day is 24 August.

From 1133 to 1855, a great fair was held annually at West Smithfield on the saint's feast day. This provides the setting for Jonson's play *Bartholomew Fair* (1614, performed 1631), in which the various protagonists visit the fair. The name 'Bartholomew' was applied to various goods on sale at the fair; a **Bartholomew baby** is a puppet or doll sold at the fair, and **Bartholomew pig** refers to the roast pork available there (one of Jonson's characters, the ranting Puritan Zeal-for-the-land Busy, has come to the fair for the express purpose of eating *Bartholomew pig*).

The **Massacre of St Bartholomew** is the name given to the massacre of Huguenots throughout France ordered by Charles IX at the instigation of his mother Catherine de Médicis, began on the morning of the feast of St Bartholomew, 24 August 1572. In Protestant writing, this became proverbial as a type of savagery and betrayal.

Dick Barton special agent hero, originally of a radio series for children, broadcast between 1946 and 1951, and later appearing on television and films; *Dick Barton* was noted for his upright moral character as well as for his struggle with a range of criminal adversaries.

Baruch the scribe of the prophet ➤ JEREMIAH; he was sent by his master to read Jeremiah's prophecies in the Temple, against the king's wishes. *Baruch* is also the name of a book of the Apocrypha, attributed in the text to his authorship.

get to first base achieve the first step towards one's objective. Originally from North American usage, in which *base* refers to each of the four points in the angles of the 'diamond' in baseball, which a player has to reach in order to score a run.

touch base with briefly make or renew contact with someone or something. Originally from North American usage, in which *base* refers to each of the four points in the

angles of the 'diamond' in baseball, which a player has to reach in order to score a run.

Basic English a simplified form of English limited to 850 selected words, intended for international communication.

St Basil (*c.*330–79), Doctor of the Church, bishop of Caesarea; known as **St Basil the Great**. Brother of St Gregory of Nyssa, he staunchly opposed Arianism and put forward a monastic rule which is still the basis of monasticism in the Eastern Church. His feast day is 14 June.

basilica a large oblong hall or building with double colonnades and a semicircular apse, used in ancient Rome as a law court or for public assemblies. The name was then applied to a building of this type used as a Christian Church; in Rome, it designated specifically the seven churches founded by Constantine. *Basilica* is also the name given to certain churches granted special privileges by the Pope.

Recorded from the mid 16th century, the word comes from Latin, literally 'royal palace', and from Greek *basilikē*, feminine of *basiliskos* 'royal', from *basileus* 'king'.

basilisk a mythical reptile with a lethal gaze or breath, hatched by a serpent from a cock's egg. In figurative or allusive use, the idea of a lethal gaze is paramount, as in **basilisk eye**, **basilisk stare**.

The name comes ultimately from Greek *basiliskos* 'little king, serpent', from *basileus* 'king', and Pliny suggests that it is so called from a spot, resembling a crown, on its head; medieval writers gave it 'a certain comb or coronet'.

Basin State informal name for Utah.

Basin Street a street in the Storyville district of New Orleans, particularly associated with early jazz, as in the title of 'Basin Street Blues' (Spencer Williams, 1928).

the Hound of the Baskervilles in Conan Doyle's story of this name (1902), a ghostly and savage hound believed to haunt, and hunt to their deaths, the Dartmoor family of Baskerville, in revenge for an ancestor's crimes. ➤ *Sherlock* HOLMES demonstrates that the legend is being exploited by an unrecognized descendant who hopes to inherit the family estate.

basket case a person or thing regarded as useless or unable to cope, originally a US slang expression for a soldier who had lost all four limbs, and was so unable to move independently.

basket of bread a basket of bread is the emblem of ➤ St NICHOLAS *of Tolentino*.

basket of fruit and flowers a basket of fruit and flowers is the emblem of ➤ St DOROTHY.

Basque a member of a people living in the Basque Country of France and Spain. Culturally one of the most distinct groups in Europe, the Basques were largely independent until the 19th century; the Basque separatist movement ETA is carrying on an armed struggle against the Spanish government. The Basque language is not known to be related to any other language.

The name comes via French from Latin *Vasco*, the same base as *Gascon*.

bassarid a Thracian bacchanal; a ➤ BACCHANT. The word comes from Greek, literally meaning 'fox', probably from the traditional dress of fox-skins.

Bastet in Egyptian mythology, a goddess usually shown as a woman with the head of a cat, wearing one gold earring.

Bastille a fortress in Paris built in the 14th century and used in the 17th–18th centuries as a state prison. Its storming by the mob on 14 July 1789 marked the start of the French Revolution; the anniversary of this event (**Bastille Day**) is kept as a national holiday in France.

The name comes (via Old French) from Provençal *bastida*, from *bastir* 'build'.

bat in poetic use, bats are often associated with the coming of night and darkness. They have also a sinister association with vampires, notably in the tradition established by Bram Stoker in *Dracula* (1897).

bat mitzvah in Judaism, a religious initiation ceremony for a Jewish girl aged twelve years and one day, regarded as the age of religious maturity. The word comes from Hebrew *baṭ miṣwāh* 'daughter of commandment', suggested by ➤ BAR *mitzvah*.

with bated breath in great suspense; very anxiously or excitedly. *Baited*, which is sometimes seen, is a misspelling, since bated in this sense is a shortened form of abated, the idea being that one's breathing is lessened under the influence of extreme suspense.

H. M. Bateman (1887–1970), Australian-born British cartoonist, who is known for the series of cartoons entitled 'The Man Who ...', which illustrated a variety of offences against established custom.

Order of the Bath (in the UK) an order of knighthood, so called from the ceremonial bath which originally preceded installation. It has four classes of membership, which are: Knight or Dame Grand Cross of the Order of the Bath (GCB), Knight or Dame Commander (KCB/DCB), and Companion (CB). (See also ➤ KNIGHT *of the Bath*.)

The herald or marshal of the Order is known as **Bath King of Arms**.

Bathsheba in the Bible, the beautiful wife of ➤ URIAH the Hittite, seen bathing by ➤ DAVID; desiring her, the king arranged for Uriah's death in battle, and married the widow. Bathsheba subsequently became the mother of David's heir, ➤ SOLOMON.

Batman an American cartoon character, by day the millionaire socialite Bruce Wayne but at night a cloaked and masked figure, the *Caped Crusader*, fighting crime in Gotham City (New York), often assisted by *Robin the Boy Wonder*. First appearing in 1939 in a comic strip by artist Bob Kane (1916–) and writer Bill Finger (1917–74), Batman has since featured in a popular 1960s TV series and two major films (1989 and 1992).

hand on the baton hand over a particular duty or responsibility. A metaphor from athletics: the *baton* is the short stick or rod passed from one runner to the next in a relay race.

Batrachomyomachia the 'battle of the frogs and mice', a short Greek mock-epic poem in Homeric style, describing a one-day war between the frogs and the mice in a story deriving from one of Aesop's fables. The fighting is brought to an end by Zeus at the request of Athena; having failed with thunderbolts, he sends crabs to quell the strife.

batten down the hatches prepare for a difficulty or crisis; literally, secure a ship's tarpaulins over the hatchways with *battens* or strips of wood or metal.

Battenberg name of a family of German counts who died out in the 14th century; in 1858, the name was revived for the offspring of a morganatic marriage of a prince of the German state of Hesse. In 1917 the members of the family who were connected with the

British royal family and lived in England, renounced the German title of prince of Battenberg and took instead the surname *Mountbatten*.

Battle Abbey an abbey founded by William the Conqueror near the site of the ➤ *Battle of* HASTINGS, in fulfilment of his vow before the battle that he would build an abbey if he achieved victory. The church was consecrated in 1094.

Battle Hymn of the Republic the title of Julia Ward Howe's poem, which became one of the most popular songs of the Union forces during the American Civil War, is said to have been suggested to her by the editor of the *Atlantic Monthly*, J. T. Fields, when both were visiting the Union troops in 1861. The 'Battle Hymn' was first published in the *Atlantic Monthly* in February, 1862.

Battle of Britain a series of air battles fought over Britain (August–October 1940), in which the RAF successfully resisted raids by the numerically superior German air force.

Battle of the Bulge an unofficial name for the campaign in the Ardennes, December 1944–January 1945, when German forces attempted to break through Allied lines and almost succeeded in doing so.

battleaxe a battleaxe is the emblem of ➤ *St* OLAF, who was killed in battle.

Battleborn State informal name for the state of Nevada, which was admitted to the Union during the American Civil War (October, 1864).

not know a B from a battledore be completely illiterate or ignorant; the saying is based on the resemblance in shape of the paddle-shaped battledore to a horn-book, from which children traditionally learned to read.

Baucis in a story told by Ovid, the wife of a good old countryman Philemon. They entertained the gods ➤ ZEUS and ➤ HERMES as hospitably as their poverty allowed when the gods, who had visited the earth in disguise, were rejected by the rich. For this, the couple were saved from a flood which covered the district, and their dwelling was transformed into a temple of which they became the first priest and priestess. They were also granted their request to die at the same time, and were then turned into trees whose boughs intertwined.

Bauhaus a school of applied arts established by Walter Gropius in Weimar in 1919 and noted for its refined functionalist approach to architecture and industrial design. The socialist principles on which Bauhaus ideas rested incurred the hostility of the Nazis and, after moving to Berlin in 1932, the school was closed in 1933.

bawbee in Scottish usage, a coin of low value, originally a silver coin worth three (later six) Scottish pennies. Recorded from the mid 16th century, the word comes from the name of the laird of *Sillebawby*, mint-master under James V of Scotland.

bay a wreath of leaves from the bay laurel or bay tree was the traditional way of marking recognition of the prowess of a victor or poet (see also ➤ POET *Laureate*). From this, bay leaves or *bays* symbolize public recognition.

Bay trees were also seen from classical times as having a protective role. In later tradition, bay trees (like ➤ ROWANS) might be planted as a protection against witches, and a bay tree withering was taken as a portent of evil.

Bay leaves have also been used as a traditional method of divination; the belief that bay leaves fastened to or placed under the pillow will result in dreaming of one's future spouse is recorded from the early 18th century.

bring someone to bay trap or corner a person or animal being hunted or chased. A medieval hunting term (Old French *tenir a bay*) referring to the position of the quarry when it is cornered by the baying hounds. And animal thus cornered is said to *stand at bay*.

Bay Psalm Book the metrical version of the Psalms produced at Cambridge, Massachusetts (the ➤ BAY *State*) in 1640, the first book to be printed in British America.

Bay State informal name for the state of Massachusetts (the original colony was sited around Massachusetts Bay).

Bay Street the moneyed interests of Toronto, especially as opposed to other regions of Canada (*Bay Street* is a street in Toronto where the headquarters of many financial institutions are located).

Bayard¹ name of the magic bright bay-coloured horse given by Charlemagne to Renaud (or Rinaldo), one of the four sons of

Aimon. *Bayard* was formerly used as a mock-heroic name for any horse, and also as a type of blind recklessness.

Bayard² the French soldier Pierre du Terrail, Chevalier de *Bayard* (1473–1524), became known as the knight 'sans peur et sans reproche' (fearless and above reproach).

Bayeux Tapestry a fine example of medieval English embroidery, executed between 1066 and 1077, probably at Canterbury, for Odo, bishop of Bayeux and half-brother of William the Conqueror, and now exhibited at Bayeux in Normandy. In seventy-nine scenes, accompanied by a Latin text and arranged like a strip cartoon, it tells the story of the Norman Conquest and the events leading up to it; these include a representation of ▶ HALLEY's comet, the appearance of which as causing predictions of disaster prior to the Battle of Hastings is noted in the Anglo-Saxon Chronicle.

Bayou State informal name for Mississippi.

Bayreuth a town in Bavaria where Wagner made his home from 1874 and where he is buried. Festivals of his operas are held regularly there in a theatre specially built (1872–6) to house performances of *Der Ring des Nibelungen*.

BC before Christ (used to indicate that the date is before the Christian era).

Beachy Head name of a chalk headland on the Sussex coast, noted for the number of suicides which have taken place by jumping over the cliff there. It is also, in Chesterton's poem 'The Rolling English Road' (1914), one of the points of the type of a rambling journey.

beacon the maintenance of a chain of beacons was one of the means of national defence against a possible Spanish invasion in late 16th-century England. From this, *beacon* came to mean a conspicuous hill suitable for the site of a signal fire (frequently occurring in place-names, as **Brecon Beacons**, **Dunkery Beacon**).
  Recorded from Old English (in form *bēacn*) meaning 'sign, portent', the word is of West Germanic origin and is related to *beckon*.

bead originally meaning 'prayer', current senses derive from the use of a rosary, each bead representing a prayer. **Beadsman** is a

historical term for a pensioner provided for by a benefactor.

beadle a ceremonial officer of a church, college, or similar institution. Originally (from Old English to the late 17th century) a person who makes a proclamation, a town crier; later (now historical), a parish officer appointed by the vestry to keep order in church and punish petty offenders.

beagle a small hound of a breed with a short coat, used for hunting hares. Recorded from the late 15th century, the word may come from Old French *beegueule* 'open-mouthed', from *beer* 'open wide' + *gueule* 'throat'.
  HMS *Beagle* was the name of the ship of ▶ Charles DARWIN's voyage of 1831–6 around the southern hemisphere; the **Beagle Channel** through the islands of Tierra del Fuego at the southern tip of South America was named after her.

beak-head a Romanesque architectural ornament consisting of a bird, animal, or human head with a beak or tongue extending downwards. Each beak-head is cut as a wedge and is designed to sit in an arch.

Beaker folk a late Neolithic and early Bronze Age European people (c.2700–1700 BC), named after distinctive waisted pots (**Beaker ware**) that were associated with their burials and appear to have been used for alcoholic drinks. It is now thought that the Beaker folk were not a separate race, but that the use of such pots spread as a result of migration, trade, and fashion.

off beam on the wrong track, mistaken. Originally (mid 20th century) referring to the radio beam or signal used to guide aircraft.

on one's beam-ends at the end of one's financial resources; *beam-ends* are the ends of a ship's beams, and a ship *on her beam-ends* is one on its side, almost capsizing.

a beam in one's eye a fault that is greater in oneself than in the person with whom one is finding fault, in allusion to *Matthew* 7:3 'Why beholdest thou the mote that is in thy brother's eye, but considerest not the beam that is in thine own eye?'

bean from early times, the broad bean was a staple foodstuff (see *beanfeast* below), and there are various traditional rhymes recommending the best time of planting. Beans as an article of diet are proverbially associated with Leicestershire.

Beans were traditionally used in casting ballots, and the Latin tag *Abstineto a fabis* 'Abstain from beans' is understood as an injunction to abstain from meddling in affairs of state by casting one's vote in an election. The followers of ➤ PYTHAGORAS abstained from eating beans, although the reason for this is not known.

A **beanfeast** is a celebratory party with plenty of food and drink; originally, an annual dinner given by an employer to his employees, at which beans and bacon were regarded as an indispensable dish. The term is recorded from the early 19th century.

Beanie Baby US trademark name for any of a variety of soft toy animals stuffed with beans, frequently treated as a collectable item, and highly popular in the 1990s.

bear[1] a *bear* is the type of an uncouth and savage creature. In medieval usage, also taken as symbolizing sloth and gluttony.

From the late 18th century, **the Bear** has been used to denote Russia.

A *bear* is the emblem of St Gall, a 7th-century Irish monk and hermit living in what is now Switzerland, and the Russian St Seraphim (1759–1833), who while living as a hermit cared for bears and other wild animals.

The **bear and ragged staff** is the crest of the Earls of Warwick, showing a bear with a staff having projecting stumps or knobs; the bear is said to derive from *Arthgal*, a legendary Earl of Warwick, who because his name meant 'bear' took the animal as his badge; the *ragged staff* refers to the story that his son killed a giant with a young ash tree, which he tore up by the roots.

The **Bear Bible**, printed at Basle in 1569, was decorated with the symbol of a bear on the title page.

A **bear garden** is a scene of uproar and confusion; a *bear garden* was originally (like the ➤ PARIS *garden*) a place set apart for baiting of bears with dogs for sport, and such areas were also often used for other rough sports. In the 18th century, **bear leader** was a humorous name for a rich young man's travelling tutor, seen as one managing a somewhat uncouth charge.

bear[2] in Stock Exchange usage, a person who sells shares hoping to buy them back again later at a lower price. The term (applied to the stock thus sold) is recorded from the early 18th century, and was common at the time of the ➤ SOUTH *Sea Bubble*. The dealer in this kind of stock was known as the **bearskin jobber**, and it seems likely that the original phrase was 'sell the bearskin', and that it derived from the proverbial advice 'not to sell the skin before one has caught the bear'. A **bear market** is a market in which share prices are falling, encouraging selling.

The associated *bull* is of later date, and may perhaps have been suggested by the existence of *bear* in this sense.

beard the lion in his den attack someone on their own ground or subject; partly from the idea of taking a lion by the tuft of hair on its chin, partly from the use of *beard* to mean 'face'.

beast from late Middle English (in Wyclif's translation of the Bible), **the Beast** was a name for Antichrist (see also ➤ *the* MARK *of the beast*, ➤ *the* NUMBER *of the beast*).

The **Beast of Belsen** was a byname for Josef Kramer (1906–45), German commandant of Belsen concentration camp from December 1944, who in 1945 was tried before a British military tribunal and executed.

The **Beast of Bodmin Moor** is the name given to a panther-like creature supposedly living in the Bodmin Moor area; despite reports of such feral cats from the early 1990s, no conclusive proof for their existence has yet been demonstrated.

The **Beast of Bolsover** is the nickname of the Labour politician Dennis Skinner (1932–), MP for Bolsover in Derbyshire and noted for his abrasive manner and left-wing views.

The **beast with two backs** is a term for a man and woman in the act of sexual intercourse; originally as a quotation from Shakespeare's *Othello* (1602–4). Earlier Rabelais had had, '*faire la bête à deux dos* [do the two-backed beast together]'.

beat about the bush discuss a matter without coming to the point; be ineffectual and waste time. A metaphor originating in the shooting or netting of birds.

beat a (hasty) retreat withdraw, typically in order to avoid something unpleasant. Formerly in a military context, a drumbeat could be used to keep soldiers in step while retreating.

beat generation a movement of young people in the 1950s and early 1960s who rejected conventional society, valuing free self-expression and favouring modern jazz. The phrase itself was supposedly coined by Jack Kerouac (1922–69) in the course of a conversation.

beat the bounds trace out the boundaries of a parish, striking certain points with rods; the custom is recorded from the late 16th century.

beat the bushes search thoroughly. A North American expression, originating in the practice of hunters who walk through undergrowth with long sticks to force birds or animals hiding in the bushes out into the open where they can be shot or netted.

beat the Dutch say or do something extraordinary; the term is recorded from the late 18th century, and is from the US.

beatific vision the first sight of the glories of heaven; the direct experience of God by those in heaven.

beatification in the Roman Catholic Church, declaration by the Pope that a dead person is in a state of bliss, constituting the first step towards canonization and permitting public veneration.

the Beatitudes the blessings listed by Jesus in the Sermon on the Mount (Matthew 3:5–11). The word *beatitude* means supreme blessedness; it is recorded from late Middle English, and comes via Old French or Latin, from Latin *beatus* 'blessed'.

the Beatles a pop and rock group from Liverpool consisting of George Harrison, John Lennon, Paul McCartney, and Ringo Starr.

beatnik a young person in the 1950s and early 1960s belonging to a subculture associated with the ➤ BEAT *generation*. The word was formed in the 1960s on the pattern of *sputnik*, perhaps influenced by US use of Yiddish *-nik*, denoting someone or something who acts in a particular way.

Beatrice name given by ➤ DANTE *Alighieri* in *Vita nuova* and *The Divine Comedy* to the woman with whom he had fallen in love at his first sight of her; in *The Divine Comedy* she is his guide for his spiritual journey. While her identity is not certainly known, she is generally identified with Bice Portinari, who married Simone de' Bardi and died in 1290.

Beatrice is also the name of the spirited heroine of Shakespeare's *Much Ado About Nothing* (1598–9).

beau a rich, fashionable young man, a dandy; sometimes used in a personal appellation, as in **Beau Brummell, Beau Nash**. Recorded from the late 17th century, the word comes from French, literally 'handsome', from Latin *bellus*.

Beau Geste was the nickname of Michael Geste (punning on *beau geste* a noble and generous act) who in P. G. Wren's romantic adventure novel (1924) of this title runs away to enlist in the French Foreign Legion to spare his family the distress of a wrongful accusation against him.

Beauty and the Beast a fairy story by the French writer for children Madame de Beaumont (1711–80), translated into English in 1757. In the story Beauty, the youngest daughter of a merchant, goes to live in the Beast's palace and agrees to marry him; she discovers that he is a prince who has been put under a spell, which is destroyed by her love for him, and her ability to see his true worth beneath the hideous exterior.

beaver[1] the *beaver* is often taken as a type of industry, from its habit of gnawing through tree-trunks to make dams. Recorded from Old English (in form *beofor*) and of Germanic origin, the word comes ultimately from an Indo-European root meaning 'brown'.

The **Beaver State** is an informal name for Oregon.

beaver[2] the lower part of the face guard of a helmet in a suit of armour. Recorded from the late 15th century, the word comes from Old French *bavier* 'bib', from *baver* 'slaver'.

bebop a type of jazz originating in the 1940s and characterized by complex harmony and rhythms.

St Thomas à Becket (c.1118–70), English prelate and statesman, Archbishop of Canterbury 1162–70. Initially a friend and supporter of Henry II, as archbishop he came into open opposition with the king, whose reported words 'Will no one rid me of this turbulent priest?' are said to have sent four knights to assassinate Becket in his cathedral. Henry was obliged to do public penance at Becket's tomb, which became a major centre of pilgrimage until its destruction under Henry VIII (1538). His feast day is 29 December.

Becky Sharp the scheming anti-heroine of Thackeray's *Vanity Fair* (1847–8), who despite her wit and charm is unscrupulous in her pursuit of material gain.

bed and breakfast sell (shares) after hours one evening and buy them back as soon as possible the following day, in order to establish a loss for tax purposes.

a bed of nails a problematic or uncomfortable situation. Originally, a board with nails pointing out of it, as lain on by Eastern fakirs and ascetics.

a bed of roses a situation that is comfortable or easy (often used in the negative).

Bedchamber Crisis on Robert Peel's first taking office as Prime Minister in 1839, he requested that some of the Whig *ladies of the bedchamber* be replaced by Tories. When Queen Victoria (as queen regnant) refused the request, Peel resigned.

St Bede (*c.*673–735), English monk, theologian, and historian, known as **The Venerable Bede**, who lived and worked at the monastery in Jarrow on Tyneside. Bede wrote *The Ecclesiastical History of the English People* (completed in 731), a primary source for early English history. His feast day is 27 May.

Bedevere in the Arthurian romances, one of the few who survives the final battle against Mordred; he was charged by the dying Arthur with the duty of throwing the sword ➤ EXCALIBUR back into the lake, and after twice failing to carry out the task, finally did so.

bedlam a scene of uproar or confusion, deriving ultimately from *Bedlam*, a corruption of *Bethlehem*, in the name of the 'Hospital of St Mary of Bethlehem', founded by the Sheriff of London in Bishopsgate in 1247 for the housing of the clergy of St Mary of Bethlehem when they visited Britain. The house is mentioned as a hospital for the sick in 1330, and lunatics are stated to have been there in 1402. On the ➤ DISSOLUTION *of the monasteries* it passed to the London civic authorities and in 1547 became a royal foundation. Its place was taken in 1675 by a new hospital in Moorfields, and this again was transferred to the Lambeth Road in 1815. The site now houses the Imperial War Museum.

The use of 'bedlam' as a general term to mean an asylum for the insane is recorded from the mid 17th century. (See also ➤ TOM o' *Bedlam*.)

Bedouin a nomadic Arab of the desert; the word comes (via Old French) from Arabic

badawīn 'dwellers in the desert', from *badw* 'desert'.

bee traditionally taken as the type of an industrious and productive worker. *Bees* are also the emblem of ➤ St AMBROSE (see also ➤ BEEHIVE) and ➤ St JOHN *Chrysostom*.

There are a number of superstitions concerning bees, including various beliefs to do with death. The tradition of 'telling the bees' that the owner of their hive has died is a long-established one; it is believed that this will avert the death or disappearance of the bees.

To have **a bee in one's bonnet** is to have an obsessive preoccupation with something, recorded from the 19th century. The expression **bees in the head** was used in the early 16th century for someone regarded as crazy or eccentric, and the alliterative version with *bonnet* is indicated by the 17th century poet Herrick's reference to a bee in his 'bonnet brave' in his poem 'Mad Maud's Song' (*Hesperides*, 1648).

beefcake attractive men with well-developed muscles; the slang term is modelled on the earlier *cheesecake* for an attractive woman.

beefeater a Yeoman Warder or Yeoman of the Guard in the Tower of London. The word is recorded from the early 17th century, originally as a derogatory term for a well-fed servant: the current sense dates from the late 17th century.

beehive a *beehive* is an emblem of ➤ St AMBROSE, from the story that a swarm of bees, symbolizing his future eloquence, settled on him as a child.

The **Beehive State** is an informal name for Utah.

beeline a straight line between two points, originally with reference to the straight line supposedly taken instinctively by a bee when returning to the hive.

Beelzebub a name for the Devil, recorded in English from early times; Milton in *Paradise Lost*, however, uses it as the name of one of the fallen angels. The name comes originally from late Latin translating a Hebrew word meaning 'lord of the flies', recorded in 2 Kings 1:2 as the name of a Philistine god, and a Greek word meaning 'the Devil', from Matthew 12:24.

been there, done that used to express past experience of or familiarity with something, especially something now regarded as boring or unwelcome; the extension 'and got the T-shirt' reinforces the notion of a jaded tourist who has relentlessly visited sites and bought souvenirs.

beer and skittles amusement; from the proverbial saying (recorded from the mid 19th century), **life isn't all beer and skittles**. The game of *skittles* is taken as the type of light-hearted entertainment.

Mrs Beeton (1836–65), English author on cookery, famous for her best-selling *Book of Cookery and Household Management* (1861), first published serially in a women's magazine, contained over 3,000 recipes and articles, as well as sections giving advice on legal and medical matters.

beg the question assume the truth of an argument or proposition to be proved, without arguing it. The original meaning belongs to the field of logic and is a translation of Latin *petitio principii*, literally meaning 'laying claim to a principle', i.e. assuming something that ought to be proved first.

beggar a person who lives by asking for money or food.
   A **beggar on horseback** is a formerly poor person made arrogant or corrupt through achieving wealth and luxury; recorded from the early 16th century, and related to the mid 17th century saying, **set a beggar on horseback and he'll ride to the devil**.
   The Beggar's Opera is a low-life ballad opera (1728) by John Gay (1685–1732), combining burlesque and political satire in its story of the highwayman ➤ MACHEATH who is betrayed by the informer ➤ PEACHUM. In the 20th century, Bertolt Brecht's version of Gay's work, *The Threepenny Opera* (*Die Dreigroschenoper*, 1928) was one of the theatrical successes of Weimar Germany.

beginner's luck good luck traditionally said to attend a beginner; the expression is recorded from the late 19th century.

Beguine a member of a lay sisterhood in the Low Countries, formed in the 12th century and not bound by vows; members were allowed to leave their societies for marriage. They are still represented by small communities existing in the Netherlands, with an organization somewhat similar to some Anglican sisterhoods.
   The name is said in a 12th-century chronicle to derive from the nickname of ➤ LAMBERT, a priest of Liège, nicknamed 'le Bègue' because he stammered.

behemoth a huge or monstrous creature. The name comes from a Hebrew word occurring several times in the Old Testament and generally translated as 'beast'; however, in Job 40:15, the Authorized Version has 'behemoth'. The animal mentioned in Job is probably the hippopotamus, but the word came to be used generally for a particularly large and strong animal.

Bel an alternative form of the name of the god ➤ BAAL, occurring most frequently in **Bel and the Dragon**, two stories included as a single item in the Apocrypha. The first relates how the prophet ➤ DANIEL convinced the Babylonian king that the offerings of food and drink which were daily set before the image of Bel were not really eaten by the god but were secretly removed by the priests. As a result, the priests were executed and the image destroyed.
   In the second story, which is apparently based on an ancient Semitic myth, Daniel obtained the king's consent to attack a dragon, and killed it by feeding it with cakes made of pitch, fat, and hair. This so enraged the people that they insisted that Daniel should be cast into a den of seven lions. With the help of the prophet Habakkuk, who was miraculously transported from Judaea to feed him, he was saved from death and freed. In consequence the king became a worshipper of Yahweh.

Sir Toby Belch in Shakespeare's *Twelfth Night* (1601), a roistering knight, disreputable uncle to Olivia, who argues for the ➤ CAKES *and ale* of life against the Puritanism of ➤ MALVOLIO.

beldam a malicious and ugly woman, especially an old one; a witch. Recorded from late Middle English (originally in the sense 'grandmother'), the word comes from Old French *bel* 'beautiful' + *dam* 'mother'.

Belgae an ancient Celtic people inhabiting Gaul north of the Seine and Marne Rivers, eventually defeated by Julius Caesar in the Gallic Wars of 58–51 BC. At the beginning of the 1st century BC some of the Belgae had crossed to southern England, where they established kingdoms around Colchester, Winchester, and Silchester.

Belial the personification of evil, used from early times as a name for the Devil, and by Milton as the name of the fallen angel who represents impurity. Following biblical use, the name is often used in the phrase *sons of*

Belial. It comes from a Hebrew word meaning 'worthlessness'.

Belisarius outstanding general of the 6th century Roman emperor ➤ JUSTINIAN, his greatest victories being the recovery of Africa from the Vandals in 533, and Italy from the Ostrogoths in 540. Towards the end of his life he fell from favour and was accused of a conspiracy against Justinian; there was a tradition that his eyes were put out and that he ended his life as a beggar on the streets of Constantinople.

bell a *bell* is the emblem of ➤ St ANTHONY *of Egypt* and the 6th-century Breton abbot St Winwaloe, of whom it was said that at the sound of his bell, fishes would follow him.

Bell, book, and candle are the formulaic requirements for laying a curse on someone, with allusion to the closing words of the rite of excommunication, 'Do to the book, quench the candle, ring the bell', meaning that the service book is closed, the candle put out (by being dashed to the floor), and the passing bell rung, as a sign of spiritual death.

St ➤ AGATHA is the patron saint of **bell-founders**, perhaps through a misinterpretation of the emblem with which she is most commonly represented, her severed breasts lying upturned on a plate.

To **bell the cat** is to take the danger of a shared enterprise upon oneself, from the fable in which mice proposed hanging a bell around a cat's neck so as to be warned of its approach; the nickname 'Bell-the-Cat' was popularly given to the 16th century Scottish Earl of Angus who is said to have used the phrase when asserting his readiness to lead the Scottish nobles in a revolt against King James III's low-born favourites.

To **ring the bell** is to be the best of the lot (in allusion to a fairground strength-testing machine).

Bellerophon in Greek mythology, an ancient Corinthian hero, said in some accounts to be the son of ➤ POSEIDON. Anteia, wife of Proetus king of Argus, fell in love with him, and when he rejected her accused him publicly of trying to seduce her (cf. ➤ POTIPHAR's wife). Proetus, unwilling to violate the laws of hospitality, sent Bellerophon to the king of Lycia, with a sealed letter requesting the king to kill Bellerophon. The king set him a number of tasks likely to prove fatal, such as killing the ➤ CHIMAERA and defeating the ➤ AMAZONS, but Bellerophon with the help of the winged horse ➤ PEGASUS was always

successful. He was finally reconciled to the king, and married his daughter.

Afterwards Bellerophon incurred the anger of the gods by his presumption in trying to ride Pegasus to heaven, but the horse threw him. He ended his life as a lonely outcast.

bellman historical term for a town crier, a man employed to go round the streets of a town and make public announcements, to which he attracted attention by ringing a bell. The *bellman* also announced deaths, and called on the faithful to pray for the souls of the departed.

Bellona the Roman goddess of war, sometimes thought of as the wife or sister of Mars; it is possible that she was associated with human sacrifice.

bells and **whistles** in computing, speciously attractive but superfluous facilities, with allusion to the various bells and whistles of old fairground organs.

ring the bells backward ring them beginning with the bass bell, in order to give alarm of fire or invasion, or express dismay; the expression is recorded from the early 16th century.

go belly up go bankrupt. The allusion is to a dead fish or other animal floating upside down in the water.

beloved disciple the anonymous and idealized disciple in St John's Gospel, described as the one 'whom Jesus loved', and traditionally often identified as St John the Evangelist.

below the belt unfair or unfairly; disregarding the rules, from the notion of an unfair and illegal blow in boxing.

below the salt at the lower end of the table, among the less distinguished guests; a large salt-cellar (the *salt*), often made of precious metal, was traditionally placed in the middle of a long dining-table, marking the division between those regarded as more or less favoured guests.

Belphegor the Septuagint and Vulgate form of the Moabitish 'Baal-peor' mentioned in Numbers 25. Machiavelli in his *Novella di Belfagor* (*c.*1518) gives the name to a devil sent into the world by Pluto to discover if it is true, as many of those arriving in hell assert, that they have been sent there by their wives, and the name *Belphegor* is sometimes used generally for a devil or demon.

Belphoebe in Spenser's *Faerie Queene*, a chaste huntress who partly symbolizes Queen Elizabeth.

Belsen a Nazi concentration camp in the Second World War, near the village of Belsen in north western Germany, the liberation of which at the end of the Second World War provided the Allied countries with horrific and graphic pictures of what had been done to its inmates. (See also ➤ BEAST *of Belsen*.)

Belshazzar's feast the feast made by Belshazzar, the son of ➤ NEBUCHADNEZZAR and the last king of Babylonia, at which his doom was foretold by the writing on the wall, interpreted by ➤ DANIEL. Belshazzar was killed in the sack of Babylon by Cyrus in 538 BC.

belt and braces twofold security. From the literal *belt* and *braces* for holding up a pair of loose-fitting trousers.

Beltane an ancient Celtic festival celebrated on May Day, marked by bonfires being kindled on the hills. Beltane was also traditionally one of the quarter-days in Scotland, the others being ➤ HALLOWMAS, ➤ CANDLEMAS, and ➤ LAMMAS. The name comes from the Celtic name for the day which marked the beginning of summer.

In recent times, *Beltane* has been celebrated as a modern Pagan festival.

The name is recorded from late Middle English, and comes from Scottish Gaelic *bealltainn*.

Beltway Washington DC, especially as representing the perceived insularity of the US government, from a transferred use by association with the ring road encircling Washington.

In US slang, a **Beltway Bandit** is a company or individual, frequently one employed by a US government agency, hired by a corporation to assist in securing government contracts.

belvedere a summer house or open-sided gallery, typically at rooftop level, commanding a fine view; the word comes (in the late 16th century) from Italian, literally 'fair sight'. (See also the *Apollo Belvedere* at ➤ APOLLO.)

The **Belvedere Torso** is the name given to a Greek sculpture fragment of a male nude, believed to have been copied by the Athenian sculptor Apollonius from a 2nd-century original; the pose of the torso influenced Michelangelo and was much studied in the Late Renaissance and Baroque periods.

bema the altar part or sanctuary in ancient and Orthodox churches. Recorded in English from the late 17th century, the word comes from Greek *bēma* 'a step or raised place', the term used for the platform from which orators spoke in ancient Athens.

ben trovato of an anecdote, invented but plausible. The phrase is Italian, and means literally 'well found'; The saying *Se non è vero, è molto ben trovato* 'if it is not true, it is a happy invention' was apparently a common saying in the 16th century.

Bench the office of a judge or magistrate, from the *bench* as a judge's seat in a law court (recorded in this sense from Middle English); from this comes the expression **raised to the Bench**, meaning, elevated to the dignity of a judge. The term **Bench and Bar** is used for judges and barristers collectively.

In the UK, a **bencher** is a senior member of any of the Inns of Court, who form for each Inn a self-elective body, managing its affairs, and traditionally possessed the privilege of 'calling to the bar'.

benchmark a standard or point of reference against which things may be compared or assessed; a *benchmark* was originally a surveyor's mark cut in a wall, pillar, or building and used as a reference point in measuring altitudes.

The mark consists of a series of wedge-shaped incisures, in the form of the 'broad-arrow' with a horizontal bar through its apex; when the spot is below sea-level, as in mining surveys, the mark is inverted. The horizontal bar is the essential part, the broad arrow being added (originally by the Ordnance Survey) as an identification. In taking a reading, an angle-iron is held with its upper extremity inserted in the horizontal bar, so as to form a temporary bracket or *bench* for the support of the levelling-staff, which can thus be placed on absolutely the same base on any subsequent occasion.

bend in heraldry, an ordinary in the form of a broad diagonal stripe from top left (dexter chief) to bottom right (sinister base) of a shield or part of one.

A **bend sinister** is a broad diagonal stripe from top right to bottom left of a shield (a supposed sign of bastardy).

the Benedicite the canticle used in the Anglican service of matins beginning 'O all ye works of the Lord, bless ye the Lord'. It is also called 'The Song of the Three Holy Children', the text being taken from that book of the Apocrypha.

Benedick a newly married man, especially one who had been regarded as a sworn bachelor, from the name of the hero in Shakespeare's *Much Ado About Nothing*, who against his own will falls in love with and marries Beatrice; the usage probably develops from the mocking question, 'How dost thou, Benedick the married man?'

St Benedict (*c*.480–*c*.550), Italian hermit. He established a monastery at ➤ MONTE *Cassino* and his *Regula Monachorum* (known as the Rule of St Benedict) formed the basis of Western monasticism. His feast day is 11 July (formerly 21 March).

Benedictine a monk or nun of a Christian religious order following the rule of St Benedict, established *c*.540. The Rule of St Benedict was gradually adopted by most Western monastic houses, sometimes with their own modifications. Benedictines were also known as *Black Monks* from the colour of their habits.

The liqueur benedictine, based on brandy, is named from its being originally made by Benedictine monks in France.

Benediction a service in which the congregation is blessed with the Blessed Sacrament, held mainly in the Roman Catholic Church.

benedictional a book containing the forms of episcopal benedictions formerly in use.

Benedictus an invocation beginning *Benedictus qui venit in nomine Domini* (Blessed is he who comes in the name of the Lord) forming a set part of the Mass.

benefit of clergy the exemption of the English clergy and nuns from the jurisdiction of the ordinary civil courts, granted in the Middle Ages but abolished in 1827.

Benjamin a Hebrew patriarch, the youngest and favourite son of ➤ JACOB, whose elder brothers were forced by their unrecognized brother ➤ JOSEPH, whom they had wronged, to take back to Egypt with them.

In Egypt, an accusation of the theft of a cup is arranged against Benjamin, and it seems that Jacob will indeed lose him; however, this is the dramatic opening to Joseph's forgiveness of, and reconciliation with, the other brothers.

Benjamin gave his name to the smallest tribe of Israel, traditionally descended from him.

Benjamin's portion is the largest portion of something, with allusion to Genesis 63:34, in which Joseph, giving food to his brothers, gives to Benjamin (the only one who is innocent of wrongdoing against him) five times the amount he has given to the others.

Beowulf a legendary Scandinavian hero whose exploits are celebrated in an eponymous Old English poem; in the first part, as a young warrior, he destroys the monster ➤ GRENDEL and Grendel's mother, and in the second part, as an old king, he kills (but is also killed by) a dragon which is ravaging his country.

Berchta a mother goddess of German mythology, typically dressed in white (her name means 'bright') and triple-headed; she was traditionally patron of spinners, because at the end of the year she was said to finish off unfinished work; however on Twelfth Night she might also spoil and tangle flax as a punishment.

Berchtesgarden a town in southern Germany in the Bavarian alps, site of Hitler's fortified retreat.

Berenice's hair the northern constellation *Coma Berenices*, named after an Egyptian queen of the 3rd century BC, wife of Ptolemy III. She dedicated her hair as an offering for the safe return of her husband from an expedition, and the hair was stolen and according to legend, placed in the heavens.

Vitus Bering (1681–1741), Danish navigator and explorer, who led several Russian expeditions aimed at discovering whether Asia and North America were connected by land. He sailed along the coast of Siberia and in 1741 reached Alaska from the east but died on the return journey; the **Bering Sea** and **Bering Strait** are named after him.

Berlin airlift an operation by British and American aircraft to airlift food and supplies to Berlin in 1948–9, while Russian forces blockaded the city to isolate it from the West and terminate the joint Allied military government of the city. After the blockade was lifted the city was formally divided into two parts: **West Berlin**, comprising the American, British, and French sectors, later a state of the Federal Republic of Germany despite forming an enclave within the German Democratic Republic; and **East Berlin**, the sector of the city occupied by the USSR and later capital of the German Democratic Republic.

Berlin Wall a fortified and heavily guarded wall built in 1961 by the communist authorities on the boundary between East and West Berlin chiefly to curb the flow of East Germans to the West. Regarded as a symbol of the division of Europe into the communist countries of the East and the democracies of the West, it was opened in November 1989 after the collapse of the communist regime in East Germany and subsequently dismantled.

Bermuda Triangle an area of the western Atlantic Ocean where a large number of ships and aircraft are said to have mysteriously disappeared; the name is recorded from the 1960s.

St Bernard of Aosta (*c.*996–*c.*1081), French monk who founded two hospices for travellers in the Alps. The St Bernard passes, where the hospices were situated, and St Bernard dogs are named after him, and he is patron saint of mountaineers. His feast day is 28 May.

St Bernard of Clairvaux (1090–1153), French theologian and monastic reformer. He was the first abbot of Clairvaux and his monastery became one of the chief centres of the Cistercian order. His feast day is 20 August.

St Bernadette (1844–79), French peasant girl, born Marie Bernarde Soubirous. Her visions of the Virgin Mary in Lourdes in 1858 led to the town's establishment as a centre of pilgrimage. Bernadette later became a nun and she was canonized in 1933. Her feast day is 18 February.

Bernadotte family name of the present royal house of Sweden, founded by Jean Baptiste Jules Bernadotte (1763–1844), French soldier, king of Sweden (as Charles XIV) 1818–44. One of Napoleon's marshals, he was adopted by Charles XIII of Sweden in 1810 and later became king.

Berne Convention an international copyright agreement of 1886, later revised. The US has never been party to it.

Bernicia an Anglian kingdom founded in the 6th century AD, extending from the Tyne to the Forth and eventually united with Deira to form Northumbria.

Berossus a priest at Babylon in the 3rd century BC who wrote a history of Babylon which transmitted Babylonian history and astronomy to the Greek world.

Berry a former province and medieval duchy of France; Jean, duc de Berry (1340–1416), son of John II of France, was the patron who commissioned the *Très riches heures du duc de Berry.*

give someone a wide berth stay well away from someone. *Berth* is a nautical term originally meaning the distance that ships should keep away from each other or from the shore, rocks, or other hazards, in order to avoid a collision.

Alphonse Bertillon (1853–1914), French criminologist. He devised a system of body measurements for the identification of criminals, which was widely used until superseded by fingerprinting at the beginning of the 20th century.

beryl in early sources taken as a type of perfect clarity.

Bes in Egyptian mythology, a grotesque god depicted as having short legs, an obese body, and an almost bestial face, who dispelled evil spirits.

besetting sin a fault to which someone is especially prone, a characterist weakness. *Beset* means literally 'surround with hostile intent', so the image is of the forces of sin besieging a person.

best bib and tucker best clothes. Originally used of items of women's dress: a *bib* is a garment worn over the upper front part of the body (as in the *bib* of an apron), and a *tucker* was a piece of lace formerly used to adorn a woman's bodice.

the best club in London traditional name for the House of Commons.

bestiary a descriptive or anecdotal treatise on various kinds of animal, especially a medieval work with a moralizing tone.

beta the second letter of the Greek alphabet (B, β), transliterated as 'b'.
    A **beta test** is a trial of machinery, software, or other products, in the final stages of its development, carried out by a party unconnected with its development.

bethel a hallowed spot, a place where God is worshipped; originally with reference to Genesis 28:19, from the story of Jacob who set up a pillar on the spot on which he had dreamed of seeing a ladder reaching up to heaven.

Bethesda in the bible (John 5:2–4), the name of a healing pool, perhaps representing *Bethzatha*, and understood to mean 'house of grace'.

Bethlehem a small town to the south of Jerusalem, first mentioned in Egyptian records of the 14th century BC. It was the native city of King David and is the reputed birthplace of Jesus. (See also ➤ BEDLAM.)

better the devil you know it is wiser to deal with an undesirable but familiar person or situation than to risk a change that might lead to something more difficult to deal with. The phrase is a shortened form of the mid 19th century proverbial saying, **better the devil you know than the devil you don't (know)**.

Betty Crocker a fictitious character, exhibiting conservative values and a consistently cheerful demeanour, purporting to be the presenter or writer of a series of radio programmes, newspaper articles, and books on cooking, distributed in the United States from 1924 onwards. The name was first used in 1921 as the signatory to letters sent to prizewinners in a promotional competition.

Beulah in the prophecies of Isaiah (ch. 62, v. 4), a name to be given to Israel when she is at one with God. *Beulah* in Hebrew means 'married'.

In Bunyan's *Pilgrim's Progress*, the **Land of Beulah** is a pleasant and fertile country beyond the Valley of the Shadow of Death, and within sight of the Heavenly City; the name may thus be used for heaven itself.

In Blake's writing, *Beulah* stands for a state of light, which is symbolized by the moon.

Bevin boy during the Second World War, a young man of age for National Service selected by lot to work as a miner; the term comes from the name of the Labour politician Ernest *Bevin* (1881–1951), Minister of Labour and National Service, 1940–5.

beyond the veil in the unknown state of being after death; the phrase is originally a figurative reference to the veil which in the Jewish Temple separated the main body of the Temple from the tabernacle, and derives particularly from Tyndale's translation of the Bible.

Bhagavadgita a sacred Hindu poem composed between the 2nd century BC and the 2nd century AD and incorporated into the ➤ MAHABHARATA. Presented as a dialogue between the Kshatriya prince Arjuna and his divine charioteer Krishna, it stresses the importance of doing one's duty and of faith in God.

Bhopal a city in central India, the capital of the state of Madhya Pradesh. In December 1984 leakage of poisonous gas from an American-owned pesticide factory in the city caused the death of about 2,500 people.

Biarritz a seaside resort in SW France, on the Bay of Biscay, which was made fashionable after 1854 by Napoleon III and the Empress Eugénie; Biarritz later became especially popular with British visitors.

the Bible the Christian scriptures, consisting of the Old and New Testaments; the Jewish scriptures, consisting of the Torah or Law, the Prophets, and the Hagiographa or Writings.

The Bible is traditionally regarded by Christians as having divine authority, though they disagree on how it should be interpreted. The medieval Catholic Church suppressed translations of the Latin text into the vernacular, and only at the Reformation did they become widely available; among English translations the Authorized or King James Version of 1611 made a lasting impression on English culture. Since the 19th century, the methods of critical scholarship have been applied to the Bible as a historical text, though fundamentalist belief in its literal truth has become prominent in the 20th century.

The **Bible Belt** denotes those areas of the southern and middle western United States and western Canada where Protestant fundamentalism is widely practised.

Bibliothèque nationale the national library of France, in Paris, which receives a copy of every book and periodical published in France.

bidding prayer a prayer in the form of an invitation by a minister or leader of a congregation to pray about something.

Bifrost in Scandinavian mythology, the bridge connecting heaven and earth.

big of considerable size or extent, in a number of names and phrases.

The **Big Apple** is an informal name for New York City.

The **big bang** was the explosion of dense matter which according to current cosmological theories marked the origin of the universe. In the beginning a fireball of radiation at extremely high temperature and density, but occupying a tiny volume, is believed to have formed. This expanded and cooled, extremely fast at first, but more slowly as subatomic particles condensed into matter which later accumulated to form galaxies and stars. The galaxies are currently still retreating from one another. What was left of the original radiation continued to cool and has been detected as a uniform background of weak microwave radiation.

In the UK, **Big Bang** is the name given to the introduction in 1986 of major changes in trading in the Stock Exchange, principally involving widening of membership, relaxation of rules for brokers, and computerization.

Big Ben is the great clock tower of the Houses of Parliament in London and its bell, named after Sir Benjamin Hall (1802–67), commissioner of public works at the time of its construction; *Big Ben* was designed by the English lawyer and mechanician Edmund Beckett, Lord Grimthorpe (1816–1905).

Big Bend National Park is a US national park in a bend of the Rio Grande, in the desert lands of southern Texas on the border with Mexico, in which were discovered, in 1975, fossil remains of the pterosaur.

Big Brother is a person or organization exercising total control over people's lives, from the head of state in George Orwell's novel *1984* (1949); his apparently benevolent but actually ruthlessly omnipotent rule is summed up by the slogan, 'Big Brother is watching you.'

In 2000, *Big Brother* became the name of a television game show in which selected contestants shared a house and were monitored by video camera. Each week one person was voted out of the house by the viewing public, and the winner was the last contestant to remain.

A **big cheese** is an important person. The phrase dates from the 1920s, and *cheese* probably comes via Urdu from Persian *čīz* 'thing'; *the cheese* was used earlier to mean 'first-rate' (i.e. *the* thing).

The **Big Smoke** is an informal term for London; also called ➤ *the* SMOKE.

A **big stick** is a display of force or power, especially in international diplomacy; the phrase is associated particularly with Theodore Roosevelt (1858–1919).

A **big white chief** is an important person, the senior member of a group; the name is a humorous one modelled on the supposed speech of American Indians.

Bigfoot a large, hairy ape-like creature resembling a yeti, supposedly found in NW America, so named because of the size of its footprints. (It is also known by the Salish name *Sasquatch*.)

Biggles a fictional aviator and war hero Major James Bigglesworth, DSO, MC in a series of books for children by Captain W. E. Johns, published between the 1930s and 1970s; he typifies the adventurous hero who is as morally upright as he is daring.

bigwig an important person, especially in a particular sphere; recorded from the early 18th century, the term comes from the large wigs worn at that period by important men.

on your bike! go away! Take action! Used as an expression of annoyance, or to urge someone to do something; in this sense, it became a 1980s catchphrase in Britain, used as an exhortation to the unemployed to look for work. This derived from a speech by the Conservative politician Norman Tebbit, who said of his unemployed father in the 1930s, 'He did not riot, he got on his bike and looked for work.'

Bikini an atoll in the Marshall Islands, in the western Pacific, used by the US between 1946 and 1958 as a site for testing nuclear weapons.

The *bikini* as a two-piece swimsuit for women was so named because of the supposed 'explosive' effect created by the garment.

bile a bitter greenish-brown alkaline fluid which aids digestion and is secreted by the liver and stored in the gall bladder, and which was formerly regarded as one of the four ➤ HUMOURS of the body.

Old Bill a grumbling veteran soldier, typically having a large moustache (with allusion to a cartoon character created during the war of 1914–18 by Bruce Bairnsfather (1888–1959), British cartoonist). Taking shelter from bombardment in a shell-hole, he advises his complaining friend, 'If you know of a better 'ole, go to it.'

Old Bill is also an informal name for the police (also **the Bill**). This may have originated from the cartoon character's being depicted in police uniform and giving advice on wartime security on posters during the war of 1939–45.

bill of health a certificate relating to the incidence of infectious disease on ship or in port at time of sailing; from this comes the phrase **a clean bill of health** to mean a declaration or confirmation that someone is healthy or that something is in good condition.

Bill of Rights a legal statement of the rights of a class of people, in particular: the English constitutional settlement of 1689, confirming the deposition of James II and the accession of William and Mary, guaranteeing the Protestant succession, and laying down the principles of parliamentary supremacy; the first ten amendments to the Constitution of the US, ratified in 1791.

Billingsgate a London fish market dating from the 16th century, traditionally noted for vituperative language.

bimbo an attractive but unintelligent or frivolous young woman. The term came into English (from Italian, 'little child, baby') in the early 1920s as a derogatory term for a person of either sex. The sense of stupid or 'loose' woman was however developing, and in the late 1980s the term enjoyed a new vogue in the media.

Bimini an island in the Bahamas, according to Indian legend the site of the ➤ FOUNTAIN of Youth.

bird used in a number of figurative and emblematic phrases.

To **give someone the bird** is to boo or jeer at someone. Earlier (early 19th century) in theatrical slang as *the big bird*, meaning a goose, because an audience's hissing an unpopular act or actor could be compared with the hissing of geese.

The bird has flown means that the prisoner or fugitive has escaped; the expression was famously used by Charles I of his failed attempt to arrest the ➤ FIVE *Members* in the House of Commons, 4 January 1642, when he found that the men had escaped.

A **bird in hand** is something that one has securely or is sure of, from the proverb alluding to bird-catching, **a bird in the hand is worth two in the bush**. The saying has been current in English since the mid 15th century, and is recorded in Latin from the 13th century.

The **Bird of Freedom** is the emblematic bald eagle of the US; the phrase is recorded from the mid 19th century.

The **bird of Jove** is the eagle, which in classical mythology was sacred to Jove. The **bird of Juno** is the peacock, which in classical mythology was sacred to Juno.

birdie in golf, a score of one stroke under par at a hole; the term comes from US slang *bird*, denoting any first-rate thing.

birds an emblem of ➤ St FRANCIS *of Assisi*.

The birds and the bees is an informal term for basic facts about sex and reproduction as told to a child.

Birds of a feather are people with similar tastes and interests. From the proverb *birds of a feather flock together*, current in this form from the late 16th century and perhaps ultimately deriving from the Apocrypha (Ecclesiasticus 27:9).

Birthday Honours in Britain, the titles and decorations awarded on a sovereign's official birthday.

bishop[1] a senior member of the Christian clergy, usually in charge of a diocese and empowered to confer holy orders.

In chess, a bishop is a piece, typically with its top shaped like a mitre, that can move in any direction along a diagonal on which it stands. Each player starts the game with two bishops, one moving on white squares and the other on black.

Recorded in Old English (in form *biscop*, *bisceop*) the word comes from Greek *episkopos* 'overseer'.

bishop[2] file and tamper with the teeth of a horse so as to deceive as to age. Recorded from the early 18th century, the term apparently comes from the name of someone initiating the practice.

Bishops' Bible an edition of the Bible published in 1568 under the direction of Archbishop Parker, and intended to counteract the popularity of the Calvinist ➤ GENEVA *Bible*.

have the bit between one's teeth be ready to tackle a problem in a determined or independent way; the allusion is to a horse which is out of its rider's control.

the bitch goddess material or worldly success; the term was coined by the philosopher William James (1842–1910) in a letter to H. G. Wells, 11 September 1906.

bite one's thumb at insult by making the gesture of biting one's thumb; in Shakespeare's *Romeo and Juliet* (1595), in a scene between two quarrelling servants, one when challenged says to the other, 'I do not bite my thumb at you, sir; but I bite my thumb, sir.'

bite the bullet behave stoically; the reference is to a wounded soldier undergoing surgery without the aid of anaesthetics.

bite the hand that feeds one injure a benefactor; the expression is recorded from the late 18th century, and is first recorded in Edmund Burke's *Thoughts on the Cause of the Present Discontents* (1770).

the biter bit a person who has done harm has been harmed in a similar way. In the late 17th century, a *biter* was a cant term for a fraudster or trickster.

to the bitter end persevering to the end, whatever the outcome. Perhaps associated with a nautical word *bitter* meaning the last part of a cable inboard of the *bitts* (strong bollards on a ship for securing mooring lines), and possibly also influenced by the biblical sentence 'her end is bitter as wormwood' (Proverbs 5:4).

black of the very darkest colour due to the absence of or complete absorption of light; the opposite of white. *Black* in western countries has traditionally been worn as a sign of mourning, and in figurative use the word has traditionally implied foreboding, evil, or melancholy. **Not as black as one is painted** means not as bad as one's reputation. It comes from the proverb *the devil is not as black as he is painted*, first recorded in English in the mid 16th century and used as a warning not to base one's fears of something on exaggerated reports.

The **Black Act** was a severe law passed in the early 18th century against poaching and trespassing (poachers who blackened their faces were known as *blacks*).

The **Black and Tans** were an armed force recruited by the British government to suppress insurrection in Ireland in 1921, so called from their wearing a mixture of black constabulary and khaki military uniforms.

Black Auster in Macaulay's *Battle of Lake Regillus* (1842) is the name of the horse belonging to Herminius.

Black Beauty is the name of the horse which is the central character in Anna Sewell's eponymous novel (1877); the book tells the story, in autobiographical form, of Black Beauty's (often careless or cruel) treatment by a variety of owners.

A **black belt** is a belt worn by an expert in judo, karate, and other martial arts. Also, a person qualified to wear this.

Black Bess is supposedly the name of the highwayman ➤ *Dick* TURPIN's horse, deriving from the version of Turpin's story given by Harrison Ainsworth in his novel *Rookwood* (1834).

black bile, in medieval science and medicine, was one of the four bodily ➤ HUMOURS, believed to be associated with a *melancholy* temperament. Recorded in English from the late 18th century, the term is a translation of Greek *melankholia* 'melancholy', from *melas*, *melan-* 'black' + *kholē* 'bile', an excess of which was formerly believed to cause depression.

A **black book** is an official book bound in black; the distinctive name of various individual books of public note, sometimes referring to the colour of the binding. It is also one in which there is a record of punishments, giving rise to the figurative phrase **to be in someone's black books**.

A **black box** is any complex piece of equipment, typically a unit in an electronic system, with contents which are mysterious to the user; specifically now, a flight recorder in an aircraft.

The **black cap** was a cap (actually a small piece of black cloth) formerly worn by a judge when passing sentence of death.

Black Carib is a language derived from Island Carib with borrowings from Spanish, English, and French, spoken in isolated parts of Central America by descendants of people transported from the Lesser Antilles.

A **black-coat worker** is a person in a clerical or professional, rather than an industrial or commercial, occupation.

The **Black Country** is a district of the Midlands with much heavy industry, traditionally regarded as blackened by the smoke and dust of the coal and iron trades.

The **Black Death** was the great epidemic of bubonic plague that killed a large proportion of the population of Europe in the mid 14th century. It originated in central Asia and China and spread rapidly through Europe, carried by the fleas of black rats, reaching England in 1348 and killing between one third and one half of the population in a matter of months. The name is modern, and was introduced in the early 19th century.

The **black dog** is a metaphorical representation of melancholy or depression, used particularly by Samuel Johnson to describe his attacks of melancholia. In the 20th century, the term has been associated with Winston Churchill, who used the phrase 'black dog' when alluding to his own periodic bouts of depression.

The **Black Douglas** was the byname of James Douglas (1286?–1330), Scottish champion and supporter of Robert Bruce, and afterwards of several senior representatives of his branch of the Douglas family.

Black earth is another name for ➤ CHERNOZEM.

The **black economy** is the part of a country's economic activity which is unrecorded and untaxed by its government.

A **Black Friar** is a ➤ DOMINICAN friar, named for the black habits worn by the order.

Black Friday is a name for various Fridays regarded as disastrous, such as 6 December 1745, when the landing of the Young Pretender was announced in London, and 11 May 1866, which saw a commercial panic at the failure of Overend, Gurney, & Co.

The **Black Hand** was a name given to several secret societies or associations, such as a Spanish revolutionary society of anarchists of the 19th century.

The **Black Hills** are a range of mountains in east Wyoming and west South Dakota, which includes the sculptured granite face of ➤ Mount RUSHMORE. The Black Hills were considered sacred territory by the Sioux; discovery of gold there in 1874, and the subsequent gold rush, led to war in 1876, and the ➤ Battle of LITTLE Bighorn.

A **black hole** is a region of space having a gravitational field so intense that no matter or radiation can escape; informally, a place where money or lost items are thought of as going, never to be seen again.

The **Black Hole of Calcutta** was a dungeon 6 metres (20 feet) square in Fort William, Calcutta, where perhaps as many as 146 English prisoners were confined overnight following the capture of Calcutta by the nawab of Bengal in 1756. Only 23 of them were still alive the next morning.

Black information is information held by banks, credit agencies, or other financial institutions about people who are considered bad credit risks.

Black Jew is another term for ➤ FALASHA.

Black letter is an early, ornate, bold style of type, distinguished from Roman type (which subsequently became established), and still in regular use in Germany.

Black magic is magic involving the supposed invocation of evil spirits for evil purposes.

A **Black Maria** is a police vehicle for transporting prisoners. The term originated (in the mid 19th century) in the US, and the name is said to come from a black woman, *Maria* Lee, who kept a boarding house in Boston and helped police in escorting drunk and disorderly customers to jail.

A **black market** is an illegal traffic or trade in officially controlled or scarce commodities.

A **black mass** is a travesty of the Roman Catholic Mass in worship of the Devil.

Black Monday is a Monday regarded as unlucky; in particular, Easter Monday (probably so called because Mondays in general were held to be unlucky; the tradition that a day of rejoicing is naturally followed by calamity may also be involved). The name is also given to Monday 19 October 1987, when massive falls in the value of stocks on Wall Street triggered similar falls in markets around the world.

A **Black Monk** is a member of the ➤ BENEDICTINES, from the black habits worn by Benedictine Orders.

A **Black Muslim** is a member of the ➤ NATION *of Islam.*

A **Black Panther** is a member of a militant political organization set up in the US in 1966 to fight for black rights. From its peak in the late 1960s it declined in the 1970s after internal conflict and the arrest of some of its leaders.

The **Black Pope** is an informal term for the General of the ➤ JESUITS, recorded from the late 19th century.

Black Power is a movement in support of rights and political power for black people, especially prominent in the US in the 1960s and 1970s.

The **Black Prince** was a name given to Edward, Prince of Wales (1330–76), eldest son of Edward III of England, who was responsible for the English victory at Poitiers in 1356. He predeceased his father, but his son became king as Richard II. The name is recorded from the mid 16th century, but although it has been suggested that it refers either to the colour of his armour or to the savagery of some of his deeds, there is no clear evidence as to the origin.

The **Black Prince's ruby** is a large red gem which is in fact a spinel with a smaller ruby inserted, now set in the Maltese cross at the front of the British imperial state crown. The jewel was given to the Black Prince by Pedro the Cruel, king of Castile, after the battle of Nájera in 1367; later, it was worn by Henry V at Agincourt in 1415.

Black Rod is the chief usher of the Lord Chamberlain's department of the royal household.

Black Sash was a women's anti-apartheid movement in South Africa, established in the late 1950s.

Black Saturday is a particularly unlucky Saturday; in Scotland, Saturday 10 September 1547, the date of the Battle of Pinkie, where an English army led by the Duke of Somerset defeated the Scots.

The **Black Sea** is a tideless almost land-locked sea bounded by Ukraine, Russia, Georgia, Turkey, Bulgaria, and Romania, connected to the Mediterranean through the Bosporus and the Sea of Marmara.

A **black sheep** is a member of a family or group who is regarded as a disgrace to it. The term is recorded from the late 18th century.

The **black spot** in Stevenson's *Treasure Island* (1883), a summons to one regarded as a traitor who is 'tipped the black spot'.

The **Black Stone** is the sacred reddish-black stone built into the outside wall of the ➤ KAABA and ritually touched by Muslim pilgrims.

In Australia, **beyond the black stump** is beyond the limits of settled, and therefore civilized, life; from the use of a fire-blackened stump as a marker when giving directions to travellers.

A **black swan** is a thing or kind of person that is extremely rare, a ➤ RARA *avis*. The phrase is originally from the *Satires* of the Roman writer Juvenal (AD *c*.60–*c*.130).

Black Thursday is a particularly unlucky Thursday; in Australia, 6 February 1851, a day on which devastating bushfires occurred in Victoria.

The **Black Watch** is a name for the Royal Highland Regiment. In the early 18th century the term *Watch* was given to certain companies of irregular troops in the Highlands; *Black Watch* referred to some of these companies raised *c*.1729–30, distinctive by their dark-coloured tartan.

Black Wednesday is a particularly unlucky Wednesday, particularly 16 September 1992, the day on which the UK withdrew sterling from the European Exchange Rate Mechanism as a result of adverse economic circumstances. Conservatives opposed to closer ties with Europe called the day *White Wednesday* to signal their pleasure at the withdrawal.

blackball reject a candidate for membership of a private club, typically by means of a secret ballot. The term is recorded from the late 18th century, and comes from the practice of registering an adverse vote by placing a black ball in a ballot box.

blackberries proverbially taken as the type of something plentiful.

In some regions, it was traditionally thought unlucky to pick blackberries after a certain date, such as Michaelmas (29 September) or All Saints' Day (1 November), as it was believed that after that date the fruit had been spoiled by the Devil or other malefic powers.

blackbird the *blackbird* is noted for its song; it is also the emblem of the 7th-century Irish monk ➤ *St* KEVIN.

In the 19th century, *blackbird* was also a slang term for a black or Polynesian captive on a slave ship.

blackboard jungle a school noted for indiscipline; the term comes from the title of a novel (1954) by Evan Hunter, later filmed.

blackguard a man who behaves in a dishonourable or contemptible way. The term originated (in the early 16th century) as two words, *black guard*, denoting a body of attendants or servants, especially the menials who had charge of kitchen utensils, but the exact significance of the epithet 'black' is uncertain. The sense 'scoundrel, villain' dates from the mid 18th century, and was formerly considered highly offensive.

blackleg a person who continues working when fellow workers are on strike. The term is recorded in this sense from the mid 19th century, but the origin of the name remains unknown.

blacklist a list of people or groups regarded as unacceptable or untrustworthy and often marked down for punishment or execution; the term is recorded from the early 17th century.

blackmail the action of demanding money from someone in return for not revealing compromising information about them; the term originally denoted protection money exacted from farmers and landowners in the English and Scottish border country in the 16th and 17th centuries.

blackshirt a member of a Fascist organization, in particular, (in Italy) a member of a paramilitary group founded in the 1920s by Benito Mussolini, and (in the UK) a supporter of Oswald Mosley's British Union of Fascists, founded in 1932.

Blackstone used informally to refer to *Commentaries on the Laws of England* (1765–9), an exposition of English law by William Blackstone (1723–80).

blackthorn winter a spell of cold weather at the time in early spring when the blackthorn flowers (the *blackthorn* is a thorny shrub which bears its white flowers before the leaves appear).

Blair Babes informal term for the record number of Labour women MPs elected to Parliament in May 1997 when Labour took office under Tony Blair.

St Blaise an Armenian bishop and martyr of the 4th century, one of the ➤ FOURTEEN *Holy Helpers*, who was said to have been martyred by being torn with combs for carding wool before he was beheaded.

He is said at the intervention of the boy's mother to have healed a boy who had a fishbone stuck in his throat; when Blaise was afterwards in prison, the woman brought him food and candles. His emblems are a comb (for carding wool) and a candle, he is the patron saint of wool-combers and those with illnesses of the throat, and his feast day is 3 February.

blank verse verse without rhyme, especially the iambic pentameter of unrhymed heroic, the regular measure of English dramatic and epic poetry.

born on the wrong side of the blanket a dated term denoting illegitimacy, recorded from the late 18th century.

Blarney Stone an inscribed stone in the wall of *Blarney* Castle, near Cork, which is difficult of access but which is said to give the gift of persuasive speech to anyone who kisses it; from this comes *blarney* as a word for flattering or cajoling talk.

blasphemy the action or offence of speaking sacrilegiously about God or sacred things; profane talk. Recorded from Middle English, the word comes via Old French and ecclesiastical Latin from Greek *blasphēmia* 'slander, blasphemy'.

a blast from the past something powerfully nostalgic, especially an old pop song.

Blatant Beast in Spenser's *Faerie Queene*, a monster, the personification of the calumnious voice of the world, begotten of Envy and Detraction.

blaxploitation the exploitation of black people, especially with regard to stereotyped roles in films.

bleed someone dry or white drain someone of all their money or resources. Since the late 17th century, *bleeding* has been a metaphor for extorting money from someone. *White* refers to the physiological effect of loss of blood.

Blenheim a battle in 1704 in Bavaria, near the village of Blindheim, in which the English, under the Duke of Marlborough, defeated the French and the Bavarians.

The name was given to the Duke of Marlborough's seat at Woodstock near Oxford, a stately home designed by Vanbrugh. The house and its estate were given to the first Duke of Marlborough in honour of his victory at *Blenheim*.

Louis Blériot (1872–1936), French aviation pioneer. Trained as an engineer, he built one of the first successful monoplanes in 1907, and on 25 July 1909 he became the first to fly the English Channel (Calais to Dover), in a monoplane of his own design.

Blessed Virgin Mary a title given to ➤ MARY as the mother of Jesus.

single blessedness a humorous expression for the state of being unmarried, originally a quotation from Shakespeare's *Midsummer Night's Dream*.

a blessing in disguise an apparent misfortune that eventually has good results, recorded from the mid 18th century.

Bletchley Park near Milton Keynes in Buckinghamshire, during the Second World War the centre of British codebreaking activity, where the ➤ ENIGMA code was broken, and the computer ➤ COLOSSUS used.

Captain Bligh the type of a naval martinet, from William *Bligh* (1754–1817), British naval officer, captain of HMS *Bounty* (see *mutiny on the Bounty* at ➤ MUTINY).

Blighty an informal and often affectionate term for Britain or England, chiefly as used by soldiers of the First and Second World Wars (in the First World War, a wound which was sufficiently serious to merit being shipped home to Britain was known as a *Blighty*).

The term was first used by soldiers serving in India, and is an Anglo-Indian alteration of Urdu *bilāyatī* 'foreign, European', from Arabic *wilāyat*, *wilāya* 'dominion, district'.

Blimp a pompous, reactionary type of person, deriving from the character, **Colonel Blimp**, invented by cartoonist David Low (1891–1963), used in anti-German or anti-government drawings before and during the Second World War.

blind ➤ St LUCY, ➤ St DUNSTAN, the archangel ➤ RAPHAEL, and ➤ St THOMAS *the Apostle* are the patron saints of the blind.

Blind as a bat, meaning completely blind, is a simile recorded from the late 16th century; earlier comparisons of this kind were to *beetles* and *moles*, the common point being that all were seen as creatures who habitually moved in darkness.

The expression **turn a blind eye**, meaning pretend not to notice, is said to be in allusion to Lord Nelson (see ➤ NELSON), who lifted a telescope to his blind eye at the Battle of Copenhagen (1801), thus not seeing the signal to 'discontinue the action'.

The blind leading the blind is used of a situation in which the ignorant or inexperienced are instructed or guided by someone equally ignorant or inexperienced. With allusion to the proverb, *When the blind lead the blind, both shall fall into the ditch*, quoting the Bible (Matthew 15:14).

blind man's buff is a game in which a blindfold player tries to catch others while being pushed about by them; *buff* here means a buffet or blow.

blind with science means confuse by the use of long or technical words or involved explanations; the expression is recorded from the 1930s.

the Blitz the German air raids on Britain in 1940; the word dates from that year, and is an abbreviation of *blitzkrieg*, an intense military campaign intended to bring about a swift victory. The word comes from German, and means literally 'lightning war'.

a new kid on the block a newcomer to a particular place or sphere of activity. Originally US; the *block* is a block of buildings between streets, hence a locality.

put one's head on the block put one's position or reputation at risk by proceeding with a particular course of action; with allusion to the *block* of wood on which a condemned person was formerly beheaded.

Blondel legendary troubador who in medieval chronicles is said to have discovered Richard I in the castle of Durrenstein, where he had been imprisoned by the Duke of Austria, by singing below the castle windows.

Blondie the curly-haired heroine of an American strip cartoon by Chic Young (1901–73) which first appeared in 1930; *Blondie* was first the girlfriend, and later the wife, of Dagwood Bumstead for whom the ➤ DAGWOOD *sandwich* is named.

Blondin (1824–97), French acrobat, famous for walking across a tightrope suspended over ➤ NIAGARA *Falls* on several occasions.

blood in medieval science and medicine, *blood* was regarded as one of the four bodily humours, believed to be associated with a confident and optimistic, or *sanguine*, temperament.

Blood is traditionally used to denote the killing of a person, or guilt for a death, as in **blood on one's hands**.

Blood and iron means military force as distinguished from diplomacy; the phrase is a translation of German *Blut und Eisen*, and is particularly associated with the German statesman Otto von Bismarck (1815–98).

Blood-and-thunder designates a story which features bloodshed and violence; the term is recorded from the mid 19th century.

Blood is thicker than water means that family loyalties are stronger than other relationships. The underlying idea is very old, but this form of the saying is only recorded from the early 19th century.

Blood on the carpet is a serious disagreement or its aftermath; used hyperbolically to suggest that there has been bloodshed.

Blood, toil, tears and sweat is Winston Churchill's summary of what in May 1940 he could offer the country for its immediate future, in the words, 'I have nothing to offer but blood, toil, tears and sweat.'

First blood is the first point or advantage gained in a contest. Also literally, 'the first shedding of blood', especially in a boxing match or formerly in duelling with swords.

To say that something is **like getting blood out of a stone** means that it is extremely difficult and frustrating; used with reference to obtaining something from someone who is unable or unwilling to provide it.

To **make one's blood curdle** is to fill one with horror. Like the alternative **make one's blood run cold**, originating in the medieval physiological scheme of the four humours in the human frame (melancholy, phlegm, blood, and choler). *Blood* was the hot, moist element, so the effect of horror or fear in making it run cold or curdling (solidifying) it was to make it unable to fulfil its proper function of supplying the body with vital heat or energy.

bloodied but unbowed proud of what one has achieved despite having suffered great difficulties or losses; originally as a quotation from W. E. Henley's poem *Invictus* (1888), 'My head is bloody, but unbowed.'

bloody covered with blood or involving bloodshed and cruelty. The adjective is used informally to express anger, annoyance, or shock; recorded in English from the mid 17th century, the origin of the term is uncertain, but it is thought to have a connection with the 'bloods' (aristocratic rowdies) of the late 17th and early 18th centuries. From the mid 18th century until quite recently, *bloody* used as a swear word was regarded as unprintable, probably from the mistaken belief that it implied a blasphemous reference to the blood of Christ, or that the word was an alteration of 'by Our Lady'; hence the shock occasioned in Shaw's play when Eliza uses the words 'Not bloody likely' (see ➤ PYGMALION).

The **Bloody Assizes** were the trials of the supporters of the Duke of Monmouth after their defeat at the Battle of Sedgemoor, held in SW England in 1685. The government's representative, Judge ➤ JEFFREYS, sentenced several hundred rebels to death and about 1,000 others to transportation to America as plantation slaves.

Bloody Friday is a name for 21 July 1972, the day when a number of people were killed and injured by bombs in Belfast.

The **Bloody Hand** in heraldry is the armorial device or ➤ RED *Hand* of Ulster.

Bloody Mary is a nickname of Mary Tudor (1516–58), in reference to the series of religious persecutions taking place in her reign.

Bloody Sunday is a name for various Sundays marked by violence and bloodshed, especially 30 January 1972 in Northern Ireland, when 13 civilians were killed during the dispersal of marchers by British troops in the Bogside.

Bloody Thursday is a name for 5 July 1934, when 3 people were killed on the San Francisco Waterfront during industrial conflict surrounding the longshoremen's strike.

The **Bloody Tower**, in the Tower of London, was supposedly the site of the murder of the ➤ PRINCES *in the Tower*.

the **bloom** is off the rose something is no longer new, fresh, or exciting. *Bloom* refers to the first freshness or beauty of something.

Bloomsbury Group a group of writers, artists, and philosophers living in or associated with Bloomsbury in the early 20th century. Members of the group, which included Virginia Woolf, Lytton Strachey, Vanessa Bell, Duncan Grant, and Roger Fry, were known for their unconventional lifestyles and attitudes and were a powerful force in the growth of modernism.

Bloomsday the 16th of June, on which celebrations take place in Ireland and other countries to mark the anniversary of the events in James Joyce's *Ulysses*.

blot one's copybook tarnish one's good reputation; a *copybook* was a book in which copies were written or printed for pupils to imitate.

blow hot and cold vacillate, be sometimes enthusiastic and sometimes unenthusiastic. With reference to a fable involving a traveller who was offered hospitality by a satyr and offended his host by blowing on his cold fingers to warm them and on his hot soup to cool it.

blow the gaff reveal a plot or secret; the term is recorded from the early 19th century, but the origin is unknown.

blow the whistle on bring an illicit activity to an end by informing on the person responsible; the term *whistleblower* for such an informant comes (in the 1970s) from this.

be **blown** off course have one's plans disrupted by some circumstance, be deflected from one's chosen path. A nautical metaphor: contrary winds deflect a sailing ship from its intended course.

blue of a colour intermediate between green and violet, as of the sky or sea on a sunny day.

Blue was traditionally seen as the colour of constancy, as well as the colour of sorrow and anguish, and of plagues and hurtful things. It is also associated with the male sex (as *pink* is with the female sex).

Politically, the colour was associated with the Scottish Presbyterian or Whig party in the 17th century, and later with the Tory, and then Conservative, party.

At Oxford and Cambridge Universities, a *blue* is a person who has represented Cambridge (a **Cambridge Blue**) or Oxford (an **Oxford Blue**) in a particular sport.

The informal sense of blue to mean 'obscene, indecent, profane' developed in the mid 19th century.

Blue blood is that which is traditionally said to flow in the veins of old and aristocratic families; the term is a translation of Spanish *sangre azul*, attributed to Castilian families who claimed to have no admixture of Moorish, Jewish, or other foreign blood. The expression may have originated in the blueness of the veins of people of fair complexion as compared with those of dark skin.

The **blue boar** was the heraldic cognizance of Richard Duke of York (1411–60), father of Edward IV and Richard III.

The **Blue Bonnets** were Scots soldiery (also called *Blue Caps*), from the broad round horizontally flattened bonnet or cap of blue woollen material, formerly widely worn in Scotland.

A **blue book** in the UK is a report bound in a blue cover and issued by Parliament or the Privy Council; in the US, an official book listing government officials.

Blue-chip denotes companies or their shares considered to be a reliable investment, though less secure than gilt-edged stock. The term comes (in the early 20th century) from the US; from the *blue chip* used in gambling games, which usually has a high value.

A **Blue Coat** is a student at a charity school with a blue uniform which represents the blue coat traditionally worn by an almoner; the name is particularly associated with Christ's Hospital School, whose uniform is a long dark blue gown fastened at the waist with a belt, and bright yellow stockings.

A **blue-collar worker** is a manual worker, particularly in industry; the term is recorded (originally in the US) from the 1950s.

A **blue-eyed boy** is a person highly regarded by someone and treated with special favour; the term is first recorded in a novel by P. G. Wodehouse in 1924.

A **blue flag** is a European award for beaches based on cleanliness and safety.

The **Blue Hen's Chickens** are inhabitants of the state of Delaware. The term is said to have come from a company in the American War of Independence, led by a Captain Caldwell of Delaware, who were known in Carolina firstly as 'Caldwell's gamecocks', and then 'the blue hen's chickens' and the 'blue chickens'. From this, the name 'Blue Hen' was given to the state.

Blue John is a blue or purple banded variety of fluorite found in Derbyshire.

In colonial New England, a **blue law** was a strict puritanical law, particularly one preventing entertainment or leisure activities on a Sunday; currently in North America, it is a law prohibiting certain activities, such as shopping, on a Sunday.

A **blue moon** is the type of something rarely seen, as a moon that is blue is something that is seldom or never seen; **once in a blue moon** means very rarely. In the early 16th century, to say 'that the moon is blue' is recorded as the type of a fantastic statement.

The **Blue Nile** is one of the two principal headwaters of the ➤ NILE. Rising from Lake Tana in NW Ethiopia, it flows some 1,600 km (1,000 miles) southwards then north-westwards into Sudan, where it meets the White Nile at Khartoum.

To **blue-pencil** is to censor or make cuts in a manuscript; a blue 'lead' pencil was traditionally used for marking corrections and deletions.

The **Blue Peter** is a blue flag with a white square in the centre, raised by a ship about to leave port. From 1958, *Blue Peter* has also been the name of a television magazine series for children which combines education and entertainment with successful charitable appeals.

The **Blue Riband** (or **Blue Ribbon**) is a badge worn by members of the Order of the Garter; it is also the name of a trophy for the ship making the fastest eastward sea crossing of the Atlantic Ocean on a regular commercial basis. The **Blue Ribbon of the turf** is the Derby; the term was used by Disraeli in his memoir *Lord George Bentinck* (1852).

In astronomy, a **blue shift** is the displacement of the spectrum to shorter wavelengths in the light coming from distant celestial objects moving towards the observer.

Blue-sky means ignoring possible difficulties; hypothetical, not yet practicable or profitable in the current state of knowledge or technological development. A **blue-sky law** is a law relating to the practice of dealing in doubtful or worthless securities. The term is recorded from the early 20th century, and is supposed to allude to a person who is ready to sell the 'blue sky' to a credulous buyer.

Bluebeard a character in a tale by Charles Perrault, who killed several wives in turn for disobeying his order to avoid a locked room which contained the bodies of his previous wives. His last wife, left in his castle on her own with her sister, explores and opens the fatal room, as Bluebead on returning discovers; in the nick of time, she is rescued by her brothers, who arrive and kill Bluebeard.

His name is often used allusively to refer to the uncontrollable curiosity which has brought them to their death.

Bluebird name of a series of boats and cars in which Malcolm Campbell (1885–1948) and his son Donald Campbell (1921–67) broke world land and water speed records. The last *Bluebird*, in which Donald Campbell had been killed over 30 years earlier attempting to break his own water speed record, was raised from Coniston Water on 8 March 2001.

Bluegrass State informal name for Kentucky; *bluegrass* here is a bluish-green grass which was introduced into North America from northern Europe, and which is widely grown for fodder, especially in Kentucky and Virginia.

Bluemantle one of four pursuivants of the English College of Arms.

blueprint a design plan or other technical drawing. The term comes (in the late 19th century) from the original process in which prints were composed of white lines on a blue ground or of blue lines on a white ground.

blues melancholic music of black American folk origin, typically in a 12-bar sequence. It developed in the rural southern US towards the end of the 19th century, finding a wider audience in the 1940s, as blacks migrated to the cities. This urban blues gave rise to rhythm and blues, and rock and roll.

the blues feelings of melancholy, sadness, or depression. The term is recorded from the mid 18th century, and comes elliptically from *blue devils* 'depression or delirium tremens'.

bluestocking an intellectual or literary woman. The term is recorded from the late 17th century and was originally used to describe a man wearing blue worsted (instead of formal black silk) stockings; extended to mean 'in informal dress'. Later the term denoted a person who attended the literary assemblies held (*c.*1750) by three London society ladies, where some of the men favoured less formal dress. The women who attended became known as **blue-stocking ladies** or **blue-stockingers**.

call someone's bluff challenge someone to carry out a stated intention, in the expectation of being able to expose it as a false pretence. In the game of poker (formerly also known as *bluff*), **calling someone's bluff** meant making an opponent show their hand in order to reveal that its value is weaker than their heavy betting suggests.

bo tree a fig tree native to India and SE Asia, regarded as sacred by Buddhists. Recorded from the mid 19th century, the name represents Sinhalese *bōgaha* 'tree of knowledge' (Buddha's enlightenment having occurred beneath such a tree), from Sanskrit *budh* 'understand thoroughly' + *gaha* 'tree'.

Boadicea another name for ➤ BOUDICCA.

Boanerges 'sons of thunder', the byname given by Jesus to James and John, the sons of Zebedee, who wanted to call down fire on the Samaritans.

boar more fully the **wild boar**, a tusked wild pig from which domestic pigs are descended; in allusive use, **the Boar** is Richard III, whose emblem was a ➤ WHITE *Boar*.
   A **boar's head** was traditionally served at a feast on Christmas day.

go by the board (of something planned or previously upheld) be abandoned, rejected, or ignored. Earlier in nautical use meaning 'fall overboard', used of a mast falling past the *board* (i.e. the side of the ship).

boat a boat is the emblem of ➤ *St* SIMON, ➤ *St* JUDE, and the 7th-century French abbot St Bertin, whose monastery of Sithiu (Saint-Bertin) in northern France was originally accessible only by water.

Boaz in the Old Testament, the name of the wealthy landowner who became the second husband of ➤ RUTH.

bob[1] a change of order in bell-ringing; used in names of change-ringing methods, as **plain bob**. The term is recorded from the late 17th century, and may be connected with *bob* meaning 'sudden movement up and down'.

bob[2] in British usage, a shilling; more generally, used with reference to a large but unspecified amount of money. The term is recorded from the late 18th century but the origin is unknown.

bob for apples try to catch floating or hanging apples with one's mouth alone, as a game, traditionally played at ➤ HALLOW'EEN.

Bob's your uncle everything is all right. Popular etymology suggests that the term derives from the political advancement of ➤ *Arthur James* BALFOUR (1848–1930), who was nephew to the Conservative statesman Robert, Lord Salisbury, and who became first Chief Secretary for Ireland and then (in 1902) Prime Minister, although the phrase is not recorded until the 1930s.

bobby informal term for a police officer, deriving (in the mid 19th century) from a pet form of *Robert*, given name of the British Conservative politician Robert Peel (1788–1850), founder of the modern police force.

Giovanni Boccaccio (1313–75), Italian writer, poet, and humanist. He is most famous for the *Decameron* (1348–58), a collection of a hundred tales told by ten young people who have moved to the country to escape the Black Death.

the Boche informal and dated term for Germans, especially German soldiers, considered collectively. The word is French soldiers' slang, originally in the sense 'rascal', later used in the First World War meaning 'German'.

Bodhgaya a village in the state of Bihar, NE India, where the Buddha attained enlightenment. A ➤ BO *tree* there is said to be a descendant of the tree under which he meditated.

bodhisattva in Mahayana Buddhism, a person who is able to reach nirvana but delays doing so through compassion for suffering beings.

bodice-ripper a sexually explicit romantic novel or film, especially one with a historical setting with a plot featuring the seduction of the heroine.

know where the bodies are buried have the security deriving from personal knowledge of an organization's confidential affairs and secrets.

Bodleian Library the library of Oxford University, one of six copyright libraries in the UK. The first library was founded in the 14th century, but was refounded by *Sir Thomas Bodley* (1545–1613), English scholar and diplomat.

body and soul the corporeal and spiritual entities that make up a person; the term is traditionally often used in the context of the difficulty of sustaining existence, as in 'keep body and soul together'.

body politic the people of a nation, state, or society considered collectively as an organized group of citizens; the term is recorded from the early 16th century.

bodyline in cricket, persistent short-pitched fast bowling on the leg side, threatening the batsman's body, especially as employed by England in the Ashes series in Australia in 1932–3.

bodysnatcher a person who illicitly disinterred corpses for dissection, for which there was no legal provision until 1832, a ➤ RESURRECTION *man*.

Boeotia a region of ancient Greece, of which the chief city was Thebes, according to legend founded by ➤ CADMUS. *Boeotia* was traditionally proverbial among Athenians for the dullness and stupidity of its inhabitants.

Boethius (*c.*480–524), Roman statesman and philosopher, best known for *The Consolation of Philosophy*, which he wrote while in prison on a charge of treason. He argued that the soul can attain happiness in affliction by realizing the value of goodness and meditating on the reality of God.

boffin informal term for a person engaged in scientific or technical research; the word is recorded from the Second World War, and seems to have been first applied by members of the Royal Air Force to scientists working on radar, but the origin is unknown.

bog-standard ordinary or basic. The term probably comes from an alteration of *box-standard*, an informal term for a motorcycle or other mechanical device which has no modifications, but which is in the condition in which it came out of the manufacturer's box.

bogey an evil or mischievous spirit. Recorded from the mid 19th century, as a proper name for the Devil, the word is probably related to *bogle*.

In golf, *bogey* denotes a score of one stroke over par at a hole, and may come from *Bogey* (the Devil) regarded as an imaginary player.

Bogomil a member of a heretical medieval Balkan sect professing a modified form of ➤ MANICHAEISM. The name is recorded from the mid 19th century, and comes from medieval Greek *Bogomilos*, from *Bogomil*, literally 'beloved of God', the name of the person who first disseminated the heresy, from Old Church Slavonic.

Bohemia a region forming the western part of the Czech Republic, originally a Slavic kingdom, later subject to Austrian rule.

In Shakespeare's *The Winter's Tale* (1610–11), ➤ PERDITA is abandoned as an infant on the coast of Bohemia, and later marries the king's son.

From the mid 19th century, *Bohemia* was also used to designate the community or milieu of social **Bohemians**, persons with informal and unconventional social habits, especially artists or writers. The usage comes (in the mid 19th century) from French *bohémien* 'gypsy', because gypsies were thought to come from Bohemia, or because they perhaps entered the West through Bohemia.

to boldly go explore freely, unhindered by fear of the unknown; from the brief given to the Starship *Enterprise* in ➤ STAR Trek, 'to boldly go where no man has gone before.'

Bollywood the Indian popular film industry, based in Bombay; the word is recorded from the 1970s, and is a blend of *Bombay* and *Hollywood*.

Bolshevik a member of the majority faction of the Russian Social Democratic Party, which was renamed the Communist Party after seizing power in the October Revolution of 1917. The name is Russian, from *bol'she* 'greater', with reference to the greater faction.

Bolshoi Ballet a Moscow ballet company, established since 1825 at the Bolshoi Theatre, where it staged the first production of Tchaikovsky's *Swan Lake* (1877).

a bolt from the blue a sudden or unexpected piece of news, with reference to the unlikelihood of a thunderbolt coming from a clear blue sky.

Bon a Japanese Buddhist festival held annually in August to honour the dead; also called *Festival of the Dead* and *Lantern Festival*.

Bona Dea a Roman fertility goddess (in Latin, the 'good goddess'), worshipped exclusively by women, and sometimes identified with ➤ FAUNA.

Bonaparte a Corsican family including the three actual or titular rulers of France named ➤ NAPOLEON; during the Napoleonic Wars, the informal *Boney* was often used as a disparaging reference to Napoleon I.

St Bonaventura (1221–74), Franciscan theologian; known as **the Seraphic Doctor**. Appointed minister general of his order in 1257, he was made cardinal bishop of Albano in 1273. His feast day is 15 (formerly 14) July.

James Bond a British secret agent in the spy novels of Ian Fleming (1908–64), and subsequently in the films based on them. *Bond*, known also by his code name 007, is noted for his daring, his sexual success, and (especially in the films) the number of gadgets with which he pursues his secret service activities.

bone as the most lasting parts of the body, *bones* are traditionally used for 'mortal remains'.

In proverbial usage, a *bone* is the type of something hard and dry.

Bones are traditionally used in enchantment or divination, and **point the bone at** means (of an Australian Aboriginal) cast a spell on someone so as to cause their sickness or death. The expression refers to an Aboriginal ritual, in which a bone is pointed at a victim. In southern Africa, to **throw the bones at** is to use divining bones (a set of carved dice or bones used by traditional healers in divination) to foretell the future or discover the source of a difficulty by studying the pattern they form when thrown on the ground.

Water foaming before a ship's bows is known as **a bone in her mouth**; the expression is recorded from the early 17th century.

A **bone of contention** is a subject or issue over which there is continuing disagreement; proverbially, a bone thrown between two dogs is the type of something which causes a quarrel.

To **make no bones about something** is to have no hesitation in stating or dealing with something, however unpleasant, awkward, or distasteful it is. The obsolete expression *find bones in* suggests how the meaning of this could have evolved: finding bones in meat or soup presents a difficulty in consuming it, but *making no bones* means that impediments are either ignored or overcome.

Boney a traditional English informal name for ➤ *Napoleon* BONAPARTE.

St Boniface (680–754), Anglo-Saxon missionary, born *Wynfrith*, known as the *Apostle of Germany*. He was sent to Frisia and Germany to spread the Christian faith and was appointed Primate of Germany in 732; he was martyred in Frisia. His emblem is an axe, as the instrument of his martyrdom, and his feast day is 5 June.

Bonnie and Clyde title of Warren Beatty's film (1967) about the 1930s American gangsters *Bonnie* Parker and her partner *Clyde* Barrow, who were eventually ambushed and shot dead at a police roadblock in 1934.

Bonnie Prince Charlie name given by his supporters to the young Charles Edward Stuart (1720–88), otherwise known as the ➤ YOUNG *Pretender*.

boogie-woogie a style of jazz played on the piano with a strong, fast beat; the term is recorded from the early 20th century (in the US, where *boogie* meant 'party'); the ultimate origin is unknown.

Boojum an imaginary dangerous animal, invented by Lewis Carroll in his nonsense poem *The Hunting of the Snark*. The name is used allusively for an otherwise unspecified danger.

book a *book* is the emblem of ➤ St ANNE, ➤ St AUGUSTINE, ➤ St BERNARD, and other saints.
  Recorded from Old English (in form *bōc*, originally meaning also 'a document or charter'), the word is of Germanic origin, and is probably related to *beech* (on which runes were carved).
  The **Book of Common Prayer** is the official service book of the Church of England, compiled by Thomas Cranmer and others, first issued in 1549, and largely unchanged since the revision of 1662.
  A **book of hours** is a book of prayers appointed for particular canonical hours or times of day, used by Roman Catholics for private devotions and popular especially in the Middle Ages, when they were often richly illuminated.
  The **Book of Kells** is an 8th-century illuminated manuscript of the Gospels, now kept in the library of Trinity College, Dublin, and produced there in the scriptorium of Iona or at *Kells* in County Meath, where the community moved after attack by Vikings in the early 9th century.
  The **book of life** is the record of those achieving salvation; originally, with biblical reference, as in Revelation 20:12.
  The **Book of the Dead** is a collection of ancient Egyptian religious and magical texts, selections from which were often written on or placed in tombs. The name (in full **Tibetan Book of the Dead**) is also given to a Tibetan Buddhist text recited during funerary rites, describing the passage from death to rebirth.

Booker Prize a literary prize awarded annually for a novel published by a British or Commonwealth citizen during the previous year, financed by the multinational company Booker McConnell.

Boolean denoting a system of algebraic notation used to represent logical propositions by means of the binary digits 0 (false) and 1 (true), especially in computing and electronics. The name comes from George *Boole* (1815–64), English mathematician, from whose ideas the study of mathematical or symbolic logic mainly developed.

boomerang a curved flat piece of wood that can be thrown so as to return to the thrower, traditionally used by Australian Aboriginals as a hunting weapon.

Betty Boop the heroine of a number of short cartoon films produced by Max Fleischer (1883–1972), and appearing in a newspaper strip from 1934; she was wide-eyed, dressed in skimpy clothing, and had a garter on her left leg. She was said to have been based on a popular singer of the 1920s, Helen Kane, known for adding 'boop-boop-a-doop' when singing 'I Wanna be Loved by You'.

boot a boot is the emblem of the English priest John Schorne (d. *c.*1315), centre of a popular cult, who was said to have trapped the Devil in his boot.

boot and saddle a cavalry signal to mount, from an alteration of French *boute-selle* 'place-saddle'.

bootlegger a smuggler of liquor. The word is recorded from the late 19th century, and comes from the smugglers' practice of concealing bottles in their boots.

by one's own bootstraps by one's own efforts. A *bootstrap* was sewn into boots to help with pulling them on. The idiom has given rise to the term *bootstrapping*, meaning to 'make use of existing resources to improve one's position', hence the computer term *booting*.

the Border the boundary and adjoining districts between Scotland and England, which especially between the 15th and the 17th centuries was a lawless area requiring particular management. The term seems to have originated in Scotland, where the border with England, being the only one it had, became known as *the* border. The political importance of the Border disappeared after James VI of Scotland inherited the English crown in 1603.

Border States in the US, an informal name for Delaware, Maryland, Virginia, Kentucky, and Missouri.

Boreas in Roman and Greek mythology, the god of the north wind.

Borgia the family name of Rodrigo *Borgia* (1431–1503), later Pope Alexander VI, and his illegitimate children Cesare (*c.*1476–1507) and Lucrezia (1480–1519); their traditional reputation was for ruthless ambition, and they were popularly believed to be skilled in poisoning.

bork obstruct (someone, especially a candidate for public office) by systematically defaming or vilifying them. The word comes from the name of Robert *Bork* (1927–), an American judge whose nomination to the Supreme Court (1987) was rejected following unfavourable publicity for his allegedly extreme views.

born in the purple born into an imperial or royal family as a ➤ PORPHYROGENITE; ➤ PURPLE was originally the dye used for fabric worn by an emperor or senior magistrate in Rome or Byzantium.

born under a lucky star naturally fortunate; a proverbial phrase reflecting belief in planetary influences on one's fortunes.

born with a silver spoon in one's mouth proverbial expression for being born in affluence.

Borobudur a Buddhist monument in central Java, built *c.*800. It consists of five square successively smaller terraces, one above the other, surmounted by three galleries and a stupa.

Battle of Borodino a battle in 1812 at Borodino, a village to the west of Moscow, at which Napoleon's forces defeated the Russian army under Prince Kutuzov (1745–1813). This allowed the French to advance to Moscow, but the heavy losses that they suffered at Borodino contributed to their eventual defeat.

borrowed plumes a borrowed display likely to make the wearer appear pretentious or laughable, often with reference to the fable in which the jay or jackdaw assumes the peacock's plumes.

the Borrowers central characters in a series of children's stories by Mary Norton, beginning with *The Borrowers* (1952); they are a family of tiny people who live under the floorboards in an old house and survive by 'borrowing' objects from the household overhead.

Borscht Belt a resort area in the Catskill Mountains, in the state of New York, frequented chiefly by Jewish people of eastern European origin.

Borsetshire the county in which the long-running radio soap opera ➤ *the* ARCHERS is set; the county town is *Borchester*, and the name is an alteration of ➤ BARSETSHIRE.

Hieronymus Bosch (*c.*1450–1516), Dutch painter. Bosch's highly detailed works are typically crowded with half-human, half-animal creatures and grotesque demons in settings symbolic of sin and folly. His individual style prefigures that of the surrealists.

Boskop a town in South Africa, in North-West Province, where a skull fossil was found in 1913. The fossil is undated and morphologically shows no primitive features. At the time this find was regarded as representative of a distinct 'Boskop race' but is now thought to be related to the San–Nama (Bushman–Hottentot) types.

Bosporus a strait connecting the Black Sea with the Sea of Marmara, and separating Europe from the Anatolian peninsula of western Asia; Istanbul (originally Byzantium and then Constantinople) is located at its south end. Its name, meaning 'cow's passage', is said to derive from the legend that ➤ Io crossed it in her flight from Hera's vengeance.

Boston a town in Lincolnshire, for which was named the state capital of Massachusetts, founded *c.*1630, known for its social exclusivity (see also ➤ BRAHMIN).
   Boston Stump is an informal name for the church tower of Boston, Lincolnshire, perhaps because, although lofty and a conspicuous sea-mark, it has no spire.
   The **Boston Tea Party** was a violent demonstration in 1773 by American colonists prior to the War of American Independence. Colonists boarded vessels in Boston harbour and threw the cargoes of tea into the water in protest at the imposition of a tax on tea by the British Parliament, in which the colonists had no representation.

Bosworth Field a battle of the Wars of the Roses fought in 1485 near Market Bosworth in Leicestershire. Henry Tudor defeated and killed the Yorkist king Richard III, enabling him to take the throne as Henry VII.

Botany Bay an inlet of the Tasman Sea in New South Wales, Australia, just south of Sydney, which was the site of Captain James

Cook's landing in 1770 and of an early British penal settlement.

It was named by Cook after the large variety of plants collected there by his companion, Sir Joseph Banks.

Sandro Botticelli (1445–1510), Italian painter, who worked in Renaissance Florence under the patronage of the Medicis. Botticelli is best known for his mythological works such as *Primavera* (*c*.1478) and *The Birth of Venus* (*c*.1480). His work had a significant influence on the Pre-Raphaelites.

bottom drawer household linen stored by a woman in preparation for her marriage, originally as in the lowest drawer of a chest of drawers; the term is recorded from the late 19th century. A corresponding US term was a ➤ HOPE *chest*.

bottomless pit an unfathomable place, Hell; in Revelation 9:11, ➤ ABADDON is called 'the angel of the bottomless pit'.

Boudicca (d. AD 62), a queen of the Britons, ruler of the Iceni tribe in eastern England; also known as **Boadicea**. Boudicca led her forces in revolt against the Romans and sacked Colchester, St Albans, and London before being defeated by the Roman governor Suetonius Paulinus.

bouncing bomb the bomb used in the ➤ DAMBUSTERS' *raid* on the Ruhr valley dams; the bomb when dropped was designed to bounce along the surface of the water before impacting on the dam itself.

one's bounden duty a responsibility regarded by oneself and others as obligatory. *Bounden* as the past participle of bind is now archaic in all contexts and seldom found except in this phrase.

Nicolas Bourbaki a pseudonym of a group of mathematicians, mainly French, attempting to give a complete account of the foundations of pure mathematics. Their first publication was in 1939.

The group was named, humorously, after a defeated French general of the Franco-Prussian War (1870–1).

Bourbon the surname of a branch of the royal family of France. The Bourbons ruled France from 1589, when Henry IV succeeded to the throne, until the monarchy was overthrown in 1848, and reached the peak of their power under Louis XIV in the late 17th century. Members of this family have also

been kings of Spain (1700–1931, and since 1975).

boustrophedon of written words, from right to left and from left to right in alternate lines. Recorded from the early 17th century, the word comes from Greek, and means literally 'as an ox turns in ploughing', from *bous* 'ox' + -*strophos* 'turning'.

born within sound of Bow Bells born within City bounds, ➤ COCKNEY; the bells referred to are those of Bow Church or St Mary-le-Bow, formerly St Mary of the Arches, in Cheapside, London, so called from the 'bows' or arches supporting its steeple.

bow down in the house of Rimmon pay lip-service to a principle, sacrifice one's principles for the sake of conformity; originally with reference to 2 Kings 5:18, the verse in which ➤ NAAMAN, believing in the God of Israel who had healed him, explained to Elijah that he must still accompany his master the king of Syria to the temple of ➤ RIMMON.

Bow Street Runner the popular name for a London policeman during the first half of the 19th century; *Bow Street* in London, near Covent Garden, is the site of the principal metropolitan police court. The *Bow Street Runners* were nicknamed *Redbreasts* for the bright scarlet waistcoats they habitually wore.

bowdlerize remove material that is considered improper or offensive from (a text), especially with the result that the text becomes weaker or less effective. The word comes from the name of Dr Thomas *Bowdler* (1754–1825), who in 1818 published an expurgated edition of Shakespeare.

bowels of mercy innate compassion; the *bowels* were traditionally regarded as the seat of tender and sympathetic emotions, as in Colossians 3:12.

Bowery a street and district in New York associated with drunks and vagrants. The name derives from the fact that it once ran through Peter Stuyvesant's farm, or *bouwerie*, as it was called by the Dutch settlers.

bowie knife a long knife with a blade double-edged at the point. It is named after the American frontiersman Jim *Bowie* (1789–1836), who shared command of the garrison that resisted the Mexican attack on the Alamo, where he died.

bowler a man's hard felt hat with a round dome-shaped crown, which since the 1920s has been a symbol of civilian life after retirement from the army; the name comes (in the mid 19th century) from William *Bowler*, the English hatter who designed it in 1850.

a shot across the bows a statement or gesture intended to frighten someone into changing their course of action. Literally, a shot fired in front of the bows of a ship, not intending to hit it but to make it stop or alter course.

bowstring the string of an archer's bow, traditionally made of three strands of hemp, and in Ottoman Turkey used for strangling offenders.

Box and Cox used to refer to an arrangement whereby people or things make use of the same accommodation or facilities at different times, according to a strict arrangement. The expression comes from the title of a play (1847) by J. M. Morton, in which two characters, John *Box* and James *Cox*, unknowingly become tenants of the same room.

box the compass recite the compass points in correct order; the phrase is recorded from the mid 18th century, and box may come from Spanish *bojar* 'sail round', from Middle Low German *bōgen* 'bend', from the base of *bow*.

Boxer[1] a member of a fiercely nationalistic Chinese secret society which flourished in the 19th century. In 1899 the society led a Chinese uprising against Western domination which was eventually crushed by a combined European force, aided by Japan and the US. The name translates Chinese *yì hé quán*, literally 'righteous harmony fists'.

Boxer[2] in Orwell's *Animal Farm* (1945), the name of the carthorse who is a type of simple and hardworking loyalty (his credo is 'I must work harder'), but who is rewarded by being sent to the knacker's when no longer physically able to work.

Boxgrove man a fossil hominid of the Middle Pleistocene period, whose fragmentary remains were found at *Boxgrove* near Chichester, SE England, in 1993 and 1995. Dated (controversially) to about 500,000 years ago, it is one of the earliest known humans in Europe.

Boxing Day the first day (strictly, the first weekday) after Christmas day, on which Christmas-boxes were traditionally given.

boy bishop one of the choirboys formerly elected at the annual 'Feast of Boys' in certain cathedrals, to walk in a procession of the boys to the altar of the Innocents or of the Holy Trinity, and perform the office on the eve and day of the Holy Innocents, the boys occupying the canons' stalls in the cathedral during the service. Provision for this is made in the Sarum Office.

The custom dates from the 13th century, and lasted until the Reformation. Boy bishops were appointed also in religious houses and in schools.

boycott withdraw from commercial or social relations with (a country, organization, or person) as a punishment or protest, from the name of Captain Charles C. *Boycott* (1832–97), an Irish land agent so treated in 1880, in an attempt instigated by the Irish Land League to get rents reduced.

Boyle's law a law stating that the pressure of a given mass of an ideal gas is inversely proportional to its volume at a constant temperature, named for Robert *Boyle* (1627–91), Irish-born scientist. A founder member of the Royal Society, Boyle put forward a view of matter based on particles which was a precursor of the modern theory of chemical elements. He is best known for his experiments with the air pump.

Battle of the Boyne a battle fought near the River Boyne in Ireland in 1690, in which the Protestant army of William of Orange, the newly crowned William III, defeated the Catholic army (including troops from both France and Ireland) led by the recently deposed James II. The battle is celebrated annually (on 12 July) in Northern Ireland as a victory for the Protestant cause.

three boys in a tub is one of the emblems of ➤ St NICHOLAS *of Myra*.

Boz the pseudonym used by Charles Dickens in his *Pickwick Papers* and contributions to the *Morning Chronicle*; in his preface to the *Pickwick Papers* (1847), Dickens explained that he had taken the name from a younger brother's mispronunciation of the nickname 'Moses'.

Bradbury a term for the former one-pound note, from the name of John S. *Bradbury*, British Secretary to the Treasury, 1913–19.

Bradshaw a timetable of all passenger trains in Britain, issued 1839–1961. It was named after its first publisher, George *Brad-shaw* (1801–53), printer and engraver.

Braganza the dynasty that ruled Portugal from 1640 until the end of the monarchy in 1910 and Brazil (on its independence from Portugal) from 1822 until the formation of a republic in 1889.

Bragi in Scandinavian mythology, the god of poetry.

Tycho Brahe (1546–1601), Danish astronomer. He built an observatory equipped with precision instruments, but despite demonstrating that comets follow sun-centred paths he adhered to a geocentric view of the planets.

Brahma the creator god in Hinduism, who forms a triad with Vishnu and Shiva. Brahma was an important god of late Vedic religion, but has been little worshipped since the 5th century AD and has only one major temple dedicated to him in India today.

Brahman a member of the highest Hindu caste, that of the priesthood.

Brahmana in Hinduism, any of the lengthy commentaries on the Vedas, composed in Sanskrit *c*.900–700 BC and containing expository material relating to Vedic sacrificial ritual.

Brahmanism the complex sacrificial religion that emerged in post-Vedic India (*c*.900 BC) under the influence of the dominant priesthood (Brahmans), an early stage in the development of Hinduism. It was largely as a reaction to Brahman orthodoxy that religions such as Buddhism and Jainism were formed.

Brahmin a socially or culturally superior person, especially one from New England, and in particular ► BOSTON.

Braille a form of written language for the blind, in which characters are represented by patterns of raised dots that are felt with the fingertips, developed by Louis *Braille* (1809–52), French educationist. Blind from the age of 3, by the age of 15 he had developed his own system of raised-point reading and writing, which was immediately accepted by his fellow students at the Institute des Jeunes Aveugles in Paris, and which was officially adopted two years after his death.

brain drain the emigration of highly trained or qualified people from a particular country; the term was used particularly in the UK in the 1960s in relation to scientists moving to the US.

Brainiac a superintelligent alien character of the 1950s ► SUPERMAN comic strip. The name represents a blend of *brain* and *maniac*.

In North America, *brainiac* is used informally for an exceptionally intelligent person.

brainwash pressurize (someone) into adopting radically different beliefs by using systematic and often forcible means; the term is recorded from the 1950s, and was particularly associated with the activities of totalitarian, and especially Communist, states.

Bran in Welsh mythology, a king of the island of Britain who, when mortally wounded, ordered that his head should be cut off and kept as it would have miraculous powers; the oracular head was said to have been buried in London, as a protection against invasion. The name *Bran* means 'raven'.

a brand from the burning a rescued person, a convert; originally with biblical allusion, as to Amos 4:11 and Zechariah 3:2.

Brand X a name used for an unidentified brand contrasted unfavourably with a product of the same type which is being promoted; the term is recorded from the 1930s.

Brandenburg Gate one of the city gates of Berlin (built 1788–91), the only one that survives. After the construction of the ► BERLIN Wall in 1961 it stood in East Berlin, a conspicuous symbol of a divided city. It was reopened in December 1989.

Brands Hatch a motor-racing circuit near Farningham in Kent.

brass traditionally taken as a type of hardness or insensitivity; impudence, effrontery, nerve.

Formerly (from late Middle English to the late 18th century), *brass* was used for copper or bronze coin; from the late 16th century, it has been used informally to mean 'cash'.

In the UK, *brass* also denotes a memorial, typically a medieval one, consisting of a flat piece of inscribed brass, laid in the floor or set into the wall of a church.

The word is recorded from Old English (in form *bræs*), but is of unknown origin.

A **brass hat** is an army officer of high rank (having gold braid on the cap); the term may be used pejoratively, to indicate someone seen as out of touch with the fighting forces.

In North America, **the brass ring** is an informal expression for success, typically regarded as a reward for ambition or hard work, originally with reference to the reward of a free ride given on a merry-go-round to the person hooking a brass ring suspended over the horses.

Cold enough to freeze the balls off a brass monkey means bitterly cold; the phrase is often said to come (in the late 19th century) from a type of brass rack or 'monkey' in which cannonballs were stored and which contracted in very cold weather, ejecting the balls. However, the term 'monkey' is not otherwise recorded in this sense, and the rate of contraction of brass in cold temperatures is unlikely to be sufficient to cause the reputed effect. The phrase is also first recorded as 'freeze the tail off a brass monkey'. It therefore seems most likely that the phrase is simply a ribald allusion to the fact that metal figures will become very cold to the touch in cold weather (and some materials will become brittle).

To **get down to brass tacks** is to come to the essential details, reach the real matter in hand; the term, which is originally US, is recorded from the late 19th century.

brave new world used to refer, often ironically, to a new and hopeful period in history resulting from major changes in society, from the title of a satirical novel by Aldous Huxley (1932), originally with reference to Miranda's words in Shakespeare's *The Tempest*, on first encountering other human beings.

Braveheart name given to the 13th-century Scottish hero William Wallace (c.1270–1305) in the film *Braveheart* (1995), in which he is shown courageously fighting and dying for Scottish independence. *Braveheart* may now be used allusively to encapsulate a view of Scottish nationalism maintained against English oppression.

the bravest of the brave nickname of Marshal Ney, from Napoleon's comment on him when Ney commanded the rearguard on the retreat from Moscow in 1812.

Vicar of Bray the protagonist of an 18th-century song who kept his benefice from Charles II's reign to George I's by changing his beliefs to suit the times.

brazen age a mythological age, said by classical writers such as the Greek poet Hesiod of the 8th century BC, to come after the silver age and before the iron age.

breach of promise the action of breaking a sworn assurance to do something, formerly especially to marry someone.

breach of the peace an act of violent or noisy behaviour that causes a public disturbance and is considered a criminal offence.

bread often taken as the type of something essential to life. **One cannot live by bread alone** means that people have spiritual as well as physical needs; originally with biblical allusion to Deuteronomy 8:3 and Matthew 4:4.

Bread and butter is used for a person's livelihood or main source of income, typically as earned by routine work; the phrase in this sense is first recorded in a letter of August 1732 by Jonathan Swift. From the early 20th century (originally in the US), the term **bread-and-butter letter** has been used for a letter conveying conventional thanks for hospitality.

Bread and circuses stands for a diet of entertainment or political policies on which the masses are fed to keep them happy; the phrase is a translation of Latin *panem et circenses* in the work of the Roman satirist Juvenal (AD c.60–c.130), 'Only two things does he [the modern citizen] anxiously wish for—bread and circuses.'

Bread and water is a frugal diet that is eaten in poverty, chosen in abstinence, or given as a punishment.

Bread and wine are the consecrated elements used in the celebration of the Eucharist; the sacrament of the Eucharist.

The **bread of idleness** is food or sustenance for which one has not worked; after Proverbs 31:27.

To **cast one's bread upon the waters** is to do good without expectation of reward; with biblical allusion to Ecclesiastes 11:1.

break a butterfly on a wheel employ disproportionate force in the achievement of an aim; the wheel here is one on which the bodies of criminals were broken as a method of execution. The phrase is first used by Pope in the line, 'Who breaks a butterfly upon a wheel?'

break one's duck in cricket, score one's first run (in allusion to the origin of ▶ DUCK as resembling a *duck's egg* in shape).

break the mould make impossible the repetition of a certain type of creation; put an end to a pattern of events or behaviour by setting markedly different standards. Originally with reference to Ariosto's *Orlando Furioso* (1532), 'Nature made him and then broke the mould'.

breaking of bread in the Christian Church, a name for the Eucharist.

Nicholas **Breakspear** name of the only English pope, ➤ ADRIAN IV.

breast *breasts* (on a dish) are the emblem of ➤ *St* AGATHA.

The *breast* is also used for a person's chest regarded as the seat of the emotions, and the repository of consciousness, designs, and secrets. The phrase **make a clean breast of**, meaning make a full disclosure or confession, is recorded from the mid 18th century.

the **breath of life** a necessity; originally with biblical allusion to the literal sense, as in Genesis 2:7.

Breeches Bible a popular name for the ➤ GENEVA *Bible*. of 1560, so named because the word *breeches* is used in Genesis 3:7 for the garments made by Adam and Eve.

Brehon law the code of law prevailing in Ireland before the English conquest; a *brehon* was a judge in ancient Ireland.

St Brendan (*c.*486–*c.*575), Irish abbot. The legend of the 'Navigation of St Brendan' (*c.*1050), describing his voyage with a band of monks to a promised land (possibly Orkney or the Hebrides), was widely popular in the Middle Ages. His emblem is a whale, and his feast day is 16 May.

Brent Spar name of the redundant oil installation which Shell UK in 1995 planned for deep sea disposal; ➤ GREENPEACE activists, claiming that toxic chemicals from the installation would damage the deep sea environment, prevented the process with the combination of a flotilla of small boats and a successful public relations campaign.

Bretwalda lord of the Britons, lord of Britain; in the Anglo-Saxon Chronicle, a title given to King Egbert, and (retrospectively) to some earlier Anglo-Saxon kings, and occasionally assumed by later ones.

breviary a book containing the service for each day, to be recited by those in orders in the Roman Catholic Church. The word is recorded from late Middle English (when it

also denoted an abridged version of the psalms), and comes from Latin *breviarium* 'summary, abridgement', ultimately from *brevis* 'short, brief'.

Brewster Sessions magistrates' sessions for the issue of licences to permit trade in alcoholic liquor (a *brewster* is a brewer, originally a female one).

Brian Boru (d. 1014), king of Munster, who after successfully establishing his dominance as high king was finally killed in battle against the Norse at Clontarf; he is seen as the type of an early Irish warrior king.

brickfielder in Australia, a dry north wind, typically accompanied by dust. Recorded from the early 19th century, the term comes from the name of *Brickfield* Hill, the site (now part of central Sydney) of a former brickworks, associated with dust.

make bricks without straw try to accomplish something without proper or adequate material, equipment, or information. With allusion to Exodus 5:6–19; 'without straw' meant 'without having straw provided' (i.e. the Israelites were required to gather the straw for themselves in order to make the bricks required by their Egyptian taskmasters). A misinterpretation has led to the current sense.

St Bride another name for ➤ *St* BRIDGET *of Ireland.*

Brides in the Bath name given in the popular press to the case of George Joseph Smith, who between 1912 and 1914 bigamously married and drowned in the bath three women, whose lives he had previously insured; arrested (initially for falsifying an entry in the marriage register) early in 1915, he was tried, convicted, and executed for murder later in the same year.

bridewell archaic term for a prison or reform school for petty offenders. Recorded from the mid 16th century, the word comes from *St Bride's Well* in the City of London, near which such a building stood.

bridge a structure carrying a road over a river or other obstacle, often in figurative use. **Bridge-building** is the promotion of friendly relations between groups.

From the 12th century, a **Bridge Fraternity** was a confraternity of laymen dedicated to the building or maintenance of a bridge, especially one carrying a pilgrimage route over a river. The best-known example of such a fraternity is that of the bridge of Avignon, founded by St-Bénézet in the late 12th century and linking Avignon with Villeneuve on the opposite bank of the Rhone.

A **bridge of boats** is a bridge formed by mooring boats side by side across a river; the *bridge of boats* over the river Rhône at Arles was in use throughout the 2nd and 3rd centuries AD.

The **Bridge of Sighs** in Venice is a bridge connecting the Doge's palace with the state prison originally crossed by prisoners on their way to torture or execution.

To **cross that bridge when one comes to it** is to deal with a problem when and if it arises; from the proverbial saying **don't cross the bridge till you come to it**, recorded from the mid 19th century.

St Bridget of Ireland (d. *c.*525), Irish abbess. She was venerated in Ireland as a virgin saint and noted in miracle stories for her compassion; her cult soon spread over most of western Europe. It has been suggested that she may represent the Irish goddess Brig. She is also called *Bride*, *Brigid*, and *Mary of the Gael*. Her emblems are a cheese and a cow, and her feast day is 1 February.

St Bridget of Sweden (*c.*1303–73), Swedish nun and visionary. She experienced her first vision of the Virgin Mary at the age of 7. After her husband's death she was inspired by further visions to devote herself to religion, and she founded the Order of *Bridgettines* (*c.*1346) at Vadstena in Sweden. She is also called *Birgitta*. Her feast day is 23 July.

Brigadoon a fictional Highland village (in the 1947 musical of this title by Lerner and Loewe), which since the 18th century has been under an enchantment so that it comes to life for only one day every hundred years; the name is used allusively for a representation of an idealized Scotland, or for something characterized by its infrequent appearance or occurrence.

bright-eyed and bushy tailed alert and lively, eager; the image is of an animal in good health and spirits.

bright young thing an enthusiastic, ambitious, and self-consciously fashionable young person, a term originally applied in the 1920s to a member of a young fashionable set noted for exuberant and outrageous behaviour.

brinkmanship the art or practice of pursuing a dangerous policy to the limits of safety before stopping, especially in politics. The term derives from an interview in 1956 with the American international lawyer and politician John Foster Dulles (1888–1959), in which he said, 'The ability to get to the verge without getting into the war is the necessary art…We walked to the brink and we looked it in the face.'

all shipshape and Bristol fashion in good order, neat and clean. Recorded from the mid 19th century, the term was originally in nautical use, referring to the commercial prosperity of Bristol, when its shipping was in good order.

Britannia the personification of Britain, usually depicted as a helmeted woman with shield and trident. The figure had appeared on Roman coins and was revived with the name *Britannia* on the coinage of Charles II (the first model being Charles's favourite Frances Stuart (1647–1702), later Duchess of Richmond).

In the 20th century, *Britannia* was the name of the British royal yacht, launched in 1953 and taken out of service in 1997.

British of or pertaining to Great Britain.

The **British Academy** is an institution founded in 1901 for the promotion of historical, philosophical, and philological studies.

The **British Expeditionary Force** was a British force made available by the army reform of 1908 for service overseas. Such forces were sent to France in 1914, at the outbreak of the First World War and 1939, early in the Second World War (this force was evacuated from Dunkirk in 1940).

The **British Library** is the national library of Britain, containing the former library departments of the British Museum. The principal copyright library, it was established separately from the British Museum in 1972, and moved into its own premises in 1997.

The **British Lion** is the lion as the national emblem of Great Britain; in figurative usage, the British nation. The term is first recorded in Dryden's *The Hind and the Panther* (1687). In sport, the *British Lions* are a touring international rugby union team representing the British Isles.

The **British Museum** is a national museum of antiquities in London. Established with public funds in 1753, it includes among its holdings the ➤ MAGNA *Carta*, the ➤ ELGIN *Marbles*, and the ➤ ROSETTA *Stone*.

broad having a distance larger than usual from side to side; wide

The **land of the broad acres** is a traditional name for Yorkshire.

A **broad arrow** is a mark resembling a broad arrowhead, formerly used on British prison clothing and other government property.

Broad Church is a name for a tradition or group within the Anglican Church favouring a liberal interpretation of doctrine; the phrase came into vogue around 1848, and according to the Master of Balliol, Benjamin Jowett, was first proposed in his hearing by the poet Arthur Hugh Clough (1819–61). In general usage, *Broad Church* means a group, organization, or doctrine which allows for and caters to a wide range of opinions and people.

Broad in the beam means fat around the hips. Originally *beam* referred to the horizontal transverse timbers of a wooden ship, hence the greatest width of a ship, from which is derived the figurative use.

Broadmoor a special hospital near Reading in southern England for the secure holding of patients regarded as both mentally ill and potentially dangerous. It was established in 1863.

the Broads a network of shallow freshwater lakes, traversed by slow-moving rivers, in Norfolk and Suffolk. They were formed by the gradual natural flooding of medieval peat diggings.

broadside a firing of all the guns from one side of a warship.

Broadway a street traversing the length of Manhattan, New York. It is famous for its theatres, and its name has become synonymous with show business (it is also known informally as the ➤ GREAT *White Way*).

Brobdingnag in Swift's *Gulliver's Travels* (1726), a land where everything is of huge size.

Brock's benefit a spectacular display of pyrotechnics, from the name of the public fireworks display held annually at the Crystal Palace, London, from 1865 to 1936, from C. T. *Brock*, firework manufacturer.

Brocken the highest of the Harz Mountains of north central Germany. It is noted for the phenomenon of the **Brocken spectre** and for witches' revels which reputedly took place there on Walpurgis night.

The *Brocken spectre* is a magnified shadow of an observer, typically surrounded by rainbow-like bands, thrown on to a bank of cloud in high mountain areas when the sun is low. The phenomenon was first reported on the Brocken.

brogue a marked accent, especially Irish or Scottish, when speaking English. Recorded from the early 18th century, the term may come allusively from *brogue* 'a rough shoe of untanned leather, formerly worn in parts of Ireland and the Scottish Highlands', referring to the rough footwear of Irish peasants.

broken reed someone not to be relied on; originally often with biblical allusion to Isaiah 36:6.

Bronze Age a prehistoric period that followed the Stone Age and preceded the Iron Age, when weapons and tools were made of bronze rather than stone.

The Bronze Age began in the Near East and SE Europe in the late 4th and early 3rd millennium BC. It is associated with the first European civilizations, the beginnings of urban life in China, and the final stages of some Meso-American civilizations, but did not appear in Africa and Australasia at all.

broom a sprig of this shrub (in Latin *planta genista*) was said to have been worn as a crest by Geoffrey of Anjou, and to be the origin of the name ➤ PLANTAGENET. The word is recorded from Old English (in the form *brōm*) and is of Germanic origin, ultimately related to *bramble*.

From late Middle English, *broom* has also meant a long-handled brush of bristles or twigs, used for sweeping; this is the emblem of ➤ St MARTHA, St Petronilla, an early Roman martyr whose fictional legend makes her the daughter of ➤ St PETER, and St Zita, a 13th-century Luccan serving-maid.

A **new broom** is a newly-appointed person who is likely to make far-reaching changes. With allusion to the proverb *a new broom sweeps clean*, current since the mid 16th century.

broomstick a brush with twigs at one end and a long handle, on which witches were traditionally said to fly.

Brother Jonathan America personified. Recorded from the early 19th century, the term is said to come from the name applied to Jonathan Trumbull, Governor of New York, by George Washington, and to have been used originally with biblical reference to 2 Samuel 1:26.

am I my brother's keeper? an expression of rejection for natural ties; originally a biblical quotation, from the response of ➤ CAIN to God when asked the whereabouts of the murdered Abel (Geneis 4:9).

Brown a common surname.

Capability Brown was the name given to the English landscape gardener Lancelot *Brown* (1716–83). He evolved an English style of natural-looking landscape parks, as at Blenheim and Chatsworth.

In the stories of G. K. Chesterton (1874–1936), **Father Brown** is a Roman Catholic priest who is also an amateur detective, and who solves crimes through apparent paradoxes and inspired common sense.

John Brown (1800–59), was an American abolitionist. In 1859 he was executed after raiding a government arsenal at Harpers Ferry in Virginia, intending to arm black slaves and start a revolt. He became a hero of the abolitionists in the Civil War.

brownie especially in Scottish folklore, a benevolent elf supposedly haunting houses and doing housework secretly. The name is a diminutive of *brown*; a 'wee brown man' often appears in Scottish ballads and fairy tales, and may be compared with the Old Norse *svartálfar*, the dark elves of the Edda.

Brownies (now **Brownie Guides**) are the junior wing of the Guides, wearing a brown uniform; the organization awards points and badges for proficiency in various activities. A **brownie point** is an imaginary award given to someone who does good deeds or tries to please.

Brownshirt a member of a Nazi militia founded by Hitler in Munich in 1921, with brown uniforms resembling those of Mussolini's Blackshirts. They aided Hitler's rise to power, but were eclipsed by the SS after the ➤ NIGHT *of the Long Knives* in June 1934.

Robert the Bruce (1274–1329), Scottish nationalist leader, from 1306, Robert I, King of Scotland.

Bruegel the name of a family of Flemish artists, Pieter Bruegel the Elder (1525–69), who produced landscapes, religious allegories, and satires of peasant life, Peter Bruegel the Younger (1564–1638), known as **Hell Bruegel**, who is noted for his paintings of devils, and Jan Bruegel (1568–1623), son of Pieter

Bruegel the Elder, known as **Velvet Bruegel**, who was a celebrated painter of flowers, landscapes, and mythological scenes.

Bruges a city in NW Belgium, capital of the province of West Flanders, which until the 15th century was a centre of the Flemish textile trade.

The **Bruges Group** was a political pressure group formed with the intention of arguing against British participation in the creation of a federal European state. The name alludes to a speech given in Bruges by Margaret Thatcher, then British Prime Minister, in September 1988.

bruin a bear, especially in children's fables; from Dutch *bruin* 'brown', used as a name for the bear in the 13th-century fable *Reynard the Fox*.

Brum an informal name for Birmingham, a shortened form of ➤ BRUMMAGEM.

Brumaire the second month of the French republican calendar (1793–1805), originally running from 22 October to 20 November. The name is French, from *brume* 'mist'.

Brummagem cheap, showy, or counterfeit. The term comes (in the mid 17th century) from a dialect form of *Birmingham*, England, with reference to counterfeit coins and cheap plated goods once made there.

Brunhild in the *Nibelungenlied*, the wife of Gunther, who instigated the murder of Siegfried. In the Norse versions she is *Brynhild*, a Valkyrie whom ➤ SIGURD (the counterpart of Siegfried) wins by penetrating the wall of fire behind which she lies in an enchanted sleep; his death comes about because he is later tricked into forgetting her and marrying the Nibelung princess Gudrun.

Isambard Kingdom Brunel (1806–59), English engineer, son of ➤ *Marc Isambard* BRUNEL. He was chief engineer of the Great Western Railway. His achievements include designing the Clifton suspension bridge (1829–30) and the first transatlantic steamship, the *Great Western* (1838), and the *Great Eastern* (1858), the world's largest ship until 1899.

St Bruno (*c.*1032–1101), German-born French churchman. In 1084 he withdrew to the mountains of Chartreuse and founded the ➤ CARTHUSIAN order at La Grande Chartreuse. His feast day is 6 October.

Brunswick a former duchy and state of Germany, mostly incorporated into Lower

Saxony, more fully **Brunswick-Wolfenbüttel**. In earlier times Hanover constituted the electorate of **Brunswick-Lüneburg**, whence the name **line of Brunswick** for English sovereigns from George I.

brush name for the bushy tail of a fox.

Brussels the capital of Belgium and of the Belgian province of Brabant; the headquarters of the European Commission is located there.

Brutus[1] legendary Trojan hero, great-grandson of Aeneas and supposed ancestor of the British people. In medieval legend he was said to have brought a group of Trojans to England and founded *Troynovant* or New Troy (London).

Brutus[2] name of an important family in ancient Rome.

Lucius Junius Brutus was the legendary founder of the Roman Republic. Traditionally he led a popular uprising after the rape of ➤ LUCRETIA, against the king (his uncle) and drove him from Rome. He and the father of Lucretia were elected as the first consuls of the Republic (509 BC).

The Roman senator **Marcus Junius Brutus** (85–42 BC), with Cassius, led the conspirators who assassinated Julius Caesar in 44. They were defeated by Caesar's supporters, Antony and Octavian, at the battle of Philippi in 42, after which he committed suicide.

Brythonic denoting, relating to, or belonging to the southern group of Celtic languages, consisting of Welsh, Cornish, and Breton. They were spoken in Britain before and during the Roman occupation, surviving as Welsh and Cornish after the Anglo-Saxon invasions, and being taken to Brittany by emigrants.

Bubbles popular name for the portrait by John Everett Millais and his grandson, William James (1881–1973) as a four-year-old boy blowing bubbles; the picture became widely known when it was used in an advertisement by Pears' soap.

bubonic plague the commonest form of plague in humans, characterized by fever, delirium, and the formation of buboes. The plague bacterium is transmitted by rat fleas. Epidemics occurred in Europe throughout the Middle Ages (notably as the ➤ BLACK *Death* and the ➤ GREAT *Plague* of 1665–6); the disease is still endemic in parts of Asia.

buccaneer a pirate, originally one operating in the Caribbean. The word is recorded from the mid 17th century, originally denoting European hunters in the Caribbean; it comes ultimately from French *boucan* 'a frame on which to cook or cure meat', from Tupi *mukem*.

Bucentaur the state barge used by the Doge of Venice for the ➤ MARRIAGE *of the Adriatic* on Ascension Day.

The name comes ultimately from Italian *bucentoro*, and may be taken from the figurehead of the vessel, representing a mythical creature, half man and half ox, perhaps from Greek *bous* 'ox' + *kentauros* 'centaur'. Alternatively, *bucentoro* may be from Venetian Italian, literally 'barge of gold'.

Bucephalus the favourite horse of Alexander the Great, who tamed the horse as a boy and took it with him on his campaigns until its death, after a battle, in 326 BC. The name in Greek means literally 'ox-headed'.

Buchenwald a Nazi concentration camp in the Second World War, near the village of Buchenwald in eastern Germany.

Buchmanism another name for ➤ MORAL *Rearmament*, from the name of Frank Buchman (1878–1961), American evangelist and founder of the Oxford Group.

buck archaic term for a fashionable and typically hellraising young man. Recorded from the early 18th century, the word initially implied spirited conduct rather than elegance of dress; the meaning of a young man regarded as being fashionable dates from the early 19th century.

pass the buck shift the responsibility for something to someone else; the *buck* here is an article placed as a reminder in front of a player whose turn it is to deal at poker.

Harry Truman (1884–1974), as President of the US, had on his desk the unattributed motto, **the buck stops here**, meaning that the responsibility for something cannot or should not be passed to someone else.

Buckeye State informal name for the state of Ohio, so called from the abundance of buckeye trees, an American tree related to the horse chestnut, with showy red or white flowers.

Buckingham Palace the London residence of the British sovereign since 1837, adjoining St James's Park, Westminster. It was built for the Duke of Buckingham in the early 18th century and bought by George III in 1761, and redesigned by John Nash for George IV *c.*1821–30; the facade facing the Mall was redesigned in 1913.

Buckley's chance in Australia, a slim chance, no chance at all. The expression is sometimes said to be from the name of William *Buckley* (died 1856), who, despite dire predictions as to his chances of survival, lived with the Aboriginals for many years.

Buddha a title given to the founder of Buddhism, Siddartha Gautama (*c.*563–*c.*460 BC). Born an Indian prince in what is now Nepal, he renounced wealth and family to become an ascetic, and after achieving enlightenment while meditating, taught all who came to learn from him.

  Buddhism, founded by him, is now a widespread Asian religion or philosophy. It has no god, and gives a central role to the doctrine of karma. The 'four noble truths' of Buddhism state that all existence is suffering, that the cause of suffering is desire, that freedom from suffering is nirvana, and that this is attained through the 'eightfold path' of ethical conduct, wisdom, and mental discipline (including meditation). There are two major traditions, Theravada and Mahayana.

Buffalo Bill (1846–1917), American showman, born *William Frederick Cody.* He gained his nickname for killing 4,280 buffalo in eight months to feed the Union Pacific Railroad workers, and subsequently devoted his life to his travelling Wild West Show.

Buffy the Vampire-Slayer in Joss Whedon's cult TV series (1997–) of this name, Buffy Summers, a Californian high-school girl who discovers that she is ➤ *the* SLAYER, with special powers to destroy vampires.

Bug Bible a name given to versions of the English Bible (Coverdale's and Matthew's) in which the words in Psalm 91:5 are translated, 'thou shalt not be afraid for any bugs by night'.

bug-eyed monster an extra-terrestrial monster with bulging eyes.

Buggins' turn a system by which appointments or awards are made in rotation rather than by merit, from *Buggins*, used to represent a typical surname.

Bugs Bunny an American cartoon rabbit with prominent teeth who first appeared in Warner Brothers' films in 1938.

bull[1] a bull is the emblem of ➤ *St* LUKE, ➤ *St* FRIDESWIDE, and ➤ *St* THOMAS *Aquinas;* **the Bull** is the zodiacal sign and constellation ➤ TAURUS.

  On the Stock Exchange, a person who buys shares hoping to sell them at a higher price later is known as a *bull;* the term is recorded from the early 18th century.

  In Egyptian mythology, the god ➤ APIS was depicted as a bull, symbolizing fertility and strength in war.

  A **bull in a china shop** is a clumsy person in a situation calling for adroit movement; the phrase is recorded from the mid 19th century.

  A **bull market** is a market in which share prices are rising, encouraging buying (compare *bear market* at ➤ BEAR[2]).

  A **bull-roarer** is a sacred object of Australian Aboriginal ceremony and ritual, so called because of a fancied resemblance to a child's toy. A *bull-roarer* consists of a flat oval carved piece of wood, pointed at each end and pierced at one end; a string is threaded through the hole so that the bull-roarer can be swung round, making a booming noise. It is also known as a *churinga.*

  Bull Run is a small river in eastern Virginia, scene of two Confederate victories, in 1861 and 1862, during the American Civil War.

  The word dates from late Old English (in form *bula*, recorded in place names), and comes from Old Norse *boli.*

  The expression **like a bull at a gate** means with the angry vigour of a bull charging a restraining ('five-barred') gate; the expression is recorded from the late 19th century.

  To **take the bull by the horns** implies that one is taking a firm grasp on a difficult issue; the expression is recorded from the early 18th century.

bull[2] a papal edict. Recorded from Middle English, the word comes via Old French from Latin *bulla* 'bubble, rounded object', in medieval Latin, 'seal or sealed document'. Also called *papal bull.*

bulldog a *bulldog* has traditionally been taken as the symbol of what are regarded as British characteristics of pluck and stubbornness, and may generally denote a person noted for courageous or stubborn tenacity.

  At Oxford and Cambridge Universities, *bulldog* is used informally for an official who assists the proctors, especially in disciplinary matters.

Bulldog Drummond is the hero of a series of novels by Sapper (H. C. McNeile, 1888–1937); the former Captain Drummond is a large, ugly, xenophobic, but charming ex-army officer who despite his apparent brainlessness defeats a succession of fiendishly clever international crooks with a blend of violence and daring.

bullseye the centre of the target in sports such as archery, shooting, and darts; a shot that hits the centre of such a target; in figurative use, something that achieves exactly the intended effect.

Bumble the beadle in Dickens's *Oliver Twist*, a type of official pomposity and fussy stupidity.

Natty Bumppo real name of *Leatherstocking*, the hero of *The Pioneers* (1823) and four other novels (the *Leatherstocking* series) of American frontier life by James Fenimore Cooper (1789–1851); his name may be used for the type of a frontiersman of the period, with particular reference to tracking skills.

Bunbury a fictitious excuse for making a visit or avoiding an obligation, from the name of an imaginary person (so used) in Oscar Wilde's *The Importance of Being Earnest*.

Buncombe the name of the county in North Carolina from which the word ➤ BUNKUM derives.

go a bundle on be very keen on or fond of. *Bundle* here is in the late 19th century US slang sense of a bundle of money, i.e. a large sum. Originally (in the early 20th century) US slang for betting a large sum of money on a horse. Now used figuratively, often with a negative.

Bunker Hill the first pitched battle (1775) of the War of American Independence (actually fought on Breed's Hill near Boston, Massachusetts). Although the British won, the good performance of the untrained Americans gave considerable impetus to the Revolution.

bunkum nonsense. Recorded from the mid 19th century, originally as *buncombe*, the word comes from *Buncombe* County in North Carolina, mentioned in an inconsequential speech made by its congressman, Felix Walker, solely to please his constituents (*c.*1820).

bunny a child's word for a rabbit.

A **bunny boiler** is a woman who takes revenge after having been spurned by her lover, with reference to the film *Fatal Attraction*, in which a jilted mistress boils her lover's pet rabbit.

A **bunny girl** is a club hostess, waitress, or photographic model, wearing a skimpy costume with ears and a tail suggestive of a rabbit.

Billy Bunter a schoolboy character, noted for his fatness and gluttony, in stories by Frank Richards (pseudonym of Charles Hamilton 1876–1961).

bunyip in Australia, a mythical amphibious monster said to inhabit inland waterways. The name comes from an aboriginal word.

burb a suburb or suburban area; the usage is recorded from the late 1970s in US English, especially in **the burbs**, a somewhat dismissive term for a location seen as conventional and boring.

burden of proof the obligation to prove one's assertion; the term (translating Latin *onus probandi* in Roman law) is recorded from the late 16th century.

Burgess Shale a stratum of sedimentary rock exposed in the Rocky Mountains in British Columbia, Canada. The bed, dated to the Cambrian period (about 540 million years ago), is rich in well-preserved fossils of early marine invertebrates, many of which represent evolutionary lineages unknown in later times.

Burgundy a region and former duchy of east central France, centred on Dijon. Under a series of strong dukes Burgundy achieved considerable independence from imperial control in the later Middle Ages, before being absorbed by France when King Louis XI claimed the duchy in 1477.

William Burke (1792–1829), Irish murderer. He was a bodysnatcher operating in Edinburgh with his accomplice *William Hare*, and was convicted of murdering those whose bodies he subsequently sold for dissection. He gave his name to the verb *burke* meaning, 'kill secretly by suffocation or strangulation', as Burke is said to have killed his victims.

Burke's Peerage a genealogical guide to peers and baronets, first published in 1826, by John *Burke* (1787–1848), Irish genealogical and heraldic writer.

Burlington Bertie the type of a man-about-town, personified in the song 'Burlington Bertie from Bow' (1915) by W. F. Hargreaves, popularized by the music-hall performer Vesta Tilley (*Burlington* refers to the luxurious *Burlington Arcade* in the fashionable area of Piccadilly, London).

Burma Road a route linking Lashi in Burma to Kunming in China. Completed in 1939, it was built by the Chinese in response to the Japanese occupation of the Chinese coast, to serve as a supply route to the interior.

burn one's boats destroy one's means of retreat, do something which makes it impossible to return to an earlier state; the term is recorded (in figurative use) from the late 19th century.

burn the candle at both ends draw on one's resources from two directions; especially, overtax one's strength by going to bed late and getting up early. The expression is recorded in English from the mid 18th century, but is found earlier in French.

burn the midnight oil read or work late into the night, supposedly by lamplight; a related image is found in the expression ➤ SMELL *of the lamp*.

burning bush in Exodus 3:2, a bush which 'burned with fire, and…was not consumed', seen by ➤ MOSES on Mount Horeb, and constituting a sign from God that he was to lead the Israelites out of Egypt.

burning fiery furnace in Daniel ch. 3, the fire into which the three Hebrew exiles in Babylon, Shadrach, Meshach, and Abednego, were cast by King Nebuchadnezzar because they refused to worship pagan images, and in which they were preserved unharmed.

Burns Night 25 January, the birthday of the Scottish poet Robert Burns (1759–96), when celebrations are held in Scotland and elsewhere.

burnt offering an offering burnt on an altar as a religious sacrifice, originally in biblical use, as in Job 1.

go for a **Burton** meet with disaster, be ruined, destroyed, or killed. Origin uncertain; the expression originated in the mid 20th century airman's slang meaning 'be killed in a crash'. Suggested references to Burton's,

the British men's outfitters, or Burton, a kind of ale, are folk etymologies, with no definite evidence to support them.

bury one's head in the sand ignore unpleasant realities; the expression alludes to the traditional belief that the ➤ OSTRICH if pursued would bury its head in the sand, through incapacity to distinguish between seeing and being seen.

bury the hatchet end a quarrel or conflict and become friendly; the allusion is to an American Indian custom of burying a hatchet or tomahawk to mark the conclusion of a peace treaty.

Busby Babes informal name given to the young football players recruited for Manchester United by Matt *Busby* (1909–94), the Scottish-born football manager. An air crash at Munich airport in 1958 killed most of the side, but he reconstructed the team and won the European Cup in 1968.

the bush wild or uncultivated country, especially in Australia or Africa (see also, ➤ SYDNEY *or the bush*). **Bush telegraph** is an informal network by means of which information is conveyed in remote areas; the term is originally Australian, and refers to bushrangers' confederates who disseminated intelligence as to the movements of the police.

bushel in Britain, a measure of capacity equal to 8 gallons (equivalent to 36.4 litres), used for corn, fruit, liquids, etc.; in the US, a measure of capacity equal to 64 US pints (equivalent to 35.2 litres), used for dry goods. The word is recorded from Middle English, and comes from Old French *boissel*, perhaps ultimately of Gaulish origin.

  The expression **hide one's light under a bushel**, meaning keep quiet about one's talents or accomplishments, originally refers to Matthew 5:15.

bushido the code of honour and morals developed by the Japanese ➤ SAMURAI. The word is Japanese, and comes from *bushi* 'samurai' + *dō* 'way'.

bushranger in 19th-century Australia, an escaped convict or outlaw living in the bush, often by resort to robbery.

bushwhacker one who lives in wild uncultivated country; in the American Civil War, an irregular combatant with a group who had taken to the woods.

buskin a thick-soled laced boot worn by an ancient Athenian tragic actor to gain height; **the buskin** denotes the style or spirit of tragic drama. The word is recorded from the early 16th century, designating a calf-length boot; it probably comes via Old French from Middle Dutch *broseken*, but the ultimate origin is unknown.

busman's holiday a holiday or form of recreation that involves doing the same thing that one does at work; the term is recorded from the late 19th century, when excursions by bus were a popular form of holiday.

busy bee an industrious person; an expression deriving from the *bee* taken as the type of a busy worker.

the butcher, the baker, the candlestick-maker people of all trades; from the nursery rhyme 'Rub-a-dub-dub, Three men in a tub.'

Butlin's popular holiday camps founded by Sir William ('Billy') Butlin (1899–1980) in 1936 at Skegness, taken as the type of an establishment offering organized leisure and entertainment.

butterfly often taken as the type of a fragile and ephemeral creature (see also ➤ BREAK *a butterfly on a wheel*).
   The **butterfly effect** is the effect of a very small change in the initial conditions of a system which makes a significant difference to the outcome; the term derives from the title of a paper (1979) by the American meteorologist Edward Lorenz (1917–), 'Predictability: Does the flap of a butterfly's wings in Brazil set off a tornado in Texas?'
   Float like a butterfly, sting like a bee is the summary of Muhammad Ali's boxing strategy (probably originated by his aide Drew 'Bundini' Brown).

Buttons a nickname for a liveried pageboy; especially, in the pantomime of ➤ CINDER-ELLA, the page who serves Cinderella's father and has an unrequited love for Cinderella herself; the character was first introduced in the 19th century, after Rossini's Cinderella opera *La Cenerentola* (1817) became well known.

buzzword a technical word or phrase that has become fashionable, typically as a slogan.

Byblos an ancient Mediterranean seaport, situated on the site of modern Jebeil, to the north of Beirut in Lebanon. An important trading centre with strong links with Egypt, it became a thriving Phoenician city in the 2nd millennium BC, and was particularly noted for the export of papyrus and cedar wood.

Byerley Turk with the ➤ GODOLPHIN *Barb* and the ➤ DARLEY *Arabian*, one of the three founding sires of the Thoroughbred, imported to improve the stock in the 18th century.

Byzantine of or pertaining to the ancient city of Byzantium, or Constantinople. The **Byzantine Empire** in SE Europe and Asia Minor was formed from the eastern part of the Roman Empire at the end of the 4th century AD. Constantinople (Byzantium) became the capital of the Eastern Empire in 476, with the fall of Rome, and in 1054 theological and political differences between Constantinople and Rome led to the breach between Eastern and Western Christianity (see ➤ GREAT *Schism*). The loss of Constantinople to the Ottoman Turks in 1453 was the end of the empire, although its rulers held Trebizond (Trabzon) until 1461.
   The term *Byzantine* denotes something regarded as typifying the politics and bureaucratic structure of the *Byzantine Empire*; in particular, (of a system or situation) excessively complicated and typically involving a great deal of administrative detail; characterized by deviousness or underhand procedure.
   Byzantine is also used to designate an ornate artistic and architectural style which developed in the Byzantine Empire and spread to Italy, Russia, and elsewhere. The art is generally rich and stylized (as in religious icons) and the architecture is typified by many-domed, highly decorated churches.

Byzantium an ancient Greek city, founded in the 7th century BC, at the southern end of the Bosporus, site of the modern city of Istanbul. It was rebuilt by Constantine the Great in AD 324–30 as Constantinople.

Cc

C the third letter of the modern English alphabet and of the ancient Roman one, originally corresponding to Greek *gamma*, Semitic *gimel*.

Ça ira French for 'things will work out', refrain of 'Carillon national', popular song of the French Revolution (*c.* July 1790), translated by William Doyle; the phrase is believed to originate with Benjamin Franklin, who may have uttered it in 1776 when asked for news of the American Revolution.

Cabal in the mid 17th century, the name given to a committee of five ministers under Charles II, whose surnames happened to begin with C, A, B, A, and L (Clifford, Arlington, Buckingham, Ashley, and Lauderdale).
   The word *cabal* (denoting the ➤ KABBALAH) is recorded from the late 16th century, and comes ultimately via French from medieval Latin *cabala*.

the Cabinet the term was first used in the early 17th century for the private room in which confidential advisers of the sovereign or chief ministers of a country meet; the current sense of a committee of senior ministers responsible for controlling government policy is recorded from the mid 17th century.

cable the chain of a ship's anchor; in nautical usage, a length of 200 yards (182.9 metres) or (in the US) 240 yards (219.4 metres).

the whole caboodle the whole number or quantity of people or things in question. Recorded from the mid 19th century (originally US), and perhaps from the phrase ➤ *the whole* KIT *and boodle*, in the same sense.

caboshed in heraldry (of the head of a stag, bull, or other animal) shown full face with no neck visible.

Cabot the name of two Italian explorers and navigators, the elder of whom, **John Cabot** (*c.*1450–*c.*98), sailed from Bristol in 1497 in search of Asia, but in fact landed on the mainland of North America (the site of his arrival is uncertain). Returning to Bristol, he undertook a second expedition in 1498 from which he never returned.

His son **Sebastian Cabot** (*c.*1475–1557) accompanied his father on his voyage in 1497 and made further voyages after the latter's death, most notably to Brazil and the River Plate (1526).

cacodemon a malevolent spirit or person. The word is recorded from the late 16th century and comes from Greek, from *kakos* 'bad' + *daimōn* 'spirit'.

cacoethes an urge to do something inadvisable; the word is recorded from the mid 16th century, and comes via Latin from Greek *kakoēthes*, from *kakos* 'bad' + *ēthos* 'disposition'.
   cacoethes scribendi is an incurable passion for writing; the phrase is originally a quotation from the Roman satirist Juvenal (AD *c.*60–*c.*130).

Brother Cadfael in the popular detective stories of Ellis Peters (1913–95), a former crusader who is a Benedictine monk of the 12th-century abbey of Shrewsbury, later home to the shrine of ➤ St WINEFRIDE; Cadfael uses his worldly knowledge and herbalist's skills, as well as his faith, to resolve mysteries in the abbey and the town.

Cadmus in Greek mythology, the brother of ➤ EUROPA and traditional founder of Thebes in Boeotia. He killed a dragon which guarded a spring, and when (on Athene's advice) he sowed the dragon's teeth there came up a harvest of armed men; he disposed of the majority by setting them to fight one another, and the survivors formed the ancestors of the Theban nobility.

caduceus an ancient Greek or Roman herald's wand, typically one with two serpents twined round it, carried by the messenger god Hermes or Mercury. The word comes from Latin, from Doric Greek *karukeion* for Greek *kērux* 'herald'.

Caedmon (7th century), Anglo-Saxon monk and poet, said to have been an illiterate herdsman inspired in a vision to compose poetry on biblical themes. The only authentic fragment of his work is a song in praise of the Creation, quoted by Bede.

Caen a city and river port in Normandy in northern France, on the River Orne, which is the burial place of William the Conqueror. The town was the scene of fierce fighting between the Germans and the Allies in June and July 1944.

Caerleon a town in South Wales, the tradional seat of Arthur, as in Tennyson's *Idylls of the King*. It is probably to be identified with *Carlioun*, which in Malory's *Morte D'Arthur* is said to be where Arthur was crowned and held his court.

Caernarfon a town in NW Wales on the shore of the Menai Strait, the birthplace of Edward II.

Caesar a title of Roman emperors, especially those from Augustus to Hadrian. Recorded from the Middle English, the word comes from Latin *Caesar*, family name of the Roman statesman ➤ *Gaius* JULIUS *Caesar*.

Caesarea an ancient port on the Mediterranean coast of Israel, founded in 22 BC by Herod the Great on the site of a Phoenician harbour and named in honour of the Roman emperor Augustus Caesar. Caesarea became one of the principal cities of Roman Palestine, but it later declined as its harbour silted up.

Caesarea Philippi a city in ancient Palestine, on the site of the present-day village of Baniyas in the Golan Heights. It was the site of a Hellenistic shrine to the god Pan and then of a temple built towards the end of the 1st century BC by Herod the Great and named in honour of the Roman emperor Augustus Caesar.

Caesarean section a surgical operation for delivering a child by cutting through the wall of the mother's abdomen. The term is recorded from the early 17th century, and the name is said to come from the story that Julius *Caesar* was delivered by this method.

Count Cagliostro assumed name of an Italian adventurer, Giuseppe Balsamo (1743–95), who posed successfully as an alchemist and magician in late 18th-century Paris society; he was banished after his involvement in the ➤ *Affair of the* DIAMOND *Necklace*. In 1789 he was arrested in Rome, and spent his final years in prison.

Caiaphas name of the Jewish high priest at the time of the trial and execution of Jesus; in John 11:50 it is Caiaphas who says, 'It is expedient for us, that one man should die for the people, and that the whole nation perish not.'

Cain in the Bible, the eldest son of Adam and Eve, and murderer of his brother Abel after Abel's offering to God of a lamb was accepted by God, while Cain's sheaves were rejected. Cain is the first murderer of humankind, and from this becomes a fugitive and outcast.

The **curse of Cain** is the fate of someone compelled to lead a wandering life, like Cain after the killing of Abel (Genesis 4:11–12).

The **land God gave to Cain** is a name for Labrador, referring to Cain's banishment by God to a desolate land 'east of Eden'. The term derives from a remark attributed to the French navigator and explorer Jacques Cartier (1491–1557), on first discovering the northern shore of the Gulf of St Lawrence (now Labrador and Quebec).

The **mark of Cain** was placed on Cain by God, initially as a sign that he should not be killed or harmed, later taken as identifying him as a murderer.

Cajun a member of any of the largely self-contained communities in the bayou areas of southern Louisiana formed by descendants of French Canadians, speaking an archaic form of French and known for their lively folk music and spicy cooking. The name comes from an alteration of *Acadian* (see ➤ ACADIA).

cakes and ale merrymaking, good things; originally, a quotation from Shakespeare's *Twelfth Night* (1601).

Calais a port in northern France. Captured by Edward III in 1347 after a long siege, it remained an English possession until it was retaken by the French in 1558.

Calamity Jane (*c*.1852–1903), American frontierswoman, noted for her skill at shooting and riding; born *Martha Jane Canary*.

Calchas in Homer's *Iliad*, the seer of the Greek forces at the siege of Troy.

caldarium a hot room in an ancient Roman bath.

Caledonia the Roman name for northern Britain, later applied poetically or rhetorically to Scotland, as in Scott's *The Lay of the Last Minstrel* (1805), 'O Caledonia! stern and wild'.

The **Caledonian Canal** is a system of lochs and canals crossing Scotland from Inverness on the east coast to Fort William on the west. Built by Thomas Telford, it was opened in

1822. It traverses the Great Glen, part of its length being formed by Loch Ness.

calends the first day of the month in the ancient Roman calendar. Recorded from Old English (denoting an appointed time) the word comes via Old French from Latin *kalendae*, *calendae* 'first day of the month' (when accounts were due and the order of days was proclaimed), and is related to Latin *calare* and Greek *kalein* 'call, proclaim'.

calfskin a calf's skin as the type of clothing worn by fools or jesters.

Caliban in Shakespeare's *The Tempest*, the brutish and degraded son of the witch Sycorax, who has been forced to serve ➤ PROSPERO; in contrast to the 'airy spirit' ➤ ARIEL, he typifies a gross and animal nature. His name may represent either 'Carib' or 'cannibal'.

Caliburn in the chronicle of Geoffrey of Monmouth, the name of King Arthur's sword; ➤ EXCALIBUR is an alteration of it.

Caligula (AD 12–41), Roman emperor 37–41, born *Gaius Julius Caesar Germanicus*. He gained the nickname *Caligula* ('little boot') as an infant on account of the miniature military boots he wore. His brief reign, which began when he succeeded Tiberius and ended with his assassination, became notorious for its tyrannical excesses.

caliph the chief Muslim civil and religious ruler, regarded as the successor of Muhammad. The caliph ruled in Baghdad until 1258 and then in Egypt until the Ottoman conquest of 1517; the title was then held by the Ottoman sultans until it was abolished in 1924.

Calliope in Greek and Roman mythology, the Muse of epic poetry. The name comes from Greek *Kalliopē*, literally 'having a beautiful voice'.

Callippic cycle a period of 76 years, equal to 4 Metonic cycles, at the end of which, by omission of one day, the phases of the moon recur at the same day and hour. It is named after *Callippus*, a Greek astronomer of the 4th century BC.

Callisto in Greek mythology, a nymph, an attendant of Artemis, who was the lover of Zeus and mother of his son Arcas; she was turned into a bear either by Zeus to save her from the anger of his wife Hera or by Hera and Artemis in vengeance; later she was placed as a constellation in the heavens by Zeus (see also ➤ URSA *Major*).

Calvary the hill outside Jerusalem on which Jesus was crucified. The name comes from late Latin *calvaria* 'skull', translation of Greek *golgotha* 'place of a skull' (Matthew 27:33).

The word calvary is also used to designate a sculpture or picture representing the scene of the Crucifixion.

Calvinism the Protestant theological system of the French Protestant theologian and reformer John Calvin (1509–64) and his successors, which develops Luther's doctrine of justification by faith alone into an emphasis on the grace of God and centres on the doctrine of predestination.

Calydon a Greek town in Aetolia, in Greek mythology ruled over by ➤ MELEAGER), and ravaged by the **Calydonian boar**, a monstrous wild boar sent by Artemis. The boar was hunted down and killed by Meleager.

Calypso in Greek mythology, a nymph who kept the shipwrecked Odysseus on her island, Ogygia, for seven years; she released him in the end on the orders of Zeus. Her name is Greek, meaning literally 'she who conceals'.

Cambria the Latin name for Wales, a variant of Cumbria, from Welsh ➤ CYMRY.

Cambyses (d.522 BC), king of Persia 529–522 BC, son of Cyrus. He is chiefly remembered for his conquest of Egypt in 525 BC, and as the subject of a play (1569) by Preston which became proverbial for its bombastic grandiloquence.

Camden Town Group a group of artists active in London in the period 1911–1913, lead by Walter Sickert and Spencer Frederick Gore, generally considered to be the earliest British exponents of post-impressionism; in 1913 they merged into the larger ➤ LONDON *Group*.

camel the *camel* can survive for long periods without food or drink, chiefly by using up the fat reserves in its hump; from this comes the name ➤ SHIP *of the desert*.

Camels are the emblem of the 4th-century Egyptian martyr St Mennas, probably because pilgrims to his shrine arrive by camel.

camelopard an archaic name for a giraffe, coming (in late Middle English) via Latin from Greek *kamēlopardalis*, from *kamēlos* 'camel' + *pardalis* 'female panther or pard';

the second element derives from the comparison of a giraffe's spotted skin to that of a leopard.

Camelot in Arthurian legend, the place where King Arthur held his court, variously identified as Caerleon in Wales, Camelford in Cornwall, Cadbury Castle in Somerset, and (by Thomas Malory) Winchester in Hampshire.

In extended usage, *Camelot* is a place associated with glittering romance and optimism; it is also often used for the White House of John Fitzgerald Kennedy's presidency (1961–3).

in camera in private, in particular taking place in the private chambers of a judge, with the press and public excluded; the term comes from late Latin, 'in the chamber'.

Camford a fictional equivalent of the universities of Oxford and Cambridge; an alternative (though less popular) term for
➤ OXBRIDGE.

Don Camillo the Italian parish priest who is the hero of a number of stories by Giovanni Guareschi (1908–68), in which he is pitted against his former Partisan ally the Communist mayor of the village.

Marcus Furius Camillus (d. *c.*365 BC), Roman statesman and general, who according to Livy was regarded as the second founder of Rome after its occupation by Brennus and his Gauls *c.*390 BC.

the Camorra a secret criminal society originating in Naples and Neapolitan emigrant communities in the 19th century. Some members later moved to the US and formed links with the Mafia. The name is Italian, and may come from Spanish *camorra* 'dispute, quarrel'.

Camp David the country retreat of the President of the US, in the Appalachian Mountains in Maryland. President Carter hosted talks there between the leaders of Israel and Egypt which resulted in the Camp David agreements (1978) and the Egypt–Israel peace treaty of 1979.

Originally established and named *Shangri-La* in 1942 by President Franklin Roosevelt, *Camp David* was renamed in 1953 by President Dwight Eisenhower after his grandson David.

Campaign for Nuclear Disarmament a British organization which campaigns for the abolition of nuclear weapons worldwide and calls for unilateral disarmament. Founded in 1958, it was revived in 1979 to oppose the siting of US cruise missiles in Britain. With the improvement in East–West relations and the break-up of the Soviet Union, the organization has had a lower public profile.

Campania territory in ancient Italy south of Latium, lying between the Apennines and the Tyrrhenian Sea, and extending south to the Surrentine promontory (Sorrento). A volcanic plain, it is exceptionally fertile, and many wealthy Romans had villas there.

St Edmund Campion (1540–81), English Jesuit priest and martyr. He was ordained a deacon in the Church of England in 1569 but went abroad, becoming a Catholic and a Jesuit priest in 1573. Returning to England in 1580, he was arrested, charged with conspiracy against the Crown, tortured, and executed. He was canonized in 1970. His feast day is 1 December.

Campus Martius in ancient Rome, a park and recreation ground (the 'field of Mars') outside the city walls which was where the Roman legions exercised. It was originally the site of an altar to Mars.

a can of worms a complex and largely uninvestigated matter (especially one likely to prove problematic or scandalous); the term is recorded from the 1960s.

Cana an ancient small town in Galilee, where Christ is said to have performed his first miracle by changing water into wine during a marriage feast (John 2:1–11).

Canaan the biblical name for the area of ancient Palestine west of the River Jordan, the Promised Land of the Israelites, who conquered and occupied it during the latter part of the 2nd millennium BC.

canard an unfounded rumour or story. Recorded from the mid 19th century, the word comes from French, literally 'duck', also 'hoax', from Old French *caner* 'to quack'. One suggested origin is the expression *vendre un canard à moitié* 'half-sell a duck', with the implication that a half-sale is no sale at all, and therefore the vendor has been fooled. Alternatively, the expression has been attributed to a made-up story about ducks, which was believed by many, and came to exemplify public credulity.

Le Canard Enchaîné ('The Chained Duck') is the title of a famous French satirical weekly newspaper, founded in 1916.

canary in the 19th century, domestic *canaries* were often kept in coal mines; by succumbing to any build up of gas, they gave warning to miners of potential danger.

Cancer in astrology, the fourth sign of the zodiac, which the sun enters at the northern summer solstice (about 21 June).

Candace in biblical times, a title of queen mothers who ruled Ethiopia; in Acts 8:27, the apostle Philip converts and baptizes the chamberlain of one of these queens.

Candide the naive hero of Voltaire's novel *Candide* (1759) who through the misfortunes he encounters rejects the unfounded optimism of his tutor Dr ➤ PANGLOSS in favour of the practical philosophy inherent in the phrase 'we must cultivate our garden.'

candle a candle is the emblem of ➤ *St* GENEVIEVE, ➤ *St* BLAISE, and ➤ *St* GUDULE.

Cannot hold a candle to means be nowhere near as good as. The positive form of this expression (recorded in the mid 16th century) makes plain the literal sense of an assistant holding a candle to provide illumination for a superior to work by. The current negative version implies that the subordinate is so far inferior as to be unfit to perform even this humble task.

In candle is an expression used of a horse chestnut tree in flower.

Not worth the candle means not justifiable because of the trouble or cost involved. The idea is that expenditure on a candle to provide light for an activity would not be recouped by the profits from that activity. The expression is of French origin, recorded from the early 17th century.

To **sell by the candle** was to dispose of by auction in which bids are received so long as a small piece of candle burns, the last bid before the candle goes out securing the article; the custom was apparently French in origin.

Candlemas a Christian festival held on 2 February to commemorate the purification of the Virgin Mary (after childbirth, according to Jewish law) and the presentation of Christ in the temple. Candles were traditionally blessed at this festival.

canephora in ancient Greece, each of the maidens who carried on their heads baskets bearing sacred objects used at certain feasts; a caryatid representing or resembling such a figure.

Cannae a village in Apulia in Italy, the scene of a great defeat inflicted on the Romans by ➤ HANNIBAL in 216 BC.

cannon a *cannon* is one of the emblems of ➤ *St* BARBARA.

A **loose cannon** is a person or thing likely to cause unintentional or misdirected damage. Literally in former times, a piece of ordnance that had broken loose from its fastening or mounting, an accident especially dangerous on wooden ships of war.

canon¹ originally, a Church decree or law; later (from late Middle English), a general law, rule, principle, or criterion by which something is judged. **Canon law** is ecclesiastical law, especially (in the Roman Catholic Church) that laid down by papal pronouncements.

Recorded from Old English, the word comes via Latin from Greek *kanōn* 'rule'; it was reinforced in Middle English by Old French *canon*. From Middle English, the word also designated (in the Roman Catholic Church) the part of the Mass containing the words of consecration (also known as the **canon of the Mass**).

From late Middle English, *canon* has also designated a collection or list of sacred books accepted as genuine; from the late 19th century the term was extended to cover the works of a particular author or artist that are recognized as genuine, and then a list of literary works considered to be permanently established as being of the highest quality.

In music, a *canon* is a piece in which the same melody is begun in different parts successively, so that the imitations overlap; **in canon** means with different parts successively beginning the same melody. This sense is recorded from the late 16th century.

In the Christian Church, **canonical age** is the age according to canon law at which a person may seek ordination or undertake a particular duty.

A **canonical hour** is each of the times of daily prayer appointed in the breviary; each of the seven offices (matins with lauds, prime, terce, sext, nones, vespers, and compline) appointed for these times. In the Church of England, it is the time (now usually between 8 a.m. and 6 p.m.) during which a marriage may lawfully be celebrated.

canon² originally (in the Roman Catholic Church), a member of certain orders of clergy that live communally according to an ecclesiastical rule in the same way as monks (also as **canon regular** or **regular canon**).

Later (from the mid 16th century), a member of the clergy who is on the staff of a cathedral, especially one who is a member of the chapter. The position is frequently conferred as an honorary one.

The word is recorded from Middle English and comes via Old French from Latin *canonicus* 'according to rule', ultimately from the base of ➤ CANON[1].

canonization in the Roman Catholic Church, the official declaration that a dead person is a saint; the process typically involves a rigorous investigation of the life and record of the prospective saint and any cult surrounding them. In the early Church, sanctity was often established through the growth of a spontaneous cult; in the late 12th century, it was declared that the formal pronouncement of the Church was required for public veneration.

Recorded from late Middle English, the word comes from late Latin *canonizare* 'admit as authoritative' (in medieval Latin 'admit to the list of recognized saints'), from Latin *canon* (see ➤ CANON[1]).

Canopic jar a covered urn used in ancient Egyptian burials to hold the entrails and other visceral organs from an embalmed body. The lids, originally plain, were later modelled as the human, falcon, dog, and jackal heads of the four sons of Horus, protectors of the jars.

The name comes (via Latin) from *Canopus*, the name of a town in ancient Egypt.

Canossa a town in Modena, Italy, where in 1077 the Emperor Henry IV (1050–1106), who had been excommunicated during his struggle with the papacy, was forced to recant and do penance before Pope Gregory VII. In 1872 Otto von Bismarck asserted **we will not go to Canossa**, in his denial of papal authority over German subjects.

Cantab of Cambridge University; the term comes from Latin *Cantabrigiensis*, from *Cantabrigia* 'Cambridge'.

Cantate Psalm 98 (97 in the Vulgate) used as a canticle (e.g. as an alternative to the Magnificat at Evening Prayer in the Church of England); *cantate* is Latin for 'sing ye', and is the first word of the psalm.

The fourth Sunday after Easter is sometimes called **Cantate Sunday** because the introit for that day is taken from the Cantate.

canteen culture in the UK, a set of conservative and discriminatory attitudes said to exist within the police force, characterized by resistance to the introduction of modern managerial standards and practices, and at its most extreme associated with male chauvinist and racist views.

canter a pace of a horse between a trot and a gallop, with not less than one foot on the ground at any time. The word is recorded from the early 18th century (as a verb), and is short for *Canterbury pace* or *Canterbury gallop* (see ➤ CANTERBURY).

At a canter means without much effort, easily. A horse-racing metaphor, implying that the horse has to make so little effort that it can win at the easy pace of a canter rather than having to gallop.

Canterbury a city in Kent, SE England, the seat of the Archbishop of Canterbury. St Augustine established a church and monastery there in 597, and it became a place of medieval pilgrimage, to the shrine of ➤ *St Thomas à* BECKET.

The **Canterbury bell**, a bellflower grown for ornament, is named with reference to the bells on pilgrims' horses.

A **Canterbury gallop** is a slow easy gallop, supposedly the pace of mounted pilgrims.

A **Canterbury tale** is a story told on a pilgrimage (originally one of Chaucer's cycle of linked tales told by a group of pilgrims); a long tedious story.

canticle a hymn or chant, typically with a biblical text, forming a regular part of a church service. The word is recorded from Middle English and comes from Latin *canticulum* 'little song'.

The **Canticles** or **Canticle of Canticles** is another name for the ➤ SONG *of Songs* (especially in the Vulgate).

Canute (d. 1035), Danish king of England 1017–35, Denmark 1018–35, and Norway 1028–35, who became king of England after Edmund Ironside's murder. He is remembered for the legend of his demonstrating to fawning courtiers his inability to stop the rising tide; this has become distorted in folklore to suggest that Canute really expected to turn back the tide.

by a canvas by a small margin. The tapered front end of a racing boat was formerly covered with canvas to prevent water being taken on board; hence the length between the tip of the bow and the first oarsman.

cap an article of headgear.

A **cap and bells** is the insignia of the professional jester.

A **cap of liberty** was a conical cap given to Roman slaves on emancipation, often used as a Republican symbol.

A **cap of maintenance** is a cap or hat worn as a symbol of dignity, or carried before a monarch on ceremonial occasions.

If the cap fits, wear it is an injunction to a hearer to take as applying to themselves a generalized remark or criticism that the speaker feels is apposite. Early citations of this saying (recorded from the mid 18th century) show that the *cap* in question was a originally a fool's cap.

Capetian name of the dynasty ruling France 987–1328, founded by Hugh *Capet* (938–96), king of France 987–96.

capital cross a Greek cross having each extremity terminated in an ornament like a Tuscan capital.

Capitol in ancient Rome, the temple of Jupiter Optimus Maximus on the Saturnian or Tarpeian (afterwards called Capitoline) Hill in ancient Rome; the name is sometimes applied to the whole hill, including the citadel. The *Capitol* in literary terms is often seen as a symbol of Rome.

In the US, *Capitol* (usually **the Capitol**) is the name of the seat of the US Congress in Washington DC. The term in an American context in fact goes back to the late 17th century, in Virginia. **Capitol Hill** is the region around the Capitol in Washington DC (often as an allusive reference to the US Congress itself).

capitulary a royal ordinance under the Merovingian dynasty. Recorded from the mid 17th century, the word comes via late Latin *capitularius*, from Latin *capitulum* in the sense 'section of a law'.

Andy Capp cloth-capped working-class hero of the popular cartoon strip, created in 1957 by the British cartoonist Reg Smythe (1917–98).

Cappadocia an ancient region of central Asia Minor, between Lake Tuz and the Euphrates, north of Cilicia. It was an important centre of early Christianity.

Capri an island off the west coast of Italy, south of Naples, to which the Roman emperor Tiberius (42 BC–AD 37) retired in AD 26, never returning to Rome.

Capricorn the tenth sign of the zodiac (the Goat), which the sun enters at the northern winter solstice (about 21 December).

Recorded from Old English, the name comes from Latin *capricornus*, from *caper*, *capr-* 'goat' + *cornu* 'horn', on the pattern of Greek *aigokerōs* 'goat-horned, Capricorn'.

Capsian of, relating to, or denoting a Palaeolithic culture of North Africa and southern Europe, noted for its microliths. It is dated to *c.*8000–4500 BC, named from Latin *Capsa* (now *Gafsa* in Tunisia) where objects from this culture were found.

Capuchin a friar belonging to a branch of the Franciscan order that observes a strict rule drawn up in 1529. The name is recorded from the late 16th century, and comes via obsolete French from Italian *cappuccino*, from *cappuccio* 'hood, cowl', from *cappa* 'covering for the head', the friars being so named because of their sharp-pointed hoods.

Capulet in Shakespeare's *Romeo and Juliet*, the name of the Veronese noble house (the Cappelletti) to which Juliet belongs, hostile to the family of the Montagues (the Montecchi).

Caracalla nickname of Aurelius Antoninus (188–217), Roman emperor 211–17; the name *Caracalla* derived from the long hooded Celtic cloak which he made fashionable.

Caradoc Celtic form of the name of the British chieftain ➤ CARATACUS.

carat a measure of the purity of gold, pure gold being 24 carats; later also, a unit of weight for precious stones and pearls, now equivalent to 200 milligrams.

Recorded from late Middle English, the word comes via French from Italian *carato*, from Arabic *kīrāt* (a unit of weight), from Greek *keration* 'fruit of the carob' (also denoting a unit of weight), diminutive of *keras* 'horn', with reference to the elongated seed pod of the carob.

Caratacus (1st century AD), British chieftain, son of Cymbeline. He took part in the resistance to the Roman invasion of AD 43 and when defeated fled to Yorkshire, where he was handed over to the Romans in AD 51. His Celtic name is *Caradoc*, and he is also known as *Caractacus*.

carbon dating the determination of the age of an organic object from the relative proportions of the carbon isotopes carbon-12 and carbon-14 that it contains. The ratio between them changes as radioactive carbon-14 decays and is not replaced by exchange with the atmosphere.

the Carboniferous the fifth period of the Palaeozoic era, between the Devonian and Permian periods. The Carboniferous lasted from about 363 to 290 million years ago. During this time the first reptiles and seed-bearing plants appeared, and there were extensive coral reefs and coal-forming swamp forests.

a card up one's sleeve a plan in reserve, a hidden advantage (see also ➤ *have an* ACE *up one's sleeve*).

cardinal¹ a leading dignitary of the Roman Catholic Church. Cardinals are nominated by the Pope, and form the Sacred College which elects succeeding popes (now invariably from among their own number). The word is recorded from Old English and comes from Latin *cardinalis*, from *cardo, cardin-* 'hinge' (see also ➤ CARDINAL²); the derivation reflects the notion of the important function of such priests as 'pivots' of church life.

Cardinals wear a deep scarlet cassock with a wide-brimmed red hat; the **cardinal's hat** is often taken as a symbol of his office, and is the emblem of ➤ St BONAVENTURA, ➤ *St* JEROME, and St Robert Bellarmine (1542–1621).

cardinal² of fundamental importance (formed as ➤ CARDINAL¹).

The **cardinal humour** are the four chief ➤ HUMOURS of the body.

A **cardinal number** is a number denoting quantity (one, two, three, etc.) as opposed to an ordinal number (first, second, third, etc.).

The **cardinal points** are the four main points of the compass (north, south, east, and west).

The **cardinal virtues** are the chief moral attributes of scholastic philosophy: justice, prudence, temperance, and fortitude, identified by the classical philosophers and adopted by Christian moral theologians.

Care Sunday the fifth Sunday in Lent; formerly also, the Sunday preceding Good Friday; *Care* here means 'sorrow, trouble, grief'.

caret a mark (^, ʌ) placed below the line to indicate a proposed insertion in a printed or written text. The word comes (in the late 17th century) from Latin, meaning literally 'is lacking'.

Mother Carey's chicken a sailors' name (now dated) for the storm petrel; it is recorded from the mid 18th century, but the origin is unknown.

Carey Street a street in London, formerly the location of the Bankruptcy Department of the Supreme Court, used allusively to indicate a state of bankruptcy.

carfax a place where four roads or streets meet (now usually in place-names). The word is recorded from Middle English, and comes ultimately, via Anglo-Norman French, Old French, and popular Latin, from Latin *quadri-* 'four' + *furca* 'fork'.

cargo cult in the Melanesian Islands, a system of belief based around the expected arrival of ancestral spirits in ships bringing cargoes of food and other goods.

Mr Carker the treacherous manager of the Dombey shipping house in Dickens's *Dombey and Son* (1848), noted for his hypocritical smile and white and glistening teeth.

Carling Sunday another name for ➤ CARE *Sunday*, the fifth Sunday of Lent, on which it was customary to eat *carlings*, dried or parched peas. The name may come ultimately from the first element in *Care Sunday*.

Carlism a Spanish conservative political movement originating in support of Don *Carlos*, brother of Fernando VII (died 1833), who claimed the throne in place of Fernando's daughter Isabella. The movement supported the Catholic Church and opposed centralized government; it was revived in support of the Nationalist side during the Spanish Civil War.

Carlovingian another term for ➤ CAROLINGIAN. The name comes from French, and is formed from *Karl* 'Charles' on the pattern of *Merovingian*.

Mount Carmel a group of mountains near the Mediterranean coast in NW Israel, which in the Bible is the scene of the defeat of the priests of Baal by the prophet ➤ ELIJAH.

Carmelite a friar or nun of a contemplative Catholic order dedicated to Our Lady. The Carmelite order of friars was founded during the Crusades *c*.1154 by St Berthold at Mount Carmel; the order of nuns was established in 1452. A reform movement in the late 16th century, led by St Teresa of Ávila and St John of the Cross, led to the formation of the stricter 'discalced' orders.

Carmen the seductive Spanish gipsy girl who is the eponymous heroine of Bizet's opera (1875).

Carnaby Street a street in the West End of London, which became famous in the 1960s as a centre of the popular fashion industry.

Carnac the site in Brittany of nearly 3,000 megalithic stones dating from the Neolithic period. They include single standing stones (menhirs), dolmens, and long avenues of grey monoliths arranged in order of height.

carnival a period of public revelry at a regular time each year, as during the week before Lent in Roman Catholic countries, involving processions, music, dancing, and the use of masquerade. Recorded from the mid 16th century, the word comes via Italian from medieval Latin *carnevelamen*, *carnelevarium* 'Shrovetide', from Latin *caro*, *carn-* 'flesh' + *levare* 'put away'.

Carolingian of or relating to the Frankish dynasty, founded by ➤ CHARLEMAGNE's father Pepin III, that ruled in western Europe from 750 to 987 in succession to the ➤ MEROVINGIAN dynasty.
   Carolingian is also used specifically to designate a style of minuscule script developed in France during the time of Charlemagne, on which modern lower-case letters are largely based.
   The **Carolingian Renaissance** was a period during the reign of Charlemagne and his successors that was marked by achievements in art, architecture, learning, and music. Credit for stimulating this renaissance is traditionally given to Charlemagne's adviser Alcuin.
   The name is an alteration of earlier ➤ CARLOVINGIAN, by association with medieval Latin *Carolus* 'Charles'.

carpe diem Latin phrase meaning 'seize the day!', used as an exclamation to urge someone to make the most of the present time and give little thought to the future; originally it is a quotation from the Roman poet Horace.

on the carpet being severely reprimanded by someone. The expression comes from the earlier meaning of *carpet* in the sense of 'table covering', referring to the 'carpet of the council table' before which one would be summoned for reprimand.

carpetbagger in the US in the 19th century, a person from the northern states who went to the South after the Civil War to profit from Reconstruction, of whom it was said that their 'property qualification' consisted merely of the contents of the carpetbag they had brought with them.
   In extended usage, the term now denotes a political candidate who seeks election in an area where they have no local connections.

Carrara a town in Tuscany in NW Italy, famous for the white marble quarried there since Roman times.

carrel a small cubicle with a desk for the use of a reader or student in a library; formerly, a small enclosure or study in a cloister. Recorded from the late 16th century, the word is apparently related to *carol* in the old sense 'ring'.

carriage trade archaic term for those customers of sufficient wealth or social standing to maintain a private carriage.

in the cart in serious trouble or difficulty, probably deriving from the historical sense of a *cart* as used for conveying convicts to the gallows and for the public exposure of offenders.

put the cart before the horse reverse the proper order of things; the expression is recorded from the early 16th century.

carte blanche complete freedom to act as one wishes, from the original literal sense (recorded from the early 18th century) of a blank sheet of paper to be filled in as a person wishes.

Cartesian of or relating to the ideas of the philosopher *Descartes*, deriving from *Cartesius*, the Latinized form of his name.
   Cartesian coordinates are numbers which indicate the location of a point relative to a fixed reference point (the origin), being its shortest (perpendicular) distances from two fixed axes (or three planes defined by three fixed axes) which intersect at right angles at the origin.

Carthage an ancient city on the coast of North Africa near present-day Tunis. Founded by the Phoenicians *c*.814 BC, Carthage became a major force in the Mediterranean, and came into conflict with Rome in the Punic Wars. It was finally destroyed by the Romans in 146 BC; at the time it was decreed that the destruction should be complete, with no houses or crops surviving (see ➤ DELENDA *est Carthago*), although in the 1st century ➤ BC it was to be refounded by Julius Caesar. A **Carthaginian peace** is a peace settlement which imposes very severe terms on the defeated side.

Carthusian a monk or nun of an austere contemplative order founded by ➤ *St* BRUNO in 1084. (See also ➤ CHARTERHOUSE.)

Sydney Carton the cynical barrister in Charles Dickens's *A Tale of Two Cities* who redeems his wastrel life by deliberately taking the place of a man sentenced to death.

cartouche an oval or oblong enclosing a group of Egyptian hieroglyphs, typically representing the name and title of a monarch.

caryatid a stone carving of a draped female figure, used as a pillar to support the entablature of a Greek or Greek-style building. The name comes (in the mid 16th century) via French and Italian from Latin *caryatides* from Greek *karuatides*, plural of *karuatis* 'priestess of Artemis at Caryae', from *Karuai* (Caryae) in Laconia.

Louis Casabianca (1755–98), a Corsican naval officer who perished with his little son at the Battle of Aboukir Bay, an event commemorated in the poem *Casabianca* (1849) by Mrs Hemans.

Giovanni Jacopo Casanova (1725–98), Italian adventurer. He is famous for his memoirs describing his sexual encounters and other exploits.

Mr Casaubon the bachelor scholar in George Eliot's *Middlemarch* (1871–2) who becomes Dorothea's husband; he is initially admired by his wife for his breadth of knowledge, but it becomes clear that his intellectual life is limited to pedantry, and that his projected great work on comparative religions will never be written.

cash for questions designating or relating to a series of incidents in the mid-1990s in which several Conservative MPs were alleged to have accepted money from private individuals in return for tabling specific questions in the House of Commons.

Casket Letters letters supposed to have been passed between Mary Queen of Scots and Bothwell, and to have established her complicity in the murder of Darnley. They were repudiated by the queen as forgeries, but it was threatened that they would be used as evidence against her. They disappeared before the end of the 16th century and have never been recovered.

Caslon a kind of roman typeface first introduced in the 18th century, named after William *Caslon* (1692–1766), English type founder.

Caspar traditionally the name of one of the three ➤ Magi.

Cassandra in Greek mythology, a daughter of the Trojan king Priam, who was given the gift of prophecy by Apollo. When she cheated him, however, he turned this into a curse by causing her prophecies, though true, to be disbelieved. After the fall of Troy, she became the slave of Agamemnon; having prophesied his death, she was killed with him by Clytemnestra.

From 1935 *Cassandra* was also the penname of the *Daily Mirror* journalist William Connor (1909–67). Cassandra's support for criticism of P. G. Wodehouse's wartime broadcasts from France while interned by the Germans was extremely influential; his 'vitriolic' style, on the other hand, often annoyed the government.

Cassiopeia in Greek mythology, the wife of Cepheus, king of Ethiopia, and mother of ➤ Andromeda. She boasted that she herself (or, in some versions, her daughter) was more beautiful than the nereids, thus incurring the wrath of Poseidon.

In astronomy, *Cassiopeia* is a constellation near the north celestial pole, recognizable by the conspicuous 'W' pattern of its brightest stars.

Gaius Cassius (d. 42 BC), Roman general, one of the main leaders of the conspiracy in 44 BC to assassinate Julius Caesar. He and Brutus were defeated by Caesar's supporters, Antony and Octavian, at the battle of Philippi, in the course of which he committed suicide.

cassock a full-length garment of a single colour worn by certain Christian clergy, members of church choirs, and others having some particular office or role in a church. The word comes (in the mid 16th century) via French *casaque* 'long coat' from Italian *casacca* 'riding coat', probably ultimately from Turkic *kazak* 'vagabond' (see ➤ Cossack).

cast the first stone be the first to make an accusation (used to emphasize that a potential critic is not wholly blameless); the original reference is to John 8:7, and the saying of Jesus to those who wanted to stone a woman who had committed adultery, 'He that is without sin among you, let him first cast a stone at her.'

Castalia a spring on Mount Parnassus, sacred in antiquity to Apollo and the Muses.

caste each of the hereditary classes of Hindu society, distinguished by relative degrees of ritual purity or pollution and of social status. Castes are traditionally defined by occupation, but may also be linked to geo-graphical location and dietary customs. There are four basic classes or *varnas* in Hindu society: *Brahman* (priest), *Kshatriya* (warrior), *Vaisya* (merchant or farmer), and *Sudra* (labourer).

Recorded in English from the mid 16th century (in the general sense 'race, breed'), the word comes from Spanish and Portu-guese *casta* 'lineage, race, breed', feminine of *casto* 'pure, unmixed', from Latin *castus* 'chaste'.

Castel Gandolfo the summer residence of the pope, situated on the edge of Lake Albano near Rome.

Castile a region of central Spain, on the central plateau of the Iberian peninsula, for-merly an independent Spanish kingdom. The marriage of Isabella of Castile to Ferdi-nand of Aragon in 1469 linked these two powerful kingdoms and led eventually to the unification of Spain.

castle a large building or group of buildings fortified against attack with thick walls, bat-tlements, towers, and in many cases a moat. The word is recorded from late Old English and comes from Anglo-Norman French and Old Northern French *castel*, from Latin *castellum*, diminutive of *castrum* 'fort'.

The Castle was a name for the former Irish viceregal government and administration, of which Dublin Castle was the seat

Castles in Spain are visionary unattainable schemes; the expression is recorded from late Middle English, and it is possible that *Spain*, as the nearest Moorish country to Christendom, was taken as the type of a re-gion in which the prospective castle-builder had no standing. An alternative expression, **castles in the air**, is recorded from the late 16th century.

Castor and Pollux in Greek mythology, the twin sons of ▶ JUPITER and ▶ LEDA and brothers of ▶ HELEN, the ▶ DIOSCURI.

casus belli an act or situation provoking or justifying war. The phrase is Latin, and comes from *casus* 'case', and *belli* 'of war'; it is recorded in English from the mid 19th cen-tury.

cat the *cat* has been traditionally associated with witchcraft, and in Christian art a cat may be shown in a picture as emblematic of sinful human nature; cat may also be used in-formally for a malicious or spiteful woman.

In ancient Egypt, cats were regarded as sac-red animals; the goddess ▶ BASTET is shown with a cat's head.

The **Cat and Mouse Act** is an informal name for the 1913 act passed, during the suf-fragette campaign, to allow for the tempor-ary release of prisoners on hunger strike and their subsequent rearrest.

A cat may look at a king means that even a person of low status or importance has rights. Used proverbially since the mid 16th century.

A **cat o' nine tails** is a rope whip with nine knotted cords, formerly used (especially at sea) to flog offenders.

Cat's cradle is a child's game in which a loop of string is put around and between the fingers and complex patterns are formed.

A **cat's paw** is a person who is used by an-other, typically to carry out an unpleasant or dangerous task, and originally with allusion to the fable of a monkey which asked a cat to extract its roasted chestnuts from the fire.

To **let the cat out of the bag** is to reveal a secret, especially carelessly or by mistake. Recorded from the mid 18th century.

To **put the cat among the pigeons** is to stir up trouble; the expression is recorded from the early 18th century, and the idea of the de-structive potential of a cat inside a pigeon-loft is explained as standing for a man getting among women.

catacomb an underground cemetery con-sisting of a subterranean gallery with re-cesses for tombs, as constructed by the ancient Romans. Recorded from Old English, the word comes from late Latin *catumbas*, the name of the subterranean cemetery under the Basilica of St Sebastian on the Appian Way near Rome, in or near which the relics of the apostles Peter and Paul were said to have been placed in the 3rd century.

The term *catacombs* was subsequently given to other subterranean cemeteries in Rome (rediscovered in the late 16th century), especially as traditional places of refuge for early Christians in times of persecution.

Catalan a Romance language closely re-lated to Castilian Spanish and Provençal, widely spoken in *Catalonia*, an autonomous region of NE Spain with a strong separatist tradition (where it has official status along-side Castilian Spanish) and in Andorra, the Balearic Islands, and parts of southern France.

in the catbird seat in a superior or advan-tageous position. A **catbird** is a long-tailed

American songbird of the mockingbird family, with catlike mewing calls, and this expression is said to be an allusion to a baseball player in the fortunate position of having no strikes and therefore three balls still to play (a reference made in James Thurber's short story *The Catbird Seat*).

catch-22 a dilemma or difficult circumstance from which there is no escape because of mutually conflicting or dependent conditions. The term comes from the title of a novel (1961) by Joseph Heller, in which the main character feigns madness in order to avoid dangerous combat missions, but finds that *Catch-22* specifies that a concern for one's own safety amid real and immediate dangers is taken to indicate a rational mind.

catchphrase a well-known sentence or phrase, typically one that is associated with a particular famous person or fictional character.

catechism a summary of the principles of Christian religion in the form of questions and answers, used for the instruction of Christians. The word is recorded from the early 16th century and comes via ecclesiastical Latin from ecclesiastical Greek *katēkhizein* 'instruct orally, make hear'.

catechumen a Christian convert under instruction before baptism. Recorded from late Middle English, the word comes via ecclesiastical Latin from ecclesiastical Greek *katēkhoumenos* 'being instructed', from *katēkhizein* 'instruct orally, make hear'.

Cathar a member of a heretical medieval Christian sect which professed a form of Manichaean dualism and sought to achieve great spiritual purity. The name is recorded in English from the mid 17th century, and comes from medieval Latin *Cathari* (plural), from Greek *katharoi* 'the pure'.

catharsis the process of releasing, and thereby providing relief from, strong or repressed emotions. The notion of 'release' through drama derives from Aristotle's *Poetics*.

The word comes from Greek *katharsis*, from *kathairein* 'cleanse', from *katharos* 'pure'.

Cathay the name by which China (also called *Khitai*) was known to medieval Europe. The name comes from medieval Latin *Cataya*, *Cathaya*, from Turkic *Khitāy*.

cathedral the principal church of a diocese, with which the bishop is officially associated. Recorded from Middle English (as an

adjective, the noun being short for *cathedral church* 'the church which contains the bishop's throne'), the word comes via Latin from Greek *kathedra* 'seat'.

St Catherine of Alexandria (d. *c*.307), early and probably legendary Christian martyr. According to tradition she opposed the persecution of Christians under the emperor Maxentius and refused to recant or to marry the emperor; when pagan philosophers were sent to dispute with her she converted them. She is traditionally regarded as one of the ► FOURTEEN *Holy Helpers*.

She is said to have been tortured on a spiked wheel (destroyed by her angelic protectors) and finally beheaded. Her emblems are a wheel (see ► CATHERINE *wheel*) and a sword, and a palm-branch as a symbol of her virginity. Her feast day is 25 November.

St Catherine of Siena (1333?–80), Sienese virgin and member of the Dominican Third Order, who was a noted spiritual leader of the 14th century, and who was popularly believed to have contributed significantly to the ending of the ► GREAT *Schism* and the return of the papacy to Rome from Avignon. She is the patron saint of Italy, and was declared a Doctor of the Church in 1970. Her usual emblem is a lily, and her feast day was 30 April; from 1969 it has been 29 April.

Catherine the Great (1729–96), empress of Russia. Born a princess of Anhalt-Zerbst, she became empress (as **Catherine II**) after her husband, Peter III, was deposed. She is taken as the type of a powerful female ruler.

Catherine wheel a firework in the form of a flat coil which spins when fixed to something solid, and lit; it is named for the spiked wheel which was one of the instruments of martyrdom of ► St CATHERINE *of Alexandria*.

Catholic of or including all Christians; of or relating to the historic doctrine and practice of the Western Church; ► ROMAN *Catholic*. The term is recorded from late Middle English and comes via Old French or late Latin from Greek *katholikos* 'universal', from *kata* 'in respect of' + *holos* 'whole'.

The **Catholic Church** is the Church universal, the whole body of Christians; also, the Church of Rome.

Catholic Emancipation is the term for the granting of full political and civil liberties to Roman Catholics in Britain and Ireland. This was effected by the Catholic Emancipation Act of 1829, which repealed restrictive laws, including that which barred Catholics from holding public office.

The **Catholic King** is a title given to the king of Spain.

The **Catholic League** in 16th-century France was the party headed by the Guise family, the ➤ HOLY *League*.

Catiline (*c*.108–62 BC), Roman nobleman and conspirator. In 63 BC his planned uprising was discovered by Cicero, and Catiline fled from Rome. In the suppression of the uprising his fellow conspirators were executed and Catiline himself died in battle in Etruria.

Marcus Porcius Cato (234–149 BC), Roman statesman, orator, and writer, known as **Cato the Elder** or **Cato the Censor**. As censor he initiated a vigorous programme of reform, and attempted to stem the growing influence of Greek culture; he was also an implacable enemey of Carthage, ending every speech he made in the Senate with the words ➤ DELENDA *est Carthago*.

Cato Street Conspiracy a plot by a group of conspirators led by Arthur Thistlewood (1770–1820) to assassinate participants at a cabinet dinner given by Lord Harrowby in February 1820, as a preliminary to revolution. The attempt failed, and Thistlewood and four of his accomplices were hanged.

Catullus (*c*.84–*c*.54 BC), Roman poet. His one book of verse contains poems in a variety of metres on a range of subjects. He is best known for his love poems.

Caucasian in the racial classification as developed by Blumenbach and others in the 19th century, *Caucasian* (or **Caucasoid**) included peoples whose skin colour ranged from light (in northern Europe) to dark (in parts of North Africa and India). Although the classification is outdated and the categories are now not generally accepted as scientific, the term *Caucasian* has acquired a more restricted meaning. It is now used, especially in the US, as a synonym for 'white or of European origin'.

Caudine Forks name given to a narrow pass in the mountains near Capua, where the Roman army was defeated by the Samnites in 321 BC.

cauldron of oil a cauldron of oil is the emblem of ➤ St JOHN *the Evangelist*.

the good old cause in 17th century England, applied particularly to Puritan beliefs and principles, as in Milton's *The Ready and*

Easy Way to Establish a Free Commonwealth (2nd ed., 1660). The usage was later reinforced by Wordsworth.

rebel without a cause a person who is dissatisfied with society but does not have a specific aim to fight for, from the title of a US film, starring James Dean, released in 1955.

causewayed camp a type of Neolithic settlement in southern Britain, visible as an oval enclosure surrounded by concentric ditches that are crossed by several causeways. It is believed that such camps may have had a ritual function.

Cavalier a supporter of Charles I in the Civil War of 1642–9, a 17th-century Royalist. The word in this sense is recorded from the mid 17th century and is a special usage of the more general, 'a horseman; a lively military man; a courtly or fashionable gentleman, a gallant, especially as an escort to a lady'; ultimately it derives (perhaps through French) from Italian *cavaliere* from Latin *caballus* 'horse'.

The term as applied to the king's supporters by their opponents was originally derogatory. It was later increasingly used to indicate a style of life and social custom opposed to the repressive practices of the ➤ ROUNDHEADS.

The **Cavalier Parliament** was a name for the first Parliament of Charles II, following the Restoration in 1660 and noted for its support of the restored monarchy.

caveat emptor the principle that the buyer alone is responsible for checking the quality and suitability of goods before a purchase is made; the phrase is Latin and means, 'let the buyer beware.'

caviar to the general a good thing unappreciated by the ignorant; the phrase is originally a quotation from Shakespeare's *Hamlet* (1601).

Cawnpore earlier variant spelling of *Kanpur* in northern India, the site of a massacre of British soldiers and European families in July 1857, during the Indian Mutiny.

William Caxton (*c*.1422–91), the first English printer. He printed the first book in English in 1474 and went on to produce about eighty other texts.

St Cecilia (2nd or 3rd century), Roman martyr. According to legend, she took a vow of celibacy but when forced to marry converted her husband to Christianity and both were martyred. She was first confined in a hot bathroom in an attempt to suffocate her; later she was beheaded. She is the patron saint of church music. She is typically shown with an organ or with a lute, and her feast day is 22 November.

celestial heavenly (ultimately from Latin *caelum* 'heaven').

In Bunyan's ➤ PILGRIM'*s Progress*, the **Celestial City** is the object of Christian's journey, heaven.

The **Celestial Empire** was the Chinese Empire; the name is recorded in English from the early 19th century.

In Christian theologoy, the **celestial hierarchy** comprises each of three divisions of angelic beings (each comprising three orders) in the ninefold celestial system described in a 4th-century work formerly attributed to Dionysius the Areopagite (see ➤ DIONYSIUS[4]) and now to ➤ PSEUDO-*Dionysius*; angels collectively, the angelic host.

Benvenuto Cellini (1500–71), Italian goldsmith and sculptor, the most renowned goldsmith of his day. His work is characterized by its elaborate virtuosity. His autobiography is famous for its racy style and its vivid picture of contemporary Italian life.

Anders Celsius (1701–44), Swedish astronomer, best known for his temperature scale. He was professor of astronomy at Uppsala, and in 1742 he advocated a metric temperature scale with 100° as the freezing point of water and 0° as the boiling point; however, the thermometer which was actually introduced at the Uppsala Observatory had its scale reversed.

Celt a member of a group of peoples inhabiting much of Europe and Asia Minor in pre-Roman times. Their culture developed in the late Bronze Age around the upper Danube, and reached its height in the La Tène culture (5th to 1st centuries BC) before being overrun by the Romans and various Germanic peoples. The language group of the Celts is **Celtic**, constituting a branch of the Indo-European family and including Irish, Scottish Gaelic, Welsh, Breton, Manx, Cornish, and several extinct pre-Roman languages such as Gaulish.

The **Celtic Church** is the Christian Church in the British Isles from its foundation in the 2nd or 3rd century until its assimilation into the Roman Catholic Church (664 in England; 12th century in Wales, Scotland, and Ireland).

A **Celtic cross** is a Latin cross with a circle round the centre.

The **Celtic fringe** is the Highland Scots, Irish, Welsh, and Cornish in relation to the rest of Britain; the term, often regarded as derogatory, is recorded from the late 19th century.

The **Celtic tiger** is the Irish economy seen as a successor to the earlier ➤ TIGER *economies*.

The **Celtic twilight** is the romantic fairy tale atmosphere of Irish folklore and literature; the term derives originally from W. B. Yeats's name for his collection of writings (1893) based on Irish folk-tales.

Cenci name of a 16th-century Italian family; the execution of **Beatrice Cenci** in 1599 for the murder of her father was the subject of Shelley's play *The Cenci* (1819–21).

cenotaph a monument to someone buried elsewhere, especially one commemorating people who died in a war; **the Cenotaph** is the name of the war memorial in Whitehall, London, designed by Sir Edwin Lutyens and erected in 1919–20. The word is recorded from the early 17th century and comes ultimately, via French and late Latin, from Greek *kenos* 'empty' + *taphos* 'tomb'.

censer a container in which incense is burnt, typically during a religious ceremony.

censor originally (in ancient Rome), either of two magistrates who held censuses and supervised public morals. Later, in extended use, an official who examines material that is about to be published, such as books, films, news, and art, and suppresses any parts that are considered obscene, politically unacceptable, or a threat to security.

centaur in Greek mythology, a creature with the head, arms, and torso of a man and the body and legs of a horse. They are said to have been defeated by the ➤ LAPITHS in the battle after the wedding of Pirithous, when they tried to carry off the bride and other women; in classical Greek thought they may have symbolized animal nature.

The name comes via Latin from Greek *kentauros*, the Greek name for a Thessalonian tribe of expert horsemen; of unknown ultimate origin.

Centennial State informal name for Colorado, which was admitted as a state in the centennial year (1876) of the existence of the United States.

centurion the commander of a century (a company, originally of a hundred men) in the ancient Roman army.

Cerberus in Greek mythology, a monstrous watchdog with three (or in some accounts fifty) heads, which guarded the entrance to Hades. Cerberus could be appeased with a cake, as by Aeneas, or lulled to sleep (as by Orpheus) with lyre music; one of the twelve labours of Hercules was to bring him up from the underworld.

cereology the study or investigation of ➤ CROP *circles*; the term is recorded from the late 20th century, and derives from ➤ CERES.

Ceres in Roman mythology, the corn goddess, the equivalent of the Greek ➤ DEMETER.
    In astronomy, *Ceres* is the name of the first asteroid to be discovered, found by G. Piazzi of Palermo on 1 January 1801.

Ceridwen in Welsh mythology, the goddess of poetic inspiration, an enchantress said to live beneath a lake; her magic cauldron conferred the gift of second sight.

Cerynitian hind a hind with gilded horns, sacred to Artemis, living in the land of the Hyperboreans, captured by Hercules as the fourth of his Labours.

Cesarewitch a horse race run annually over two miles at Newmarket, England. The name comes from Russian *tsesarevich* 'heir to the throne', in honour of the Russian Crown prince (later Alexander II) who attended the inaugural race in 1839.

Chad in full **Mr Chad**. The figure of a human head looking over a wall, with a caption protesting against some omission or shortage, and usually beginning 'Wot, no—?'

St Chad (d. 672), first bishop of Mercia and Lindsey at Lichfield, for whom there was an early and popular cult; it was said by Bede that if the faithful put dust from his shrine into water, the drink was medicinal for people and animals. His feast day is 2 March.

chaff the husks of corn or other seed separated by winnowing or threshing; traditionally taken as the type of something worthless. To **be caught with chaff** is to be easily deceived (as in the proverb, *you cannot catch old birds with chaff*). To **separate the wheat from the chaff** is to distinguish valuable people or things from worthless ones.
    Recorded from Old English (in the form *cæf*, *ceaf*), the word probably comes from a Germanic base meaning 'gnaw'.

Chagatai name of a dynasty founded by *Chaghatai*, a son of Genghis Khan, which reigned in Transoxiana 1227–1358, later used to designate the literary Turkic language of central Asia between the 15th and 19th centuries.

chain a jointed measuring line consisting of linked metal rods; the length of such a measuring line (66 ft).

Council of Chalcedon the fourth ecumenical council of the Christian Church, held in 451 at Chalcedon, a former city on the Bosporus in Asia Minor, now part of Istanbul.
    A **Chalcedonian** was a person upholding the decrees of the Council of Chalcedon (AD 451), especially those regarding the nature of Christ, which were eventually accepted by all except the ➤ MONOPHYSITE Churches.

chalcedony a microcrystalline type of quartz occurring in several different forms including onyx and agate. The word comes (in late Middle English) from Latin *chalcedonius* (often believed to mean 'stone of Chalcedon', but this is doubtful), which in the Vulgate represents Greek *khalkēdōn*, the name (in Revelation 21:19) of the precious stone forming the third foundation of the New Jerusalem.

Chaldea an ancient country in what is now southern Iraq, inhabited by the **Chaldeans**, an ancient people who lived in Chaldea *c.*800 BC and ruled Babylonia 625–539 BC. They were renowned as astronomers and astrologers.
    The name comes from Greek *Khaldaia*, from Akkadian *Kald*, the name of a Babylonian tribal group.

chalice a chalice is the emblem of St Richard of Chichester (1197–1253), who is said once to have dropped the chalice at Mass without the wine being spilt, ➤ St HUGH *of Lincoln*, and other saints.

not by a long chalk by no means, not at all, with reference to the chalk used for marking up scores in competitive games.

chalk and cheese the types of two completely different things; the proverbial contrast between these two substances is recorded from late Middle English.

Challenger Disaster the accident in which the US space shuttle *Challenger* was destroyed on takeoff in January 1986, exploding in mid-air and killing all seven astronauts on board (the crew members included a science teacher who had won a national competition to participate, and who had been going to give a lesson from space to her class). Shuttle missions were subsequently suspended until September 1988, while more rigorous safety systems were instituted.

Chamber of Horrors the name given in the mid 19th century to a room in Madame Tussaud's waxwork exhibition which showed especially notorious murderers and their victims as well as scenes of execution.

chameleon from this lizard's highly developed ability to change colour, it has become the type of a changeable or inconstant person.

The name is recorded from Middle English, and comes via Latin from Greek *khamaileōn*, from *khamai* 'on the ground' + *leōn* 'lion'.

Champ de Mars the park in Paris by the Seine, laid out in 1765, and named after the Roman ➤ CAMPUS *Martius*.

champagne a white sparkling wine from Champagne in NE France, first produced there in about 1700, and regarded as a symbol of luxury and associated with celebration.

Champagne Charlie is a name for a man noted for living a life of luxury and excess, from the name of a popular song, first performed in 1868.

In the UK, **champagne socialist** is a derogatory term for a person who espouses socialist ideals while enjoying a wealthy and luxurious lifestyle.

Champs Élysées an avenue in Paris, leading from the Place de la Concorde to the Arc de Triomphe. It is noted for its fashionable shops and restaurants.

Charlie Chan fictional Chinese-American detective working for the Honolulu police force, created by the American writer Earl Derr Biggers (1884–1933).

Chan Chan the capital of the pre-Inca civilization of the Chimu. Its extensive adobe ruins are situated on the coast of north Peru.

chancel the part of a church near the altar, reserved for the clergy and choir, and typically separated from the nave by steps or a screen. The word is recorded from Middle English, and comes (via Old French) from Latin *cancelli* 'crossbars'.

Chancery in the UK, the Lord Chancellor's court, the highest court of judicature next to the House of Lords; but, since the Judicature Act of 1873 a division of the High Court of Justice. It formerly consisted of two distinct tribunals, one ordinary, being a court of common law, the other extraordinary, being a court of equity. To the former belonged the issuing of writs for a new parliament, and of all original writs. The second proceeded upon rules of equity and conscience, moderating the rigour of the common law, and giving relief in cases where there was no remedy in the common-law courts; it is in this role that it is shown in Dickens's *Bleak House*, presiding over the apparently interminable case of the ➤ JARNDYCE estate, and entangling the many hopeless claimants who expect a judgement shortly.

The expression **in chancery**, referring to the head of a boxer or wrestler held under an opponent's head and being pummelled, derives from the tenacity and absolute control which the Court of Chancery was believed to exert, and to the certainty of cost and loss to property which was 'in chancery'.

Chandleresque in the style of Raymond *Chandler* (1888–1959), American novelist, remembered as the creator of the private detective ➤ *Philip* MARLOWE, and noted for his tough realistic style and settings ranging across social boundaries.

changeling a child believed to have been secretly substituted by fairies for the parents' real child in infancy; the term is first recorded from the late 16th century.

ring the changes vary the ways of expressing, arranging, or doing something, with allusion to bell-ringing and the different orders in which a peal of bells may be rung.

Channel Tunnel a railway tunnel under the English Channel, linking the coasts of England and France, opened in 1994 and 49 km (31 miles) long. The name considerably predates the actual tunnel, as the idea was discussed in the 19th century. The humorous blend *Chunnel*, referring to such a project, is found from the 1920s.

chanson de geste a medieval French historical verse romance, typically one connected with ➤ CHARLEMAGNE. The phrase is French, and means literally 'song of heroic deeds', from *chanson* 'song' and *geste* from Latin *gesta* 'actions, exploits'.

Chanticleer a name given to a domestic cock, especially in fairy tales and medieval poems. The name is recorded from Middle English, and comes from Old French *Chantecler*, the name of the cock in the fable *Reynard the Fox*, from *chanter* 'sing, crow' + *cler* 'clear'.

chantry a chapel, altar, or other part of a church endowed for a priest or priests to celebrate masses for the founder's soul; a chapel, altar, or other part of a church endowed for such a purpose. The word is recorded from late Middle English, and comes from Old French *chanterie*, from *chanter* 'to sing'.

chaos originally, denoting a gaping void or chasm, later extended to formless primordial matter; in current usage, complete disorder and confusion. In Greek mythology, *Chaos* is sometimes personified as the first created being, from which came the primeval deities Gaia, Tartarus, Erebus, and Nyx.

Chaos theory is the branch of mathematics that deals with complex systems whose behaviour is highly sensitive to slight changes in conditions, so that small alterations can give rise to strikingly great consequences, as in the ➤ BUTTERFLY *effect*.

Recorded from the late 15th century, the word comes via French and Latin from Greek *khaos* 'vast chasm, void'.

chapbook a small pamphlet containing tales, ballads, or tracts, sold by pedlars; (chiefly in North America) a small paper-covered booklet, typically containing poems or fiction. The term is recorded from the early 19th century, and the first element comes from *chapman*, archaic term for a pedlar.

chapel a small building for Christian worship; part of a large church or cathedral with its own altar and dedication. The word is recorded from Middle English and comes via Old French from medieval Latin *cappella*, diminutive of *cappa* 'cap or cape' (the first chapel being a sanctuary in which ➤ St MARTIN's cloak was preserved).

A **chapel of ease** is a chapel situated for the convenience of parishioners living a long distance from the parish church; the term is recorded from the mid 16th century.

The **Chapel Royal** is the body of clergy, singers, and musicians employed by the English monarch for religious services, now based at St James's Palace, London. Among members of the Chapel Royal have been

Thomas Tallis, William Byrd, and Henry Purcell.

chaplain a member of the clergy attached to a private chapel, institution, ship, regiment, etc. The word comes (in Middle English via Old French) from medieval Latin *cappellanus*, originally denoting a custodian of the cloak of St Martin, from *cappella*, originally 'little cloak' (see also ➤ CHAPEL).

Chaplinesque in the style of Charlie *Chaplin* (1889–1977), English film actor and director. He directed and starred in many short silent comedies, mostly playing a bowler-hatted tramp, a character which was his trademark for more than twenty-five years.

Chappaquiddick Island a small island off the coast of Massachusetts, the scene of a car accident in 1969 involving Senator Edward Kennedy in which his assistant Mary Jo Kopechne drowned.

chapter[1] the governing body of a religious community, especially a cathedral, or a knightly order. The term is recorded from Middle English, and comes via Old French from Latin *capitulum*, diminutive of *caput* 'head'.

A **chapter house** is a building used for the meetings of the canons of a cathedral or other religious community.

chapter[2] the main division of a book.

Chapter and verse is an exact reference or authority; originally, the exact reference to a passage of Scripture (the usage is recorded from the early 17th century). **Chapter and verse** divisions to the scriptures are of comparatively late date; Jewish scholars of the 6th to 10th centuries AD (*Masoretes*) divided books into verses, and the New Testament was divided into chapters by Stephen Langton (*c*.1150–1228). Verses appeared in the Greek and Latin editions of the New Testament produced in Geneva in 1551, and then in the English ➤ GENEVA *Bible* of 1560.

A **chapter of accidents** is a series of unfortunate events; the term is recorded from the late 18th century.

charge in heraldry, a device or bearing placed on a shield or crest.

Charge of the Light Brigade a British cavalry charge in 1854 during the Battle of Balaclava in the Crimean War. A misunderstanding between the commander of the Light Brigade and his superiors led to the British cavalry being destroyed. The charge was immortalized in verse by Alfred Tennyson.

Charing Cross a locality in the City of Westminster, London, containing the site of a cross erected to commemorate the last resting place of the coffin of Eleanor of Castile, queen of Edward I, on its journey from Nottinghamshire, where she died in 1290, to Westminster.

The original cross (the final one of 12 which marked the stages of the coffin's journey) was destroyed in the 17th century, and an equestrian statue of Charles I now stands in its place. A bronze plaque in the pavement behind the statue (placed there in 1955) marks the official centre of London, from which mileages are measured.

Charing represents a name recorded from the Anglo-Saxon period, rather than an alteration of *chère reine*, as is sometimes suggested.

charivari a cacophonous mock serenade, typically performed by a group of people in derision of an unpopular person or in celebration of a marriage. The term is recorded from the mid 17th century, and comes from French (of unknown origin); it was taken as the title of a Parisian satirical journal, of which the full title of *Punch* (1841) was an imitation, 'Punch, or the London Charivari'.

charlatan a person falsely claiming to have a special knowledge or skill. The word is recorded from the early 17th century, denoting an itinerant seller of supposed remedies; it comes via French from Italian *ciarlatano*, from *ciartare* 'to babble'.

Charlemagne (742–814), king of the Franks 768–814 and Holy Roman emperor (as Charles I) 800–814; the name comes from *Carolus Magnus* 'Charles the Great'. As the first Holy Roman emperor Charlemagne promoted the arts and education, and his court became the cultural centre of the ➤ CAROLINGIAN *Renaissance*, the influence of which outlasted his empire.

Charles's Wain the Plough in Ursa Major. It is called in Old English *Carles wægn* 'the wain of Carl (Charlemagne)', perhaps because the star Arcturus was associated with King Arthur, with whom Charlemagne was connected in legend.

Charleston a city and port in South Carolina; the bombardment in 1861 of Fort Sumter, in the harbour, by Confederate troops marked the beginning of the American Civil War.

The *charleston*, a lively dance of the 1920s which involved turning the knees inwards and kicking out the lower legs, was named for the city.

Charlotte Dundas a paddle steamer launched in 1802 on the River Clyde, the first vessel to use steam propulsion commercially.

Charon in Greek mythology, an old man who ferried the souls of the dead across the Rivers ➤ STYX and ➤ ACHERON to ➤ HADES; he received a fee of one obol for each soul.

Charterhouse archaic term for a ➤ CARTHUSIAN monastery; in the UK, *Charterhouse* is now the name of a charitable institution, later a public school, founded on the site of the Carthusian monastery in London (later moved to Godalming, Surrey).

The name is recorded from late Middle English, and comes ultimately from (Old) French *Chartreuse* (from medieval Latin *Carthusia*), with assimilation of the second element to *house*.

Chartism a UK parliamentary reform movement of 1837–48, the principles of which were set out in a manifesto called *The People's Charter* (the name is first used in an address of 1838 by the Chartist William Lovett, 1800–77). This document called for universal suffrage for men, equal electoral districts, voting by secret ballot, abolition of property qualifications for MPs, and annual general elections.

Chartres a city in northern France, noted for its Gothic cathedral with fine stained glass.

Chartreuse in France and French-speaking countries, a ➤ CARTHUSIAN monastery.

The drink *chartreuse*, a pale green or yellow liqueur made from brandy and aromatic herbs, is named after *La Grande Chartreuse*, the Carthusian monastery near Grenoble, where the liqueur was first made.

Charybdis in Greek mythology, a dangerous whirlpool in a narrow channel of the sea, opposite the cave of the sea-monster ➤ SCYLLA.

chase the dragon take heroin by heating it on a piece of folded tin foil and inhaling the fumes. The term is said to be translated from Chinese, and to arise from the fact that the fumes and the molten heroin powder move up and down the piece of tin foil with an undulating movement resembling the tail of the dragon in Chinese myths.

chastity belt historical term for a garment or device designed to prevent the woman wearing it from having sexual intercourse.

chasuble a sleeveless outer vestment worn by a Catholic or High Anglican priest when celebrating Mass, typically ornate and having a simple hole for the head. Recorded from Middle English, the word comes via Old French from late Latin *casubla*, alteration of *casula* 'hooded cloak or little cottage', diminutive of *casa* 'house'.

chattering classes educated people, especially those in academic, artistic, or media circles, considered as a social group given to the expression of liberal opinions about society and culture. The term is recorded from the 1980s.

Lady Chatterley a sexually promiscuous woman, especially one attracted to a man considered socially inferior, with allusion to the character in D. H. Lawrence's novel *Lady Chatterley's Lover* (originally published in Italy in 1928, but not available in England in unexpurgated form until 1960), which tells the story of Constance Chatterley's affair with the gamekeeper Mellors.

Geoffrey Chaucer (*c.*1342–1400), English poet. His most famous work, the *Canterbury Tales* (*c.*1387–1400), is a cycle of linked tales told by a group of pilgrims. His skills of characterization, humour, and versatility established him as the first great English poet.

chauvinism exaggerated or aggressive patriotism; excessive or prejudiced support or loyalty for one's own cause, group, or sex. The word dates from the late 19th century and is named after Nicolas *Chauvin*, a Napoleonic veteran noted for his extreme patriotism, popularized as a character by the Cogniard brothers in *Cocarde Tricolore* (1831).

Chavín a civilization that flourished in Peru *c.*1000–200 BC, uniting a large part of the country's coastal region in a common culture. It is named after the town and temple complex of *Chavín* de Huantar in the northern highlands, where the civilization was centred.

Checkers name of a spaniel belonging to Richard Nixon's children, which became famous when in 1952 Nixon was accused of surreptitiously accepting money for his vice-presidential campaign. In a high-profile speech on television Nixon asserted his family's modest means and financial independence and probity, but admitted accepting a spaniel as a gift. The **Checkers speech** may be referred to as a type of political broadcast resting on a personal appeal.

checkmate in chess, a position in which a player's king is directly attacked by an opponent's piece or pawn and has no possible move to escape the check. The attacking player thus wins the game.

Recorded from Middle English, the term comes from Old French *eschec mat*, from Arabic *šāh mā*, from Persian *šāh māt* 'the king is dead'.

checks and balances counterbalancing influences by which an organization or system is regulated, typically those ensuring that power in political institutions is not concentrated in the hands of particular individuals or groups. The term is first recorded in the writings of the American statesman John Adams (1735–1826).

turn the other cheek refrain from retaliating when one has been attacked or insulted, originally with biblical allusion to Matthew 5:39.

cheese a *cheese* is the emblem of St Juthwara, a reputed British virgin martyr with a cult in the south west of England, and ➤ St BRIDGET *of Ireland*.

chela a follower and pupil of a guru; the word comes from Hindi *celā*.

Chelsea pensioner in the UK, an inmate of the Chelsea Royal Hospital for old or disabled soldiers; the hospital was originally founded by Charles II in 1682, and the pensioners are characterized by their scarlet coats.

Chenab a river of northern India and Pakistan, which rises in the Himalayas and flows through Himachal Pradesh and Jammu and Kashmir, to join the Sutlej River in Punjab. It is one of the five rivers that gave Punjab its name.

Cheops (fl. early 26th century BC), Egyptian pharaoh of the 4th dynasty; Egyptian name *Khufu*. He commissioned the building of the Great Pyramid at Giza.

Chequers a Tudor mansion in Buckinghamshire which serves as a country seat of the British Prime Minister in office; it was left to the nation for this purpose by the British politician and philanthropist Lord Lee of Fareham (1868–1947).

Chernobyl a town near Kiev in Ukraine where, in April 1986, an accident at a nuclear power station resulted in a serious escape of radioactive material, and the subsequent contamination of Ukraine, Belarus, and other parts of Europe. (See also ➤ CULTURAL *Chernobyl*.)

cherry taken as the type of something pleasant and desirable. The **cherry on the cake** is a desirable feature perceived as a pleasing but inessential addition to something that is already worth having. A **bowl of cherries** is a very pleasant or enjoyable situation (now usually with negative). Often with reference to the 1931 song-title 'Life is just a bowl of cherries' by Lew Brown (1893–1958).

To **cherry-pick** is to choose selectively (as the most beneficial or profitable items or opportunities) from what is available. The expression is probably a back-formation from *cherry picker*, a hydraulic crane with a platform at the end, for raising and lowering people working at a height, with the idea of someone being raised to a position of advantage for picking the best fruit on a tree. As the term has become more familiar there has been a further shift in emphasis: a **cherry-picker** may now be a person who selects favourable figures and statistics in order to present biased data.

Chersonese ancient name for the Gallipoli peninsula; the name (recorded from the early 17th century) comes via Latin from Greek *khersonēsos* 'peninsula', from *khersos* 'dry' + *nēsos* 'island'. It survives also in more modern poetic use.

cherub a winged angelic being described in biblical tradition as attending on God, represented in ancient Middle Eastern art as a lion or a bull with eagles' wings and a human face and regarded in Christian angelology as an angel of the second highest order of the ninefold celestial hierarchy; the plural form is **cherubim**.

In art, the word denotes a representation of a cherub, depicted as a chubby, healthy-looking child with wings; the plural form is **cherubim** or **cherubs**.

Recorded from Old English (in form *cherubin*), the word comes ultimately, via Latin and Greek, from Hebrew *kĕrūb*, plural *kĕrūḇīm*. A rabbinic folk etymology, which explains the Hebrew singular form as representing Aramaic *kĕ-raḇyā* 'like a child', led to the representation of the cherub as a child.

Cheshire cat a cat depicted with a broad fixed grin, as popularized through Lewis Carroll's *Alice's Adventures in Wonderland* (1865). The origin is unknown, but it is said that *Cheshire* cheeses used to be marked with the face of a smiling cat.

chess a board game of strategic skill for two players, played on a chequered board. Each player begins the game with a king, a queen, two bishops, two knights, two rooks (or 'castles'), and eight pawns, which are moved and capture opposing pieces according to precise rules. The object is to put the opponent's king under a direct attack from which escape is impossible (*checkmate*). Recorded from Middle English, the word comes from Old French *esches*, plural of *eschec* 'a check'.

old chestnut a joke, story, or subject that has become tedious and uninteresting because of its age and repetition; the expression is recorded from the late 19th century and the origin is unknown, although it has been suggested that it derives from a scene in W. Dimond's *The Broken Sword* (1816), 'this is the twenty-seventh time I have heard you relate this story, and you invariably said, a chestnut, till now.'

pull someone's chestnuts out of the fire succeed in a hazardous undertaking for someone else's benefit, with reference to the fable of a monkey using a ➤ CAT's *paw* to extract roasting chestnuts from a fire.

chevalier historical term for a knight; a member of certain orders of knighthood or of modern French orders such as the Legion of Honour. Recorded from late Middle English (denoting a horseman or mounted knight) the word comes via Old French and medieval Latin, from Latin *caballus* 'horse'.

The **Young Chevalier** was a name given to Charles Edward Stuart (1720–88), son of James Francis Edward Stuart, and otherwise known as the ➤ YOUNG *Pretender*.

The **Chevalier de St George** was a name given to James Francis Edward Stuart (1688–1766), father of Charles Edward Stuart, and otherwise known as the *Chevalier* and the ➤ OLD *Pretender*.

chevet in large churches, an apse with an ambulatory giving access behind the high altar to a series of chapels set in bays. The style was developed in 12th-century France.

The term is recorded from the early 19th century, and comes from French, literally 'pillow', from Latin *capitium*, from *caput* 'head'.

chi-ro a monogram of *chi* (X) and *rho* (P) as the first two letters of Greek *Khristos* Christ.

chiaroscuro the treatment of light and shade in drawing and painting; an effect of contrasted light and shadow created by light falling unevenly or from a particular direction on something. Recorded from the mid 17th century, the word comes from Italian, from *chiaro* 'clear bright' (from Latin *clarus*) + *oscuro* 'dark, obscure' (from Latin *obscurus*).

Chichén Itzá a site in northern Yucatán, Mexico, the centre of the Mayan empire after AD 918.

chicken a *chicken* may symbolize something in need of shelter and protection, as in Jesus's lament for Jerusalem (see ➤ HEN), and Macduff's grief for his children in Shakespeare's *Macbeth* (see ➤ at one FELL swoop); it is also a type of timidity. The word is recorded from Old English (in form *cīcen*, *cȳen*), and is of Germanic origin, probably related to *cock*.

The phrase **chicken-and-egg** denotes a situation in which each of two things appears to be necessary to the other. Either it is impossible to say which came first or it appears that neither could ever exist.

Chicken Little is a name for an alarmist, a person who panics at the first sign of a problem; from the name of a character in a nursery story who repeatedly warns that the sky is falling down.

Why did the chicken cross the road? is a traditional puzzle question, to which the answer is, to get to the other side; recorded from the mid 19th century.

chickens come home to roost one's past mistakes or wrongdoings will eventually be the cause of trouble. With allusion to the proverb, **curses, like chickens, come home to roost**.

child on a boar a child on a boar is the emblem of ➤ *St* CYRICUS.

childe archaic or literary word for a youth of noble birth, typically forming part of a name, as *Childe Harold*. The word is recorded from late Old English, and is a variant of *child*.

Childe Roland is the hero of a poem by Browning, 'Childe Roland to the Dark Tower came', the title deriving from a snatch of song recited by Edgar in Shakespeare's *King Lear*; in the poem, the narrator is a knight errant crossing a nightmare landscape who finally reaches the Dark Tower and sets the ➤ SLUGHORN to his lips, but the outcome and the reason for his journey are unknown.

Childermas old name for the feast of the Holy Innocents, 28 December. The name is recorded from Old English, in form *childramæsse*, from *cildra* 'of children' and *mæsse* 'Mass'.

Children of Israel The Jewish people, as people whose descent is traditionally traced from the patriarch Jacob (also called *Israel*), each of whose twelve sons became the founder of a tribe.

the Children's Crusade a movement in 1212 in which tens of thousands of children (mostly from France and Germany) embarked on a crusade to the Holy Land. Most of the children never reached their destination; arriving at French and Italian ports, many were sold into slavery.

Chillingham name of a park in Northumberland, one of several parks in Britain in which white ➤ PARK *cattle* are maintained.

Chillon a castle on the lake of Geneva in which the ➤ PRISONER *of Chillon* was held in captivity.

Chiltern Hundreds in the UK, a Crown manor, whose administration is a nominal office for which an MP applies as a way of resigning from the House of Commons.

The holding of an office of profit under the Crown became a disqualification in 1707, and in 1740 the Stewardship of a royal manor was used in order to create a disqualification. In January 1750-51 John Pitt, MP for Wrexham, took the Stewardship of the *Chiltern Hundreds*, which has come to be the ordinary form.

chimera in Greek mythology, a fire-breathing female monster with a lion's head, a goat's body, and a serpent's tale; any mythical animal with parts taken from various animals. In extended usage, the term may be used for a thing which is hoped or wished for but in fact is illusory or impossible to achieve.

Chimera is also now used in biology for an organism containing a mixture of genetically different tissues, formed by processes such as fusion of early embryos, grafting, or mutation.

China syndrome a hypothetical sequence of events following the meltdown of a nuclear reactor, in which the core melts through its containment structure and deep into the earth. It takes its name from *China* as being on the opposite side of the earth from a reactor in the US.

china wedding in the US, a 20th wedding anniversary.

Chindit a member of the Allied forces behind the Japanese lines in Burma (now Myanmar) in 1943–5. The name comes from Burmese *chinthé*, a mythical creature.

Chinese of or pertaining to China.

A **Chinese wall** is an insurmountable barrier to understanding (alluding to the ➤ GREAT *Wall of China*); on the Stock Exchange, a prohibition against the passing of confidential information from one department of a financial institution to another.

The **Chinese water torture** is a form of torture whereby a constant drip of water is caused to fall on to the victim's head.

chinoiserie the imitation or evocation of Chinese motifs and techniques in Western art, furniture, and architecture, especially in the 18th century.

a chip off the old block someone resembling their father or mother, especially in character and behaviour; the term is recorded from the early 17th century.

a chip on one's shoulder a deeply ingrained grievance, typically about a particular thing. The phrase (originally US) is recorded from the 19th century, and may originate in a practice described in the *Long Island Telegraph* (Hempstead, New York), 20 May 1830, 'When two churlish boys were *determined* to fight, a *chip* would be placed on the shoulder of one, and the other demanded to knock it off at his peril.'

chips gambling chips with which a stake is placed; to **have had one's chips** is to be beaten, be finished. **When the chips are down** means when it comes to the point.

Mr Chips nickname of the schoolmaster hero, Mr Chipping, of James Hilton's novel *Good-bye, Mr Chips* (1934); he spends his professional life in the same school, and despite his unimpressive looks and manner is in the end regarded with respect and affection by pupils and colleagues.

Chiron in Greek mythology, a learned ➤ CENTAUR who acted as teacher to Jason, Achilles, and many other heroes.

chivalry the medieval knightly system with its religious, moral, and social code; knights, noblemen, and horsemen of that system collectively. Recorded from Middle English, the word comes, via Old French *chevalerie* and medieval Latin, from late Latin *caballarius* 'horseman' (see ➤ CHEVALIER).

Chladni figures the patterns formed when a sand-covered surface is made to vibrate. The sand collects in the regions of least motion. They are named (in the early 19th century) after Ernst *Chladni* (1756–1827), German physicist.

Chloe in the classical Greek story by Longus, the shepherdess loved by ➤ DAPHNIS.

Choctaw the Muskogean language of an American Indian people now living mainly in Mississippi, closely related to Chickasaw and now almost extinct, sometimes taken as the type of an unknown or difficult language.

choir an organized body of singers performing or leading in the musical parts of a church service; that part of a church appropriated to singers; especially the chancel of a cathedral, minster, or large church.

Choir may also denote a company of angels, especially any of the nine orders in medieval angelology.

The word is recorded from Middle English (in form *quer*, *quere*), from Old French *quer*, from Latin *chorus*. The spelling change in the 17th century, which means that now the older variant *quire* is found only in the reference in the Book of Common Prayer to 'Quires and Places where they sing', was due to association with Latin *chorus* and modern French *choeur*.

choler in medieval science and medicine, one of the four bodily ➤ HUMOURS, identified with bile, believed to be associated with a peevish or irascible, or *choleric*, temperament. Also known as *yellow bile*.

Recorded from late Middle English (also denoting diarrhoea), the word comes from Old French *colere* 'bile, anger', from Latin *cholera* 'diarrhoea' (from Greek *kholera*), which in late Latin acquired the senses 'bile or anger', from Greek *kholē* 'bile'.

not much chop no good; not up to much. The sense of *chop* here originated in the Hindi word *chāp* (in English since the early

17th century) meaning 'official stamp'. As used by Europeans in the Far East, the word was extended to cover documents such as passports to which an official stamp or impression was attached and in China to mean 'branded goods'. From this the sense developed in the late 19th century to mean something that has 'class' or has been validated as genuine or good.

chop and change change one's tactics, vacillate, be inconstant; an alliterative phrase in which *chop* has lost its original meaning of 'barter' and is now taken as 'change, alter'.

chopsocky kung fu or a similar martial art, especially as depicted in violent action films. The term dates from the 1970s, and may be a humorous formation on *chop suey*.

chorus in ancient Greek tragedy, a group of performers who comment on the main action, typically speaking and moving together; a single character who speaks the prologue and other linking parts of the play, especially in Elizabethan drama.

The word is recorded from the mid 16th century (denoting a character speaking the prologue and epilogue in a play and serving to comment on events), and comes via Latin from Greek *khoros*.

chosen people those selected by God for a special relationship with him, especially the people of Israel, the Jews.

Chouan a member of an irregular force maintaining a partisan resistance in the west of France against the Republican and Bonapartist governments. The name may be from that of Jean *Chouan*, said to be one of their leaders, or from *chouan* as an older form of *chat-huant* a species of owl.

chrism a mixture of oil and balsam, consecrated and used for anointing at baptism and other rites of the Catholic, Orthodox, and Anglican Churches. The word is recorded from Old English, and comes via medieval and ecclesiastical Latin from Greek *khrisma* 'anointing', from *khriein* 'anoint'.

chrisom a white robe put on a child at baptism, and used as its shroud if it died within the month. The word is recorded from Middle English and is an alteration of *chrism*, representing a popular sound with two syllables.

Christ the title, also treated as a name, given to Jesus of Nazareth; the Messiah as

prophesied in the Hebrew scriptures. The name is recorded in Old English (in form *Crīst*), from Latin *Christus*, from Greek *Khristos*, noun use of an adjective meaning 'anointed', from *khriein* 'anoint', translating Hebrew *māšīaḥ* 'Messiah'.

Christ's cross me speed is a formula said before repeating the alphabet; the figure of a cross preceded the alphabet in horn-books (see also ➤ CRISS-*cross*).

Christ's thorn is a thorny shrub popularly supposed to have formed Christ's crown of thorns, in particular either of two shrubs related to the buckthorn.

Christendom the worldwide body or society of Christians; the Christian world. The word is recorded from Old English (in form *crīstendōm*), and comes from *crīsten* 'Christian' + -*dōm* 'domain'.

Christian the name of the central character of the first part of Bunyan's ➤ *The* PILGRIM's *Progress* (1678–84), which recounts the story of his journey to the Celestial City.

Fletcher Christian (*c*.1764–*c*.1793), English seaman and mutineer. As first mate under Captain Bligh on HMS *Bounty*, in April 1789 Christian seized the ship and cast Bligh and others adrift. In 1790 the mutineers settled on Pitcairn Island, where Christian was probably killed by Tahitians.

Christian Brothers a Roman Catholic lay teaching order, originally founded in France in 1684.

Christian science the beliefs and practices of the Church of Christ Scientist, a Christian sect founded by Mary Baker Eddy in 1879. Members hold that only God and the mind have ultimate reality, and that sin and illness are illusions which can be overcome by prayer and faith.

Christiana the central character of the second part of Bunyan's ➤ *The* PILGRIM's *Progress*, the wife of Christian, who with her children sets out to follow her husband's path to the Celestial City.

Christianity the religion based on the person and teachings of Jesus of Nazareth, or its beliefs and practices. It originated among the Jewish followers of Jesus of Nazareth, who believed that he was the promised Messiah (or 'Christ'), but the Christian Church soon became an independent organization, largely through the missionary efforts of St Paul. In 313 Constantine ended official persecution in the Roman Empire and in 380

Theodosius I recognized it as the state religion.

Christingle a lighted candle symbolizing Christ as the light of the world, held by children especially at a special Advent service originating in the Moravian Church. Recorded from the 1950s, the name probably comes from German dialect *Christkindl* 'Christ-child, Christmas gift'.

Christmas the annual Christian festival celebrating Christ's birth, held on 25 December (one of the quarter days in England, Wales, and Ireland); the name is recorded from Old English, in form *Cristes* 'Christ's' *mæsse* 'Mass'.

A **Christmas box** was originally a box, usually of earthenware, in which contributions of money were collected at Christmas by apprentices; the box being broken when full and the money shared. Later, a present or gratuity given at Christmas to tradespeople or those held to have performed a regular service (such as delivering post) for a person without direct payment from them. The practice gave rise to the name ➤ BOXING *Day* for the day on which such presents were generally given.

A **Christmas card** is a decorative greetings card sent at Christmas; the custom began in England in the 1860s. The term may be used to refer to a conventionally pretty scene reminiscent of such a card.

Christmas Day is the day on which the festival of Christmas is celebrated, 25 December.

A **Christmas stocking** is a real or ornamental stocking hung up by children on Christmas Eve for Father Christmas to fill with presents.

A **Christmas tree** is an evergreen (especially spruce) or artificial tree set up and decorated with lights, tinsel, and other ornaments as part of Christmas celebrations. The custom was originally German, but spread to England after its introduction into the royal household in the early years of the reign of Queen Victoria.

St Christopher a legendary 3rd-century Christian martyr, adopted as the patron saint of travellers, since it is said that he once carried Christ in the form of a child across a river; he was traditionally a giant, and is often shown as such in art, carrying the Christ-child on his shoulder. He is also one of the ➤ FOURTEEN *Holy Helpers*.

His image was often placed in wall-paintings on the north wall of churches opposite the porch so that he would be seen by those who entered; there was a tradition that anyone seeing an image of the saint would not die that day, and he was invoked against water, tempest, plague, and sudden death. His feast day is 25 July.

Christopher Robin name of the little boy in A. A. Milne's stories about the bear ➤ WINNIE-*the-Pooh* and other toys, shown in the illustrations with long hair and wearing a smock; the original *Christopher Robin* was Milne's son.

Christy Minstrels name of a troupe of minstrels imitating black musicians, originated in New York in the late 19th century by George *Christy*.

Chronicles the name of two books of the Bible, recording the history of Israel and Judah until the return from Exile (536 BC).

chrysanthemum a favourite funeral flower in some parts of Europe, and thus associated with All Souls' Day. In Japan, it is the crest of the imperial family.

The **Chrysanthemum Throne** is the throne of Japan.

chrysoprase a golden-green precious stone, mentioned in the New Testament (Revelation 21:20) as one of the precious stones in the wall of the New Jerusalem, perhaps a variety of beryl; in the Middle Ages, believed to have the faculty of shining in the dark. Now, an apple-green variety of chalcedony containing nickel, used as a gemstone.

The word is recorded from Middle English, and comes via Old French and Latin from Greek *khrusoprasos*, from *khrusos* 'gold' + *prason* 'leek'.

chthonic concerning, belonging to, or inhabiting the underworld. The word is recorded from the late 19th century, and comes from Greek *khthōn* 'earth'.

Chunnel from the late 1920s, a humorous name for the projected ➤ CHANNEL *Tunnel*.

church a building used for public Christian worship. Also (with upper case initial) a particular Christian organization, typically one with its own clergy, buildings, and distinctive doctrines; **the Church**, the hierarchy of clergy of such an organization, especially the Church of England or the Roman Catholic Church.

The **Church Militant** is the whole body of living Christian believers, regarded as striving to combat evil here on earth.

A **church mouse** is a mouse living in a church, proverbially taken as a type of poverty, as in **poor as a church mouse**.

The **Church of England** is the English branch of the Western Christian Church, which combines Catholic and Protestant traditions, rejects the Pope's authority, and has the monarch as its titular head. The English Church was part of the Catholic Church until the Reformation of the 16th century; after Henry VIII failed to obtain a divorce from Catherine of Aragon he repudiated papal supremacy, bringing the Church under the control of the Crown.

The **Church of Scotland** is the the national (Presbyterian) Christian Church in Scotland. In 1560 John Knox reformed the established Church along Presbyterian lines, but there were repeated attempts by the Stuart monarchs to impose episcopalianism, and the Church of Scotland was not finally established as Presbyterian until 1690.

Church Slavonic is the liturgical language used in the Orthodox Church in Russia, Serbia, and some other countries. It is a modified form of Old Church Slavonic.

The word is recorded from Old English (in form *cir(i)ce, cyr(i)ce*), ultimately based on medieval Greek *kurikon*, from Greek *kuriakon (dōma)* 'Lord's (house)', from *kurios* 'master or lord'.

Churching of Women the formal thanksgiving by women after childbirth, based on the Jewish rite of Purification and first mentioned in a letter of St Augustine of Canterbury to St Gregory the Great.

Churrigueresque of or relating to the lavishly ornamented late Spanish baroque style, characteristic or suggestive of the architecture of José Benito *Churriguera* (1650–1723), a Spanish architect who worked in this style.

ci-devant in the language of Revolutionary France, a person of rank, a former nobleman or noblewoman. The expression is from French, and is used to indicate that someone or something once possessed a specified characteristic but no longer does so; it means literally, 'heretofore'.

ciborium a receptacle shaped like a shrine or a cup with an arched cover, used in the Christian Church for the reservation of the Eucharist. Also, a canopy over an altar in a church, standing on four pillars. Recorded from the mid 16th century, the word comes via medieval Latin from Greek *kibōrion* 'seed vessel of the water lily or a cup made from it';

it is probably also influenced by Latin *cibus* 'food'.

Marcus Tullius Cicero (106–43 BC), Roman statesman, orator, and writer. As an orator and writer Cicero established a model for Latin prose; his surviving works include speeches, treatises on rhetoric, philosophical works, and letters. He was a supporter of Pompey against Julius Caesar. In the *Philippics* (43 BC) he attacked Mark Antony, who had him put to death.

El Cid (*c.*1043–99), Count of Bivar, Spanish soldier. A champion of Christianity against the Moors, in 1094 he captured Valencia, which he went on to rule. He is immortalized in the Spanish *Poema del Cid* (12th century) and in Corneille's play *Le Cid* (1637).

close but no cigar of an attempt which is almost but not quite successful, referring to a cigar offered in congratulation.

Cinderella a girl in various traditional European fairy tales. In the version by Charles Perrault she is exploited as a servant by her stepmother and stepsisters but enabled by a fairy godmother to attend a royal ball. She meets and captivates ➤ PRINCE *Charming* but has to flee at midnight, leaving the prince to identify her by the glass slipper which she leaves behind.

Cinque Ports a group of medieval ports in Kent and East Sussex in SE England, which were formerly allowed trading privileges in exchange for providing the bulk of England's navy. The five original Cinque Ports were Hastings, Sandwich, Dover, Romney, and Hythe; later Rye and Winchelsea were added.

cinquecento the 16th century as a period of Italian art, architecture, or literature, with a reversion to classical forms. The term comes from Italian, literally '500' (shortened from *milcinquecento* '1500') used with reference to the years 1500–99.

cinquefoil an ornamental design of five lobes arranged in a circle, as in architectural tracery or heraldry.

cipher a secret or disguised way of writing; a code. The term comes (in late Middle English, in the senses 'symbol for zero' and 'arabic numeral') from Old French, based on Arabic *ṣifr* 'zero'.

Circe in Greek mythology, an enchantress who lived with her wild animals on the island of Aeaea. When Odysseus visited the island his companions were changed into pigs by her potions, but he protected himself with the herb ➤ MOLY, and forced her to restore his men into human beings.

the wheel has come full circle the situation has returned to what it was in the past, as if completing a cycle, with reference to Shakespeare's *King Lear*, by association with the wheel fabled to be turned by Fortune and representing mutability.

circulating library a library with books lent for a small fee to subscribers; the first circulating library was set up in Edinburgh in the early 18th century, and in the 18th and 19th centuries the system proved extremely popular, with the rise of such establishments as Mudie's Lending Library. The *circulating library* was particularly associated with a taste for popular fiction.

Circumlocution Office the type of a government department, satirized in Dickens's *Little Dorrit* (1857), in which the establishment is shown as run purely for the benefit of its incompetent and obstructive officials, typified by the Barnacle family.

a three-ring circus an uproar, an ostentatious event. The idea is of a circus on a grand enough scale to have three show rings; the figurative use dates from the US in the mid 19th century.

cisalpine on this (the Roman) side of the Alps; south of the Alps.

Cistercian a member of an order founded as a stricter branch of the Benedictines, the reforms being particularly associated with the influence of ➤ St BERNARD *of Clairvaux*, who was particularly critical of elaborate decoration in ecclesiastical buildings. The monks are now divided into two observances, the strict observance, whose adherents are known popularly as Trappists, and the common observance, which has certain relaxations.

The name comes (via French) from *Cistercium*, the Latin name of *Cîteaux* near Dijon in France, where the order was founded.

Cities of the Plain Sodom and Gomorrah; the original reference is to Genesis 13:12.

City of God Paradise, perceived as an ideal community in Heaven; the Christian Church. The phrase is a translation of Latin *Civitas Dei*, by St Augustine.

City of London the part of London situated within the ancient boundaries and governed by the Lord Mayor and the Corporation; the financial and commercial institutions located there are known as **the City**.

civic crown in ancient Rome, a garland of oak leaves and acorns, given to one who saved the life of a fellow-citizen in war; the phrase is a translation of Latin *corona civica*.

the end of civilization as we know it the complete collapse of ordered society; supposedly a cinematic cliché, and actually used in the film *Citizen Kane* (1941).

civis Romanus sum Latin for, 'I am a Roman citizen', the formal statement of Roman citizenship.

Civvy Street in British informal usage, civilian as opposed to Service life.

Clactonian of, relating to, or denoting a Lower Palaeolithic culture represented by flint implements found at Clacton-on-Sea in SE England, dated to about 250,000–200,000 years ago.

Claddagh ring a ring in the form of two hands clasping a heart, traditionally given in Ireland as a token of love. It is called after a small fishing village on the edge of Galway city.

clam a marine bivalve mollusc with shells of equal size which is the type of something which silently withdraws into itself from contact with another. The name is recorded from the early 16th century and apparently comes from earlier *clam* 'a clamp', from Old English *clam*, *clamm* 'a bond or bondage'.

In North American usage, **happy as a clam at high tide** means very happy.

clan a group of close-knit and interrelated families (especially associated with families in the Scottish Highlands). The word is recorded from late Middle English, and comes from Scottish Gaelic *clann* 'offspring, family', from Old Irish *cland*, from Latin *planta* 'sprout'.

A **clan badge** is a sprig of a plant worn as the symbol of a particular clan.

The **Clan Na Gael** was an Irish-American revolutionary organization formed to pursue Irish independence after the defeat of the Fenian rising of 1867.

Clapham a district in south-west London.

The **man on the Clapham omnibus** as the type of the average man; the phrase is attributed to the English judge Lord Bowen (1853–94).

The **Clapham Sect** was an early 19th-century group noted for evangelical opinions and philanthropic activity; some of the chief members lived at *Clapham*.

like the clappers very fast; *the clappers* are a contrivance in a mill for striking or shaking the hopper so as to make the grain move down to the millstones.

claptrap nonsense; originally from a theatrical device of the 18th century designed to elicit applause. The term in its current sense is first recorded in Byron's *Don Juan* (1819).

claque a group of people hired to applaud (or heckle) a performer or public speaker; a group of sycophantic followers. The word comes (in the mid 19th century) from French, from *claquer* 'to clap'; the practice of paying members of an audience for their support originated at the Paris opera.

St Clare of Assisi (1194–1253), Italian saint and abbess. With St Francis she founded the order of Poor Ladies of San Damiano ('Poor Clares'), of which she was abbess. In 1958 she was declared the patron saint of television, on the grounds that she miraculously experienced the Christmas midnight mass in the Church of St Francis in Assisi when on her deathbed.

She is often shown with a pyx or monstrance, in reference to the story that when Assisi was in danger from the army of the Emperor Frederick II, which included Saracen troops, Clare (who was ill) was carried to the wall of the city holding a pyx with the Sacrament, and the attacking forces fled. Her feast day is 11 (formerly 12) August.

Clarenceux in heraldry, (in the UK) the title given to the second King of Arms, with jurisdiction south of the Trent. Recorded from Middle English and coming from Anglo-Norman French, the position is named after the dukedom of *Clarence* created for the second son of Edward II, married to the heiress of *Clare* in Suffolk.

Constitutions of Clarendon a body of propositions drawn up at the Council of *Clarendon* in the reign of Henry II (1164), defining the limits of civil and ecclesiastical jurisdiction in England.

Clarendon Code the common name of four Acts passed in England when Edward Hyde, Lord *Clarendon* (1609–74), was Charles II's chief adviser, all intended to curb the powers and liberties of dissenters and nonconformists.

Clarendon Press an imprint of Oxford University Press, named from the Clarendon Building which was designed by Hawksmoor as the new printing-house (Lord *Clarendon* (1609–74) was Chancellor of Oxford University 1660–7). The imprint was first used in 1713 for a selection of verses in honour of Queen Anne.

classic race in the UK, each of the five main flat races of the horse-racing season, namely the Two Thousand and the One Thousand Guineas, the Derby, the Oaks, and the St Leger.

the classics the works of ancient Greek and Latin writers and philosophers.

Clause Four a clause in the Labour Party constitution containing an affirmation of the Party's commitment to the common ownership of industry and services (this specific point was originally introduced in 1918 as clause 3d and revised in 1929 under Clause 4, which has thereafter dealt also with the Party's other aims).

In 1995, the modernization of ➤ NEW *Labour* reached the point at which (despite left-wing opposition) *Clause Four* could be replaced.

claymore a broadsword used by Scottish Highlanders, either two-edged, or basket-hilted and single-edged (a form introduced in the 16th century). The name comes from Gaelic *claidheamh* 'sword' + *mór* 'great'.

Clayton's in Australian and New Zealand usage, largely illusory; existing in name only. The expression comes (in the 1980s) from the proprietary name of a soft drink marketed using the line 'It's the drink I have when I'm not having a drink'.

make a clean breast of confess fully one's mistakes or wrongdoings. The breast was popularly supposed in former times to be the dwelling of a person's conscience.

clear blue water the ideological gap between the British Conservative and Labour parties. The phrase, from a blend of *clear water*, the distance between two boats, and *blue water*, the open sea, with a play on *blue* as the traditional colour of the British Conservative party, is recorded from 1994.

clear the decks prepare for a particular event or goal by dealing with anything beforehand that might hinder progress. In the literal sense, obstacles or superfluous items were removed from the decks of a ship before a battle at sea.

be in a cleft stick be in a difficult situation when any action one takes will have adverse consequences. *Cleft* is a form of the past participle of cleave, in its basic meaning of 'to divide with a cutting blow' or 'split'.

St Clement of Alexandria (*c.*150–*c.*215), Greek theologian. He was head of the catechetical school at Alexandria (*c.*190–202), but was forced to flee from Roman imperial persecution. His main contribution to theological scholarship was to relate the ideas of Greek philosophy to the Christian faith. His feast day is 5 December.

St Clement of Rome (1st century AD), pope (bishop of Rome) *c.*88–*c.*97, probably the third after St Peter; he wrote an epistle *c.*96 to the Church at Corinth, insisting that certain deposed presbyters be reinstated.

In later tradition he became the subject of a variety of legends; one held that he was martyred by being thrown into the sea with an anchor round his neck. His feast day is 23 November.

Cleopatra (69–30 BC), queen of Egypt from 47 BC, the last Ptolemaic ruler. After a brief liaison with Julius Caesar she formed a political and romantic alliance with Mark Antony. Their ambitions ultimately brought them into conflict with Rome, and she and Antony were defeated at the battle of Actium in 31. She is reputed to have committed suicide by allowing herself to be bitten by an asp.

Cleopatra's nose is taken as the type of a single feature a change in which would have been of immeasurable influence; the reference is to a comment by the French mathematician, physicist, and moralist Blaise Pascal (1623–62), 'Had Cleopatra's nose been shorter, the whole face of the world would have changed.'

Cleopatra's Needles are a pair of granite obelisks erected at Heliopolis by Tuthmosis III *c.*1475 BC. They were taken from Egypt in 1878, one being set up on the Thames Embankment in London and the other in Central Park, New York. They have no known historical connection with Cleopatra.

clerestory the upper part of the nave, choir, and transepts of a large church, containing a series of windows. It is clear of the roofs of the aisles and admits light to the central parts of the building.

clergy the body of all people ordained for religious duties, especially in the Christian

Church. Recorded from Middle English, the word comes via Old French, based on ecclesiastical Latin *clericus* 'clergyman', from Greek *klērikos* 'belonging to the Christian clergy', from *klēros* 'lot, heritage' (Acts 1:26, 'And they gave forth their lots, and the lot fell upon Matthias', in the account of the choosing of a twelfth apostle to replace Judas).

clerihew a short comic or nonsensical verse in two rhyming couplets with lines of unequal length, and referring to a famous person; the term dates from the 1920s, and the form is named after the English writer Edmund *Clerihew* Bentley (1875–1956), who invented it.

Clerk of the Closet in the UK, the sovereign's principal chaplain.

click a speech sound produced as a type of plosive by sudden withdrawal of the tongue from the soft palate, front teeth, or back teeth and hard palate, occurring in some southern African and other languages. A **click language** is one in which such sounds are used.

cliffhanger a dramatic and exciting ending to an episode of a serial, leaving the audience in suspense and anxious not to miss the next episode; originally (in the US in the 1930s) a *cliffhanger* was a serial film in which each episode ended in a desperate situation.

climb on the bandwagon seek to join the party or group that is likely to succeed.

clink an informal word for prison, recorded from the early 16th century and originally denoting a particular prison in Southwark, London.

Clio in Greek mythology, the Muse of history; the name comes from Greek *kleiein* 'celebrate'.

clip the wings of prevent someone from acting freely; check the aspirations of. From the practice of trimming the feathers of a bird so as to disable it from flight.

clipper a fast sailing ship, especially one of 19th-century design with concave bows and raked masts.

Clipper chip a microchip developed by the US Government, and proposed as a compulsory standard for data encryption technology, which inserts an identifying code into encrypted transmissions that allows them to be deciphered by a third party with access to a Government-held key.

Clitumnus a spring near Spoleto, renowned in classical antiquity; it was described by Virgil and the younger Pliny, and visited by the emperors Caligula and Flavius Honorius.

Cliveden Set the group of right-wing politicians and journalists who met regularly in the 1930s at *Cliveden*, Lord Astor's country house.

Cloacina name for a supposed Roman goddess of the sewers; in ancient Rome, the *Cloaca Maxima* was the main sewer (originally an open watercourse but later covered over).

cloak a cloak is the emblem of ➤ St MARTIN *of Tours*.
  Cloak-and-dagger means involving or characteristic of mystery, intrigue, or espionage; the term is recorded from the early 19th century as a translation of French *de cape de d'épée* or Spanish *de capa y espada*, relating particularly to dramas or stories of intrigue or melodramatic adventure, in which the principal characters are likely to be cloaked and armed with swords or daggers.

cloister a covered walk in a convent, monastery, college, or cathedral, often with a wall on one side and a colonnade open to a quadrangle on the other. The word is recorded from Middle English (in the sense 'place of religious seclusion', and comes via Old French from Latin *claustrum, clostrum* 'lock, enclosed place', from *claudere* 'to close'.

Clonmacnoise the remains in county Galway, above the Shannon river, of one of the most important Irish monasteries, founded in the mid-6th century, which by the 8th century was a major centre of art and learning.

Close Encounter term used for a supposed encounter with a UFO, and divided into categories, from a **Close Encounter of the First Kind** (sighting but no physical evidence), through Second (physical evidence left) and Third (extra-terrestrials beings observed) to a **Close Encounter of the Fourth Kind**, which involves abduction by aliens. The expression was popularized by the science-fiction film *Close Encounters of the Third Kind* (1977).

close season a period between specified dates when fishing or the killing of particular game is officially forbidden.

out of the closet out into the open; *closet* (the North American word for *cupboard*) typifies privacy and seclusion in biblical usage.

Come out of the closet means 'cease hiding a secret about oneself'; from the late 20th century it has particularly been used in reference to making public one's homosexuality.

the cloth the clergy, the clerical profession; the expression is recorded from the early 18th century, and derives from the earlier (mid 17th century) use of *cloth* to mean the profession of a minister or clergyman, as marked by their professional garb.

cloth of state an embroidered cloth erected over a throne or chair as a sign of rank, a canopy.

Clotho in Greek Mythology, one of the three ➤ FATES; the name in Greek means literally 'she who spins', and traditionally Clotho spun the thread of life, which was then measured by Lachesis, and cut by Atropos.

cloud cuckoo land a state of unrealistic or absurdly over-optimistic fantasy. The phrase is recorded in English from the late 19th century, and is a translation of Greek *Nephelokokkugia*, the name of the city built by the birds in Aristophanes' comedy *Birds*, from *nephelē* 'cloud' + *kokkux* 'cuckoo'.

on cloud nine extremely happy, with reference to a notional ten-part classification of clouds in which 'nine' was next to the highest.

cloven hoof a divided hoof, as that of a goat, ascribed to a satyr, the god Pan, or to the Devil; in extended usage, the mark of an inherently evil nature.

clover a plant whose leaves which are typically three-lobed; a **four-leaved clover** is a traditional symbol of luck.
  To be **in clover** is to be in ease and luxury. This sense of the phrase, dating from the early 18th century, refers to clover's being particularly attractive to livestock.

Clovis¹ (465–511), king of the Franks from 481. He extended Merovingian rule to Gaul and Germany after victories at Soissons (486) and Cologne (496), making Paris his capital. After his conversion to Christianity he championed orthodoxy against the Arian Visigoths, finally defeating them in the battle of Poitiers (507). He is traditionally regarded as founder of the French nation, and *Louis* as the Christian name of many early kings of France derives from *Clovis*.

Clovis² a Palaeo-Indian culture of Central and North America, dated to about 11,500–11,000 years ago and earlier. The culture is distinguished by heavy leaf-shaped stone spearheads (**Clovis points**), often found in conjunction with the bones of mammoths. The culture was first found near *Clovis* in eastern New Mexico, US.

club a thick heavy stick or staff for use as a weapon; **prentices and clubs** is recorded from the mid 16th century as the rallying cry of London apprentices.

A club is the emblem of ➤ St CHRISTOPHER, ➤ St JUDE, ➤ St MAGNUS, ➤ St SIMON, and ➤ St JAMES *the Less*.

In cards, *clubs* form one of the four suits, marked with the conventional reprentation of a trefoil leaf in black; *club* here is a translation of the Spanish name *basto*, or Italian *bastone*, the symbol shown on Spanish cards; the design on English cards is taken from the French, where the name is *trèfle* 'trefoil'.

clue a piece of evidence or information used in the detection of a crime or the solving of a mystery; ultimately a variant of *clew* meaning 'a ball of thread', and in particular that used by Theseus to guide himself through the ➤ LABYRINTH.

Cluedo trademark name for a board game based on solving a murder committed in country house by one of a set of stock characters, invented by Anthony E. Platt in 1944; the six potential murderers are, ➤ *Reverend* GREEN, ➤ *Colonel* MUSTARD, ➤ *Mrs* PEACOCK, ➤ *Professor* PLUM, ➤ *Miss* SCARLETT, and ➤ *Mrs* WHITE, and players are required to accuse a named character in a specific location and with a particular weapon.

Cluniac of or relating to a reformed Benedictine monastic order founded at *Cluny* in eastern France in 910.

Cluny a Benedictine monastery in eastern France, founded in 910 and introducing a period of monastic reform based on strict observance of the Benedictine Rule; the abbey was subject only to the pope, and all future Cluniac foundations, or priories, remained directly subject to the original mother house.

The abbey church, built between 1088 and 1130, and famous for its size and magnificence, was badly damaged in the French Revolution and effectively demolished in the 19th century.

Clyde a river in western central Scotland which flows from the Southern Uplands to the Firth of Clyde, formerly famous for the shipbuilding industries along its banks.

Clytemnestra in Greek mythology, the wife of ➤ AGAMEMNON. She conspired with her lover Aegisthus to murder Agamemnon on his return from the Trojan War, and was murdered in retribution by her son Orestes and her daughter Electra.

Clytie in classical mythology, a water nymph who fell in love with Apollo; pining away, she became rooted in the ground, and her face became a sunflower, following the sun on its daily course.

drive a coach and horses through make (legislation) useless; the idea of a coach and six horses as the type of something very large which could fill or make a hole is recorded from the late 17th century.

coals pieces of (burning) coal.

To **carry coals to Newcastle** is to provide a commodity already in abundant supply; the expression 'as common as coals from Newcastle' is recorded from the early 17th century, and 'carry coals to Newcastle' from the mid 17th century.

To **haul someone over the coals** is to reprimand someone severely; the original reference is to the treatment of heretics, as in a comment attributed to Cardinal Allen (1532–94).

To **heap coals of fire on a person's head** is to cause remorse by returning good for evil; the reference is originally biblical, to Romans 12:20.

the coast is clear there is no danger of being observed or caught; the expression is recorded from the 16th century, and refers to the expectation that a sea-coast would be guarded against landing or attack.

coat of arms a coat or vest embroidered with heraldic arms, a herald's tabard; the distinctive heraldic bearings or shield of a person, family, corporation, or country.

coat of many colours in the Bible, given to ➤ JOSEPH by his father Jacob. The gift increased the jealousy of his brothers, who sold him into slavery and showed the torn and bloodstained coat to Jacob as a proof that Joseph was dead.

let the cobbler stick to his last people should only concern themselves with things they know something about (proverbial saying translating Latin *ne sutor ultra crepidam*).

cock proverbially protective of its hens and noted for aggression; the cock traditionally crows at first light or ➤ COCKCROW, and is used in ➤ COCKFIGHTING.

A *cock* is the emblem of ➤ St PETER and ➤ St VITUS.

Cock-a-doodle-doo is used to represent the sound made by a cock when it crows, and from this is also a child's name for a cock.

A **cock and bull story** is an incredible tale, a false story; the expression 'talk of a cock and a bull' is recorded from the early 17th century, and apparently refers to an original story or fable, now lost.

Cock of the North, in a Jacobite song of *c.*1715, is a nickname given to the Duke of Gordon.

The **cock-of-the-walk**, reflecting the dominance of the male bird, is a person whose supremacy in a particular circle or sphere is undisputed; the phrase is recorded from the mid 19th century.

Cock robin is a familiar name for a male robin, especially in nursery rhymes.

That cock won't fight means that won't do; the expression, which refers to cockfighting, is recorded from the late 18th century.

cock-a-hoop extremely and obviously pleased, especially about a triumph or success; the expression dates from the mid 17th century, and comes from the phrase *set cock a hoop*, of unknown origin, apparently denoting the action of turning on the tap and allowing liquor to flow (prior to a drinking session).

Cockaigne an imaginary land of idleness and luxury. Recorded from Middle English, the word comes from Old French *cocaigne*, as in *pais de cocaigne* 'fool's paradise', ultimately from Middle Low German *kokenje* 'small sweet cake', diminutive of *koke* 'cake'.

cockatrice a ➤ BASILISK; in heraldry, a mythical animal depicted as a two-legged dragon (or ➤ WYVERN) with a cock's head.

Recorded from late Middle English, the word comes via Old French from Latin *calcatrix* 'tracker' (from *calcare* 'to tread or track'), translating Greek *ikhneumōn* 'tracker', see ➤ ICHNEUMON.

cockcrow a poetic or literary term for dawn, as signalled by the crowing of a cock; reference may also be made to the story of ➤ St PETER's denial, of which Jesus had

warned him (Matthew 26:34), 'before the cock crow, thou shalt deny me thrice.'

according to Cocker reliably, correctly; recorded from the early 19th century, and deriving from the name of Edward *Cocker* (1631–75), English arithmetician, reputed author of a popular text, *Arithmetick*.

cockle the ribbed mollusc shell which became the symbol of St ➤ JAMES *the Great* and his shrine of ➤ SANTIAGO *de Compostela*.

A **cockle-hat** was a hat with a cockle-shell or scallop-shell in it, worn by pilgrims, especially those travelling to Santiago.

cockles of one heart one's deepest feelings; recorded from the late 17th century, and perhaps deriving from a perceived resemblance in shape between a heart and a cockle-shell.

Cockney a native of East London, traditionally one born within hearing of Bow Bells; the dialect or accent typical of such a person (see also ➤ MOCKNEY).

The word is recorded from late Middle English, denoting a pampered child; the origin is uncertain, but it is apparently not the same word as Middle English *cokeney* 'cock's egg', denoting a small misshapen egg (probably from cock + obsolete *ey* 'egg'). A later sense was 'a town-dweller regarded as affected or puny', from which the current sense arose in the early 17th century.

cockpit a place for holding cockfights; in figurative usage, the place where a contest is fought out. The word is also recorded from the late 16th century used for a theatre, in Shakespeare's *Henry V* (1599).

The Cockpit was the name of a 17th-century London theatre, built on the site of a cockpit, and was later used for a block of buildings on or near the site of a cockpit built by Henry VII, used from the 17th century as government offices, and from this used informally for 'the Treasury' and 'the Privy Council chambers'.

In the early 18th century the term was in nautical use, denoting an area in the aft lower deck of a man-of-war where the wounded were taken, later coming to mean the 'pit' or well in a sailing yacht from which it was steered.

The **cockpit of Europe** is a name for Belgium, as a part of Europe on which European conflicts have frequently been fought; the idea is first recorded in the writings of the Anglo-Welsh man of letters James Howell (*c.*1594–1666).

cocksure presumptuously or arrogantly confident, the first element from archaic *cock* as a euphemism for *God*.

Cocytus in Greek mythology, one of the rivers of Hades. It was also the name of a tributary of the Acheron in Epirus.

Code Napoléon the French legal code drawn up under Napoleon I in 1804.

codex an ancient manuscript text in book form. The word comes (in the late 16th century, denoting a collection of statutes or set of rules) from Latin, literally 'block of wood', later denoting a block split into leaves or tablets for writing on, hence a book.

codswallop nonsense. Recorded from the 1960s, and sometimes said to be named after Hiram *Codd*, who invented a bottle for fizzy drinks (1875); the derivation remains unconfirmed.

coelacanth a large bony marine fish with a three-lobed tail fin and fleshy pectoral fins, found chiefly around the Comoro Islands near Madagascar. It is thought to be related to the ancestors of land vertebrates and was known only from fossils until one was found alive in 1938.

The name is recorded from the mid 19th century, and comes via the modern Latin genus name from Greek *koîlos* 'hollow' + *akantha* 'spine' (because its fins have hollow spines).

coenobite a member of a monastic community; the word is recorded from late Middle English and comes via Old French or ecclesiastical Latin, and late Latin, from Greek *koinobion* 'convent', from *koinos* 'common' + *bios* 'life'.

Coeur de Lion nickname (French, literally 'heart of a lion') of Richard I of England (1157–99).

coffin corner in American football, the corner formed by the goal line and sideline.

Coffin Texts texts inscribed on the inside of coffins during the Middle Kingdom in Egypt.

the cogito in philosophy, the principle establishing the existence of a being from the fact of its thinking or awareness.

The word in Latin means 'I think', and comes from the formula, **cogito, ergo sum** 'I think or am thinking, therefore I am' of the French philosopher and mathematician René Descartes (1596–1650). The formulation was first made in French, as *'Je pense, donc je suis'* in *Le Discours de la méthode* (1637); it is now generally quoted from the 1641 Latin edition.

cognizance in heraldry, a distinctive device or mark, especially an emblem or badge formerly worn by retainers of a noble house.

shuffle off this mortal coil die; originally a quotation from Shakespeare's *Hamlet* (1601).

Colchis an ancient region south of the Caucasus mountains at the eastern end of the Black Sea. In classical mythology it was the goal of Jason's expedition for the ➤ GOLDEN *Fleece*, and the home of ➤ MEDEA.

cold at a low temperature (literally and figuratively); **in cold blood** means without feeling or mercy, ruthlessly. According to medieval physiology, blood was naturally hot, so this phrase refers to an unnatural state in which someone can do a (hot-blooded) deed of passion or violence without the normal heating of the blood.

Cold comfort is poor or inadequate consolation, with reference to a traditional view that charity is often given in a perfunctory or uncaring way. **Cold Comfort Farm** is the title of a novel (1932) by Stella Gibbons, which depicts the fated, poverty-stricken, and generally uncomfortable rural lives of the Starkadder family and their matriarch, Aunt Ada Doom (see also ➤ *something* NASTY *in the woodshed*); the book was written as a parody of the work of such regional writers as Mary Webb (1881–1927).

Cold dark matter is matter consisting of massive particles of low energy, which is believed by some scientists to exist in the universe but which has not yet been directly observed.

Cold fusion is nuclear fusion occurring at or close to room temperature. Claims for its discovery in 1989 are generally held to have been mistaken.

Cold turkey is the abrupt and complete cessation of taking a drug to which one is addicted; the phrase derives from one of the symptoms, the development of 'goose-flesh' on the skin from a sudden chill, caused by this.

Cold war is a state of political hostility existing between the Soviet bloc countries and the Western powers after the Second World

War, characterized by threats, violent propaganda, subversive activities, and other measures short of open warfare.

Colditz a medieval castle near Leipzig in Germany, used as a top-security camp for Allied prisoners in the Second World War.

collaboration traitorous cooperation with an enemy; the term was particularly used of those in occupied countries who cooperated with the Axis forces in the Second World War.

collect in church use, a short prayer, especially one assigned to a particular day or season. The word is recorded from Middle English, and comes via Old French from Latin *collecta* 'gathering', feminine past participle of *colligere* 'gather together'.

College of Arms in the UK, a corporation which officially records and grants armorial bearings. Formed in 1484, it comprises three Kings of Arms, six heralds, and four pursuivants.

Collins a letter of thanks for hospitality or entertainment, sent by a departed guest, from such a letter sent by **Mr Collins**, the pompous young clergyman in Jane Austen's *Pride and Prejudice* (1813), to the Bennet family.

Cologne a German city on the Rhine, famous in the Middle Ages for its shrine of the Wise Men of the East, commonly called the **Three Kings of Cologne** (see ➤ *the* THREE *Kings*).

colophon a publisher's emblem or imprint, especially one on the title page of a book; formerly also, a statement at the end of a book, typically with a printer's emblem, giving information about its authorship and printing.

The word is recorded from the early 17th century (denoting a finishing touch), and comes via late Latin from Greek *kolophōn* 'summit or finishing touch'.

Colosseum the name since medieval times of the *Amphitheatrum Flavium*, a vast amphitheatre in Rome, begun *c.*75 AD; the name is Latin, and is the neuter of *colosseus* 'gigantic'.

Epistle to the Colossians a book of the New Testament, an epistle of St Paul to the Church at Colossae in Phrygia.

colossus a person or thing of enormous size, importance or ability; the word in this

sense is recorded from the early 17th century, and derives from the ➤ COLOSSUS *of Rhodes.*

Colossus was the name given to the electronic digital computer, one of the first of its kind, which was developed at ➤ BLETCHLEY *Park* in the Second World War to break German codes, the use of which was said to have shortened the war by two years.

Colossus of Rhodes a huge bronze statue of the sun god Helios, one of the Seven Wonders of the World. Built *c.*292–280 BC, it stood beside the harbour entrance at Rhodes for about fifty years. *Colossus* comes via Latin from Greek *kolossos*, applied by Herodotus to the statues of Egyptian temples.

St Columba (*c.*521–97), Irish abbot and missionary. He established the monastery at Iona in *c.*563, and converted the Picts to Christianity. St Columba contributed significantly to the literature of Celtic Christianity. His feast day is 9 June.

Columbine a character in Italian *commedia dell'arte*, the mistress of ➤ HARLEQUIN; the name comes via French from Italian *Colombina*, feminine of *colombino* 'dovelike', from *colombo* 'dove'.

Christopher Columbus (1451–1506), Italian-born Spanish explorer. He persuaded the Spanish monarchs, Ferdinand and Isabella, to sponsor an expedition to sail across the Atlantic in search of Asia and to prove that the world was round. In 1492 he set sail with three small ships and discovered the New World (in fact various Caribbean islands).

Columbus Day in the US is a legal holiday commemorating the discovery of the New World by Christopher Columbus in 1492. It is observed by most states on the second Monday of October.

comb a comb (for carding wool) is the emblem of ➤ *St* BLAISE.

Comédie Française the French national theatre (used for both comedy and tragedy), in Paris, founded in 1680 by Louis XIV, and reconstituted by Napoleon I in 1803. It is organized as a cooperative society in which each actor holds a share or part-share.

comedy professional entertainment consisting of jokes and satirical sketches, intended to make an audience laugh. Recorded from late Middle English (as a genre of drama, also denoting a narrative poem with a happy ending, as in Dante's *Divine Comedy*), the word comes via Old French and Latin from Greek *kōmōidia*, from *kōmōidos* 'comic poet', from *kōmos* 'revel' + *aoidos* 'singer'.

Commander of the Faithful one of the titles of a caliph, first assumed (*c.*640) by Omar I.

commando a soldier specially trained for carrying out raids; a unit of such troops. The term is recorded from the late 18th century (denoting a militia, originally consisting of Boers in South Africa); it comes ultimately from Portuguese *commandar* 'to command'.

commedia dell'arte an improvised kind of popular comedy in Italian theatres in the 16th–18th centuries, based on stock characters. Actors adapted their comic dialogue and action according to a few basic plots (commonly love intrigues) and to topical issues.

Committee of Public Safety a French governing body set up in April 1793, during the Revolution. Consisting of nine (later twelve) members, it was at first dominated by Danton, but later came under the influence of Robespierre, when it initiated the Terror. The Committee's power ended with the fall of Robespierre in 1794, and it was dissolved in 1795.

common shared by a number of people; belonging to or affected by the whole of a community.

Common law is the part of English law that is derived from custom and judicial precedent rather than statutes, and often contrasted with *statute law*; the body of English law as adopted and adapted by the different States of the US.

The **common man** is a representative of the general populace or the masses. The **century of the common man** is the 20th century; the term derives from a speech by the American Democratic politician Henry Wallace (1888–1965), made during the Second World War.

The **Common Market** was a name for the European Economic Community or European Union, used especially in the 1960s and 1970s.

Common or garden means ordinary. The phrase is recorded in it literal sense ('the Common or Garden Nightshade') from the mid 17th century; this extended usage dates from the late 19th century.

Common Prayer is the Church of England liturgy, originally set forth in the ➤ BOOK *of Common Prayer*.

Common sense was originally an 'internal' sense which was regarded as the common

bond or centre of the five senses, in which the various impressions received were reduced to the unity of a common consciousness.

the Commons in historical usage, the common people regarded as a part of a political system, especially in Britain. In the UK, *the Commons* is also short for **the House of Commons**, the elected chamber of Parliament.

commonwealth the body politic; a nation, viewed as a community in which everyone has an interest. The term is recorded from late Middle English, originally as two words, denoting public welfare.

The **Commonwealth** is the name given to the republican period of government in Britain between the execution of Charles I in 1649 and the Restoration of Charles II in 1660.

Commonwealth (also called **Commonwealth of Nations**) is also now used for an international association consisting of the UK together with states that were previously part of the British Empire, and dependencies. The British monarch is the symbolic head of the Commonwealth.

Commonwealth Day is the second Monday in March, celebrating the British Commonwealth. It was instituted to commemorate assistance given to Britain by the colonies during the Boer War (1899–1902).

the **commonwealth of learning** is learned people collectively; the phrase is recorded from the mid 17th century.

the Commune the group which seized the municipal government of Paris in the French Revolution and played a leading part in the Reign of Terror until suppressed in 1794.

The Commune is also the name given to the municipal government organized on communalistic principles elected in Paris in 1871. Its adherents were known as **Comunards**. It was soon brutally suppressed by government troops. Also called **the Paris Commune**.

communion the service of Christian worship at which bread and wine are consecrated and shared; the ➤ EUCHARIST.

communion of saints a fellowship between Christians living and dead.

community charge (in the UK) a tax, introduced by the Conservative government in 1990 (1989 in Scotland), levied locally on every adult in a community. It was replaced in 1993 by the council tax. Informally called the ➤ POLL *tax*.

Comnenus name of an imperial Byzantine dynasty of the 11th and 12th centuries.

compass the use of the compass for navigation at sea was reported from China *c*.1100, western Europe 1187, Arabia *c*.1220, and Scandinavia *c*.1300, although it probably dates from much earlier. Since the early 20th century the magnetic compass has been superseded by the gyrocompass as primary equipment for ships and aircraft.

The word is recorded in Middle English in various senses ('measure', 'artifice', 'circumscribed area', and 'pair of compasses') which also occur in Old French, from which the word comes, but their development and origin are uncertain. The transference of sense to the magnetic compass is held to have occurred in the related Italian word *compasso*, from the circular shape of the compass box.

See also ➤ BOX *the compass*.

compline the seventh and last of the daytime canonical hours of prayer; the office, originally directed to be said immediately before retiring for the night, appointed for this hour.

Compostela the Spanish city of ➤ SANTIAGO *de Compostela*, which has been in the medieval period a pilgrimage centre for its shrine of ➤ St JAMES *the Great*.

Comus revelry personified; the term comes from Milton's *Masque of Comus* (1637), in which Comus himself is a pagan god of Milton's invention.

Conan the Barbarian sword and sorcery fantasy hero, otherwise known as **Conan of Cimmeria**, noted for his strength, fighting skills, and enjoyment of physical pleasures; the character was originally created by the American writer Robert E. Howard (1906–36), and in the 1982 film was played by Arnold Schwarzenegger.

the Concert of Europe the chief European powers acting together, used particularly of post-Napoleonic Europe; the term was used by Gladstone in a speech at Midlothian (1880).

conch a shell of this kind blown like a trumpet is often depicted as played by Tritons and other mythological figures.

conclave in the Roman Catholic Church, the assembly of cardinals for the election of a pope; the meeting place for such an assembly. The word is recorded from late Middle English (denoting a private room) and comes via French from Latin *conclave* 'lockable room', from *con-* 'with' + *clavis* 'key'.

concordance an alphabetical list of the words (especially the important ones) present in a text or body of texts, usually with citations of the passages concerned or with the context displayed on a computer screen.

Concorde a supersonic airliner, the only one to have entered operational service, able to cruise at twice the speed of sound. Produced through Anglo-French cooperation, it made its maiden flight in 1969 and has been in commercial service since 1976.

concrete jungle a city or an area of a city with a high density of large, unattractive, modern buildings and which is perceived as an unpleasant living environment.

conduct unbecoming unsuitable or inappropriate behaviour; the phrase comes from *Articles of War* (1872) 'Any officer who shall behave in a scandalous manner, unbecoming the character of an officer and a gentleman shall…be CASHIERED'; the Naval Discipline Act, 10 August 1860 uses the words 'conduct unbecoming the character of an Officer'.

coney a rabbit; originally the preferred term (now superseded by *rabbit*) and still in use in heraldry, and for the animal's fur. In the 16th and 17th centuries, **coney-catching** was a term for duping or deceiving a gullible victim.

Coney Island a resort and amusement park on the Atlantic coast in Brooklyn, New York City, on the south shore of Long Island.

Confederate States the eleven Southern states, Alabama, Arkansas, Florida, Georgia, Louisiana, Mississippi, North Carolina, South Carolina, Tennessee, Texas, and Virginia, which seceded from the United States in 1860–1, thus precipitating the American Civil War.

Conference on Disarmament a committee with forty nations as members that seeks to negotiate multilateral disarmament. It was constituted in 1962 as the **Committee on Disarmament** (with eighteen nations as members) and adopted its present title in 1984. It meets in Geneva.

confessio a tomb in which a martyr or confessor is buried, and, by extension, the whole structure erected over it; also, the crypt or shrine under the high-altar, or the part of the altar, in which the relics are placed.

confession a formal admission of one's sins with repentance and desire of absolution, especially privately to a priest as a religious duty.

Confession is also used for a statement of faith setting out essential religious doctrine (also called **confession of faith**); (with capital initial) the religious body or Church sharing a confession of faith.

confetti small pieces of coloured paper traditionally thrown over a bride and bridegroom by their wedding guests after the marriage ceremony has taken place. The term is recorded from the early 19th century, and originally denoted the real or imitation sweets thrown during Italian carnivals; it comes from Italian, literally 'sweets', from Latin *confectum* 'something prepared'.

Confiteor a form of prayer confessing sins, used in the Roman Catholic Mass and some other sacraments. The word is Latin, 'I confess', from the formula *Confiteor Deo Omnipotenti* 'I confess to Almighty God'.

confraternity a brotherhood, especially with a religious or charitable purpose.

Confucianism a system of philosophical and ethical teachings founded by the Chinese philosopher *Confucius* (551–479 BC). His ideas about the importance of practical moral values, collected by his disciples in the *Analects*, and developed by Mencius, formed the basis of *Confucianism*.

confusable a word or phrase that is easily confused with another in meaning or usage, such as *mitigate*, which is often confused with *militate*.

confusion worse confounded complete confusion, deriving from a usage by Milton in *Paradise Lost* (1667).

Congress the national legislative body of the United States, which meets at the Capitol in Washington DC; it was established by the Constitution of 1787 and is composed of the Senate and the House of Representatives.

a name to conjure with a person who is important within a particular sphere of activity, with reference to the magical practice of summoning a spirit to do one's bidding by invoking a powerful name or using a spell.

Connacht a province in the south-west of Ireland; with Ulster, Munster, and Leinster one of the traditional four divisions of the island. Also called *Connaught*.

Hell or Connaught is a summary of the choice offered to the Catholic population of Ireland, transported to the western counties of *Connacht* to make room for settlers, traditionally attributed to Oliver Cromwell.

Conqueror an epithet of various rulers, especially William, duke of Normandy and (after 1066) king of England (see ➤ NORMAN *Conquest*).

The phrase **came over with the Conqueror**, when applied to a family, means old and distinguished; supposedly, identified as one of the Norman families accompanying William of Normandy to England.

conquistador a conqueror, especially one of the Spanish conquerors of Mexico and Peru in the 16th century.

prisoner of conscience a person detained or imprisoned because of his or her religious or political beliefs; the term is recorded from the early 1960s, and is particularly associated with the campaigns of ➤ AMNESTY *International*.

conscientious objector a person who for reasons of conscience refuses to conform to the requirements of law, especially one who objects to serving in the armed forces. The term is recorded from the late 19th century, but came to prominence with national conscription in the First World War, when those claiming to be *conscientious objectors* had to establish their status before a tribunal; the derogatory shortening *conchy* dates from this period.

conscript fathers the body of Roman senators; a translation of Latin *patres conscripti*, the collective title by which the Roman senators were addressed (used also as a title by the Venetian senate).

age of consent the age at which a person's consent to sexual intercourse is valid in law.

consenting adult an adult who willingly agrees to engage in a sexual act.

consolamentum the spiritual baptism of the Cathars.

Consols British government securities without redemption date and with fixed annual interest; the term dates from the late 18th century, and is a contraction of *consolidated annuities*.

conspicuous by one's absence obviously not present in a place where one or it should be, from a speech made in 1859 by the British Whig statesman Lord John Russell (1792–1878). Lord John attributed the coinage to a passage in Tacitus, relating to the funeral procession in AD 22, of Junia, sister of Brutus and widow of Cassius, in which the effigies of the two men were said to be most conspicuous because they were not to be seen.

a conspiracy of silence an agreement to say nothing about an issue that should be generally known. The phrase appears to have originated with the French philosopher Auguste Comte (1798–1857).

Council of Constance the 16th ecumenical council of the Roman Catholic Church (1414–18), which brought to an end the ➤ GREAT *Schism*.

Constantine (*c*.274–337), Roman emperor; known as **Constantine the Great**. He was the first Roman emperor to be converted to Christianity and in 324 made Christianity a state religion, though paganism was also tolerated. In 330 he moved his capital from Rome to Byzantium, renaming it *Constantinopolis* (➤ CONSTANTINOPLE). In the Orthodox Church he is venerated as a saint.

Constantinople the former name for Istanbul from AD 330 (when it was given its name by Constantine the Great) to the capture of the city by the Turks in 1453. *Constantinople* is the anglicized form of *Constantinopolis*, 'city of Constantine'.

Constituent Assembly the parliamentary assembly of revolutionary France, set up in 1789 under the formal name of *Assemblée Nationale Constituante*; it was replaced by the Legislative Assembly in 1791.

The name Constituent Assembly was subsequently used for the body elected in 1917 in the first phase of the Russian Revolution; it was dissolved in 1918 by the Bolsheviks.

the Constitution the basic written set of principles and precedents of federal government in the US, which came into operation in 1789 and has since been modified by twenty-six amendments.

The **Constitution State** is an informal name for Connecticut, where the draft US Constitution was ratified in 1788.

consubstantiation the doctrine, especially in Lutheran belief, that the substance of the bread and wine coexists with the body and blood of Christ in the Eucharist. It was formulated in opposition to the doctrine of ➤ TRANSUBSTANTIATION.

consul in ancient Rome, one of the two annually elected chief magistrates who jointly ruled the republic; any of the three chief magistrates of the first French republic (1799–1804). The word derives ultimately from Latin *consulere* 'take counsel'.

contango on the British Stock Exchange, the normal situation in which the spot or cash price of a commodity is lower than the forward price; formerly, a percentage paid by a buyer of stock to postpone transfer to a future settling day. On the British Stock Exchange, **contango day** is the eighth day before a settling day.

Recorded from the mid 19th century, the word is probably an arbitrary formation on the pattern of Latin verb forms ending in -*o* in the first person singular, perhaps with the idea 'I make contingent'.

contemplative a person whose life is devoted primarily to prayer, especially in a monastery or convent.

contempt of court the offence of being disobedient to or disrespectful of a court of law and its officers.

Continental Congress in the US, each of the three congresses held by the American colonies in revolt against British rule in 1774, 1775, and 1776 respectively. The second Congress, convened in the wake of the battles at Lexington and Concord, created a Continental Army, which fought and eventually won the ➤ *War of* AMERICAN *Independence*.

Continental Divide the main series of mountain ridges in North America, chiefly the crests of the Rocky Mountains, which form a watershed separating the rivers flowing eastwards into the Atlantic Ocean or the Gulf of Mexico from those flowing westwards into the Pacific.

continental drift the gradual movement of the continents across the earth's surface through geological time.

The reality of continental drift was confirmed in the 1960s, leading to the theory of plate tectonics. It is believed that a single supercontinent called Pangaea broke up to form Gondwana and Laurasia, which further split to form the present-day continents.

continuous creation the creation of matter as a continuing process throughout time, especially as postulated in steady state theories of the universe.

conundrum a question asked for amusement, typically one with a pun in its answer; a riddle; a confusing and difficult problem or question. The word is of unknown origin, but is first recorded (in the late 16th century) in a work by Thomas Nashe, as a term of abuse for a crank or pedant, later coming to denote a whim or fancy, also a pun. Current senses date from the late 17th century.

conventicle a secret or unlawful religious meeting of people with nonconformist views; the **Conventicles Acts** were two acts of Charles II, 'to prevent and suppress seditious Conventicles'.

conversus former term for a lay-brother in a Benedictine monastery.

Convocation in the Church of England, a representative assembly of clergy of the province of Canterbury or York.

Captain James Cook (1728–79), English explorer. On his first expedition to the Pacific (1768–71), he charted the coasts of New Zealand and New Guinea as well as exploring the east coast of Australia and claiming it for Britain. He made two more voyages to the Pacific before being killed in a skirmish with native people in Hawaii.

cook someone's goose spoil someone's plans; cause someone's downfall. The underlying idea seems to be that a goose was cherished and fattened up for a special occasion.

Cook's tour a rapid tour of many places; named after the travel firm founded by the English businessman Thomas *Cook* (1808–92). In 1841 he organized the first publicly advertised excursion train in England; the success of this venture led him to organize further excursions both in Britain and abroad.

cookie in North America, a sweet biscuit; the **Cookie Monster**, a a member of the ► MUPPETS, was a large blue friendly creature characterized by its sweet tooth and voracious appetite.

The way the cookie crumbles means, how things turn out. It is often used retrospectively, to suggest that the position is undesirable but unalterable.

too many cooks spoil the broth proverbial saying, meaning that if too many people are involved in a task or activity, it will not be done well; it is recorded from the late 16th century. The allusive phrase *too many cooks* is also used.

cool as a cucumber completely calm; the term is recorded from the mid 18th century.

Cool Britannia Britain, perceived as a stylish and fashionable place; especially (in the late 1990s) as represented by the international success of and interest in contemporary British art, popular music, film, and fashion.

Copenhagen name of the Duke of Wellington's chestnut charger, which he rode during the Peninsular campaign and at Waterloo. *Copenhagen*, who was the grandson of the famous racehorse ► ECLIPSE, was buried at Stratfield Saye with full military honours. He figures in the equestrian statue of Wellington opposite the entrance of Apsley House in London.

Copernican system the theory that the sun is the centre of the solar system, with the planets (including the earth) orbiting round it, formulated by the Polish astronomer Nicolaus *Copernicus* (1473–1543). He proposed a model of the solar system in which the planets orbited in perfect circles around the sun, and his work ultimately led to the overthrow of the established geocentric cosmology. He published his astronomical theories in *De Revolutionibus Orbium Coelestium* (1543).

King Cophetua a legendary African king who fell in love with and married a beggar girl; the story is told in one of the ballads in Percy's *Reliques* (1765), and was the subject of one of Burne-Jones's paintings, *King Cophetua and the Beggar Maid* (1884).

copper the earliest metal to be used by humans; the **Copper Age** is the Chalcolithic period, especially in SE Europe, when weapons were made of copper. *Copper* was also associated by alchemists with the planet Venus.

  copper-bottomed means thoroughly reliable, certain not to fail; figuratively, from earlier usage referring to the copper sheathing of the bottom of a ship.

Recorded from Old English (in form *copor*, *coper*), the word is ultimately based on late Latin *cuprum*, from Latin *cyprium aes* 'Cyprus metal', so named because Cyprus was the chief source.

copperhead in the US, this venomous snake has become the type of secret or unexpected hostility, since unlike the rattlesnake it strikes without warning. During the American Civil War, *Copperhead* was a derogatory nickname among Unionists for a Northern sympathizer with the Secessionists of the South.

Copt a native Egyptian in the Hellenistic and Roman periods; a member of the Coptic Church. **Coptic**, the language of the Copts, represents the final stage of ancient Egyptian. It now survives only as the liturgical language of the **Coptic Church**, the native Christian Church in Egypt, traditionally founded by St Mark, and adhering to the Monophysite doctrine rejected by the Council of Chalcedon. Long persecuted after the Muslim Arab conquest of Egypt in the 7th century, the Coptic community now make up about 5 per cent of Egypt's population.

The name comes via French *Copte* or modern Latin *Coptus*, from Arabic *al-kibt*, *al-kubt* 'Copts', and ultimately (via Coptic) from Greek *Aiguptios* 'Egyptian'.

copybook a book containing models of handwriting for learners to imitate.

copyright the exclusive legal right, given to the originator or their assignee for a fixed number of years, to print, publish, perform, film, or record literary, artistic, or musical material, and to authorize others to do the same.

A **copyright library** is a library entitled to a free copy of each book published in the UK. The copyright libraries in the British Isles are the British Library, the Bodleian Library, Cambridge University Library, the National Library of Wales, the National Library of Scotland, and the library of Trinity College, Dublin.

Coral Sea a part of the western Pacific lying between Australia, New Guinea, and Vanuatu, the scene of a naval battle between US and Japanese carriers in 1942.

corban an offering or sacrifice made to God by the ancient Hebrews; the treasury of the Temple at Jerusalem (the earliest sense in English) as where such offerings were

placed. The word comes ultimately via popular Latin and New Testament Greek from Hebrew *qorbān* 'offering'.

corbel a projection jutting out from a wall to support a structure above it; a **corbel table** is a projecting course of bricks or stones resting on corbels. Recorded from late Middle English, the word comes from Old French, diminutive of *corp* 'crow', from Latin *corvus* 'raven', perhaps because of the shape of a corbel, resembling a crow's beak.

corbie in Scottish usage, a raven, crow, or rook; the word is recorded from late Middle English, and comes, like ➤ CORBEL, from Old French *corp* 'crow'.

A **corbie messenger** is one who returns too late or not at all, with reference to Genesis 8:7, and the raven sent out from the ark.

Corcovado a high peak on the south side of Rio de Janeiro; a gigantic statue of Christ, 40 m (131 ft) high, named 'Christ the Redeemer', stands on its summit.

Charlotte Corday 1768–93), French political assassin. She became involved with the Girondists and in 1793 assassinated the revolutionary leader Jean Paul Marat in his bath; she was found guilty of treason and guillotined four days later.

Cordelia in Shakespeare's play, the youngest of the three daughters of King ➤ LEAR, who is rejected by her father as ungrateful when she refrains from extravagant statements of her love for him, but who unlike her elder sisters is loyal to him; she is seen as a figure of loving duty and self-sacrifice.

Cordelier a Franciscan Observant; so named from the knotted cord (Old French *cordelle* 'small rope') which these friars wore around the waist.

The *Cordeliers* were one of the political clubs of the French Revolution; the name derived from the meeting-place of the club, a former convent of the Franciscan Cordeliers.

Cordoba a city in Andalusia, southern Spain. Founded by the Carthaginians, it was under Moorish rule from 711 to 1236, and as capital of the most powerful of the Arab states in Spain, it was a centre of learning and culture, and was renowned for its architecture, particularly the Great Mosque. (See also ➤ CORDOVAN.)

cordon bleu a cook of the highest class. The term (in French, literally 'blue ribbon') is recorded from the mid 18th century; the blue ribbon once signified the highest order of chivalry in the reign of the Bourbon kings.

cordon sanitaire a guarded line preventing anyone from leaving an area infected by a disease and thus spreading it; the term is recorded from the 19th century.

cordovan a kind of soft leather made originally from goatskin and now from horsehide; the word is recorded from the late 16th century, and comes from *Cordova*, a variant of ➤ CORDOBA, where it was originally made.

cordwainer a shoemaker (still used in the names of guilds); the word is recorded from Middle English, and comes ultimately from Old French *cordewan* 'of Cordoba' (see ➤ CORDOVAN).

Corinth a city on the north coast of the Peloponnese, Greece, a prominent city state in ancient Greece, which was celebrated for its artistic adornment, and which became a type of luxury and licentiousness.

From the proverbial luxury and licentiousness of Corinth, **Corinthian** was used from the late 16th century for a wealthy (and profligate) man. In the early 19th century the term was extended to mean a man of fashion, and finally, a wealthy amateur of sport.

Corinthian also means relating to or denoting the lightest and most ornate of the classical orders of architecture (used especially by the Romans), characterized by flared capitals with rows of acanthus leaves.

Corinthian brass, an alloy produced at Corinth, said to be of gold, silver, and copper, was much prized in ancient times as the material of costly ornaments.

Epistle to the Corinthians either of two books of the New Testament, epistles of St Paul to the Church at Corinth.

Gaius Marcius Coriolanus (5th century BC), Roman general, who got his name from the capture of the Volscian town of Corioli, but whose pride, despite his military prowess and fame, was so offensive to the people of Rome that he was banished. According to legend, he subsequently led a Volscian army against the city and was only turned back by the pleas of his mother and wife.

cormorant this large diving bird is taken as the type of an insatiably greedy or rapacious person. The name is recorded from Middle English, and comes via Old French

from medieval Latin *corvus marinus* 'sea-raven'.

corn the chief cereal crop of a district, especially (in England) wheat or (in Scotland) oats.

A **corn dolly** is a symbolic or decorative model of a human figure, made of plaited straw.

Corn in Egypt means a plentiful supply; from Genesis 42:2.

In the UK, the **Corn Laws** were a series of 19th-century laws introduced to protect British farmers from foreign competition by allowing grain to be imported only after the price of home-grown wheat had risen above a certain level. They had the unintended effect of forcing up bread prices and were eventually repealed in 1846.

fight one's corner defend one's position or interests. A boxing metaphor; opponents take diagonally opposite corners of the ring.

cornerstone a stone that forms the base of a corner of a building, joining two walls; an important quality or feature on which a particular thing depends or is based (often in biblical allusions, as in Isaiah 28:16).

Cornhusker State an informal name for Nebraska.

cornucopia a symbol of plenty consisting of a goat's horn overflowing with flowers, fruit, and corn. The word comes (in the early 16th century) from late Latin, from Latin *cornu copiae* 'horn of plenty', a mythical horn able to provide whatever is desired, in Greek mythology supposedly the horn of the goat ➤ AMALTHEA which suckled Zeus.

Duchy of Cornwall an estate vested in the Prince of Wales, consisting of properties in Cornwall and elsewhere in SW England.

coronach in Scotland or Ireland, a funeral song; the word is recorded from the early 16th century and was originally Scots, denoting the outcry of a crowd, from Scottish Gaelic *corranach* (Irish *coranach*), from *comh-* 'together' + *rànach* 'outcry'.

Coronation stone another name for the ➤ STONE *of Scone*.

Coronation Street a fictitious street in, and the title of, a television soap opera (1960–) set in a working-class street in the middle of an industrial city in the north of England.

coronet a relatively simple crown, now especially as worn by lesser royalty and peers or peeresses.

corposant an appearance of ➤ St ELMO's *fire* on a mast, rigging, or other structure; the word is recorded from the mid 16th century and comes from Old Spanish, Portuguese, and Italian *corpo santo* 'holy body'.

corpus a collection of written texts, especially the entire works of a particular author or a body of writing on a particular subject. The word (Latin, literally 'body') is recorded from late Middle English denoting an animal or human body; the textual sense dates from the early 18th century.

Corpus is now also used for a collection of written or spoken material in machine-readable form, assembled for the purpose of studying linguistic structures and frequencies.

Corpus Christi a feast of the Western Christian Church commemorating the institution of the Eucharist, observed on the Thursday after Trinity Sunday. The name is Latin, and means literally, 'body of Christ'.

the corridors of power the senior levels of government or administration, where covert influence is regarded as being exerted and significant decisions are made, from the title of C. P. Snow's novel (1964).

corroboree an Australian Aboriginal dance ceremony which may take the form of a sacred ritual or an informal gathering. The word comes from Dharuk *garaabara*, denoting a style of dancing.

corruption of blood the effect of attainder by which the person attainted could neither inherit, retain, nor transmit land.

corsair a privateer, especially one operating along the southern shore of the Mediterranean in the 17th century; the word comes (in the mid 16th century, via French) from medieval Latin *cursarius*, from *cursus* 'a raid, plunder'.

Byron's poem *The Corsair* (1814) told the story of a pirate chief, Conrad, whose chivalry and courage in the end outweigh his vices; the poem had great popular success.

the Corsican a name for Napoleon Bonaparte, who was born in Corsica; he was also called by his enemies the **Corsican ogre**.

Hernando Cortés (1485–1547), first of the Spanish conquistadores. Cortés overthrew the Aztec empire, conquering its capital,

Tenochtitlán, in 1519 and deposing the emperor, Montezuma. In the poem 'On First Looking into Chapman's Homer' (1817), Keats takes him as the type of an explorer looking at previously unknown lands, although in fact it was ➤ BALBOA rather than Cortés who was the first European to see the Pacific Ocean.

Corunna a port in NW Spain. It was the point of departure for the Armada in 1588 and the site of a battle in 1809 in the Peninsular War, at which British forces under Sir John Moore defeated the French. Moore, who was killed in the battle, was buried in the city.

Corybant a priest of the fertility and nature goddess Cybele, whose worship involved wild dances and ecstatic states; the word **corybantic**, meaning wild, frenzied, derives from the name.

Corydon a shepherd who figures in the *Idylls* of Theocritus and the *Eclogues* of Virgil, and whose name has become conventional in pastoral poetry.

Cosa Nostra a US criminal organization resembling and related to the Mafia. The name is Italian, meaning literally 'our affair'.

Cosmati name of a family of architects, sculptors, and mosaicists living in Rome in the 13th century; **Cosmati work**, a style of mosaic in which marble slabs are surrounded with borders made up of small pieces of marble and glass, is named after them.

cosmos the universe seen as a well-ordered whole; from the the Greek word *kosmos* 'order, ornament, world, or universe', so called by Pythagoras or his disciples from their view of its perfect order and arrangement.

Cossack a member of a people of southern Russia, Ukraine, and Siberia, noted for their horsemanship and military skill. The Cossacks had their origins in the 15th century when refugees from religious persecution, outlaws, adventurers, and escaped serfs banded together in settlements for protection. Under the tsars they were allowed considerable autonomy in return for protecting the frontiers; with the collapse of Soviet rule Cossack groups have reasserted their identity in both Russia and Ukraine.

The name comes through Russian from Turkic *kazak* 'vagabond, nomad', a word which is ultimately also the base of ➤ CAS-SOCK.

costermonger a dated British term for a person who sells goods, especially fruit and vegetables, from a handcart in the street. The word is recorded from the early 16th century, when it denoted an apple seller, and comes from *costard*, a kind of cooking apple of large ribbed variety.

King Cotton cotton as the dominant commercial crop of the southern American states personified; the **Cotton State** is an informal name for Alabama.

Cottonopolis was a nickname for the city of Manchester, in NW England, once a centre of the British cotton trade.

couch potato a person who takes little or no exercise and watches a lot of television. The term was coined in the US from a pun on *boob tube* as a slang expression for television; someone given to continuous viewing was a *boob tuber*, and the cartoonist Robert Armstrong drew the most familiar tuber, a potato, reclining on a couch watching TV. Following this, a club was formed called The Couch Potatoes, and the name was later registered as a trademark. (See also *mouse potato* at ➤ MOUSE.)

couchant in heraldry, (of an animal) lying with the body resting on the legs and the head raised.

counsel of perfection advice designed to guide one towards moral perfection (sometimes with reference to Matthew 19:21; ideal but impracticable advice.

count a foreign nobleman whose rank corresponds to that of an earl; the term is recorded from late Middle English, and comes via Old French from Latin *comes, comit-* 'companion, overseer, attendant', in late Latin, 'person holding a state office'.

The **Count of Britain** and the **Count of the Saxon Shore** were the two generals of the Roman province of Britannia in the 4th century.

count one's chickens treat something that has not yet happened as a certainty. With reference to the proverbial admonition *don't count your chickens before they're hatched*, recorded from the late 16th century.

Counter-Reformation the reform of the Church of Rome in the 16th and 17th centuries which was stimulated by the Protestant Reformation. Measures to oppose the spread of the Reformation were resolved on at the ➤ *Council of* TRENT (1545–63) and the Jesuit order became the spearhead of the Counter-Reformation, both within Europe and abroad. Although most of northern Europe remained Protestant, southern Germany and Poland were brought back to the Roman Catholic Church.

go to the country test public opinion by dissolving Parliament and holding a general election; the term is first recorded in Disraeli's novel *Sybil* (1845).

courant in heraldry, (of an animal) represented as running.

court card a playing card that is a king, queen, or jack of a suit. The term dates from the mid 17th century, and is an alteration of *coat card*, so named because of the decorative dress of the figures depicted.

court hand a notoriously illegible style of handwriting used in English law courts until banned in 1731.

court martial a judicial court for trying members of the armed services accused of offences against military law.

court of love an institution said to have existed in southern France in the Middle Ages, a tribunal composed of lords and ladies deciding questions of love and gallantry; such an institution in medieval literature.

Court of St James's the British sovereign's court; St James's Palace was the chief royal residence between 1660 and 1837, when Queen Victoria moved to Buckingham Palace. It is currently the official London residence of the Prince of Wales.

Courtauld Institute of Art founded by the English industrialist Samuel *Courtauld* (1876–1947). He was a collector of French Impressionist and post-Impressionist paintings. He presented his collection to the University of London, endowed the *Courtauld Institute*, and bequeathed to it his house in Portman Square, London.

courtly love a highly conventionalized medieval tradition of love between a knight and a married noblewoman, first developed by the troubadours of Southern France and extensively employed in European literature of the time. The love of the knight for his lady was regarded as an ennobling passion

and the relationship was typically uncon-
summated.

coven a group or gathering of witches who
meet regularly; the word is a variant of *covin*
(archaic term for fraud, deception; in Middle
English, denoting a company or band), and
comes via Old French from Latin *convenium*,
from *convenire* 'assemble'.

covenant in theology, an agreement which
brings about a relationship of commitment
between God and his people. The Jewish
faith is based on the biblical covenants made
with Abraham, Moses, and David. In Christian theology, the **New Covenant** is the covenant between God and the followers of
Christ, and the **Old Covenant** is the covenant
between God and Israel in the Old Testament.

Covenanter an adherent of the National
Covenant (1638) or the Solemn League and
Covenant (1643), upholding the organization
of the Scottish Presbyterian Church.

Covent Garden a district in central London, originally the convent garden of the
Abbey of Westminster. It was the site for 300
years of London's chief fruit and vegetable
market, which in 1974 was moved to Nine
Elms, Battersea. The first Covent Garden Theatre was opened in 1732; and was several
times destroyed and reconstructed. Since
1946 it has been the home of the national
opera and ballet companies, based at the
Royal Opera House (built 1888).

send to Coventry refuse to associate with
or speak to, perhaps deriving from the extreme unpopularity of soldiers stationed in
Coventry, who were cut off socially by the citizens, or because Royalist prisoners were
sent there, the city being staunchly Parliamentarian.

Coverdale's Bible the first complete
printed English Bible (1535), translated by
Miles *Coverdale* (1488–1568), English biblical
scholar. His translation was published in
Zurich while he was in exile for preaching
against confession and images. He also
edited the Great Bible of 1539 by the printer
Richard Grafton.

cow a *cow* is the emblem of ➤ St BRIDGET *of
Ireland* and St Perpetua, a 3rd-century martyr
of Carthage, who was gored by a mad heifer
in her martyrdom.
   In Egyptian mythology, the goddess
➤ HATHOR may be represented as a cow; in

Greek mythology, ➤ Io was turned into a
heifer by Zeus to protect her from Hera.

Cowes a town on the Isle of Wight, southern England, which is internationally famous as a yachting centre.

cowl a large loose hood, especially one
forming part of a monk's habit. Recorded
from Old English (in form *cugele*, *cūle*) the
word comes from ecclesiastical Latin *cuculla*,
from Latin *cucullus* 'hood of a cloak'.

coxcomb a vain and conceited man, ultimately from a variant of *cockscomb*, and referring to the design of a jester's cap.

coxswain the steersman of a ship's boat
(originally the *cock* or *cockboat*).

Coyote State an informal name for South
Dakota.

CQD the original ➤ SOS for shipping, used
in the last signals sent by the ➤ TITANIC.

Crab the zodiacal sign or constellation
➤ CANCER.

crack of dawn very early in the morning;
the term (originally US) is recorded from the
late 19th century.

crack of doom a thunder peal announcing
the Day of Judgement; originally often as a
quotation from Shakespeare's *Macbeth*.

cracker-barrel in North American usage
(especially of a philosophy), plain, simple,
and unsophisticated; with reference to the
barrels of soda crackers once found in country stores, around which informal discussions would take place between customers.

the Craft the brotherhood of ➤ FREE-
MASONS; the expression is recorded from late
Middle English.

crannog an ancient fortified dwelling constructed in a lake or marsh in Scotland or Ireland. The name is recorded from the early
17th century and comes from Irish *crannóg*,
Scottish Gaelic *crannag* 'timber structure',
from *crann* 'tree, beam'.

the Creation the bringing into of existence of the universe, especially when regarded as an act of God.

creation science the reinterpretation of
scientific knowledge in accord with belief in

the literal truth of the Bible, especially regarding the origin of matter, life, and humankind.

creationism the belief that the universe and living organisms originate from specific acts of divine creation, as in the biblical account, rather than by natural processes such as evolution.

Battle of Crécy a battle between the English and the French in 1346 near the village of Crécy-en-Ponthieu in Picardy, at which the forces of Edward III defeated those of Philip VI. It was the first major English victory of the Hundred Years War.

credit where credit is due praise should be given when it is deserved (often used in the context of conceding that praise is appropriate, even if one is reluctant to give it). Recorded from the mid 19th century, but earlier in the form 'honour where honour is due', following the rendering of Romans 13:8 in the Authorized Version and Rhemish Bible.

credo a statement of the beliefs or aims which guide someone's actions; (with capital initial) a creed of the Christian Church in Latin. The word is Latin, literally 'I believe'.

the Creed a formal statement of Christian beliefs, especially the ➤ APOSTLES' *Creed*, the ➤ ATHANASIAN *Creed*, or the ➤ NICENE *Creed*.

make one's flesh creep cause to feel disgust or revulsion; indicating that there is a physical sensation of something crawling over the skin, and causing goose-pimples.

creeping to the Cross an informal term for the Adoration of the Cross, in the Roman Catholic Service for Good Friday.

Creole a person of mixed European and black descent, especially in the Caribbean; descendant of Spanish or other European settlers in the Caribbean or Central or South America; a white descendant of French settlers in Louisiana and other parts of the southern US.

Creole also denotes a mother tongue formed from the contact of a European language (especially English, French, Spanish, or Portuguese) with local languages (especially African languages spoken by slaves in the W. Indies), usually through an earlier pidgin stage.

The name comes via French and Spanish, probably from Portuguese *crioulo* 'black person born in Brazil, home-born slave', from *criar* 'to breed', from Latin *creare* 'produce, create'.

Creon name (meaning 'prince') given to several figures in Greek myth, especially the king of Corinth with whom Jason and Medea took refuge, and the brother of ➤ JOCASTA, who became ruler of Thebes, and who as king was responsible for the death of ➤ ANTIGONE.

crescent the curved sickle shape of the waxing or waning moon; in heraldry, the representation of this as a charge or a cadence mark for a second son in England.

The **Crescent** symbolizes the political power of Islam or of the Ottoman Empire.

Crescent City is a name for New Orleans, which is built on a curve of the Mississippi.

Cressida in medieval legends of the Trojan War, the daughter of Calchas, a Trojan priest. She was faithless to her lover Troilus, a son of Priam.

Cresta Run a hazardously winding, steeply banked channel of ice built each year at the Cresta Valley, St Moritz, Switzerland, as a tobogganing course, on which competitors race on light toboggans in a characteristic head-first position. Such a run was first built in 1884.

Crete a Greek island in the eastern Mediterranean, noted for the remains of the Minoan civilization which flourished there in the 2nd millennium BC.

The **Cretan bull** was the bull captured by Hercules as the seventh of his Labours; it may have been either the bull which became the father of the ➤ MINOTAUR, or the one which carried ➤ EUROPA to Crete.

the Admirable Crichton name for the Scottish adventurer James *Crichton* (1560–*c*.85), an accomplished swordsman, poet, and scholar. He served in the French army and made a considerable impression on French and Italian universities with his skills as a polyglot orator. The epithet is recorded from 1652.

The Admirable Crichton was used as the title of a play by James Barrie (1914), in which the manservant Crichton, cast away with his employers on a desert island, becomes the natural leader of the party through his innate authority and skills.

not cricket in this informal phrase, *cricket* is taken as exemplifying fairness and rectitude.

Crimean War a war (1853–6) between Russia and an alliance of Great Britain, France, Sardinia, and Turkey. Russian aggression against Turkey led to war, with Turkey's European allies intervening to destroy Russian naval power in the Black Sea in 1854 and eventually capture the fortress city of Sebastopol in 1855 after a lengthy siege. In Britain the war was chiefly remembered for the deficiencies in the British army's medical services exposed by the work of Florence Nightingale and others.

Doctor Crippen familiar name for Hawley Harvey *Crippen* (1862–1910), American-born British murderer, who having poisoned his wife and concealed her body at their London home, sailed to Canada with his former secretary. His arrest on board ship was achieved through the intervention of radio-telegraphy, the first case of its use in apprehending a criminal. Crippen was later hanged, and his name is used allusively as the type of a notorious murderer.

St Crispin 3rd-century martyr, probably of Roman origin, who according to his legend preached in Gaul with his brother **Crispinian**; they are said to have supported themselves by shoemaking, and became patron saints of cobblers, shoemakers, and leather-workers. Their feast day is 25 October.

St Crispin's day, 25 October, on which the Battle of Agincourt took place, and which is referred to by Henry V in Shakespeare's play.

Cro-Magnon man the earliest form of modern human in Europe, associated with the Aurignacian flint industry. Their appearance *c.*35,000 years ago marked the beginning of the Upper Palaeolithic and the apparent decline and disappearance of Neanderthal man; the group persisted at least into the Neolithic period. The name comes from *Cro-Magnon*, a hill in the Dordogne, France, where remains were found in 1868.

Crockford informal name for **Crockford's Clerical Directory**, a reference book of Anglican clergy in the British Isles first issued in 1860.

crocodile a person making a hypocritical or malicious show of sorrow, often by weeping **crocodile tears**. These are said to be named from a belief that crocodiles wept while devouring or alluring their prey.

In Barrie's *Peter Pan*, ➤ *Captain* HOOK is stalked by, and finally falls victim to, the crocodile which has previously bitten off his hand.

Croesus (6th century BC), last king of Lydia *c.*560–546 BC. Renowned for his great wealth, he subjugated the Greek cities on the coast of Asia Minor before being overthrown by Cyrus the Great.

cromlech in Wales, a megalithic tomb consisting of a large flat stone laid on upright ones, a ➤ DOLMEN. In Brittany, the term denotes a circle of standing stones. The name comes via French from Breton *krommlec'h*.

Cronus in Greek mythology, the supreme god until dethroned by ➤ ZEUS. The youngest son of Uranus (Heaven) and Gaia (Earth), Cronus overthrew and castrated his father and then married his sister Rhea. Because he was fated to be overcome by one of his male children, Cronus swallowed all of them as soon as they were born, but when Zeus was born, Rhea deceived him and hid the baby away.

crony a close friend or companion. Recorded from the mid 17th century (originally as Cambridge university slang) the word comes from Greek *khronios* 'long-lasting' (here used to mean 'contemporary'), from *khronos* 'time'.

The word gained a high profile in the summer of 1998, when the Conservative leader William Hague used it in the House of Commons to describe what he saw as lobbyists with an undesirable influence as 'Featherbedding, pocket-lining, money-grabbing cronies.'

crop circle an area of standing crops which has been flattened in the form of a circle or more complex form. No general cause of *crop circles* has been identified although various natural and unorthodox explanations have been put forward; many are known to have been hoaxes.

crop-eared of a Roundhead in the English Civil War, having the hair cut very short; the term was probably intended by their opponents to associate them with those whose ears had been cut off as a punishment.

Croppy a supporter of the Irish Insurrection of 1798, whose short hair signalled his sympathy with the French Revolution; the term is recorded from *c*.1798, especially as a derogatory term in Loyalist songs.

cross a mark, object, or figure formed by two short intersecting lines or pieces; especially (with capital initial), **the Cross** on which Christ was crucified, or a representation of this.

A *cross* is the emblem of ➤ St HELENA and ➤ St PHILIP.

The **cross of Lorraine** is another term for the ➤ LORRAINE *cross*.

A **cross saltire** is a cross shaped like the letter X; this is the emblem of ➤ St ANDREW.

A **cross upside down** is the emblem of ➤ St PETER, who was crucified head downwards.

To **have one's cross to bear** is to suffer the troubles that life brings. The allusion is to Jesus (or Simon of Cyrene) carrying the Cross to Calvary for the Crucifixion. The expression is also used metaphorically in Matthew 10:38.

cross keys keys borne crosswise, as in the papal arms.

cross-legged of the effigy of a knight shown with one leg laid over the other; the popular tradition that this represents a crusader, although long-enduring, is unhistorical, since the first such effigies are not found until *c*.1250 (when the era of the Crusades was drawing to a close), and the style continued for another 80 or so years.

cross someone's palm with silver pay someone before having one's fortune told, originally by describing a cross on the fortune-teller's hand with a silver coin.

cross the floor in the British House of Commons, to change one's party allegiance, literally by moving across the *floor* or open space which divides the Government and the Opposition benches.

crossbill this finch's red plumage is said in a medieval fable to derive from the bird's having attempted to pull the nails from the cross at Christ's crucifixion.

get one's wires crossed have a misunderstanding. Originally with reference to a wrong telephone connection ('a crossed line'), which resulted in another call or calls being heard.

caught in the crossfire suffer damage or harm inadvertently as the result of the adversity of two other parties. Also very often used

in the literal sense of 'be trapped (and perhaps killed) by being between two opposing sides who are shooting at each other.'

crossroads the place where two roads cross or intersect, formerly used as a burial-place for suicides.

crossword a puzzle consisting of a grid of squares and blanks into which words crossing vertically and horizontally are written according to clues. It is said to have been invented by the journalist Arthur Wynne, whose puzzle (called a 'word-cross') appeared in a Sunday newspaper, the *New York World*, on 21 December 1913.

crow figurative uses may refer to carrion *crows* feeding on the bodies of the dead, and the bird is also taken as a type of blackness.

A *crow* is the emblem of ➤ St ANTHONY *of Egypt* and St Paul the first hermit (see ➤ St PAUL[2]), who were brought a loaf of bread by a crow or raven.

A **white crow** is a rare thing or event, a *rara avis*; the expression is recorded from the 16th century.

The phrase **as the crow flies** means 'as directly as possible' the expression is recorded from the early 19th century.

crow steps are the steplike projections on the sloping part of a gable, common in Flemish architecture and 16th- and 17th-century Scottish buildings.

crown a *crown* is the emblem of ➤ St LOUIS, ➤ St OLAF, ➤ St WENCESLAS, and other royal saints.

The expression **the Crown** is used for the reigning monarch representing a country's government, or the power or authority residing in the monarchy.

The **Crown jewels** comprise the crown and other ornaments and jewellery worn or carried by the sovereign on certain state occasions; the phrase is first recorded in English in the 17th century, in Milton's *Eikonoklastes* (1649).

The **Crown of St Stephen** is the crown of the sovereigns of Hungary, which according to tradition was presented to ➤ St STEPHEN *of Hungary* by Pope Sylvester II.

The **crown of thorns** is the circlet of thorns with which Christ was crowned in mockery, as recounted in John 19:2. The *crown of thorns* is one of the ➤ *Instruments of the* PASSION, and may be used figuratively to indicate undeserved humiliation and suffering.

The word is recorded from Middle English, and comes ultimately (via Anglo-Norman

French and Old French) from Latin *corona* 'wreath, chaplet'.

crowning glory a woman's hair; perhaps originally with an echo of 1 Corinthians 11:15, 'if a woman have long hair, it is a glory unto her.'

crozier a hooked staff carried by a bishop as a symbol of pastoral office, originally denoting the person who carried a processional cross in front of an archbishop. Recorded from Middle English, the word comes partly from Old French *croisier* 'cross-bearer', from *croix* 'cross' based on Latin *crux*; reinforced by Old French *crocier* 'bearer of a bishop's crook'.

cru in France, a vineyard or group of vineyards, especially one of recognized superior quality. The word comes from French *crû*, literally 'growth'.

crucifer a person carrying a cross or crucifix in a procession.

crucifix a representation of a cross with a figure of Christ on it. The word is recorded from Middle English and comes via Old French and ecclesiastical Latin, from Latin *cruci fixus* 'fixed to a cross'.

crucifixion the execution of a person by nailing or binding them to a cross; practised by the ancient Greeks and Romans, and considered particularly ignominious; **the Crucifixion**, the killing of Jesus Christ in such a way.

Cruden's Concordance a name for the *Biblical Concordance* first published by Alexander Cruden (1701–70) in 1737.

cruel and unusual punishment a term for punishment which is seen to exceed the bounds of what is regarded as an appropriate penal remedy for a civilized society; it derives from the Eighth Amendment (1791) to the Constitution of the United States.

be cruel to be kind act towards someone in a way which seems harsh but will ultimately be of benefit; often with reference to Hamlet's explanation of his outspoken condemnation to his mother of her second marriage.

Cruella De Vil the wicked central character of Dodie Smith's *One Hundred and One Dalmatians* (1956), who steals Dalmatian puppies for their fur.

cruets are the emblems of ➤ St JOSEPH *of Arimathea* and ➤ St VINCENT *of Saragossa*.

Cruft's the annual dog show of the British Kennel Club, named for the English showman Charles Cruft (1852–1939), who in 1886 initiated the first dog show in London.

cruise missile a low-flying missile which is guided to its target by an on-board computer; the deployment of *cruise missiles* at the US airbase at ➤ GREENHAM *Common*, Berkshire, became the focus for continuing protest in the 1970s and 1980s.

cruising for a bruising heading or looking for trouble (chiefly North American).

crumbs from the rich man's table an unfair and inadequate or unsatisfactory share of something. The allusion is biblical, from to the story of the beggar Lazarus 'desiring to be fed with the crumbs which fell from the rich man's table' (Luke 16:21).

when it comes to the crunch when (or if) a point is reached or an event occurs such that immediate and decisive action is required; recorded from the late 1930s.

Crusade a medieval military expedition, one of a series made by Europeans to recover the Holy Land from the Muslims in the 11th, 12th, and 13th centuries. The First Crusade (1096–9) resulted in the capture of Jerusalem and the establishment of **Crusader** states in the Holy Land, but the second (1147–9) failed to stop a Muslim resurgence, and Jerusalem fell to Saladin in 1187. The third (1189–92) recaptured some lost ground but not Jerusalem, while the fourth (1202–4) was diverted against the Byzantine Empire, which was fatally weakened by the resultant sack of Constantinople. The fifth (1217–21) was delayed in Egypt, where it accomplished nothing, and although the sixth (1228–9) resulted in the return of Jerusalem to Christian hands the city was lost to the Turks in 1244. The seventh (1248–54) ended in disaster in Egypt, while the eighth and last (1270–1) petered out when its leader, Louis IX of France, died on his way east.

The transferred use of *crusade* to mean a vigorous movement or enterprise against poverty or a similar social evil dates from the late 18th century. However, George W. Bush's use of the word to describe the projected 'war on terrorism' in the aftermath of 11 September, 2001 caused considerable unease.

Caped Crusader a name for the cartoon character ➤ BATMAN in his role as fearless crimefighter.

Robinson Crusoe the hero of Daniel Defoe's novel *Robinson Crusoe* (1719), who survives a shipwreck and lives on a desert island; the story is said to be based on that of the Scottish sailor Alexander Selkirk (1676–1721), who was marooned alone on one of the uninhabited Juan Fernandez Islands, 1704–9

crutch a crutch is the emblem of ➤ St GILES, who was traditionally lame.

Crutched Friars an order of mendicant friars established in Italy by 1169, which spread to England, France, and the Low Countries in the 13th century and was suppressed in 1656; the name comes (from obsolete *crouch* 'cross') from their bearing or wearing a cross, first on the top of their staves, and then on their habits, first in scarlet and then in blue.

crux a cross (from Latin); the term is recorded from the mid 17th century, chiefly in *crux ansata* ('cross with a handle'), a word for ➤ ANKH. From the early 18th century, the figurative use of the decisive or most important point at issue is recorded.

in full cry expressing an opinion loudly and forcefully. *Full cry* originated as a hunting expression referring to a pack of hounds all baying in pursuit of their quarry.

cry stinking fish disparage one's own efforts or products. From the practice of street vendors crying their wares (shouting and praising their goods) to attract customers.

cryonics the practice or technique of deep-freezing the bodies of those who have died of an incurable disease, in the hope of a future cure. The term is a contraction of cryogenics, the branch of physics dealing with the production and effects of very low temperatures.

cryptography the art of writing or solving codes; the term is recorded from the mid 17th century.

crystal originally, ice, or a clear and transparent mineral resembling ice; a form of quartz (especially **rock-crystal**) having these qualities, which in ancient and medieval belief was thought to be congealed water or ice which had been 'petrified' by some natural process. *Crystal* was believed to have magic powers, and is taken as the type of something characterized by purity and clarity. The word is recorded from late Old English, and

comes via French and Latin from Greek *krustallos* 'ice, crystal'.

From the early 17th century, *crystal* developed the sense in chemistry of a piece of a homogeneous solid substance having a natural geometrically regular form with symmetrically arranged plane faces.

crystal-gazing is looking intently into a crystal ball with the aim of seeing images relating to future or distant events.

crystal healing is the use of the supposed healing powers of crystals in alternative medicine.

The **Crystal Palace** was a large building of prefabricated iron and glass resembling a giant greenhouse, designed by Joseph Paxton for the Great Exhibition of 1851 in Hyde Park, London, and re-erected at Sydenham near Croydon; it was accidentally burnt down in 1936.

In the US, a **crystal wedding** is a 15th wedding anniversary.

crystalline sphere in ancient and medieval astronomy, a transparent sphere of the heavens postulated to lie between the fixed stars and the ➤ PRIMUM MOBILE and to account for the precession of the equinox and other motions.

Cuban Missile Crisis an international crisis in October 1962, the closest approach to nuclear war at any time between the US and the USSR. When the US discovered Soviet nuclear missiles on Cuba, President John F. Kennedy demanded their removal and announced a naval blockade of the island; the Soviet leader Khrushchev acceded to the US demands a week later.

cubism an early 20th-century style and movement in art, especially painting, in which perspective with a single viewpoint was abandoned and use was made of simple geometric shapes, interlocking planes, and, later, collage.

cubit an ancient measure of length, approximately equal to the length of a forearm. It was typically about 18 inches or 44 cm, though there was a **long cubit** of about 21 inches or 52 cm. The word comes (in Middle English) from Latin *cubitum* 'elbow, forearm, cubit'.

Cuchulain in Irish mythology, ➤ RED *Branch* hero of the Ulster cycle, and nephew of Conchubar; he defends Ulster against the forces of the queen of Connaught, but at last (through the enmity of the ➤ MORRIGAN) is killed fighting heroically against over-whelming odds.

cuckold the husband of an adulteress, often regarded as an object of derision, ultimately derived from Old French *cucu* 'cuckoo', from the cuckoo's habit of laying its egg in another bird's nest.

cuckoo many cuckoos lay their eggs in the nests of small songbirds; the cuckoo fledgling, once hatched, pushes the songbird fledglings out of the nest, giving rise to the phrase **cuckoo in the nest** for an unwelcome intruder in a place or situation.

In Britain the first call of the cuckoo (a migratory bird) is traditionally a sign of spring.

Culdee an Irish or Scottish monk of the 8th to 12th centuries, living as a recluse usually in a group of thirteen (on the analogy of Christ and his Apostles). The tradition ceased as the Celtic Church was brought under Roman Catholic rule.

The name is recorded from late Middle English, and comes from medieval Latin *culdeus*, alteration, influenced by Latin *cultores Dei* 'worshippers of God' of *kelledei* (plural, found in early Scottish records), from Old Irish *céle dé*, literally 'companion of God'.

Cullinan diamond the largest diamond known, presented by the people of the Transvaal to Edward VII as a birthday gift in 1907; two sections of it were set in the king's crown. The stone was named after Sir Thomas *Cullinan*, who had discovered the mine three years earlier.

Battle of Culloden the last pitched battle on British soil, and the final engagement of the Jacobite uprising of 1745–6, fought on *Culloden* moor near Inverness. The Hanoverian army under the Duke of Cumberland crushed the small and poorly supplied Jacobite army of Charles Edward Stuart, and a ruthless pursuit after the battle effectively prevented any chance of saving the Jacobite cause.

cultivate one's garden attend to one's own affairs; after Voltaire (1694–1778) '*Il faut cultiver notre jardin* [We must cultivate our garden]', typifying the practical philosophy adopted by ➤ CANDIDE.

cultural Chernobyl a cultural disaster; an event which is considered to be detrimental to the culture of a particular country, used originally and chiefly with reference to the opening of the Euro Disney theme park near Paris in April 1992. The phrase is a translation of French *Tchernobyl Culturel* (as used by the theatre director Ariane Mnouchkine) from the name ➤ CHERNOBYL, site of a serious nuclear accident in the Ukraine in 1986.

Cultural Revolution a political upheaval in China 1966–8 intended to bring about a return to revolutionary Maoist beliefs. Largely carried forward by the ➤ RED *Guard*, it resulted in attacks on intellectuals, a large-scale purge in party posts, and the appearance of a personality cult around Mao Zedong. It led to considerable economic dislocation and was gradually brought to a halt by premier Zhou Enlai.

Cumaean designating the ➤ SIBYL of Virgil's *Aeneid*, who had her seat near Cumae, an ancient city on the Italian coast near Naples.

Cumbria an ancient kingdom of northern Britain; since 1974 the name has been used for a modern county of NW England, formed largely from the former counties of Westmorland and Cumberland.

Cunarder a ship belonging to the *Cunard* Line, founded by Samuel Cunard (1787–1865) as the first regular steamship line for transatlantic passenger traffic.

cuneiform denoting or relating to the wedge-shaped characters used in the ancient writing systems of Mesopotamia, Persia, and Ugarit, surviving mainly impressed on clay tablets. The name comes ultimately (via French or modern Latin) from Latin *cuneus* 'wedge'.

cup a cup is the emblem of ➤ St JOHN *the Evangelist* and ➤ St BENEDICT.

cup-and-ring denoting marks cut in megalithic monuments consisting of a circular depression surrounded by concentric rings.

let this cup pass from me an appeal to be released from an ordeal; the allusion is to Christ in the Garden of Gethsemane, and his prayer 'If it be possible, let this cup pass from me' (Matthew 26:39). The implication is generally that the ordeal cannot be escaped, and must be endured.

cupboard love affection that is feigned in order to obtain something; the expression is recorded from the mid 18th century, but there is a mid-17th century example of 'all for the love of a cupboard', in which the *cupboard* represents the food it contains.

Cupid in Roman mythology, the god of love, son of Venus. He is represented as a naked winged boy with a bow and arrows, with which he wounds his victims.

Cupid's bow is a shape like that of the double-curved bow often shown carried by Cupid, especially at the top edge of a person's upper lip.

curate a member of the clergy engaged as assistant to a vicar, rector, or parish priest. The word is recorded from Middle English, and comes from medieval Latin *curatus*, from Latin *cura* 'care'.

A **curate's comfort** was a cake-stand with two or more tiers.

A **curate's egg** is a thing that is partly good and partly bad, from a cartoon in *Punch* (1895) depicting a meek curate who, given a stale egg at the bishop's table, assures his host that 'parts of it are excellent'.

curfew a regulation requiring people to remain indoors between specified hours, typically at night. Originally denoting a regulation requiring people to extinguish fires at a fixed hour in the evening, or a bell rung at that hour, from Old French *cuevrefeu*, from *cuvrir* 'cover' + *feu* 'fire'. The current sense dates from the late 19th century.

Curia the papal court at the Vatican, by which the Roman Catholic Church is governed. It comprises various Congregations, Tribunals, and other commissions and departments.

The word is recorded from the mid 19th century, and comes from Latin *curia*, denoting a division of an ancient Roman tribe, also (by extension) the senate of cities other than Rome; later the term came to denote a feudal or Roman Catholic court of justice, whence the current sense.

curiosa curiosities, especially erotic or pornographic books or articles.

curiouser and curiouser more and more curious, increasingly strange (originally as a quotation from Lewis Carroll's *Alice in Wonderland* (1865).

the Curragh a level stretch of open ground in County Kildare, Ireland, famous for its racecourse and military camp.

The **Curragh mutiny** is an informal name for the event at the Curragh camp in March 1914, when 60 cavalry officers stationed

there resigned their commissions in the belief that they were to be used to force Ulster to accept Home Rule.

curry favour ingratiate oneself with someone through obsequious behaviour, from an alteration of Middle English *curry favel*, from the name (*Favel* or *Fauvel*) of a chestnut horse in a 14th-century French romance who became a symbol of cunning and duplicity; hence 'to rub down Favel' meant to use the cunning which he personified.

curse of Scotland a name given to the nine of diamonds in a pack of cards, perhaps because it resembled the armorial bearings of Lord Stair, nine lozenges on a saltire, the number and shape of the spots being identical, and their arrangement similar. The first Earl of Stair was the object of much execration for his share in sanctioning the Massacre of Glencoe in 1692, and subsequently for the influential part played by him in bringing about the Union with England in 1707.

cursive written with the characters joined. The term dates from the late 18th century, and comes via medieval Latin from Latin *curs-* 'run'.

Cursor Mundi a northern poem dating from about 1300, surviving in seven manuscripts of about 24,000 short lines. It is founded on the works of late 12th-century Latin writers who wrote various pseudo-histories made up of hagiographic, legendary, and biblical material.

curtana the unpointed sword carried in front of English sovereigns at their coronation to represent mercy. The name is recorded from Middle English and comes from Anglo-Latin *curtana (spatha)* 'shortened (sword)', from Old French *cortain*, the name of a sword belonging to ▶ ROLAND (the point of which was damaged when it was thrust into a block of steel), from *cort* 'short', from Latin *curtus* 'cut short'.

curule denoting or relating to the authority exercised by the senior magistrates in ancient Rome, chiefly the consul and praetor, who were entitled to use the *sella curulis* ('curule seat', a kind of folding chair).

The word is recorded from the early 17th century and comes from Latin *curulis*, from *currus* 'chariot' (in which the chief magistrate was conveyed to the seat of office), from *currere* 'to run'.

Cush in the Bible, the eldest son of Ham and grandson of Noah (Genesis 10:6).

Cush is also the name of the southern part of ancient Nubia, first mentioned in Egyptian records of the Middle Kingdom. In the Bible it is the country of the descendants of Cush.

cusp in astrology, the initial point of an astrological house.

Custer's Last Stand popular name for the fight between the American cavalry and the Sioux at Little Bighorn in Montana in 1876, in which George Armstong *Custer* was killed.

custumal a written account of the customs of a manor or other local community or large establishment.

cut and run make a speedy or sudden departure from an awkward or hazardous situation rather than confront it or deal with it. Originally (in the early 18th century) a nautical phrase, meaning 'sever the anchor cable because of some emergency and make sail immediately'.

the cut of someone's jib the appearance or look of someone. Originally a nautical expression suggested by the prominence and characteristic form of the jib (a triangular sail set forward of the foremast) as the identifying characteristic of a ship. Used in this metaphorical sense since the early 19th century.

cut the mustard chiefly in North America, succeed; come up to expectations, meet requirements; *mustard* means the real thing, the genuine article.

cut to the chase come to the point (North American usage). *Cut* here is in the sense 'move to another part of the film', expressing the notion of ignoring any preliminaries and coming immediately to the most important part.

St Cuthbert (d. 687), English monk, who lived as a hermit on Farne Island before becoming bishop of Lindisfarne. After Viking raids on Lindisfarne at the end of the 9th century, Cuthbert's body was taken by the monks seeking a new home for the community; after years of travel, they settled at Durham, where Cuthbert's shrine now is. His feast day is 20 March.

St Cuthbert's beads are detached and perforated joints of fossil crinoids found along the Northumbrian coast.

St Cuthbert's duck is a name for the eider duck, which breeds on the Farne Islands.

cutpurse an archaic term for a pickpocket, with reference to stealing by cutting purses suspended from a waistband. **Moll Cutpurse** was the nickname of Mary Frith (1584–1659), on whose life Middleton and Dekker's *The Roaring Girl* (1611) was based.

Cutty Sark the only survivor of the British tea clippers, launched in 1869 and now preserved as a museum ship at Greenwich, London.

The name comes from Robert Burns's *Tam o' Shanter*, a poem about a Scottish farmer chased by a young witch who wore only her 'cutty sark' (= short shift).

Cybele a mother goddess worshipped especially in Phrygia and later in Greece (where she was associated with Demeter), Rome, and the Roman provinces, with her consort ➤ ATTIS.

Cyberia the space of virtual reality, especially viewed as a 'global village' or sphere of spiritual human interaction. The name comes from *cyber-*, combining form meaning, 'relating to electronic communications networks and virtual reality', suggested by *Siberia*.

Cyclades a large group of islands in the southern Aegean Sea, regarded in antiquity as circling around the sacred island of Delos.

Cyclops a member of a race of savage one-eyed giants, said to have been the builders of the walls of Mycenae. In the Odyssey, ➤ ODYSSEUS escaped death by blinding the one-eyed ➤ POLYPHEMUS. The name comes via Latin from Greek *Kuklōps*, literally 'round-eyed', from *kuklos* 'circle' + *ōps* 'eye'.

The term **cyclopean** is used to denote a type of ancient masonry made with massive irregular blocks, by association with the great size of the Cyclops.

cygnet a young swan; the word comes (in late Middle English) from Anglo-Norman French *cignet*, diminutive of Old French *cigne* 'swan', based on Latin *cycnus*, from Greek *kuknos*.

Cymru the Welsh name for Wales.

Cymry the Welsh name for the Welsh.

Cynewulf (late 8th–9th centuries), Anglo-Saxon poet. Modern scholarship attributes four poems to him: *Juliana*, *Elene*, *The Fates of the Apostles*, and *Christ II*. Each of these is inscribed with his name in runes in Anglo-Saxon collections.

Cynic a member of a school of ancient Greek philosophers founded by Antisthenes, marked by an ostentatious contempt for ease and pleasure. The movement flourished in the 3rd century BC and revived in the 1st century AD.

The name is recorded in English from the mid 16th century, and comes via Latin *cynicus*, from Greek *kunikos*; probably originally from *Kunosarges*, the name of a gymnasium where Antisthenes taught, but popularly taken to mean 'doglike, churlish', *kuôn*, *kun-*, 'dog' becoming a nickname for a Cynic.

Cynthia a name for ➤ ARTEMIS or Diana, from Mount Cynthus in Delos, where Artemis was born, and used poetically to denote the moon.

cypress this evergreen coniferous tree is traditionally a symbol of mourning.

St Cyprian (d. 258), Carthaginian bishop and martyr. The author of a work on the nature of true unity in the Church in its relation to the episcopate, he was martyred in the reign of the Roman emperor Valerian. His feast day is 16 September.

Cyrano de Bergerac (1619–55), French soldier, duellist, and writer. He is chiefly remembered for the large number of duels that he fought (many on account of his proverbially large nose), as immortalized in a play by Edmond Rostand (*Cyrano de Bergerac*, 1897).

Cyrene an ancient Greek city in North Africa, near the coast in Cyrenaica, which from the 4th century BC was a great intellectual centre, with a noted medical school.

See also ➤ SIMON *of Cyrene*.

St Cyricus reputed 4th-century martyr, said to have been put to death as a child with his mother Julitta, and traditionally counted as one of the ➤ FOURTEEN *Holy Helpers*. He may be shown as a naked child riding a boar, reflecting the story that he appeared to Charlemagne in a dream promising to save his life on a boar-hunt if the king would clothe him; this was interpreted by the bishop of Nevers as meaning that the king should repair the roof of the cathedral of St Cyr. His feast day is 16 June (15 July in the Eastern Church).

St Cyril (826–69), Greek missionary. He and his brother, St *Methodius*, were sent to Moravia where they taught in the vernacular, which they adopted also for the liturgy, and circulated a Slavic version of the scriptures. His feast day (in the Eastern Church) is 11 May; (in the Western Church) is 14 February.

The invention of the **Cyrillic alphabet**, used by many Slavic peoples, chiefly those with a historical allegiance to the Orthodox Church, is ascribed to him. Ultimately derived from Greek uncials, it is now used for Russian, Bulgarian, Serbian, Ukrainian, and some other Slavic languages.

Cyrus the Great (d. *c*.530 BC), king of Persia 559–530 BC and founder of the Achaemenid dynasty, father of Cambyses. He defeated the Median empire in 550 BC and went on to conquer Asia Minor, Babylonia, Syria, Palestine, and most of the Iranian plateau. He is said to have ruled with wisdom and moderation, maintaining good relations with the Jews (whom he freed from the Babylonian Captivity) and the Phoenicians.

Cytherea another name for ➤ APHRODITE, from Latin *Cythera* 'Kithira', the name of an Ionian island.

Dd

D the fourth letter of the modern English alphabet and of the ancient Roman one, corresponding to Greek *delta*, Hebrew *daleth*.

D-Day the day on which a particular operation is scheduled to begin; especially, (an anniversary of) 6 June 1944, when Allied forces invaded German-occupied northern France.

In Britain, *D-Day* was later also used for 15 February 1971, the day on which decimal currency came into official use.

Vasco da Gama (*c*.1469–1524), Portuguese explorer. He led the first European expedition round the Cape of Good Hope in 1497, sighting and naming Natal on Christmas Day before crossing the Indian Ocean and arriving in Calicut in 1498.

Dachau a Nazi concentration camp in southern Bavaria, from 1933 to 1945, in allusive use, a place of desolation; the slogan *'Arbeit macht frei* [Work liberates]' was inscribed on its gates (and later on those of ➤ AUSCHWITZ).

Dacia an ancient country of SE Europe in what is now NW Romania. It was annexed by Trajan in AD 106 as a province of the Roman Empire.

dactyl a metrical foot consisting of one stressed syllable followed by two unstressed syllables or (in Greek and Latin) one long syllable followed by two short syllables. Recorded from late Middle English, the word comes via Latin from Greek *daktulos*, literally 'finger', the three bones of the finger corresponding to the three syllables.

Dad's Army a name for the Second World War ➤ HOME *Guard*, from the title of the popular television series, written by Jimmy Perry and David Croft and first appearing in 1968, featuring the Home Guard of 'Walmington-on-Sea', led by the pompous bank manager Captain Mainwaring and his upper-class subordinate Sergeant Wilson, and featuring a range of men from the elderly butcher Corporal Jones to the young and naive Private Pike.

Dada an early 20th-century international movement in art, literature, music, and film, repudiating and mocking artistic and social conventions and emphasizing the illogical and absurd. Dada was launched in Zurich in 1916 by Tristan Tzara and others, soon merging with a similar group in New York. It favoured montage, collage, and the ready-made, which all emphasize the anti-rational and the arbitrariness of creative form. The name is French, literally 'hobby-horse', the title of a review which appeared in Zurich in 1916.

Daedalus in Greek mythology, a craftsman, considered the inventor of carpentry, who is said to have built the ➤ LABYRINTH for Minos, king of Crete. Minos imprisoned him and his son ➤ ICARUS, but they escaped using wings which Daedalus made and fastened with wax. Icarus, however, flew too near the sun and was killed.

daemon in ancient Greek belief, a divinity or supernatural being of a nature between gods and humans; an inner or attendant spirit or inspiring force. The word is recorded from the mid 16th century, and until the 19th century represented the common spelling of *demon*.

Daemon is the term used by Rudyard Kipling for his authorial inspiration.

daffodil in poetry, the bright yellow flowers of the *daffodil* are associated with the approach of spring. The name is recorded from the mid 16th century and comes from late Middle English *affodill* (the initial *d-* is unexplained), from medieval Latin *affodilus*, a variant of Latin *asphodilus* (see ➤ ASPHODEL).

dagger a short knife with a pointed and edged blade, used as a weapon, which is the emblem of ➤ St EDWARD *the Martyr*, St Peter the Martyr, a 13th-century Dominican friar and priest born in Verona, who was attacked and killed while travelling from Como to Milan (he was wounded in the head with an axe, while the friar who was with him was stabbed), St Olaf (see ➤ OLAF *II Haraldsson*), and ➤ St WENCESLAS.

In printing, *dagger* is another name for an ➤ OBELUS.

Dagobert the name of several ➤ MEROVINGIAN kings.

Dagon in the Bible, a national deity of the ancient Philistines, represented as a fish-tailed man. The name comes via Latin and Greek from Hebrew *dāgōn*, perhaps from *dāgān* 'corn', but said (according to folk etymology) to be from *dāg* 'fish'.

Dagwood sandwich in North America, a thick sandwich with a variety of fillings, named (in the 1970s) after *Dagwood* Bumstead, a comic-strip character, suitor and later husband of ➤ BLONDIE, who makes and eats this type of sandwich.

Black Dahlia name given in press reports to the victim of a notorious and unsolved American murder case, in which the mutilated body of a young actress was discovered in Los Angeles in 1947.

daisy the white-petalled, yellow-centred flowers of this plant are associated with spring (as in a 19th-century saying, **it is not spring until you can plant your foot upon twelve daisies**). In informal use (chiefly US) a *daisy* is something regarded as first-rate or charming.

Dalai Lama the spiritual head of Tibetan Buddhism and, until the establishment of Chinese communist rule, the spiritual and temporal ruler of Tibet. Each Dalai Lama is believed to be the reincarnation of the bodhisattva Avalokitesvara, reappearing in a child when the incumbent Dalai Lama dies. The present Dalai Lama, the fourteenth incarnation, escaped to India in 1959 following the invasion of Tibet by the Chinese and was awarded the Nobel Peace Prize in 1989.

The name is from Tibetan, literally 'ocean monk', so named because he is regarded as 'the ocean of compassion'.

Dalek in science fiction, a member of a race of hostile alien machine-organisms which appeared in the BBC television serial *Dr Who* from 1963; they are characterized by their staccato mechanical utterance, and their catch-phrase, 'Exterminate! Exterminate!'

The name is an invented word, coined by the author Terry Nation after a volume of an encyclopedia covering the alphabetical sequence *dal–lek*.

Arthur Daley Cockney con-man noted for his cunning and frequently unsuccessful deals, a central character in the TV series *Minder* (1979–85 and 1988–94).

Dallas a city in NE Texas where President John F. Kennedy was assassinated in November 1963.

Dallas was also the title of a glitzy US soap (1978–91) featuring members of the warring and oil-rich Ewing family of Southfork Ranch, Texas.

Dalmatia an ancient region in what is now SW Croatia, comprising mountains and a narrow coastal plain along the Adriatic, together with offshore islands, which once formed part of the Roman province of Illyricum. *Dalmatian* dogs are so named because they are believed to have originated in Dalmatia in the 18th century.

dalmatic a wide-sleeved long, loose vestment open at the sides, worn by deacons and bishops, and by monarchs at their coronation. Recorded from late Middle English, the word comes via Old French *dalmatique* or late Latin *dalmatica*, from *dalmatica (vestis)* '(robe) of (white) Dalmatian wool', from *Dalmaticus* 'of Dalmatia'.

Dalriada an ancient Gaelic kingdom in northern Ireland whose people (the Scots) established a colony in SW Scotland from about the late 5th century. By the 9th century Irish Dalriada had declined but the people of Scottish Dalriada gradually acquired dominion over the whole of Scotland.

Damascene of or relating to the city of ➤ DAMASCUS, and particularly used in the phrase **Damascene conversion**, in allusion to the conversion of St Paul on the ➤ road to DAMASCUS.

Damascus was famous for its metalworking, and *damascene* is also used to mean relating to or denoting a process of inlaying a metal object with gold or silver decoration.

Damascus a city (now capital of Syria) which has existed for over 4,000 years (see also ➤ DAMASCENE). In the Bible, it was while Saul of Tarsus was travelling to Damascus in pursuit of Christians that he experienced a vision from God, and was temporarily struck blind; when he recovered his sight, he became a convert (see ➤ St PAUL[1]) to the cause which he had formerly persecuted. The term **road to Damascus** is now used for a sudden and complete personal conversion to a cause or principle which one has formerly rejected.

Damascus steel is steel made with a wavy surface pattern produced by hammer-welding strips of steel and iron followed by repeated heating and forging, used chiefly for knife and sword blades. Such items were often marketed, but not necessarily made, in Damascus during the medieval period.

damask a figured, lustrous woven fabric, with a pattern visible on both sides, originally produced in ➤ DAMASCUS.

A **damask rose** is a sweet-scented rose of an old variety (or hybrid) that is typically pink or light red in colour. The petals are very soft and velvety and are used to make attar.

Dambusters' raid informal name for the Second World War raid by 617 Squadron of the RAF, May 1943, on the Möhne and Eder dams in the Ruhr valley in Germany, using the ➤ BOUNCING *bomb* designed by Barnes Wallis.

damn in Christian belief, to be **damned** is to be condemned by God to suffer eternal punishment in hell. The word comes (in Middle English, via Old French) from Latin *dam(p)nare* 'inflict loss on', from *damnum* 'loss, damage'.

To **damn with faint praise** is to commend so feebly as to imply disapproval; from Pope's 'An Epistle to Dr Arbuthnot' (1735).

Damocles a legendary courtier who extravagantly praised the happiness of Dionysius I, ruler of Syracuse. To show him how precarious this happiness was, Dionysius seated him at a banquet with a sword hung by a single hair over his head. The **sword of Damocles** is now used to refer to a precarious situation.

Damon a legendary Syracusan of the 4th century whose friend *Pythias* (also called Phintias) was sentenced to death by Dionysius I. Damon stood bail for Pythias, who returned just in time to save him, and was himself reprieved.

damsel archaic or poetic term for a young unmarried woman; also in the humorous **damsel in distress** for a young woman in difficulties. Recorded from Middle English, the word comes from Old French *dam(e)isele*, based on Latin *domina* 'mistress'.

Dan in the Bible, a Hebrew patriarch, son of Jacob and Bilhah, or the the tribe of Israel traditionally descended from him. *Dan* is also the name of an ancient town in the north of Canaan, where the tribe of Dan settled.

The proverbial expression **from Dan to Beersheba** is used to indicate a farthest extremity; in biblical times *Dan* marked the farthest northern point of the ancient Hebrew kingdom, and *Beersheba* the southern point.

Danae in Greek mythology, the daughter of Acrisius, king of Argos. An oracle foretold that she would bear a son who would kill her father, and in an attempt to evade this, Acrisius imprisoned her. Zeus visited her in the form of a shower of gold and she conceived ➤ PERSEUS, who killed Acrisius by accident.

Danaids in Greek mythology, the daughters of Danaus, king of Argos, who were compelled to marry the sons of his brother Aegyptus. Apart from one, Hypermnestra, who helped her husband to escape, the sisters murdered their husbands on the wedding night, and were punished in Hades by being set to fill a leaky jar with water.

dance of death a medieval allegorical representation in which a personified Death leads people to the grave, designed to emphasize the equality of all before death.

Dane a Viking invader of the British Isles in the 9th–11th centuries; the term in this sense, broadly covering all Norse invaders of the period and not just those coming from Denmark, is recorded from Old English.

Danegeld was a land tax levied in Anglo-Saxon England during the reign of King Ethelred to raise funds for protection against Danish invaders; the term is also given to taxes collected for national defence by the Norman kings until 1162. The word is now often used allusively with reference to the likelihood that buying off an enemy will ensure their return for further payment, a view popularized in a poem by Kipling, 'What Dane-geld means' (1911).

The **Danelaw** was the part of northern and eastern England occupied or administered by Danes from the late 9th century until after the Norman Conquest.

Daniel a Hebrew prophet (6th century BC), who spent his life as a captive at the court of Babylon. In the Bible he interpreted the dreams of ➤ NEBUCHADNEZZAR and was delivered by God from the lions' den into which he had been thrown as the result of a trick.

In the apocryphal Book of ➤ SUSANNA he is portrayed as a wise judge.

Dannebrog the national flag of Denmark. The word is Danish, and means literally 'Danish cloth'.

The **Order of Dannebrog** is a Danish order of knighthood, founded in 1219, revived in 1671, and regulated by various later statutes.

danse macabre another (French) term for the ➤ DANCE *of death*.

Dante Alighieri (1265–1321), Italian poet, whose reputation rests chiefly on *The Divine Comedy* (*c*.1309–20), an epic poem describing his spiritual journey through Hell and Purgatory and finally to Paradise. His love for *Beatrice* Portinari is described in *Vita nuova* (*c*.1290–4).

Daphne in Greek mythology, a nymph who was turned into a laurel bush to save her from the amorous pursuit of Apollo.

Daphnis in Greek mythology, a Sicilian shepherd who, according to one version of the legend, was struck with blindness for his infidelity to the nymph Echenais. He consoled himself with pastoral poetry, of which he was the inventor.

Darby and Joan a devoted old married couple, living in placid domestic harmony, from a poem (1735) in the *Gentleman's Magazine*.

Dardanelles a narrow strait between Europe and Asiatic Turkey (called the ➤ HELLESPONT in classical times), linking the Sea of Marmara with the Aegean Sea, which in 1915 was the scene of an unsuccessful attack on Turkey by Allied troops (see ➤ GALLIPOLI).

Dardanus in Greek mythology, ancestor of the kings of Troy, son of Zeus and Electra, daughter of the Titan Atlas. In the Trojan war, the enmity of Zeus' wife Hera towards the Trojans in part originated from her jealousy of Electra.

Dan Dare in a comic strip (1950–67) in *The Eagle*, the heroic Space Fleet Colonel who defended the universe against the ➤ MEKON and his evil allies.

Virginia Dare (1587–?), first English child born in North America. Born on ➤ ROANOKE *Island*, Virginia, she disappeared with the other members of the ➤ LOST *Colony*.

Darien a sparsely populated province of eastern Panama, but originally designating the whole of the Isthmus of Panama; famously mentioned by Keats in his reference to 'stout Cortes…Silent upon a peak in Darien' (although it was ➤ BALBOA and not ➤ CORTÉS who was the first to see the Pacific here).

Darius (*c*.550–486 BC), king of Persia 521–486 BC, known as **Darius the Great**. He divided the empire into provinces, governed by satraps, developed commerce, built a network of roads, and connected the Nile with the Red Sea by canal. After a revolt by the Greek cities in Ionia he invaded Greece but was defeated at ➤ MARATHON.

Darius was also the name of the last Achaemenid king of Persia (553–330 BC), defeated and dethroned by Alexander the Great (see ➤ ALEXANDER[1]).

dark often used figuratively to mean unenlightened or ominous.

The **Dark Ages** are the period in western Europe between the fall of the Roman Empire and the high Middle Ages, *c*.500–1100 AD, during which Germanic tribes swept through Europe and North Africa, often attacking and destroying towns and settlements. It is traditionally viewed as being a time of unenlightenment, though scholarship was kept alive in the monasteries and learning was encouraged at the courts of Charlemagne and Alfred the Great.

The **dark and bloody ground** is a name for Kentucky, popularized by the American poet Theodore O'Hara (1820–67) in the poem 'The Bivouac of the Dead' (1847). The phrase is sometimes said to be the meaning of Kentucky as an Indian term, but this has been questioned; alternatively, it is said to derive from a warning given by a Cherokee chief in the late 18th century, that the land was already 'a bloody ground' from earlier hunting and fighting, and that it would be dark for prospective settlers.

The **Dark Continent** was a name given to Africa at a time when it was little known to Europeans, first recorded in H. M. Stanley's *Through the Dark Continent* (1878).

A **dark horse** is a person about whom little is known, especially someone whose abilities or potential for success is concealed. The term is originally racing slang, denoting a horse about whose racing powers little is known, and is first recorded in the mid 19th century.

The **Dark Lady** is the woman to whom a number of Shakespeare's sonnets were written; the Elizabethan scholar A. L. Rowse suggested that she may have been Emilia Lanier (1569–1645), but she has never been certainly identified; an alternative name is that of Mary Fitton (1578–1647).

It was a dark and stormy night is one variant of an opening line intended to convey a threatening and doom-laden atmosphere; in this form used by the novelist Edward

Bulwer-Lytton (1803–73) in his novel *Paul Clifford* (1830).

Darley Arabian with the Byerley Turk and the Godolphin Barb, one of the three founding sires of the Thoroughbred, imported to improve the stock in the 18th century.

Mr Darling father of Wendy and her brothers, whose neglect of his children leads to their temporary loss in the Never-Never Land when they follow ➤ PETER *Pan*.

D'Artagnan the young and dashing Gascon in Dumas' novel *Les Trois Mousquetaires* (1844), who despite initially giving offence by his impetuous ways is befriended by the ➤ THREE *Musketeers*, Athos, Porthos, and Aramis, and with their help defeats the machinations of Cardinal Richelieu.

Darth Vader in the ➤ STAR *Wars* trilogy, the former ➤ JEDI who has betrayed his allegiance to serve the Empire, and who is the father of ➤ LUKE *Skywalker*; he is characterized by his ruthless aggression, and by the black cloak, armour, and concealing vizor in which he is always clothed. Although he is initially the villain of the trilogy, he is ultimately redeemed, turning his destructive powers on the Emperor to save his son.

Darwinism the theory of the evolution of species by natural selection advanced by the English natural historian and geologist Charles *Darwin* (1809–82). Darwin was the naturalist on HMS *Beagle* for her voyage around the southern hemisphere (1831–6), during which he collected the material which became the basis for his ideas on natural selection. His works *On the Origin of Species* (1859) and *The Descent of Man* (1871) had a fundamental effect on our concepts of nature and humanity's place within it.

Daughters of the American Revolution in the US, a patriotic society whose aims include encouraging education and the study of US history and which tends to be politically conservative. Membership is limited to female descendants of those who aided the cause of independence. It was first organized in 1890.

dauphin title of the eldest son of the king of France, from the family name of the lords of the *Dauphiné* (first used in this way in the 14th century), ultimately a nickname meaning 'dolphin'.

David (d. *c.*962 BC), king of Judah and Israel. In the biblical account he was the youngest son of Jesse, who killed the Philistine Goliath and, on ➤ SAUL's death, became king, making Jerusalem his capital; he was the father of ➤ ABSALOM and (by his marriage with ➤ BATHSHEBA), ➤ SOLOMON. He is traditionally regarded as the author of the Psalms, though this has been disputed.

It was a traditional Jewish belief that the Messiah would be descended from David, and in Matthew 9:27 two blind men seeking healing from Jesus address him as 'Son of David'.

St David (6th century), Welsh monk, who since the 12th century has been regarded as the patron saint of Wales. Little is known of his life, but it is generally accepted that he transferred the centre of Welsh ecclesiastical administration from Caerleon to Mynyw (now St David's); he also established a number of monasteries and churches. His feast day is 1 March.

Davy Jones's locker the bottom of the sea, especially regarded as the grave of those drowned at sea, from an extension of the early 18th-century *Davy Jones*, denoting the evil spirit of the sea.

dawn raid in Stock Exchange usage, an attempt to acquire a substantial portion of a company's shares at the start of a day's trading, typically as a preliminary to a takeover bid.

dawn redwood a coniferous tree with deciduous needles, known only as a fossil until it was found growing in SW China in 1941.

don't give up the day job don't recklessly abandon steady work with the idea of making a fortune by pursuing a hobby or alternative interest. Used as a humorous way of recommending someone not to pursue an alternative (and perhaps more glamorous) career at which they are unlikely to be successful.

day of reckoning the time when past mistakes or misdeeds must be punished or paid for, a testing time when the degree of one's success or failure will be revealed; with allusion to Judgement Day, on which (in some beliefs) the judgement of mankind is expected to take place.

day-star the morning star, (in poetic use) the sun; figuratively, someone or something regarded as the precursor of a new era.

daylight saving the achieving of longer evening daylight, especially in summer, by setting the clocks an hour ahead of the standard time; the originator of the system was the English builder William Willett (1865–1915). The first Daylight Saving Bill was introduced into the House of Commons in the following March, but did not become law until (as a wartime measure) 1916.

days of grace the period of time allowed by law for the payment of a bill of exchange or an insurance premium after it falls due.

dayspring a poetic and literary term for dawn; sometimes with biblical reference to an allusion to the nativity of John the Baptist in Luke 1:78.

Dayton Accord an agreement on measures to achieve the ending of hostilities in former Yugoslavia, reached in Dayton, Ohio, on 21 November 1995 and signed by the Presidents of Bosnia, Croatia, and Serbia on 14 December 1995 in Paris.

de profundis a heartfelt cry of appeal expressing one's deepest feelings of sorrow and anguish, from the opening words (Latin, 'from the depths') of Psalm 130. *De Profundis* was the title of Oscar Wilde's prose apologia, begun while he was in prison as a letter to Lord Alfred Douglas, and published in 1905.

deacon in Catholic, Anglican, and Orthodox Churches, an ordained minister ranking below that of priest (now, except in the Orthodox Church, typically in training for the priesthood). In some Protestant Churches, a *deacon* is a lay officer appointed to assist a minister, especially in secular affairs; in the early Church, a deacon was an appointed minister of charity.

The word is recorded from Old English (in form *diacon*) and comes via ecclesiastical Latin from Greek *diakonos* 'servant', in ecclesiastical Greek 'Christian minister'.

a dead cat bounce a misleading sign of vitality in something that is really moribund. A dead cat will not bounce, although if dropped from a sufficient height it might appear to do so. The expression was coined in the late 20th century by Wall Street traders for the situation when a stock or company on a long-term, irrevocable downward trend suddenly shows a small temporary improvement.

dead in the water unable to function effectively. Originally used of a ship, meaning 'unable to move'.

dead man walking in the United States, a condemned prisoner making the final journey to the execution chamber.

Dead Sea a salt lake or inland sea in the Jordan valley, on the Israel–Jordan border. Its surface is 400 m (1,300 ft) below sea level. The name is recorded from Middle English, and is a translation of Latin *mare mortuum*, Greek (in the writings of Aristotle) *hē nekra thalassa*. The term was used by the Greeks and Romans for the Arctic Ocean in the North of Europe, perhaps because it was regarded as devoid of life or movement.

Dead Sea fruit is a name for a legendary fruit, of attractive appearance, which dissolved into smoke and ashes when held (also called *apple of Sodom*); figuratively, a hollow disappointing thing. The fruit are described in the *Travels* attributed to the 14th-century John de Mandeville.

The **Dead Sea Scrolls** are a collection of Hebrew and Aramaic manuscripts discovered in pottery storage jars in caves near Qumran between 1947 and 1956. Thought to have been hidden by the Essenes or a similar Jewish sect shortly before the revolt against Roman rule AD 66–70, the scrolls include texts of many books of the Old Testament; they are some 1,000 years older than previously known versions.

dead white European male a writer, philosopher, or other significant figure whose importance and talents may have been exaggerated by virtue of his belonging to a historically dominant gender and ethnic group. The acronym **DWEM** is also used.

deadline historical term for a line drawn around a prison, beyond which prisoners were liable to be shot.

dean the head of the chapter of a cathedral or collegiate church. Recorded from Middle English, the word comes via Old French from late Latin *decanus* 'chief of a group of ten', from *decem* 'ten'.

Dear John letter a letter from a woman to a man, terminating a personal relationship.

deasil in Scotland, in the direction of the sun's apparent course, considered as lucky; clockwise; the opposite of ► WIDDERSHINS. Recorded from the late 18th century, the word comes from Scottish Gaelic.

death often (as *Death*) represented in art and literature as a skeleton or an old man holding a scythe, the personification of the power that destroys life. A **death's head** is a human skull as a symbol of mortality.

Death in the pot is a biblical phrase, from the story of a famine during which a pottage containing poisonous herbs was made by Elisha's servant for the sons of the prophets; when they cried out, 'O thou man of God, there is death in the pot' (2 Kings 5:40), Elisha added meal to the dish, and they were able to eat it safely.

Death row especially with reference to the US, a prison block or section for prisoners sentenced to death.

Till death us do part means for as long as each of a couple live, from the marriage service in the *Book of Common Prayer*.

Deborah a biblical prophet and leader who inspired the Israelite army to defeat the Canaanites. The 'Song of Deborah', a song of victory attributed to her, is thought to be one of the oldest sections of the Bible.

Debrett's familiar name for *The Peerage of England, Scotland, and Ireland*, compiled by the English publisher John *Debrett* and first issued in 1803, which is regarded as the authority on the British nobility.

Decalogue another name for the ➤ TEN *Commandments*; the name is recorded from late Middle English, and comes via French and ecclesiastical Latin from Greek *dekalogos (biblos)* '(book of) the Ten Commandments', from *hoi deka logoi* 'the Ten Commandments' (literally 'the ten sayings').

Decameron a work by Boccaccio, written between 1348 and 1358, containing a hundred tales supposedly told in ten days by a party of ten young people who had fled from the Black Death in Florence. The work was influential on later writers such as Chaucer and Shakespeare.

decanal relating to or denoting the south side of the choir of a church, the side on which the dean sits.

Decapolis in biblical times, a league of 10 ancient Greek cities formed in Palestine after the Roman conquest of 63 BC; the cities were Scythopolis, Hippos, Gadara, Raphana, Dion, Pelia, Gerasa, Philadelphia, Canatha, and Damascus.

December the twelfth month of the year, in the northern hemisphere usually considered the first month of winter. The name is recorded from Middle English, and comes from Latin, from *decem* 'ten', being originally the tenth month of the Roman year.

The **Decembrists** were a group of Russian revolutionaries who in December 1825 led an unsuccessful revolt against Tsar Nicholas I. The leaders were executed and later came to be regarded as martyrs by the Left.

decimate kill one in every ten of (a group of people) as a punishment for the whole group; kill, destroy, or remove a large proportion of. In Middle English the term *decimation* denoted the levying of a tithe, and later the tax imposed by Cromwell on the Royalists (1655). The verb *decimate* originally alluded to the Roman punishment of executing one man in ten of a mutinous legion.

Historically, the meaning of the word *decimate* is 'kill one in every ten of (a group of people)'. This sense has been more or less totally superseded by the later, more general sense 'kill or destroy (a large proportion of)', as in *the virus has decimated the population*. Some traditionalists argue that this and other later senses are incorrect, but it is clear that this is now part of standard English.

Declaration of Independence a document declaring the US to be independent of the British Crown, signed on 4 July 1776 by the Congressional representatives of thirteen states, including Thomas Jefferson, Benjamin Franklin, and John Adams.

Declaration of Rights a statute passed by the English parliament in 1689, which first established the joint monarchy of William and Mary and which was designed to ensure that the Crown would not act without Parliament's consent. It was later incorporated into the Bill of Rights.

Decorated denoting a stage of English Gothic church architecture typical of the 14th century (between Early English and Perpendicular), with increasing use of decoration and geometrical, curvilinear, and reticulated tracery.

decretal the collection of papal decrees forming part of canon law.

Decretum a collection of decisions and judgements in canon law. The word is from Latin, literally 'something decreed'.

Feast of Dedication another name for ➤ HANUKKAH.

the Deep South the south-eastern region of the US regarded as embodying traditional Southern culture and traditions.

Deep Throat codename (from the title of a pornographic film, 1972) given in the

➤ WATERGATE affair to the journalists' principal anonymous informant; from this, *deep
throat* is used to mean a person working for
an organization who anonymously supplies
information on misconduct to an outside
source. The original *Deep Throat* has never
been publicly identified.

deer sometimes taken as a type of swiftness. (See also ➤ DOE, ➤ HART, ➤ STAG.)

Defender of the Faith a title conferred on
Henry VIII by Pope Leo X in 1521. It was recognized by Parliament as an official title of the
English monarch in 1544, and has been
borne by all subsequent sovereigns.

Defenestration of Prague in 1618, the
throwing by Protestant citizens of Catholic
officials from the windows of Hradčany Castle, an event which contributed to the outbreak of the Thirty Years War.

defrock deprive (a person in holy orders) of
ecclesiastical status.

prohibited degrees the number of steps
of consanguinity or affinity within which
marriage is not allowed.

Deianira in Greek mythology, the wife of
➤ HERCULES, who was tricked into smearing
poison on a garment which caused his death.

Deira a northern Anglo-Saxon kingdom in
Britain which at the end of the 7th century
AD united with Bernicia to form Northum-
bria.

Deirdre in Irish mythology, a tragic heroine
(**Deirdre of the Sorrows**) of whom it was
prophesied that her beauty would bring ban-
ishment and death to heroes. King
Conchubar of Ulster wanted to marry her,
but she fell in love with Naoise, son of
Usnach, who with his brothers carried her
off to Scotland. They were lured back by
Conchubar and treacherously slain, and
Deirdre took her own life.

Delectable Mountains in Bunyan's ➤ PIL-
GRIM'S *Progress*, the country within sight of
the Celestial City.

delenda est Carthago the words, calling
for the complete destruction of ➤ CARTHAGE,
with which ➤ CATO the Elder ended every
speech in the Senate.

Delian League an alliance of ancient
Greek city states, dominated by Athens, that

joined in 478–447 BC against the Persians.
The league was disbanded on the defeat of
Athens in the Peloponnesian War (404 BC),
but again united under Athens' leadership
against Spartan aggression in 377–338 BC.
Also called the *Athenian empire*.

Delian problem the problem of finding
geometrically the side of a cube having twice
the volume of a given cube (from the Delian
oracle's pronouncement that a plague in Athens would cease if the cubical altar to Apollo
were doubled in size).

Delilah in the Bible, a woman who betrayed her husband ➤ SAMSON to the Philistines by revealing to them that the secret of
his strength lay in his long hair.

Della Cruscan of or relating to the Academy della Crusca in Florence, an institution
established in 1582, with the purity of the
Italian language as its chief interest. The
name *Accademia della Crusca* 'Academy of the
bran' referred to the 'sifting' of the language.

Delos a small Greek island in the Aegean
Sea, regarded as the centre of the Cyclades.
In classical times it was considered to be sacred to Apollo, and according to legend was
the birthplace of Apollo and Artemis.

Delphi one of the most important religious
sanctuaries of the ancient Greek world, dedicated to Apollo and situated on the lower
southern slopes of Mount Parnassus above
the Gulf of Corinth. It was thought of as the
navel of the earth.
    The **Delphic oracle** was the oracle of
Apollo at Delphi, regarded as particularly
holy; the characteristic riddling responses to
a wide range of questions were delivered by
the ➤ PYTHIA, and have given rise to the use
of *Delphic* to mean deliberately obscure or
ambiguous.

delta the fourth letter of the Greek alphabet (Δ, δ), transliterated as 'd'.
    The word is used for a triangular tract of
sediment deposited at the mouth of a river,
typically where it diverges into several out-
lets. Originally (in the mid 16th century) the
term was applied specifically as **the Delta** (of
the River Nile), from the shape of the Greek
letter.
    Delta Force is the name of an elite Ameri-
can military force whose main responsibilities are rescue operations and special forces
work.

the Deluge another name for the biblical
➤ FLOOD, recorded in Genesis ch. 6–8.

delusions of grandeur a false impression
of one's own importance. Current in English
since the early 20th century, the equivalent
of the earlier French phrase (borrowed into
English) *folie de grandeur*.

Demeter in Greek mythology, the corn
goddess, daughter of Cronus and Rhea, and
mother of ➤ PERSEPHONE. She is associated
with Cybele, and her symbol is an ear of
corn. The Eleusinian mysteries were held in
honour of her. Roman equivalent ➤ CERES.

demon an evil spirit or devil, especially one
thought to possess a person or act as a tor-
mentor in hell; the word is recorded from
Middle English, and comes partly via medieval Latin and Latin from Greek *daimōn*
'deity, genius', and partly (in this sense) from
Latin *daemonium* 'lesser or evil spirit', from
Greek diminutive of *daimōn*.

From late Middle English, the word was
also used for a divinity or supernatural being
(in ancient Greek belief) of a nature between
gods and humans, an inner or attendant
spirit or inspiring force, for which ➤ DAEMON
is now the standard spelling.

Demos the common people of an ancient
Greek state; the populace as a political unit,
especially in a democracy.

Demosthenes (384–322 BC), Athenian orator and statesman, who according to Plutarch overcame an initial stammer by
training himself to speak with pebbles in his
mouth. He is best known for his political
speeches on the need to resist the aggressive
tendencies of Philip II of Macedon (the *Philippics*). The Greeks were defeated by Philip at
the battle of Chaeronea in 338 BC and Demosthenes committed suicide after the failure of
an Athenian revolt against Macedon.

denarius an ancient Roman silver coin, originally worth ten asses.

St Denis (died *c*.250), Italian-born French
bishop, patron saint of France; Roman name
Dionysius. According to tradition he was one
of a group of seven missionaries sent from
Rome to convert Gaul; he became bishop of
Paris and was martyred in the reign of the
emperor Valerian. He was martyred by being
beheaded, and according to legend subsequently walked two leagues carrying his own

head. He is taken as one of the ➤ FOURTEEN
Holy Helpers. His feast day is 9 October.

Denmark Street the world of composers
and publishers of popular music, Tin Pan
Alley, from the name of a street in London.

Dennis the Menace a cartoon character
introduced in 1951 in the children's comic
the *Beano*, a destructive boy with black-and-
red striped jersey, boots, and black hair, who
with his dog Gnasher terrorizes teachers,
other children, and anyone else they may encounter.

In contrast, a US *Dennis the Menace*, created
by Hank Ketcham and also appearing in 1951,
is a dynamic five-year-old who is not aggressive and who exhausts his parents only by his
energy; disasters which ensue are accidental
rather than planned.

deodand historical term for a thing forfeited to the Crown for a religious or charitable use, as having caused a human death.
The word comes ultimately from Latin *Deo
dandum* 'thing to be given to God'.

the Deposition the taking down of the
body of Christ from the Cross.

the Depression the financial and industrial slump of 1929 and subsequent years,
also known as **the Great Depression**.

Derby an annual flat horse race for three-
year-olds, founded in 1780 by the 12th Earl of
Derby. The race is run on Epsom Downs in
England on **Derby Day** in late May or early
June. In North American usage, a *derby* is a
bowler hat, said to be from American de-
mand for a hat of the type worn at the Epsom
Derby.

A **Derby Dog** is a dog appearing on the
racecourse after this has been cleared; taken
proverbially as something sure to turn up or
come in the way. The term is recorded from
the mid 19th century.

derrick a kind of crane with a movable
pivoted arm for moving and lifting heavy
weights, originally meaning a hangman or
the gallows, from *Derrick* the surname of a
London hangman.

derring-do action displaying heroic courage. The term comes (in the late 16th century) from late Middle English *dorryng do*
'daring to do', used by Chaucer, and, in a passage by Lydgate based on Chaucer's work,
misprinted in 16th-century editions as

derrynge do; this was misinterpreted by Spenser to mean 'manhood, chivalry', and subsequently taken up and popularized by Sir Walter Scott.

dervish a Muslim (specifically Sufi) religious man who has taken vows of poverty and austerity. Dervishes first appeared in the 12th century; they were noted for their wild or ecstatic rituals. The name comes via Turkish from Persian *darvīš* 'religious mendicant'.

desert a dry, barren area of land, especially one covered with sand, that is characteristically desolate, waterless, and without vegetation.
   The **Desert Fathers** were the hermits living an ascetic life in 4th-century Egypt, whose lives became the pattern for Christian community monasticism.
   Desert Island Discs is a popular radio programme (1942–), originally created by Roy Plomley (1914–85), in which the chosen celebrity 'castaway' chooses eight records with which to be marooned on a desert island, together with one luxury and one book besides the Bible and Shakespeare.
   Operation **Desert Storm** was the name of the Allied Forces' land campaign in the 1991 Gulf War; **Desert Storm syndrome** is another term for ➤ GULF *War Syndrome*.
   See also *ship of the desert* at ➤ SHIP.

Desperate Dan the enormous stubble-chinned cowboy in a cartoon strip in the *Dandy* comic, noted for his fondness for cow pies containing the whole animal.

Deucalion in Greek mythology, the son of ➤ PROMETHEUS. With his wife Pyrrha he survived a flood sent by Zeus to punish human wickedness; they were then instructed to throw stones over their shoulders, and these turned into humans to repopulate the world.

deuce a thing representing, or represented by, the number two; the word is recorded from the late 15th century, and comes from Old French *deus* 'two', from Latin *duos*.
   In tennis, *deuce* is the score of 40 all in a game, at which each player needs two consecutive points to win the game.

deus ex machina an unexpected power or event saving a seemingly hopeless situation, especially as a contrived plot device in a play or novel. The phrase is modern Latin, a direct translation of Greek *theos ek mēkhanēnēs* 'god from the machinery', since in Greek theatre, actors representing gods were suspended above the stage, the denouement of the play being brought about by their intervention.

Deutero-Isaiah the supposed later author of Isaiah 40–55 (from Greek *deuteros* 'second').

Deuteronomy the fifth book of the Bible, containing a recapitulation of the Ten Commandments and much of the Mosaic law.

Devanagari the alphabet used for Sanskrit, Hindi, and other Indian languages. The name comes from Sanskrit, literally 'divine town script', from *deva* 'god' + *nāgarī* (from *nagara* 'town'), an earlier name of the script.

Devi in Hindu mythology, the supreme goddess, often identified with Parvati and Sakti.

leave someone to their own devices leave someone to do as they wish without supervision. *Device* in the sense of 'inclination' or 'fancy' is now obsolete in the singular, and in the plural survives only in this expression and in the phrase *devices and desires* in the General Confession in the Book of Common Prayer.

devil in Christian and Jewish belief, the supreme spirit of evil, Satan. The Devil is traditionally represented with horns, cloven hooves, and a forked tail, all signs of his demonic origin. The name is recorded from Old English (in form *dēofol*) and comes ultimately via late Latin from Greek *diabolos* 'accuser, slanderer' (used in the Septuagint to translate late Hebrew *śāṭān* 'Satan'), from *diaballein* 'to slander'.
   A **devil's advocate** is a person appointed by the Roman Catholic Church to challenge a proposed beatification or canonization, or the verification of a miracle.
   The **devil's bones** are dice, a name recorded from the mid 17th century.
   The **devil's dozen** is thirteen.
   Devil's Island is a rocky island off the coast of French Guiana, used from 1852 as a penal settlement, especially for political prisoners. The last prisoner was released in 1953.
   The **devil's picture books** are playing cards; a name recorded from the late 18th century.

dew pond a shallow pond, especially an artificial one, occurring on downs where the water supply from springs or surface drainage is inadequate; so named because such ponds were originally thought to be fed by dew.

Dewey decimal classification an internationally applied decimal system of library classification which uses a three-figure code from 000 to 999 to represent the major branches of knowledge, and allows finer classification to be made by the addition of further figures after a decimal point. It is named after the American librarian Melvil *Dewey* (1851–1931).

dexter in heraldry, of, on, or towards the right-hand side (in a coat of arms, from the bearer's point of view, i.e. the left as it is depicted). The opposite of ➤ SINISTER. The term is recorded from the mid 16th century and comes from Latin, 'on the right'.

dharma in Indian religion, the eternal law of the cosmos, inherent in the very nature of things. In Hinduism, *dharma* is seen as the cosmic law both upheld by the gods and expressed in right behaviour by humans, including adherence to the social order. In Buddhism, it is interpreted as universal truth or law, especially as proclaimed by the Buddha. In Jainism, it is conceived both as virtue and as a kind of fundamental substance, the medium of motion.

The word comes from Sanskrit, literally 'decree or custom'.

diaconicon a building or room adjoining a church, where vestments, ornaments, and other things used in the church service are kept; a sacristy. The word comes from Greek *diakonikon*, from the base of ➤ DEACON.

diadem a jewelled crown or headband worn as a symbol of sovereignty. Recorded from Middle English, the word comes via Old French and Latin from Greek *diadēma* 'the regal headband of the Persian kings', from *diadein* 'bind round'.

Diadochi the six Macedonian generals of Alexander the Great (Antigonus, Antipater, Cassander, Lysimachus, Ptolemy, and Seleucus), among whom his empire was eventually divided after his death in 323 BC. The word comes from Greek *diadokhoi* 'successors'.

dialectic enquiry into metaphysical contradictions and their solutions. The ancient Greeks used the term to refer to various methods of reasoning and discussion in order to discover the truth. More recently, Kant applied the term to the criticism of the contradictions which arise from supposing knowledge of objects beyond the limits of experience, e.g. the soul. Hegel applied the term to the process of thought by which apparent contradictions (which he termed

thesis and antithesis) are seen to be part of a higher truth (synthesis).

The word is recorded from late Middle English, and comes via Old French or Latin from Greek *dialektikē (tekhnē)* '(art) of debate', from *dialegesthai* 'converse with'.

Dialectical materialism is the Marxist theory (adopted as the official philosophy of the Soviet communists) that political and historical events result from the conflict of social forces and are interpretable as a series of contradictions and their solutions. The conflict is seen as caused by material needs.

dialogue of the deaf a discussion in which each party is unresponsive to what the others say; the expression is a translation of French *dialogue de sourds*.

diamond a precious stone consisting of a clear and colourless crystalline form of pure carbon, the hardest naturally occurring substance, taken as a type of brilliance or excellence. The word is recorded from Middle English, and comes via Old French from medieval Latin *diamas, diamant-*, variant of Latin *adamans*, from the base of adamant.

Diamond is also used for a figure with four straight sides of equal length forming two opposite acute angles and two opposite obtuse angles, a rhombus, and *diamonds* are thus one of the four suits in a conventional pack of playing cards, denoted by a red figure of such a shape.

Diamond was the name of Isaac Newton's dog, which according to a (probably apocryphal) story knocked over a candle which set fire to some papers and thereby destroyed the finished work of some years.

A **diamond jubilee** is the 60th anniversary of a notable event, especially a sovereign's accession or the foundation of an organization.

A **diamond necklace** was at the centre of the **Affair of the Diamond Necklace** in 18th century France. Queen Marie Antoinette was said to have purchased a valuable necklace and subsequently denied any knowledge of the matter. Although the affair was an attempt by a French adventuress to acquire the necklace by a pretence of acting on behalf of the Queen, and Marie Antoinette was not involved, the Queen's innocence was not believed, and the scandal contributed materially to her unpopularity.

The **Diamond Sculls** are an annual single-scull race at Henley Royal Regatta, instituted in 1844, for which the prize was a gold pin ornamented with gold sculls and a drop diamond.

The **Diamond State** is an informal name for the state of Delaware, said to be so named because it was seen as small in size but of great importance.

A **diamond wedding** is the sixtieth anniversary of a wedding.

Diana of Ephesus a statue of the goddess particularly venerated at Ephesus; her Temple there was one of the ➤ SEVEN *Wonders of the World*.

In the Bible (Acts 19:28) **great is Diana of the Ephesians** was the cry of a crowd at Ephesus protesting against the preaching of the apostles Paul and Barnabas; according to the account given in Acts, the people had been worked up by a silversmith named Demetrius, who traded in silver models of Diana's shrine and was concerned for his livelihood.

the diaspora Jews living outside Israel; the dispersion of the Jews beyond Israel.

The main diaspora began in the 8th–6th centuries BC, and even before the sack of Jerusalem in AD 70 the number of Jews dispersed by the diaspora was greater than that living in Israel. Thereafter, Jews were dispersed even more widely throughout the Roman world and beyond (for example, into India). The term embraces concerns about cultural assimilation and loss of Jewish identity which are at the centre of the movement of Zionism.

The word is Greek, and comes from *diaspeirein* 'disperse', from *dia* 'across' + *speirein* 'scatter'. The term originated in the Septuagint (Deuteronomy 28:25) in the phrase *esē diaspora en pasais basileias tēs gēs* 'thou shalt be a dispersion in all kingdoms of the earth'.

diatessaron an arrangement of the four Gospels as one narrative; the word comes via Old French and Latin from Greek *dia tessarōn* 'composed of four'.

dice a small cube with each side having a different number of spots on it, ranging from one to six, thrown and used in gambling and other games involving chance.

The word is originally the plural of *die*, recorded from Middle English and coming via Old French from Latin *datum* 'something given or played'. (See also ➤ *the* DIE *is cast.*)

dice with death take serious risks; *dice with* is here used in the general sense of 'play a game of chance with'.

dictatorship of the proletariat the Communist ideal of proletarian supremacy following the overthrow of capitalism and preceding the classless state.

Dido in the *Aeneid*, the queen and founder of Carthage, who fell in love with the shipwrecked Aeneas and killed herself when he deserted her.

Didyma an ancient sanctuary of Apollo, site of one of the most famous oracles of the Aegean region, close to the west coast of Asia Minor; the name is said to come from Greek 'twin', and to refer to the two springs there.

Didymus the Greek word for 'twin', an epithet of St Thomas the apostle.

die hard disappear or change very slowly; the expression seems to have been used first in the 18th century of criminals who died resisting to the last on the Tyburn gallows in London. At the battle of Albuera in 1811 during the Peninsular War, the commander of the British 57th Regiment of Foot exhorted his men to 'die hard'; as a result of their heroism, the Regiment was nicknamed the **Diehards**. The term was later applied to political groups particularly resistant to change.

Dien Bien Phu a village in NW Vietnam, in 1954 the site of a French military post which was captured by the Vietminh after a 55-day siege; a significant defeat for French forces in the war (1946–54) in Indo-China.

Dieppe Raid an unsuccessful amphibious raid on *Dieppe*, a channel port in northern France, made in August 1942 by a joint force of British and Canadian troops to destroy the German-held port and airfield. The raid ended disastrously, with two thirds of the Allied troops being killed.

Dies Irae a Latin hymn sung in a Mass for the dead; from the opening words (literally, 'day of wrath') of the hymn.

Diet of Worms a meeting of the Holy Roman emperor Charles V's imperial diet at Worms in 1521, at which Martin Luther was summoned to appear. Luther committed himself there to the cause of Protestant reform, and his teaching was formally condemned in the Edict of Worms.

Dieu et mon droit French phrase meaning, God and my right, the motto of the British monarchs from the time of Henry VI.

Digambara a member of one of two principal sects of Jainism, which was formed as a result of doctrinal schism in about AD 80 and continues today in parts of southern India. The sect's adherents reject property ownership and usually do not wear clothes.

Digger a member of a group of radical dissenters formed in England in 1649 as an offshoot of the ➤ LEVELLERS, believing in a form of agrarian communism in which common land would be made available to the poor; they first asserted their principles at St George's Hill, Walton-on-Thames, in Surrey in 1649, where they began to dig up the land and plant crops. The Diggers were suppressed by the authorities, and their leader, Gerrard Winstanley (fl. 1648–52) imprisoned.

digger in Australia and New Zealand, an informal term for a man, especially a private soldier. The term derived (in the early 20th century) from *digger* 'miner', reinforced by association with the digging of trenches on the battlefields.

dilemma a situation in which a difficult choice has to be made between two or more alternatives, especially ones that are equally undesirable (see also ➤ *on the* HORNS *of a dilemma*). The word is recorded from the early 16th century, denoting a form of argument involving a choice between equally unfavourable alternatives; it comes via Latin from Greek *dilēmma*, from *di-* 'twice' + *lēmma* 'premise'.

the law of diminishing returns the principle by which, after a certain point, the level of profits or benefits to be gained is reduced to less than the amount of money or energy invested. Originating in the early 19th century with reference to the profits from agriculture, this expression is predominantly used in economics.

dimissory in the Christian Church, denoting formal permission from a bishop (**letters dimissory**) for a person from one diocese to be ordained in another, or (formerly) for an ordained person to leave one diocese for another.

The word is recorded (as a plural noun) from late Middle English, and comes from late Latin *dimissorius*, from *dimiss-* 'sent away'. The adjective dates from the late 16th century, the original sense being 'valedictory'.

dinosaur a fossil reptile of the Mesozoic era, often reaching an enormous size; in extended usage, a person or thing that is outdated or has become obsolete because of failure to adapt to changing circumstances.

Dinosaurs were all extinct by the end of the Cretaceous period (65 million years ago), the most popular theory being that the extinctions were in fact the result of the impact of a large meteorite.

The word is recorded from the mid 19th century, and comes from modern Latin *dinosaurus* from Greek *deinos* 'terrible' + *sauros* 'lizard'. It was coined by the English anatomist and palaeontologist Richard Owen (1804–92).

Diocletian (245–313), Roman emperor 284–305. Faced with mounting military problems, in 286 he divided the empire between himself in the east and Maximian in the west. Diocletian insisted on the maintenance of Roman law in the provinces and launched the final persecution of the Christians (303); he abdicated in 305.

Diogenes (*c*.400–*c*.325 BC), Greek philosopher. The most famous of the ➤ CYNICS, he lived ascetically in Athens (according to legend, he lived in a tub) and was accordingly named *Kuōn* ('the dog'), from which the Cynics were then said to have derived their name. According to one story, he used to walk round Athens by day with a light, explaining that he was looking for an honest man. He emphasized self-sufficiency and the need for natural, uninhibited behaviour, regardless of social conventions.

Diomedes in Greek mythology, one of the ➤ SEVEN *against Thebes*, who was later one of the leaders of the Greek forces in the Trojan War; in medieval developments of the story, it is Diomedes with whom ➤ CRESSIDA falls in love and betrays Troilus.

horses of Diomedes in Greek mythology, the man-eating horses of *Diomedes*, a Thracian and son of Ares, which were captured as one of the ➤ *Labours of* HERCULES.

Dione in Greek mythology, a Titan, the mother by Zeus of Aphrodite.

Dionne Quintuplets five Canadian sisters, Émilie, Yvonne, Cécile, Marie, and Annette, who were born on 28 May 1934; they were the first documented set of quintuplets to survive birth. In 1935 they were made wards of the Canadian government, and in their early years were international celebrities and a major tourist attraction.

Dionysius the name of two rulers of Syracuse. Dionysius I (*c*.430–367 BC, ruled 405–367) was known as **Dionysius the Elder**. A tyrannical ruler, he waged three wars against the Carthaginians for control of Sicily, later becoming the principal power in Greek Italy after the capture of Rhegium (386) and other Greek cities in southern Italy. His son, Dionysius II (*c*.397–*c*.344 BC, ruled 367–357 and 346–344) was known as **Dionysius the Younger**. He lacked his father's military ambitions and signed a peace treaty with Carthage in 367. Despite his patronage of philosophers, he resisted the attempt by Plato to turn him into a philosopher king.

Dionysius the Areopagite (1st century AD), Greek churchman. His conversion by St Paul is recorded in Acts 17:34 and according to tradition he went on to become the first bishop of Athens. He was later confused with St Denis and with a mystical theologian, Pseudo-Dionysius the Areopagite, who exercised a profound influence on medieval theology.

Dionysus in Greek mythology, a god, son of ➤ ZEUS and Semele; his worship entered Greece from Thrace *c*.1000 BC. Originally a god of the fertility of nature, associated with wild and ecstatic religious rites, in later traditions he is a god of wine who loosens inhibitions and inspires creativity in music and poetry. Also called ➤ BACCHUS.

Dioscuri in Greek and Roman mythology the twins Castor and Pollux, born to ➤ LEDA after her seduction by Zeus, and brothers of ➤ HELEN. Castor was mortal, but Pollux was immortal; at Pollux's request they shared his immortality between them, spending half their time below the earth in Hades and the other half on Olympus. They are often identified with the constellation Gemini.

The name comes from Greek *Dioskouroi* 'sons of Zeus'.

diphthong a sound formed by the combination of two vowels in a single syllable, in which the sound begins as one vowel and moves towards another (as in *coin*, *loud*, and *side*). Also, a digraph representing the sound of a diphthong or single vowel (as in *feat*); a compound vowel character; a ligature (such as æ).

Recorded from late Middle English, the word comes via French and late Latin from Greek *diphthongos*, from *di-* 'twice' + *phthongos* 'voice, sound'.

diplomatic edition an edition exactly reproducing an original version. *Diplomatic* in this sense is recorded from the late 18th century, and is probably due to the publication of the *Codex Juris Gentium Diplomaticus* (1695), a collection of public documents, many of which dealt with international affairs.

the Dipper in the US, an informal name for *the Plough* (see ➤ PLOUGH), taking its shape to represent a ladle for dipping up water.

diptych an ancient writing tablet consisting of two hinged leaves with waxed inner sides for writing on with a stylus; the word is recorded in English in this sense from the early 17th century.

Diptychs in the early Church were tablets recording a list of the living and the dead who were prayed for at the Eucharist; the word also denoted the names themselves, and the intercessions in the course of which they were introduced.

From the early 19th century, *diptych* has been used for a painting, especially an altarpiece, on two hinged wooden panels which may be closed like a book.

The word comes via late Latin from late Greek *diptukha* 'pair of writing tablets', from Greek *diptukhos* 'folded in two'.

the Directory the French revolutionary government in France 1795–9, comprising two councils and a five-member executive. It maintained an aggressive foreign policy, but could not control events at home and was overthrown by Napoleon Bonaparte.

The neoclassical decorative style intermediate between the more ornate Louis XVI style and the Empire style, prevalent during *the Directory*, is known as **Directoire**.

dirge a lament for the dead, especially one forming part of a funeral rite. The word comes (in Middle English, denoting the Office for the Dead), from Latin *dirige!* (imperative) 'direct!', the first word of an antiphon (Psalm 5:8) used in the Latin Office for the Dead.

dirty work at the crossroads dishonourable, illicit, or underhand behaviour. The term (recorded from the early 20th century) may reflect a view of *crossroads* as a sinister place, where suicides were traditionally buried.

Dis in Roman mythology, the ruler of the Underworld, equivalent of the Greek Pluto (see ➤ PLUTO[1]) or Hades; the name, as coming from *Dives* 'rich', may be a translation for *Pluto*.

discalced denoting or belonging to one of several strict orders of Catholic friars or nuns who go barefoot or are shod only in sandals.

The word is recorded from the mid 17th century, and is a variant, influenced by French, of earlier *discalceated*, and from Latin *discalceatus*, from *dis-* (expressing removal) + *calceatus* (from *calceus* 'shoe').

disciple a personal follower of Christ during his life, especially one of the twelve Apostles (see also ➤ BELOVED *disciple*.). The word is recorded from Old English, and comes from Latin *discipulus* 'learner', from *discere* learn.

age of discretion the age at which one is considered fit to manage one's affairs or take responsibility for one's actions; the phrase is recorded from the mid 19th century.

Discworld the universe which provides the setting for the fantasy novels of Terry Pratchett (1948–), a disc resting on the backs of four elephants, in turn standing on the shell of a giant turtle swimming through space.

disjecta membra scattered fragments, especially of a written work; the phrase is Latin, an alteration of *disjecti membra poetae*, as used by the poet Horace, 'in our case you would not recognize, as you would in the case of Ennius, the limbs, even though you had dismembered him, of a poet.'

the dismal science economics; a humorous term coined by Thomas Carlyle (1795–1881).

Dismas traditionally, the name of the penitent thief (the unrepentant thief is said to have been named *Gestas*) crucified with Jesus, to whom the promise was made in Luke 23:43, 'Today shalt thou be with me in paradise.' The name is found in the apocryphal Gospel of Nicodemus.

Disneyland a fantastic or fanciful place, a never-never land, from the name of the large amusement park set up by the Disney Corporation near Los Angeles.

the Dispatch Box a box in the British House of Commons for official documents next to which Ministers stand when speaking.

mentioned in dispatches distinguished by having one's actions commended in an official military dispatch.

dissociation of sensibility T. S. Eliot's term for a separation of thought from feeling which he held to be first manifested in poetry of the later seventeenth century.

dissolution of the monasteries the abolition of monasteries in England and Wales by Henry VIII under two Acts (1536, 1539), in order to replenish his treasury by vesting monastic assets in the Crown and to establish royal supremacy in ecclesiastical affairs.

distaff a stick or spindle on to which wool or flax is wound for spinning; in extended usage, used as modifier, as in **distaff side** 'the female side of a family' to mean of or concerning women. The word is recorded from Old English (in form *distæf*); the first element is apparently related to Middle Low German *dise*, *disene* 'distaff, bunch of flax', the second is *staff*. The extended sense arose because spinning was traditionally done by women.

St Distaff's day was the day after Twelfth Day or the Feast of the Epiphany, on which day (7 January) women resumed their spinning and other ordinary employments after the holidays.

go the distance complete a difficult task or endure an ordeal. A metaphor from boxing, meaning when used of a boxer, 'complete a match without being knocked out', and of a boxing match, 'last the scheduled length'. In the US there is an additional baseball-related sense, 'pitch for the entire length of an inning'.

Dives a poetic or literary term for a rich man, deriving (in late Middle English) from late Latin, used in the Vulgate translation of the Bible, in the story in Luke ch. 16 of the rich man and the beggar Lazarus (see ➤ LAZARUS).

divide and rule the policy of maintaining supremacy over one's opponents by encouraging dissent between them, thereby preventing them from uniting against one. Since the early 17th century, the saying has often been wrongly attributed to the Italian political philosopher Niccolò Machiavelli (1469–1527).

The Divine Comedy an epic poem, by ➤ DANTE (*c*.1309–20) describing his spiritual journey through Hell and Purgatory (with Virgil as guide) and finally to Paradise (with Beatrice as guide).

Divine Office in the Christian Church, the series of services of prayers and psalms said (or chanted) daily by Catholic priests, members of religious orders, and other clergy.

divine right of kings the doctrine that kings derive their authority from God not their subjects, from which it follows that rebellion is the worst of political crimes. It was enunciated in Britain in the 16th century under the Stuarts and is also associated with the absolutism of Louis XIV of France.

divining rod a stick or rod, typically forked, used for ➤ DOWSING.

Diwali a Hindu festival with lights, held in the period October to November, to celebrate the new season at the end of the monsoon. It is particularly associated with Lakshmi, the goddess of prosperity, and marks the beginning of the financial year in India.

The name comes from Hindi *dīvālī*, from Sanskrit *dīpāvali* 'row of lights', from *dīpā* 'lamp' + *vali* 'row'.

Dixie an informal name for the Southern states of the US. It was used in the song 'Dixie' (1859), a marching song popular with Confederate soldiers in the American Civil War. The ultimate origin is uncertain, although it has been suggested that the name comes from French *dix* 'ten' on ten-dollar notes printed before the Civil War by the Citizens Bank of Louisiana, and circulating in the Southern States. (See also ➤ HEART *of Dixie*.)

To **whistle Dixie** is to engage in unrealistic fantasies, waste one's time.

Dixieland is a kind of jazz with a strong two-beat rhythm and collective improvisation, which originated in New Orleans in the early 20th century.

djinn an alternative spelling for ➤ JINN.

dobbin a dated pet name for a draught horse or farm horse; recorded from the late 16th century, it is a pet form of the given name *Robert*.

In Thackeray's *Vanity Fair* (1847–8), William *Dobbin* is the name of Amelia's steadfast admirer, seen as a figure of patience and long-suffering.

doctor originally (in Middle English) a person skilled in, and therefore entitled to teach or speak authoritatively on, any branch of knowledge, a learned person; the word comes via Old French from Latin *doctor* 'teacher', from *docere* 'teach'.

From this developed the senses of **Doctor of the Church**, and (with capital initial) a person holding the highest university degree; the sense of *doctor* as an authority on medicine or surgery gave rise to the current meaning of a qualified medical practitioner.

The title *Doctor of the Church* was given to any of the early Christian theologians regarded as especially authoritative in the Western Church (particularly St Augustine of Hippo, St Jerome, St Ambrose, and St Gregory the Great), or those later so designated by the Pope (e.g. St Thomas Aquinas, St Teresa of Ávila).

Doctors' Commons is (the site of) a London building occupied by the former College of Doctors of Laws, in which legal business relating to wills, marriage licences, and divorce proceedings was transacted. The name referred originally to the common table and dining-hall of the Association or College of Doctors of Civil Law in London, formed in 1509 by civilians entitled to plead in the Court of Arches.

dodge the column shirk a duty, avoid work; *column* here means the usual formation of troops for marching.

dodo a large extinct flightless bird with a stout body, which was found on Mauritius until the end of the 17th century. The name, recorded from the early 17th century, comes from Portuguese *doudo* 'simpleton', because the bird had no fear of man and was easily killed.

doe a doe is the emblem of St Withburga (d. *c*.743), an English princess who was said to have founded a community at East Dereham, and who was buried there; according to William of Malmesbury, she had a tame doe which gave her milk.

John Doe chiefly in the US, an anonymous party, typically the plaintiff, in a legal action. Recorded from the 18th century, *John Doe* was originally in legal use as a name of a fictitious plaintiff, corresponding to *Richard Roe*, used to represent the defendant.

dog a *dog* is the emblem of ➤ St DOMINIC, ➤ St ROCH, ➤ St EUSTACE, ➤ St HUBERT, and ➤ St BERNARD *of Aosta*.

A **dog and pony show** is an elaborate display or performance designed to attract people's attention (chiefly North American).

The nickname of ➤ DIOGENES was **the Dog**.

The **dog days** are the hottest period of the year (reckoned in antiquity from the heliacal rising of ➤ SIRIUS, the **Dog Star** (see below).

Dog does not eat dog proverbial saying, mid 16th century, meaning that people of the same profession should not attack each other. A similar idea is found in *De Lingua Latina* by the Roman scholar and satirist Varro

((116–27 BC), '*canis caninam non est* [a dog does not eat a dog's flesh].'

A **dog in the manger** is a person who is inclined to prevent others from having or using things that one does not need oneself, from the fable of the dog that lay in a manger to prevent the ox and horse from eating the hay.

The term **dog Latin** for a debased form of Latin is recorded from the late 18th century, and represents a derogatory use of *dog*.

The **dog rose** is a delicately scented Eurasian wild rose with pink or white flowers, which commonly grows in hedgerows, the root of which was in classical times thought to cure the bite of a mad dog.

The **Dog Star** is the star ➤ SIRIUS. The name is a translation of Greek *kuon* or Latin *canicula* 'small dog', both names of the star; so named as it appears to follow at the heels of Orion (the hunter).

The term **dog-tooth** is given to a small pointed architectural ornament or moulding forming one of a series radiating like petals from a raised centre, typical of Romanesque and Early English styles.

Dogberry a foolish constable in Shakespeare's *Much Ado About Nothing* (1598–9), used allusively for an ignorant and self-important official.

doge formerly the chief magistrate of Venice or Genoa. The word is recorded from the mid 16th century, and comes via French from Venetian Italian *doze*, based on Latin *dux, duc-* 'leader'.

doggerel comic verse composed in irregular rhythm; verse or words that are badly written or expressed. Recorded from late Middle English (as an adjective describing such verse), apparently from *dog* used contemptuously, as in ➤ DOG Latin.

the dogs of war the havoc accompanying military conflict, originally a quotation from Shakespeare's *Julius Caesar* (1599), 'Cry, "Havoc!" and let slip the dogs of war.'

dogwatch either of two short watches on a ship (4–6 or 6–8 pm); the name refers to the light sleeping of dogs, and the difficulty of telling whether, when their eyes are shut, they are asleep or not.

doh the first and eighth note of a major scale.

doldrums the condition of a ship making no headway; a region of calms, sudden storms, and light unpredictable winds near the Equator; in figurative usage, a state or period of little activity or progress in affairs. The word is recorded (as *doldrum* 'dull, sluggish person') from the late 18th century, and may come from *dull*, on the pattern of *tantrums*.

Dolly name given to the lamb which in 1997 was successfully cloned by British scientists.

dolmen a megalithic tomb with a large flat stone laid on upright ones, found chiefly in Britain and France. The word is recorded from the mid 19th century and comes from French, perhaps via Breton from Cornish *tolmen* 'hole of a stone'.

dolphin used for a dolphin-like creature depicted in heraldry or art, typically with an arched body and fins like a fish; in early Christian art, used as an emblem of love, diligence, or swiftness.

Dom a title prefixed to the name of some Roman Catholic dignitaries and Benedictine and Carthusian monks, coming from Latin *dominus* 'master'.

Millennium Dome a large building resembling a giant dome erected at Greenwich in London to house a national exhibition celebrating British achievements at the millennium. *The Dome* was formally opened to visitors by invitation on New Year's Eve 1999, and subsequently to the general public; it closed a year later.

Dome of the Rock an Islamic shrine in Jerusalem, for Muslims the third most holy place after Mecca and Medina. Built in the area of Solomon's temple, the shrine dates from the end of the 7th century. It surrounds the sacred rock on which, according to tradition, Abraham prepared to sacrifice his son Isaac and from which the prophet Muhammad made his miraculous midnight ascent into heaven (the Night Journey).

Domesday Book a comprehensive record of the extent, value, ownership, and liabilities of land in England, made in 1086 by order of William I. The name was apparently a popular one applied during the 12th century because the book was regarded as a final authority (with allusion to *doomsday* 'the Day of Judgement'); it is sometimes referred to as *Doomsday Book*.

dominations (in traditional Christian angelology) the fourth-highest order of the ninefold ➤ CELESTIAL *hierarchy*.

St Dominic (c.1170–1221), Spanish priest and friar; Spanish name *Domingo de Guzmán*. In 1216 he founded the Order of Friars Preachers at Toulouse in France; its members became known as **Dominicans** or Black Friars. In art his usual emblems are a lily or a black and white dog, from the punning *Domini canis* 'hound of God'. His feast day is 8 August.

domino any of 28 small oblong pieces marked with 0–6 pips in each half, used to play the game of **dominoes**, in which each piece is laid down to form a line, each player in turn trying to find and lay down a piece with a value matched by that of a piece at either end of the line already formed. This meaning dates from the early 19th century; in an earlier sense, the word meant a loose cloak, worn with a mask for the upper part of the face at masquerades. It is originally recorded in the late 17th century, from French, denoting a hood worn by priests in winter, and is probably ultimately based on Latin *dominus* 'lord, master'.

The **domino theory** is the theory that a political event in one country will cause similar events in neighbouring countries, like a falling domino causing an entire row of upended dominoes to fall (the **domino effect**). The term derives from a speech by President Eisenhower in 1954 on the possibility of the spread of communist rule.

don a university teacher, especially a senior member of a college at Oxford or Cambridge; originally, a transferred colloquial use of the word as a Spanish title prefixed to a male forename.

Donald Duck a Walt Disney cartoon character, an irascible duck with a high quacking voice who likes his own way; he first appeared in 1934, and Clarence Nash (1904–85) spoke the soundtrack for his voice.

Donation of Constantine the grant by which the emperor ▸ CONSTANTINE supposedly conferred on Pope Sylvester I (314–35) and his successors spiritual supremacy over the other Christian patriarchs; the document was a forgery of the 9th century, but in the Middle Ages was widely regarded as important to claims of papal power in Europe.

Donation of Pepin the undertaking by the Carolingian king Pepin III to win for the papacy lands which had been conquered by

the Lombards; these lands became the foundation of the Papal States.

Donatist a member of a schismatic Christian group in North Africa, formed in 311, who held that only those living a blameless life belonged to the Church. They survived until the 7th century, and were named after *Donatus* (d. c.355), a Christian prelate in Carthage and the group's leader.

Aelius Donatus (4th century), Roman grammarian. The *Ars Grammatica*, containing his treatises on Latin grammar, was the sole textbook used in schools in the Middle Ages.

donjon the great tower or innermost keep of a castle. The word is recorded from Middle English, and is a variant of *dungeon*.

donkey the *donkey* was used as a beast of burden, and traditionally taken as a type of stupidity.

A *donkey*, representing the deliberate eschewing of a horse that might have symbolized martial and worldly power, was the animal on which Jesus rode into Jerusalem on Palm Sunday.

The word was originally pronounced to rhyme with *monkey*, and may come from *dun* 'dull greyish-brown', or from the given name *Duncan*.

Donkeys' years is an informal expression for a very long time, recorded from the early 20th century, and with punning allusion to the length of a donkey's ears.

Donner Pass a site in the Sierra Nevada in north-eastern California where some members of an 1844 emigrant party (the **Donner Party**, named from the *Donner* family) survived a blizzard partly by eating the dead.

Donnybrook Fair an annual fair once held in a what is now a suburb of Dublin; *donnybrook* may now be used to indicate uproar and confusion.

doom death, destruction, or some other terrible fate; in Christian belief, an archaic name for the Last Judgement. The word is recorded from Old English (in form *dōm*), and originally denoted 'statute, judgement'; it is of Germanic origin, from a base meaning 'put in place'.

Doomsday is the last day of the world's existence; Judgement Day. **Doomsday Book** is sometimes found as a variant of Domesday Book.

doppelgänger an apparition or double of a living person. The word (recorded from the

mid 19th century) comes from German, literally 'double-goer'.

Dorcas name of a woman in Acts 9:36, described as 'full of good works and almsdeeds
which she did', after whom the **Dorcas society** of women in a church whose aim is to
make and provide clothing for the poor is
named.

Dorian a member of a Hellenic people
speaking the Doric dialect of Greek, thought
to have entered Greece from the north *c.*1100
BC. They settled in the Peloponnese and later
colonized Sicily and southern Italy.

Dorian mode the mode represented by the
natural diatonic scale D-D (containing a
minor 3rd and minor 7th).

Doric[1] relating to or denoting a classical
order of architecture characterized by a
plain, sturdy column and a thick square abacus resting on a rounded moulding.

Doric[2] the ancient Greek dialect of the Dorians, and in extended usage, any broad or
rustic dialect, especially that spoken in the
north-east of Scotland.

Dormition in the Orthodox Church, the
passing of the Virgin Mary from earthly life;
the feast held in honour of this on 15 August,
corresponding to the Assumption in the
Western Church.

dormouse the *dormouse*, some kinds of
which are noted for spending long periods of
hibernation, is used from the mid 16th century as the type of a sleepy or dozing person,
and sleepiness is the overriding characteristic of the Dormouse in Carroll's *Alice in Wonderland*. The first element of the word is
associated with French *dormir* or Latin
dormire 'to sleep'.

St Dorothy (d. *c.*313), a virgin martyr during the persecution of Diocletian. She is said
to have been taunted on her way to execution by Theophilus, a young lawyer who
asked her to send him fruits from the paradise to which she believed she was going. She
agreed to do so, and after her death an angel
brought him a basket holding three apples
and three roses; this converted him, and he
too was executed. Her emblem is a basket of
fruit and flowers, and her feast day is 6 February.

dot the i's and cross the t's ensure that all
details are correct; the phrase is recorded
from the mid 19th century.

Dotheboys Hall in Dickens's *Nicholas
Nickleby* (1839), the harsh and desolate school
of which Mr Squeers is the headmaster.

Douay Bible an English translation of the
Bible formerly used in the Roman Catholic
Church, completed early in the 17th century
at Douai, in northern France, which at that
time was a centre for English Roman Catholics in exile.

double Dutch language that is impossible
to understand, gibberish. The term is recorded from the late 19th century, although
high Dutch, in the same sense, is earlier.

double helix a pair of parallel helices intertwined about a common axis, especially that
in the structure of the DNA molecule; the
structure was originally proposed by Francis
Crick (1916–) and James D. Watson (1928–),
broadly explaining how genetic information
is carried in living organisms and how genes
replicate.

double whammy a twofold blow or set-
back; a figurative use of 'two blows resulting
in a knockout'. The original (US) sense of
whammy was 'an evil influence', and in the
1950s was particularly associated with the
comic strip L'il Abner; a *double whammy* in
this context was an intense and powerful
look which had a stunning effect on its victims.
  Double whammy in its current sense entered
the language through modern politics, being
given a high profile by Conservative campaigning in the British general election of
1992, with campaign posters on tax policy
using the slogan, 'Labour's double whammy'.

doublethink the acceptance of or mental
capacity to accept contrary opinions or beliefs at the same time, especially as a result of
political indoctrination, coined by George
Orwell in his novel *Nineteen Eighty-Four* (1949).

Doubting Castle in Bunyan's *Pilgrim's Progress* (1678), the castle of Giant Despair.

doubting Thomas a person who is sceptical and refuses to believe something without proof, from biblical allusion to the
apostle ➤ *St* THOMAS, who declared that he
would not believe that Christ had risen unless he had seen and touched his wounds.

dove this bird is traditionally a symbol of
peace.
  In Christian art, a *dove* often stands for the
Holy Spirit, as in Luke 3:22, in the account of
Jesus being baptized by John in Jordan, 'And

the Holy Spirit descended in a bodily shape like a dove upon him.' The dove in biblical terms is also associated with an olive branch as a messenger of peace and deliverance, as in the account in Genesis 8:8–12, of the dove sent out from the ark by Noah, which returned from its second flight with an olive leaf in its beak, 'so Noah knew that the waters were abated from the earth'.

A dove is the emblem of ➤ *St* AMBROSE, ➤ *St* DAVID, ➤ *St* GREGORY, and the Welsh-born St Samson, 6th-century bishop of Dol in Brittany.

In 20th century political usage, a *dove* is a person who (unlike a *hawk*) advocates peaceful or conciliatory policies, especially in foreign affairs.

Treaty of Dover made in 1670 between Charles II and Louis XIV; there were in fact two treaties, in the second and secret one of which Charles promised to declare himself a Catholic in return for a French subsidy.

Dow Jones Index an index of figures indicating the relative price of shares on the New York Stock Exchange, based on the average price of selected stocks. It is named from *Dow Jones & Co, Inc.*, a financial news agency founded by Charles H. *Dow* (1851–1902) and Edward D. *Jones* (c.1855–1920), American economists whose company compiled the first average of US stock prices in 1884.

Downing Street a street in Westminster, London, between Whitehall and St James's Park. No. 10 (since the time of Sir Robert Walpole) is the official residence of the Prime Minister; No. 11 is the home of the Chancellor of the Exchequer, and the Foreign and Commonwealth Office is also situated in the street. *Downing Street* is often used to personify the Prime Minister's immediate circle as distinct from the Parliamentary party.

The **Downing Street Declaration** is a joint agreement between the British and Irish governments, formulated in 1993, forming the basis of a peace initiative in Northern Ireland.

dowsing a technique for searching for underground water, minerals, ley lines, or anything invisible, by observing the motion of a pointer (traditionally a forked stick or *divining rod*, now often paired bent wires) or the changes in direction of a pendulum, supposedly in response to unseen influences.

doxology a liturgical formula of praise to God. The word is recorded from the mid 17th century, and comes via medieval Latin from Greek *doxologia*, from *doxa* 'appearance, glory', from *dokein* 'seem'.

dozen a group or set of twelve. Recorded from Middle English, the word comes ultimately (via Old French) from Latin *duodecim* 'twelve'.

Drachenfels a hill in western Germany on the east bank of the Rhine, which in German legend was the home of the dragon killed by ➤ SIEGFRIED.

Draco (7th century BC), Athenian legislator. His codification of Athenian law was notorious for its severity in that the death penalty was imposed even for trivial crimes, giving rise to the adjective **draconian**.

Dracula the Transylvanian vampire in Bram Stoker's novel *Dracula* (1897). The name is a variant of *Drakula*, *Dragwlya*, names given to Vlad Țepeș (Vlad the Impaler), a 15th-century prince of Wallachia renowned for his cruelty.

dragon a mythical monster like a giant reptile. In European tradition the dragon is typically fire-breathing and tends to symbolize chaos or evil, whereas in the Far East it is usually a beneficent symbol of fertility, associated with water and the heavens.

In medieval Norse and Germanic legends, *dragons* are often shown as guardians of treasure-hoards terrorizing the surrounding countryside; the dragon killed by ➤ BEOWULF in his final battle is a typical example.

A *dragon* is the emblem of ➤ St GEORGE, ➤ *St* MARGARET *of Antioch*, ➤ *St* MARTHA, St Sylvester (d. 335), Pope from 314 to 335, and the 6th-century Welsh-born St Armel, Breton abbot who is said to have captured a dragon and disposed of it by ordering it to plunge into the river below Mont-Saint-Armel.

Dragon is also used for any of (originally) four Asian countries, South Korea, Taiwan, Singapore, and Hong Kong, which developed booming economies based on high-technology exports.

The word is recorded from Middle English (also denoting a large serpent), and comes via Old French and Latin from Greek *drakōn* 'serpent'.

A **dragon boat** is a traditional type of Chinese rowing boat, decorated at the prow and stern with figures of the head and tail of a dragon, used in racing at an annual Spring festival, said to originate in ancient China.

A **Dragon Lady** is a domineering, powerful, or belligerent woman; from the name of a villainous Asian female character in the comic strip 'Terry and the Pirates', drawn by the American cartoonist Milton Caniff (1907-1988).

A **dragon ship** was a Viking longship ornamented with a beaked prow.

The **dragon's teeth** were the teeth of the dragon killed by ➤ CADMUS in Greek legend, which when sown in the ground sprouted up as armed men; the expression **sow dragon's teeth**, meaning take action that (perhaps unintentionally) brings trouble about, derives from this.

here be dragons alluding to a traditional indication of early map-makers that a region was unexplored and potentially dangerous.

dramatic unities the three dramatic principles requiring limitation of the supposed time of a drama to that occupied in acting it or to a single day (**unity of time**), use of one scene throughout (**unity of place**), and concentration on the development of a single plot (**unity of action**). The principles are derived from a Renaissance interpretation of Aristotle's *Poetics*.

Drang nach Osten the former German policy of eastward expansion, especially that espoused under Nazi rule. The phrase is German, literally 'pressure towards the east'.

Draupnir in Scandinavian mythology, the gold ring belonging to ➤ ODIN which produced nine further rings every night.

draw the longbow make exaggerated statements about one's own achievements, boast; the term is recorded from the early 19th century.

dreadlocks a Rastafarian hairstyle in which the hair is washed but not combed and twisted while wet into tight braids or ringlets hanging down on all sides.

dreadnought a type of battleship introduced in the early 20th century, larger and faster than its predecessors and equipped entirely with large-calibre guns. The term comes from the name of Britain's HMS *Dreadnought*, which was the first to be completed (1906).

City of Dreaming Spires a name for Oxford, deriving originally from 'Thyrsis' (1866), a poem by Matthew Arnold, which refers to 'that sweet City with her dreaming Spires.'

dree one's weird submit to one's destiny; *dree*, a Scottish or archaic word meaning 'endure', is recorded from Old English (in form

drēogan) and is of Germanic origin; related to Old Norse *drȳgja* 'practise, perpetrate'.

Dresden a city in eastern Germany, the capital of Saxony, on the River Elbe. Famous for its baroque architecture, it was almost totally destroyed by Allied bombing in 1945, and is sometimes referred to as a type of complete destruction of this kind.

Dresden is also associated with porcelain ware with elaborate decoration and delicate colourings, made originally at Dresden and (since 1710) at nearby Meissen.

dress-down Friday in the US a day, typically a Friday, on which it is considered acceptable for office workers to dress more casually ('dress down') in the workplace.

Dreyfusard a supporter of the French army officer of Jewish descent Alfred *Dreyfus* (1859–1935), who in 1894 was falsely accused of providing military secrets to the Germans; his trial and imprisonment caused a major political crisis in France. He was eventually rehabilitated in 1906.

drive-by shooting a shooting carried out from a passing vehicle; the term is recorded in the US from the early 1980s, and was linked particularly with rival teenage gangs and with the drug culture. The term *drive-by* soon began to be used figuratively, especially in implying a hit-and-run approach to a subject, as in **drive-by documentary** and **drive-by journalism**.

driven snow snow piled into drifts or made smooth by the wind, taken as a type of purity.

Drogheda a port in the NE Republic of Ireland, where in 1649 the inhabitants were massacred after refusing to surrender to Oliver Cromwell's forces.

droit de seigneur the alleged right of a medieval feudal lord to have sexual intercourse with a vassal's bride on her wedding night. The phrase is French, literally 'lord's right'.

drone a male bee in a colony of social bees, which does no work but can fertilize a queen; in figurative usage (from the early 16th century), a person who does no useful work and lives off others.

In the stories of P. G. Wodehouse, the **Drones Club** was the club frequented by Bertie Wooster and his friends.

a drop in the ocean a very small amount compared with what is needed. Wyclif's translation (1382) of Isaiah has an earlier version, 'a drope of a boket' [a drop of a bucket], and this was used also in the Authorized Version. A **drop in the bucket** is now also current.

Drottningholm the winter palace of the Swedish royal family, on an island to the west of Stockholm. It was built in 1662 for Queen Eleonora of Sweden.

a drug on the market an unsaleable or valueless commodity. Drug in the sense of 'a commodity for which there is no demand' is recorded from the mid 17th century, but its history does not make it unequivocally clear that it is the same word as the medicinal substance. The phrase is recorded from the mid 19th century (earlier also as **a drug in the market**).

Druid a priest, magician, or soothsayer in the ancient Celtic religion; the word is first recorded from the mid 16th century in English sources, in Golding's translation of Caesar's *Martiall Exploytes in Gallia* (1565), and comes from Latin *druidae, druides* (plural), from Gaulish, related to Irish *draoidh* 'magician'.

According to Pliny the elder, *mistletoe* was the sacred plant of the Druids, who cut it ritually with a golden sickle as part of their sacrificial ceremonies. The popular association of druids with oak groves derives largely from Pliny's account.

The use of *Druid* for a member of a group claiming to represent or be derived from this religion is recorded from the early 18th century.

drumhead court martial carried out by an army in the field, originally round an up-turned drum, for summary treatment of offences during military operations.

drunken Helot in allusion to the statement by Plutarch that Helots were, on certain occasions, forced to appear in a state of drunkenness as an object lesson to Spartan youth.

Drury Lane the site in London of the Theatre Royal, one of London's most famous theatres, where Nell Gwynn (1650–87) is said to have sold oranges. While under Sheridan's managment in the late 18th century, it was demolished and rebuilt; the new theatre, however, burned down in 1809.

The present and fourth theatre on this site, dating from 1812, was not particularly successful until the 1880s, when it became famous for its melodramas and spectacles.

Druze a member of a political and religious sect of Islamic origin, living chiefly in Lebanon and Syria. The Druze broke away from the Ismaili Muslims in the 11th century; they are regarded as heretical by the Muslim community at large.

The name comes from French, and derives from Arabic *durūz* (plural), from the name of one of their founders, Muhammad ibn Ismail al-Darazī (died 1019).

dryad in folklore and Greek mythology, a nymph inhabiting a tree, especially an oak tree, or a wood; the word comes via Old French and Latin from Greek *druas, druad-*, from *drus* 'tree'.

Dr Jonas Dryasdust a fictional antiquarian to whom Sir Walter Scott pretended to dedicate *Ivanhoe* (1819) and other novels; from this, a writer or student of antiquities, history, or statistics, who is concerned with the driest and most uninteresting details.

the Dual Monarchy Austria-Hungary, especially between 1867 and 1918.

ducat a gold coin formerly current in most European countries. The origin is Italian *ducato*, referring to a silver coin minted by the Duke of Apulia in 1190.

Duccio (*c.*1255–*c.*1320), Italian painter, founder of the Sienese school of painting, building on elements of the Byzantine tradition. The only fully documented surviving work by him is the *Maestà* for the high altar of Siena cathedral (completed 1311).

duck in cricket, a batsman's score of nought. From a shortening of *duck's egg*, used for the figure 0 because of its similar outline.

duck and cover in the US, take action to protect oneself from danger, especially where such action is likely to prove completely inadequate; with reference to a civil-defence slogan used in the US *c.*1950.

ducking stool a chair fastened to the end of a pole, used formerly to plunge offenders into a pond or river as a punishment, and used particularly for disorderly women, scolds, and dishonest tradesmen.

ducks and drakes a game of throwing flat stones so that they skim along the surface of water; in figurative use, **play ducks and drakes with** trifle with; treat frivolously or wastefully.

get one's ducks in a row get one's facts straight or have everything organized; the reference is to lining up one's targets.

Duessa in Spenser's *Faerie Queene*, the daughter of Deceit and Shame, standing for falsity in general, but in particular alluding to the Roman Catholic Church and Mary, Queen of Scots; she is contrasted with ➤ UNA, who stands for single-minded adherence to true religion.

Dulcinea the name given by ➤ *Don* QUIX-OTE to his mistress in Cervantes's romance; more generally, a sweetheart, a lover.

dun make persistent demands on (someone), especially for payment of a debt. First recorded (in the early 17th century) as a noun, from *Dunkirk* privateer. An alternative (18th-century) explanation derived it from the name of *Joe Dun*, said to have been a bailiff in Lincoln.

Book of the Dun Cow a fragmentary Irish manuscript of the 11th century, containing stories from Irish mythology, and in particular the deeds of Cuchulain.

Dunblane a town in Scotland which in March 1996 was the scene of a tragedy when sixteen pupils of the local primary school with their teacher were shot to death by a ➤ SPREE *killer*.

dunce a foolish or ignorant person; originally an epithet for a follower of ➤ *John* DUNS *Scotus*, whose adherents were ridiculed by 16th-century humanists and reformers as enemies of learning.

A **dunce's cap** is a paper cone formerly put on the head of a *dunce* at school as a mark of disgrace; the expression is recorded from the mid 19th century.

Dunfermline a city in Fife, Scotland, near the Firth of Forth. A number of Scottish kings, including Robert the Bruce, are buried in its Benedictine abbey.

Dunkirk a port of northern France, which in the Middle Ages was a centre of privateering activity. In modern times, *Dunkirk* was the scene of the evacuation of the British Expeditionary Force in 1940. Forced to retreat to the Channel by the German breakthrough at Sedan, 335,000 Allied troops were evacuated by warships, requisitioned civilian ships, and a host of small boats, under constant attack from the air.

The expression **Dunkirk spirit** is used (sometimes ironically) for the refusal to surrender or despair in a time of crisis.

Dunmow flitch a side of bacon awarded at Great Dunmow in Essex on Whit Monday to any married couple who will swear that they have not quarrelled or repented of their marriage vows for at least a year and a day. The custom was instituted in Great Dunmow; the earliest evidence for it is 1244, though its origin may be earlier.

John Duns Scotus (*c.*1265–1308), Scottish theologian and scholar. A profoundly influential figure in the Middle Ages, he was the first major theologian to defend the theory of the Immaculate Conception, and opposed ➤ *St* THOMAS *Aquinas* in arguing that faith was a matter of will rather than something dependent on logical proofs.

In the 16th century his name, through his followers the *Scotists*, became associated with a scholasticism characterized by hair-splitting and useless distinctions, which was seen as inimical to the new learning; from this developed the word ➤ DUNCE.

St Dunstan (*c.*909–88), Anglo-Saxon prelate. As Archbishop of Canterbury he introduced the strict Benedictine rule into England and succeeded in restoring monastic life. He is traditionally said to have been a metalworker. He is sometimes shown holding the devil by the nose with a pair of tongs, and his feast day is 19 May.

duodecimo a size of book in which each leaf is one twelfth of the size of the printing sheet. The word is recorded from the mid 17th century, and comes from Latin *(in) duodecimo* '(in) a twelfth'.

Auguste Dupin detective created by Edgar Allan Poe in *The Murders in the Rue Morgue* (1841) and other stories, noted for his powers of logic and deduction.

Dame Durden from a traditional song, a name for a housewife; in Dickens's *Bleak House* (1853), when Esther Summerson takes over the household keys, she is nicknamed *Dame Durden*.

Durga in Hindu mythology, a fierce goddess, wife of Shiva, often identified with Kali. She is usually depicted riding a tiger or lion and slaying the buffalo demon, and with eight or ten arms.

Durindana the sword of Roland or Orlando, which had been that of Hector of Troy. Also called *Durandal*.

Dussehra the tenth and final day of the Hindu festival of Navaratri. In southern India it especially commemorates the victory of the god Rama over the demon king Ravana.

dust and ashes used to convey a feeling of great disappointment of disillusion about something; originally with allusion to the legend of the ➤ DEAD *Sea fruit*.

shake the dust off one's feet depart indignantly or disdainfully; originally with allusion to Matthew 10:14.

dusty answer an unsatisfactory reply; perhaps originally as a quotation from George Meredith's *Modern Love* (1862).

Dutch uncle a person giving firm but benevolent advice; the expression is recorded from the mid 19th century, and may imply only that the person concerned is not an actual relative.

Dutchman's breeches a small patch of blue sky, traditionally said by sailors to be just enough to make a pair of breeches for a Dutchman.

dwarf in folklore or fantasy, a member of a mythical race of short, stocky human-like creatures who are generally skilled in mining and metalworking.

dybbuk in Jewish folklore, a malevolent wandering spirit that enters and possesses the body of a living person until exorcized.

dyed in the wool unchanging in a particular belief or opinion, originally with allusion to the fact that yarn was dyed in the raw state, producing a more even and permanent colour.

put one's finger in the dyke attempt to stem the advance of something undesirable, from a story of a small Dutch boy who saved his community from flooding, by placing his finger in a hole in a dyke.

Ee

E the fifth letter of the modern English alphabet. and of the ancient Roman one, representing the Semitic ∃ (= *h*), but adopted by the Greeks (and from them by the Romans) as a vowel.

In the Second World War, an **E-boat** was an enemy torpedo boat.

An **E-number** is a code number preceded by the letter E, denoting food additives numbered in accordance with EU directives.

eagle this large bird of prey, renowned for its keen sight and powerful soaring flight, is traditionally regarded as the ➤ KING *of birds*. In the 15th-century *Boke of St Albans*, the eagle is listed in falconry as the bird for an emperor.

An *eagle* is the emblem of ➤ St JOHN *the Evangelist*.

The figure of an eagle was used as an ensign in the Roman and French imperial armies; a figure of a **bald eagle** is the emblem of the United States, from which **the Eagle** may mean the US.

The **two-headed eagle** was the emblem of the empires of Austria and Russia.

Ealing Studios a film studio in Ealing, West London, active 1929–55, but remembered chiefly for the comedies it made in the post-war decade.

Early English denoting the earliest stage of English Gothic church architecture, typical of the late 12th and 13th centuries and marked by the use of pointed arches and simple lancet windows without tracery.

the earthly paradise the garden of Eden; an ideal or idyllic place, typically one of great natural beauty.

earthquake in Greek mythology, ➤ POSEIDON was god of earthquakes, and one of his epithets was 'earth-shaker'.

east the direction towards the point of the horizon where the sun rises at the equinoxes, on the right-hand side of a person facing north, or the point on the horizon itself.

In a Christian church, *east* designates the end that contains the (high) altar, traditionally but not necessarily the geographical east.

The word is recorded from Old English (in form *ēst-*) and is of Germanic origin; it comes ultimately from an Indo-European root shared by Latin *aurora*, Greek *auōs* 'dawn'.

The **East End** is the part of London east of the City as far as the River Lea, including the Docklands; traditionally having a high immigrant population, and marked by poverty.

The **East India Company** was a trading company (informally, ➤ JOHN *Company*) formed in 1600 to develop commerce in the newly colonized areas of SE Asia and India. In the 18th century it took administrative control of Bengal and other areas of India, and held it until the British Crown took over in 1858 in the wake of the Indian Mutiny. An **East Indiaman** was a trading ship belonging to the East India Company.

The **East Indies** is an archaic name for the whole of SE Asia to the east of and including India.

The **East Side** is a part of Manhattan in New York City, lying between the East River and Fifth Avenue.

Easter the most important and oldest festival of the Christian Church, celebrating the resurrection of Christ and held (in the Western Church) between 21 March and 25 April, on the first Sunday after the first full moon following the northern spring equinox.

The name is recorded from Old English (in form *ēastre*) and is of Germanic origin, related to *east*. According to Bede the word is derived from *Ēastre*, the name of a goddess associated with spring.

An **Easter egg** is an artificial chocolate egg or decorated hard-boiled egg given at Easter, especially to children.

The **Easter Rising** was the uprising in Dublin and other cities in Ireland against British rule, Easter 1916. It ended with the surrender of the protesters, and the execution of their leaders.

An **Easter Sepulchre** was a recess in certain medieval churches for keeping the Eucharistic elements from Good Friday until the Easter festivities.

Easter term is a term in the courts of law, formerly movable and occurring between Easter and Whitsuntide, but now fixed within a certain period; in the older universities, a term formerly occurring between Easter and Whitsuntide and now included in the Trinity term; in some universities and schools, the term between Christmas and Easter.

Eastern Church another name for the ➤ ORTHODOX *Church*.

Eastern Empire the eastern part of the Roman Empire, after its division in AD 395.

eat crow in North American usage, be humiliated by having to admit one's mistakes or defeats.

eat humble pie make a humble apology and accept humiliation. *Humble pie* is from a pun based on *umbles* 'offal', considered as inferior food.

eat one's terms in the course of studying for the Bar, be required to dine a certain number of times in the Hall of one of the Inns of Court.

Ebenezer the name of the memorial stone set up by Samuel after the victory of Mizpeh, when the Israelites recovered the ark of the Lord from the Philistines (1 Samuel 7–12); in Hebrew the name means 'the stone of help', and from this the term has come to be used for a Nonconformist chapel.

Ebla a city in ancient Syria, situated to the south-west of Aleppo. It became very powerful in the mid 3rd millennium BC, when it dominated a region corresponding to modern Lebanon, northern Syria, and SE Turkey. It was a thriving trading city and centre of scholarship, as testified in some 15,000 cuneiform tablets discovered among the city's ruins in 1975.

Eblis in William Beckford's *Vathek* (1786), the prince of darkness to whose realm Vathek is banished after he has impiously challenged Mohammed and brought about his own damnation; in later literature, the term 'son of Eblis' is found as an objurgation. The name probably represents ➤ IBLIS.

Ebonics American black English regarded as a language in its own right rather than as a dialect of standard English; the name is a blend of *ebony* and *phonics*.

ebony a heavy blackish or very dark brown wood, traditionally taken as the type of intense blackness. The name is recorded from late Middle English and comes from earlier *ebon* (via Old French and Latin from Greek

ebenos 'ebony tree'), perhaps on the pattern of *ivory*.

Eboracum Roman name for York; from this, the ecclesiastical title of the Archbishop of York is *Ebor*.

Ecce Homo a representation of Christ wearing the crown of thorns, from the words of Pontius Pilate to the Jews, 'behold the man', after Jesus was crowned with thorns (John 19:5).

Ecclesia the Church, especially as personified in medieval art.

Ecclesiastes a book of the Bible traditionally attributed to Solomon, consisting largely of reflections on the vanity of human life.

Ecclesiastical Commissioners the members of a body, subordinate to the Privy Council, which managed the estates and revenues of the Church of England from 1835 to 1948.

Ecclesiasticus a book of the Apocrypha containing moral and practical maxims, probably composed or compiled in the early 2nd century BC.

Echo in Greek mythology, a nymph deprived of speech by Hera in order to stop her chatter, and left able only to repeat what others had said; she fell in love with ➤ NARCISSUS, and on being rejected by him, wasted away with grief until there was nothing left of her but her voice. In another account she was vainly loved by the god Pan, who finally caused some shepherds to go mad and tear her to pieces; Earth hid the fragments, which could still imitate other sounds.

Eclipse a famous racehorse of the 18th century and one of the ancestors of all thoroughbred racehorses throughout the world. The **Eclipse Stakes**, run annually at Sandown Park near London since 1886, is named in the horse's honour. (See also ➤ COPENHAGEN.)

economical with the truth used euphemistically to describe a person or statement that lies or deliberately withholds information. The expression comes from a statement given in evidence by Sir Robert Armstrong, British cabinet secretary, in the 'Spycatcher' trial (1986), conducted to prevent publication of a book by a former MI5 employee, 'It contains a misleading impression, not a lie. It was being economical with the truth.'

The theological phrase *economy of truth* (i.e. sparing use of truth) is of long-standing, and was used by the 18th-century politician Edmund Burke.

ectoplasm a supernatural viscous substance that is supposed to exude from the body of a medium during a spiritualistic trance and form the material for the manifestation of spirits.

ecumenical originally (from the late 16th century), belonging to the universal Church; later, promoting or relating to unity among the world's Christian Churches, as in **ecumenical movement**, a movement for the reunification of the various branches of the Christian Church worldwide.

The word comes via late Latin from Greek *oikoumenikos* from *oikoumenē* 'the (inhabited) earth'.

Edda either of two 13th-century Icelandic books, the **Elder** or **Poetic Edda** (a collection of Old Norse poems on Norse legends) and the **Younger** or **Prose Edda** (a handbook to Icelandic poetry by Snorri Sturluson). The Eddas are the chief source of knowledge of Scandinavian mythology.

Eddystone Rocks a rocky reef off the coast of Cornwall, SW of Plymouth. The reef was the site of the earliest lighthouse (1699) built on rocks fully exposed to the sea.

Eden the place (more fully, the **Garden of Eden**) where Adam and Eve lived in the biblical account of the Creation, from which they were expelled for disobediently eating the fruit of the tree of knowledge.

The name comes from late Latin (Vulgate), Greek *Edēn* (Septuagint), and Hebrew *'Eden*, perhaps related to Akkadian *edinu*, from Sumerian *eden* 'plain, desert', but believed to be related to Hebrew *'ēḏen* 'delight'.

set someone's teeth on edge cause someone to feel intense discomfort or irritation. An expression used in the Bible (Jeremiah 31:30) of the unpleasant sensation caused by eating something bitter or sour.

Battle of Edgehill the first pitched battle of the English Civil War (1642), fought at the village of Edgehill in the west Midlands. The Parliamentary army attempted to halt the Royalist army's march on London; the battle ended with no clear winner and with heavy losses on both sides.

Edict of Milan a proclamation made by the Emperor Constantine in 313 by which Christianity was given legal status within the Empire.

Edict of Nantes an edict issued by Henry IV of France in 1598, granting toleration to the Protestants (revoked by Louis XIV in 1685).

Edinburgh Festival an international festival of the arts held annually in Edinburgh since 1947. In addition to the main programme a flourishing fringe festival has developed.

St Edmund the Martyr (*c*.841–70), king of East Anglia 855–70. After the defeat of his army by the invading Danes in 870, tradition holds that he was captured and shot with arrows for refusing to reject the Christian faith or to share power with his pagan conqueror. Arrows, for his martyrdom, and a wolf, said to have guarded the saint's head after his death, are the emblems of St Edmund. His feast day is 20 November.

Edward male forename; name of two English saints.

St Edward the Confessor (*c*.1003–66), was the son of Ethelred the Unready and his second wife Emma of Normandy, king of England 1042–66. Famed for his piety, Edward rebuilt Westminster Abbey, where he was eventually buried. He is sometimes shown with a ring which according to legend he gave to a beggar; subsequently English pilgrims in the Holy Land (or India) encountered an old man who said that he was St John the Apostle, and who gave them back the ring, telling them to return it to the king, and warn him that he would die in six months' time. His feast day is 13 October.

St Edward the Martyr (*c*.963–78), was the son of Edgar, king of England 975–8. Edward was faced by a challenge for the throne from supporters of his half-brother, Ethelred, who eventually had him murdered at Corfe Castle in Dorset. His emblem is a dagger, symbol of his martyrdom. His feast day is 18 March.

Edwardian of, relating to, or characteristic of the reign of King *Edward* VII (1841–1910), king from 1901.

Egeria in Roman religion, an Italian water-nymph, to whom pregnant women sacrificed to secure easy delivery, and who was said to be the consort and adviser of Numa Pompilius, the legendary second king of Rome (715–673 BC), whom she used to meet by night at the Porta Capena and instruct in statesmanship and religion.

egg it was traditionally thought that if a hen laid a very small egg it was unlucky; it was sometimes called a *cock's egg*, and believed capable of hatching a cockatrice or basilisk. Superstition also attached to the question of which end of a boiled egg should be opened; Sir Thomas Browne in *Vulgar Errors* (1650) notes that it was thought unlucky to crack an egg at the smaller end.

Egg Saturday and **Egg Sunday** are former names for the Saturday and Sunday before Shrove Tuesday, traditionally a time of celebration before the rigours of Lent.

kill the goose that lays the golden eggs destroy a reliable and valuable source of income; the allusion is to one of Aesop's fables, in which a man killed the goose which laid a single golden egg each day in the belief that he would find a number of eggs inside it, and instead through greed lost his source of wealth. (See also ➤ GOLDEN *goose*.)

putting all one's eggs in one basket risking everything on the success of one venture. The warning against doing this was first noted as a proverbial expression in English in the mid 17th century.

eggshell traditionally a type of worthlessness or fragility. *Eggshells* were also believed to be used in casting spells, and it was thought necessary to crush or break them to prevent this, as recorded by Pliny the Elder (23–79). In the late 16th century, Scot in his *Discoverie of Witchcraft* (1584) recorded the belief that witches could sail in eggshells.

ego a person's sense of self-esteem or self-importance; in metaphysics, a conscious thinking subject; in psychoanalysis, the part of the mind that mediates between the conscious and the unconscious and is responsible for reality testing and a sense of personal identity. The term is recorded from the early 19th century, and comes from Latin, literally 'I'.

egotistical sublime a phrase coined by Keats in a letter of 27 October 1818 to describe his version of Wordsworth's distinctive genius.

Egypt the ancient kingdoms of Upper and Lower Egypt were ruled successively by thirty-one dynasties, which may be divided into the Old Kingdom, the Middle Kingdom, and the New Kingdom. Egypt was a centre of Hellenistic culture and then a Roman province before coming under Islamic rule and then becoming part of the Ottoman Empire (modern Egypt became independent in 1922).

Gypsies derive their name from the popular belief that they originated in Egypt, and ➤ St MARY *of Egypt* was sometimes referred to informally as *Mary Gypsy*.

To **spoil the Egyptians** means to profit from the wealth or belongings of another (*spoil* here means plunder or despoil); with biblical allusion to Exodus 12:37.

Eiffel Tower a wrought-iron structure erected in Paris for the World Exhibition of 1889, designed and built by the French engineer Alexandre Gustave *Eiffel* (1832–1923). With a height of 300 metres (984 ft), it was the tallest man-made structure for many years.

Eiger a mountain peak in the Bernese Alps in central Switzerland, the north face of which is often taken as the type of something bleak and forbidding.

eight the word is recorded from Old English (in form *ehta*, *eahta*) and is of Germanic origin; it comes from an Indo-European root shared by Latin *octo* and Greek *oktō*.

The Eight is the name given to a group of American realist painters who exhibited together in 1908, united by a concern to involve painting with the realities of contemporary, especially urban, life.

The expression **behind the eight ball** means (chiefly in North America) at a disadvantage; in a variety of the game of pool, the black ball is numbered eight.

eightfold path in Buddhism, the path to nirvana, comprising eight aspects in which an aspirant must become practised.

Eikon Basilike a book, published about the date of his execution (1649), claiming to be meditations by Charles I, and for a long time so regarded; the title is Greek, and means literally 'royal image'. It was exceedingly popular, going through 49 editions, to the extent that a reply by Parliament was thought necessary, and ➤ EIKONOKLASTES published in the same year.

Eikonoklastes a book, 'the Imagebreaker', by John Milton, issued in 1649 by Parliament as a detailed refutation of the picture of Charles I given in ➤ EIKON *Basilike*.

Eire the Gaelic name for Ireland, the official name of the Republic of Ireland from 1937 to 1949.

Eirene in Greek mythology, the goddess of peace; her Roman equivalent is Pax.

eisteddfod a competitive festival of music and poetry in Wales, in particular the annual **National Eisteddfod**. The word is from Welsh, and means literally 'session', from *eistedd* 'sit'.

Battle of El Alamein a battle of the Second World War fought in 1942 at El Alamein in Egypt, 90 km (60 miles) west of Alexandria. The German Afrika Korps under Rommel was halted in its advance towards the Nile by the British 8th Army under Montgomery, giving a decisive British victory.

El Dorado the name of a fictitious country or city abounding in gold, formerly believed to exist somewhere in the region of the Orinoco and Amazon Rivers; the name is first recorded in English in the title of Raleigh's *Discoverie of Guiana, with a relation of the Great and Golden City of Manoa (which the Spanish call El Dorado)* (1596).

The belief, which led Spanish conquistadors to converge on the area in search of treasure and Sir ➤ *Walter* RALEIGH to lead his second expedition up the Orinoco, appears to have originated in rumours of an Indian ruler who ritually coated his body with gold dust and then plunged into a sacred lake while his subjects threw in gold and jewels. The name comes from Spanish, and means literally 'the gilded one'.

Elaine in Arthurian romances, the name of the maiden who falls in love with Lancelot and dies of unrequited love; in Malory's *Morte D'Arthur* she is the *Maid of Astolat* (Tennyson's *Lady of Shalott*).

Elba a small island off the west coast of Italy, famous as the place of Napoleon's first exile (1814–15).

elder according to legend, ➤ JUDAS *Iscariot* hanged himself on an elder, and the tree, which is associated with witches, is sometimes believed to be unlucky. Pliny's *Natural History*, on the other hand, says that elder has prophylactic and curative properties, and it was also believed that elder could protect against lightning.

Eleanor Cross any of the stone crosses erected by Edward I to mark the stopping places of the cortège that brought the body of his queen, Eleanor of Castile (1246–90), from Nottinghamshire to London in 1290. Three of the twelve crosses survive.

Elector a German prince entitled to take part in the election of the Holy Roman Emperor. There were originally seven Electors; subsequently electorates were created for Bavaria (1623–1778), Hanover (from 1708), and Hesse-Kassel (from 1803). The role officially terminated with the abolition of the ➤ HOLY *Roman Empire* in 1806.

electoral college a body of electors chosen or appointed by a larger group, as, the princes who elected the Holy Roman Emperor, or (in the US) a body of people representing the states of the US, who formally cast votes for the election of the President and Vice-President.

Electra in Greek mytholgy, the daughter of ➤ AGAMEMNON and ➤ CLYTEMNESTRA, sister of Orestes. She persuaded her brother Orestes to kill Clytemnestra and Aegisthus (their mother's lover) in revenge for the murder of Agamemnon. Her name is used in **Electra complex**, a dated term in psychoanalysis for the Oedipus complex as manifested in young girls.

Electra is also the name of one of the ➤ PLEIADES, daughter of the Titan Atlas and mother by Zeus of ➤ DARDANUS, ancestor of the kings of Troy.

elegy in Greek and Roman poetry, a poem written in elegiac couplets, as notably by Catullus and Propertius; in modern literature, a poem of serious reflection, typically a lament for the dead. The word is recorded from the early 16th century and comes via French or Latin from Greek *elegeia*, from *elegos* 'mournful poem'.

element any of the four substances (earth, water, air, and fire) regarded as the fundamental constituents of the world in ancient and medieval philosophy. The word is recorded from Middle English (denoting fundamental constituents of the world or celestial objects) and comes via Old French from Latin *elementum* 'principle, rudiment', translating Greek *stoikheion* 'step, component part'.

In late Middle English, *elements* denoted the letters of the alphabet; from this developed the sense of the rudiments of learning, the first principles of a subject.

From the mid 16th century, *element* (usually in plural) has also denoted the bread or wine used in the Christian Eucharist.

Elementary, my dear Watson supposedly said by Sherlock Holmes to ➤ *Dr* WATSON, although the remark in this form is not found in any of Conan Doyle's stories;

the nearest thing to it is an exchange in *The Memoirs of Sherlock Holmes* (1894). '"Excellent," I cried. "Elementary," said he.' The misquotation 'Elementary, my dear Watson' is first recorded in P. G. Wodehouse's *Psmith, Journalist* (1915).

elenchus the Socratic method of eliciting truth by question and answer, especially as used to refute an argument (also called **Socratic elenchus**).

elephant the *elephant* is the largest living land animal, and is taken as a type of something of great size and weight. The Indian elephant was traditionally used as a beast of burden and in the ancient world (as, notably, by ➤ HANNIBAL when he crossed the Alps in 219–18 BC) as a mount in war.

Elephant is also used for a size of paper, typically 28 x 23 inches (approximately 711 x 584 mm).

In the US, the elephant is the emblem of the Republican Party.

The word is recorded from Middle English, and comes via Old French and Latin from Greek *elephas, elephant-* 'ivory, elephant'.

The **elephant and castle** is a public-house sign which has given its name to the main crossroads of Southwark in London; it is popularly said to be a corruption of *Infanta de Castile*, but in fact is probably adopted from the arms of the Worshipful Company of Cutlers, whose trade included the importation of elephants' tusks (in heraldry, the elephant is shown with a crenellated round tower on its back).

The **Elephant Man** was the nickname of Joseph Carey Merrick (1862–90), who as a result of what is now thought to be Proteus syndrome had an enormous head with bone protruding from his forehead and mouth, and folds of spongy flesh covered with skin resembling a cauliflower hanging from his head, chest, and back.

The **Order of the Elephant** is the highest Danish order of knighthood. It was first founded in the 12th century. The Order was originally associated with an Order dedicated to the Virgin Mary, with a medallion of the Virgin and a smaller medallion with three nails of the Cross, on a chain of alternate elephants and spurs.

In the US, the expression **see the elephant** means see the world, get experience of life; an *elephant* is taken here as the type of something remarkable.

Eleusis a village near Athens which in classical times was a town famous for its cult of the corn goddess Demeter. The annual rites performed there by the ancient Greeks in honour of Demeter and Persephone are known as the **Eleusinian Mysteries**.

elevation in the Christian Church, the raising of the consecrated elements for adoration at Mass.

eleven the word is recorded from Old English (in form *endleofon*), and comes from the base of *one* + a second element, probably expressing the sense 'left over' and occurring also in *twelve*. The phrase **the Eleven** is used to designate the original Apostles, without ➤ JUDAS.

In the UK, the **eleven-plus** is an examination taken at the age of 11–12 to determine the type of secondary school a child should enter; the examination is now limited to a few local education authority areas.

The slogan **give us back our eleven days** was used in protest against the adoption of the Gregorian Calendar in 1752.

Up to eleven is an informal expression meaning, up to maximum volume; with reference to a scene in the film *This is Spinal Tap* (1984), featuring a supposedly louder amplifier with control knobs having 11 rather than 10 as the top setting.

eleventh that is number eleven in a sequence.

At the eleventh hour means at the latest possible moment; originally with reference to the story in Matthew ch. 20 of the labourers who were hired 'about the eleventh hour' to work in the vineyard, and who were given the same payment as those who had worked all day.

The **eleventh commandment** is a humorous term for a rule to be observed as strictly as the ten commandments, recorded from the mid 19th century, and often defined as, 'Thou shalt not be found out.'

elf a supernatural creature of folk tales, typically represented as a small, delicate, elusive figure in human form with pointed ears, magical powers, and a capricious nature. The word is recorded from Old English and is of Germanic origin; related to German *Alp* 'nightmare'.

An **elf-arrow** is a name for a flint arrowhead (regarded as an elves' weapon). The term **elf-locks** is used for a tangled mass of hair, as said to have been tangled by supernatural agency.

Elgin Marbles a collection of classical Greek marble sculptures and architectural fragments, chiefly from the frieze and pediment of the ➤ PARTHENON in Athens, brought to England by the diplomat and art connoisseur Thomas Bruce (1766–1841), the 7th Earl of Elgin. Their original exhibition in London had an enormous impact, it being the first time authentic classical Greek sculpture had been on public display.

Eli in the Bible, the priest who acted as a teacher to the prophet ➤ SAMUEL, and whose successor Samuel became.

Elia the pseudonym adopted by ➤ *Charles* LAMB in his *Essays of Elia* (1823) and *Last Essays of Elia* (1833); the name was that of an Italian clerk who had formerly worked at the South Sea House with Lamb's brother John.

Elijah (9th century BC), a Hebrew prophet in the time of ➤ AHAB and Jezebel who maintained the worship of Jehovah against that of Baal and other pagan gods. He is said to have been miraculously fed by ravens, to have raised a widow's son from the dead, and to have been carried to heaven in a chariot of fire (1 Kings 17–2 Kings 2).

His successor as the prophet of Israel was ➤ ELISHA, something signalled in 2 Kings 2:13, when after Elisha had seen the fiery chariot go up to heaven, 'He took up also the mantle of Elijah that fell from him.'

Elisha (9th century BC), a Hebrew prophet, disciple and successor of ➤ ELIJAH, who invited ➤ JEHU to lead the revolt against the house of Ahab, and who healed ➤ NAAMAN of his leprosy.

elixir a magical or medicinal potion; in alchemy, a preparation which was supposed to be able to change metals into gold. The word is recorded from late Middle English and comes via medieval Latin from Arabic *al-'iksīr*, and ultimately from Greek *xērion* 'powder for drying wounds'.

The **elixir of life** was an alchemical preparation supposedly able to prolong life indefinitely; the phrase is a translation of medieval Latin *elixir vitae*.

Elizabeth female forename, name of two saints.

in the Bible, **St Elizabeth** is the wife of ➤ ZACHARIAS and mother of John the Baptist; she is said to have been the cousin of the Virgin Mary (see ➤ *the* VISITATION). Her feast day (jointly with Zacharias) is 5 November.

St Elizabeth of Hungary (1207–31), princess. Married happily to the Landgrave of Thuringia and early widowed, she devoted her life to the poor. Roses are her emblem. Her feast day is 17 (formerly 19) November.

elk test a test of the stability and handling of a motor vehicle when swerving sharply, as if to avoid a sudden obstruction in the road; the term is recorded from the late 1990s as describing a practice in Scandinavian countries.

ell a former measure of length (equivalent to six hand breadths) used mainly for textiles, locally variable but typically about 45 inches in England and 37 inches in Scotland.

The word is recorded from Old English (in form *eln*) and is of Germanic origin, from an Indo-European root shared by Latin *ulna* ('humerus'). Like the ➤ CUBIT, the measure was originally linked to the length of the human arm or forearm.

Ellis Island an island in the bay of New York, formerly the site of a fort, that from 1892 until 1943 served as an entry point for immigrants to the US, and later (until 1954) as a detention centre for people awaiting deportation. The island is named after Samuel Ellis, a Manhattan merchant who owned it in the 1770s.

St Elmo another name for ➤ *St* ERASMUS (d. *c*.300).

St Elmo's fire is a phenomenon in which a luminous electrical discharge appears on a ship or aircraft during a storm, regarded as a sign of protection given by St Elmo.

Elohist the postulated author or authors of parts of the Hexateuch in which God is regularly named Elohim.

St Eloi (*c*.588–660), bishop of Noyon, pioneer apostle in much of Flanders. He was a skilled metalworker. His main emblem is a horseshoe, though like ➤ *St* DUNSTAN he is also shown holding the Devil by the nose with a pair of pincers. His feast day is 1 December, and the feast of his translation is 25 June.

Elsinore a port on the NE coast of the island of Zealand, Denmark. It is the site of the 16th-century Kronborg Castle, which is the setting for Shakespeare's *Hamlet*.

Elysée Palace a building in Paris which has been the official residence of the French President since 1870. It was built in 1718 for the Comte d'Evreux and was occupied by Madame de Pompadour, Napoleon I, and Napoleon III.

Elysium in Greek mythology, the place at the ends of the earth to which certain favoured heroes were conveyed by the gods after death. The name comes via Latin from Greek *Elusion* (*pedion*) '(plain) of the blessed'. It is also known as **the Elysian fields**.

em in printing, a unit for measuring the width of printed matter, equal to the height of the type size being used.

Emancipation Proclamation (in the American Civil War) the announcement made by President Lincoln on 22 September 1862 emancipating all black slaves in states still engaged in rebellion against the Federal Union with effect from the beginning of 1863. Although implementation was strictly beyond Lincoln's powers, the declaration turned the war into a crusade against slavery.

embarras de richesse(s) a superfluity of something, more than one needs or wants; a French phrase, meaning 'embarrassment of riches', from *L'embarras des richesses* (1726), title of comedy by Abbé d'Allainval.

Ember day any of a number of days reserved for fasting and prayer in the Western Christian Church. *Ember days* traditionally comprise the Wednesday, Friday, and Saturday following St Lucy's Day (13 December), the first Sunday in Lent, Pentecost (Whitsun), and Holy Cross Day (14 September), though other days are observed locally. They date back at least to 5th-century Rome, probably originating in agricultural festivals, though they have long been associated with ordinations.

Ember is recorded from Old English (in form *ymbren*), perhaps an alteration of *ymbryne* 'period', from *ymb* 'about' + *ryne* 'course', perhaps influenced in part by ecclesiastical Latin *quatuor tempera* 'four periods' (on which the equivalent German *Quatember* is based).

emblem a heraldic device or symbolic object as a distinctive badge of a nation, organization, or family. The word is recorded from the late 16th century (as a verb), and comes from Latin *emblema* 'inlaid work, raised ornament', from Greek *emblēma* 'insertion', from *emballein* 'throw in, insert'.

An **emblem book** is a book of a kind popular in medieval and Renaissance Europe, containing drawings accompanied by allegorical interpretations.

emerald this bright green precious stone is a type of brilliant green. In heraldry, *emerald* is the name given to the tincture vert in the fanciful blazon of arms of peers. Recorded from Middle English, the word comes via Old French and Latin from Greek *(s)maragdos* from Hebrew *bāreqet* 'emerald', from *bāraq* 'flash, sparkle'.

The **Emerald Isle** is a name a name for Ireland, perhaps from the prevailing green of its countryside; first recorded in the nationalist poem *Erin* (1795) by William Drennan (1754–1820).

éminence grise a person who exercises power or influence in a certain sphere without holding an official position. The term was originally applied to Cardinal Richelieu's grey-cloaked private secretary, Père Joseph (1577–1638). (See also ➤ GREY *eminence*.)

Emmanuel the name (also **Immanuel**) given to Christ as the deliverer of Judah prophesied by Isaiah, as in Isaiah 7:14, Isaiah 8:8, and Matthew 1:23, 'Behold, a virgin shall be with child, and shall bring forth a son, and they shall call his name Emmanuel, which being interpreted is, God with us.'

Emmy in the US, a statuette awarded annually to an outstanding television programme or performer. Recorded from the 1940s, the name is said to be from *Immy*, short for *image orthicon tube* (a kind of television camera tube).

emoticon a representation of a facial expression such as a smile or frown, formed by various combinations of keyboard characters and used in electronic communications to convey the writer's feelings or intended tone. The word is recorded from the 1990s, and is a blend of *emotion* and *icon*.

Empedocles (*c*.493–*c*.433 BC), Greek philosopher, born in Sicily. He taught that the universe is composed of fire, air, water, and earth, which mingle and separate under the influence of the opposing principles of Love and Strife. According to legend he leapt into the crater of Mount Etna in order that he might be thought a god.

Empire City informal name for New York City.

Empire State informal name for the state of New York.

Empire State Building a skyscraper on Fifth Avenue, New York City, which was for several years the tallest building in the world. When first erected, in 1930–1, it measured 381 m (1,250 ft); the addition of a television mast in 1951 brought its height to 449 m (1,472 ft).

Empire State of the South informal name for the state of Georgia.

Empire style a style of furniture, decoration, or dress fashionable during the First or (less commonly) the Second Empire in France. The decorative style was neoclassical but marked by an interest in Egyptian and other ancient motifs probably inspired by Napoleon's Egyptian campaigns.

Empty Quarter alternative name for Rub' al Khali, a vast desert in the Arabian peninsula, extending from central Saudi Arabia southwards to Yemen and eastwards to the United Arab Emirates and Oman.

Empusa in classical mythology, an evil spirit or demon supposed to be sent by Hecate.

the empyrean heaven, in particular the highest part of heaven, thought by the ancients to be the realm of pure fire and by early Christians to be the abode of God and the angels. The word is recorded from late Middle English (as an adjective, meaning belonging to or deriving from heaven), and comes via medieval Latin from Greek *empurios*, from *en-* 'in' + *pur* 'fire' The noun dates from the mid 17th century.

en in printing, a unit of measurement equal to half an em and approximately the average width of typeset characters, used especially for estimating the total amount of space a text will require.

Encaenia an annual celebration at Oxford University in memory of founders and benefactors. The name is recorded from the late 17th century, and comes via Latin from Greek *enkainia* 'dedication festival' (based on *kainos* 'new').

Enceladus in Greek mythology, a giant killed by Athena. His name was used for a satellite of Saturn, the eighth closest to the planet and probably composed mainly of ice, discovered by W. Herschel in 1789.

enclosure the process or policy of fencing in waste or common land so as to make it private property, as pursued in much of Britain in the 18th and early 19th centuries.

pour encourager les autres French expression meaning, as an example to others;

originally, a quotation from Voltaire on the execution of Admiral John Byng in 1757, for neglect of duty in failing to relieve Minorca when blockaded by a French fleet.

encyclical a papal letter sent to all bishops of the Roman Catholic Church. The word is recorded (as an adjective) from the mid 17th century, and comes via late Latin from Greek *enkuklios* 'circular, general'.

the end justifies the means wrong or unfair methods may be used if the overall goal is good. Very commonly used in the negative.

the end of civilization as we know it the complete collapse of ordered society. Supposedly a cinematic cliché, and actually used in the film *Citizen Kane* (1941). Often used ironically.

the end of one's tether having no patience, resources, or energy left to cope with something. The image is that of a grazing animal tethered on a rope that allows it a certain range in which to move but which at full stretch prohibits further movement.

Endura the physical privations (frequently fatal) undergone by the Cathars after *consolamentum* to prevent recontamination of the soul.

Endymion a remarkably beautiful young man, loved by the Moon (Selene); well-known tradition claims that he had fifty daughters by Selene. According to one story, he was put in an eternal sleep by Zeus for having fallen in love with Hera, and was then visited every night by Selene.

English Pale that part of Ireland (see ▶PALE[1]) over which England exercised jurisdiction before the whole country was conquered. Centred on Dublin, it varied in extent at different times from the reign of Henry II until the full conquest under Elizabeth I. The term was also used for a small area round Calais, the only part of France remaining in English hands after the Hundred Years War. It was recaptured by France in 1558.

enigma a riddle, usually one involving metaphor; in figurative usage, a person or thing that is mysterious, puzzling, or difficult to understand; the word is recorded from the mid 16th century, and comes via Latin from Greek *ainigma*, from *ainissesthai* 'speak allusively', from *ainos* 'fable'. It was famously used by Winston Churchill in a broadcast of 1941 to describe Russia, 'a riddle wrapped in a mystery inside an enigma'.

Enigma was the name of the German encoding machines used for vital strategic messages in the Second World War; with the assistance of a machine smuggled out of Germany, British cryptographers working at ➤ BLETCHLEY *Park* on the project codenamed *Ultra* broke the German codes. The story of Enigma remained an official secret until the ban on publication was lifted in 1974. See also ➤ COLOSSUS.

Eniwetok an uninhabited island in the North Pacific, one of the Marshall Islands. Cleared of its native population, it was used by the US as a testing ground for atom bombs from 1948 to 1954.

the Enlightenment a European intellectual movement of the late 17th and 18th centuries emphasizing reason and individualism rather than tradition. It was heavily influenced by 17th-century philosophers such as Descartes, Locke, and Newton, and its prominent exponents include Kant, Goethe, Voltaire, Rousseau, and Adam Smith.

Enoch[1] in the Bible, the eldest son of Cain, and the first city built by Cain (Genesis 4:17), named after him.

Enoch[2] a Hebrew patriarch, father of Methuselah; he is said in the Bible to have lived for 365 years, and may be cited as a type of extreme longevity.

Enoch is also said to have ascended to heaven without dying, as in Genesis 5:24. By this story he is sometimes linked with ➤ ELIJAH, who ascended to heaven in a fiery chariot, and ➤ St JOHN *the Evangelist*, whose later legend also says that he was taken up to heaven without dying.

Two works ascribed to him, the *Book of Enoch* and the *Book of the Secrets of Enoch*, date from the 2nd–1st centuries BC and 1st century AD respectively. A third treatise likewise dates from the Christian era.

Enola Gay name of the B-29 bomber used in the atomic destruction of Hiroshima.

the Entente Cordiale the understanding between Britain and France reached in 1904, forming the basis of Anglo-French cooperation in the First World War.

Eocene of, relating to, or denoting the second epoch of the Tertiary period, between the Palaeocene and Oligocene epochs. The Eocene epoch lasted from 56.5 to 35.4 million years ago. It was a time of rising temperatures, and there was an abundance of mammals, including the first horses, bats, and whales.

The term is recorded from the mid 19th century, and comes from Greek *ēōs* 'dawn' + *kainos* 'new'.

Eolithic of, relating to, or denoting a period at the beginning of the Stone Age, preceding the Palaeolithic and characterized by the earliest crude stone tools.

The term is recorded from the late 19th century, and comes via French from Greek *ēōs* 'dawn' + *lithikos* (from *lithos* 'stone').

Eos in Greek mythology, the goddess of the dawn, whose Roman equivalent was ➤ AURORA.

épater les bourgeois shock people who have attitudes or views perceived as conventional or complacent; the comment '*Il faut épater le bourgeois* [One must astonish the bourgeois]' is attributed to Baudelaire; the phrase is also attributed to Privat d'Anglemont (*c.*1820–59) in the form '*Je les ai épatés, les bourgeois* [I flabbergasted them, the bourgeois].'

ephemera things that exist or are used or enjoyed for only a short time; items of collectable memorabilia, typically written or printed ones, that were originally expected to have only short-term usefulness or popularity.

Recorded in English from the late 16th century as the plural of *ephemeron*, from Greek, neuter of *ephēmeros* 'lasting only a day'. As a singular noun the word originally denoted a plant said by ancient writers to last only one day, or an insect with a short lifespan, and hence was applied (late 18th century) to a person or thing of short-lived interest. Current use has been influenced by plurals such as *trivia* and *memorabilia*.

Epistle to the Ephesians a book of the New Testament ascribed to St Paul consisting of an epistle to the Church at Ephesus.

Ephesus an ancient Greek city on the west coat of Asia Minor, in present-day Turkey, site of the temple of Diana (see ➤ DIANA *of Ephesus*), one of the Seven Wonders of the World. It was an important centre of early Christianity; St Paul preached there and St John is traditionally said to have lived there.

ephor in ancient Greece, any of the five senior Spartan magistrates; the word comes from Greek *ephoros* 'overseer'.

epic a long poem, typically one derived from ancient oral tradition, narrating the deeds and adventures of heroic or legendary figures or the past history of a nation. The word comes via Latin from Greek *epikos*, from *epos* 'word, song', related to *eipein* 'say'.

Epicureanism an ancient school of philosophy, founded in Athens by the Greek philosopher *Epicurus* (341–270 BC). His physics is based on Democritus' theory of a materialist universe composed of indestructible atoms moving in a void, unregulated by divine providence.

The school rejected determinism and advocated hedonism (pleasure as the highest good), but of a restrained kind: mental pleasure was regarded more highly than physical, and the ultimate pleasure was held to be freedom from anxiety and mental pain, especially that arising from needless fear of death and of the gods.

Epidaurus an ancient Greek city and port on the NE coast of the Peloponnese, site of a temple dedicated to Asclepius and a well-preserved Greek theatre dating from the 4th century BC.

epigram a pithy saying or remark expressing an idea in a clever and amusing way; a short poem, especially a satirical one, having a witty or ingenious ending.

Epimenides a semi-legendary Cretan poet and prophet supposedly living between the 7th and 6th centuries BC, and credited with the creation of ➤ *the* LIAR *paradox*. He is said to be the person referred as having made the assertion that all Cretans were liars in Titus 1:12 'One of themselves; even a prophet of their own'.

the Epiphany the manifestation of Christ to the Gentiles as represented by the ➤ MAGI; the festival commemorating this on 6 January. The name is recorded from Middle English, and comes ultimately from Greek *epiphainein* 'reveal'.

episcopacy the government of a Church by bishops. The word comes (in the mid 17th century) from ecclesiastical Latin *episcopatus* 'episcopate, the office of a bishop', on the pattern of *prelacy*.

Episcopal Church the Anglican Church in Scotland and the US.

Epistle in the Christian Church, a book of the New Testament in the form of a letter from an Apostle.

Epistle also denotes an extract from an Epistle (or another New Testament book not a Gospel) that is read in a church service.

The **Epistle side** in a church is the south end of an altar, from which the Epistle is traditionally read (opposite to the north or *Gospel* side).

epitaph a phrase or form of words written in memory of a person who has died, especially as an inscription on a tombstone. The word is recorded from late Middle English, and comes via Old French and Latin from Greek *epitaphion* 'funeral oration'.

epithalamium a song or poem celebrating a marriage. The word is recorded from the late 16th century, and comes via Latin from Greek *epithalamion*, from *epi* 'upon' + *thalamos* 'bridal chamber'.

Epsom Downs site of the racecourse, near the town of *Epsom* in Surrey, where the annual Derby and Oaks horse races are held.

Equality State an informal name for Wyoming, the first state in the US to introduce women's suffrage.

equator a line notionally drawn on the earth equidistant from the poles, dividing the earth into northern and southern hemispheres and constituting the parallel of latitude 0°. The term is recorded from late Middle English, and comes from medieval Latin *aequator*, in the phrase *circulus aequator diei et noctis* 'circle equalizing day and night'.

equinox the time or date (twice each year) at which the sun crosses the celestial equator, when day and night are of equal length (about 22 September and 20 March).

St Erasmus 4th-century bishop of Formiae and martyr, also known as ➤ *St* ELMO; he is one of the ➤ FOURTEEN *Holy Helpers*. His emblem is a windlass; the iconography was later misunderstood, and it was thought to be an instrument of torture with which his intestines were wound out of him. His feast day is 2 June.

Erato in Greek and Roman mythology, the Muse of lyric poetry and hymns. The name is Greek, and means literally 'lovely'.

Erebus in Greek mythology, the primeval god of darkness, son of Chaos; also taken as the proper name of a dark region between

Earth and Hades, and as such a type of a place of blackness and gloom.

Erebus was also the name of one of the two ships of Sir James Ross's expedition to the Antarctic in 1838 (the other was called *Terror*); Mount Erebus, a volcanic peak on Ross Island, Antarctica, the world's most southerly active volcano, is named for it.

Erech biblical name for ➤ URUK.

Erechtheum a marble temple of the Ionic order built on the Acropolis in Athens c.421–406 BC, with shrines to Athene, Poseidon, and Erechtheus, a legendary king of Athens. A masterpiece of the Ionic order, it is most famous for its southern portico, in which the entablature is supported by six caryatids.

eremite a Christian hermit or recluse; the word is recorded from Middle English, and comes via Old French from late Latin *eremita*, from the base of ➤ HERMIT.

Erewhon an anagram of 'nowhere', used as the title of a satirical novel by Samuel Butler published anonymously in 1872; *Erewhon* in the story is the name of a previously undiscovered country, in which morality is equated with health and good looks, and crime with illness.

Eridanus a long straggling southern constellation (the River), said to represent the river into which ➤ PHAETHON fell when struck by Zeus' thunderbolt.

Lake Erie one of the five Great Lakes of North America, situated on the border between Canada and the US. It is linked to Lake Huron by the Detroit River and to Lake Ontario by the Welland Ship Canal and the Niagara River, which is its only natural outlet.

Erin a poetic and literary name for Ireland, derived ultimately from *Érainn*, a name given to one of the ancient peoples of Ireland, which was extended to include the population of the whole island.

Erinyes in Greek mythology, the Furies.

erl-king in Germanic mythology, a bearded giant or goblin believed to lure little children to the land of death. The term comes from German 'alder-king', a mistranslation of Danish *ellerkonge* 'king of the elves'.

ermine a stoat, especially in its white winter coat. The word comes through Old French, and probably derives ultimately from medieval Latin *(mus) Armenius* 'Armenian (mouse)'.

Ermine also denotes the white fur of the stoat, used for trimming garments, especially the ceremonial robes of judges or peers; in heraldry, it is fur represented as black spots on a white ground, as a heraldic tincture (the spots represent the dark tips of the ermines' tails, and are usually elaborated into short vertical lines with small curved projections, often with (usually three) smaller dots above).

Eros in Greek mythology, the god of love, son of Aphrodite; his Roman equivalent is ➤ CUPID. The name comes via Latin from Greek, literally 'sexual love'.

A winged statue of *Eros* over the fountain in Piccadilly Circus, London, made by Sir Alfred Gilbert (1854–1934), was erected as a memorial to the philanthropist the Earl of Shaftesbury, and unveiled in 1893.

Erse the Scottish or Irish Gaelic language; the name is an early Scots form of *Irish*.

Erymanthian boar a monstrous boar, living on Mount Erymanthus in Arcadia and ravaging the surrounding countryside, which Hercules captured as the second of his Labours.

Esau in the Bible, the elder of the twin sons of Isaac and Rebecca, who sold his birthright to his brother Jacob for a ➤ MESS *of pottage*, and was later tricked out of his father's blessing by his brother. The smooth-skinned Jacob deceived Isaac, who was blind, by using animal skins so that to his father's touch he felt like Esau, a 'hairy man'; despite Isaac's words, 'The voice is Jacob's voice, but the hands are the hands of Esau', he gave the blessing to his younger son.

eschatology the part of theology concerned with death, judgement, and the final destiny of the soul and of humankind (the ➤ FOUR *last things*).

Escorial a monastery and palace in central Spain, near Madrid, built in the late 16th century by Philip II, and encompassing the royal mausoleum.

escutcheon a shield or emblem bearing a coat of arms. The word comes (in the late 15th century) from Anglo-Norman French *escuchon*, based on Latin *scutum* 'shield'.

A **blot on one's escutcheon** is a stain on one's reputation or character; a figurative phrase recorded from the late 17th century.

Esdras either of two books of the Apocrypha. The first is mainly a compilation from Chronicles, Nehemiah, and Ezra; the second is a record of angelic revelation.

Esperanto an artificial language devised in 1887 as an international medium of communication, based on roots from the chief European languages. The name *Dr Esperanto* was used as a pen-name by the inventor of the language, Ludwik L. Zamenhof (1858–1917), Polish physician; the literal sense is 'one who hopes' (based on Latin *sperare* 'to hope').

esprit de l'escalier used to refer to the fact that a witty remark or retort often comes to mind after the opportunity to make it has passed. The (French) phrase means literally 'wit of the staircase' (i.e. a witty remark coming to mind on the stairs leading away from a gathering), and was coined by the French philosopher and man of letters Denis Diderot (1713–84).

Esquipulas a town in SE Guatemala. Noted for the image of the 'Black Christ of Esquipulas' in its church, the town is a centre of pilgrimage.

Essene a member of an ancient Jewish ascetic sect of the 2nd century BC–2nd century AD in Palestine, who lived in highly organized groups and held property in common. The Essenes are widely regarded as authors of the Dead Sea Scrolls.

Essex a county in the south-east of England.
 Essex girl is a derogatory term applied to a type of young woman, supposedly to be found in and around Essex, and variously characterized as unintelligent, promiscuous, and materialistic. While **Essex man** is regarded primarily as a type of political supporter, *Essex girl* is seen primarily in social terms, and is typically the butt of politically incorrect jokes.
 Essex man is characterized as a brash, amoral, self-made young businessman, of right-wing views and few or no cultural or intellectual interests, devoted to the acquisition of goods and material wealth.

the Establishment a group in a society exercising power and influence over matters of policy or taste, and seen as resisting change. The term is recorded intermittently from the 1920s, but in British English derives its current use from an article by the journalist Henry Fairlie in the *Spectator* of 1955.

the three estates in Britain, the three groups traditionally constituting Parliament, now the Lords Spiritual (the heads of the Church), the Lords Temporal (the peerage), and the Commons.

Esther in the Bible, a Jewish woman chosen on account of her beauty by the Persian king Ahasuerus (generally supposed to be Xerxes I) to be his queen. She used her influence with him to save her kinsman ➤ MORDECAI and the Israelites in captivity from persecution, particularly at the hands of the king's chief minister, ➤ HAMAN.
 Esther is also the book of the Bible containing an account of these events; a part survives only in Greek and is included in the Apocrypha.

Estuary English in the UK, a type of accent identified as spreading outwards from London and containing features of both received pronunciation and London speech.

ET a creature from outer space, stranded on earth, who is befriended by Californian children in Spielberg's film (1982) of that name; the letters stand for *extra-terrestrial*.

the Eternal City a name for the city of Rome; a translation of Latin *urbs aeterna*, occurring in Ovid and Tibullus, and frequently found in the official documents of the Empire.

eternal triangle a relationship between three people, typically a couple and the lover of one of them, involving sexual rivalry.

eth an Old English letter, ð or Ð. It was superseded by the digraph *th*, but is now used as a phonetic symbol.

St Etheldreda (d. 679), English princess and queen, foundress and abbess of Ely. She is the patron saint of Ely, and the word *tawdry* derives from a contraction of *St Audrey*, a later form of her name, in reference to the cheap laces and other finery sold at the annual fair in her honour. It is said that in a time of famine the Ely community was supplied with milk by two does, and Etheldreda may be shown with them. Her feast day is 23 June.

ethical foreign policy the conduct of foreign policy according to ethical as well as national considerations; the phrase has been particularly associated with the incumbency of the Labour politician Robin Cook as Foreign Secretary (1997–2001).

ethnic cleansing the mass expulsion or killing of members of one ethnic or religious group in an area by those of another. The term has been in use since the early 1990s, as conflict spread in the former Yugoslavia; it became particularly associated with the bitter fighting between Bosnian Serbs and Bosnian Muslims in Bosnia, and later with events in ➤ Kosovo.

Mount Etna a volcano in eastern Sicily, which is the highest and most active volcano in Europe; it was traditionally said to be Vulcan's workshop, and in classical times eruption were also explained as the struggles of giants imprisoned by Zeus beneath the mountain.

Etruria an ancient state of western Italy, situated between the Rivers Arno and Tiber and corresponding approximately to modern Tuscany and parts of Umbria. It was the centre of the Etruscan civilization, which was at its height *c.*500 BC and was an important influence on the Romans, who had subdued the Etruscans by the end of the 3rd century BC.

   Etruscan, the language of ancient Etruria, was written in an alphabet derived from Greek but is not related to any known language.

Etzel in the *Nibelungenlied* the equivalent of the Norse ➤ ATLI.

Eucharist the Christian service, ceremony, or sacrament commemorating the Last Supper, in which bread and wine are consecrated and consumed. Also, the consecrated elements, especially the bread.

   From the earliest times Christians have blessed and shared bread and wine in commemoration of the Last Supper (recorded in the first three Gospels and 1 Corinthians 10–11) and of the self-sacrifice of Christ. The bread and wine are referred to as the body and blood of Christ, though much theological controversy has focused on how substantially or symbolically this is to be interpreted.

   The word is recorded from late Middle English, and comes via Old French, based on ecclesiastical Greek *eukharistia* 'thanksgiving'.

Euclid (*c.*300 BC), Greek mathematician. His great work *Elements of Geometry*, which covered plane geometry, the theory of numbers, irrationals, and solid geometry, was the standard work until other kinds of geometry were discovered in the 19th century.

   Euclidean geometry is the geometry of ordinary experience, based on the axioms of Euclid, especially the one stating that parallel lines do not meet.

Till Eulenspiegel a German peasant (in English, *Owlglass*) of the 14th century whose jokes were the subject of a 16th-century collection of satirical tales.

Eumenides in Greek mythology, a name given to the Furies. The Eumenides ('the Kindly Ones') probably originated as well-disposed deities of fertility, whose name was given to the Furies either by confusion or euphemistically.

eunuch a man who has been castrated, especially (in the past) one employed to guard the women's living areas at an oriental court. The word is recorded from Old English, and comes via Latin from Greek *enoukhos*, literally 'bedroom work'.

euphemism a mild or indirect word or expression substituted for one considered to be too harsh or blunt when referring to something unpleasant or embarrassing. The word is recorded from the late 16th century, and comes from Greek *euphēmismos*, from *euphēmizein* 'use auspicious words'.

euphuism an artificial, highly elaborate way of writing or speaking. Recorded from the late 16th century, the word comes from late 16th century: from *Euphues*, the name of a character in John Lyly's prose romance of the same name (1578–80), from Greek *euphuēs* 'well endowed by nature'. It originally referred to a conversational and literary style popular in the late 16th and early 17th centuries in imitation of Lyly's work.

eureka a cry of joy or satisfaction when one finds or discovers something. Recorded from the early 17th century, and said to have been uttered by Archimedes when he hit upon a method of determining the purity of gold (Greek *heurēka* 'I have found it').

   Eureka was the name given to a lode in the Ballarat goldfield. This was the site of the **Eureka stockade**, scene of a clash between gold-miners and the police and military at Ballarat in 1854, now a symbol of republicanism. The **Eureka flag** is a blue flag bearing a white cross with a star at the end of each arm, first raised at the *Eureka stockade*; it is also known as the *Southern Cross*.

Euripides (480–*c.*406 BC), Greek dramatist. His nineteen surviving plays show important innovations in the handling of traditional myths, such as the introduction of realism, an interest in feminine psychology, and the portrayal of abnormal and irrational states of mind.

euro the single European currency, introduced in parts of the European Union in 1999.

Europa in Greek mythology, a princess of Tyre who was courted by Zeus in the form of a bull. She was carried off by him to Crete, where she bore him three sons (Minos, Rhadamanthus, and Sarpedon). The continent of *Europe* is said to be named after her, although Herodotus thinks this is unlikely since she was a Phoenician, and not from mainland Europe.

Euryale the name of one of the three ➤ GORGONS.

Eurydice in Greek mythology, the wife of ➤ ORPHEUS. After she was killed by a snake Orpheus secured her release from the underworld on the condition that he did not look back at her on their way back to the world of the living. When he did so, Eurydice disappeared.

Eusebius (*c.*264–*c.*340 AD), bishop and Church historian; known as **Eusebius of Caesaria**. His *Ecclesiastical History* is the principal source for the history of Christianity (especially in the Eastern Church) from the age of the Apostles until 324.

St Eustace a possibly legendary martyr who is traditionally regarded as one of the ➤ FOURTEEN *Holy Helpers*; he is shown (like ➤ St HUBERT) confronting a hart or stag with a crucifix in its antlers.
According to his unhistorical legend, he was a Roman general named Placidas who in the time of Trajan became a convert to Christianity and changed his name to Eustace; with his wife and children he was martyred by being roasted to death in a brazen bull. His feast day is 20 September (in the East, 2 November).

Euterpe in Greek and Roman mythology, the Muse of flutes. The name is Greek, and means literally 'well-pleasing'.

euthanasia the painless killing of a patient suffering from an incurable and painful disease or in an irreversible coma. The practice is illegal in most countries, although euthanasia in cases where the patient has given active consent is accepted in practice in the Netherlands.
The word is recorded from the early 17th century (in the sense 'easy death'), and comes from Greek, from *eu* 'well' + *thanatos* 'death'.

evangelical of or according to the teaching of the gospel or the Christian religion; in particular, of or denoting a tradition within Protestant Christianity emphasizing the authority of the Bible, personal conversion, and the doctrine of salvation by faith in the Atonement.

Evangelist the writer of one of the four Gospels (Matthew, Mark, Luke, or John); ➤ *St* JOHN is also known as **St John the Evangelist**.

evangelistary a book containing the portions of the Gospels that form part of the liturgy.

Eve in the Bible, the first woman, companion of ➤ ADAM and mother of Cain and Abel; she was formed by God from a rib from Adam's side, and is shown in Genesis as yielding to the temptation of the serpent, and subsequently persuading Adam to eat the fruit of the tree of knowledge. (See also ➤ AFRICAN *Eve hypothesis*.)

evensong in the Christian Church, a service of evening prayers, psalms, and canticles, conducted according to a set form, especially that of the Anglican Church. The word is recorded from Old English (in form *æfensang*), originally applied to the pre-Reformation service of vespers.

Dame Edna Everage Australian 'Housewife Superstar', a character created by the comedian Barry Humphries (1934–), first appearing on British television in the late 1970s, and noted for her flamboyant outfits and self-adulatory accounts of her lifestyle and family.

Mount Everest a mountain in the Himalayas, on the border between Nepal and Tibet. Rising to 8,848 m (29,028 ft), it is the highest mountain in the world; it was first climbed in 1953 by Sir Edmund Hillary and Tenzing Norgay.

Everglades a vast area of marshland and coastal mangrove in southern Florida, part of which is protected as a national park.

Evergreen State informal name for the State of Washington.

every man for himself everyone must take care of themselves and their own interests and safety. Originally a proverbial saying in its own right, and recorded from Middle English, but from the mid 16th century often expanded to **every man for himself, and the devil take the hindmost** or, less commonly, **every man for himself and God for us all**.

Everyman the name of the principal character in a 15th-century morality play, to whom Knowledge makes the promise, 'Everyman, I will go with thee, and be thy guide.'

the Evil Empire a term for the former Soviet Union, deriving from a speech by Ronald Reagan in 1983. The name is often used allusively of a political approach focusing exclusively on the perceived dangers from a particular direction.

the evil eye a gaze or stare superstitiously believed to cause material harm; the expression in this sense is recorded from the late 18th century.

ewe lamb a person's most cherished possession; originally with biblical allusion to 2 Samuel 12, 'But the poor man had nothing, save one little ewe lamb', the words with which the prophet Nathan rebuked ➤ DAVID for taking the wife of Uriah the Hittite from him.

Ewing name of the dysfunctional oil-rich Texas family around whom the television soap ➤ DALLAS was centred.

ex cathedra with the full authority of office (especially that of the Pope, implying infallibility as defined in Roman Catholic doctrine). The phrase is Latin, 'from the teacher's chair', from *ex* 'from' and *cathedra* 'seat' (from Greek *kathedra*).

Exaltation of the Cross a feast observed in the Roman Catholic and Orthodox Churches on 14 September in honour of the Cross of Christ, to commemorate either the exposition of the supposed True Cross in 629 after its recovery from the Persians, or the dedication by Constantine in 335 of the basilica built on the site of the Holy Sepulchre.

Excalibur in Arthurian legend, King Arthur's magic sword, which according to legend he drew from the stone in which it was embedded to prove that he was the true king; by another account, it was given him by the Lady of the Lake. In Malory's *Morte D'Arthur*, when the king is mortally wounded, he tells Sir Bedivere to throw the sword back into the lake; when he finally obeys, an arm in white samite emerges from the water to catch and take the sword.

excelsior the Latin motto ('higher') on the seal of the State of New York (adopted by the senate of that state 16 March 1778), the accompanying device being a rising sun. From this New York State is known informally as **the Excelsior State**.

In his poem 'Excelsior' (1841), the American poet Henry Wadsworth Longellow used the word as a refrain meaning 'upwards', as an injunction or aspiration ('A voice replied, far up the height, Excelsior!'). When it was pointed out that this was not grammatically correct, he is said to have suggested that the word might stand for a longer phrase, '*Scopus meus excelsior est* [My goal is higher].'

Exchequer in the UK, the former government office responsible for collecting revenue and making payments on behalf of the sovereign, auditing official accounts, and trying legal cases relating to revenue. The original sense was 'chessboard', and current senses derive from the department of state established by the Norman kings to deal with the royal revenues, named *Exchequer* from the chequered tablecloth on which accounts were kept by means of counters.

The **Exchequer Chamber** denotes any of a number of former courts of appeal whose functions were amalgamated in the Court of Appeal in 1873. Formerly also, an assembly of all the judges to decide points of law, defunct since the 18th century.

Exclusion Bill a bill of 1680 seeking to bar James Duke of York (the future James II, brother of Charles II) from the succession, on the grounds of his being a Roman Catholic; those opposed to him supported Charles's illegitimate son, the ➤ *Duke of* MONMOUTH, as representing a Protestant succession.

excommunicate officially exclude someone from participation in the sacraments and services of the Christian Church. The word is recorded from late Middle English, and comes from ecclesiastical Latin *excommunicat-* 'excluded from communication with the faithful'.

The Exeter Book a major manuscript of Old English poetry, containing some of the most famous shorter poems, such as *The Wanderer* and The *Seafarer*; it dates from *c*.940, and was given by Bishop Leofric (d. 1072) to Exeter Cathedral, where it remains.

exhibit A the most important piece of evidence relating to a matter in question. From legal usage, denoting the first exhibit submitted as evidence in a trial.

existentialism a philosophical theory or approach which emphasizes the existence of the individual person as a free and responsible agent determining their own development through acts of the will.

The term denotes recurring themes in modern philosophy and literature rather than a single school of thought. Generally taken to originate with Kierkegaard and Nietzsche, existentialism tends to be atheistic (although there is a strand of Christian existentialism deriving from the work of Kierkegaard), to disparage scientific knowledge, and to deny the existence of objective values, stressing instead the reality and significance of human freedom and experience.

Exocet a French-made guided anti-ship missile, used particularly in the Falklands War, and sometimes in figurative use; the name comes (in the 1970s) from French, from Greek *ekōkoitos* 'fish that comes up on the beach' (literally 'out of bed').

Exodus the second book of the Bible, which recounts the departure of the Israelites from slavery in Egypt, their journey across the Red Sea and through the wilderness led by ➤ MOSES, and the giving of the ➤ TEN *Commandments*. The events have been variously dated by scholars between about 1580 and 1200 BC.

exorcize originally, conjure up or command an evil spirit; later, drive out or attempt to drive out an evil spirit from a person or place in which it is believed to be present. Recorded from late Middle English, the word comes via French or ecclesiastical Latin from Greek *exorkizein*, from *ex-* 'out' + *horkos* 'oath'. The specific sense of driving out an evil spirit dates from the mid 16th century.

expressionism a style of painting, music, or drama in which the artist or writer seeks to express emotional experience rather than impressions of the external world. Expressionists characteristically reject traditional ideas of beauty or harmony and use distortion, exaggeration, and other non-naturalistic devices in order to emphasize and express the inner world of emotion.

extropy the pseudoscientific principle that life will expand indefinitely and in an orderly, progressive way throughout the entire universe by the means of human intelligence and technology; the word (recorded from the 1980s) comes from *ex-* 'out' + a shortened form of *entropy*.

Exultet the Latin hymn beginning *Exultet jam angelica turba caelorum*, sung in the Roman Catholic Church at the blessing of the paschal candle on Easter Eve.

Exxon Valdez name of the oil tanker which ran aground off the Alaskan coast in 1989, causing considerable environmental damage and giving rise to the development of the ➤ VALDEZ *Principles*.

eye *eyes* (on a dish) are the emblem of ➤ St LUCY, who was blinded during her martyrdom.

All my eye and Betty Martin is nonsense; said in a letter of 1781 to be 'a sea phrase', although the identity of *Betty Martin* is unexplained.

In 18th-century landscape design, an **eye-catcher** was an architectural feature such as a sham ruin or a monument, intended to draw the eye in a particular direction.

An eye for an eye and a tooth for a tooth is used to refer to the belief that retaliation in kind is the appropriate way to deal with an offence or crime, with biblical allusion to Exodus 21:23–4.

The **eye of a needle** is the type of a minute gap through which it is difficult to pass; mainly with echoes of Jesus's saying, 'it is easier for a camel to go through the eye of a needle, than for a rich man to enter into the kingdom of heaven' (Matthew 19:24).

The **eye of the storm** is the calm region at the centre of a storm, often used figuratively.

An eye to the main chance means consideration for one's own interests; *main chance* literally, in the game of hazard, a number (5, 6, 7, or 8) called by a player before throwing the dice.

eyeball to eyeball face to face with someone, especially in an aggressive way; the expression is particularly associated with the US politician Dean Rusk (1909–94) as Secretary of State on the ➤ CUBAN *Missile Crisis*, 24 October 1962, 'We're eyeball to eyeball, and I think the other fellow just blinked.'

Ezekiel a Hebrew prophet of the 6th century BC who prophesied the forthcoming destruction of Jerusalem and the Jewish nation and inspired hope for the future well-being of a restored state. Also, a book of the Bible containing his prophecies.

Ezra a Jewish priest and scribe who played a central part in the reform of Judaism in the 5th or 4th century BC, continuing the work of Nehemiah and forbidding mixed marriages. Also, a book of the Bible telling of Ezra, the return of the Jews from Babylon, and the rebuilding of the Temple.

F the sixth letter of the modern English alphabet and of the ancient Roman one, corresponding to Greek *digamma* (Ϝ), Semitic *waw*.

Peter Carl Fabergé (1846–1920), Russian goldsmith and jeweller, of French descent. He is famous for the intricate Easter eggs that he made for Tsar Alexander III and other royal households.

Fabius (d. 203 BC), Roman general and statesman, known as **Fabius Cunctator** ('the Delayer'). After Hannibal's defeat of the Roman army at Cannae in 216 BC, Fabius successfully pursued a strategy of caution and delay in order to wear down the Carthaginian invaders.

George Washington, whose tactics were likened to those of the Roman general, was named **the American Fabius**, and the **Fabian Society**, an organization of socialists aiming at the gradual rather than revolutionary achievement of socialism, founded in 1884, was also named after Fabius.

fable a short story, typically with animals as characters, conveying a moral; a story, typically a supernatural one incorporating elements of myth and legend. Recorded from Middle English, the word comes via Old French from Latin *fabula* 'story', from *fari* 'speak'.

fabliau a metrical tale, typically a bawdily humorous one, of a type found chiefly in early French poetry.

the face that launched a thousand ships the face of ➤ HELEN, seeing her as the cause of the Trojan War; originally as a quotation from Marlowe's *Doctor Faustus* (1604).

Factory Acts (in the UK) a series of laws regulating the operation of factories, designed to improve the working conditions of employees, especially women and children. The most important was that of 1833, which set a minimum age of 9 years and a maximum of eight hours a day for child employees and which also instituted inspectors to ensure compliance with these regulations.

faerie a poetic or literary word for fairyland, a pseudo-archaism introduced by Edmund Spenser (*c.*1552–99) in his allegorical poem *The Faerie Queene*, celebrating Queen Elizabeth.

Fafnir in Scandinavian and Germanic mythology, in the story of the Volsungs and Nibelungs, the dragon who guards a hoard of gold and is killed by ➤ SIGURD (Siegfried).

Fagin in Dickens's *Oliver Twist* (1838), the master of the gang of pickpockets led by the ➤ ARTFUL *Dodger*; his name is used allusively for a criminal who systematically recruits and organizes child thieves.

Fahrenheit of or denoting a scale of temperature on which water freezes at 32° and boils at 212° under standard conditions, named (in the mid 18th century) after Gabriel Daniel *Fahrenheit* (1686–1736), German physicist.

a fair field and no favour equal conditions in a contest, not unduly favouring or hindering either side.

a fair-weather friend someone who cannot be relied on for continuing support in a difficult situation, especially when one is attacked or criticized.

fairy a small imaginary being of human form that has magical powers, especially a female one. The word is recorded from Middle English (denoting fairyland, or fairies collectively), and comes via Old French from Latin *fata* 'the Fates'.

Fairies were traditionally seen as impinging on the mortal world with dangerous effect, but the perception of them as powerful beings inhabiting a parallel world to that of humankind gradually dwindled, and by the 17th century they were largely figures of a literary tradition.

In the 20th century, the question of whether fairies might exist was raised by Arthur Conan Doyle, who published *The Coming of the Fairies* (1921), based on the experiences of two Yorkshire schoolgirls from Cottingley who had apparently been visited by, and taken photographs of, fairies. Conan Doyle, a keen believer in the supernatural, was convinced, although (as was revealed in 1983 by the original authors) the photographs had in fact been faked by the two girls.

A **fairy godmother** is a female character in some fairy stories who has magical powers and brings unexpected good fortune to the hero or heroine; the term is recorded from the mid 19th century.

Fairy money is money or gold given by fairies to mortals, which is said to turn to dried leaves and crumble rapidly away; John Locke uses the image in his *Essay concerning Human Understanding* (1690).

A **fairy ring** is a circular area of grass that is darker in colour than the surrounding grass due to the growth of certain fungi. They were popularly believed to have been caused by fairies dancing.

St Faith (3rd century?), virgin and martyr; her shrine at Conques was a popular centre, and she was invoked by Crusaders and pilgrims. She is shown with a sword or a bundle of rods, and her feast day is 6 October.

faith will move mountains see ➤ *move* MOUNTAINS.

Fala name of a Scotch terrier belonging to Franklin Roosevelt, which in 1944 was in the news when it was reported that the dog had been left on an Aleutian island and that a destroyer had been sent back for it. Roosevelt (in his dog's name) firmly countered stories of the waste of taxpayers' money, saying publicly that while he did not resent attacks on his family, Fala did.

Falange the Spanish Fascist movement that merged with traditional right-wing elements in 1937 to form the ruling party, the Falange Española Tradicionalista, under General Franco. It was formally abolished in 1977. The name is Spanish, and comes from Latin *phalang-*, *phalanx* 'body of infantry, phalanx'.

Falasha a member of a group of people in Ethiopia who hold the Jewish faith but use Ge'ez rather than Hebrew as a liturgical language. The Falashas were not formally recognized as Jews until 1975, and many of them were airlifted to Israel in 1984–5 and after. Also called ➤ BLACK *Jew*.

The name is Amharic, and means literally 'exile, immigrant'.

falcon in Egyptian mythology, the god ➤ HORUS is represented as having the head of a falcon.

The name is recorded from Middle English (in form *faucon*, originally denoting any diurnal bird of prey used in falconry), and comes via Old French, from late Latin *falco*, from Latin *falx*, *falc-* 'scythe' (or of Germanic origin, related to Dutch and German). The *-l-* was added in the 15th century to conform with the Latin spelling.

Falklands War an armed conflict between Britain and Argentina in 1982, which came about when on the orders of General Galtieri's military junta, Argentinian forces invaded the *Falkland Islands*, a group of islands in the South Atlantic, forming a British Crown Colony, originally occupied and colonized by Britain in 1832–3, following the expulsion of an Argentinian garrison. In response Britain sent a task force of ships and aircraft, which forced the Argentinians to surrender six weeks after its arrival.

the Fall the lapse of humankind into a state of sin, ascribed in traditional Jewish and Christian theology to the disobedience of Adam and Eve as described in Genesis; also called **the Fall of Man**.

In North America, **the Fall** means autumn; the expression derives from the earlier **fall of the leaf**, first recorded in Roger Ascham's *Toxophilus* (1545).

fall by the wayside fail to persist in an endeavour or undertaking; with biblical allusion to the ➤ *parable of the* SOWER, in which some of the seed 'fell by the way side' and was eaten by birds.

fall on stony ground of words or a suggestion be ignored or badly received; with biblical allusion to the ➤ *parable of the* SOWER, in which some seed 'fell upon stony places' and withered away.

fallen angel in Christian, Jewish, and Muslim tradition, an angel who rebelled against God and was cast out of heaven.

falling sickness an archaic term for epilepsy; in Shakespeare's *Julius Caesar*, the expression is used of Caesar.

false friend a word or expression that has a similar form to one in a person's native language, but a different meaning (for example English *magazine* and French *magasin* 'shop').

false memory an apparent recollection of an event which did not actually occur, especially one of childhood sexual abuse arising from suggestion during psychoanalysis; in the 1990s the question of whether buried memory of this kind could be recovered through psychoanalysis was strongly debated, with proponents of the theory using the term *recovered memory* to demonstrate the belief that such recollections could be rooted in fact.

familiar a demon (also called a **familiar spirit**) supposedly attending and obeying a witch, often said to assume the form of an animal.

selling off the family silver parting with a valuable resource for immediate advantage. The reference is to a speech by former British Conservative Prime Minister, Harold Macmillan, to the Tory Reform Group in 1985 on privatization (the selling off of nationalized industries to private companies was likened to the sale of family assets by impoverished landowners, 'First of all the Georgian silver goes…')

the Famous Five four children, Julian, Dick, Anne, and their cousin 'George' (Georgina), with their dog Timmy, in a series of adventure stories (1942–63) by the popular children's writer Enid Blyton.

famous for fifteen minutes enjoying a brief period of fame before fading back into obscurity; coined by the American artist Andy Warhol, who predicted in 1968 that 'In the future everybody will be world famous for fifteen minutes.'

sweet Fanny Adams a nautical term for tinned meat or stew; apparently from the name of a murder victim, Fanny Adams, *c*.1870, whose body was said to have been mutilated.

trip the light fantastic humorous term meaning, to dance; originally, with allusion to Milton's 'L'Allegro' (1645), 'Come, and trip it as ye go On the light fantastic toe.'

bet the farm in North American usage, risk all that one owns by backing a particular project or investment.

Farnese the Italian family ruling the duchy of Parma and Piacenza from 1545 to 1731. The **Farnese Hercules**, a copy (by Glycon of Athens) of the statue of Hercules by Lysippus, Greek sculptor of the 4th century BC, excavated in 1540 from the Baths of Caracalla in

Rome, was initially in the possession of the family.

farthing a former monetary unit and coin of the UK, withdrawn in 1961, equal to a quarter of an old penny. Recorded from Old English (in form *fēorthing*), the word comes from *fēortha* 'fourth', perhaps on the pattern of Old Norse *fjórthungr* 'quarter'.

fasces in ancient Rome, a bundle of rods with a projecting axe blade, carried by a lictor as a symbol of a magistrate's power; the word is Latin, plural of *fascis* 'rod'.

fascism an authoritarian and nationalistic right-wing system of government and social organization.

The term Fascism was first used of the totalitarian right-wing nationalist regime of Mussolini in Italy (1922–43), and the regimes of the Nazis in Germany and Franco in Spain were also Fascist. Fascism tends to include a belief in the supremacy of one national or ethnic group, a contempt for democracy, an insistence on obedience to a powerful leader, and a strong demagogic approach.

The name comes from Italian *fascismo*, from *fascio* 'bundle, political group', from Latin *fascis* 'rod'.

fat cat a wealthy and powerful person, especially a businessman or politician; the term is recorded from the late 1920s in the US, but has become frequent in the UK since the early 1990s, in relation particularly to what are perceived as inflated salaries paid to senior executives of formerly nationalized industries.

the fat is in the fire something has been said or done that is about to cause trouble or anger. In this current sense with reference to the sizzling and spitting resulting from a spillage of cooking fat into an open flame. The expression is recorded from the mid 16th century in the sense that something has gone irretrievably wrong.

the fat of the land the best of everything as one's resource for living; originally with reference to Genesis 45:18, 'Ye shall eat the fat of the land.'

Fata Morgana a mirage; originally (in Italian) 'fairy Morgan', referring to a mirage seen in the Strait of Messina between Italy and Sicily and attributed to ▶ MORGAN *le Fay*, whose legend and reputation were carried to Sicily by Norman settlers.

a fate worse than death rape; the term is recorded from the early 19th century, although earlier in the mid 17th century Dorothy Osborne in a letter refers to 'the Roman courage, when they killed themselves to avoid misfortunes that were infinitely worse than death'.

the Fates in Greek and Roman mythology, the three goddesses who preside over the birth, life, and death of humans. Each person was thought of as a spindle, around which the three Fates (Clotho, Lachesis, and Atropos) would spin the thread (eventually to be measured off and cut) of human destiny.

father a male parent.

Father Christmas is an imaginary figure said to bring presents for children on the night before Christmas Day. He is conventionally pictured as a jolly old man from the far north, with a long white beard and red garments trimmed with white fur, an image which is comparatively recent. In late medieval Europe he became identified with St Nicholas (Santa Claus); in England Father Christmas was a personification of Christmas in many 16th-century masques and in mummers' plays. There was a great revival of the celebration of Christmas in the 19th century and Father Christmas acquired (from St Nicholas) the association of present-bringing.

The **Father of English Poetry** is a name for ➤ *Geoffrey* CHAUCER, given him by John Dryden.

The **Father of History** is a name for ➤ HERODOTUS.

The **Father of Lies** is a name for the Devil; originally with biblical allusion to John 8:44.

In the UK, the **father of the chapel** is the shop steward of a printers' trade union; a *chapel* in this sense was originally a printers' workshop or printing office, and then a meeting or association of the journeymen in a printing office for arranging affairs and settling disagreements among themselves.

Father of the Faithful is a name for the patriarch Abraham, after Romans 4:11. In Muslim usage, it is a title for the Caliph.

The **Father of the House of Commons** is the member with the longest continuous service.

The **Father of Waters** is an informal name for the the Mississippi.

Father's Day is a day of the year on which fathers are particularly honoured by their children, especially with gifts and greetings cards. It was first observed in the state of Washington in 1910; in the US and Britain, it is usually the third Sunday in June, in Australia, the first Sunday in September.

the Fatherland Germany, especially during the period of Hitler's control.

the Fathers of the Church early Christian theologians (in particular of the first five centuries) whose writings are regarded as especially authoritative.

Fatiha the short first sura of the Koran, used by Muslims as an essential element of ritual prayer. The word comes from Arabic *al-Fātiḥah* 'the opening (sura)'.

Fatima[1] (*c.*606–32 AD), youngest daughter of the prophet Muhammad and wife of the fourth caliph, Ali. The descendants of Muhammad trace their lineage through her; she is revered especially by Shiite Muslims as the mother of the imams Hasan and Husayn.*

The **Fatimid** dynasty, which ruled in parts of northern Africa, Egypt, and Syria from 909 to 1171, and founded Cairo as its capital in 969, is said to descend from her.

Fatima[2] name of the last and surviving wife of ➤ BLUEBEARD.

Fátima[3] a village in Portugal, where in 1917 it was reported that apparitions of the Virgin Mary appeared; it is now the site of a Marian shrine.

kill the fatted calf produce one's best food to celebrate, especially at a prodigal's return, with biblical allusion to the story of the **prodigal son** (see ➤ PRODIGAL), in which the father, welcoming the return of his son with a feast, tells his servants, 'bring hither the fatted calf, and kill it' (Luke 15:23).

fatwa a ruling on a point of Islamic law given by a recognized authority. In 1989 a fatwa calling for the death of the British novelist Salman Rushdie was issued by Ayatollah Khomeini following the publication of Rushdie's novel *The Satanic Verses*.

faun in Roman mythology, one of a class of lustful rural gods, represented as a man with a goat's horns, ears, legs, and tail. The word is recorded from late Middle English, and comes from the name of the pastoral god ➤ FAUNUS.

fauna the animals of a particular region, habitat, or geological period. The term is recorded from the late 18th century, and is a modern Latin application of *Fauna*, the name of a rural goddess, sister of ➤ FAUNUS.

Faunus in Roman mythology, an ancient Italian pastoral god, grandson of Saturn, associated with wooded places.

Faust (d. *c.*1540), German astronomer and necromancer. Reputed to have sold his soul to the Devil, he became the subject of dramas by Marlowe and Goethe, an opera by Gounod, and a novel by Thomas Mann.

fauvism a short-lived but influential style of painting with vivid expressionism and non-naturalistic use of colour that flourished in Paris from 1905.
   The name comes from French *fauvisme*, from *fauve* 'wild beast'. The name originated from a remark of the French art critic Louis Vauxcelles at the Salon of 1905; coming across a quattrocento-style statue in the midst of works by Matisse and his associates, he is reputed to have said, '*Donatello au milieu des fauves!*' ('Donatello among the wild beasts').

most **favoured** nation the nation to which a State has granted by treaty and other agreements the greatest political or commercial privileges, especially that to which the State accords the lowest scale of import duties.

Guy Fawkes (1570–1606), English conspirator, who was hanged for his part in the ➤ GUNPOWDER *Plot* of 5 November 1605. The occasion is commemorated annually on Bonfire Night with fireworks, bonfires, and the burning of a *guy*, named after Guy Fawkes.

Fayum the name of a province in upper Egypt used to designate articles discovered there, in particular funerary portraits of the early Christian period.

feast of reason intellectual discussion, as complementary to genial conversation; the phrase comes originally from Pope's *Satires of Horace* (1733), 'the feast of reason and the flow of soul'.

show the white **feather** behave in a cowardly fashion (a white feather in the tail of a game bird is a mark of bad breeding). During the First World War, *white feathers* were sometimes sent or given to men as a sign that they should be on active service.

a **feather** in one's cap something to be proud of. Originally (in the late 17th century) taken as a sign of folly, but by the mid 18th century it was acquiring its current laudatory sense.

feather one's own nest make money, usually illicitly and at someone else's expense. With reference to the habit of some birds of using feathers (their own or another bird's) to line the interior of their nests. This figurative use is recorded from the late 16th century.

featherweight a weight in boxing and other sports intermediate between bantamweight and lightweight. In the amateur boxing scale it ranges from 54 to 57 kg.

February the second month of the year in the northern hemisphere, usually considered the last month of winter. The name is recorded from Middle English (in form *feverer*), and comes via Old French from Latin *februarius*, from *februa*, the name of a purification feast held in this month. The spelling change in the 15th century was due to association with the Latin word.
   The traditional name **February fill-dyke** comes from a 16th-century saying **February fill dyke be it black or be it white**, meaning that February is a month likely to bring heavy rain (black) or snow (white).
   The **February Revolution** was the first phase of the ➤ RUSSIAN *Revolution*.

Federal designating the Northern States in the American Civil War.

Federal Bureau of Investigation an agency of the US federal government that deals principally with internal security and counter-intelligence and that also conducts investigations in federal law enforcement. It was established in 1908 as a branch of the Department of Justice, but was substantially reorganized under the controversial directorship (1924–72) of J. Edgar Hoover.

fee-faw-fum the first line of doggerel spoken by the giant in the fairy tale 'Jack the Giant Killer' (➤ JACK *and the Beanstalk*) on seeing Jack.

feeding frenzy an aggressive and competitive group attack on prey by a number of sharks or piranhas; in figurative use, an episode of frantic competition or rivalry for something, often referring to media excitement over a news story.

the **Feeding of the Five Thousand** in the Bible (Mark ch. 6), the miracle by which Jesus fed the five thousand who had gathered to hear him on the only food which they had, five loaves and two fishes; when everyone had eaten, the fragments filled twelve baskets.

feel-good causing a feeling of happiness and well-being, especially in material contexts.

   Feel-good in its current sense is recorded from the early 1970s, but prior to that Dr *Feelgood* had been a name adopted in 1962 by the blues pianist 'Piano Red' (William Perryman).

feet of clay a fundamental flaw or weakness in a person otherwise revered, with biblical allusion to a dream of ➤ NEBUCHADNEZZAR, in which a magnificent idol has feet 'part of iron and part of clay'; Daniel interprets this to signify a future kingdom that will be 'partly strong, and partly broken', and will eventually fall.

felix culpa the sin of Adam viewed as fortunate, because it brought about the blessedness of the Redemption; the phrase is Latin, and means 'happy fault'.

at one fell swoop at a single blow, in one go. *Swoop* here denotes the sudden pouncing of a bird of prey from a height on its quarry, especially with allusion to Shakespeare's *Macbeth* (1606).

felo de se suicide. From Anglo-Latin, literally 'felon of himself'; suicide was formerly a criminal act in the UK.

sit on the fence avoid making a decision or choice. The two sides of a fence are seen in this and related idioms as representing the two opposing or conflicting positions or interests involved in a particular debate or situation.

feng shui in Chinese thought, a system of laws considered to govern spatial arrangement and orientation in relation to the flow of energy (*chi*), and whose favourable or unfavourable effects are taken into account when siting and designing buildings.

   The term is Chinese, from *fēng* 'wind' and *shuǐ* 'water'.

Fenian a member of the Irish Republican Brotherhood, a 19th-century revolutionary nationalist organization among the Irish in the US and Ireland. The name comes from Old Irish *fēne*, the name of an ancient Irish people, confused with *fiann*, *fianna* 'band of warriors', the partial source of the name of the modern party *Fianna Fáil*.

Fenrir in Norse mythology, the wolf, son of Loki, which will devour Odin at ➤ RAGNARÖK. Fenrir was originally shackled by the gods, in the process of which he bit off the hand of ➤ TYR, but at Ragnarök he will break his bonds to join in the attack on the gods.

Fermat's last theorem a conjecture by the French mathematician Pierre de Fermat (1601–65), that if n is an integer greater than 2, the equation $x^n + y^n = z^n$ has no positive integral solutions. Fermat apparently noted in the margin of his copy of *Diophantus' Arithmetica* 'I have a truly marvellous demonstration of this proposition which this margin is too narrow to contain', but his proof has never been found, and *Fermat's last theorem* may be cited as an example of an unsolved problem. In 1995 a general proof was published by the Princeton-based British mathematician Andrew Wiles.

fess in heraldry, an ordinary in the form of a broad horizontal stripe across the middle of the shield; **in fess**, across the middle third of the field.

Festival of Britain a festival celebrated with lavish exhibitions and shows throughout Britain, especially at the South Bank in London (see ➤ SKYLON) in May 1951, to mark the centenary of the ➤ GREAT *Exhibition* of 1851.

fetterlock a D-shaped fetter for tethering a horse by the leg, now only as represented as a heraldic charge; the **falcon and fetterlock** was one of the badges of the House of York.

in fine fettle in very good condition. *Fettle* was recorded in a mid 18th-century glossary of Lancashire dialect as meaning 'dress, case, condition'.

feudalism the dominant social system in medieval Europe, in which the nobility held lands from the Crown in exchange for military service, and vassals were in turn tenants of the nobles, while the peasants (villeins or serfs) were obliged to live on their lord's land and give him homage, labour, and a share of the produce, notionally in exchange for military protection.

the Few in Britain, the RAF pilots who took part in the Battle of Britain; the name alludes to a speech made by Winston Churchill on the Battle of Britain in the House of Commons, 20 August 1940.

fey originally (in Old English, in form *fǣge*) fated to die soon; the word is of Germanic origin, and related to German *feige* 'cowardly'.

The original meaning is still current in Scottish usage, but from the early 19th century the word has developed a more general sense of giving an impression of vague unworldliness, having supernatural powers of clairvoyance.

St Fiacre (d. *c.*670), Irish-born hermit living in France; he is said to have been a skilled horticulturist, but to have been of a misogynistic nature. His emblem is a spade. His feast day is 30 August (1 September in France and Ireland).

Fiacre is the name of a small four-wheeled carriage for public hire, named after the *Hôtel de St Fiacre* in Paris, where such vehicles were first hired out.

fiddle while Rome burns be concerned with relatively trivial matters while ignoring the serious or disastrous events going on around one; the original reference is to the behaviour of the emperor Nero, who according to Suetonius sang the whole of 'The Sack of Ilium' in his preferred stage costume to celebrate the beauty of the flames as Rome burned.

The first use of *fiddle* in this allusion is found in George Daniel's *Trinarchodia* (1649).

Field of the Cloth of Gold the scene of a meeting between Henry VIII of England and Francis I of France near Calais in 1520, for which both monarchs erected elaborate temporary palaces, including a sumptuous display of golden cloth. Little of importance was achieved, although the meeting symbolized Henry's determination to play a full part in European dynastic politics.

The Fifteen a name for the Jacobite rebellion of 1715.

fifth that is number five in a series.

A **fifth column** is a group within a country at war who are sympathetic to or working for its enemies. The term dates from the Spanish Civil War, when General Mola, leading four columns of nationalist troops towards Madrid in 1936, declared that he had a *fifth column* inside the city.

The **fifth force** is a hypothetical force counteracting or modifying the effect of gravity, postulated to explain some apparently anomalous observations. Recent experiments have suggested that it does not exist.

Fifth-generation denotes a proposed new class of computer or programming language employing artificial intelligence.

The **Fifth Monarchy** is the last of the five great kingdoms predicted in the Book of Daniel (Daniel 2:44); in the 17th century, this was identified with the millennial reign of Christ predicted in the apocalypse.

To **smite under the fifth rib** is to strike to the heart, kill; originally with biblical allusion to 2 Samuel 2:23.

in the US, to **take the fifth** is to exercise the right guaranteed by the Fifth Amendment (1791) to the Constitution of refusing to answer questions in order to avoid incriminating oneself.

fig in a number of phrases, such as *not give a fig for*, taken as the type of something of little value.

In Mark ch. 11, Jesus sees a fig-tree with leaves but no fruit and says to it, 'No man eat fruit of thee hereafter for ever'; the tree subsequently withers. It is in fact usual for the leaves of this tree to appear before the fruit; but the 'barren fig tree' is being used as an image of Israel's failure to respond spiritually to God.

A **fig leaf** is often used for concealing the genitals in paintings and sculpture, with particular reference to the story of Adam and Eve, when having eaten of the tree of the knowledge of good and evil and become ashamed of their nakedness, 'they sewed fig leaves together, and made themselves aprons' (Genesis 3:7).

Figaro the central character, a barber turned valet who both assists and circumvents his master Count Almaviva, of *The Barber of Seville* (1775) and *The Marriage of Figaro* (1784) by the French dramatist Pierre de Beaumarchais (1732–99); they inspired operas by Rossini and Mozart. Figaro was popularly seen as resisting the aristocratic abuse of personal power.

The French daily newspaper *Le Figaro*, originally founded in Paris in 1826 to comment on the arts, was named after him.

filibuster an action such as prolonged speaking which obstructs progress in a legislative assembly in a way that does not technically contravene the required procedures.

The word comes from French *flibustier*, first applied to pirates who pillaged the Spanish colonies in the West Indies. In the mid 19th century (via Spanish *filibustero*), the term denoted American adventurers who incited revolution in several Latin American states.

The verb was used to describe tactics intended to sabotage US congressional proceedings.

Filioque the word inserted in the Western version of the Nicene Creed to assert the doctrine of the procession of the Holy Ghost from the Son as well as from the Father, which is not admitted by the Eastern Church. It was one of the central issues in the Great Schism of 1054.

Filioque is Latin, literally 'and from the Son'.

fin de siècle French phrase meaning relating to or characteristic of the end of a century, especially the 19th century, seen as characteristically advanced, modern, or decadent.

finders keepers (losers weepers) whoever finds something by chance is entitled to keep it (and the person who lost it will just have to lament its loss). Mainly used humorously, this expression has been current since the early 19th century, although the idea goes back much further and is found in the Roman dramatist Plautus. A variant sometimes heard is **findings keepings**.

fine feathers beautiful clothes. Alluding to the proverb *fine feathers make fine birds*, meaning that an eye-catching appearance makes an undistinguished person seem beautiful or impressive. Recorded in English from the late 19th century, but earlier (early 16th century) in French.

one's finest hour the time of one's greatest achievement; now particularly associated with a speech of 18 June 1940 by Winston Churchill, 'If the British Empire and its Commonwealth lasts for a thousand years, men will still say, "This was their finest hour." '

Fingal a character in an epic poem by the Scottish poet James Macpherson (1736–96), based on the legendary Irish hero ➤ FINN *mac Cool* but fictionally transformed and depicted as fighting both the Norse invaders and the Romans (under Caracalla) from an invented kingdom in NW Scotland.

Fingal's Cave is the name of a cave on the island of Staffa in the Inner Hebrides, noted for the clustered basaltic pillars that form its cliffs. It is said to have been the inspiration of Mendelssohn's overture *The Hebrides* (also known as *Fingal's Cave*), but in fact he noted down the principal theme before his visit to Staffa.

have a finger in every pie be involved in a large and varied number of activities or enterprises; the expression in this form is recorded from the late 19th century, but the image of a finger (earlier hand) in a pie indicating involvement dates back to the mid 16th century.

be all fingers and thumbs be clumsy or awkward in handling something, lack all manual dexterity. An obsolete earlier (mid 16th-century) variant is, **each finger is a thumb**; in the 19th century, the expression **all thumbs** was used.

Huckleberry Finn name of the character created by Mark Twain, introduced in *The Adventures of Tom Sawyer* (1876), and central to its sequel, *The Adventures of Huckleberry Finn* (1884). Son of the town drunkard, Huckleberry Finn is shown as brave and resourceful, but cramped by the confines of civilization.

Finn mac Cool in Irish mythology, the warrior hero of a cycle of legends about a band of warriors defending Ireland. Father of the legendary Irish warrior and bard ➤ OSSIAN, he is supposed to have lived in the 3rd century AD.

fire one of the four elements in ancient and medieval philosophy and in astrology (considered essential to the nature of the signs Aries, Leo, and Sagittarius).

Fire and brimstone is torment in hell; often with biblical allusion, as in Revelation 19:20.

The **Fire of London** was the huge and devastating fire which destroyed some 13,000 houses over 400 acres of London between 2 and 6 September 1666, having started in a bakery in Pudding Lane in the City of London.

To **go through fire and water** is to face any peril. Originally with reference to the medieval practice of trial by ordeal, which could take the form of making an accused person hold or walk on red-hot iron or of throwing them into water.

To **set the world on fire** is to do something remarkable or sensational (often in negative contexts). A variant in British English is, **set the Thames on fire**.

fireside chats in the US, the informal broadcasts made by Franklin Roosevelt (1882–1945) during his presidency on topics of national interest.

firing on all (four) cylinders working or functioning at a peak level. A metaphor from an internal-combustion engine; a cylinder is said to be firing when the fuel inside it is ignited.

first often used to mean of pre-eminent importance.

First Consul was the title held by Napoleon Bonaparte (see ➤ NAPOLEON) from 1799 to 1804, when he became Emperor of France.

The **First Fleet** comprised the eleven British ships under the command of Arthur Phillip (1738–1814), sailor and first governor of New South Wales, which arrived in Australia in January 1788.

A **first-foot** is the first person to cross a threshold in the New Year, in accordance with a Scottish custom; it is traditionally thought lucky for the *first-foot* to be a dark-haired man.

The **First Four Ships** were the first European settlers' ships that arrived in New Zealand in 1840.

First fruits are the first agricultural produce of a season, especially when given as an offering to God; originally with biblical allusion as to Numbers 18:12.

The **First Lady** is the wife of the President of the US; the term is recorded from the mid 19th century, and has gradually come into official use.

First past the post means winning a race (especially a horse-race) by being the first to reach the finishing line; a **first-past-the-post** electoral system is one, as in Britain, in which a candidate or party wins an election by achievement of a simple majority.

The **First State** is an informal name for Delaware.

The **First World** is the industrialized capitalist countries of western Europe, North America, Japan, Australia, and New Zealand.

The **First World War** was a war (1914–18) in which the Central Powers (Germany and Austria–Hungary, joined later by Turkey and Bulgaria) were defeated by an alliance of Britain and its dominions, France, Russia, and others, joined later by Italy and the US.

fish in Christian art, a *fish* is a symbol of Christ, and sometimes also of the newly baptized and of the Eucharist; it is often found in paintings in the catacombs. The reason for the symbolism is not wholly clear, although it may derive from the Greek letters of 'Jesus Christ, Son of God, Saviour' read as *ikhthus* 'fish'.

A *fish* is an emblem of ➤ St ANTHONY *of Padua* and other saints.

The **Fish** or **The Fishes** are names given to the zodiacal sign or constellation Pisces.

Something which is described as **neither fish nor fowl nor good red herring** is of indefinite character and difficult to identify or classify; with original reference to dietary restrictions in times of fasting and abstinence.

There are plenty more fish in the sea means that there are many other people in the world, used especially as a consolatory remark to someone whose romantic relationship has ended. With allusion to the proverb *there are as good fish in the sea as ever came out of it*, recorded from the late 16th century.

Fisher King in medieval legends of the ➤ *Holy* GRAIL, a wounded king in whose castle the Grail is kept, and who will only be healed when the right question about the Grail is asked.

fisher of men an evangelist; originally with biblical allusion to Matthew 4:19.

the Fisherman's ring a seal-ring worn by the Pope, showing St Peter drawing in his net full of fish.

fishwife a woman who sells fish, taken as typified by a coarse-mannered woman who is prone to shouting and abuse (the association of fish-selling with vituperative language is also found in ➤ BILLINGSGATE).

five the cardinal number that is one more than four.

in Sikh belief, the **five Ks** are five signs, *kangha* (comb), *kara* (steel bangle), *kesh* (uncut hair, covered by a turban, and beard), *kirpan* (short sword) and *kuccha* (short trousers, originally for riding) which show allegiance to the ➤ KHALSA.

The **Five Members** were the members of the Long Parliament, Pym, Hampden, Haselrig, Holles, and Strode, whose arrest was unsuccessfully attempted by Charles I on 4 January 1642 in the House of Commons; having been warned in advance, they had escaped. The event contributed materially to the final break between king and Parliament.

The **Five Pillars of Islam** are the five duties expected of every Muslim—profession of the faith in a prescribed form, observance of ritual prayer, giving alms to the poor, fasting during the month of Ramadan, and performing a pilgrimage to Mecca.

fix someone's wagon in the US, bring about someone's downfall, spoil someone's chances of success.

get a fix on assess or determine the nature or facts of; obtain a clear understanding of. From the action of determining the position of an aircraft, ship, or body of troops by visual or radio bearings or astronomical observation.

flag a national flag is often taken as the essential symbol of the country concerned, as in the US *Pledge of Allegiance*.

In the US, 14 June, the anniversary of the adoption of the ➤ STARS *and Stripes* in 1777, is known as **Flag Day**.

A **flag of convenience** is a flag of a country under which a ship is registered in order to avoid financial charges or restrictive regulations in the owner's country.

To **fly the flag** is (of a ship) to be registered to a particular country and sail under its flag; in figurative use, to represent or demonstrate support for one's country, political party, or organization, especially when one is abroad.

To **show the flag** is to make a gesture of support for or solidarity with one's country, political party, or organization, especially when one is abroad or among outsiders. Used literally of a naval vessel making an official visit to a foreign port, especially as a show of strength.

To **wrap oneself in the flag** is to make an excessive show of patriotism, especially for political ends (chiefly in North American usage).

run something up the flagpole recorded as an established expression in the 1960s, suggesting the testing of a new idea or product; the full expression is, *let's run it up the flagpole and see if anyone salutes it.*

put the flags out celebrate publicly. Evelyn Waugh's novel *Put Out More Flags* (1942) had an epigraph from the Chinese, part of which reads, 'a drunk military man should order gallons and put out more flags in order to increase his military splendour.'

flamboyant of or denoting a style of French Gothic architecture marked by wavy flamelike tracery and ornate decoration.

flaming sword traditionally held by the angel in the expulsion from Paradise, originally as in Genesis 3:24.

Flanders a region in the south-western part of the Low Countries, now divided between Belgium (where it forms the provinces of East and West Flanders), France, and the

Netherlands. It was a powerful medieval principality and the scene of prolonged fighting during the First World War, when Allied troops held the sector of the Western Front round the town of Ypres.

The **Flanders Mare** was a nickname of Anne of Cleves (1515–57), fourth wife of Henry VIII, whom the king divorced; according to Smollett's *A Complete History of England* (3rd ed., 1759), 'The King found her so different from her picture…that…he swore they had brought him a Flanders mare.'

The **Flanders poppy** is a red poppy, used as an emblem of the Allied soldiers who fell in the First World War.

flapper in the 1920s, a fashionable young woman intent on enjoying herself and flouting conventional standards of behaviour.

Flapper vote was a derogatory term for the parliamentary vote granted to women of 21 and over in 1928.

Flash Gordon spaceman hero of the comic strip created by the American cartoonist Alex Raymond in 1934, who in order to save the world from extinction is sent to the planet Mongo to defeat the forces of the evil emperor Ming.

a flash in the pan a thing or person whose sudden but brief success is not repeated or repeatable. With allusion to the priming of a firearm, the flash being from an explosion of gunpowder within the lock.

Flashman a character in *Tom Brown's Schooldays* (1857) by Thomas Hughes, revived from 1969 in a series of humorous novels by George Macdonald Fraser. Flashman is a bully and a coward (as in the original novel), and his reputation as a hero is entirely undeserved, but his saving grace appears to be that he is free from the hypocrisy of many of the more moral characters around him.

flatline die; with reference to the continuous straight line displayed on a heart monitor, indicating death. The term is recorded in a medical context in the early 1980s, but came to general prominence with the release of the film *The Flatliners* (1990). The film tells the story of a group of medical students who dangerously exploit their ability to control the heart rate by helping each other to *flatline* in order to experience the first few seconds after the moment of death, before being revived (the participants, or **flatliners**, were considerably chastened by the experience).

Flavian a member of a dynasty (AD 69–96) of Roman emperors including ➤ VESPASIAN and his sons Titus and Domitian.

flavour of the month a person or thing that enjoys a short period of great popularity; the term originated as a marketing ploy in US ice-cream parlours in the 1940s, when a particular ice-cream flavour would be singled out for the month or week for special promotion.

flea the *flea* is taken as the type of something small and contemptible, or as a sign of dirt and degradation.

the Fleet a stream (now covered) flowing into the Thames between Ludgate Hill and Fleet Street, and the nearby **Fleet prison**, a former London prison in the neighbourhood of the present Farringdon Street, alongside the Fleet river. It was built in the time of Richard I, and long afterwards served as a place of imprisonment for persons condemned by the Star Chamber. After the abolition of the latter in 1640, it served mainly as a debtors' prison, until demolished in 1848.

The term **Fleet marriage** was used for a wedding performed clandestinely by a **Fleet parson**, any of a number of disreputable clergymen to be found in or around the Fleet prison ready to perform such marriages.

Fleet Street, often used to refer to the British Press, is a street in central London in which the offices of national newspapers were located until the mid 1980s.

fleur-de-lis a stylized lily composed of three petals bound together near their bases. It is especially known from the former royal arms of France, in which it appears in gold on a blue field. Recorded from Middle English, the term comes from Old French *flour de lys* 'flower of the lily'.

flocks and herds sheep and cattle, one's possessions generally; originally often with biblical allusion, as in Genesis 46:32.

Battle of Flodden (Field) a decisive battle of the Anglo-Scottish war of 1513, at Flodden, a hill near the Northumbrian village of Branxton. A Scottish army under James IV was defeated by a smaller but better-led English force under the Earl of Surrey (sent northwards by Henry VIII, who was on campaign in France) and suffered heavy losses, including the king and most of his nobles.

the Flood the biblical flood said in Genesis ch. 6–9 to have been brought by God upon earth because of the wickedness of the human race, and from which only ➤ NOAH and his family were saved; in extended usage, marking a period of time preceded by extreme antiquity, as in *antediluvian, before the Flood*.

Flora in Roman mythology, the goddess of flowering plants.

Floréal the eighth month of the French Republican calendar (1793–1805), originally running from 20 April to 19 May. The name is French, and comes from Latin *floreus* 'flowery'.

florin an English gold coin of the 14th century, worth six shillings and eight old pence; a former British coin and monetary unit worth two shillings.

The word comes via Old French from Italian *fiorino*, diminutive of *fiore* 'flower', from Latin *flos, flor-*. The word originally denoted a gold coin issued in Florence, bearing a *fleur-de-lis* (the city's emblem) on the reverse.

Florizel the prince of Bohemia, in Shakespeare's *The Winter's Tale*; as a young man, George, Prince of Wales, afterwards George IV, signed his letters to the actress Mary Robinson (see ➤ PERDITA) 'Florizel'.

flotsam the wreckage of a ship or its cargo found floating on or washed up by the sea (as distinguished from ➤ JETSAM, goods or material thrown overboard and washed ashore). **Flotsam and jetsam** is used generally for useless or discarded objects.

flourish like a green bay tree develop vigorously in a congenial environment, whether or not this is deserved; originally with reference to Psalm 37:5 in the Book of Common Prayer.

flow of soul genial conversation, as complementary to intellectual discussion; the phrase comes originally from Pope's *Satires of Horace* (1733), 'the feast of reason and the flow of soul'.

no flowers by request an intimation that no flowers are desired at a funeral; the writer and humorist Alfred Ainger (1837–1904) used the phrase at a dinner for contributors in 1897 to sum up the principles on which the *Dictionary of National Biography* was being compiled.

flutter the dovecotes cause alarm, throw into confusion or excitement; perhaps originally as a quotation from Shakespeare's *Coriolanus* (1608).

fly often taken as the type of something unimportant and trivial.

A **fly in amber** is a curious relic of the past, preserved into the present; alluding to the fossilised bodies of insects often found trapped in amber. The image was given a different slant by Michael Crichton's thriller *Jurassic Park* (1990) and the Spielberg film based on it, in which the DNA essential to the recreation of dinosaurs was retrieved from the animal's blood supposedly fossilized with the insect that had fed from it.

A **fly in the ointment** is a minor irritation that spoils the success or enjoyment of something; originally with biblical allusion to Ecclesiastes 10:1, 'Dead flies cause the ointment of the apothecary to send forth a stinking savour.'

A **fly on the wall** is an unnoticed observer of a particular situation. Very often as a modifier, as in **fly-on-the-wall documentary**, which refers to a film-making technique whereby events are merely observed and presented realistically with minimum interference rather than acted out under direction.

A **fly on the wheel** is a person who overestimates their own influence. With reference to Aesop's fable of a fly sitting on the axletree of a moving chariot and saying, 'See what a dust I raise.'

fly a kite make a kite rise and remain suspended in the air; in figurative usage, try something out to test opinion. This meaning derives ultimately from the historical sense 'raise money by an accommodation bill', i.e., raise money on credit, and this sense of testing public opinion of one's creditworthiness gave rise to the current figurative usage. In the US, **go fly a kite!** means 'go away!'

flying that flies; in a number of phrases.

a **flying bishop** is an informal term in the Anglican Church in the UK for a bishop opposed to the ordination of women priests, who is authorized to act as bishop to clergy outside his own diocese, should they be similarly opposed, and their own bishop willing to ordain women.

The **Flying Dutchmen** is a legendary spectral ship supposedly seen in the region of the Cape of Good Hope and presaging disaster; the name is also used for the captain of this ship, said to have been condemned to sail the seas for ever.

A **flying saucer** is a disc-shaped flying craft supposedly piloted by aliens, a UFO; the term is recorded from the late 1940s.

The **Flying Scotsman** is an LNER steam locomotive of Sir Nigel Gresley's A3 Pacific design, once used as the daily express train between London (King's Cross) and Edinburgh, and now preserved.

A **flying squad** is a division of a police force or other organization which is capable of reaching an incident quickly; the term is recorded from the late 1920s, and the rhyming slang *Sweeney Todd* from the mid 1930s.

With flying colours means with distinction. In former military parlance, *flying colours* meant having the regimental flag flying as a sign of success or victory; a conquered army usually had to *lower (or strike) its colours*.

Foggy Bottom in the US, a nickname for the State Department, from the traditional name of a swampy piece of land in Washington near Hamburg village.

Folies-Bergère a variety theatre in Paris, opened in 1869, known for its lavish productions featuring nude and semi-nude female performers.

folio an individual leaf of paper or parchment, either loose as one of a series or forming part of a bound volume, which is numbered on the recto or front side only.

Recorded from late Middle English, the word comes from Latin, ablative of *folium* 'leaf', in medieval Latin used in references to mean 'on leaf so-and-so'. The original sense of *in folio* (from Italian *in foglio*) was 'in the form of a full-sized sheet or leaf folded once (designating the largest size of book)'.

folly a costly ornamental building with no practical purpose, especially a tower or mock-Gothic ruin built in a large garden or park.

Folsom a Palaeo-Indian culture of Central and North America, dated to about 10,500–8,000 years ago. The culture is distinguished by fluted stone projectile points or spearheads (**Folsom points**), the discovery of which (in 1926) forced a radical rethinking of the date at which humans first inhabited the New World. The name comes (in the early 20th century) from *Folsom*, New Mexico, the area where remains were first found.

Fontevraud in France, the site of a major Benedictine abbey of the 11th and 12th centuries; Henry II of England, Eleanor of Aquitaine, and their son Richard I are buried there.

Fonthill Abbey the Gothic house in Wiltshire of the English writer and collector William Beckford (1759–1844); he is said to have spent over a quarter of a million on it in the course of sixteen years, but he was forced through debts in 1822 to sell the property.

All Fools' Day a humorous term for 1 April as a day for testing the credulity of others; recorded from the early 18th century, and probably modelled on *All Saints' Day* and *All Souls' Day*.

foolscap a size of paper, about 330 x 200 (or 400) mm. It is said to be named from a former watermark representing a fool's cap.

foot a unit of linear measure equal to 12 inches (30.48 cm), so named because it was originally based on the length of a man's foot.

a foot in both camps have an interest or stake in two parties or sides without commitment to either (with allusion to the military sense of forces in encampment).

footloose and fancy-free without commitments or responsibilities; free to act or travel as one pleases. Footloose used literally in the late 17th century to mean 'free to move the feet', and was originally US (late 19th century) in this sense. The collocation with *fancy-free* (*fancy* in the sense of 'love' or 'object of one's affections') is recorded from the mid 20th century.

Forbidden City an area of Beijing (Peking) containing the former imperial palaces, to which entry was forbidden to all except the members of the imperial family and their servants.

The name *Forbidden City* is also given to Lhasa in Tibet, which as the centre of Tibetan Buddhism was closed to foreign visitors until the 20th century.

forbidden fruit the fruit forbidden to Adam in the garden of Eden; with reference to Genesis 2:17. The term *forbidden fruit*, recorded from the mid 17th century, often implies its attraction.

foreign devil in China, a foreigner, especially a European, a translation of Chinese *(faan) kwai ló* '(foreign) devil fellow'; the term is recorded in English from the mid 19th century.

Foreign Legion a military formation of the French army founded in the 1830s to fight France's colonial wars. Composed, except for the higher ranks, of non-Frenchmen, the Legion was famed for its audacity and endurance. Its most famous campaigns were in French North Africa in the late 19th and early

20th centuries. Although its original purpose has been lost, it is still in existence, in greatly reduced form.

In the 19th and early 20th centuries, the *Foreign Legion* provided the background for a number of romantic British adventure stories, as Ouida's *Under Two Flags* (1867) and P. G. Wren's *Beau Geste* (1924), in which upper-class Englishmen wrongly suspected of crime joined the ranks of the Legion under an alias.

forelock a lock of hair growing just above the forehead.

To **take time by the forelock** is to seize an opportunity. The Latin fabulist Phaedrus described Opportunity or Occasion as being bald except for a long forelock, a personification that was illustrated in Renaissance emblem books and was also applied to Time.

To **touch one's forelock** is to indicate respect or deference. From the action of raising a hand to one's forehead in deference when meeting a person of higher social rank (also **tug one's forelock**).

Forest Lawn in California, a large cemetery outside Los Angeles, noted for its landscaping and elaborate statuary; the name is sometimes used allusively.

the Forgotten Army the British army in Burma after the fall of Rangoon in 1942 and the evacuation west, and the subsequent cutting by the Japanese of the supply link from India to Nationalist China, said to derive from Lord Louis Mountbatten's encouragement to his troops after taking over as supreme Allied commander in South-East Asia, 'You are not the Forgotten Army—no one's even heard of you.'

the Forgotten Man a phrase coined by William Graham Sumner in a speech at Yale University in 1885, in which he said, 'The forgotten man works and votes—generally he prays—but his chief business in life is to pay…Who and where is the forgotten man in this case, who will have to pay for it all?' The term was later used by Franklin Roosevelt.

form follows function guiding principle taught by proponents of the architectural Modernist movement; the phrase was coined by the American architect Louis Henri Sullivan (1856–1924).

Formosa former name for Taiwan, an island off the south-east coast of China where the Nationalist Chinese State was set up by ➤ CHIANG *Kai-shek* in 1949; the name is from

Portuguese and means 'beautiful'. The literary impostor ➤ *George* PSALMANAZAR (1679?–1763) presented himself as a native of *Formosa*, compiling a catechism in its supposed language.

Formula One an international form of motor racing, whose races are called Grand Prix.

Fort Knox a US military reservation in Kentucky, famous as the site of the depository (built in 1936) which holds the bulk of the nation's gold bullion in its vaults.

Fortean of, relating to, or denoting paranormal phenomena; the word comes from the name of Charles H. *Fort* (1874–1932), American student of paranormal phenomena.

painting the Forth Bridge the steel structure of the *Forth Bridge* in Scotland has required constant repainting; this is consequently an expression for undertaking a task that can never be completed.

Fortune chance or luck as a power in human affairs, often personified as a goddess; the word comes (in Middle English, via Old French) from Latin *Fortuna*, the name of a goddess personifying luck or chance. Fortune's emblem, the ➤ WHEEL *of Fortune*), indicates mutability.

forty the name **The Forty** is given to the members of the Académie Française; also called **the Forty Immortals**.
   The **Forty-five** is an informal name for the Jacobite rebellion of 1745.
   The **Forty Martyrs of England and Wales** is the name given to a group of English and Welsh Roman Catholics canonized in 1970 as representing those martyred for their faith between 1535 and 1679. Their feast day is 25 October.
   A **forty-niner** was a seeker for gold in the Californian gold rush of 1849.
   The **forty-ninth parallel** is the parallel of latitude 49° north of the equator, especially as forming the boundary between Canada and the US west of the Lake of the Woods.
   Forty years on are the opening words of the Harrow school song by the English schoolmaster E. E Bowen (1836–1901). The words were used by Alan Bennett as the title of a satirical comedy (1968) set in an English public school.

forum in an ancient Roman city, a public square or marketplace used for judicial and other business.

Fosse Way an ancient road in Britain, so called from the *fosse* or ditch that used to run along each side of it. It ran from Axminster to Lincoln, via Bath and Leicester (about 300 km, 200 miles), and marked the limit of the first stage of the Roman occupation (mid 1st century AD).

Foucault's pendulum the huge pendulum hung from the roof of the Panthéon in Paris in 1851 by the French physicist Jean Bernard Léon Foucault (1819–68), to demonstrate the rotation of the earth.

foul anchor an anchor that has become entangled with a rope or cable, as the badge of the British Admiralty.

foul one's own nest do something damaging or harmful to oneself or one's own interests. From the proverbial condemnation, current in English since the early 15th century and before that in Latin, of a person who vilifies their own country or family, *It's an ill bird that fouls its own nest.*

Founding Father a member of the convention that drew up the constitution of the US in 1787. Early use of the phrase is particularly associated with US president Warren G. Harding (1865–1923), who in his inaugural address of 1921 referred to his 'belief in the divine inspiration of the founding fathers'.

Fountain of Youth a mythical fountain which according to legend had the power of renewing youth; it was said in the 12th-century French work *Roman d'Alisandre* to have been a sidestream of the Euphrates in which Alexander the Great and his army bathed, and were restored to the prime of life.
   The belief in the existence of such a fountain was widespread in the Middle Ages. After the discovery of America it was said to be in the Bahamas, and the Spanish explorer ➤ *Juan* PONCE *de León*, discoverer of Florida, was authorized in 1512 to look for and settle ➤ BIMINI, the island where the *Fountain of Youth* was said to be.

four equivalent to the product of two and two, one more than three.
   A **four-colour problem** is a mathematical problem to prove that any plane map can be coloured with only four colours so that no two same-coloured regions have a common boundary.
   The **four freedoms** are the four essential human freedoms as proclaimed in a speech to Congress by Franklin D. Roosevelt in 1941: freedom of speech and expression, freedom

of worship, freedom from want, and freedom from fear.

The **Four Horsemen of the Apocalypse** are War, Famine, Death, and Pestilence; they are traditionally identified with the riders of the white, red, black, and pale horses seen in Revelation.

In Christian belief, the **four last things** are death, judgement, heaven, and hell, as studied in eschatology.

A **four-letter word** is any of several short words referring to sexual or excretory functions, regarded as coarse or offensive; the term is recorded from the 1920s.

The **four noble truths** are the four central beliefs containing the essence of Buddhist teaching; they are that human life is characterized by frustration and suffering, that the cause of this is desire and greed, that desire must therefore be got rid of, and that following the ➤ EIGHTFOLD *path* is the way to achieve this.

fourteen equivalent to the product of seven and two; one more than thirteen.

The **Fourteen Holy Helpers** are a group of saints, also known as the *Auxiliary Saints*, whose intercessory powers in human affairs, especially illness, were regarded as particularly effective; their collective cult was especially strong in the Rhineland between the 14th and 16th centuries.

The **Fourteen Points** were set out by US President Woodrow Wilson (1856–1924) in a speech to the US Congress, 8 January 1918, as the basis for peace negotiations in the First World War.

fourth constituting number four in a sequence.

The **fourth dimension** is a postulated spatial dimension additional to those determining length, area, and volume; the phrase is recorded from the late 19th century, and is now also used in physics to denote time as analogous to linear dimensions.

The **fourth estate** is the press; a group regarded as having power in the land equivalent to that of one of the three Estates of the Realm, the Crown, the House of Lords, and the House of Commons. The term derives from a usage by Thomas Babington Macaulay (1800–59), 'The gallery in which the reporters sit has become a fourth estate of the realm.'

The **Fourth of July** in the US is ➤ INDEPENDENCE *Day*.

The **Fourth of June** is the birthday of George III (1738–1820), speech day at Eton because of his interest in the school.

The **Fourth World** comprises those countries and communities considered to be the poorest and most underdeveloped of the Third World.

fox the *fox* is proverbial for its artfulness and cunning; in Ben Jonson's play, the miser who deceives those around him with promises of wealth is named *Volpone* (in Italian, 'Fox'). It figures in a number of fables, such as that giving rise to the expression ➤ SOUR *grapes*. In the story in which the fox and the crane entertain one another the fox meets his match: the long-beaked crane serves food in a deep-necked jar from which the fox cannot eat.

In the stories of 'Uncle Remus', **Brer Fox** is the determined enemy of ➤ *Brer* RABBIT, who despite his own strength and cunning is in the end always outwitted by the rabbit.

Foxe's Martyrs informal name for *Actes and Monuments*, the martyrology by the Protestant divine John *Foxe* (1516–87).

Francesca see ➤ PAOLO *and Francesca*.

Francis male forename, name of two saints.

St Francis de Sales (1567–1622), French bishop, was one of the leaders of the Counter-Reformation. The Salesian order (founded in 1859) is named after him. His feast day is 24 January.

St Francis of Assisi, (c.1181–1226), Italian monk, was founder of the Franciscan order. Born into a wealthy family, he renounced his inheritance and devoted himself to his religious calling. He soon attracted followers, founding the Franciscan order in 1209 and drew up its original rule (based on complete poverty). He is revered for his generosity, simple faith, humility, and love of nature, and is often shown preaching to the birds. His feast day is 4 October.

The extremely austere rule written by him in 1209 for the **Franciscan** order was modified in 1221 and received papal approval in 1223, but divergences of practice led to the separation of the Friars Minor of the Observance (the Observants) and the Friars Minor Conventual (the Conventuals) in 1517, and to the foundation of the stricter Friars Minor Capuchin (the ➤ CAPUCHINS) in 1529. The order of Franciscan nuns was founded by ➤ *St* CLARE (c.1212) under the direction of St Francis; they are known as 'Poor Clares'. There is also a third order of lay associates (tertiaries), and a Franciscan order within the Anglican Church.

Franco-Prussian War the war of 1870–1 between France (under Napoleon III) and Prussia, in which Prussian troops advanced into France and decisively defeated the French at Sedan. The defeat marked the end of the French Second Empire. For Prussia, the proclamation of the new German Empire at Versailles was the climax of Bismarck's ambitions to unite Germany.

Frank a member of a Germanic people that conquered Gaul in the 6th century and controlled much of western Europe for several centuries afterwards. Also (in the eastern Mediterranean region), a person of western European nationality or descent.
    The name is recorded from Old English (in form *Franca*) and is of Germanic origin, perhaps from the name of a weapon and related to Old English *franca* 'javelin'; it is ultimately related to *France* and *French*.

Frankenstein a character in the novel *Frankenstein, or the Modern Prometheus* (1818) by Mary Shelley. Baron Frankenstein is a scientist who creates and brings to life a manlike monster which eventually turns on him and destroys him; *Frankenstein* is not the name of the monster itself, as is often assumed, and sometimes suggested in allusive use.
    In the 1990s, the name has been used by opponents of the development of genetically-modified crops in the expressions **Frankenstein food** or **Frankenfood**.

frankincense an aromatic gum resin obtained from an African tree and burnt as incense; traditionally used in the Jewish Temple. It was one of the gifts, with gold and myrrh, brought by the ➤ MAGI to the infant Jesus, and because it was also used by magicians and sorcerers may symbolize their submission to him.
    The word is recorded from late Middle English, and comes from Old French *franc encens*, literally 'high-quality incense'.

frater historical term for the dining room or refectory of a monastery; the word is recorded from Middle English and comes from Old French, from a shortening of *refreitor*, from late Latin *refectorium* 'refectory'.

Free Church a Christian Church which has dissented or seceded from an established Church; the term is recorded from the mid 16th century.
    The **Free Church of Scotland** is a strict Presbyterian Church organized by dissenting

members of the established Church of Scotland in 1843. In 1900 its majority amalgamated with the United Presbyterian Church to form the United Free Church; its name was retained by the minority group, nicknamed the *Wee Free Kirk*.

Free French an organization of French troops and volunteers in exile formed under General de Gaulle in 1940. Based in London, the movement continued the war against the Axis Powers after de Gaulle appealed by radio from London for French resistance to the Franco-German armistice. Its French National Committee (established in 1941) eventually developed into a provisional government for liberated France. The Free French were also involved in the liberation of Paris in 1944.

freedom ride in the US, an organized ride in buses or other public transport as a demonstration against racial segregation; the term was used particularly in the context of civil rights demonstrations of the 1960s.

Freedom Trail a historic route through Boston, Massachusetts, which begins and ends at Faneuil Hall, where Bostonians met to protest against British 'taxation without representation' (see ➤ BOSTON *Tea Party*) in the months preceding the War of American Independence.

Freemason a member of an international order established for mutual help and fellowship, which holds elaborate secret ceremonies.
    The original *free masons* were itinerant skilled stonemasons of the 14th century, who are said to have recognized fellow craftsmen by secret signs. while the *accepted masons* were honorary members of the fraternity who began to be admitted early in the 17th century. Modern freemasonry is usually traced to the formation of the Grand Lodge in London in 1717; members are typically professionals and businessmen. Freemasons have sometimes been criticized for their secrecy, for supposed occult elements in their rituals, or for alleged corruption in business, professional, or government matters.

French of or pertaining to France.
    French leave is absence from work or duty without permission, said to derive from the French custom of leaving a dinner or ball without saying goodbye to the host or hostess. The phrase was first recorded in the late

18th century; the equivalent French expression is *filer à l'Anglaise*, literally 'to escape in the style of the English'.

The **French Republican Calendar** was a reformed calendar officially introduced by the French Republican government on 5 October 1793, and taken to have started on the equinox of 22 September 1792, the day of the proclamation of the Republic. It had twelve months of thirty days each (divided into three weeks of ten days), *Vendemiaire*, *Brumaire*, *Frimaire*, *Nivose*, *Pluviose*, *Ventose*, *Germinal*, *Floréal*, *Prairial*, *Messidor*, *Thermidor*, and *Fructidor*, and with five days of festivals at the year's end (six in leap years). It was abandoned under the Napoleonic regime and the Gregorian calendar was formally reinstated on 1 January 1806.

The **French Revolution** was the overthrow of the Bourbon monarchy in France (1789–99). The Revolution began with the meeting of the legislative assembly (the States General) in May 1789, when the French government was already in crisis; the Bastille was stormed in July of the same year. The Revolution became steadily more radical and ruthless with power increasingly in the hands of the Jacobins and Robespierre. Louis XVI's execution in January 1793 was followed by Robespierre's Reign of Terror (September 1793–July 1794). The Directory, the last of several different forms of republican administration, was overthrown by Napoleon in 1799.

The **French Wars of Religion** were a series of religious and political conflicts in France (1562–98) involving the Protestant Huguenots on one side and Catholic groups on the other. The wars were complicated by interventions from Spain, Rome, England, the Netherlands, and elsewhere, and were not brought to an end until the defeat of the Holy League and the settlement of the Edict of Nantes.

fresco a painting done rapidly in watercolour on wet plaster on a wall or ceiling, so that the colours penetrate the plaster and become fixed as it dries; this method of painting, used in Roman times and by the great masters of the Italian Renaissance including Giotto, Masaccio, Piero della Francesca, Raphael, and Michelangelo.

The word is recorded from the late 16th century and comes from Italian, literally 'cool, fresh'. It was first recorded in the phrase *in fresco*, representing Italian *affresco* 'on the fresh (plaster)'.

fresh fields and pastures new new areas of activity, from a misquotation of Milton's 'Lycidas' (1638), 'Tomorrow to fresh woods and pastures new.'

Freudian slip an unintentional error regarded as revealing subconscious feelings, named after the Austrian neurologist and psychotherapist Sigmund *Freud* (1856–1939). He was the first to emphasize the significance of unconscious processes in normal and neurotic behaviour, and was the founder of psychoanalysis as both a theory of personality and a therapeutic practice.

Frey in Scandinavian mythology, the god of fertility and dispenser of rain and sunshine. His sister **Freya** is the goddess of love and of the night.

friar a member of any of certain religious orders of men, especially the four mendicant orders, Augustinians, Carmelites, Dominicans, and Franciscans (the Franciscans, who regard themselves of humbler rank than members of other orders, are known as the **Friars Minor**). The word is recorded from Middle English, and comes via Old French from Latin *frater* 'brother'.

Friday the day of the week before Saturday and following Thursday, recorded in Old English and named for the Germanic goddess *Frigga*, as a translation of the late Latin *Veneris dies* 'day of the planet Venus'.

Friday, in memory of ➤ GOOD *Friday*, was traditionally a day of fasting and abstinence in the Christian Church; it is also often traditionally regarded as an unlucky day, with Friday 13th being particularly perilous.

In Islamic belief, Friday is regarded as the day of the week on which Adam was created (as in Genesis 1:26–7).

See also ➤ BLACK *Friday*, ➤ BLOODY *Friday*.

St Frideswide (*c*.680–727), Anglo-Saxon princess, virgin and patron of Oxford; she was first abbess of a double monastery founded on the site of what is now Christ Church Cathedral. Her cult was locally popular and her shrine was restored under Mary I, but in 1558 it was desecrated when through the agency of a Calvinist divine who wished to suppress the cult, her relics were mixed with those of the wife of one of the fellows. Her feast days are 19 October and 12 February (the date of her translation).

Friend a member of the ➤ RELIGIOUS *Society of Friends*, a Quaker; the name is recorded from the late 17th century.

friend of Dorothy a term for a gay man for whom Dorothy in the *Wizard of Oz* (1939), as portrayed by Judy Garland, is an icon.

friendly fire weapon fire coming from one's own side that causes accidental injury or death to one's own forces.

Friends of the Earth an international pressure group established in 1971 to campaign for a better awareness of and response to environmental problems.

Frigga in Scandinavian mythology, the wife of Odin and goddess of married love and of the hearth, sometimes identified with ➤ FREYA. ➤ FRIDAY is named after her.

frigidarium a cold room in an ancient Roman bath.

Frimaire the third month of the French Republican calendar (1793–1805), originally running from 21 November to 20 December. The name comes from the French *frimas* 'hoar frost'.

Frisia an ancient region of NW Europe, consisting of the Frisian Islands and parts of the mainland corresponding to the modern provinces of Friesland and Groningen in the Netherlands and the regions of Ostfriesland and Nordfriesland in NW Germany. *Frisian* is the Germanic language most closely related to English and Dutch.

Frodo forename of the ➤ HOBBIT Frodo Baggins, who is one of the central characters of Tolkien's *The Lord of the Rings*, and who ultimately succeeds in his quest to destroy the One Ring.

frog the word *frog* was used as as a general term of abuse in Middle English, and was applied specifically to the Dutch in the 17th century; its application to the French (late 18th century) is partly alliterative, partly from the reputation of the French for eating frogs' legs.

Allusions are also found to a traditional fairy story, recorded by the ➤ GRIMM brothers, in which a frog in a pool returns a princess's lost golden ball in return for her promise that he may live with and be loved by her. When he claims the reward her father makes her keep her promise; the frog eats from her plate and sleeps in her room. In the original story it is when she has thrown him against the wall that he turns into his real shape, that of a handsome prince, who is now her lover and husband; the usual version is that it is when she kisses him that the enchantment is broken and he is restored.

Jean Froissart (1333?–*c*.1400), French chronicler and poet, whose chronicles record the chivalric exploits of the nobles of England and France from 1325 to 1400.

Fronde a series of civil wars in France 1648–53, in which the nobles whose power had been weakened by the policies of Cardinal Richelieu rose in rebellion against Mazarin and the court during the minority of Louis XIV. The word comes from the name for a type of sling used in a children's game played in the streets of Paris at this time.

front bench in the UK, the foremost seats in the House of Commons, occupied by the members of the cabinet and shadow cabinet.

Fructidor the twelfth month of the French Republican calendar (1793–1805), originally running from 18 August to 16 September. Also, the purge of conservative deputies that took place on the eighteenth day of this month (4 September) in 1797.

out of the frying pan into the fire from a bad situation to one that is worse; leap out of the frying pan into the fire is recorded in a mid 16th-century collection of English proverbs and epigrams.

Dr Fu Manchu a moustached Chinese master-criminal created by the British writer Sax Rohmer (1883?–1959), first appearing in the novel *Dr Fu Manchu* (1913).

fudge factor a figure included in a calculation to account for some unquantified but significant phenomenon or to ensure a desired result. *Fudge*, apparently originating in the mid 18th century as an exclamation of disgust or irritation, acquired a specific verbal sense in printers' jargon of the late 18th century, meaning to 'do work imperfectly or as best one can with the materials available'.

Führer 'Leader', the title assumed by Adolf Hitler in 1934.

Mount Fuji a dormant volcano in the Chubu region of Japan, with a symmetrical, conical, snow-capped peak. Regarded by the Japanese as sacred, it has been celebrated in art and literature for centuries.

Fulbright Act a US act of 1946, named for the American senator William Fulbright (1905–95), which authorized funds from the sale of surplus war materials overseas to be used to finance exchange programmes of students and teachers between the US and other countries. The scheme was later supported by grants from the US government.

fundamentalism a form of Protestant Christianity which upholds belief in the strict and literal interpretation of the Bible, including its narratives, doctrines, prophecies, and moral laws. Also, strict maintenance of ancient or fundamental doctrines of any religion or ideology, notably Islam.

the Furies in Greek mythology, spirits of punishment, often represented as one of three goddesses (Alecto, Megaera, and Tisiphone) with hair composed of snakes, who executed the curses pronounced upon criminals, tortured the guilty with stings of conscience, and inflicted famines and pestilences. The Furies were identified at an early date with the ➤ EUMENIDES.

furlong an eighth of a mile, 220 yards. Recorded from Old English (in form *furlang*), the word comes from *furh* 'furrow' + *lang* 'long'. The word originally denoted the length of a furrow in a common field (formally regarded as a square of ten acres). It was also used as the equivalent of the Roman *stadium*, one eighth of a Roman mile, whence the current sense.

furphy in Australia and New Zealand, a rumour or story, especially one that is untrue or absurd. The word comes from the First World War, from the name painted on water and sanitary carts manufactured by the *Furphy* family of Shepparton, Victoria.

futhark the runic alphabet; from its first six letters, *f, u, th, a* (or *o*), *r, k*.

future shock a state of distress or disorientation due to rapid social or technological change; coined by the American writer Alvin Toffler (1928–) in *Horizon* Summer 1965.

fyrd the English militia before 1066.

Gg

G the seventh letter of the modern English alphabet and of the ancient Roman one, originally corresponding to a differentiated form of C.

A **G-man** is an FBI agent; *G* is here the initial letter of *government*.

A **G-string** is a garment consisting of a narrow strip of cloth that covers the genitals and is attached to a waistband, worn as underwear or by striptease performers.

Gabriel in the Bible, the archangel who foretold the birth of Jesus to the Virgin Mary (Luke 1:26–38), and who also appeared to Zacharias, father of John the Baptist, and to Daniel; in Islam, the archangel who revealed the Koran to the Prophet Muhammad.

From their yelping call, wild geese are sometimes known as **Gabriel's hounds**.

Gadarene swine the pigs into which Jesus cast the demons that had possessed a madman (see ➤ LEGION), and which as a result ran down a steep cliff into the sea and were killed; from this, *Gadarene* means involving or engaged in a headlong or potentially disastrous rush to do something.

Gadarene comes from New Testament Greek *Gadarēnos* 'inhabitant of Gadara' (see Mark ch. 8).

Gaelic a Celtic language spoken in the highlands and islands of western Scotland, brought from Ireland in the 5th and 6th centuries AD and now spoken by about 40,000 people; also (more fully **Irish Gaelic**) another term for the Irish language.

The **Gaelic League** was founded in 1893 to revive Irish language and culture.

the Gaeltacht a region of Ireland in which the vernacular language is Irish.

Gaia in Greek mythology, the Earth personified as a goddess, daughter of Chaos. She was the mother and wife of Uranus (Heaven); their offspring included the Titans and the Cyclops.

The **Gaia hypothesis** is the theory, put forward by the English scientist James Lovelock (1919–) in 1969, that living matter on the earth collectively defines and regulates the material conditions necessary for the continuance of life.

Gaiety Girl a chorus girl or performer in a musical show, originally and especially at the *Gaiety*, a former London theatre famous for its musicals.

the gaiety of nations general gaiety or amusement; originally as a quotation from Samuel Johnson on the death of the actor David Garrick in *Lives of the Poets* (1779–81).

Galahad the noblest of King Arthur's knights, son of ➤ *Sir* LANCELOT, renowned for immaculate purity and destined to find the Holy Grail.

Galatea in Greek mythology, the name both of a sea nymph courted by the Cyclops ➤ POLYPHEMUS, who in jealousy killed his rival Acis, and that given to the statue fashioned by ➤ PYGMALION and brought to life.

Galatia an ancient region in central Asia Minor, settled by invading Gauls (the **Galatians**) in the 3rd century BC. It later became a protectorate of Rome and then (with some further territories) a province of the Roman Empire.

The **Epistle to the Galatians** is a book of the New Testament, an epistle of St Paul to the Church in Galatia.

galaxy a system of millions or billions of stars, together with gas and dust, held together by gravitational attraction; **the Galaxy**, the galaxy of which the solar system is a part, the ➤ MILKY *Way*; in figurative usage, a large or impressive group of people.

The name is recorded from Middle English, referring to the Milky Way, and comes via Old French and medieval Latin from Greek *galaxias (kuklos)* 'milky (vault)', from *gala, galakt-* 'milk'.

Galba (*c.*3 BC–AD 69), Roman emperor AD 68–9. The successor to Nero, he aroused hostility by his severity and parsimony and was murdered in a conspiracy organized by his successor Otho in the *Year of the Four Emperors*.

Galen (129–99), Greek physician. He attempted to systematize the whole of medicine, making important discoveries in anatomy and physiology. His works became influential in Europe when retranslated from Arabic in the 12th century. The word **galenical**, meaning (of a medicine) made of natural rather than synthetic components, derives from his name.

Galilee a northern region of ancient Palestine, west of the River Jordan, associated with the ministry of Jesus.

The word *galilee* is also used for a porch or chapel at the entrance to a church; perhaps alluding to Galilee as an outlying portion of the Holy Land, or with reference to the phrase in Matthew 4:15, 'Galilee of the Gentiles'.

The designation **the Galilaean** is applied to Jesus as an inhabitant of *Galilee*, often with derogatory implication.

Galileo Galilei (1564–1642), Italian astronomer and physicist, one of the founders of modern science. He discovered the constancy of a pendulum's swing, formulated the law of uniform acceleration of falling bodies, and described the parabolic trajectory of projectiles. He applied the telescope to astronomy and observed craters on the moon, sunspots, Jupiter's moons, and the phases of Venus. His acceptance of the Copernican system was rejected by the Catholic Church, and under threat of torture from the Inquisition he publicly recanted his heretical views.

The **Galilean moons** are the four largest satellites of Jupiter (Callisto, Europa, Ganymede, and Io), discovered by ➤ GALILEO in 1610 and independently by the German astronomer Simon Marius (1573–1624).

gall bile; proverbial for its bitterness, and in biblical allusion associated with ➤ WORMWOOD; the **gall of bitterness** is the extremity of bitterness.

Gallia the Latin name for Gaul, as in Caesar's *De Bello Gallico*, '*Gallia est omnis divisa in partes tres* [Gaul as a whole is divided into three parts]'.

Gallic Wars Julius Caesar's campaigns 58–51 BC, which established Roman control over Gaul north of the Alps and west of the River Rhine (Transalpine Gaul). During this period Caesar twice invaded Britain (55 and 54 BC). Largely disunited, the Gauls combined in 53–52 BC under the chieftain Vercingetorix (d. *c.*46 BC) but were eventually defeated.

Gallio a person who is indifferent, from the name of a Roman proconsul of Achaia, whose refusal to take action is recorded in Acts 18:17.

Gallipoli a major campaign of the First World War which took place on the Gallipoli peninsula, on the European side of the Dardanelles, in 1915–16.

In early 1915, after a naval attempt to force the Dardanelles had failed, the Allies (with heavy involvement of troops from Australia and New Zealand) invaded the peninsula, hoping to remove Turkey from the war and open supply lines to Russia's Black Sea ports. The campaign reached stalemate and became bogged down in trench warfare. After each side had suffered a quarter of a million casualties, the Allies evacuated the peninsula without further loss in January 1916.

Gallup poll trademark name for an assessment of public opinion by the questioning of a representative sample, typically as a basis for forecasting votes in an election. It is named after George H. *Gallup* (1901–84), the American statistician who devised the method.

the only game in town the best or most important of its kind; the only thing worth concerning itself with.

the Gamecock State an informal name for South Carolina; a *gamecock* is a cock bred and trained for cockfighting, traditionally a type of aggressive competition.

gamesmanship the art of winning games by using various ploys and tactics to gain a psychological advantage. The term derives from the title of Stephen Potter's humorous book (1947), 'The theory and practice of gamesmanship or the art of winning games without actually cheating'.

gammon nonsense, rubbish. First recorded in the early 18th century; the origin is uncertain, but the term was first used in criminals' slang in *give gammon* 'give cover to (a pickpocket)' and *keep in gammon* 'distract (a victim) for a pickpocket'.

The phrase **gammon and spinach** means 'nonsense, humbug'; with a pun on *gammon* 'bacon, ham'. The words *gammon and spinach* are part of the refrain to the song 'A frog he would a-wooing go', and the term is used by Dickens: Miss Mowcher in *David Copperfield* (1850) says, 'What a world of gammon and spinnage it is, though, ain't it!'.

Sarah Gamp in Dickens's *Martin Chuzzlewit* (1844), a monthly nurse with a fondness for gin who carried a large cotton umbrella; *gamp* from this is a dated British term for an umbrella, especially a large unwieldy one.

gamut a complete scale of musical notes; the compass or range of a voice or instrument. Earlier, a scale consisting of seven overlapping hexachords, containing all the recognized notes used in medieval music, covering almost three octaves from bass G to treble E. The word comes from medieval Latin *gamma ut*, originally the name of the lowest note in the medieval scale (bass G an octave and a half below middle C), then applied to the whole range of notes used in medieval music. The Greek letter Γ (gamma) was used for bass G, with *ut* indicating that it was the first note in the lowest of the hexachords or six-note scales.

Notes in each hexachord were named using syllables of a Latin hymn for St John the Baptist's Day, in which each line began on the next note of the scale: '*Ut* queant laxis *re*sonare fibris *Mi*ra gestorum *fa*muli tuorum, *Sol*ve polluti *la*bii reatum, Sancte Iohannes.' A seventh note, *si*, was added later, from the initial letters of Sancte Iohannes. The scheme was adapted in the 19th century to form solmization systems such as the Tonic Sol-fa.

The system of naming the notes of a scale by syllables is attributed to the Italian Benedictine monk and musical theorist Guido d'Arezzo (*c*.990–1050).

To **run the gamut** is to experience, display, or perform the complete range of something.

Ganesh in Hinduism, an elephant-headed deity, son of Shiva and Parvati. Worshipped as the remover of obstacles and patron of learning, he is invoked at the beginning of literary works, rituals, or any new undertaking. He is usually depicted coloured red, with a pot belly and one broken tusk, riding a rat. He is also known as *Ganapati*.

Ganges a river of northern India and Bangladesh, rising in the Himalayas and flowing south-east to the Bay of Bengal. The river is regarded by Hindus as sacred.

Ganymede in Greek mythology, a Trojan youth who was so beautiful that he was carried off to be Zeus' cup-bearer.

Garamond a typeface much used in books, named (in the mid 19th century) after Claude Garamond (1499–1561), French type founder.

garden often used in phrases designating a fertile, beautiful, and peaceful place. **Everything in the garden is lovely**, meaning all is well, is an early 20th-century catchphrase, originating in a song popularized by the English music-hall artiste Marie Lloyd (1870–1922) used as an expression of general satisfaction and contentment.

The **Garden of Earthly Delights** is the title of a painting by ➤ *Hieronymous* BOSCH, a triptych showing (with many surreal images) the lost earthly paradise with the creation of Eve followed by the Temptation and finally the Fall.

The **Garden of England** is an informal name for the English counties of Kent and Worcestershire, in recognition of their fertility.

The **Garden State** is an informal name for New Jersey.

Gargantua a voracious giant in Rabelais' book of the same name (1534); *gargantuan*, meaning enormous, is derived from the name.

garlic traditionally a protection against evil, especially (perhaps since the publication of Bram Stoker's *Dracula*) vampires.

The name is recorded from Old English (in form *gārlēac*), from *gār* 'spear (because the shape of a clove resembles the head of a spear) + *lēac* 'leek'.

All Sir Garnet all as it should be, highly satisfactory; the term, recorded from the late 19th century, refers to the British soldier Sir Garnet Wolseley (1833–1933). The leader of several successful military expeditions, he was regarded as the ideal of the modern professional soldier, and was the model for the 'modern Major-General' in Gilbert and Sullivan's *The Pirates of Penzance* (1879).

Alf Garnett central character of the television series *Till Death Us Do Part* (1964–74), characterized by the extremity of his right-wing, xenophobic, and racist views, and intolerance of any opinion but his own.

garter a band worn around the leg to keep up a stocking or sock. The word is recorded from Middle English and comes from Old French, from *garet* 'bend of the knee, calf of the leg', probably of Celtic origin.

The **Order of the Garter** is the highest order of English knighthood, founded by Edward III *c*.1344. According to tradition, the garter was that of the Countess of Salisbury, which the king placed on his own leg after it fell off while she was dancing with him. The king's comment to those present, '*Honi soit qui mal y pense*' (shame be to him who thinks evil of it), was adopted as the motto of the order.

The *Garter* as the badge of the Order is a ribbon of dark-blue velvet, edged and buckled with gold, and bearing the above words embroidered in gold, and is worn below the left knee; garters also form part of the ornament of the collar worn by the Knights. Presentation is in the sovereign's personal gift.

In the UK, **Garter King of Arms** is the principal King of Arms of the English ➤ COLLEGE *of Arms*.

Garuda in Hindu mythology, an eagle-like being that serves as the mount of ➤ VISHNU.

all gas and gaiters a satisfactory state of affairs; originally recorded in Dickens's *Nicholas Nickleby* (1839) 'All is gas and gaiters.'

Gascony a region and former province of SW France, in the northern foothills of the Pyrenees, which having united with Aquitaine in the 11th century, was held by England between 1154 and 1453.

Gascons were traditionally said to be braggarts and boasters as well as impetuous (➤ D'ARTAGNAN in *The Three Musketeers* is a Gascon). **Gasconade** is a poetic and literary term for extravagant boasting, and comes ultimately from French *gasconner* 'talk like a Gascon, brag'.

-gate combining form used in nouns denoting an actual or alleged scandal, especially one involving a cover-up. The usage derives from the ➤ WATERGATE scandal in the US, 1972.

gate of horn in Greek mythology, the gate through which true dreams pass (as opposed to the ➤ IVORY *gate* for false dreams).

Gatha any of seventeen poems attributed to Zoroaster which are the most ancient texts of the Avesta.

gaudy a celebratory dinner or entertainment held by a college for old members. The term is recorded in the mid 16th century (in the sense 'rejoicing, a celebration') from Latin *gaudium* 'joy', or from *gaude* 'rejoice!'.

gaudy night a ➤ GAUDY; originally as a quotation from Shakespeare's *Antony and Cleopatra* (1606–7), 'Let's have one other gaudy night', and reinforced by the title of Dorothy L. Sayers's detective novel (1935), set in a fictional Oxford women's college.

Gaul an ancient region of Europe, corresponding to modern France, Belgium, the south Netherlands, SW Germany, and northern Italy. The area south of the Alps was conquered in 222 BC by the Romans, who called it **Cisalpine Gaul**. The area north of the Alps, known as **Transalpine Gaul**, was taken by Julius Caesar between 58 and 51 BC; the southern province of Transalpine Gaul became known as **Gallia Narbonensis**.

throw down the gauntlet issue a challenge, from the medieval custom of issuing a challenge by throwing one's *gauntlet*, or armoured glove, to the ground; whoever picked it up (**take up the gauntlet**) was deemed to have accepted the challenge.

Siddhartha Gautama name of the ➤ BUDDHA.

Gawain in Arthurian legend, one of the knights of the Round Table who sought for the Holy Grail. He is Arthur's nephew, and is the hero of the medieval poem *Sir Gawain and the Green Knight*.

gay homosexual; a sense of the word recorded from the 1930s and becoming established in the 1960s as the term preferred by homosexual men to describe themselves. It is now the standard accepted word throughout the English-speaking world.

The term **gay gene** is used for a sequence or sequences of DNA which, when present in the human X-chromosome, may predispose towards homosexuality. Whether such a gene in fact exists is still a matter of debate, as are the moral and ethical questions attendant on research in this area.

Gaza Strip a strip of territory in Palestine, on the SE Mediterranean coast, including the town of Gaza. Administered by Egypt from 1949, and occupied by Israel from 1967, it became a self-governing enclave under the PLO–Israeli accord of 1994 and elected its own legislative council in 1996.

all one's geese are swans one characteristically exaggerates the merits of undistinguished persons or things; the use of *goose* and *swan* to point up such a contrast dates back to the 16th century (in early use, *crow* was also used in place of *goose*).

Gehazi in the Bible, the servant of Elisha who, when his master has healed ➤ NAAMAN of leprosy, surreptitiously follows the Syrian to claim the reward which the prophet has refused; he is punished for his dishonesty by himself becoming a leper.

Gehenna in Judaism and the New Testament, hell. The name comes via ecclesiastical Latin from Greek *geenna*, from Hebrew *gē' hinnōm* 'hell', literally 'valley of Hinnom', a place near Jerusalem where children were sacrificed to Baal, as in Jeremiah 19:6.

Gemara a rabbinical commentary on the Mishnah, forming the second part of the Talmud. The name comes from Aramaic *gĕmārā* 'completion'.

Gem State an informal name for Idaho.

Gemini a northern constellation (the Twins), said to represent the twins Castor and Pollux, the ➤ DIOSCURI, whose names are given to its two brightest stars. Also, in astrological thought, the third sign of the zodiac, which the sun enters about 21 May.
  Gemini was also the name of a series of twelve manned American orbiting spacecraft, launched in the 1960s in preparation for the Apollo programme.
  Gemini comes from Latin, and means 'twins'.

genealogy a line of descent traced continuously from an ancestor. The word is recorded from Middle English and comes via Old French and late Latin from Greek *genealogia*, from *genea* 'race, generation'.

General Strike the strike of May 1926 in the UK, called by the Trades Union Congress in support of the mineworkers.

General Synod the highest governing body of the Church of England, an elected assembly of three houses (bishops, clergy, and laity).

General Thanksgiving a form of thanksgiving in the Book of Common Prayer or the Alternative Service Book.

the generation gap differences of outlook or opinion between people of different generations; the term is recorded from the 1960s.

Generation X the generation born after that of the ➤ BABY *boomers* (roughly from the early 1960s to mid 1970s), typically perceived to be disaffected and directionless. The term was popularized by Douglas Coupland's book *Generation X: tales for an accelerated culture* (1991), although it had been coined much earlier, in the title of a book (1964) by Charles Hamblett and Jane Deverson.

Genesis the first book of the Bible, which includes the stories of the creation of the world, ➤ NOAH's *ark*, the ➤ *Tower of* BABEL, and the patriarchs ➤ ABRAHAM, Isaac, ➤ JACOB, and Joseph.
  The name, recorded from late Old English, comes via Latin from Greek, 'generation, creation, nativity, horoscope', from the base of *gignesthai* 'be born or produced'. The name was given to the first book of the Old Testament in the Greek translation (the Septuagint), hence in the Latin translation (the Vulgate).

genetic engineering the deliberate modification of the characteristics of an organism by manipulating its genetic material. The phrase is recorded from 1969, and in 1980 the US Supreme Court ruled that engineered living organisms were patentable.

genetic fingerprinting the analysis of DNA from samples of body tissues or fluids in order to identify individuals. Patterns can be identified which are believed to be specific to the person or animal from which the sample came.

Geneva a city in Switzerland, noted in the 17th century for its Protestantism.
  Geneva bands are two white cloth strips attached to the collar of some Protestants' clerical dress, as originally worn by Calvinists in Geneva.
  The **Geneva Bible** is an English translation of the Bible published in 1560 by Protestant scholars working in Europe.
  The **Geneva Convention** is an international agreement first made at Geneva in 1864 and later revised, governing the status and treatment of captured and wounded military personnel and civilians in wartime.

St Genevieve (d. *c.*500), French nun, and patroness of Paris, who is said to have helped save the city from Attila and the Huns by fasting and prayer. Her emblem is a candle, sometimes shown with the devil, who is said to have blown it out when she went to pray in the church at night. Her feast day is 3 January.

Genghis Khan (1162–1227), founder of the Mongol empire; born *Temujin*. He took the name Genghis Khan ('ruler of all') in 1206 after uniting the nomadic Mongol tribes, and by the time of his death his empire extended from China to the Black Sea; his grandson Kublai Khan completed the conquest of China. In allusive use his name stands for a figure of savage conquest.

genie a spirit of Arabian folklore, as traditionally depicted imprisoned within a bottle or oil lamp, and capable of granting wishes when summoned; figuratively, an agent of power or change which is or may be released from containment.

To **let the genie out of the bottle** is to let loose or lose control of an unpredictable force, start an uncontrollable chain of events. Sometimes in the form, **you can't put the genie back in the bottle**.

Recorded from the mid 17th century (denoting a guardian or protective spirit), the word comes via French from Latin base of ➤ GENIUS. *Génie* was adopted in the current sense by the 18th-century French translators of *The Arabian Nights' Entertainments*, because of its resemblance in form and sense to Arabic *jinnī* ➤ JINN.

genius loci the presiding god or spirit of a particular place; originally with reference to Virgil *Aeneid* 'He prays to the spirit of the place and to Earth'; later with *genius* taken as referring to the body of associations connected with or inspirations derived from a place, rather than to a tutelary deity.

Alexander Pope in *Epistles to Several Persons* (1731) has a related phrase, 'Consult the genius of the place in all.'

Genizah a room attached to an ancient synagogue in Cairo, where vast quantities of fragments of biblical and other Jewish manuscripts were discovered in 1896–8.

genocide the deliberate killing of a large group of people, especially those of a particular race or nation. The term is recorded from the 1940s, in relation to Nazi rule in occupied Europe.

Gentile a person who is not Jewish. The name is recorded from late Middle English and comes from Latin *gentilis* 'of a family or nation, of the same clan' (used in the Vulgate to refer to non-Jews) from *gens, gent-* 'family, race', from the root of *gignere* 'to beget'.

gentleman's agreement an arrangement or understanding which is based upon the trust of both or all parties, rather than being legally binding.

genuflect lower one's body briefly by bending one knee to the ground, typically in worship or as a sign of respect. The word comes from ecclesiastical Latin *genuflectere*, from Latin *genu* 'knee' + *flectere* 'to bend'.

Geoffrey of Monmouth (*c.*1100–*c.*1154), Welsh chronicler. His *Historia Regum Britanniae* (*c.*1139; first printed in 1508), an account of the kings of Britain, was a major source for English literature but is now thought to contain little historical fact.

geomancy divination from the configuration of a handful of earth or random dots.

The term is also used for the art of placing or arranging buildings or other sites auspiciously.

geometry the branch of mathematics concerned with the properties and relations of points, lines, surfaces, solids, and higher dimensional analogues; in the Middle Ages, one of the subjects of the ➤ QUADRIVIUM.

George male forename; St George is patron saint of England. He is reputed in legend to have slain a dragon, and may have been martyred near Lydda in Palestine some time before the reign of Constantine. His cult did not become popular until the 6th century, and he probably became patron saint of England in the 14th century. He is taken as one of the ➤ FOURTEEN *Holy Helpers*. His feast day is 23 April.

The George, a jewel bearing the image of the saint, forms part of the insignia of the ➤ *Order of the* GARTER. **St George's cross** is a red vertical cross on a white background.

In the UK and Commonwealth countries, the **George Cross** is a decoration for bravery awarded especially to civilians, instituted in 1940 by King George VI and taking precedence over all other medals and decorations except the Victoria Cross. **George Cross Island** is a name for Malta, which was awarded the George Cross in recognition of the bravery of its inhabitants in the Second World War.

In the UK and Commonwealth countries, the **George Medal** is a medal for bravery awarded especially to civilians, instituted with the George Cross in 1940.

Gerald of Wales English name for ➤ GIRALDUS *Cambrensis*.

John Gerard (1545–1612), English herbalist. Gerard was qualified as a barber-surgeon in London and soon developed an interest in plants, particularly those with medicinal properties. He was curator of the physic garden of the College of Surgeons and published his *Herball*, containing over 1,800 woodcuts, in 1597. It became the best-known English herbal.

St Germanus of Auxerre (d. 446), bishop of Auxerre; he was leader of the British force which won the ➤ HALLELUJAH *Victory* over the Picts and Saxons, and his shrine became a famous pilgrimage centre.

Germinal the seventh month of the French Republican calendar (1793–1805), originally running from 21 March to 19 April. The name is French, from Latin *germen*, *germin-* 'sprout, seed'.

Geronimo (*c.*1829–1909), Apache chief. He led his people in resistance to white encroachment on tribal reservations in Arizona before surrendering in 1886.

His name is used as an exclamation to express exhilaration, especially when leaping from a great height or moving at speed. The expression dates from the Second World War, and was adopted as a slogan by American paratroopers.

gerrymander manipulate the boundaries (of an electoral constituency) so as to favour one party or class. Recorded from the early 19th century, and deriving from the name of Governor Elbridge *Gerry* of Massachusetts + *salamander*, from the supposed similarity between a salamander and the shape of a new voting district on a map drawn when he was in office (1812), the creation of which was felt to favour his party: the map (with claws, wings, and fangs added), was published in the Boston *Weekly Messenger*, with the title *The Gerry-Mander*.

St Gertrude of Nivelles (626–59), daughter of Pepin of Landen, abbess of Nivelles. She is represented in art with mice as her emblem, and has been invoked against pests of rats and mice, by travellers and pilgrims, and as a patroness of the recently dead, on the popular belief that the journey to the next world took three days, the first night of which was spent under the care of Gertrude. Fine weather on her feast-day was regarded as a signal for beginning garden work. Her feast day is 17 March.

Geryon in Greek mythology, a three-headed or three-bodied giant, living on an island in the far west; he owned a great herd of fine cattle, and it was one of the ➤ *Labours of* HERCULES to steal them and drive them back to Greece.

Gessler the tyrannical Austrian governor in the story of the legendary Swiss hero ➤ *William* TELL.

gestalt in psychology, an organized whole that is perceived as more than the sum of its parts; the word is German (recorded in English from the 1920s), and means literally 'form, shape'.

Gestalt psychology is a movement in psychology founded in Germany in 1912, seeking to explain perceptions in terms of gestalts rather than by analysing their constituents.

Gestalt psychotherapy is a psychotherapeutic approach developed by Fritz Perls (1893–1970). It focuses on insight into gestalts in patients and their relations to the world, and often uses role playing to aid the resolution of past conflicts.

Gestapo the German secret police under Nazi rule. It ruthlessly suppressed opposition to the Nazis in Germany and occupied Europe and sent Jews and others to concentration camps. From 1936 it was headed by Heinrich Himmler. The name is German, from *Geheime Staatspolizei* 'secret state police'.

Gestas traditionally the name of the impenitent thief, who with the penitent ➤ DISMAS was crucified with Jesus.

don't get mad, get even used to advise in favour of revenge rather than fruitless rage. A saying popularized by the US President John F. Kennedy.

Garden of Gethsemane a garden between Jerusalem and the Mount of Olives, where Jesus went with his disciples after the Last Supper, and where he was betrayed; in allusion, a place of suffering and endurance. (See also ➤ *the* AGONY *in the Garden*.)

Battle of Gettysburg a decisive battle of the American Civil War, fought near the town of Gettysburg in Pennsylvania in July 1863. A Union army under General Meade repulsed the Confederate army of General Lee and forced him to abandon his invasion of the north.

The **Gettysburg address** was a speech delivered on 19 November 1863 by President Abraham Lincoln at the dedication of the national cemetery on the site of the Battle of Gettysburg, opening with the words, 'Fourscore and seven years ago our fathers brought forth upon this continent a new nation, conceived in liberty, and dedicated to the proposition that all men are created equal.'

ghat a level place on the edge of a river where Hindus cremate their dead. Also called **burning-ghat**.

Ghaznavid a member of a Turkish Muslim dynasty founded in Ghazna, Afghanistan, in AD 977. The dynasty extended its power into Persia and the Punjab, but in the 11th century fragmented under pressure from the Seljuk Turks, and was finally destroyed in 1186.

Ghent a city in Belgium, capital of the medieval principality of Flanders, which was formerly known in English as Gaunt (surviving in names, e.g. ➤ JOHN *of Gaunt*).

ghetto a part of a city, especially a slum area, occupied by a minority group or groups; originally, the Jewish quarter in a city. Recorded from the early 17th century, the word may come from Italian *getto* 'foundry' (because the first ghetto was established in 1516 on the site of a foundry in Venice), or from Italian *borghetto*, diminutive of *borgo* 'borough'.

Ghibelline a member of one of the two great political factions in Italian medieval politics, traditionally supporting the Holy Roman emperor against the Pope and his supporters, the Guelphs, during the long struggle between the papacy and the Empire. The name may come ultimately from German *Waiblingen*, an estate belonging to Hohenstaufen emperors.

ghost an apparition of a dead person which is believed to appear or become manifest to the living, typically as a nebulous image and attempting to right a wrong done in life; this sense of the word is recorded from late Middle English.

The word is recorded from Old English (in form *gāst*) in the sense 'spirit, soul', and is of Germanic origin; the *gh-* spelling occurs first in Caxton, and was probably influenced by Flemish *gheest*.

The **Ghost Dance** was an American Indian religious cult of the second half of the 19th century, based on the performance of a ritual dance, lasting sometimes for several days, which, it was believed, would drive away white people, bring the dead back to life, and restore the traditional lands and way of life. Advocated by the Sioux chief Sitting Bull, the cult was central to the uprising that was crushed at the Battle of Wounded Knee.

The **ghost in the machine** is the mind viewed as distinct from the body, a term coined in 1949 by the philosopher Gilbert Ryle for a viewpoint which he regarded as completely misleading.

A **ghost town** is a deserted town with few or no remaining inhabitants; typically one which was previously at the centre of a gold-mining site where the vein is now exhausted.

The ghost walks means that money is available and salaries will paid. The phrase has been has been explained by the story that an actor playing the ghost of Hamlet's father refused to 'walk again' until the cast's overdue salaries had been paid.

A **ghost word** is a word recorded in a dictionary or other reference work which is not actually used. The term is first recorded in a paper entitled 'Report upon "Ghost-words"' by the philologist W. W. Skeat (1835–1912), in which he warned against such inclusions.

ghoul an evil spirit or phantom, especially one supposed to rob graves and feed on dead bodies. Recorded from the late 18th century, the word comes from Arabic *gūl*, a desert demon believed to rob graves and devour corpses.

GI a private soldier in the US army, originally (denoting equipment supplied to US forces) an abbreviation of *government issue* (or *general issue*).

giant an imaginary or mythical being of human form but superhuman size, often seen as at war with the gods; in Greek mythology, it was the giants who rebelled unsuccessfully against ➤ ZEUS and the gods of Olympus, and in Scandinavian mythology, the frost giants were the particular enemies of ➤ THOR.

In astronomy, *giant* is the name for a star of relatively great size and luminosity compared to ordinary stars of the main sequence, and 10–100 times the diameter of the sun.

In Bunyan's *Pilgrim's Progress*, **Giant Despair** imprisons Christian and Hopeful in ➤ DOUBTING *Castle*.

In architecture, a **giant order** is an order whose columns extend through more than one storey.

The **Giant's Causeway** is a geological formation of basalt columns, dating from the Tertiary period, on the north coast of Northern Ireland. It was once believed to be the end of a road made by a legendary giant to Staffa in the Inner Hebrides, where there is a similar formation.

giaour archaic and derogatory term for a non-Muslim, especially a Christian.

Rock of Gibraltar a rocky headland at the eastern end of the Strait of Gibraltar, captured by the British during the War of the Spanish Succession in 1704 and formally ceded by the Peace of Utrecht (1713–14); traditionally one of the ➤ PILLARS *of Hercules*.

Gibson Desert a desert region in Western Australia, to the south-east of the Great Sandy Desert. The first European to cross it (1876) was Ernest Giles, who named it after his companion Alfred *Gibson*, who went missing on an earlier expedition.

Gibson girl a girl typifying the fashionable ideal of the late 19th and early 20th centuries, as represented in the work of Charles D. *Gibson* (1867–1944), American artist and illustrator.

Gideon in the Bible, an Old Testament warrior and judge of Israel, under whose leadership (Judges ch. 6–8) the Midianites were conquered.

look a gift horse in the mouth find fault with what has been given or be ungrateful for an opportunity. The Latin version of the proverb *don't look a gift horse in the mouth* was known to St Jerome in the early 5th century AD. The 16th-century English form was *do not look a given horse in the mouth*.

Gigantomachy in Greek mythology, the struggle between the gods and the giants, ending with the defeat of the giants.

Gigantopithecus a very large fossil Asian ape of the Upper Miocene to Lower Pleistocene.

Gilbertine a member of the English religious order for men and women founded by St *Gilbert* of Sempringham (*c*.1083–1189).

gild the lily embellish excessively, add ornament where none is needed, from an alteration of a quotation from Shakespeare's *King John*, 'To gild refinèd gold, to paint the lily'. The conflated expression *gild the lily* is recorded from the early 20th century.

gild the pill make something unpleasant seem more acceptable (pills were traditionally coated with gilt to make them more attractive).

Gildas British historian of the 6th century whose Latin work, *De Excidio et Conquestu Britanniae*, refers to the British victory over the Saxons at the ➤ Battle of BADON Hill (although he does not mention Arthur).

St Giles (d. *c*.710), hermit, living in Provence, whose shrine became an important pilgrimage centre in the Middle Ages. According to his legend, a hind that was being hunted took refuge with him; Giles was wounded and lamed by the arrow shot at it.

Many churches, including St Giles at Cripplegate in London, were dedicated to him, and there were two annual medieval fairs, at Winchester and Oxford, of which St Giles' Fair Oxford survives as a funfair, set up for two days each year in the wide street of St Giles' in the city centre.

In Germany, he was regarded as one of the ➤ FOURTEEN *Holy Helpers*. His feast day is 1 September.

Gilgamesh a legendary king of the Sumerian city state of Uruk who is supposed to have ruled sometime during the first half of the 3rd millennium BC. He is the hero of the Babylonian epic of Gilgamesh, one of the best-known works of ancient literature, which recounts his exploits in an ultimately unsuccessful quest for immortality. It contains an account of a flood that has close parallels with the biblical story of Noah.

gilt-edged relating to or denoting stocks or securities ('paper') that are regarded as extremely reliable investments; *gilt-edged* was originally used literally of writing-paper or the pages of books.

take the gilt off the gingerbread strip something of its attractions; *gingerbread*, cake made with treacle or syrup and flavoured with ginger, was traditionally made in decorative forms which were then gilded.

ginger group a highly active faction within a party or movement that presses for stronger action on a particular issue. An old horse-coper's trick (recorded from the late 18th century) to make a broken-down animal look lively was to insert ginger into its anus. Hence the metaphorical phrase to **ginger up**, meaning 'to put spirit or mettle into', which is what a *ginger group* does.

Ginnunagap in Scandinavian mythology, the abyss between Niflheim and Muspelheim.

Gioconda smile an enigmatic smile, reminiscent of *La Gioconda*, a portrait (also known as *Mona Lisa*) by Leonardo da Vinci (1452–1519) of the wife of Francesco del *Giocondo*, noted for the sitter's enigmatic smile.

Giotto (*c*.1267–1337), Italian painter. He rejected the flat, formulaic, and static images of Italo-Byzantine art in favour of a more naturalistic style showing human expression. Notable works include the frescoes in the

Arena Chapel, Padua (1305–8) and the church of Santa Croce in Florence (c.1320).

Giotto's O is the perfect circle supposedly drawn freehand by Giotto.

Giraldus Cambrensis (c.1146–1220), Welsh cleric and chronicler; he is the author of *Topographia Hibernica*, which covers the natural history, marvels, and early events of Ireland, and the *Iterarium Cambriae* on the topography of Wales. He is also known as **Gerald of Wales**.

gird up one's loins prepare and strengthen oneself for what is to come; originally with biblical allusion, as in 2 Kings 4:29.

girl Friday a female helper, especially a junior office worker or a personal assistant to a business executive; recorded from 1940, as an alteration of ➤ MAN *Friday*.

Girondist a member of the French moderate republican Party in power during the Revolution 1791–3, so called because the party leaders were the deputies from the department of the *Gironde* in SW France.

Giza a city south-west of Cairo in northern Egypt, on the west bank of the Nile, site of the Pyramids and the Sphinx.

gladiator in ancient Rome, a man trained to fight with weapons against other men or wild animals in an arena; usually a slave or prisoner trained for the purpose. The word is Latin, and comes from *gladius* 'sword'; it was used by Cicero as a term of abuse in his denunciation of Catiline.

Glagolitic denoting or relating to an alphabet based on Greek minuscules, formerly used in writing some Slavic languages. The alphabet is of uncertain origin, and was introduced in the 9th century, at about the same time as the Cyrillic alphabet, which has superseded it except in some Orthodox Church liturgies.

glasnost in the former Soviet Union, the policy or practice of more open consultative government and wider dissemination of information, initiated by leader Mikhail Gorbachev from 1985.

The word comes from Russian *glasnost'*, literally 'the fact of being public'.

glass ceiling an unacknowledged barrier to advancement in a profession, especially affecting women and members of minorities. The term was originally (in the early 1980s) coined to denote an invisible but impenetrable barrier enshrining prejudices which were not openly admitted, but as the concept became more familiar, the figurative associations were developed: a *glass ceiling* was taken as something that could be broken.

Glastonbury a town in Somerset which is the legendary burial place of King Arthur and Queen Guinevere, and the site of a ruined abbey held by legend to have been founded by ➤ JOSEPH *of Arimathea*. It was identified in medieval times with the mythical ➤ AVALON.

The **Glastonbury thorn** is a winter-flowering form of hawthorn, said to have sprung up at Glastonbury from the staff of ➤ JOSEPH *of Arimathea*; it is traditionally said to flower on Christmas Day according to the Old Style calendar.

Gleipnir in Scandinavian mythology, name of the magic shackle with which ➤ FENRIR was bound by the gods; it was forged by the dwarfs from the sound of a cat's footfall, the beard of a woman, the roots of a mountain, the sinews of a bear, the breath of a fish, and the spittle of a bird.

Massacre of Glencoe a massacre in 1692 of members of the Jacobite MacDonald clan by Campbell soldiers, which took place near Glencoe in the Scottish Highlands.

The MacDonald clan failed to swear allegiance to William III, making them liable to military punishment. Soldiers from the Campbell clan, who had been billeted on the MacDonalds for twelve days, murdered the MacDonald chief and about thirty of his followers, while the rest of the clan escaped. The chief of the Campbell clan, which had a long-standing feud with the MacDonalds, was held responsible, although the massacre was almost certainly instigated by the government.

Glendalough in Wicklow, the remains, consisting of a round tower, a ruined cathedral, and several stone churches, of an important early monastic settlement, founded by ➤ St KEVIN in the 7th century.

Owen Glendower (c.1354–c.1417), Welsh chief. He proclaimed himself Prince of Wales and led a national uprising against Henry IV, allying himself with Henry's English opponents, including Henry Percy. He continued fighting against the English until his death.

glimpses of the moon the earth by night, sublunary scenes (originally with reference to the scene in Shakespeare's *Hamlet* in which Hamlet refers to his father's ghost's revisiting 'the glimpses of the moon'.

glittering generalities platitudes, clichés, superficially convincing but empty phrases; the phrase is first recorded in a letter from the American lawyer Rufus Choate (1799–1859).

global warming the gradual increase in the overall temperature of the earth's atmosphere due to the greenhouse effect caused by increased levels of carbon dioxide, CFCs, and other pollutants.

globe a globe is the emblem of ➤ St LOUIS.
A **globe of fire** is the emblem of ➤ St MARTIN *of Tours*.
The **Globe Theatre is** a theatre in Southwark, London, erected in 1599, where many of Shakespeare's plays were first publicly performed by Richard Burbage and his company. Shakespeare had a share in the theatre and also acted there; it has been suggested that the reference in Prospero's speech in *The Tempest* to 'the great globe itself' may contain a punning allusion to the theatre.
The theatre caught fire in 1613 from a discharge of stage gunfire during a play, and was destroyed, although it was rebuilt in 1614 and used until all London theatres were closed on the outbreak of the Civil War in 1642. Its site was rediscovered in 1989 and a reconstruction of the original theatre was opened in 1997.

Gloria a Christian liturgical hymn or formula beginning (in the Latin text) with *Gloria* 'Glory'.
Gloria in excelsis is the hymn beginning *Gloria in excelsis Deo* ('Glory to God in the highest'), forming a set part of the Mass.
Gloria Patri is the doxology beginning *Gloria Patris* ('Glory be to the Father'), used after psalms and in formal prayer, such as the rosary.

Gloriana a name for Queen Elizabeth I, which is used for the character representing her in Spenser's *Faerie Queene*. Benjamin Britten's opera composed for the coronation of Elizabeth II (1952), was entitled *Gloriana*.

the Glorious Revolution the events (1688–9) that led to the replacement, in 1689, of James II by his daughter Mary II and her husband William of Orange (who became William III) as joint monarchs. The bloodless 'revolution' greatly enhanced the constitutional powers of Parliament, with William and Mary's acceptance of the conditions laid down in the Bill of Rights.
The term is first recorded in a sermon preached on 5 November 1716, which coupled the discovery of the ➤ GUNPOWDER *Plot* with the *Glorious Revolution* as examples of divine intervention.

the Glorious Twelfth 12 August, on which the grouse-shooting season opens; the term is recorded from the late 19th century.

glossolalia the phenomenon of (apparently) speaking in an unknown language, especially in religious worship. It is practised especially by Pentecostal and charismatic Christians.

glove traditionally as a token of a pledge, or a challenge to battle, as in **throw down the glove**, **take up the glove** (a *glove* here is a gauntlet).
A *glove* as a type of something that fits or suits perfectly is recorded from the late 18th century.
The expressions **handle without gloves** and **take the gloves off**, recorded from the early 19th century and meaning, treat without mercy or forbearance, refer to boxing-gloves, and the notion of bare-knuckle fighting as being particularly vicious.

a glutton for punishment a person who is always eager to undertake hard or unpleasant tasks. *Glutton of—* was used figuratively from the early 18th century for someone who is inordinately fond of the thing specified, especially translating the Latin phrase *helluo librorum* 'a glutton of books'. The current usage may originate with early 19th-century sporting slang.

Glyndebourne Festival an annual festival of opera, held at the estate of Glyndebourne near Lewes, EAST SUSSEX. The original opera house was built by the owner of the estate, John Christie (1882–1962), who founded the festival in 1934. A new opera house was opened in 1994.

gnash one's teeth feel or express anger or fury. Often in association with *weeping* or *wailing*, as used in the Bible *passim* to express a mixture of remorse and rage (e.g. in Matthew 8:12).

gnome a legendary dwarfish creature supposed to guard the earth's treasures underground; now popularly represented in a small garden ornament in the form of a bearded man with a pointed hat.

The word is recorded from the mid 17th century, and comes via French from modern Latin *gnomus*, a word used by Paracelsus as a synonym of *Pygmaeus*, denoting a mythical race of very small people said to inhabit parts of Ethiopia and India.

The **gnomes of Zurich** is an informal term for Swiss financiers, regarded as having a sinister influence; the phrase was popularized by the British Labour statesman Harold Wilson (1916–95).

gnomic expressed in or of the nature of short, pithy maxims or aphorisms. Recorded from the early 19th century (**gnomical** in the same sense dates from the early 16th century), the word comes from Greek *gnōmikos*, ultimately formed as English *gnome* (late 16th century), 'thought, judgement, opinion', from Greek *gnōme* in same sense, from *gnōmai* 'sayings, maxims', from the base of *gignōskein* 'know'.

gnosis knowledge of spiritual mysteries. Recorded from the late 16th century, the word comes from Greek *gnōsis* 'knowledge', related to *gignōskein* 'know'.

Gnosticism a prominent heretical movement of the 2nd-century Christian Church, partly of pre-Christian origin. Gnostic doctrine taught that the world was created and ruled by a lesser divinity, the demiurge, and that Christ was an emissary of the remote supreme divine being, esoteric knowledge (*gnosis*) of whom enabled the redemption of the human spirit.

go see also ➤ *go to the* COUNTRY.

go the extra mile make an extra effort, do more than is strictly asked or required. In a revue song (1957) by Joyce Grenfell, but perhaps ultimately in allusion to Matthew 5:41 'And whosoever shall compel thee to go a mile, go with him twain.'

goal see ➤ *score an* OWN *goal*.

goalposts see ➤ MOVE *the goalposts*.

goat the *goat* is taken as the symbol of a (damned) sinner (often with biblical allusion to Matthew 25:32–3, as in ➤ SEPARATE *the sheep from the goats*); it is also traditionally a type of lustfulness and folly.

The **Goat** is a name for the zodiacal sign Capricorn or the constellation Capricornus.

The word is recorded from Old English (in form *gāt*, meaning 'female goat'), and is of Germanic origin, ultimately related to Latin *haedus* 'kid'.

Gobi Desert a barren plateau of southern Mongolia and northern China; in allusive use, a type of remote emptiness and desolation.

goblin a mischievous, ugly, dwarf-like creature of folklore. The word is Middle English and from Old French *gobelin*, possibly related to German (see ➤ KOBOLD) or Greek *kobalos* 'mischievous goblin'. In medieval Latin *Gobelinus* occurs as the name of a mischievous spirit, said to haunt Évreux in northern France in the 12th century.

God in Christianity and other monotheistic religions, the creator and ruler of the universe and source of all moral authority, the supreme being. In certain other religions (with lower-case initial), a superhuman being or spirit worshipped as having power over nature or human fortunes; a deity.

An **act of God** is an instance of uncontrollable natural forces in operation (often used in insurance claims, as being exempted from cover given).

The expression **God of the gaps** denotes God as an explanation for phenomena not yet explained by science; God thought of as acting only in those spheres not otherwise accounted for. The phrase itself is recorded from the mid 20th century, deriving from earlier (critical) accounts of this mode of thought.

God save the Queen (or King) is the British national anthem. Evidence suggests a 17th-century origin for the complete words and tune of the anthem. The ultimate origin is obscure: the phrase 'God save the King' occurs in various passages in the Old Testament, while as early as 1545 it was a watchword in the navy, with 'long to reign over us' as a countersign.

godfather in literal use, a male godparent, who presents a child at baptism, responding on their behalf and promising to take responsibility for their religious education; the term is recorded from Old English, and in late Middle English was extended to a male sponsor at the consecration of a church bell.

From the 1960s, the word has also denoted a person directing an illegal organization, especially a leader of the American mafia; the usage derives from the film *The Godfather* (1972) by Francis Ford Coppola, based on the novel (1969) by Mario Puzo, and centring on *Don Corleone*, the sinister head of a Mafia 'family'.

Godfrey of Bouillon (d. 1100), duke of lower Lorraine and leader of the First Crusade in which Jerusalem was captured; he is often taken as the type of a Christian knight and war-leader, and is traditionally one of the ▶ NINE *Worthies*.

Lady Godiva (d. 1080), English noblewoman, wife of Leofric, Earl of Mercia. According to a 13th-century legend, she agreed to her husband's proposition that he would reduce unpopular taxes only if she rode naked on horseback through the marketplace of Coventry. In later versions of the story, all the townspeople refrained from watching, except for *Peeping Tom*, who was struck blind in punishment.

the Godolphin Barb with the ▶ BYERLEY *Turk* and the ▶ DARLEY *Arabian*, one of the three founding sires of the Thoroughbred, imported to improve the stock in the 18th century.

Godzilla a Jurassic dinosaur which has survived by living in the depths of the ocean, and which has been disturbed and mutated by atom bomb tests into a dragonlike monster capable of devastating Tokyo. *Godzilla* (originally called *Gojira*) appeared in 1955, in the first of a series of Japanese films.

what goes around comes around the consequences of one's actions will have to be dealt with eventually. A late 20th-century saying of US origin.

Gog and Magog in the Bible, the names of enemies of God's people. In Ezekiel 38–9, Gog is apparently a ruler from the land of Magog, while in Revelations 20:8, **Gog and Magog** are nations under the dominion of Satan.

In medieval legend, **Gog and Magog** are opponents of Alexander the Great, living north of the Caucasus.

The names are also used for two giant statues standing in Guildhall, London, from the time of Henry V (destroyed in 1666 and 1940; replaced in 1708 and 1953), representing either the last two survivors of a race of giants supposed to have inhabited Britain before Roman times, or *Gogmagog*, chief of the giants, and Corineus, an ally of the legendary Trojan hero ▶ BRUTUS.

Goidelic of, relating to, or denoting the northern group of Celtic languages, including Irish, Scottish Gaelic, and Manx. Speakers of the Celtic precursor of the Goidelic languages are thought to have invaded Ireland from Europe *c.*1000 BC, spreading into Scotland and the Isle of Man from the 5th century AD onwards.

Golconda a source of wealth, advantages, or happiness; from the name of a city near Hyderabad, India, famous for its diamonds.

gold a yellow precious metal, the chemical element of atomic number 79, valued especially for use in jewellery and decoration, and to guarantee the value of currencies; taken as a type of something that is precious, beautiful, or brilliant.

The bullseye of an archery target is known as the *gold*.

The word is recorded from Old English, and is of Germanic origin, from an Indo-European root shared by *yellow*.

A **crock of gold** is a large but distant or imaginary reward, with allusion to the story of a *crock of gold* supposedly to be found by anyone reaching the end of a rainbow.

Chiefly in the US, a **gold brick** is a thing that looks valuable, but is in fact worthless; from the confidence trickster's practice of preparing a block of base metal with a corner of gold to look like a brick-shaped piece of gold.

The **Gold Coast** is a former name (until 1957) for Ghana, so called because it was an important source of gold.

The **Gold Collar** is a classic greyhound race, inaugurated in 1933, run annually in September at the Catford track in south London, originally in May, now in September.

A **gold disc** is a framed golden disc awarded to a recording artist or group for sales of a recording exceeding a specified high figure. The figure varies from year to year and between countries; typical recent figures are, for a single, 500,000 in the UK or one million in the US, and for an album, 250,000 in the UK or 500,000 in the US.

The **gold standard** was the system by which the value of a currency was defined in terms of gold, for which the currency could be exchanged. The gold standard was generally abandoned in the Depression of the 1930s.

In the UK, **Gold Stick** is a ceremonial officer in the Sovereign's household, entitled to carry a gilt rod on state occasions. The office is now held by the colonels of the senior household regiments in England and Scotland.

golden often used figuratively to convey an idea of supremely special quality.

A **golden age** is an idyllic, often imaginary past time of peace, prosperity, and happiness; originally, the Greek and Roman poets' name for the first period of history, when the human race lived in an ideal state, and which was succeeded by the silver, brazen, and iron ages.

In Greek mythology, a *golden apple* may be a fruit from the apples of the ➤ HESPERIDES, the ➤ APPLE *of discord*, or one of the apples thrown down to distract ➤ ATALANTA.

The Golden Ass is a prose narrative (*Metamorphoses*) of the 2nd century by ➤ APULEIUS, a picaresque novel which recounts the adventures of a man who is transformed into an ass, and which depicts in particular the practices of ancient religious mysteries.

Three golden balls were the traditional sign of a pawnbroker, sometimes said to be derived from the coat of arms of the Medici family, or from the three bags of gold given to three girls for dowries by ➤ St NICHOLAS *of Myra*.

The Golden Bough is the title of a book (1890–1915) by the Scottish anthropologist James George Frazer, proposing an evolutionary theory of the development of human thought, from the magical and religious to the scientific, and focusing particularly on the figure of the sacrificial king who dies and is reborn. The title came from Virgil's *Aeneid*, 'the double tree that bears the golden bough' in Dryden's translation (1697); Aeneas is told by the Sibyl that he must find and pick the branch before he can safely journey to the underworld.

The golden bowl is broken is a biblical metaphor for death, deriving from Ecclesiastes, 'Or ever the silver cord be loosed, or the golden bowl be broken, or the pitcher be broken at the fountain, or the wheel broken at the cistern.'

In the Bible, the **golden calf** is an image of gold in the shape of a calf, made by Aaron in response to the Israelites' plea for a god while they awaited Moses' return from Mount Sinai, where he was receiving the ➤ TEN *Commandments* (Exodus 32), and which Moses destroyed; in extended usage, a false god, especially wealth as an object of worship.

In Greek mythology, the **Golden Fleece** is the fleece of the golden-fleeced ram which rescued Helle and her brother (see ➤ HELLESPONT), which was guarded by an unsleeping dragon, and sought and won by ➤ JASON with the help of ➤ MEDEA. The **Order of the Golden Fleece** was an order of knighthood instituted at Bruges in 1430 by Philip the Good, duke of Burgundy. The right of investiture in the order of the Golden Fleece belonged (after 1700) to the sovereigns of Austria and Spain.

The **Golden Gate** is a deep channel connecting San Francisco Bay with the Pacific Ocean, spanned by the Golden Gate suspension bridge (completed 1937).

In some soccer and hockey competitions, a **golden goal** is the first goal scored during extra time which ends the match and gives victory to the scoring side.

In a traditional fairytale, the **golden goose** was a goose which laid golden eggs; it was killed in an attempt to possess the source of this wealth, which as a result was lost. The phrase is now used for a continuing source of wealth or profit that may be exhausted if it is misused.

A **golden handshake** is a substantial payment given to someone who is made redundant or retires early.

The **Golden Horde** was the Tartar and Mongol army, led by descendants of ➤ GENGHIS *Khan*, that overran Asia and parts of eastern Europe in the 13th century and maintained an empire until around 1500 (so called from the richness of the leader's camp).

The **Golden Horn** is a curved inlet of the Bosporus forming the harbour of Istanbul.

In medical usage, the **golden hour** is the first hour after the occurrence of a traumatic injury, considered the most critical for successful emergency treatment.

A **golden jubilee** is the fiftieth anniversary of a significant event, in particular, a sovereign's accession.

The **Golden Legend** is a medieval collection of saints' lives and similar stories, written in the 13th century by Jacobus de Voragine (1230–98), Archbishop of Genoa; an English version was published by Caxton in 1483. The title is a translation of Latin *Legenda Aurea*.

The **golden mean** is the ideal moderate position between two extremes; originally as a translation of Latin *aurea mediocritas*, from Horace's *Odes*.

The **golden number** is the number showing a year's place in the ➤ METONIC *cycle* and used to fix the date of Easter for that year; the *golden number* for any year AD is found by adding 1 to the number of the year and dividing the result by 19; the remainder is the golden number for that year (if there is no remainder, the golden number is 19). The term is a translation of medieval Latin *aureus* *numerus*, so called from its importance in calculating the date of Easter, and not as sometimes suggested because it appeared in calendars in letters of gold.

A **golden rose** is an ornament of wrought gold, blessed by the pope on the fourth Sunday in Lent, and usually sent as a mark of favour to some notable Roman Catholic personage, city, or church. The ornament has been of various forms; the design finally adopted is a thorny branch with several leaves and flowers, surmounted by a principal rose—all of pure gold. The *Golden Rose* is also an award presented at the International Television Festival at Montreux for successful light entertainment programmes.

The **golden rule** is a basic principle which should always be followed to ensure success in general or in a particular activity; the term is sometimes specifically used of the injunction given by Jesus in Matthew 7:12, 'whatsoever ye would that men should do to you, do ye even so to them.'

The **golden section** is the division of a line so that the whole is to the greater part as that part is to the smaller part (i.e. in a ratio of 1 to ½ ($\sqrt{5}$ + 1)), a proportion which is considered to be particularly pleasing to the eye. Although the proportion has been known since the 4th century BC, and occurs in Euclid, the name *golden section* (now the usual term) is not recorded before the 19th century.

The **Golden State** is an informal name for California.

The **Golden Temple** is the Sikh temple at Amritsar in the Punjab, the holiest of the Sikh faith and an important pilgrimage site, which in 1919 was the scene of a riot in which 400 people were killed by British troops. In 1984 the building was occupied by a group of Sikh extremists, and sustained some damage when they were forcibly removed by Indian troops.

A **golden wedding** is the fiftieth anniversary of a wedding.

See also ➤ *kill the goose that lays the golden* EGGS.

Goldilocks heroine of the children's story *The Three Bears*, in which she eats and sleeps in their house without leave, and chooses the possessions of the smallest bear as being neither too large nor too small for her, but 'just right'; the essential story goes back to 1837, but the version in which *Goldilocks* is first named as the intruder is in John Hassall's *Old Nursery Stories and Rhymes* (*c*.1904).

Goldilocks is now used allusively to designate something regarded as falling in the centre of a range of possible values or conditions, rather than leaning to one extreme or the other.

golem in Jewish legend, a clay figure brought to life by magic; an automaton or robot. The word is recorded from the late 19th century, and comes via Yiddish from Hebrew *gōlem* 'shapeless mass'.

Golgotha the site of the crucifixion of Jesus; Calvary. The name comes from late Latin, via Greek from an Aramaic form of Hebrew *gulgoleth* 'skull'; as in Matthew 27:33.

Goliath in the Bible, a Philistine giant and warrior, according to legend killed by David (1 Samuel 17) armed only with a sling and 'five smooth stones'; the contest between the young David and Goliath is often taken as a type of apparently unequal combat.

According to another tradition, the giant killed by David was originally unnamed, and Goliath was killed by Elhanan (2 Samuel 21:19).

golliwog a soft doll with bright clothes, a black face, and fuzzy hair. From *Golliwogg*, the name of a doll character in books by Bertha Upton (died 1912), American writer, perhaps a blend of the exclamation *golly* and *pollywog* 'tadpole'.

Gollum in Tolkien's *The Hobbit* and ➤ LORD *of the Rings*, a repulsive but pitiful figure, the former hobbit who, having come into possession of the One Ring (his 'precious') is possessed by it. When he is tricked out of the ring he is reduced to an entity obsessively bent on recovery; in the end he is destroyed with it.

Gomorrah a town in ancient Palestine, probably south of the Dead Sea. According to Genesis 19:24, it was destroyed by fire from heaven, along with ➤ SODOM, for the wickedness of its inhabitants.

Gondwana a vast continental area believed to have existed in the southern hemisphere and to have resulted from the break-up of Pangaea in Mesozoic times. It comprised the present Arabia, Africa, South America, Antarctica, Australia, and the peninsula of India.

The name is recorded from the late 19th century, originally denoting any of a series of rocks in India, especially fluviatile shales and sandstones, from the name of a region in central northern India, from Sanskrit *gondavana* 'forest of Gond'.

gone with the wind from Ernest Dowson 'I have forgot much, Cynara, gone with the wind' (1896); subsequently popularized by the title of Margaret Mitchell's novel (1936) on the American Civil War.

good of particular (especially moral) worth. The question **can any good thing come out of Nazareth?** alludes to the question asked by ➤ NATHANIEL (John 1: 46) on being told of the ministry of Jesus, 'Can there any good thing come out of Nazareth?'

Good Friday is the Friday before Easter Sunday, on which the Crucifixion of Christ is commemorated in the Christian Church. It is traditionally a day of fasting and penance.

The **Good Friday agreement** is an agreement between the British and Irish governments and the main political parties of Northern Ireland, reached at Stormont Castle, Belfast, on Good Friday (10 April) 1998, and passed by public referenda in Northern Ireland and the Irish Republic on 22 May 1998, setting out proposals for the securing of peace in Northern Ireland.

In the US, a **good ol' boy** is a (typically white) male from the Southern States of America, regarded as one of a group conforming to a social and cultural masculine stereotype.

The **Good Shepherd** is a name for Jesus Christ, with allusion to John 10:16 (see also ➤ SHEPHERD).

See also ➤ *the good old* CAUSE, ➤ *good* SA-MARITAN, ➤ *good* WINE *needs no bush*, ➤ *the* GREAT *and the good*, ➤ *you've* NEVER *had it so good*.

goodfella a gangster, especially a member of a Mafia 'family'; the term was popularized by the film *Goodfellas* (1990) by Martin Scorsese, in which a reliable member of the Mafia is seen as a *good fellow* by his associates.

goods and chattels all kinds of personal property; a *chattel* is a movable possession.

Goodwood a racecourse in West Sussex, near Chichester, which is the scene of an annual summer race meeting.

Goody Two-shoes a nursery story dating from the 18th century, in which the orphaned heroine survives adversity, and while setting a constant good example becomes both rich and beloved. The term is used

today for a girl or woman who is regarded as priggishly moral.

googly in cricket, an off break bowled with an apparent leg-break action. The word is recorded from the early 20th century, but the origin is unknown.

Goon any of the members of the cast of a British radio show of the 1950s and 1960s, the **Goon Show**, including Spike Milligan, Harry Secombe, and Peter Sellers, noted for its zany and surrealist humour.

Goon is recorded from the mid 19th century meaning 'a silly, foolish, or eccentric person', perhaps from dialect *gooney* 'booby', influenced by the subhuman cartoon character 'Alice the *Goon*', created by E. C. Segar (1894–1938), American cartoonist. Allied prisoners-of-war in the Second World War referred to their German guards as 'goons'.

goose the *goose* is proverbially contrasted with the *swan* as being the clumsier, less elegant, and less distinguished bird; it is also traditionally taken as a type of stupidity and folly.

A *goose* is the emblem of St Werburga, a Mercian princess and nun (d. *c.*700), who in her legend is said to have brought a goose back to life, ➤ St BRIDGET *of Ireland*, and ➤ *St* MARTIN *of Tours*.

A **goose-girl** is a girl employed to tend geese, in fairy stories the type of the peasant girl who marries a prince.

The **goose-step** is a military marching step in which the legs are not bent at the knee, especially associated with German militarism.

See also ➤ *all one's* GEESE *are swans*, ➤ GOLDEN *goose*, and ➤ *kill the goose that lays the golden* EGGS.

gooseberry as the first fruit of the summer, *gooseberries* were often traditionally eaten at Whitsun or at village feasts and celebrations.

Children were traditionally told that babies were found under gooseberry bushes.

In British informal use, someone who *plays gooseberry* is a third person who stays in the company of two people, especially lovers, who would prefer to be alone; the usage comes from *gooseberry-picker*, referring to an activity as a pretext for the lovers to be together.

The word is recorded from the mid 16th century; the first element perhaps from *goose*, or based on Old French *groseille*, altered because of an unexplained association with the bird.

gopher a burrowing rodent of North and Central America. The word may come from Canadian French *gaufre* 'honeycomb', because the gopher 'honeycombs' the ground with its burrows.

Gopher is the name of a menu-based system which allows users of the Internet to search for and retrieve documents on topics of interest. The name comes from the gopher mascot of the University of Minnesota, US, where the system was invented.

The **Gopher State** is an informal name for Minnesota.

gopura in southern India, the great pyramidal tower over the entrance gate to a temple precinct. The name comes from Sanskrit *gopura* 'city gate', from *go* 'cow, cattle' + *pura* 'city, quarter'.

Gorbals a district of Glasgow on the south bank of the River Clyde, formerly noted for its slums and tenement buildings.

Gordium an ancient city of Asia Minor (now NW Turkey), the capital of Phrygia in the 8th and 9th centuries BC. According to legend the city was founded by Gordius, who tied the knot cut by Alexander the Great during his expedition of 334 BC.

The expression **cut the Gordian knot**, used to mean solve or remove a problem in a direct or forceful way, rejecting gentler or more indirect methods, comes from the legend that *Gordius*, king of Gordium, tied an intricate knot and prophesied that whoever untied it would become the ruler of Asia. It was cut through with a sword by Alexander the Great.

Gordon Bennett expressing surprise, incredulity, or exasperation. The word is probably an alteration of gorblimey, after James *Gordon Bennett* (1841–1918), American publisher and sports sponsor.

Gordon Riots a series of anti-Catholic riots in London in June 1780 in which about 300 people were killed. The riots were provoked by a petition presented to Parliament by Lord George *Gordon* (1751–93) against the relaxation of restrictions on the holding of landed property by Roman Catholics.

one's gorge rises one is sickened or disgusted. *Gorge* is an obsolete term from falconry, meaning 'a meal for a hawk'; from this derives the more general sense of the contents of the stomach.

Gorgon in Greek mythology, each of three sisters, Stheno, Euryale, and Medusa, with snakes for hair, who had the power to turn anyone who looked at them to stone. ➤ MEDUSA was killed by Perseus, and the winged horse ➤ PEGASUS is said to have sprung from her blood.

In extended usage, *gorgon* is used for a fierce, frightening, or repulsive woman.

Gorsedd a council of Welsh or other Celtic bards and Druids, especially as meeting daily before the eisteddfod. The word is Welsh, and means 'mound, throne, assembly'.

Goschens a colloquial name for consols after their conversion from 3 to 2¾ per cent by G. J. *Goschen* (Chancellor of the Exchequer) in 1888 (later to 2½).

Goschen had been appointed as Chancellor in 1886 when Lord Randolph Churchill suddenly resigned the office; Churchill afterwards said ruefully, 'All great men make mistakes. Napoleon forgot Blücher, I forgot Goschen.'

Goshen a place of plenty or of light, from the name of the fertile land allotted to the Israelites in Egypt, in which (Exodus 10:23 implies) there was light during the plague of darkness.

Gospel the record of Christ's life and teaching in the first four books of the New Testament; each of these books. The four Gospels ascribed to St Matthew, St Mark, St Luke, and St John all give an account of the ministry, crucifixion, and resurrection of Christ, though the Gospel of John differs greatly from the other three. There are also several apocryphal gospels of later date.

The word comes from Old English *gōdspel* 'good news', translating ecclesiastical Latin *bona annuntiatio* used to gloss *evangelium*, from Greek *euangelion* 'good news'; after the vowel was shortened in Old English, the first syllable was mistaken for *god* 'God'.

In a church, the **Gospel side** is the north side of the altar, at which the Gospel is read, opposite to the ➤ EPISTLE *side*.

Goth a member of a Germanic people that invaded the Roman Empire from the east between the 3rd and 5th centuries. The eastern division, the Ostrogoths, founded a kingdom in Italy, while the Visigoths went on to found one in Spain.

Gotham a village in Nottinghamshire associated with the folk tale *The Wise Men of*

Gotham, in which the inhabitants of the village demonstrated cunning by feigning stupidity.

Gotham is now also a nickname for New York City, used originally by Washington Irving and later associated with the ➤ BATMAN stories.

Gothic of or in the style of architecture prevalent in western Europe in the 12th–16th centuries (and revived in the mid 18th to early 20th centuries), characterized by pointed arches, rib vaults, and flying buttresses, together with large windows and elaborate tracery. English Gothic architecture is divided into Early English, Decorated, and Perpendicular.

The word comes via French or late Latin from *Gothi* 'the Goths', and was used in the 17th and 18th centuries to mean 'not classical' (i.e. not Greek or Roman), and hence to refer to medieval architecture which did not follow classical models and a typeface based on medieval handwriting.

The **gothic novel** is an English genre of fiction popularized in the 18th to early 19th centuries by Mrs Radcliffe and others, characterized by an atmosphere of mystery and horror and having a pseudo-medieval setting; in Jane Austen's *Northanger Abbey* (1818), the heroine Catherine Morland's fondness for such novels leads her to suspect her lover's father of having murdered his wife.

The **Gothic revival** designates the reintroduction of a Gothic style of architecture towards the middle of the 19th century.

Gothic type is a typeface with lettering derived from the angular style of handwriting with broad vertical downstrokes used in western Europe from the 13th century, including Fraktur and black-letter typefaces.

Gothick a pseudo-archaic spelling of ➤ GOTHIC in the sense belonging to or redolent of the Dark Ages; portentously gloomy or horrifying.

Götterdammerung in Germanic mythology, the downfall of the gods. The word comes from German, literally 'twilight', popularized by Wagner's use of the word as the title of the last opera of the Ring cycle.

gourd see ➤ JONAH'S *gourd*.

gown the members of a university as distinct from the permanent residents of a town; usually in ➤ TOWN *and gown*.

the Gracchi Tiberius Sempronius *Gracchus* (*c.*163–133 BC) and his brother Gaius

Sempronius (*c.*153–121 BC), Roman tribunes. They were responsible for radical social and economic legislation, especially concerning the redistribution of land to the poor. This led eventually to their deaths, as the legislation was passed against the wishes of the senatorial class.

grace in Christian belief, the free and unmerited favour of God, as manifested in the salvation of sinners and the bestowal of blessings.

Grace in Christian usage also denotes a short prayer of thanks said before or after a meal.

The word is also used as a form of description or address for a duke, duchess, or archbishop: **Her Grace, the Duchess of Omnium, Your Grace**.

An **act of grace** is a privilege or concession that cannot be claimed as a right.

The phrase **grace and favour** denotes accommodation occupied by permission of a sovereign or government.

A **grace note** is an extra note added as an embellishment and not essential to the harmony or melody.

The expression **by the grace of God** means through God's favour, especially (translating Latin *Dei gratia* appended to the formal statement of a monarch's title, and formerly to that of some ecclesiastical dignitaries.

Gradgrind a person lacking warm feelings and imagination and interested only in facts, seen as resembling Thomas *Gradgrind*, character in Charles Dickens's novel *Hard Times* (1854).

gradual in the Western Christian Church, a response sung or recited between the Epistle and Gospel in the Mass; the name comes (in the mid 16th century) from the earlier *gradual* adjective, from medieval Latin *gradualis*, from Latin *gradus* 'step'. The original sense of the adjective was 'arranged in degrees'; the noun refers to the altar steps in a church, from which the antiphons were sung.

Holy Grail in medieval legend, the cup or platter (also called simply the *Grail*) used by Christ at the Last Supper, and in which Joseph of Arimathea received Christ's blood at the Cross. Quests for it undertaken by medieval knights are described in versions of the Arthurian legends written from the early 13th century onward; it is the immaculately pure ➤ GALAHAD, accompanied by Bors and Perceval, who is destined to find the *Holy Grail*. In figurative usage, the term is used for a thing which is being earnestly pursued or sought after.

The word comes via Old French *graal*, from medieval Latin *gradalis* 'dish'.

Grainne in the legends relating to the Irish hero Finn, the daughter of King Cormac. Finn, though a great warrior and hunter, was unfortunate in love. He sought to marry Grainne, but she fell in love with Finn's nephew Diarmait O'Duibhne and eloped with him. The long story of their flight and Finn's unsuccessful pursuit ends in Finn's temporary acceptance of the situation; but Finn finally caused the death of Diarmait.

grain see ➤ *grain of* MUSTARD *seed*.

gramarye originally (in Middle English), grammar; (from the late 15th century), occult learning; magic, necromancy. The word was revived in literary use by Sir Walter Scott, and comes via Anglo-Norman French from the base of *grammar*.

grammar the whole system and structure of a language or of languages in general, usually taken as consisting of syntax and morphology (including inflections) and sometimes also phonology and semantics; *grammar* was one of the ➤ SEVEN *liberal arts*.

Recorded from late Middle English, the word comes via Old French and Latin from Greek *grammatikē (tekhnē)* '(art) of letters', from *gramma, grammat-* 'letter of the alphabet, thing written'.

Grammy each of a number of annual awards given by the American National Academy of Recording Arts and Sciences for achievement in the record industry.

Granada a city in Andalusia in southern Spain. Founded in the 8th century, it became the capital of the Moorish kingdom of Granada in 1238, and was the last Moorish stronghold to fall in the reconquest of Spain in 1492. It is the site of the Alhambra palace.

grand often used to designate something of major size and importance.

The **Grand Canyon** is a deep gorge in Arizona, formed by the Colorado River, which is about 440 km (277 miles) long, 8 to 24 km (5 to 15 miles) wide, and, in places, 1,800 m (6,000 ft) deep. **Grand Canyon State** is an informal name for Arizona.

The **Grand Fleet** is the main British naval fleet, either that based at Spithead in the 18th century or that based at Scapa Flow in the First World War.

Grand Guignol is a dramatic entertainment of a sensational or horrific nature, originally a sequence of short pieces as performed at the *Grand Guignol* theatre in Paris. From the name of the bloodthirsty puppet ➤ GUIGNOL.

The **Grand National** is an annual horse race established in 1839, a steeplechase run over a course of 4 miles 856 yards (about 7,200 metres) with thirty jumps, at Aintree, Liverpool, in late March or early April.

The **Grand Prix (de Paris)** is an international horse race for three-year-olds, founded in 1863 and run annually in June at Longchamps, Paris.

A **grand slam** is the winning of each of a group of major championships or matches in a particular sport in the same year, in particular in tennis, golf, or rugby union; *grand slam* here is a transferred use from cards, especially bridge, referring to the bidding and winning of all thirteen tricks.

The **grand tour** was a cultural tour of Europe conventionally undertaken, especially in the 18th century, by a young man of the upper classes as a part of his education.

Grande Armée Napoleon's main army, from the campaign of 1805 to that of 1814.

teach one's grandmother to suck eggs presume to advise a more experienced person. Proverbial expression from the saying *don't teach your grandmother to suck eggs*, used since the early 18th century as a caution against any attempt by the ignorant or inexperienced to instruct someone wiser or more knowledgeable.

Granger States an informal name for Wisconsin, Illinois, Minnesota, and Iowa, referring to their capacity for producing grain.

Granite City informal name for Aberdeen.

Granite State informal name for New Hampshire.

Grantha a southern Indian alphabet dating from the 5th century AD, used by Tamil brahmans for the Sanskrit transcriptions of their sacred books.

on the grapevine referring to the circulation of rumours and unofficial information; the term apparently derives a usage in the American Civil War, and is a shortening of 'a dispatch by grapevine telegraph'.

grasp the nettle tackle a difficulty boldly (in allusion to the fact that a nettle stings when touched lightly, but not when grasped firmly); the idea of the *nettle* representing a difficult or perilous situation is found in Shakespeare's 2 Henry IV (1597).

grass taken as a type of something green; the word may also mean the season when the grass grows, spring and early summer.

In literary or poetic use, *grass* is often referred to as growing over and covering graves and battlefields. The image may also cover the idea of grass growing in the streets of a formerly prosperous community returning to the wilderness.

The word is recorded in Old English (in form *græs*) and is of Germanic origin, ultimately related to *green* and *grow*.

The term **grass roots** is used for the most basic level of an activity or organization, a figurative use recorded from the early 20th century, and now particularly applied in politics to the rank-and-file of a political organization.

A **grass widow** is a woman whose husband is away often or for a prolonged period. In the early 16th century, the word denoted an unmarried woman with a child, perhaps from the idea of the couple having lain on the *grass* instead of in bed. The current sense dates from the mid 19th century.

The **grass is always greener** means that other people's lives or situations always seem better than one's own. A shortened form of the saying *the grass is always greener on the other side of the fence*, often used as a caution against dissatisfaction with one's own lot in life. There are a number of similar sayings, for example *blue are the hills that are far away*.

Put out to grass means force to retire, make redundant. Used literally of putting a horse or other animal out to graze. In figurative use since the late 16th century, the earlier form of the expression was with *turn (out)* rather than *put out*.

grasshopper the *grasshopper*, with its chirping sound, is sometimes taken as a type of something frivolous and trivial.

In biblical translations, *grasshopper* is sometimes used for locust, as in Ecclesiastes 12:1, 'the grasshopper shall be a burden, and desire shall fail.'

A *grasshopper* was also the personal emblem of the 16th-century financier Thomas Gresham (see ➤ GRESHAM's *law*); his house in Lombard Street was known as 'the Sign of the Grasshopper', and the badge was later used by Martin's Bank, which originated in Gresham's trading there.

grassy knoll in conspiracy theories of the death of John Fitzgerald Kennedy, it is suggested that the real assassin was an unidentified gunman on a *grassy knoll* overlooking the route of the motorcade in ➤ DALLAS.

graven image an idol, in allusion to the second commandment in Exodus 20:2, 'Thou shalt not make unto thee any graven image.'

graveyard shift a work shift that runs through the early morning hours, typically covering the period between midnight and 8 a.m.; a group of employees working such a shift. The term is originally nautical, and has been explained as referring to the number of disasters that occur during this time.

board the gravy train obtain access to an easy source of financial gain. *Gravy* is slang for 'money easily acquired', and *gravy train* may be an alteration of *gravy boat*, a boat-shaped vessel for serving gravy.

Gray's Inn one of the Inns of Court in London, originating in the late 13th century with those who came to study law under Reginald de Grey of Wilton; his manor house, just outside the City of London, became the first hostel of the society. The precise date at which the Honourable Society of Gray's Inn was founded is not known, but by the 16th century it was well established, with such notable members as William Cecil, Lord Burleigh and Francis Walsingham.

greasy pole a pole covered with an oily substance to make it more difficult to climb or walk along, used especially as a form of entertainment; used to refer to the difficult route to the top of someone's profession.

great often used to indicate status as well as size.

The **great and the good** are people in a given sphere regarded as particularly worthy and admirable; the term is first recorded in the mid 19th century , but is now often used ironically.

In astronomy, the **Great Bear** is the constellation ➤ URSA *Major*, named from the story in Greek mythology that the nymph Callisto was turned into a bear and placed as a constellation in the heavens by Zeus.

The **Great Bible** is the edition of the English Bible which Thomas Cromwell ordered in 1538 to be set up in every parish church. It was the work of Miles Coverdale, and was first issued in 1539.

The **Great Divide** is another name for the ➤ CONTINENTAL *Divide* or Great Dividing Range.

The **Great Exhibition** was the first international exhibition of the products of industry, promoted by Prince Albert and held in the Crystal Palace in London in 1851.

The **great game** is spying; the term in this sense is first recorded in Rudyard Kipling's *Kim* (1901).

A **great gulf fixed** is an unbridgeable difference; originally with biblical allusion to Luke 16:26, in the words of Abraham to ➤ DIVES in the story of the rich man and Lazarus, the beggar.

The **Great Lakes** are a group of five large interconnected lakes in central North America, consisting of Lakes Superior, Michigan, Huron, Erie, and Ontario, and constituting the largest area of fresh water in the world. Lake Michigan is wholly within the US, and the others lie on the Canada–US border. Connected to the Atlantic Ocean by the St Lawrence Seaway, the Great Lakes form an important commercial waterway. The **Great Lake State** is an informal name for Michigan.

The **Great Leap Forward** was an unsuccessful attempt made under Mao Zedong in China 1958–60 to hasten the process of industrialization and improve agricultural production by reorganizing the population into large rural collectives and adopting labour-intensive industrial methods.

The **great majority** is the dead; often in **join the great majority**, die, originally from the poet Edward Young (1683–1765) 'Death joins us to the great majority.' The same idea is found earlier in the writing of the 1st-century AD Roman satirist Petronius, '*Abiit ad plures* [He's gone to join the majority].'

The **Great Mother** is another name for the ➤ MOTHER *Goddess*.

The **Great Plague** is a serious outbreak of bubonic plague in England in 1665–6, in which about one fifth of the population of London died, and which was the last major outbreak in Britain.

The **Great Schism** is the breach between the Eastern and the Western Churches, traditionally dated to 1054 and becoming final in 1472. The excommunications of 1054 were abolished as an ecumenical gesture in 1965. The name is also used for the period 1378–1417, when the Western Church was divided by the creation of antipopes.

The **Great Spirit** is the supreme god in the traditional religion of many North American Indians, a translation of Ojibwa *kitchi manitou*.

The **Great Trek** was the northward migration 1835–7 of large numbers of Boers, discontented with British rule in the Cape, to the areas where they eventually founded the Transvaal Republic and Orange Free State.

The **great unwashed** is a derogatory term for the lower classes, the rabble, recorded from the mid 19th century.

The **Great Wall of China** is a fortified wall in northern China, extending some 2,400 km (1,500 miles) from Kansu province to the Yellow Sea north of Beijing. It was first built *c*.210 BC, as a protection against nomad invaders. The present wall dates from the Ming dynasty. Although principally a defensive wall, it served also as a means of communication: for most of its length it was wide enough to allow five horses to travel abreast.

The **Great War** is another name for the ➤ FIRST *World War*; the term in this sense is recorded from 1914.

The **Great Wen** is an archaic nickname for London, a phrase originally coined by William Cobbett in *Rural Rides* (1821).

The **Great White Way** is a nickname for Broadway in New York City, with reference to the brilliant street illumination.

Great Zimbabwe is a complex of stone ruins in a fertile valley in Zimbabwe, south of Harare, discovered by Europeans in 1868. They are the remains of a city which was the centre of a flourishing civilization in the 14th and 15th centuries. The buildings consist of an acropolis, a stone enclosure, and other scattered remains. The circumstances of its eventual decline and abandonment are unknown.

the Greatest Show on Earth the title under which the American showman Phineas Taylor Barnum (1810–91) billed his circus when it opened in 1871.

Greek of or pertaining to Greece.

To say that something is **all Greek to me** is to say it is completely unintelligible. *Greek* for unintelligible language or gibberish is recorded from from the late 16th century, as in Shakespeare's *Julius Caesar* (1599) when Casca, having said that Cicero spoke Greek, adds, 'for mine own part, it was Greek to me.'

The phrase **at the Greek calends** means never; the *Greek Calends* will never come as the Greeks did not use calends in reckoning time. The term is recorded from the mid 17th century.

A **Greek cross** is a cross of which all four arms are of equal length.

Greek fire was a combustible composition emitted by a flame-throwing weapon, and used to set light to enemy ships, which was first used by the Greeks besieged in Constantinople (673–8). It ignited on contact with water, and was probably based on naphtha and quicklime.

A **Greek gift** is a gift made to conceal an act of treachery; the allusion is to the ▶ TROJAN *Horse*, and to the warning *timeo Danaos et dona ferentes* 'I fear the Greeks even when they bring gifts.'

A **Greek key** is a pattern of interlocking right-angled spirals.

The **Greek Orthodox Church** is the Eastern Orthodox Church which uses the Byzantine rite in Greek, in particular the national Church of Greece.

green traditionally the colour of jealousy, *green* is also taken to symbolize youth and immaturity.

In 20th century use, *green* (often with a capital initial) means concerned with or supporting protection of the environment as a political principle.

The **Reverend Green** is one of the six stock characters constituting the murderer and suspects in the game of ▶ CLUEDO.

The **green belt** is an area of open land around a city, on which building is restricted. A *green belt* also marks a level of proficiency in judo, karate, or other martial arts below that of a brown belt.

A **Green Beret** is a British commando or a member of the US Army Special Forces.

In England and Wales, the **Green Book** is a book setting out the procedural rules of the county courts, bound in green.

In the US, a **green card** is a permit allowing a foreign national to live and work permanently in the US.

The **green-eyed monster** is jealousy personified; originally from Iago's warning in Shakespeare's *Othello*, 'O! beware, my lord, of jealousy; It is the green-eyed monster which doth mock The meat it feeds on.'

The term **green fingers** is used for natural ability in growing plants; recorded from the 1930s.

A **green light** is taken as a signal that one may proceed with one's chosen course; often in **give the green light to**. The allusion is to a green light in traffic signals.

The **green man** is a man dressed up in greenery to represent a wild man of the woods or seasonal fertility. A carved image of this is often seen in medieval English churches, as a human face with branches and foliage growing out of the mouth.

The **Green Mountain State** is an informal name for Vermont.

In the UK, a **Green Paper** is a preliminary report of government proposals that is published in order to provoke discussion.

A **Green Party** is an environmentalist political party. Green Parties arose in Europe in the early 1970s, since when they have achieved a certain amount of electoral success, particularly in Germany. The Green Party in Britain was founded in 1973 as the Ecology Party, changing its name in 1985.

The **green room** is a room in a theatre or studio in which performers can relax when they are not performing. The name probably derives from the room's originally being painted green. The first reference to it is in *Love Makes a Man* (1701), a play by Colley Cibber.

The term **green shoots** is used for signs of growth or renewal, especially of economic recovery. The expression in this context derives from a misquotation, 'the green shoots of recovery', of a speech made by the Conservative politician Norman Lamont when Chancellor in 1991, when he said that, 'The green shoots of economic spring are appearing once again.'

Green Thursday is another name for Maundy Thursday, perhaps referring to the practice of giving green branches to penitents who had made their confession on Ash Wednesday.

greenery-yallery of or in the style of the 19th-century Aesthetic Movement (used to convey the idea of affectation); originally as a quotation from Gilbert and Sullivan's *Patience* (1881).

Greenham Common a village near Newbury, Berkshire, the site of a US cruise missile base which became a focus for anti-nuclear protests in the 1980s.

greenhouse effect the trapping of the sun's warmth in a planet's lower atmosphere due to the greater transparency of the atmosphere to visible radiation from the sun than to infrared radiation emitted from the planet's surface.

Greenpeace an international organization that campaigns actively but non-violently for conservation of the environment and the preservation of endangered species. The name is said to have been coined when the Canadian environmentalist Bill Darnell said, 'Make it a *green* peace.'

Greenwich a London borough on the south bank of the Thames, the original site of the Royal Greenwich Observatory. The buildings at Greenwich, together with many of the old instruments, now form part of the National Maritime Museum, and reclaimed land at Greenwich forms the site of the ➤ *Millennium* DOME.

Greenwich Mean Time is the mean solar time at the Greenwich meridian, adopted as the standard time in a zone that includes the British Isles.

The **Greenwich meridian** is the prime meridian, which passes through the former Royal Observatory at Greenwich. It was adopted internationally as the zero of longitude in 1884.

Greenwich Village a district of New York City on the lower west side of Manhattan, traditionally associated with writers, artists, and musicians.

Gregorian calendar the calendar introduced in 1582 by Pope Gregory XIII, as a modification of the Julian calendar.

To bring the calendar back into line with the solar year, 10 days were suppressed, and centenary years were only made leap years if they were divisible by 400. Scotland adopted the Gregorian calendar in 1600, but England and Wales did not follow suit until 1752 (by which time 11 days had to be suppressed). At the same time New Year's Day was changed from 25 March to 1 January, and dates using the new calendar were designated 'New Style'.

Gregorian chant church music sung as a single vocal line in free rhythm and a restricted scale (plainsong), in a style developed for the medieval Latin liturgy, and named after St Gregory the Great, who is said to have standardized it.

Gregory VII (*c.*1020–85), pope from 1073, who asserted the power of the papacy and hierarchy and insisted on clerical celibacy; in his conflict with the Holy Roman Emperor Henry IV (1050–1106) he was at first successful, so that Henry was forced to do penance at ➤ CANOSSA in 1077; finally deposed in 1084, Gregory died at Salerno, his last words being, 'I have loved justice and hated iniquity; therefore I die in exile.'

St Gregory of Tours (*c.*540–94), Frankish bishop and historian. He was elected bishop of Tours in 573; his writings provide the chief authority for the early Merovingian period of French history. His feast day is 17 November.

St Gregory the Great (*c.*540–604), pope (as Gregory I) from 590 and Doctor of the Church. An important reformer, he did much to establish the temporal power of the papacy. He sent St Augustine to England to lead the country's conversion to Christianity, and is also credited with the introduction of Gregorian chant. His feast day is 12 March.

gremlin an imaginary mischievous sprite regarded as responsible for an unexplained problem or fault, especially a mechanical or electronic one. From the 1940s, originally as RAF slang, and perhaps suggested by *goblin*.

Grendel in the Old English epic poem *Beowulf*, the water monster who nightly attacks Heorot, the hall built by Hrothgar, king of Denmark, and each night kills and eats one of Hrothgar's thanes. Grendel is of the race of ➤ CAIN, living away from humankind but drawn by savagery and greed to the hall where the king's men feast.

He ravages Heorot over many years, but is mortally wounded in his fight with the hero ➤ BEOWULF and his severed arm nailed up as a trophy. Grendel's mother then comes to Heorot to avenge her son; she kills Hrothgar's most valued thane, but is in her turn destroyed by Beowulf in her underwater lair.

Gresham's Law the tendency for money of lower intrinsic value to circulate more freely than money of higher intrinsic and equal nominal value (often expressed as 'Bad money drives out good'). It is named for the English financier Thomas Gresham (*c.*1519–79), who founded the Royal Exchange in 1566 and served as the chief financial adviser to the Elizabethan government. Gresham's emblem, a ➤ GRASSHOPPER, was later used by Martin's Bank.

Gretchen in Goethe's *Faust* (1808), name of the simple girl seduced by Faust; in extended usage, a girl held to resemble her, a typically German girl or woman.

Gretna Green a village in Scotland just north of the English border near Carlisle, formerly a popular place for runaway couples from England to be married without the parental consent required in England for people under a certain age.

Place de Grève in Paris, the former site of public executions; the first guillotine was erected there in April 1792.

grey of the colour grey, between white and black.

A **grey area** is an area of law or morality which does not fall into any predefined category and which is a matter of uncertainty. In the 1960s, *grey areas* in British planning parlance referred to places that were not in as desperate a state as slums but which were in decline and in need of rebuilding.

A **Grey Friar** is a Franciscan friar, so named because of the colour of the order's habit.

Grey matter is the darker tissue of the brain and spinal cord, consisting mainly of nerve cell bodies and branching dendrites; informally, intelligence. The phrase **little grey cells** was used by Agatha Christie's detective ➤ *Hercule* POIROT to describe his intelligence.

See also ➤ MEN *in (grey) suits.*

gridiron a gridiron is the emblem of ➤ *St* LAWRENCE and ➤ *St* VINCENT *of Saragossa.*

gridlock a traffic jam affecting a whole network of intersecting streets, which in the early 1990s developed the figurative use of a situation in which no progress can be made. In US politics it was used particularly to denote the situation in which legislation makes no progress, either because of conflicts within Congress, or because of disagreements between Congress and the Administration.

griffin a mythical creature with the head and wings of an eagle and the body of a lion, typically depicted with pointed ears and with the eagle's legs taking the place of the forelegs. The ancient Greeks believed that they lived in Scythia, guarding the gold for which that country was renowned.

Grim Reaper a personification of death in the form of a cloaked skeleton wielding a large scythe; *reaper* in this sense is recorded from the mid 19th century.

Grimaldi name of the ruling dynasty of the principality of Monaco.

Grimm surname of two brothers, Jacob (1785–1863) and Wilhelm (1786–1859) *Grimm*, German philologists and folklorists. In 1852 the brothers jointly inaugurated a dictionary of German on historical principles, which was eventually completed by other scholars in 1960. They also compiled an anthology of German fairy stories, based on oral folk tales, which appeared in three volumes between 1812 and 1822, and their name may be used

allusively in this context to indicate a somewhat sinister atmosphere of magic and danger.

Grimm's law is the observation that certain Indo-European consonants (mainly stops) undergo regular changes in the Germanic languages which are not seen in others such as Greek or Latin. Examples include *p* becoming *f* so that Latin *pedem* corresponds to English *foot* and German *Fuss*. The principle was set out by Jacob Grimm in his German grammar (2nd edition, 1822).

grimoire a book of magic spells and incantations. Recorded from the mid 19th century, the word comes from French, and is an alteration of *grammaire* 'grammar'.

grin and bear it deal with one's pain or misfortune in a stoical manner. In earlier use, *grin* here meant not 'smile broadly' but 'show the teeth' or 'snarl'. From the mid 17th to the mid 18th centuries, *grin* was generally used derogatorily or in contrast to a cheerful *smile.*

keep one's nose to the grindstone work hard and continuously. A *grindstone* was a thick revolving disc of stone on which knives were sharpened and tools ground. In various forms since the mid 16th century, this idiom originally referred to getting mastery over someone else by compelling them to toil unremittingly, holding them like a knife-blade against the grindstone.

grisaille a method of painting in grey monochrome, typically to imitate sculpture; a painting or stained-glass window in this style. The word comes (in the mid 19th century) from French, from *gris* 'grey'.

Griselda the heroine of Chaucer's *Clerk's Tale*, the model of a patient wife who is persecuted and ultimately apparently rejected by her husband. The story comes from Boccaccio.

grist to the mill experience, material, or knowledge which can be turned to good use. Grist in the sense of 'corn that is to be ground' is current now only in this phrase (used metaphorically since the late 16th century) and in the proverb *all is grist that comes to the mill*. The world is related to Old Saxon *gristgrimmo* meaning 'gnashing of teeth'.

groat any of various medieval European coins, in particular an English silver coin worth four old pence, issued between 1351 and 1662; often taken as the type of something of little or no value, as in *not care a groat*.

The word comes from Middle Dutch *groot* or Middle Low German *grōte* 'great, thick', hence 'thick penny'.

grog spirits (originally rum) mixed with water. The word, which is mid 18th century, is said to be from *Old Grog*, the reputed nickname (because of his grogram cloak) of Admiral Vernon (1684–1757), who in 1740 first ordered diluted (instead of neat) rum to be served out to sailors.

Gromit name of the faithful and silent dog belonging to the cheese-loving inventor ➤ WALLACE in Nick Park's claymation films of his two plasticine figures; despite his inability to speak, *Gromit* ably conveys his views through expression and the movement of his long dark ears.

ground zero the ground under an exploding (nuclear) bomb; in the US, used to designate the site of the World Trade Center after it was destroyed by terrorist action, 11 September 2001.

groundhog North American term for the woodchuck, a marmot with a heavy body and short legs.

In the US, **Groundhog Day** is 2 February, when the groundhog is said to come out of its hole at the end of hibernation. If the animal sees its shadow—i.e. if the weather is sunny—it is said to portend six weeks more of winter weather.

groundling a spectator or reader of inferior taste; originally a member of the part of a theatre audience that traditionally stood in the pit beneath the stage, with reference to Hamlet's words to the players in Shakespeare's *Hamlet* (1601).

groves of academe the academic world; originally as a quotation from the *Epistles* of the 1st-century AD Roman poet Horace, '*Atque inter silvas Academi quaerere verum* [And seek for truth in the groves of Academe].'

Grub Street used in reference to a world or class of impoverished journalists and writers, from the name of a street (later Milton Street) in Moorgate, London, inhabited by such authors in the 17th century.

Mrs Grundy a person with very conventional standards of propriety, from the name of a person repeatedly mentioned in T.

Morton's comedy *Speed the Plough* (1798), often in the phrase 'What will Mrs Grundy say?', which became a popular catchphrase.

Guadalcanal an island in the western Pacific, the largest of the Solomon Islands, which during the Second World War was the scene of the first major US offensive against the Japanese (August 1942).

guardian angel a spirit that is thought to watch over and protect a person or place; recorded from the mid 17th century.

Gudrun in Norse legend, sister of Gunnar, the wife of ➤ SIGURD and later of Atli (Attila the Hun); the Norse equivalent of Kriemhild in the *Nibelungenlied*. In both Norse and Germanic versions of the story, she is ultimately a figure of vengeance, bringing about the death of the brothers who have killed her husband.

In saga literature, *Gudrun* is also the name of the remorseless heroine of the Old Icelandic *Laxdæla Saga*, who is loved by Kjartan but marries his foster-brother Bolli, and who in the end incites Bolli to kill Kjartan.

St Gudule (*c.*648–712), virgin, patron of Brussels. She habitually prayed in the early morning, and it was said that when she was praying the devil blew out the candle, which was then reignited by divine power; she is often shown with a candle. Her feast day is 8 January.

Guelph a member of one of two great factions in Italian medieval politics, traditionally supporting the Pope against the Holy Roman emperor (supported by the ➤ GHIBELLINES). The name comes through Italian *Guelfo* from Middle High German *Welf*, the name of the founder of one of the two great rival dynasties in the Holy Roman Empire, a princely family of Swabian origin from which the British royal house is descended through George I.

The name *Welf* is believed to have been adopted into political use in Italy from its reputed use as a war cry (at the battle of Weinsburg in 1140) by partisans of Henry the Lion, Duke of Bavaria, who belonged to this family, and fought against the Emperor Conrad III; it was thus adopted as a name for the adversaries of the Hohenstaufen emperors.

Guernica a town in the Basque Provinces of northern Spain, to the east of Bilbao. Formerly the seat of a Basque parliament, it was bombed in 1937, during the Spanish Civil

War, by German planes in support of Franco, an event depicted in a famous painting by Picasso.

Guignol the bloodthirsty chief character in a French puppet show of that name which is similar to Punch and Judy, which has given its name to ➤ GRAND *Guignol*.

guild a medieval association of craftsmen or merchants, often having considerable power.

Guilds are first mentioned in Old English pre-Conquest documents, but they had a strong religious focus, with their objects including the provision of masses for the souls of deceased members, and the payment of *wergild* in cases of justifiable homicide. **Merchant guilds**, incorporated societies of the merchants of a town or city, having exclusive rights of trading within the town, are not found in pre-Conquest England, although they were known on the Continent, and were later introduced to England (in many English towns, and in the royal burghs of Scotland, the merchant guild became the governing body of the town).

The **trade guilds**, which in England came to prominence in the 14th century, were associations of persons exercising the same craft, formed for the purpose of protecting and promoting their common interests. They are historically represented in London by the Livery Companies, although these are not ordinarily known as guilds.

guillotine a machine with a heavy blade sliding vertically in grooves, used for beheading people. The device was named after Joseph-Ignace *Guillotin* (1738–1814), the French physician who recommended its use for executions in 1789; its introduction was intended as a humanitarian measure for relatively painless killing (previously the right to death by decapitation had been limited to the nobility). The first guillotine was set up in the ➤ Place de GRÈVE in Paris. It was informally called *Louison* and *Louisette*, after Dr Antoine *Louis* who designed the machine; later it became known also as *la Veuve* 'the Widow'.

The term *guillotine* is used in parliament for a procedure used to prevent delay in the discussion of a legislative bill by fixing times at which various parts of it must be voted on.

guinea a former British gold coin that was first minted in 1663 from gold imported from West Africa, with a value that was later fixed at 21 shillings. It was replaced by the sovereign from 1817.

It was named after *Guinea* in West Africa as being intended for the *Guinea trade* and made with gold from that source; the first coins were minted 'in the name and for the use of the Company of Royal Adventurers of England trading with Africa'; these pieces were to bear for distinction the figure of a little elephant.

guinea pig a person or thing used as a subject for experiment; no longer occurring in the wild, the *guinea pig* is now typically kept as a pet or for laboratory research.

Guinevere in Arthurian legend, the wife of King ➤ ARTHUR and lover of ➤ LANCELOT. In the Arthurian cycle she is seen through her love for Lancelot as one of the key factors in the ultimate destruction of Arthur's kingdom, by providing an opening which can be exploited by the traitor ➤ MORDRED. Guinevere, who survives her husband's death, traditionally repented her sins and became a nun.

Gulag a system of labour camps maintained in the Soviet Union from 1930 to 1955 in which many people died. Besides ordinary criminals, inmates included dissident intellectuals, political opponents, and members of ethnic minorities; the word became widely known in the west in the 1960s and 1970s with the translation of Alexander Solzhenitsyn's works, notably *The Gulag Archipelago*.

The word is Russian, from *G(lavnoe) u(pravlenie ispravitel'no-trudovykh) lag(ereĭ)* 'Chief Administration for Corrective Labour Camps'.

gules red, as a heraldic tincture. The word comes (in Middle English) from Old French *goles* (plural of *gole* 'throat', from Latin *gula*), used to denote pieces of red-dyed fur used as a neck ornament.

Gulf War the war of January and February 1991 in which an international coalition of forces assembled in Saudi Arabia under the auspices of the United Nations forced the withdrawal of Saddam Hussein's Iraqi forces from Kuwait, which they had invaded and occupied in August 1990.

Gulf War Syndrome is a medical condition affecting many veterans of the 1991 Gulf War, causing fatigue, chronic headaches, and skin and respiratory disorders. Its origin is uncertain, though it has been attributed to exposure to a combination of pesticides, vaccines, and other chemicals.

gull a credulous person, a dupe, a fool, possibly a transferred used of the word meaning 'an unfledged bird'.

Gullah a member of a black people living on the coast of South Carolina and nearby islands. Also, the Creole language of this people, having an English base with elements from various West African languages. The name may come from a shortening of *Angola*, or from *Gola*, the name of an agricultural people of Liberia and Sierra Leone.

Gummidge a peevish, self-pitying, and pessimistic person, given to complaining, from the name of Mrs *Gummidge*, a character in Dickens's *David Copperfield* (1850).

Worzel Gummidge a talking scarecrow with straw hair who is the central character of a series of children's books by Barbara Euphan Todd (d. 1976); the stories were later televised.

gunboat diplomacy foreign policy that is supported by the use or threat of military force, a term now associated particularly with British imperial power.

Gunga Din central character in the poem (1892) by Kipling, the Indian water-carrier who is killed bringing water to fighting soldiers; allusive use typically refers to the line, 'You're a better man that I am, Gunga Din!'

Gunnar in Norse legend, the brother of Gudrun; eqivalent of Gunther in the *Nibelung-enlied*. In the Norse stories, he brings about the death of his brother-in-law ➤ SIGURD, who having helped him by magic to win Brynhild has betrayed the secret, and is himself killed by Atli, at the instigation of Gudrun.

gunner's daughter the gun to which a sailor, especially a boy serving on a warship, was lashed for flogging (see also ➤ KISS *the gunner's daughter*).

gunpowder the introduction of *gunpowder* can be taken as a type of technological advance; Francis Bacon in *Novum Organum* (1620) said of 'printing, gunpowder, and the mariner's needle [the compass]' that 'these three have changed the whole face and state of things throughout the world'. Thomas Carlyle in 1838 wrote of 'The three great elements of modern civilization, Gunpowder, Printing, and the Protestant Religion.'

The **Gunpowder Plot** was a conspiracy by a small group of Catholic extremists to blow up James I and his Parliament on 5 November 1605. The plot was uncovered when Lord Monteagle was sent an anonymous letter telling him to stay away from the House on the appointed day. Guy Fawkes was arrested in the cellars of the Houses of Parliament the day before the scheduled attack and betrayed his colleagues under torture. The leader of the plot, Robert Catesby, was killed resisting arrest and the rest of the conspirators were captured and executed. The plot is commemorated by the traditional searching of the vaults before the opening of each session of Parliament, and by bonfires and fireworks, with the burning of an effigy of ➤ *Guy* FAWKES, one of the conspirators, annually on 5 November.

stick to one's guns refuse to compromise or change, despite criticism. With allusion to maintaining one's position under enemy fire.

according to Gunter in the US, reliably, correctly; the allusion is to the English mathematician Edmund *Gunter* who devised **Gunter's chain**, a former measuring instrument 66 ft (20.1 m) long, subdivided into 100 links, each of which is a short section of wire connected to the next link by a loop. It has now been superseded by the steel tape and electronic equipment.

Gunter's a famous London confectioner's and caterer's, established in the reign of George III and noted particularly for their ice-creams.

Gunther in the *Nibelungenlied*, the husband of Brunhild and brother of Kriemhild, by whom he was beheaded in revenge for Siegfried's murder; equivalent of the Norse ➤ GUNNAR.

Gurkha a member of any of several peoples of Nepal noted for their military prowess; in particular, a member of a regiment in the British army established specifically for Nepalese recruits in the mid 19th century. *Gurkha* is the name of a locality, from the Sanskrit word for 'cowherd', used as an epithet of their patron deity.

Gurmukhi the script used by Sikhs for writing Punjabi; the word comes via Punjabi from Sanskrit *guru* 'teacher' + *mukha* 'month'.

guru a Hindu spiritual teacher. Also, each of the ten first leaders of the Sikh religion. The word comes from Sanskrit meaning 'weighty, grave', hence 'elder, teacher'.

Gutenberg Bible the edition of the Bible (Vulgate version) printed by the German printer Johannes Gutenberg (*c.*1400–68). He was the first in the West to print using movable type, introduced typecasting using a matrix, and was the first to use a press. The *Gutenberg Bible* was completed in about 1455 in Mainz, Germany. Printed in Latin in three volumes in 42-line columns, it is the first complete book extant in the West and is also the earliest to be printed from movable type. There are about forty copies still in existence. Also called the *Forty-two-line Bible*.

St Guthlac (*c.*673–714), hermit of Crowland, whose cult had great popularity in pre-Conquest England. He is represented with a scourge, as a weapon against diabolical attacks. His feast day is 11 April; the date of his translation is 30 August.

gutter press reporters or newspapers engaging in sensational journalism, especially accounts of the private lives of public figures; the usage is recorded from the late 19th century.

guy a figure representing ➤ *Guy* FAWKES, burnt on a bonfire on Guy Fawkes' Night,

and often displayed by children begging for money for fireworks.

The original *guys* were figures paraded about in the streets on the anniversary of the ➤ GUNPOWDER *Plot*.

Guy Fawkes Night is another name for ➤ BONFIRE *Night*.

Gwynedd a former principality of North Wales. Powerful in the mid 13th century under Llewelyn, it was finally subjugated by the English forces of Edward I in 1282, following Llewelyn's death.

gypsy a member of a travelling people with dark skin and hair, speaking a language (Romany) related to Hindi, and traditionally living by seasonal work, itinerant trade, and fortune telling. Gypsies are now found mostly in Europe, parts of North Africa, and North America, but are believed to have originated in the Indian subcontinent. They have at various times been subjected to persecution and forced migration, notably in Nazi Germany.

The word (originally *gipcyan*) dates from the mid 16th century, and is short for *Egyptian*, because gypsies were popularly supposed to have come from Egypt.

Hh

H the eighth letter of the modern English alphabet and of the ancient Roman one, representing a Semitic letter adopted by Greek as H, originally the eighth and later, after the omission of F, the seventh letter of the alphabet.

ha-ha a ditch with a wall on its inner side below ground level, forming a boundary to a park or garden without interrupting the view. Recorded from the early 18th century, from French, it is said to represent a cry of surprise on suddenly encountering such an obstacle.

Habakkuk a Hebrew minor prophet, probably of the 7th century BC; also, a book of the Bible containing his prophecies.

habeas corpus a writ requiring a person under arrest to be brought before a judge or into court, especially to secure the person's release unless lawful grounds are shown for their detention.
  Recorded from late Middle English, the phrase is from Latin, literally 'thou shalt have the body (in court)'.

habit a long, loose garment worn by a member of a religious order; **the habit** is used to mean the monastic order or profession.

Habsburg one of the principal dynasties of central Europe from medieval to modern times.
  Taking their name from a castle in Aargau, Switzerland, the family established a hereditary monarchy in Austria in 1282, and secured the title of Holy Roman emperor from 1452, reaching its peak of power under Emperor Charles V. Austrian and Spanish branches were created when Charles divided the territories between his son Philip II and his brother Ferdinand; the Habsburgs ruled Spain 1504–1700, while Habsburg rule in Austria ended with the collapse of Austria–Hungary in 1918.
  The **Habsburg lip** is a term for the prominent lower lip and chin characteristic of the Habsburg family, and said to be the result of inbreeding.

hack a writer or journalist producing dull, unoriginal work. *Hack* is recorded in this

sense from the late 17th century, and comes from the use of the word to mean 'a horse for ordinary riding'; ultimately, it is an abbreviation of ➤ HACKNEY.

one's hackles rise the hairs on the back of one's neck are thought of as being raised in anger or hostility; *hackles* are the long feathers on the neck of a fighting cock, or the erectile hairs along the back of a dog, which rise when the animal is angry.

hackney a horse or pony of a light breed with a high-stepping trot, used in harness. The word is Middle English, and probably comes from *Hackney* in East London, where horses were pastured. The term originally denoted an ordinary riding horse (as opposed to a war horse or draught horse), especially one available for hire.
  The word is the origin of **hackneyed** meaning 'unoriginal and trite', and ultimately of ➤ HACK for a dull and uninspired journalist.

Hades in Greek mythology, the underworld; the abode of the spirits of the dead. Also, the god of the underworld (also called *Pluto*, see ➤ PLUTO¹), one of the sons of Cronus.

Hadith a collection of traditions containing sayings of the prophet Muhammad which, with accounts of his daily practice (the Sunna), constitute the major source of guidance for Muslims apart from the Koran. The name comes from Arabic ḥadīt 'tradition'.

Hadrian (AD 76–138), Roman emperor from 117. The adopted successor of ➤ TRAJAN, he toured the provinces of the Empire and secured the frontiers.
  The building of **Hadrian's Wall**, a Roman defensive wall across northern England, stretching from the Solway Firth in the west to the mouth of the River Tyne in the east (about 120 km, 74 miles), was begun just after his visit to Britain, to defend the province of Britain against invasions by tribes from the north. The wall was built of stone and was 2.5–3 m thick, with forts and fortified posts at intervals along its length. After Hadrian's

death the frontier was advanced to the ➤ AN-TONINE *Wall*, which the Romans proved unable to hold; after being overrun and restored several times Hadrian's Wall was abandoned c.410 AD.

hag a witch, especially one in the form of an ugly old woman. The word is Middle English, and is perhaps from an Old English word related to Dutch *heks* and German *Hexe* 'witch'.

Haganah an underground defence force comprising a group of Jewish settlers in Palestine and playing a leading part in the creation of the State of Israel in 1948.

Hagar in the Bible and in Islamic tradition, the Egyptian slave who is mother of ➤ ISH-MAEL (Ismail) by Abraham. Driven out of Abraham's household by his wife Sarah, she and her son take flight into the desert, where their lives are saved by an angel who reveals to them the existence of a well.

Haggadah the text recited at the Seder on the first two nights of the Jewish Passover, including a narrative of the Exodus. Also, a legend, parable, or anecdote used to illustrate a point of the Law in the Talmud.
The name comes from Hebrew *Haggādāh* 'tale, parable'.

Haggai a Hebrew minor prophet of the 6th century. Also, a book of the Bible containing his prophecies of a glorious future in the Messianic age.

haggard a hawk caught for training as a wild adult of more than twelve months. Recorded from the mid 16th century (used in falconry), the word comes from French, and is perhaps related to *hedge*, later influenced by *hag*.
The original notion was of a bird which had fended for itself and might be half-starved as well as untamed; from this developed the usage of *haggard* to mean looking exhausted and unwell.

Hagia Sophia another name for ➤ SANTA *Sophia*. The name is Greek, literally 'holy wisdom'.

hagigah in Judaism, the peace-offering brought by pilgrims to the Temple at the three great feasts of Passover, Pentecost, and Tabernacles.

Hagiographa the books of the Bible comprising the last of the three major divisions of the Hebrew scriptures, other than the Law

and the Prophets. The books of the Hagiographa are: Ruth, Psalms, Job, Proverbs, Ecclesiastes, Song of Solomon, Lamentations, Daniel, Esther, Ezra–Nehemiah, and Chronicles. Also called *the Writings*.

hagiography the writing of the lives of saints; a biography idealizing its subject. The word comes ultimately from Greek *hagios* 'holy, saintly'.

hagioscope another term for ➤ SQUINT in a church.

haiku a Japanese poem of seventeen syllables, in three lines of five, seven, and five, traditionally evoking images of the natural world. The form originated in the 16th century.

Hail Mary a prayer to the Virgin Mary used chiefly by Roman Catholics, beginning with part of Luke 1:28. Also called ➤ AVE *Maria*.
In American football, a **Hail Mary pass** is a play in which the ball is thrown far down the field; in transferred usage, a high-risk manoeuvre, especially one undertaken at a very late stage.

Haile Selassie (1892–1975), emperor of Ethiopia 1930–74. In exile in Britain during the Italian occupation of Ethiopia (1936–41), he was restored to the throne by the Allies and ruled until deposed by a military coup. He is revered by the ➤ RASTAFARIAN religious sect.

hair a hair is traditionally used as the type of something of extremely small magnitude, value, or measure, the slightest thing, the least degree. The sword over ➤ DAMOCLES'S head is suspended by a single hair.
In classical and biblical stories a person's hair may have sacred significance; ➤ BERENI-CE'S *hair* was dedicated as an offering for her husband's safe return from war, and Nisus, king of Megara (see ➤ NISUS[1]) was vulnerable to betrayal when his daughter Scylla cut off his lock of purple hair. In the Bible, ➤ SAMSON's strength lay in his hair, and ➤ ABSALOM, admired for his long hair, was able to be killed when it caught in the branches of a tree.
A **hair of the dog that bit you** is an alcoholic drink taken to cure a hangover, from the former belief that such a hair was an efficacious remedy against the bite of a mad dog.
A **hair shirt** was a shirt of haircloth, formerly worn by penitents and ascetics.

hajj the Muslim pilgrimage to Mecca which takes place in the last month of the year, and which all Muslims are expected to make at least once during their lifetime. The word comes from Arabic *(al-) ḥajj* '(the Great) Pilgrimage'. A Muslim who has been to Mecca as a pilgrim is known as a **haji**.

haka a Maori ceremonial war dance involving chanting, an imitation of which is performed by New Zealand rugby teams before a match.

Richard Hakluyt (*c.*1552–1616), English geographer and historian. He compiled *Principal Navigations, Voyages, and Discoveries of the English Nation* (1598), a collection of accounts of great voyages of discovery which inspired further discovery and colonization.

halal denoting or relating to meat prepared as prescribed by Muslim law. The word comes (in the mid 19th century) from Arabic *ḥalāl* 'according to religious law'.

halcyon days a period of time in the past that was idyllically happy and peaceful. The *halcyon* is a mythical bird said by ancient writers to breed in a nest floating at sea at the winter solstice, charming the wind and waves into calm.

Hale–Bopp a periodic comet which passed close to the sun in the spring of 1997 and was one of the brightest of the 20th century. It was exceptionally large and active, has a period of just over 4,000 years, and was the first comet to exhibit a sodium tail. Named after Alan Hale and Thomas Bopp, the American astronomers who discovered it (independently of each other).

half a loaf not as much as one wants, but better than nothing. With allusion to the proverb, current since the mid 16th century, *half a loaf is better than no bread*.

half mast the position of a flag which is being flown some way below the top of its staff as a mark of respect for a person who has died.

Halicarnassus an ancient Greek city on the SW coast of Asia Minor, at what is now the Turkish city of Bodrum. It was the birthplace of the historian Herodotus and is the site of the Mausoleum of Halicarnassus (see ➤ MAUSOLEUM), one of the ➤ SEVEN *Wonders of the World*.

Hall of Mirrors one of the rooms (in French, the *Galerie des Glaces*) in the State Apartments of the palace of Versailles, constructed at the end of the 17th century with 17 mirrors opposite 17 windows, and lit by glass chandeliers; it was in the ➤ HALL *of Mirrors* that the ➤ *Treaty of* VERSAILLES was signed in 1919.

Hallel a portion of the service for certain Jewish festivals, consisting of Psalms 113–118. The word comes from Hebrew *hallēl* 'praise'.

hallelujah God be praised (uttered in worship or as an expression of rejoicing). From Old English, via ecclesiastical Latin from Greek *allēlouia* (in the Septuagint), or (from the 16th century) directly from Hebrew *hallĕlūyāh* 'praise ye the Lord'.

The **Hallelujah Chorus** is a musical composition based on the word 'hallelujah', especially that in the oratorio 'Messiah' by G. F. Handel (1685–1759), German-born musician.

The **Hallelujah Victory** was supposedly that gained over a pagan army by newly converted Bretons, led by ➤ GERMANUS, bishop of Auxerre, in 429; their battle-cry was 'Hallelujah!'

Halley's Comet a periodical comet with an orbital period of about 76 years, its reappearance in 1758–9 having been predicted by the English astronomer and mathematician Edmond Halley (1656–1742), who identified it. It was first recorded in 240 BC and last appeared, rather faintly, in 1985–6, when the European space probe Giotto took close-up photographs of the nucleus.

hallmark a mark stamped on articles of gold, silver, or platinum by the British assay offices, certifying their standard of purity. Recorded from the early 18th century, the word refers to *Goldsmiths' Hall* in London, where articles were tested and stamped with such a mark.

Halloween the night of 31 October, the eve of All Saints' Day. Halloween is of pre-Christian origin, being associated with the Celtic festival Samhain, when ghosts and spirits were thought to be abroad. Adopted as a Christian festival, it gradually became a secular rather than a Christian observance, involving dressing up and the wearing of masks. These secular customs were popularized in the US in the late 19th century and later developed into the custom of children playing trick or treat.

The name is recorded from the late 18th century, and is a contraction of *All Hallows*

Even 'All Saints Eve'; *hallow* here means a holy person or saint.

Hallstatt a cultural phase of the late Bronze Age and early Iron Age in Europe (*c.*1200–600 BC in temperate continental areas), preceding the La Tène period. It is generally equated with the Urnfield complex and is associated with the early Celts.

halo a disc or circle of light shown surrounding the head of a saint or holy person to represent their holiness, recorded in this sense from the mid 19th century. (From the 6th century, living persons were shown with a square halo.) The word dates from the mid 16th century (denoting a circle of light round the sun), and comes via medieval Latin and Latin from Greek *halōs* 'disc of the sun and moon'.

Ham in the Bible, a son of Noah, traditional ancestor of the Hamites and the people of Canaan. In Genesis Ham is said (in contrast to his brothers) to have mocked his father when Noah was drunk; in return Noah prophesied that he would be 'the lowest of slaves' to his brothers.

ham an excessively theatrical actor. The term (originally US, from the late 19th century) may be from the first syllable of *amateur* (compare with the US slang term *hamfatter* 'inexpert performer').

hamadryad in Greek and Roman mythology, a nymph who lives in a tree and dies when the tree dies. The word comes via Latin from Greek *Hamadruas*, from *hama* 'together' + *drus* 'tree'.

Haman in the Bible, the chief minister of ➤ AHASUERUS, who plotted a massacre of the Jews and was hanged on the gallows he prepared for the ➤ MORDECAI (Esther 7:10); the gallows was said to be fifty cubits high, and the expression **hang as high as Haman** became proverbial.

hamartia a fatal flaw leading to the downfall of a tragic hero or heroine. Recorded from the late 18th century, the word comes from Greek meaning 'fault, failure, guilt'; it was used in Aristotle's *Poetics* with reference to ancient Greek tragedy.

Hamas a Palestinian Islamic fundamentalist movement that has become a focus for Arab resistance in the Israeli-occupied territories. It opposes peace with Israel and has

come into conflict with the more moderate Palestine Liberation Organization.

Hamelin a medieval market town in Lower Saxony, which in the legend of the ➤ PIED *Piper* was infested with a plague of rats.

Hamite a member of a group of North African peoples, including the ancient Egyptians and Berbers, supposedly descended from ➤ HAM, son of Noah.

Hamitic of or denoting a hypothetical language family formerly proposed to comprise Berber, ancient Egyptian, the Cushitic languages, and the Chadic languages. These are now recognized as independent branches of the Afro-Asiatic family.

Hamlet a legendary prince of Denmark, hero of a tragedy by Shakespeare. The story is based on one in Saxo Grammaticus's *Historiae Danicae*, in which the young prince is opposed to the usurping uncle who has murdered Hamlet's father and married his mother.

In Shakespeare's play, Hamlet, adjured by his father's ghost to seek revenge, is torn between hatred of his usurping uncle and love for his mother; in allusive use, his name may indicate not only tragedy but also an ultimately fatal indecision.

The expression **Hamlet without the prince** is used for a performance or event taking place without the principal actor or central figure. The phrase derives from an account given in the *Morning Post* of September 1775, of a theatrical company in which the actor who was to play the hero ran off with the innkeeper's daughter; when the play was announced, the audience was told 'the part of Hamlet to be left out, for that night.'

hammer a hammer is the emblem of St Apollonia, a 3rd-century martyr whose sufferings included having her teeth wrenched from her jaws, and ➤ St ELOI.

In Scandinavian mythology, a hammer, *Mjǫllnir*, was the weapon of the god ➤ THOR.

The Hammer was a personal epithet (translating ➤ MARTEL) of a number of military and political figures of the Middle Ages.

A **hammer and sickle** are the symbols of the industrial worker and the peasant used as the emblem of the former USSR and of international communism.

Hammer and tongs means with great energy and noise, with reference to a blacksmith's blows on the hot iron taken with the tongs from the fire of the forge. Often **go at something hammer and tongs**.

be hammered on the Stock Exchange, be declared a defaulter, from the practice of striking three strokes with a mallet on the side of a rostrum in the Stock Exchange before a formal declaration of default.

Hampton Court a palace on the north bank of the Thames in the borough of Richmond-upon-Thames, London. It was built by Cardinal Wolsey as his private residence but later presented by him to Henry VIII, and was a favourite royal residence until the reign of George II.
The **Hampton Court Conference** was held by James I at Hampton Court in January 1604 with the Anglican bishops and representatives of puritan ministers.

hand from the mid 16th century, a linear measure, now used only of a horse's height, and equal to four inches; a hand-breadth.
From hand to mouth means satisfying only one's immediate needs because of lack of money for future plans and investments; recorded from the early 16th century.
The **hand of glory** was originally a French charm made from a mandrake root; the phrase is a translation of French *main de gloire*, an alteration of the original *mandragore* 'mandrake'. Later, the term came to mean a charm made from the hand of an executed criminal.
The expression **hands across the sea** meaning promoting closer international links is recorded from the late 19th century.
To **put one's hand to the plough** is to set out on a task from which one will not be deflected; originally with biblical allusion to Luke 9:62, 'No man, having put his hand to the plough, and looking back, is fit for the kingdom of God.'

handsome is as handsome does character and behaviour are more important than good looks. Proverbial saying dating in this form from the mid 17th century. *Handsome* describing behaviour is properly 'chivalrous' or 'genteel', though in the context of this proverb is taken to refer to good looks. The original sense is made clear in the earlier (late 16th-century) *goodly is he that goodly doth*.

Hang Seng index a figure indicating the relative price of shares on the Hong Kong Stock Exchange, named after the *Hang Seng Bank* in Hong Kong, where it was devised.

hang someone out to dry leave someone in a difficult or vulnerable situation (chiefly North American); the idea is of wet washing suspended from a washing-line, flapping in the wind.

hanged, drawn, and quartered in allusion to the traditional mode of execution for traitors, by which prisoners were drawn on a hurdle to the place of execution, and after being hanged were disembowelled while still alive; their bodies were then quartered, for display in different places.

the Hanging Gardens of Babylon legendary terraced gardens at Babylon, watered by pumps from the Euphrates, whose construction was ascribed to Nebuchadnezzar (*c.*600 BC). They were one of the ➤ SEVEN *Wonders of the World*.

Hannibal (247–182 BC), Carthaginian general. In the second Punic War he attacked Italy via the Alps, which he crossed with elephants; he repeatedly defeated the Romans, but failed to take Rome itself. After being recalled to Africa he was defeated at Zama by Scipio Africanus in 202.

Hanoi Jane nickname given to the American actress Jane Fonda (1937–), who campaigned against American involvement in the Vietnam War, and who in 1972 visited Hanoi to denounce the US bombing campaigns against North Vietnam.

Hanover a former state and province in northern Germany. It was an electorate of the Holy Roman Empire 1692–1806, ruled by the Guelph dynasty, and from 1866 until 1945 was a province of Prussia. In 1714 the Elector of Hanover succeeded to the British throne as George I, and from then until the accession of Victoria (1837) the same monarch ruled both Britain and Hanover.
With the accession of Victoria (1837) to the British throne, however, Hanover passed to her uncle, Ernest, Duke of Cumberland (1771–1851). The British royal house from 1714 to the death of Queen Victoria in 1901 was known as **the House of Hanover**, and its members as the **Hanoverians**.
The heraldic badge of Hanover, a *white horse*, was formerly represented in the ➤ ROYAL *Arms* of the United Kingdom.

Hansard the official verbatim record of debates in the British, Canadian, Australian, or New Zealand parliament. It is named after Thomas C. *Hansard* (1776–1833), an English printer whose company originally printed it.

Hanse a medieval guild of merchants; **the Hanse** or **Hanseatic League**. The word is recorded from Middle English, and comes from Old French *hanse* 'guild, company', from Old High German *hansa* 'company, troop'.

The *Hanseatic League* was a medieval association of north German cities, formed in 1241 and surviving until the 19th century. In the later Middle Ages it included over 100 towns and functioned as an independent political power, but it began to collapse in the 17th century, and only Hamburg, Bremen, and Lübeck remained when it disbanded in the 19th century.

Hanukkah a lesser Jewish festival, lasting eight days from the 25th day of Kislev (in December) and commemorating the rededication of the Temple in 165 BC by the Maccabees after its desecration by the Syrians. It is marked by the successive kindling of eight lights.

Hanuman a semi-divine being of monkeylike form, whose exploits are described in the ➤ RAMAYANA; he helps Rama rescue his wife Sita from the demon king of Lanka.

The name *hanuman* also denotes a pale-coloured langur monkey of the Indian subcontinent, venerated by Hindus.

hapax legomenon a term of which only one instance of use is recorded. The phrase comes (in the mid 17th century) from Greek 'a thing said once', from *hapax* 'once' and the passive participle of *legein* 'to say'.

happy-clappy belonging to or characteristic of a Christian group whose worship is marked by enthusiasm and spontaneity; the term is an informal and mildly disparaging one for a style of worship associated with the evangelical movement.

happy families a children's card game played with special cards in sets of four, each depicting members of a 'family', the object being to acquire as many sets as possible.

happy hunting ground a place where success or enjoyment is obtained, originally referring to the optimistic hope of American Indians for good hunting grounds in the afterlife.

hara-kiri ritual suicide by disembowelment with a sword, formerly practised in Japan by samurai as an honourable alternative to disgrace or execution; figuratively, ostentatious or ritualized self-destruction. The word comes (in the mid 19th century) from colloquial Japanese, from *hara* 'belly' + *kiri* 'cutting'.

haram a Muslim sacred place, forbidden to non-Muslims; the word comes from Arabic *ḥarām* 'forbidden'.

play hardball deal with matters in an uncompromising or ruthless manner, especially in politics; the expression comes in North American usage from a term for baseball, especially as contrasted with softball.

hard-boiled denoting a tough, realistic style of detective fiction set in a world permeated by corruption and deceit.

hare taken as a type of a fleet-footed and timid animal, the *hare* was traditionally supposed to sleep with its eyes open; hares were also associated with witchcraft, and witches were believed to be able to take the shape of a hare.

Hare and hounds is a game, especially a paperchase, in which a group of people chase another person or group across the countryside.

The **hare and the tortoise**, in one of Aesop's fables, typify the defeat of ability by persistence; the hare lost the race between them through over-confidence in its superiority of speed, because it allowed itself over the course of the race to be distracted from reaching the goal.

To **start a hare** is to raise a topic of conversation or argument. The rapid twisting and running of a hunted hare is here a metaphor for the pursuit of a topic in an animated conversation, especialy one in which the participants hold strong views.

Hare Krishna a member of the International Society for Krishna Consciousness, a religious sect based mainly in the US and other Western countries. Its devotees typically wear saffron robes, favour celibacy, practise vegetarianism, and chant mantras based on the name of the Hindu god Krishna.

Haredi a member of any of various Orthodox Jewish sects characterized by strict adherence to the traditional form of Jewish law and rejection of modern secular culture, many of whom do not recognize the modern state of Israel as a spiritual authority. The name is from Hebrew, literally 'one who trembles (in awe at the word of God)'.

harem the separate part of a Muslim household reserved for wives, concubines, and female servants; the women living there. In extended usage, the word also denotes the wives (or concubines) of a polygamous man, and thus a group of female animals sharing a single mate.

The word comes (in the mid 17th century) from Arabic *ḥaram*, *ḥarīm*, literally 'prohibited, prohibited place', and from this 'sanctuary, women's quarters, women'.

Harijan a member of a hereditary Hindu group of the lowest social and ritual status, an ➤ UNTOUCHABLE. The word comes from Sanskrit *harijana*, literally 'a person dedicated to Vishnu', from *Hari* 'Vishnu' + *jana* 'person'. The term was adopted and popularized by Mahatma Gandhi.

Harlem a district of New York City, situated to the north of 96th Street in NE Manhattan. It has a large black population and in the 1920s and 1930s was noted for its nightclubs and jazz bands.

The **Harlem Renaissance** was a movement in US literature in the 1920s which centred on Harlem and was an early manifestation of black consciousness in the US.

Harlequin a mute character in traditional pantomime, typically masked and dressed in a diamond-patterned costume, in the Italian *commedia dell' arte* the lover of ➤ COLUMBINE.

The name (recorded from the 16th century) comes from obsolete French, from earlier *Herlequin* (or *Hellequin*), the name of the leader of a legendary troop of demon horsemen; perhaps ultimately related to Old English *Herla cyning* 'King Herla', a mythical figure sometimes identified with Woden.

The **harlequinade** is the section of a traditional pantomime in which Harlequin played a leading role. It originated in the Italian *commedia dell'arte* as a sequence of narrative dances, but became a mere epilogue to the presentation of a fairy tale, which eventually displaced it altogether.

Harley Street a street in central London where many eminent physicians and surgeons have consulting rooms.

harmony an arrangement of the four Gospels, or of any parallel narratives, which presents a single continuous narrative text.

Harpers Ferry a small town in Jefferson County, West Virginia, at the junction of the Potomac and Shenandoah Rivers. It is famous for a raid in October 1859 in which ➤ John BROWN and a group of abolitionists captured a Federal arsenal located there.

harpy in Greek and Roman mythology, a rapacious monster described as having a woman's head and body and a bird's wings and claws or (as in Virgil's *Aeneid*) depicted as a bird of prey with a woman's face; in extended usage, a grasping unscrupulous woman.

under the harrow in distress. A *harrow* is a heavy frame set with iron teeth or tines, drawn over ploughed land to break up clods and root up weeds. The situation of a frog (late 14th century) or toad (early 19th century) beneath the tines is the epitome of misery.

Harrowing of Hell in medieval Christian theology, the defeat of the powers of evil and the release of its victims by the descent of Christ into hell after his death. It is a subject of mystery plays and of Orthodox icons; in medieval religious art Christ is shown treading down the gates of hell to release the souls of the faithful who have died before his Coming.

Harrowing here comes from *harrow*, a by-form of the verb *to harry*.

hart in Christian iconography, the hart can symbolize a soul longing for the water of baptism, in allusion to Psalm 42. A hart can also stand as an image of Christ as the adversary of Satan, since the Bestiaries attribute to deer the power of finding and killing snakes.

A *hart* (or stag), sometimes with a cross in its antlers, is the emblem of ➤ St EUSTACE and ➤ St HUBERT.

A **hart royal** was traditionally a hart that had been hunted by a king or queen and had escaped.

See also ➤ WHITE *hart*.

Harun ar-Rashid (763–809), fifth Abbasid caliph of Baghdad 786–809. The most powerful of the Abbasid caliphs, he was made famous by his portrayal in the *Arabian Nights*, and is known particularly for his custom of walking the streets of his city in disguise.

Harvard University the oldest American university, founded in 1636 at Cambridge, Massachusetts. It is named after John *Harvard* (1607–38), an English settler who bequeathed his library and half his estate to the university.

harvest the gathering in of crops.

A **harvest festival** is a celebration of the annual harvest, especially (in Britain) one held in schools and as a service in Christian churches, to which gifts of food are brought for the poor.

A **harvest home** is (a festival marking) the gathering in of the final part of the year's harvest.

A **harvest moon** is the full moon that is seen nearest to the time of the autumn equinox.

Harz Mountains a range of mountains in central Germany, the highest of which is the ➤ BROCKEN. The region is the source of many legends about witchcraft and sorcery.

Hashemite a member of an Arab princely family claiming descent from *Hashim*, great-grandfather of Muhammad; the official name for Jordan, ruled by a branch of this dynasty, is the **Hashemite Kingdom of Jordan**.

Hasid a member of a strictly orthodox Jewish sect in Palestine in the 3rd and 2nd centuries BC which opposed Hellenizing influences on their faith and supported the Maccabean revolt. The name comes from Hebrew *ḥāsīḏ* 'pious'.

Hasidism a mystical Jewish movement founded in Poland in the 18th century in reaction to the rigid academicism of rabbinical Judaism. The movement, which emphasized the importance of religious enthusiasm, had a strong popular following. Denounced in 1781 as heretical, the movement declined sharply in the 19th century, but fundamentalist communities developed from it, and *Hasidism* is still influential in Jewish life, particularly in Israel and New York.

more haste, less speed one makes better progress with a task if one does not try to do it too quickly. The primary meaning of 'speed' in this proverbial saying was 'success in the performance of an activity' rather than 'rapidity of movement', though it is the latter that is now generally assumed to be meant.

Battle of Hastings a decisive battle which took place in 1066, on a ridge called *Senlac*, just north of the town of Hastings, East Sussex. William the ➤ CONQUEROR (William I) defeated the forces of the Anglo-Saxon king Harold II; Harold died in the battle, leaving the way open for William to seize London and the vacant throne and leading to the subsequent Norman Conquest of England. ➤ BATTLE *Abbey* was founded by William to give thanks for his victory.

hat-trick three successes of the same kind, especially consecutive ones within a limited period, originally referring in cricket to the club presentation of a new hat (or some equivalent) to a bowler taking three wickets successively.

hatchment a large tablet, typically diamond-shaped, bearing the coat of arms of someone who has died, displayed in their honour. The word is recorded from the early 16th century, and probably comes from obsolete French *hachement*, from Old French *acesmement* 'adornment'.

Hathor in Egyptian mythology, a sky goddess, the patron of love and joy, represented variously as a cow, with a cow's head or ears, or with a solar disc between a cow's horns. Her name means 'House of Horus'.

Hatshepsut (d. 1482 BC), Egyptian queen of the 18th dynasty, reigned *c*.1503–1482 BC. On the death of her husband Tuthmosis II she became regent for her nephew Tuthmosis III; she then named herself Pharaoh and was often portrayed as male.

Hau-Hauism a 19th-century Maori religion promising eternal salvation from the white man.

Lord Haw-haw nickname given to William Joyce (1906–46), who made propaganda broadcasts in English from Nazi Germany; the nickname referred to his drawling nasal delivery, thought to mimic the 'haw-haw' quality supposedly typical of upper-class speech.

hawk in falconry, any diurnal bird of prey, used in falconry.

Hawk is also used to denote a person who advocates an aggressive or warlike policy, especially in foreign affairs; the opposite of a *dove*.

To **know a hawk from a handsaw** is to have ordinary discernment, chiefly with allusion to Shakespeare's *Hamlet*, when ➤ HAMLET, who has been feigning madness, says, 'I am but mad north-north-west; when the wind is southerly, I know a hawk from a handsaw.' (*Handsaw* is generally taken as an alteration of *heronshaw*, a heron.)

Hawkeye nickname of the tracker ➤ *Natty* BUMPPO in J. Fenimore Cooper's novels of American frontier life. **Hawkeye Pierce** is the name of one of the surgeons depicted in ➤ MASH.

Hawkeye State informal name for Iowa.

Hawkshaw name of a detective in the play *The Ticket-of-Leave Man* by Tom Taylor (1817–80), English dramatist; also portrayed in the comic strip *Hawkshaw the Detective* by Augustus Charles ('Gus') Mager (1878–1956), American cartoonist.

hawthorn in Britain, it was traditionally believed that bringing hawthorn blossom, or *may*, into the house was unlucky.

He Bible the first of two issues of the Bible printed in 1611, in which the last words of Ruth 3:15 are, 'and he went into the city', where the ➤ SHE *Bible* has, 'and she went into the city'.

head a *head* (held in the hands) is the emblem of ➤ St DENIS, ➤ St OSWALD, and other saints who were beheaded at martyrdom.

the Headless Man in British use, an anonymous figure featuring in photographs at the centre of the Argyll divorce case in the 1960s; in August 2000, a presumed identification of the man with Douglas Fairbanks Jnr was made public for the first time.

heart the *heart* is traditionally regarded as the centre of a person's thoughts and emotions, especially love or compassion.

The heart is stylistically represented by two equal curves meeting at a point at the bottom and a cusp at the top; such *hearts* are emblematic of love.

Hearts are one of the four suits in a conventional pack of playing cards, denoted by a stylized red figure of a heart.

The **heart of darkness** is a place of savagery and barbarism, from the title of Joseph Conrad's novel (1902).

Heart of Dixie is an informal name for Alabama.

The **Heart of Midlothian** is a name for the old Edinburgh Tolbooth, or prison, taken by Scott as the title of a novel (1818), set in 18th-century Edinburgh and opening with the ➤ PORTEOUS *riot*.

The phrase **heart of oak** is used for the solid central part of an oak tree as the traditional timber for ships. The phrase was popularized by the 18th-century song, 'Heart of oak are our ships, heart of oak are our men.'

Heart's blood is an archaic term for the blood, as being necessary for life; vital energy or force.

just a heartbeat away from the Presidency the vice-president's position; from a reference by Adlai Stevenson (1900–65) to the Republican Vice-Presidential nominee Richard Nixon, in a speech at Cleveland, Ohio, 23 October 1952.

hearts and minds people as represented by their emotions and intellect; originally with biblical allusion to Philippians 4:7, 'And the peace of God, which passeth all understanding, shall keep your hearts and minds through Christ Jesus.'

The term is now used to denote emotional or intellectual support or commitment. In the 20th century the phrase was used particularly in the context of public opposition to the Vietnam War.

Heath Robinson ingeniously or ridiculously over-complicated in design or construction; the term comes from the name of the English cartoonist and illustrator William Heath *Robinson* (1872–1944), who lampooned the machine age by inventing absurdly complicated 'Heath Robinson contraptions' to perform elementary or ridiculous actions.

take to the heather in Scottish usage, become an outlaw.

heaven a place regarded in various religions as the abode of God (or the gods) and the angels, and of the good after death, often traditionally depicted as being above the sky.

Hebe in Greek mythology, the daughter of Hera and Zeus, and cup-bearer of the gods.

Hebrew a member of an ancient people living in what is now Israel and Palestine and, according to biblical tradition, descended from the patriarch Jacob, grandson of Abraham. After the Exodus (*c.*1300 BC) they established the kingdoms of Israel and Judah, and their scriptures and traditions form the basis of the Jewish religion. Also, the Semitic language of this people, in its ancient or modern form.

Hebrew Bible the sacred writings of Judaism, called by Christians the Old Testament, and comprising the Law (Torah), the Prophets, and the Hagiographa or Writings.

Epistle to the Hebrews a book of the New Testament, traditionally included among the letters of St Paul but now generally held to be non-Pauline.

Hebron a Palestinian city on the West Bank of the Jordan. It is one of the most ancient cities in the Middle East, probably founded in the 18th century BC, and as the home of Abraham it is a holy city of both Judaism and Islam.

hecatomb in ancient Greece or Rome, a great public sacrifice, originally of a hundred oxen; figuratively, an extensive loss of life for some cause. The word comes (in the late 16th century, via Latin) from Greek *hekatombē* (from *hekaton* 'hundred' + *bous* 'ox').

Hecuba in Greek mythology, queen of Troy, the wife of ➤ PRIAM and mother of children including ➤ HECTOR, Paris, Cassandra, and Troilus; after the fall of Troy and the death of Priam she became a slave. She is taken as the type of a bereft and mourning woman.

hedge one's bets try to minimize the risk of being wrong or incurring loss by pursuing two courses of action at the same time. *Hedging* (formerly *hedging in* or *hedging off*) one's financial liabilities, especially bets, meant limiting potential losses by putting money on the other side in such a way as more or less to balance any potential loss on the first transaction. In betting terms this means in practice putting money on more than one runner in a race.

hedgehog in the Bestiaries it is said to gather fruit for its young by impalement on its spines; it may thus be taken to exemplify prudence, or as an image of the Devil harvesting unwary souls.

Uriah Heep obsequious and treacherous character in Dickens's *David Copperfield* (1850), characterized by exaggerated self-denigration.

Hegira ➤ MUHAMMAD's departure from Mecca to Medina in AD 622, prompted by the opposition of the merchants of Mecca and marking the consolidation of the first Muslim community. The name comes (via medieval Latin) from Arabic *hijra* 'departure', from *hajara* 'emigrate'.

The abbreviation *AH* (from Latin *anno Hegirae*) means 'in the year of the Hegira', and is used in the Muslim calendar for reckoning years from the departure from Mecca.

Heidelberg man a type of prehistoric man indicated by a prehistoric jaw found at Mauer near Heidelberg in 1907.

Heil Hitler used by the Germans or their supporters during the Nazi regime as a greeting or an acclamation of the supremacy of Hitler.

Heimdall in Scandinavian mythology, the watchman of the gods, said to have been the son of nine mothers.

Heimskringla the sagas of the Norse kings, compiled by the Icelandic historian and poet ➤ SNORRI *Sturluson* (1179–1241); the

stories cover the period from mythical times to the late 12th century. The title is taken from *Kringla heimsins* 'orb of the world', the opening words of the book.

Hel in Scandinavian mythology, the underworld and the goddess who ruled it, daughter of ➤ LOKI, and sister of ➤ FENRIR and the ➤ MIDGARD's *serpent*.

Helen in Greek mythology, the daughter of Zeus and Leda, born from an egg. In the Homeric poems she was the outstandingly beautiful wife of ➤ MENELAUS, and her abduction by Paris (to whom she had been promised, as a bribe, by Aphrodite) led to the Trojan War. Helen has a non-Greek name and is probably in origin an ancient pre-Hellenic goddess connected with vegetation and fertility.

St Helena (*c*.255–*c*.330 AD), Roman empress and mother of Constantine the Great. In 326 she visited the Holy Land and founded basilicas on the Mount of Olives and at Bethlehem. She is credited with the finding of the cross on which Christ was crucified. Her feast day is 21 May in the Eastern Church, and 18 August in the Western Church.

Mount Helicon a mountain in Boeotia, central Greece, to the north of the Gulf of Corinth, which was believed by the ancient Greeks to be the home of the Muses.

Heliogabalus (AD 204–22), Roman emperor 218–22. He took his name from the Syro-Phoenician sun god *Elah-Gabal*, of whom he was a hereditary priest. He became notorious for his dissipated lifestyle and neglect of state affairs.

Heliopolis an ancient Egyptian city situated near the apex of the Nile delta at what is now Cairo. It was an important religious centre and the centre of sun worship, and was the original site of the obelisks known as Cleopatra's Needles. The name is Greek, from *hēlios* 'sun' + *polis* 'city'.

Heliopolis was also the ancient Greek name for ➤ BAALBEK.

Helios in Greek mythology, the sun personified as a god, father of ➤ PHAETHON. He is generally represented as a charioteer driving daily from east to west across the sky.

hell a place regarded in various religions as a spiritual realm of evil and suffering, often traditionally depicted as a place of perpetual fire beneath the earth where the wicked are punished after death.

The **Hell-fire Clubs** were associations of reckless and profligate young ruffians who were a nuisance to London chiefly in the early 18th century. There was a later and more famous Hell-fire Club, founded about 1745, at Medmenham Abbey.

A **Hell's Angel** is a member of any of a number of gangs ('chapters') of male motorcycle enthusiasts, first formed in California in the 1950s and originally notorious for lawless behaviour.

Hellas Greek name for Greece.

Hellene an ancient Greek; said to be descended from *Hellen*, in Greek mythology, the son or brother of Deucalion.

Hellenic the branch of the Indo-European language family comprising classical and modern Greek.

Hellenistic of or relating to Greek history, language, and culture from the death of Alexander the Great to the defeat of Cleopatra and Mark Antony by Octavian in 31 BC. During this period Greek culture flourished, spreading through the Mediterranean and into the Near East and Asia and centring on Alexandria in Egypt and Pergamum in Turkey.

Hellespont the ancient name for the Dardanelles, named after the legendary Helle, who fell into the strait and was drowned while escaping with her brother Phrixus from their stepmother, Ino, on a golden-fleeced ram (see ➤ *the* GOLDEN *Fleece*).

helot a member of a class of serfs in ancient Sparta, intermediate in status between slaves and citizens. The name comes via Latin from Greek *Heilōtes* (plural), traditionally taken as referring to Helos, a Laconian town whose inhabitants were enslaved.

hemlock in ancient Greece, the poison obtained from this plant was a method of execution; ➤ SOCRATES was put to death in this way.

hemp the fibre of the cannabis plant, extracted from the stem and used to make rope, especially with reference to execution by hanging. The name is recorded from Old English (in form *henep, hænep*) and is of Germanic origin; it is related to Greek *kannabis*.

hen while a hen may be taken as the type of a foolish woman (to be **like a hen with one chick** is to be absurdly fussy and over-anxious), a hen with her chickens may symbolize Christ, in allusion to Jesus's words in Matthew ch. 23, 'O Jerusalem, Jerusalem…how often would I have gathered thy children together, even as a hen gathereth her chickens under her wings.'

To be **as scarce as hen's teeth** is to be very rare; as he's do not possess teeth, the implication is that something is rare to the point of non-existence. Originally (mid 19th century) a US colloquialism.

Hengist and Horsa (d. 488 and d. 455), semi-mythological Jutish leaders. According to Bede the brothers were invited to Britain by the British king ➤ VORTIGERN in 449 to assist in defeating the Picts and later established an independent Anglo-Saxon kingdom in Kent.

Henley Royal Regatta the oldest rowing regatta in Europe, inaugurated in 1839 at Henley-on-Thames, Oxfordshire, as a result of the interest aroused locally by the first Oxford and Cambridge Boat Race, which took place at Henley in 1829. The regatta is held annually in the first week in July.

Hephaestus in Greek mythology, the god of fire and of craftsmen, son of Zeus and Hera, and husband of Aphrodite. He was a divine metalworker who was lame as the result of having interfered in a quarrel between his parents. His Roman equivalent is ➤ VULCAN.

heptarchy the seven kingdoms of the Angles and the Saxons believed to have been established in Britain in the 7th–8th century.

The term appears to have been introduced by 16th century historians, in accordance with their notion that there were seven Angle and Saxon kingdoms so related that one of their rulers had always the supreme position of King of the Angles.

Heptateuch the first seven books of the Bible (Genesis to Judges) collectively.

heptathlon an athletic event, in particular one for women, in which each competitor takes part in the same prescribed seven events (100 metres hurdles, high jump, shotput, 200 metres, long jump, javelin, and 800 metres).

Hera in Greek mythology, a powerful goddess, the wife and sister of Zeus and the daughter of Cronus and Rhea. She was worshipped as the queen of heaven and as a marriage goddess. Her Roman equivalent is ➤ JUNO. Her name comes from Greek *Hēra* 'lady', feminine of *hērōs* 'hero', perhaps used as a title.

Heracles Greek form of ➤ HERCULES.

Heraclitus (*c*.500 BC), Greek philosopher. He believed that fire is the origin of all things and that permanence is an illusion, everything being in a (harmonious) process of constant change.

Heraclius (d. 641), emperor of the Eastern Empire from 610, who defeated the Persian Chosroes and recaptured the wood of the Cross; he became through this a hero of medieval legend.

herald an official employed to oversee state ceremonial, precedence, and the use of armorial bearings, and (historically) to make proclamations, carry ceremonial messages, and oversee tournaments.

In the UK, a *herald* is an official of the ➤ COLLEGE *of Arms* (also known as the **Heralds' College**) or the Lyon Court ranking above a pursuivant.

Heraldry is the system by which coats of arms and other armorial bearings are devised, described, and regulated.

herb of grace the plant rue; the name is supposed to derive (like the synonymous *herb of repentance*), from the coincidence of the name with the noun and verb rue 'repent, repentance'. The name is probably now best-known from Shakespeare, as in *Richard II*: 'I'll set a bank of rue, sour herb of grace.'

Herculaneum an ancient Roman town, near Naples, on the lower slopes of Vesuvius. The volcano's eruption in AD 79 buried it deeply under volcanic ash, along with Pompeii, and thus largely preserved it until its accidental rediscovery by a well-digger in 1709. The first excavations were begun in 1738.

ex pede Herculem inferring the whole of something from an insignificant part; alluding to the story that Pythagoras calculated Hercules's height from the size of Hercules's foot.

Hercules in Greek and Roman mythology, a hero (the Greek form of his name is *Heracles*) of superhuman strength and courage; he is usually armed with a club. The son of Zeus and Alcmene, in his cradle he strangled two snakes which Hera had sent to kill him; in adult life he performed twelve immense tasks or 'labours' imposed on him, and after death was ranked among the gods. He died when the dying centaur Nessus, whom he had killed, tricked Hercules's wife Deianeira into smearing his blood on her husband's robe. The centaur's blood was a poison which consumed Hercules with fire.

The **Labours of Hercules** in order comprise the ➤ NEMEAN *lion*, the ➤ HYDRA, the ➤ ERYMANTHIAN *boar*, the ➤ CERYNITIAN *hind*, the ➤ STYMPHALIAN *birds*, the ➤ AUGEAN *stables*, the ➤ CRETAN *bull*, the ➤ *horses of* DIOMEDES, the girdle of the ➤ AMAZON, the cattle of ➤ GERYON, the golden apples of the ➤ HESPERIDES, and the capture of ➤ CERBERUS.

heresy belief or opinion contrary to orthodox religious (especially Christian) doctrine. Recorded from Middle English, the word comes via Old French and Latin from Greek *hairesis* 'choice' (in ecclesiastial Greek 'heretical sect'), from *haireomai* 'choose'.

heretic a person believing in or practising religious heresy. The word (recorded from Middle English) comes from Old French via ecclesiastical Latin from Greek *hairetikos* 'able to choose'.

Hereward the Wake (11th century), semi-legendary Anglo-Saxon rebel leader. A leader of Anglo-Saxon resistance to William I's new Norman regime, he is thought to have been responsible for an uprising centred on the Isle of Ely in 1070. *The Wake* apparently means 'the watchful one'.

herm a squared stone pillar with a carved head on top (typically of ➤ HERMES), used in ancient Greece as a boundary marker or a signpost.

Hermaphrodite in Greek mythology, a son of Hermes and Aphrodite, with whom the nymph Salmacis fell in love and prayed to be forever united. As a result Hermaphroditus and Salmacis became joined in a single body which retained characteristics of both sexes.

hermeneutics the branch of knowledge that deals with interpretation, especially of the Bible or literary texts.

Hermes in Greek mythology, the son of Zeus and Maia, the messenger of the gods, and god of merchants, thieves, and oratory. He was portrayed as a herald equipped for travelling, with broad-brimmed hat, winged shoes, and a winged rod. His Roman equivalent is ➤ MERCURY.

He was also associated with fertility, and from early times was represented by a stock or stone (a ➤ HERM), generally having a human head carved at the top and a phallus halfway up it. As patron of flocks and herds, he may be shown carrying a lamb or a calf, and thus may be taken as the equivalent of Christ as the Good Shepherd.

Hermes Trismegistus is a legendary figure regarded by Neoplatonists and others as the author of certain works on astrology, magic, and alchemy. Latin *Trismegistus* means 'thrice-greatest Hermes', in reference to ➤ THOTH, identified with *Hermes*.

Hermetic of or relating to an ancient occult tradition encompassing alchemy, astrology, and theosophy; the word comes in the mid 17th century from the name of ➤ HERMES, identified with ➤ THOTH, regarded as the founder of alchemy and astrology.

A **hermetic seal** is an airtight seal (originally as used by alchemists).

hermit a person living in solitude as a religious discipline; the word is recorded from Middle English, and comes via Old French and late Latin, from Greek *erēmitēs*, from *erēmos* 'solitary'.

Hero in Greek mythology, priestess of Aphrodite at Sestos on the European shore of the Hellespont, whose lover Leander, a youth of Abydos on the opposite shore, swam the strait nightly to visit her. One stormy night he was drowned and Hero in grief threw herself into the sea.

Herod (*c*.74–4 BC), ruled 37–4 BC, known as **Herod the Great**. He built the palace of Masada and rebuilt the Temple in Jerusalem. According to the New Testament, Jesus was born during his reign, and he ordered the ➤ MASSACRE *of the Innocents* (Matthew 2:16). (See also ➤ OUT-*Herod Herod*.)

Of his descendants, his grandson **Herod Agrippa I** (10 BC–AD 44), imprisoned St Peter and put St James the Great to death. **Herod Agrippa II** (AD 27–*c*.93), son of Herod Agrippa I, presided over the trial of St Paul (Acts 25:13 ff.).

Herod Antipas (22 BC–*c*.40 AD), son of Herod the Great, married ➤ HERODIAS and was responsible for the beheading of John the Baptist. According to the New Testament (Luke 23:7), Pilate sent Jesus to be questioned by him before the Crucifixion.

Herodias in the Bible, the wife of Herod Antipas, by a second marriage denounced as incestuous by John the Baptist, and mother of Salome.

Herodotus (5th century BC), Greek historian. Known as 'the Father of History'. He was the first historian to collect his materials systematically, test their accuracy to a certain extent, and arrange them in a well-constructed and vivid narrative.

heroic age the period in Greek history and legend before the Trojan War and its aftermath, in which the legends of the heroes were set.

herringbone an arrangement or design consisting of registers of short parallel lines, with all the lines in one register sloping one way and all the lines in the next register sloping the other way so as to resemble the bones in a fish, used especially in the weave of cloth or the placing of bricks.

herstory history viewed from a female or specifically feminist perspective. The term is recorded from the 1970s.

Hesiod (*c*.700 BC), Greek poet. One of the earliest known Greek poets, he wrote the *Theogony*, a hexametric poem on the genealogies of the gods, and *Works and Days*, which gave moral and practical advice and was the chief model for later ancient didactic poetry.

the Hesperides a group of nymphs, the daughters of Hesperus (or, in earlier versions, of Night and Hades), who were guardians, with the aid of a watchful dragon, of a tree of *golden apples* (given to Hera by Gaia) in a garden located beyond the Atlas Mountains at the western border of Oceanus, the river encircling the world. One of the labours of ➤ HERCULES was to fetch the golden apples.

Hesperus the planet Venus, the evening star.

hetaera a courtesan or mistress, especially one in ancient Greece akin to the modern geisha.

hex a magic spell, a curse. The word comes (in the mid 19th century, as a verb) via Pennsylvanian German, from German *hexen* (verb), *Hexe* (noun).

Hexateuch the first six books of the Bible (Genesis to Joshua) collectively.

Hezbollah an extremist Shiite Muslim group which has close links with Iran, created after the Iranian revolution of 1979 and active especially in Lebanon. The name comes from Arabic ḥizbullāh 'Party of God'.

Hiawatha a legendary 16th-century North American Indian teacher and chieftain, hero of a narrative poem by Henry Wadsworth Longfellow called *The Song of Hiawatha* (1855).

hibakusha in Japan, a survivor of either of the atomic explosions at Hiroshima or Nagasaki in 1945.

Hibernia Latin name for Ireland, from an alteration of *Iverna*, from Greek *I(w)ernē*, of Celtic origin; related to Irish *Éire*, *Éirinn* 'Ireland'.

hic jacet literary term for an epitaph; Latin for 'here lies', the first two words of a Latin epitaph.

hide a former measure of land used in England, typically equal to between 60 and 120 acres, being the amount that would support a family and its dependants.

hieroglyph a stylized picture of an object representing a word, syllable, or sound, as found in ancient Egyptian and certain other writing systems.

higgledy-piggledy in confusion or disorder. The expression comes (in the late 16th century) from a rhyming jingle, probably with reference to the irregular herding together of pigs.

high often used figuratively.
  High Church means of or adhering to a tradition within the Anglican Church emphasizing ritual, priestly authority, sacraments, and historical continuity with Catholic Christianity.
  High German is the standard literary and spoken form of German, originally used in the highlands in the south of Germany. The establishment of this form as a standard language owes much to the biblical translations of Martin Luther in the 16th century.
  High Mass is a Roman Catholic or Anglo-Catholic mass with full ceremonial, including music and incense and typically having the assistance of a deacon and subdeacon.
  The **high priest** was the chief priest of the historic Jewish religion.
  The **high seas** are the open ocean, especially that not within any country's jurisdiction.
  A **high table** is a table in a dining hall, typically on a platform, for the most important people, such as the fellows of a college.

High treason is the crime of betraying one's country, ➤ TREASON against the sovereign or state.

the Highlands the mountainous part of Scotland, to the north of Glasgow and Stirling, often associated with Gaelic culture
  The **Highland clearances** is the term given to the forced removal of crofters from their land in the Highlands of Scotland in the late 18th and early 19th centuries. The clearances, carried out by landlords wanting to install sheep and deer on their estates, led to extreme hardship as well as to widespread emigration to North America and elsewhere.
  Highland Games are a meeting for athletic events, playing of the bagpipes, and dancing, held in the Scottish Highlands or by Scots elsewhere. The most famous gathering is that held annually at Braemar.

highwayman a man, typically on horseback, who held up travellers at gunpoint in order to rob them; ➤ *Dick* TURPIN is a famous example. The term is recorded from the mid 17th century.

St Hilary (*c*.315–*c*.367), French bishop. In *c*.350 he was appointed bishop of Poitiers, in which position he became a leading opponent of Arianism; he was named a Doctor of the Church in 1851. His feast day is 13 January.
  Hilary term is a university term beginning in January; a term or session of the High Court beginning in January.

St Hilda (614–80), English abbess. Related to the Anglo-Saxon kings of Northumbria, she founded a monastery for both men and women at Whitby around 658, and was one of the leaders of the Celtic Church delegation at the Synod of Whitby, but accepted the decision in favour of Roman rather than Celtic customs. Her feast day is 17 November.

St Hildegard of Bingen (1089–1179), German abbess, scholar, composer, and mystic. A nun of the Benedictine order, she became Abbess of Diessem in 1136, later moving her community to Bingen. She wrote scientific works, poetry, and music, and described her mystical experiences in *Scivias*. Her feast day is 17 September.

the Hill in North America, informal name for the US Senate, or the Canadian federal parliament or government.

hillbilly an unsophisticated country person, as associated originally with the remote regions of the Appalachians.

as old as the hills of very long standing or great age. *Hills* in the Bible are a metaphor for permanence.

Hillsborough a football stadium in Sheffield, England, home of Sheffield Wednesday Football Club, which was the scene of Britain's worst sports disaster when, on 15 April 1989, 95 Liverpool fans died in a crush at an FA Cup semi-final match between Liverpool and Nottingham Forest.

Hinayana a name given by the followers of Mahayana Buddhism to the more orthodox schools of early Buddhism. The tradition died out in India, but it survived in Ceylon (Sri Lanka) as the Theravada school and was taken from there to other regions of SE Asia.

hind a *hind* is the emblem of ➤ St EUSTACE, ➤ St GILES, and ➤ St HUBERT; ➤ St ETHELDREDA, who is said to have been brought milk by two does, may also be shown with them.

Hindenburg a German airship (named for the German soldier and statesman Paul von *Hindenburg*, 1847–1934), the largest ever built, intended to provide a luxury passenger service across the Atlantic; on 6 May 1937, while landing in New Jersey from its inaugural flight, the *Hindenburg* burst into flames and was completely destroyed, with 36 of the 97 people aboard being killed.

Hindenburg Line in the First World War, a German fortified line of defence on the Western Front to which Field Marshal Paul von *Hindenburg* (1847–1934) directed retreat and which was not breached until near the end of the war; it was also called the ➤ SIEGFRIED *Line*.

Hinduism a major religious and cultural tradition of the Indian subcontinent, which developed from Vedic religion.

Hinduism is a diverse family of devotional and ascetic cults and philosophical schools, all sharing a belief in reincarnation and involving the worship of one or more of a large pantheon of gods and goddesses, including ➤ BRAHMA, ➤ SHIVA, and ➤ VISHNU (incarnate as Rama and Krishna), ➤ KALI, Durga, Parvati, and ➤ GANESH. Hindu society was traditionally based on a caste system.

Hinnom the valley of *Hinnom* is the literal name of the biblical ➤ GEHENNA.

smite hip and thigh punish unsparingly, originally with biblical allusion to Judges 15:8 of Samson and the Philistines.

hippocampus a mythical sea-monster, half horse and half fish or dolphin, represented as drawing the chariot of Neptune.

Hippocrates (*c.*460–377 BC), Greek physician, traditionally regarded as the father of medicine. His name is attached to a body of ancient Greek medical writings, probably none of which was written by him.

The **Hippocratic oath** is an oath stating the obligations and proper conduct of doctors, formerly taken by those beginning medical practice. Parts of the oath are still used in some medical schools.

Hippocrene the name of a fountain (literally, 'the fountain of the horse') on Mount Helicon sacred to the Muses, which according to legend was produced by a stroke of ➤ PEGASUS' hoof; *Hippocrene* allusively means poetic inspiration.

hippodrome in ancient Greece or Rome, a course for chariot or horse races.

hippogriff a mythical creature with the body of a horse and the wings and head of an eagle, born of the union of a male griffin and a filly.

Hippolyta queen of the Amazons given in marriage to ➤ THESEUS by ➤ HERCULES, who had conquered her and taken away her girdle, the achievement being one of his twelve labours. She had a son by Theseus called ➤ HIPPOLYTUS. According to another version she was slain by Hercules, and it was her sister Antiope who was the wife of Theseus.

Hippolytus the son of Theseus and ➤ HIPPOLYTA, banished and cursed by his father after being accused by his stepmother ➤ PHAEDRA of rape. He was killed when a sea monster, sent by Poseidon in response to the curse, frightened his horses as he drove his chariot along a seashore.

hippy especially in the 1960s, a person of unconventional appearance, typically having long hair and wearing beads, associated with a subculture involving a rejection of conventional values and the taking of hallucinogenic drugs. The name comes from *hip* meaning 'following the latest fashion, understanding, aware'.

Hiram in the Bible, name of a king of Tyre, who supplied many of the building materials for Solomon's Temple.

Hiram is also the name of a skilled worker in the building of the Temple of Solomon, a figure in the legends of freemasonry.

historiated of carved or drawn figural scenes, especially applied to an initial letter in an illuminated manuscript, decorated with designs representing scenes from the text.

the rest is history used to indicate that the events succeeding those already related are so well known that they need not be counted again.

hit the ground running proceed at a fast pace from the start with enthusiasm and dynamism. Recorded from the late 20th century, and probably referring to military personnel disembarking rapidly from a ship or helicopter.

hitch one's wagon to a star set oneself high aspirations; first recorded in Ralph Waldo Emerson's *Society and Solitude* (1870).

Hitler derogatory term for an overbearing and officious person, held to resemble the Nazi leader and German Führer Adolf *Hitler* (1889–1945).
In April 1983, it was announced that the **Hitler diaries** had been discovered. Initially accepted as genuine (extracts were published in the *Sunday Times*), it was soon demonstrated that they were forgeries.
A **Hitler moustache** is a small square moustache like that worn by Adolf Hitler.

Hittite a member of an ancient people who established an empire in Asia Minor and Syria that flourished from c.1700 to c.1200 BC. Also, a subject of this empire or one of their descendants, including a Canaanite or Syrian people mentioned in the Bible (11th to 8th century BC).

hob a sprite or hobgoblin. In Middle English the word meant 'country fellow', and was a pet form of *Rob*, short for *Robin* or *Robert*, often referring specifically to ➤ ROBIN *Goodfellow*.

hobbit a member of an imaginary race similar to humans, of small size and with hairy feet, in stories by J. R. R. Tolkien. The name was invented by Tolkien, and said by him to mean 'hole-dweller'.

hobby horse a model of a horse or a horse's head, typically of wicker, used in morris dancing or pantomime; traditionally, the framework was fastened about the waist of one of the morris dancers, so that the *hobby horse* became one of the characters.

Hobby here represents a pet form of the given name *Robin*, originally in the sense 'a small horse or pony'.

hobgoblin in mythology and fairy stories, a mischievous imp or sprite; fearsome mythical creature, a bogey.

Hobson-Jobson assimilation of adopted foreign words to the sound-pattern of the adopting language, from the title of a famous collection (1886) of Anglo-Indian words by Yule & Burnell, representing an alteration (by British hearers) of Arabic *Yā Ḥasan! Yā Husayn!* O Hasan! O Husain!, a cry used by Muslims at the ceremonies held at ➤ MUHARRAM.

Hobson's choice a choice of taking what is available or nothing at all, named (in the mid 17th century) after Thomas *Hobson* (1554–1631), a Cambridge carrier who hired out horses, giving the customer the 'choice' of the one nearest the door or none at all.

Hock designating days of or events connected with the beginning of the second week after Easter, formerly important for the payment of rents, the collection of **Hock money** (often by roughly humorous methods) for parish purposes, and as the beginning of the summer half of the rural year. The origin of the name is unknown.
Hock Monday and **Hock Tuesday** are names for the second Monday and Tuesday after Easter Sunday. **Hocktide** is the period comprising these days.

hocus-pocus deception, trickery (words often used by a person performing conjuring tricks). The expression comes (in the early 17th century)from *hax pax max Deus adimax*, a pseudo-Latin phrase used as a magic formula by conjurors.

Hodegetria an iconographical depiction of the Virgin and Child in which the Virgin with her right hand indicates the Child, who is on her left arm; the word is Greek, and means 'The Indicator of the Way'.
According to tradition the arrangement follows that of a painting originally attributed to St Luke, but the earliest surviving example is probably to be assigned to the 7th century.

hog a domesticated pig, especially a castrated male reared for slaughter; often taken as a type of undiscriminating greed. The word is recorded from Old English (in form *hogg, hocg*), perhaps of Celtic origin and related to Welsh *hwch* and Cornish *hoch* 'pig, sow'.

Go the whole hog is an informal expression meaning, do something completely or thoroughly; of several origins suggested, one interprets *hog* as the American slang term for a ten cent piece; another refers the idiom to one of William Cowper's poems (1779), which discusses Muslim uncertainty about which parts of the pig are acceptable as food, leading to the 'whole hog' being eaten, because of confusion over Muhammad's teaching.

Hogmanay in Scotland, New Year's Eve, and the celebrations that take place at this time. Also, a gift of cake etc. demanded by children at Hogmanay. The word is recorded from the early 17th century, and perhaps comes from an Anglo-Norman French form of Old French *aguillanneuf* 'last day of the year, new year's gift'.

Hogwarts in the books of J. K. Rowling, the school for wizards attended by ➤ *Harry* POT-TER.

Hohenstaufen a German dynastic family, some of whom ruled as Holy Roman emperors between 1138 and 1254, among them ➤ FREDERICK I (Barbarossa).

Hohenzollern a German dynastic family from which came the kings of Prussia from 1701 to 1918 and German emperors (of whom the last was Kaiser Wilhelm II) from 1871 to 1918.

hoi polloi the masses; the common people; from Greek (literally, 'the many'; *hoi* is the Greek word for the definite article 'the').

Holi a Hindu spring festival celebrated in February or March in honour of Krishna.

holier than thou characterized by an attitude of self-conscious virtue and piety, from Isaiah 65:5.

Raphael Holinshed (d. *c.*1580), English chronicler. Although the named compiler of *The Chronicles of England, Scotland, and Ireland* (1577), Holinshed wrote only the *Historie of England* and had help with the remainder. The revised (1587) edition was used by Shakespeare.

hollow square a body of infantry drawn up in a square with a space in the middle.

holly the branches, dark-green foliage, and red berries of this plant are traditionally used as decorations at Christmas.

The holly as an evergreen tree is used as an image of fidelity.

Hollywood a district of Los Angeles, the principal centre of the American film industry; the American film industry and the lifestyles of the people associated with it.

Sherlock Holmes an extremely perceptive private detective in stories by Arthur Conan Doyle (1859–1930). Presented through the eyes of his friend and colleague ➤ *Dr* WAT-SON, Holmes is shown as embodying the powers of rational deduction, unaffected by his occasional indulgence in cocaine. His duel with his arch-enemy Professor ➤ MORIARTY appeared to lead to his death in the ➤ REICHENBACH *Falls*, but Doyle was forced by popular demand to allow the detective to emerge unscathed. (See also ➤ SHERLOCK.)

the Holocaust the mass murder of Jews under the German Nazi regime during the period 1941–45. More than 6 million European Jews, as well as members of other persecuted groups, such as gypsies and homosexuals, were murdered at concentration camps such as Auschwitz. The term **Holocaust denial** is now used for the mistaken belief or assertion that the Holocaust did not happen, or was greatly exaggerated.

The word holocaust was originally recorded in Middle English denoting a Jewish sacrificial offering which is burnt completely on an altar; from this it was extended to mean a sacrifice on a large scale, and then a complete destruction or massacre. (It comes ultimately from Greek *holokauston*, from *holos* 'whole' + *kaustos* 'burnt'.) The specific application was introduced by historians during the 1950s, probably as an equivalent to Hebrew *hurban* and *shoah* 'catastrophe' (used in the same sense); but it had been foreshadowed by contemporary references to the Nazi atrocities as a 'holocaust' in the sense of slaughter on a large scale.

Holofernes in the Apocrypha, the Assyrian general of Nebuchadnezzar's forces, who was killed by ➤ JUDITH.

holy sacred (often in Christian phraseology).

The **Holy City** is Jerusalem; (in Christian tradition) Heaven.

Holy Cross Day is the day on which the feast of the ➤ EXALTATION *of the Cross* is held, 14 September.

A **holy day** is a day consecrated or set apart for religious observance; also called **holy day of obligation**.

The **Holy Door** is the door in the facade of St Peter's, Rome, which is nearest to the Vatican. It is normally sealed with brickwork, except during the *Holy Year*, when it is opened for the passage of those wishing to gain the Indulgence of the Holy Year.

The **Holy Family** is Christ as a child with Mary and Joseph (and often also others such as John the Baptist or St Anne), especially as a subject for a painting.

The **Holy Father** is a name for the Pope.

The **Holy Ghost** is another term for the *Holy Spirit*. The **Order of the Holy Ghost** was a French order of Knighthood (*ordre du Saint-Esprit*), instituted by Henry III in 1578.

Holy Innocents' Day is a Christian festival commemorating the ➤ MASSACRE *of the Innocents*, 28 December.

Holy Island is another name for ➤ LINDISFARNE, which from the 7th century until its sack by Vikings was an important religious centre. It is also the name of a small island off the western coast of ➤ ANGLESEY in North Wales.

The **Holy Land** is a region on the eastern shore of the Mediterranean, in what is now Israel and Palestine, revered by Christians as the place in which Christ lived and taught, by Jews as the land given to the people of Israel, and by Muslims.

The **Holy League** was any of various European alliances sponsored by the papacy during the 15th, 16th, and 17th centuries. They include the League of 1511–13, formed by Pope Julius II to expel Louis XII of France from Italy, the French Holy League (also called the Catholic League) of 1576 and 1584, a Catholic extremist league formed during the French Wars of Religion, and the Holy (or Catholic) League of 1609, a military alliance of the German Catholic princes.

The **Holy Name** is the name of Jesus as an object of formal devotion, especially in the Catholic Church.

The **holy of holies** was the inner chamber of the sanctuary in the Jewish Temple in Jerusalem, separated by a veil from the outer chamber. It was reserved for the presence of God and could be entered only by the High Priest on the Day of Atonement.

The **Holy Office** was the ecclesiastical court of the Roman Catholic Church established as the final court of appeal in trials of heresy. Formed in 1542 as part of the Inquisition, it was renamed the Sacred Congregation for the Doctrine of the Faith in 1965.

The **Holy Roman Empire** was the empire set up in western Europe following the coronation of Charlemagne as emperor in the year 800. It was created by the medieval papacy in an attempt to unite Christendom under one rule. At times the territory of the empire was extensive and included Germany, Austria, Switzerland, and parts of Italy and the Netherlands. The title of emperor, which had largely belonged to German dynasties since Otto I's coronation in 962, was formally abolished in 1806.

Holy Scripture is the sacred writings of Christianity contained in the Bible.

The **Holy See** is the papacy or the papal court; those associated with the Pope in the government of the Roman Catholic Church at the Vatican.

The **Holy Sepulchre** was the place in which the body of Jesus was laid after being taken down from the Cross. Also, the church in Jerusalem erected over the traditional site of this tomb.

The **Holy Spirit**, in Christian belief, is the third person of the Trinity; God as spiritually active in the world. In Christian art, the Holy Spirit is often represented as a ➤ DOVE.

Holy water is water blessed by a priest and used in religious ceremonies.

Holy Week is the week before Easter, starting on Palm Sunday.

Holy Writ is the Bible; writings or sayings of unchallenged authority.

A **Holy Year** in the Roman Catholic Church is a period of remission from the penal consequences of sin, granted under certain conditions for a year usually at intervals of twenty-five years. It is also locally applied to certain pilgrimages, notably Santiago de Compostela, when the feast day of the patronal saint falls on a Sunday.

hom the juice of the soma plant as a sacred drink of the Parsees.

Home Counties the English counties surrounding London, into which London has extended. They comprise chiefly Essex, Kent, Surrey, and Hertfordshire.

Home Guard the British citizen army organized in 1940 to defend the UK against invasion, finally disbanded in 1957.

home of lost causes a name for Oxford; originally a quotation from Matthew Arnold's *Essays in Criticism* (1865).

home rule the government of a colony, dependent country, or region by its own citizens, in particular as advocated for Ireland 1870–1914. The campaign for Irish home rule was one of the dominant forces in British politics in the late 19th and early 20th centuries.

Homer (8th century BC), Greek epic poet. He is traditionally held to be the author of the *Iliad* and the *Odyssey*, though modern scholarship has revealed the place of the Homeric poems in a pre-literate oral tradition. In later antiquity Homer was regarded as the greatest poet, and his poems were constantly used as a model and source by others.
   Homeric can be used of Bronze Age Greece as described in these poems.

Homo the genus of primates of which modern humans (*Homo sapiens*) are the present-day representatives. The genus *Homo* is believed to have existed for at least two million years, of which *H. sapiens* has occupied perhaps the last 400,000 years, and modern humans (*H. sapiens sapiens*) first appeared in the Upper Palaeolithic. Among several extinct species are *H. habilis*, *H. erectus*, and *H. neanderthalensis*, known from remains found at Olduvai Gorge in East Africa, and elsewhere.
   Homo sapiens is the primate species to which modern humans belong; humans regarded as a species.

homonym each of two or more words having the same written form but of different meaning and origin.

honest broker an impartial mediator in international, industrial, or other disputes. Recorded from the late 19th century, the term is a translation of German *ehrlicher Makler* as applied to himself by the German statesman Otto von Bismarck (1815–98).

honi soit qui mal y pense French phrase meaning, 'shame on him who thinks evil of it' (the motto of the ➤ *Order of the* GARTER).

honours of war privileges granted to a capitulating force, for example that of marching out with colours flying.

Captain Hook the dark and sinister pirate captain with a steel hook in place of his right hand, who in Barrie's *Peter Pan* is the mortal enemy of Peter, but who in the end falls victim to the crocodile which stalks him.

hook, line, and sinker used to emphasize that someone has been completely deceived or tricked (with allusion to the taking of bait by a fish).

by hook or by crook by one means or another; the expression is of longstanding, but there is no clear evidence for the origin.

Hoosier State informal name for Indiana; Hoosier (of unknown origin) means a native or inhabitant of Indiana.

Hooverville in the US, a shanty town built by unemployed and destitute people during the Depression of the early 1930s, named after Herbert *Hoover* (1874–1964), during whose presidency such accommodation was built.

hop-o'-my-thumb a dwarf, a pygmy; the original *Hop o' my Thumb* was the central character of a fairy story by Perrault, the minute youngest child of a poor faggot-maker who through his wit and daring saves his six elder (and larger) brothers from an ogre, and who steals the ogre's ➤ SEVEN-*league boots*.

Hopalong Cassidy a limping fictional cowboy, created by the writer Clarence E. Mulford, who wearing black clothes and riding a white horse was played in a series of films (and later a television series) by the American actor William Boyd (1898–1972).

hope one of the three theological virtues.
   Hope springs eternal means that it is human nature always to find fresh cause for optimism. A shortened version of Alexander Pope's line 'Hope springs eternal in the human breast' (*Essay on Man*, 1734).

Horace (65–8 BC), Roman poet of the Augustan period. A notable satirist and literary critic, he is best known for his *Odes*, much imitated by later ages, especially by the poets of 17th-century England.

horn in biblical and derived uses a *horn* is taken as an emblem of power and might, a means of defence or resistance.
   In Christian iconography (except as in the *horns of Moses*), the representation of *horns* on the head of a person or supernatural being are a sign of evil. *Horns* were also fancifully said to be worn by a cuckold.
   Recorded from Old English and of Germanic origin, the word comes from an Indo-European root shared by Latin *cornu* and Greek *keras*.
   A **horn of plenty** is another name for a ➤ CORNUCOPIA.

The **horns of Moses** in traditional art appear in representations of Moses in which he is shown with horns, based on a misreading of the passage describing his descent from Mount Sinai, in which the Hebrew word for 'rays of light' as surrounding his head has been mistranslated.

The **horns of the altar** are the projections, resembling a horn, at each corner of the altar in the Jewish Temple.

To be **on the horns of a dilemma** is to be faced with a decision involving equally unfavourable alternatives (a mid 16th-century source described ➤ DILEMMA as 'a horned argument (after scholastic Latin *argumentum cornutum*), the idea being that avoidance of one 'horn' of the argument resulted in impalement on the other.

Cape Horn the southernmost point of South America, on a Chilean island south of Tierra del Fuego. The region is notorious for its storms, and until the opening of the Panama Canal in 1914 constituted the only sea route between the Atlantic and Pacific Oceans. It was named after *Hoorn*, the birthplace of the Dutch navigator William C. Schouten who discovered it in 1616.

hornbook a former teaching aid consisting of a leaf of paper showing the alphabet, and often the ten digits and the Lord's Prayer, mounted on a wooden tablet and protected by a thin plate of horn.

horoscope in astrology, a forecast of a person's future, typically including a delineation of character and circumstances, based on the relative positions of the stars and planets at the time of that person's birth. The word comes ultimately from Greek *hōroskopos*, from *hōra* 'time' + *skopos* 'observer'.

horse the *horse*, used for riding, racing, and to carry and pull loads, is taken as a type of strength. (See also ➤ HORSES.)

The name of the **horse chestnut** (which is late 16th century) translates (now obsolete) botanical Latin *Castanea equina*; its fruit is said to have been an Eastern remedy for chest diseases in horses.

In the UK, the **Horse Guards** are the mounted squadrons provided from the Household Cavalry for ceremonial duties.

The **horse latitudes** are a belt of calm air and sea occurring in both the northern and southern hemispheres between the trade winds and the westerlies.

The **Horse-marines** is a name for the 17th Lancers, two troops of whom were once employed as marines during fighting in the West Indies (see also, ➤ TELL *that to the horse marines*).

horseleech in figurative use, a rapacious, insatiable person, sometimes with biblical allusion, as to Proverbs 30:15, 'The horse-leech hath two daughters, crying Give, give.'

horsepower an imperial unit of power equal to 550 foot-pounds per second (about 750 watts); the power of an engine measured in terms of this.

horses ➤ St GILES and St Hippolytus, a Roman martyr of the 3rd century are said to have been torn apart by wild *horses*. The expression **wild horses won't drag someone to something**, meaning that nothing will make someone go to a particular place, is an emphatic assertion referring to the traditional punishment of tying someone to one or more wild horses to be dragged to death or pulled apart.

To **change horses in midstream** is to change one's mind or tactics midway through a course of action. Recorded from the mid 19th century, quoted by Abraham Lincoln as the saying of 'an old Dutch farmer', and often as proverbial saying, *don't change horses in midstream*.

horseshoe a shoe for a horse, traditionally regarded as bringing good luck.

Horus in Egyptian mythology, a god regarded as the protector of the monarchy, and typically represented as a falcon-headed man. He assumed various aspects: in the myth of Isis and Osiris he was the posthumous son of the latter, whose murder he avenged, and in this aspect he was known to the Greeks as Harpocrates, most often represented as a chubby infant with a finger held to his mouth.

hosanna especially in biblical, Judaic, and Christian use, used to express adoration, praise, or joy. The word comes via Greek from Rabbinical Hebrew *hōšaʿnā*, abbreviation of biblical *hōšīʿā-nnā* 'save, we pray' (Psalm 118:25).

Hosea a Hebrew minor prophet of the 8th century BC; a book of the Bible containing his prophecies.

hospital originally, a house for the reception and entertainment of pilgrims, travellers, or strangers; any of the establishments of the ➤ KNIGHTS *Hospitallers*. Also, a charitable institution for the housing and maintenance of the needy; an asylum for the destitute, infirm, or aged (now chiefly in surviving proper names).

Hospital blues was a name for the uniform worn by wounded soldiers in the wars of 1914–18 and 1939–45.

Hospital Sunday is the Sunday nearest to St Luke's day (18 October).

hospitaller a member of a charitable order, originally the ➤ KNIGHTS *Hospitallers*.

host the bread (often **the Host**) consecrated in the Eucharist.

A *host* (in a monstrance) is the emblem of ➤ St CLARE *of Assisi*.

Recorded from Middle English, the word comes via Old French from Latin *hostia* 'victim'. •

a hostage to fortune an act, commitment, or remark which is regarded as unwise because it invites trouble or could prove difficult to live up to. The original *hostages to fortune* were a man's family, with allusion to Francis Bacon's *Essays* (1625).

hot button having a high temperature, in literal and figurative use.

A **hot button** is a topic or issue that is highly charged emotionally or politically; the term is recorded in the US as a marketing term from the early 1970s.

A **hot cross bun** is a bun marked with a cross and containing dried fruit, traditionally eaten on ➤ GOOD *Friday*.

Hot-desking is the practice in an office of allocating desks to workers when they are required or on a rota system, rather than giving each worker their own desk; the usage as a working practice is recorded from the early 1990s.

A **hot potato** is a controversial issue or situation which is awkward or unpleasant to deal with.

In North American usage, **hot-stove** denotes a discussion about a favourite sport carried on during the off season; the expression (recorded from the 1950s) is associated with discussions conducted around a heater in the winter.

Hotspur archaic term for a rash or reckless person; first recorded and best known as, the nickname of Henry Percy (1364–1403), son of the Earl of Northumberland, who was killed in battle at Shrewsbury during a rebellion against Henry IV.

Hottentot used to refer to Khoikhoi peoples of South Africa and Namibia. The term comes from Dutch, perhaps a repetitive formula in a Nama dancing-song, transferred by Dutch sailors to the people themselves, or from German *hotteren-totteren* 'stutter' (with reference to their click language).

The word *Hottentot* is first recorded in the late 17th century and was a name applied by white Europeans to the Khoikhoi. It is now regarded as offensive with reference to people and should always be avoided in favour of *Khoikhoi* or the names of the particular peoples. The only standard use for *Hottentot* in modern use is in the names of animals and plants.

houri a beautiful young woman, especially one of the virgin companions of the faithful in the Muslim Paradise. The word (recorded from the 18th century) comes through Persian from Arabic, meaning 'having eyes with a marked contrast of black and white'.

a house divided a group or organization weakened by internal dissensions, and thus unable to withstand external pressure. Alluding to Matthew 12:25.

the House that Jack built a nursery accumulation of great antiquity, possibly based on an old Hebrew original, a hymn in Sepher Haggadah, beginning 'A kid my father bought for two pieces of money', 'then came the cat and ate the kid, etc.', 'then came the dog and bit the cat, etc.', ending with the Angel of Death who killed the butcher who slew the ox, etc.; and the Holy One who slew the Angel of Death. That the English version is an early one is indicated by the reference to the 'priest, all shaven and shorn'.

Houston an inland port of Texas, linked to the Gulf of Mexico by the Houston Ship Canal. Since 1961 it has been a centre for space research and manned space flight, and is the site of the NASA Space Centre.

It is named after Samuel *Houston* (1793–1863), an American politician and military leader who led the struggle to win control of Texas and make it part of the US.

Houyhnhnm the name (intended to suggest the neigh of a horse) of a fictional race of reasoning horses in Swift's *Gulliver's Travels* (1726).

according to Hoyle according to plan or the rules. The expression comes (in the early 20th century) from Edmond *Hoyle* (1672–1769), English writer on card games.

Hubble Space Telescope an orbiting astronomical observatory launched in 1990. The telescope's fine high-resolution images are far better than can be obtained from the earth's surface.

Hubble's law a law stating that the red shifts in the spectra of distant galaxies (and hence their speeds of recession) are proportional to their distance, proposed by the American astronomer Edwin *Hubble* (1889–1953), who studied galaxies and devised a classification scheme for them.

Hubble's constant is the ratio of the speed of recession of a galaxy (due to the expansion of the universe) to its distance from the observer. The reciprocal of the constant is called *Hubble time* and represents the length of time for which the universe has been expanding, and hence the age of the universe.

St Hubert (d. 727), bishop of Maastricht and Liège; he is said to have converted to Christianity when, hunting on a Good Friday, he found himself confronted by a stag with a crucifix in its antlers (a similar story is told of ➤ St EUSTACE). His supposed hunting-horn is in the Wallace Collection. His feast day is 30 May, and his translation 3 November.

hubris in Greek tragedy, excessive pride towards or defiance of the gods, leading to ➤ NEMESIS; in extended usage, excessive pride or self-confidence.

Henry Hudson (*c.*1565–1611), English explorer. He discovered the North American bay, river, and strait which bear his name. In 1610 he attempted to winter in Hudson Bay, but his crew mutinied and set Hudson and a few companions adrift, never to be seen again.

Hudson's Bay Company a British colonial trading company set up in 1670 and granted all lands draining into Hudson Bay for purposes of commercial exploitation, principally trade in fur. The company amalgamated with the rival North-West Company in 1821 and handed over control to the new Canadian government in 1870; it is now a Canadian retail and wholesale operation.

A **Hudson's Bay blanket** is a durable woollen blanket, typically with a coloured border, originally sold by the Company, and frequently used as material for coats.

hue and cry a loud cry calling for the pursuit and capture of a criminal. In former English law, the cry had to be raised by the inhabitants of a hundred in which a robbery had been committed, if they were not to become liable for the damages suffered by the victim.

Hugh male forename, name of three saints.

Little St Hugh (d. 1255), also known as **Hugh of Lincoln**, was a boy of nine whose murdered body was discovered in a well; the rumour spread that he had been the victim of ritual murder carried out by the Jewish community in Lincoln, and as a result 19 Jews were executed. The story represents a popular form of anti-Semitic belief of the period. His feast day is 27 August.

St Hugh of Cluny (1024–1109), was abbot of ➤ CLUNY. A monk at Cluny from about *c.*1040, he became abbot in 1049, and it was during the period of his rule that the great expansion of Cluny took place. His feast day is 29 April.

St Hugh of Lincoln (*c.*1140–1200), was a Carthusian monk and bishop, noted for his scholarship, who revived the learning of the Lincoln schools. He was proverbial for his justice, as for his care for the sick and oppressed; he was also the friend and critic of three Angevin kings, Henry II, Richard, and John.

He is sometimes shown with a tame swan (from his manor at Stow), and with a chalice ornamented with the child Jesus. His feast day is 17 November and his translation, 6 October.

Huguenot a French Protestant of the 16th–17th centuries. Largely Calvinist, the Huguenots suffered severe persecution at the hands of the Catholic majority, and many thousands emigrated from France.

The name is French, an alteration (by association with the name of a Geneva burgomaster, Besançon *Hugues*) of *eiguenot*, from Dutch *eedgenot*, from Swiss German *Eidgenoss* 'confederate', from *Eid* 'oath' + *Genoss* 'associate'.

Hulda in Germanic mythology, the goddess of marriage and fertility; an aspect of the triple mother goddess who may also be personified as ➤ BERCHTA and *Mother Holle*, the ancient goddess of death.

the hulks old ships stripped of fittings and permanently moored, which during the 18th and 19th centuries were used as prisons.

Human Genome Project an international project to study the entire genetic material of a human being.

Humanae Vitae encyclical issued by Pope Paul VI in 1968, condemning artificial means of birth control.

humanism an outlook or system of thought attaching prime importance to human rather than divine or supernatural matters. Humanist beliefs stress the potential value and goodness of human beings, emphasize common human needs, and seek solely rational ways of solving human problems.

Humanism (often with capital initial) denotes a Renaissance cultural movement which turned away from medieval scholasticism and revived interest in ancient Greek and Roman thought. Among some contemporary writers, the term also denotes a system of thought criticized as being centred on the notion of the rational, autonomous self and ignoring the unintegrated and conditioned nature of the individual.

humanities learning or literature concerned with human culture, especially literature, history, art, music, and philosophy.

Humbert Humbert the stepfather of ➤ LO-LITA, in Nabokov's novel, who has an affair with his sexually precocious stepdaughter.

humours in medieval science and medicine, the four chief fluids of the body, ➤ BLOOD, ➤ PHLEGM, *yellow bile* (➤ CHOLER), and ➤ BLACK *bile* (*melancholy*), that were thought to determine a person's physical and mental qualities by the relative proportions in which they were present. Also called ➤ CARDINAL *humours*.

Sir Humphrey Appleby in the television series *Yes Minister* (1980–2) and *Yes Prime Minister* (1986–88) by Jonathan Lynn and Antony Jay, the subtle Permanent Secretary (and ultimately Cabinet Secretary) whose Civil Service wiles usually thwart the political initiatives of the Minister (and later Prime Minister) Jim Hacker, to whom he is nominally responsible.

Humpty-Dumpty the egg-like nursery-rhyme character who fell off a wall and could not be put together again; the rhyme was originally a riddle to which the answer was 'egg', and is recorded from the first half of the 19th century. *Humpty-Dumpty* is a character in Carroll's *Through the Looking-Glass* (1872).

Hun a member of a warlike Asiatic nomadic people who invaded and ravaged Europe in the 4th–5th centuries; their famous leader was ➤ ATTILA.

In extended usage, *Hun* denotes a reckless or uncivilized destroyer of something; it is also (especially in military contexts during the First and Second World Wars) a derogatory term for a German.

hundred the number equivalent to the product of ten and ten; ten more than ninety.

In Anglo-Saxon England, a *hundred* was a subdivision of a county or shire, having its own court.

The **Hundred Days** were the period of the restoration of Napoleon Bonaparte, after his escape from Elba, ending with his abdication on 22 June 1815; the immediate source was a speech delivered by Louis de Chabrol de Volvic, prefect of Paris, to Louis XVIII in 1815.

Hundred-eyed in Greek mythology is the epithet of ➤ ARGUS.

The **Hundred Flowers** are a period of debate in China 1956–7, when, under the slogan 'Let a hundred flowers bloom and a hundred schools of thought contend', citizens were invited to voice their opinions of the communist regime. It was forcibly ended after social unrest and fierce criticism of the government, with those who had voiced their opinions being prosecuted.

The **Hundred Years War** was a war between France and England, conventionally dated 1337–1453. The war consisted of a series of conflicts in which successive English kings attempted to dominate France, and began when Edward III claimed the throne of France following the death of the last Capetian king. Despite a number of English military successes, most notably Crécy, Poitiers, and (in 1415) Agincourt, the English were unable to consolidate their advantages. Under the regency of Henry VI, control of conquered territory was gradually lost to French forces, revitalized in the first instance by Joan of Arc. With the exception of Calais, all English conquests had been lost by 1453.

A **hundredweight** is a unit of weight equal to one twentieth of an imperial or metric ton.

hunger march a march undertaken by a group of people in protest against unemployment or poverty, especially any of those by unemployed workers in Britain during the 1920s and 1930s.

Hungerford a country town in Berkshire, England, where in August 1987 a survivalist named Michael Ryan killed fourteen people before committing suicide; the event is sometimes taken as the type of a massacre by a ➤ SPREE *killer*.

hunter-gatherer a member of a nomadic people who live chiefly by hunting and fishing, and harvesting wild food. All humans probably lived in this way before the Neolithic period, but now only a few groups remain.

hunter's moon the first full moon after a harvest moon.

hunting pink scarlet as worn by foxhunters; a scarlet riding-coat or the material from which it is made. It has been suggested that huntsmen took the colour because Henry II declared foxhunting a royal sport.

Huntington Beach a city on the Pacific coast, to the south of Long Beach, in southern California, which is noted as a surfing locality.

Huon of Bordeaux hero of a French 13th-century *chanson de geste*, who kills the son of Charlemagne in an affray, and to redeem his life has to make a journey to Babylon; he is assisted by the magic powers of ➤ OBERON.

Hussite a member or follower of the religious movement begun by the Bohemian religious reformer John *Huss* (*c.*1372–1415). A rector of Prague University, he supported the views of Wyclif, attacked ecclesiastical abuses, and was excommunicated in 1411. He was later tried and burnt at the stake.

After Huss's execution the Hussites took up arms against the Holy Roman Empire and demanded a set of reforms that anticipated the Reformation. Most of the demands were granted (1436), and a Church was established that remained independent of the Roman Catholic Church until 1620. An early Protestant group that arose among the Hussites, the Bohemian Brethren, is thought to have formed the basis of the Moravian Church.

hussy an impudent or immoral girl or woman; the original late Middle English sense was 'housewife', of which the word is a contraction.

Hy Brasil in Irish mythology, the name of a magical island situated off the west coast of Ireland.

hyacinth the flower of the hyacinth is supposed to have sprung from the blood of **Hyacinthus**, a beautiful boy whom the god Apollo loved but killed accidentally with a discus. From his blood Apollo caused the hyacinth to spring up.

Hyades in Greek mythology, the daughters of Atlas and sisters of the Pleiades who nursed the infant Dionysus; as a reward, they were placed as stars in the head of the constellation Taurus. In another version of the story, they were changed into stars by Zeus out of compassion for their bitter mourning for their brother Hyas.

The name of the constellation comes from Greek *Huades*, by folk etymology from *huein* 'to rain' (in reference to their weeping), but perhaps from *hus* 'pig', the Latin name of the constellation being *Suculae* 'little pigs'.

Hyblean sweet, mellifluous; from the name of *Hybla*, a town in Sicily celebrated for the honey produced on the neighbouring hills.

Mr Hyde the evil personality assumed by ➤ *Dr* JEKYLL in R. L. Stevenson's story 'Strange Case of Dr Jekyll and Mr Hyde' (1886).

Hyde Park the largest British royal park, in west central London, between Bayswater Road and Kensington Road. It contains the Serpentine, Marble Arch, the Albert Memorial, and Speakers' Corner.

Hydra in Greek mythology, a many-headed snake whose heads grew again as they were cut off, killed by ➤ HERCULES as the second of his Labours; in figurative usage, a thing which is hard to overcome or resist because of its pervasive or enduring quality or its many aspects.

hyena the expression **laugh like a hyena**, which has become proverbial, refers to the animal's characteristic cry, and it may also be taken as a type of contemptible and repellent creature.

Recorded from Middle English, the word comes via Latin from Greek *huaina*, feminine of *hus* 'pig'; the transference of the term probably being because the animal's mane was thought to resemble a hog's bristles.

Hygeia in Greek mythology, the goddess of health, daughter of Asclepius.

Hyksos a people of mixed Semitic and Asian descent who invaded Egypt and settled in the Nile delta *c.*1640 BC. They formed the 15th and 16th dynasties of Egypt and ruled a large part of the country until driven out *c.*1532 BC.

The name comes from Greek *Huksōs* (interpreted by Manetho as 'shepherd kings' or 'captive shepherds'), from Egyptian *heqa khoswe* 'foreign rulers'.

Hylas in Greek mythology, a king's son taken as his companion on the expedition of the Argonauts by Hercules; he was drowned when a water-nymph who had fallen in love with him drew him into her fountain.

Hymen originally a cry (*Hymen Hymeniae*) used at ancient Greek weddings, and understood (rightly or wrongly) as an invocation of a handsome young man of that name who had been happily married.

Mount Hymettus a mountain in Attica, famous in ancient times for its honey and marble.

hymn a religious song or poem, typically of praise to God or a god. Recorded from Old English, the word comes via Latin from Greek *humnos* 'ode or song in praise of a god or hero', used in the Septuagint to translate various Hebrew words, and hence in the New Testament and other Christian writings. (See also ➤ SING *from the same hymn sheet.*)

Hypatia (*c.*370–415), Greek philosopher, astronomer, and mathematician. Head of the Neoplatonist school at Alexandria, she wrote several learned treatises as well as devising inventions such as an astrolabe. She was murdered by a Christian mob opposed to her Neoplatonist philosophy.

Hyperborean in Greek mythology, a member of a race worshipping Apollo and living in a land of sunshine and plenty beyond the north wind.

Hyperion in Greek mythology, one of the Titans, father of the sun, moon, and dawn.

Hypermnestra in Greek mythology, one of the ➤ DANAIDS, the only one who did not murder her husband on their wedding night.

Hypnos in Greek mythology, the god of sleep, son of Nyx (Night).

hypostatic union in Christian theology, the combination of divine and human natures in the single person of Christ.

Hyrcanian of or pertaining to Hyrcania, an ancient region bordering the Caspian Sea which was noted for its wildness.

hyssop in biblical use, a wild shrub of uncertain identity whose twigs were used for sprinkling in ancient Jewish rites of purification.

I the ninth letter of the modern English alphabet, representing the Semitic consonant *yod*, which was adopted by Greek as *iota*, representing a vowel. In the 17th century a differentiation was made in the Roman alphabet, the consonant being represented by J, j (in its origin merely a variant form of I, i in certain positions), and the vowel by I, i.

I Ching an ancient Chinese manual of divination based on eight symbolic trigrams and sixty-four hexagrams, interpreted in terms of the principles of yin and yang. It was included as one of the 'five classics' of Confucianism. Its English name is *Book of Changes*, a translation of the original Chinese *yijing*.

Iago in Shakespeare's *Othello* (1602–4), the Machiavellian villain who as an apparently loyal subordinate so poisons ➤ OTHELLO's mind that he kills his innocent wife and attempts to have her supposed lover murdered. Allusions to *Iago* refer to his single-minded desire for negativism and destruction, as well as to the malice and innuendo with which he achieves his ends.

iambus a metrical foot consisting of one short (or unstressed) syllable followed by one long (or stressed) syllable. The word, which is Latin, comes from Greek *iambos* 'iambus, lampoon', from *iaptein* 'attack verbally' (because the iambic trimeter was first used by Greek satirists).

ibis a large wading bird with a long downcurved bill, long neck, and long legs, in Egyptian mythology, associated particularly with the god ➤ THOTH.

Iblis in Muslim belief, the Devil; the name means one who has nothing to expect from the mercy of God. (See also ➤ EBLIS.)

Icarus in Greek mythology, the son of ➤ DAEDALUS, who escaped from Crete using wings made by his father but was killed when he flew too near the sun and the wax attaching his wings melted so that he fell into the sea, and was drowned. *Icarus* is used allusively to denote someone who is over-ambitious in their aspirations.

Ice Age the series of glacial episodes during the Pleistocene period.

iceman a name for a prehistoric human or hominid, the frozen remains of whom are discovered preserved in (especially) glacial ice; the term has been particularly associated with the body of a man discovered in 1991 in the mountains of the Tyrol on the Italo-Austrian border.

The first newspaper reports suggested that it was the body of a medieval man; initial archaeological views selected the Bronze Age. However, carbon dating, and the analysis of skin and bone samples, soon made it clear that *Iceman* came from a much earlier period, perhaps as early as 3300 BC.

Iceni a tribe of ancient Britons inhabiting an area of SE England in present-day Norfolk and Suffolk. Their queen, ➤ BOUDICCA, led an unsuccessful rebellion against the Romans in AD 60.

Ich dien German, meaning 'I serve'; the motto of the Prince of Wales, adopted with the crest of ostrich feathers after the battle of Crécy (1346), from John of Luxembourg, King of Bohemia, who was killed in the battle.

The motto is spelt *ich diene* on the tomb of the Black Prince, Edward Prince of Wales, at the time of his burial at Canterbury in 1376.

Ichabod in the Bible, the name given by ➤ ELI's daughter-in-law to her son, used as an expression of regret, in allusion to 1 Samuel (she named the child Ichabod, saying, 'the glory is departed from Israel'), in the account of the capture of the ➤ ARK *of the Covenant* of God by the Philistines.

ichor in Greek mythology, the fluid which flows like blood in the veins of the gods.

Ichthus Latin transliteration of Greek for 'fish', which in its Greek form is an acrostic standing for 'Jesus Christ, Son of God, Saviour'.

Icknield Way an ancient pre-Roman track which crosses England in a wide curve from Wiltshire to Norfolk.

icon a painting of Christ or another holy figure, typically in a traditional style on wood, venerated and used as an aid to devotion in the Byzantine and other Eastern Churches.

In computing, an *icon* is a symbol or graphic representation on a VDU screen of a program, option, or window, especially one of several for selection.

The word is recorded from the mid 16th century in the sense 'simile' and from the late 16th century in the sense 'likeness, image' (see ➤ EIKON *Basilike*); it comes via Latin from Greek *eikōn* 'likeness, image'. Current senses date from the mid 19th century onwards.

iconoclast a destroyer of images used in religious worship, in particular, a supporter of the 8th- and 9th-century movement in the Byzantine Church which sought to abolish the veneration of icons and other religious images. The word is recorded from the mid 17th century, and comes via medieval Latin from ecclesiastical Greek *eikonoklastēs*, from *eikōn* 'likeness' + *klan* 'to break'. The title of Milton's *Eikonoklastes* (1649) can be seen as an early use.

In extended use, the word denotes someone who attacks cherished beliefs or institutions.

id the part of the mind in which innate instinctive impulses and primary processes are manifest. The word comes from Latin (literally, 'that'), translating German *es*. It was first used in this sense by Freud, following use in a similar sense by his contemporary, Georg Groddeck.

Ida a mountain in central Crete, the highest peak in the island associated in classical times with the god Zeus, who is said in some legends to have been born in a cave there.

Ida was also the name of a range of mountains in southern Phrygia where Paris of Troy was exposed as a child, in an attempt to avert the destruction he was prophesied to bring on Troy; he was brought up by shepherds there.

ides in the ancient Roman calendar, a day falling roughly in the middle of each month (the 15th day of March, May, July, and October, and the 13th of other months) from which other dates were calculated.

According to Plutarch, **beware the Ides of March** was a warning given by a soothsayer to Julius Caesar that he would be in great danger on the Ides of March; Caesar was assassinated on that day.

idol an image or representation of a god used as an object of worship; in extended usage, a person or thing that is greatly admired, loved, or revered. Recorded from Middle English, the word comes via Old French from Latin *idolum* 'image, form', used in ecclesiastical Latin in the sense 'idol', ultimately from Greek *eidos* 'form, shape'.

The **idols of the tribe, cave, market, and theatre** are four classes of fallacies referred by Bacon (1620) respectively to limitations of human mind, prejudices of idiosyncrasy, influence of words, philosophical and logical prepossessions.

Idomeneus in Greek mythology, king of Crete, son of Deucalion and descendant of Minos. He was forced to kill his son after vowing to sacrifice the first living thing that he met on his return from the Trojan war.

Idun in Scandinvian mythology, the goddess who was the guardian of the magic apples of youth; when (through the machinations of ➤ LOKI) she and her apples were captured by the giants, the gods began to age, until Loki was forced to rescue Idun.

St Ignatius Loyola (1491–1556), Spanish theologian and founder of the Society of Jesus, who after sustaining a leg wound as a soldier, renounced military life and turned to prayer and mortification. In 1534 he founded the Society of Jesus and became its first general. His *Spiritual Exercises* (1548), an ordered scheme of meditations, is still used in the training of ➤ JESUITS. His feast day is 31 July.

ignis fatuus a ➤ WILL-O'-*the*-wisp. Recorded in English from the mid 16th century, the phrase is modern Latin, literally 'foolish fire' (because of its erratic movement).

Igraine in Arthurian legend, the mother by ➤ UTHER *Pendragon* of ➤ ARTHUR; she was the wife of Gorlois of Cornwall, and Uther took on the form of Gorlois by Merlin's magic.

IHS Jesus; the letters, from late Latin, represent Greek as an abbreviation of the name of Jesus used in manuscripts and also as a symbolic or ornamental monogram. Later they are often taken as an abbreviation of various Latin phrases, notably *Iesus Hominum Salvator* 'Jesus Saviour of Men', *In Hoc Signo (vinces)* 'in this sign (thou shalt conquer)', and *In Hac Salus* 'in this (cross) is salvation'.

Iliad a Greek hexameter epic poem in twenty-four books, traditionally ascribed to Homer.

The poem tells of the climax of the Trojan War between Greeks and Trojans. The greatest of the Greek heroes, ➤ ACHILLES, retires to his tent enraged by a perceived insult. In his absence his close friend Patroclus is killed by the Trojan hero Hector; at this the grief-stricken Achilles takes the field and kills Hector.

The phrase **Iliad in a nutshell** is an allusion to a copy of Homer's *Iliad* which was supposedly small enough to be enclosed in the shell of a nut; it is used to suggest great condensation, brevity, or limitation.

Ilium the alternative name for ➤ TROY, especially the 7th-century BC Greek city.

of that ilk in Scottish usage, of the place or estate of the same name, as in *Sir Iain Moncreiffe of that Ilk*; the word is recorded from Old English (in the form *ilca*, in sense 'same'), and is of Germanic origin, related to *alike*.

Illyria an ancient region along the east coast of the Adriatic Sea, including Dalmatia and what is now Montenegro and northern Albania, subsequently the Roman province of *Illyricum*, and later divided into the provinces of Dalmatia and Pannonia. It was overrun by the Huns and the Visigoths between the 3rd and 5th centuries AD.

The name was revived, as the **Illyrian Provinces**, in 1809 after Napoleon's defeat of the Austrians and the annexation of the region to France. The region was reclaimed by Austria in 1814, retaining its identity as the kingdom of Illyria until 1849.

Imam a title of various Muslim leaders, especially of one succeeding Muhammad as leader of Shiite Islam. The word comes from Arabic *'imām* 'leader', from *'amma* 'lead the way'.

Imbolc an ancient Celtic festival celebrated on the second day of February. The name is a Celtic word, literally 'in the belly or womb', the festival being dedicated to women and fertility.

Imhotep (fl. 27th century BC), Egyptian architect and scholar. He probably designed the step pyramid built at Saqqara for the 3rd-dynasty pharaoh Djoser. Later deified, he was worshipped as the patron of architects, scribes, and doctors, while in Greece he was identified with the god ➤ ASCLEPIUS.

Imitation of Christ English name for ➤ THOMAS *à Kempis*'s manual of spiritual devotion *De Imitatione Christi*.

Immaculate Conception the doctrine that God preserved the Virgin Mary from the taint of original sin from the moment she was conceived. The belief was much disputed in the Middle Ages, but was generally accepted by Roman Catholics from the 16th century; it was defined as a dogma of the Roman Catholic Church in 1854. The **Feast of the Immaculate Conception** is celebrated on 8 December.

Immaculate Heart of Mary the heart of the Virgin Mary as an object of devotion in the Roman Catholic Church.

the Immortals a title for the royal bodyguard of ancient Persia, because their number was always the same.

imp a small, mischievous devil or sprite. The word is recorded in Old English (in form *impa, impe*) in the sense 'young shoot, scion', *impian* 'to graft', based on Greek *emphuein* 'to implant'. In late Middle English, the noun denoted a descendant, especially of a noble family, and later a child of the devil or a person regarded as such; hence a 'little devil' or mischievous child (early 17th century).

The verb *imp* in falconry, meaning repair a damaged feather in (the wing or tail of a trained hawk) by attaching part of a new feather, retains the original meaning 'to graft'.

impale in heraldry, display (a coat of arms) side by side with another on the same shield, separated by a vertical line; (of a coat of arms) adjoin (another coat of arms) in this way.

imperial of, relating to, or denoting the system of non-metric weights and measures (the ounce, pound, stone, inch, foot, yard, mile, acre, pint, gallon, etc.) formerly used for all measures in the UK, and still used for some. Also, (of a size of paper) measuring (in the UK) 762×559 mm (30×22 inches).

Imphal the capital of the state of Manipur in the far north-east of India, lying close to the border with Burma (Myanmar), which was the scene of an important victory in 1944 by Anglo-Indian forces over the Japanese.

impluvium the square basin in the centre of the atrium of an ancient Roman house, which received rainwater from an opening in the roof.

Impressionism a style or movement in painting originating in France in the 1860s, characterized by a concern with depicting the visual impression of the moment, especially in terms of the shifting effect of light and colour. The Impressionist painters repudiated both the precise academic style and the emotional concerns of Romanticism, and their interest in objective representation, especially of landscape, was influenced by early photography.

imprimatur an official licence issued by the Roman Catholic Church to print an ecclesiastical or religious book; from the Latin 'let it be printed'.

in extremis at the point of death; Latin, from *in* 'in' + *extremis*, ablative plural of *extremus* 'outermost'.

in memoriam in memory of (a dead person); Latin. The phrase was used by Tennyson in *In Memoriam A. H. H.*, a poem, published in 1850, written in memory of his friend Arthur Hallam, who died suddenly in 1833 at the age of 22.

Inca a member of a South American Indian people living in the central Andes before the Spanish conquest. Also, the supreme ruler of this people.
    The Incas arrived in the Cuzco valley in Peru *c.*1200 AD. When the Spanish invaded in the early 1530s, the Inca empire covered most of modern Ecuador and Peru, much of Bolivia, and parts of Argentina and Chile. Inca technology and architecture were highly developed despite a lack of wheeled vehicles and of writing. Their descendants, speaking Quechua, still make up about half of Peru's population.

the Incarnation in Christian theology, the embodiment of God the Son in human flesh as Jesus Christ; the word comes ultimately from ecclesiastical Latin *incarnat-* 'made flesh', from *in-* 'into' + *caro, carn-* 'flesh'.

inch a unit of linear measure equal to one twelfth of a foot. The word is recorded in late Old English (in form *ynce*) and comes from Latin *uncia* 'twelfth part', from *unus* 'one' (probably denoting a unit).

Inchcape Rock a sandstone reef in the North Sea, off the mouth of the River Tay in Scotland. A lighthouse designed by the Scottish civil engineers Robert Stevenson (1772–1850) and John Rennie was built there in 1807–*c.*1811.

incipit a manuscript, early printed book, or chanted liturgical text; the word is Latin, literally '(here) begins'.

Incitatus the name of ➤ CALIGULA's horse, made a consul by the emperor.

incline one's ear listen favourably; originally often with biblical allusion, as to Psalms 17:6.

incognito an assumed or false identity. The word comes (in the mid 17th century) from Italian, literally 'unknown'.

incubation in ancient Greece, the practice of sleeping in a temple or sacred place in the expectation of visions or revelations.

incubus a male demon believed to have sexual intercourse with sleeping women. Recorded from Middle English, the word is a late Latin form of Latin *incubo* 'nightmare', from *incubare* 'lie on'.

incunabula the early stages of the development of something; in particular, early printed books, especially those printed before 1501. The word comes from Latin, meaning literally 'swaddling clothes'.

act of indemnity a parliamentary act granting exemption from the penalties attached to any unconstitutional or illegal proceeding; in English history, applied particularly to acts of 1660 and 1690, exempting those who had taken arms or acted against Charles II and William III respectively from any penal consequences.

Independence Day another term for ➤ FOURTH *of July*.

Independence Hall a building in Philadelphia where the US Declaration of Independence was proclaimed and outside which the Liberty Bell is kept.

Index Expurgatorium a list of passages to be deleted from a book before it was considered fit for reading by Roman Catholics; a list of authors considered fit to read only after the removal of objectionable matter from their works, later included in the *Index Librorum Prohibitorum*.

Index Librorum Prohibitorum an official list of books which Roman Catholics were forbidden to read or which were to be read only in expurgated editions, as contrary to Catholic faith or morals. The first Index was issued in 1557; it was revised at intervals until abolished in 1966.

Indiaman a ship engaged in trade with India or the East or West Indies, especially an *East Indiaman* (see ➤ EAST).

Indian Mutiny a revolt of Indians against British rule, 1857–8.

Discontent with British administration resulted in widespread mutinies in British garrison towns, with accompanying massacres of white soldiers and inhabitants. After a series of sieges (most notably that of Lucknow) and battles, the revolt was put down; it was followed by the institution of direct rule by the British Crown in place of the ➤ EAST *India Company* administration.

Indian rope-trick the supposed feat, performed in the Indian subcontinent, of climbing an upright, unsupported length of rope.

Indian summer a period of unusually dry, warm weather occurring in late autumn. The name is generally attributed to the fact that the region in which the meteorological conditions in question were originally noticed was still occupied by indigenous American peoples, although other more specific explanations have been attempted.

Indianapolis name of an American heavy cruiser which in 1945 was torpedoed in Japanese waters and sank; of 1,196 men aboard, only 316 survived, many of them dying by dehydration or shark attack through the ensuing five days before they were rescued. The *Indianapolis* involved the greatest loss of life in American naval history.

Indies an archaic term for the East Indies.

Indo-European of or relating to the family of languages spoken over the greater part of Europe and Asia as far as northern India.
   The Indo-European languages have a history of over 3,000 years. Their unattested, reconstructed ancestor, Proto-Indo-European, is believed to have been spoken well before 4000 BC in a region somewhere to the north or south of the Black Sea. The family comprises twelve branches: Indic (including Sanskrit and its descendants), Iranian, Anatolian (including Hittite and other extinct languages), Armenian, Hellenic (Greek), Albanian (or Illyrian), Italic (including Latin and the Romance languages), Celtic, Tocharian (an extinct group from central Asia), Germanic (including English, German, Dutch, and the Scandinavian languages), Baltic, and Slavic (including Russian, Czech, Bulgarian, and Serbo-Croat).

Indra in Hinduism, the warrior king of the heavens, god of war and storm, to whom many of the prayers in the Rig Veda are addressed. His weapons are the thunderbolt and lightning, his helpers are the Maruts. His role in later Hinduism is small.

induct formally introduce (a member of the clergy) into possession of a benefice. The word (recorded from late Middle English) comes from Latin *inducere* 'to lead in'.

indulgence in the Roman Catholic Church, a grant by the Pope of remission of the temporal punishment in purgatory still due for sins after absolution. The unrestricted sale of indulgences by ➤ PARDONERS was a widespread abuse during the later Middle Ages.

Indus a river of southern Asia, flowing from Tibet through Kashmir and Pakistan to the Arabian Sea. Along its valley an early civilization flourished from *c.*2600 to 1760 BC, whose economic wealth was derived from well-attested sea and land trade with the rest of the Indian subcontinent. In the early 2nd millennium its power declined, probably because of incursions by the Aryans.

Industrial Revolution the rapid development of industry that occurred in Britain in the late 18th and 19th centuries, brought about by the introduction of machinery.

Indy a form of motor racing in which cars are driven round a banked, regular oval circuit which allows for racing at exceptionally high speeds. It takes place chiefly in the US, and is named (from the 1950s) from *Indianapolis* in Indiana, where the principal *Indy* event, an annual 500-mile (804.5-km) motor race, known as the **Indy 500**, is held.

Ine (d. 726), king of Wessex, who extended the prestige and power of the throne and developed an extensive legal code.

infallibility in the Roman Catholic Church, the doctrine (also called **papal infallibility**) that in specified circumstances the Pope is incapable of error in pronouncing dogma; the assertion that infallibility attached to his definitions in matters of faith and morals was made by the Vatican Council of 1870.

infangthief in Anglo-Saxon law, the right of the lord of a manor to try and to punish a thief caught within the limits of his demesne. Recorded from Old English (in form *infangenþēof*) the word means literally 'thief seized within'.

infanticide the killing of a newborn child, which in some societies (as in ancient Greece, by exposure) has in certain circumstances been sanctioned; in law, the crime of a mother killing her child within a year of birth.

infantry soldiers marching or fighting on foot; foot soldiers collectively.

inferiority complex an unrealistic feeling of general inadequacy caused by actual or supposed inferiority in one sphere, sometimes marked by aggressive behaviour in compensation.

Inferno hell (with reference to Dante's ➤ DIVINE *Comedy*).

infidel a person who does not believe in religion or who adheres to a religion other than one's own. The word originally denoted a person of a religion other than one's own, specifically a Muslim (to a Christian), a Christian (to a Muslim), or a Gentile (to a Jew).

infula in the Christian Church, either of the two ribbons on a bishop's mitre. The term comes (in the early 17th century) from Latin, denoting a woollen fillet worn by a priest or placed on the head of a sacrificial victim.

inkhorn term a word or expression used only in academic writing.

Inner Temple one of the two ➤ INNS *of Court* on the site of the Temple in London, the other being the ➤ MIDDLE *Temple*.

innings in cricket, each of two or four divisions of a game during which one side has a turn at batting; in transferred use, a period during which a person or group is active or effective.

the Innocents the young children killed by Herod in the ➤ MASSACRE *of the Innocents* after the birth of Jesus.

   Innocents' Day is a Christian festival commemorating the ➤ MASSACRE *of the Innocents*, 28 December.

Inns of Chancery the buildings in London formerly used as hostels for law students.

Inns of Court the four legal societies having the exclusive right of admitting people to the English bar; the sets of buildings in London occupied by these societies.

the Inquisition an ecclesiastical tribunal established by Pope Gregory IX c.1232 for the suppression of heresy, at a time when certain heretical groups were regarded by the Church as enemies of society. It was active chiefly in northern Italy and southern France, becoming notorious for the use of torture; condemned heretics who refused to recant were handed over to the civil authorities and could be burned at the stake. In 1542 the papal Inquisition was reinstituted to combat Protestantism, eventually becoming an organ of papal government.

   The **Inquisitor General** was the head of the ➤ SPANISH *Inquisition*.

INRI an abbreviation for Jesus of Nazareth, King of the Jews (a traditional representation in art of the inscription over Christ's head at the Crucifixion). The letters are the initials of the Latin phrase *Iesus Nazarenus Rex Iudaeorum*.

insider dealing the illegal practice of trading on the stock exchange to one's own advantage through having access to confidential information.

add insult to injury act in a way that makes a bad or displeasing situation worse. From Edward Moore's The Foundling (1748), 'This is adding insult to injuries.'

integer a whole number; a number which is not a fraction. The word is recorded from the early 16th century, as an adjective meaning 'entire, whole', and comes from Latin, 'intact, whole'.

intelligence quotient a number representing a person's reasoning ability (measured using problem-solving tests) as compared to the statistical norm or average for their age, taken as 100. Abbreviated as **IQ**.

intelligentsia intellectuals or highly educated people as a group, especially when regarded as possessing culture and political influence. The word comes (in the early 20th century) from Russian *intelligentsiya*, from Polish *inteligencja*, from Latin *intelligentia*.

intercalary of a day or month, inserted in the calendar to harmonize it with the solar year, e.g. 29 February in leap years.

interdict in the Roman Catholic Church, a sentence debarring a person, or especially a place, from ecclesiastical functions and privileges; in English history, referring particularly to the papal interdict laid on England in 1208.

International any of four associations founded to promote socialist or communist action.

   The First International was formed by Karl Marx in London in 1864 as an international working men's association and was dissolved twelve years later after internal wrangling between Marxists and anarchists. The Second International was formed in Paris in 1889 to celebrate the 100th anniversary of the French Revolution and, although gravely weakened by the First World War, still survives as a loose association of social democrats.

The Third International, also known as the Comintern, was formed by the Bolsheviks in 1919 to further the cause of world revolution. Active if seldom effective between the wars, it was abolished in 1943 as a gesture towards the Soviet Union's war allies. The Fourth International, a body of Trotskyist organizations, was formed in 1938 in opposition to the policies of the Stalin-dominated Third International.

International Brigade a group of volunteers (mainly from Europe and the US) which was raised internationally by foreign communist parties and which fought on the Republican side in the Spanish Civil War.

International Court of Justice a judicial court of the United Nations which replaced the Cour Permanente de Justice in 1945 and meets at The Hague.

International Phonetic Alphabet an internationally recognized set of phonetic symbols developed in the late 19th century, based on the principle of strict one-to-one correspondence between sounds and symbols.

the Internationale a revolutionary song composed in France in the late 19th century. It was adopted by French socialists and subsequently by others, and was the official anthem of the USSR until 1944.

Internet an international computer network providing electronic mail and information from computers in educational institutions, government agencies, and industry, accessible to the general public via modem links.

Interpol an organization based in Paris that coordinates investigations made by the police forces of member countries into crimes with an international dimension. Originally, the name was the telegraphic address of the International Criminal Police Commission, founded in 1923.

the Interregnum the period in English history from the execution of Charles I in 1649 to the Restoration of Charles II in 1660.

intestines intestines are the emblem of ➤ *St* ERASMUS.

intifada the Palestinian uprising against Israeli occupation of the West Bank and Gaza Strip, beginning in 1987. The word comes from Arabic *intifāḍa* 'an uprising' (literally 'a jumping up as a reaction to something') from *intifaḍa* 'be shaken, shake oneself'.

the Intolerable Acts derogatory term for four measures enacted by the British Parliament in 1774 against the American colonies, by which the harbour of Boston was closed until restitution was made for the tea destroyed at the ➤ BOSTON *Tea Party*, the charter of the Massachusetts colony was abrogated, British officials charged with capital offences as a result of carrying out law enforcement could elect to go to England or another colony for trial, and new arrangements for billeting British troops on American households were made.

Inuit the members of an indigenous people of northern Canada and parts of Greenland and Alaska.

The peoples inhabiting the regions from NW Canada to western Greenland prefer to be called *Inuit* rather than *Eskimo*, and this term now has official status in Canada. By analogy, the term *Inuit* is also used, usually in an attempt to be politically correct, as a synonym for *Eskimo* in general. However, this latter use, in including people from Siberia who are not Inupiaq-speakers, is, strictly speaking, not accurate.

Les Invalides founded by Louis XIV in 1670 as a military hospital, and later the resting place of Napoleon Bonaparte and others.

Invention of the Cross a festival, held on 3 May (Holy Rood Day), commemorating the reputed finding of the Cross of Christ by ➤ *St* HELENA, mother of the emperor Constantine, in AD 326 (*invention* here meant 'coming upon, finding').

invincible ignorance in theological terms, ignorance which the person concerned does not have the means to overcome; the term is a translation of scholastic Latin *ignorantia invinciblis*, in the *Summa Theologiae* of ➤ THOMAS *Aquinas*.

invisibility in a number of legends, conferred on the wearer by an article of clothing, as a ring or helmet.

The **Invisible Man** was the central character of H. G. Wells's novel of that name (1897), about a scientist who discovers (in the end, disastrously for himself) how to make himself invisible; because he can only appear visible by wearing clothing, the typical image of him is shrouded in a big coat with hat and heavy gloves.

The **invisible hand** is the doctrine of laissez-faire economics, as formulated by Adam Smith.

invita Minerva when one is not in the mood; without inspiration (a Latin phrase meaning 'Minerva (the goddess of wisdom) unwilling').

Io in Greek mythology, a priestess of Hera who was loved by ➤ ZEUS. Trying to protect her from the jealousy of Hera, Zeus turned Io into a heifer. Hera sent a gadfly to torture the heifer, which then fled across the world and finally reached Egypt, where Zeus turned her back into human form.

The *Bosporus* ('cow's passage') and the *Ionian* Sea are reputed to have been crossed by Io, and derive their names from her story.

Iona a small island in the Inner Hebrides, off the west coast of Mull. It is the site of a monastery founded by St Columba in about 563, which became the centre for Celtic Christian missions in Scotland.

Ionia in classical times, the central part of the west coast of Asia Minor, which had long been inhabited by Hellenic people (the Ionians) and was again colonized by Greeks from the mainland from about the 8th century BC.

Ionian a member of an ancient Hellenic people inhabiting Attica, parts of western Asia Minor, and the Aegean islands in preclassical times. They were apparently displaced from some areas by the Dorians in the 11th or 12th century BC but retained their settlements in Attica, especially Athens, where they were responsible for some of the greatest achievements of classical Greece. They also colonized the islands that became known as the Ionian Islands.

Ionian mode in music, the mode represented by the natural diatonic scale C–C (the major scale).

Ionic relating to or denoting a classical order of architecture characterized by a column with scroll shapes (volutes) on either side of the capital.

iota the ninth (and smallest) letter of the Greek alphabet (I, ι), transliterated as 'i'.

Often used, as in **not one iota**, to mean an extremely small amount.

Iphigenia in Greek mythology, the daughter of ➤ AGAMEMNON, who was obliged to offer her as a sacrifice to Artemis when the Greek fleet was becalmed on its way to the Trojan War. However, in some accounts, Artemis saved her life and took her to Tauris in the Crimea, where she became a priestess until rescued by her brother Orestes.

ipsissima verba the precise words; the phrase is Latin.

IRA abbreviation for the *Irish Republican Army*, the military arm of Sinn Fein, aiming for union between the Republic of Ireland and Northern Ireland. The IRA was formed during the struggle for independence from Britain in 1916–21.

Irgun a right-wing Zionist organization founded in 1931. During the period when it was active (1937–48) it carried out violent attacks on Arabs and Britons in its campaign to establish a Jewish state; it was disbanded after the creation of Israel in 1948.

Iris in Greek mythology, the goddess of the rainbow, who acted as a messenger of the gods.

Irish Free State the name for southern Ireland from 1921 until 1937.

iron often in figurative use to mean stern and unyielding.

The **iron age** was originally the Greek and Roman poets' name for the last and worst period of human history, succeeding the gold, silver, and brazen ages; in allusive reference, an age of wickedness, cruelty, or oppression.

In archaeology, the *Iron Age* denotes a prehistoric period that followed the Bronze Age, when weapons and tools came to be made of iron. It is conventionally taken as beginning in the early 1st millennium BC, but iron-working began with the Hittites in Anatolia in *c*.1400 BC. Its arrival in Britain was associated with the first Celtic immigrants in about the 6th century BC. In much of Europe it ended at the Roman period, but outside the Roman Empire it continued to the 4th–6th centuries AD.

The **Iron Chancellor** was the nickname of the German statesman Otto von Bismarck (1815–98), Chancellor of the German Empire (1871–90).

The **Iron Cross** is the highest German military decoration for bravery, originally awarded in Prussia (instituted 1813) and revived by Hitler in 1939.

The **Iron Crown of Lombardy** was the hereditary crown of the ancient kings of Lombardy, so called from having a circlet of iron inserted, reputed to have been made from one of the nails of the Cross.

The **Iron Curtain** was a notional barrier separating the former Soviet bloc and the West prior to the decline of communism that followed the political events in eastern Europe in 1989. The phrase is particularly associated with a speech by Winston Churchill in 1946, 'From Stettin in the Baltic to Trieste in the Adriatic an iron curtain has descended across the Continent,' although the term in relation to the Soviet Union and her sphere of influence is recorded intermittently from 1920.

The **Iron Duke** was a nickname of the Duke of Wellington (1769–1852), recorded from the mid 19th century.

The iron entered into someone's soul means that someone became deeply and permanently affected by imprisonment or illtreatment. It comes from the Latin *ferrum pertransit animam ejus*, a mistranslation in the Vulgate of the Hebrew, literally 'his person entered into the iron', i.e., he was placed in chains or fetters.

An **iron hand in a velvet glove** is ruthlessness disguised by courtesy; recorded in Carlyle's *Latter-day Pamphlets* (1850) as defined by Napoleon.

The **Iron Lady** is the nickname of Margaret Thatcher (1925–), given her in January 1976 by the Soviet defence ministry newspaper *Red Star*, which accused her of trying to revive the Cold War.

The **iron mask** was that worn by the **Man in the Iron Mask**, a political prisoner in France at the time of Louis XIV, said by some to be a brother of the king, who was made to wear a mask supposedly of iron; he died in the Bastille in 1703, and his identity is still disputed.

An **iron triangle** is a grouping of three power bases for mutual defence and support, as for example the Pentagon, the defence industry, and Congress.

ironclad a 19th-century warship with armour plating; the term was originally used particularly of such ships during the American Civil War (see ➤ MONITOR).

Ironside nickname of Edmund II, king of England (c.998–1016); the name is noted in the *Anglo-Saxon Chronicle* as given him for his bravery.

Ironsides a nickname for the Parliamentary leader Oliver Cromwell (1599–1658). In the English Civil War, Cromwell's cavalry troopers were called *Ironsides* by their Royalist opponents in allusion to their hardiness in battle.

Isaac in the Bible, a Hebrew patriarch, son of ➤ ABRAHAM and Sarah and father of ➤ JACOB and Esau, whom Abraham was commanded by God to sacrifice. Because of his obedience to God, Isaac was spared; a ram caught in a thicket nearby was substituted for the boy.

Isaiah a major Hebrew prophet of Judah in the 8th century BC, who taught the supremacy of the God of Israel and emphasized the moral demands on worshippers. Also, a book of the Bible containing his prophecies (and, it is generally thought, those of at least one later prophet).

Iseult a princess in medieval legend. According to one account, she was the sister or daughter of the king of Ireland, the wife of King Mark of Cornwall, and loved by ➤ TRISTRAM. In another account, she was the daughter of the king of Brittany and wife of Tristram.

Ishmael in the Bible, a son of ➤ ABRAHAM and ➤ HAGAR, his wife Sarah's maid, driven away with his mother after the birth of Isaac (Genesis 16:12). *Ishmael* (or Ismail) is also important in Islamic belief as the traditional ancestor of Muhammad and of the Arab peoples. In allusive use, *Ishmael* denotes an outcast.

Ishtar a Babylonian and Assyrian goddess of love and war whose name and functions correspond to those of the Phoenician goddess ➤ ASTARTE.

Isidore male forename, name of two saints.

St Isidore of Seville (c.560–636), was a Spanish archbishop and Doctor of the Church. He is noted for his *Etymologies*, an encyclopedic work used by many medieval authors. His feast day is 4 April.

St Isidore the farmer (c.1080–1130), is the Spanish patron of Madrid, and of farmers; he worked as a labourer on a farm near Madrid, and according to one legend was once seen being assisted in his ploughing by a second team of white oxen driven by angels. His emblem is a sickle, and his feast day is 15 May.

Isis in Egyptian mythology, a goddess of fertility, wife of Osiris and mother of ➤ HORUS. Her worship spread to western Asia, Greece, and Rome, where she was identified with various local goddesses, and became the focus of one of the major mystery religions, involving enactment of the myth of the death and resurrection of ➤ OSIRIS.

Islam the religion of the Muslims, a monotheistic faith regarded as revealed through Muhammad as the Prophet of Allah.

Founded in the Arabian peninsula in the 7th century AD, Islam is now the professed faith of nearly a billion people worldwide, particularly in North Africa, the Middle East, and parts of Asia. The ritual observances and moral code of Islam were said to have been given to Muhammad as a series of revelations, which were codified in the Koran. Islam is regarded by its adherents as the last of the revealed religions, and Muhammad is seen as the last of the prophets, building on and perfecting the examples and teachings of Abraham, Moses, and Jesus. There are two major branches in Islam, ➤ SUNNI and ➤ SHIA.

The name comes from Arabic *'islām* 'submission', from *'aslama* 'submit (to God)'.

Islands of the Blessed (in classical mythology) a land, traditionally located near the place where the sun sets, to which the souls of the good were taken to enjoy a life of eternal bliss.

Islington person a term used to denote a middle-class, socially aware person with left-wing views, characteristics supposedly typical of Islington residents, and harking back to the *parlour pink* of a previous generation. *Islington person* is seen as a typical supporter of ➤ NEW *Labour* who, while rejecting the brash self-interest of ➤ ESSEX *man*, is nevertheless similarly insulated by material wealth from the harshest pressures of modern society.

Ismaili a member of a branch of Shiite Muslims that seceded from the main group in the 8th century because of their belief that Ismail, the son of the sixth Shiite imam, should have become the seventh imam. The Ismailis eventually split into many sects, of which the best known is the Nizari sect, headed by the ➤ AGA *Khan*.

Israel the Hebrew nation or people. According to tradition they are descended from the patriarch Jacob (also named *Israel*), whose twelve sons became founders of the twelve tribes. Also called **children of Israel**.

Israel was also used as the name of the northern kingdom of the Hebrews (*c.*930–721

BC), formed after the reign of Solomon, whose inhabitants were carried away to captivity in Babylon.

The name comes from Hebrew *Yiśrā'ēl* 'he that strives with God', from the story of Jacob's wrestling at Penuel with a man by whom he was given an angelic blessing, in Genesis 32:28, 'Thy name shall be no more Jacob, but Israel.'

Israfel in Muslim tradition, the angel of music, who will sound the trumpet on the Day of Judgement.

Issachar in the Bible, a Hebrew patriarch, son of Jacob and Leah (Genesis 30:18); the tribe of Israel traditionally descended from him.

issuant in heraldry, (of the upper part of an animal) shown rising up or out from another bearing, especially from the bottom of a chief or from behind a fess.

it sex appeal; the term is first recorded of the mysterious 'Mrs Bathurst' in Kipling's *Traffics and Discoveries* (1904). The usage was reinforced by the romantic novelist Elinor Glyn in her novel *It* (1927).

The American actress Clara Bow (1905–65), who starred in the film of Glyn's novel, was subsequently known as the **It Girl**. The term came to be used for an actress or model, regarded as vivacious and outgoing, and having particular sex appeal; in later use, it also denotes a young woman typifying the latest fashion and social success.

italic of the sloping kind of typeface used especially for emphasis or distinction and in foreign words; (of handwriting) modelled on 16th-century Italian handwriting, typically cursive and sloping and with elliptical or pointed letters.

Ithaca an island off the western coast of Greece in the Ionian Sea, the legendary home of ➤ ODYSSEUS.

ITMA title of a British radio comedy series (1939–49); *ITMA* was originally the acronym for a *Daily Express* headline of 2 May 1939, 'It's that man again…! At the head of a cavalcade of seven black motor cars Hitler swept out of his Berlin Chancellery last night on a mystery journey.'

Ivan the Terrible name given to Ivan IV (1530–84), grand duke of Muscovy and first tsar of Russia. He captured Kazan, Astrakhan, and Siberia, but the Tartar siege of Moscow and the Polish victory in the

Livonian War (1558–82) left Russia weak and divided. In 1581 he killed his eldest son Ivan in a fit of rage, the succession passing to his mentally handicapped second son Fyodor.

Ivanhoe the hero of Scott's novel (1819) of that name, a knight of noble Saxon lineage at the time of the Crusades; he becomes a friend and supporter of Richard the Lionheart, despite the traditional enmity between Normans and Saxons, which Scott presents as having survived from the 11th century.

ivory this hard creamy-white substance composing the main part of the tusks of an elephant, walrus, or narwhal, was formerly used to make ornaments and other articles.

In classical belief, the **ivory gate** was the gate through which false dreams pass; in Virgil's *Aeneid*, it is said that the spirits of the dead send false dreams to humankind through the *ivory gate*, and true dreams through the *gate of horn*.

An **ivory tower** is a state of privileged seclusion or separation from the facts and practicalities of the real world; the term is recorded from the early 20th century, translating French *tour d'ivoire*, used by the writer Sainte-Beuve (1804–69).

ivy in classical times, the *ivy* was sacred to Bacchus (the ➤ THYRSUS was sometimes wreathed with ivy). A branch or bush of ivy was the traditional sign of a vintner's shop or tavern, giving rise to the expression ➤ *Good* WINE *needs no bush.*

Ivy was sometimes regarded as unlucky, and is traditionally opposed to the *holly* at times of celebration.

The **Ivy League** is a group of long-established universities in the eastern US having high academic and social prestige. It includes Harvard, Yale, Princeton, and Columbia. The term refers to the ivy traditionally growing over the walls of these establishments.

Iwo Jima a small volcanic island, the largest of the Volcano Islands in the western Pacific. During the Second World War it was the heavily fortified site of a Japanese airbase, and its attack and capture in 1944–5 was one of the severest US campaigns. It was returned to Japan in 1968.

The photograph of the American Marines raising the flag at Iwo Jima on 23 February 1945 became one of the most famous images of the Pacific War; the event is commemorated by the Marines' Memorial near ➤ AR-LINGTON.

Ixion in Greek mythology, a king punished by Zeus for attempting to seduce Hera by being pinned to a fiery wheel that revolved unceasingly through the underworld.

Izvestia a Russian daily newspaper founded in 1917 as the official organ of the Soviet government. It has continued to be published independently since the collapse of communist rule and the break-up of the Soviet Union. The name is from Russian *izvestiya* 'news'.

Jj

J the tenth letter of the modern English alphabet, originally a modification of the letter I. In the 17th century the two forms of the letter came to be differentiated, i remaining for the vowel and j being used for the consonant, with the capital form of the latter, J, being introduced.

jabberwocky invented or meaningless language, nonsense, from the title of a nonsense poem in Lewis Carroll's *Through the Looking Glass* (1871), about the monstrous *Jabberwock*.

J'accuse title of the open letter written by Émile Zola to the President of the French Republic protesting at the trial and conviction of Alfred Dreyfus (see ➤ DREYFUSARD).

jacinth in early use, a gem of a blue colour, probably a sapphire, mentioned in Exodus 28:19 as being in the high priest's breastplate, and in Revelation 21:20 a stone in the wall of the New Jerusalem; the name comes (in Middle English) from an Old French or medieval Latin alteration of Latin *hyacinthus* 'hyacinth'. In modern usage, *jacinth* denotes a reddish-orange gem variety of zircon.

Jack pet name of the given name John. The term was originally (in late Middle English) used to denote an ordinary man, and in the mid 16th century, a youth, hence the ➤ KNAVE in cards, and the use of the word to denote a male animal. The word is also used for a number of devices saving human labour, as if one had a helper. The general sense of 'labourer' arose in the early 18th century, and since the mid 16th century, the notion of 'smallness' has arisen.

Jack and Jill is a nursery rhyme, in which *Jack* and *Jill*, who go up a hill for water, both fall down, with Jack breaking his crown and Jill tumbling after; it has been suggested that the origin is political, with Jack and Jill representing Henry VII's ministers Empson and Dudley, who were executed soon after Henry VIII's accession. An alternative explanation is that the rhyme is of Scandinavian origin, in the story of two children (Hjuki and Bil) who were stolen by the moon while drawing water. In North American usage, a

Jack and Jill party is a party held for a couple soon to be married, to which both men and women are invited.

Jack and the Beanstalk is a fairy story, recorded from the mid 18th century, about a poor boy who sells his mother's cow for a handful of beans; she throws them angrily away, but the ones that have fallen into the garden root and grow into an enormous plant. Jack climbs the beanstalk, and discovers a ferocious giant; with magic help, he first steals from the giant and then by a trick contrives his death. A beanstalk is proverbially fast-growing, but in this story it may also represent the Norse world-ash ➤ YGGDRASIL.

Jack Frost is a personification of frost; recorded from the early 19th century.

Jack Horner is a nursery-rhyme character, 'Little Jack Horner', said to have 'pulled out a plum' from a 'Christmas pie'; it has been suggested that this refers to a real Jack Horner who cheated his way into property at the dissolution of the monasteries.

A **jack-in-office** is a self-important minor official; the term is recorded from the early 18th century.

A **jack-in-the-box** is a toy consisting of a box containing a figure on a spring which pops up when the lid is opened; the term is recorded from the early 18th century.

A **Jack-in-the-green** is a man or boy enclosed in a wooden or wicker pyramidal framework covered with leaves, in traditional May Day celebrations.

A **jack of all trades and master of none** is a traditional expression (from the early 17th century) for a person who tries to master too many skills and thus learns none of them properly.

A **jack-o'lantern** was originally a man with a lantern, a night watchman; from this, an ignis fatuus or ➤ WILL-*o-the-wisp*. The term in these senses is recorded from the 17th century. From the mid 19th century, *jack-o'-lantern* has also been used (originally in the US) for a lantern made from a hollowed-out pumpkin or turnip in which holes are cut to represent facial features, typically made at Halloween.

A **Jack Russell** is a terrier of a small working breed with short legs, named after the

Revd John (*Jack*) *Russell* (1795–1883), an English clergyman famed in fox-hunting circles as a breeder of such terriers.

Jack Sprat, in the 16th and 17th centuries, was a name for a very small man, a dwarf; in the nursery rhyme, recorded from the late 17th century, *Jack Sprat* is the husband who 'could eat no fat', while his wife 'could eat no lean'.

Jack tar is an informal name for a sailor, recorded from the late 18th century.

Jack the Giant-killer is a nursery tale of Northern origin, known in England from very early times. Jack was the son of a Cornish farmer, and lived in the days of King Arthur, who by his ingenuity acquired a coat that made him invisible, shoes which gave him great speed in running, and a magic sword. With the help of these, he destroyed all the giants in the land.

Jack the Ripper was an unidentified 19th-century English murderer. In 1888 at least six prostitutes were brutally killed in the East End of London, the bodies being mutilated in a way that indicated a knowledge of anatomy. The authorities received taunting notes from a person calling himself *Jack the Ripper* and claiming to be the murderer, but the cases remain unsolved despite a wide variety of names being suggested.

jackal the *jackal* was traditionally supposed to go in front of the lion and hunt up prey for him, and from this was called **the lion's provider**.

The name is recorded in English from the early 17th century; by the end of the century, it was used to denote a person seen as behaving like a jackal, especially one in a subservient relation to another. More recently, it has acquired connotations of cunning and treachery.

jackass a male ass or donkey; the word is recorded from the early 18th century, and from the early 19th century has also denoted a stupid person, a fool.

jackboot a large leather military boot reaching to the knee, used as a symbol of cruel or authoritarian behaviour or rule, and now particularly associated with German soldiers during the Nazi regime.

jackdaw noted for its inquisitiveness, its ability to mimic the sound of words, and its propensity to steal bright objects. It is also mentioned allusively in reference to the fable of a jackdaw which decked itself out in peacock's feathers to impress the other birds.

jackpot a large cash prize in a game or lottery, especially one that accumulates until it is won. The term was originally used in a form of poker, where the pool or pot accumulated until a player could open the bidding with two jacks or better.

jackrabbit a hare found on the prairies and steppes of North America, sometimes taken as a type of swift-footedness. The name is a contraction of *jackass-rabbit*, so called from its long ears.

Jacob in the Bible, a Hebrew patriarch, the younger of the twin sons of ➤ ISAAC and Rebecca, who persuaded his brother ➤ ESAU to sell him his birthright and tricked him out of his father's blessing (Genesis 25, 27).

Jacob married his cousin ➤ RACHEL and (through the deception of their father, his uncle ➤ LABAN) her sister Leah; it was Rachel's children, his youngest sons ➤ JOSEPH and ➤ BENJAMIN who were dearest to him. His twelve sons became the founders of the twelve tribes of ancient Israel.

The piebald **Jacob sheep** was named originally from the story in Genesis 30:40, in which Jacob, who has herded his uncle Laban's cattle and sheep, is given the speckled and brown animals for his portion.

Jacob's ladder was a ladder reaching up to heaven, seen in a dream by Jacob (Genesis 28:12), when he saw the angels of God ascending and descending; it was in the same dream that God spoke to him and promised to him and his descendants the land on which he was then lying. When he woke in the morning he set up the stone which had been his pillow to mark the place, which was later named ➤ BETHEL.

Jacob's stone is a name given to the ➤ STONE *of Scone*, said to have been the stone used by Jacob for a pillow when he had the dream of *Jacob's ladder*.

Jacobean of or relating to the reign (1603–25) of James I of England; (of furniture) in the style prevalent during the reign of James I, especially being the colour of dark oak.

Jacobin a member of a democratic club established in Paris in 1789. The Jacobins were the most radical and ruthless of the political groups formed in the wake of the French Revolution, and in association with Robespierre they instituted the Terror of 1793–4.

The term was applied to the Dominicans in Old French from their church in Paris, St Jacques (Latin, *Jacobus*), near which they built their first convent; the latter eventually became the headquarters of the French revolutionary group.

Jacobite a supporter of the deposed James II and his descendants in their claim to the British throne after the Revolution of 1688. Drawing most of their support from Catholic clans of the Scottish Highlands, Jacobites made attempts to regain the throne in 1689–90, 1715, 1719, and 1745–6, finally being defeated at the Battle of Culloden.

Jacobus de Voragine (*c.*1230–*c.*98), archbishop of Genoa and author of the ➤ GOLDEN *Legend*.

jacquerie a communal uprising or revolt, especially the revolt of the peasants of northern France against the nobles in 1357–8; the term is recorded from the early 16th century, and comes from Old French, literally 'villeins', from *Jacques*, a given name formerly used to mean 'peasant' in France.

jade a hard, typically green stone used for ornaments and implements and consisting of the minerals jadeite or nephrite. The word is recorded from the late 16th century, and comes via French from Spanish *piedra de ijada* 'stone of the flank' (i.e., stone for colic, which it was believed to cure).

Jael in the Bible (Judges 4:17) the woman who killed the commander of the Canaanite army, Sisera; when he was in flight after a defeat, she sheltered him in her tent, but when he was asleep she killed him by hammering a nail into his temples.

Jagannatha another name for ➤ JUGGER- NAUT.

Jainism a non-theistic religion founded in India in the 6th century BC by the Jina Vardhamana Mahavira as a reaction against the teachings of orthodox Brahmanism, and still practised there. The Jain religion teaches salvation by perfection through successive lives, and non-injury to living creatures, and is noted for its ascetics.

The name *Jain*, for an adherent of Jainism, comes via Hindi from Sanskrit *jaina* 'of or concerning a *Jina* (a great Jain teacher or holy man, literally 'victor')', from *ji-* 'conquer' or *iyā* 'overcome'.

Jairus's daughter in the New Testament, a synagogue leader's daughter who was raised from the dead by Jesus.

jam tomorrow a pleasant thing which is often promised but rarely materializes. From Lewis Carroll's *Through the Looking-Glass* (1871), 'The rule is jam to-morrow and jam yesterday—but never jam today.'

James male forename, name of two saints.

St James the Great was an Apostle, son of Zebedee and brother of John. He was put to death by Herod Agrippa I; afterwards, according to a Spanish tradition, his body was taken to ➤ SANTIAGO *de Compostela*, which became a major pilgrimage centre. He is traditionally seen in Spanish iconography as leading the Christian Reconquest against the Moors. His emblems are a scallop shell and a pilgrim's hat, and his feast day is 25 July.

St James the Less was also an Apostle; he is said to have been martyred by being beaten to death with a fuller's club. He may be identical with the James who was a leader of the early Christian Church at Jerusalem, also known as *the Lord's brother*. His emblem is a fuller's club, and his feast day (in the Eastern Church) is 9 October; (in the Western Church) is 1 May.

Jameson Raid an abortive raid into Boer territory made in 1895–6 by pro-British extremists led by Dr L. S. Jameson (1853–1917) in an attempt to incite an uprising among recent, non-Boer immigrants. The raid seriously heightened tension in South Africa and contributed to the eventual outbreak of the Second Boer War.

Jamshid a legendary early king of Persia, reputed inventor of the arts of medicine, navigation, and iron-working. According to legend he was king of the peris (or fairies) who was condemned to assume human form for boasting of his immortality, and ruled Persia for 700 years.

Jane the heroine of a *Daily Mirror* strip cartoon created by Norman Pett, originating in 1932, but particularly remembered for her Second World War adventures (which often involved loss of her clothing).

janissary a member of the Turkish infantry forming the Sultan's guard between the 14th and 19th centuries. The word is recorded from the early 16th century, and comes from French *ianissaire*, based on Turkish *yeniçeri*, from *yeni* 'new' + *çeri* 'troops'.

Jansenism a Christian movement of the 17th and 18th centuries, based on the writings of the Flemish Roman Catholic Cornelius Otto *Jansen*(1585–1638), a strong opponent of the Jesuits who proposed a reform of Christianity through a return to St Augustine. *Jansenism* was characterized by moral rigour and asceticism. It was the subject of papal condemnation and of persecution in France, but was tolerated in the Netherlands. Its most famous adherent was Pascal.

St Januarius (d. *c.*305), bishop of Benevento and martyr. He is patron saint of Naples, where his relics are preserved; they include a phial of his blood which is said to liquefy. His feast day is 16 November.

January the first month of the year, in the northern hemisphere usually considered the second month of winter. The name (recorded from Old English) comes from Latin *Januarius (mensis)* 'month of Janus', the Roman god who presided over doors and beginnings.

Janus in Roman mythology, an ancient Italian deity, guardian of doorways and gates and protector of the state in time of war; he is usually represented with two faces, so that he looks both forwards and backwards. In ancient Rome the doors of the shrine of Janus in the Forum were closed in times of peace; according to Livy between the time of ➤ NUMA and his own day, this happened only twice, once after the First Punic War (241 BC) and after Octavian's victory at Actium (31 BC).

Japheth in the Bible, a son of Noah, traditional ancestor of the peoples living round the Mediterranean. His name is probably to be connected with that of *Iapetus*, a Titan in Greek mythology.

jar of ointment a jar of ointment is the emblem of ➤ St MARY *Magdalene* and ➤ St MARY *of Egypt*.

jargon special words or expressions used by a particular profession or group that are difficult for others to understand. The word is recorded from late Middle English, originally in the sense 'twittering, chattering', later 'gibbering' (from Old French, of unknown origin). The modern sense dates from the mid 17th century.

Jarndyce v. Jarndyce the Chancery suit around which the plot of Dickens's *Bleak House* (1853) revolves, and which over the years has destroyed the happiness and lives of most members of the family involved as they become obsessed with pursuing their claims and waiting for the long-expected judgement; in the end, the costs of the case

are found to have consumed the whole property.

Jarrow a town in NE England, on the Tyne estuary. From the 7th century until the Viking invasions its monastery was a centre of Northumbrian Christian culture; the Venerable Bede lived and worked there. Its name is associated with a series of hunger marches to London by the unemployed during the Depression of the 1930s.

Jason in Greek mythology, the son of the king of Iolcos in Thessaly, and leader of the ➤ ARGONAUTS in the quest for the ➤ GOLDEN *Fleece*, during which Jason has to perform such tasks as yoking a pair of fire-breathing bulls for ploughing, and sowing the dragon's teeth of ➤ CADMUS, from which spring up armed men. Assisted by the sorceress ➤ MEDEA, whom he marries, he is successful in his quest, but later when he deserts her for Creusa, daughter of the king of Corinth, Medea takes vengeance by killing the princess as well as her own children by Jason.

jasper originally, any bright-coloured chalcedony other than carnelian; now, an opaque reddish-brown variety of chalcedony. In the Bible, jasper is the name of a stone in the high-priest's breastplate (Exodus 28:20); it is also one of the stones in the wall of the New Jerusalem (21:18).

Jataka any of the various stories of the former lives of the Buddha found in Buddhist literature. The name comes from Sanskrit *jātaka* 'born under'.

jaundiced affected or tinged with jealousy or resentment, bitter; the usage, recorded from the early 18th century, related to the early belief that jealousy was associated with the medical condition *jaundice*, characterized by yellowing of the skin.

Java man a fossil hominid of the Middle Pleistocene period, whose remains were found in Java in 1891.

jazz a type of music of black American origin characterized by improvisation, syncopation, and usually a regular or forceful rhythm, emerging at the beginning of the 20th century. Brass and woodwind instruments and piano are particularly associated with jazz, although guitar and occasionally violin are also used; styles include Dixieland, swing, bebop, and free jazz.

Jedi in ➤ STAR *Wars*, the name given to the mystical knightly order, trained to use the

Force, whose powers have been misused and their order almost destroyed by the renegade ➤ DARTH Vader.

Jeeves the resourceful and influential valet of ➤ Bertie WOOSTER in the novels of P. G. Wodehouse.

Judge Jeffreys (c.1645–89), Welsh judge and Chief Justice of the King's Bench from 1683, who took part in the ➤ POPISH Plot prosecutions and later became infamous for his brutal sentencing at the ➤ BLOODY Assizes.

Jehoshaphat a king of Judah in the mid 9th century BC.

Jehovah a form of the Hebrew name of God used in some translations of the Bible. The name comes from medieval Latin Iehouah, Iehoua, from Hebrew YHWH or JHVH, the consonants of the name of God, with the inclusion of vowels taken from 'ăḏōnāy 'my lord'.

A **Jehovah Witness** is a member of a fundamentalist Christian sect (the Watch Tower Bible and Tract Society) founded in the US by Charles Taze Russell (1852–1916), denying many traditional Christian doctrines (including the divinity of Christ) but preaching the Second Coming of Christ, and refusing military service and blood transfusion on religious grounds.

Jehu (842–815 BC), king of Israel, who at the invitation of Elisha led the revolt against the house of Ahab and had ➤ JEZEBEL killed; he was noted for his furious chariot-driving.

Dr Jekyll the central character of Robert Louis Stevenson's story The Strange Case of Dr Jekyll and Mr Hyde (1886). He discovers a drug which creates a separate personality (appearing in the character of ➤ Mr HYDE) into which Jekyll's evil impulses are channelled. The term **Jekyll-and-Hyde** is often used to describe someone with violent and unpredictable changes of mood and personality.

War of Jenkins's Ear a naval war between England and Spain (1739). It was precipitated by a British sea captain, Robert Jenkins, who appeared before Parliament to produce what he claimed was his ear, cut off by the Spanish while they were carrying out a search of his ship in the Caribbean. His story was probably at least partially fabricated.

Jephthah in the Bible, a judge of Israel who sacrificed his daughter in consequence of a vow that if victorious in battle he would sacrifice the first living thing that met him

on his return. A similar rash promise was made by ➤ IDOMENEUS in Greek mythology.

Jeremiah (c.650–c.585 BC), a Hebrew major prophet who foresaw the fall of Assyria, the conquest of his country by Egypt and Babylon, and the destruction of Jerusalem. The biblical ➤ LAMENTATIONS are traditionally ascribed to him.

In extended usage, a Jeremiah is a person who complains continually or foretells disaster. A jeremiad is a long, mournful complaint or lamentation, a list of woes, as uttered by the prophet.

Jericho a town in Palestine, in the West Bank north of the Dead Sea, which has been occupied from at least 9000 BC. According to the Bible, Jericho was a Canaanite city destroyed by the Israelites after they crossed the Jordan into the Promised Land; its walls were flattened by the shout of the army and the blast of the trumpets.

jeroboam a wine bottle with a capacity four times larger than that of an ordinary bottle. It is named after Jeroboam, a king of Israel 'who made Israel to sin'.

St Jerome (c.342–420), Doctor of the Church. He was secretary to Pope Damasus in Rome (382–5) before settling in Bethlehem, where he ruled a newly founded monastery and devoted his life to study. He is chiefly known for his compilation of the ➤ VULGATE.

In art Jerome is often shown in cardinal's dress, or with the lion from whose paw (according to legend) he removed a thorn; he may also have a stone in his hand as a sign of penance. His feast day is 30 September.

Jerry informal term for a German (especially in military contexts); the word is recorded from 1919.

jerry-built badly or hastily built with materials of poor quality. The term is mid 19th century, and is sometimes said to be from the name of a firm of builders in Liverpool, or to allude to the walls of Jericho, which fell down at the sound of Joshua's trumpets.

Jerusalem the holy city of the Jews, sacred also to Christians and Muslims, lying in the Judaean hills about 30 km (20 miles) from the River Jordan.

The city was captured from the Canaanites by King David of the Israelites (c.1000 BC), who made it his capital. As the site of the Temple, built by Solomon (957 BC), it became also the centre of the Jewish religion. Since then it has shared the troubled history of the area—destroyed by the Babylonians in 586 BC and by the Romans in AD 70, refounded by Hadrian as a Gentile city (AD 135) under the name of Aelia Capitolina, destroyed again by the Persians in 614, and fought over by Saracens and Crusaders in the Middle Ages.

From 1099 it was the capital of a Crusader kingdom, which persisted as a political entity until 1291, even though Jerusalem itself was captured by Saladin in 1187. Suleiman the Magnificent rebuilt its walls (1542). From 1947 the city was divided between the states of Israel and Jordan until the Israelis occupied the whole city in June 1967 and proclaimed it the capital of Israel. It is revered by Christians as the place of Christ's death and resurrection, and by Muslims as the site of the Dome of the Rock.

The **Jerusalem Bible** is a modern English translation of the Bible by mainly Roman Catholic scholars, published in 1966 and revised (as the **New Jerusalem Bible**) in 1985.

The **Jerusalem Chamber** is a room in Westminster Abbey in which Henry IV died, 20 March 1413.

A **Jerusalem cross** is a cross with arms of equal length each ending in a bar; a cross potent.

Jesse in the Bible, the father of ➤ DAVID (1 Samuel 16), represented as the first in the genealogy of Jesus Christ.

A **Jesse tree** is a representation in carving or stained glass of the genealogy of Jesus as a tree with Jesse at the base and intermediate descendants on branching scrolls of foliage. A **Jesse window** is a church window showing Jesus' descent from Jesse, typically in the form of a *Jesse tree*.

Jesu archaic form of ➤ JESUS, coming (in Middle English) from Old French. *Jesus* became the usual spelling in the 16th century, but *Jesu* was often retained in translations of the Bible, reflecting Latin vocative use.

Jesuit a member of the *Society of Jesus*, a Roman Catholic order of priests founded by ➤ St IGNATIUS *Loyola*, St Francis Xavier, and others in 1534, to do missionary work. The order was zealous in opposing the Reformation. Despite periodic persecution it has retained an important influence in Catholic thought and education.

By their enemies the Jesuits were accused of teaching that the end justifies the means, and the lax principles of casuistry put forward by a few of their moralists were ascribed to the order as a whole, thus giving rise to **jesuitical** in the sense dissembling or equivocating, in the manner once associated with Jesuits.

Jesuits' bark is an archaic term for cinchona bark, introduced into Europe from the Jesuit Missions in South America.

Jesus the central figure of the Christian religion. He conducted a mission of preaching and healing (with reported miracles) in Palestine in about AD 28–30, which is described in the Gospels, as are his arrest, death by crucifixion, and Resurrection from the dead. His followers considered him to be the Christ or Messiah and the Son of God, and belief in his Resurrection became a central tenet of Christianity.

The name comes from Christian Latin *Iesus*, from Greek *Iēsous*, from a late Hebrew or Aramaic analogous formation based on *Yĕhōšûaʿ* 'Joshua'.

jetsam unwanted material or goods that have been thrown overboard from a ship and washed ashore, especially material that has been discarded to lighten the vessel. Recorded from the late 16th century, originally as *jetson*: a contraction of *jettison*.

Jew a member of the people and cultural community whose traditional religion is Judaism and who trace their origins to the ancient Hebrew people of Israel.

The name is Middle English and comes via Old French and Latin from Greek *Ioudaios*, via Aramaic from Hebrew *yĕhūdī*, from *yĕhūḏāh* 'Judah'.

jewel in the crown the best in a particular class of assets, traditionally used in the context of British colonial possessions.

Jewish calendar a complex ancient calendar in use among Jewish people. It is a lunar calendar adapted to the solar year, normally consisting of twelve months but having thirteen months in leap years, which occur seven times in every cycle of nineteen years. The years are reckoned from the Creation (which is placed at 3761 BC); there are 12 months, with an intercalary month (First Adar) being added in leap years. The religious year begins with Nisan and ends with Adar, while the civil year begins with Tishri and ends with Elul.

Jewish New Year another term for ➤ ROSH *Hashana*.

Jewry Jews collectively; formerly also, a Jewish quarter in a town or city.

Jezebel (fl. 9th century BC), a Phoenician princess, traditionally the great-aunt of ➤ DIDO and in the Bible the wife of ➤ AHAB king of Israel. She was denounced by Elijah for introducing the worship of Baal into Israel, and was finally killed at the order of ➤ JEHU (2 Kings 10:30–37).

According to the story, when Jezebel heard that Jehu had come, she 'painted her face, and tired her head' and looked down from the window at him. At Jehu's order, she was thrown down from the window, and (following a prophecy made by Elijah) the dogs ate her body all except her skull, her feet, and the palms of her hands.

Jezreel in the Bible, the capital of Israel in the reign of Ahab; Naboth's vineyard was near to it, and it was in Jezreel that Jezebel was put to death. ➤ HOSEA later prophesied (Hosea 1:5) that guilt for the blood of Jezreel would fall on the house of Jehu, and that the nation of Israel would be destroyed in the valley of Jezreel.

Jhelum a river which rises in the Himalayas and flows through the Vale of Kashmir into Punjab, where it meets the Chenab River. It is one of the five rivers that gave Punjab its name. In ancient times it was called the Hydaspes.

jihad a holy war undertaken by Muslims against unbelievers. The name comes from Arabic *jihād*, literally 'effort', expressing, in Muslim thought, struggle on behalf of God and Islam.

Jim Crow the name of a black character in a 19th-century plantation song, with the refrain 'Wheel about and turn about and jump Jim Crow'; the name was also used in the stage presentation of a song and dance act first performed by Thomas D. Rice (1808–60). From the mid 20th century, *Jim Crow* was also used to denote racial discrimination, especially through segregation of black people in the US.

Jim Crow laws were laws which formerly ensured the segregation of black people in the US.

Jina in ➤ JAINISM, a great teacher who has attained liberation from karma; a carving or statue of such a teacher.

jingo a dated, chiefly derogatory expression for a vociferous supporter of policy (**jingoism**) favouring war, especially in the name of patriotism.

Originally (in the late 17th century) a conjuror's word, *by jingo* occurred in a popular song adopted by those supporting the sending of a British fleet into Turkish waters to resist Russia in 1878. The chorus ran: 'We don't want to fight, yet by Jingo! if we do, We've got the ships, we've got the men, and got the money too'.

jinn in Arabian and Muslim mythology, an intelligent spirit of lower rank than the angels, able to appear in human and animal forms and to possess humans, and having supernatural powers.

The name influenced the adoption from French of ➤ GENIE.

jive a lively style of dance popular especially in the 1940s and 1950s, performed to swing music or rock and roll.

Recorded from the 1920s (in the US, originally denoting meaningless or misleading speech).

Joab in the Bible, commander of ➤ DAVID's army, who put ➤ ABSALOM to death.

St Joachim in Christian tradition, the husband of St Anne and father of the Virgin Mary. He is first mentioned in an apocryphal work of the 2nd century, and then rarely referred to until much later times; scenes such as the marriage of Joachim and Anne are shown in medieval art.

In the Eastern Church the feast of St Joachim and St Anne is on 9 September; in the Western Church the feast of St Joachim was on 16 August, but is now (with St Anne) on 26 July.

Pope Joan according to a legend widely believed in the Middle Ages, a woman in male disguise who (*c.*1100) became a distinguished scholar and then pope, reigned for more than two years, and died after giving birth to a child during a procession.

St Joan of Arc (*c.*1412–31), French national heroine, known as the **Maid of Orleans**. She led the French armies against the English in the Hundred Years War, relieving besieged Orleans (1429) and ensuring that Charles VII could be crowned in previously occupied Reims. Captured by the Burgundians in 1430, she was handed over to the English, convicted of heresy, and burnt at the stake. She was canonized in 1920, and her feast day is 30 May.

Job in the Bible, a prosperous man whose patience and piety were tried by undeserved misfortunes, and who, in spite of his bitter lamentations, remained confident in the goodness and justice of God; also, the book of the Bible recounting his story.

Job is shown initially as a man who is wealthy and upright, surrounded by his family; he is reduced from this to sitting among ashes scraping with potsherds at the boils that afflict him, while his wife urges him to 'Curse God, and die.' Despite this, and despite the comforting of his friends which only aggravates his sense of despair, he remains true to his belief in God, and is in the end restored and justified.

The expression **poor as Job** means very poor. Job after his possessions are taken from him becomes a type of abject poverty; proverbial allusions to him are recorded from late Middle English.

A **Job's comforter** is a person who aggravates distress under the guise of giving comfort, with allusion to the story of the biblical patriarch, in which three friends who came to comfort him only increased his sense of injustice and wrong.

jobsworth an official who upholds petty rules even at the expense of humanity or common sense. The expression comes from the supposedly characteristic response of such a person, 'It's more than my job's worth (not) to'.

Jocasta in Greek mythology, a Theban woman, the wife of ➤ LAIUS and mother and later wife of ➤ OEDIPUS. When she discovered that she had committed incest with her son, she hanged herself.

Jockey Club an organization whose stewards are the central authority for the administration of horse racing in Britain. It was founded in 1750.

Jodrell Bank the site in Cheshire of one of the world's largest radio telescopes, with a fully steerable dish 76 m (250 ft) in diameter.

Joe an ordinary man (pet form of the given name *Joseph*); the usage is recorded from the mid 19th century.

In British usage, **Joe Bloggs** is a name for a hypothetical average man. The equivalent in North America is **Joe Blow**.

Joe Public is a name for a hypothetical representative member of the general public, or the general public personified.

Joe Sixpack is a name, chiefly in the US, for a hypothetical ordinary working man; *Sixpack* refers to a pack of six cans of beer held together with a plastic fastener.

Joel a Hebrew minor prophet of the 5th or possibly 9th century BC; a book of the Bible containing his prophecies.

St John¹ an Apostle, son of Zebedee and brother of ➤ St JAMES *the Great*; also known as **St John the Evangelist** or **St John the Divine**, said to have been persecuted under Domitian but to have survived into old age.

St John was present at the Crucifixion and it was to him that care of the Virgin Mary was confided by the dying Jesus; he is traditionally identified with the ➤ BELOVED *disciple*.

He has traditionally been credited with the authorship of the fourth Gospel, Revelation, and three epistles of the New Testament.

In Christian art he is represented with a book (for the Gospel) and his symbol of an eagle; he may also be shown with a cup holding a viper, recalling the challenge to him by a priest of Diana at Ephesus to drink poisoned wine. His feast day is 27 December.

St John² usually known as **John the Baptist**. A Jewish preacher and prophet, son of ➤ St ELIZABETH and ➤ ZACHARIAS, seen as the forerunner of Jesus: 'There was a man sent from God, whose name was John…He was not that Light, but was sent to bear witness of that Light' (John 1:6–8).

In *c.*27 AD he was preaching and baptizing on the banks of the River Jordan, and among those whom he baptized was Christ; John is reported to have said, 'I saw the Spirit descending like a dove, and it abode with him' (John 1:32).

He was beheaded by Herod Antipas after denouncing the latter's marriage to Herodias, the wife of Herod's brother Philip, and at the request of Herodias's daughter ➤ SALOME.

During his ministry John is said to have lived in the desert wearing camel's hair and eating locusts and wild honey (Matthew 3:4), and this is how he is typically represented. His feast day is 24 June.

St John³ there are a number of other saints of this name.

St John Chrysostom (*c.*347–407), bishop of Constantinople, is a Doctor of the Church. He attempted to reform the corrupt state of the court, clergy, and people; this offended many, including the Empress Eudoxia, who banished him in 403. His name means 'golden-mouthed' in Greek. His emblem is a bee, and his feast day is 27 January.

St John of God (1495–1550), is the Portuguese founder of the Brothers Hospitallers, who fought as a mercenary for Spain against the French and Turks and later worked as a shepherd and a pedlar. His feast day is 8 March.

St John of Nepomuk (c.1345–93), priest and martyr, was put to death by Wenceslas IV of Bohemia by being thrown into the river Moldau. He was later regarded as a martyr for the seal of the confession, since the story grew up that he had incurred the king's anger for refusing to reveal the contents of the queen's confession. His feast day is 16 May.

St John of the Cross (1542–91), was a Spanish mystic and poet. A Carmelite monk and priest, he joined with St Teresa of Ávila in founding the 'discalced' Carmelite order in 1568. He also wrote mystical poems. His feast day is 14 December.

John Barleycorn a personification of barley, or of malt liquor; the term is recorded from the early 17th century, in the title of a ballad of 'the bloody murther of Sir John Barleycorn'.

John Bull a personification of England or the typical Englishman, represented as a stout red-faced farmer in a top hat and high boots. The name is that of a character representing the English nation in John Arbuthnot's satire *Law is a Bottomless Pit; or, the History of John Bull* (1712).

John Company a nickname for the ➤ EAST India Company, taken over from the name *Jan Kompanie*, by which the Dutch East India Company and Dutch government were traditionally known in the East Indies; a translation (1785) of Sparrman's *Voyage to the Cape of Good Hope* notes that the Dutch as traders in this area had represented their company as 'one individual powerful prince, by the Christian name of *Jan* or *John*', and that from this the writer had told his interpreter to say 'that we were the children of *Jan Company*'.

John Hancock informal American expression for a personal signature, perhaps from the American Revolutionary leader *John Hancock* (1737–93), the first of the signatories to the ➤ DECLARATION *of Independence*.

Johnny Reb in the American Civil War, a Unionist name for a Confederate soldier.

Dr Johnson familiar name for the English lexicographer Samuel *Johnson* (1709–84), writer, critic, and conversationalist. His *A Dictionary of the English Language*, published in 1755, was and remains a landmark of lexicography.

Jean de Joinville (c.1224–1317), French chronicler, author of the *Histoire de Saint Louis*, which provides a detailed account of the Seventh Crusade (1248–54).

joker a playing card, typically bearing the figure of a jester, used in some games as a wild card; in the US, *joker* denotes a clause unobtrusively inserted in a bill or document and affecting its operation in a way not immediately apparent.

In the ➤ BATMAN stories, the *Joker* is one of Batman's villainous opponents.

A **joker in the pack** is a person whose behaviour is unexpected or unpredictable.

Jolly Roger a pirate's flag with a white skull and crossbones on a black background; the term is recorded from the late 18th century.

Jonah in the Bible, a Hebrew minor prophet, who was called by God to preach in Nineveh, but disobeyed and attempted to escape by sea; in a storm he was thrown overboard as a bringer of bad luck and swallowed by a great fish (traditionally, a whale), only to be saved and finally succeed in his mission.

The name *Jonah* is proverbially used for someone likely to bring bad luck, particularly at sea.

In the Authorized Version and other translations, a plant which grows quickly to shade the prophet is called a *gourd*; this may be referred to as **Jonah's gourd**.

Jonathan in the Bible, a son of ➤ SAUL, noted for his friendship with ➤ DAVID and killed with his father at the battle of Mount Gilboa by the Philistines. (See also ➤ BROTHER *Jonathan*.)

Indiana Jones an archaeologist, played by Harrison Ford in the film *Raiders of the Lost Ark* (1981, by Steven Spielberg) and its two sequels. A mild-mannered academic in the classroom, on the trail of a lost treasure such as the ➤ ARK *of the Covenant* or the ➤ HOLY *Grail* he is transformed into a daring adventurer armed with a bullwhip.

Inigo Jones (1573–1652), English architect and stage designer. He introduced the Palladian style to England; notable buildings include the Queen's House at Greenwich (1616) and the Banqueting Hall at Whitehall (1619). He also pioneered the use of the proscenium arch and movable stage scenery in England.

keep up with the Joneses try to maintain the same social and material standards as one's friends and neighbours; the expression derives from a comic-strip title, 'Keeping up with the Joneses—by Pop' in the New York *Globe*, 1913.

jongleur in the Middle Ages, an itinerant minstrel. The word is French, a variant of *jougleur* 'juggler', earlier *jogleor* 'pleasant, smiling', from Latin *joculator* 'joker'.

Jordan a river flowing southward for 320 km (200 miles) from the Anti-Lebanon Mountains through the Sea of Galilee into the Dead Sea. John the Baptist baptized Christ in the River Jordan. It is regarded as sacred not only by Christians but also by Jews and Muslims.

The crossing of Jordan is taken figuratively (after Numbers 33:51, in reference to the Israelites passing over Jordan to the land of Canaan) to symbolize death; the usage was reinforced by John Bunyan in the second part of *Pilgrim's Progress* (1684) in the story of Mr Standfast's crossing the river.

Jorvik Viking name for York; the name is now used in the title of the *Jorvik Viking Centre*, founded by the York Archaelogical Trust and recreating for visitors the streets of the Viking city of York as established through archaeological exploration.

Joseph in the Bible, a Hebrew patriarch, son of ➤ JACOB. He was given a coat of many colours by his father, whose favourite he was, and he exacerbated his brothers' jealousy by dreams which predicted his dominance over them, as by their sheaves in the harvest field bowing down to the sheaf of Joseph.

Sold by them into captivity in Egypt and at risk from the machinations of ➤ POTIPHAR'S wife, he attained high office in Egypt, finding favour with Pharaoh by his interpretation of the dream of seven fat and seven lean cattle, and seven full and seven thin ears of corn, as a warning against a coming famine.

The story is ultimately one of reconciliation, when his brothers come to Egypt to buy corn and are in Joseph's power; in the end the whole family of Jacob settles in Egypt.

St Joseph husband of the Virgin Mary. A carpenter of Nazareth, and by later tradition already elderly, he was betrothed to Mary at the time of the Annunciation. In Christian art, representations of the Nativity often show St Joseph a little apart from the main group, with his chin on his hand. His feast day is 19 March.

Joseph of Arimathea a member of the council at Jerusalem who, after the Crucifixion, asked Pilate for Christ's body, which he

buried in his own tomb. He is also known from the medieval story that he came to England with the ➤ HOLY *Grail* and built the first church at ➤ GLASTONBURY.

Josephine (1763–1814), Empress of France 1804–9. She married Napoleon in 1796. Their marriage proved childless and she was divorced by Napoleon in 1809. She is remembered in the (probably apocryphal) words attributed to Napoleon, 'Not tonight, Josephine' (the phrase, current by the early 20th century, does not appear in contemporary sources).

Flavius Josephus (*c*.37–*c*.100), Jewish historian, general, and Pharisee. His *Jewish War* gives an eyewitness account of the events leading up to the Jewish revolt against the Romans in 66, in which he was a leader. His *Antiquities of the Jews* is a history running from the Creation to 66.

Joshua (fl. *c*.13th century BC), the Israelite leader who succeeded ➤ MOSES; he led his people into the Promised Land, and captured ➤ JERICHO. Also, the sixth book of the Bible, named for him, telling of the conquest of Canaan and its division among the twelve tribes of Israel.

A **Joshua tree** is a yucca which grows as a tree and has clusters of spiky leaves, native to arid regions of south-western North America. The name apparently comes (in the mid 19th century) from the plant's being likened to a man brandishing a spear, with reference to Joshua 8:18 ('and Joshua stretched out his hand with the spear towards the city').

Josiah in the Bible, a king of Judah who put an end to the worship of idols and restored strict religious observance.

jot a very small amount; via Latin, from Greek *iōta*, the smallest letter of the Greek alphabet.

The phrase **not one jot or tittle** means not the smallest amount; after Matthew 5:18; *tittle* here comes from the medieval Latin for 'small stroke, accent' (see ➤ TITTLE).

Jotun in Scandinavian mythology, a member of the race of giants, enemies of the gods, dwelling in their region of **Jotunheim**.

Jove another name for ➤ JUPITER; the name comes from Latin *Jov-*, stem of Old Latin *Jovis*, replaced later by *Jupiter*. The dated English exclamation **by Jove** is recorded from the late 16th century.

Joyous Gard the castle of Lancelot in Arthurian legend. It is situated somewhere in the north, and Malory says it has been variously identified as Alnwick or Bamburgh (near Berwick-on-Tweed). Tristram once keeps Iseult there for three years; after Lancelot has to surrender Guinevere it is renamed 'Dolorous Gard'.

Don Juan legendary Spanish lover and hero of a number of stories, the type of a heartless seducer. According to a Spanish story first dramatized by Gabriel Téllez (1584–1641), he was Don Juan Tenorio of Seville.

jube a rood-loft or screen and gallery dividing the choir of a church from the nave. The word comes from Latin meaning 'bid' or 'order', and is said to be from the words *Jube, domine, benedicere*, said from it by the deacon before the reading of the Gospel.

Jubilate Psalm 100, beginning *Jubilate deo* 'rejoice in God', especially as used as a canticle in the Anglican service of matins.

jubilee a special anniversary of an event, especially one celebrating twenty-five or fifty years of a reign or activity.

In Jewish history, a jubilee is a year of emancipation and restoration, kept every fifty years; in the Roman Catholic Church, it is a period of remission from the penal consequences of sin, granted by the Roman Catholic Church under certain conditions for a year, usually at intervals of twenty-five years.

Recorded from late Middle English, the word comes via Old French from late Latin *jubilaeus (annus)* '(year) of jubilee', based on Hebrew *yōḇēl*, originally 'ram's-horn trumpet', with which the jubilee year was proclaimed.

Judaea the southern part of ancient Palestine, corresponding to the former kingdom of Judah. The Jews returned to the region after the Babylonian Captivity, and in 165 BC the Maccabees again established it as an independent kingdom. It became a province of the Roman Empire in 63 BC, and was subsequently amalgamated with Palestine.

Judah in the Bible, a Hebrew patriarch, the fourth son of Jacob. Also, the tribe of Israel traditionally descended from him, the most powerful of the twelve tribes of Israel.

Judah is also the name given to the southern part of ancient Palestine, occupied by the tribe of Judah. After the reign of Solomon

(*c.*930 BC) it formed a separate kingdom from Israel.

Judaism the monotheistic religion of the Jews. For its origins Judaism looks to the biblical covenant made by God with Abraham, and to the laws revealed to Moses and recorded in the Torah (supplemented by the rabbinical Talmud), which established the Jewish people's special relationship with God.

Since the destruction of the Temple in Jerusalem in AD 70, the rituals of Judaism have centred on the home and the synagogue, the chief day of worship being the Sabbath (sunset on Friday to sunset on Saturday), and the annual observances including Yom Kippur and Passover.

Judas one of the twelve Apostles; full name **Judas Iscariot**, who betrayed Christ to the Jewish authorities in return for ➤ THIRTY *pieces of silver*; the Gospels leave his motives uncertain. Overcome with remorse, he later committed suicide by hanging, and was buried in the ➤ POTTER's *field*.

The **Judas Bible** is an early 17th century translation in which *Judas* appears as a misprint for *Jesus*.

Judas-coloured means, of hair, red, from the medieval tradition that Judas Iscariot had red hair and beard.

A **Judas goat** is an animal used to lead others in a flock or herd to destruction, as in a slaughterhouse.

A **Judas kiss** is an act of betrayal, especially one disguised as a gesture of friendship, with biblical allusion to the betrayal of Christ, when in ➤ GETHSEMANE Judas identified their quarry to the soldiers with a kiss of greeting.

A **Judas tree** is a Mediterranean tree of the pea family, with purple flowers that typically appear before the rounded leaves; according to popular belief, Judas hanged himself on a tree of this kind.

A **Judas window** is a small aperture in a door (in some old houses, or in prison cells), through which a person can look without being noticed from the other side; a peephole.

Judas Maccabaeus (d. *c.*161 BC), Jewish leader. Leading a Jewish revolt in Judaea against Antiochus IV Epiphanes from around 167, he recovered Jerusalem and dedicated the Temple anew, and protected Judaism from Hellenization. He is the hero of the two books of the Maccabees in the Apocrypha.

St Jude an Apostle, supposed brother of James; also known as *Judas*. Thaddaeus (mentioned in St Matthew's Gospel) is traditionally identified with him. According to tradition, he was martyred in Persia with St Simon.

He may be shown holding a club, as the instrument of his martyrdom; otherwise he is seen holding a fish (while St Simon has a ship). His feast day (with St Simon) is 28 October.

judge proverbially taken as a type of gravity and sobriety.

The office of a judge is referred to as the ➤ BENCH; in the UK, a judge formally wears scarlet robes trimmed with ermine, sometimes alluded to as symbolizing the office.

In ancient Israel, a *judge* was a leader having temporary authority in the period between Joshua and the kings.

The word comes (in Middle English, via Old French) from Latin *judex*, *judic-*, from *jus* 'law' + *dicere* 'to say'.

Judgement Day the time of the ➤ LAST *Judgement*; the end of the world.

Judgement of Solomon in the Bible, the arbitration of king ➤ SOLOMON over a baby claimed by two women. He proposed cutting the baby in half, and then gave it to the woman who showed concern for its life, recognizing that the true mother was the one who would relinquish the child rather than have it harmed.

Judges the seventh book of the Bible, describing the conquest of Canaan under the leaders called 'judges' in an account that is parallel to that of the Book of Joshua and is probably more accurate historically. The book includes the stories of Deborah, Jael, Gideon, Jephthah, and Samson.

Judges' Rules in English law, rules regarding the admissibility of an accused's statements as evidence.

Judith in the Apocrypha, a rich Israelite widow who saved the town of Bethulia from Nebuchadnezzar's army by seducing the besieging general ➤ HOLOFERNES and cutting off his head while he slept. Also, a book of the Apocrypha recounting the story of Judith.

Judy the wife of Punch in the ➤ PUNCH *and Judy* show.

Juggernaut in Hinduism, the form of Krishna worshipped in Puri, Orissa, where in the annual festival his image is dragged through the streets on a heavy chariot; devotees are said formerly to have thrown themselves under its wheels.

The word *juggernaut*, meaning a large heavy vehicle, comes in extended usage from this.

The name comes via Hindi from Sanskrit *Jagannātha* 'Lord of the World'.

Jugurtha (d.104 BC), joint king of Numidia *c*.118–104. His attacks on his royal partners prompted intervention by Rome and led to the outbreak of the **Jugurthine War** (112–105). He was eventually captured by the Roman general Marius and executed in Rome.

Julian calendar a calendar introduced by the authority of Julius Caesar in 46 BC, in which the **Julian year** consisted of 365 days, every fourth year having 366 days. It was superseded by the Gregorian calendar, though it is still used by some Orthodox Churches. Dates in the Julian calendar are sometimes designated 'Old Style'.

Julian of Norwich (*c*.1342–*c*.1413), English mystic. She is said to have lived as a recluse outside St Julian's Church, Norwich. She is chiefly associated with the *Revelations of Divine Love* (*c*.1393), a description of a series of visions she had in which she depicts the Holy Trinity as Father, Mother, and Lord.

Julian the Apostate (*c*.331–63 AD), Roman emperor from 360 AD. He restored paganism as the state cult in place of Christianity, but this move was reversed after his death on campaign against the Persians; his last words are said to have been, *vicisti, Galilaee* ['you have conquered, Galilean').

Juliet the heroine of Shakespeare's *Romeo and Juliet* (1595), sometimes taken as a type of doomed young love.

A **Juliet cap** is a type of women's small ornamental cap, typically made of lace or net and often worn by brides. Recorded from the early 20th century, it is so named because it forms part of the traditional costume of the heroine of Shakespeare's *Romeo and Juliet*.

Julius Caesar (100–44 BC), Roman general and statesman. He established the First Triumvirate with ➤ POMPEY and Crassus (60), and became consul in 59, obtaining command of the provinces of Illyricum, Cisalpine Gaul, and Transalpine Gaul. Between 58 and 51 he fought the Gallic Wars, subjugating Transalpine Gaul and defeating ➤ VERCINGETORIX, invading Britain (55–54), and acquiring immense power.

Resentment at this on the part of Pompey and other powerful Romans led to civil war; in 49 BC Caesar crossed the ➤ RUBICON into Italy, and next year Pompey was defeated at Pharsalia in Thessaly.

Julius Caesar was made dictator of the Roman Empire and initiated a series of reforms, including the introduction of the Julian calendar; in Egypt he had a brief liaison with ➤ CLEOPATRA. Hostility to Caesar's autocracy culminated in his murder on the ➤ IDES (15th) of March in a conspiracy led by ➤ BRUTUS and Cassius.

July the seventh month of the year, in the northern hemisphere usually considered the second month of summer. The name is recorded from Middle English, and comes from Latin *Julius (mensis)* '(month) of July', named after Julius Caesar.

The **July monarchy** is a name for the monarchy (1830–48) of Louis Philippe, king of the French, who became king in the July Revolution of 1830.

The **July Revolution** was the revolution of 1830 in which Charles X of France was overthrown and by which Louis Philippe gained the throne as king of the French.

Jumbo name of an elephant at London Zoo, sold in 1882 to the Barnum and Bailey circus; the word had originally denoted a large and clumsy person.

Jumna a river of northern India, which rises in the Himalayas and flows in a large arc southwards and south-eastwards, through Delhi, joining the Ganges below Allahabad. Its source (Yamunotri) and its confluence with the Ganges are both Hindu holy places. Its Hindu name is *Yamuna*.

June the sixth month of the year, in the northern hemisphere usually considered the first month of summer. Recorded from Middle English, the word comes via Old French from Latin *Junius (mensis)* '(month) of June', variant of *Junonius* 'sacred to Juno'.

The **June War** is the Arab name for the ➤ SIX *Day War*.

Juneteenth Day in the US, 19 June, originally a holiday in Texas marking the day on which slaves there were emancipated.

Juno in Roman mythology, the most important goddess of the Roman state, wife of ➤ JUPITER. She was originally an ancient Italian goddess. Her Greek equivalent is ➤ HERA.

Jupiter in Roman mythology, the chief god of the Roman state religion, giver of victory, originally a sky god associated with thunder and lightning. His wife was Juno. Also called *Jove*. His Greek equivalent is ➤ ZEUS. The name is Latin, from *Jovis pater*, literally 'Father Jove'.

In astronomy, *Jupiter* is the name given to the largest planet in the solar system, a gas giant which is the fifth in order from the sun and one of the brightest objects in the night sky.

Jupiter Ammon was a deity worshipped in the Egyptian western desert, where the cult of the Egyptian god ➤ AMUN was linked with Jupiter.

Jurassic the second period of the Mesozoic era, between the Triassic and Cretaceous periods. The Jurassic lasted from about 208 to 146 million years ago. Large reptiles, including the largest known dinosaurs, were dominant on both land and sea. Ammonites were abundant, and the first birds (including Archaeopteryx) appeared.

The name comes from French *jurassique*, from the Jura mountains on the border of France and Switzerland.

Jurassic Park was the title of a thriller (1990) by Michael Crichton and the Spielberg film based on it, in which dinosaurs were cloned from fossil DNA to stock a theme park; the result was carnage as the systems for control and safety failed. *Jurassic Park* is now referred to as a type of environment where savagery prevails.

jury a body of people (typically twelve in number, giving rise to the expression ➤ TWELVE *good men and true*) sworn to give a verdict in a legal case on the basis of evidence submitted to them in court. The word is recorded from late Middle English, and comes from Old French *juree* 'oath, inquiry', from Latin *jurata*, feminine past participle of *jurare* 'swear'.

The expression **the jury is still out** means that the final decision has not been given; referring to the custom that a jury in court retires to consider its verdict.

just war in the Middle Ages, a debate among moral theologians on the circumstances in which participation in war by Christians could be justified led to St Thomas Aquinas's laying down three conditions which a *just war* must meet: it had to be authorized by the sovereign, the cause must be just, and those engaging in it must have the intention of advancing good or avoiding evil. In the 16th century a fourth condition was added by the Spanish theologian Francisco de Vitoria (d. 1546), saying that the war must be fought by 'proper means'. The phrase is recorded in English from the late 15th century.

Justinian (483–565), Byzantine emperor 527–65, husband of ➤ THEODORA. Through his general ➤ BELISARIUS he regained North Africa from the Vandals, Italy from the Ostrogoths, and Spain from the Visigoths. He codified Roman law in ➤ *the* DIGEST (529) and carried out a building programme throughout the Empire, of which St Sophia at Constantinople (532) was a part.

Jute a member of a Germanic people that (according to Bede) joined the Angles and Saxons in invading Britain in the 5th century, settling in a region including Kent and the Isle of Wight. They may have come from Jutland.

Battle of Jutland a major naval battle in the First World War, fought between the British Grand Fleet under Admiral Jellicoe and the German High Seas Fleet in the North Sea west of Jutland on 31 May 1916. Although the battle was indecisive the German fleet never again sought a full-scale engagement, and the Allies retained control of the North Sea.

Juvenal (*c*.60–*c*.140), Roman satirist. His sixteen verse satires present a savage attack on the vice and folly of Roman society, chiefly in the reign of the emperor Domitian.

Kk

K the eleventh letter of the modern English alphabet and the tenth of the ancient Roman one, corresponding to Greek *kappa*, Phoenician and general Semitic *kaph*.

K2 the highest mountain in the Karakoram range, on the border between Pakistan and China. It is the second-highest peak in the world, and was discovered in 1856 and named K2 because it was the second peak to be surveyed in the Karakoram range. It was also formerly known as *Mount Godwin-Austen* after Col. H. H. Godwin-Austen, who first surveyed it.

ka in ancient Egypt, the supposed spiritual part of an individual human being or god, which survived (with the soul) after death and could reside in a statue of the person.

Kaaba a square stone building in the centre of the Great Mosque at ➤ MECCA, the site most holy to Muslims and towards which they must face when praying. It stands on the site of a pre-Islamic shrine said to have been built by Abraham, and a sacred Black Stone is set in its south-eastern corner.

Kabbalah the ancient Jewish tradition of mystical interpretation of the Bible, first transmitted orally and using esoteric methods (including ciphers). It reached the height of its influence in the later Middle Ages and remains significant in ➤ HASIDISM.

Kaddish an ancient Jewish prayer sequence regularly recited in the synagogue service, including thanksgiving and praise and concluding with a prayer for universal peace; a form of this prayer sequence recited for the dead. The word comes from Aramaic *qaddīš* 'holy'.

Kairouan a city in NE Tunisia which is a Muslim holy city and a place of pilgrimage.

kaiser the German Emperor, the Emperor of Austria, or the head of the Holy Roman Empire; in British usage, **the Kaiser** refers particularly to Wilhelm II of Germany (1859–1941), especially in the context of the First World War.

The word is originally recorded from Middle English (in form *cayser*), from Old Norse

keisari, based on Latin *Caesar*; the modern English form (early 19th century) derives from German *Kaiser*.

The **Kaiser's War** is a name for the First World War.

Kalahari Desert a high, vast, arid plateau in southern Africa north of the Orange River, comprising most of Botswana with parts in Namibia and South Africa.

Kalevala a collection of Finnish legends transmitted orally until published in the 19th century, and now regarded as the Finnish national epic.

Kaleyard School a group of late 19th-century fiction writers, including J. M. Barrie, who described local town life in Scotland in a romantic vein and with much use of the vernacular.

Kaleyard in Scots means literally 'kitchen garden'.

Kalgoorlie a gold-mining town in Western Australia. Gold was discovered there in 1887, leading to a gold rush in the 1890s.

Kali in Hinduism, the most terrifying goddess, wife of ➤ SHIVA, often identified with Durga, and in her benevolent aspect with Parvati. She is typically depicted as black, naked, old, and hideous, with a necklace of skulls, a belt of severed hands, and a protruding bloodstained tongue. The ➤ THUGS were her devotees.

Union of the Kalmar the treaty which joined together the Crowns of Denmark, Sweden, and Norway in 1397, dissolved in 1523.

kalpa in Hindu and Buddhist tradition, an immense period of time, reckoned as 4,320 million human years, and considered to be the length of a single cycle of the cosmos (or 'day of Brahma') from creation to dissolution.

Kama the Hindu god of love, typically represented as a youth with a bowl of sugar cane, a bowstring of bees, and arrows of flowers.

Kama Sutra an ancient Sanskrit treatise on the art of love and sexual technique; the name comes from Sanskrit, from *kāma* 'love' + *sūtra* 'thread'.

kamerad especially in the First World War, used by a German-speaking soldier notifying to an enemy a wish to surrender; the word is German for 'comrade'.

kamikaze in the Second World War, a Japanese aircraft loaded with explosives and making a deliberate suicidal crash on an enemy target. The word, which is Japanese, comes from *kami* 'divinity' + *kaze* 'wind', originally referring to the gale that, in Japanese tradition, destroyed the fleet of invading Mongols in 1281.

Kandy a city in Sri Lanka, which was the capital (1480–1815) of the former independent kingdom of Kandy and contains one of the most sacred Buddhist shrines, the Dalada Maligava (Temple of the Tooth).

kangaroo court an unofficial court held by a group of people in order to try someone regarded, especially without good evidence, as guilty of a crime or misdemeanour.

kangha a comb worn in the hair as one of the five distinguishing signs of the Sikh ➤ KHALSA, symbolizing cleanliness.

Kanpur a city in Uttar Pradesh, northern India, on the River Ganges, also known as *Cawnpore*. It was the site of a massacre of British soldiers and European families in July 1857, during the Indian Mutiny.

kara a steel bangle worn on the right wrist as one of the five distinguishing signs of the Sikh ➤ KHALSA, symbolizing loyalty, commitment, and unity with God.

Karakorum an ancient city in central Mongolia, now ruined, which was the capital of the Mongol empire, established by Genghis Khan in 1220. The capital was moved by Kublai Khan to Khanbaliq (modern Beijing) in 1267, and Karakorum was destroyed by Chinese forces in 1388.

Karbala a city in southern Iraq, which is a holy city for Shiite Muslims, being the site of the tomb of Husayn, grandson of Muhammad, who was killed there in AD 680.

Anna Karenina the tragic heroine of Tolstoy's novel of that name (1875–7), whose unhappy love affair with Count Vronsky, and the pressures of a hypocritical society, end in her killing herself by throwing herself in front of a train.

karma in Hinduism and Buddhism, the sum of a person's actions in this and previous states of existence, viewed as deciding their fate in future existences. The word comes from Sanskrit *karman* 'action, effect, fate'.

In Hinduism, **karma yoga** is the discipline of selfless action as a way to perfection.

Karnak a village in Egypt on the Nile, now largely amalgamated with Luxor. It is the site of the northern complex of monuments of ancient Thebes, including the great temple of ➤ AMUN.

Fred Karno's army a type of chaotic organization, named for the comedian Fred *Karno* (1866–1941); his 'Army' was the company which gave a solid start or valuable experience to many comedians. 'We are Fred Karno's army, the ragtime infantry', perhaps referring to 'Kitchener's Army', was one of the trench songs of the First World War.

the kasbah in a North African city, the area surrounding the citadel, typically the old part of a city; the word figures in a famous supposed film line, *Come with me to the Casbah*.

Katzenjammer Kids cartoon drawn by Rudolf Dirks in 1897 for the *New York Journal*, featuring Hans and Fritz, two incorrigible children; the name *Katzenjammer* came from German *Katzen* (combining form of *Katze* 'cat') + *Jammer* 'distress'.

Kedar in the Bible, the name of a son of ➤ ISHMAEL, and of the nomadic tribe descended from him.

keelhaul in former naval practice, punish someone by dragging them through the water under the keel of a ship, either across the width or from bow to stern.

Kellogg Pact a treaty renouncing war as an instrument of national policy, signed in Paris in 1928 by representatives of fifteen nations. It grew out of a proposal made by the French Premier Aristide Briand (1862–1932) to Frank B. Kellogg (1856–1937), US Secretary of State. Also called **Kellogg–Briand Pact**.

game as Ned Kelly very brave; Ned *Kelly* (1855–80) was an Australian outlaw. Leader of a band of horse and cattle thieves and bank raiders operating in Victoria, he was eventually hanged in Melbourne. He became a folk hero.

Kelmscott the name of *Kelmscott* House, Hammersmith (named after Kelmscott Manor, Kelmscott, Oxfordshire), the home of William Morris (1834–1896), used in the name of the Kelmscott Press, which was founded there by him in 1890 and worked until 1898, printing limited editions of fine books.

kelpie a water spirit of Scottish folklore, typically taking the form of a horse, reputed to delight in the drowning of travellers. The word (recorded from the late 17th century) may come from Scottish Gaelic *cailpeach*, *colpach* 'bullock, colt'.

The later derived sense of a sheepdog of an Australian breed, originally bred from a Scottish collie, apparently comes from the name of a particular bitch, *King's Kelpie* (*c.*1879).

St Kenelm (d. 812 or 821), a prince of the Mercian royal family, who may have died in battle against the Welsh, and was buried at Winchcombe. In the later **Kenelm Legend** of the 11th century, he is said to have been murdered in infancy on the orders of a jealous sister; the whereabouts of his body was later revealed by a document in Old English, dropped by a dove on to the high altar of St Peter's, Rome, which was read by English pilgrims. His feast day is 17 July.

Kensal Green the first London cemetery (as distinct from a churchyard), opened in 1832, and used allusively as a symbol of death and burial.

Kent one of the kingdoms of Anglo-Saxon England, probably covering much the same area as the modern county in SE England.

Man of Kent a native or inhabitant of the county of Kent living to the east of the River Medway; distinguished from a **Kentish man**, a native or inhabitant of Kent living west of the River Medway.

St Kentigern (d. 612), monk and bishop, evangelist of Strathclyde and Cumbria, and associated particularly with Glasgow; he is said to have been the illegitimate grandson of a British prince, and is also known by his pet name of *Mungo*. His later legends include the story that when the queen was told by her husband to find within three days a ring which he had thrown out to sea, he comforted her by telling her that the ring had been returned in a salmon caught by one of his monks; from this, a ring and a fish appear on the arms of the city of Glasgow. His feast day is 13 January.

Kentucky Derby an annual horse race for three-year-olds at Louisville, Kentucky. First held in 1875, it is the oldest horse race in the US.

Kermit the Frog the name of the bright green frog who is one of the central characters of ➤ *the* Muppets.

kesh the uncut hair and beard worn as one of the five distinguishing signs of the Sikh ➤ Khalsa, symbolizing dedication.

kestrel figuratively (in archaic use), a contemptible person. In falconry, a *kestrel* is traditionally the bird flown by a knave.

Jack Ketch (1663–86), public executioner. His name became notorious on account of his barbarity at a number of executions, and from that (and perhaps partly also from association with the verb *catch*) it was given to the hangman in the puppet-play of Punchinello, which was introduced from Italy shortly after his death; finally, *Jack Ketch* became a generic term for an executioner.

kettle of fish originally (in late 18th-century Scotland) an expression for a kettle of fish cooked during a boating excursion or picnic, and thus applied to the picnic itself. The ironical use **a pretty kettle of fish!** is likely to be an extension of this.

St Kevin (d. *c.*618), founder and abbot of the monastic settlement ➤ Glendalough in County Wicklow. One later legend associates him with a blackbird, which is said to have laid one of her eggs on his outstretched hands while he was at prayer; Kevin remained in the same position until the egg had hatched. His feast day is 3 June.

Kew Gardens the Royal Botanic Gardens at Kew, in Richmond, London. Developed by the mother of George III with the aid of Sir Joseph Banks, the gardens were presented to the nation in 1841 and are now an important botanical institution.

kewpie American trademark name for a type of doll (also called **kewpie doll**) characterized by a large head, big eyes, chubby cheeks, and a curl or topknot on top of its head. The name comes (in the early 20th century) from an alteration of *Cupid*.

key a key (representing one's own key to a house) is often used as a symbol on a coming-of-age card.

Keys are the emblem of ➤ St Peter, St Petronilla, an early Roman martyr whose fictional legend makes her the daughter of ➤ *St*

PETER, ➤ *St* MARTHA, and St Zita, a 13th-century Luccan serving-maid.

Keystone Kops bumbling police characters in films made by Keystone, a US film company formed in 1912, remembered for its silent slapstick comedy films.

Keystone State informal name for Pennsylvania, as being the seventh or central one of the original thirteen states.

khaki a textile fabric of a dull brownish-yellow colour, in particular a strong cotton fabric used in military clothing. Dating from the mid 19th century, the word comes from an Urdu word meaning 'dust-coloured'.
  The **Khaki Election** was an informal name for the British general election of 1900, used in reference to the South African War of 1899–1902, and later also applied to the general elections, such as 1918, in which military action was a key issue.

Khalistan the name given by Sikh nationalists to a proposed independent Sikh state; the name may be compared with Arabic *khālsa* 'pure, real, proper'.

Khalsa the body or company of fully initiated Sikhs, to which devout orthodox Sikhs are ritually admitted at puberty. The Khalsa was founded in 1699 by the last Guru (Gobind Singh). Members show their allegiance by five signs (called the *five Ks*). Men take the additional name *Singh* 'lion', and women the name *Kaur* 'princess'.

Khartoum established in 1821 as an Egyptian army camp at the junction of the Blue Nile and the White Nile, and later a garrison town. In 1885 a British and Egyptian force under the command of ➤ *General* GORDON was besieged in Khartoum for ten months by the Mahdists, who eventually stormed the garrison, killing most of the defenders, including Gordon.

Khmer an ancient kingdom in SE Asia which reached the peak of its power in the 11th century, when it ruled over the entire Mekong valley from the capital at Angkor. It was destroyed by Siamese conquests in the 12th and 14th centuries.

Khmer Rouge a communist guerrilla organization which opposed the Cambodian government in the 1960s and waged a civil war from 1970, taking power in 1975. Under Pol Pot the Khmer Rouge undertook a forced reconstruction of Cambodian society, involving mass deportations from the towns to the countryside and mass executions (see ➤ KILLING *field*).

Khonsu a moon god worshipped especially at Thebes, a member of a triad as the divine son of Amun and Mut. His name means 'he who crosses'.

Khyber Pass a mountain pass in the Hindu Kush, on the border between Pakistan and Afghanistan. The pass was for long of great commercial and strategic importance, the route by which successive invaders entered India, and was garrisoned by the British intermittently between 1839 and 1947.

kibbutz a communal settlement in Israel, typically a farm.

kiblah the direction of the ➤ KAABA (the sacred building at Mecca), to which Muslims turn at prayer. The word comes (in the mid 17th century) from Arabic *ḳibla* 'that which is opposite'.

kick something into touch remove something from the centre of attention. In football, the touchlines mark the sides of the playing area, and if the ball is kicked beyond them (into touch) it is no longer in play.

kid a young goat, taken as a type of young and frisky animal; in extended usage (from the 17th century) a child, a young person.

kidnap take someone away illegally by force, typically to obtain a ransom; the word dates from the late 17th century, and the second element represents the slang *nap* 'nab, seize'.

kidney temperament, nature, as in **of the same kidney**. The *kidneys* were anciently thought to control disposition and temperament.

Mount Kilimanjaro an extinct volcano in northern Tanzania. It has twin peaks, the higher of which, Kibo, is the highest mountain in Africa.

Kilkenny cats two cats from Kilkenny in Ireland which, according to legend, fought until only their tails remained.

kill two birds with one stone achieve two aims at once; proverbial, recorded from the mid 17th century.

killing field a place where a heavy loss of life has occurred, typically as the result of massacre or genocide during a time of warfare or violent civil unrest. The term is particularly associated with Cambodia under the rule of Pol Pot and the ➤ KHMER *Rouge* in the late 1970s, where mass deportations from the towns to the countryside were followed by mass executions in what became known as *the killing fields*. It was with the release in 1984 of the film *The Killing Fields* that the phrase passed into the language.

Kilroy mythical person, popularized by American servicemen in the Second World War, who left such inscriptions as 'Kilroy was here' on walls all over the world.

Of the many unverifiable accounts of the source of the term, one claims that James J. *Kilroy* of Halifax, Massachusetts, a shipyard employee, wrote 'Kilroy was here' on sections of warships after inspection; the phrase is said to have been reproduced by shipyard workers who entered the armed services.

kilt a knee-length skirt of pleated tartan cloth, traditionally worn by men as part of Scottish Highland dress (and now also worn by women and girls). The wearing of the *kilt* was proscribed for a time after the Jacobite rising of 1745, as part of the policy to erode distinctive Highland practices.

Kim hero of Kipling's picaresque novel of that name (1901), the orphaned son of an Irish soldier, who grows up as an Indian. He becomes the chela of a Buddhist lama from Tibet as well as being (through his father's old regiment) educated as a European and later recruited into the British secret service.

Kim's game is a memory-testing game in which players try to remember as many as possible of a set of objects briefly shown to them; from the game with jewels played by *Kim* in Kipling's novel.

Kimberley a city in South Africa, in the province of Northern Cape, which has been a diamond-mining centre since the early 1870s.

king the male ruler of an independent state, especially one who inherits the position by right of birth.

In chess, the king is the most important piece, of which each player has one, which the opponent has to checkmate in order to win. The king can move in any direction, including diagonally, to any adjacent square that is not attacked by an opponent's piece or pawn. In cards, the king is the highest-ranking court card.

The phrase **king and country**, denoting the objects of allegiance for a patriot whose head of State is a king, is recorded from the early 17th century. **Your King and Country need you** was the caption for a recruiting advertisement of 1914, showing Lord Kitchener with pointing finger. The recruiting slogan was coined by Eric Field, July 1914.

King Charles's head is an obsession resembling that of Dickens's character 'Mr Dick' in *David Copperfield* (1850), who 'had been for upwards of ten years endeavouring to keep King Charles the First out of the Memorial; but he had been constantly getting into it, and was there now.'

The **King James Bible** is another name for the ➤ AUTHORIZED *Version*, dedicated to James I.

King Kong is a huge ape-like monster featured in the film *King Kong* (1933); captured and brought to New York, it escapes, climbing the Empire State Building with Fay Wray in its grasp before being shot down from besieging aeroplanes.

In the UK, a **King of Arms** is a chief herald. Those now at the College of Arms are the Garter, Clarenceux, and Norroy and Ulster Kings of Arms; the Lyon King of Arms has jurisdiction in Scotland.

The **king of beasts** is a name for the lion; its supposed rank in the hierarchy of animals is recorded from classical times. The **king of birds** is the eagle (used in reference to the bird's perceived grandeur); one of Aesop's fables tells how the ➤ WREN attempted to steal the title.

In the Christian Church, **King of Kings** is used as a name or form of address for God. Also, a title assumed by certain kings who rule over lesser kings.

King of Rome was the title born by the son (1811–32) of Napoleon I, who had gone into exile as a child with his mother, Marie-Louise of Austria, and died young; he was latterly known by the Austrian title of Duke of Reichstadt.

The **King of the Romans** was the prospective head of the ➤ HOLY *Roman Empire*; the title was assumed after selection by the seven Electors and coronation at Aachen, but prior to coronation as Emperor by the Pope at Rome.

The **King over the Water** is the Jacobite name for the exiled James II, 'over the water' in France, and later for his son and grandson, the ➤ OLD *Pretender* and the ➤ YOUNG *Pretender*. Jacobites were said to drink a secret toast to the Stuart king by passing their glasses over a bowl of water as a signal.

The **king's evil** is a name for scrofula, in England and France formerly held to be curable by the royal touch. The practice of touching for the *king's evil* continued from the time of Edward the Confessor to the death of Queen Anne in 1714. The Office for the ceremony has not been printed in the Prayer-book since 1719.

The **king's shilling** was a shilling formerly given to a recruit when enlisting in the army during the reign of a king.

the Kingmaker nickname of Richard Neville, Earl of *Warwick* (1428–71), English statesman. During the Wars of the Roses he fought first on the Yorkist side, helping Edward IV to gain the throne (1461), and then on the Lancastrian side, briefly restoring Henry VI to the throne (1470). Warwick was killed at the battle of Barnet.

Kings the name of two books of the Bible, recording the history of Israel from the accession of Solomon to the destruction of the Temple in 586 BC. In the Septuagint and Vulgate, these are called the third and fourth books of Kings, the two books of Samuel being called the first and second books of Kings.

the Kirk (of Scotland) the Church of Scotland as distinct from the Church of England or from the Episcopal Church in Scotland.

The **Kirk Session** is the lowest court in the Church of Scotland, composed of the minister and elders of the parish.

kirpan a short sword or knife with a curved blade, worn (sometimes in miniature form) as one of the five distinguishing signs of the Sikh ➤ KHALSA, symbolizing power and freedom.

kismet fate, destiny. The word comes (in the early 19th century, via Turkish) from Arabic *ḳismat* 'division, portion, lot', from *ḳasama* 'to divide'.

kiss and tell recount one's sexual exploits, especially to the media regarding a famous person; in US politics from the mid 1970s, the revealing of confidential information gained through any close or privileged relationship.

the kiss of death a seemingly kind or well-intentioned action, look, or association, which brings disastrous consequences; the association is with the kiss of betrayal given to Jesus by ➤ JUDAS.

kiss of peace a ceremonial kiss as part of a religious ceremony, especially in the Eucharist.

kiss the gunner's daughter be lashed to the breech of a gun for flogging, an old naval punishment.

kissing bough a Christmas wreath or ball of evergreens hung from the ceiling, under which a person may be kissed.

kissing cousin a relative who is not a close cousin, but who is known well enough to be given a kiss in greeting.

kissing gate a small gate hung in a U- or V-shaped enclosure, letting one person through at a time.

when the kissing has to stop when the honeymoon period finishes; when one is forced to recognize harsh realities, originally with reference to the line in Browning's 'A Toccata of Galuppi's' (1855).

kit-cat a canvas of a standard size (typically 36 × 28 inches, 91.5 × 71 cm), especially as used for a life-size portrait showing the sitter's head, shoulders, and one or both hands. The name comes from a series of portraits of the members of the **Kit-Cat Club**, an association of prominent Whigs and literary figures founded in the early part of the 18th century. It was named after *Kit* (= Christopher) *Cat* or *Catling*, who kept the pie house in Shire Lane, by Temple Bar, the original meeting place of the club.

kitchen cabinet a group of unofficial advisers (originally of the president of the US, in the mid 19th century) popularly believed to have greater influence than elected or appropriate officials; a private or unofficial group of advisers thought to be unduly influential.

kitchen-sink in art forms, characterized by great realism in the depiction of drab or sordid subjects. The term is most used of post-war British drama, such as John Osborne's *Look Back in Anger* (1956), which used working-class domestic settings rather than the drawing rooms of conventional middle-class drama.

kite from the mid 16th century, the name of this bird of prey was used figuratively for a person preying on others, a rapacious person, a sharper. The name is recorded from Old English (in form *cȳta*), and is probably of imitative origin and related to German *Kauz* 'screech owl'.

kith and kin one's relations. The word kith is Old English, and the original senses were 'knowledge', 'one's native land', and 'friends and neighbours'. The phrase *kith and kin* originally denoted one's country and relatives; later one's friends and relatives.

kitsch art, objects, or design considered to be in poor taste because of excessive garishness or sentimentality, but sometimes appreciated in an ironic or knowing way. The word comes (in the 1920s) from German.

Kitty Hawk a town on a narrow sand peninsula on the Atlantic coast of North Carolina. It was there that, in 1903, the Wright brothers made the first powered aeroplane flight.

kiwi a flightless New Zealand bird with hairlike feathers, having a long downcurved bill with sensitive nostrils at the tip, a national emblem of New Zealand; from the early 20th century, used informally for a New Zealander.

Klondike a tributary of the Yukon River, in Yukon Territory, NW Canada, which rises in the Ogilvie mountains and flows 160 km (100 miles) westwards to join the Yukon at Dawson. It gave its name to the surrounding region, which became famous when gold was found in nearby Bonanza Creek in 1896. In the ensuing gold rush of 1897–8 thousands settled in the area to mine gold. and the town of Dawson was established. Within ten years the area was exhausted and the population dramatically decreased.

Klosters a fashionable Alpine winter-sports resort in eastern Switzerland, near the Austrian border.

knave another term for the 'jack' in cards. The word originally (in Old English) meant 'boy, servant', and then generally someone of low social status; in Middle English, the sense of 'dishonest or unscrupulous man' developed. The playing-card sense is recorded from the middle of the 16th century.

Knickerbocker a New Yorker, taken as a descendant of the original Dutch settlers in New York. The term comes from Diedrich *Knickerbocker*, pretended author of W. Irving's *History of New York* (1809).

The term *knickerbockers* for loose-fitting breeches gathered at the knee or calf is said to have arisen from the resemblance of knickerbockers to the knee breeches worn by Dutch men in Cruikshank's illustrations in Irving's book.

knife a knife is the emblem of ➤ St BARTHOLOMEW, St Peter the Martyr, a 13th-century Dominican friar and priest born in Verona, who was attacked and killed while travelling from Como to Milan (he was wounded in the head with an axe, while the friar who was with him was stabbed), and ➤ St WILLIAM *of Norwich*.

knight in the Middle Ages, a man who served his sovereign or lord as a mounted soldier in armour; a man raised by a sovereign to honourable military rank after service as a page or a squire.

In the UK, a *knight* is a man awarded a nonhereditary title by the sovereign in recognition of merit or service and entitled to use the honorific 'Sir' in front of his name.

Knight is also a dated term for a member of the class of equites in ancient Rome, or a citizen of the second class in ancient Athens (called *hippeus* in Greek), seen in comparison with medieval knights.

In chess, a *knight* is a piece, typically with its top shaped like a horse's head, that moves by jumping to the opposite corner of a rectangle two squares by three. Each player starts the game with two knights.

The word is recorded from Old English (in the form *cniht*, denoting 'boy, youth, servant') and is of West Germanic origin.

A **knight errant** was a medieval knight wandering in search of chivalrous adventures.

A **Knight of Columbus** is a member of a society of Roman Catholic men founded at New Haven, Connecticut, in 1882.

A **Knight of the Round Table** was a member of the brotherhood of knights who were followers of ➤ *King* ARTHUR.

The **Knight of the Rueful Countenance** is another name for ➤ *Don* QUIXOTE.

A **knight of the shire** is a gentleman representing a shire or county in Parliament, originally, a parliamentary member chosen from those holding the rank of knight.

In the Middle Ages, **knight service** was the tenure of land by a knight on condition of performing military service.

Knights Hospitallers a military and religious order founded as the Knights of the Order of the Hospital of St John of Jerusalem in the 11th century.

Originally protectors of pilgrims, they also undertook the care of the sick. During the Middle Ages they became a powerful and wealthy military force, with foundations in various European countries; their military power ended when Malta was surrendered to

Napoleon (1798). In England, the order was revived in 1831 and was responsible for the foundation of the St John Ambulance Brigade in 1888.

Knights Templars a religious and military order for the protection of pilgrims to the Holy Land, founded as the Poor Knights of Christ and of the Temple of Solomon in 1118.

The order became powerful and wealthy, but its members' arrogance towards rulers, together with their wealth and their rivalry with the Knights Hospitallers, led to their downfall; the order was suppressed in 1312, many of its possessions being given to the Hospitallers. The Inner and Middle Temple in London are on the site of the Templars' English headquarters.

knobkerrie a short stick with a knobbed head, traditionally used as a weapon by the indigenous peoples of South Africa.

Knossos the principal city of Minoan Crete, the remains of which are situated on the north coast of Crete. Excavations by Sir Arthur Evans from 1900 onwards revealed the remains of a luxurious and spectacularly decorated complex of buildings, which he named the Palace of Minos, with frescoes of landscapes, animal life, and the sport of bull-leaping. The city site was occupied from Neolithic times until c.1200 BC; Crete was overrun by the Mycenaeans in c.1450 BC, but the palace survived until the 14th or early 13th century BC.

knot a unit of speed equivalent to one nautical mile per hour, used especially of ships, aircraft, or winds. This comes from the use of the word to mean a length marked by knots on a log line, as a measure of speed.

knot garden a formal garden laid out in an intricate design; *knot* was used from the late 15th century to denote a flower-bed laid out in a fanciful or ornate shape.

know the ropes be thoroughly acquainted with the way in which something is done, an expression deriving from the days of sailing ships, when skill in handling ropes was essential for any sailor.

kobold in Germanic mythology, a spirit who haunts houses or lives underground in caves or mines.

Koh-i-noor a famous Indian diamond, one of the treasures belonging to Aurangzeb, which has a history going back to the 14th century. It passed into British possession on the annexation of Punjab in 1849, and was set in the queen's state crown for the coronation of George VI (1937). The name comes from Persian, meaning 'mountain of light'.

Kohima Memorial memorial at Kohima in the far north-east of India to the Burma campaign of the Second World War; it carries the epitaph, 'When you go home, tell them of us and say, "For your tomorrow we gave our today." '

Theo Kojak a New York policeman played by Telly Savalas (1924–94) in the television series (1973–8) of that name, characterized by his wisecracking, bald head, and habit of sucking lollipops, as by his catchphrase, 'Who loves ya, baby?'

Kol Nidre an Aramaic prayer annulling vows made before God, sung by Jews at the opening of the Day of Atonement service on the eve of ➤ YOM *Kippur*. The name comes from Aramaic *kol niḏrē* 'all the vows' (the opening words of the prayer).

Kon-Tiki the raft made of balsa logs in which Thor Heyerdahl sailed from the western coast of Peru to the islands of Polynesia in 1947. It was named after an Inca god.

Konya an ancient Phrygian settlement, which became the capital of the Seljuk sultans towards the end of the 11th century.

the Kop a high bank of terracing at certain soccer grounds where spectators formerly stood, notably at Liverpool Football Club. The name comes from *Spion Kop*, site of a Boer War battle in which troops from Lancashire led the assault (Liverpool then being part of Lancashire).

Koran the Islamic sacred book, believed to be the word of God as dictated to Muhammad by the archangel Gabriel and written down in Arabic. The Koran consists of 114 units of varying lengths, known as *suras*; the first sura is said as part of the ritual prayer. These touch upon all aspects of human existence, including matters of doctrine, social organization, and legislation. The Koran was traditionally held by Muslims to be untranslatable, although versions or interpretations in other languages are available.

kore an archaic Greek statue of a young woman, standing and clothed in long loose robes. The word comes from Greek *korē* 'maiden'.

Korean War the war of 1950–3 between North and South Korea. UN troops, dominated by US forces, countered the invasion of South Korea by North Korean forces by invading North Korea, while China intervened on the side of the North.

Koreish the tribe which inhabited Mecca in the time of Muhammad and to which he belonged.

koru a stylized fern-leaf motif in Maori carving and tattooing.

kosher of food, or premises in which food is sold, cooked, or eaten, satisfying the requirements of Jewish law.

Restrictions on the foods suitable for Jews are derived from rules in the books of Leviticus and Deuteronomy. Animals must be slaughtered and prepared in the prescribed way, in which the blood is drained from the body, while certain creatures, notably pigs and shellfish, are forbidden altogether. Meat and milk must not be cooked or consumed together, and separate utensils must be kept for each. Strict observance of these rules is today confined mainly to Orthodox Jews.

The word comes (in the mid 19th century) from Hebrew *kāšēr* 'proper'.

Kosovo an autonomous province of Serbia bordering on Albania, the majority of whose people are of Albanian descent, and which in 1999 was subjected to ➤ ETHNIC *cleansing* by Serbian paramilitary forces, resulting in the bombing of Belgrade by Nato.

kouros an archaic Greek statue of a young man, standing and often naked. The word is from Greek, the Ionic form of *koros* 'boy'.

kowtow kneel and touch the ground with the forehead in worship or submission as part of traditional Chinese custom. The word comes from Chinese *kētóu*, from *kē* 'knock' + *tóu* 'head'.

Krakatoa a small volcanic island in Indonesia, lying between Java and Sumatra, scene of a great eruption in 1883 which destroyed most of the island.

kraken an enormous mythical sea monster said to appear off the coast of Norway.

the Kremlin the citadel in Moscow housing the Russian and (formerly) USSR government. The name is recorded from the mid 17th century, and comes via French from Russian *kreml'* 'citadel'.

The study and analysis of Soviet or Russian policies was known as **Kremlinology**.

Kriemhild in the *Nibelungenlied*, a Burgundian princess, wife of Siegfried and later of Etzel (Attila the Hun), whom she marries in order to be revenged on her brothers for Siegfried's murder. Her Norse equivalent is ➤ GUDRUN.

Krishna in Hindu belief, one of the most popular gods, the eighth and most important avatar or incarnation of Vishnu.

He is worshipped in several forms: as the child god whose miracles and pranks are extolled in the Puranas; as the divine cowherd whose erotic exploits, especially with his favourite, Radha, have produced both romantic and religious literature; and as the divine charioteer who preaches to Arjuna on the battlefield in the *Bhagavadgita*.

Kriss Kringle in parts of the US, Santa Claus; the name is probably an alteration of German *Christkindl* 'Christmas present, (informal) Christ-child'.

Kristallnacht the occasion of concerted violence by Nazis throughout Germany and Austria against Jews and their property on the night of 9–10 November 1938. The (German) word means literally 'night of crystal', referring to the broken glass produced by the smashing of shop windows.

Kruger telegram sent by Kaiser Wilhelm II of Germany to President Kruger of Transvaal, 3 January 1896, after the failure of the ➤ JAMESON *Raid*; the intention was to demonstrate to Britain the dangers of political isolation, but the effect was to arouse considerable anti-German feeling.

Kshatriya a member of the second of the four great Hindu castes, the military caste. The traditional function of the Kshatriyas is to protect society by fighting in wartime and governing in peacetime.

Ku Klux Klan an extremist right-wing secret society in the US. The Ku Klux Klan was originally founded in the southern states after the Civil War to oppose social change and black emancipation by violence and terrorism. Although disbanded twice, it re-emerged in the 1950s and 1960s and continues at a local level. Members disguise themselves in white robes and hoods, and often use a burning cross as a symbol of their organization.

Kuan Yin in Chinese Buddhism, the goddess of compassion.

Kublai Khan (1216–94), Mongol emperor of China, grandson of Genghis Khan. With his brother Mangu (then Mongol Khan) he conquered southern China (1252–9). After Mangu's death in 1259 he completed the conquest of China, founded the Yuan dynasty, and established his capital on the site of the modern Beijing.

kuccha short trousers ending above the knee, worn as one of the five distinguishing signs of the Sikh ► KHALSA, symbolizing loyalty and discipline.

kudos praise and honour received for an achievement. Recorded from the late 18th century, the word is Greek and means 'praise'.

Kufic an early angular form of the Arabic alphabet found chiefly in decorative incriptions. Recorded from the early 18th century, the word comes from the name *Kufa*, a city south of Baghdad, because the script was attributed to the city's scholars.

kulak a peasant in Russia wealthy enough to own a farm and hire labour. Emerging after the emancipation of serfs in the 19th century the kulaks resisted Stalin's forced collectivization, but millions were arrested, exiled, or killed.

Kumbh Mela a Hindu festival and assembly, held once every twelve years at four locations in India, at which pilgrims bathe in the waters of the Ganges and Jumna Rivers. The name comes from Sanskrit, meaning literally 'pitcher festival'.

kumkum a red powder used ceremonially, especially by Hindu women to make a small distinctive mark on the forehead.

Kuomintang a nationalist party founded in China under Sun Yat-sen in 1912, and led by Chiang Kai-shek from 1925. It held power from 1928 until the Communist Party took power in October 1949 and subsequently formed the central administration of Taiwan.

kurdaitcha in Australia, the use among Aboriginals of a bone in spells intended to cause sickness or death; a man empowered to point the bone at a victim.

kurgan a prehistoric burial mound or barrow of a type found in southern Russia and the Ukraine.

Kursk a Russian nuclear submarine lost with all hands in the Barents Sea in August 2000; for a number days it was thought that at least some of the crew had survived and could be rescued.

kusti a cord worn round the waist by Parsees, consisting of seventy-two threads to represent the chapters of one of the portions of the Zend-Avesta.

Kwanzaa a secular festival observed by many African Americans from 26 December to 1 January as a celebration of their cultural heritage and traditional values. The name comes from Kiswahili *matunda ya kwanza*, literally 'first fruits (of the harvest)'.

kylin a mythical composite animal, often figured on Chinese and Japanese ceramics. Recorded from the mid 19th century, the name comes from Chinese *qilin*, from *qi* 'male' + *lin* 'female'.

Kyrie a short repeated invocation (in Greek or in translation) used in many Christian liturgies, especially at the beginning of the Eucharist or as a response in a litany. The word comes from Greek *Kuriē eleēson* 'Lord, have mercy'.

L1

L the twelfth letter of the modern English alphabet and the eleventh of the ancient Roman one, corresponding to Greek *lambda* and ultimately Semitic *lamed*.

L is the Roman numeral for 50. Originally, this was a symbol identified with the letter *L* because of coincidence of form. In ancient Roman notation, *L* with a stroke above denoted 50,000.

L is also the sign for pounds sterling, from the initial letter of Latin *librae* 'pounds'.

La Rochelle a port on the Atlantic coast of western France, which in the 17th century was a noted Huguenot stronghold. Having supported the English invasion of Ré, La Rochelle was besieged and finally conquered by the forces of Louis XIII and Richelieu. Many of its inhabitants starved to death during the siege.

La Scala an opera house in Milan built 1776–8 by the Empress Maria Theresa (at the time of Austria's control of Milan) on the site of the church of Santa Maria della Scala.

laager a camp or encampment formed by a circle of wagons; an entrenched position or viewpoint that is defended against opponents. The word comes from Afrikaans and ultimately from Dutch *leger*, *lager* 'camp'.

Laban in the Bible, the father of Leah and ➤ RACHEL and uncle of ➤ JACOB, who tricked his nephew into marrying the elder sister Leah, and having to serve another seven years for Rachel.

labarum Constantine the Great's imperial standard, which bore Christian imagery (a monogram of the first two letters of Greek *Christos*) fused with the military symbols of the Roman Empire.

labour of love work undertaken either from fondness for the work itself, or from desire to benefit persons whom one loves. The term was originally used (in the late 17th century) as a direct quotation from St Paul's Epistle to the Thessalonians.

labours of the month in the Middle Ages, seasonal occupations associated with particular months, and often represented in sculpture and illumination. The traditional representations are: January, Janus (sometimes also sitting at a table feasting); February, a man warming himself by a fire; March, pruning (usually vines); sometimes also digging; April, a man in foliage; May, a knight on horseback; June, mowing (haymaking); July, harvesting (reaping); August, threshing grain (occasionally fruit-picking); September, treading grapes (occasionally picking grapes); October, beating acorns from trees (sometimes filling casks); November, slaughtering hogs (sometimes animals feeding from a manger); December, feasting.

labrys the sacred double-headed axe of ancient Crete.

the Labyrinth in Greek mythology, the intricate maze constructed by ➤ DAEDALUS for the Cretan king Minos to house the ➤ MINOTAUR; Theseus, using a ball of thread, made his way through its passages to kill the monster.

Lacedaemon an area of ancient Greece comprising the city of Sparta and its surroundings; **Lacedaemonian** thus means Spartan, or (of speech or correspondence) laconic.

Lachesis in Greek mythology, one of the three ➤ FATES. Traditionally, *Clotho* holds the distaff, *Lachesis* spins the thread of life, and *Atropos* cuts the thread.

laconic (of a person, speech, or style of writing) using very few words. The term comes (in the mid 16th century, in the sense 'Laconian, Spartan) via Latin from Greek from *Lakōn* 'Sparta', the Spartans being known for their terse speech.

lacuna an unfilled space or interval; a gap; a missing portion in a book or manuscript. The word comes (in the mid 17th century) from Latin, 'pool', from *lacus* 'lake'.

ladder a ladder is the emblem of the monk and abbot *St John Climacus* (d. 649), author of the treatise *The Ladder of Paradise* from which his name comes (*Climacus* means 'ladder'), in which he developed the concept of the ladder as an image of spiritual life.

To **kick down the ladder** is to reject or disown the friends or associates who have helped one to rise in the world, especially with the idea of preventing them from attaining a similar position.

ladies who lunch women who organize and take part in fashionable lunches to raise funds for charitable projects, from 'The Ladies who Lunch', 1970 song by Stephen Sondheim (1930–).

Ladies' Gallery a public gallery in the House of Commons, reserved for women to attend debates.

Ladino the language of some Sephardic Jews, especially formerly in Mediterranean countries. It is based on medieval Spanish, with an admixture of Hebrew, Greek, and Turkish words, and is written in modified Hebrew characters.

ladle a *ladle* is the emblem of ➤ St MARTHA, seen as the epitome of housewifely virtues.

lady in Old English the word (in the form *hlǣfdīge*) denoted a woman to whom homage or obedience is due, such as the wife of a lord or the mistress of a household, and also (specifically) the Virgin Mary (**Our Lady**); it comes from *hlāf* 'loaf' + a Germanic base meaning 'knead', related to *dough*.

It isn't over till the fat lady sings means that there is still time for a situation to change. With allusion to the saying *the opera isn't over till the fat lady sings*, originating in the US in the late 20th century.

A **Lady Bountiful** is a patronizingly generous woman, named from a character in Farquhar's *The Beaux' Stratagem*.

A **Lady Chapel** is a chapel in a church or cathedral, typically to the east of the high altar in a cathedral, to the south in a church, dedicated to the Virgin Mary.

Lady Day is 25 March (the feast of the Annunciation), a quarter day in England, Wales, and Ireland.

The **Lady of Shalott** was the name given by Tennyson to ➤ ELAINE, the Maid of Astolat, who died of unrequited love for Lancelot. In Tennyson's poem she is imprisoned in her tower by a magic spell, which compels her to watch in a mirror the scenes outside which she then depicts in her weaving. The mirror cracks, and the curse falls on her, when she looks directly out of the window, and sees Lancelot; she dies as her barge carries her down the river to Camelot.

The **Lady of the Lake** in the Arthurian romances, is the sorceress who gives the sword Excalibur to Arthur.

The **Lady of the Lamp** is a popular name for Florence Nightingale (1820–1910), referring to her work as a nurse in the Crimean War; this image of her in the wards at night is first alluded to by Longfellow in *The Courtship of Miles Standish* (1858), 'A Lady with a Lamp shall stand in the great history of the land, A noble type of good, Heroic womanhood.'

ladybird the *ladybird* is traditionally regarded as lucky, and its name ('Our Lady's bird') associates it with the Virgin Mary.

Ladysmith a town in eastern South Africa, founded in the early 19th century and named after the wife of the governor of Natal, Sir Harry Smith (1787–1860). It was subjected to a four-month siege by Boer forces during the Second Boer War, and was finally relieved on 28 February 1900 by Lord Roberts.

Laertes in Greek mythology, the father of Odysseus, who survives to see his son come home to Ithaca.

In Shakespeare's *Hamlet*, *Laertes* is the name of ➤ OPHELIA's brother, who avenges his sister's death by killing Hamlet in the duel in which he himself is also killed.

Laetare Sunday the fourth Sunday of Lent. The name comes from Latin *Laetare* 'Rejoice', the opening word of the Introit, and the day marks the point at which the rigours of Lent are temporarily relaxed. It is also known as Mothering Sunday and Refreshment Sunday.

Lag b'Omer a Jewish festival held on the 33rd day of the Omer (the period between Passover and Pentecost), traditionally regarded as celebrating the end of a plague in the 2nd century.

laissez-faire a policy or attitude of leaving things to take their own course, without interfering; abstention by governments from interfering in the workings of the free market.

The remark '*Laissez-nous-faire* [Allow us to do it]', dated *c.*1664, is recorded in a source of the mid 18th century, as a reply to the French statesman Jean Baptiste Colbert (1619–83), who had asked what could be done for commerce. The expression became particularly associated with 18th-century political economists, as d'Argenson and Quesnay.

Laius in Greek mythology, a king of Thebes, husband of Jocasta and father of ➤ OEDIPUS, of whom it was prophesied that he would be killed by his own son. Laius accordingly ordered that the child should be exposed, but Oedipus was rescued and brought up in ignorance of his birth. When a man, he met Laius, quarrelled with him, and killed him; he subsequently married the widowed Jocasta.

Lake Poets the poets Samuel Taylor Coleridge, Robert Southey, and William Wordsworth, who lived in and were inspired by the Lake District; they are also known as the *Lake School*. Both terms are first recorded in the *Edinburgh Review* of 1816; the pejorative *Lakers*, however, antedates them by two years.

Lakshmi in Hindu belief, the goddess of prosperity, consort of Vishnu. She assumes different forms (e.g. ➤ RADHA, ➤ SITA) in order to accompany her husband in his various incarnations.

Lallans a distinctive Scottish literary form of English, based on standard older Scots. The name comes (as an adjective in the early 18th century) from a Scots variant of *Lowlands*, with reference to a central Lowlands dialect.

lama an honorific title applied to a spiritual leader in Tibetan Buddhism, whether a reincarnate lama (such as the ➤ DALAI *Lama*) or one who has earned the title in life.

Lamarckism the theory of the origin of species proposed by the French naturalist Jean Baptiste de *Lamarck* (1744–1829), French naturalist. He was an early proponent of organic evolution, although his theory is not widely accepted today. He suggested that species could have evolved from each other by small changes in their structure, and that the mechanism of such change (not now generally considered possible) was that characteristics acquired in order to survive could be passed on to offspring.

lamb a *lamb* symbolizes youth and innocence; in Christian art it is emblematic of Jesus Christ (the **Lamb of God**, see John 1:29).

A *lamb* is the emblem of ➤ St AGNES and ➤ St JOHN the Baptist.

St Lambert (*c.*635–*c.*705), bishop of Maastricht and patron of Liège; he was venerated as a martyr because his violent death was attributed by later biographers to his having reproved the Frankish ruler Pepin II

(687–714) for adultery. His feast day is 17 September.

Lambeth Palace a palace in the London borough of Lambeth, the residence of the Archbishop of Canterbury since 1197.

lame duck an ineffectual or unsuccessful person or thing, originally (in the mid 18th century) Stock Exchange slang for one who could not meet his financial engagements, a defaulter. The term is first recorded in a letter from Horace Walpole of 1761.

Lamentations a book of the Bible (in full **the Lamentations of Jeremiah**) telling of the desolation of Judah after the fall of Jerusalem in 586 BC.

lamia a mythical monster supposed to have the body of a woman, and to prey on human beings and suck the blood of children. The word is used in early translations of the Bible for Isaiah 34:15 (where the Authorized Version has 'screech owl', with marginal alternative 'night monster' and Lamentations 4:3 (where the Authorized Version has 'sea monsters' or 'sea calves'). *Lamia* comes via Latin from Greek, denoting a carnivorous fish or mythical monster.

In Keats's poem of this name, the serpent *Lamia* is transformed into a beautiful woman and wins the love of Lycius. At their wedding feast in Corinth her real nature is recognized by the sage Apollonius: he challenges her by her name, and she reverts to her true form, vanishing with a shriek of anguish.

Lammas the first day of August (also called **Lammas Day**), formerly observed as harvest festival, and one of the quarter-days in Scotland. The first element represents Old English *hláf* 'loaf', but the word was later interpreted as if it represented *lamb* + *mass*.

lamplighter a person employed to light street gaslights by hand, often used allusively with reference to the rapidity with which the lamplighter ran on his rounds, or climbed the ladders formerly used to reach the street lamps.

lampoon a speech or text criticizing someone or something by using ridicule, irony, or sarcasm. The word comes (in the mid 17th century) from French, said to be from *lampons* 'let us drink' (used as a refrain), from *lamper* 'gulp down', nasalized form of *laper* 'to lap (liquid)' It is first recorded in the *Memoirs* (1645) of John Evelyn.

lamprey a surfeit of this as a food fish is traditionally said to have caused the death of

Henry I, according to a contemporary account quoted by Fabyan's *New Chronicles of England and France* (1516).

House of Lancaster the English royal house descended from ➤ JOHN *of Gaunt*, Duke of Lancaster, that ruled England from 1399 (Henry IV) until 1461 (the deposition of Henry VI) and again on Henry's brief restoration in 1470–1. With the red rose as its emblem it fought the Wars of the Roses with the ➤ *House of* YORK, both houses being branches of the Plantagenet line. Lancaster's descendants, the Tudors, eventually prevailed through Henry VII's accession to the throne in 1485.

The **Duchy of Lancaster** is now an estate vested in the Crown, consisting of properties in Lancashire and elsewhere in England.

Lancaster House Agreement an agreement which brought about the establishment of the independent state of Zimbabwe, reached in September 1979 at Lancaster House in London.

lance a lance is the emblem of ➤ *St* JUDE, ➤ *St* THOMAS *the Apostle*, St Gereon, a 4th-century martyr of Cologne, and ➤ *St* MAURICE.

Lancelot in Arthurian legend, the most famous of Arthur's knights, father of ➤ GALAHAD; he is one of the most significant figures of the cycle, since it is the revelation of his adulterous love for ➤ GUINEVERE that forces him into exile and allows the traitor ➤ MORDRED opportunity to rebel against Arthur.

Lancelot is seen as a type of flawed courage; he is one of Arthur's greatest knights, but he is not judged pure enough to find the ➤ HOLY *Grail* which will be his son's reward.

land¹ an area of ground, as characterized by its physical features. The phrase **how the land lies** means, what the state of affairs is. **The lie of the land** (late 17th century) is used both literally, for the way in which the features or characteristics of an area present themselves, or figuratively.

In informal American usage, to **do a land-office business** means to do a lot of successful trading. The expression looks back to the period at which new lands were being made available to settlers, and land-offices dealing with sales and settlement of new lands accordingly did a great deal of business.

In the UK, **from Land's End to John o'Groats** means from one end of Britain to the other; *Land's End* is a rocky promontory in SW Cornwall, forming the westernmost point of England, and by road is approximately 876 miles from *John o'Groats*, a village at the extreme NE point of the Scottish mainland.

in the UK, a **land girl** is a woman doing farm work, especially during the Second World War.

The **Land League** was an Irish organization formed in 1879 to campaign for tenants' rights. Its techniques included the use of the boycott against anyone taking on a farm from which the tenant had been evicted.

land² a country or state.

Land of Hope and Glory is the song written by A. C. Benson (1862–1925) to a melody by Edward Elgar. Benson's song was written to be sung as the Finale to Elgar's *Coronation Ode* (1902); it became very popular as a patriotic song, and is now particularly associated with the Last Night of the Proms.

In the Bible, the **land of milk and honey** is the land promised to the Israelites, 'a land flowing with milk and honey' (Exodus 3:8). A *land of milk and honey* may now be used generally to suggest a place of prosperity and contentment, but there may also be a suggestion that this is a future state to be achieved.

In the Bible, the **Land of Nod** was the place in which the exiled Cain lived after the murder of Abel. From the mid 18th century, the phrase has been used punningly to mean sleep; the place of Cain's exile, and its desolate nature, is more likely to be described as ➤ *the land God gave to* CAIN.

The **Land of the Free** is an informal name for the United States, taken from the poem 'The Star-Spangled Banner' by the American lawyer and verse-writer Francis Scott Key (1779–1843), which was adopted as the US national anthem in 1931.

The **Land of the Little Sticks** is Canada (from Chinook *stik* 'wood, tree, forest', the subarctic tundra region of northern Canada, characterized by its stunted vegetation).

The **Land of the Long White Cloud** is New Zealand (translating the Maori name ➤ AOTEAROA).

The **Land of the Midnight Sun** is any of the most northerly European countries, where the sun can be seen at midnight during the summer.

The **Land of the Rising Sun** is Japan; a translation of Japanese *Nippon*, which comes from *nichi* 'the sun' + *pon, hon* 'source'. *Nippon* is recorded in English from the early 17th century, but *Land of the Rising Sun* is not found until the mid 19th century.

langue d'oc the form of medieval French spoken south of the Loire, generally characterized by the use of *oc* to mean 'yes', and forming the basis of modern Provençal.

langue d'oïl the form of medieval French spoken north of the Loire, generally characterized by the use of *oïl* to mean 'yes', and forming the basis of modern French.

lantern a lantern is the emblem of ➤ *St* LUCY and ➤ *St* GUDULE.

Laocoon in Greek mythology, a Trojan priest who, with his two sons, was crushed to death by two great sea serpents as a penalty for warning the Trojans against the ➤ TROJAN *Horse*. A marble sculpture in the Vatican Museum, attributed by Pliny to Agesander, Athenodorus, and Polydurus of Rhodes, depicts the death of Laocoon and his sons, and in allusive use his name often reflects the idea of someone struggling within enveloping coils.

the laogai in China, a system of labour camps, many of whose inmates are political dissidents. The name comes from Chinese, meaning 'reform through labour', and is recorded from English from the 1990s.

in the lap of the gods beyond human control; from Homer *The Iliad* 'It lies in the lap of the gods.'

Lapith in Greek mythology, a member of a Thessalian people who fought and defeated the centaurs; the battle between them after the wedding feast of the Lapith king Pirithous, when the centaurs tried to carry off the bride and other Lapith women, was a favourite topic for Greek sculptors.

lapwing traditional allusions to the *lapwing* refer to its crested head, its technique of distracting an enemy from its nest by crying loudly at a distance from it, or by offering itself as quarry to be followed, and to the belief that the newly-hatched lapwing runs about with its head in the shell.

lares gods of the household worshipped in ancient Rome in conjunction with Vesta and the penates; the phrase **lares and penates** is used to mean the home.

lark the lark's song is delivered on the wing, and traditional allusions refer to its early singing, the strength and sweetness of its song, and the height to which it soars above its nest.

Larry the Lamb in the ➤ TOYTOWN stories of S. G. Hulme Beatman (1886–1932), the well-meaning but ineffectual lamb whose customary bleating apology is, 'I'm only a little lamb.'

Las Vegas a city in southern Nevada noted for its casinos and nightclubs.

Lascaux the site of a cave in the Dordogne, France, which is richly decorated with Palaeolithic wall paintings of animals dated to the Magdalenian period. Discovered in 1940, the cave was closed in 1963 to protect the paintings, a replica later being opened nearby.

Lassie name of the loyal and intelligent collie which is the central character in a series of films, originally created by Eric Knight in the children's story *Lassie Come Home* (1940), in which a poor Yorkshire couple have to sell their son's much-loved collie.

last final.
　In the **last chance saloon** means having been allowed one final opportunity to improve or get things right, from the fanciful idea of a saloon bar with this name.
　A **last hurrah** is the final act in a politician's career, a final performance or effort, a swansong, from the title of *The Last Hurrah*, a novel (1956) by Edwin O'Connor.
　The **Last Judgement** is the judgement of humankind expected in some religious traditions to take place at the end of the world.
　The **last post** in the British armed forces is the second of two bugle calls giving notice of the hour of retiring at night, played also at military funerals and acts of remembrance.
　In the Christian Church, the **last rites** are those administered to a person who is about to die.
　The **Last Supper** was the supper eaten by Jesus and his disciples on the night before the Crucifixion, as recorded in the New Testament and commemorated by Christians in the Eucharist.
　The **last trump** is the trumpet blast that in some religious beliefs is thought will wake the dead on Judgement Day.
　See also the ➤ FOUR *last things*.

Lateran the site in Rome containing the cathedral church of Rome (a basilica dedicated to St John the Baptist and St John the Evangelist, originally founded in the 4th century by ➤ CONSTANTINE) and the **Lateran Palace**, where the popes resided until the 14th century.

The **Lateran Council** is any of five general councils of the Western Church held in the Lateran Palace in 1123, 1139, 1179, 1215, and 1512–17. The council of 1215 condemned the ➤ ALBIGENSES as heretical and clarified the Church doctrine on transubstantiation, the Trinity, and the Incarnation.

The **Lateran Treaty** is a concordat signed in 1929 in the Lateran Palace between the kingdom of Italy (represented by Mussolini) and the Holy See (represented by Pope Pius XI), which recognized as fully sovereign and independent the papal state under the name Vatican City.

Latin the language of ancient Rome and its empire, widely used historically as a language of scholarship and administration.

Latin is a member of the Italic branch of the Indo-European family of languages. After the decline of the Roman Empire it continued to be a medium of communication among educated people throughout the Middle Ages in Europe and elsewhere, and remained the liturgical language of the Roman Catholic Church until the reforms of the second Vatican Council (1962–5); it is still used for scientific names in biology and astronomy. The Romance languages are derived from it.

The **Latin Church** is the Christian Church which originated in the Western Roman Empire, giving allegiance to the Pope of Rome, and historically using Latin for the liturgy; the Roman Catholic Church as distinguished from Orthodox and Uniate Churches.

A **Latin cross** is a plain cross in which the vertical part below the horizontal is longer than the other three parts.

Latium an ancient region of west central Italy, west of the Apennines and south of the River Tiber. Settled during the early part of the 1st millennium BC by a branch of the Indo-European people known as the *Latini*, it had become dominated by Rome by the end of the 4th century BC; it is now part of the modern region of Lazio.

Latona in Roman mythology, ➤ LETO.

Latter-Day Saints the Mormons' name for themselves.

lauds a service of morning prayer in the Divine Office of the Western Christian Church, traditionally said or chanted at daybreak, though historically it was often held with matins on the previous night.

Recorded from Middle English, the name comes from the frequent use, in Psalms 148–150, of the Latin imperative *laudate!* 'praise ye!'

laugh all the way to the bank make a great deal of money with very little effort. Often used ironically.

laugh to scorn ridicule someone or something; a biblical idiom, as in Job 12:4 and Matthew 9:24.

Laughing Cavalier popular name for a portrait of an unknown man by the Dutch painter Franz Hals (*c*.1580–1666); the name is not contemporary, but began to be used in the late 19th century.

laughing gas a non-technical term for nitrous oxide. The gas, originally discovered by Sir Humphrey Davy (1778–1829), which was used particularly in dentistry as an anaesthetic, produces exhilaration when first inhaled.

Laura ➤ PETRARCH's name for the woman in praise of whom his sonnet sequence is written.

Laurasia a vast continental area believed to have existed in the northern hemisphere and to have resulted from the break-up of Pangaea in Mesozoic times. It comprised the present North America, Greenland, Europe, and most of Asia north of the Himalayas.

laurel the foliage of the bay tree woven into a wreath or crown and worn on the head as an emblem of victory or mark of honour in classical times. The word is often found in the plural, as in **look to one's laurels**, be concerned about losing one's pre-eminence, and **rest on one's laurels**, cease to strive for further glory.

In classical times (as recorded by Pliny), laurel was believed to avert lightning.

Laurel may also be used in numismatics to designate an English gold coin, first coined in 1619, on which the sovereign's head was shown with a wreath of laurel.

Laurence laziness personified, a lazy person (**lazy Laurence** is also used); this association of the personal name with the quality is first recorded in the proverbial **Laurence bids wages**, meaning that the attractions of idleness are tempting.

It has been suggested that there is an allusion to the heat prevalent around the time of the feast of ➤ St LAWRENCE (10 August). Another conjecture is that there was a joke to the effect that when the martyr St Lawrence told his torturers to turn him round on his gridiron, it was because he was too lazy to move by himself.

In the US, *laurence* is also used for the shimmering effect that can be seen on a road or other surface on a hot day; this may again derive from the association of St Lawrence with heat.

lavabo (in the Roman Catholic Church) a towel or basin used for the ritual washing of the celebrant's hands at the offertory of the Mass. The word comes (in the mid 18th century) from Latin, literally 'I will wash', in *Lavabo inter innocentes manus meas* 'I will wash my hands in innocence' (Psalm 26:6), which was recited at the washing of hands in the Roman rite.

lavender the flowers and stalks of *lavender* were customarily placed among linen or other clothes as a preservative against moths during storage, and from this comes the phrase **lay up in lavender**, meaning preserve carefully for future use.

Lavender and old lace, used to denote a gentle and old-fashioned style, was originally the title of a novel (1902) by Myrtle Reed, later dramatized; the phrase was reworked in Joseph Kesselring's play *Arsenic and Old Lace* (1941), featuring two respectable spinster sisters who are given to poisoning their lodgers.

The **lavender list** was an informal name for the draft of Harold Wilson's last honours list, supposedly first drawn up by his secretary Marcia Falkender on a sheet of lavender notepaper, and later regarded as having some names of questionable merit.

laver a basin or similar container used for washing oneself; (in biblical use) a large brass bowl for Jewish priests' ritual ablutions.

law the system of rules recognized by a country or community.

In the United Kingdom, a **law lord** is a member of the House of Lords qualified to perform its legal work; a term first recorded in a letter of Edmund Burke's of 1773.

The **law of averages** is the supposed principle that future events are likely to turn out so that they balance any past deviation from a presumed average. The term is recorded from the 19th century, and derives initially from a comment by the historian Henry Thomas Buckle (1821–62). The first (sceptical) reference to 'Mr Buckle's "Law of Averages" ' is found in 1875, and from then on the term became established.

The **law of nations** is international law, a body of rules established by custom or treaty and recognized by nations as binding in their relations with one another. *Law of nations*, a translation of the Latin phrase *jus gentium*, was originally used to denote rules common to the law of all nations. The transition to the current sense developed particularly through the appeal to 'the law of nations' in such matters as the treatment of ambassadors or the obligation to observe treaties.

The **law of the jungle** is the supposed code of survival in jungle life, originally shown favourably in Kipling's *Jungle Books*, 'Now this is the Law of the Jungle—as old and as true as the sky.' The term is now used to embody the principle that those who are strong and apply ruthless self-interest will be most successful.

The **Law Society** is the professional body responsible for regulating solicitors in England and Wales, established in 1825.

lawn fine linen or cotton fabric used for making clothes, especially the sleeves of a bishop, from which it is used allusively. It is probably named from the French city of *Laon*, important for linen manufacture.

St Lawrence (d.258), Roman martyr and deacon of Rome. According to tradition, Lawrence was ordered by the prefect of Rome to deliver up the treasure of the Church; when in response to this order he presented the poor people of Rome to the prefect, he was roasted to death on a gridiron. His traditional emblem is a gridiron, and his feast day is 10 August.

laws of war the rules and conventions, recognized by civilized nations, which limit belligerents' action.

lay not ordained into or belonging to the clergy. Recorded from Middle English, the word comes from Old French via late Latin and ultimately from Greek *laos* 'people'.

A **lay brother** is a man who has taken the vows of a religious order but is not ordained or obliged to take part in the full cycle of liturgy and is employed in ancillary or manual work.

In the Anglican Church, a **lay reader** is a layperson licensed to preach and to conduct some religious services, but not licensed to celebrate the Eucharist.

A **lay sister** is a woman who has taken the vows of a religious order but is not obliged to take part in the full cycle of liturgy and is employed in ancillary or manual work.

laying on of hands in religious usage, the deliberate touching of someone in blessing or ordination.

Lazarus in the Bible, the brother of Martha and Mary, raised from the dead by Jesus. According to the story in John, ch. 11, Lazarus had died and been buried before Jesus reached him; he was raised not just from the dead, but from the tomb, and has thus become a type for an unlooked-for resurrection.

In Luke 16:20, *Lazarus* is also the name of a beggar covered with sores, who was refused help by the rich man Dives, but who on death entered heaven when Dives was denied. The archaic term for a leper, *lazar*, comes from his name.

Le Mans an industrial town in NW France, which is the site of a motor-racing circuit, on which a 24-hour endurance race (established in 1923) is held each summer.

lead in alchemy, this metal is associated with Saturn, and is proverbial for its heaviness and low value.

To **go down like a lead balloon** is to fail, be a flop, (especially of a speech or suggestion) be poorly received. The idea of something plummeting as heavily as a balloon made of lead is recorded from the mid 20th century.

Leadenhall Street the East India Company, from the name of a street in the City of London, which from 1648 to 1861 contained the Company's headquarters.

turn over a new leaf improve one's conduct or performance. The *leaf* here is the page of a book. Recorded from the late 16th century, it now always means to alter for the better, but could previously also mean just to alter or even alter for the worse.

the League of Nations an association of countries established in 1919 by the Treaty of Versailles to promote international cooperation and achieve international peace and security. Although the League greatly assisted post-war economic reconstruction, it failed in its prime purpose through the refusal of member nations to put international interests before national ones, It was powerless to stop Italian, German, and Japanese expansionism leading to the Second World War, and was replaced by the United Nations in 1945.

Leah in the Bible, the eldest daughter of ➤ LABAN and sister of ➤ RACHEL, who by a trick became the first wife of ➤ JACOB.

Leander in Greek mythology, a young man, the lover of the priestess Hero, who swam nightly across the Hellespont to visit her, and who was drowned while so doing.

The **Leander Club** is the oldest amateur rowing club in the world, founded early in the 19th century, and now based in Henley-on-Thames.

Leaning Tower of Pisa the circular bell tower of Pisa cathedral, which leans about 5 m (17 ft) from the perpendicular over its height of 55 m (181 ft).

a leap in the dark a daring step or enterprise whose consequences are unpredictable; in Vanbrugh's The Provoked Wife (1697), one of the characters, contemplating marriage, says: 'So, now I am in for Hobbes's voyage, a great leap in the dark.' The allusion is to the attributed last words of the English philosopher Thomas Hobbes (1588–1679), 'I am about to take my last voyage, a great leap in the dark.'

leap year a year, occurring once every four years, which has 366 days including 29 February as an intercalary day. The term, recorded from late Middle English, probably comes from the fact that feast days after February in such a year fell two days later than in the previous year, rather than one day later as in other years, and could be said to have 'leaped' a day.

According to tradition, a woman may propose to a man on 29 February.

Lear a legendary early king of Britain, the central figure in Shakespeare's tragedy *King Lear*, mentioned by the chronicler Geoffrey of Monmouth. In Shakespeare's play, Lear divides his kingdom between his two elder daughters, Goneril and Regan, and is driven to madness by their neglect and mistreatment of him. He may be taken as the proverbial figure of a parent faced with an ungrateful child.

least said, soonest mended a difficult situation will be resolved more quickly if there is no more discussion of it. Proverbial in a number of versions since the mid 15th century, and in this form from the late 18th century.

leatherneck an informal term for a US marine, with allusion to the leather lining inside the collar of a marine's uniform.

Leatherstocking nickname of ➤ *Natty* BUMPPO, the hero of *The Pioneers* (1823) and four other novels of American frontier life by James Fenimore Cooper (1789–1851).

leave no stone unturned try every possible expedient; the expression is used by Pliny in his Letters. The term was said by the sophist Zenobius to derive from a story of hidden Persian treasure.

leaven in figurative use, a pervasive influence that modifies something or transforms it for the better, as in Matthew 13:33. Although the term is now used to denote a force for good, it was originally used also to warn against bad influences, as in Matthew 16:6.

The phrase **of the same leaven** designates someone of the same sort or character.

Lebensraum literally, space for living; the term used for territory which many German nationalists in the mid 20th century claimed was needed for the survival and healthy development of the nation.

Hannibal Lecter the psychopathic genius who is the serial-killer anti-hero of *The Silence of the Lambs* (1988, film 1991) and other books by Thomas Harris (1940–). Dr Lecter is otherwise known as **Hannibal the Cannibal**, and his 'I'm having an old friend for dinner' is to be taken in its literal sense.

lectern a tall stand with a sloping top to hold a book or notes, and from which someone, typically a preacher or lecturer, can read while standing up. Recorded from Middle English, the word comes via Old French from medieval Latin *lectrum*, from *legere* 'to read'.

lectionary a list or book of portions of the Bible appointed to be read at divine service.

Leda in Greek mythology, the wife of Tyndareus king of Sparta. She was loved by Zeus, who visited her in the form of a swan; among her children were the ➤ DIOSCURI, ➤ HELEN, and Clytemnestra.

lee shore a shore lying on the leeward side of a ship (the side sheltered from the wind), on to which a ship could be blown in foul weather.

leech[1] a term (now archaic or humorous) for a doctor or healer. Recorded from Old English, the word was later often understood as a transferred use of ➤ LEECH[2], sometimes with an indication of rapacity.

Leechcraft is similarly used for the art of healing.

leech[2] an aquatic or terrestrial annelid worm with suckers at both ends. Many species are bloodsucking parasites, especially of vertebrates (*leeches* were traditionally used in medicine to draw off blood) and others are predators, giving rise to the transferred sense of a person who extorts profit from or sponges on others.

leek the *leek* is a national emblem of Wales, and is traditionally worn on St David's day (1 March). No clear reason for the association with ➤ St DAVID has been identified, although some sources suggest that it derives from a battle in which Welsh forces led by David wore leeks as a badge, and Fluellen in Shakespeare's *Henry V* explains it as a memorial to a battle fought in France under the Black Prince, in which 'Welshmen did good service in a garden where leeks did grow, wearing leeks in their Monmouth caps'.

Proverbial usages refer to it as the type of something worthless (as in **not worth a leek**) or allude to its colour.

left on, towards, or relating to the side of a human body or of a thing which is to the west when the person or thing is facing north. The original meaning (in Old English) was 'weak', the left-hand side being regarded as the weaker side of the body.

Left also means of or relating to a person or group favouring radical, reforming, or socialist views. The usage is first recorded in English in Carlyle's account (in *The French Revolution*, 1837), and originated in the French National Assembly of 1789, in which the nobles were seated on the President's right and the commons on his left; this ceremonial grouping soon came to reflect political views.

The **Left Bank** is a district of the city of Paris, situated on the left bank of the River Seine, to the south of the river, an area noted for its intellectual and artistic life.

In baseball, **left field** is the part of the outfield to the left of the batter when facing the pitcher; in extended usage, it is a surprising or unconventional position or style (as in **out of left field**), or a position of ignorance, error, or confusion.

A **left-handed marriage** was a morganatic marriage (it was customary, in such marriages in Germany, for the bridegroom to give the bride his left hand instead of his right).

legate a member of the clergy, especially a cardinal, representing the Pope.

legend a traditional story sometimes popularly regarded as historical but not authenticated. This sense dates from the early 17th century; in Middle English, the word was used to denote the story of a saint's life, and came via Old French from medieval Latin *legenda* 'things to be read'.

A **legend in their own lifetime** is a very famous or notorious person; someone whose fame is comparable to that of a hero of legend or about whom similar stories are told.

legion a division of 3,000–6,000 men, including a complement of cavalry, in the ancient Roman army.

Legion is also used to mean great in number, many, as in **their name is legion**. This usage dates from the late 17th century, from the story in Mark 5:9 of the madman healed by Jesus, who when asked his name had replied, 'My name is Legion, for we are many.'

leitmotif a recurrent theme throughout a musical or literary composition, associated with a particular person, idea, or situation, originally associated particularly with the musical drama of Wagner.

lemming a small, short-tailed, thickset rodent of the Arctic tundra. The Norway lemming is noted for its fluctuating populations and periodic mass migrations, and from this *lemming* is used to denote a person who unthinkingly joins a mass movement, especially a headlong rush to destruction.

Lemnos a Greek island in the northern Aegean Sea, where in Greek mythology Hephaestus is said to have fallen when thrown out of heaven; its extinct volcano was said to be his forge.

In later legend, Lemnos was associated with two massacres. Firstly, the women of Lemnos offended Aphrodite and in consequence were deserted by their husbands; in revenge, they killed all the men on the island, and married the ➤ ARGONAUTS who spent a year on Lemnos in their travels; their children became the next generation on the island. Secondly, the Pelasgians settled in Lemnos when driven out of Attica; they brought a number of captive Athenian women with them who bore their children. The children grew up speaking the Attic dialect with their mothers, and the Pelasgians grew suspicious of them: the women and children were murdered by them.

lemon the type of something unsatisfactory, perhaps referring to the least valuable symbol in a fruit machine; **the answer is a lemon** means that the response is unsatisfactory.

In the US, **lemon law** is an informal term for a law designed to provide redress for buyers of faulty or substandard cars; the expression **hand someone a lemon**, meaning pass off a sub-standard article as being of good value, is recorded from the early 20th century.

Lemuria a hypothetical continent stretching from Africa to south-east Asia, formerly supposed to have existed in the Jurassic period.

Lend-Lease an arrangement made in 1941 whereby the US supplied military equipment and armaments to the UK and its allies, originally as a loan in return for the use of British-owned military bases.

Leningrad between 1924 and 1991, the name given to St Petersburg in honour of Vladimir Ilich *Lenin* (1870–1924), the principal figure in the Russian Revolution and first Premier of the Soviet Union 1918–24.

Lent the period preceding Easter which in the Christian Church is devoted to fasting, abstinence, and penitence in commemoration of Christ's fasting in the wilderness. In the Western Church it runs from Ash Wednesday to Holy Saturday, and so includes forty weekdays. The name comes from a Middle English abbreviation of ➤ LENTEN.

The **lent lily** is the European wild daffodil, which typically has pale creamy-white outer petals.

In the UK, **Lent term** is the university term in which Lent falls.

Lenten of, in, or appropriate to Lent. Old English *lencten* 'spring, Lent', of Germanic origin, is related to *long*, perhaps with reference to the lengthening of the day in spring; it is now interpreted as coming directly from *Lent* + the suffix *-en*.

Lenten fare is food appropriate to Lent, especially that without meat.

A **Lenten rose** is a hellebore that is cultivated for its flowers which appear in late winter or early spring.

Leo a large constellation (the Lion), said to represent the lion slain by Hercules. *Leo* is also the fifth sign of the zodiac, which the sun enters about 23 July.

St Leo (d. 461), pope from 440 and Doctor of the Church; known as **Leo the Great**. He defined the doctrine of the Incarnation at the Council of Chalcedon (451) and extended the power of the Roman see to Africa, Spain, and Gaul. He persuaded the Huns to retire beyond the Danube and secured concessions from the Vandals when they captured Rome.

His feast day is (in the Eastern Church) 18 February; (in the Western Church) 11 April.

St Leonard (?6th century), Frankish noble and hermit, who became one of the most popular saints of western Europe in the Middle Ages. He was patron especially of pregnant women and captives such as prisoners of war, and his feast day is 6 November.

Leonidas king of Sparta, commander of the Greeks at the battle of ➤ THERMOPYLAE in 480 BC, where he and all his men were killed.

leopard the leopard was originally (as in Pliny's *Natural History*) regarded as a hybrid between a lion and a 'pard'. In heraldry, *leopard* means both the spotted leopard as a heraldic device, and a lion passant guardant as in the arms of England.

Battle of Lepanto a naval battle fought in 1571 close to the port of Lepanto at the entrance to the Gulf of Corinth. The Christian forces of Rome, Venice, and Spain, under the leadership of Don John of Austria, defeated a large Turkish fleet, ending for the time being Turkish naval domination in the eastern Mediterranean.

leper a person suffering from leprosy; in figurative use, a person who is avoided or rejected by others for moral or social reasons. The word comes ultimately via French and Latin from Greek *lepra*, feminine of *lepros* 'scaly'.

leprechaun in Irish folklore, a small mischievous sprite. The word is Irish, and comes ultimately from Old Irish *lu* 'small' + *corp* 'body'.

leprosy now mainly confined to tropical Africa and Asia, *leprosy* was common in medieval Europe, and those afflicted by it were forced to live apart from the community.

Traditional allusions tend to refer to the pallor of the skin in someone suffering from the illness.

Leptis Magna an ancient seaport and trading centre on the Mediterranean coast of North Africa, near present-day Al Khums in Libya. Founded by the Phoenicians, it became one of the three chief cities of Tripolitania and was later a Roman colony under Trajan. Most of its impressive remains date from the reign of Septimius Severus (AD 193–211), a native of the city.

Lesbian from or relating to Lesbos, a Greek island in the eastern Aegean, off the coast of NW Turkey; its artistic golden age of the late 7th and early 6th centuries BC produced the poets Alcaeus and ➤ SAPPHO, and the sense of *lesbian* to mean a homosexual woman derives from the association with Sappho, who expressed affection for women in her poetry.

lese-majesty the insulting of a monarch or other ruler; treason. Recorded from Middle English, the phrase comes directly from French *lèse-majesté*, and ultimately from Latin *laesa majestas* 'injured sovereignty'.

Lethe in Greek mythology, a river in Hades whose water when drunk made the souls of the dead forget their life on earth. The name comes via Latin from Greek *lēthē* 'forgetfulness'.

Leto in Greek mythology, the daughter of a Titan, mother (by Zeus) of ➤ ARTEMIS and ➤ APOLLO. Her Roman name is *Latona*.

a dead letter a law or practice no longer observed. Originally with reference to biblical passages in which St Paul compares the life-giving spirit of the New Testament with what he sees as the dead 'letter' of the Mosaic Law. Also, until the late 19th century, **Dead-letter Office** was the name given to the organization dealing with unclaimed and misdirected mail.

letter of marque a licence to fit out an armed vessel and use it in the capture of enemy merchant shipping and to commit acts which would otherwise have constituted piracy.

letters patent an open document issued by a monarch or government conferring a patent or other right.

lettre de cachet a warrant issued in the France of the *ancien régime* for the imprisonment of a person without trial at the pleasure of the monarch.

the Levant an archaic name for the eastern part of the Mediterranean with its islands and neighbouring countries. The name comes from French, literally 'rising', the present participle of *lever* 'to lift', used as a noun in the sense 'point of sunrise, east'. Recorded from the late 15th century, the word originally meant more generally the countries of the east, with **High Levant** another term for the Far East.

The archaic term *levant* 'run away, typically leaving unpaid debts' may come from this; there is a comparable expression in French *faire voile en Levant*, literally 'set sail for the Levant.'

A **levanter** is a strong easterly wind in the Mediterranean region.

level playing field a state or condition of parity or impartiality, fair play (a playing field which is not level may be held to offer unfair advantages to the home side). In the 1980s the image became increasingly popular in the worlds of business and politics, although a number of instances suggest scepticism that the implied equality of opportunity is to be readily achieved.

Leveller an extreme radical dissenter in the English Civil War (1642–9), wishing to *level* all differences of rank, and calling for the abolition of the monarchy, social and agrarian reforms, and religious freedom; they were ultimately suppressed by Cromwell.

leveret a young hare in its first year. Recorded from late Middle English, the world comes from an Anglo-Norman French diminutive of *levre* 'hare'.

Levi (in the Bible) a Hebrew patriarch, son of Jacob and Leah (Genesis 29:34); the ➤ LE-VITES, the tribe of Israel traditionally descended from him.

leviathan in biblical use, a sea monster, identified in different passages with the whale and the crocodile (e.g. Job 41, Psalm 74:14), and with the Devil (after Isaiah 27:1). The word is also used allusively for an absolute monarch or state, from the title of Thomas Hobbes's 1651 political study *Leviathan*.

Levite a member of the Hebrew tribe of Levi, especially of that part of it which provided assistants to the priests in the worship in the Jewish temple.

Leviticus the third book of the Bible, containing details of law and ritual; in Judaism, the **Levitical** rules concerning conduct and temple rituals are derived from this book. The **Levitical degrees** are the degrees of consanguinity within which marriage is forbidden in Leviticus 18:6–18.

Lexington a residential town north-west of Boston, Massachusetts, which was the scene in 1775 of the first battle in the War of American Independence.

ley line a supposed straight line connecting three or more prehistoric or ancient sites, sometimes regarded as the line of a former track and associated by some with lines of energy and other paranormal phenomena. Recorded from the 1920s, *ley* is a variant of *lea* 'an open area of grassy or arable land'.

the liar paradox the paradox involved in a speaker's statement that he or she is lying or is a (habitual) liar, as in the statement by a Cretan that all Cretans are liars; by this definition, if he is a Cretan, then what he says cannot be true, and Cretans are honest.

liberty freedom.
The **Liberty Bell** is a bell in Philadelphia first rung on 8 July 1776 to celebrate the first public reading of the Declaration of Independence. It bears the legend 'Proclaim liberty throughout all the land unto all the inhabitants thereof' (Leviticus 25:10). It cracked irreparably when rung for George Washington's birthday in 1846 and is now housed near Independence Hall, Philadelphia.
Liberty Hall is a place where one may do as one likes. The phrase comes originally from Goldmith's *She Stoops to Conquer* (1773).
The **Statue of Liberty** is a statue at the entrance to New York harbour, a symbol of welcome to immigrants, representing a draped female figure carrying a book of laws in her left hand and holding aloft a torch in her right; it is inscribed with lines by the American poet Emma Lazarus (1849–87). Dedicated in 1886, it was designed by Frédéric-Auguste Bartholdi and was the gift of the French, commemorating the alliance of France and the US during the War of American Independence. The formal title of the statue is *Liberty Enlightening the World*.

Libra the seventh sign of the zodiac, the Scales or Balance, which the sun enters at the northern autumnal equinox (about 23 September).

Library of Congress the US national library, in Washington DC. It was established in 1800, originally for the benefit of members of the US Congress, and was at first housed in the Capitol, moving to its present site in 1897.

lick into shape make presentable, originally with reference to the supposed practice of bears with their young. According to early bestiaries, bear-cubs were born without form, and were then licked into shape by their mothers; a bear may thus be taken as a symbol of the Church shaping human nature.

lictor in ancient Rome, an officer attending the consul or other magistrate, bearing the fasces, and executing sentence on offenders.

light at the end of the tunnel a long-awaited indication that a period of hardship or adversity is nearing an end.

the Light of the World Jesus Christ, *Lux Mundi*; the phrase is biblical, as in John 8:12; it was famously used by the Pre-Raphaelite artist Holman Hunt as the title of his picture (1851–3) of Jesus Christ, illustrating Revelation 3:20.

light year a unit of astronomical distance equivalent to the distance that light travels in one year, which is 9.4607×10^{12} km (nearly 6 million million miles); often used figuratively.

lighthouse the ➤ PHAROS of Alexandria was one of the Seven Wonders of the World.

In early Christian iconography, in which the Church is often portrayed as a ship, a *lighthouse* is a symbol for the safe guidance of the soul through life.

lightning never strikes twice calamity never occurs twice; a proverbial allusion to the folk belief that lightning never strikes the same spot twice.

Li'l Abner an American cartoon character created by Al Capp in 1934; the good-natured but simple Abner and his hillbilly family, including a much-loved pig, counterpoint the commonly encountered human failings of stupidity and greed.

Lili Marlene a German song (1917) by Hans Leip (1893–1983) which was popular with both German and Allied soldiers during the Second World War. The song, with its image of Lili Marlene standing beneath the lantern by the barrack gate, became known to Allied troops after it was broadcast to them by Nazi propaganda radio in North Africa in 1941, and an English version of the lyrics was written by Tommie Connor. Leip said that the song was based on two girls he knew called Lili and Marlene.

Lilith a female demon of Jewish folklore, who tries to kill newborn children. In the Talmud she is the first wife of Adam, dispossessed by Eve.

Lilliburlero an anti-Jacobite song ridiculing the Irish, popular at the end of the 17th century especially among soldiers and supporters of William III during the Revolution of 1688; the refrain of the song is 'Lilli burlero bullen a la'.

Lilliput in Swift's *Gulliver's Travels*, the imaginary country inhabited by people 6 inches (15 cm) high; the term **Lilliputian** for a trivial or very small person or thing derives from this.

When Gulliver is shipwrecked on the island of Lilliput, the inhabitants attempt to constrain him by tying him down with a network of ropes; this image is often referred to in allusions to Gulliver and Lilliput.

lily a white *lily* stands for purity, and an orange lily is an emblem of the ➤ ORANGE *Order*. In heraldry, the lilies of the ➤ FLEUR-*de-lis* represent France.

A *lily* is the emblem of ➤ St ANTHONY *of Padua*, ➤ St CATHERINE *of Siena*, and ➤ St DOMINIC. In representations of the ➤ ANNUNCI-ATION, Gabriel is often shown holding a lily.

In biblical translations, the **lilies of the field** may be any of a number of conspicuous Palestinian flowers, variously identified as a lily, tulip, anemone, and gladiolus.

in the Bible, **lily of the valley** is used to translate the Vulgate's *lilium convallium* (Song of Solomon), an unidentified plant.

limbo in some Christian beliefs, the supposed abode of the souls of unbaptized infants, and of the just who died before Christ's coming.

The name is recorded from late Middle English, and comes from the medieval Latin phrase *in limbo*, from *limbus* 'hem, border, limbo'. From the mid seventeenth century the use of the term widened to cover a place or situation resembling limbo; it is now generally used for an uncertain period of awaiting a decision or resolution; an intermediate state or condition.

limerick a humorous five-line poem with a rhyme scheme *aabba*, popularized by the English humorist Edward Lear (1812–88) and closely associated with him. It is said to be named from the chorus 'will you come up to Limerick?', sung between improvised verses at a gathering.

Limey an American and Australian informal derogatory term for a British person. It dates from the late 19th century, and is said to derive from the former enforced consumption of lime juice in the British navy in order to prevent scurvy.

Lincoln Memorial a monument in Washington DC to the American Republican statesman Abraham Lincoln (1809–65), designed by Henry Bacon (1866–1924) and dedicated in 1922. Built in the form of a Greek temple, the monument houses a large statue of Lincoln.

Lincoln's Inn one of the Inns of Court in London, on the site of what was originally the palace of Ralph Neville (d. 1244), bishop of Chichester and Chancellor, and which later became the property of Henry de Lacy, earl of Lincoln (1249?–1311). When the property was made available to students of the law it was thus called *Lincoln's Inn*.

Lindbergh law in the US, a law making kidnapping a federal offence if the victim is taken across a state line or if ransom demands are sent by post. The law was passed by Congress in response to the kidnapping and death of the infant son of the American aviator Charles Lindbergh (1902–74).

Lindisfarne a small island off the coast of Northumberland, north of the Farne Islands. Linked to the mainland by a causeway exposed only at low tide, it is the site of a church and monastery founded by St Aidan in 635, which was a missionary centre of the Celtic Church. The sacking of Lindisfarne at the end of the 8th century was one of the first indicators of the coming Viking raids on Britain.

The **Lindisfarne Gospels** are a manuscript of the four gospels which was probably written to mark the canonization of St Cuthbert in 698; the illuminations and decorative capitals show elements of Celtic and Byzantine design.

Linear A the earlier of two related forms of writing discovered at Knossos in Crete between 1894 and 1901, found on tablets and vases dating from *c.*1700 to 1450 BC and still largely unintelligible.

Linear B a form of Bronze Age writing discovered on tablets in Crete, dating from *c.*1400 to 1200 BC. In 1952 it was shown by Michael Ventris and John Chadwick to be a syllabic script composed of linear signs, derived from Linear A and older Minoan scripts, representing a form of Mycenaean Greek.

wash one's dirty linen in public discuss or argue about one's personal affairs in public. Early 19th century in English; the equivalent French prohibition on publicizing *linge sale* is attributed to Napoleon.

lingam a symbol of divine generative energy, especially a phallus or phallic object as a symbol of Shiva. The word comes from Sanskrit *linga*, literally 'mark, (sexual) characteristic'.

Lingua Franca a mixture of Italian with French, Greek, Arabic, and Spanish, formerly used in the Levant; *lingua franca* now denotes a language that is adopted as a common language between speakers whose native languages are different.

Recorded from the late 17th century, the phrase comes from Italian, and means literally 'Frankish tongue'.

Linnaean system the classification system for plants and animals devised by the Swedish botanist Carolus Linnaeus (1707–78). He devised an authoritative classification system for flowering plants involving binomial Latin names (later superseded by that of Antoine Jussieu), and also a classification method for animals.

lion the *lion* is traditionally taken as the type of strength, majesty, and courage, the 'king of beasts', and has been used as an epithet of successful and warlike rulers. (See also ➤ TWIST *the lion's tail*.)

A *lion* is the emblem of ➤ *St* MARK and ➤ *St* JEROME; the **lion of St Mark** is a winged lion emblematic of St Mark the Evangelist; one of the four animals of the ➤ TETRAMORPH.

The expression **a lion in the way** for a danger or obstacle likely to be imaginary comes from Proverbs 26:13. **The lion's mouth** is a place of great danger, as in Proverbs 22:21.

The **lion's provider** is the ➤ JACKAL, from the traditional belief that the jackal went before the lion to hunt up his prey.

The **lion's share** of something is the largest share.

The **Lions Club** is a worldwide charitable society devoted to social and international service, taking its membership primarily from business and professional groups.

To **throw to the lions** is to put in an unpleasant or dangerous situation, originally with reference to the practice in imperial Rome of throwing religious and political dissidents, especially Christians, to wild beasts as a method of execution. The earliest use in English appears to be in a 17th-century sermon. The Latin phrase *Christianos ad leones* 'Throw the Christians to the lions' is recorded in Tertullian's *Apologeticus*.

pay lip service to express approval or support for something without taking any significant action.

Lipizzaner a horse of a fine white breed used especially in displays of dressage. The name comes (in the early 20th century) from German, from *Lippiza*, site of the former Austrian Imperial stud near Trieste; the stud is now based in Vienna.

the Litany in the Christian Church, a series of petitions for use in church services or processions, usually recited by the clergy and responded to in a recurring formula by the people.

litotes ironical understatement in which an affirmative is expressed by the negative of its contrary (e.g. *I shan't be sorry* for *I shall be glad*). Recorded from the late 16th century, the word comes via late Latin from Greek, ultimately from *litos* 'plain, meagre'.

little of small extent or size.

The **Battle of Little Bighorn** was a battle in which General George Custer and his forces were defeated by Sioux warriors on 25 June 1876, popularly known as ➤ CUSTER's *Last Stand*. It took place in the valley of the Little Bighorn River in Montana.

A **Little Englander** is a person who opposes an international role or policy for England (or, in practice, for Britain). The term dates from the late 19th century, and is currently often used in relation to opposition to Europe.

The **little gentleman in black velvet** is the mole, as a Jacobite toast, referring to the belief that William III's death resulted from the king's being thrown from his horse when it stumbled on a molehill.

A **little green man** is an imaginary being from outer space. The expression is not recorded until the mid-20th century; the earliest literal use of the phrase, in Kipling's *Puck of Pook's Hill* (1906), refers to a Pictish warrior who is tattooed green.

The phrase **little local difficulties** was used by Harold Macmillan (1894–1986) as Prime Minister, before leaving for a Commonwealth tour in January 1958, referring to the resignation of the Chancellor of the Exchequer and other members of the Cabinet.

Little Lord Fauntleroy is the boy hero of Frances Hodgson Burnett's novel *Little Lord Fauntleroy* (1886), who wore velvet suits with lace collars, and had his hair in ringlets.

Little Red Riding-hood is the heroine of the nursery story by the French writer Charles Perrault (1628–1703), in which a woodcutter's daughter is menaced by a wolf which has eaten her grandmother and is lying in wait, disguised as the grandmother, for Red Riding Hood herself.

liturgy a form or formulary according to which public religious worship, especially Christian worship, is conducted. **The Liturgy** designates the Communion office of the Orthodox Church, and is also an archaic term in the Anglican Church for the Book of Common Prayer. Recorded from the mid 16th century, the word comes via French or late Latin from Greek *leitourgia* 'public service, worship of the gods'.

Liturgical colours are the colours used in ecclesiastical vestments and hangings for an altar, varying according to the season, festival, or kind of service. These have varied over the centuries, but now generally conform to the system established in 1570, with violet for Advent and Lent, white and gold for Christmas, Epiphany, Easter Sunday, and Trinity Sunday, red for Passion Sunday and Pentecost, and green for the rest of the year.

live and let live you should tolerate the opinions and behaviour of others so that they will similarly tolerate your own. First recorded in English in the early 17th century, and referred to there as a Dutch proverb.

live to fight another day survive a certain experience or ordeal. The idea, found in the Greek comic dramatist Menander, is expressed in the English proverbial jingle *He who fights and runs away Lives to fight another day.*

liver the *liver* was anciently supposed to be the seat of love and violent emotion; it was the source of one of the four humours (➤ CHOLER) of early physiology.

A light coloured liver was traditionally supposed to show a deficiency of choler, and thus indicate a lack of spirit or courage; the expressions **white-livered** and **yellow-livered**, meaning cowardly, derive from this.

In the ancient world, the liver of a sacrificed animal was examined for omens.

livery a special uniform worn by a servant, an official, or a member of a City Company. The original sense was 'the dispensing of food, provisions, or clothing to servants', and the sense of a special uniform arose because medieval nobles provided matching clothes to distinguish their own servants from those of others.

In the UK, a **livery company** is any of the London City companies, which formerly had distinctive costumes. Descended from medieval craft guilds, the companies are now largely social and charitable organizations; none is now a trading company, though some still have some involvement with the operation of their original trade; several support public schools (e.g. Merchant Taylors, Haberdashers), and collectively they are involved in various forms of technical education. A member of such a company is known as a **liveryman**.

Dr Livingstone, I presume the words with which in 1871 Henry Morton Stanley (1841–1904) greeted the Scottish missionary and explorer David Livingstone (1813–73), who in 1866 had gone in search of the source of the Nile. As a newspaper correspondent Stanley was sent in 1869 to central Africa to find Livingstone; he discovered him two years later in poor health at Lake Tanganyika.

Lloyd's an incorporated society of insurance underwriters in London, made up of private syndicates. Founded in 1871, Lloyd's originally dealt only in marine insurance. It is named after the coffee house of Edward Lloyd (fl. 1688–1726), in which underwriters and merchants congregated and where **Lloyd's List**, a daily newsletter relating to shipping, was started in 1734.

Lloyd's Register, also called **Lloyd's Register of Shipping**, is a classified list of merchant ships over a certain tonnage, published annually in London.

Loathly Lady a traditional ballad figure, an apparently ugly woman whose beauty is restored when at last she has found a husband and the enchantment laid on her is dispelled. The story is told by the ➤ Wife *of Bath* in the *Canterbury Tales*; the knight who has married the *loathly lady* has to answer the question, 'what do women most desire?', and his wife regains youth and beauty at the correct answer, 'sovereignty'.

loaves and fishes personal profit as a motive for religious profession or public service, with biblical allusion to John 6:26, and the story of the miracle by which Jesus and his disciples fed a crowd of five thousand with 'five loaves, and two fishes'.

loaves of bread the emblem of ➤ St Philip and ➤ St Nicholas *of Tolentino*.

lobby in the UK, any of several large halls in the Houses of Parliament in which MPs may meet members of the public. The verb *to lobby*, meaning to seek to influence a politician or public official on an issue, derives (originally in the US) from the practice of frequenting the lobby of a house of legislature

to influence its members into supporting a cause.

A **lobby correspondent** in the UK is a senior political journalist of a group receiving direct but unattributable briefings from the government.

Loch Ness Monster a large creature alleged to live in the deep waters of Loch Ness. Reports of its existence date from the time of St Columba (6th century); the number of sightings increased after the construction of a major road alongside the loch in 1933, but, despite recent scientific expeditions, there is still no proof of its existence.

Lochinvar the hero of a ballad included in the fifth canto of Scott's *Marmion*. His fair Ellen is about to be married to 'a laggard in love and a dastard in war', when the brave Lochinvar arrives at the bridal feast, claims a dance with her, and, as they reach the door, swings the lady on to his horse, and rides off with her.

Lockerbie a town in SW Scotland, in Dumfries and Galloway, where in 1988 the wreckage of an American airliner, destroyed by a terrorist bomb, crashed on the town, killing all those on board and eleven people on the ground.

locust taken as a type of devouring and destructive propensities. The phrase **locust years** for years of poverty and hardship was coined by Winston Churchill in his *History of the Second World War* (1948) to describe Britain in the 1930s. The allusion is biblical, to Joel 2:25.

lodestar a star that is used to guide the course of a ship, especially the pole star. The word is recorded from Middle English, and the first element means 'way, course'. The figurative use developed early and was popular up to the 17th century; it was then revived in the early 19th century.

lodestone a piece of magnetite or other naturally magnetized mineral, able to be used as a magnet. Recorded from the early 16th century, the word means literally 'waystone', from the use of the magnet in guiding mariners.

King Log in Aesop's fable, the antithesis of ➤ *King* Stork in his rule over the frogs. According to the story, the frogs asked for a king, and were first of all given a log by Jupiter. Demanding a more active king, they were given a stork, who ate many of them.

The two kings are referred to allusively as types of inertia and excessive activity.

log cabin a hut built of whole or split logs; in North America taken (as typical of a settler's cabin) as symbolizing the humblest origins from which a person might rise to eminence.

logic reasoning conducted or assessed according to strict principles of validity; a particular system or codification of the principles of proof and inference. In the Middle Ages, *logic* was one of the ➤ SEVEN *liberal arts*.

In computing, a **logic bomb** is a set of instructions secretly incorporated into a program so that if a particular condition is satisfied they will be carried out, usually with harmful effects.

Logic chopping is the practice of engaging in excessively pedantic argument. The expression *chop logic* is recorded from the early 16th century, and originally meant 'exchange or bandy logical arguments'; in later use, *chop* was wrongly understood as meaning 'cut, split'.

logical positivism a form of positivism, developed by members of the Vienna Circle, which considers that the only meaningful philosophical problems are those which can be solved by logical analysis.

logion a saying attributed to Christ, especially one not recorded in the canonical Gospels. The word comes from Greek, 'oracle', from *logos* 'word'.

Logos in theology, the Word of God, or principle of divine reason and creative order, identified in the Gospel of John with the second person of the Trinity incarnate in Jesus Christ.

In Jungian psychology, *Logos* is used for the principle of reason and judgement, associated with the animus.

logrolling the practice of exchanging favours, especially in politics by reciprocal voting for each other's proposed legislation. Recorded from the early 19th century, the expression is North American, and derives from the proverbial phrase *you roll my log and I'll roll yours.*

Lohengrin in medieval French and German romances, the son of Perceval (Parsifal). He was summoned from the temple of the Holy Grail in a boat drawn by swans to Antwerp, where he rescued Elsa of Brabant from a forced marriage; he was ready to marry her himself, providing that she did not ask who he was. Elsa broke this condition and he was carried away in the swan-boat back to the Grail castle.

loiter with intent stand or wait around with the intention of committing an offence. A legal phrase derived from an 1891 Act of Parliament, it is also used figuratively and humorously of anyone who is waiting around for some unspecified purpose.

Loki in Scandinavian mythology, a mischievous and sometimes evil god who contrived the death of Balder and was punished by being bound to a rock. He was the father of Fenrir, the Midgard's serpent, and Hel.

Lolita the sexually precocious heroine of Nabokov's novel (1958) who has an affair with her stepfather Humbert Humbert.

Lollard a follower of John Wyclif. The Lollards believed that the Church should aid people to live a life of evangelical poverty and imitate Christ. Official attitudes to the Lollards varied considerably, but they were generally held to be heretics and often severely persecuted.

The word was originally a derogatory term, derived from a Dutch word meaning 'mumbler', based on *lollen* 'to mumble'.

Lombard a member of a Germanic people who invaded Italy in the 6th century, and who settled in what became **Lombardy**. The name of this people comes from Italian *lombardo*, representing late Latin *Langobardus*, of Germanic origin, from the base of the adjective *long* + the ethnic name *Bardi*. The name *Longobard* is now also used by modern scholars.

In the Middle Ages, the term *Lombard* was used for bankers and money-lenders from Lombardy, and from this was applied generally to anyone engaged in banking and money-lending. **Lombard Street** in the City of London, containing many of the principal London banks, was so named because it was formerly occupied by bankers from Lombardy.

The expression **all Lombard Street to a China Orange**, denoting very long odds against, dates from the early 19th century, although a *China orange* taken as the type of something worthless is recorded earlier.

London Eye name given to the *Millennium Wheel*, an observation wheel erected on the banks of the Thames in London between County Hall and Jubilee Gardens and opened to the public in February 2000; its passenger-carrying capsules are designed to give a 25-mile view across the London skyline.

London particular a dense fog of a kind formerly affecting London; *London fog* had been used by Maria Edgeworth in a letter of 1830, but *London particular* is first recorded in Dickens's *Bleak House* (1853).

lone solitary, single.

The **Lone Ranger** was a character created originally for American radio in 1933, as a masked enforcer of law in the American West, who (assisted by the Indian *Tonto*) constantly intervenes on the side of right, but never reveals his identity. Episodes ended with his call to his white horse, 'Hi-yo, Silver, away!'

The **Lone Star State** is an informal name for Texas.

A **lone wolf** is a wolf living by itself rather than in a pack, and thus a person who prefers to act alone. In its literal sense, the term may well have been popularized by the character of the wolf Akela in Kipling's *Jungle Books*.

long of notable distance or duration.

Long John Silver is the one-legged pirate who is the anti-hero of Stevenson's *Treasure Island* (1883).

The **Long March** was the epic withdrawal of the Chinese communists from SE to NW China in 1934–5, over a distance of 9,600 km (6,000 miles). 100,000 people, led by Mao Zedong, left the communist rural base (the Jiangxi Soviet) after it was almost destroyed by the Kuomintang; 20,000 people survived the journey to reach Yan'an in Shaanxi province.

The **Long Parliament** was the English Parliament which sat from November 1640 to March 1653, was restored for a short time in 1659, and finally voted its own dissolution in 1660. It was summoned by Charles I and sat through the English Civil War and on into the interregnum which followed.

Long pig is a translation of a term formerly used in some Pacific Islands for human flesh as food.

longbow a large bow drawn by hand and shooting a long feathered arrow. It was the chief weapon of English armies from the 14th century until the introduction of firearms. (See also ➤ DRAW *the longbow*.)

Longchamp in Paris, the racecourse at the end of the Bois de Boulogne, where the Prix de l'Arc de Triomphe is run.

Longinus traditionally the name of the Roman soldier who pierced Jesus in the side with his spear at the Crucifixion.

looking-glass being or involving the opposite of what is normal or expected; the allusion is to Lewis Carroll's *Through the Looking Glass* (1871), in which Alice climbs through the looking glass and encounters the Red and White Queens and other chessboard characters.

loony tunes crazy or deranged (people), from *Looney Tunes*, a US animated cartoon series beginning in the 1930s, featuring Bugs Bunny and other characters.

in the loop aware of information known to only a privileged few.

lord a man of noble rank or high office, a peer. In the UK, the **House of Lords** is the chamber of Parliament which until 1999 was composed of hereditary and life peers and bishops; reform of the method of selecting the chamber is currently under way.

Our Lord is a name for Christ, and the **Lord's Prayer** is the prayer taught by Jesus to his disciples, as recorded in Matthew 6:9–13; the term is a translation of Latin *oratio Dominica*, and is first recorded in the Book of Common Prayer of 1549.

The **Lord Mayor's Day** is 9 November, the day on which the Lord Mayor of London goes in procession with the Aldermen and other city dignitaries to and from Westminster, where he receives from the Lord Chancellor the assent of the Crown to his election. The procession is known as the **Lord Mayor's show**.

The **Lord of Hosts** is God; a title of Jehovah in the Old Testament, sometimes referring to the heavenly hosts, and sometimes to the armies of Israel.

The **Lord of the Isles** was a title of the early lords of Argyll as rulers of the Western Isles; the title forfeited in 1493, and was merged in the Crown of Scotland in 1540.

The **Lord of the Rings** in Tolkien's trilogy of that name (1954–5), is a title of Sauron, the Dark Lord, referring to the rings of power made for dwarves, elves, and men, and especially to the One Ring which confers magical powers, including invisibility, on its holder.

The **Lord Protector of the Commonwealth** was a title of Oliver Cromwell, established in an Act of 1653.

Lord's a cricket ground in St John's Wood, north London, headquarters since 1814 of the

Marylebone Cricket Club (MCC), named after the cricketer Thomas Lord (1755–1832).

Lorelei in German legend, a beautiful woman with long blonde hair who sat on the *Lorelei* rock on the bank of the Rhine, in the Rhine gorge near Sankt Goarshausen, and with her singing lured boatmen to distraction. The name is often used allusively.

Lorelei is also the name of the gold-digging heroine of Anita Loos's comic novel *Gentlemen Prefer Blondes* (1925).

Loreto a town in eastern Italy, near the Adriatic coast to the south of Ancona, which is the site of the **House of Loreto** (or *Holy House*), said to be the home of the Virgin Mary and to have been brought from Nazareth by angels in 1295.

Lorraine a medieval kingdom (corresponding to the modern region of NE France) which extended from the North Sea to Italy. The name comes from Latin *Lotharingia*, from *Lothair*, the name of a Frankish king (825–69).

Lorraine later became an important French duchy of the House of Guise.

The **Lorraine cross** (or **cross of Lorraine**) is a cross with one vertical and two horizontal bars. It was the symbol of Joan of Arc, and in the Second World War was adopted by the Free French forces of General de Gaulle.

Los Alamos a town in northern New Mexico, which has been a centre for nuclear research since the 1940s, when it was the site of the development of the first atomic and hydrogen bombs.

lost used in literal and figurative phrases.

The **Lost Colony** is a name for the first English settlement in America, birthplace of ▶ Virginia DARE, which was established on Roanoke Island in 1585 and had mysteriously disappeared by 1591.

The **lost generation** were the generation reaching maturity during and just after the First World War, a high proportion of whose men were killed during those years. The expression was applied by Gertrude Stein to disillusioned young American writers who went to live in Paris in the 1920s.

The **Lost Leader** was the title of a poem by Robert Browning (1845) on Wordsworth's acceptance of the office of Poet Laureate, condemning the poet's abandonment of radical principles with the lines.

The **Lost Tribes of Israel** were the ten tribes of Israel taken away *c.*720 BC to captivity in Assyria (2 Kings 17:6), from which they

are believed never to have returned, while the tribes of Benjamin and Judah remained.

Lot in the Bible, the nephew of Abraham, who was allowed to escape from the destruction of Sodom (Genesis 19). His wife, who disobeyed orders and looked back, was turned into a pillar of salt.

Lotharingia an ancient duchy of northern Europe, situated between the Rhine and the Scheldt from Frisia to the Alps. The name ▶ LORRAINE derives from this.

Lothario a man who behaves selfishly and irresponsibly in his sexual relationships with women, from a character in Rowe's *Fair Penitent* (1703).

lotus in Greek mythology, a legendary plant whose fruit induces a dreamy forgetfulness and an unwillingness to depart.

Lotus is also the name of either of two large water lilies, a red-flowered Asian lily, the flower of which is a symbol in Asian art and religion, and a white- or blue-flowered lily regarded as sacred in ancient Egypt.

The word is recorded from the late 15th century, denoting a type of clover or trefoil described by Homer as food for horses; it comes via Latin from Greek *lōtos*, and is of Semitic origin. The term was used by classical writers to denote various trees and plants. This legendary plant, mentioned by Homer, was thought by later Greek writers to be *Ziziphus lotus*, a relative of the jujube.

A **lotus-eater** is a person who spends their time indulging in pleasure and luxury rather than dealing with practical concerns. The *lotus-eaters* or *Lotophagi* in Greek mythology were a people who lived on the fruit of the lotus, said to cause a dreamy forgetfulness and an unwillingness to depart. *Lotophagi* is recorded in English from the early 17th century, but the first use of *lotus-eater* is in the title of a poem by Tennyson, *The Lotos-eaters* (1832)

The **lotus position** is a cross-legged position for meditation, with the feet resting on the thighs.

The **Lotus Sutra** is one of the most important texts in Mahayana Buddhism, significant particularly in China and Japan and given special veneration by the Nichiren sect.

Louis the name of eighteen kings of France, etymologically representing the name of ▶ CLOVIS, who as king of the Franks was seen as founder of the French kingdom.

St Louis (1214–70), king of France (as **Louis IX** from 1226), built the ▶ SAINTE *Chapelle* in

Paris as a shrine for the relic of Christ's Crown of Thorns. His feast day is 25 August.

Louisiana Purchase the territory sold by France to the US in 1803, comprising the western part of the Mississippi valley and including the modern state of Louisiana. The area had been explored by France, ceded to Spain in 1762, and returned to France in 1800.

Lourdes a town in SW France, at the foot of the Pyrenees, which has been a major place of Roman Catholic pilgrimage since in 1858 a young peasant girl, Marie Bernarde Soubirous (St Bernadette), claimed to have had a series of visions of the Virgin Mary.

Louvre the principal museum and art gallery of France, in Paris, housed in the former royal palace built by Francis I and later extended. (Philip Augustus had first established a royal residence here in the late 12th century.) The royal collections, from Francis I onwards and greatly increased by Louis XIV, formed the nucleus of the national collection.

love (in tennis, squash, and some other sports) a score of zero; nil. This usage apparently comes from the phrase *play for love* (i.e. the love of the game, not for money); folk etymology has connected the word with French *l'oeuf* 'egg', from the resemblance in shape between an egg and a zero.

love in a cottage expression for a marriage made for love without sufficient means to sustain a household. The expression is recorded from the early 19th century, and probably derives from *The Clandestine Marriage* (1766) by George Colman the Elder (1732–94) and David Garrick (1717–79).

lovely jubbly expressing delight or affirmation, especially in response to an anticipated success. The phrase derives ultimately from *lubbly Jubbly*, a 1950s advertising slogan for *Jubbly*, an orange-flavoured soft drink; it was recoined in the BBC television series *Only Fools and Horses* (1981–96) as a characteristic expression of Derek Trotter, or 'Del Boy', a Peckham market trader.

Low Sunday the Sunday after Easter, perhaps so named in contrast to the high days of Holy Week and Easter.

Loyalist a colonist of the American revolutionary period who supported the British cause.

The name *Loyalist* is also given in Northern Ireland to a supporter of the union with Great Britain.

lozenge in heraldry, a charge in the shape of a solid diamond, in particular one on which the arms of an unmarried or widowed woman are displayed.

Lubyanka a building in Moscow used as a prison and as the headquarters of the KGB and other Russian secret police organizations since the Russian Revolution.

Lord Lucan a British peer who disappeared in mysterious circumstances in 1974 following an attack on his wife and the murder of the family nanny. Speculation about his survival and whereabouts continues to this day, and his name may be used allusively.

Lucifer the rebel archangel whose fall from heaven was supposed to be referred to in Isaiah 14:12; *Lucifer* was traditionally interpreted as the name of Satan before his fall, and gives rise to the expression **proud as Lucifer**.

The name comes (in Old English) from Latin, 'light-bringing morning star'. In literary use, *Lucifer* may designate the morning star, the planet Venus appearing in the sky before sunrise.

lucre money, especially when regarded as sordid or distasteful or gained in a dishonourable way; the phrase **filthy lucre** is with biblical allusion to Titus 1:11.

Lucretia in Roman legend, a woman who was raped by a son of Tarquinius Superbus and took her own life; this led to the expulsion of the Tarquins from Rome by a rebellion under Brutus.

Lucullan (especially of food) extremely luxurious, from the name of Licinius Lucullus, Roman general of the 1st century BC, famous for giving lavish banquets.

lucus a non lucendo a paradoxical or otherwise absurd derivation; something of which the qualities are the opposite of what its name suggests. Recorded in English from the early 18th century, this Latin phrase means 'a grove (so called) from the absence of *lux* (light)'; that is, a grove is named from the fact of its not shining, a proposition discussed by the Roman rhetorician Quintillian (AD c.35–c.96) in his *Institutio Oratoria*.

St Lucy (d. 304), virgin and martyr, who died at Syracuse in the persecution of Diocletian; her eyes, reputed to have been put out and miraculously restored, are her usual emblem. Her feast day, 13 December, was the shortest day of the year according to the Julian calendar. Especially in Sweden, **St Lucy's day** is associated with a festival of light.

Luddite a member of any of the bands of English workers who destroyed machinery, especially in cotton and woollen mills, which they believed was threatening their jobs (1811–16). The name probably comes from Ned *Lud*, one of the participants in the destruction of machinery.

Lughnasa in Ireland, 1 August, the first day of autumn and one of the four traditional quarter days. The name means 'festival of *Lug*', in Irish mythology, the god who embodies the type of sacred kingship and who is associated with the sun, and would originally have been sacred to this god. In modern times *Lughnasa* has been associated with fairs; legends concerned with the day relate to St Patrick's defeat of paganism.

St Luke an evangelist, closely associated with St Paul and traditionally the author of the third Gospel and the Acts of the Apostles. A physician, he was possibly the son of a Greek freedman of Rome.

His emblem is an ox, one of the animals of the Tetramorph, and he may be portrayed painting the Virgin, or shown with surgical instruments. His feast day is 18 October.

Luke Skywalker in the ➤ STAR *Wars* trilogy the boy who, unknown to himself, is the last inheritor of ➤ JEDI powers, and who in the end destroys the Empire and redeems his father ➤ DARTH *Vader*.

lumpenproletariat (especially in Marxist terminology) the unorganized and unpolitical lower orders of society who are not interested in revolutionary advancement. The word was originally used by Karl Marx, the first element representing German *Lumpen* 'rag, rogue'.

there's no such thing as a free lunch one never gets something for nothing; any benefit received has eventually to be paid for. Originally (mid 20th century) a US axiom relating to economics and finance.

Lupercalia an ancient Roman festival of purification and fertility, held annually on 15 February. Chosen celebrants, wearing the skins of sacrificed animals, ran through the streets, and for a woman to be struck by one of them was to increase her fertility.

The festival was held in honour of *Lupercus*, the equivalent of the Greek god Pan. It is likely that his name is connected with *lupus* 'wolf', and that he was seen as a protector of flocks from wolves.

leave in the lurch leave someone abruptly and without assistance or support when they are in a difficult situation. *Lurch* as a noun meaning 'a state of discomfiture', recorded from the mid 16th century, has long been obsolete except in this idiom.

Lusitania a Cunard liner which was sunk by a German submarine in the Atlantic in May 1915 with the loss of over 1,000 lives; the event was a factor in bringing the US into the First World War. *Lusitania* was originally an ancient Roman province in the Iberian peninsula, corresponding to modern Portugal.

Lutetia the Roman name for what is now the city of Paris. It has given its name to **lutetium**, the chemical element of atomic number 71, a rare silvery-white metal of the lanthanide series, which was discovered in the early 20th century, and which was named for the home of its discoverer.

Lutheran Church the Protestant Church following the teachings of the German Protestant theologian Martin Luther (1483–1546), and accepting the Augsburg Confession of 1530, with justification by faith alone as a cardinal doctrine. The Lutheran Church is the largest Protestant body, with substantial membership in Germany, Scandinavia, and the US.

Lutine Bell a bell kept at Lloyd's in London and rung whenever there is an important announcement to be made to the underwriters. It was salvaged from HMS *Lutine*, which sank in 1799 with a large cargo of gold and bullion, which loss was borne by the underwriters, who were members of Lloyd's.

Lux Mundi Latin for the ➤ LIGHT *of the World.*

Luxor a city in eastern Egypt, on the east bank of the Nile, which is the site of the southern part of ancient Thebes and contains the ruins of the temple built by Amenhotep III and of monuments erected by Ramses II.

lycanthropy the supernatural transformation of a person into a wolf, as recounted in folk tales. *Lycanthropy* is recorded from the late 16th century, as a supposed form of madness involving the delusion of being a wolf.

The word comes from modern Latin *lycanthropia*, and ultimately from Greek *lukos* 'wolf' + *anthropos* 'man'.

Lyceum the garden at Athens in which Aristotle taught philosophy; Aristotelian philosophy and its followers. The name comes via Latin from Greek *Lukeion*, neuter of *Lukeios*, epithet of Apollo (from whose neighbouring temple the Lyceum was named).

The *Lyceum* was also the name of a theatre near the Strand in London, noted for the melodramatic productions staged there by Henry Irving and others.

lychgate a roofed gateway to a churchyard, formerly used at burials for sheltering a coffin until the clergyman's arrival; a **lychway** is a path along which a corpse has been carried to burial, which was supposed in some districts to establish a right of way. The first element comes from Old English *līc* 'body'.

Lycurgan harsh or severe; originally, referring to the constitutional innovations, of *Lycurgus*, 9th-century BC Spartan lawgiver, who is traditionally held to have been the founder of the constitution and military regime of ancient Sparta.

Lydia an ancient region of western Asia Minor, south of Mysia and north of Caria. It

became a powerful kingdom in the 7th century BC but in 546 its final king, Croesus, was defeated by Cyrus and it was absorbed into the Persian empire. Lydia was probably the first realm to use coined money.

In music, the **Lydian mode** is the mode represented by the natural diatonic scale F–F (containing an augmented 4th).

lynch law the punishment or execution of alleged criminals by a group of people without a legal trial. It is named after Captain William *Lynch* (1742–1820), head of a self-constituted judicial tribunal in Virginia *c.*1780.

lynx traditionally alluded to for its keenness of sight; the expression **lynx-eyed** is recorded from the late 16th century.

Lyon the chief herald of Scotland, also called **Lord Lyon**, **Lyon King of Arms**, who presides over the **Lyon Court**. *Lyon* is recorded from late Middle English, and is an archaic variant of *lion*, named from the lion on the royal shield.

Lyonesse in Malory, the region of origin for Tristram; the name is also geographical in Tennyson who makes it the place of the last battle between Arthur and Mordred. It is traditionally said to be a tract of land between Land's End and the Scilly Isles, now submerged.

Mm

M the thirteenth letter of the modern English alphabet and the twelfth of the ancient Roman one, corresponding to Greek *mū*, Semitic *mēm*.

In the ➤ *James* BOND novels and films, *M* is the initial by which the head of the Secret Service is known.

ma nishtana in the Passover Haggadah, the questions traditionally asked by the youngest member of a Jewish household on Seder Night; this part of the Passover celebrations. The name comes from the formulaic beginning of the questions, meaning 'What makes this night different from all other nights?', and the questions are, 'What is the meaning of the precepts, statutes, and laws which the Lord our God has given you?' (Deuteronomy 6:20), 'Why is this rite observed by you?' (Exodus 12:26), and 'What is this?' (Exodus 13:14).

Maastricht Treaty a treaty on European economic and monetary union, agreed by the heads of government of the twelve member states of the European Community at a summit meeting in Maastricht in December 1991. Ratification was completed in October 1993.

Maat in Egyptian mythology, the goddess of truth, justice, and cosmic order, daughter of Ra. She is depicted as a young and beautiful woman, standing or seated, with a feather on her head.

Mabinogion a collection of Welsh prose tales of the 11th–13th centuries, dealing with Celtic legends and mythology, and preserved in The White Book of Rhydderch (1300–25) and The Red Book of Hergest (1375–1425). The four main stories cover events in the life and death of the legendary hero Pryderi, son of Pwyll.

These stories, together with a number of other tales from the Red Book of Hergest, were translated and published by Lady Charlotte Guest as the *Mabinogion* (1838–49).

Lady Macbeth a remorseless or melodramatic woman, especially one leading or assisting a weak man, with allusion to the scene in Shakespeare's *Macbeth* in which Macbeth balks at returning to the room in which he has murdered Duncan to replace the daggers with which he killed the king, and so ensure that Duncan's attendants are believed to be his murderers. His wife undertakes the task, with the words 'Infirm of purpose! Give me the daggers'.

Maccabee a member or supporter of a Jewish family of which ➤ JUDAS *Maccabaeus* was the leading figure, which led a religious revolt in Judaea against the Syrian Seleucid king Antiochus IV *c.*167 BC, as recorded in the Books of the ➤ MACCABEES. The term is occasionally found in extended use, the earliest of which as applied to the Methodists is recorded by John Wesley.

The **Maccabees** are four books of Jewish history and theology, of which the first two are included in the Apocrypha.

McCarthyism a vociferous campaign against alleged communists in the US government and other institutions carried out under the American Republican politician Senator Joseph *McCarthy* (1909–57) in the period 1950–4. Many of the accused were blacklisted or lost their jobs, though most did not in fact belong to the Communist Party. The campaign ended when McCarthy received public censure in December 1954.

mace a staff of office, especially that which lies on the table in the House of Commons when the Speaker is in the chair, regarded as a symbol of the authority of the House. The *mace* is an ornamental version of a medieval weapon which consisted of a heavy staff or club, typically of metal and with a spiked head; the word comes from Old French *masse* 'large hammer'.

McGuffin an object or device in a film or a book which serves merely as a trigger for the plot. Recorded from the late 20th century, the word is a Scottish surname, said to have been borrowed by the English film director, Alfred Hitchcock, from a humorous story involving such a pivotal factor.

Captain Macheath the dashing highwayman who is the central character of John Gay's *The Beggar's Opera* (1728); he is betrayed by the informer ➤ PEACHUM, but ultimately escapes from Newgate.

Machiavellian cunning, scheming, and unscrupulous, especially in politics or in advancing one's career. The word derives from Niccolò *Machiavelli* (1469–1527), Italian statesman and political philosopher, whose best-known work *The Prince* (1532) advises rulers that the acquisition and effective use of power may necessitate unethical methods.

mackerel sky a sky dappled with rows of small white fleecy (typically cirrocumulus) clouds, like the pattern on a mackerel's back, recorded from the mid 17th century. It is traditionally believed to herald a change in the weather.

Machu Picchu a fortified Inca town in the Andes in Peru, which the invading Spaniards never found. Although it was not an important fortress, it is famous for its dramatic position, perched high on a steep-sided ridge. It contains a palace, a temple to the sun, and extensive cultivation terraces. Discovered in 1911, it was named after the mountain that rises above it.

McNaghten rules rules or criteria for judging criminal responsibility where there is a question of insanity. The name applied to the answers given in the House of Lords in 1843 after the trial of Daniel McNaghten for the murder of Sir Robert Peel's secretary, Edward Drummond, when five questions were put respecting crimes alleged to have been committed by persons suffering from insanity.

According to the rules, the defendant must show that he or she is suffering from a defect of reason arising out of 'a disease of the mind', and that, as a result of this defect, was unaware of the 'nature and quality' of his or her acts.

mad mentally ill, insane.

Mad as a hatter means completely mad. Hat-makers sometimes suffered from mercury poisoning as a result of the use of mercurous nitrate in the manufacture of felt hats, and the idea was personified in one of the two eccentric hosts (the **Mad Hatter**) at the 'mad tea party' in Lewis Carroll's *Alice's Adventures in Wonderland* (1865).

Mad as a March hare means completely mad; the allusion here is to the running and leaping of hares in the breeding season, and again was reinforced by the character created by Lewis Carroll in *Alice's Adventures in Wonderland* (1865).

far from the madding crowd secluded or removed from public notice. In allusion to the phrases's use in Gray's *Elegy in a Country Churchyard*, and later also taken as the title of a novel by Thomas Hardy.

Madison Avenue a street in New York City, centre of the American advertising business, often used in allusion to the world of American advertising agents.

Madog a 12th-century Welsh prince who in some stories is said to have been the discoverer of America. He does not appear in contemporary sources, and is first mentioned by a 15th-century bard in connection with a mysterious voyage. The claim that he discovered America was first made in the 16th century.

Madonna the Virgin Mary, a name (from Italian, meaning 'my lady') recorded in English from the mid 17th century.

Mae West an inflatable life jacket, originally as issued to RAF personnel during the Second World War, from the name of the American film actress Mae West, noted for her large bust.

Maeldune in early Irish literature, the hero of *Immram Curaig Máele Dúin* [*Voyage of Máel Dúin's Boat*], one of the stories of fabulous sea voyages (*immrams*) written in Ireland between the late 8th and 11th centuries.

maelstrom a powerful whirlpool in the sea or a river, named (in the late 17th century, from early modern Dutch) after a mythical whirlpool supposed to exist in the Arctic Ocean, west of Norway. The use of *maelstrom* as a proper name seems to come from Dutch maps, for example in Mercator's *Atlas* (1595).

maenad in ancient Greece, a female follower of Bacchus, traditionally associated with divine possession and frenzied rites. Recorded from the late 16th century, the word comes via Latin from Greek *Mainas, Mainad-*, from *mainesthai* 'to rave'.

Maeve in Irish legend, the legendary and sexually voracious queen of Conacht (*Medb*), who is the implacable enemy of ➤ CUCHULAIN, and who instigates the cattle-raid on Ulster to capture the Brown Bull of Cuailgne (see ➤ TAIN-BO-CUAILGNE).

Mafeking a town in South Africa, in North-West Province. In 1899–1900, during the Second Boer War, a small British force under the command of Baden-Powell was besieged there by the Boers for 215 days; its eventual relief was greeted in Britain with widespread celebration.

Mafia an organized international body of criminals, operating originally in Sicily and now especially in Italy and the US and having a complex and ruthless behavioural code, developed during the 18th–19th centuries. The word comes from Italian (Sicilian dialect), originally in the sense 'bragging'.

the Magdalen ➤ *St* MARY *Magdalen*; also called **the Magdalene**. The name comes, in late Middle English, via ecclesiastical Latin from Greek *(Maria hē) Magdalēnē* 'Mary of *Magdala*' (to whom Jesus appeared after his resurrection, as recounted in John 20:1–18).

She was commonly identified (probably wrongly) with the sinner of Luke 8:37, and was traditionally represented in hagiology as a reformed prostitute elevated to sanctity by repentance and faith; from this come the archaic uses of *magdalen* to mean a reformed prostitute and a house for reformed prostitutes.

Magdalenian of, relating to, or denoting the final Palaeolithic culture in Europe, following the Solutrean and dated to about 17,000–11,500 years ago. It is characterized by a range of bone and horn tools, and by highly developed cave art.

The name comes from French *Magdalénien* 'from La Madeleine', a site in the Dordogne, France, where objects from this culture were found.

Magellan an American space probe, launched in 1989 to map the surface of Venus, using radar to penetrate the dense cloud cover, and was deliberately burned up in Venus's atmosphere in 1994.

The probe was named for the Portuguese explorer Ferdinand Magellan (*c*.1480–1521), whose expedition of 1519–22 was the first to circumnavigate the globe, although Magellan himself was killed in a skirmish before completing the journey.

Magen David a hexagram used as a symbol of Judaism. Recorded from the early 20th century, the term comes from Hebrew, and means literally 'shield of David', with reference to David, king of Israel.

Magi the 'wise men' from the East, often referred to as the **Three Magi**, who brought gifts to the infant Jesus (Matthew 2:1), said in later tradition to be kings named Caspar,

Melchior, and Balthasar who brought gifts of gold, frankincense, and myrrh. Recorded from Old English, the word is the plural form of ➤ MAGUS.

magic bullet a medicine or other remedy with wonderful or highly specific properties, especially one that has not yet been discovered. Recorded from the mid 20th century, the term may come from German *Zauberkugel*, attributed to Paul Ehrlich (1854–1915), German medical scientist, in connection with his search for a cure for syphilis.

German folklore includes a number of stories in which magic bullets of supernatural accuracy play a prominent role. The best-known is the legend of a marksman or 'freeshooter' who makes a pact with the powers of evil to obtain bullets which will go wherever he chooses; the story forms the basis for the opera *Die Freischütz* (1821) by Carl Maria von Weber (1784–1824).

magic circle an inner group of politicians viewed as choosing the leader of the Conservative Party before this became an electoral matter. The phrase was coined by Iain Macleod in a critical article in the *Spectator* of 17 January 1964 on the 'emergence' of Alec Douglas-Home in succession to Harold Macmillan in 1963.

Maginot Line a system of fortifications constructed by the French along their eastern border between 1929 and 1934, widely considered impregnable, but outflanked by German forces in 1940. It was named after André *Maginot* (1877–1932), a French minister of war. The *Maginot Line* may now be referred to allusively to indicate a preoccupation with what is an illusory means of defence.

Magna Carta a charter of liberty and political rights obtained from King John of England by his rebellious barons at Runnymede in 1215. Although often violated by medieval kings, it came to be seen as the seminal document of English constitutional practice, as shown by a comment of the English jurist Edward Coke (1552–1634) on the Lords' Amendment to the Petition of Right, 17 May 1628.

Magna Graecia the ancient Greek cities of southern Italy, founded from *c*.750 BC onwards by colonists from Euboea, Sparta, and elsewhere in Greece. The name is Latin, and means literally 'Great Greece'.

magna mater Latin meaning 'great mother'; a mother-goddess; a fertility goddess, especially ➤ CYBELE.

Magnificat a canticle used in Christian liturgy, especially at vespers and evensong, the text being the hymn of the Virgin Mary (Luke 1:46–55). The literal meaning of *Magnificat* in Latin is 'magnifies', and the opening words of the canticle translate as 'my soul magnifies the Lord'.

magnolia especially associated with the southern states of the US, and Mississippi, which has the flower for its emblem, is known as the **Magnolia State**. The term **Steel Magnolia**, epitomizing a southern woman who has a steely character beneath a feminine and apparently fragile exterior, was applied particularly to Rosalynn Carter, First Lady of the US, 1977–81.

The tree is named after Pierre Magnol (1638–1715), French botanist.

St Magnus of Orkney (*c.*1075–1116), convert to Christianity and martyr; he was put to death by his cousin Haakon, co-earl of Orkney, accepting his violent death and praying for his killers. He was regarded as a martyr and became an important Scottish saint; he is said to have appeared promising victory to Robert Bruce on the night before Bannockburn. His emblem is an axe, and his feast day is 16 April.

magpie the *magpie* is used in similes or comparisons to refer to a person who collects things, especially things of little use or value, or a person who chatters idly, and in traditional belief was sometimes regarded as a bird of ill-omen.

The name is recorded from the late 16th century, and is probably a shortening of dialect *maggot the pie*, *maggoty-pie*, from *Magot* (Middle English pet form of the given name *Marguerite*) + *pie* (ultimately from Latin *pica* 'magpie').

magus a member of a priestly caste in ancient Persia (of Akkadian or Median origin), which through its official status in western Iran became the principal protagonist of Zoroastrianism. The term was then extended to denote a person skilled in eastern magic and astrology; a magician or sorcerer.

Mahabharata one of the two great Sanskrit epics of the Hindus (the other is the *Ramayana*), that evolved over centuries, existing in its present form since *c.*400 AD. Probably the longest single poem in the world, it describes the civil war waged between the five Pandava brothers and their one hundred stepbrothers at Kuruksetra near modern Delhi; the numerous interpolated episodes include the *Bhagavadgita*.

Mahayana one of the two major traditions of Buddhism, now practised in a variety of forms especially in China, Tibet, Japan, and Korea. The tradition emerged around the 1st century AD and is typically concerned with personal spiritual practice and the ideal of the bodhisattva.

Mahdi in popular Muslim belief, a spiritual and temporal leader who will rule before the end of the world and restore religion and justice. Not part of orthodox doctrine, the concept of such a figure was introduced into popular Islam through Sufi channels influenced by Christian doctrine. Notable among those claiming to be this leader was Muhammad Ahmad of Dongola in Sudan (1843–85), whose revolutionary movement captured Khartoum and overthrew the Egyptian regime.

Mahomet an archaic form of ➤ MUHAMMAD, recorded from late Middle English; the alternative *Mahound* is also found.

If the mountain will not come to Mahomet, Mahomet must go to the mountain is a proverbial saying, early 17th century, used in the context of an apparently insoluble situation. The saying refers to a story of Muhammad recounted by Bacon in his *Essays*, in which the Prophet called a hill to him, and when it did not move, made this remark.

Mahomet's coffin refers to the legend current in European sources and recorded from the medieval period, that the coffin of Muhammad was suspended without visible supports, but by magnets or lodestones, from the ceiling of his tomb.

Maia in Greek mythology, the daughter of Atlas and mother of Hermes.

In Roman mythology, *Maia* is a goddess associated with Vulcan and also (by confusion with the Greek goddess) with Mercury, the Roman equivalent of Hermes. She was worshipped on 1 May and 15 May; that month is named after her.

Maiden Castle a prehistoric site in Dorset, consisting of an enormous Iron Age earthwork surrounded by a series of ramparts; excavations in 1934–7 show that settlement there dated back to the Neolithic period.

maiden speech the first speech delivered in the House of Commons or House of Lords by a Member, an expression dating from the early 18th century.

Commissaire Maigret the pipe-smoking French detective in a series of novels by Georges Simenon (1903–89) beginning in 1931; Maigret relies on his understanding of the criminal's motives rather than scientific deduction to solve crimes and the novels show considerable insight into human psychology.

mailed fist the threat or show of armed force, the display of political ruthlessness. Translating German *mit gepanzerter Faust*, the phrase is recorded from the late 19th century, as a report in the *Times* of 17 December 1897 of a speech by Emperor Wilhelm II of Germany.

Main Street chiefly in the US, used in reference to the materialism, mediocrity, or parochialism regarded as typical of small-town life, from the title of a novel (1920) by Sinclair Lewis.

Maison Carrée a Roman temple at Nîmes in France, which according to an inscription was dedicated to Gaius and Lucius Caesar, grandsons and adopted heirs of the Emperor ➤ AUGUSTUS.

Maitreya the Buddha who will appear in the future; a representation of this Buddha. The word is Sanskrit, from *mitra* 'friend or friendship'.

Major Prophet each of the prophets, Isaiah, Jeremiah, and Ezekiel, for whom the three longer prophetic books of the Old Testament are named and whose prophecies they record.

majuscule large lettering, either capital or uncial, in which all the letters are the same height. The name comes (in the early 18th century) via French from Latin *majuscula (littera)* 'somewhat greater (letter)'. (Compare ➤ MINUSCULE.)

make someone's day often used ironically as a warning that an action will give pleasure to someone hostile, as in 'Go ahead, make my day', spoken in *Sudden Impact* (1983 film) by Clint Eastwood.

Malabar Christians a group of Christians of SW India who trace their foundation to a mission of St Thomas the Apostle and have historically used a Syriac liturgy. Many now

form a Uniate (Catholic) Church; others have links to the Syrian Orthodox or the Anglican Church.

Malachi a book of the Bible belonging to a period before Ezra and Nehemiah. The word in Hebrew means literally 'my messenger'; *Malachi* is probably not a personal name, though often taken as such.

Malakoff a fort near Sevastopol captured by the French in 1855 in the Crimean War; the French general, Pélissier, took the title of Duc de Malakoff, and the name was also used for a suburb of Paris.

malaprop the mistaken use of a word in place of a similar-sounding one, often with unintentionally amusing effect, from the name of Mrs *Malaprop* in Sheridan's play *The Rivals* (1775).

malice aforethought in law, the intention to kill or harm which is held to distinguish unlawful killing from murder.

Malignant a person who is disaffected towards constituted authority, a malcontent; especially (in Parliamentarian terminology), a supporter of the royalist cause during the English civil war. This may ultimately derive from established usage of the adjective in 16th-century Protestant polemic, as in the phrase **Church malignant**.

Malleus Maleficarum (or *Hexenhammer*), the 'Hammer of Witches', published in 1484 by Jakob Sprenger, the Dominican inquisitor of Cologne, and Heinrich Krämer, prior of Cologne. It was the textbook of the day on witchcraft, setting out how it may be discovered and how it may be punished.

malmsey now, a fortified Madeira wine of the sweetest type. Originally, a strong, sweet white wine imported from Greece and the eastern Mediterranean islands. The word came into English from Middle Dutch via Old French from *Monemvasia*, the name of a port in SE mainland Greece.

George, Duke of Clarence (1449–78), brother of Edward IV, was said by contemporary chroniclers to have been drowned in a butt of malmsey while prisoner in the Tower of London.

Battle of Malplaquet a battle in 1709 during the War of the Spanish Succession, near the village of Malplaquet in northern France, on the border with Belgium. A force of allied

British and Austrian troops under the Duke of Marlborough won a victory over the French.

Maltese cross a cross with arms of equal length which broaden from the centre and have their ends indented in a shallow V-shape, so named because it was formerly worn by the Knights Hospitallers or *Knights of Malta* who were based on the island.

Malthusian of or pertaining to the theories of the English economist and clergyman Thomas Robert *Malthus* (1766–1834), who in *Essay on Population* (1798) argued that without the practice of 'moral restraint' the population tends to increase at a greater rate than its means of subsistence, resulting in the population checks of war, famine, and epidemic.

Malvolio in Shakespeare's *Twelfth Night* (1601), the Puritan steward of Olivia who through his consciousness of moral superiority and personal worth is tricked by ➤ *Sir Toby* BELCH and his companions into believing that Olivia is in love with him; the behaviour into which they persuade him leads to his being confined for insanity.

Mameluke a member of a regime that formerly ruled parts of the Middle East. Descended from slaves brought from the Caucasus and central Asia as bodyguards by the caliphs and sultans of Egypt, they ruled Syria (1260–1516) and Egypt (1250–1517), and continued as a ruling military caste in Ottoman Egypt until massacred by the viceroy Muhammad Ali in 1811.

The name comes from French *mameluk*, from Arabic *mamlūk* (passive participle used as a noun meaning 'slave'), from *malaka* 'possess'.

Mammon wealth regarded as an evil influence or false object of worship and devotion. It was taken by medieval writers as the name of the devil of covetousness, and revived in this sense by Milton.

The phrase **the mammon of unrighteousness** comes Luke 16:19.

mammoth a large extinct elephant of the Pleistocene epoch, typically hairy with a sloping back and long curved tusks. Recorded from the early 18th century, the word comes from Russian *mamo(n)t*, and is probably of Siberian origin. The adjectival use meaning 'huge' developed in the early 19th century.

The **Mammoth Cave** in Kentucky is the largest known cave system in the world, consisting of over 480 km (300 miles) of charted passageways and containing some spectacular rock formations.

man a male person.

A **man for all seasons** is a person who is ready for any situation or contingency, or adaptable to any circumstance; originally, as a description of St Thomas More by Robert Whittington in *Vulgaria* (1521). Erasmus had applied the idea earlier, describing More in *In Praise of Folly* (1509) as 'a man of all hours'.

Man Friday in Daniel Defoe's novel *Robinson Crusoe* (1719) is Crusoe's servant, to whom he usually refers as 'my man Friday', named for the day on which Crusoe saved his life. From the early 19th century the term has been used to designate a (male) helper or follower.

The **man in the moon** is a mythical person supposed to live in the moon. Inhabitants of the moon were postulated in ancient and Hellenistic Greek texts; the use in English, recorded from Middle English, derives from the imagined semblance of a person or a human face in the disc of the (full) moon. By the mid 16th century, the *man in the moon* had become proverbial as the type of someone too distant to have any understanding or knowledge of a person's circumstances.

The **Man of Sorrows** is a name for Jesus Christ, deriving from a prophecy in Isaiah 53:3; in art represented as an image of Christ surrounded by instruments of the Passion.

mana especially in Polynesian, Melanesian, and Maori belief, pervasive supernatural or magical power.

Manannán the son of Lir, a highly popular god of the old Gaelic pantheon, the subject of many legends and the patron of sailors and merchants. The Isle of Man was his favourite abode, and is said to take its name from him. There he has degenerated into a legendary giant, with three legs (seen revolving in the coat of arms of the island).

Manasseh in the Bible, a Hebrew patriarch, son of Jacob. Also, the tribe descended from him.

Manchester Martyrs three Fenians, William O'Meara Allen, Michael Larkin, and William O'Brien, who were hanged at Manchester in 1867, for their part in the rescue of Thomas Kelly and Timothy Deasy, two leading Fenians, in the course of which a police sergeant was shot dead.

Manchu a member of a people originally living in Manchuria, who formed the last imperial dynasty of China (1644–1912). The name is from the Manchu language, and means literally 'pure'.

Manchukuo name given in 1932 to Manchuria, a mountainous region forming the NE portion of China, which was declared an independent state by Japan; it was restored to China in 1945.

Mancunian a native or inhabitant of Manchester; the name comes (in the early 20th century) from *Mancunium*, the Latin name of Manchester.

mandala a circular figure representing the universe in Hindu and Buddhist symbolism; in psychoanalysis, such a symbol in a dream, representing the dreamer's search for completeness and self-unity. The word comes from Sanskrit *maṇḍala* 'disc'.

mandarin an official in any of the senior grades of the former imperial Chinese civil service. *Mandarins* were chosen by examination, and there were nine grades, each of which was distinguished by the material from which the round ornament or 'button' on top of the official headgear was made. From the early 18th century, *Mandarin* has also been used for the standard literary and official form of Chinese.

Recorded in English in the late 16th century, the word comes from Portuguese *mandarim*, via Malay, from Hindi *mantrī* 'counsellor'. The current transferred meaning of a powerful official or senior bureaucrat, especially one perceived as reactionary and secretive, developed in the early 20th century.

The **mandarin orange** may be named from the colour of the fruit being likened to the official yellow robes of a *mandarin*.

Mandelbrot set a particular set of complex numbers which has a highly convoluted fractal boundary when plotted. It is named after the Polish-born French mathematician Benoit Mandelbrot (1924–), who is known as the pioneer of fractal geometry.

mandorla another term for ➤ VESICA *piscis*. The word is Italian, and means literally 'almond', referring to the pointed oval shape of the figure.

mandrake a Mediterranean plant of the nightshade family, with white or purple flowers and large yellow berries. It has a forked fleshy root which supposedly resembles the human form and was formerly widely used in medicine and magic, being thought to promote conception. It was reputed to shriek when pulled from the ground and to cause the death of whoever uprooted it (a dog being therefore traditionally employed for the purpose). Recorded from Middle English, the name comes from medieval Latin *mandragora*, associated with man (because of the shape of its root) + *drake* in the Old English sense 'dragon'.

the Manhattan Project the code name for the American project set up in 1942 to develop an atom bomb. The project culminated in 1945 with the detonation of the first nuclear weapon, at White Sands in New Mexico.

Manichaeism a dualistic religious system with Christian, Gnostic, and pagan elements, founded in Persia in the 3rd century by Manes (*c.*216–*c.*276). The system was based on a supposed primeval conflict between light and darkness. It spread widely in the Roman Empire and in Asia, and survived in Chinese Turkestan until the 13th century.

Manifest Destiny the 19th century doctrine or belief that the expansion of the United States throughout the American continents was both justified and inevitable.

maniple In the Western Church, a vestment formerly worn by a priest celebrating the Eucharist, consisting of a strip hanging from the left arm. The *maniple* is generally thought to derive from the folded napkin or handkerchief carried by Roman consuls as a rank ornament.

Maniple is also used (from the mid 16th century) for a subdivision of a Roman legion, containing either 120 or 60 men.

Recorded from late Middle English, the term comes via Old French from Latin *manipulus* 'handful, troop', from *manus* 'hand'.

manitou (among certain Algonquian North American Indians) a good or evil spirit as an object of reverence. The name comes in the late 17th century via French from an Algonquian language.

manna in the Bible, the substance miraculously supplied each day as food to the Israelites in the wilderness (Exodus 16). Its supposed nature has been debated. It has thus been suggested that what was denoted was an exudation of the tamarisk, the word for which in Aramaic is *mannā*.

The extended use of *manna* to mean 'an unexpected or gratuitous benefit' (frequently in **manna from heaven**) is recorded from the early 17th century.

to the manner born naturally fitted for some position or employment; originally, as a quotation from Shakespeare's *Hamlet*.

Manoa a fabulous city in South America; in his *Discoverie of Guiana* (1596), Walter Raleigh refers to it as 'the great and Golden Citie of Manoa (which the Spaniards call El Dorado)'.

the Mansion House the official residence of the Lord Mayor of London; it was built between 1739 and 1753.

manticore a mythical beast typically depicted as having the body of a lion (occasionally a tiger), the face of a man, porcupine's quills, and the sting of a scorpion. Recorded from late Middle English, the name comes via Old French and Latin from Greek *mantikhōras*, corrupt reading in Aristotle for *martikhoras*, from an Old Persian word meaning 'maneater'.

In heraldry, the *manticore* is represented as a monster with the body of a beast of prey, the head of a man, sometimes with spiral or curved horns, and sometimes with the feet of a dragon.

mantle the prophet ➤ ELIJAH marked Elisha as his successor as prophet of Israel (2 Kings 2:13) by casting his mantle about Elisha's shoulders.

mantra originally in Hinduism and Buddhism, a word or sound repeated to aid concentration in meditation. Also, a Vedic hymn. The word is Sanskrit and means literally 'instrument of thought', from *man* 'think'.

Manu the archetypal first man of Hindu mythology, survivor of the great flood and father of the human race. He is also the legendary author of one of the most famous codes of Hindu religious law, the *Manusmriti* (Laws of Manu), composed in Sanskrit and dating in its present form from the 1st century BC.

Manx cat a cat of a breed having no tail or an extremely short one, originating on the Isle of Man.

many-headed monster the people, the populace; after Horace *Epistles* 'the people are

a many-headed beast.' The term is recorded in English since the 16th century. The expression was popularized by Pope in *Epistles of Horace* (1737).

maple leaf the leaf of the maple, used as an emblem of Canada.

Mappa Mundi a map of the world of a kind produced in the medieval and early Renaissance periods, typically depicting Jerusalem at its centre, and featuring details of cosmology, mythology, and history. A famous example is a 13th-century circular map, preserved in Hereford Cathedral in England. The name comes from medieval Latin, literally 'sheet of the world'.

maquis dense scrub vegetation consisting of hardy evergreen shrubs and small trees, characteristic of coastal regions in the Mediterranean. The French resistance movement during the German occupation (1940–5), **the Maquis**, took their name from this.

Maranatha in biblical translations, a word representing an Aramaic phrase occurring in 1 Corinthians 16:22 and usually left untranslated, its exact interpretation being variously understood by scholars and translators. Current scholarship favours the interpretation 'Come, O Lord!'; the most widely advocated alternative being 'Our Lord has come.' It has also often erroneously been regarded as forming part of a formula of imprecation in ➤ ANATHEMA *maranatha*.

Maratha a member of the princely and military castes of the former Hindu kingdom of Maharashtra in central India. The Marathas rose in rebellion against the Muslim Moguls and in 1674 established their own kingdom under the leadership of Shivaji. They came to dominate southern and central India but were later subdued by the British.

Marathon in ancient Greece, the scene of a victory over the Persians in 490 BC; the modern race (strictly one of 26 miles 38 yards or 42.195 km.) is based on the tradition that a messenger ran from Marathon to Athens (22 miles) with the news. The original account by Herodotus told of the messenger Pheidippides running 150 miles from Athens to Sparta before the battle, seeking help; on reaching Athens, he gasped out his dying words, 'Greetings, we win!'

Maravedi a name applied to the North African Berber rulers of Muslim Spain, from the late 11th century to 1145; the word is from Arabic meaning 'holy men', and came to mean a medieval Spanish copper coin and monetary unit.

Marble Arch a large arch with three gateways at the NE corner of Hyde Park in London, near the site of which ➤ TYBURN gallows once stood. Designed by John Nash, it was erected in 1827 in front of Buckingham Palace and moved in 1851 to its present site.

March the third month of the year, in the northern hemisphere usually considered the first month of spring. The name comes from Latin *Martius*, short for *mensis Martius* 'month of Mars', and at ancient Rome several festivals of Mars took place in March, presumably in preparation for the campaigning season, since Mars was a god of war.

A **March hare** is a brown hare in the breeding season, noted for its leaping, boxing, and chasing in circles, and taken as the type of something mad (see also ➤ MAD *as a March hare*).

march to a different drum conform to different principles and practices from those around one; ultimately from Henry David Thoreau *Walden* (1854).

marching season a season of processions or parades traditionally held annually throughout Northern Ireland from 12 July to 12 August, in which members of the ➤ ORANGE *Order* march in celebration of the defeat of the Catholic James II by William III at the Battle of the Boyne in 1690.

Marconi scandal in 1912, it was suggested that Lloyd George, chancellor of the exchequer, and Rufus Isaacs, attorney general, had used inside knowledge to buy shares in the American Marconi company at a favourable rate. In the following year a House of Commons select committee acquitted both ministers of acting otherwise than in good faith, but the reputations of both men suffered.

Mardi Gras a carnival held in some countries on Shrove Tuesday, most famously in New Orleans. The (French) phrase means literally 'fat Tuesday', alluding to the last day of feasting before the fast and penitence of Lent.

Marduk the chief god of Babylon, who became lord of the gods of heaven and earth after conquering Tiamat, the monster of primeval chaos.

mare's nest an illusory discovery, originally in the phrase *to have found* (or *spied*) *a mare's nest* (i.e. something that does not exist), used in the sense 'to have discovered something amazing'. The expression is recorded from the late 16th century.

Marengo a decisive French victory of Napoleon's campaign in Italy in 1800, close to the village of Marengo, near Turin. After military reverses had all but destroyed French power in Italy, Napoleon crossed the Alps to defeat and capture an Austrian army, a victory which led to Italy coming under French control again.

Marengo also designates chicken or veal sautéed in oil, served with a tomato sauce, and traditionally garnished with eggs and crayfish. The dish is said to have been served to Napoleon after his victory at Marengo.

Margaret female forename, name of two saints.

St Margaret of Antioch was the centre of much popular devotion in the Middle Ages, but probably never existed as a historical person. She is recognized as one of the ➤ FOURTEEN *Holy Helpers*. Also called *Marina*. Her feast day is on 13 July in the Eastern Church, and 20 July in the Western Church. She is often depicted spearing a dragon.

St Margaret of Scotland (*c*.1046–93), was an English princess and Scottish queen, wife of Malcolm III. She exerted a strong influence over royal policy during her husband's reign, and was instrumental in the reform of the Scottish Church. Feast day, 16 November.

Maid Marian in English folklore, the lover of ➤ ROBIN *Hood*; she is also traditionally a female character in the morris dance and May game, and (in modern use) a named character in the Horn dance performed annually at Abbots Bromley in Staffordshire. Her appearance in later forms of the story of Robin Hood may be attributable to the fact that both were represented in the May Day pageants.

Marianne the French Republic personified; a proclamation of the Republic of 22 September 1792 announced that the symbol of the new regime would be a female figure representing the goddess of liberty. The name *Marianne* came popularly to be applied to the figure, typically represented wearing a Phrygian cap. The image of *Marianne*, appearing on stamps and coins and as a bust in town halls, has since the 1960s been modelled on a living person (the first, in 1969, was inspired by Brigitte Bardot).

The reason for the adoption of the name is not known. *La garisou de Marianno* is the name of an Occitan song composed by the Republican poet Guillaume Lavabre, probably in 1792; a song called *La Marianno* is said to have been sung at festivals in the mid 19th century in the town of Castres (Tarn), in front of a statue of the Republic known locally as 'La Marianno'.

Marie Celeste erroneous form of the name ➤ MARY *Celeste*.

Mariolatry excessive reverence for the Virgin Mary, to the point of idolatrous worship. Recorded from the early 17th century, the term was coined as part of the vocabulary of Protestant polemic.

Mark in Arthurian legend, king of Cornwall, husband of ➤ ISEULT and uncle of ➤ TRISTRAM. In different versions of the story of Tristram and Iseult, he is represented as a noble king and trusting husband, or as the type of treachery and cowardice.

St Mark an Apostle, companion of St Peter and St Paul, traditional author of the second Gospel, sometimes identified with the John Mark whose mother's house in Jerusalem was a meeting-place for the Apostles. He is also sometimes said to have been the young man who according to Mark 14:51 followed Jesus after he had been arrested, but escaped capture.

Mark is patron of Venice, to which his body was brought in the 9th century. His symbol as an evangelist is a lion, one of the ➤ TETRAMORPH, and his feast day is 25 April.

the mark of the beast in Revelation 16:2, a sign placed on followers or worshippers of Antichrist. In extended use, the phrase was first used to mean an indicator or symptom of heresy, and then more generally a sign of infamy.

Marlboro Man a cowboy character appearing in advertising campaigns for *Marlboro* cigarettes, often used allusively (and ironically) to denote the type of a tough outdoors man. **Marlboro Country** is similarly used for the natural home of such a person.

Jacob Marley in Dickens's *A Christmas Carol*, Scrooge's late partner, whose chained ghost appears to Scrooge and warns him to change his miserly ways. **Marley's ghost** denotes the type of such a spectre.

Philip Marlowe a fictional detective, created by Raymond Chandler, who embodies the 'private eye' qualities described by Chandler in the comment, 'Down these mean streets a man must go who is not himself mean, who is neither tarnished nor afraid.'

Marne a river of east central France. Its valley was the scene of two important battles in the First World War. The first battle (September 1914) halted and repelled the German advance on Paris; the second (July 1918) ended the final German offensive.

Maro, Prophet of the Gentiles in the Middle Ages, the name under which the Roman poet ➤ VIRGIL (Publius Vergilius *Maro*) was commemorated at the Christmas Mass at Rouen and elsewhere; the allusion is to the passage in his *Eclogues* which was taken as an unconscious but divinely inspired prophecy of Christ.

Maronite a member of a Christian sect of Syrian origin, living chiefly in Lebanon and in communion with the Roman Catholic Church. Maronites have been prominent in Lebanese politics and traditionally hold the office of President. The name comes ultimately from the name of John *Maro*, a 7th-cent. Syrian religious leader, who may have been the first Maronite patriarch.

Maroon a member of a group of black people living in the mountains and forests of Suriname and the West Indies, descended from runaway slaves. The name comes (in the mid 17th century) from French *marron* meaning 'feral', from Spanish *cimarrón* 'wild', (as a noun) 'runaway slave'.

Miss Marple a fictional detective created by Agatha Christie (1890–1976), whose apparently gentle existence as an elderly spinster in an English village (St Mary Mead) is belied by her frequent and successful investigations into murder and other crimes. She typically solves mysteries by comparing actions and events with her knowledge and experience of village life.

Marrano (in medieval Spain) a christianized Jew or Moor, especially one who merely professed conversion in order to avoid persecution. The name is Spanish, and is of unknown origin, although various explanations have been suggested; these include the earlier (10th-century) Spanish *marrano* 'hog', assuming the word to be used as a particularly offensive term of abuse, or Spanish Arabic *muharram* 'excommunicate'. This suggestion is based on the view that Jewish and Muslim converts would be suspected of practising their former religion in private, and would thus be excommunicates.

Marriage of the Adriatic a ceremony formerly held on Ascension Day in Venice to symbolize the city's sea power, during which the doge dropped a ring into the water from his official barge.

Mars in Roman mythology, the god of war and the most important Roman god after Jupiter. He was probably originally an agricultural god, and the month of March is named after him. His Greek equivalent is ➤ ARES. Legends of Mars include the story of his love for Venus, and the trap made for them by her husband Vulcan, and from early times this became a favourite subject for artists. The wolf and the woodpecker were regarded as sacred to Mars, and the **field of Mars** is another name for the ➤ CAMPUS *Martius* of ancient Rome. The **hill of Mars** is the ➤ AREOPAGUS ('hill of Ares') of ancient Athens.

Mars is the name given to a small reddish planet which is the fourth in order from the sun and is periodically visible to the naked eye. From its distinctive colour, which comes from its iron-rich minerals, it is known informally as the *red planet*. In astrological belief, the influence of the planet is associated with combative, aggressive, or masculine qualities.

Marseillaise the national anthem of France, written by Rouget de Lisle in 1792 on the declaration of war against Austria, and first sung in Paris by volunteer army units from Marseilles.

Marshall Plan a programme of financial aid and other initiatives, sponsored by the US, designed to boost the economies of western European countries after the Second World War. It was originally advocated by Secretary of State George C. Marshall and passed by Congress in 1948.

marshalsea in England, a court formerly held before the steward and the knight *marshal* of the royal household, originally to hear cases between the monarch's servants, but afterwards with wider jurisdiction. It was abolished in 1849.

The **Marshalsea** was the name of a former prison in Southwark, London, originally the prison of the Court of the Marshalsea, under the control of the knight marshal, and in later years used for the imprisonment of debtors. It was abolished in 1842. The *Marshalsea* is the setting for a substantial part

of Charles Dickens's *Little Dorrit* (1857), in which the imprisonment of Mr Dorrit lasts for so many years that he becomes known as the **Father of the Marshalsea**.

Battle of Marston Moor a battle of the English Civil War, fought in 1644 on Marston Moor near York, in which the Royalist armies of Prince Rupert and the Duke of Newcastle suffered a defeat by the English and Scottish Parliamentary armies which fatally weakened Charles I's cause.

Marsyas in Greek mythology, a satyr who challenged Apollo to a contest in flute playing and was flayed alive when he lost; the river Marsyas in Asia Minor is said to have sprung either from his blood, or from the tears of his mourners. The episode is the subject of one of Titian's best-known paintings, *The Flaying of Marsyas* (c.1570–6).

Martello tower any of numerous small circular forts that were erected for defence purposes along the SE coasts of England during the Napoleonic Wars. The name comes from Cape *Mortella* in Corsica, site of a small circular fort which was recaptured with some difficulty by the English fleet on 8 February 1794; its design was then used as a basis for fortifications in the British Isles from 1804.

St Martha in the New Testament, the sister of Lazarus and Mary and friend of Jesus. She is taken as the type of a woman who is constantly busied with domestic affairs, from the story in Luke 10 in which she is seen as concerned with household chores while Mary sits and talks with Jesus.

According to medieval legend, Martha, Mary, and Lazarus travelled to Provence after the death of Jesus. Martha is said to have overcome a dragon at Tarascon by sprinkling it with holy water and tying her girdle about its neck; she then led it to Arles, where it was killed. She may be shown with a ladle, a broom, or a bunch of keys, for her housewifely skills, or with the dragon which she overcame. Her feast day is 29 July in the West.

Martian a hypothetical or fictional inhabitant of the planet ➤ MARS, later taken as the type of someone unfamiliar with what is generally considered to be normal or usual.

Martin male forename, name of two saints.
St Martin de Porres (1579–1639), a Dominican lay brother, was the illegitimate son of a Spanish grandee and a freed black slave from

Lima in Peru. He was noted for his dedication to the poor as for his undiscriminating charity to those of all races. His feast day is 5 November.

St Martin of Tours ((d.397), was a French bishop, and is a patron saint of France. When giving half his cloak to a beggar he received a vision of Christ, after which he was baptized. He joined St Hilary at Poitiers and founded the first monastery in Gaul. St Martin is often shown dividing his cloak with the beggar, or with a globe of fire above his head, seen one day when he said Mass. Another emblem, from the 15th century, is a goose, the migration of which often coincides with his feast. His feast day (➤ MARTINMAS) is 11 November, and **St Martin's summer** is a season of fine, mild weather occurring about this time.

martinet a strict disciplinarian, especially in the armed forces. Recorded from the late 17th century, the word originally denoted a system of drill invented by Jean *Martinet* (d. 1672), a French soldier whose attention to drill and training as Inspector-General of the infantry helped to shape the regular army of Louis XIV.

Martinmas St *Martin*'s Day, 11 November, in Scotland, one of the two term-days recognized by common law. In many parts of England it was traditionally the time for hiring servants, and the day on which hiring fairs were held. It was also the time at which cattle and other farm animals were slaughtered, to be salted for the winter, and the phrases **Martinmas beef** and **Martinmas meat** refer to this, as does the proverbial saying, **every hog has its Martinmas**.

martlet in heraldry, a bird like a swallow without feet, borne (typically with the wings closed) as a charge or a mark of cadency for a fourth son.

martyr a person who is killed because of their religious or other beliefs. In the Roman Catholic liturgy, martyrs rank before all other saints. Recorded from Old English, the word comes via ecclesiastical Latin from Greek *martur* 'witness' (in Christian use, 'martyr').

The Martyr King is Charles I, a title reflecting the beliefs of those members of the Anglican Church who regard his execution as an act of religious persecution; 30 January was formally instituted as a fast in his memory in 1660 (it was suppressed in 1859, although a lesser festival was reinstated in 1980).

Captain Marvel cartoon character in American comics from 1940; a red-costumed superhero (resembling Superman), who has undergone a similar transformation. In real life he was Billy Batson, an orphan who was transformed into *Captain Marvel* with the utterance of the magic word ➤ SHAZAM.

Marx Brothers a family of American comedians, consisting of the brothers Chico (1886–1961), Harpo (1888–1964), Groucho (1890–1977), and Zeppo (1901–79). Their films, which are characterized by their anarchic humour, include *Duck Soup* (1933) and *A Night at the Opera* (1935).

Marxism the political and economic theories of the German political philosopher and economists Karl Marx (1818–83) and Friedrich Engels (1820–95), later developed by their followers to form the basis for the theory and practice of communism.

Central to Marxist theory is an explanation of social change in terms of economic factors, according to which the means of production provide the economic *base* which influences or determines the political and ideological *superstructure*. Marx and Engels predicted the revolutionary overthrow of capitalism by the proletariat and the eventual attainment of a classless communist society.

Mary female forename, name of three saints.

Mary was the mother of Jesus, known as **the (Blessed) Virgin Mary**, **St Mary**, or **Our Lady**. According to the Gospels she was a virgin betrothed to Joseph at the time of the Annunciation and conceived Jesus by the power of the Holy Spirit. She has been venerated by Catholic and Orthodox Churches from the earliest Christian times, and her feast days are, 1 January (Roman Catholic Church), 25 March (Annunciation), 15 August (Assumption), 8 September (Nativity), 8 December (Immaculate Conception).

In the New Testament, **St Mary Magdalene** was a woman of Magdala in Galilee. She was a follower of Jesus, who cured her of evil spirits (Luke 8:2), and was present at the Crucifixion. She went with other women to anoint his body in the tomb and found it empty; she is the first of those in the Gospels to whom the risen Christ appeared. *Mary Magdalene* is also traditionally identified with the 'sinner' of Luke 7:37 who anointed Jesus's feet with oil, and with Mary the sister of ➤ MARTHA and ➤ LAZARUS. Although the identification is now rejected in the Roman

Calendar, it is implicit in traditional legends and representations. She may be shown with a jar of ointment, or in a scene of the Crucifixion, and her feast day is 22 July.

St Mary of Egypt was a 5th-century Egyptian saint who, according to her legend, after living as a prostitute was converted on a visit to Jerusalem and became a hermit. Taking three loaves for food, she withdrew to live in the desert, where she remained for the rest of her life, surviving on dates and berries. When she died, a lion helped to bury her body. She was sometimes referred to informally as **Mary Gypsy**. Her usual emblems are the three loaves, and the lion, and her feast day is usually 2 April, but may be celebrated on 9 or 10 April.

Mary Bell order a court order prohibiting the publication of information which might lead to the identification of a ward of court, from the name of *Mary Bell* (1957–), who in 1968 was convicted of the manslaughter of two younger children. Released from custody and living under another name, she gave birth to a daughter in 1984, and in order to protect the child's anonymity, the High Court made an order forbidding public identification of Mary Bell or her whereabouts.

Mary Celeste an American brig that was found in the North Atlantic in December 1872 in perfect condition but abandoned. The fate of the crew and the reason for the abandonment of the ship remain a mystery. She is sometimes referred to incorrectly as the *Marie Celeste*.

Mary Rose a heavily armed ship, built for Henry VIII, that in 1545 sank with the loss of nearly all her company when going out to engage the French fleet off Portsmouth. The hull, with some of the ship's contents, was raised in 1982, and is now on public display in Portsmouth dockyard.

marzipan layer the stockbroking executives ranking immediately below the partners in a firm. The expression, recorded from the early 1980s, makes figurative use of the layer of almond paste lying beneath the sugar icing of a cake. Although it is not the top layer, it is nevertheless rich and somewhat luxurious.

Masada the site, on a steep rocky hill, of the ruins of a palace and fortification built by Herod the Great on the SW shore of the Dead Sea in the 1st century BC. It was a Jewish stronghold in the Zealots' revolt against the Romans (AD 66–73) and was the scene in AD 73 of mass suicide by the Jewish defenders when the Romans breached the citadel after a siege of nearly two years. The name may be used allusively of a readiness to anticipate threatened defeat by bringing about one's own destruction first.

Mash from a novel (1968) by the American writer Richard Hooker, subsequently a film and (1973–84) a highly successful television series; *Mash* shows an American *Mobile Army Surgical Hospital* during the Korean War, staffed by *Hawkeye Pierce* and his colleagues. It is characterized by an irreverent and anti-militaristic spirit, and a realistic sense of the urgency, and capacity for invention and compromise, required in medical staff dealing with battlefield casualties.

mason a builder or worker in stone; with capital initial, from the mid 17th century, a ➤ FREEMASON. In Scotland, a **mason word** is the secret password of a Freemason.

A **mason's mark** is a distinctive device carved on stone by the mason who dressed it.

Perry Mason in the detective novels of the American writer Erle Stanley Gardner (1889–1970), a notably successful criminal lawyer who always appeared for the defence, and who revealed the true criminal in an exciting courtroom scene. Perry Mason was played in a long-running television series (1957–66) by the actor Raymond Burr.

Mason–Dixon Line in the US, the boundary between Maryland and Pennsylvania, taken as the northern limit of the slave-owning states before the abolition of slavery; it is named after Charles *Mason* (1730–87) and Jeremiah *Dixon* (1733–77), English astronomers, who defined most of the boundary between Pennsylvania and Maryland by survey in 1763–7.

the Masorah the collection of information and comment on the text of the traditional Hebrew Bible by the **Masoretes**, Jewish scholars of the 6th to 10th centuries AD who contributed to the establishment of a recognized text of the Hebrew Bible, with pointing and accents to indicate its pronunciation, and to the compilation of the *Masorah*.

masque a form of amateur dramatic entertainment, popular among the nobility in 16th- and 17th-century England, which consisted of dancing and acting performed by masked players, originally in dumbshow and later with metrical dialogue.

Mass the Christian Eucharist or Holy Communion, especially in the Roman Catholic Church. *Mass* was also formerly used for the feast day or festival of a specified saint; this usage now survives only as a suffix, as in *Candlemas*, *Christmas*, *Lammas*, and *Michaelmas*.

Recorded from Old English, the word comes from ecclesiastical Latin *missa*, from Latin *miss-* 'dismissed', from *mittere*, perhaps from the last words of the service, '*Ite, missa est* [Go, it is the dismissal]'.

Massacre of the Innocents the killing by order of Herod the Great, after the birth of Jesus, of all boy children under two years old (▶ the INNOCENTS) in Bethlehem. In the 19th-century British parliament, the phrase was also used informally for measures which had to be 'sacrificed' at the end of a session for want of time.

Masters Tournament a prestigious US golf competition, held in Augusta, Georgia, in which golfers (chiefly professionals) compete only by invitation on the basis of their past achievements. It has been held annually since 1934.

go to the mat vigorously engage in an argument or dispute, typically on behalf of a particular person or cause; alluding to the thick mat in a gymnasium on which wrestling is practised.

Mata Hari the type of a beautiful and seductive female spy, from the Dutch dancer and secret agent (1876–1917) whose pseudonym this was. She became a professional dancer in Paris in 1905 and probably worked for both French and German intelligence services before being executed by the French in 1917.

mater dolorosa the Virgin Mary sorrowing for the death of Christ, especially as a representation in art. The phrase is Latin, and may originate in the verses ascribed to the Franciscan lay brother Jacopone da Todi (*c.*1230–1306) and others, '*Stabat mater dolorosa luxta crucem lacrimosa* [At the cross her station keeping, stood the sorrowful mother weeping].'

materia medica the body of remedial substances used in the practice of medicine; the study of the origin and properties of these substances. Recorded from the late 17th century, the phrase is modern Latin, translating Greek *hulē iatrikē* 'healing material', the title of a work by the 1st century Greek physician and pharmacologist Dioscorides.

matins a service forming part of the traditional Divine Office of the Western Christian Church, originally said (or chanted) at or after midnight, but historically often held with lauds on the previous evening. Also, a service of morning prayer in various Churches, especially the Anglican Church.

matsuri a solemn festival celebrated periodically at Shinto shrines in Japan.

Matterhorn a mountain in the Alps, on the border between Switzerland and Italy, first climbed in 1865 by the English mountaineer Edward Whymper. It may be taken as the type of a difficult and dangerous ascent.

St Matthew an Apostle, a tax-gatherer from Capernaum in Galilee, traditional author of the first Gospel. Matthew may be represented in art as the author of one of the Gospels, in which case his symbol is an angel, one of the ▶ TETRAMORPH. He may alternatively be shown with the instruments of his martyrdom (a spear, sword, or halberd), or with a money-bag or money-box as a sign of his occupation as tax-gatherer. He may also be shown wearing spectacles, perhaps so as to read his accounts. His feast day is 21 September in the West and 16 November in the East.

The term **Matthew principle** means that more will be given to those who are already provided for. The allusion is to Matthew 25:29.

St Matthias an Apostle, chosen by lot after the Ascension to replace Judas. He may be shown with an axe or a halberd as instruments of his martyrdom. His feast day is 14 May in the Western Church and 9 August in the Eastern Church.

matzo a crisp biscuit of unleavened bread, traditionally eaten by Jews during Passover.

Mau Mau an African secret society originating among the Kikuyu that in the 1950s used violence and terror to try to expel European settlers and end British rule in Kenya. The British eventually subdued the organization, but Kenya gained independence in 1963. The term is Kikuyu, and in probably an application of *mau-mau* used to describe voracious devouring.

maudlin self-pityingly or tearfully sentimental. In Middle English *Maudlin* denotes ▶ St MARY Magdalene, and comes from Old French *Madeleine*, from ecclesiastical Latin *Magdalena*. The sense of the current adjective derives from allusion to pictures of Mary Magdalene weeping.

Maundy in the UK, a public ceremony on the Thursday before Easter (**Maundy Thursday**) at which the monarch distributes **Maundy money**, specially minted silver coins distributed by the British sovereign on Maundy Thursday. The number of recipients and the face value in pence of the amount they each receive traditionally correspond to the number of years in the sovereign's age. In the original form of this ceremony, a sovereign, senior cleric, or other eminent person washed the feet of a number of poor people (in commemoration of Christ's washing the Apostles' feet at the Last Supper: John 13), and usually distributed clothing, food, or money.

Recorded from Middle English, the word comes via Old French from Latin *mandatum* 'commandment'. The words 'A new commandment (*mandatum novum*) (John 13:34), from the discourse which followed the washing of the apostles' feet, were adopted as the first antiphon sung at the commemorative observance.

St Maurice 3rd-century soldier-saint, said to have been leader of the ➤ THEBAN *Legion* and martyred with them for refusing to sacrifice to the pagan gods. In medieval iconography he is often shown as an African. His feast day is 22 September.

Maurya a dynasty which ruled northern India 321–c.184 BC. It was founded by Chandragupta *Maurya*, who introduced a centralized government and uniform script, and developed a highway network which led to Mauryan control of most of the Indian subcontinent. The oldest extant Indian art dates from this era.

mausoleum a building, especially a large and stately one, housing a tomb or tombs. The word comes via Latin from Greek *Mausōlos*, the name of a king of Caria (4th century BC), to whose tomb in Halicarnassus, erected by his queen Artemisia and considered one of the ➤ SEVEN *Wonders of the World*, the name was originally applied.

maverick an unorthodox or independent-minded person; a person refusing to conform to a particular party or group. The word comes from the North American term for an unbranded calf or yearling, and dates in that sense from the mid 19th century, from the name of Samuel A. *Maverick* (1803–70), a Texas

engineer and rancher who did not brand his cattle.

Maxim gun the first fully automatic water-cooled machine gun, designed in Britain in 1884 and used especially in the First World War. In a satiric verse by Hilaire Belloc (1870–1953), it is seen as typifying the military power of a developed nation.

Maxim's a fashionable restaurant in the rue Royale, Paris, opened in 1893, and forming a social and cultural centre.

Maxwell's demon a hypothetical being imagined as controlling a hole in a partition dividing a gas-filled container into two parts, and allowing only fast-moving molecules to pass in one direction, and slow-moving molecules in the other. This would result in one side of the container becoming warmer and the other colder, in violation of the second law of thermodynamics. It is named after the Scottish physicist James Clerk *Maxwell* (1831–79).

May the fifth month of the year, in the northern hemisphere usually considered the last month of spring and harbinger of summer. From the late 16th century, *May* in poetic use also denotes one's bloom or prime. **May and January** may mean a young woman and an old man as husband and wife, as in Chaucer's *Merchant's Tale* (c.1395). (See also *the 3rd of May* at ➤ THIRD.)

Recorded from Old English, the name comes from Latin *Maius*, probably from the name of a deity cognate with the name of the goddess *Maia* and with *magnus* 'great'.

May balls at the University of Cambridge are held during **May Week** (see below).

May Day is 1 May, celebrated in many countries as a traditional springtime festival or as an international day honouring workers.

A **May game** is a performance or entertainment (typically involving the characters of Robin Hood and Maid Marian) forming part of celebrations held on *May Day*; the merrymaking and sports associated with this. The term is recorded from the early 16th century; by the middle of the century, the phrase **make a May game of**, meaning make a laughing-stock of someone, had developed.

A **May meeting** was each of a succession of annual meetings of various religious and philanthropic societies formerly held during the month of May in Exeter Hall, London, and other buildings.

A **May Queen** is a pretty girl chosen and crowned with flowers in traditional celebrations of May Day; in 1591 an allegorical entertainment showing the *May Queen* being met by her nymphs was presented before Queen Elizabeth I.

May Week at Cambridge University is a week in late May or early June when intercollegiate boat races are held.

Maya¹ the mother of Siddhartha Gautama, the ➤ BUDDHA. According to Buddhist legend, the birth of her son was foretold in a dream in which she saw a white elephant with six tusks entering her side; she later gave birth in the wooded garden of Lumbini, standing with her right hand on the branch of a sal tree, while the child emerged from her right hip. The scenes of Maya and the elephant, and the birth of the Buddha, are frequently depicted in Buddhist art.

Maya² an American Indian people of Yucatán and elsewhere in Central America, with a civilization which developed over an extensive area of southern Mexico, Guatemala, and Belize from the 2nd millennium BC, reaching its peak *c.*300–*c.*900 AD. Its remains include stone temples built on pyramids and ornamented with sculptures. The Mayas had a cumbersome system of pictorial writing and an extremely accurate calendar system.

maya in Hinduism, the supernatural power wielded by gods and demons; in Hinduism and Buddhism, the power by which the universe becomes manifest; the illusion or appearance of the phenomenal world. The word comes from Sanskrit *māyā* 'create'.

Mayday an international radio distress signal used by ships and aircraft. Recorded from the 1920s, the word represents a pronunciation of French *m'aider*, from *venez m'aider* 'come and help me'. (See also ➤ CQD, ➤ SOS.)

Mayfair a fashionable and opulent district in the West End of London which includes the site of a fair which was held annually from the 17th century to the end of the 18th century in Brook fields near Hyde Park Corner; the area takes its name from this. **Mayfair boy** is a dated term for a gentleman crook of the 1930s.

Mayflower the ship in which the Pilgrim Fathers sailed from England to America. It arrived at Cape Cod on 21 November 1620 after a voyage of sixty-six days. The **Mayflower Compact** was a document signed by 41 of the male passengers prior to their landing at Plymouth; it formed the signatories into a body politic for the purpose of establishing a government.

mayfly this short-lived insect is proverbial for its brief existence.

Maynooth a village in County Kildare in the Republic of Ireland, which is the site of St Patrick's College, a Roman Catholic seminary founded in 1795.

Mayor of the Palace in the Frankish kingdoms, a nominal subordinate wielding the power of his titular superior, originally in the Frankish kingdoms under the later Merovingian kings. The title represents French *maire du palais* and post-classical Latin *major palatii*.

maypole a tall pole, traditionally decorated with flowers or greenery and often with painted spiral stripes, set up on a green or other open space, around which people dance during May or springtime celebrations; in the 17th century, it was one of the symbols of secular revelry particularly disliked by Puritans. The tradition of dancers holding long ribbons attached to the top of the pole dates from the 19th century.

MCC Marylebone Cricket Club, founded in 1787, which has its headquarters at Lord's Cricket Ground in London. The tacitly accepted governing body of cricket until 1969, it continues to have primary responsibility for the game's laws.

mea culpa an acknowledgement of one's guilt or responsibility for an error; a Latin phrase, meaning literally '(through) my own fault', from the prayer of confession in the Latin liturgy of the Church.

Mecca a city in western Saudi Arabia, an oasis town in the Red Sea region of Hejaz, east of Jiddah, considered by Muslims to be the holiest city of Islam. It was the birthplace in AD 570 of the prophet ➤ MUHAMMAD, and was the scene of his early teachings before his emigration to Medina in 622 (the ➤ HEGIRA). On Muhammad's return to Mecca in 630 it became the centre of the new Muslim faith. It is the site of the Great Mosque and the ➤ KAABA, and is a centre of Islamic ritual, including the haj pilgrimage which leads thousands of visitors to the city each year.

Mede a member of an Indo-European people who inhabited ancient Media, establishing an extensive empire during the 7th century BC, which was conquered by Cyrus the Great of Persia in 550 BC.

The phrase **law of the Medes and Persians** means a law, or system of laws, that cannot be altered. The reference is biblical, to Daniel 6:15, 'the law of the Medes and Persians is, That no decree nor statute which the king establisheth may be changed.'

Medea in Greek mythology, princess of ➤ COLCHIS and a sorceress, traditionally with a knowledge of poisons. She helped ➤ JASON to obtain the ➤ GOLDEN *Fleece* from her father Aeetes, and married him; assisting the Argonauts to escape from Colchis, she murdered her younger brother. When Jason deserted her for Creusa, the daughter of King Creon of Corinth, she took revenge by killing Creon, Creusa, and her own children, and fled to Athens. She is taken as the type of a vengeful and ruthless woman.

Medici a powerful Italian family of bankers and merchants whose members effectively ruled Florence for much of the 15th century, and to whom belonged four popes, including Leo X (1513–21) and Clement VII (1523–34), and two queens of France; from 1569 they were grand dukes of Tuscany.

Medicean designates any of the four largest moons of Jupiter (Io, Europa, Ganymede, or Callisto), named by their discoverer Galileo in honour of his patron Cosimo II de' Medici.

Medina a city in western Saudi Arabia, which was the refuge of Muhammad's infant Muslim community from its removal from Mecca in AD 622 until its return there in 630. It was renamed Medina, meaning 'city', by Muhammad and made the capital of the new Islamic state until it was superseded by Damascus in 661. It is Muhammad's burial place and the site of the first Islamic mosque, constructed around his tomb. It is considered by Muslims to be the second most holy city after Mecca, and a visit to the prophet's tomb at Medina often forms a sequel to the formal pilgrimage to Mecca.

Medmenham Abbey a ruined Cistercian abbey on the Thames near Marlow, rebuilt as a residence and notorious in the 18th century as the meeting-place of a convivial club known as the *Franciscans* or *Hell-fire Club*, founded by Francis Dashwood. Its motto '*Fay ce que voudras*' was adopted from that of Rabelais's abbey of Thélème.

Medusa the only one of the three ➤ GORGONS who was mortal, the sight of her head was so terrible that even after her death anyone who saw it was turned to stone. With the help of the gods, she was killed by ➤ PERSEUS; the winged horses ➤ PEGASUS and Chrysaor sprang from her blood as it was shed. Her name is used allusively with reference to her snaky hair and stony gaze.

Megaera in Greek mythology, one of the ➤ FURIES.

megalith a large stone that forms a prehistoric monument (e.g. a standing stone) or part of one (e.g. a stone circle or chambered tomb).

Megan's law a law passed in New Jersey, US, in 1994 which permits police to notify families if a convicted sex offender moves into their area; also, designating similar (proposed) laws in other states or countries, especially national legislation passed in the US in 1996, which makes notification of residents obligatory.

It was named after *Megan* Kanka, a 7-year-old girl who was murdered in 1994 in New Jersey, US, by a convicted child sex offender living near her home.

Megiddo an ancient city of NW Palestine, situated to the south-east of Haifa in present-day Israel. Its commanding location made the city the scene of many early battles, and from its name the word *Armageddon* ('hill of Megiddo') is derived. It was the scene in 1918 of the defeat of Turkish forces by the British under General Allenby.

Megillah a book of the Hebrew scriptures (the Song of Solomon, Ruth, Lamentations, Ecclesiastes, and Esther) appointed to be read on certain Jewish notable days, especially the Book of Esther, read at the festival of Purim.

The whole megillah is an informal expression for something in its entirety, especially a complicated set of arrangements or a long-winded story. The phrase, which represents Yiddish *a gantse megile*, alludes to the length of the Megillah.

Meiji the period when Japan was ruled by the emperor Meiji Tenno (1868–1912), marked by the modernization and westernization of the country.

Mein Kampf 'My Struggle', title of Hitler's autobiography, first published in German in two volumes in 1925 and 1927, and later widely translated. It embodies the principles of National Socialism which the author was later to put into practice.

meiosis in rhetoric, another term for ➤ LI-TOTES. Recorded from the mid 16th century, the word comes via modern Latin, from Greek *meiōsis*, from *meioun* 'lessen', from *meiōn* 'less'.

Meissen fine hard-paste porcelain produced in Meissen, a city in Saxony, eastern Germany, since 1710, in Britain often called Dresden china. The name may be used allusively for the type of a woman whose looks evoke the delicacy of a Meissen figurine.

Meistersinger a member of one of the guilds of German lyric poets and musicians which flourished from the 12th to 17th century. Their technique was elaborate and they were subject to rigid regulations, as depicted in Wagner's opera *Die Meistersinger von Nürnberg* (1868).

the Mekon in the *Eagle* comic strip from *c*.1950, the adversary of ➤ Dan DARE, who constantly plots to dominate the solar system. His name is used allusively both for his cunning and powerful brain, and for his bald head.

mela in the Indian subcontinent, a fair or Hindu festival.

melancholy a deep, pensive, and long-lasting sadness. In the Middle Ages, *melancholy* was also synonymous with ➤ black BILE, one of the four bodily humours.
    The word comes ultimately from Greek *melas* 'black' + *kholē* 'bile', an excess of which was formerly believed to cause depression.

Melba the name of the Australian operatic soprano Dame Nellie Melba (1861–1931), used in a number of figurative and allusive contexts. In Australia, the informal expression **do a Melba** refers to the repeated 'farewell' appearances made by her.

Melchior the traditional name of one of the ➤ MAGI, represented as a king of Nubia.

Melchizedek in the Bible, a priest and king of Salem (which is usually identified with Jerusalem). He was revered by Abraham, who paid tithes to him (Genesis 14:18), and he is described as bringing out bread and wine; this was later taken in the Christian Church as prefiguring the Eucharist.

Meleager in Greek mythology, a hero at whose birth the Fates declared that he would die when a brand then on the fire was consumed. His mother Althaea seized the brand and kept it, but threw it back into the fire when he quarrelled with and killed her

brothers in a hunting expedition, whereupon he died.
    He is said to have hunted down and killed the ➤ CALYDONIAN *boar*, in the company of ➤ ATALANTA, with whom he was in love, and who first wounded the boar. He gave the spoils of the chase to her, and it was the attempt of his uncles to deprive her of them that brought about their deaths.

melodrama originally, a stage-play (typically romantic and sensational in plot and incident) with songs interspersed and action accompanied by appropriate orchestral music. As the musical element ceased to be regarded as essential, the word came to mean a sensational dramatic piece with exaggerated characters and exciting events intended to appeal to the emotions.
    Recorded from the early 19th century, the word comes via French from Greek *melos* 'music' + French *drame* 'drama'.

Melos a Greek island in the Aegean Sea, in the south-west of the Cyclades group. It was the centre of a flourishing civilization in the Bronze Age and is the site of the discovery in 1820 of a Hellenistic marble statue of Aphrodite, the Venus de Milo.

Melpomene in classical mythology, the Muse of tragedy. Her name, which is Greek, means literally 'singer'.

meltdown an accident in a nuclear reactor in which the fuel overheats and melts the reactor core or shielding; in figurative use, a disastrous event, especially a rapid fall in share prices.

melting pot a place where different elements, such as peoples, styles, or theories, are mixed together. The term is used particularly of a country seen as one in which diverse races and cultures are assimilated.

Melungeon a member of a people of mixed Black, White, and Amerindian descent inhabiting the southern Appalachian mountains in the eastern US. The name may be an alteration of *mélange*.

Mélusine in French medieval legend, a fairy, connected with various French princely houses, as the house of Lusignan. According to legend, although she appeared as a beautiful woman, she had the tail of a serpent.

memento mori an object serving as a warning or reminder of death, such as a skull. Recorded from the late 16th century, the Latin phrase means literally, 'remember (that you have) to die'.

Memnon a mythical king of the Ethiopians, son of Aurora and Tithonus, who fought for the Trojans at the siege of Troy and was killed by Achilles. He was associated by the ancients with various eastern lands, and in the 17th century **Memnonian** was used to mean 'oriental, Persian', as in Milton's *Paradise Lost* Susa is described as the 'Memnonian Palace' of Xerxes.

In the ancient world a colossus of Amenophis III at Thebes in Egypt was believed by the Greeks to be a statue of *Memnon*; it was said to give forth a musical sound when touched by the dawn.

Memorial Day in the US, a day on which those who died on active service are remembered, usually the last Monday in May, but on other days in some Southern states; it was originally a Union holiday after the Civil War of 1861–5.

down memory lane recalling a pleasant past; from *Down Memory Lane* (1949), the title of a compilation of Mack Sennett comedy shorts.

Memphis an ancient city of Egypt, whose ruins are situated on the Nile about 15 km (nearly 10 miles) south of Cairo. It is thought to have been founded as the capital of the Old Kingdom of Egypt *c*.3100 BC by Menes, the ruler of the first Egyptian dynasty, who united the kingdoms of Upper and Lower Egypt. Associated with the god Ptah, it remained one of Egypt's principal cities even after Thebes was made the capital of the New Kingdom *c*.1550 BC. It is the site of the pyramids of Saqqara and Giza and the Sphinx.

Memphis is also the name of a river port on the Mississippi in the extreme south-west of Tennessee, named after the ancient city on the Nile because of its river location. Founded in 1819, it was the home in the late 19th century of blues music, the scene in 1968 of the assassination of Martin Luther King, and the childhood home and burial place of Elvis Presley.

men male people.

In the US, **men in black** are dark-clothed men of unknown identity or origin, who supposedly visit those who have seen a UFO or reported an alien encounter, in order to suppress any public account of the incident.

Men in (grey) suits are powerful men within an organization who exercise their influence or authority anonymously.

Men in white coats is a humorous term for psychiatrists or psychiatric workers (used to imply that somebody is mad or mentally unbalanced).

mend one's fences make peace with a person; originally US, in the late 19th century, with reference to a member of Congress returning to his home to keep in touch with the voters and to look after his interests there.

Mendelism the theory of hereditiy as formulated by the Moravian monk Gregor Johann *Mendel* (1822–84), the father of genetics. From systematically breeding peas he demonstrated the transmission of characteristics in a predictable way by factors (genes) which remain intact and independent between generations and do not blend, though they may mask one another's effects.

mendicant a member of a Christian religious order originally relying solely on alms, a **mendicant friar**. The most important of these orders in the Western Church (often referred to as the *Four Orders*) were the Franciscans, Dominicans, Carmelites, and Augustinian Hermits. Recorded from later Middle English, the term comes from Latin *mendicant-* 'begging', from the verb *mendicare*, from *mendicus* 'beggar', from *mendum* 'deficiency'.

From the early 17th century, the term was extended to Buddhists and members of other religions who lived a wandering life, relying upon alms.

Menelaus in Greek mythology, king of Sparta, husband of ➤ HELEN and brother of ➤ AGAMEMNON. Helen was stolen from him by Paris, an event which provoked the Trojan War. They were reunited after the fall of Troy.

menhir a tall upright stone of a kind erected in prehistoric times in western Europe. The word comes from Breton *men* 'stone' + *hir* 'long'.

Menin Gate a gateway to the town of ➤ YPRES which is a memorial to British soldiers of the First World War; on it are inscribed the names of those who have no known grave.

Mennonite chiefly in the US and Canada, a member of a Protestant sect originating in Friesland in the 16th century, emphasizing adult baptism and rejecting Church organization, military service, and public office. It is named after its founder, *Menno* Simons (1496–1561).

menologion a calendar of the Greek Orthodox Church, containing biographies of the saints. The name comes from ecclesiastical Greek, from Greek *mēn* 'month' + *logos* 'account'.

the Menorah a sacred candelabrum with seven branches used in the Temple in Jerusalem, originally that made by the craftsman Bezalel and placed in the sanctuary of the Tabernacle (Exodus 37:17 ff.). The Menorah framed by two olive branches is the emblem of the state of Israel.

The name *menorah* also denotes a candelabrum used in Jewish worship, especially one with eight branches used at Hanukkah.

mens sana in corpore sano Latin tag from the *Satires* of Juvenal (AD *c*.60–*c*.130) meaning 'a rational mind in a healthy body', quoted in English from the early 17th century, and frequently given as the ideal of education.

Mensa an international organization founded in England in 1945 whose members must achieve very high scores in IQ tests to be admitted. The name comes from Latin for 'table', with allusion to a round table at which all members have equal status.

Menshevik a member of the non-Leninist wing of the Russian Social Democratic Workers' Party, which proposed moderate reforms and opposed the Bolsheviks' advocacy of revolutionary action by a small political elite. They were defeated by the Bolsheviks after the overthrow of the tsar in 1917.

The name comes from Russian *Men'shevík* 'a member of the minority' from *men'she* 'less'. Lenin coined the name at a time when the party was (untypically) in the minority for a brief period.

Mentor in Homer's *Odyssey*, the character in whose guise Athena appears to the young Telemachus and acts as his guide and adviser; the familiarity of the story was reinforced by *Les Aventures des Télémaque* (1699) by the French theologian and writer Fénélon. From the mid 18th century, *mentor* has been used to mean an experienced and trusted adviser.

In the 18th and 19th centuries, *Mentor* was frequently used in book titles to denote a guide-book or book of advice.

Mephistopheles an evil spirit to whom Faust, in the German legend, sold his soul.

The origin of the name, which appears first in German in the late 16th century, is uncertain.

Mercator projection a projection of a map of the world on to a cylinder in such a way that all the parallels of latitude have the same length as the equator, invented by the Flemish geographer and cartographer Gerardus *Mercator* (1512–94). It was first published in 1569 and used especially for marine charts and certain climatological maps.

Merchant Adventurers an English trading guild which was involved in trade overseas, principally with the Netherlands (and later Germany) during the 15th–18th centuries. Established in 1407, it engaged chiefly in the lucrative business of exporting woollen cloth. It was formally disbanded in 1806.

Mercia a former kingdom of central England. It was established by invading Angles in the 6th century AD in the border areas between the new Anglo-Saxon settlements in the east and the Celtic regions in the west.

Mercury in Roman mythology, the Roman god of eloquence, skill, trading, and thieving, herald and messenger of the gods, presider over roads, and conductor of departed souls to Hades, who was identified with ➤ HERMES. He is usually represented in art as a young man with winged sandals and a winged hat, and bearing the caduceus.

His function as a messenger gave rise to the use of his name in the titles of newspapers and journals, as *The Scotch Mercury* of 1643. (The '*English Mercury* (1588)', sometimes cited as the earliest English newspaper, was in fact an 18th-century forgery.)

From late Middle English, *mercury* was used to denote the chemical element of atomic number 80, a heavy silvery-white metal (also called *quicksilver*) which is liquid at ordinary temperatures. This application probably arose from an analogy between the fluidity of the metal at room temperature and the rapid motion held to be characteristic of the classical deity.

Mercurial was formerly used to designate those born under the planet Mercury; having the qualities (identical with those assigned to or supposed to be inspired by the god Mercury) considered to be a consequence of this, as eloquence, ingenuity, aptitude for commerce. In current usage, it means subject to sudden or unpredictable changes of mood or mind; although these qualities were originally associated with the god, the allusion is now generally understood as referring to the properties of mercury as a metal.

mercy seat the golden covering placed upon the Ark of the Covenant, regarded as the resting-place of God; the throne of God in Heaven. The term is found in Exodus 25:17.

meridian a circle of constant longitude passing through a given place on the earth's surface and the terrestrial poles; in astronomy, a circle passing through the celestial poles and the zenith of a given place on the earth's surface.

Recorded from late Middle English, the word comes via Old French from Latin *meridianum* (neuter, used as a noun) 'noon', from *medius* 'middle' + *dies* 'day'. The use in astronomy is due to the fact that the sun crosses a meridian at noon.

Merlin in Arthurian legend, the powerful magician who protected Arthur in childhood and was later his chief counsellor; he was eventually entrapped by the enchantress ➤ VIVIEN.

mermaid a fictitious or mythical half-human sea creature with the head and trunk of a woman and the tail of a fish, conventionally depicted (especially in heraldry) as beautiful and with long flowing golden hair, holding in the right hand a comb and in the left a mirror. In early use, the *mermaid* is often identified with the siren of classical mythology. Recorded from Middle English, the word comes from *mere* with the obsolete sense 'sea' + *maid*.

The **Mermaid Tavern**, which stood in Bread Street, London, was frequented by Shakespeare, Donne, and other literary figures.

Merovingian a member of the Frankish dynasty founded by Clovis and reigning in Gaul and Germany *c*.500–750. The word comes from the medieval Latin *Merovingi* 'descendants of Merovich' (semi-legendary 5th-century Frankish leader said to be the grandfather of ➤ CLOVIS).

merry cheerful and lively; in a number of fixed phrases.

Merry England is England, originally as characterized by a pleasant landscape; (sometimes ironically, and with the pseudo-archaic spelling **merrie England**) England characterized by the cheerfulness or animation of its people, especially in a past golden age.

In the legends of Robin Hood, the **merry men** are his followers.

A **Merry Widow** is an amorous or designing widow, from the English name of Franz Lehár's operetta *Die Lustige Witwe*, first produced in German in Vienna in 1905, and in English in London, 1907. The musical-comedy actress Lily Elsie (1886–1962), appearing in London in the title role, wore an ornate wide-brimmed hat designed by Lucy, Lady Duff Gordon ('Lucile'); **Merry Widow hats** are named from this.

Mersey the name of a river flowing to the Irish Sea near Liverpool, used (as in **Mersey beat**) to designate the kind of popular music associated with the Beatles and other groups from that area.

the Mesolithic the Middle Stone Age, which in Europe falls between the end of the last glacial period (*c*.8500 BC) and the beginnings of agriculture. Mesolithic people lived by hunting, gathering, and fishing, and the period is characterized by the use of microliths and the first domestication of an animal (the dog).

mess of pottage in the biblical story, the dish of lentils for which the hungry ➤ ESAU sold his birthright to his younger brother Jacob (Genesis 25); the expression is proverbial for a ridiculously small amount offered or taken for something of real value.

Although the proverbial use is recorded from 1526, it does not occur in the Authorized Version of 1611; it does however appear in the heading of chapter 25 in the Bibles of 1537 and 1539, and in the Geneva Bible of 1560.

Messalina (*c*.22–48 BC), Roman empress, third wife of Claudius. She became notorious in Rome for the murders she instigated and for her extramarital affairs, and was executed on Claudius' orders, after the disclosure of her secret marriage with one of his political opponents. Her name is used for the type of a licentious and scheming woman.

shoot the messenger treat the bearer of bad news as if they were to blame for it; often in the form, *don't shoot the messenger!* Being the bearer of bad tidings has been a traditionally thankless task, as in Sophocles' *Antigone*, 'No man loves the messenger of ill.'

the Messiah the promised deliverer of the Jewish nation prophesied in the Hebrew Bible; Jesus regarded by Christians as the

Messiah of the Hebrew prophecies and the saviour of humankind.

Recorded from Old English (in the form *Messias*), the name comes via late Latin and Greek from Hebrew *māšiaḥ* 'anointed'.

From the mid 17th century, the word has developed a transferred use to denote an expected liberator or saviour of an oppressed people, country, or cause.

Messidor the tenth month of the French Republican calendar (1793–1805), originally running from 19 June to 18 July. The name comes (in French) from Latin *messis* 'harvest' + Greek *dōron* 'gift'.

metal metals were traditionally divided into *noble* or *precious* metals (gold, silver, and platinum, which resist corrosion) and *base* or *imperfect* metals (such as lead). In heraldry, *metal* is used for the tinctures or (gold) and argent (silver).

Recorded from Middle English, the word comes via Old French or Latin, from Greek *metallon* 'mine, quarry, metal'.

metaphor a figure of speech in which a word or phrase is applied to an object or action to which it is not literally applicable. Recorded from the late 15th century, the word comes via French and Latin from Greek *metaphora*, from *metapherein* 'to transfer'.

metaphysical poets a group of 17th-century poets whose work is characterized by the use of complex and elaborate images or conceits, typically using an intellectual form of argumentation to express emotional states. Members of the group include John Donne, George Herbert, Henry Vaughan, and Andrew Marvell.

The application of *metaphysical* to these poets is first recorded from the mid 18th century. The genesis of the specific use, however, can be found a century earlier, in a reference by William Drummond of Hawthornden (1585–1649) to 'Metaphysicall Ideas'.

metaphysics the branch of philosophy that deals with the first principles of things, including abstract concepts such as being, knowing, substance, cause, identity, time, and space. Metaphysics has two main strands: that which holds that what exists lies beyond experience (as argued by Plato), and that which holds that objects of experience constitute the only reality (as argued by Kant, the logical positivists, and Hume). Metaphysics has also concerned itself with a discussion of whether what exists is made of one substance or many, and whether what exists is inevitable or driven by chance.

Recorded from the mid 16th century, the word represents medieval Latin *metaphysica* (neuter plural), based on Greek *ta meta ta phusika* 'the things after the Physics', referring to the sequence of Aristotle's works: the title came to denote the branch of study treated in the books, later interpreted as meaning 'the science of things transcending what is physical or natural'.

metempsychosis the supposed transmigration at death of the soul of a human being or animal into a new body of the same or a different species, chiefly in Pythagoreanism and certain Eastern religions.

method acting a technique of acting in which an actor aspires to complete emotional identification with a part, based on the system evolved by Stanislavsky and brought into prominence in the US in the 1930s.

method in one's madness sense or reason in what appears to be foolish or abnormal behaviour; from Shakespeare's *Hamlet* (1601) in the scene in which Hamlet feigns insanity, 'Though this be madness, yet there is method in't.'

Methodist a member of a Christian Protestant denomination originating in the 18th-century evangelistic movement of Charles and John Wesley and George Whitefield. The Methodist Church grew out of a religious society established within the Church of England, from which it formally separated in 1791. It is particularly strong in the US and now constitutes one of the largest Protestant denominations worldwide, with more than 30 million members. Methodism has a strong tradition of missionary work and concern with social welfare, and emphasizes the believer's personal relationship with God.

The original reason for the name is not clear, but it probably reflects the use of *Methodist* to mean someone who advocates a particular method or system of theological belief, especially with reference to doctrinal disputes about grace and justification.

Methuselah in the Bible, a patriarch, the grandfather of Noah, who is said to have lived for 969 years. His name is used allusively as the type of a very old person, and the expression **as old as Methuselah** is recorded from the early 16th century.

The name *methuselah* is used for a wine bottle of eight times the standard size.

Metroland the area around London served by the underground railway, especially as viewed nostalgically as an ideal suburban environment of the 1920s and 1930s. Evelyn Waugh used the name *Margot Metroland* for a key character in *Decline and Fall*, *Vile Bodies*, and other satiric novels.

metropolitan in the Christian Church, a bishop having authority over the bishops of a province, in particular (in many Orthodox Churches) one ranking above archbishop and below patriarch.

be on one's mettle be ready or forced to prove one's ability to cope well with a demanding situation. *Mettle* here derives from a specialized spelling (used for figurative senses) of *metal*.

Mexican wave an effect resembling a moving wave produced by successive sections of the crowd in a stadium standing up, raising their arms, lowering them, and sitting down again. It is so named because of the repeated practice of this movement at the 1986 soccer World Cup finals in Mexico City.

mezuzah a parchment inscribed with religious texts and attached in a case to the doorpost of a Jewish house as a sign of faith. Recorded from the mid 17th century, the word comes from Hebrew *mĕzūzāh* 'doorpost'.

mezzanine financing financing which involves unsecured, higher-yielding loans that are subordinate to bank loans and secured loans but rank above equity. The usage is recorded from the mid 1970s, and represents a transference of *mezzanine* to mean a low storey between two others in a building.

Micah (in the Bible) a Hebrew minor prophet. Also, a book of the Bible bearing his name, foretelling the destruction of Samaria and of Jerusalem.

Wilkins Micawber a character in Dickens's novel *David Copperfield* (1850), an eternal optimist who, despite evidence to the contrary, continues to have faith that 'something will turn up'.

St Michael one of the archangels (Jude 9) whose role is divine messenger and executor of God's judgements. His name means 'Who is like unto God?' In Revelations 12:7 he is shown as a warrior leading the hosts of

heaven, 'There was war in heaven, Michael and his angels fought against the dragon.'

He is typically represented slaying a dragon, and he may also be shown weighing souls, sometimes as part of the Last Judgement. His feast day (St Michael and All Angels, or ➤ MICHAELMAS *Day*) is 29 September.

In the UK, the **Order of St Michael and St George** is an order of knighthood instituted in 1818, divided into three classes: Knight or Dame Grand Cross of the Order of St Michael and St George (GCMG), Knight or Dame Commander (KCMG/DCMG), and Companion (CMG).

Michaelmas the feast of St ➤ MICHAEL and All Angels, 29 September, one of the quarter days in England, Ireland, and Wales. **Old Michaelmas** is the day that would have been called 29 September if the Old Style calendar had not been corrected.

A **Michaelmas goose** is traditionally eaten at a feast on this day, and a **Michaelmas summer** is a period of warm weather before the onset of winter, associated with this time.

Mickey Finn a surreptitiously drugged or doctored drink given to someone so as to make them drunk or insensible. Recorded from the 1920s, the origin of the expression is unknown, but it is sometimes said to be the name of a notorious Chicago saloon-keeper (*c.*1896–1906).

Mickey Mouse a Walt Disney cartoon character, who first appeared as Mortimer Mouse in 1927, becoming Mickey in 1928. During the 1930s he became established as the central Disney character, with Disney himself speaking the soundtrack for Mickey's voice. He is perhaps the most famous of the Disney cartoon characters.

Mickey Mouse is also used informally to indicate that something is of inferior quality.

Midas a king of Phrygia, who, according to one story, was given by Dionysus the power of turning everything he touched into gold. Unable to eat or drink, he prayed to be relieved of the gift and was instructed to wash in the River Pactolus. According to another story, he declared Pan a better flute player than Apollo, who thereupon gave him ass's ears. Midas tried to hide them but his barber whispered the secret to some reeds, which repeat it whenever they rustle in the wind.

middle at an equal distance from the extremities of something.

The **Middle Ages** are the period of European history from the fall of the Roman Empire in the West (5th century) to the fall of Constantinople (1453), or, more narrowly, from c.1000 to 1453.

Middle America is the middle class in the United States, especially when regarded as a conservative political force; the Midwest of the United States regarded as the home of such people.

Middle England is the middle classes in England outside London, especially as representative of conservative political views.

The **Middle Kingdom** is a period of ancient Egyptian history (c.2040–1640 BC, 11th–14th dynasty).

Middle Kingdom is also a former term for China or its eighteen inner provinces. The name is a translation of Chinese *zhongguo* 'central state', originally the name given to the imperial state, in contrast to the dependencies surrounding it; from 1911 onwards, part of the official name of the Chinese state.

Middle Kingdom is also used for the central region consisting of the Low Countries, Alsace, Lorraine, Burgundy, Provence, and Lombardy, and much of central Italy given to the Frankish king Lothair I by the Treaty of Verdun in 843.

The **middle passage** was the sea journey undertaken by slave ships from West Africa to the West Indies, seen as the middle part of the journey of the transportation of a slave from Africa to America. The term is first recorded in *An Essay on the Impolicy of the African Slave Trade* (1788) by the abolitionist Thomas Clarkson (1760–1846).

The **Middle Temple** is one of the two Inns of Court on the site of the ➤ TEMPLE in London, England, the other being the ➤ INNER *Temple*.

Middletown in the US, an archetypal middle-class community. The term was popularized by R. S. and H. M. Lynd's *Middletown: a study in contemporary American culture* (1929), said to be based on Muncie, Indiana.

Midgard in Scandinavian mythology, the region, encircled by the sea, in which human beings live; the earth.

The **Midgard**'s serpent was a monstrous serpent, the offspring of ➤ LOKI, which was thrown by Odin into the sea, where, with its tail in its mouth, it encircled the earth.

midnight appointment in US politics, an appointment made during the last hours of an administration, originally with particular reference to those made by the 2nd President

John Adams (1735–1826) in a letter by Thomas Jefferson of January 1811.

midnight Mass a Mass celebrated at or shortly before midnight, especially on Christmas Eve.

Midrash an ancient commentary on part of the Hebrew scriptures, attached to the biblical text. The earliest Midrashim come from the 2nd century AD, although much of their content is older.

Midsummer another term for the Summer Solstice, and the period of time immediately surrounding it.

Midsummer Day is 24 June, the feast of the Nativity of St John the Baptist, a quarter day in England, Wales, and Ireland, originally coinciding with the summer solstice and in some countries marked by a summer festival.

Battle of Midway in 1942, off the Midway Islands in the central Pacific, a decisive sea battle in which the US navy repelled a Japanese invasion fleet, sinking four aircraft carriers. This defeat marked the end of Japanese expansion in the Pacific during the Second World War.

midwife toad a European toad, the male of which carries the developing eggs wrapped around his hind legs. The Austrian zoologist Paul Kammerer (1880–1926) showed specimens of the animal which appeared to support the evolutionary theories of ➤ LAMARCKISM, but the apparent development of nuptial pads on the forefeet was shown to be fraudulent.

might is right those who are powerful can do what they wish unchallenged, even if their action is in fact unjustified. An observation made by both Greek and Latin writers and known in this form in English since the late medieval period.

mighty hunter in the Bible, an epithet applied to ➤ NIMROD.

mihrab a niche in the wall of a mosque, at the point nearest to Mecca, towards which the congregation faces to pray.

mikado a title formerly given to the emperor of Japan. The word comes from Japanese *mi* 'august' + *kado* 'gate'; the title is a tranferred use of 'gate (to the Imperial palace)', an ancient place of audience.

It was usual for European writers prior to the Meiji Restoration of 1868 to describe the *Mikado* as a 'spiritual' emperor and the

➤ SHOGUN (who was the *de facto ruler* until 1867) as a second or 'temporal' ruler.

mile a unit of linear measure equal to 1,760 yards (approximately 1.609 kilometres); originally, a Roman measure of 1,000 paces (approximately 1,620 yards).

Recorded from Old English (in the form *mīl*) the word is based on Latin *mil(l)ia*, plural of *mille* 'thousand'; the original Roman unit of distance was *mille passus* 'a thousand paces'.

Milesian¹ of or pertaining to ancient ➤ MILETUS, a city in Asia Minor, especially in ➤ MILESIAN *tale*.

A **Milesian tale** is an erotic short story of a type produced by ancient Greek and Roman novelists; the term derives from the title of a collection of stories by Aristides (2nd century BC); probably so called because *Miletus* in Asia Minor was the traditional setting for the genre.

Milesian² a native or inhabitant of ancient Ireland, from the legend that the ancient kingdom was conquered and reorganized about 1300 BC by the sons of *Milesius* (Miledh), a fabulous Spanish king.

Miletus an ancient city of the Ionian Greeks in SW Asia Minor. In the 7th and 6th centuries BC it was a powerful port, from which more than sixty colonies were founded on the shores of the Black Sea and in Italy and Egypt. It was the home of the philosophers Thales, Anaximander, and Anaximenes. It was conquered by the Persians in 494 BC. By the 6th century AD its harbours had become silted up by the alluvial deposits of the Menderes River.

Milice in France, a force employed by the Vichy government of 1940–44 to repress internal dissent.

Militant a Trotskyite political organization in Britain, which publishes the weekly newspaper *Militant*. During the early 1980s it attempted to infiltrate and express its views from within the Labour Party.

military-industrial complex a country's military establishment and those industries producing arms or other military materials, regarded as a powerful vested interest. The term derives from a speech by US President Eisenhower in 1961.

militia a military force that is raised from the civil population to supplement a regular army in an emergency.

Recorded from the late 16th century in the sense 'a system of military discipline and organization', in the 17th century the word came to be applied to the name of various military units and forces raised locally from the citizen body of an area, and distinguished from professional standing armies as these developed. The usage may derive from such instances as the 'Ordinance for settling the Militia of London' (1642, where the word was taken to refer specifically to the trained bands of London affected by the order).

Subsequently *militia* also developed the sense of a military force that engages in rebel or terror activities, typically in opposition to a regular army; most recently, this has been applied to the militias of East Timor.

milk for babes something easy and pleasant to learn; especially in allusion to 1 Corinthians.

milk of human kindness compassion, sympathy; originally from Shakespeare's *Macbeth* (1606), in Lady Macbeth's expression of her anxiety that her husband lacked the necessary ruthlessness to kill King Duncan and seize the throne.

Milky Way a faint band of light crossing the sky, clearly visible on dark moonless nights and discovered by Galileo to be made up of vast numbers of faint stars. It corresponds to the plane of our Galaxy, in which most of its stars are located.

The *Milky Way* was sometimes named from famous pilgrimage routes; as ➤ WALSINGHAM *Way* and the *Way of St James* (the road to Santiago de Compostela).

Millbank a building on the embankment of the north side of the River Thames in Westminster, London, which since 1980 has been the headquarters of the British Labour Party, and which is particularly associated with the centralized control seen as typifying ➤ NEW *Labour*.

millenarianism the doctrine of or belief in a future (and typically imminent) thousand-year age of blessedness, beginning with or culminating in the Second Coming of Christ. It is central to the teaching of groups such as Plymouth Brethren, Adventists, Mormons, and Jehovah's Witnesses.

The term may also be used more generally for belief in a future golden age of peace, justice, and prosperity.

millennium a period of a thousand years, especially when calculated from the traditional date of the birth of Christ. In the Christian Church, the term is also used for the period of one thousand years during which (according to one interpretation of Revelation 20:1–5), Christ will reign in person on earth.

Recorded from the mid 17th century, the word is modern Latin, from *mille* 'thousand', on the pattern of *biennium*.

The **millennium bug** was the informal name for a problem with some computers arising from an inability of the software to deal correctly with dates of 1 January 2000 or later, through the misinterpretation of a two-digit number (as 87, 99) used to represent a year without specifying the century concerned.

Mills and Boon trademark name used to denote idealized and sentimental romantic situations of the kind associated with the type of fiction published by Mills & Boon Limited.

millstone each of two circular stones used for grinding corn; in figurative use, a heavy and inescapable responsibility, often with reference to Matthew 18:6. A **millstone round one's neck** also refers to a method of executing people by throwing them into deep water with a heavy stone attached to them, a fate believed to have been suffered by several early Christian martyrs.

Milo of Croton a famous wrestler who lived towards the end of the 6th century BC. He is said to have died when his hand became trapped in the trunk of a tree which he was trying to split with his fist; held fast, he was eaten by wild animals.

Caspar Milquetoast a cartoon character created by H. T. Webster in 1924 and named after the American dish *milk toast*. *Milquetoast* is now used as a term for a person who is timid or submissive.

Mimir in Scandinavian mythology, the wisest of the Aesir and guardian of the sacred well, to whom Odin sacrificed one eye in exchange for poetic inspiration; when he was killed by the Vanir, Odin preserved his decapitated head, which became oracular.

minaret a slender tower, typically part of a mosque, with a balcony from which a muezzin calls Muslims to prayer. Recorded from the late 17th century, the word comes from

French or Spanish and ultimately, via Turkish, from Arabic *manār(a)* 'lighthouse, minaret', based on *nār* 'fire or light'.

mind one's P's and Q's be careful or particular in one's words or behaviour. The expression is recorded from the late 18th century, and may refer to the difficulty found by a child learning to write in distinguishing between the tailed letters *p* and *q*.

In the early 17th century, the dramatist Thomas Dekker has 'Now thou art in thy pee and cue'; *pee* here is a kind of coat, and *cue* means either a queue of hair, or possibly cue as a tail; it might however indicate an early currency of this expression through a punning allusion.

Minerva in Roman mythology, the goddess, originally of weaving and other crafts, later of wisdom, creativity, and prowess in war, from ancient times identified with the Greek ➤ ATHENE; her symbol is an owl. She is said to have been born fully-armed from the head of Jupiter. (See also ➤ INVITA *Minerva*.)

Ming the dynasty ruling China 1368–1644. Also, Chinese porcelain made during the rule of the Ming dynasty, characterized by elaborate designs and vivid colours.

ministering angel a kind-hearted person, especially a woman, who nurses or comforts others. Recorded from the early 17th century, particularly with allusion to Shakespeare's *Hamlet* (1603), the image of a tender and nurturing woman in this guise was reinforced by Scott in *Marmion* (1808).

Minnehaha in Longfellow's *The Song of Hiawatha* (1855), the beautiful Dakota girl whom Hiawatha marries, taken as the type of an American Indian woman.

Minnesinger a German lyric poet and singer of the 12th–14th centuries, who performed songs of courtly love. The name comes (in the early 19th century) from German *Minnesinger* 'love-singer'.

minnow this small freshwater fish, which typically forms large shoals, is often taken as the type of something which though great in number is weak in strength.

Minoan of, relating to, or denoting a Bronze Age civilization centred on Crete (*c.*3000–1050 BC), its people, or its language. This civilization had reached its zenith by the beginning of the late Bronze Age; impressive remains reveal the existence of large urban centres dominated by palaces. It is also noted for its script (see ➤ LINEAR *A*) and distinctive art and architecture, and greatly influenced the Mycenaeans, who succeeded the Minoans in control of the Aegean *c.*1400 BC.

It is named after the legendary king ➤ MINOS, to whom a palace excavated at Knossos was attributed.

Minor Prophet any of the twelve prophets after whom the shorter prophetic books of the Bible, from Hosea to Malachi, are named.

Minos in Greek mythology, a legendary king of Crete, son of Zeus and Europa. His wife Pasiphaë gave birth to the bull-headed ➤ MINOTAUR, which was kept in the ➤ LABYRINTH constructed by Daedalus. Minos exacted an annual tribute from Athens in the form of young people to be devoured by the monster; this came to an end when Theseus, son of the king of Athens, who had volunteered himself as one of the tribute party, killed the Minotaur.

The **Palace of Minos** is a complex of buildings excavated and reconstructed by Arthur Evans at Knossos, which yielded local coins portraying the labyrinth as the city's symbol and a ➤ LINEAR *B* religious tablet which refers to the 'lady of the labyrinth'.

Minotaur in Greek mythology, a creature who was half-man and half-bull, the offspring of Pasiphaë, wife of ➤ MINOS, and a bull with which she fell in love. Confined in Crete in a labyrinth made by ➤ DAEDALUS and fed on human flesh, it was eventually slain by Theseus.

minstrel a medieval singer or musician, especially one who sang or recited lyric or heroic poetry to a musical accompaniment for the nobility. Recorded from Middle English, the word comes from Old French *menestral* 'entertainer, servant', via Provençal for late Latin *ministerialis* 'servant'.

mint a place where money is coined, especially under state authority. Recorded from Old English (in form *mynet* 'coin', and of West Germanic origin) the word is related to Dutch *munt* and German *Münze*, from Latin *moneta* 'money'.

The **Mint** was a name given to a place of privilege formerly existing near the King's or Queen's Bench Prison in Southwark abolished by statute in 1723; to **send someone to the Mint** was to ruin them. The place took its name from a house which had been a 'mint of coynage' for Henry VIII, and so subject to royal privilege. Because it acted as a shelter for debtors it attracted a large number of

poor and destitute people, and in mid-18th century poetry it was put on a similar level with Bedlam and Newgate.

minuscule of or in a small cursive script of the Roman alphabet, with ascenders and descenders, developed in the 7th century AD. The name comes (in the early 18th century) via French from Latin *minuscula (littera)* 'somewhat smaller (letter)'. (Compare ➤ MAJUSCULE.)

Miocene of, relating to, or denoting the fourth epoch of the Tertiary period, between the Oligocene and Pliocene epochs. This epoch lasted from 23.3 to 5.2 million years ago. During this time the Alps and Himalayas were being formed and there was diversification of the primates, including the first apes.

Mir a Soviet space station, launched in 1986 and designed to be permanently manned. The name is Russian, literally 'peace'.

mirabile dictu Latin phrase, meaning 'wonderful to relate', perhaps originally as a tag from Virgil's *Georgics*.

miracle a surprising and welcome event that is not explicable by natural or scientific laws and is therefore considered to be the work of a divine agency. Recorded from Middle English, the word comes via Old French from Latin *miraculum* 'object of wonder', from *mirari* 'to wonder', from *mirus* 'wonderful'.

A **miracle play** is a dramatization based on events in the life of Jesus or the legends of the saints, popular in the Middle Ages, a ➤ MYSTERY *play*.

all done with mirrors an apparent achievement with an element of trickery, alluding to explanations of the art of a conjuror.

miser a person who hoards wealth and spends as little money as possible. Recorded from the late 15th century (as an adjective in the sense 'miserly'), the word comes from Latin, meaning literally 'wretched'.

miserere a psalm in which mercy is sought, especially Psalm 51 (50 in the Vulgate), beginning '*Miserere mei Deus* [Have mercy upon me, O God]', or the music written for it.

misericord a ledge projecting from the underside of a hinged seat in a choir stall which, when the seat is turned up, gives support to someone standing. Medieval misericords were often decorated with elaborate and sometimes bawdy scenes from secular or religious life, visible when the seat was raised.

Dating in this sense from the early 16th century, *misericord* (denoting pity) is recorded from Middle English, and comes ultimately from Latin *misericordia*, from *misericors* 'compassionate', from the stem of *misereri* 'to pity' + *cor, cord-* 'heart'. Other early uses in English include an apartment in a monastery in which some relaxations of the monastic rule were permitted, and a small dagger used to deliver a death stroke to a wounded enemy.

Mishnah an authoritative collection of exegetical material embodying the oral tradition of Jewish law and forming the first part of the Talmud. The name is from Hebrew *mišnāh* and means 'teaching by repetition'.

misper police slang for a *missing person*, a phrase recorded from the 19th century.

Lord of Misrule traditionally a man presiding over games and other revelry over the Christmas season, especially in a wealthy household, at the Inns of Court, at Oxford and Cambridge Colleges, and at civic entertainments. Also called *Abbot of Misrule, Master of Misrule*.

missal a book containing the texts used in the Catholic Mass throughout the year. Recorded from Middle English, the word comes from medieval Latin *missale*, neuter of ecclesiastical Latin *missalis* 'relating to the Mass', from *missa* 'Mass'.

missing link a hypothetical fossil form intermediate between two living forms, especially between humans and apes, especially as sought by early evolutionary biologists. The term may also be applied pejoratively to a person held to resemble such a creature.

mission statement a formal summary of the aims and values of a company, organization, or individual; a concept which won an important place in the business jargon of the 1990s, although opinions were divided as to the effective value of such expressions of aspiration.

missionary a person sent on a religious mission, especially one sent to promote Christianity in a foreign country.

The **missionary position** is a position for sexual intercourse in which a couple lie face to face with the woman underneath the man, said to be so named because early missionaries advocated the position as 'proper' to primitive peoples, to whom the practice was unknown.

Missolonghi a city in western Greece, on the north shore of the Gulf of Patras. It is noted as the place where the poet Byron, who had joined the fight for Greek independence from the Turks, died of malaria in 1824.

Missouri Compromise an arrangement made in 1820 which provided that Missouri should be admitted to the Union as a slave state, but that slavery should not be allowed in any new state lying north of 36° 30′.

mistletoe according to Pliny the Elder, mistletoe was sacred to the druids, and it has a number of traditional and pagan associations. It is traditionally used in England to decorate houses at Christmas, when it is associated with the custom of **kissing under the mistletoe**.

In Scandinavian mythology, the shaft which Loki caused the blind Hod to throw at Balder, killing him, was tipped with mistletoe, which was the only plant that could harm him.

Recorded from Old English (in form *misteltā*), the word comes from *mistel* 'mistletoe' (of Germanic origin) + *tān* 'twig'.

The Mistletoe Bough was a ballad by Thomas Bayly (1839), which recounts the story of a young bride who during a game hides herself in a chest with a spring-lock and is then trapped there; many years later her skeleton is discovered. Bayly based the ballad on a passage in Samuel Rogers' poem *Italy*.

Mitanni an ancient kingdom which flourished in northern Mesopotamia in the 15th–14th centuries BC, thought to have had a Hurrian population but Indo-Iranian rulers.

Mitchell principles six recommendations arising from the investigations of the group chaired by George J. Mitchell (1933–), US lawyer and senator (1980–94), who from 1995–6 chaired a group investigating procedures by which disarmament in Northern Ireland could be achieved. The recommendations urged all sides involved in the conflict in Northern Ireland to renounce violence and to agree to a process of disarmament before entering into all-party negotiations.

Mithraeum a sanctuary or temple of the god ➤ MITHRAS.

Mithras a god of light, truth, and honour, the central figure of the cult of **Mithraism** but probably of Persian origin; he is often shown slaying the sacred bull. He was also associated with merchants and the protection of warriors.

Mithraism became popular among Roman soldiers of the later empire, and was the main rival to Christianity in the first three centuries AD. The sacrifice of a bull formed an important part of cult worship.

mithridatize render immune against a poison by administering gradually increasing doses of the poison. The word comes from the name of *Mithridates* the Great, king of Pontus 120–63, who was said to have rendered himself proof against poisons by the constant use of antidotes.

Mitla an ancient city in southern Mexico, to the east of the city of Oaxaca, now a noted archaeological site. Believed to have been established as a burial site by the Zapotecs, it was eventually overrun by the Mixtecs in about AD 1000.

mitre a tall headdress worn by bishops and senior abbots as a symbol of office, tapering to a point at front and back with a deep cleft between. Recorded from late Middle English, the word comes from Old French via Latin from Greek *mitra* 'belt or turban'.

In the Anglican Church after the Reformation down to the time of George III, while the mitre was theoretically part of the episcopal insignia, it was generally only worn at coronations. More recently, however, its use has been revived for ceremonial occasions.

Three *mitres* are the emblem of ➤ St BERNARDINO *of Siena*.

Walter Mitty a person who fantasizes about a life much more exciting and glamorous than their own life, from the name of the hero of James Thurber's short story *The Secret Life of Walter Mitty* (1939); the 1947 film was probably influential in popularizing the word.

Mizpah designating a ring, locket, or other piece of jewellery, given as an expression or token of association or remembrance, originally and especially one with 'Mizpah' inscribed on it. The allusion is biblical; in Genesis 31:49 Jacob and Laban give this name to a place as a sign that God should keep watch between them ('The Lord watch between me and thee').

Mizpah comes from Hebrew *Mispah* watchtower, used as the name of several places in ancient Palestine.

mnemonic a device such as a pattern of letters, ideas, or associations which assists in remembering something. Recorded from the mid 18th century (as an adjective), the word comes ultimately from Greek *mnēmonikos*, from *mnēmōn* 'mindful'.

Mnemosyne in Greek mythology, the mother of the Muses; one of the Titans, and the personification of memory.

moa a large extinct flightless bird resembling the emu, formerly found in New Zealand. One species, *Dinornis maximus* is the tallest known bird at over 3 m, but *Megalapteryx didinus*, which may have survived until the early 19th century, was much smaller. The name is from Maori.

Moab an ancient region east of the Dead Sea, the inhabitants of which, the **Moabites**, were said to be incestuously descended from Moab, son of Lot and Lot's daughter. There was regular contact between the Israelites and Moabites, and Naomi's daughter-in-law ➤ RUTH was a **Moabitess**.

In 19th-century slang, *Moab* was used for a kind of turban-shaped hat; the reference being to Psalms 40:8, 'Moab is my washpot' referring to the shape of the hat.

The **Moabite Stone** is a monument erected by Mesha, king of Moab, in c.850 BC which describes (in an early form of the Hebrew language) the campaign between Moab and ancient Israel (2 Kings 3), and furnishes an early example of an inscription in the Phoenician alphabet. It is now in the Louvre in Paris.

mob a large crowd of people, especially one that is disorderly and intent on causing trouble or violence. The word is recorded from the late 17th century and is an abbreviation of the archaic *mobile*, short for Latin *mobile vulgus* 'excitable crowd'.

From the early 20th century, **the Mob** has been an informal term for the Mafia.

Moby Dick the great white whale in Herman Melville's novel of that name (1851), which is hunted by the vengeful Captain Ahab, and which eventually destroys the whaling ship the *Pequod*. The name is used allusively for something on a vast scale.

mockney a form of speech perceived as an affected imitation of cockney in accent and vocabulary. The name, which is a blend of *mock* and *Cockney*, is recorded from the late 1980s as a form of pseudo-Cockney often deliberately adopted to conceal a speaker's privileged background.

Moesia an ancient country of southern Europe, corresponding to parts of modern Bulgaria and Serbia. It became a province of Rome in AD 15, remaining part of the Roman Empire until the 7th century.

Mogul a member of the Muslim dynasty of Mongol origin founded by the successors of Tamerlane, which ruled much of India from the 16th to the 19th century.

Mohács a river port and industrial town on the Danube in southern Hungary, close to the borders with Croatia and Serbia, which was the site of a battle in 1526 in which the Hungarians were defeated by a Turkish force under Suleiman I; as a result, Hungary became part of the Ottoman Empire. A site nearby was the scene of a further decisive battle fought in 1687 during the campaign that swept the Turks out of Hungary.

Mohawk a member of an American Indian people, originally inhabiting parts of what is now upper New York State. Recorded in English from the mid 17th century, the name comes from Narragansett *mohowawog*, literally 'maneaters'; an early variant spelling survives in ➤ MOHOCK.

From the 1980s in North America, *Mohawk* has also been used to denote a Mohican haircut.

Mohican a member of an Algonquian people formerly inhabiting part of Connecticut, or their language; a Mohegan. Although the spelling *Mohegan* is now preferred, *Mohican* is also found in modern use after J. Fenimore Cooper's usage in *The Last of the Mohicans* (1826) and other novels. In these stories, the American Indian Uncas is the last survivor of his people; the phrase **last of the Mohicans** is now used for the sole survivor of a noble race or kind.

From the 1960s, *Mohican* has been used to designate a hairstyle with the head shaved except for a strip of hair from the middle of the forehead to the back of the neck, typically stiffened to stand erect or in spikes. The style imitates a traditional deer-hair topknot worn by males of certain northeastern American Indian peoples, and is probably so named from conventional illustrations of the writings of J. Fenimore Cooper.

Mohock a member of a band of aristocratic ruffians who roamed the streets of London at night in the early 18th century. The name was originally an extended use of ➤ MOHAWK, using a variant spelling.

mole in proverbial use often referred to as the type of a blind creature. The mole was also toasted by Jacobites as the ➤ LITTLE *gentleman in black velvet*, in reference to the death of William III, said to have been caused by a fall from his horse which had stumbled on a molehill.

From the early 1920s, *mole* has been used allusively to designate a spy who achieves over a long period an important position within the security defences of a country, or someone within an organization who anonymously betrays confidential information.

moline in heraldry, (of a cross) having each extremity broadened, split, and curved back (a **cross moline**). The word comes from Anglo-Norman French *moliné*, from *molin* 'mill', because of a resemblance to the iron support of a millstone.

Mollweide projection a projection of a map of the world on to an ellipse, with lines of latitude represented by straight lines (spaced more closely towards the poles) and meridians represented by equally spaced elliptical curves. This projection distorts shape but preserves relative area. It is named after Karl B. *Mollweide* (1774–1825), German mathematician and astronomer, who first used it.

Moloch a Canaanite idol to whom children were sacrificed; in extended usage, a tyrannical object of sacrifices. The Rabbinical story that children were burnt alive (being placed in the arms of the idol, whence they fell into the flames) appears to be unfounded, but is widely known, and has influenced the extended use. The deity is represented by Milton in *Paradise Lost* as one of the devils.

Molotov cocktail a crude incendiary device typically consisting of a bottle filled with flammable liquid and with a means of ignition. The production of similar grenades was organized by Vyacheslav *Molotov* (1890–1986), during the Second World War.

moly a mythical herb with white flowers and black roots, endowed with magic properties, and said by Homer to have been given by Hermes to Odysseus as a charm against Circe. The name comes via Latin from Greek *mōlu*.

the moment of truth a crisis, a turning-point; a testing situation; from Spanish *el momento de la verdad* the time of the final sword-thrust in a bullfight.

Momus a person likened to *Momus*, the Greek god of censure and ridicule, who for his censures upon the gods was banished from heaven; a fault-finder, a captious or carping critic. Often in allusions to the story that when Hephaistos (or Zeus) had made a man, Momus blamed him for not having put a window in his breast.

Mona Lisa a painting (now in the Louvre in Paris) executed 1503–6 by Leonardo da Vinci. The sitter was the wife of Francesco del Giocondo; her enigmatic smile has become one of the most famous images in Western art.

Monday the day of the week before Tuesday and following Sunday. Recorded from Old English (in form *Mōnandæg*), the name originally meant 'day of the moon', a translation of late Latin *lunae dies*.

The **Monday club** is a right-wing political club, formed in 1961, that originally held its meetings on Mondays.

In North America, a **Monday morning quarterback** is a person who passes judgement on and criticizes something after the event, an armchair critic.

Saint Monday is used with reference to the practice among workmen of being idle on Monday, as a consequence of drunkenness on the Sunday, chiefly in the phrase **to keep Saint Monday**.

mondo used in reference to something very striking or remarkable of its kind (often in conjunction with a pseudo-Italian noun or adjective). The term comes from Italian *Mondo Cane*, literally 'dog's world', the title of a film (1961) depicting bizarre behaviour.

money *money* comes from Latin *moneta* 'mint', originally a title of a goddess (in classical times regarded as identical with Juno), in whose temple in Rome money was minted.

A **money box** (or **moneybag**) is the emblem of ➤ St MATTHEW and ➤ St NICHOLAS *of Myra*.

A **money changer** is an archaic term for a person whose business was the exchanging of one currency for another; often with biblical allusion, as to Matthew 21:12.

Money for jam is money or reward earned for little or no effort; the allusion is said to be to the prevalence of jam in Army rations in the early 20th century. **Money for old rope** is an alternative, giving another type of a virtually worthless item.

Mongol a native or national of Mongolia, a Mongolian. In the 13th century AD the Mongol empire under Genghis Khan extended across central Asia from Manchuria in the east to European Russia in the west. Under Kublai Khan China was conquered and the Mongol capital moved to Khanbaliq (modern Beijing). The Mongol empire collapsed after a series of defeats culminating in the destruction of the Golden Horde by the Muscovites in 1380.

The term *mongol* was adopted in the late 19th century to refer to a person suffering from *Down's syndrome*, owing to the similarity of some of the physical symptoms of the disorder with the normal facial characteristics of East Asian people. In modern English, this use is now unacceptable and considered offensive.

St Monica (332–*c*.387), mother of ➤ St AUGUSTINE *of Hippo*. She is often regarded as the model of Christian mothers for her patience with her son's spiritual crises, which ended with his conversion in 386. Her feast day is 27 August (formerly 4 May).

monitor former term for a shallow-draught warship mounting one or two heavy guns for bombardment, named for a vessel developed by Swedish engineer John Ericsson for the Union forces. In a letter of 1862 he said that he proposed to name the new battery *Monitor* on the ground that 'The ironclad intruder will thus prove a severe monitor [that is, something providing guidance to moral conduct] to those leaders [of the Southern rebellion].'

This prototype vessel engaged the Confederate ironclad *Virginia* in Chesapeake Bay in a battle that drew worldwide attention; after this a number of similar warships were built by the Union. The original *Monitor*, however, went down off Cape Hatteras in 1862.

monk a member of a religious community of men typically living under vows of poverty, chastity, and obedience; the earliest such communities were groups of hermits living in the desert. In England, the term was not applied before the Reformation to members of the mendicant orders, who were always called *friars*, but since that period the usage has widened to include members of those orders.

Recorded from Old English (in form *munuc*), the word is based on Greek *monakhos* 'solitary', from *monos* 'alone'.

monkey a *monkey* is proverbially taken as the type of a clever, artful, or amusing person. Monkeys were often in the past kept as domestic pets, and proprietors of barrel-organs were typically accompanied by a monkey, giving rise to an extended metaphor in which the monkey stands for the junior member of a disparaged partnership.

Recorded from the mid 16th century, the word is of unknown origin, perhaps from Low German; in the Middle Low German version of *Reynard the Fox* (1498), *Moneke* appears once as the name of the son of Martin the Ape.

A **Monkey Trial** is a trial of a teacher for teaching evolutionary theories, contrary to the laws of certain States of the US, specifically that of J. T. Scopes in Dayton, Tennessee (10–21 July, 1925), with William Jennings Bryan for the prosecution, and Clarence Darrow for the defence. Scopes was convicted, and fined $100 dollars.

See also *cold enough to freeze the balls off a brass monkey* at ➤ BRASS.

three wise monkeys a conventional sculptured group of three monkeys; used allusively to refer to a person who chooses to ignore or keep silent about wrongdoing. One monkey is depicted with its paws over its mouth (taken as connoting 'speak no evil'), one with its paws over its eyes ('see no evil'), and one with its paws over its ears ('hear no evil').

Monophysite a person who holds that there is only one inseparable nature (partly divine, partly and subordinately human) in the person of Christ, contrary to a declaration of the Council of Chalcedon (451).

Monopoly trademark name for a board game in which players engage in simulated property and financial dealings using imitation money. It was invented in the US and the name was coined by Charles Darrow *c*.1935.

Monopoly money is the imitation money provided in the game of Monopoly; in extended usage, currency having or perceived as having no real existence or value.

Monroe doctrine a principle of US policy, originated by James *Monroe* (1758–1831), American Democratic Republican statesman, 5th President of the US 1817–25. The *Monroe doctrine* states that any intervention by external powers in the politics of the Americas is a potentially hostile act against the US.

Mons a town in southern Belgium, the scene in August 1914 of the first major battle of the First World War between British and German forces (see also ➤ ANGELS *of Mons*).

Mons Gaudi the name (in post-classical Latin of the 10th century), meaning 'Mount of Joy', given by pilgrims to the mountain Rama, to the north-west of Jerusalem. The name was later applied to other elevations from which the holy city could be seen, and finally to any vantage point. See also ➤ MONTJOIE.

Monsieur a title of the second son or the next younger brother of the King of France. The word in French means literally 'my lord'.

monstrance in the Roman Catholic Church, an open or transparent receptacle in which the consecrated Host is exposed for veneration. Recorded from late Middle English (also in the sense 'demonstration or proof'), the word comes via medieval Latin from Latin *monstrare* 'show'.

A monstrance is the emblem of ➤ St CLARE and St Norbert, founder of the ➤ PREMONSTRATENSIANS.

Monte Albán an ancient city, now in ruins, in Oaxaca, southern Mexico. Occupied from the 8th century BC, it was a centre of the Zapotec culture from about the 1st century BC to the 8th century AD, after which it was occupied by the Mixtecs until the Spanish conquest in the 16th century.

Monte Carlo a resort in Monaco, forming one of the four communes of the principality; it is famous as a gambling resort and as the terminus of the annual Monte Carlo rally.

The **Monte Carlo method** is a technique in which a large quantity of randomly generated numbers are studied using a probabilistic model to find an approximate solution to a numerical problem that would be difficult to solve by other methods. It is named after Monte Carlo with reference to its gambling casino.

Monte Cassino a hill in central Italy near the town of Cassino, the site of the principal monastery of the Benedictines, founded by St Benedict *c*.529. The monastery and the town were destroyed in 1944 during bitter fighting between Allied and German forces, but have since been restored.

Montessori a system of education for young children that seeks to develop natural interests and activities rather than use formal teaching methods, based on the ideas of the Italian educationist Maria Montessori (1870–1952).

month recorded from Old English (in form mōnaþ), and of Germanic origin, the word is related to ➤ MOON, and the primitive calendar month of many early civilizations began on, or on the day after, the day of the full moon.

In the Christian Church, a **month's mind** is the commemoration of a dead person by the celebration of a requiem mass or (later more widely) special prayers on the day one month after the date of the death or funeral.

Montjoie in medieval French tradition, Charlemagne's ensign and war cry, representing ➤ MONS *Gaudi* from which Jerusalem was seen by pilgrims. *Montjoie* is the cry of Charlemagne's forces in the *Song of Roland*, and **Montjoie St Denis** (which appears in the old royal arms of France) was the national war-cry of the French.

The term was also used for the crosses erected to mark stations on the route between Aigues Mort and Paris, along which the body of Louis IX (St Louis) was taken, following his death in 1270.

Montmartre a district in northern Paris, on a hill above the Seine, much frequented by artists in the late 19th and early 20th centuries when it was a separate village.

Montreux a resort town in SW Switzerland, at the east end of Lake Geneva, which since the 1960s has hosted annual festivals of both jazz and television; Golden, Silver, and Bronze Roses are awarded to winners at the light entertainment festival.

Montserrat a mountain in the NW of Barcelona, known for an ancient wooden statue of the Virgin and Child, which had supposedly been carved by St Luke and brought to Spain by St Peter, and which was concealed in a cave there during the period of Moorish rule.

the full monty the full amount expected, desired, or possible. Of unknown origin, the phrase has only been recorded recently. Among various (unsubstantiated) theories, one cites the phrase *the full Montague Burton*, apparently meaning 'Sunday-best three-piece suit' (from the name of a tailor of made-to-measure clothing in the early 20th

century); another recounts the possibility of a military usage, *the full monty* being 'the full cooked English breakfast' insisted upon by Field Marshal Montgomery.

Monty Python's Flying Circus an influential British television comedy series (1969–74), noted especially for its absurdist or surrealist style of humour and starring, among others, John Cleese.

monument the word *monument* is recorded from Middle English, and originally denoted a burial place rather than the statue or building over it or commemorating a person or event; the word comes via French from Latin *monumentum*, from *monere* 'remind'.

The Monument is a Doric column 202 feet in height, built in the City of London (1671–7) according to the design of Sir Christopher Wren, to commemorate the great fire of London of 1666, which originated in a house 202 feet from the site of the column.

moon the constantly recurring changes and phases of the moon have caused it to be taken as a type of changeableness and inconstancy; they were also traditionally supposed to influence the health of body and mind, and to cause insanity.

The *moon* may also be personified as a goddess (for example, *Diana* or *Cynthia*), and as such symbolizes virginity.

Recorded from Old English (in form mōna) and of Germanic origin, related to *month*, the word comes from an Indo-European root shared by Latin *mensis* and Greek *mēn* 'month', and also Latin *metiri* 'measure' (the moon being used to measure time).

To **believe that the moon is made of green cheese** is to believe an absurdity, an expression recorded from the 16th century. The origin is not clear, but may refer to the mottled appearance of a cheese like sage Derby being held to resemble the variegated surface of the moon.

The **Moon Festival** is a Chinese festival held in the middle of the autumn, originally a family gathering after the completion of the harvest.

Moonie informal and often derogatory term for a member of the Unification Church, from the name of its founder, Sun Myung *Moon*.

moonlight the light of the moon; when the moon is shining.

Moonlight and roses means romance; from the title of a song by Black and Moret, 1925.

A **moonlight flit** is a hurried departure by night, especially to avoid paying a debt.

moonlighting in 19th-century Ireland, the perpetration by night of violence against the persons or property of tenants who had incurred the hostility of the Land League.

The term is now generally used for the practice of having a second job, typically secretly and at night, in addition to one's regular employment.

moonshine from late Middle English, *moonshine* has been taken as the type of something insubstantial or unreal (originally, in the phrase **moonshine in the water**). Later, the term was extended to mean foolish, nonsensical, or fanciful talk or ideas.

In North America, from the late 18th century, *moonshine* has been used to designate illicitly distilled or smuggled liquor.

Moor a member of a NW African Muslim people of mixed Berber and Arab descent. In the 8th century they conquered the Iberian peninsula, but were finally driven out of their last stronghold in Granada at the end of the 15th century.

In the Middle Ages, and as late as the 17th century, the Moors were commonly supposed to be mostly black or very darkskinned; the name was thus sometimes used in the sense 'a black person'.

The name comes from Old French *More*, via Latin from Greek *Mauros* 'inhabitant of Mauretania'.

Moore's law an observation and prediction originally made in 1965 by Gordon Earle Moore (1929–), US microchip manufacturer, stating that a new type of microprocessor chip is released every 12 to 24 months, with each new version having approximately twice as many logical elements as its predecessor, and that this trend is likely to continue.

Moors Murders name given to the sadistic serial killings of children carried out by Ian Brady (1938–) and his accomplice Myra Hindley (1942–), for which they were convicted in 1966; the name derived from their having buried the bodies of their victims on Saddleworth Moor in the Pennines.

moot an assembly of people, especially one for judicial or legislative purposes. Chiefly associated with national and local administration from the Anglo-Saxon to the Early Modern period.

From the early 16th century, the term has also been used to designate a mock trial set up to examine a hypothetical case as an academic exercise. It was revived in the Inns of Court in the 19th century after falling into disuse, and introduced into universities where law is studied.

The use of *moot* as an adjective meaning 'subject to debate, dispute, or uncertainty, and typically not admitting a final decision' derives from the use of **moot court** to designate this kind of mock trial.

Recorded from Old English and of Germanic origin, the word is ultimately related to *meet*.

Moral Majority the name of a political movement of evangelical Christians, founded in the US in 1979 by the Reverend Jerry Falwell, that advocates an ultra-conservative political and social agenda, especially on issues such as abortion and religious education. The choice of name may have been influenced by the title of Westely and Egstien's book *The Silent Majority* (1969).

Moral Rearmament an organization founded by the American Lutheran evangelist Frank Buchman (1878–1961) and first popularized in Oxford in the 1920s (hence until about 1938 called the *Oxford Group Movement*). It emphasizes personal integrity and confession of faults, cooperation, and mutual respect, especially as a basis for social transformation.

morality play a kind of drama with personified abstract qualities as the main characters and presenting a lesson about good conduct and character, popular in the 15th and early 16th centuries.

Moravian a member of a Protestant Church founded in Saxony by emigrants from Moravia, and continuing the tradition of the Unitas Fratrum, a body holding Hussite doctrines, which had its chief seat in Moravia and Bohemia.

The virtual founder of the body was Count Zinzendorf (1700–60), who was the patron of the Moravian refugees, and embraced their doctrines. The Moravians early obtained many adherents in England and colonial North America.

Mordecai in the Bible, the cousin of Esther who is taken into favour by the king after the execution of his enemy ➤ HAMAN, the previously favoured counsellor. In the biblical story (Esther 5:13) Haman's hatred of Mordecai is represented as obsessive.

Mordred (in Arthurian legend) the nephew of King Arthur who abducted Guinevere and raised a rebellion against Arthur.

St Thomas More (1478–1535), English scholar and statesman, Lord Chancellor 1529–32. His *Utopia* (1516), describing an ideal city state, established him as a leading humanist of the Renaissance. He was imprisoned in 1534 after opposing Henry's marriage to Anne Boleyn, and beheaded for opposing the Act of Supremacy. Feast day, 22 June.

Morgan le Fay (in Arthurian legend) an enchantress, sister of King Arthur.

morganatic of or denoting a marriage in which neither the spouse of lower rank, nor any children, have any claim to the possessions or title of the spouse of higher rank.
    Recorded from the early 18th century, the word comes from modern Latin *morganaticus*, from medieval Latin *matrimonium ad morganaticum* 'marriage with a morning gift', because a morning gift, given by a husband to his wife on the morning after the marriage, was the wife's sole entitlement in a marriage of this kind.

Morgiana in the Arabian Nights, the slave of ➤ ALI *Baba* who discovers the forty thieves in the oil jars, and contrives their deaths.

Moriarty in Conan Doyle's stories of ➤ *Sherlock* HOLMES, the arch criminal who is Holmes's implacable enemy. His final attempt to murder Holmes resulted in their both falling into the abyss of the ➤ REICHENBACH *Falls*, apparently to their deaths, although the popularity of the character forced Conan Doyle to resurrect Holmes.

Mormon a member of the Church of Jesus Christ of Latter-Day Saints, a religion founded in the US in 1830 by Joseph Smith Jr.
    Smith claimed to have found and translated *The Book of Mormon* by divine revelation. It tells the story of a group of Hebrews who migrated to America *c.*600 BC, and is taken as scriptural alongside the Bible. The Mormons came into conflict with the US government over their practice of polygamy (officially abandoned in 1890) and moved their headquarters from Illinois to Salt Lake City, Utah, in 1847 under Smith's successor, Brigham Young.

morning star a planet, especially Venus, when visible in the east before sunrise; figuratively, someone or something regarded as the precursor of a new era. The term is particularly applied to Christ, after Revelation 22:16.

Mornington Crescent the name of a station (closed for a number of years) on the London Underground, taken as the title of a spoof panel game on the BBC Radio comedy programme *I'm Sorry, I Haven't a Clue.* Panellists (according to a set of undisclosed rules) name places within Greater London in turn, the apparent aim being to reach *Mornington Crescent.*

Morpheus in Roman mythology, the son of Somnus (god of sleep), the god of dreams and, in later writings, also god of sleep. The phrase **in the arms of Morpheus** is recorded from the late 18th century.

morris dance a lively traditional English dance performed out of doors by groups known as 'sides'. Dancers wear a distinctive costume that is mainly black and white and has small bells attached, and often carry handkerchiefs or sticks. At least one of the dancers is likely to represent a symbolic or legendary figure, as the fool, hobby horse, or Maid Marian.
    The phrase is recorded from late Middle English; *morris* comes from a variant of *Moorish*, but the association with the Moors remains unexplained.

Morse an alphabet or code in which letters are represented by combinations of long and short light or sound signals, named (in the mid 19th century) after Samuel F. B. *Morse* (1791–1872), American inventor.

Inspector Morse music-loving, beer-drinking Oxford policeman who is the central character in a series of detective novels by the British crime writer Colin Dexter (1930–).

mortal sin in Christian theology, a grave sin that is regarded as depriving the soul of divine grace, often contrasted with a ➤ VE-NIAL *sin.*

Le Morte D'Arthur the title, meaning 'the Death of Arthur', generally given to the lengthy cycle of Arthurian legends by Malory, finished in 1470 and printed by Caxton in 1485.

Morticia a member of the ghoulish ➤ AD-DAMS *Family,* noted for her white complexion and shock of black hair.

Morton's Fork an argument used by the English prelate and statesman John *Morton* (c.1420–1500), as Chancellor in demanding gifts for the royal treasury: if a man lived well he was obviously rich and if he lived frugally then he must have savings. The phrase in this form dates from the mid 19th century, but Francis Bacon in his *Historie of the Raigne of King Henry the Seventh* (1622) says that, 'There is a tradition of a dilemma that Bishop Morton…used to raise up the benevolence to higher rates; and some called it his Fork.' The term is now found in wider allusive use.

Moses (fl. *c.*14th–13th centuries BC), Hebrew prophet and lawgiver, brother of Aaron. According to the biblical account, he was born in Egypt, and to escape a massacre was hidden by his mother in a basket among the bulrushes; found there by Pharaoh's daughter, he was adopted and brought up by her. Grown to manhood, he led the Israelites away from servitude in Egypt, across the desert towards the Promised Land. During the journey he was inspired by God on Mount Sinai to write down the ➤ TEN *Commandments* on tablets of stone (Exodus 20). In allusive use, the name may be used to denote someone held to resemble Moses, especially in his character of lawgiver or leader.

The **Law of Moses** or *Mosaic Law* is the system of moral and ceremonial precepts contained in the Pentateuch; the ceremonial portion of the system considered separately.

A **Moses basket** is a carrycot or small portable cot made of wickerwork, with allusion to the biblical story of Moses, left in a basket among the bulrushes (Exodus 2:3).

Grandma Moses (1860–1961), name given to the American painter Anna Mary Robertson *Moses*, who took up painting as a hobby when widowed in 1927, producing more than a thousand paintings in naive style, mostly of American rural life.

mosque a Muslim place of worship. Mosques consist of an area reserved for communal prayers, frequently in a domed building with a minaret, and with a niche (mihrab) or other structure indicating the direction of Mecca. There may also be a platform for preaching (minbar), and an adjacent courtyard in which water is provided for the obligatory ablutions before prayer. Since representations of the human form are forbidden, decoration is geometric or based on Arabic calligraphy.

The **Great Mosque** at ➤ MECCA is the mosque established by Muhammad as a place of worship and later extended; it was given its final form in the years 1572–7 in the reign of Sultan Selim II.

mosstrooper a person who lived by plundering property in the Scottish Borders during the 17th century, making raids across the 'mosses' or peatbogs.

a mote in a person's eye a fault observed in another person by a person who ignores a greater fault of his or her own; a *mote* is an irritating particle in the eye, and the allusion is to Matthew 7:3.

mother the word is of Germanic origin, from an Indo-European root shared by Latin *mater* and Greek *mētēr*.

Mother Church is the Church considered as a final arbiter.

Mother Earth is the earth considered as the source of all its living beings and inanimate things, a phrase representing a personification recorded from the mid 16th century.

Mother Goose is an old woman said to be the source of traditional nursery rhymes; she is often depicted as flying on the back of a gander. The name first appears in the title of *Mother Goose's Melody; or Sonnets from the Cradle*, published by John Newbery in 1781, but probably compiled around 1760. The ultimate origin is likely to be a fairy tale by Charles Perrault, *Contes de ma mère l'oye* [Tales of Mother Goose], a French expression meaning 'old wives' tale'. The American tradition that the real *Mother Goose* was an Elizabeth Goose, of Boston, is not substantiated.

The **Mother of God** is a name given to the Virgin Mary (as mother of the divine Christ).

The **Mother of Parliaments** is the British parliament, an expression coined by the English liberal politician and reformer John Bright (1811–89).

Mother-of-pearl is a smooth shining iridescent substance forming the inner layer of the shell of some molluscs, especially oysters and abalones, used in ornamentation.

Mother's Day is a day of the year on which mothers are particularly honoured by their children. In North America it is the second Sunday in May; in Britain it has become another term for *Mothering Sunday*.

Mothering Sunday mid-Lent Sunday, traditionally the day on which children visited and gave presents to their parents.

Motown music released on or reminiscent of the US record label Tamla Motown, the first black-owned record company in the US, founded in Detroit in 1959 (the name comes from a shortening of *Motor Town*).

Tamla Motown was important in popularizing soul music.

motte-and-bailey denoting a castle consisting of a fort on a motte, or mound, surrounded by a bailey.

motto a short sentence or phrase chosen as encapsulating the beliefs or ideals guiding an individual, family, or institution; in heraldry, a phrase or sentence accompanying a coat of arms or crest, typically on a scroll. Recorded from the late 16th century, the word is from Italian 'word'.

Moulin Rouge a cabaret in Montmartre, Paris, a favourite resort of poets and artists around the end of the 19th century. Toulouse-Lautrec immortalized its dancers in his posters. In French, the literal meaning of the name is 'red mill'.

Mount Vernon a property in NE Virginia, on a site overlooking the Potomac River. Built in 1743, it was the home of George Washington from 1747 until his death in 1799.

mountain in figurative use, something of great size. To **make a mountain out of a molehill** is a traditional description of laying unnecessary stress on a small matter, recorded from the 16th century. (See also *if the mountain will not come to Mahomet* at ➤ Mahomet.)

A **mountain in labour** is great effort expended on little outcome, an allusion to the words of the Roman poet Horace (65–8 BC) in his *Ars Poetica*, '*Parturient montes, nascetur ridiculus mus* [Mountains will go into labour, and a silly little mouse will be born].'

The **Mountain State** is an informal name for Vermont.

See also ➤ *move* MOUNTAINS, ➤ MOUNTAINS *of the Moon*.

mountaineers a mountaineers' stick is the emblem of ➤ St BERNARD *of Aosta*.

move mountains achieve spectacular and apparently impossible results; make every possible effort. Often referring to the saying *faith will move mountains*, ultimately with biblical allusion, as to Matthew 17:20.

Mountains of the Moon the type of a very remote place; further than one can imagine, the ends of the earth. The term is also used by Ptolemy as the supposed source of the Nile, and is thought there to designate the Ruwenzori mountain range in central Africa.

mountebank a person who deceives others, especially in order to trick them out of their money; a charlatan; a person who sold patent medicines in public places.

Recorded from the late 16th century, the word comes from Italian *montambanco*, from the imperative phrase *monta in banco!* 'climb on the bench!', with allusion to the raised platform used to attract an audience.

mouse in proverbial use, the *mouse* is often taken as the type of something small, weak, or insignificant, especially as contrasted with a larger, stronger animal.

A *mouse* is the emblem of ➤ St GERTRUDE *of Nivelles*.

In computing, a *mouse* is the name given to a small hand-held device which is moved over a flat surface to produce a corresponding movement of a pointer on a VDU screen.

A **country mouse** is a person from a rural area unfamiliar with urban life; the allusion is to one of Aesop's fables which contrasts the *country mouse* with the urban-dwelling **town mouse**. In the fable each mouse visits the other, but is in the end convinced of the superiority of its own home.

Mouse and man is an alliterative phrase for every living thing; it was probably popularized by Robert Burns in *To a Mouse* (1785), 'The best laid plans o' Mice an' Men, Gang aft agley.'

A **mouse potato** is a person who spends large amounts of leisure or working time operating a computer. An alteration of ➤ COUCH *potato*, the phrase is one of a cluster of terms which in the 1980s and 1990s developed in reference to an all-absorbing interest in computing.

a better mousetrap an improved version of a well-known article; from an observation (1889) attributed to Ralph Waldo Emerson, though also claimed by Elbert Hubbard, 'If a man…make a better mouse-trap than his neighbour…the world will make a beaten path to his door.'

Mousterian of, relating to, or denoting the main culture of the Middle Palaeolithic period in Europe, between the Acheulian and Aurignacian periods (chiefly 80,000–35,000 years ago). It is associated with Neanderthal peoples and is typified by flints worked on one side only.

The name comes (in the late 19th century) from *Le Moustier*, a cave in SW France where objects from this culture were found.

out of the mouths of babes— proverbial saying, late 19th century, meaning that young children may sometimes speak with disconcerting wisdom; with biblical allusion to Psalm 8, verse 2 (*Book of Common Prayer*), and Matthew 21:16.

movable feast a religious feast day that does not occur on the same calendar date each year. The term refers most often to Easter Day and other Christian holy days whose dates are related to it.

move the goalposts unfairly alter the conditions or rules of a procedure during its course. The term has been current since the late 1980s, and provides a useful image for the idea of making an important (and usually unheralded) alteration to terms and conditions previously agreed.

mover and shaker a person who influences things, a person who gets things done; earliest in Arthur O'Shaughnessy's poem 'Ode' (1874).

Mowgli in Kipling's *Jungle Books*, the boy who is reared with wolves.

Mozarabic of or relating to the Christian inhabitants of Spain under the Muslim Moorish kings. Recorded from the late 17th century, the word comes via Spanish from Arabic *musta'rib*, literally 'making oneself an Arab'.

The term **Mozarab** is used to designate a person who continued to practice Christianity, but who adopted many aspects of Islamic culture, including language.

The **Mozarabic liturgy** denotes the ancient ritual of the Christian Church in the Iberian peninsula from the earliest times until the 11th century; a modified form of it is still used in some chapels in Spain.

muckraking the figurative use of *muckraking* to denote the searching out and publicizing of something discreditable can be traced back to Bunyan's description in *Pilgrim's Progress* (1684) of 'the Man with the Muck-rake' as an emblem of worldly gain; this was then alluded to and extended by Theodore Roosevelt in a speech of 1906.

Mudejar a subject Muslim during the Christian reconquest of the Iberian peninsula from the Moors (11th–15th centuries) who, until 1492, was allowed to retain Islamic laws and religion in return for loyalty to a Christian monarch. After 1492 such people were treated with less toleration,

dubbed Moriscos, and forced to accept the Christian faith or leave the country.

The name is now used to designate a partly Gothic, partly Islamic style of architecture and art prevalent in Spain in the 12th to 15th centuries.

Mudejar is Spanish, and comes from Arabic *mudajjan* 'allowed to stay'.

muezzin a man who calls Muslims to prayer from the minaret of a mosque. Recorded from the late 16th century, the word is a dialect variant of Arabic *mu'aḍḍin*, active participle of *aḍḍana* 'proclaim'.

mufti[1] a Muslim legal expert who is empowered to give rulings on religious matters. Recorded from the late 16th century, the word comes from Arabic *muftī*, active participle of *'aftā* 'decide a point of law'.

In the Ottoman Empire, the *Mufti* (or **Grand Mufti**) was the name given to the official head of religion within the state, or to a deputy appointed by him as chief legal authority for a large city.

mufti[2] plain clothes worn by a person who wears a uniform for their job, such as a soldier or police officer. Recorded from the early 19th century, the word may come humorously from ➤ MUFTI[1], in a reference to a costume of dressing-gown, smoking-cap, and slippers, suggesting the appearance of a stage 'mufti'.

Muggletonian a member of a small Christian sect founded in England *c.*1651 by Lodowicke Muggleton (1609–98) and John Reeve (1608–58), who claimed to be the two witnesses mentioned in the book of Revelation (Revelations 11:3–6).

mugwump in North America, a person who remains aloof or independent, especially from party politics. The term comes (in the mid 19th century) from Algonquian *mugquomp* 'great chief'.

Muhammad (*c.*570–632), Arab prophet and founder of ➤ ISLAM. He was born in Mecca, where *c.*610 he received the first of a series of revelations which, as the ➤ KORAN, became the doctrinal and legislative basis of Islam. His sayings (the *Hadith*) and the accounts of his daily practice (the *Sunna*) constitute the other main sources of guidance for most Muslims.

In the face of opposition to his preaching he and his small group of supporters were forced to flee to Medina in 622; this flight,

known as the ➤ HEGIRA), is of great significance in Islam, and the Islamic calendar
(which is based on lunar months) is dated
from AD 622 (= 1 AH). (See also ➤ MAHOMET.)

Muharram the first month of the year in
the Islamic calendar, and an annual celebration in this month commemorating the
death of Husayn, grandson of Muhammad,
and his retinue. The name comes from
Arabic *muḥarram* 'inviolable'.

Mulberry harbour code name for the prefabricated harbour used in the invasion of
continental Europe by Allied forces in 1944.

mule the offspring of a donkey and a horse
(strictly, a male donkey and a female horse),
typically sterile and used as a beast of burden. It is also proverbially taken as the type
of obstinacy.

Since the 1980s, *mule* has also been the informal name for a person (typically a young
woman in need of money) recruited by a
drug trafficker to carry drugs through air-
ports and other customs points.

mullah a Muslim learned in Islamic theology and sacred law. Recorded from the
early 17th century, the word comes from Persian, Turkish, and Urdu *mullā*, from Arabic
mawlā.

cover a multitude of sins conceal or
gloss over many problems or defects; with
biblical reference to 1 Peter 4:8.

mumbo-jumbo language or ritual causing
or intended to cause confusion or bewilderment. This sense dates from the late 19th
century, and derives from the mid 18th-cen-
tury form *Mumbo Jumbo*, name of a supposed
African idol.

mummers' play a traditional English folk
play, of a type often associated with Christmas and popular in the 18th and early 19th
centuries. The plot typically features Saint
George and involves the miraculous resurrection of a character, possibly recalling
pagan agricultural ceremonies.

Mummerset an imitation rustic West
Country accent used by actors, from the
name of an imaginary or idealized rustic
county in the West of England. The name
probably comes from *mummer*, on the pattern of *Somerset*.

mummy especially in ancient Egypt, a
body of a human being or animal that has

been ceremonially preserved by removal of
the internal organs, treatment with natron
and resin, and wrapping in bandages. In
Egypt the preservation of the body was regarded as important for the afterlife.

The idea of a mummy whose rest has been
disturbed becoming an active and malevolent entity has become a staple of horror
books and films, as in the Hammer Films
Curse of the Mummy's Tomb (1964).

The word is recorded from late Middle
English, denoting a substance taken from
embalmed bodies and used in medicines; it
comes from French *momie*, from medieval
Latin *mumia* and Arabic *mūmiyā* 'embalmed
body', perhaps from Persian *mūm* 'wax'.

mumpsimus a traditional custom or notion adhered to although shown to be unrea-
sonable; a person who obstinately adheres to
such a custom or notion. The word represents an erroneous version of Latin
sumpsimus in *quod in ore sumpsimus* 'which we
have taken into the mouth' (Eucharist), in a
story of an illiterate priest who, when corrected, replied 'I will not change my old
mumpsimus for your new sumpsimus'.

Baron Munchausen the hero of a book of
fantastic travellers' tales (1785) written in
English by a German, Rudolph Erich Raspe.
The original Baron Munchausen is said to
have lived 1720–97, to have served in the Russian army against the Turks, and to have related extravagant tales of his prowess.

His name is used for **Munchausen's syndrome**, a mental disorder in which a person
repeatedly feigns severe illness so as to obtain hospital treatment. **Munchausen's syndrome by proxy** is the term given to a
mental disorder in which a person seeks attention by inducing or feigning illness in another person, typically a child.

Munchkin in the children's fantasy *The
Wizard of Oz*, by L. Frank Baum (1856–1919),
US writer: any of a race of small, child-like
creatures who help Dorothy in her quest for
the city of Oz; the term is used allusively for a
small or mischievous person or a child.

St Mungo another name for ➤ *St*
KENTIGERN; *mungo* in Celtic means 'my dear
friend'.

Munich Agreement an agreement between Britain, France, Germany, and Italy,
signed at Munich on 29 September 1938,
under which the Sudetenland was ceded to

Germany; Neville Chamberlain, on his return, famously and erroneously declared that he believed that he was bringing back 'peace for our time'. In extended use (and allusively as *Munich*), it may denote an agreement held to resemble this pact in representing mistaken or dishonourable appeasement.

Munro any of the 277 mountains in Scotland that are at least 3,000 feet high (approximately 914 metres), named (in the early 20th century) after Hugh Thomas *Munro* (1856–1919), who published a list of all such mountains in the *Journal of the Scottish Mountaineering Club* for 1891.

the Munsters monster family in an American TV series of the mid 1960s, of whom *Herman Munster* resembles ➤ FRANKENSTEIN's monster, his wife is a vampire, and their son a werewolf.

the Muppets a group of glove and rod puppets and marionettes, chiefly representing animals, and including such characters as ➤ KERMIT *the Frog* and ➤ *Miss* PIGGY, created by Jim Henson (1936–90). First popularized in the children's television programme *Sesame Street* (1969), they later appeared in *The Muppet Show* (1976–81).

Murder, Inc. in the US of the 1930s, originally and especially in New York, a network of gangsters controlling organized crime and carrying out assassinations for money.

murder will out murder cannot remain undetected; proverbial from late Middle English.

Murphy's Law a supposed law of nature, expressed in various humorous popular sayings, to the effect that anything that can go wrong will go wrong. It is named for Captain Edward A. *Murphy*, who performed studies on deceleration for the US Air Force in 1949 (during which he noted that if things could be done wrongly, they would be).

murrey the deep purple-red colour of a mulberry; in heraldry, another term for ➤ SANGUINE. Recorded from late Middle English, the word comes via Old French from medieval Latin *moratus*, from *morum* 'mulberry'.

Mururoa a remote South Pacific atoll in the Tuamotu archipelago, in French Polynesia, used as a nuclear testing site since 1966.

Muscovy a medieval principality in west central Russia, centred on Moscow, which formed the nucleus of modern Russia. As Muscovy expanded, princes of Muscovy became the rulers of Russia; in 1472 Ivan III, grand duke of Muscovy, completed the unification of the country, and in 1547 Ivan the Terrible became the first tsar of Russia.

muscular Christianity a Christian life of brave and cheerful physical activity, especially as popularly associated with the writings of Charles Kingsley (1819–75) and with boys' public schools of the Victorian British Empire. The term is first recorded in the *Saturday Review* of 21 February 1857.

Muse (in Greek and Roman mythology) each of nine goddesses, the daughters of Zeus and Mnemosyne, who preside over the arts and sciences.

mushroom the type of a person or thing that appears or develops suddenly or is ephemeral.
   A **mushroom cloud** is a mushroom-shaped cloud of dust and debris formed after a nuclear explosion.

music of the spheres the harmonious sound supposed to be produced by the motion of the concentric, transparent, hollow globes imagined by the older astronomers as revolving round the earth and respectively carrying with them the several heavenly bodies (moon, sun, planets, and fixed stars).

musketeer a member of the household troops of the French king in the 17th and 18th centuries. (See also the *Three Musketeers* at ➤ THREE.)

Muslim a follower of the religion of Islam. Recorded from the early 17th century, the word comes from Arabic, the active participle of '*aslama* 'submit oneself to the will of God' (see also ➤ ISLAM).
   The **Muslim Brotherhood** is an Islamic religious and political organization dedicated to the establishment of a nation based on Islamic principles. Founded in Egypt in 1928, it has become a radical underground force in Egypt and other Sunni countries, promoting strict moral discipline and opposing Western influence, often by violence.
   The **Muslim calendar** is that according to which the Islamic year is reckoned.
   The **Muslim League** is one of the main political parties in Pakistan. It was formed in

1906 in India to represent the rights of Indian Muslims; its demands from 1940 for an independent Muslim state led ultimately to the establishment of Pakistan.

Muspelheim in Scandinavian mythology, the home of the fire-giant Surt.

Mussulman an archaic name (from Persian) for a ➤ MUSLIM.

mustard originally prepared with 'must' (new wine). It is frequently used to evoke ideas of warmth and enthusiasm, as in **keen as mustard**.

Colonel Mustard is one of the six stock characters constituting the murderer and suspects in the game of ➤ CLUEDO.

A **grain of mustard seed** is a proverbial expression for something which, while small in itself, is capable of great development; the allusion is to Matthew 13:31, in which the kingdom of heaven is likened to a grain of mustard seed, tiny when it is sown, but becoming a tree when grown. (The plant referred to is thought to be the black mustard plant, which in Palestine grows to a great height.)

See also ➤ CUT *the mustard*.

pass muster be accepted as adequate or satisfactory; in origin a military expression, meaning 'come through a review or inspection without censure'.

Mut in Egyptian mythology, a goddess who was the wife of Amun and mother of Khonsu.

mutatis mutandis (used when comparing two or more cases or situations) making necessary alterations while not affecting the main point at issue. The Latin tag, recorded in English from the early 16th century, means literally 'things having been changed that have to be changed'.

mutiny an open rebellion against the proper authorities, especially by soldiers or sailors against their officers. The word comes (in the mid 16th century) from obsolete *mutine* 'rebellion', from French *mutin* 'mutineer', based on Latin *movere* 'to move'.

The **mutiny on the Bounty** was a mutiny which took place in 1789 on the British navy ship HMS *Bounty*, when part of the crew, led by Fletcher Christian, mutinied against their commander, William Bligh, and set him adrift in an open boat with eighteen companions. Although a number of the mutineers were captured and executed, others (including Christian) reached the ➤ PITCAIRN *Islands*, where they settled.

Mycenae an ancient city in Greece, situated near the coast in the NE Peloponnese, the centre of the late Bronze Age Mycenaean civilization. The capital of King Agamemnon, it was at its most prosperous in the period *c*.1400–1200 BC, which saw construction of the palace and the massive walls of Cyclopean masonry, including the 'Lion Gate', the entrance to the citadel (*c*.1250 BC). Systematic excavation of the site began in 1840, although the major discoveries were made by Heinrich Schliemann in the 1870s.

The **Myceneans** controlled the Aegean after the fall of the Minoan civilization *c*.1400 BC. They spoke a form of Greek, written in a distinctive script (see ➤ LINEAR *B*), and their culture is identified with that portrayed in the Homeric poems. Their power declined during widespread upheavals at the end of the Mediterranean Bronze Age, around 1100 BC.

Myrmidon a member of a warlike Thessalian people whom, according to a Homeric story, Achilles led to the siege of Troy. In extended usage, the term is used for a hired ruffian or unscrupulous subordinate; **myrmidon of the law** is recorded as a derogatory term for a police officer or a minor administrative legal official.

myrrh a fragrant gum resin obtained from certain trees and used, especially in the Near East, in perfumery, medicines, and incense. In early use (the word is recorded from Old English) it is almost always found with reference to the offering of *myrrh* made by the Magi to the infant Jesus, a gift which prefigured his death and entombment.

Myrrha in Greek mythology, the mother of ➤ ADONIS by her own father Cinyras; when Cinyras, finding that he had taken part in incest, was about to kill her, she was turned by the gods into a *myrrh*-tree.

myrtle sacred to the goddess Venus, *myrtle* was used as an emblem of love.

mysteries the secret rites of Greek and Roman pagan religion, or of any ancient or tribal religion, to which only initiates are admitted.

mystery something that is difficult or impossible to understand or explain; chiefly in Christian theology, a religious belief based on divine revelation, especially one regarded as beyond human understanding; an incident in the life of Jesus or of a saint as a focus of devotion in the Roman Catholic Church, especially each of those commemorated during recitation of successive decades of the rosary.

In secular reference, a handicraft or trade, especially when referred to in indentures; the practices, skills, or lore peculiar to a particular trade or activity and regarded as baffling to those without specialized knowledge.

Recorded from Middle English (in the sense 'mystic presence, hidden religious symbolism', the word comes via Old French and Latin from Greek *mustērion*, related to ➤ MYSTIC.

A **mystery play** is a popular medieval play based on biblical stories or the lives of the saints. Mystery plays were performed by members of trade guilds in Europe from the 13th century, in churches or later on wagons or temporary stages along a route, frequently introducing apocryphal and satirical elements. Several cycles of plays survive in association with particular English cities and towns.

A **mystery religion** is a religion centred on secret or mystical rites for initiates, especially any of a number of cults popular during the late Roman Empire.

mystic a person who seeks by contemplation and self-surrender to obtain unity with or absorption into the Deity or the absolute, or who believes in the spiritual apprehension of truths that are beyond the intellect.

Recorded from Middle English (in the sense 'mystical meaning'), the word comes via Old French or Latin from Greek *mustikos*, from *mustēs* 'initiated person' from *muein* 'close the eyes or lips', also 'initiate'. This sense of the noun dates from the late 17th century.

myth a traditional story, especially one concerning the early history of a people or explaining some natural or social phenomenon, and typically involving supernatural beings or events.

Nn

N the fourteenth letter of the modern English alphabet and the thirteenth of the ancient Roman one, representing the Greek *nū* and the Semitic *nūn*.

N or M is the answer to the first question in the Catechism, 'What is your name?'

The **N-word** is sometimes used to refer to the word 'nigger', which as a contemptuous term for a black person is one of the most racially offensive words in the language.

Naaman in the Bible, the Syrian soldier who is healed of leprosy by the prophet ➤ ELISHA, who tells him to wash in the river of Jordan. Naaman does so, despite his initial protest (2 Kings 5:12); being healed, he declares that henceforth he will worship the god of Israel, although he will still have to accompany his master the king to the temple of Rimmon.

Nabataean a member of an ancient Arabian people who from 312 BC formed an independent kingdom with its capital at Petra (now in Jordan). The kingdom was allied to the Roman Empire from AD 63 and incorporated as the province of Arabia in AD 106.

Naboth in the Bible, the owner of a vineyard coveted by king Ahab; when Naboth refused to sell it, Ahab's wife ➤ JEZEBEL caused him to be falsely accused of blasphemy and stoned to death. On taking possession of the vineyard, Ahab was warned by ➤ ELIJAH that the sin would bring disaster on his dynasty and on Jezebel. The story is referred to allusively for situations in which one who is already wealthy covets the single possession of another.

Nacht und Nebel a situation characterized by mystery or obscurity, specifically the name of a decree issued in Nazi Germany in December 1941, under which offending nationals in occupied countries disappeared suddenly and without trace, frequently during the night. The phrase, which is German, means 'night and fog'.

Nader's Raiders popular name for researchers working for the American lawyer and reformer Ralph *Nader* (1934–). He campaigned on behalf of public safety and prompted legislation concerning car design (in 1965 he published a book with the title *Unsafe at Any Speed*), radiation hazards, food packaging, and insecticides.

nadir the point on the celestial sphere directly below an observer; in general use, the lowest point in the fortunes of a person or organization. Recorded from late Middle English (in the astronomical sense) the word comes via French from Arabic *naẓīr (as-samt)* 'opposite (to the zenith)'.

Nagasaki a city and port in SW Japan, on the west coast of Kyushu island. It was the target of the second atom bomb, dropped by the United States on 9 August 1945, which resulted in the deaths of about 75,000 people and devastated one third of the city.

Nahum (in the Bible) a Hebrew minor prophet. Also, a book of the Bible containing his prophecy of the fall of Nineveh (early 7th century BC).

naiad (in classical mythology) a water nymph said to inhabit a river, spring, or waterfall. The name comes via Latin from Greek *Naias, Naiad-*, from *naein* 'to flow'.

naiant (in heraldry, of a fish or marine creature) swimming horizontally. The word comes (in the mid 16th century) from Anglo-Norman French, variant of Old French *noiant* 'swimming'.

nail in devotion or meditation, *nails*, as used for the crucifixion of Jesus, are taken as symbolizing the Passion.

Nails are the emblem of ➤ St JOSEPH *of Arimathea*, ➤ St LOUIS, and ➤ St WILLIAM *of Norwich*.

Livy records the belief in ancient Rome that a plague could be checked by the dictator driving a nail into the ➤ CAPITOL.

A **nail in the coffin** is an action or event regarded as likely to have a detrimental or destructive effect on a situation, enterprise, or person.

To **nail one's colours to the mast** is to refuse to admit defeat; declare openly which side one favours. The allusion is to a sea-battle in which the colours nailed to the mast cannot be lowered in defeat.

On the nail means immediately, at once (usually referring to the payment of money). The explanations associating this phrase with certain pillars of the Exchange at Limerick or Bristol are too late to be of any authority in deciding the question.

Najaf a city in southern Iraq, on the Euphrates, which contains the shrine of Ali, the prophet Muhammad's son-in-law, and is a holy city for the Shiite Muslims.

naked ape the human being, especially as viewed from a biological perspective. *The Naked Ape* was the title of a book (1967) by Desmond Morris.

naked truth the plain truth, perhaps originally with allusion to Horace's *nudaque veritas* (Odes), or to any of a number of fables in which Truth is shown personified as a naked woman in contrast to the elaborately dressed Falsehood.

Nam informal name for Vietnam in the context of the ➤ VIETNAM *War*.

name recorded from Old English and of Germanic origin, the word comes ultimately from a root shared by Latin *nomen* and Greek *onoma*.
To **have one's name and number on it** (of a bullet) is to be destined to kill one; another version of ➤ *every* BULLET *has its billet*; the number here referred to is a military number.
To **name and shame** is to make public details of failure, wrongdoing, or other shortcoming on the part of a specified person, institution, or organization, with the purpose of embarrassing them into improving their behaviour.
A **name day** is the feast day of a saint after whom a person is named.
Their name liveth for evermore comes from the Apocrypha, and is used as the standard inscription on the Stone of Sacrifice in each military cemetery of World War One. Its use was proposed by Rudyard Kipling as a member of the War Graves Commission.

Nana in Barrie's *Peter Pan* (1911), name of the dog which is the children's nurse. Because Mr Darling has ordered Nana to be shut outside in her kennel, the nursery is left unguarded.

Nanak (1469–1539), Indian religious leader and founder of Sikhism; known as **Guru Nanak**. In 1499 he underwent a religious experience and became a wandering preacher. Not seeking to create a new religion, he preached that spiritual liberation could be achieved through meditating on the name of God. His teachings are contained in a number of hymns which form part of the ➤ ADI *Granth*.

Nancy a city in NE France, chief town of Lorraine, site of the battle in 1477 in which Charles le Téméraire, Duke of Burgundy, was defeated and killed.

nancy story in the West Indies, a traditional African folk tale about ➤ ANANCY the spider, who overcomes others by cunning rather than physical strength.

Nandi in Hinduism, a bull which serves as the mount of ➤ SHIVA and symbolizes fertility.

Nanjing a city in eastern China, on the Yangtze River, formerly *Nanking*, which was the capital of various ruling dynasties and of China from 1368 until replaced by Beijing in 1421.

nanny state government institutions and practices of the Welfare State collectively, perceived as overprotective, interfering, or excessively authoritarian, a term apparently coined by the Conservative politician Iain Macleod (1913–70) in the *Spectator* in 1965.

Nansen passport a document of identification issued to stateless people after the First World War, named after the Norwegian arctic explorer Fridtjof *Nansen* (1861–1930), who was responsible for its issue. He received the Nobel Peace Prize in 1922 for organizing relief work among victims of the Russian famine.

Nantucket an island off the coast of Massachusetts, south of Cape Cod and east of Martha's Vineyard. First visited by the English in 1602, it was settled by the Quakers in 1659, and was an important whaling centre in the 18th and 19th centuries.

naos the inner chamber or sanctuary of a Greek or other ancient temple. The term can also be applied to the main body or nave of a Byzantine church.

napalm a highly flammable sticky jelly used in incendiary bombs and flame-throwers, consisting of petrol thickened with special soaps; the use of *napalm* is associated particularly with the ➤ VIETNAM *War*.

Naphtali (in the Bible) a Hebrew patriarch, son of Jacob and Bilhah (Genesis 30:7–8);

also, the tribe of Israel traditionally descended from him.

Napoleon the name of three rulers of France, of the Bonaparte dynasty established by the Corsican-born Napoleon Bonaparte (1769–1821), emperor 1804–14 and 1815.

The name *Napoleon* is used particularly in allusion to someone who has the strategic and military capacities of Napoleon I; the belief on someone's part that they are Napoleon is sometimes cited as a type of derangement.

Napoleonic Wars a series of campaigns (1800–15) of French armies under Napoleon I against Austria, Russia, Great Britain, Portugal, Prussia, and other European powers. They ended with Napoleon's defeat at the Battle of Waterloo.

Nara a city in central Japan, on the island of Honshu, which was the first capital of Japan (710–84) and an important centre of Japanese Buddhism.

Narcissus in Greek mythology, a beautiful youth who rejected the nymph Echo and fell in love with his own reflection in a pool. He pined away and was changed into the flower that bears his name. The term **narcissism** is thus used for excessive or erotic interest in oneself and one's physical appearance.

Narmada a river which rises in Madhya Pradesh, central India, and flows generally westwards to the Gulf of Cambay; it is regarded by Hindus as sacred.

Narnia the fictional magic kingdom which is the setting for the Christian allegory of seven children's books by C. S. Lewis (1898–1963); in the first book, *The Lion, the Witch, and the Wardrobe* (1950) four children who reach Narnia through the back of a wardrobe are able, with the help of the lion ➤ ASLAN, to break the power of the witch Jadis and redeem Narnia from perpetual winter.

narthex an antechamber, porch, or distinct area at the western entrance of some early Christian churches, separated off by a railing and used by catechumens, penitents, and others; an antechamber or large porch in a modern church. Recorded from the late 17th century, the word comes via Latin from Greek *narthēx*.

narwhal a small Arctic whale, the male of which has a long forward-pointing spirally twisted tusk developed from one of its teeth;

in the past this tusk was sometimes represented as or believed to be a unicorn's horn, with its magic properties.

NASA in the US, the National Aeronautics and Space Administration.

Naseby a major battle of the English Civil War, which took place in 1645 near the village of Naseby in Northamptonshire. The Royalist army of Prince Rupert and King Charles I was decisively defeated by the New Model Army under General Fairfax and Oliver Cromwell. Following this defeat Charles I's cause collapsed completely.

Nashville the state capital of Tennessee, noted for its music industry and the Country Music Hall of Fame.

something nasty in the woodshed a traumatic experience or a concealed unpleasantness in a person's background. The phrase comes from Stella Gibbons' comic novel *Cold Comfort Farm* (1932), in which Ada Doom's dominance over her family is maintained by constant references to her having 'seen something nasty in the woodshed' in her youth; the details of the experience remain unexplained.

Nathan in the Bible, a prophet of the time of ➤ DAVID, who rebuked the king for taking the wife of Uriah (see ➤ EWE *lamb*).

Nathaniel in the Bible, a disciple of whom Jesus said, 'Behold an Israelite indeed, in whom is no guile!' (John 1:47). He is sometimes identified with ➤ BARTHOLOMEW.

Nation of Islam an exclusively black Islamic sect proposing a separate black nation, founded in Detroit *c*.1930. It came to prominence under the influence of the American political activist Malcolm X (1925–65).

national common to or characteristic of a whole nation.

A **national anthem** is a solemn patriotic song officially adopted by a country as an expression of national identity. The term is first recorded as the title of a poem by Shelley, 'A New National Anthem' (1819); by the mid 19th century, it referred to a specific song.

The **national debt** is the total amount of money which a country's government has borrowed, by various means. A government may raise money by means such as the selling of interest-bearing bonds to the public or borrowing from foreign creditors, often in order to support the national currency, pay for social programmes, or avoid the need to raise taxes.

The **National Gallery** is an art gallery in Trafalgar Square, London, holding one of the chief national collections of pictures. The collection began in 1824, when Parliament voted money for the purchase of thirty-eight pictures from the J. J. Angerstein collection, and the present main building was opened in 1838 and has been extended several times, most recently by the addition of the Sainsbury wing (opened 1991).

A **national government** is a coalition government, especially one subordinating party differences to the national interest in a time of crisis, as in Britain under Ramsay MacDonald in 1931–5.

The **National Trust** is a trust for the preservation of places of historic interest or natural beauty in England, Wales, and Northern Ireland, founded in 1895 and supported by endowment and private subscription. The National Trust for Scotland was founded in 1931.

the Nativity the birth of Jesus Christ, celebrated in the Christian Church on 25 December; traditional representations of this show the stable, Mary and Jesus, Joseph (often a little to one side), an ox and an ass, and often the shepherds kneeling in adoration. Recorded from Middle English, the word comes via Old French from Latin, ultimately from *nativus* 'arisen by birth'.

Natufian of, relating to, or denoting a late Mesolithic culture of the Middle East, dated to about 12,500–10,000 years ago, which provides evidence for the first settled villages, and is characterized by the use of microliths and of bone for implements. The name comes from Wadi *an-Natuf*, the type site (a cave north-west of Jerusalem).

natural science a branch of science which deals with the physical world, e.g. physics, chemistry, geology, biology; the branch of knowledge which deals with the study of the physical world.

natural selection the process whereby organisms better adapted to their environment tend to survive and produce more offspring. The theory of its action was first fully expounded by Charles Darwin and it is now believed to be the main process that brings about evolution.

nature the phenomena of the physical world collectively, including plants, animals, the landscape, and other features and products of the earth, as opposed to humans or human creations; the physical force regarded as causing and regulating these phenomena, especially as personified as **Dame Nature**, **Mother Nature**.

Nature is also used for the basic or inherent features of something, especially when seen as characteristic of it; the innate or essential qualities or character of a person or animal. In the Middle Ages, and since in some theological use, these features were seen as given by God and arising out of his creation.

Recorded from Middle English (denoting the physical power of a person), the word comes via Old French from Latin *natura* 'birth'.

The phrase **nature and nurture** is used to mean heredity and environment as influences on, or the determinants of, personality or behaviour; there has been a long debate on which, if either, is dominant. The phrase in this form is recorded from the late 19th century, but Shakespeare's *Tempest* juxtaposes the concepts in the description of Caliban.

The **nature of the beast** is the (undesirable but unchangeable) inherent or essential quality or character of the thing; an expression recorded from the late 17th century.

Nature red in tooth and claw is a ruthless personification of the creative and regulative physical power conceived of as operating in the material world; the phrase is originally from Tennyson's *In Memoriam* (1850).

naughty nineties the 1890s, regarded as a time of liberalism and permissiveness, especially in Britain and France; the term is first recorded in 1925.

Nausicaa in Greek mythology, the daugher of Alcinous, king of the Phaecians, who is found by the shipwrecked Odysseus playing at ball with her maids.

Nautilus a name given to Robert Fulton's 'diving boat' (1800), also to the fictitious submarine in Jules Verne's *Twenty Thousand Leagues under the Sea*. It became the name of the first nuclear-powered submarine, launched in 1954.

Nautilus is a Latin word, from Greek *nautilos*, literally 'sailor'.

Navaratri a Hindu autumn festival extending over the nine nights before Dussehra. It is associated with many local observances, especially the Bengali festival of the goddess ► DURGA. The name comes from Sanskrit, meaning literally 'nine nights'.

Battle of Navarino a decisive naval battle in the Greek struggle for independence from the Ottoman Empire, fought in 1827 in the Bay of Navarino off Pylos in the Peloponnese. Britain, Russia, and France sent a combined fleet which destroyed the Egyptian and Turkish fleet.

Navarre an autonomous region of northern Spain, on the border with France; capital, Pamplona. It represents the southern part of the former kingdom of Navarre, which was conquered by Ferdinand in 1512 and attached to Spain, while the northern part passed to France in 1589 through inheritance by Henri IV, king of France 1589–1610.

nave the central part of a church building, intended to accommodate most of the congregation. In traditional Western churches it is rectangular, separated from the chancel by a step or rail, and from adjacent aisles by pillars. Recorded from the late 17th century, the word comes from Latin *navis* 'ship'.

Naxos a Greek island in the southern Aegean, the largest of the Cyclades, where according to some legends ➤ ARIADNE was abandoned by Theseus.

Nazareth a historic town in lower Galilee, in present-day northern Israel. Mentioned in the Gospels as the home of Mary and Joseph, it is closely associated with the childhood of Jesus and is a centre of Christian pilgrimage.

A **Nazarene** is a native or inhabitant of Nazareth or (chiefly in Jewish or Muslim use) a Christian; Jesus Christ is referred to as **the Nazarene**. The name is also used for a member of an early sect or faction of Jewish Christians, especially one in 4th-century Syria using an Aramaic version of the Gospels and observing much of the Jewish law.

Nazca Lines a group of huge abstract designs, including representations of birds and animals, and straight lines on the coastal plain north of Nazca in southern Peru, clearly visible from the air but almost indecipherable from ground level. Made by exposing the underlying sand, they belong to a pre-Inca culture, and their purpose is uncertain; some hold the designs to represent a vast calendar or astronomical information. They have been preserved by the extreme dryness of the region.

Nazi a member of the National Socialist German Workers' Party, formed in Munich after the First World War. It advocated right-wing authoritarian nationalist government, and developed a racist ideology based on anti-Semitism and a belief in the superiority of 'Aryan' Germans. Its leader, Adolf Hitler, who was elected Chancellor in 1933, established a totalitarian dictatorship, rearmed Germany in support of expansionist foreign policies in central Europe, and so precipitated the Second World War.

A **Nazi salute** is a gesture or salute in which the right arm is inclined upwards, with the hand open and the palm down.

Nazirite an Israelite consecrated to the service of God, under vows to abstain from alcohol, let the hair grow, and avoid defilement by contact with corpses (Numbers 6).

ne plus ultra Latin, meaning 'not further beyond', the supposed inscription on the Pillars of Hercules prohibiting passage by ships.

Neanderthal an extinct human that was widely distributed in ice age Europe between *c.*120,000–35,000 years ago, with a receding forehead and prominent brow ridges. The Neanderthals were associated with the Mousterian flint industry of the Middle Palaeolithic.

In figurative use, the name may be applied to someone considered uncivilized, unintelligent, or uncouth.

The name comes (in the mid 19th century) from *Neanderthal*, the name of a region in Germany, where remains of Neanderthal man were found.

neap tide a tide just after the first or third quarters of the moon when there is least difference between high and low water. Recorded from late Middle English, *neap* was originally an adjective, from Old English *nēp*, first element of *nēflōd*, of unknown origin.

near-death experience an unusual experience taking place on the brink of death and recounted by a person on recovery, typically an out-of-body experience or a vision of a tunnel of light.

Nebuchadnezzar (*c.*630–562 BC), king of Babylon 605–562 BC. He rebuilt the city with massive walls, a huge temple, and a ziggurat, and extended his rule over neighbouring countries. In 586 BC he captured and destroyed Jerusalem and deported many Israelites in what is known as the ➤ BABYLONIAN *Captivity*.

The name *Nebuchadnezzar* is given to a very large wine bottle, equivalent in capacity to about twenty regular bottles.

Battle of Nechtansmere a battle which took place in 685 at Nechtansmere, near Forfar, Scotland, in which the Picts defeated the Northumbrians, stopping their expansion northward and forcing their withdrawal.

neck or nothing risking everything on success, with allusion to the idea of falling and breaking one's neck through reckless riding.

the same neck of the woods a particular area or locality; neck in the sense of 'narrow strip of woodland' is recorded from the late 18th century.

necklace in Christian iconography, a *necklace* is the emblem of ➤ St ETHELDREDA.

In South Africa in the 1970s, *necklace* was used for a tyre doused or filled with petrol, placed round a victim's neck and set alight.

necromancy the supposed practice of communicating with the dead, especially in order to predict the future. The word comes from Middle English *nigromancie*, via Old French from medieval Latin *nigromantia*, changed (by association with Latin *niger* 'black') from late Latin *necromantia*, where the first element represented Greek *nekros* 'corpse'.

The translator ➤ *Philemon* HOLLAND (1552–1637) gave the name *Necromancy* to that part of the *Odyssey* (book 6) which describes Odysseus' visit to Hades.

nectar in Greek and Roman mythology, the drink of the gods. The word comes from Greek *nektar*, the ultimate origin of which is unexplained.

needle see also ➤ EYE *of a needle*.

look for a needle in a haystack proverbial expression for attempting an impossible task; earlier versions (recorded from the mid 16th century) are **look for a needle in a meadow** and **look for a needle in a bottle of hay**.

needs must an unwelcome course of action is or was necessary or unavoidable; a shortened form of the proverb *needs must when the Devil drives*.

Nefertiti (fl. 14th century BC), Egyptian queen, wife of ➤ AKHENATEN. She initially supported Akhenaten's religious reforms, although she may have withdrawn her support in favour of the new religion promoted by her half-brother Tutankhamen. She is best known from the painted limestone bust of her, now in Berlin, in which she is shown with a long and slender neck.

Nehemiah (5th century BC) a Hebrew leader who supervised the rebuilding of the walls of Jerusalem (*c.*444) and introduced moral and religious reforms (*c.*432). His work was continued by ➤ EZRA.

Nelson name of the British admiral Horatio *Nelson* (1758–1805), used in a number of phrases.

To **turn a Nelson eye** is to turn a blind eye to, overlook, pretend ignorance of. The allusion is to the battle of Copenhagen in 1801, when the signal 'discontinue the action' was hoisted; Nelson is said to have clapped his telescope to his blind eye, and declared that he could not see the signal.

The **Nelson touch** is a masterly or sympathetic approach to a problem, with allusion to the skills of Admiral Horatio Nelson. The expression was coined by Nelson himself, in a letter of 25 September 1805.

Nelson's blood was rum, as formerly officially issued in the Navy.

Nelson's Column is a memorial to Lord Nelson in Trafalgar Square, London, consisting of a column 58 metres (170 feet) high surmounted by his statue.

Nelson's Pillar is a monument in Dublin, erected 1808–9, which was blown up by Republicans in 1966.

Nemean lion in Greek mythology, a monstrous lion which terrorized the Nemea, a wooded district near Argos in ancient Greece, until killed by Hercules as the first of his twelve labours.

Nemesis in Greek mythology, a goddess usually portrayed as the agent of divine punishment for wrongdoing or presumption (hubris). She is often little more than the personification of retribution or righteous indignation, although she is occasionally seen as a deity pursued amorously by Zeus and taking various non-human forms to evade him.

Nennius (fl. *c.*800), Welsh chronicler. He is traditionally credited with the compilation or revision of the *Historia Britonum*, which includes one of the earliest known accounts of King Arthur.

neoclassicism the revival of a classical style or treatment in art, literature, architecture, or music. As an aesthetic and artistic style this originated in Rome in the mid 18th century, combining a reaction against the late baroque and rococo with a new interest in antiquity. In music, the term refers to a return by composers of the early 20th century to the forms and styles of the 17th and 18th centuries, as a reaction against 19th-century Romanticism.

Neolithic of, relating to, or denoting the later part of the Stone Age, when ground or polished stone weapons and implements prevailed. In the Neolithic period farm animals were first domesticated and agriculture was introduced, beginning in the Near East by the 8th millennium BC and spreading to northern Europe by the 4th millennium BC. Neolithic societies in NW Europe left such monuments as causewayed camps, henges, long barrows, and chambered tombs.

neologism a newly coined word or expression. Recorded from the early 19th century, the word comes from French *néologisme*.

Neoplatonism a philosophical and religious system developed by the followers of Plotinus in the 3rd century AD. Neoplatonism combined ideas from Plato, Aristotle, Pythagoras, and the Stoics with oriental mysticism. Predominant in pagan Europe until the early 6th century, it was a major influence on early Christian writers, on later medieval and Renaissance thought, and on Islamic philosophy. It envisages the human soul rising above the imperfect material world through virtue and contemplation towards knowledge of the transcendent One.

Neoptolemus in Greek mythology, the son of Achilles and killer of Priam after the fall of Troy; in Homer's *Odyssey* he is said to have returned safely to his home at Scyros, and to have married Hermione, daughter of Menelaus and Helen.

nepenthes a drug described in Homer's *Odyssey* as banishing grief or trouble from a person's mind; the name may thus be applied to any drug or potion bringing welcome forgetfulness.

nepotism the practice among those with power or influence of favouring relatives or friends, especially by giving them jobs. Recorded from the mid 17th century, the word comes via French from Italian *nepotismo*, from *nipote* 'nephew', with reference to privileges bestowed on the 'nephews' of popes, who were in many cases their illegitimate sons.

Neptune in Roman mythology, the god of the water and of the sea; his Greek equivalent is ➤ POSEIDON.

From the early 19th century, the traditional shipboard ceremony held when crossing the equator has included a sailor dressed as Neptune.

Neptunism was a theory propounded by A. G. Werner that the rocks of the earth's crust were formed primarily by crystallization from the sea, rather than by solidification of magma. The theory was popular at the end of the 18th and the beginning of the 19th century, but is now rejected.

nerd a foolish or contemptible person who lacks social skills or is boringly studious. Fashionable in the early 1980s, the word dates from the 1950s, but its origin is unknown.

Nereus in Greek mythology, an old sea god. Like Proteus he had the power of assuming various forms. His daughters were the **Nereids**, sea-nymphs who included ➤ THETIS, mother of Achilles.

Nero (AD 37–68), Roman emperor, whose patronage of the arts extended to appearing himself upon the stage. Infamous for his cruelty, he ordered the murder of his mother Agrippina in 59 and wantonly executed leading Romans. His reign witnessed a fire which destroyed half of Rome in 64; in Suetonius's *Lives of the Caesars*, it is said that after watching the fire, Nero dressed himself in his tragedian's costume and sang *The Fall of Ilium*. This story gave rise to the expression ➤ *to* FIDDLE *while Rome burns* (although Nero's instrument would have been the lyre).

A wave of uprisings in 68 led to his flight from Rome and his eventual suicide.

Nessie informal name for the ➤ LOCH *Ness monster*.

Nessus a centaur who was killed by Hercules; when dying, he told Hercules' wife Deianeira that if she ever doubted her husband's love, a robe smeared with Nessus's blood would ensure his constancy. Deianeira followed this advice, but the centaur's blood was a poison that consumed Hercules with fire.

The phrase **shirt of Nessus** is used for a destructive or expurgatory force or influence.

nest egg a sum of money saved for the future; originally, a real or artificial egg left in a nest to induce hens to lay eggs there.

Nestor a king of Pylos in the Peloponnese, who in old age led his subjects to the ➤ TROJAN *War*. His wisdom and eloquence were proverbial.

net a net is the emblem of ➤ *St* PETER and ➤ *St* ANDREW.

the Net informal term for the ➤ INTERNET.

nether millstone the lower of a pair of millstones, as the type of something hard and unyielding, originally with biblical allusion to Job 41:24.

Neustria the western part of the Frankish empire in the Merovingian period. The name probably represents an unrecorded Frankish toponym meaning 'new western dominion', referring to the Franks' conquest of northern Gaul in the 5th century.

you've never had it so good a phrase associated with the Conservative politician Harold Macmillan (1894–1986), referring to a speech as Prime Minister on 20 July 1957, when he said, 'Let us be frank about it: most of our people have never had it so good.' 'You Never Had It So Good' was the Democratic Party slogan during the 1952 US election campaign.

Never-Never in Australia, the unpopulated northern part of the Northern Territory and Queensland; the desert country of the interior of Australia, the remote outback. Recorded from the mid 19th century, the name has been variously explained as implying that one may never return from it, or will never wish to go back to it; it has also been suggested that the phrase is really a corruption of the Comeleroi *nievah vahs* signifying 'unoccupied land'.

Never-Never land an imaginary, illusory, or Utopian place, often with allusion to the ideal country in J. M. Barrie's *Peter Pan*.

new often in place names, or denoting significant cultural or political change.

    New Age is a broad movement of the late 20th century, originating California and the West Coast of the US, which is characterized by alternative approaches to traditional Western culture, with an interest in spirituality, mysticism, holism, and environmentalism.

    The **New Deal** is a name for the economic measures introduced by Franklin D. Roosevelt (1882–1945) in 1933 to counteract the effects of the Great Depression. It involved a massive public works programme, complemented by the large-scale granting of loans, and succeeded in reducing unemployment by between 7 and 10 million.

    The **New Forest** is an area of heath and woodland in southern Hampshire (*forest* here

has the specialized sense of an area, typically owned by the sovereign and partly wooded, kept for hunting and having its own laws). It has been reserved as Crown property since 1079, originally by William I as a royal hunting area.

    The **New Jerusalem** is the abode of the blessed in heaven, with reference to Revelation 21:2.

    The **New Kingdom** is a period of ancient Egyptian history (*c.*1550–1070 BC, 18th–20th dynasty).

    New Labour refers to that section of the Labour Party which actively supported the internal reforms initiated by Neil Kinnock (party leader, 1983–1992) and carried through by John Smith (party leader 1992–1994) and Tony Blair (party leader 1994–, Prime Minister 1997–); the Labour Party as a whole after the implementation of those reforms.

    The **new learning** was the studies, especially that of the Greek language, introduced into England in the 16th century. Also, the doctrines of the Reformation.

    The **New Look** was a style of women's clothing introduced in 1947 by Christian Dior, featuring calf-length full skirts and a generous use of material in contrast to wartime austerity.

    In Christian theology from the late Middle English period, the term **new man** has been used to designate someone regarded as morally or spiritually reformed or renewed, often with explicit biblical allusion, as to Ephesians 4:24. In the 1980s, **New Man** began to be used in a secular sense to designate a man rejecting sexist attitudes and the traditional male role, especially in the context of domestic responsibilities and childcare.

    The **New Model Army** was a disciplined and well-trained army created in 1645 by Oliver Cromwell to fight for the Parliamentary cause in the English Civil War. It later came to possess considerable political influence.

    New Style refers to the method of calculating dates using the ➤ GREGORIAN *calendar*, which in England and Wales superseded the use of the Julian calendar in 1752.

    The **New Testament** is the second part of the Christian Bible, written originally in Greek and recording the life and teachings of Christ and his earliest followers. It includes the four Gospels, the Acts of the Apostles, twenty-one Epistles by St Paul and others, and the book of Revelation.

    The **New World** was North and South America regarded collectively in relation to Europe. The term was first applied to the

Americas (also to other areas, e.g. Australia), especially after the early voyages of European explorers.

The **New World Order** is a vision of a world ordered differently from the way it is at present; in particular, an optimistic view of the world order or balance of power following the end of the Cold War. The term was given prominence in a speech in March 1991 by George Bush (1924–) when President of the US.

New Year's Day is the first day of the year; in the modern Western calendar, 1 January, although before the adoption of the ➤ GREGORIAN *calendar* in the 18th century, the legal beginning of the year was 25 March. **New Year's Eve** is 31 December in the modern Western calendar.

Newgate a former London prison, originally the gatehouse of the main west gate to the city, first used as a prison in the early Middle Ages. whose unsanitary conditions became notorious in the 18th century before the building was burnt down in the Gordon Riots of 1780. A new edifice was erected on the same spot but was demolished in 1902 to make way for the Central Criminal Court.

The **Newgate Calendar** was a publication issued from *c.*1774 until the mid 19th century that dealt with notorious crimes as committed by those who were prisoners in Newgate.

newspeak the name of an artificial official language in George Orwell's *Nineteen Eighty-Four* (1949), now used to denote ambiguous euphemistic language used chiefly in political propaganda.

Newton's laws of motion three fundamental laws of classical physics, established by the English mathematician and physicist Isaac *Newton* (1642–1727). The first states that a body continues in a state of rest or uniform motion in a straight line unless it is acted on by an external force. The second states that the rate of change of momentum of a moving body is proportional to the force acting to produce the change. The third states that if one body exerts a force on another, there is an equal and opposite force (or reaction) exerted by the second body on the first.

Newton is considered the greatest single influence on theoretical physics until Einstein. In his *Principia Mathematica* (1687), Newton gave a mathematical description of the laws of mechanics and gravitation, and applied these to planetary motion. According to tradition, the idea of universal gravitation

occurred to him while watching an apple fall from a tree; this story is given in Voltaire's *Philosophie de Newton*, where the source is said to have been Newton's step-niece, Mrs Conduitt.

next year in Jerusalem! traditionally the concluding words of the Jewish Passover service, expressing the hope of the ➤ DIASPORA that Jews dispersed throughout the world would once more be reunited.

Niagara Falls the waterfalls on the Niagara River, consisting of two principal parts separated by Goat Island: the Horseshoe Falls adjoining the west (Canadian) bank, which fall 47 m (158 ft), and the American Falls adjoining the east (American) bank, which fall 50 m (167 ft). They are a popular tourist venue, especially for honeymooners, and an attraction for various stunts.

Nibelung in Germanic mythology, a member of a Scandinavian race of dwarfs, owners of a hoard of gold and magic treasures, who were ruled by *Nibelung*, king of Nibelheim (land of mist). The treasure was eventually taken by Siegfried, hero of the ➤ NIBELUNGENLIED.

Nibelungenlied a 13th-century German poem, embodying a story found in the (Poetic) Edda, telling of the life and death of Siegfried, a prince of the Netherlands. There have been many adaptations of the story, including Wagner's epic music drama *Der Ring des Nibelungen* (1847–74).

➤ SIEGFRIED kills the dragon Fafner to seize the treasure of the Nibelungs; he then marries the Burgundian princess Kriemhild and uses trickery to help her brother Gunther win Brunhild, but is killed by Gunther's retainer Hagen. His wife Kriemhild agrees to marry Etzel (Attila the Hun) in order to be revenged, and beheads Hagen herself.

Nicaea an ancient city in Asia Minor, on the site of modern Iznik, which was important in Roman and Byzantine times. It was the site of two ecumenical councils of the early Christian Church (in 325 and 787). The first, the **Council of Nicaea** in 325, condemned Arianism and produced the Nicene Creed. The second, in 787, condemned the iconoclasts.

nice work if you can get it expressing envy of what is perceived to be another's more favourable situation, from a song (1937) by Ira Gershwin.

Nicene Creed a formal statement of Christian belief which is very widely used in Christian liturgies, based on that adopted at the first Council of ➤ NICAEA in 325.

Nichiren a Japanese Buddhist sect founded by the religious teacher Nichiren (1222–82) with the Lotus Sutra as its central scripture. There are more than 30 million followers in more than forty subsects, the largest now being Nichiren-Shoshu, which is connected with the religious and political organization Soka Gakkai.

Nicholas male forename, name of two saints.

St Nicholas of Myra was a 4th-century Christian prelate, said to have been bishop of Myra in Lycia; his relics were translated to Bari in Italy in 1087.

Legends of the saint include the stories that he gave three bags of gold as dowries to three girls about to be sold into prostitution, and that he restored to life three boys who had been murdered and pickled in a brine tub; he also saved from death three men who had been unjustly condemned, and three sailors off the coast of Turkey. He is patron saint of children, sailors, Greece, and Russia; of pawnbrokers (from the connection made between the ➤ *three* GOLDEN *balls* of a pawnbroker's sign and the three bags of gold given as dowries); and of perfumiers (because a fragrant substance is said to have been emitted from his shrine at Bari). The cult of *Santa Claus* (a corruption of his name) comes from the Dutch custom of giving gifts to children on his feast day.

Three boys in a tub, three moneybags, and a ship, are all emblems of St Nicholas. His feast day is 6 December.

St Nicholas of Tolentino (1245–1305), was an Augustinian friar, born in Ancona, and named for St Nicholas of Myra; he was renowned as a preacher, and for his care of the sick and destitute. His usual emblems are a basket of loaves of bread (traditionally given to the sick, or to women in labour) and a star, and his feast day is 10 September.

nickname a familiar or humorous name given to a person or thing instead of or as well as the real name. The word is recorded from late Middle English, and comes from *an eke name* (*eke* meaning 'addition') misinterpreted, by wrong division, as *a neke name*.

Nicodemus in the Bible, the Pharisee and member of the council of the Sanhedrin who visited Jesus by night, and later assisted in Jesus's burial.

Niflheim in Scandinavian mythology, an underworld of eternal cold, darkness, and mist inhabited by those who died of old age or illness, and ruled over by the goddess ➤ HEL.

Night Journey in Muslim tradition, the journey through the air made by Muhammad, guided by the archangel Gabriel. They flew first to Jerusalem, where Muhammad prayed with earlier prophets including Abraham, Moses, and Jesus, before entering the presence of Allah in heaven.

night of the long knives a treacherous massacre or betrayal, especially the massacre of the Brownshirts on Hitler's orders in June 1934. Traditionally, the phrase is used to refer to the (legendary) massacre of the Britons by Hengist in 472, described by Geoffrey of Monmouth in his *Historia Regum Britanniae*.

The term has also been used to describe Harold Macmillan's dismissal of seven of his Cabinet on 13 July 1962.

nightingale in Greek mythology, ➤ PHILOMELA was transformed into a nightingale.

nightmare a frightening or unpleasant dream. In Middle English, the word denoted a female evil spirit thought to lie upon and suffocate sleepers.

nihilism the rejection of all religious and moral principles, often in the belief that life is meaningless; extreme scepticism maintaining that nothing in the world has a real existence. This was the doctrine of an extreme Russian revolutionary party *c.*1900, which found nothing to approve of in the established social order.

Nike in Greek mythology, the goddess of victory; a winged statue representing this goddess.

Nile a river in eastern Africa, the confluence of the ➤ BLUE *Nile* and the ➤ WHITE *Nile*, which flows northwards through Sudan and Egypt to the Mediterranean, and which is the longest river in the world; the search to discover the true source of the Nile was pursued by a number of 19th-century explorers. It was in the course of such a journey that David Livingstone (see ➤ *Dr* LIVINGSTONE, *I presume*) was for a time lost.

Nile is one of the oldest geographical names in the world, and comes via Latin from ancient Greek, and probably ultimately from Semitic–Hamitic *nagal* 'river'. It was called *Ar* or *Aur* 'black' by the ancient Egyptians, referring to the colour of the sediment when it is in full flood.

nimbus a luminous cloud or a halo surrounding a supernatural being or a saint. Recorded from the early 17th century, the word is Latin, and means literally 'cloud, aureole'.

Nimby a person who objects to the siting of something perceived as unpleasant or hazardous in their own neighbourhood, especially while raising no such objections to similar developments elsewhere. Recorded from the 1980s, the word is an acronym from the words *not in my back yard*.

Nimrod a skilful hunter, from the name of the great-grandson of Noah, traditional founder of the Babylonian dynasty, described in Genesis as 'a mighty hunter before the Lord'. The Hebrew name *Nimrōd*, literally 'let us rebel' or 'we will rebel', is probably a distortion of the name of the Mesopotamian war-god *Ninurta*, a mighty hunter and warrior.

nine in medieval angelology there were traditionally *nine* orders to the ➤ CELESTIAL *hierarchy*; cats proverbially have *nine* lives; *nine* days or nights is the period during which a novelty is supposed to attract attention.

The **Nine Days' Queen**, a name for Lady Jane Grey (1537–54), Queen of England for nine days following the death of Edward VI. She was quickly deposed by forces loyal to Edward's (Catholic) sister Mary, who had popular support, and executed the following year.

A **nine days' wonder** is a person who or thing which is briefly famous.

In American usage, **Nine-eleven** (written 9/11) refers to the terrorist action of 11 September 2001, in which hijacked passenger planes were flown into the ➤ WORLD *Trade Center* and the Pentagon, and a fourth hijacked plane crashed near Pittsburgh.

Nine men's morris is a game, also known as *merrill*, played on a board between two players, each with an equal number of pebbles, discs of wood or metal, pegs, or pins.

The **Nine Worthies** were nine famous personages of ancient Jewish history and classical and medieval Christian history and legend (Joshua, David, and Judas Maccabaeus; Hector, Alexander, and Julius Caesar; and King Arthur, Charlemagne, and Godfrey of Bouillon).

Nineveh an ancient city located on the east bank of the Tigris, opposite the modern city of Mosul, to which ➤ JONAH was sent to preach. It was the oldest city of the ancient Assyrian empire and its capital during the reign of Sennacherib until it was destroyed by a coalition of Babylonians and Medes in 612 BC.

St Ninian (*c.*360–*c.*432), Scottish bishop and missionary. According to Bede he founded a church at Whithorn in SW Scotland (*c.*400) and from there evangelized the southern Picts. His feast day is 26 August.

Niobe the daughter of Tantalus, and mother of a large family. Apollo and Artemis, enraged because Niobe boasted herself superior to their mother Leto (who had only two children), slew her children and turned Niobe herself into a stone, and her tears into streams that trickled from it.

Nippon the Japanese name for Japan, literally 'land where the sun rises or originates'.

nirvana a transcendent state in which there is neither suffering, desire, nor sense of self, and the subject is released from the effects of karma. It represents the final goal of Buddhism.

The word comes from Sanskrit *nirvāṇa*, from *nirvā* 'be extinguished'.

nisei in North America, an American or Canadian whose parents were immigrants from Japan. The word comes (in the 1940s) from Japanese, meaning literally 'second generation'.

nitre an early name for natron or saltpetre; used allusively with reference to natron employed as a cleansing agent, as in Jeremiah 22:2.

From the 17th century, *nitre* was also the name of a supposed volatile substance related to or present in saltpetre, formerly presumed to be present in the air and rain. It was used with reference to the use of saltpetre in gunpowder, or to the supposition that thunder and lightning were caused by nitre in the air.

Nivose the fourth month of the French Republican calendar (1793–1805), originally running from 21 December to 19 January. The name comes from Latin *nivosus* 'snowy'.

nix a water sprite; the word comes (in the mid 19th century) from German, and is related to archaic English *nicker*. A **nixie** is a female water sprite.

Nizari a member of a Muslim sect that split from the Ismaili branch in 1094 over disagreement about the succession to the caliphate. The majority of Nizaris now live in the Indian subcontinent; their leader is the Aga Khan. Originally based in Persia, the Nizaris were known to those whom they opposed as *Hashshishin* or 'Assassins'.

Njord in Scandinavian mythology, the god of the wind and sea, father of ➤ FREY and ➤ FREYA.

no-man's-land disputed ground between the front lines or trenches of two opposing armies; used particularly with reference to the First World War.

no surrender! Protestant Northern Irish slogan originating with the defenders of Derry against the Catholic forces of James II in 1689.

Noah (in the Bible) a Hebrew patriarch represented as tenth in descent from Adam. According to a story in Genesis he made the ark which saved his family and specimens of every animal from the Flood, and his sons Ham, Shem, and Japheth were regarded as ancestors of all the races of humankind (Genesis 5–10). The tradition of a great flood in very early times is found also in other countries.
   Noah's ark is the ship in which Noah, his family, and the animals were saved from the Flood, according to the biblical account (Genesis 6–8); a children's toy representing this.

Nobel Prize any of six international prizes awarded annually for outstanding work in physics, chemistry, physiology or medicine, literature, economics, and the promotion of peace. The Nobel Prizes, first awarded in 1901, were established by the will of the Swedish chemist and engineer Alfred *Nobel* (1833–96), who made a large fortune from his invention of dynamite (1866), gelignite, and other high explosives. The prizes are traditionally awarded on 10 December, the anniversary of his death. The awards are decided by members of Swedish learned societies or, in the case of the peace prize, the Norwegian Parliament.

noble a former English gold coin first issued in 1351.

the noble art boxing.

noble gas any of the gaseous elements helium, neon, argon, krypton, xenon, and radon, occupying Group 0 (18) of the periodic table. They were long believed to be totally unreactive but compounds of xenon, krypton, and radon are now known.

the noble savage a representative of primitive mankind as idealized in Romantic literature, symbolizing the innate goodness of humanity when free from the corrupting influence of civilization. The phrase itself comes from Dryden's *Conquest of Granada* (1672).

noblesse oblige French phrase meaning, privilege entails responsibility.

Noddy a character in the stories (1949–) of Enid Blyton, a toy figure of a boy with a head that nods when he speaks, whose brightly coloured clothes include a distinctive long blue cap with a bell at the tip, and whose simplicity and good intentions often lead to trouble.

Noel Christmas, especially as a refrain in carols and on Christmas cards. Recorded from the early 19th century, the word comes from French *Noël* 'Christmas'.

Noh traditional Japanese masked drama with dance and song, evolved from Shinto rites. Noh dates from the 14th and 15th centuries, and its subject matter is taken mainly from Japan's classical literature. Traditionally the players were all male, with the chorus playing a passive narrative role.

noli me tangere a painting representing the appearance of Jesus to Mary Magdalen at the sepulchre (John 20:17), when the newly-risen Jesus warned his disciple 'do not touch me'.

Nome a city in western Alaska, on the south coast of the Seward Peninsula. Founded in 1896 as a gold-mining camp, it became a centre of the Alaskan gold rush at the turn of the century.

nomen in Roman history, the second personal name of a citizen of ancient Rome that indicates the gens to which he or she belonged, e.g. Marcus *Tullius* Cicero.

nominalism in philosophy, the doctrine that universals or general ideas are mere names without any corresponding reality. Only particular objects exist, and properties, numbers, and sets are merely features of the way of considering the things that exist. Important in medieval scholastic thought, nominalism is associated particularly with William of Occam (see ➤ OCCAM's razor).

nonce (of a word or expression) coined for one occasion. The word derives (in Middle English) from *then anes* 'the one (purpose)', from *then* (obsolete form of *the*) + *ane* 'one', altered by misdivision.

Nonconformist originally (in the early part of the 17th century) a person adhering to the doctrine but not the usages of the Church of England; the first recorded usage relates to a defence of the surplice, the sign of the cross after baptism, and the custom of kneeling to receive Holy Communion. Later (especially after the passing of the ➤ *Act of* UNIFORMITY in 1662, and the consequent ejection from their livings of those ministers who refused to conform), a member of a Protestant Church which dissents from the established Church of England.

nones in the ancient Roman calendar, the ninth day before the ides by inclusive reckoning, i.e. the 7th day of March, May, July, October, the 5th of other months. Recorded from late Middle English, the word comes via Old French from Latin *nonas*, feminine accusative plural of *nonus* 'ninth'.

In the Christian Church, *nones* is the name for the fifth of the canonical hours of prayer, originally appointed for the ninth hour of the day (about 3 p.m.), and the office appointed for this hour.

Nonjuror a member of the clergy who refused to take the oath of allegiance to William and Mary in 1689.

nonpareil an unrivalled or matchless person or thing; in printing, an old type size equal to six points (larger than ruby).

Nonsuch Palace a Tudor palace near Cheam in Surrey, built by Henry VIII. It was not completed until 1557, but the name is first mentioned in the Exchequer Accounts for 1538. In the 17th century, the English Catholic priest Richard Lassels (1603?–68), in his posthumously published *The Voyage of Italy*, referred to Fontainebleu as 'the Nonsuch of France'. *Nonsuch Palace* was demolished in 1670.

noon twelve o'clock in the day; midday. In Old English, *nōn* means 'the ninth hour from

sunrise', i.e. approximately 3 p.m., from Latin *nona (hora)* 'ninth hour'.

It was traditionally believed that the change in the time denoted by *noon*, from about 3 o'clock to about 12 o'clock, probably resulted from anticipation of the ecclesiastical office or of a meal hour; this view was based on the belief that the canonical hours were counted starting at 6 o'clock, and that in the Benedictine order *nones* would ordinarily be held at about 3 o'clock. Recent research, however, suggests that in the Benedictine order in Italy nones would have been held closer to 12 o'clock, and it is possible that this became the usual time for nones in several orders.

Norbertine another term for ➤ PREMONSTRATENSIAN. The name comes (in the late 17th century) from St *Norbert* (*c*.1080–1134), founder of the order.

Norman a member of a people of mixed Frankish and Scandinavian origin who settled in Normandy from about AD 912 and became a dominant military power in western Europe and the Mediterranean in the 11th century, in particular, any of the Normans who conquered England in 1066 or their descendants.

The **Norman Conquest** is the conquest of England by William of Normandy (William the Conqueror) after the Battle of Hastings in 1066. Most of the Saxon nobles had been dispossessed or killed and the population was heavily taxed (the Domesday Book was compiled in 1086). Norman institutions and customs (such as feudalism) were introduced, and Anglo-Norman French and Latin adopted as the languages of literature, law, and government.

Norman French is the northern form of Old French spoken by the Normans; the variety of this used in English law courts from the 11th to 13th centuries; Anglo-Norman French.

the Norns in Scandinavian mythology, the three virgin goddesses of destiny (Urd or Urdar, Verdandi, and Skuld), who sit by the well of fate at the base of the ash tree ➤ YGGDRASIL and spin the web of fate.

Norroy (in the UK) the title (in full **Norroy and Ulster**) given to the third King of Arms, with jurisdiction north of the Trent and (since 1943) in Northern Ireland. The name comes (in late Middle English) from Old French *nord* 'north' + *roi* 'king'.

north the direction in which a compass needle normally points, towards the horizon on the left-hand side of a person facing east, or the part of the horizon lying in this direction.

In 19th-century America, **the North** was used for those northern states of the United States which were opposed to slavery in the Civil War, and which fought on the side of the Union. In current usage, **the North** often designates the industrialized and economically advanced nations of the world.

The **North-East Passage** is a passage for ships along the northern coast of Europe and Asia, from the Atlantic to the Pacific via the Arctic Ocean, sought for many years as a possible trade route to the East. It was first navigated in 1878–9 by the Swedish Arctic explorer Baron Nordenskjöld (1832–1901).

The **North Pole** is the northern geographical pole of the earth, situated on the Arctic ice-cap; the northern celestial or magnetic pole.

The **North Star** is the Pole Star, and the North Star Sate is an informal name for Minnesota.

The **North-West Passage** is a sea passage along the northern coast of the American continent, through the Canadian Arctic from the Atlantic to the Pacific. It was (like the *North-East Passage*) sought for many years as a possible trade route; it was first navigated in 1903–6 by Roald Amundsen.

Northern Lights another name for the aurora borealis.

Northumbria an ancient Anglo-Saxon kingdom in NE England extending from the Humber to the Forth. The name comes from obsolete *Northumber*, denoting a person living beyond the Humber.

nostalgie de la boue a desire for degradation and depravity. The French phrase, meaning literally 'mud nostalgia', was coined by the French poet and dramatist Émile Augier (1820–89), in *Le Mariage d'Olympe* (1855). In response to the comment that a duck placed on a lake with swans will miss his pond and eventually return to it, the character Montrichard replies, '*La nostalgie de la boue!* [Longing to be back in the mud!]'

nostoc a micro-organism composed of beaded filaments which aggregate to form a gelatinous mass, growing in water and damp places and able to fix nitrogen from the atmosphere. It was formerly believed to be an emanation from the stars, and the name was invented by ➤ PARACELSUS.

Nostradamus (1503–66), French astrologer and physician; Latinized name of *Michel de Nostredame*. His cryptic and apocalyptic predictions in rhyming quatrains appeared in two collections (1555; 1558) and their interpretation continues to be the subject of controversy.

not in my backyard expressing an objection to the siting of something regarded as unpleasant in one's own locality, while by implication finding it acceptable elsewhere. The expression originated in the United States in derogatory references to the anti-nuclear movement, and in Britain was particularly associated with reports of the then Environment Secretary Nicholas Ridley's opposition in 1988 to housing developments near his home; the acronym NIMBY derives from this.

you ain't seen nothing yet there is something even more extreme or impressive in store. Often with allusion to Al Jolson's 'you ain't heard nuttin' yet,' used as an aside in the 1927 film *The Jazz Singer*.

Notre-Dame a Gothic cathedral church in Paris, dedicated to the Virgin Mary, on the Île de la Cité (an island in the Seine). It was built between 1163 and 1250 and is especially noted for its innovatory flying buttresses and sculptured facade. The French phrase means literally 'our lady'.

Notting Hill a district of NW central London, the scene of an annual Caribbean-style street carnival.

Nova Scotia a province of eastern Canada, originally settled by the French in the early 18th century as *Acadia*, which became one of the original four provinces in the Dominion of Canada in 1867.

November the eleventh month of the year, in the northern hemisphere usually considered the last month of autumn. Recorded from Old English, the name comes from Latin, from *novem* 'nine', being originally the ninth month of the Roman year.

November is used allusively with reference to the short, damp, cold, or foggy days regarded as characteristic of the northern hemisphere.

novena (in the Roman Catholic church) a form of worship consisting of special prayers or services on nine successive days. Recorded from the mid 19th century, the phrase comes from medieval Latin, from Latin *novem* 'nine'.

Novgorod a city in NW Russia, on the Volkhov River at the northern tip of Lake Ilmen, which is Russia's oldest city; it was settled by the Varangian chief Rurik in 862 and ruled by Alexander Nevsky between 1238 and 1263, when it was an important centre of medieval eastern Europe.

noyade an execution carried out by drowning, especially a mass execution by drowning as carried out in France at Nantes in 1794. The word comes from French, and means literally 'drowning', from the verb *noyer*, from Latin *necare* 'kill without a weapon', later 'drown'.

nth denoting an unspecified member of a series of numbers or enumerated items; (in general use) denoting an unspecified item or instance in a series, typically the last or latest in a long series.

nuclear winter a period of abnormal cold and darkness predicted to follow a nuclear war, caused by a layer of smoke and dust in the atmosphere blocking the sun's rays.

nul points no points scored in a contest, especially as a hypothetical mark awarded for a failure or dismal performance. *Nul points* is the lowest score attainable by an entry in the Eurovision Song Contest, in which the compèring is delivered in both English and French.

null and void having no legal or binding force.

In a statistical test, a **null hypothesis** is the hypothesis that there is no significant difference between specified populations, any observed difference being due to sampling or experimental error.

Nullarbor Plain a vast arid plain in SW Australia, stretching inland from the Great Australian Bight. It contains no surface water, has sparse vegetation, and is almost uninhabited, from Latin *nullus arbor* 'no tree'.

Numa Numa Pompilius (traditionally 715–673 BC), legendary second king of Rome, who claimed to have received instruction from the water goddess ➤ EGERIA; the name may be used allusively for someone likened to him, especially as a lawgiver.

number an arithmetical value, expressed by a word, symbol, or figure, representing a particular quantity and used in counting and

making calculations and for showing order in a series or for identification.

The number of the beast is the number 666, numerologically representing the name of the Antichrist of the Revelation 13:18, 'Let him that hath understanding count the number of the beast: for it is the number of a man; and his number is Six hundred threescore and six.' It has been suggested that the number given could be a coded reference to Nero: the numerical value of *Nero Caesar*, written in Hebrew letters, adds up to 666.

Number Ten is a name for 10 Downing Street, the official London home of the British Prime Minister.

Numbers the fourth book of the Bible, relating the experiences of the Israelites in the wilderness after Moses led them out of Egypt. It is named in English from the book's accounts of a census; the title in Hebrew means 'in the wilderness'.

by numbers following simple instructions identified by numbers or as if identified by numbers; the allusion is to *painting by numbers*, a painting kit with a canvas on which numbers have been marked to indicate which colour of paint should be applied in which place.

Numidia an ancient kingdom, later a Roman province, situated in North Africa in an area north of the Sahara corresponding roughly to present-day Algeria.

nun a member of a religious community of women, typically one living under vows of poverty, chastity, and obedience. The word comes (in Old English) from ecclesiastical Latin *nonna*, feminine of *nonnus* 'monk', reinforced by Old French.

Nunc Dimittis the Song of Simeon (Luke 2:29–32) used as a canticle in Christian liturgy, especially at compline and evensong. The phrase is Latin, and represents the opening words of the canticle, '(Lord), now you let (your servant) depart'. In extended usage, *nunc dimittis* may now mean departure, dismissal.

nuncio in the Roman Catholic Church, a papal ambassador to a foreign court or government. Recorded from the early 16th century, the word comes from Italian, from Latin *nuntius* 'messenger'.

Nuremberg a city in southern Germany, in Bavaria, which in the 15th and 16th centuries was a leading cultural centre and was the home of Albrecht Dürer and Hans Sachs. After the Second World War the city centre was carefully reconstructed, as its cobbled streets and timbered houses had been reduced to rubble by Allied bombing.

The **Nuremberg laws** in Nazi Germany were laws promulgated in 1935 barring Jews from German citizenship and forbidding intermarriage between Aryans and Jews.

A **Nuremberg rally** was a mass meeting of the German Nazi party, held annually in Nuremberg from 1933 to 1938, notable for their carefully stage-managed effects.

A **Nuremberg trial** was any of a series of trials of former Nazi leaders for alleged war crimes, crimes against peace, and crimes against humanity, presided over by an International Military Tribunal representing the victorious Allied Powers and held in Nuremberg in 1945–6.

nursery rhyme a simple traditional song or poem for children. The term is first recorded in 1816, and probably derives from the title of Ann and Jane Taylor's *Rhymes for the Nursery* of 1806.

nut in Middle English a *nut* was sometimes taken as the type of something small and of little value; the English anchoress and mystic Julian of Norwich (1343–1416), in her *Revelations of Divine Love*, uses the image of a hazelnut in this way, as the type of something insignificant which is still loved by God.

The children's nursery rhyme 'I had a little nut tree' relates that 'the King of Spain's daughter' came to visit the nut-tree's owner; it has been suggested that this is a reference to the visit to Henry VII's court made in 1506 by Juana of Castile, sister of Catherine of Aragon.

The hard shell of a nut also gives rise to expressions such as **a hard nut to crack** for a difficult problem.

Nutcracker man the nickname of a fossil hominid with massive jaws and molar teeth, the maker of the oldest stone tools known, especially the original specimen found near Olduvai Gorge in 1959 by Mary Leakey.

Nutmeg State informal name for Connecticut (see ➤ WOODEN *nutmeg*).

nymph a mythological spirit of nature imagined as a beautiful maiden inhabiting rivers, woods, or other locations. Recorded from late Middle English, the word comes via Old French and Latin from Greek *numphē* 'nymph, bride', and is related to Latin *nubere* 'be the wife of'.

In literary use from the early 17th century, *nymph* may be used for a river or stream.

A **nymphaeum** is a grotto or shrine dedicated to a nymph or nymphs; a building or part of a building built to represent such a shrine.

Nyx in Greek mythology, the female personification of the night, daughter of Chaos.

Oo

O the fifteenth letter of the modern English alphabet and the fourteenth of the ancient Roman one, corresponding to Greek *o*, representing the sixteenth letter of the Phoenician and ancient Semitic alphabet.

O' a prefix in Irish patronymic names such as *O'Neill*; recorded from the mid 18th century, it represents Irish *ó, ua* 'descendant'.

oak allusion is often made to the hardness and durability of the oak, and to the traditional use of oak timber for ships. In traditional rhymes, it may be linked and compared with other trees, as the *ash* and the *thorn*.

Oak-apple Day is the anniversary of Charles II's restoration (29 May), when oak-apples or oak-leaves used to be worn in memory of his hiding in an oak after the battle of Worcester.

the Oaks an annual flat horse race for three-year-old fillies run on Epsom Downs, over the same course as the Derby. It was first run in 1779, and is so called from the estate of the 12th Earl of Derby, owner of the first winner.

oakum loose fibre obtained by untwisting old rope, used especially in caulking wooden ships. **Picking oakum** was a task formerly assigned to convicts and inmates of workhouses.

Recorded from Old English in the form *ācumbe*, literally 'off-combings', the current sense dates from Middle English.

Obadiah (in the Bible) a Hebrew minor prophet; the shortest book of the Bible, bearing his name.

obeah a kind of sorcery practised especially in the Caribbean. Recorded from the mid 18th century, the word comes from Twi, from *bayi* 'sorcery'.

obelisk a stone pillar, typically having a square or rectangular cross section, set up as a monument or landmark, originally in ancient Egypt. Recorded from the mid 16th century, the word comes via Latin from Greek *obeliskos*, diminutive of *obelos* 'pointed pillar'.

obelus in printing, a symbol (†) used as a reference mark in printed matter, or to indicate that a person is deceased; also called *dagger*. *Obelus* is also the name for a mark (– or ÷) used in ancient manuscripts to mark a word or passage as spurious, corrupt, or doubtful.

Recorded from late Middle English, the word comes via Latin from Greek *obelos* 'pointed pillar', also 'critical mark'.

Oberammergau a village in the Bavarian Alps of SW Germany, which is the site of the most famous of the few surviving passion plays, which has been performed by the villagers every tenth year (with few exceptions) from 1634 as a result of a vow made during an epidemic of plague.

Oberon name of the king of the fairies, husband of Titania in Shakespeare's *A Midsummer Night's Dream*; originally *Auberon*, the king of the elves who in the medieval French poem uses his magic powers to help ➤ HUON *of Bordeaux*. The spelling *Oberon* is used in Lord Berners's translation of *Huon de Bordeaux* (*c.*1530). (See also ➤ ALBERICH.)

Obi-Wan Kenobi in the first film of the ➤ STAR *Wars* trilogy, the ➤ JEDI master who finds and trains the young ➤ LUKE *Skywalker*, enabling him to set out on his quest.

oblate a person dedicated to a religious life, but typically having not taken full monastic vows. In earlier times, *oblate* was also used for a child dedicated by their parents to a religious house and placed there to be brought up.

Recorded from the late 17th century, the word comes via French from medieval Latin *oblatus*, past participle (used as a noun) of Latin *offerre* 'to offer'.

obol an ancient Greek coin worth one sixth of a drachma, traditionally the coin placed in the mouth of the dead as a fee for ➤ CHARON to ferry them across the Styx. The word originally meant 'spit' or 'nail', and came to be used for a type of coin as in early times nails were used as money.

Occam's razor the principle (attributed to the English philosopher and Franciscan friar

William of *Occam*, *c*.1285–1349) that in explaining a thing no more assumptions should be made than are necessary. The principle is often invoked to defend reductionism or nominalism.

Occident formal or poetic name for the countries of the West, especially Europe and America. Recorded from late Middle English, the name comes via Old French from Latin *occident-* 'going down, setting' (referring to the sun), from the verb *occidere*.

Occitan the medieval or modern language of Languedoc, including literary Provençal of the 12th–14th centuries.

the occult supernatural, mystical, or magical beliefs, practices, or phenomena. Recorded from the late 15th century (as a verb, meaning 'to conceal'), the word comes from Latin *occultare* 'secrete', and is ultimately based on *celare* 'to hide'.

Oceanus in Greek mythology, the son of Uranus (Heaven) and Gaia (Earth), brother and husband of ➤ TETHYS, the personification of the great river believed to encircle the whole world.

An **Oceanid** is a sea nymph, any of the daughters of Oceanus and Tethys.

Octavian early name (until 27 BC) of Augustus (63 BC–AD 14), first Roman emperor.

octavo a size of book page that results from folding each printed sheet into eight leaves (sixteen pages). The name comes from the Latin phrase *in octavo*, used to designate such a book.

October the tenth month of the year, in the northern hemisphere usually considered the second month of autumn. Recorded from late Old English, the name comes from Latin, from *octo* 'eight', being originally the eighth month of the Roman year.

The **October Revolution** was the Russian Bolshevik revolution in November (October Old Style) 1917, in which the provisional government was overthrown, leading to the establishment of the USSR.

In the US, an **October surprise** is an unexpected but popular political act or speech made just prior to a November election in an attempt to win votes, used especially with reference to an alleged conspiracy in which members of the 1980 Republican campaign team are said to have made an arms deal with Iran to delay the release of US hostages in Iran until after the election.

The **October War** is the Arab name for the ➤ YOM *Kippur War*.

Oddfellow a member of a fraternity organized under this name, typically for social or benevolent purposes. The name 'Odd Fellows' appears to have been originally assumed by local social clubs formed in various parts of England during the 18th century, usually with rites of initiation, passwords, and secret ceremonies, supposed to imitate those of Freemasonry.

ode a lyric poem, typically one in the form of an address to a particular subject, written in varied or irregular metre; a classical poem of a kind originally meant to be sung.

In classical times, odes written by Pindar were generally dignified or exalted in subject and style and were based on the odes sung by the chorus (choral odes) in Greek tragedy. Those written in Latin by Horace provide a simpler, more intimate model.

Recorded from the late 16th century, the word comes via French and late Latin from Greek *ōidē*, Attic form of *aoidē* 'song'.

ODESSA an organization arranging the escape from Germany of high-ranking Nazis at the end of World War II. The name is an acronym from the initials of the German *Organisation der Ehemaligen SS Angehörigen* Organization of former SS members, after *Odessa*, the name of a city and port on the south coast of the Ukraine.

Odin in Scandinavian mythology, the supreme god and creator, god of victory and the dead, married to Freya (Frigga) and usually represented as a one-eyed old man of great wisdom. He is said to have won the ➤ RUNES for humankind by hanging himself for nine nights and days on the world tree ➤ YGGDRASIL (because of which he is god of the hanged); he gave one eye to Mimir, guardian of the well of wisdom, in exchange for poetic inspiration.

odour of sanctity a sweet or balsamic odour reputedly emitted by the bodies of saints at or near death, and regarded as evidence of their sanctity.

Odysseus in Greek mythology, the king of Ithaca, renowned for his cunning and resourcefulness; in Latin, he is known as *Ulysses*.

He is the central figure of the *Odyssey*, a Greek hexameter epic poem traditionally ascribed to Homer, describing the travels of

Odysseus during his ten years of wandering after the sack of Troy. He eventually returned home to Ithaca and killed the suitors who had plagued his wife Penelope during his absence.

Oedipus in Greek mythology, the son of ➤ JOCASTA and of Laius, king of Thebes. Left to die on a mountain by Laius, who had been told by an oracle that he would be killed by his own son, the infant Oedipus was saved by a shepherd. Returning eventually to Thebes, Oedipus solved the riddle of the sphinx, but unwittingly killed his father and married Jocasta; their children were ➤ ANTIGONE, Ismene, ➤ POLYNICES, and Eteocles. On discovering what he had done he put out his own eyes in a fit of madness, while Jocasta hanged herself.

In Freudian theory, an **Oedipus complex** is the complex of emotions aroused in a young child, typically around the age of four, by an unconscious sexual desire for the parent of the opposite sex and wish to exclude the parent of the same sex. (The term was originally applied to boys, the equivalent in girls being called the *Electra complex*.)

oeil-de-boeuf the name of an octagonal vestibule lighted by a small round window (a 'bull's eye') in the palace at Versailles; the expression has thus come to mean a small vestibule or antechamber in a palace, and figuratively, a royal household or court.

Oenone a nymph of Mount Ida and lover of Paris, prince of Troy, who deserted her for Helen.

off-Broadway (of a theatre, play, or performer) located in, appearing in, or associated with an area of New York other than Broadway, typically with reference to experimental and less commercial productions. The term **off-off-Broadway** is now used for productions regarded as even more experimental, avant-garde, and informal.

Offa (d.796), king of Mercia 757–96. He organized the construction of Offa's Dyke. After seizing power in Mercia he expanded his territory to become overlord of most of England south of the Humber.

Offa's dyke is the name given to a series of earthworks marking the traditional boundary between England and Wales, running from near the mouth of the Wye to near the mouth of the Dee, originally constructed by Offa in the second half of the 8th century to mark the boundary established by his wars with the Welsh.

Official Secrets Act in the UK, the legislation that controls access to confidential information important for national security; the Act itself was passed in 1889.

in the offing likely to happen or appear soon; *offing* here means literally 'the more distant part of the sea in view'.

Oflag former term for a German prison camp for captured enemy officers; the name is German, and is a contraction of *Offizier(s)lager* 'officers' camp'.

ogee in architecture, showing in section a double continuous S-shaped curve. The word comes (in late Middle English) from ➤ OGIVE, with which it was then synonymous; the current sense developed in the late 17th century.

ogham an ancient British and Irish alphabet, dating from the 4th century BC and consisting of twenty characters formed by parallel strokes on either side of or across a continuous line. Recorded from the early 18th century, the word comes from Irish *ogam*, connected with *Ogma*, the name of its mythical inventor.

Ogier the Dane in French medieval poetry, a hero (in Danish, *Holger Danske*) who is supposedly the son of the Danish king Gaufray, and who firsts fights against Charlemagne and then becomes one of his followers, noted for his skill in battle.

ogive a pointed or Gothic arch; the term is recorded from late Middle English, and comes from French, of unknown origin (see also ➤ OGEE).

Ogopogo a water monster alleged to live in Okanagan Lake, British Columbia. The name is an invented word, and is said to be from a British music hall song (1924) by C. Clark, although no contemporary copy of this has been traced.

OGPU an organization for investigating and combating counter-revolutionary activities in the former Soviet Union, existing from 1922 (1922–3 as the GPU) to 1934 and replacing the Cheka.

ogre in folklore, a man-eating giant. The word comes from French, and was used by Charles Perrault in 1697; ultimately it derives from Latin *Orcus*, a name for Hades, god of the underworld; of unknown origin. In English, it is found first in an 18th-century translation of the *Arabian Nights*.

oil used in several phrases relating to oil as a smooth and viscous liquid.

Oil and water are taken as a type of two elements, factors, or people that do not agree or blend together.

To **oil someone's palm** is to bribe a person.

To **oil the wheels** is to help something go smoothly.

See also ➤ POUR *oil on troubled waters*.

OK used to express assent, agreement, or acceptance. Recorded from the mid 19th century (originally US), it is probably an abbreviation of *orl korrect*, humorous form of *all correct*, popularized as a slogan during President Martin Van Buren's re-election campaign of 1840 in the US; his nickname *Old Kinderhook* (derived from his birthplace) provided the initials.

Okhrana an organization set up in 1881 in Russia after the assassination of Alexander II to maintain State security and suppress revolutionary activities, replaced after the Revolution of 1917 by the Cheka.

Okie a derogatory term for a migrant agricultural worker from Oklahoma who had been forced to leave a farm during the depression of the 1930s.

St Olaf (*c*.995–1030), king of Norway as Olaf II Haraldsson, reigned 1016–30, canonized for his attempts to spread Christianity in his kingdom. He was forced into exile by a rebellion in 1028 and killed in battle at Stiklestad while attempting to return. He is the patron saint of Norway. Feast day, 29 July.

old in a number of names, or indicating an established and unchanging system.

The **Old Bailey** is the Central Criminal Court in London, formerly standing in an ancient bailey of the London city wall. The present court was built in 1903–6 on the site of Newgate Prison.

An **old boy network** is an informal system of support and friendship through which men are thought to use their positions of influence to help others who went to the same school or university as they did, or who share a similar social background.

Old Church Slavonic is the oldest recorded Slavic language, as used by the apostles Cyril and Methodius and surviving in texts from the 9th–12th centuries. It is related particularly to the Southern Slavic languages.

The **Old Colony** is an informal name for Massachusetts.

The **Old Contemptibles** were the veterans of the British Expeditionary Force sent to France in the First World War (1914), so named because of the German Emperor's alleged exhortation to his soldiers to 'walk over General French's contemptible little army'.

The **Old Dominion** is an informal name for the state of Virginia.

Old English is the language of the Anglo-Saxons (up to about 1150), an inflected language with a Germanic vocabulary, very different from modern English.

Old Faithful is the name of a geyser in Yellowstone National Park, Wyoming, noted for the regularity of its eruptions.

Old Glory is an informal name for the US national flag, otherwise known as the ➤ STARS *and Stripes*. It is attributed to Captain William Driver (1803–86), when saluting a new flag flown on his ship, the *Charles Dogget*, on leaving Salem, Massachusetts for the South Pacific in 1831.

The **old guard** are the original or long-standing members of a group or party, especially ones who are unwilling to accept change or new ideas.

The **Old Hundredth** is a hymn tune which first appeared in the Geneva psalter of 1551 and was later set to Psalm 100 in the 'old' metrical version of the Geneva Psalter (hymn 166 in 'Hymns Ancient and Modern'); the psalm itself.

The **Old Kingdom** is a period of ancient Egyptian history (*c*.2575–2134 BC, 4th–8th dynasty).

Old Labour is the Labour Party before the introduction of the internal reforms initiated by Neil Kinnock (party leader, 1983–1992) and carried through by John Smith (party leader 1992–1994) and his successor Tony Blair (Prime Minister 1997–); the term is now used for that section of the Labour Party which argues that the aims and ideals of *New Labour* represent an abandonment of socialist principles.

The **Old Lady of Threadneedle Street** is the nickname of the Bank of England, which stands in this street. The term dates from the late 18th century, as a caption to James Gillray's cartoon of 22 May 1797, 'Political Ravishment, or The Old Lady of Threadneedle-Street in danger!'

In Christian tradition, the **old leaven** refers to traces of the unregenerate state or prejudices that may be held by religious converts, referred to in 1 Corinthians 5:7.

The **Old Line State** is an informal name for Maryland.

The **old man of the mountains** was a name applied to the founder of the Assassins, who established a base for the sect at a mountain fortress in the region of what is now northern Iran, and his successors.

In the story of Sinbad the Sailor in the *Arabian Nights*, the **old man of the sea** was the sea-god who forced Sinbad to carry him on his shoulders for many days and nights until he was thwarted by being made so drunk that he toppled off.

Old Man River is an informal name for the Mississippi.

An **old master** is a great artist of former times, especially of the 13th–17th century in Europe; the term is first recorded in 1696 in the diary of John Evelyn.

The **old moon** is the moon in its last quarter, before the new moon.

Old Mother Hubbard is a nursery-rhyme character who found her cupboard bare when she went to fetch her dog a bone; the story is given in Sarah Catherine Martin's *The Comic Adventures of Old Mother Hubbard* (1805), based on a traditional rhyme. The character of *Mother Hubbard* is well-known in popular mythology since at least the late 16th century. Early nursery-rhyme illustrations often depicted *Mother Hubbard* in a loose-fitting cloak or dress, and her name was thus applied to this kind of garment. In allusive use, however, reference is likely to be made to the complete lack of resources typified by her empty cupboard, whereby 'the poor dog had none'.

Old Nick is an informal name for the Devil, recorded from the mid 17th century. The name is unexplained, although it was once suggested to refer to the forename of *Niccolò* Macchiavelli (see ➤ MACCHIAVELLIAN). It has also been suggested that *Nick* may be a shortened form of *Iniquity*, another term for the Vice in the early modern English morality play.

The **Old North State** is an informal name for North Carolina.

The **Old Pretender** was James Francis Edward Stuart (1688–1766), son of James II, whose birth as a Catholic male heir was a contributory cause to his father's being driven into exile. Referred to initially in anti-Jacobite circles as the *pretended Prince of Wales*, supposedly introduced into the Queen's bed in a ➤ WARMING *pan*, he then became known as **the Pretender**, a usage which Bishop Burnet attributes to James's half-sister Queen Anne. The name *Old Pretender* developed later to distinguish James from his son, Charles Edward Stuart (1720–80), the *Young Pretender*.

Old Sarum is a hill in southern England north of Salisbury, the site of an ancient Iron Age settlement and hill fort, and later of a Norman castle and town. It fell into decline after the new cathedral and town of Salisbury were established in 1220, and the site was deserted. As a famous ➤ ROTTEN *borough*, it returned two MPs until 1832.

An **old school tie** is a necktie with a characteristic pattern worn by the former pupils of a particular school, especially a public school; in transferred used, the behaviour and attitudes usually associated with the wearing of such a tie, especially conservatism and group loyalty.

An **old Spanish custom** is an irregular practice in a company aimed at decreasing working hours or increasing financial rewards or perquisites. Recorded from the 1930s, the origin of the term has not been explained.

Old Style is the method of calculating dates using the ➤ JULIAN *calendar*, which in England and Wales was superseded by the use of the Gregorian calendar in 1752.

The **Old Testament** is the first part of the Christian Bible, comprising thirty-nine books and corresponding approximately to the Hebrew Bible. Most of the books were written in Hebrew, some in Aramaic, between about 1200 and 100 BC. They comprise the chief texts of the law, history, prophecy, and wisdom literature of the ancient people of Israel.

An **old wives' tale** is a widely held traditional belief that is now thought to be unscientific or incorrect. The phrase (and its earlier variant *old wives' fable*) is recorded from the 16th century, with the earliest example being from Tyndale's translation of the Bible (1526), in 1 Timothy 4:7.

The **Old World** is Europe, Asia, and Africa, regarded collectively as the part of the world known before the discovery of the Americas; the term is recorded from the late 16th century, in the poetry of John Donne.

Oldowan of, relating to, or denoting an early Lower Palaeolithic culture of Africa, dated to about 2.0–1.5 million years ago. It is characterized by primitive stone tools that are associated chiefly with *Homo habilis*. The name comes (in the 1930s) from *Oldoway*, alteration of ➤ OLDUVAI *Gorge*.

oldspeak normal English usage as opposed to technical or propagandist language, from George Orwell's *Nineteen Eighty-Four* (see ➤ NEWSPEAK).

Olduvai Gorge a gorge in northern Tanzania, in which the exposed strata contain numerous fossils (especially hominids) spanning the full range of the Pleistocene period.

Olivant name of Roland's horn, which was made of ivory (*oliphant*, or elephant ivory), and with which he finally summoned Charlemagne's army to Roncesvalles.

olive branch the branch of an olive tree, traditionally regarded as a symbol of peace (in allusion to the story of Noah in Genesis 8:1, in which a dove returns with an olive branch after the Flood).

Oliver the companion of Roland in the *Chanson de Roland* and one of the paladins, who at Roncesvalles finally persuades his friend to summon Charlemagne to their aid by blowing the ivory horn ➤ OLIVANT.

Mount of Olives the highest point in the range of hills to the east of Jerusalem, a holy place for both Judaism and Christianity and frequently mentioned in the Bible. It was said to have been the site of Christ's ascension, and the Garden of Gethsemane is located nearby. Its slopes have been a sacred Jewish burial ground for centuries. It is also known as *Olivet*.

Olympia a plain in Greece, in the western Peloponnese. In ancient Greece it was the site of the chief sanctuary of the god Zeus, the place where the original Olympic Games were held. An **Olympiad** was a period of four years between Olympic Games, used by the ancient Greeks in dating events.

Olympic Games an ancient Greek festival with athletic, literary, and musical competitions held at Olympia every four years, traditionally from 776 BC until abolished by the Roman emperor Theodosius I in AD 393.

In modern times, the phrase designates a sports festival held every four years in different venues, instigated by the Frenchman Baron de Coubertin (1863–1937) in 1896. Athletes representing nearly 150 countries now compete for gold, silver, and bronze medals in more than twenty sports.

An **Olympic village** is the place where the competitors in the modern Olympic games are housed for the duration of the event.

Olympus in Greek mythology, the home of the twelve greater gods and the court of Zeus, identified in later antiquity with Mount Olympus in Greece.

om in Hinduism and Tibetan Buddhism, a mystic syllable, considered the most sacred mantra. It appears at the beginning and end of most Sanskrit recitations, prayers, and texts. The word comes from Sanskrit, and is sometimes regarded as three sounds, *a-u-m*, symbolic of the three major Hindu deities.

Omar I (*c*.581–644), Muslim caliph 634–44. Converted to Islam in 617, after becoming caliph he conquered Syria, Palestine, and Egypt, in the course of which (*c*.641) the library at Alexandria was burnt.

Omdurman a city in central Sudan, on the Nile opposite Khartoum, which in 1885, following the victory of the Mahdi (Muhammad Ahmad) and his forces over the British, was made the capital of the Mahdist state of Sudan. In 1898 it was recaptured by the British after the Battle of Omdurman, Kitchener's decisive victory over the Mahdi's successor, which marked the end of the uprising.

omega the last letter of the Greek alphabet (Ω, ω), transliterated as 'o' or 'ō'; figuratively, the last of a series, the final development. (See also ➤ ALPHA *and omega*.)

omen an event regarded as a portent of good or evil. Recorded from the late 16th century, the word comes from Latin, but its ultimate origin is unknown.

Omer in Judaism, a sheaf of corn or omer of grain presented as an offering on the second day of Passover; the period of 49 days between this day and Pentecost. The name comes from Hebrew '*ōmer*, an ancient Hebrew dry measure, the tenth part of an ephah.

omertà (as practised by the Mafia) a code of silence about criminal activity and a refusal to give evidence to the police. Recorded from the late 19th century, the word is Italian, and is either a regional variation of Italian *umiltà* 'humility' (with reference to the Mafia code which enjoins submission of the group to the leader as well as silence on all Mafia concerns), or Old Spanish *hombredad* 'manliness'.

omnium gatherum a collection of miscellaneous people or things. Recorded from the early 16th century, the phrase is mock Latin, from Latin *omnium* 'of all' and *gather* + the Latin suffix *-um*.

omphalos a conical stone (especially that at Delphi) representing the navel of the earth in ancient Greek mythology.

on-message in accordance with a planned or intended message; (of the actions or statements of a political party member) in accordance with official party policy; an expression recorded from the early 1990s.

Onan in the Bible, a son of Judah (Genesis 38:9), who was ordered by his father to beget children with the wife of his brother who had died childless. He did not wish to beget children who would not belong to him, so he did not complete copulation but 'let his seed fall on the ground', for which God punished him with death. Although Onan's sin is taken by modern biblical scholars to have been his failure to fulfil the obligation of marrying his brother's widow, this passage has frequently been taken in the Christian (as in the Jewish) tradition to show divine condemnation of autoeroticism.

once bitten, twice shy a bad experience makes one wary of the same thing happening again. Proverbial, late 19th century in this form.

One Nation a nation not divided by social inequality; in Britain in the 1990s, especially regarded as the objective of a branch of or movement within the Conservative Party, seen as originating in the paternalistic form of Toryism advocated by Benjamin Disraeli.

In 1950 a group of Conservative MPs, then in opposition, published under the title *One Nation* a pamphlet asserting their view of the necessity of greater commitment by their party to the social services; these ideas had great influence when the party returned to government in the following year.

In the 1990s, *One Nation* returned to prominence in the debate between the right and left wings of the Conservative Party on the effect of the Thatcherite policies of the 1980s.

the one that got away traditional angler's description of a large fish that just eluded capture, from the comment 'you should have seen the one that got away.'

onion dome a dome which bulges in the middle and rises to a point, used especially in Russian church architecture.

onomatopoeia the formation of a word from a sound associated with what is named (e.g. *cuckoo*, *sizzle*). Recorded from the late 16th century, the term comes from Greek *onomatopoiia* 'word-making'.

ontology the branch of metaphysics dealing with the nature of being. Recorded from the early 18th century, the word comes from modern Latin ontologia, from Greek *ōn*, *ont-* 'being', + the suffix *-logy* denoting a subject of study or interest.

In philosophy, the **ontological argument** is the argument that God, being defined as most great or perfect, must exist, since a God who exists is greater than a God who does not.

onyx a semi-precious variety of agate with different colours in layers. In the Bible it is one of the precious jewels said in Exodus 28:20 to have been set in the high priest's breastplate, and in Revelation 21:20 it is said to be one of the twelve jewels set in the wall of the New Jerusalem.

opal a gemstone which is typically semi-transparent and showing many small points of shifting colour against a pale or dark ground; it is often referred to allusively to evoke the idea of changing colours.

The belief that opals are unlucky is recorded from the 19th century, and may originate with Walter Scott's novel *Anne of Geierstein* (1829), in which an opal brings ill fortune on its owner.

open sesame in the tale of ➤ ALI *Baba* and the Forty Thieves, the magic words by which the door of the robbers' cave was made to fly open; the phrase is thus used for a means of securing access to what would normally be inaccessible.

Ophir (in the Bible) an unidentified region, perhaps in SE Arabia, famous for its fine gold and precious stones.

opium a reddish-brown heavy-scented addictive drug prepared from the juice of the opium poppy and used illicitly as a narcotic; opium addiction is a strong theme in 19th century literature. In 1822 Thomas De Quincey had published his autobiographical *Confessions of an Opium Eater*. From the 17th century, the word has also been in figurative use.

Recorded from late Middle English, the word comes via Latin from Greek *opion* 'poppy juice', from *opos* 'juice', from an Indo-European root meaning 'water'.

Opium of the people is something regarded as inducing a false and unrealistic sense of contentment among people. The term originated as a translation of German *Opium des Volks*, used by Karl Marx.

The **Opium Wars** were two wars involving China regarding the question of commercial rights. That between Britain and China (1839–42) followed China's attempt to prohibit the illegal importation of opium from British India into China. The second, involving Britain and France against China (1856–60), followed Chinese restrictions on foreign trade. Defeat of the Chinese resulted in the ceding of Hong Kong to Britain and the opening of five 'treaty ports' to traders.

opportunity knocks a chance of success occurs; from the proverb *opportunity never knocks twice at any man's door*, meaning that a chance once offered must be taken at the time.

the Opposition in the UK, the principal parliamentary party opposed to that in office. The term 'His Majesty's Opposition' was first used in a debate by the radical politician John Cam Hobhouse (1786–1869), later Lord Broughton, 10 April 1826.

Ops in Roman mythology, goddess of abundance and harvest, associated with Saturn. She is referred to in *Paradise Lost* as Saturn's consort, and in Keats's *Hyperion* as one of the fallen Titans.

opus Alexandrinum a pavement mosaic work widely used in Byzantium in the 9th century and later in Italy, consisting of coloured stone, glass, and semiprecious stones arranged in intricate geometric patterns.

opus anglicanum the fine pictorial embroidery produced in England in the Middle Ages, especially between c.1100 and c.1350, characterized by the depiction of lively human and animal figures, and the use of gold cloth, and used especially for ecclesiastical vestments.

opus Dei in the Christian Church, liturgical worship regarded as man's primary duty to God. The Latin phrase, meaning literally 'the work of God', is attributed to St Benedict but is attested from the 5th century in the sense of Divine Office or worship.

or gold or yellow, as a heraldic tincture. Recorded from the early 16th century, the word comes via French from Latin *aurum* 'gold'. It is one of the two metals used in heraldry, the other being ➤ ARGENT.

oracle a priest or priestess acting as a medium through whom advice or prophecy was sought from the gods in classical antiquity, or a place at which such advice or prophecy was sought; in extended use, the term may be used for a person or thing regarded as an infallible authority or guide on something. *Oracle* is also used to denote the response or message provided by such a source, especially one that is ambiguous or obscure.

Recorded from late Middle English, the word comes via Old French from Latin *oraculum*, from *orare* 'speak'.

Oracle bones are the bones of a ritually-killed animal, carved with script and used in ancient China for divination.

Oradour a French village west of Limoges, in full *Oradour-sur-Glane*, which in June 1944 was surrounded by the SS division *Das Reich*. All but a few of the inhabitants were massacred, and the village was subsequently burnt. Oradour has never been rebuilt, and its ruins still stand.

Oral Law the part of Jewish religious law believed to have been passed down by oral tradition before being collected in the Mishnah.

House of Orange the Dutch royal house, originally a princely dynasty of the principality centred on the town of Orange in France in the 16th century.

Members of the family held the position of stadtholder or magistrate from the mid 16th until the late 18th century. In 1689 William of Orange became King William III of Great Britain and Ireland and the son of the last stadtholder became King William I of the United Netherlands in 1815.

orange blossom flowers from an orange tree, traditionally worn by the bride at a wedding; *orange blossom* may thus be taken as a symbol of marriage. The custom appears to have been introduced to Britain in the 1820s from France, where it was said to be customary for a bride to wear a crown of orange buds and blossoms.

Orange Order a Protestant political society in Ireland, especially in Northern Ireland; members are known as **Orangemen**. The Orange Order was formed in 1795 (as the Association of Orangemen) for the defence of Protestantism and maintenance of Protestant ascendancy in Ireland, and was probably named from the wearing of orange badges as a symbol of adherence to William III (William of Orange), who defeated the Catholic James II at the Battle of the Boyne in 1690.

oratorio a large-scale, usually narrative musical work for orchestra and voices, typically on a sacred theme, performed without costume, scenery, or action. The form arose in the early 17th century, from the services of the ➤ ORATORY.

Oratory in the Roman Catholic Church, a religious society of secular priests founded in Rome in 1564 to provide plain preaching and popular services and established in various countries.

The Oratory of St Philip Neri was constituted at Rome in 1564 and recognized by the Pope in 1575. It was so named from the small chapel or oratory built over one of the aisles of the Church of St Jerome, in which St Philip Neri (1515–95) and his followers, 'Fathers of the Oratory', carried on their work for six years before 1564. In 1577 the congregation moved to the new church (*Chiesa Nuova*) of the Valicella, in which were conducted the musical services thence called, in Italian, ➤ ORATORIO.

Oratory meaning 'a small chapel, especially for private worship', is recorded from Middle English, and comes ultimately from Latin *orare* 'pray, speak'.

orb a golden globe surmounted by a cross, forming part of the regalia of a monarch. Recorded from late Middle English in the sense 'circle', the word comes from Latin *orbis* 'ring'.

orc in fantasy literature and games, a member of an imaginary race of human-like creatures, characterized as ugly, warlike, and malevolent. The word (denoting an ogre) is recorded from the late 16th century, perhaps from Latin *orcus* 'hell' or Italian *orco* 'demon, monster', influenced by obsolete *orc* 'ferocious sea creature' and by Old English *orcneas* 'monsters'. The current sense is due to the use of the word in Tolkien's fantasy adventures. See also ➤ OGRE.

Orcus in Roman mythology, a name (of unknown origin) for Dis, the god of the Underworld, or the Underworld itself; ultimately origin of the word ➤ OGRE and perhaps ➤ ORC.

ordeal an ancient test of guilt or innocence, especially among Germanic peoples, by subjection of the accused to severe pain, survival of which was taken as divine proof of innocence. In Anglo-Saxon and Norman England, until its abolition in 1215, it took four forms: fire ordeal, hot water ordeal, cold water ordeal, and trial by combat; later applied to analogous modes of determining innocence or guilt found in other societies.

Recorded in Old English and of Germanic origin, the word is related to German *urteilen* 'give judgement', from a base meaning 'share out'. The word is not found in Middle English (except once in Chaucer's *Troilus*); the modern use begins in late 16th-century accounts of these traditional tests.

Order! a call for silence or the observance of the prescribed procedures by someone in charge of a meeting or legislative assembly, such as the Speaker of the House of Commons.

Order Paper in the United Kingdom and Canada, a paper on which the day's business for a legislative assembly is entered; in the House of Commons, members traditionally wave their order papers to signify support for a speaker.

ordinal number a number defining a thing's position in a series, such as 'first', 'second', or 'third'. Ordinal numbers are used as adjectives, nouns, and pronouns.

ordinary in heraldry, any of the simplest principal charges used in coats of arms, usually having a basic geometrical shape (especially chief, pale, bend, fess, bar, chevron, cross, saltire).

ordnance mounted guns, cannon; from the late 15th century, the branch of government service dealing especially with military stores and materials, under the control of the **Master of the Ordnance**. (The word was originally a variant of *ordinance*, and comes via Old French and medieval Latin from Latin *ordinare* 'put in order'.)

In the UK, the **Ordnance Survey** is an official survey organization, originally under the direction of the Master of the Ordnance, preparing large-scale detailed maps of the whole country; it originated in a topographic survey (1784) of the Trigonometric Society.

oread in Greek and Roman mythology, a nymph believed to inhabit high mountains. The name comes ultimately from Greek *oros* 'mountain'.

Oregon Trail a route across the central US, from the Missouri to Oregon, some 3,000 km

(2,000 miles) in length. It was used chiefly in the 1840s by settlers moving west.

Orestes the son of ➤ AGAMEMNON and ➤ CLYTEMNESTRA, and brother of ➤ ELECTRA. Having grown to manhood in exile, he returned to Argos and killed his mother and her lover Aegisthus to avenge the murder of Agamemnon; pursued by the avenging Furies for the crime of matricide he fled to the shrine of Apollo at Delphi, where ultimately he was pardoned by Athena. The story is the subject of Aeschylus's trilogy, the *Oresteia*.

organ an organ is the emblem of ➤ St CECILIA, patron saint of music.

orgies secret rites used in the worship of Bacchus, Dionysus, and other Greek and Roman deities, celebrated with dancing, drunkenness, and singing. Recorded from the early 16th century, the word comes via French and Latin from Greek *orgia* 'secret rites or revels'.

Oriana a name frequently applied by poets to Elizabeth I; in the medieval Spanish or Portuguese romance *Amadis of Gaul*, the princess of Britain with whom the hero Amadis is in love is named *Oriana*.

orichalc a yellow metal prized in ancient times, probably a form of brass or a similar alloy, although some writers treated it as a fabulous metal. The name comes (in late Middle English, via Latin) from Greek *oreikhalkon*, literally 'mountain copper'.

oriel a large polygonal recess in a building, typically built out from an upper storey and supported from the ground or on corbels; a window in such a structure.

the Orient a poetic and literary name for the countries of the East, especially east Asia. The word comes (in late Middle English, via Old French) from Latin *orient-* 'rising or east', from *oriri* 'to rise'.

Orient Express a train which ran between Paris and Istanbul and other Balkan cities, via Vienna, from 1883 to 1977; the name is also used for a successor to this train, following part of the original route.

Oriflamme the sacred scarlet silk banner of St Denis given to early French kings on setting out for war by the abbot of St Denis; in extend use, a principle or ideal that serves as a rallying point in a struggle. Recorded from late Middle English, the word comes via Old French from Latin *aurum* 'gold' + *flamma* 'flame'.

Origen (*c.*185–*c.*254), Christian scholar and theologian, probably born in Alexandria. His most famous work was the *Hexapla*, an edition of the Old Testament with six or more parallel versions. His Neoplatonist theology, which taught the pre-existence of souls, and that all rational beings, including the fallen angels, have free will and will ultimately be saved through God's love, was ultimately rejected by Church orthodoxy.

original sin the tendency to evil supposedly innate in all human beings, held to be inherited from Adam in consequence of the Fall. The concept of original sin was established by the writings of St Augustine and the view of some early theologians that the human will is capable of good without the help of divine grace was branded a heresy.

Orion in Greek mythology, a giant and hunter who was changed into a constellation at his death. His association with the constellation is very early, being mentioned in Homer.

The constellation itself, said to represent a hunter holding a club and shield, lies on the celestial equator and contains many bright stars, including a line of three that form **Orion's Belt**. **Orion's hound** is another name for the ➤ DOG *Star*.

Orkhon any of a number of 8th-century stone monuments discovered in northern Mongolia in 1889; the extinct Turkic language in which inscriptions on these monuments are written.

Orlando the Italian form of ➤ ROLAND, a hero of the romances of Charlemagne. *Orlando Furioso* is a poem by Ariosto, published in its complete form in 1532, designed to exalt the house of Este and its legendary ancestor Rogero (Ruggiero). It continues the story of the love of Orlando (➤ ROLAND in the Charlemagne romances) for Angelica, princess of Cathay, begun in *Orlando Innamorato*, a poem by Boiardo, published in 1487.

Orleanist a person supporting the claim to the French throne of the descendants of the Duke of *Orleans* (1640–1701), younger brother of Louis XIV, especially Louis Philippe (1830–48), known as the ➤ CITIZEN *King*.

Orleans a city in central France on the Loire which in 1429 was the scene of Joan of Arc's first victory over the English during the Hundred Years War; *Orleans* was also one of the main royal duchies of medieval France, originally created in 1344 for the younger son of

Philip VI of France, and associated particularly with the ➤ ORLEANIST dynasty descended from Louis XIV's younger brother.

Ormazd another name for ➤ AHURA *Mazda*.

Orosius (fl. early 5th century), a priest of Tarragona in Spain, disciple of St Augustine and friend of St Jerome, author of the *Historia Adversos Paganos*, a universal history and geography which was translated by the circle of King Alfred in the 890s.

Orpheus in Greek mythology, a poet who could entrance wild beasts with the beauty of his singing and lyre playing. He went to the underworld after the death of his wife Eurydice and secured her release from the dead, but lost her because he failed to obey the condition that he must not look back at her until they had reached the world of the living. It was said that when he was killed by being torn to pieces by maenads, his severed head floated down the river Hebrus and reached the island of Lesbos, which became the home of lyric poetry.

   Orphism was a mystic religion of ancient Greece, originating in the 7th or 6th century BC and based on poems (now lost) attributed to Orpheus, emphasizing the mixture of good and evil in human nature and the necessity for individuals to rid themselves of the evil part of their nature by ritual and moral purification throughout a series of reincarnations.

orphrey an ornamental stripe or border, especially one on an ecclesiastical vestment such as a chasuble. Recorded from Middle English, the word comes via Old French from a medieval Latin alteration of *auriphrygium*, from Latin *aurum* 'gold' + *Phrygius* 'Phrygian' (also used in the sense 'embroidered').

orrery a clockwork model of the solar system, or of just the sun, earth, and moon. It is named after Charles Boyle (1676–1731), fourth Earl of *Orrery*, for whom a copy of the machine invented by George Graham *c*.1700 was made by the instrument-maker John Rowley.

Orthodox Church a Christian Church or federation of Churches originating in the Greek-speaking Church of the Byzantine Empire, not accepting the authority of the Pope of Rome, and using elaborate and archaic forms of service.

   The chief Orthodox Churches (often known collectively as the **Eastern Orthodox Church**) include the national Churches of Greece, Russia, Bulgaria, Romania, and Serbia. The term is also used by other ancient Churches, mainly of African or Asian origin, e.g. the Coptic, Syrian, and Ethiopian Churches.

Orthodox Judaism a major branch within Judaism which teaches strict adherence to rabbinical interpretation of Jewish law and its traditional observances. There are more than 600 rules governing religious and everyday life. Orthodox Jews maintain the separation of the sexes in synagogue worship.

Orwellian characteristic or reminiscent of the world of *Nineteen Eighty-four* (1949), a dystopian account of a future state in which every aspect of life is controlled by Big Brother, by the British novelist George Orwell (1903–50).

Oscan an extinct Italic language of southern Italy, related to Umbrian and surviving in inscriptions mainly of the 4th to 1st centuries BC.

Oscar the nickname (a trademark in the US) for a gold statuette given as an Academy award. One of the several speculative stories of its origin claims that the statuette reminded Margaret Herrick, an executive director of the Academy of Motion Picture Arts and Sciences, of her uncle Oscar.

Osiris in Egyptian mythology, a god originally connected with fertility, husband of Isis and father of Horus. He is known chiefly through the story of his death at the hands of his brother Seth and his subsequent restoration to a new life as ruler of the afterlife. Under Ptolemy I his cult was combined with that of Apis to produce the cult of Serapis.

Ossa a mountain in Thessaly, NE Greece, south of Mount Olympus. In Greek mythology the giants were said to have piled Mount Olympus and Mount Ossa on to Mount Pelion in an attempt to reach heaven and destroy the gods.

Ossi in Germany, an informal (often derogatory) term for a citizen of the former German Democratic Republic. The name is probably an abbreviation of *Ostdeutsche* 'East German'.

Ossian a legendary Irish warrior and bard, whose name became well known in 1760–3 when the Scottish poet James Macpherson (1736–96) published his own verse as an alleged translation of 3rd-century Gaelic tales. His Irish name is *Oisin*.

Ossining Correctional Facility official name for the American prison of ➤ SING Sing.

ossuary a container or room into which the bones of dead people are placed. Recorded from the mid 17th century, the word comes from late Latin *ossuarium*, formed irregularly from Latin *os* 'bone'.

Ostia an ancient city and harbour which was situated on the western coast of Italy at the mouth of the River Tiber. It was the first colony founded by ancient Rome and was a major port and commercial centre.

ostracize in ancient Greece, banish (an unpopular or too powerful citizen) from a city for five or ten years by popular vote. The word comes ultimately from Greek *ostrakon* 'shell or potsherd', on which names were written in such votes.

ostrich it was once popularly believed that ostriches bury their heads in the sand if pursued, through incapacity to distinguish between seeing and being seen, and this supposed habit is often referred to allusively. *Ostriches* are also proverbial for their indiscriminate voracity and liking for hard substances (which are swallowed to assist the gizzard in its functions).

Ostrogoth a member of the eastern branch of the Goths, who conquered Italy in the 5th–6th centuries AD.

Oswald male forename, name of two saints.
  St Oswald (d. 642), was king of Northumbria and martyr, killed in battle against the pagan king Penda of Mercia; his body was mutilated as a sacrifice to Odin, and his relics were subsequently dispersed. His head was buried at Lindisfarne, and was taken with the body of ➤ CUTHBERT when the monks evacuated the island in 875.
  Oswald was venerated as a warrior king who combined traditional Anglo Saxon heroism with Christian fortitude and sacrifice; his feast day was celebrated from the late 7th century. He is a patron saint of soldiers, and his emblems are a head and a raven. His feast day is 5 August.
  St Oswald of York (d. 992), was an English prelate and Benedictine monk. As Archbishop of York, he founded several monasteries and, with St Dunstan, revived the Church and learning in 10th-century England. His feast day is 28 February.

Othello the 'Moor of Venice', central character of Shakespeare's tragedy (1602–4), shown as a great man and successful soldier who is driven by the machinations of ➤ IAGO to believe that his young wife Desdemona has been unfaithful to him; he kills her, and attempts to have her supposed lover murdered. *Othello* may be alluded to as a type of morbid jealousy.

otter *otters* are the emblem of ➤ St CUTHBERT.

Ottoman of or relating to the Turkish dynasty of *Osman* (*Othman*) I (1259–1326), Turkish conqueror. He reigned as sultan of the Seljuk Turks from 1288, conquering NW Asia Minor.
  The **Ottoman Empire** was the Turkish empire, established in northern Anatolia by Osman I at the end of the 13th century and expanded by his successors to include all of Asia Minor and much of SE Europe. After setbacks caused by the invasion of the Mongol ruler Tamerlane in 1402, Constantinople was captured in 1453 and the empire reached its zenith under Suleiman in the mid 16th century. It had greatly declined by the 19th century and collapsed after the First World War; in its declining years it was nicknamed the ➤ SICK *Man of Europe*.

oubliette a secret dungeon with access only through a trapdoor in its ceiling. Recorded from the late 18th century, the word comes from French, from *oublier* 'forget'.

Battle of Oudenarde a battle which took place in 1708 during the War of the Spanish Succession, near the town of Oudenarde in eastern Flanders, Belgium. A force of allied British and Austrian troops under the Duke of Marlborough and the Austrian general Prince Eugene of Savoy defeated the French.

Ouija board a board with letters, numbers, and other signs around its edge, to which a planchette, movable pointer, or upturned glass points supposedly in answer to questions from people at a seance. The word comes (in the late 19th century) from French *oui* 'yes' + German *ja* 'yes'.

ounce a unit of weight of one sixteenth of a pound avoirdupois (approximately 28 grams); a unit of one twelfth of a pound troy or apothecaries' measure, equal to 480 grains (approximately 31 grams). Recorded from Middle English, the word comes via Old French from Latin *uncia* 'twelfth part (of a pound or foot)', also the base of ➤ INCH.

out-Herod Herod outdo Herod in cruelty, evil, or extravagance. The reference is to the figure of Herod in the traditional mystery play, represented as a blustering tyrant, and the phrase is first used in Shakespeare's *Hamlet* in the scene in which Hamlet speaks to the Players and warns them against this kind of acting.

Outremer a name applied to the medieval French crusader states, including Armenia, Antioch, Tripoli, and Jerusalem, from French *outre* 'beyond' + *mer* 'sea'.

the Oval the cricket ground at Kennington in London which is the headquarters of Surrey Cricket Club. In extended use, *oval* is thus used for an oval sports field, and (in Australia) a ground for Australian Rules football.

Oval Office the office of the US President in the west wing of the White House; in extended use, the Presidency.

over-egg the pudding used to suggest that one has gone too far in embellishing, exaggerating, or doing something (excessive quantities of egg in a pudding could either make it too rich or cause it not to set correctly).

Overlord the codename (in full, **Operation Overlord**) for the allied invasion of German-occupied Normandy in June 1944 (➤ D-*Day*).

overplay one's hand (in a card game) play or bet on one's hand with a mistaken optimism; figuratively, spoil one's chance of success through excessive confidence in one's position.

Ovid (43 BC–*c.*17 AD), Roman poet. He is particularly known for his elegiac love poems (such as the *Amores* and the *Ars Amatoria*) and for the *Metamorphoses*, a hexametric epic which retells Greek and Roman myths.

owl the *owl* is taken as a symbol of wisdom (and was the emblem of ➤ ATHENE), but if a person is described as looking **owlish** it may imply that their solemn appearance is not matched by an inward intelligence or alertness. See also ➤ STUFFED *owl*.

Till Owlglass the English name for ➤ *Till* EULENSPIEGEL.

score an own goal do something which has the unintended effect of harming one's own interests; an *own goal* is a goal scored by mistake against the scorer's own side.

ox the *ox* is proverbially a type of strength and fortitude, and of stupidity.

The **black ox** means misfortune, adversity, old age (originally in the traditional saying, **the black ox has trod on his foot**), recorded from the 16th century.

An **ox-bone** is the emblem of ➤ St ALPHEGE, who was pelted to death with them by the Danes.

Ox-eyed means having large dark protuberant eyes like those of an ox; in references to classical literature, a particular epithet of ➤ JUNO.

Oxbridge Oxford and Cambridge universities regarded together; the expression is first recorded in Thackeray's novel *Pendennis* (1849).

Oxford a city in central England on the River Thames; site of **Oxford University**, the oldest English university, comprising a federation of thirty-nine colleges, the first of which, University College, was formally founded in 1249. The university was established at Oxford soon after 1167, perhaps as a result of a migration of students from Paris. The first women's college, Lady Margaret Hall, was founded in 1878.

Oxford English is a name for spoken English marked by affected utterance, popularly supposed to be characteristic of members of Oxford University.

The **Oxford English Dictionary** is the largest dictionary of the English language, prepared in Oxford and originally issued in instalments (originally as the *New English Dictionary*) between 1884 and 1928. A second edition was published in 1989, and a third edition is being prepared.

The **Oxford Group** was a Christian movement popularized in Oxford in the late 1920s, advocating discussion of personal problems by groups. It was later known as ➤ MORAL REARMAMENT.

The **Oxford Movement** was a Christian movement started in Oxford in 1833, seeking to restore traditional Catholic teachings and ceremonial within the Church of England. Its leaders were John Keble, Edward Pusey, and (until he became a Roman Catholic) John Henry Newman. It formed the basis of the present Anglo-Catholic (or High Church) tradition.

Oxus ancient name for the Amu Darya river.

oxymoron a figure of speech in which apparently contradictory terms appear in conjunction (e.g. *faith unfaithful kept him falsely* *true*). Recorded from the mid 17th century, the word comes from Greek *oxumōron*, neuter (used as a noun) of *oxumōros* 'pointedly foolish', from *oxus* 'sharp' + *mōros* 'foolish'.

oyster taken proverbially as the type of someone who is reserved and uncommunicative. (See also ➤ *the* WORLD *is one's oyster*.)

Oz the name of the fictional city and land in the children's fantasy *The Wonderful Wizard of Oz* by the US writer L. Frank Baum (1856–1919), widely popularized by the 1939 film *The Wizard of Oz*; in extended usage, any place thought to resemble Baum's city, especially any fantastic, ideal, or imaginary domain. (See also ➤ WIZARD *of Oz*.)

Ozymandias a corruption (*Osymandias*) of the prenomen of Ramses II of Egypt (*c*.1304–*c*.1237 BC), of whom a colossal 57-foot statue, now surviving only in fragments, once stood at Thebes. The name became widely known from Shelley's sonnet of 1817 entitled *Ozymandias*, in which the poet refers to the original inscription, 'My name is Ozymandias, king of kings: Look on my works, ye Mighty, and despair!'

Pp

P the sixteenth letter of the modern English alphabet and the fifteenth of the ancient Roman one, corresponding to Greek *pi*, Phoenician and Semitic *pe*.

paddle one's own canoe be independent and self-sufficient; figurative sense recorded from the early 19th century.

Paddy an informal and chiefly offensive name for an Irishman; the name is an Irish pet-form of *Padraig* or *Patrick*, and is recorded in this usage from the late 18th century.

paean a song of praise or thanksgiving. Recorded from the late 16th century, the word comes via Latin from Greek *paian* 'hymn of thanksgiving to Apollo' (evoked by the name *Paian*, originally the Homeric name for the physician of the gods).

pagan a person holding religious beliefs other than those of the main world religions. The word comes (in late Middle English) from Latin *paganus* 'villager, rustic' from *pagus* 'country district'. Latin *paganus* also meant 'civilian', becoming in Christian Latin 'heathen' (i.e. one not enrolled in the army of Christ).

Page Three a British trademark term for a feature which formerly appeared daily on page three of the *Sun* newspaper and included a picture of a topless young woman.

pagoda a Hindu or Buddhist temple or sacred building, typically a many-tiered tower, in India and the Far East. Recorded from the late 16th century, the word comes from Portuguese *pagode*, perhaps based on Persian *butkada* 'temple of idols', influenced by Prakrit *bhagodī* 'divine'.
   A **pagoda-tree** was a mythical tree humorously supposed to produce *pagodas*, in this sense gold or silver coins formerly current in southern India; the expression **shake the pagoda-tree** meant to make a fortune in India under the East India Company.

Pahlavi an Aramaic-based writing system used in Persia from the 2nd century BC to the advent of Islam in the 7th century AD. It was also used for the recording of ancient Avestan sacred texts.

no pain, no gain suffering is necessary in order to achieve something. There has been a proverbial association between *pain* and *gain* since at least the late 16th century, but this form probably originated as the slogan of fitness classes in the late 20th century.

like watching paint dry (of an activity or experience) extremely boring.

paint the town red enjoy oneself flamboyantly; an informal expression recorded first in the US in the mid 19th century.

paladin any of the twelve peers of Charlemagne's court, of whom the *Count Palatine* was the chief; later, a knight renowned for heroism and chivalry. The word comes through Italian from Latin *palatinus* '(officer) of the palace'.

Palaeolithic the early phase of the Stone Age, lasting about 2.5 million years, when primitive stone implements were used. The Palaeolithic period extends from the first appearance of artefacts to the end of the last ice age (about 8,500 years BC). The period has been divided into the **Lower Palaeolithic**, with the earliest forms of humankind and the emergence of hand-axe industries (ending about 120,000 years ago), the **Middle Palaeolithic**, the era of Neanderthal man (ending about 35,000 years ago), and the **Upper Palaeolithic**, during which only modern Homo sapiens is known to have existed.

Count Palatine in the later Roman Empire, a count (*comes*) attached to the imperial palace, and having supreme judicial authority in all causes that came to the king's immediate audience; later, a feudal lord having royal authority within a region of a kingdom; a high official of the Holy Roman Empire with royal authority within his domain.
   A **palatinate** was a territory under the jurisdiction of a Count Palatine; **the Palatinate** was a territory of the German Empire ruled by the Count Palatine of the Rhine.

pale[1] former term for an area within determined bounds, or subject to a particular jurisdiction, as in **the Pale**, used to designate the ➤ ENGLISH *Pale* in medieval Ireland, the territory of Calais in northern France when under English jurisdiction, and those areas of Tsarist Russia to which Jewish residence was restricted (known more fully as the **Pale of Settlement**).

The expression **beyond the pale**, meaning 'outside the bounds of acceptable behaviour', is recorded from the mid 19th century.

Pale in Middle English, meaning a wooden stake used as an upright along with others to form a fence, comes via Old French from Latin *palus* 'stake'.

pale² in heraldry, a broad vertical stripe down the middle of a shield.

pale horse the creature on which Death rides in the vision in Revelation 6:8.

paleface a name supposedly used by the North American Indians for a white person. The term is recorded from the early 19th century.

Palenque the site of a former Mayan city in SE Mexico, south-east of present-day Villahermosa. The well-preserved ruins of the city, which existed from about AD 300 to 900, include notable examples of Mayan architecture and extensive hieroglyphic texts. The city's ancient name has been lost and it is now named after a neighbouring village.

palfrey archaic term for a docile horse used for ordinary riding, especially by women. Recorded from Middle English, the word comes via Old French from medieval Latin alteration of late Latin *paraveredus*, from Greek *para* 'beside, extra' + Latin *veredus* 'light horse'.

Pali an Indic language, closely related to Sanskrit, in which the sacred texts of southern Buddhism are written. Pali developed in northern India in the 5th–2nd centuries BC. As the language of the Buddhist sacred texts, it was brought to Sri Lanka and Burma (Myanmar), and, though not spoken there, became the vehicle of a large literature of commentaries and chronicles.

palimony compensation made by one member of an unmarried couple to the other after separation. The word comes (in the 1970s) from a blend of *pal* and *alimony*.

palimpsest a manuscript or piece of writing material on which later writing has been superimposed on effaced earlier writing; in figurative use, something reused or altered but still bearing visible traces of its earlier form. Recorded from the mid 17th century, the word comes via Latin from Greek *palimpsēstos*, from *palin* 'again' and *psēstos* 'rubbed smooth'.

palindrome a word, phrase, or sequence that reads the same backwards as forwards, e.g. *madam*, *nurses run*, or (in relation to Napoleon) *able was I ere I saw Elba*.

Palio a traditional horse race held in Siena twice a year, in July and August. The name is Italian, and comes from Latin *pallium* 'covering', with reference to the cloth, a banner of silk or velvet, given as the prize.

pall a cloth spread over a coffin, hearse, or tomb. The word is recorded in Old English as *pæll* 'rich (purple) cloth', 'cloth cover for a chalice', and comes from Latin *pallium* 'covering, cloak'. A **pall-bearer** at a funeral, now a person either helping to carry or officially escorting the coffin, was originally someone who held up the edges of the pall.

Pall Mall a street in London built on the site of an alley for playing *pall-mall*, a 16th- and 17th-century game in which a boxwood ball was driven through an iron ring suspended at the end of a long alley.

Palladian of, relating to, or denoting the neoclassical style of the Italian architect Andrea *Palladio* (1508–80), who led a revival of classical architecture, in particular promoting the Roman ideals of harmonic proportions and symmetrical planning. *Palladian* is used in particular with reference to the phase of English architecture from *c*.1715, when there was a revival of interest in Palladio and his English follower, Inigo Jones, and a reaction against the baroque.

Palladium in Greek legend, an image of the goddess Pallas (Athene), on which the safety of Troy was believed to depend; it was later said to have been taken to Rome.

Pallas in Greek mythology, one of the names (of unknown meaning) of ➤ ATHENE.

pallium a woollen vestment conferred by the Pope on an archbishop, consisting of a narrow circular band placed round the shoulders with a short lappet hanging from front and back.

From the mid 16th century, the term has also been used to denote a man's large rectangular cloak, especially as worn by Greek philosophical and religious teachers.

Recorded from Old English, the word is Latin, and means literally 'covering'.

palm an unbranched evergreen tree with a crown of very long feathered or fan-shaped leaves, and typically having old leaf scars forming a regular pattern on the trunk. The leaf of this tree was traditionally awarded as a prize or viewed as a symbol of victory or triumph.

In Christian symbolism, the *palm* is used as a festive emblem on Palm Sunday, and was also the sign of a pilgrim who was returning or had returned from the Holy Land (a **palmer**). In northern countries, *palm* may be used for other shrubs, such as sallow or pussy willow, which are used on Palm Sunday. A palm is also a symbol of virginity.

Recorded in Old English and of Germanic origin, the word is ultimately related to Latin *palma* 'palm (of a hand)', its leaf being likened to a spread hand.

A **Palm Court** is a large room or patio, especially in a hotel, decorated with palm trees; the term **Palm Court music** is used to designate light orchestral music of a kind frequently played in a *Palm Court*.

Palm Sunday is the Sunday before Easter, on which Christ's entry into Jerusalem is celebrated in many Christian churches by processions in which branches of palms are carried. The name is recorded from Old English.

Palmetto State informal name for South Carolina; its flag bears the figure of a cabbage palmetto tree.

palmistry the art or practice of supposedly interpreting a person's character or predicting their future by examining the lines and other features of the hand, especially the palm and fingers.

Palmyra an ancient city of Syria, an oasis in the Syrian desert north-east of Damascus on the site of present-day Tadmur. First mentioned in the 19th century BC, Palmyra was an independent state in the 1st century BC, becoming a dependency of Rome between the 1st and 3rd centuries AD. A flourishing city on a trade route between Damascus and the Euphrates, it regained its independence briefly under ➤ ZENOBIA. The name is a Greek form of the city's modern and ancient pre-Semitic name *Tadmur* or *Tadmor*, meaning 'city of palms'.

Palookaville an imaginary town characterized by mediocrity, ineptitude, or stupidity. *Palooka* as a term for a stupid, clumsy, or ineffectual person, and in particular a mediocre prizefighter, has been current since 1920, and *Palookaville*, as the natural home of

such a person, is found in Budd Schulberg's script for the film *On the Waterfront*, in the phrase, 'A one-way ticket to Palookaville'.

paly in heraldry, divided into equal vertical stripes. Recorded from late Middle English, the word comes from Old French *pale* 'divided by stakes', from *pal* 'pale, stake'.

Pamplona a city in northern Spain, capital of the former kingdom and modern region of Navarre, noted for the fiesta of San Fermin, held there in July, which is celebrated with the running of bulls through the streets of the city.

Pan in Greek mythology, a god of flocks and herds, native to Arcadia, typically represented with the horns, ears, and legs of a goat on a man's body. He was thought of as loving mountains, caves, and lonely places and as playing on the pan pipes. His sudden appearance was supposed to cause terror similar to that of a frightened and stampeding herd, and the word *panic* is derived from his name. He was identified by the Romans with ➤ FAUNUS.

Plutarch relates that during the reign of Tiberius (AD 14–37), passengers in a ship off the west coast of Greece heard a voice calling that the god Pan was dead; this story was associated in Christian legend with the birth and resurrection of Christ.

The name *Pan* was probably originally in the sense 'the feeder' (i.e. herdsman), although the name was regularly associated with Greek *pas* or *pan* (= 'all'), giving rise to his identification as a god of nature or the universe.

The **pan pipes** are a musical instrument made from a row of short pipes of varying length fixed together and played by blowing across the top, originally associated with the god.

go down the pan reach a stage of abject failure or uselessness; *pan* here is short for *lavatory pan*.

panacea a solution or remedy for all difficulties or diseases. Recorded from the mid 16th century, the word comes via Latin from Greek *panakeia*, for *panakēs* 'all-healing'. In Spenser's *Faerie Queene*, the name *panacea* is given to a plant reputed to heal all ills (all-heal or woundwort).

Panama Canal a canal across the Isthmus of Panama, connecting the Atlantic and Pacific Oceans. Its construction, begun by Ferdinand de Lesseps in 1881 but abandoned in

1889, was completed by the US between 1904 and 1914. Control of the canal remained with the US until 1999, the date of its reversion to Panama.

Pancake Day Shrove Tuesday, when pancakes are traditionally made to use up eggs and fat before the beginning of Lent.

Panchen Lama a Tibetan lama ranking next after the Dalai Lama. The name comes from Tibetan *panchen*, abbreviation of *pandi-tachen-po* 'great learned one'. The Panchen Lama identifies the new Dalai Lama.

St Pancras (d. early 4th century), martyr, supposedly a Phrygian orphan brought to Rome and converted there. Relics of the saint were sent by the pope to Oswy, king of Northumbria, in the 7th century, and from this his name appears in Bede's martyrology. Six ancient churches in England were dedicated to St Pancras; the one in North London gave its name to the railway station. His feast day is 12 May.

Pandarus a Lycian fighting on the side of the Trojans, described in the *Iliad* as breaking the truce with the Greeks by wounding Menelaus with an arrow. The role as the lovers' go-between that he plays in Chaucer's (and later Shakespeare's) story of Troilus and Cressida originated with Boccaccio and is also the origin of the word ➤ PANDER.

pandemonium wild and noisy disorder or confusion; uproar. Originally (in Milton's *Paradise Lost*) it denoted the capital of hell, containing the council chamber of the evil spirits.

In extended use, *pandemonium* was used first for any place resembling this, and then more generally for wild and noisy disorder or confusion, uproar.

pander a person who assists the baser urges or evil designs of others. The term developed from the name of ➤ PANDARUS.

Pandora in Greek mythology, the first mortal woman. In one story she was created by Zeus and sent to earth with a jar or box of evils in revenge for Prometheus' having brought the gift of fire back to the world. Prometheus' simple brother Epimetheus married her despite his brother's warnings, and Pandora let out all the evils from the jar to infect the earth; hope alone remained to assuage the lot of humankind. In another account the jar contained all the blessings which would have been preserved for the world had they not been allowed to escape.

Pandora's box is a term for a process that generates many complicated problems as the result of unwise interference in something.

Pangaea a vast continental area or super-continent comprising all the continental crust of the earth, which is postulated to have existed in late Palaeozoic and Mesozoic times before breaking up into Gondwana and Laurasia.

The name is frequently stated to have been coined by A. Wegener 1914, in *Die Entstehung der Kontinente und Ozeane*, but it has not been found in the 1st edition of that book (actually published in 1915); *Pangäa* does occur in ed. 2 (1920), but with no indication that it is a coinage.

Pangloss name of the tutor and philosopher in Voltaire's *Candide* (1759), given to optimism regardless of circumstances.

panjandrum a person who has or claims to have a great deal of authority or influence. The word comes from *Grand Panjandrum*, an invented phrase in a nonsense passage composed in 1755 by the English actor and dramatist Samuel Foote (1720–77) to test the vaunted memory of the actor Charles Macklin (1697?–1797).

Panopticon the name given by Jeremy Bentham in 1790 to his proposal for an institutional building, especially a prison, of circular shape with the area occupied by the inmates disposed round and fully open to view from a central vantage point. A scheme for a penitentiary on these lines was accepted by Parliament in 1794, and a site at Millbank, London, was chosen, but, in the event, the new penitentiary (which opened in 1816) was not built to Bentham's plan. Among later prisons constructed on the panopticon principle, the Stateville Penitentiary at Joliet, Illinois, is still in use.

The word comes from Greek *pan* 'all' + *optikon*, neuter of *optikos* 'optic', and is recorded from the mid 18th century as a word for a kind of telescope.

Pantagruel the name of the last of the giants in Rabelais's *Pantagruel* (1532), represented as an extravagant and coarse humorist who deals satirically with serious subjects; **Pantagruelian** in extended usage means enormous, gigantic.

St Pantaleon 4th-century physician who was martyred under Diocletian; he is considered one of the ➤ FOURTEEN *Holy Helpers*, and from his cult in Venice his name may be the origin of ➤ PANTALOON. His feast day is 27 July.

Pantaloon a Venetian character in Italian *commedia dell'arte*, typically represented as a foolish old man wearing spectacles, pantaloons, and slippers; in harlequinade or pantomime, he is shown as an old man, alternately foolish and scheming, who abets the clown in his tricks and provides a butt for his jokes.

Traditionally Pantaloon had the same role in both Italian and English harlequinade, as the father or guardian of the heroine (Columbine) who attempts to prevent her marriage to the hero (Harlequin).

The loose breeches extended below the knee, fashionable in the period following the Restoration, were known as *pantaloons*; the diarist John Evelyn (1620–1706) commented in 1661 that they had been taken by the French from the costume of the stage character of the period.

Recorded in English from the late 16th century, the name comes originally via French from Italian *pantalone* 'a kind of mask on the Italian stage, representing the Venetian', supposed ultimately to be derived from the name of *San Pantaleone* or *Pantalone*, formerly a favourite saint of the Venetians.

Pantechnicon a building in Belgrave Square, London, constructed in the early 19th century to house an exhibition and sale of various arts and crafts, and later used as a furniture warehouse; it was destroyed by fire, with its contents, in 1874. From this the term was extended to mean any building housing a collection of shops or stalls offering a range of merchandise, and finally a large van for transporting furniture.

Panthalassa a universal sea or single ocean, such as would have surrounded Pangaea.

pantheism a doctrine which identifies God with the universe, or regards the universe as a manifestation of God.

Pantheon a large circular temple in Rome, dedicated to all the gods. It was begun by Agrippa *c.*25 BC as a conventional rectangular temple, but rebuilt as a larger, circular, domed building in the 2nd and 3rd centuries by Hadrian, Severus, and Caracalla. It was consecrated as a Christian church (Santa Maria Rotonda) in 609.

From this specific use the word was extended to mean a temple dedicated to all the gods (especially in ancient Greece and Rome) or a building in which the illustrious dead of a nation are buried or honoured. The term is now used for the gods of a people or religion collectively, or for a group or set of people particularly respected, famous, or important.

panther a leopard, especially a black one; originally, an exotic spotted wild cat believed to be distinct from the leopard. Fabulous accounts included the belief that the animal was a hybrid between the lion and the 'pard', and that the panther exhaled a sweet fragrance. In later literary use, the *panther* is also taken as the type of a fierce, powerful, and elusive creature.

Pantocrator a title of Christ represented as the ruler of the universe, especially in Byzantine church decoration. The name (recorded in English from the late 19th century) comes via Latin from Greek, 'ruler over all'.

pantomime a theatrical entertainment, mainly for children, which involves music, topical jokes, and slapstick comedy and is based on a fairy tale or nursery story, usually produced around Christmas. Modern British pantomime developed from the harlequinade and the cast typically includes a man in the chief comic female role ('principal dame'), a woman in the main male role ('principal boy'), and an animal played by actors in comic costume.

Pantomime is recorded from the late 16th century, and was first used in the Latin form and in the sense of an actor in Roman mime expressing meaning through gestures accompanied by movement. The current use developed in English in the mid 18th century.

Paolo and Francesca a type of doomed and sinful pair of lovers. *Francesca*, the wife of Giovanni Malatesta of Rimini, fell in love with her husband's younger brother *Paolo* and was put to death with him; her story is told in the fifth canto of Dante's *Inferno*.

papal of or relating to a pope or to the papacy; recorded from late Middle English, the word comes via Old French and medieval Latin from ecclesiastical Latin *papa* 'bishop of Rome'.

The **Papal States** were the temporal dominions belonging to the Pope, especially in central Italy, over which he exercised sovereignty from the 7th to the 19th centuries.

The **papal tiara** is an ornate cap with three coronets, used in the coronation of the Pope and as a symbol of the Pope's authority.

paparazzo a freelance photographer who pursues celebrities to get photographs of them. The name comes (in the mid 20th century, from Italian) from the name of a character in Fellini's film *La Dolce Vita* (1960).

paper over the cracks use a temporary expedient, or to create a mere semblance of order. The phrase is a translation of a German expression used by Otto von Bismarck in a letter of 1865, and early uses refer to this.

paper tiger a person or thing that appears threatening but is ineffectual. The expression became well-known in the West from its use by Mao Zhe Dong in an interview in 1946.

Paphian of or relating to Paphos, a Cypriot city held to be the birthplace of Aphrodite or Venus and formerly sacred to her; *Paphian* in literary use can thus mean relating to love and sexual desire, and the goddess may be referred to as the **Paphian Goddess** or **Paphian Queen**.

papyrus a material prepared in ancient Egypt from the pithy stem of the water plant *papyrus*, a tall aquatic sedge native to central Africa and the Nile valley, used in sheets throughout the ancient Mediterranean world for writing or painting on and also for making articles such as rope, sandals, and boats.

To form a sheet of writing material, the stem of the papyrus plant was sliced into thin strips which were laid side by side, with another layer of similar strips crossing them, usually followed by a third parallel to the first. The whole was then soaked in water, pressed, and dried.

parable a simple story used to illustrate a moral or spiritual lesson, as told by Jesus in the Gospels. Recorded from Middle English, the word comes via Old French from an ecclesiastical Latin sense 'discourse, allegory' of Latin *parabola* 'comparison', from Greek *parabolē* 'placing side by side, application'. Stories told by Jesus are often referred to by specific titles referring to their subjects, such as the **parable of the sower**.

Paracelsus (*c.*1493–1541), Swiss physician: born Theophrastus Phillipus Aureolus Bombastus von Hohenheim. He developed a new approach to medicine and philosophy based on observation and experience. He saw illness as having a specific external cause (rather than an imbalance of the bodily humours), and introduced chemical remedies to replace traditional ones. Paracelsus' progressive view was offset by his overall occultist perspective.

Paraclete (in Christian theology) the Holy Spirit as advocate or counsellor (John 14:26, 'the Comforter, which is the Holy Ghost'). The name comes via late Latin from Greek *paraklētos* 'called in aid'.

Paradise heaven as the ultimate abode of the just; the abode of Adam and Eve before the Fall in the biblical account of the Creation; the garden of Eden. Recorded from Middle English, the word comes via Old French and ecclesiastical Latin from Greek *paradeisos* 'royal (enclosed) park', from Avestan *pairidaēza* 'enclosure, park'. The word was used first in Greek by Xenophon for a Persian enclosed park, orchard, or pleasure ground.

From late Middle English, *Paradise* was also used for an enclosed garden or orchard, or an enclosed area or court in front of a building, especially a church, and in the Middle Ages particularly a court in front of St Peter's, Rome. ➤ PARVIS derives from the same base as this.

Paradise Lost is the title of Milton's epic poem (1667), which in twelve books relates the story of the Fall of Man, and which in its own words is intended to 'justify the ways of God to man'. *Paradise Regained* (1671), its sequel, relates in four books the story of the temptation of Jesus in the wilderness.

paradox a statement or proposition which, despite sound (or apparently sound) reasoning from acceptable premises, leads to a conclusion that seems senseless, logically unacceptable, or self-contradictory; a seemingly absurd or self-contradictory statement or proposition which when investigated or explained may prove to be well founded or true.

Recorded from the mid 16th century (originally denoting a statement contrary to accepted opinion), the word comes via late Latin from Greek *paradoxon* 'contrary (opinion)'.

Paralympics an international athletic competition for disabled athletes, modelled on the Olympic Games, established during the 1950s. The name comes from a blend of *paraplegic* and *Olympics*.

Paranthropus a genus name often applied to robust fossil hominids first found in South Africa in 1938, and now usually included in the species *Australopithecus robustus*.

Parcae in Roman mythology, the ➤ FATES.

pass the parcel a children's game in which a parcel is passed around to the accompaniment of music, the child holding the parcel when the music stops being allowed to unwrap a layer.

parchment a stiff, flat, thin material of a yellowish colour made from the prepared skin of an animal, usually a sheep or goat, and used as a durable writing surface in ancient and medieval times. Recorded from Middle English, the word comes via Old French from a blend of late Latin *pergamina* 'writing material from Pergamum' and *Parthica pellis* 'Parthian skin' (a kind of scarlet leather).

parclose a screen or railing in a church enclosing a tomb or altar or separating off a side chapel.

pard poetic or literary term for a leopard; in heraldry, a representation of this animal. (In early use, the *pard* was sometimes thought to be a different animal from a leopard or panther.).

pardoner a person who was licensed to sell papal pardons or indulgences; in the Middle Ages, *pardoners* such as the character in Chaucer's *Canterbury Tales* were often represented as figures of dubious moral probity.

pariah a member of a low caste or of no caste in southern India. The word comes in the 17th century from Tamil 'hereditary drummer', from *parai* a drum (*pariahs* not being allowed to join in with a religious procession).

From the early 19th century, the term has been in general use for someone who is despised and shunned, an outcast.

Parian of or relating to ➤ PAROS or the fine white marble for which it is renowned; denoting a form of fine white unglazed hardpaste porcelain likened to Parian marble.

The **Parian chronicle** is an inscribed marble stele, originally set up on ➤ PAROS, giving a record of ancient Greek history from the reign of Cecrops, the legendary first king of Athens, to the archonship of Astyanax at Paros and of Diognetus at Athens (*c.*264 BC);

two fragments survive, one kept in the Ashmolean Museum at Oxford, the other on Paros itself.

Paris in Greek mythology, a Trojan prince, the son of Priam and Hecuba. Appointed by the gods to decide who among the three goddesses Hera, Athene, and Aphrodite should win a prize for beauty, he awarded it to Aphrodite, who promised him the most beautiful woman in the world—Helen, wife of Menelaus king of Sparta. He abducted Helen, bringing about the Trojan War, in which he killed Achilles but was later himself killed.

parish (in the Christian Church) a small administrative district typically having its own church and a priest or pastor. Also, a small country district; the smallest unit of local government, constituted only in rural areas.

The **parish pump** was the pump supplying water to a parish, regarded as an informal place for meeting and discussion; used allusively to refer to matters of limited scope and interest, especially in politics.

Park Avenue name of a street in New York city, used allusively to denote the kind of fashionable and wealthy lifestyle typified by it.

park cattle animals of a breed of primitive cattle that are maintained in a semi-wild state in several parks in Britain, e.g. at Chillingham in Northumberland. They are typically white in colour with dark ears and muzzles. Also called **white park cattle**.

Park Lane name of a street in the West End of London, running alongside Hyde Park, used allusively to refer to the wealthy and aristocratic lifestyle traditionally typified by it.

Parkhurst a top-security British prison at Newport on the Isle of Wight, which was initially opened in 1838 as a model penal establishment for young offenders, taking boys who were later to be transported from the ➤ HULKS at Portsmouth.

Parkinson's law the notion that work expands so as to fill the time available for its completion. It is named after the English historian and journalist Cyril Northcote *Parkinson* (1909–93), who proposed it.

Parliament in the UK, the highest legislature, consisting of the Sovereign, the House of Lords, and the House of Commons; the members of this legislature for a particular period, especially between one dissolution and the next; a similar legislature in other nations and states. Recorded from Middle English, the word comes from Old French *parlement* 'speaking', from the verb *parler*.

parlour a room in a monastery or convent that is set aside for conversation. Recorded from Middle English, the word comes from Anglo-Norman French *parlur* 'place for speaking'.

Mount Parnassus a mountain in central Greece, just north of Delphi. Held to be sacred by the ancient Greeks, as was the spring of ➤ CASTALIA on its southern slopes, it was associated with Apollo and the Muses and regarded as a symbol of poetry.
   Parnassian means of or belonging to Mount Parnassus as the source of literary (especially poetic) inspiration. The name was also given to a group of French poets of the late 19th century who rejected Romanticism and emphasized strictness of form, named from the anthology *Le Parnasse contemporain* (1866).

parody an imitation of the style of a particular writer, artist, or genre with deliberate exaggeration for comic effect. Recorded from the late 16th century, the word comes via late Latin from Greek *parōidia* 'burlesque poem'.

Paros a Greek island in the southern Aegean, in the Cyclades. It is noted for the translucent white Parian marble which has been quarried there since the 6th century BC.

parricide the killing of a parent or other near relative. The word comes (in the late 16th century) via French from Latin *parricidium* 'murder of a parent', with first element of unknown origin, but for long associated with Latin *pater* 'father' and *parens* 'parent'.

Parsee an adherent of Zoroastrianism, especially a descendant of those Zoroastrians who fled to India from Muslim persecution in Persia during the 7th–8th centuries. The name comes from Persian *pārsī* 'Persian'.

Parthenon the temple of Athene Parthenos, built on the Acropolis in 447–432 BC by Pericles to honour Athens' patron goddess and to commemorate the recent Greek victory over the Persians. It was designed by Ictinus and Callicrates with sculptures by Phidias, including a colossal gold and ivory statue of Athene. It remains standing, despite being severely damaged by Venetian

bombardment in 1687. (See also ➤ ELGIN *Marbles*.)

Parthenope in Greek mythology, one of the sirens. The name was also that of a Greek colony from Cumae on the site of the modern Naples, and the **Parthenopean Republic** was the short-lived republic established in Naples by French revolutionary forces in 1799.

Parthia an ancient kingdom which lay SE of the Caspian Sea in present-day Iran. From *c.*250 BC to *c.*230 AD the Parthians ruled an empire stretching from the Euphrates to the Indus. Established by the Parthians' rebellion against the Seleucids, the empire reached the peak of its power around the 2nd century BC. It was eventually eclipsed by the Sassanians. The Parthians were skilled horsemen, with a culture that contained a mixture of Greek and Persian elements.
   A **Parthian shot** is a parting shot, so named because of the trick used by Parthians of shooting arrows backwards while in real or pretended flight.

the parting of the ways the moment at which a choice must be made or at which two people must separate; after Ezekiel 21:21.

Dame Partlet a name for a hen, traditionally the mate of ➤ CHANTICLEER. The name comes from Old French *Pertelote*, a female proper name.

the party's over a period of success or good fortune has come to an end; title of a song (1956) by Betty Comden and Adolph Green.

Parvati in Hindu mythology, a benevolent goddess, wife of Shiva, mother of Ganesha and Skanda, often identified in her malevolent aspect with Durga and Kali. The name comes from Sanskrit *Pārvatī*, literally 'daughter of the mountain'.

parvis an enclosed area in front of a cathedral or church, typically one that is surrounded with colonnades or porticoes. The word is based on late Latin *paradisus* 'paradise', in the Middle Ages denoting a court in front of St Peter's, Rome.

Pascalian of or relating to the French mathematician, physicist, and religious philosopher Blaise *Pascal* (1623–62), who before the age of 20 had proved a geometric theorem and constructed the first mechanical calculator to be offered for sale. He founded the theory of probabilities and developed a forerunner of integral calculus, but is best known for deriving the principle that the pressure of a fluid at rest is transmitted equally in all directions.

Pascal's triangle is a triangular array of numbers in which those at the ends of the rows are 1 and each of the others is the sum of the nearest two numbers in the row above (the apex, 1, being at the top).

Pascal's wager is the argument that it is in one's own best interest to behave as if God exists, since the possibility of eternal punishment in hell outweighs any advantage in believing otherwise.

paschal of or relating to Easter or to the Jewish Passover. The word comes (in late Middle English) from Old French, from ecclesiastical Latin *paschalis*, from *pascha* 'feast of Passover', via Greek and Aramaic from Hebrew *Pesaḥ* 'Passover'.

A **paschal candle** is a large candle blessed and lighted in the service of Holy Saturday and placed by the altar until Pentecost or (formerly) Ascension Day.

The **Paschal Lamb** is Christ; allusively, from the term for a lamb sacrificed at Passover.

Paschaltide in the Christian Church is the period following Easter Sunday.

pasha former title for a Turkish officer of high rank. There were three grades of pashas, distinguished by the number of horsetails they wore: three tails indicated a rank corresponding to commanding general; two, a rank corresponding to general of division; one, a rank corresponding to general of brigade; from this come the expressions **pasha of three tails** and **pasha of two tails**.

Recorded from the 17th century, the word comes from Turkish *paşa*.

Pasiphaë in Greek mythology, the wife of Minos and mother of the ➤ MINOTAUR, and of ➤ ARIADNE and Phaedra.

pasque flower a spring-flowering European plant related to the anemones, with purple flowers and fern-like foliage. Recorded (as *passeflower*) from the late 16th century, the name comes from French *passe-fleur*. The change in spelling of the first word was due to association with archaic *pasque* 'Easter' (because of the plant's early flowering).

pass one's sell-by date reach a point where one is useless or worn out. With allusion to the date marked on a perishable product indicating the recommended time by which it should be sold.

pass on the torch pass on a tradition; the expression comes originally from the Roman poet Lucretius (*c*.94–55 BC) in *De Rerum Natura*. The reference is to the *torch-race* of classical antiquity, in which the runners carried lighted torches and (in some cases) passed them on to other runners stationed at certain points.

passage grave a prehistoric megalithic burial chamber of a type found chiefly in western Europe, with a passage leading to the exterior. Passage graves were originally covered by a mound, which in many cases has disappeared, and most date from the Neolithic period.

passant in heraldry, (of an animal) represented as walking, with the right front foot raised. The animal is depicted in profile facing the dexter (left) side with the tail raised, unless otherwise specified (e.g. as 'passant guardant').

Battle of Passchendaele a prolonged episode of trench warfare involving appalling loss of life during the First World War in 1917, near the village of Passchendaele in western Belgium. It is also known as the third Battle of Ypres.

passing bell in early use, a bell rung for a dying person at the point of death, as a signal for prayers for the departing soul; later, a bell rung immediately after a person's death.

the Passion the suffering and death of Jesus, sometimes including his agony in Gethsemane. Recorded from Middle English, the word comes via Old French from late Latin *passio(n-)* (chiefly a term in Christian theology), from Latin *pati* 'suffer'.

The **Instruments of the Passion** are the objects associated with Christ's Passion, such as the Cross, the crown of thorns, and the nails.

A **passion flower** is an evergreen climbing plant of warm regions, which bears distinctive flowers with parts that supposedly resemble Instruments of the Passion. The three stigmas are said to correspond to the nails, the five stamens to the wounds, the corona to the crown of thorns, and the ten perianth segments to the apostles. The lobed leaves and tendrils of the plant were also said to represent the hands and scourges of Jesus' torturers.

A **passion play** is a dramatic performance representing Jesus's Passion from the Last Supper to the Crucifixion.

Passion Sunday is the fifth Sunday in Lent, the beginning of Passiontide; the Sunday before Palm Sunday. In the Roman Catholic Church this was suppressed as a separate observance in the Second Vatican Council's revision of the Calendar in 1969; instead, the Passion is regarded as commemorated on Palm Sunday, now properly called Passion (Palm) Sunday. **Passion Week** is the week between Passion Sunday and Palm Sunday; formerly also, the week immediately before Easter, Holy Week.

Passover the major Jewish spring festival which commemorates the liberation of the Israelites from Egyptian bondage, lasting seven or eight days from the 15th day of Nisan. The name comes from *pass over* 'pass without touching', with reference to the biblical story in Exodus 12 of how the Israelites escaped by marking their doorposts with the blood of a lamb, when the plague which destroyed their firstborn fell on the Egyptians.

pastoral a form of literature portraying an idealized version of country life, the earliest example of which is found in the Idylls of the Greek poet ➤ THEOCRITUS (*c*.310–*c*.250 BC). The *pastoral* became popular during the Renaissance, and inspired particularly such prose romances as Sidney's *Arcadia*.

The word comes ultimately from Latin *pastor* 'shepherd'; in late Middle English, *pastoral* denoted a book on the cure or care of souls, often with reference to the title of St Gregory the Great's *Cura Pastoralis* ('Pastoral Care'), which had been translated into English by King Alfred.

The **Pastoral Epistles** are the books of the New Testament comprising the two letters of Paul to Timothy and the one to Titus, which deal chiefly with the duties of those charged with the care of souls.

A **pastoral letter** is an official letter from a bishop to all the clergy or members of his or her diocese, and a **pastoral staff** is a bishop's crozier.

Pastoral theology is Christian theology that considers religious truth in relation to spiritual needs.

stand pat stick stubbornly to one's opinion or decision; in the card games poker and blackjack *standing pat* is retaining one's hand as dealt, without drawing other cards.

patent a government authority or licence to an individual or organization conferring a right or title for a set period, especially the sole right to make, use, or sell some invention. Recorded from late Middle English, the word comes via Old French from Latin *patent-* 'lying open'.

A **patent roll** is a parchment roll containing the ➤ LETTERS *patent* issued in Britain (or formerly in England) in any one year.

paternoster (in the Roman Catholic Church) the Lord's Prayer, especially in Latin. Also, any of a number of special beads occurring at regular intervals in a rosary, indicating that the Lord's Prayer is to be recited. The name comes from Latin '*Pater noster* [our Father]', the first two words of the prayer in Latin.

Paternoster Row is a street in London near St Paul's, traditionally the site of booksellers and publishers.

pathetic fallacy the attribution of human feelings and responses to inanimate things or animals, especially in art and literature. The term was coined by the critic John Ruskin in *Modern Painters* (1856).

Pathfinder in the novels of James Fenimore Cooper, one of the names given to ➤ *Natty* BUMPPO.

Pathfinder was also the name of an unmanned American spacecraft which landed on Mars in 1997, deploying a small robotic rover (Sojourner) to explore the surface and examine the rocks.

Patmos a Greek island in the Aegean Sea, one of the Dodecanese group. It is believed that St John was living there in exile (from AD 95) when he had the visions described in Revelation.

patriarch the male head of a family or tribe; a person regarded as the oldest or most venerable of a group. The name is used particularly to denote any of those biblical figures regarded as fathers of the human race, especially ➤ ABRAHAM, ➤ ISAAC, and ➤ JACOB, and their forefathers, or the sons of Jacob.

Patriarch is also used for the title of a most senior Orthodox or Catholic bishop, in particular, a bishop of one of the most ancient Christian sees (Alexandria, Antioch, Constantinople, Jerusalem, and formerly Rome), and the head of an autocephalous or independent Orthodox Church.

Recorded from Middle English, the word comes via Old French and ecclesiastical Latin from Greek *patriarkhēs*, from *patria* 'family' + *arkhēs* 'ruling'.

patrician a member of a noble family or class in ancient Rome. The rank was originally hereditary, but in Imperial Rome patricians could be appointed by the emperor. In the later Roman Empire and Byzantine Empire, *patrician* was an honorific title bestowed by the Emperor at Byzantium, introduced by Constantine I; it was also used for an officer, originally bearing this distinction, sent or appointed as representative of the Byzantine Emperor to administer the provinces of Italy and Africa.

In extended use, an aristocrat or nobleman, a member of a long-established wealthy family. Recorded from late Middle English, the word comes via Old French from Latin *patricius* 'having a noble father'.

St Patrick (5th century), Apostle and patron saint of Ireland. His *Confession* is the chief source for the events of his life. Of Romano-British parentage, he was taken as a slave to Ireland, where he experienced a religious conversion; having escaped to Britain, where he received training for the priesthood, he returned to Ireland to preach the Gospel *c.*435. He founded the archiepiscopal see of Armagh in about 454.

Legends of the saint include the tradition that he used the shamrock to explain the nature of the Trinity, and that he was responsible for banishing snakes from Ireland. His feast day is 17 March.

The **Order of St Patrick** is a former British order of knighthood instituted in 1783; its special epithet is 'most illustrious'.

St Patrick's cross is a red diagonal cross on a white ground.

St Patrick's Purgatory is a cavern on an island in Lough Derg, Co. Donegal, Ireland, where according to legend Christ appeared to St Patrick, and showed him a deep pit in which whoever spent one day and one night could see the torments of hell and the joys of heaven.

Patriots' Day in the US, the anniversary of the Battle of Lexington and Concord in the American War of Independence, 19 April 1775, observed since 1894 as a legal holiday in Maine and Massachusetts.

patristics the branch of Christian theology that deals with the lives, writings, and doctrines of the early Christian theologians or Fathers of the Church.

Patroclus a Greek hero of the Trojan War, the close friend of Achilles. The *Iliad* describes how Patroclus' death at the hands of Hector led ➤ ACHILLES to return to battle,

and to avenge his friend by killing Hector and dragging his body round the walls of Troy.

patron saint a saint chosen or regarded as the special protector of or intercessor for a person, place, country, occupation, or institution. A **patronal festival** is the festival of a patron saint, especially the saint to whom a church is dedicated.

patronymic a name derived from the name of a father or ancestor, e.g. *Johnson*, *O'Brien*, *Ivanovich*.

St Paul[1] (d. *c.*64), missionary of Jewish descent; known as *Paul the Apostle*, or *Saul of Tarsus*, or *the Apostle of the Gentiles*. He first opposed the followers of Jesus, assisting at the martyrdom of St Stephen, but while travelling to Damascus he experienced a vision (and was temporarily struck blind), after which he was converted to Christianity; he became one of the first major Christian missionaries and theologians, and his epistles form part of the New Testament.

After a number of missionary journeys, Paul was arrested in Jerusalem for preaching against the Jewish Law; as a Roman citizen, he appealed to Caesar, and was sent for trial to Rome. He was martyred there during the persecution of Nero, traditionally on the same day as ➤ *St* PETER.

Paul's experience on the ➤ road to DAMASCUS has become proverbial as a life-changing revelation.

Paul's emblem is the sword with which he is said to have been executed. His feast day is 29 June; the feast of the Conversion of St Paul is 16 January.

St Paul[2] (d. *c.*345), said to have been the first Christian hermit, who had gone into the desert to escape persecution, and lived there for many years; Anthony of Egypt visited him there. A raven is said to have dropped a loaf of bread beside them at their meeting. According to legend, his grave was dug by two lions at Anthony's request, and in art Paul is often shown with them, a crow or raven, or with the palm-tree from which he gained food and shelter. His feast day is 10 January in the Western Church and 5 or 15 January in the Eastern Church.

Paul Pry an inquisitive person, from the name of a character in a US song of 1820.

Pausanias (2nd century), Greek geographer and historian. His *Description of Greece* (also called the *Itinerary of Greece*) is a guide to the topography and remains of ancient Greece and is still considered an invaluable source of information.

Pavlovian of or relating to classical conditioning as described by the Russian physiologist Ivan *Pavlov* (1849–1936). He showed by experiment with dogs how the secretion of saliva can be stimulated not only by food but also by the sound of a bell associated with the presentation of food.

pawn a chess piece of the smallest size and value, that moves one square forwards along its file if unobstructed (or two on the first move), or one square diagonally forwards when making a capture. Each player begins with eight pawns on the second rank, and can promote a pawn to become any other piece (typically a queen) if it reaches the opponent's end of the board. In figurative use, a *pawn* is a person used by others for their own purposes.

Recorded from late Middle English, the word comes via Anglo-Norman French from medieval Latin *pedo* 'foot-soldier', from Latin *pes, ped-* 'foot'.

pax the Latin word for peace; *Pax* in Roman mythology was the goddess of peace, equivalent of the Greek goddess Eirene. In the Christian Church, the *pax* is the kissing by all the participants at a mass of a tablet depicting the Crucifixion or other sacred object; the kiss of peace.

The **Pax Romana** was the peace which existed between nationalities within the Roman Empire. It is generally regarded as operating from the beginning of Augustus's reign (27 BC) to the death of Marcus Aurelius (AD 180), and in extended usage may apply to a widespread state of peace maintained under any jurisdiction. From the 19th century, various terms modelled on this are recorded, as **Pax Americana** and **Pax Britannica**.

In the Christian Church, **pax vobis** means 'peace be with you', reflecting Christ's greeting to the Apostles after his resurrection as recounted in John 20.

paynim archaic term for a pagan; a non-Christian, especially a Muslim. Recorded from Middle English, the word comes ultimately from ecclesiastical Latin *paganismus* 'heathenism'.

payola in the US, the practice of bribing someone to use their influence or position to promote a particular product or interest. Recorded from the 1930s, the word comes from

pay + *Victrola*, the name of a make of gramophone.

he who pays the piper calls the tune the person who provides the money for something has the right to determine how it's spent; proverbial saying from the late 19th century.

you pays your money and you takes your choice used to convey that there is little to choose between one alternative and another; originally as a *Punch* joke of 1846.

PC 49 the central character of a children's radio series, 1946–53, *PC 49* was an untypical British police constable whose name was Archibald Berkeley Willoughby. From 1955 he appeared in a strip cartoon in the *Eagle*.

peace freedom from or cessation of war.

In the US, the **Peace Corps** is an organization (created by the Peace Corps Act of 1961) which sends young people to work as volunteers in developing countries.

The **peace dividend** is a (financial) benefit from reduced defence spending; a sum of public money which may become available for other purposes when spending on defence is reduced. The term was first recorded in the US in the late 1960s, at a time when the potential benefits of withdrawal from the war in Vietnam were increasingly acknowledged, and gained a high profile again in the early 1990s following the breakup of the Soviet Union.

The **Peace Garden State** is an informal name for North Dakota.

Peace in our time comes originally from the *Book of Common Prayer* (1662), 'Give peace in our time, O Lord.' The phrase was famously used by Neville Chamberlain (1869–1940) on his return from Munich in September 1938.

A **peace process** is a series of initiatives, talks, and negotiations, designed to bring about a negotiated settlement between warring or disputing parties; in the 1990s, the term has been used with particular reference to attempts at a settlement in Northern Ireland.

Peace with honour is a phrase recorded from the 17th century, but used most famously by Benjamin Disraeli, Lord Beaconsfield, on his return from the Congress of Berlin in July 1878.

Peach State informal name for the US state of Georgia.

Peachum the receiver and informer who betrays the highwayman ➤ MACHEATH in John Gay's *The Beggar's Opera* (1728); his name comes from the informal verb *peach* 'inform on', a shortening of the archaic *appeach*, ultimately from the French base of *impeach*.

peacock a male peafowl, which has brilliant blue and green plumage and very long tail feathers that have eye-like markings and can be erected and expanded in display like a fan; in Greek mythology, the 'eyes' were those of the hundred-eyed ➤ ARGUS, placed there by Hera after Hermes killed him. The bird is proverbially taken as the type of an ostentatious, proud, or vain person; it may also be taken as a bird of ill-omen.

In the fable of the ➤ BORROWED *plumes*, a jay or jackdaw is said to have decked itself in peacock's feathers in an unsuccessful attempt to impress.

In Hindu tradition, a peacock may be shown as the mount of the war-god ➤ SKANDA.

Mrs Peacock is one of the six stock characters constituting the murderer and suspects in the game of ➤ CLUEDO.

Peacock Alley is the main corridor of the original Waldorf-Astoria Hotel in New York, so called because fashionable people paraded there.

In heraldry, a **peacock in his pride** is a peacock represented as facing the spectator with the tail expanded and the wings drooping.

The **Peacock Throne** was the former throne of the Kings of Delhi, later that of the Shahs of Iran, adorned with precious stones forming an expanded peacock's tail. The throne was taken to Persia by Nadir Shah (1688–1747), king of Persia, who in 1739 captured Delhi and with it the *Peacock Throne* and the *Koh-i-noor* diamond.

A **peacock's feather** is one of the long tail feathers of the peacock, used figuratively as a symbol of ostentation or vainglory. It was traditionally believed that to bring a peacock's feather into the house would invite ill-luck.

Peak District a limestone plateau in Derbyshire, at the southern end of the Pennines, rising to 636 m (2,088 ft) at Kinder Scout. A large part of the area was designated a national park in 1951.

Peanuts name of the comic strip (1950–99) by the American cartoonist Charles Schulz (1922–2000), featuring a range of characters including the likeable loser Charlie Brown,

his dog ➤ SNOOPY, bossy Lucy, and the philosophical Linus.

go pear-shaped go wrong. Originally RAF slang, perhaps referring to the distorted shape of an aircraft that has crashed nose-first.

pearl in figurative use, a precious, noble, or fine thing, the finest or best member or part. There is also a tradition that pearls may portend tears; they were supposed to be unlucky for brides, and in Webster's *Duchess of Malfi* (c.1623), the doomed Duchess dreams that the diamonds in her coronet are changed to pearls.

In heraldry, *pearl* is used for the tincture argent in the fanciful blazon of arms of peers.

Recorded from late Middle English, the word comes from Old French *perle*, perhaps based on Latin *perna* 'leg', extended to denote a leg-of-mutton shaped bivalve.

Pearl Harbor is a harbour on the island of Oahu, in Hawaii, the site of a major American naval base, where a surprise attack on 7 December 1941 by Japanese carrier-borne aircraft inflicted heavy damage and brought the US into the Second World War. The name may now be used allusively for a sudden and disastrous attack, mounted without warning.

The **Pearl Mosque** is a white marble mosque at Agra in Uttar Pradesh, northern India, built in the 17th century by the emperor Akbar (1542–1605).

pearls before swine valuable things offered or given to people who do not appreciate them, with biblical allusion to Matthew 7:6.

Pearly Gates informal name for the gates of heaven; the term is first recorded in a hymn by Isaac Watts (1674–1748), and refers originally to Revelation 21:21.

pearly king (also **pearly queen**), a London costermonger wearing traditional ceremonial clothes covered with pearl buttons.

Peasants' Revolt an uprising in 1381 among the peasant and artisan classes in England, particularly in Kent and Essex. The rebels marched on London, occupying the city and executing unpopular ministers, but after the death of their leader, Wat Tyler, they were persuaded to disperse by Richard II, who granted some of their demands, though the government later went back on its promises.

not the only pebble on the beach (especially of a former lover) not unique or irreplaceable; from a song-title (1897), 'You're Not the Only Pebble on the Beach.'

peck a measure of capacity for dry goods, equal to a quarter of a bushel (2 imperial gallons = 9.092 l, or 8 US quarts = 8.81 l). The word is recorded from Middle English (used especially as a measure of oats for horses) and comes from Anglo-Norman French *pek*, of unknown origin.

Peck's bad boy an unruly or mischievous child, from the name of a fictional character created by George Wilbur *Peck* (1840–1916).

pecking order a hierarchy of status seen among members of a group of people or animals, originally as observed among hens.

Pecksniff a hypocritical character in Dickens's novel *Martin Chuzzlewit* (1844); the name is used to denote an unctuous hypocrite who preaches morality while serving his own ends.

peculiar a parish or church exempt from the jurisdiction of the diocese in which it lies, through being subject to the jurisdiction of the monarch or an archbishop. Recorded from late Middle English (in the sense 'particular, special'), the word comes from Latin *peculiaris* 'of private property', and ultimately from *pecu* 'cattle' (cattle being private property). The current sense 'odd' dates from the early 17th century.

pedagogue a teacher, especially a strict or pedantic one. The word comes via Latin from Greek *paidagōgos*, denoting a slave who accompanied a child to school.

pedlar a person who goes from place to place selling small goods. Recorded from Middle English, the word may be an alteration of synonymous dialect *pedder*, apparently from dialect *ped* 'pannier'.

peel a small square defensive tower of a kind built in the 16th century in the border counties of England and Scotland. The word comes from Anglo-Norman French *pel* 'stake, palisade', from Latin *palus* 'stake'.

Emma Peel cat-suited heroine of the television thriller series *The Avengers* (1961–8), played by Diana Rigg.

peeler a dated term for a police officer, from the name of the British Conservative statesman Robert *Peel* (1788–1950), who as Home Secretary (1828–30) established the Metropolitan Police Force.

Peeping Tom the man said to have watched Lady ➤ GODIVA ride naked through Coventry; his character is in fact a 17th-century addition to the story. From the late 18th century, *peeping Tom* has been used to denote a person who gets sexual pleasure from secretly watching people undressing or engaging in sexual activity; in the US, an act outlawing intrusive voyeurism is known as a **peeping Tom statute**.

Pegasus in Greek mythology, a winged horse which sprang from the blood of ➤ MEDUSA when Perseus cut off her head. Pegasus was ridden by ➤ PERSEUS in his rescue of Andromeda, and by Bellerophon when he fought the ➤ CHIMERA; the spring ➤ HIPPOCRENE arose from a blow of his hoof.

peine forte et dure a medieval form of torture in which the body was pressed with heavy weights, to death if necessary. It was used in England on prisoners who refused to accept jury trial; St Margaret Clitherow (1558–86), arrested for harbouring priests, refused to enter a plea, and died while undergoing this torture. The phrase is French, and means literally 'strong and hard suffering'.

Peking earlier form of transliteration of the name of the Chinese capital Beijing.

Peking man is the name given to a fossil hominid of the middle Pleistocene period, identified from remains found near Beijing in 1926.

Peking opera is a stylized Chinese form of opera dating from the late 18th century, in which speech, singing, mime, and acrobatics are performed to an instrumental accompaniment.

Pelagius (*c*.360–*c*.420), British or Irish monk. He denied the doctrines of original sin and predestination, defending innate human goodness and free will. His beliefs were opposed by St Augustine of Hippo and condemned as heretical by the Synod of Carthage in about 418.

Pelasgian relating to or denoting an ancient people inhabiting the coasts and islands of the Aegean Sea and eastern Mediterranean before the arrival of Greek-speaking peoples in the Bronze Age (12th century BC).

Pele in Hawaiian mythology, the goddess of volcanoes. **Pele's hair** is the name given to fine threads of volcanic glass, formed when a spray of lava droplets cools rapidly in the air.

Peleus in Greek mythology, a king of Phthia in Thessaly, who was given as his wife the sea nymph Thetis; their child was ➤ ACHILLES.

pelican the *pelican* is traditionally said to have fed its young on its own blood. (The story is told by Epiphanius and St Augustine; it appears to be of Egyptian origin, and to have referred originally to a different bird.)

Recorded from late Old English, the word comes via late Latin from Greek *pelekan*, probably based on *pelekus* 'axe', with reference to its bill.

In the UK, a **pelican crossing** is a pedestrian crossing with traffic lights operated by pedestrians. The name comes (in the 1960s) from *pe(destrian) li(ght) con(trolled)*, altered to conform with the bird's name.

The **Pelican flag** is the state flag of Louisiana, which depicts a pelican.

In heraldry and Christian art, a **pelican in her piety** is the depiction of a pelican pecking its own breast as a symbol of Christ.

The **Pelican State** is an informal name for Louisiana.

Pelion a wooded mountain in Greece, near the coast of SE Thessaly, which in Greek mythology was held to be the home of the centaurs, and the giants were said to have piled Mounts ➤ OLYMPUS and ➤ OSSA on its summit in their attempt to reach heaven and destroy the gods. This story has given rise to the phrase **pile Pelion on Ossa**, meaning to add an extra difficulty or task to something which is already difficult or onerous.

Peloponnesian War the war of 431–404 BC fought between Athens and Sparta with their respective allies, occasioned largely by Spartan opposition to the Delian League. It ended in the total defeat of Athens and the transfer, for a brief period, of the leadership of Greece to Sparta.

Pelops in Greek mythology, the son of ➤ TANTALUS, brother of ➤ NIOBE, and father of ➤ ATREUS. He was killed by his father and served up as food to the gods, but only one shoulder was eaten, and he was restored to life with an ivory shoulder replacing the one that was missing.

Penal Laws various statutes passed in Britain and Ireland during the 16th and 17th centuries that imposed harsh restrictions on Roman Catholics. People participating in Catholic services could be fined and imprisoned, while Catholics were banned from voting, holding public office, owning land, and teaching. The laws were repealed by various Acts between 1791 and 1926.

penates in ancient Rome, household gods worshipped in conjunction with ➤ VESTA and the ➤ LARES; the name comes from Latin *penus* 'provision of food', related to *penes* 'within'.

Pendragon a title given to an ancient British or Welsh prince holding or claiming supreme power. The word, which is Welsh, meant literally 'chief war-leader', from *pen* 'head' + *dragon* 'standard'.

Penelope in Greek mythology, the wife of ➤ ODYSSEUS, who was beset by suitors when her husband did not return after the fall of Troy. She put them off by saying that she would marry only when she had finished the piece of weaving (➤ *Penelope's* WEB) on which she was engaged, and every night unravelled the work she had done during the day.

penguin the *penguin*, noted for its wings developed into flippers for swimming under water, may be referred to in relation to a clumsy, waddling walk; the black and white plumage has also given rise to the informal **penguin suit** to denote a man's evening dress of black dinner jacket worn with a white shirt.

Penguin Books is the name of the paperback publishing imprint founded by Allen Lane in 1935; the first ten titles, published in 1936 and priced at sixpence each, included titles by Agatha Christie, Ernest Hemingway, and André Maurois.

Peninsular War a campaign waged on the Iberian peninsula between the French and the British, the latter assisted by Spanish and Portuguese forces, from 1808 to 1814 during the Napoleonic Wars. The French were finally driven back over the Pyrenees in an expedition led by Wellington.

penitent in the Christian Church, a person who confesses their sins to a priest and submits to the penance imposed; originally, this might include the performance of a punishment or discipline as an outward expression or token of repentance for and expiation of a sin. Those doing public penance might wear ➤ SACKCLOTH, or (when doing penance for fornication) be dressed in a white sheet.

The **Penitential Psalms** are seven psalms (6, 32, 38, 51, 102, 130, 143) which express penitence.

pennies from heaven unexpected (financial) benefits, from a song with this title by the American songwriter Johnny Burke (1908–64).

Pennsylvania Dutch a name for the German-speaking inhabitants of the US state of Pennsylvania, descendants for the most part of 17th- and 18th-century Protestant immigrants from the Rhineland.

penny a British bronze coin and monetary unit equal (since decimalization in 1971) to one hundredth of a pound; formerly, to one twelfth of a shilling.

The penny has its origins in the Roman denarius. The English silver penny first appeared in the late 8th century and was the only coin in circulation for several centuries. The penny was minted in copper from 1797 and in bronze from 1860; coining of silver pennies ceased with the reign of Charles II, apart from a small regular issue as ➤ Maundy *money*.

Recorded from Old English and of Germanic origin, the word may be related to *pawn* 'deposit an object for money' and (with reference to its shape) *pan* 'a metal container for cooking'.

Not have a penny to bless oneself with means be completely impoverished; alluding to the cross on an old silver penny or to the practice of crossing a person's palm with silver for luck.

The **penny black** was the world's first adhesive postage stamp, issued in Britain in 1840. It was printed in black with an effigy of Queen Victoria, and had a value of one penny.

A **penny dreadful** was a cheap, sensational comic or storybook, so named because the original cost (in the 19th century) was one penny.

The phrase **the penny drops** means understanding dawns (referring to the mechanism of a penny-in-the-slot machine).

A **penny-farthing** was an early type of bicycle, made in Britain, with a very large front wheel and a small rear wheel, current from the early 1870s to the mid 1890s, and often known as the *ordinary*.

Penny wise and pound foolish means careful and economical in small matters while being wasteful or extravagant in large ones. Proverbial saying from the early 17th century.

To **spend a penny** is to urinate (used euphemistically); with reference to the coin-operated locks of public toilets.

pennyweight a unit of weight, 24 grains or one twentieth of an ounce troy.

pentacle a talisman or magical object, typically disc-shaped and inscribed with a pentagram or other figure, and used as a symbol of the element of earth. *Pentacles* are also one of the suits in some tarot packs, corresponding to *coins* in others.

Recorded from the late 16th century, the word comes from medieval Latin *pentaculum*, apparently based on Greek *penta-* 'five'.

the Pentagon the pentagonal building serving as the headquarters of the US Department of Defense, near Washington DC. It was built in 1941–3. **Pentagonese** is euphemistic or cryptic language supposedly used among high-ranking US military personnel.

The **Pentagon Papers** were a confidential report on US involvement in Indochina, commissioned in 1967 by Robert McNamara as Secretary of Defense, which in 1971 were leaked to the *New York Times* by the military defense analyst Daniel Ellsberg.

pentagram a five-pointed star that is formed by drawing a continuous line in five straight segments, often used as a mystic and magical symbol.

In the Middle Ages, pentagrams were sometimes inscribed in clothing or hung in doors and windows to keep away evil spirits and the effects of witchcraft. The pentagram is now used as a symbol of Wicca and other neo-pagan movements, the five points often being taken to represent earth, water, air, fire, and spirit.

Pentateuch the first five books of the Old Testament (Genesis, Exodus, Leviticus, Numbers, and Deuteronomy), relating the early history of the world and of the Hebrews up to the death of Moses, and including the Jewish law. Traditionally ascribed to Moses, it is now held by scholars to be a compilation from texts of the 9th to 5th centuries BC, incorporating older oral traditions.

pentathlon an athletic event comprising five different events for each competitor, in particular, in ancient Greece, leaping, running, discus-throwing, spear-throwing, and wrestling; now, (also **modern pentathlon**) an event involving fencing, shooting, swimming, riding, and cross-country running.

Pentecost the Christian festival celebrating the descent of the Holy Spirit on the disciples of Jesus after his Ascension, held on the seventh Sunday after Easter. *Pentecost* also denotes the Jewish festival or Shavuoth.

Recorded in Old English, the word comes via ecclesiastical Latin from Greek *pentēkostē* (*hēmera*) 'fiftieth (day)', because the Jewish festival is held on the fiftieth day after the second day of Passover.

In the Church of England, a **pentecostal** is an offering formerly made at Whitsuntide by a parishioner to a priest, or by an inferior church to its mother church.

The **Pentecostal Church** comprises any of a number of Christian sects and individuals emphasizing baptism in the Holy Spirit, evidenced by 'speaking in tongues', prophecy, healing, and exorcism. Pentecostal sects are often fundamentalist in doctrine and are uninhibited and spontaneous in worship.

Penthesilea the queen of the Amazons, who came to the help of Troy after the death of Hector and was killed by Achilles.

Pepin (*c.*714–68), known as **Pepin the Short**, son of Charles Martel and father of Charlemagne; he became the first king of the Frankish Carolingian dynasty on the deposition of the Merovingian Childeric III. (See also ➤ DONATION *of Pepin*.)

peppercorn rent a very low or nominal rent, from the (formerly common) practice of stipulating the payment of a peppercorn as a nominal rent; the usage dates from the early 17th century.

Pepysian of or relating to the English diarist and naval administrator Samuel *Pepys* (1633–1703), whose *Diary* (1660–9) describes events such as the Great Plague and the Fire of London as well as details of his personal life. Written in cipher, it was not deciphered until 1825.

Perceval a legendary figure dating back to ancient times, found in French, German, and English poetry from the late 12th century onwards. He is the father of Lohengrin and the hero of a number of legends, some of which are associated with the Holy Grail. Also called *Parsifal*.

perch former name for a measure of length, especially for land, equal to a quarter of a chain or 5½ yards (approximately 5.029 m). Recorded from Middle English, the word

comes via Old French from Latin *pertica* 'measuring rod, pole'.

Perdita in Shakespeare's *Winter's Tale*, the lost daughter of Leontes and Hermione who is brought up as a shepherdess; her name means 'the lost one'.

The actress Mary Robinson (1758–1800), mistress of George, Prince of Wales, afterwards George IV, was known as *Perdita* after her success in the part.

Père Lachaise in Paris, the great cemetery on the site of a Jesuit foundation of 1626, which had been enlarged by Père Lachaise (1624–1709), confessor to Louis XIV. In May 1871, the forces of the Paris Commune made their last stand there against government troops.

perestroika (in the former Soviet Union) the policy or practice of restructuring or reforming the economic and political system. First proposed by Leonid Brezhnev in 1979 and actively promoted by Mikhail Gorbachev, *perestroika* originally referred to increased automation and labour efficiency, but came to entail greater awareness of economic markets and the ending of central planning. The word is Russian, and means literally 'restructuring'.

perfect number a number which is equal to the sum of its factors (not including itself).

Perfidious Albion England or Britain considered as treacherous in international affairs, in a rendering of the French phrase *la perfide Albion*, said to have been first used by the Marquis de Ximenès (1726–1817). Both terms are recorded in English from the mid 19th century.

Pergamum a city in ancient Mysia, in western Asia Minor, situated to the north of Izmir on a rocky hill close to the Aegean coast. The capital in the 3rd and 2nd centuries BC of the Attalid dynasty, it was one of the greatest and most beautiful of the Hellenistic cities and was famed for its cultural institutions, especially its library, which was second only to that at Alexandria. The word ➤ PARCHMENT derives partly from its name.

peri (in Persian mythology) a mythical superhuman being, originally represented as evil but subsequently as a good or graceful genie or fairy. The name comes ultimately from Avestan (Zend) *pairīkā*, any of several beautiful but malevolent female demons employed by Ahriman to bring comets and eclipses, prevent rain, and cause failure of crops and dearth.

Pericles (c.495–429 BC), Athenian statesman and general. A champion of Athenian democracy, he pursued an imperialist policy and masterminded Athenian strategy in the Peloponnesian War. He commissioned the building of the Parthenon in 447 and promoted the culture of Athens in a golden age that produced such figures as Aeschylus, Socrates, and Phidias.

perish the thought used, often ironically, to show that one finds a suggestion or idea completely ridiculous; the phrase probably derives from *perish that thought!* in Colley Cibber's *Richard III* (1700).

permissive society the form of society supposed to have prevailed in the West since the mid-1960s (associated especially with the late 1960s and early 1970s), characterized by greater tolerance and more liberal attitudes in areas such as sexuality, abortion, drug use, and obscenity.

Perpendicular denoting the latest stage of English Gothic church architecture, prevalent from the late 14th to mid 16th centuries and characterized by broad arches, elaborate fan vaulting, and large windows with vertical tracery.

perpetual motion the motion of a hypothetical machine which, once activated, would run forever unless subject to an external force or to wear; although impossible according to the first and second laws of thermodynamics, the development of such a mechanism has been attempted by many inventors. The Dutch philosopher and inventor Cornelis Drebbel (1572–1634), in England in the early 17th century, was said to have perfected such a device, which he presented to the king, and which became one of the sights of the day.

Persephone in Greek mythology, a goddess, the daughter of Zeus and Demeter. She was carried off by Hades and made queen of the underworld. Demeter, vainly seeking her, refused to let the earth produce its fruits until her daughter was restored to her, but because Persephone had eaten some pomegranate seeds in the other world, she was obliged to spend part of every year there. Her story symbolizes the return of spring and the life and growth of corn. Her Roman name is *Proserpina*.

Persepolis a city in ancient Persia, situated to the north-east of Shiraz. It was founded in the late 6th century BC by Darius I as the ceremonial capital of Persia under the Achaemenid dynasty. The city's impressive ruins include functional and ceremonial buildings and cuneiform inscriptions in Old Persian, Elamite, and Akkadian. It was partially destroyed in 330 BC by Alexander the Great, and though it survived as the capital of the Seleucids it began to decline after this date.

Perseus in Greek mythology, the son of Zeus and ➤ DANAË, a hero celebrated for many achievements. Aided by gifts from the gods (a helmet which conferred invisibility from Pluto, wings for his feet from Hermes, and a mirror so that he could look indirectly at the gorgon from Athene) he cut off the head of the gorgon Medusa and gave it to Athene; riding the winged horse ➤ PEGASUS which sprang from the gorgon's blood, he rescued and married Andromeda, and he became king of Tiryns in Greece.

A prophecy had said that he would kill his grandfather; this happened in Thessaly when his grandfather, who was attending some games there, was accidentally killed by a discus thrown by Perseus.

Persia a former country of SW Asia, now called Iran. The ancient kingdom of Persia, corresponding to the modern district of Fars in SW Iran, became in the 6th century BC the domain of the Achaemenid dynasty, and under Cyrus the Great became the centre of a powerful empire which included all of western Asia, Egypt, and parts of eastern Europe; it was eventually overthrown by Alexander the Great in 330 BC.

The **Persian Wars** were the wars fought between Greece and Persia in the 5th century BC, in which the Persians sought to extend their territory over the Greek world.

Peshitta the ancient Syriac version of the Bible, used in Syriac-speaking Christian countries from the early 5th century and still the official Bible of the Syrian Christian Churches.

hoist with one's own petard have one's plans to cause trouble for others backfire on one, from Shakespeare's *Hamlet*; *hoist* is in the sense 'lifted and removed', and a *petard* is a small bomb made of a metal or wooden box filled with powder, used to blast down a door or make a hole in a wall.

Peter¹ male forename; the name given to the Apostle originally called Simon. *Peter* ('stone') is the name given him by Jesus, signifying the rock on which he would establish his Church, although he also fulfilled Jesus's prophecy that 'before the cock crow twice, thou shalt deny me thrice' (Mark 14:30).

He is regarded by Roman Catholics as the first bishop of the Church at Rome, where he is said to have been martyred in about AD 67, traditionally by being crucified upside down. He is often represented as the keeper of the door of heaven, and his emblem is a pair of keys. His feast day is 29 June.

Peter's pence was an annual tax of one penny from every householder having land of a certain value, paid to the papal see at Rome from Anglo-Saxon times until discontinued in 1534 after Henry VIII's break with Rome. In the Roman Catholic Church, it is a name given to the collection taken in churches on the feast of St Peter and St Paul.

St Peter ad Vincula is a church dedication meaning 'St Peter in chains', the reference is to the story in Acts 12, which tells of Peter's imprisonment 'bound with two chains', and of how he was miraculously released from his chains by an angel.

St Peter's fish is any of several fishes having a mark on each side of the body, alluding to the touch of St Peter's thumb and finger when he caught the fish whose mouth contained the tribute-money (Matthew 17:27).

St Peter's keys are the cross keys (one gold and one silver, representing the power to bind and loose) borne in the papal coat of arms.

Peter² male forename, name of a number of other real and fictional people.

Peter Pan is the hero of J. M. Barrie's play of the same name (1904), a motherless boy with magical powers who never grew up, and who takes the Darling children, Wendy and her brothers, from their unguarded nursery to Never Never Land where he and the Lost Boys struggle against the pirates and ► Captain Hook. After many adventures, the children go home, but Peter remains in Never Never Land, and Wendy visits him each year to spring-clean the house which he and the Lost Boys had built around her.

Peter Pan's name is used allusively for someone who retains youthful features, or who is immature.

Peter Rabbit is the blue-coated rabbit who is one of the main characters in the series of children's stories by Beatrix Potter; *The Tale of Peter Rabbit* (published privately in 1900) was the first of these.

Peter the Great is the name given to Peter I (1672–1725), tsar of Russia 1682–1725. Peter modernized his armed forces before waging the Great Northern War (1700–21) and expanding his territory in the Baltic. His extensive administrative reforms were instrumental in transforming Russia into a significant European power.

Peter the Hermit (*c.*1050–1115), was a French monk. His preaching on the First Crusade was a rallying cry for thousands of peasants throughout Europe to journey to the Holy Land; most were massacred by the Turks in Asia Minor. Peter later became prior of an Augustinian monastery in Flanders.

Peter Principle the principle that members of a hierarchy are promoted until they reach the level at which they are no longer competent; named after Laurence J. *Peter* (1919–90), the American educationalist who put forward the theory.

Peterloo massacre an attack by Manchester yeomanry on 16 August 1819 against a large but peaceable crowd. Sent to arrest the speaker at a rally of supporters of political reform in St Peter's Field, Manchester, the local yeomanry charged the crowd, killing 11 civilians and injuring more than 500.

Peters projection a world map projection in which areas are shown in correct proportion at the expense of distorted shape, using a rectangular decimal grid to replace latitude and longitude. It was devised in 1973 to be a fairer representation of equatorial (i.e. mainly developing) countries, whose area is under-represented by the usual projections such as ► Mercator's.

Petition of Right a parliamentary declaration of rights and liberties of the people presented to Charles I in a petition in 1627 and assented to by the monarch in 1628. Although not a formal statute or ordinance, this has traditionally been invested with the full force of law.

A **Petitioner** is any of those who signed the address to Charles II in 1680, petitioning for the summoning of Parliament (a move opposed by the *Abhorrers*).

Petra an ancient city of SW Asia, in present-day Jordan. The city, which lies in a hollow surrounded by cliffs, is accessible only through narrow gorges. Its extensive ruins include temples and tombs hewn from the red sandstone cliffs. It was the capital of the country of the Nabataeans from 312 BC until 63 BC, when they became subject to Rome.

Petrarch (1304–74), Italian poet. His reputation is chiefly based on the *Canzoniere* (*c.*1351–3), a sonnet sequence in praise of a woman he calls Laura. Petrarch was also an important figure in the rediscovery of Greek and Latin literature; he wrote most of his works in Latin. In 1341 Petrarch was crowned Poet Laureate.

Petrarchan denotes a sonnet of the kind used by him, with an octave rhyming *abbaabba*, and a sestet typically rhyming *cdcdcd* or *cdecde*.

Petrushka name of a traditional Russian puppet (resembling Punch), who is the central figure in Stravinsky's ballet of that name.

Petticoat Lane popular name for Middlesex Street (formerly Hog Lane) in the City of London, a centre for dealers in second-hand clothes and other commodities.

Phaedra in Greek mythology, the daughter of Minos of Crete and wife of ➤ THESEUS. She fell in love with her stepson ➤ HIPPOLYTUS, who rejected her, whereupon she hanged herself, leaving behind a letter which accused him of raping her. Theseus would not believe his son's protestations of innocence and banished him, leading to his death.

Phaethon in Greek mythology, the son of Helios the sun god. He asked to drive his father's solar chariot for a day, but could not control the immortal horses and the chariot plunged too near to the earth until Zeus killed Phaethon with a thunderbolt in order to save the earth from destruction.

phalanx (in ancient Greece) a body of Macedonian infantry drawn up in close order with shields touching and long spears overlapping.

phallus a penis, especially when erect (typically used with reference to male potency or dominance); an image or representation of an erect penis, typically symbolizing fertility or potency.

pharaoh a ruler in ancient Egypt; specifically in early use, any of those mentioned in the Old Testament and Hebrew Scriptures, under whom Joseph flourished and in whose time the oppression and Exodus of the Israelites took place.

Recorded from Middle English, the word comes via ecclesiastical Latin from Greek *Pharaō*, from Hebrew *par'ōh*, from Egyptian *pr-'o* 'great house'.

A **Pharaoh ant** is a small yellowish African ant that has established itself worldwide, living as a pest in heated buildings, so named because such ants were believed (erroneously) to be one of the plagues of ancient Egypt.

A **Pharaoh hound** is a hunting dog of a short-coated tan-coloured breed with large, pointed ears, so named because the breed is said to have been first introduced to Gozo and Malta by Phoenician sailors.

Pharaoh's serpent is an indoor firework that produces ash in a coiled, serpentine form as it burns, named by association with Aaron's staff which turned into a serpent before Pharaoh (Exodus 7:9).

Pharisee a member of an ancient Jewish sect, distinguished by strict observance of the traditional and written law, and commonly held to have pretensions to superior sanctity; they are mentioned only by Josephus and in the New Testament. Unlike the Sadducees, who tried to apply Mosaic law strictly, the Pharisees allowed some freedom of interpretation. Although in the Gospels they are represented as the chief opponents of Christ they seem to have been less hostile than the Sadducees to the nascent Church, with which they shared belief in the Resurrection.

In general use, especially with allusion to the story in Luke of the Pharisee who gave thanks that he was 'not as other men', a self-righteous person, a hypocrite.

Recorded in Old English in the form *fariseus*, the word comes via ecclesiastical Latin from Greek *Pharisaios*, from Aramaic *prīšayyā* 'separated ones'.

pharm a place where genetically modified plants or animals are grown or reared in order to produce pharmaceutical products. The word is recorded from 1990, and was formed from the first syllable of *pharmaceutical* with a punning play on *farm*.

pharmacopoeia a book, especially an official publication, containing a list of medicinal drugs with their effects and directions for their use.

Pharos a lighthouse, often considered one of the ➤ SEVEN *Wonders of the World*, erected by Ptolemy II (308–246 BC) in *c.*280 BC on the island of Pharos, off the coast of Alexandria. It was destroyed in 1375.

Pheidippides (5th century BC), Athenian messenger, who was sent to Sparta to ask for help after the Persian landing at ➤ MARATHON in 490 and is said to have covered the 250 km (150 miles) in two days on foot.

A second (probably legendary) story says that he ran from Athens to Marathon to take part in the battle, and then returned with news of the victory to Athens, making the announcement with the dying words, 'Greetings, we win!' This story is the basis of the modern marathon race.

the infant phenomenon in Dickens's *Nicholas Nickleby* (1839), the girl actress Ninetta Crummles; the expression is found in extended (and ironic) usage.

Phi Beta Kappa (in the US) an honorary society of undergraduates and some graduates to which members are elected on the basis of high academic achievement. The name comes from the initial letters of a Greek motto *philosophia biou kubernētēs* 'philosophy is the guide to life'.

phial of oil is the emblem of ➤ *St* REMIGIUS, ➤ *St* JANUARIUS, and the 8th-century English nun St Walburga.

Phidias (5th century BC), Athenian sculptor. He is noted for the Elgin marbles and his vast statue of Zeus at Olympia (c.430), which was one of the ➤ SEVEN *Wonders of the World.*

Philadelphia lawyer (chiefly in the US), a very shrewd lawyer who is expert in the exploitation of legal technicalities. Originally with reference to Andrew Hamilton of Philadelphia, who successfully defended John Zenger (1735), an American journalist and publisher, from libel charges.

philander (of a man) readily or frequently enter into casual sexual relationships with women, from the earlier noun *philander* 'man, husband', often used in literature as the given name of a lover.

Philemon in Greek mythology, husband of ➤ BAUCIS .

Epistle to Philemon a book of the New Testament, an epistle of St Paul to a well-to-do Christian living probably at Colossae in Phrygia.

Philip male forename, name of two early saints.

St Philip was an Apostle. In art he is shown either with a cross as the instrument of his martyrdom, or with loaves of bread as symbolizing his part in the feeding of the five thousand. His feast day (with St James the Less) is 1 May.

St Philip the Evangelist was one of seven deacons appointed to superintend the secular business of the Church at Jerusalem (Acts 6:5–6). His feast day is 6 June.

Philippi a city in ancient Macedonia, the scene in 42 BC of two battles in which Mark Antony and Octavian defeated Brutus and Cassius. The ruins lie close to the Aegean coast in NE Greece, near the port of Kaválla (ancient Neapolis).

Epistle to the Philippians a book of the New Testament, an epistle of St Paul to the Church at Philippi in Macedonia.

philippic a bitter attack or denunciation, especially a verbal one; from (via Latin) Greek *philippikos*, the name given to Demosthenes' speeches against Philip II of Macedon, also to those of Cicero against Mark Antony.

Philistine a member of a non-Semitic people of southern Palestine in ancient times, who came into conflict with the Israelites during the 12th and 11th centuries BC. The Philistines, from whom the country of Palestine took its name, were one of the ➤ SEA *Peoples* who, according to the Bible, came from Crete and settled the southern coastal plain of Canaan in the 12th century BC.

The word (usually in the form *philistine*) has come to mean a person who is hostile or indifferent to culture and the arts, or who has no understanding of them. This sense arose as a result of a confrontation between town and gown in Jena, Germany, in the late 17th century; a sermon on the conflict quoted: 'the Philistines are upon you' (Judges 16), which led to an association between the townspeople and those hostile to culture.

Philoctetes in Greek mythology, a famous archer, who by shooting Paris helped to bring about the fall of Troy. Although he had originally set out for Troy with the other Greeks, he had been bitten by a snake at Tenedos, and because of the smell of the suppurating wound that resulted he had been left by his companions on the desolate coast of Lesbos. After a prophecy that Troy would not fall without Philoctetes he was brought to the siege; his wound was healed and he killed Paris.

Philomel the daughter of Pandion, king of Athens. She was turned into a swallow and her sister Procne into a nightingale (or, in Latin versions, into a nightingale with Procne the swallow) when they were being pursued by the cruel Tereus, who had married Procne and raped Philomel.

philosopher a person engaged or learned in philosophy, especially as an academic discipline.

In the political theory of Plato, the **philosopher kings** are the elite whose knowledge enables them to rule justly.

The **philosopher's stone** is a mythical substance supposed to change any metal into gold or silver and, according to some, to cure all diseases and prolong life indefinitely. Its discovery was the supreme object of alchemy.

Phiz pseudonym of the English illustrator Hablot Knight Browne (1815–82), who in 1836 was chosen to illustrate Dickens's *Pickwick Papers*, and took his pseudonym to complement Dickens's 'Boz'.

Phlegethon the name of a mythological river of fire, one of the five rivers of Hades.

phlegm in medieval science and medicine, one of the four bodily ➤ HUMOURS, believed to be associated with a calm, stolid, or apathetic temperament; the adjective *phlegmatic* derives from this.

Recorded from late Middle English, the word comes via Old French from late Latin *phlegma* 'clammy moisture (of the body)', from Greek *phlegma* 'inflammation', from *phlegein* 'to burn'.

phlogiston a substance supposed by 18th-century chemists to exist in all combustible bodies, and to be released in combustion. The **phlogiston theory** was discredited when Antoine Lavoisier showed the true nature of oxygen.

St Phocas a 4th-century saint and martyr of Sinope on the Black Sea; a hermit, he was noted as a gardener, and used his produce to feed pilgrims. He is the patron saint of gardeners and agricultural workers, and sailors (perhaps because his name resembles Greek *phoce* 'a seal'), and his emblem is a spade. His feast day is celebrated on various dates, especially, 22 September or 14 July.

Phoebus an epithet of Apollo, used in contexts where the god was identified with the sun. The name comes from Greek *Phoibos*, literally 'bright one'.

Phoenicia an ancient country on the shores of the eastern Mediterranean, corresponding to modern Lebanon and the coastal plains of Syria. It consisted of a number of city states, including Tyre and Sidon, and was a flourishing centre of Mediterranean trade and colonization during the early part of the 1st millennium BC.

The **Phoenicians**, a Semitic people inhabiting ancient Phoenicia and its colonies, prospered from trade, and their trading contacts extended throughout Asia, and reached westwards as far as Africa (where they founded Carthage), Spain, and possibly Britain. They continued to thrive until the capital, Tyre, was sacked by Alexander the Great in 332 BC. The Phoenicians invented an alphabet which was borrowed by the Greeks and passed down into Western cultural tradition.

phoenix (in classical mythology) a unique bird, resembling an eagle but with rich red and gold plumage, that lived for five or six centuries in the Arabian desert (it is also known as the *Arabian bird*), after this time burning itself on a funeral pyre ignited by the sun and fanned by its own wings, and rising from the ashes with renewed youth to live through another cycle.

A variation of the myth stated that the phoenix burnt itself on the altar of the temple of Helios (the Sun) at Heliopolis (Egypt), and that a worm emerged from the ashes and became the young phoenix.

A **phoenix company** is a derogatory term for an insolvent company which is placed into voluntary liquidation by its directors, trading being resumed soon afterwards under a different company name. The usage is recorded from the early 1990s.

The **Phoenix Park Murders** is the name given the murder in Phoenix Park, Dublin, with surgical knives, of the newly arrived Irish chief secretary, Lord Frederick Cavendish, and under-secretary T. H. Burke, by Irish Invincibles in 1882.

phoney war the period of comparative inaction at the beginning of the Second World War between the German invasion of Poland (September 1939) and that of Norway (April 1940).

phossy jaw informal term for gangrene of the jawbone caused by phosphorus poisoning; recorded from the late 19th century, this industrial disease often affected workers in match factories.

Phrygia an ancient region of west central Asia Minor, to the south of Bithynia. Centred on the city of Gordium, it dominated Asia Minor after the decline of the Hittites in the 12th century BC, reaching the peak of its power in the 8th century under King Midas. It was eventually absorbed into the kingdom of Lydia in the 6th century BC.

A **Phrygian bonnet** is a conical cap with the top bent forwards, worn in ancient times and now identified with the ➤ CAP *of liberty*. Also called *Phrygian cap*.

The **Phrygian mode** is the mode represented by the natural diatonic scale E–E (containing a minor 2nd, 3rd, 6th, and 7th). Said to be warlike in character, it is supposed to have been derived from the ancient Phrygians.

Phryne name of a famous Greek courtesan of the 4th century BC, noted for her beauty and said to have been the model for Apelles's painting of Aphrodite Anadyomene and Praxiteles's statue of Aphrodite.

phylactery a small leather box containing Hebrew texts on vellum, worn by Jewish men at morning prayer as a reminder to keep the law.

The two boxes are worn on the arm (usually the left) and the forehead, with the same four texts inserted into each. These are Deuteronomy 6:4–9 and 13–21 and Exodus 13:1–10 and 11–16.

Recorded from late Middle English, the word comes via late Latin from Greek *phulaktērion* 'amulet', from *phulassein* 'to guard'.

the beloved physician in the Bible, the epithet of St Luke, as used by Paul in Colossians 4:14. Luke is thus a patron saint of doctors.

pi the sixteenth letter of the Greek alphabet (Π, π), transliterated as 'p'. Also, the numerical value of the ratio of the circumference of a circle to its diameter (approximately 3.14159).

Picardy a region and former province of northern France, centred on the city of Amiens, which was the scene of heavy fighting in the First World War. One of the soldiers' songs of the First World War was entitled 'Roses of Picardy' (1916).

picaresque of or relating to an episodic style of fiction dealing with the adventures

of a rough and dishonest but appealing hero. The picaresque novel originated in Spain in the 16th century, *La Vida de Lazarillo de Tormes* (*c.*1554) usually being cited as the earliest example. In English, the genre is associated particularly with 18th-century writers.

Recorded from the early 19th century, the word comes via French from Spanish *picaresco*, from *picaro* 'rogue'.

Pickwickian of or like Mr Pickwick in Dickens's *Pickwick Papers*, especially in being jovial, plump, or generous. *Pickwickian* can also refer to a word being used misunderstood or misused, especially to avoid offence.

Pict a member of an ancient people inhabiting northern Scotland in Roman times. Roman writings of around 300 AD apply the term *Picti* to the hostile tribes of the area north of the Antonine Wall. Their origins are uncertain, but they may have been a loose confederation of Celtic tribes. According to chroniclers the Pictish kingdom was united with that of the southern Scots under Kenneth I in about 844, and the name of the Picts as a distinct people gradually disappeared. The name comes from late Latin *Picti*, perhaps from *pict-* 'painted, tattooed', or perhaps influenced by a local name.

A **Picts' house** is any of various ancient dwellings in northern Scotland and the northern and western Isles, formerly thought to have been built by the Picts.

pidgin a grammatically simplified form of a language, typically English, Dutch, or Portuguese, with a limited vocabulary, some elements of which are taken from local languages, used for communication between people not sharing a common language. Pidgins are not normally found as native languages, but arise out of language contact between speakers of other languages. The word comes from a late 19th-century Chinese simplification of English *business*.

pie used in names of birds that resemble the magpie, especially in having black-and-white plumage, e.g. **sea-pie**, **tree pie**. Recorded from Middle English, the word comes via Old French from Latin *pica* 'magpie', related to Latin *picus* 'green woodpecker'.

Pie meaning a baked dish with a top and base of pastry and a filling of fruit or meat and vegetables is probably the same word, the various combinations of ingredients being compared to objects randomly collected by a magpie.

Pie is also used to mean a confused mass of printers' type; recorded from the mid 17th century, the term may represent a transferred use of *pie* as a cooked dish, with reference to its miscellaneous contents.

Pie in the sky is something that is pleasant to contemplate but is very unlikely to be realized, from a song by the American labour leader Joe Hill (1879–1915).

piece of eight a Spanish dollar, equivalent to 8 reals, and marked with the figure 8. The phrase is notably associated with Robert Stevenson's *Treasure Island* (1883); ➤ LONG John Silver's parrot constantly repeats 'Pieces of eight! Pieces of eight!' as a reminder of the pirates' treasure.

Pied Piper the central character of *The Pied Piper of Hamelin*, a poem by Robert Browning (1842), based on an old German legend. The piper, dressed in particoloured costume, rid the town of Hamelin (Hameln) in Brunswick of rats by enticing them away with his music, and when refused the promised payment he lured away the children of the citizens.

In extended usage, the term is used for a person who entices people to follow, especially to their doom.

Pierian belonging to Pieria, a district in northern Thessaly, that in classical mythology was reputed home of the Muses and the location of a spring sacred to them; in figurative usage, the **Pierian spring** is the source of poetic inspiration.

Pierrot a stock male character in French pantomime, usually played as a sentimental lovesick youth with a sad white-painted face, a loose white costume with a neck ruff, and a pointed hat. The character derives from *Pedrolino* of the Italian *Commedia dell'Arte*; originally a robust but simple-minded servant, the victim of pranks practised by his fellow comedians, he was gradually transformed by his interpretation in the French theatre.

pietà a picture or sculpture of the Virgin Mary holding the dead body of Christ on her lap or in her arms. The word is Italian, and comes from Latin *pietas* 'dutifulness'.

pig the pig family is descended from the wild boar and was domesticated over 8,000 years ago; the *pig* is proverbial as a type of obstinacy and greed. (See also ➤ PIGS.)

A *pig* is the emblem of ➤ St ANTHONY *of Egypt* (see also ➤ TANTONY *pig*).

A **pig in a poke** is something that is bought or accepted without knowing its value or seeing it first (a *poke* here is a bag).

Pig Latin is an invented language formed by systematic distortion of a source language; a secret language formed from English by transferring the initial consonant or consonant cluster of each word to the end of the word and adding a vocalic syllable (usually *-ay*): so *igpay atinlay*.

To **squeal like a stuck pig** is to squeal or yell loudly and shrilly; a *stuck pig* is one that is being butchered by having its throat cut.

pigeon in allusion to its harmlessness and to the fact that it is easily caught, *pigeon* in extended use means a person who is easily swindled, a dupe.

A **pigeon-hole** is a small compartment, open at the front and forming part of a set, where letters or messages may be left for someone, resembling a roosting recess in a loft for domestic pigeons; in figurative use, a category to which someone or something is assigned. In verbal use, to *pigeon-hole* may now apply assignment to a category or class in a manner that is too rigid or exclusive.

A **pigeon pair** is a name for a boy and girl as twins, or as the only children in a family.

Pigeon's blood is a type of precious stone (usually a ruby or opal) of a dark red colour.

be someone's pigeon be a person's particular responsibility or business; *pigeon* here is an archaic spelling of *pidgin* representing Chinese pronunciation of English *business*.

piggy a child's word for a pig

Miss Piggy is the flamboyant and demanding ➤ MUPPET whose conviction of her own attractions is not always shared by her companions.

A **piggy bank** is a money box, especially one shaped like a pig; savings. In the past, children's *piggy banks* were often made of earthenware with a small slot for inserting coins, and had to be smashed in order to retrieve the savings.

Bay of Pigs a bay on the SW coast of Cuba, scene of an unsuccessful attempt in 1961 by US-backed Cuban exiles to invade the country and overthrow the regime of Fidel Castro.

pigs might fly impossible, an impossibility; used ironically to express disbelief. *Pigs fly in the air with their tails forward* was a proverbial saying in the 17th century.

Pike in California and other Pacific states of the US, a name given in the 19th century to a perceived class of poor white migrants from the southern states of the US; the name comes from *Pike County*, Missouri, from which the first people of this kind were said to have come to California.

come down the pike in North America, appear on the scene, come to notice; *pike* here is short for *turnpike* 'highway'.

Pontius Pilate (d. *c*.36 AD), Roman procurator of Judaea *c*.26–*c*.36. He is remembered for presiding at the trial of Jesus Christ and authorizing his crucifixion, as recorded in the New Testament, although ritually washing his hands to show that he was innocent of Jesus's blood. *Pilate* appeared as a character in medieval mystery plays, and from this his name was used as a term of reproach for a corrupt or lax person, or one evading responsibility for their actions.

Pilate was later recalled to Rome following a massacre of Samaritans in 36. According to one tradition he subsequently committed suicide.

pilgrim a person who journeys to a sacred place for religious reasons. The word comes (in Middle English) from Provençal *pelegrin*, from Latin *peregrinus* 'foreign' (cf. *peregrine*).

The **Pilgrim Fathers** were the pioneers of British colonization of North America. A group of 102 people led by English Puritans fleeing religious persecution sailed in the *Mayflower* and founded the colony of Plymouth, Massachusetts, in 1620.

A **pilgrim's hat** is a type of broad-brimmed hat as worn by pilgrims, the emblem of ➤ St JAMES *the Great*. It may be ornamented with a **pilgrim's shell** or ➤ SCALLOP *shell*, carried by a pilgrim as a sign of having visited a shrine, in particular that of ➤ St JAMES *the Great* at Compostela in Spain.

The Pilgrim's Progress is an allegorical story (1678–84) by John Bunyan, of which the first part tells of the journey of Christian to the Celestial City, and the second the journey of his wife Christiana, guided by Greatheart. The story takes the form of a dream in which the narrator sees Christian (accompanied by Faithful) fleeing from the City of Destruction, and passing through such snares of the world as the Slough of Despond, Vanity Fair (where Faithful is put to death), the Valley of the Shadow of Death, and Doubting Castle, before reaching the Celestial City. Sustained by Evangelist, and his later companion Hopeful, he faces Giant Despair, Apollyon, and many enemies on his way.

pilgrimage a journey made to some sacred place, as an act of religious devotion.

The **Pilgrimage of Grace** is the name given to a series of popular risings in northern England in 1536 and 1537 opposing the dissolution of the monasteries and other features of the Reformation.

pillar a tall vertical structure of stone, wood, or metal used as a support for a building or as an ornament or monument; a *pillar* as that to which Jesus was bound during the Flagellation is thus one of the symbols of the ➤ PASSION.

In the 16th and 17th centuries, a *pillar* denoted a small column carried as a symbol of dignity or office; this was used by Cardinal Wolsey (*c*.1475–1530) and Cardinal Pole (1500–1558), but not recorded elsewhere. Representations of Wolsey's pillars appear in the decorations of Christ Church, Oxford. Those of Pole are represented in the illumination on the first page of his Register of Wills at Somerset House; they appear as Corinthian columns with capital and base, about the size of Roman fasces.

In the Bible, the wife of Lot (see ➤ LOT[1]) turned back to look at Sodom, from which they were fleeing before its destruction; for this disobedience, she was turned into a **pillar of salt**.

A **pillar of society** is a person regarded as a particularly responsible citizen, a mainstay of the social fabric. *Pillar* in the sense of a person regarded as a mainstay or support for something is recorded from Middle English; *Pillars of Society* was the English title (1888) of a play by Ibsen.

From pillar to post means from one place to another in an unceremonious or fruitless manner. The phrase (in its earlier form **from post to pillar**) originally referred to the rapid movement of a ball around the court in real tennis. The rhyming constructions with *tost* or *tossed* which are found in a number of early uses make reference to this.

Pillars of Hercules an ancient name for two promontories on either side of the Strait of Gibraltar (the Rock of Gibraltar and Mount Acho in Ceuta), held by legend to have been parted by the arm of Hercules.

pillory a wooden framework with holes for the head and hands, in which an offender was imprisoned and exposed to public abuse. In Great Britain the punishment of the pillory was abolished, except for perjury, in 1815, and totally in 1837. In Delaware, US, it was not abolished till 1905.

Recorded from Middle English, the word comes from Old French *pilori*, and probably from Provençal *espilori* (associated by some with a Catalan word meaning 'peephole', of uncertain origin).

pilot the word came into English in the early 16th century, denoting a person who steers a ship, via French from medieval Latin *pilotus*, an alteration of *pedota*, based on Greek *pēdon* 'oar' (plural) 'rudder'.

To **drop the pilot** is to abandon a trustworthy adviser; after a cartoon by John Tenniel in *Punch* 20 March 1890 depicting the recent dismissal of Bismarck from the Chancellorship of Germany by the new young German Emperor William II; the caption read 'dropping the pilot'.

Piltdown man a fraudulent fossil composed of a human cranium and an ape jaw, allegedly discovered near *Piltdown*, a village in East Sussex, and presented in 1912 as a genuine hominid of the early Pleistocene, but shown to be a hoax in 1953.

Mount Pinatubo a volcano on the island of Luzon, in the Philippines. It erupted in 1991, killing more than 300 people and destroying the homes of more than 200,000.

pincers are the emblem of St Apollonia, a 3rd-century martyr whose sufferings included having her teeth wrenched from her jaws, ➤ St AGATHA, ➤ St DUNSTAN, and ➤ St ELOI.

Pine Tree State informal name for the state of Maine (so called from its extensive pineforests).

pink[1] a plant with sweet-smelling pink or white flowers and slender, typically greygreen leaves. The name may be short for *pink eye*, literally 'small or half-shut eye'; compare with the synonymous French word *oeillet*, literally 'little eye'.

In figurative usage, *pink* denotes the finest example of excellence, as in Shakespeare's *Romeo and Juliet*, 'I am the very pink of courtesy'; from this developed **in the pink of condition** to denote the best possible state of health and spirits.

pink[2] of a colour intermediate between red and white, as of coral or salmon. The word comes (in the mid 17th century) from ➤ PINK[1], the early use of the adjective being to describe the colour of the flowers of this plant.

Politically, *pink* is used as a mildly derogatory informal term for a person of left-wing tendencies.

Pink elephants are hallucinations supposedly typical of those experienced by a person who is drunk.

The **pink pound** is a term for the perceived buying power of homosexuals as a consumer group, recognized in the 1980s; by the 1990s, the **pink economy** was seen as a substantial element of the business world.

The **pink triangle** was a triangular piece of pink cloth sewn on to clothing to identify homosexual men in Nazi concentration camps; in later use, a symbol indicating support for homosexual freedom and rights.

The **Pink 'Un** was the informal name for the *Sporting Times* (1865–1931), which from April 1876 was printed on pink paper.

Pinocchio puppet hero of the story by the Italian author and journalist Carlo Lorenzini (1824–90), in 1940 the subject of one of Disney's cartoons. *Pinocchio* has longings to be human; one of his characteristics is that whenever he tells a lie, his nose grows longer.

pint a unit of liquid or dry capacity equal to one eighth of a gallon, in Britain equal to 0.568 litre and in the US equal to 0.473 litre (for liquid measure) or 0.551 litre (for dry measure); in **pint-sized**, taken as the type of something very small.

Pinyin the standard system of romanized spelling for transliterating Chinese, which superseded the earlier ➤ WADE–*Giles* system. Recorded from the 1960s, the term comes from Chinese *pīn-yīn*, literally 'spell-sound'.

pioneer a person who is among the first to explore or settle a new country or area. Recorded from the early 16th century (as a military term denoting a member of the infantry), the word comes ultimately (via French) from Latin *pedo*, the same base as ➤ PAWN.

Pioneer is the name of a series of American space probes launched between 1958 and 1973, two of which provided the first clear pictures of Jupiter and Saturn (1973–79).

pip emma post meridiem: First World War signallers' name for the letters pm.

pip someone at the post defeat someone at the last moment by a small margin; *post* here is the winning post in a race.

pipe of peace a North American Indian peace pipe; a ➤ CALUMET; the term is first recorded in the late 17th century.

Pipe Roll the annual accounts kept by the Exchequer from the 12th to the 19th century;

apart from an isolated roll in 1130, the series begins in 1156 and continues with a few interruptions until 1832. The name probably derives from the subsidiary documents having been rolled in pipe form.

St Piran (d. *c*.480), monk from Ireland or Wales who settled in north Cornwall, giving his name to Perranporth. He was the patron of Cornish tin-miners. His feast day is 5 March.

Pisces a large constellation (the Fish or Fishes), said to represent a pair of fishes tied together by their tails. In Astrology, the twelfth sign of the zodiac, which the sun enters about 20 February.

piscina a stone basin near the altar in Catholic and pre-Reformation churches for draining water used in the Mass.

Pisgah the name of a mountain range east of Jordan, used with allusion to Deuteronomy 3:27, in which Moses is allowed to view the Promised Land, which he himself will not enter, from Mount Pisgah.

dig a pit for try to trap; a common biblical metaphor, as in Jeremiah 18:20.

Pitcairn Islands a British dependency comprising a group of volcanic islands in the South Pacific, east of French Polynesia. Pitcairn Island was discovered in 1767, and remained uninhabited until settled in 1790 by mutineers from HMS *Bounty* and their Tahitian companions, some of whose descendants still live there.

Pithecanthropus a former genus name applied to some fossil hominids found in Java in 1891. Also called *Java man*. The term was originally coined as a name for a hypothetical creature bridging the gap in evolutionary development between apes and man, and came from Greek *pithēkos* 'ape' + *anthropos* 'man'.

Pitman shorthand a system invented by Isaac *Pitman* (1813–97), published as *Stenographic Sound Hand* (1837). *Pitman shorthand* is still widely used in the UK and elsewhere.

Pitti an art gallery and museum in Florence, housed in the Pitti Palace (built 1440–*c*.1549). Its contents include masterpieces from the Medici collections and Gobelin tapestries.

pixie a supernatural being in folklore and children's stories, typically portrayed as small and human-like in form, with pointed ears and a pointed hat.

place in the sun a position of favour or advantage. The phrase is traceable to Pascal *Pensées*, translated by J. Walker in 1688.

In later use, it is associated with the German Chancellor Bernhard von Bülow (1849–1929), and Germany's imperial ambitions.

placebo a pill, medicine, or procedure prescribed more for the psychological benefit to the patient of being given a prescription than for any physiological effect.

Placemakers' Bible the second edition of the ➤ Geneva *Bible*, 1562, with 'placemakers' misprinted for 'peacemakers' in the Beatitudes.

plagiarism the practice of taking someone else's work or ideas and passing them off as one's own. Recorded from the early 17th century, the word comes from Latin *plagiarius* 'kidnapping'.

plague a contagious bacterial disease characterized by fever and delirium, typically with the formation of buboes (as ➤ BUBONIC *plague*; see also ➤ GREAT *Plague*). Recorded from late Middle English, the word comes from Latin *plaga* 'stroke, wound', probably from Greek (Doric dialect) *plaga*, from a base meaning 'strike'.

➤ *St* ROCH and ➤ *St* SEBASTIAN are traditionally invoked against plague.

A plague on all their houses! is an animadversion echoing the words of the mortally wounded Mercutio in Shakespeare's *Romeo and Juliet*.

A **plague-pit** was a deep pit for the common burial of plague victims.

The **Plagues of Egypt** are the ten plagues, described in Exodus 7 to Exodus 12, visited on the Egyptians to persuade them to release the Israelites.

plain simple, uncomplicated.

Plain as a pikestaff means very plain. The phrase was originally (in the mid 16th century) **plain as a packstaff**, a *packstaff* being the staff on which a pedlar supported his wares while resting.

Plain living and high thinking denotes a frugal and philosophic lifestyle; the original allusion is to Wordsworth's lines 'Plain living and high thinking are no more: The homely beauty of the good old cause Is gone.'

The **Plain People** are the Amish, the Mennonites, and the Dunkers, three strict Christian sects emphasizing a simple way of life.

Plain sailing is used to describe a process or activity which goes well and is easy and uncomplicated. The phrase, which is mid 18th century, is probably a popular use of *plane sailing*, denoting the practice of determining a ship's position on the theory that it is moving on a plane.

plainsong unaccompanied church music sung in unison in medieval modes and in free rhythm corresponding to the accentuation of the words, which are taken from the liturgy. Recorded from late Middle English, the word is a translation of Latin *cantus planus*.

planchette a small board supported on castors, typically heart-shaped and fitted with a vertical pencil, used for automatic writing and in seances.

Planck's law a law, forming the basis of quantum theory, announced by the German theoretical physicist Max *Planck* (1858–1947). *Planck's law* states that electromagnetic radiation from heated bodies is not emitted as a continuous flow but is made up of discrete units or quanta of energy, the size of which involve a fundamental physical constant (**Planck's constant**), equal to the energy of a quantum of electromagnetic radiation divided by its frequency, with a value of 6.626×10^{-34} joules.

planet a celestial body moving in an elliptical orbit round a star; originally, each of the seven major celestial bodies visible from the earth which move independently of the fixed stars and were believed to revolve the earth in concentric spheres centred on the earth (in order of their supposed distance from the earth in the Ptolemaic system, the moon, Mercury, Venus, the sun, Mars, Jupiter, and Saturn). In astrology, a celestial body distinguished from the fixed stars by having an apparent motion of its own (including the moon and sun), especially with reference to its supposed influence on people and events.

The nine planets of the solar system are either gas giants—Jupiter, Saturn, Uranus, and Neptune—or smaller rocky bodies—Mercury, Venus, Earth, Mars, and Pluto.

Recorded from Middle English, the word comes via Old French and late Latin from Greek *planētēs* 'wanderer, planet', from *planan* 'wander'.

Plantagenet name of the English royal dynasty which held the throne from the accession of Henry II in 1154 until the death of Richard III in 1485. The name comes from Latin *planta genista* 'sprig of broom', said to be worn as a crest by and given as a nickname to Geoffrey, count of Anjou, the father of Henry II. The name is first recorded in late Middle English, in the Chronicle of Robert of Gloucester, where mention is made of Geoffrey's death.

Plantation colonization or the settlement of English and then Scottish families in Ireland in the 16th–17th centuries under government sponsorship. A settler in one of these colonies was known as a **Planter**.

plantation an estate on which crops such as coffee, sugar, and tobacco are grown, especially in former colonies and as once worked by slaves.

A **plantation song** is a song of the kind formerly sung by black slaves on American plantations.

Plantin designating any of a class of old-face types based on a 16th century Flemish original, named after Christophe *Plantin* (1514–89), printer, of Antwerp. The first of these types was designed by F. H. Pierpont for the Monotype Corporation in 1913.

Plassey a village in NE India, in West Bengal, north-west of Calcutta. It was the scene in 1757 of a battle in which a small British army under Robert Clive defeated the forces of the nawab of Bengal, establishing British supremacy in Bengal.

plaster saint a person who makes a show of being without moral faults or human weakness, especially in a hypocritical way. Recorded from the late 19th century, the allusion is to a plaster statuette of a saint.

Battle of Plataea a battle in 479 BC, during the Persian Wars, in which the Persian forces were defeated by the Greeks near the city of Plataea in Boeotia.

the Battle of the River Plate a naval battle in 1939 in which the British defeated the Germans in the pocket battleship *Graf Spee*.

plateresque (especially of Spanish architecture) richly ornamented in a style suggesting silverware. The term comes from Spanish *plateresco*, from *platero* 'silversmith', from *plata* 'silver'.

Plato (*c*.429–*c*.347 BC), Greek philosopher. A disciple of Socrates and the teacher of Aristotle, he founded the Academy in Athens. An integral part of his thought is the theory of 'ideas' or 'forms', in which abstract entities or *universals* are contrasted with their objects or *particulars* in the material world. His philosophical writings are presented in the form of dialogues, with Socrates as the principal speaker; they include the *Symposium* and the *Timaeus*. Plato's political theories appear in the *Republic*, in which he explored the nature and structure of a just society.

Platonic love is love which is intimate and affectionate but not sexual. The term is recorded in English from the mid 17th century; the equivalent Latin term *amor platonicus* was used synonymously with *amor socraticus* by Ficinus (the Florentine Marsilio Ficino, 1433–99), president of Cosmo de' Medici's *Accademia Platonica*, to denote the kind of interest in young men with which Socrates was credited.

A **Platonic solid** is one of five regular solids (i.e., having all sides and all angles equal), a tetrahedron, cube, octahedron, dodecahedron, or icosahedron. Formerly also called **Platonic body**.

A **Platonic year** is a cycle, imagined by some ancient astronomers, in which the heavenly bodies were supposed to go through all their possible movements and return to their original relative positions, after which, according to some, all history would repeat itself (sometimes identified with the period of precession of the equinoxes, about 25,800 years). Also called *great year*.

Platonism is the philosophy of Plato or his followers; any of various revivals of Platonic doctrines or related ideas, especially ➤ NEO-PLATONISM and Cambridge Platonism (a 17th-century attempt to reconcile Christianity with humanism and science).

Plattdeutsch another term for ➤ Low *German*. The name comes via German from Dutch *Platduitsch*, from *plat* 'low' + *Duitsch* 'German'.

Titus Maccius Plautus (*c*.250–184 BC), Roman comic dramatist. Fantasy and imagination are more important than realism in the development of his plots, and his stock characters, which follow Greek types, are often larger than life and their language is correspondingly exuberant.

play it again, Sam popular misquotation of Humphrey Bogart's words 'If she can stand it, I can. Play it!' in the film *Casablanca* (1942), subsequently used as the title of a play (1969) and film (1972) by Woody Allen.

play the—card introduce a specified (advantageous) factor; the term derives from a comment made in 1886 by Lord Randolph Churchill on Gladstone's handling of the Irish Home Rule question, that 'the Orange card would be the one to play'.

play the game behave in a fair or honourable way; abide by the rules or conventions. Recorded from the late 19th century, the phrase is particularly associated with the appeal to public-school values enshrined in Henry Newbolt's poem 'Vita Lampada' (1897).

play to the gallery act in an exaggerated or histrionic manner, especially in order to appeal to popular taste; the *gallery* here is the highest of the galleries in a theatre, containing the cheapest seats.

play within a play a play acted as part of the action of another play; often with reference to *Hamlet*, in which Hamlet arranges for the Players to perform a play ('the Mousetrap') which shows the circumstances of his father's murder.

plebeian (in ancient Rome) a commoner, as opposed to the patricians, senators, and knights. Recorded from the mid 16th century, the word comes from Latin *plebs*, *pleb-* 'the common people'.

Pledge of Allegiance (in the US) a solemn oath of loyalty to the United States, declaimed as part of flag-saluting ceremonies, composed by the American clergyman and editor Francis Bellamy (1856–1931).

Pleiades the seven daughters of the Titan Atlas and the Oceanid Pleione, the eldest of whom, Merope, was 'the lost Pleiad', and not represented by a star. They were pursued by the hunter Orion until Zeus changed them into stars. Their name has been given to a cluster of stars (usually spoken of as seven and also called ➤ SEVEN *Sisters*) in the constellation Taurus; six stars are visible to the naked eye but there are actually some five hundred present, formed very recently in stellar terms.

Plimsoll line a marking on a ship's side showing the limit of legal submersion when loaded with cargo under various sea conditions. It is named after Samuel *Plimsoll* (1824–98), the English politician whose agitation in the 1870s resulted in the Merchant Shipping Act of 1876, ending the practice of sending to sea overloaded and heavily insured old ships, from which the owners profited if they sank.

Plinian relating to or denoting a type of a volcanic eruption in which a narrow stream of gas and ash is violently ejected from a vent to a height of several miles. The word comes (in the mid 17th century) from Italian *pliniano*, with reference to the eruption of

Vesuvius in AD 79, in which Pliny the Elder died.

Pliny the Elder (23–79), Roman statesman and scholar. His *Natural History* (77) is a vast encyclopedia of the natural and human worlds and is one of the earliest known works of its kind. He died while observing the eruption of Vesuvius.

Pliny the Younger (*c.*61–*c.*112), Roman senator and writer, nephew of Pliny the Elder. He is noted for his books of letters which deal with both public and private affairs and which include a description of the eruption of Vesuvius in 79 which destroyed the town of Pompeii and in which his uncle died. The letters also contain one of the earliest descriptions of non-Christian attitudes towards Christians.

lose the plot lose one's ability to understand or cope with what is happening, lose touch with reality.

the plot thickens the situation becomes more difficult and complex; from George Villiers *The Rehearsal* (1671).

Plotinus (*c.*205–70), philosopher, probably of Roman descent. He was the founder and leading exponent of Neoplatonism; his writings were published after his death by his pupil Porphyry.

plough often used emblematically, as in **follow the plough** meaning be a ploughman or farmer.
     From late Middle English, **the Plough** has been the name given to a prominent formation of seven stars in the constellation Ursa Major (the Great Bear), containing the Pointers that indicate the direction to the Pole Star. Also called (in North America) the *Big Dipper* and (formerly, in Britain) *Charles's Wain*.
     To **plough a lonely furrow** is to carry on without help or companionship. The earliest recorded form of this phrase is found in a speech by Lord Rosebery of July 1901.
     Plough Monday is the first Monday after Epiphany, formerly marked by popular festivals or observances in some regions, especially the north and east of England, named from the custom of dragging a plough through the streets to mark the beginning of the ploughing season.
     To **plough the sands** is to undertake an impossible or pointless task; first recorded in Robert Greene's *Never Too Late* (1590).

A **ploughshare** is the main cutting blade of a plough, often with biblical allusion to Isaiah 2:4.

pluck spirited and determined courage; recorded as a term in boxing from the 18th century, and deriving from the literal sense of the word 'the heart, liver, and lungs of an animal'.

Professor Plum one of the six stock characters constituting the murderer and suspects in the game of ➤ CLUEDO.

plumed serpent a mythical creature depicted as part bird, part snake, in particular Quetzalcóatl, a god of the Toltec and Aztec civilizations having this form.

plunder steal goods from (a place or person), typically using force and in a time of war or civil disorder. The word comes (in the mid 17th century) from German *plündern*, literally 'rob of household goods', from Middle High German *plunder* 'household effects'.
     Early use of the verb was with reference to the Thirty Years War (reflecting German usage); on the outbreak of the Civil War in 1642, the word and activity were associated with the forces under Prince Rupert.
     The well-known comment 'What a place to plunder!' is a misquotation (*was für plündern*) of the comment of the Prussian Field-Marshal Blücher (1742–1819) on London, 'Was für Plünder! [What rubbish!]'

E Pluribus Unum Latin phrase, 'out of many, one', selected as the motto for the American national seal in 1776 by a committee consisting of Thomas Jefferson, John Adams, and Benjamin Franklin.

plus royaliste que le roi a French phrase meaning 'more of a royalist than the king', now used in a number of variants to indicate that a person has adopted or developed the characteristics of a specified group or individual to an exaggerated degree.

Plutarch (*c.*46–*c.*120), Greek biographer and philosopher. He is chiefly known for *Parallel Lives*, a collection of biographies of prominent Greeks and Romans in which the moral character of his subjects is illustrated by a series of anecdotes.

Pluto¹ in Greek mythology, the god of the underworld, ➤ HADES; *Pluto* is the Latin form (used in English) of the Greek name *Ploutōn*, meaning 'wealth-giver', because wealth is seen as coming from the earth.

The name *Pluto* was given to the most re-mote known planet of the solar system, ninth in order from the sun, discovered in 1930 by Clyde Tombaugh.

Pluto was also the name of the black car-toon dog which made its first appearance with Mickey Mouse in Walt Disney's *The Chain Gang*, 1930.

Plutonian means of or associated with the underworld or the god Pluto; infernal; gloomy and dark.

Pluto² (the code-name for) a system of pipe-lines laid in 1944 to carry petrol supplies from Britain to Allied forces in France. The name is an acronym for *Pipe Line Under The Ocean*.

Plutus in Greek mythology, the personifica-tion of wealth, son of Demeter and Iasion. His name can be used allusively to indicate great riches; a character in Shakespeare's *Timon of Athens* (1616).

Pluviose the fifth month of the French Re-publican calendar (1793–1805), originally running from 20 January to 18 February. The name comes via French from Latin *pluviosus* 'rainy'.

Plymouth Brethren a strict Calvinistic re-ligious body formed at Plymouth in Devon *c*.1830, having no formal creed and no official order of ministers. Its teaching emphasizes an expected millennium and members re-nounce many secular occupations, allowing only those compatible with New Testament standards. As a result of doctrinal and other differences, a split in 1849 resulted in the for-mation of the Exclusive Brethren and the Open Brethren.

Plymouth Rock a granite boulder at Ply-mouth, Massachusetts, on to which the Pil-grim Fathers are said to have stepped from the *Mayflower*.

poacher turned gamekeeper someone who now protects the interests they previ-ously attacked (often using the knowledge gained in their earlier role).

Pocahontas (*c*.1595–1617), American In-dian princess, daughter of an Algonquian chief in Virginia. According to an English col-onist, John Smith, Pocahontas rescued him from death at the hands of her father. In 1613 she was seized as a hostage by the English and she later married another colonist, John Rolfe. In 1616 she and her husband visited England, where she died.

Podsnappery the behaviour or outlook characteristic of Dickens's Mr *Podsnap* in *Our Mutual Friend* (1864–5); insular complacency and blinkered self-satisfaction.

Podunk in the US, informal name for a hypothetical small town regarded as typic-ally dull or insignificant. Recorded from the mid 19th century, it is a place name of south-ern New England, of Algonquian origin.

Poet Laureate an eminent poet appointed as a member of the British royal household. The first Poet Laureate in the modern sense was Ben Jonson, but the title became estab-lished with the appointment of John Dryden in 1668. The Poet Laureate was formerly ex-pected to write poems for state occasions, but since Victorian times the post has carried no specific duties.

poetaster a paltry or inferior poet; a writer of poor or trashy verse. The word, which is modern Latin, was coined by Erasmus in a letter of 1521; it is first found in English in Ben Jonson's *Fountain of Self-Love* (1599).

poetic justice the fact of experiencing a fit-ting or deserved retribution for one's ac-tions; the phrase is often found as an allusion to Pope's *The Dunciad* (1728).

poetic licence the freedom to depart from the facts of a matter or from the conven-tional rules of language when speaking or writing in order to create an effect; origin-ally, as a quotation from Byron's *Don Juan* (1819).

Poets' Corner the part of the south tran-sept of Westminster Abbey where several dis-tinguished poets are buried or commemorated; the name is recorded from the mid 18th century, but *poetical quarter* in the same sense is recorded in 1711.

pogrom an organized massacre of a par-ticular ethnic group, in particular that of Jews in Russia or eastern Europe. The word comes (in the early 20th century) from Rus-sian, meaning literally 'devastation'.

poilu informal historical term for an infan-try soldier in the French army, especially one who fought in the First World War. The word is French, and means literally 'hairy', by ex-tension 'brave', whiskers being associated with virility.

ask someone point-blank ask directly; *point-blank* (*blank* probably 'the white spot in the centre of a target') refers to a shot or bullet fired from very close to its target.

win on points in boxing, win by scoring more points than one's opponent (as awarded by the judges and/or the referee) rather than by a knockout.

Hercule Poirot a fictional Belgian private detective, living in England, in the crime stories of Agatha Christie; Poirot is notable for his dapper appearance, his waxed moustaches, and his powers of deduction using his ➤ *little* GREY *cells*.

poison pen letter an anonymous letter that is libellous, abusive, or malicious; the term *poison pen* is recorded from the early 20th century.

poison pill a tactic used by a company threatened with an unwelcome takeover bid to make itself unattractive to the bidder. The use arose in the US financial markets in the early 1980s, and was allegedly coined by the US lawyer Martin Lipman in his defence of El Paso Natural Gas in 1982; it was shortly afterwards adopted as a device and a term on the British Stock Exchange.

poisoned chalice an assignment, award, or honour which is likely to prove a disadvantage or source of problems to the recipient; the phrase is found originally in Shakespeare's *Macbeth* (1606), in a speech in which Macbeth flinches from the prospective murder of Duncan.

Poisson d'Avril in France, the equivalent of April Fool (literally, 'April fish').

Poitiers a city in west central France, capital of the former province of Poitou. It was the site in AD 507 of the defeat of the Visigoths by Clovis and in 732 of Charles Martel's victory over the invading Muslims. In 1356 the city fell to the English forces of Edward, the Black Prince, but was reclaimed by the French some thirteen years later.

poker a card game played by two or more people who bet on the value of the hands dealt to them. A player wins the pool either by having the highest combination at the showdown or by forcing all opponents to concede without a showing of the hand, sometimes by means of bluff. Recorded from the mid 19th century, the word is of US origin, and may be related to German *pochen* 'to brag'.

A **poker-face** is an impassive expression that hides one's true feelings, as typical of a poker player.

Polack (now chiefly in North America), a derogatory term for a person from Poland or of Polish descent. The name is recorded from the late 16th century.

Polaris the Pole Star; the name comes (in the mid 19th century) from medieval Latin *polaris* 'heavenly', from Latin *polus* 'end of an axis'.
   Polaris was also the name of a type of submarine-launched ballistic missile designed to carry nuclear warheads, formerly in service with the US and British navies.

pole¹ a long, slender, rounded piece of wood or metal, typically used with one end placed in the ground as a support for something; from the late 15th century, of definite length, and used as a measure. From this, *pole* came to mean a measure of length, equivalent to a ➤ PERCH. Recorded from Old English, the word is of Germanic origin, ultimately based on Latin *palus* 'stake'.

pole² either of the two locations (**North Pole** or **South Pole**) on the surface of the earth (or of a celestial object) which are the northern and southern ends of the axis of rotation. Recorded from late Middle English, the name comes from Latin *polus* 'end of an axis', from Greek *polos* 'pivot, axis, sky'.

pole position the most favourable position at the start of a motor race, from a 19th-century use of *pole* in horse racing, denoting the starting position next to the inside boundary fence.

Pole Star a fairly bright star located within one degree of the celestial north pole, in the constellation Ursa Minor; in figurative usage, something which serves as a guide or governing principle, a lodestar.

policy wonk someone who takes an unnecessary interest in minor details of policy. The term is recorded from the mid 1980s, in terms of the American political scene, and there is often an implication that the high level of theoretical knowledge involved has unfitted the *policy wonk* for dealing with practical matters.

political animal a person viewed as living and acting with others; a follower of or participant in politics, translating Greek *politikon zōon*, in the *Politics* of Aristotle.

political correctness the avoidance of forms of expression or action that are perceived to exclude, marginalize, or insult groups of people who are socially disadvantaged or discriminated against.

Politically correct meaning 'appropriate to the prevailing political or social circumstances' has been recorded from the late 18th century, but did not become a fixed phrase until the early 1970s, when it received a dramatic impetus in the feminist literature of the time, and the campaign against a perceived gender bias. However, by the late 1980s the view also developed that this in itself could represent a puritanical approach which was a potential enemy to freedom of thought and expression.

By the early 1990s, use of the term political correctness was nearly always pejorative, while the labels **politically incorrect** and **political incorrectness** often suggested the notion that the idea or statement described was bravely formulated. The abbreviation **PC** is nearly always pejorative or ironic.

poll the process of voting in an election. The word is recorded from Middle English in the sense 'head', and hence 'an individual person among a number', from which developed the sense 'number of people ascertained by counting of heads' and then 'counting of heads or of votes' (17th century).

A **poll tax** is a tax levied on every adult, without reference to their income or resources. Poll taxes have often been extremely unpopular because they weigh disproportionately heavily on poorer people. Such taxes were levied in England in 1377, 1379, and 1380; the last of these is generally regarded as having contributed to the 1381 Peasants' Revolt. From the mid 1980s, the term was used informally for the ► COMMUNITY *charge*, a usage which reflected the tax's deep unpopularity.

Pollux in Greek mythology, the twin brother of Castor (see ► CASTOR *and Pollux*); also called *Polydeuces*.

Pollyanna an excessively cheerful or optimistic person, from the name of the optimistic heroine created by Eleanor Hodgman Porter (1868–1920), American author of children's stories.

Marco Polo (*c*.1254–*c*.1324), Italian traveller. With his father and uncle he travelled to China and the court of Kublai Khan via central Asia (1271–75). He eventually returned home (1292–5) via Sumatra, India, and Persia. His book recounting his travels spurred the European quest for Eastern riches.

Polonius in Shakespeare's *Hamlet*, the sententious lord chamberlain who is the father of ► OPHELIA and Laertes, and whose good intentions and well-meant advice do nothing to avert the tragedy to his family.

Poltava a city in east central Ukraine which was besieged unsuccessfully in 1709 by Charles XII's Swedish forces; they were defeated by the Russians under Peter the Great.

poltergeist a ghost or other supernatural being supposedly responsible for physical disturbances such as making loud noises and throwing objects about. The term comes (in the mid 19th century) from German *Poltergeist*, from *poltern* 'create a disturbance' + *Geist* 'ghost'.

Polybius (*c*.200–*c*.118 BC), Greek historian. After an early political career in Greece he was deported to Rome. His forty books of *Histories* (only partially extant) chronicled the rise of the Roman Empire from 220 to 146 BC.

St Polycarp (*c*.69–*c*.155), Greek bishop of Smyrna in Asia Minor. The leading Christian figure in Smyrna, he was arrested during a pagan festival, refused to recant his faith, and was burnt to death. His followers wrote an account of his martyrdom, one of the oldest such records to survive. His feast day is 23 February.

Polyclitus (5th century BC), Greek sculptor, known for his statues of idealized male athletes. Two Roman copies of his works survive, the *Doryphoros* (spear-bearer) and the *Diadumenos* (youth fastening a band round his head).

Polydeuces another name for ► POLLUX.

Polyglot Bible edited in 1653–7 by Brian Walton (?1600–61), bishop of Chester, with the help of many scholars. It contains various oriental texts of the Bible with Latin translations, and a critical apparatus.

Polyhymnia the ► MUSE of the art of mime. The name comes via Latin from Greek, and means literally 'she of many hymns'.

Polynices in Greek mythology, son of ► OEDIPUS and Jocasta, and leader of the ► SEVEN *against Thebes*; his sister ► ANTIGONE was sentenced to death by their uncle Creon for burying his ritually unburied body.

Polyphemus in Greek mythology, a Cyclops who trapped Odysseus and some of his companions in a cave, from which they escaped by putting out his one eye while he slept. In another story Polyphemus loved the sea nymph Galatea, and in jealousy killed his rival ➤ ACIS.

pomegranate the *pomegranate*, which is a symbol of fertility, was the badge of Catherine of Aragon (1485–1536), first wife of Henry VIII.

In Greek mythology, ➤ PERSEPHONE was forced to remain for half the year in the Underworld, because during her captivity there she had eaten some pomegranate seeds.

Recorded from Middle English, the word comes from Old French *pome granate*, from *pome* 'apple' + *grenate* 'pomegranate' (from Latin *(malum) granatum* '(apple) having many seeds', from *granum* 'seed').

Pommy in Australia, an informal (derogatory) term for a British person. It is said by some to derive from *pomegranate*, as a near rhyme to *immigrant*, but evidence is lacking.

Pomona in Roman mythology, the goddess of fruit and fruit-trees, wife of Vortumnus.

Pompeii an ancient city in western Italy, south-east of Naples. The city was buried by an eruption of Mount Vesuvius in 79 AD in which ➤ PLINY *the Elder* was killed; excavations of the site began in 1748, revealing well-preserved remains of buildings, mosaics, furniture, and the personal possessions of the city's inhabitants.

Pompey (106–48 BC), Roman general and statesman, known as **Pompey the Great**. He founded the First Triumvirate, but later quarrelled with ➤ *Julius* CAESAR, who defeated him at the battle of Pharsalus. He then fled to Egypt, where he was murdered.

Pompidou Centre a modern art gallery, exhibition centre, and concert hall in Paris, designed by Richard Rogers and the Italian architect Renzo Piano (1937–) and opened in 1977. The design features brightly coloured pipes, ducts, and elevators, on the outside of the exterior walls, giving the building an industrial appearance. It is named after the French statesman Georges Pompidou (1911–74).

the pomps and vanities of this wicked world ostentatious display as a type of worldly temptation; after the answer in the *Catechism*. *Pomps* here meant originally the public shows and spectacles associated with or sanctioned by pagan worship, then, more vaguely, any 'shows' held to be under the patronage of the devil, and finally (from the 17th century) tacitly transferred to those of 'the world' and associated with its 'vanities'.

pons asinorum the point at which many learners fail, especially a theory or formula that is difficult to grasp. The term is Latin for 'bridge of asses', taken from the fifth proposition of the first book of Euclid.

Pont du Gard an arched structure built by the Romans c.14 AD over the River Gard in southern France as part of an aqueduct carrying water to Nîmes. Three tiers of limestone arches of diminishing span support the covered water channel at a height of 55 metres (180 ft) above the valley. In the 18th century the lowest tier was widened to form a road bridge, which is still in use.

Pontifex Maximus (in ancient Rome) the head of the principal college of priests; (in the Roman Catholic Church) a title of the Pope. The title means literally in Latin 'supreme high priest'.

pontiff the Pope. The name comes (in the late 17th century) via French from Latin *pontifex* 'high priest'.

Pontus an ancient region of northern Asia Minor, on the Black Sea coast north of Cappadocia. It reached its height between 120 and 63 BC under Mithridates VI, when it dominated the whole of Asia Minor; by the end of the 1st century BC it had been defeated by Rome and absorbed into the Roman Empire.

Pony Express (in the US) a system of mail delivery operating from 1860–1 between St Joseph in Missouri and Sacramento in California, using continuous relays of horse riders. Buffalo Bill (William Cody) was one of its riders.

pooh-bah a person having much influence or holding many offices at the same time, especially one perceived as pompously self-important, from the name of a character in W. S. Gilbert's *The Mikado* (1885).

Poona a city in Maharashtra, western India, which was a military and administrative centre under British rule; the name is used allusively for Army officers supposedly typical of that period.

Poor Clare a member of an order of Franciscan nuns founded by St ➤ CLARE *of Assisi* in *c.*1212; the name is recorded from the early 17th century.

Poor Law a law relating to the support of the poor. Originally the responsibility of the parish, the relief and employment of the poor passed over to the workhouses in 1834. In the early 20th century the Poor Law was replaced by schemes of social security.

poor little rich girl a girl or young woman whose wealth brings her no happiness; mainly from the title of a song (1925) by Noel Coward; although the phrase had been used earlier in the title, *The Poor Little Rich Girl*, of a film (1917) starring Mary Pickford, and based on a play with the same title (1913) by Eleanor Gates.

Pooter a person resembling Charles Pooter, whose mundane and trivial lifestyle is the subject of George and Weedon Grossmith's *Diary of a Nobody* (1892); a narrow, fastidious, or self-important person.

Pop goes the weasel refrain of a popular song now regarded as a children's rhyme: 'Up and down the City Road, In and out the Eagle, That's the way the money goes—Pop goes the weasel!' The Eagle was a public house in the City Road, London.

In the mid 19th century, **Pop goes the weasel** was also the name of a popular country dance, in which one dancer would dance under the arms of the others to his or her partner to the tune of the rhyme.

Pope title of the Bishop of Rome as head of the Roman Catholic Church, and seen as in direct succession from St Peter; in extended use, a person who assumes or is credited with a position, authority, or infallibility like that of the Pope.

Recorded from Old English, the word comes via ecclesiastical Latin from ecclesiastical Greek *papas* 'bishop', patriarch', variant of Greek *pappas* 'father'.

➤ St PETER and ➤ St GREGORY *the Great* are the patron saints of popes.

Popeye cartoon character created by Elzie Segar in 1926 for the cartoon strip originating as 'Thimble Theatre' in 1919 and featuring *Olive Oyl, J. Wellington Wimpy*, and *Eugene the Jeep*. *Popeye*, the sailor whose immense strength derived from eating spinach, became Olive's accepted suitor after defeating various rivals.

popinjay a parrot; in archery, a target made of bunches of plumage fixed to a pole of different heights. From the early 16th century, *popinjay* is used, with reference to the bird's gaudy plumage, for a vain or conceited person, especially one who dresses or behaves extravagantly.

The word comes (in Middle English) from Old French *papingay*, via Spanish from Arabic *babbagā*. The change in the ending was due to association with *jay*.

Popish Plot a fictitious Jesuit plot concocted by Titus Oates in 1678, involving a plan to kill Charles II, massacre Protestants, and put the Catholic Duke of York on the English throne. The 'discovery' of the plot led to widespread panic and the execution of about thirty-five Catholics.

Mary Poppins the brisk fictional nanny with magic powers created by P. L. Travers in *Mary Poppins* (1934), and further popularized by the Walt Disney film of the same name in 1964.

poppy the type of something where the showy look is not matched by real worth.

References are also made to the story of the legendary Roman king Tarquin the Proud (see ➤ TARQUINIUS), who is said to have demonstrated how to deal with presumption or rebellion by silently striking off the heads of a row of poppies.

From the 19th century, the scarlet poppy has been seen as emblematic of those who have died in war. In the 20th century, the *poppy* as a symbol has been associated particularly with the dead of the two World Wars.

Poppy Day is another name for ➤ REMEMBRANCE *Sunday*.

poppy head an ornamental top on the end of a church pew. The term is recorded from late Middle English, and although it has been suggested that the first element represents French *poupée* 'baby, puppet', or English *poppet, puppet*, this appears to be without foundation.

the Porch another name for ➤ *the* STOA, the public ambulatory in the agora of ancient Athens in which the philosopher Zeno and his pupils met.

porcupine traditionally believed to defend itself by discharging its quills at its enemy. The *porcupine* was the personal badge of Louis XII, king of France (1462–1515).

Recorded from late Middle English, the name comes via Old French and Provençal from Latin *porcus* 'pig' + *spina* 'thorn'. An early variant, *porpentine*, is now likely to be known from its use by Shakespeare, as in *Hamlet*.

pork barrel in North America, used in reference to the use of government funds for projects designed to please voters or legislators and win votes. The term, which is recorded from the early 20th century in this sense, refers to the use of such a barrel by farmers, to keep a reserve supply of meat.

Person from Porlock according to his note on 'Kubla Khan', the casual visitor who was responsible for Coleridge's being unable to finish the poem, since he was unable to recall the opium dream on which it had been based.

porphyria a rare hereditary disease in which there is abnormal metabolism of the blood pigment haemoglobin. Porphyrins are excreted in the urine, which becomes dark; other symptoms include mental disturbances and extreme sensitivity of the skin to light. It has been suggested that George III suffered from *porphyria*.

porphyrogenite a member of the imperial family at Constantinople, reputedly born in a purple-hung or porphyry chamber. Later, a child born after his or her father's accession to a throne; a member of an imperial or royal reigning family; belonging to the highest or most privileged ranks of an organization.

porphyry a hard igneous rock containing crystals of feldspar in a fine-grained, typically reddish groundmass, used in ancient Egypt as a building stone. The word comes (in late Middle English) via medieval Latin from Greek *porphurītēs*, from *porphura* 'purple'.

Lars Porsena (6th century BC), a legendary Etruscan chieftain, king of the town of Clusium. Summoned by Tarquinius Superbus after the latter's overthrow and exile from Rome, Porsena subsequently laid siege to the city, but did not succeed in capturing it; during this period the exploits of ➤ SCAEVOLA and ➤ HORATIUS took place.

port the side of a ship or aircraft that is on the left when one is facing forward; the opposite of ➤ STARBOARD. Originally it probably meant the side turned towards the port.

any port in a storm in adverse circumstances any source of relief or escape is welcome; saying recorded from the mid 18th century.

Porte in full, the **Sublime Porte** or the **Ottoman Porte**: the Ottoman court at Constantinople. The name dates from the early 17th century, and comes from French *la Sublime Porte* 'the exalted gate', translation of the Turkish title of the central office of the Ottoman government.

Porthos name of one of the ➤ THREE *Musketeers* who befriend ➤ D'ARTAGNAN in Dumas' novel.

Portia name of the heroine in Shakespeare's *Merchant of Venice*, who, dressed in men's clothes, successfully defends her husband's friend Antonio from the prosecution of ➤ SHYLOCK; her name may be used allusively for a female advocate or barrister.

Portland vase a dark blue Roman glass vase with white decoration, dating from around the 1st century AD. Acquired in the 18th century by the Duchess of *Portland*, it is now in the British Museum; smashed in 1845, it was skilfully and carefully restored.

portmanteau word a word blending the sounds and combining the meanings of two others, for example *motel* or *brunch*. The term was coined by Lewis Carroll in *Through the Looking-glass* (1872).

Porton Down the British Ministry of Defence's chemical and biological research establishment near Salisbury in Wiltshire.

Poseidon in Greek mythology, the god of the sea, water, earthquakes, and horses, son of Cronus and Rhea and brother of Zeus. He is often depicted with a trident in his hand. His Roman equivalent is ➤ NEPTUNE.

positive vetting a process of exhaustive inquiry into the background and character of a candidate for a Civil Service post that involves access to secret material.

positivism a philosophical system which holds that every rationally justifiable assertion can be scientifically verified or is capable of logical or mathematical proof, and which therefore rejects metaphysics and theism.

play possum pretend to be asleep or unconscious when threatened (in allusion to the opossum's habit of feigning death when threatened or attacked); recorded from the early 19th century.

post-bellum occurring or existing after a war, in particular the American Civil War.

post-haste with great speed or immediacy; from the direction 'haste, post, haste', formerly given on letters; in this direction, *post* means the courier who was carrying the letters.

post-Impressionism the work or style of a varied group of late 19th-century and early 20th-century artists including Van Gogh, Gauguin, and Cézanne. They reacted against the naturalism of the Impressionists to explore colour, line, and form, and the emotional response of the artist, a concern which led to the development of expressionism.

post meridiem after midday; between noon and midnight; abbreviated as *pm*. The expression is first recorded in the mid 17th century.

post-mortem an examination of a dead body to determine the cause of death; figuratively, an analysis or discussion of an event held soon after it has occurred, especially in order to determine why it was a failure. The use is recorded from the mid 19th century, and derives from the mid 18th century use of the Latin phrase meaning literally 'after death'.

post-traumatic stress disorder a condition of persistent mental and emotional stress occurring as a result of injury or severe psychological shock, typically involving disturbance of sleep and constant vivid recall of the experience, with dulled responses to others and to the outside world.

Post-traumatic stress disorder was identified as a specific syndrome in the early 1970s; the term entered the general language in the 1980s, especially in relation to Vietnam War veterans suffering from stress-related illnesses.

go postal in the US, become irrational and violent, especially from stress; with reference to cases in which postal employees have run amok and shot colleagues.

posy a short motto or line of verse inscribed inside a ring, typically in patterned language such as an acrostic. The word is a contraction (in late Middle English) of *poesy*.

the pot calling the kettle black used to convey that the criticisms a person is aiming at someone else could equally well apply to themselves.

pot-hook a curved stroke in handwriting, especially as made by children learning to write.

Potato Famine the famine which occurred in Ireland in 1846–7, after the failure of the potato crop, which resulted in widescale deaths; the government's failure or inability to alleviate conditions remained a long-standing source of bitterness.

Potemkin transliteration of the name of Grigori Aleksandrovich *Potyomkin*, a favourite of Empress Catherine II of Russia, who reputedly gave the order for sham villages to be built for the empress's tour of the Crimea in 1787.

The **Potemkin** was a battleship whose crew mutinied in the Russian Revolution of 1905 when in the Black Sea, bombarding Odessa before seeking asylum in Romania. The incident, commemorated in Eisenstein's 1925 film *The Battleship Potemkin*, persuaded the tsar to agree to a measure of reform.

Potiphar (in the Bible) an Egyptian officer whose wife tried to seduce ➤ JOSEPH and then falsely accused him of attempting to rape her (Genesis 39).

Potomac a river of the eastern US, which rises in the Appalachian Mountains and flows through Washington DC into Chesapeake Bay. The report 'All quiet along the Potomac' is attributed to the Union general George B. McClellan (1826–85) at the time of the Civil War, although the words are also found in 'The Picket Guard' (1861), a poem by Ethel Lynn Beers (1827–79).

Potsdam a city in eastern Germany, the capital of Brandenburg, situated just southwest of Berlin on the Havel River. It is the site of the rococo Sans Souci palace built for Frederick II between 1745 and 1747, and is associated particularly with the military strength of Prussia.

The **Potsdam Conference** was a meeting held in Potsdam in the summer of 1945 between US, Soviet, and British leaders, which established principles for the Allied occupation of Germany following the end of the Second World War. From this conference an ultimatum was sent to Japan demanding unconditional surrender.

potsherd a broken piece of ceramic material, especially one found on an archaeological site.

Harry Potter hero of the children's fantasy stories by J. K. Rowling, *Harry Potter*, who has been grudgingly brought up by his aunt and uncle, attends ➤ HOGWARTS, a boarding school for wizards, to learn how to fight the evil Lord Voldemort who has caused his parents' death.

potter's field a burial place for paupers and strangers, with biblical allusion to Matthew 27:7. The field was bought with the thirty pieces of silver paid to Judas for the betrayal of Jesus by the priests, which the repentant and despairing Judas had returned to them. It is also called *Aceldama*.

the Potteries the area around Stoke-on-Trent, Staffordshire, where the English pottery industry is based.

pound a unit of weight equal to 16 oz. avoirdupois (0.4536 kg), or 12 oz. troy (0.3732 kg); the basic monetary unit (also **pound sterling**) of the UK, equal to 100 pence (prior to decimalization, 20 shillings or 240 pence). Recorded from Old English, the word is of Germanic origin, and comes ultimately from Latin *(libra) pondo*, denoting a Roman 'pound weight' of 12 ounces.

In the UK in the late 20th century the *pound* as a monetary unit has become emblematic of a desire to preserve British currency from the European standardization already applied by metrication to weights and measures.

One's pound of flesh is something one is strictly or legally entitled to, but which it is ruthless or inhuman to demand. The allusion is to Shakespeare's *Merchant of Venice*, and the bond between Antonio and ➤ SHYLOCK by which Antonio pledges a pound of his own flesh if he defaults on the bill. Shylock's insistence (defeated by Portia) on holding to the letter of the agreement is taken as a type of rapacity and ferocity.

pour oil on troubled waters proverbial expression, mid 19th century; try to settle a disagreement or dispute with words intended to placate or pacify those involved. In 1774 the *Philosophical Transactions* of the Royal Society included a paper headed 'of the stilling of waves by means of oil'; the paper referred to an account given by Pliny of how seamen in his time poured oil into the water in the belief that this would calm the waves in a storm.

powder one's nose (of a woman) go to the toilet (used as a euphemism).

power of attorney a document, or clause in a document, giving a person the authority to act for another person in specified or all legal or financial matters.

powers in traditional Christian angelology, the sixth-highest order of the ninefold celestial hierarchy.

the powers that be the authorities concerned, the people exercising political or social control, with allusion to Romans 13:1.

Powys a former Welsh kingdom. At its most powerful in the early 12th century, Powys was divided in 1160 into two principalities. It was conquered by the English in 1284 after the death of the Welsh Prince Llewelyn in 1282.

practice makes perfect used to convey that regular exercise of an activity or skill is the way to become proficient in it, especially when encouraging someone to persist in it; proverbial saying, mid 16th century.

practise what you preach proverbial saying, late 14th century, meaning that you should follow the advice you give to others.

Prado the Spanish national art gallery in Madrid, established in 1818. The name came originally from Spanish *Prado* (from Latin *pratum* 'meadow'), the proper name of the public park of Madrid.

praetor in ancient Rome, originally, the consul commanding the army; after BC 366, the annually elected magistrate; later, each of two magistrates ranking below consul.

Praetorian Guard in ancient Rome, the bodyguard of the Roman praetor or (later) emperor; in extended use, a group using its power and influence to support or defend a leader or central figure, or an established system.

Pragmatic Sanction a document drafted in 1717 by the Emperor Charles VI providing for his daughter Maria Theresa to succeed to all his territories should he die without a son. It was accepted by Austria, Hungary, and the Austrian Netherlands in 1720–3, but opposition to it led to the War of the Austrian Succession on Charles's death in 1740.

pragmatism a philosophical approach that assesses the truth of meaning of theories or beliefs in terms of the success of their practical application.

Prague the capital of the Czech Republic, which was the capital of Bohemia from the 14th century, and the scene of much religious conflict.

The **Prague School** is the name of a group of linguists established in Prague in 1926 who developed distinctive feature theory in phonology and communicative dynamism in language teaching. Leading members were Nikolai Trubetzkoy (1890–1938) and Roman Jakobson.

The **Prague Spring** was a brief period of liberalization in Czechoslovakia, ending in August 1968, during which a programme of political, economic, and cultural reform was initiated.

Prairial the ninth month of the French Republican calendar (1793–1805), originally running from 20 May to 18 June. The name, which is French, comes from *prairie* 'meadow'.

prairie a large open area of grassland, especially in North America; the word comes (in the late 18th century) via French from Latin *pratum* 'meadow'.

A **prairie schooner** is a covered wagon used by the 19th-century pioneers in crossing the North American prairies.

In Canada, the **Prairie Province** is the province of Manitoba, and the **Prairie Provinces** are the provinces of Manitoba, Saskatchewan, and Alberta.

In the US, the **Prairie State** is an informal name for the state of Illinois, and the **Prairie States** are the States of Illinois, Wisconsin, Iowa, Minnesota, and others to the south.

Pravda a Russian daily newspaper, founded in 1912 and from 1918 to 1991 the official organ of the Soviet Communist Party. Banned twice under President Yeltsin, the paper is now regarded as being broadly representative of the views of communists in Russia. The name is Russian, and means literally 'truth'.

praxis practice, as distinguished from theory; accepted practice or custom. Recorded from the late 16th century, the word comes via medieval Latin from Greek, literally 'doing'.

Praxiteles (mid 4th century BC), Athenian sculptor, only one of whose works, *Hermes Carrying the Infant Dionysus*, survives. He is also noted for a statue of Aphrodite, of which there are only Roman copies.

Prayer of Manasses a book of the Apocrypha consisting of a penitential prayer put into the mouth of Manasseh, king of Judah. His life and reign are described at 2 Kings 21:1–18.

prayer wheel a small revolving cylinder inscribed with or containing prayers, a revolution of which symbolizes the repetition of a prayer, used by Tibetan Buddhists.

Pre-Raphaelite a member of a group of English 19th-century artists, including Holman Hunt, Millais, and D. G. Rossetti, who consciously sought to emulate the simplicity and sincerity of the work of Italian artists from before the time of Raphael. The **Pre-Raphaelite Brotherhood** was founded in 1848 by seven young English artists and writers as a reaction against the slick sentimentality and academic convention of much Victorian art.

prebuttal in politics, a response formulated in anticipation of a criticism, a pre-emptive rebuttal. The term was spoken of as a ► MILLBANK technique during the 1997 British election.

preceptory a subordinate community of the Knights Templar; the provincial estate or manor supporting such a community; the buildings in which such a community was housed.

precious blood the blood of Jesus, as shed for the redemption of humankind; the phrase (first recorded in Wyclif's translation of the Bible) is frequently used in the names of religious orders and feast days.

predella a step or platform on which an altar is placed; also, a raised shelf above an altar, a painting or sculpture on this, typically forming an appendage to an altarpiece. The word is Italian, and means literally 'stool'.

predestination (as a doctrine in Christian theology) the divine foreordaining of all that will happen, especially with regard to the salvation of some and not others. It has been particularly associated with the teachings of St Augustine of Hippo and of Calvin.

predynastic of or relating to a period before the normally recognized dynasties, especially in ancient Egypt before about 3000 BC.

prelapsarian in theology, or poetic and literary use, characteristic of the time before the Fall of Man; innocent and unspoilt.

prelate a bishop or other high ecclesiastical dignitary. Recorded from Middle English, the word comes, via Old French, from medieval Latin *praelatus* 'civil dignitary', and ultimately from Latin *praeferre* 'carry before', also 'place before in esteem'.

Premonstratensian a member of an order of regular canons founded at Prémontré in France in 1120, or of the corresponding order of nuns. The Premonstratensians wear white habits and follow a strict form of the Augustinian rule, combining contemplative life with active ministry. The order had several abbeys in Britain before the Reformation and still exists in Europe.

The name comes from medieval Latin *Praemonstratensis*, from *Praemonstratus* (literally 'foreshown'), the Latin name of the abbey of Prémontré, so named because the site was prophetically pointed out by the order's founder, St Norbert, (*c.*1080–1134).

preppy (chiefly in the US), an informal term for a pupil or graduate of an expensive preparatory school or a person resembling such a pupil in dress or appearance.

Presbyterianism a form of Protestant Church government in which the Church is administered locally by the minister with a group of elected elders of equal rank, and regionally and nationally by representative courts of ministers and elders. *Presbyterianism* was first introduced in Geneva in 1541 under John Calvin, on the principle that all believers are equal in Christ and in the belief that it best represented the pattern of the early church.

presenteeism the practice of being present at one's place of work for more hours than is required by one's terms of employment. The term is recorded intermittently from the 1930s, but current usage is associated with the anxieties of the 1990s, when increasing job insecurity has appeared to result in some employees working for much longer hours than required by their contractual obligations.

press gang in the 18th and 19th centuries, a body of men employed to enlist men forcibly into service in the army or navy.

Prester John a legendary medieval Christian king of Asia, said to have defeated the Muslims and to be destined to bring help to the Holy Land. The legend spread in Europe in the mid 12th century. He was later identified with a real king of Ethiopia; another theory identifies him with a Chinese prince who defeated the sultan of Persia in 1141.

Battle of Prestonpans a battle in 1745 near the town of Prestonpans just east of Edinburgh, the first major engagement of the Jacobite uprising of 1745–6. The Jacobites routed the Hanoverians, leaving the way clear for Charles Edward Stuart's subsequent invasion of England.

Priapus in Greek mythology, a god of fertility, whose cult spread to Greece (and, later, Italy) from Turkey after Alexander's conquests. He was represented as a distorted human figure with enormous genitals. He was also a god of gardens and the patron of seafarers and shepherds.

everyone has their price everyone can be won over by money, no-one is incorruptible.

prick-eared in the 17th century, designating a person with ears made prominent or conspicuous as a result of the hair being short and close-cropped, in a style favoured by Puritan supporters of Parliament in the English Civil War; later, in figurative usage, priggish, puritanical.

pricking of one's thumbs an intuitive feeling, a foreboding, often with allusion to the words of the Second Witch in Shakespeare's *Macbeth* (1606).

It was customary to fold the thumb into the palm of the hand as a precaution against the supernatural; Ovid's *Fasti* refers to a person pointing 'with his closed fingers, and his thumb Put in the midst, lest ghosts should near him come.'

kick against the pricks hurt oneself by persisting in useless resistance or protest; with biblical allusion to Acts 9:5.

pride unbridled self esteem; in this sense, counted as the first of the ➤ SEVEN *deadly sins*.

Pride goes before a fall means that if you're too conceited or self-important, something will happen to make you look foolish; proverbial saying, late 14th century, originally with biblical allusion to Proverbs 16:18.

A **pride of lions** is a group of lions forming a social unit; the term is recorded in late Middle English, and was revived in the early 20th century.

In falconry, **pride of place** is the high position from which a falcon or similar bird swoops down on its prey; the term is first recorded in Shakespeare's *Macbeth* (1606).

Pride's Purge the exclusion or arrest of about 140 members of parliament likely to vote against a trial of the captive Charles I by soldiers under the command of Colonel

Thomas *Pride* (d.1658) in December 1648. Following the purge, the remaining members, known as the ➤ RUMP *Parliament*, voted for the trial which resulted in Charles's execution.

prie-dieu a piece of furniture for use during prayer, consisting of a kneeling surface and a narrow upright front with a rest for the elbows or for books. Recorded from the mid 18th century, the phrase is French and means literally 'pray God'.

priest's hole a hiding place for a Roman Catholic priest during times of religious persecution; these secret cupboards and passages, constructed especially in the Elizabethan period in the houses of Catholic gentry, were intended to provide refuge if necessary for days and even weeks.

prima donna the chief female singer in an opera or opera company; in extended use, a very temperamental person with an inflated view of their own talent or importance.

primal scene (in Freudian theory) the occasion on which a child becomes aware of its parents' sexual intercourse, the timing of which is thought to be crucial in determining predisposition to future neuroses.

primary colour any of a group of colours from which all other colours can be obtained by mixing. The primary colours for pigments are red, blue, and yellow. The primary additive colours for light are red, green, and blue; the primary subtractive colours (which give the primary additive colours when subtracted from white light) are magenta, cyan, and yellow.

primate in the Christian Church, the chief bishop or archbishop of a province. In England both the archbishops are primates, the Archbishop of Canterbury being entitled **Primate of All England** and the Archbishop of York **Primate of England**. In Ireland, both the Roman Catholic and the Anglican Archbishops of Armagh are styled **Primate of All Ireland**. Before the Reformation, the Archbishop of St Andrews was (from 1487) **Primate of Scotland**. In France there were formerly three primates, the archbishops of Lyons, Bourges, and Rouen.

prime¹ in the Christian Church, a service forming part of the Divine Office of the Western Church, traditionally said (or chanted) at the first hour of the day (i.e. 6 a.m.), but now little used. In monastic rules such as the *Regula Magistri* and the Rule of St Benedict

(both dating from the 6th century), *prima* is the first of the Little Hours (the others are *tierce*, *sext*, and *none*). It is believed to have been introduced by Cassian at his monastery in Bethlehem in the late 4th century. *Prime* is not included in the reordered breviary of the Divine Office issued by Pope Paul VI in 1971.

Recorded in Old English (in the form *prim*), the word comes from Latin *prima (hora)* 'first (hour)'.

prime² a state or time of greatest strength, vigour, or success in a person's life. This derives from the use of *prime* to mean the first season of the year (when this began at the vernal equinox); spring; from this developed the phrase *the prime of youth*, the time of early adulthood as the springtime of a person's life.

prime minister the head of an elected government; the principal minister of a sovereign or state. In Britain Robert Walpole is regarded as having been the first Prime Minister in the modern sense. By the middle of the 19th century the term had become common in informal use, and in 1905 it was formally recognized.

prime number a number that is divisible only by itself and unity (e.g. 2, 3, 5, 7, 11). Formerly also, the ➤ GOLDEN *number*.

prime the pump stimulate or support the growth or success of something by supplying it with money.

Primitive Church the Christian Church in its earliest times.

right of primogeniture the right of succession belonging to the firstborn child, especially the feudal rule by which the whole real estate of an intestate passed to the eldest son. The word comes (in the early 17th century) from medieval Latin *primogenitura*, from Latin *primo* 'first' + *genitura* 'geniture'.

primordial soup a solution rich in organic compounds in the primitive oceans of the earth, from which life is thought to have originated. Also called *primeval soup*.

primrose in early figurative use, this yellow springtime flower is taken as the type of the first and best.

The name is recorded from late Middle English, and means literally 'first rose'.

Primrose Day is the anniversary of the death of Benjamin Disraeli (19 April 1881), whose favourite flower was reputedly the primrose.

The **Primrose League** was a political association, formed in memory of Benjamin Disraeli in 1883, to promote and sustain the principles of Conservatism as represented by him.

The **primrose path** is the pursuit of pleasure, especially when it is seen to bring disastrous consequences. The original allusion is to the reference in Shakespeare's *Hamlet* to 'the primrose path of dalliance'.

primum mobile (in the medieval version of the Ptolemaic system) an outer sphere supposed to move round the earth in 24 hours carrying the inner spheres with it. The name comes from medieval Latin, meaning literally 'first moving thing'.

prince the son of a monarch; a close male relative of a monarch, especially a son's son; a male royal ruler of a small state, actually, nominally, or originally subject to a king or emperor. The word comes (in Middle English) via Old French from Latin *princeps*, *princip-* 'first, chief, sovereign', from *primus* 'first' + *capere* 'take'.

Prince Charming is a fairy-tale hero who first appears as in French *Roi Charmant*, hero of the Comtesse d'Aulnoy's *L'Oiseau Bleu* (1697), and in English as *King Charming* or *Prince Charming* by James Robinson Planché (1796–1880). The name was later adopted for the hero of various fairy-tale pantomimes, especially the *Sleeping Beauty* and *Cinderella*.

The **Prince Imperial** was the title of the heir apparent (1854–79) of ➤ NAPOLEON III. Exiled with his parents after his father's abdication, in 1879 he joined the British expedition to Zululand, where he was killed.

The **Prince of Darkness** is a name for the Devil, recorded from the early 17th century; in recent usage, it has been taken as a humorous appellation for the Labour politician Peter Mandelson (1953–), in tribute to his perceived mastery of the 'black art' of spin-doctoring.

The **Prince of Peace** is a title given to Jesus Christ, in allusion to the prophecy in Isaiah 9:6.

The **Prince of the Asturias** is the title of the heir to the throne of Spain.

The **Prince of Wales** is a a title traditionally granted to the heir apparent to the British throne (usually the eldest son of the sovereign) since Edward I of England gave the title to his son in 1301 after the conquest of Wales. The **Prince of Wales' feathers** are a plume of three ostrich feathers, first adopted as a crest by the eldest son of Edward III, Edward Plantagenet (1330–76), the ➤ BLACK *Prince*.

A **Prince Regent** is a prince who acts as regent, in particular the title of the future George IV, who was regent from 1811 until he became king in 1820.

Princely States in the Indian subcontinent, any of those States that were ruled by an Indian prince before the Indian Independence Act of 1947.

Princes in the Tower the young sons of Edward IV, namely Edward, Prince of Wales (b.1470) and Richard, Duke of York (b.1472), supposedly murdered in the Tower of London in or shortly after 1483 (in that year Edward reigned briefly as Edward V on the death of his father but was not crowned). They were taken to the Tower of London by their uncle (the future Richard III) and are generally assumed to have been murdered, but whether at the instigation of Richard III (as Tudor propagandists claimed) or of another is not known; two skeletons discovered in 1674 are thought to have been those of the princes.

the princess and the pea a fairy-story by Hans Christian Andersen (1805–75), about a princess who can feel a pea even beneath twelve mattresses; she is taken allusively as a type of extreme sensitivity who is irked unbearably by something.

Princess Royal the eldest daughter of a reigning monarch (especially as a title conferred by the British monarch).

princesse lointaine an ideal but unattainable woman. The expression is French, literally 'distant princess', and comes from the title of a play by Edmond Rostand (1868–1918), based on a theme of the poetry of the 12th-century troubadour Jaufré Rudel.

principal boy the leading male role in a pantomime, especially when played by a woman; the phrase is recorded from the late 19th century.

principalities (in traditional Christian angelology) the fifth-highest order of the ninefold celestial hierarchy.

printer's devil an errand-boy or junior assistant in a printing office; a *devil* is a person employed in a subordinate position to work under the direction of or for a particular person.

Printers' Bible an early 18th century edition with the misreading 'Printers have persecuted me without a cause' in Psalm 119, 'printers' being substituted for 'princes'.

Printing House Square a small square in London, the former site of the *Times* newspaper office.

prior the male head of a house or group of houses of certain religious orders, in particular, the man next in rank below an abbot, the head of a house of friars. Recorded from late Old English, the word comes from a medieval Latin noun use of Latin *prior* 'elder, former'.

St Prisca a Roman lady of the early centuries, traditionally venerated as a martyr; she is sometimes shown with two lions, who according to her Acts refused to attack her. Her feast day is 18 January.

Priscian (6th century AD), Byzantine grammarian. His *Grammatical Institutions* became one of the standard Latin grammatical works in the Middle Ages.

prisoner ➤ *St* DISMAS, ➤ *St* LEONARD, and ➤ *St* ROCH are the patron saints of prisoners.

The **Prisoner of Chillon** was the anti-Savoyard Genevan patriot François Bonivard (1493–1570), who was imprisoned for 6 years in the castle of Chillon; he was the subject of a poem by Byron, *The Prisoner of Chillon*, published in 1816.

A **prisoner of conscience** is a person who has been put in prison for holding political or religious views that are not tolerated in the state in which they live; originally used by Amnesty International.

In game theory, the **prisoner's dilemma** is a situation in which two players each have two options whose outcome depends crucially on the simultaneous choice made by the other, often formulated in terms of two prisoners separately deciding whether to confess to a crime.

In the armed services, the **prisoner's friend** is an officer who represents a defendant at a court martial; the term is recorded from the early 20th century.

To **take no prisoners** is to be ruthlessly aggressive or uncompromising in the pursuit of one's objectives.

Private Eye title of a British satirical magazine, founded in 1962; some of its ironical euphemisms, such as *Ugandan affairs* and *tired and emotional*, have passed into the language.

private eye a private detective. The term is first recorded in a story (1938) by Raymond Chandler. It has been suggested that the origin of the expression was the American detective agency founded by Allan Pinkerton;

their motto (*c.*1855) was 'We never sleep', and the agency was informally known as 'The Eye'.

privateer between the 17th and 19th centuries, an armed ship owned and officered by private individuals holding a government commission and authorized for use in war, especially in the capture of merchant shipping. The word is recorded from the mid 17th century, and is formed from *private*, on the pattern of *volunteer*.

Privy Council a body of advisers appointed by a sovereign or a Governor General (now chiefly on an honorary basis and including present and former government ministers).

In Britain, the Privy Council originated in the council of the Norman kings. A select body of officials met regularly with the sovereign to carry on everyday government, known from the 14th century as the Privy (= 'private') Council. In the 18th century the importance of the cabinet, a smaller group drawn from the Privy Council, increased and the full Privy Council's functions became chiefly formal.

privy seal in the UK, a seal affixed to documents that are afterwards to pass the Great Seal or that do not require it. Recorded from Middle English, the name means 'private seal'.

prix the French word for 'prize'. (See also the *Grand Prix* at ➤ GRAND.)

The **Prix de Rome** is a prize awarded annually by the French government in a competition for artists, sculptors, architects, and musicians; it was founded by Louis XIV in 1666 for painters and sculptors, and extended in 1720 to include architects, and in 1803 musicians and engravers. The name, literally 'prize of Rome', was given because the winner of the first prize in each category is funded for a period of study in Rome.

The **Prix Goncourt** is an award given annually for a work of French literature, named after the de Goncourt brothers, French novelists and critics of the 19th century.

prize court a naval court that adjudicated on the distribution of ships and property captured in the course of naval warfare. **Prize money** was money realized by the sale of a prize, especially a ship or ship's cargo taken in war, and distributed among the captors.

pro bono publico Latin, meaning for the public good; recorded in English from the late 17th century.

In North America, the phrase (usually in form *pro bono*) denotes work undertaken for the public good without charge, especially legal work for a client on a low income.

proclaim from the housetops announce loudly, originally with biblical allusion, from Luke 12:3 'that which ye have spoken in the ear in closets shall be proclaimed upon the housetops'.

Procne in Greek mythology, the sister of ➤ PHILOMEL and wife of Tereus; when her sister was raped by Tereus, Procne in vengeance murdered her son Itys and served his flesh to her husband.

proconsul a governor of a province in ancient Rome, having much of the authority of a consul.

In 1933, the name *Proconsul* was given to a fossil hominoid primate found in Lower Miocene deposits in East Africa, one of the last common ancestors of both humans and the great apes.

Procopius (*c.*500–*c.*562), Byzantine historian, born in Caesarea in Palestine. He accompanied Justinian's general Belisarius on his campaigns between 527 and 540. His principal works are the *History of the Wars of Justinian* and *On Justinian's Buildings*. The authenticity of his attack on Justinian, the *Secret History*, has often been doubted but is now generally accepted.

Procrustes in Greek mythology, a robber who forced travellers to lie on a bed and made them fit it by stretching their limbs or cutting off the appropriate length of leg; ➤ THESEUS eventually killed him with his own device.

proctor an officer (usually one of two) at certain universities, appointed annually and having mainly disciplinary functions; the word is a late Middle English contraction of *procurator*.

procurator an agent representing others in a court of law in countries retaining Roman civil law; (in Scotland) a lawyer practising before the lower courts. The word is recorded from Middle English (denoting a steward), and comes ultimately from Latin, meaning 'administrator, finance agent'.

In Scotland, the **procurator fiscal** is a local coroner and public prosecutor.

prodigal a person (also **prodigal son** or **prodigal daughter**) who leaves home and behaves extravagantly and wastefully, but later makes a repentant return. The allusion is to the parable in Luke 15: 11–32, in which the younger son of a wealthy man wastes his substance abroad. Returning, repentant, to his home, he finds that while his elder brother grudges the welcome offered, his father rejoices and ➤ *kills the* FATTED *calf* to make a celebratory feast.

the oldest profession the practice of working as a prostitute; politics or the law is sometimes jocularly awarded the status of 'second oldest profession', with the sarcastic implication that their practitioners are as immoral and mercenary as society traditionally considered prostitutes to be.

profiling the recording and analysis of a person's psychological and behavioural characteristics, so as to assess or predict their capabilities in a certain sphere or to assist in identifying a particular subgroup of people.

In the 1980s and 1990s, profiling became a staple of forensic investigation, with the technique of **DNA profiling**, or *genetic fingerprinting*, frequently employed to establish the unique physical characteristics of an individual. More controversially, *psychological profiling* has been used to build up an outline of the likely offender.

the Profumo affair events surrounding the resignation of the British Conservative politician John Profumo (1915–), British Conservative politician, as Secretary of State for War. In 1963 news broke of his relationship with the mistress of a Soviet diplomat, Christine Keeler, raising fears of a security breach. He resigned after it became apparent that his formal denial of the relationship to the House of Commons could not stand.

Prohibition the prevention by law of the manufacture and sale of alcohol, especially in the US between 1920 and 1933. In the US, it was forbidden by the 18th Amendment to the Constitution, but led to widespread bootlegging of illicit liquor by organized gangs, and was repealed by the 21st Amendment.

proletarian revolution (in Marxist theory) the predicted stage of political development when the proletarians overthrow capitalism.

proletariat the lowest class of citizens in ancient Rome; workers or working-class people, regarded collectively (often used with reference to Marxism).

promenade concert a concert of classical music at which a part of the audience stands in an area without seating, for which tickets are sold at a reduced price. The most famous series of such concerts is the annual BBC Promenade Concerts (known as **the Proms**), instituted by Sir Henry Wood in 1895 and held since the Second World War chiefly in the Albert Hall in London.

Prometheus a demigod, one of the Titans, who was worshipped by craftsmen; he is said in one legend to have made humankind out of clay. When Zeus hid fire away from man Prometheus stole it by trickery and returned it to earth. As punishment Zeus chained him to a rock where an eagle fed each day on his liver, which (since he was immortal) grew again each night; he was eventually rescued by Hercules.

In extended usage, **Promethean fire** is inspiration.

the Promised Land in the Bible, the land of Canaan, as promised by God to Abraham and his descendants in Genesis 12:7. In extended usage, *the Promised Land* is often used with the implication that it remains just out of reach.

the proof of the pudding is in the eating the real value of something can be judged only from practical experience or results and not from appearance or theory. Proverbial saying, early 14th century; *proof* here means 'test' rather than the more normal 'verification, proving to be true.'

propaganda originally (as *Propaganda*) a committee of cardinals of the Roman Catholic Church responsible for foreign missions, founded in 1622 by Pope Gregory XV. The word is Italian and comes from modern Latin *congregatio de propaganda fide* 'congregation for propagation of the faith'.

In the early 20th century what is now the main current sense developed: information, especially of a biased or misleading nature, used to promote or publicize a particular political cause or point of view.

prophet a person regarded as an inspired teacher or proclaimer of the will of God; among Muslims, **the Prophet** means Muhammad, and among Mormons, Joseph Smith or one of his successors. The word comes (in Middle English) via Old French and Latin from Greek *prophētēs* 'spokesman'.

In Christian use, **the Prophets** designates the books of Isaiah, Jeremiah, Ezekiel, Daniel, and the twelve minor prophets; in Jewish use, **the Prophets** is one of the three canonical divisions of the Hebrew Bible, distinguished from the Law and the Hagiographa, and comprising the books of Joshua, Judges, Samuel, Kings, Jeremiah, Ezekiel, Isaiah, and the twelve minor prophets.

The **Law and the Prophets** are the Old Testament Scriptures or their content (especially as referred to in the New Testament).

proscenium the part of a theatre stage in front of the curtain; the stage of an ancient theatre.

proselyte a person who has converted from one opinion, religion, or party to another, especially recently. Recorded from late Middle English, the word comes via late Latin from Greek *prosēluthos* 'stranger'.

Proserpina in Roman mythology, the Roman name for ➤ PERSEPHONE.

Prospero in Shakespeare's *The Tempest*, the exiled Duke of Milan who exercises magical powers over the island on which he lives, and over ➤ ARIEL and ➤ CALIBAN who are constrained to serve him. At the end of the play, preparing to return to Milan, he promises to break his staff and drown his book: symbols of his magical prowess.

Protector a regent in charge of a kingdom during the minority, absence, or incapacity of the sovereign. The term in this sense is recorded from late Middle English, at the time of the minority of Henry VI (1421–71), and was later used by Richard of Gloucester (1452–85), before assuming the throne in 1483 as Richard III, and Oliver Cromwell, 1653–8.

Protestant a member or follower of any of the Western Christian Churches that are separate from the Roman Catholic Church in accordance with the principles of the Reformation, including the Baptist, Presbyterian, and Lutheran Churches.

Protestants are so called after the declaration (*protestatio*) of Martin Luther and his supporters dissenting from the decision of the Diet of Spires (1529), which reaffirmed the edict of the Diet of Worms against the Reformation. All Protestants reject the authority of the papacy, both religious and political, and find authority in the text of the Bible, made available to all in vernacular translation.

The **Protestant Ascendancy** was the domination by the Anglo-Irish Protestant minority in Ireland, especially in the 18th and 19th centuries. The phrase is first recorded in a letter of 1792 by Edmund Burke.

The **Protestant ethic** is the view that a person's duty and responsibility is to achieve success through hard work and thrift. The term renders German *die protestantische Ethik*, coined (1904) by the economist Max Weber in his thesis on the relationship between the teachings of Calvin and the rise of capitalism.

Proteus in Greek mythology, a minor sea god, son of Oceanus and Tethys, who had the power of prophecy but who would assume different shapes to avoid answering questions; his name can be applied allusively to a changing, varying, or inconstant person or thing.

In 1989, the name *Proteus* was given to a satellite of Neptune, the sixth closest to the planet, discovered by the Voyager 2 space probe.

prothalamium a song or poem celebrating a forthcoming wedding, from *Prothalamion* (1596), title of a poem by Edmund Spenser, on the pattern of *epithalamium*.

protocol the official procedure or system of rules governing affairs of state or diplomatic occasions. The word is recorded from late Middle English, denoting the original minute of an agreement, forming the legal authority for future dealings relating to it; it comes via Old French and medieval Latin from Greek *prōtokollon* 'first page, flyleaf'.

The current sense also derives directly from French *protocole*, the collection of set forms of etiquette to be observed by the French head of state, and the name of the government department responsible for this (in the 19th century).

Protocols of the Learned Elders of Zion a fraudulent, anti-Semitic document printed in Russia in 1903 and purporting to be a report of a series of meetings held in 1897 to plan the overthrow of Christian civilization by Jews and Freemasons.

protomartyr the first martyr for a cause, especially the first Christian martyr, St Stephen.

not proven in Scots law, a verdict that there is insufficient evidence to establish guilt or innocence.

Provençal a Romance language closely related to French, Italian, and Catalan; it is sometimes called *langue d'oc* (or *Occitan*), though strictly speaking it is one dialect of

this. In the 12th–14th centuries it was the language of the troubadours and cultured speakers of southern France, but the spread of the northern dialects of French led to its decline.

Provence, on the Mediterranean coast east of the Rhône, was settled by the Greeks in the 6th century BC. In the 1st century BC, the area around Marseilles became part of the Roman colony of Gaul. It was united with France under Louis XI in 1481.

proverb a short pithy saying in general use; a concise sentence, often metaphorical or alliterative in form, stating a general truth or piece of advice.

Proverbs is a book of the Bible containing maxims attributed mainly to Solomon.

prunes and prisms a phrase spoken aloud in order to form the mouth into an attractive shape, from the advice offered by Mrs General in Dickens's *Little Dorrit* (1857). From this, the phrase is used allusively to designate a prim and affected speech, look, or manner.

Przewalski's horse a stocky wild Mongolian horse with a dun-coloured coat and a dark brown erect mane, now extinct in the wild. It is the only true wild horse, and is the ancestor of the domestic horse. It is named after Nikolai M. *Przheval'sky* (1839–88), Russian explorer.

psalm a sacred song or hymn, in particular any of those contained in the biblical Book of Psalms and used in Christian and Jewish worship. Recorded from Old English, the word comes via ecclesiastical Latin from Greek *psalmos* 'song sung to harp music', from *psallein* 'pluck'.

Psalms is a book of the Bible comprising a collection of religious verses, many of which are traditionally ascribed to King David; their numbering varies between the Hebrew, Latin, and Greek versions of the Bible.

Psalter the Book of Psalms; a copy of the biblical Psalms, especially for liturgical use.

pschent the double crown of ancient Egypt, combining the white crown of Upper Egypt with the red crown of Lower Egypt, used after the union of the two kingdoms under ➤ MENES (*c*.3000 BC). The word came into use through the discovery of the ➤ ROSETTA *Stone* in 1798, and derives through Greek from Egyptian *sekhet*.

pseudepigrapha spurious or pseudonymous writings, especially Jewish writings ascribed to various biblical patriarchs and prophets but composed within approximately 200 years of the birth of Christ.

Pseudo-Dionysius (6th century AD), the unidentified author of important theological works formerly attributed to *Dionysius the Areopagite* (see ➤ DIONYSIUS⁴).

Psmith name of an elegant, imperturbable character created by P. G. Wodehouse; *Psmith*, who first appears as a schoolboy in *Mike* (1909), explains that he has created this version of the name as best suited to his style and character.

Psyche in Greek mythology, a Hellenistic personification of the soul as female, or sometimes as a butterfly. The allegory of Psyche's love for Cupid is told in *The Golden Ass* by Apuleius.

In the story, Cupid, who had become Psyche's lover, visited her in the dark and forbade her to try to see him; when (urged on by her sisters) she disobeyed, he left her in anger. Psyche, searching for him, had to perform superhuman tasks set by his mother, Venus, before she could be reunited with her lover; in achieving the final task, she opened a casket said to contain beauty, and was overcome by a deadly sleep. Finally rescued by the intervention of Jupiter, she was brought to heaven to be married to Cupid. Allusions to Psyche often refer to the curiosity which brings her into danger.

psyche the human soul, mind, or spirit. The word comes (in the mid 17th century) via Latin from Greek *psukhē* 'breath, life, soul'.

Ptah in Egyptian mythology, an ancient deity of Memphis, creator of the universe, god of artisans, and husband of Sekhmet. He became one of the chief deities of Egypt, and was identified by the Greeks with ➤ HEPHAESTUS.

Ptolemaic system the theory (see ➤ PTOLEMY²) that the earth is the stationary centre of the universe, with the planets moving in epicyclic orbits within surrounding concentric spheres.

Although heliocentric models of planetary motion had been proposed before Ptolemy, his geocentric model was so accurate in predicting the positions of the planets that it became the standard model until challenged by Copernicus. A heliocentric system was not generally accepted until the German astronomer Johannes Kepler (1571–1630) developed

his laws of planetary motion, and the Ptolemaic system was only finally disproved following Galileo's observations of the phases of the planet Venus.

Ptolemy¹ the name of all the Macedonian rulers of Egypt, a dynasty founded by Ptolemy, the close friend and general of Alexander the Great, who took charge of Egypt after the latter's death and declared himself king (Ptolemy I) in 304 BC. The dynasty ended with the death of Cleopatra in 30 BC.

Ptolemy² (2nd century), Greek astronomer and geographer. His teachings had enormous influence on medieval thought, the geocentric view of the cosmos (the ➤ PTOLEMAIC *system* outlined in his major work *Almagest*) being adopted as Christian doctrine until the late Renaissance. Ptolemy's *Geography*, giving lists of places with their longitudes and latitudes, was also a standard work for centuries, despite its inaccuracies.

public enemy number one a person who poses the greatest threat to the welfare or security of a community or nation; (especially in the US), the first on a list of notorious wanted criminals. The term is first recorded in the *Chicago Tribune* in 1931 in reference to Al Capone.

publican in ancient Roman and biblical times, a collector or farmer of taxes. The word is used chiefly in biblical translations and allusions, as in reference to Matthew 11:9, 'Why eateth your Master with publicans and sinners?'

publish or perish used to refer to an attitude or practice existing within academic institutions, whereby researchers are under pressure to publish material in order to retain their positions or to be deemed successful.

Puck another name for ➤ ROBIN *Goodfellow*; more generally (from the Old English period), *puck* meant a mischievous and evil sprite. The use of the name for one particular spirit seems to derive from the character in Shakespeare's *Midsummer Night's Dream* (1600), and has been reinforced by Kipling's *Puck of Pook's Hill* (1906).

Captain Pugwash rotund pirate hero of the children's cartoon of this name.

Pugwash conferences a series of international conferences first held in Pugwash (a village in Nova Scotia) in 1957 by scientists to promote the peaceful application of scientific discoveries.

pukka of or appropriate to high or respectable society. The word, which comes from Hindi *pakkā* 'cooked, ripe, substantial', is used first (in the mid 17th century) of a weight or measure, meaning full, good; in extended usage, this came (in the late 18th century) to mean sure, certain, reliable. The expression **pukka sahib** came to be used for a person of good family and credentials whose behaviour is beyond reproach.

Pulitzer Prize an award for an achievement in American journalism, literature, or music, of which there are thirteen made each year. The Pulitzer Prizes were established by provisions in the will of the Hungarian-born American newspaper proprietor and editor Joseph *Pulitzer* (1847–1911).

pull see ➤ *pull someone's* CHESTNUTS *out of the fire.*

pull strings make use of one's influence and contacts to gain an advantage unofficially or unfairly; the image is of a puppeteer manipulating a marionette by means of strings.

Pullman a railway carriage affording special comfort, typically with a lounge interior and meals service at the passengers' seats. It is named after the designer, George F. *Pullman* (1831–97) of Chicago.

pulpit a raised enclosed platform in a church or chapel from which the preacher delivers a sermon. The word comes (in Middle English) from Latin *pulpitum* 'scaffold, platform', in medieval Latin 'pulpit'.

The term **bully pulpit** for a public office or position of authority that provides its occupant with an outstanding opportunity to speak out on any issue derives from Theodore Roosevelt's comment as US President, 'I have got such a bully pulpit!'

pumpkin in the fairy-story of *Cinderella*, the golden coach provided by the fairy godmother was a transformed pumpkin, which on the stroke of midnight would turn back into the fruit.

It is traditional at ➤ HALLOW'EEN to make a lantern from a hollowed-out pumpkin with holes cut for eyes, nose, and mouth so that it resembles a face.

The **pumpkin papers** is a name given to microfilm records of classified documents found in 1948 in a hollowed-out pumpkin on a farm in Maryland which belonged to the journalist Whittaker Chambers; Chambers alleged that they had been given to him by Alger Hiss, and the revelation played an important part in Hiss's trial and eventual conviction.

Pumpkin pie is traditionally eaten on ➤ THANKSGIVING *day* in the US and Canada.

pun a joke exploiting the different possible meanings of a word or the fact that there are words which sound alike but have different meanings. Recorded from the mid 17th century, the word may be an abbreviation of obsolet *pundigrion*, as a fanciful alteration of *punctilio*, a fine or petty point of conduct or procedure.

Punch a grotesque, hook-nosed humpbacked buffoon, the chief male character of the **Punch and Judy** show. Punch is the English variant of a stock character derived ultimately from Italian *commedia dell'arte* (he is also called *Punchinello*), and his self-satisfaction in his doings have given rise to the expressions **as pleased as Punch** and **as proud as Punch**.

Punch also gave his name to the title of the weekly comic magazine first published in London in 1841 as *Punch, or the London Charivari*; 'Mr Punch' was the supposed editor of the journal.

The *Punch and Judy* show is an English puppet show presented on the miniature stage of a tall collapsible booth traditionally covered with striped canvas. The show was probably introduced from the Continent in the 17th century. Punch is on the manipulator's right hand, remaining on stage all the time, while the left hand provides a series of characters—baby, wife (Judy), priest, doctor, policeman, hangman—for him to nag, beat, and finally kill. His live dog, Toby, sits on the ledge of the booth.

punch a drink made from wine or spirits mixed with water, fruit juices, and spices, and typically served hot. Recorded from the mid 17th century, the word apparently comes from Sanskrit *pañca* 'five, five kinds of', because the drink had five ingredients (water, fruit juices, spices, fruit, and sugar).

punch above one's weight engage in an activity or contest perceived as being beyond one's capacity or abilities. The allusion is to boxing, in which contests are arranged between opponents of nearly equal weight.

pundit an expert in a particular subject or field who is frequently called upon to give their opinions about it to the public. The word comes from Sanskrit *paṇḍita* 'learned'.

Punic of or relating to ancient Carthage; the word comes from Latin *Punicus* (earlier *Poenicus*), and ultimately from Greek *Phoinix* 'Phoenician'.

Punic faith is a term for treachery, from the character attributed to the Carthaginians by the Romans.

The **Punic Wars** were three wars between Rome and Carthage, which led to the un-questioned dominance of Rome in the west-ern Mediterranean. In the first Punic War (264–241 BC), Rome secured Sicily from Car-thage and established herself as a naval power; in the second (218–201 BC), the defeat of Hannibal put an end to Carthage's pos-ition as a Mediterranean power; the third (149–146 BC) ended in the total destruction of the city of Carthage.

Punjab a region of NW India and Pakistan, a wide, fertile plain traversed by the Indus and the five tributaries which gave the re-gion its name (from Hindi *panj* 'five' + *āb* 'waters').

punk an admirer or player of a loud, fast-moving, and aggressive form of rock music popular in the late 1970s, typically character-ized by coloured spiked hair and clothing decorated with safety pins or zips; also, this form of music. The terms **punk rocker** and **punk rock** are also used.

The word is recorded from the late 17th century in the sense 'soft crumbly wood that can be used as timber', and from the early 20th century in the sense 'a worthless per-son'; it may also be related to archaic *punk* 'prostitute' and *spunk*, 'courage'.

sell someone a pup swindle someone, es-pecially by selling something worthless. The idea is that the purchaser has been given an inflated perception of a useless object's po-tential or future value.

Purana any of a class of Sanskrit sacred writings on Hindu mythology and folklore of varying date and origin, the most ancient of which dates from the 4th century AD. The name comes from Sanskrit *purāna* 'ancient (legend)'.

Purbeck marble a hard limestone from *Purbeck* in Dorset, which is polished and used for decorative parts of buildings, fonts, and effigies.

purdah the practice among women in cer-tain Muslim and Hindu societies of living in a separate room or behind a curtain, or of dressing in all-enveloping clothes, in order to stay out of the sight of men or strangers. The word comes (in the early 19th century) from Urdu and Persian *parda* 'veil, curtain'.

purgatory (in Catholic doctrine) a place or state of suffering inhabited by the souls of sinners who are expiating their sins before going to heaven. Recorded from Middle Eng-lish, the word ultimately comes (via Anglo-Norman French or medieval Latin) from late Latin *purgatorius* 'purifying'.

Purification (of the Virgin Mary) the purification of the Virgin Mary after the birth of Jesus, culminating in her presenta-tion of Jesus in the temple; the feast (2 Febru-ary, also called *Candlemas*) commemorating this.

Purim a lesser Jewish festival held in spring (on the 14th or 15th day of Adar) to commem-orate the defeat of ➤ HAMAN's plot to mas-sacre the Jews as recorded in the book of Esther. The name is a Hebrew word, plural of *pūr*, explained in the book of Esther (3:7, 9:24) as meaning 'lot', with allusion to the casting of lots by Haman to select the day on which the Jews were to be killed.

Puritan a member of a group of English Protestants of the late 16th and 17th centur-ies who regarded the Reformation of the Church under Elizabeth as incomplete and sought to simplify and regulate forms of wor-ship.

Oppressed under James I and Charles I, in particular by Archbishop Laud, many (such as the Pilgrim Fathers) emigrated to the Netherlands and America. The Civil War of the 1640s led to the temporary pre-eminence of Puritanism. Soon, however, the move-ment fragmented into sects, and the term *Puritan* began to be less used; after the Restor-ation such people tended to be called Dis-senters or Nonconformists.

purple originally, a crimson dye obtained from some molluscs, formerly used for fabric worn by an emperor or senior magistrate in ancient Rome or Byzantium; in figurative use, imperial, royal. In later use, *purple* came to be used for a colour intermediate between red and blue.

Purple as a colour has symbolic connota-tions of penitence and mourning, especially as an ecclesiastical colour; in literary and poetic use, it may refer to the colour of blood.

Recorded from Old English (describing the clothing of an emperor) the word comes via Latin *purpura* 'purple' from Greek *porphura*, denoting molluscs that yielded a crimson dye, or cloth dyed with this.

In the US, the **Purple Heart** is a decoration for those wounded or killed in action, established in 1782 and re-established in 1932. *Purple heart* was also a slang term for amphetamines (from their colour and shape) in the 1960s.

A **purple passage** is an elaborate or excessively ornate passage in a literary composition; an alternative name is **purple patch**. The term is a translation of Latin *purpureus pannus*, and comes from the Roman poet Horace's *Ars Poetica*, 'Works of serious purpose and grand promises often have a purple patch or two stitched on, to shine far and wide.'

purse a purse is the emblem of St Antoninus of Florence (389–1459), who as a Christian moralist taught that money invested in commerce was true capital, and that therefore interest could be claimed on it without the sin of usury, ➤ St LAWRENCE, and St John the Almsgiver (fl. *c*.620), patriarch of Alexandria.

pursuivant an officer of the College of Arms ranking below a herald. The four ordinary pursuivants are *Rouge Croix*, *Bluemantle*, *Rouge Dragon*, and *Portcullis*. The word is recorded from late Middle English, denoting a junior heraldic officer, and comes ultimately from Old French *pursivre* 'follow after'.

From the early 16th century, *pursuivant* denoted a royal or State messenger with power to execute warrants; it refers especially in the 16th and 17th centuries to those who pursued the Catholic priests harboured by ➤ RECUSANTS.

Puseyite a follower or supporter of the English theologian Dr E. B. *Pusey* (1800–82) and his associates in the Oxford Movement who advocated the revival of Catholic doctrine and observance in the Church of England.

when push comes to shove when one must commit oneself to an action or decision, if the worst comes to the worst.

push the envelope approach or extend the limits of what is possible, originally as aviation slang, relating to graphs of aerodynamic performance on which the *envelope* is the boundary line representing an aircraft's capabilities.

pushmi-pullyu an imaginary creature resembling a llama or an antelope, but with a head at both ends, as invented by Hugh Lofting (1886–1947) in *Doctor Dolittle* (1922); in extended usage, something which is ambivalent or incoherent.

puss recorded from the mid 16th century, a word common to a number of Germanic languages, usually as a call-name for a cat. From the mid 17th century, the word has also been applied to a hare.

Puss in Boots is the central character of a story by Perrault, in which a miller bequeaths his three sons respectively his mill, his ass, and his cat. The youngest, who inherits the cat, laments his ill-fortune. But the resourceful cat, by a series of unscrupulous ruses, in which he represents his master to the king as the wealthy marquis of Carabas, secures for him the hand of the king's daughter.

putsch a violent attempt to overthrow a government; a coup. The word is Swiss German, originally 'knock, thrust, blow', and is recorded from the early 20th century; it is used particularly in connection with Hitler's unsuccessful attempt at an uprising in Munich, 1923–4.

Pwyll in Welsh mythology, prince of Dyfed and 'Head of Hades', the subject of the first story in the *Mabinogion*, in which he changes places for a year with ➤ ARAWN.

Pygmalion in Greek mythology, a king of Cyprus who fashioned an ivory statue of a beautiful woman and loved it so deeply that in answer to his prayer Aphrodite gave it life. The woman (later named *Galatea*) bore him a daughter, Paphos.

Pygmalion was used as the name of a play (1916; the musical *My Fair Lady* was based on it) by George Bernard Shaw, in which the phonetician Henry Higgins teaches the Cockney flower-seller Eliza Doolittle to pass herself off as a society woman. Before her transformation is fully achieved, Eliza utters the words 'not bloody likely', which caused a public sensation at the time of the first London production; as a result, *Pygmalion* became a humorous euphemism for 'bloody'.

pygmy originally (in late Middle English) denoting a mythological race of small people; in later use, a member of certain peoples of very short stature in equatorial Africa and parts of SE Asia. The word comes via Latin from Greek *pugmaios* 'dwarf', from *pugmē* 'the length measured from elbow to knuckles'.

pylon a monumental gateway to an ancient Egyptian temple formed by two truncated pyramidal towers.

In the early 20th century, the term was extended to cover a tall tower-like structure used for carrying electricity cables high above the ground; the word may be used (as in **Pylon Poets**) to designate those poets of the 1930s (chiefly W. H. Auden, C. Day Lewis, Louis MacNeice, and Stephen Spender) who used industrial scenes and imagery as themes of their poetry, after Spender's poem *The Pylons* (1933).

The word comes (in the early 19th century) from Greek *pulōn*, from *pulē* 'gate'.

pyramid a monumental structure with a square or triangular base and sloping sides that meet in a point at the top, especially one built of stone as a royal tomb in ancient Egypt.

Pyramids were built as tombs for Egyptian pharaohs from the 3rd dynasty (*c*.2649 BC) until *c*.1640 BC. The early step pyramid, with several steps and a flat top, developed into the true pyramid, such as the three largest at Giza near Cairo (**the Pyramids**, including the Great Pyramid of Cheops) which were one of the Seven Wonders of the World. Monuments of similar shape are associated with the Aztec and Maya civilizations of *c*.1200 BC–AD 750, and, like those in Egypt, were part of large ritual complexes.

Pyramus a Babylonian youth, lover of Thisbe. Forbidden to marry by their parents, who were neighbours, the lovers conversed through a chink in a wall and agreed to meet at a tomb outside the city. There, Thisbe was frightened away by a lioness coming from its kill, and Pyramus, seeing her bloodstained cloak and supposing her dead, stabbed himself. Thisbe, finding his body when she returned, threw herself upon his sword. Their blood stained a mulberry tree, whose fruit has ever since been black when ripe, in sign of mourning for them.

The story of Pyramus and Thisbe is the subject of the mechanicals' play in Shakespeare's *Midsummer Night's Dream*.

Pyrrhus (*c*.318–272 BC), king of Epirus *c*.307–272. After invading Italy in 280, he defeated the Romans at Asculum in 279, but sustained heavy losses; the term **Pyrrhic victory**, meaning a victory gained at too great a cost, derives from this.

Pythagoras (*c*.580–500 BC), Greek philosopher; known as **Pythagoras of Samos**. Pythagoras sought to interpret the entire physical world in terms of numbers, and founded their systematic and mystical study; he is best known for the theorem of the right-angled triangle. His analysis of the courses of the sun, moon, and stars into circular motions was not set aside until the 17th century.

Pythagoras also founded a secret religious, political, and scientific sect in Italy: the Pythagoreans held that the soul is condemned to a cycle of reincarnation, from which it may escape by attaining a state of purity.

Pythagoras' theorem is the theorem attributed to Pythagoras that the square on the hypotenuse of a right-angled triangle is equal in area to the sum of the squares on the other two sides.

The **Pythagorean letter** is the Greek letter Y, used by Pythagoras as a symbol of the two divergent paths of virtue and of vice.

The **Pythagorean system** is the system of astronomy proposed by Pythagoras, in which all celestial bodies, including the earth, were held to revolve around a central fire (not the sun, but presumably identified with the sun, resulting in the system being assumed identical with the Copernican system).

Pythia the priestess of Apollo at Delphi in ancient Greece. The name comes from Greek *Puthō*, a former name of Delphi.

Pythias in Greek mythology, the friend and companion of ➤ DAMON.

python the name of this snake comes from Greek *Puthōn*, a huge serpent killed by Apollo near Delphi; in some legends, it was the original guardian of the oracle there.

Pythonesque after the style of or resembling the absurdist or surrealist humour of ➤ MONTY *Python's Flying Circus*, a British television comedy series (1969–74).

pythoness a female soothsayer or conjuror of spirits. Recorded from Middle English, the term comes via Old French from late Latin *pythonissa*, based on Greek *puthōn* 'soothsaying'.

pyx in the Christian Church, the container in which the consecrated bread of the Eucharist is kept.

In the UK, a *pyx* is also a box at the Royal Mint in which specimen gold and silver coins are deposited to be tested annually at the **trial of the pyx** by members of the Goldsmiths' Company.

Qq

Q the seventeenth letter of the modern English alphabet and the sixteenth of the ancient Roman one, in the latter an adoption of the κ (*koppa*) of some of the early Greek alphabets, in turn derived from the Phoenician letter used to represent voiced uvular.

Q was the pseudonym of the English writer and critic Arthur Quiller-Couch (1863–1944), which he originally adopted as a student at Oxford when writing parodies of English poets for the *Oxford Magazine*.

Q also denotes the hypothetical source of the passages shared by the gospels of Matthew and Luke, but not found in Mark; Q here probably comes from German *Quelle* 'source'.

In the James Bond films, Q is the name of the elderly technician responsible for the development of Bond's customized cars and other gadgets.

See also ➤ MIND *one's P's and Q's*.

QED abbreviation for ➤ QUOD *erat demonstrandum*.

Qin a dynasty that ruled China 221–206 BC and was the first to establish rule over a united China. The construction of the Great Wall of China was begun during this period. Also *Ch'in*.

Qing a dynasty established by the Manchus that ruled China 1644–1912. Its overthrow in 1912 by Sun Yat-sen and his supporters ended imperial rule in China. Also *Ch'ing*.

quack a person who dishonestly claims to have special knowledge and skill in some field, typically in medicine. The word is recorded from the mid 17th century and is an abbreviation of earlier *quacksalver*, from Dutch, probably from obsolete *quacken* 'prattle' + *salf*, *zalf* 'salve, ointment'. A *quacksalver* may have been someone who 'quacked' or boasted about the virtues of his remedies; it has however been suggested that *quack-* may mean 'to work incompetently'.

Quadragesima the forty days of ➤ LENT. The name comes from ecclesiastical Latin, ultimately from Latin *quadraginta* 'forty'.

  Quadragesima Sunday is the first Sunday in Lent.

quadrivium a medieval university course involving the 'mathematical arts' of arithmetic, geometry, astronomy, and music; with the ➤ TRIVIUM comprising grammar, rhetoric, and logic, these subjects formed the ➤ SEVEN *liberal arts*. The name is Latin, and means literally 'the place where four roads meet'.

Quai d'Orsay a riverside street on the left bank of the Seine in Paris; the French ministry of foreign affairs, which has its headquarters in this street.

Quaker a member of the Religious Society of Friends, a Christian movement founded by George Fox *c.*1650 and devoted to peaceful principles. Central to the Quakers' belief is the doctrine of the 'Inner Light', or sense of Christ's direct working in the soul. This has led them to reject both formal ministry and all set forms of worship.

The name may refer to George Fox's direction to his followers to 'tremble at the name of the Lord', or from fits supposedly experienced by worshippers when moved by the Spirit, and this is suggested by a passage in his journal; however, there is a record of 1647 of the name having previously been applied to members of a foreign religious sect, a group of women who were 'called Quakers, and these swell, shiver, and shake'. *Quaker* is not used by the Friends themselves, but is not now regarded as derogatory.

Members of the Society of Friends typically wore very plain clothes, and this may be referred to allusively.

quango chiefly derogatory term for a semi-public administrative body outside the civil service but with financial support from and senior appointments made by the government. Recorded from the 1970s, the term is an acronym from *quasi* (or *quasi-autonomous*) *non-government(al) organization*.

quarantine a state, period, or place of isolation in which people or animals that have arrived from elsewhere or been exposed to infectious or contagious disease are placed. The use developed in the 17th century, from the original (early 16th-century) meaning of a period of forty days during which a widow who is entitled to a dower has the right to remain in her deceased husband's main dwelling.

quark in physics, any of a number of sub-atomic particles carrying a fractional electric charge, postulated as building blocks of the hadrons. Quarks have not been directly observed but theoretical predictions based on their existence have been confirmed experimentally. The name (originally *quork*) was invented in the 1960s by Murray Gell-Mann; it was changed by association with the line 'Three quarks for Muster Mark' in Joyce's *Finnegans Wake* (1939).

quarry an animal which is being hunted. Originally, the term denoted the parts of a deer that were placed on the hide and given as a reward to the hounds; the word comes (in Middle English) from Old French *cuiree*, an alteration, influenced by *cuir* 'leather' and *curer* 'clean, disembowel', of *couree*, based on Latin *cor* 'heart'.

quarter a fourth part; in heraldry, each of four or more roughly equal divisions (*dexter chief*, *sinister chief*, *dexter base*, and *sinister base*) of a shield separated by vertical and horizontal lines; a square charge which covers the top left (dexter chief) quarter of the field.

The **quarter days** are each of four days fixed by custom as marking off the quarters of the year, on which some tenancies begin and end and quarterly payments of rent and other charges fall due. In England and Ireland the quarter days are Lady Day (March 25), Midsummer Day (June 24), Michaelmas (September 29), and Christmas (December 25). The name is also sometimes applied to the Scottish terms of Candlemas (Feb. 2), Whit Sunday (May 15), Lammas (August 1), and Martinmas (November 11).

quarterdeck the part of a ship's upper deck near the stern, traditionally reserved for officers. The term was originally (in the early 17th century) used for a smaller deck situated above the *half-deck*, covering about a quarter of the vessel.

quarto a size of book page resulting from folding each printed sheet into four leaves (eight pages). Quarto-sizes range from 15 × 11 inches (**imperial quarto**) to 7⅝ × 6⅛ (**pot quarto**), according to the size of the original sheet.

Quasimodo name of the hunchback bell-ringer in Victor Hugo's novel *Notre-Dame de Paris* (1831), sometimes taken as a type of

courage and kindness behind an unattractive exterior.

From the 1960s, *Quasimodo* has been used in surfing for an act of riding on a wave in a crouched position with one arm forward and one arm back.

Quasimodo Sunday the Sunday after Easter, Low Sunday, from Latin *quasi modo*, the first words of the introit for this day, *quasi modo geniti infantes* 'as if new-born babes'.

quatrefoil an ornamental design of four lobes or leaves as used in architectural tracery, resembling a flower or clover leaf.

queen the female ruler of an independent state, especially one who inherits the position by right of birth; the wife of a king. The word is recorded from Old English (in form *cwēn*) and is of Germanic origin.

Queen and country are the objects of allegiance for a patriot whose head of State is a queen. The term is first recorded in Farquhar's *The Recruiting Officer* (1706), 'I endeavour by the example of this worthy gentleman to serve my Queen and country at home', from the reign of Queen Anne (1665–1714).

Queen Anne is dead is a phrase implying stale news; it is first recorded in the mid 19th century, in Barham's *Ingoldsby Legends* (1840), series 1, 'Lord Brougham, it appears, isn't dead, though Queen Anne is'; an earlier variant appears in Swift's *Complete Collection of Genteel and Ingenious Conversation* (1738), 'Why, Madam, Queen Elizabeth's dead'.

A **queen bee** is the single reproductive female in a hive or colony of honeybees; in extended usage, the chief or dominant woman in an organization or social group.

A **queen consort** is the wife of a reigning king, and a **queen dowager** the widow of a king. A **queen mother** is the widow of a king and mother of the sovereign. A **queen regnant** is a queen ruling in her own right.

Queen of glory and **Queen of Heaven** are epithets of the Virgin Mary.

Queen of Hearts was the nickname of Elizabeth of Bohemia (1598–1662), daughter of James I of England, who with her husband Frederick (the 'Winter King') had briefly occupied the throne of Bohemia before being driven into exile.

The *Queen of Hearts* is a well-known nursery-rhyme character dating from the late 18th century; in the 19th century she becomes one of the leading playing-card characters in Lewis Carroll's *Alice's Adventurers in*

Wonderland (1865); her favourite exclamation is 'Off with his (or her) head!'

In classical antiquity, **queen of love** is an epithet of Aphrodite or Venus.

The **queen of tides** is the moon; the phrase is first recorded in Byron's *Childe Harold* (1812).

Queensberry Rules the standard rules of boxing, originally drawn up in 1867 to govern the sport in Britain, named after John Sholto Douglas (1844–1900), 8th Marquess of *Queensberry*, who supervised the preparation of the rules; in figurative use, standard rules of polite or acceptable behaviour.

Queer Nation the name of a campaigning lesbian and gay rights organization founded in the US in 1990, reflecting a militant form of gay activism which set out deliberately to reclaim the contemptuous slang use of queer to mean a homosexual by transmuting what was originally regarded as pejorative into a force for asserting the rights of the group concerned.

Queer Street an imaginary street where people in difficulties are supposed to reside; the term is recorded from the early 19th century, and is now used particularly in relation to financial difficulty.

the **Questing Beast** in *Le Morte d'Arthur*, a monstrous creature hunted by Palomydes the Saracen; the name refers to its making a noise like that of a pack of hounds.

Quetzalcóatl the plumed serpent god of the Toltec and Aztec civilizations. Traditionally the god of the morning and evening star, he later became known as the patron of priests, inventor of books and of the calendar, and as the symbol of death and resurrection. His worship involved human sacrifice. Legend said that he would return in another age, and when Montezuma, last king of the Aztecs, received news of the landing of Cortés and his men in 1519, he thought that Quetzalcóatl had returned.

quetzalcoatlus a giant pterosaur of the late Cretaceous period, which was the largest ever flying animal with a wingspan of up to 15 m.

the **quick and the dead** the living and the dead; the phrase comes from the Apostles' Creed in the *Book of Common Prayer* (1662).

quicksilver the liquid metal mercury, used in similes and metaphors to describe something that moves or changes very quickly, or that is difficult to hold or contain.

quiddity the inherent nature or essence of someone or something; a distinctive feature or peculiarity. Recorded from late Middle English, the word comes from medieval Latin *quidditas*, from Latin *quid* 'what'.

quidnunc an archaic term for an inquisitive and gossipy person; someone who is always asking 'What now?' or 'What's new'. Recorded from the early 18th century, the word comes from Latin *quid* 'what' + *nunc* 'now'.

quiet American a person suspected of being an undercover agent or spy; with allusion to Graham Greene's *The Quiet American* (1955).

Quietism (in the Christian faith) devotional contemplation and abandonment of the will as a form of religious mysticism. Recorded from the late 17th century, the term originally denoted the religious mysticism based on the teachings of the Spanish priest Miguel de Molinos (c.1640–97); also called *Molinism*.

quietus death or something that causes death, regarded as a release from life. The expression dates from late Middle English, and represents an abbreviation of medieval Latin *quietus est* 'he is quit', originally used as a form of receipt or discharge on payment of a debt.

quincunx in astrology, an aspect of 150°, equivalent to five zodiacal signs, first referred by the English astrologer William Lilly (1602–81).

Quincunx is also used for an arrangement of five objects with four at the corners of a square or rectangle and the fifth at its centre, used for the five on a dice or playing card, and in planting trees (this sense, which is also found in Latin, apparently derives from the use of five dots or dashes, arranged in this way, to denote five twelfths of an *as*), an ancient Roman copper coin.

The word is Latin, and means literally 'five twelfths'.

Quinquagesima Sunday the Sunday before the beginning of Lent. *Quinquagesima* comes from medieval Latin, from Latin *quinquagesimus* 'fiftieth', on the pattern of ➤ QUADRAGESIMA, because it is ten days before the forty penitential days of Lent.

quinquereme an ancient Roman or Greek galley of a kind believed to have had three banks of oars, the oars in the top two banks being rowed by pairs of oarsmen and the oars in the bottom bank being rowed by single oarsmen.

The word comes from Latin, from *quinque* 'five' + *remus* 'oar'; the significance of the number five continues to be debated. In current usage, *quinquereme* may be employed to evoke a romantic vision of the ancient world.

the quintain the medieval military exercise of tilting at a post set up as a mark in tilting with a lance, typically with a sandbag attached that would swing round and strike an unsuccessful tilter. Recorded from late Middle English, the word comes from Old French *quintaine*, and is perhaps based on Latin *quintana*, a street in a Roman camp separating the fifth and sixth maniples, where military exercises were performed (from *quintus* 'fifth').

quintessence (in classical and medieval philosophy) a fifth substance in addition to the four elements, thought to compose the heavenly bodies and to be latent in all things; it was believed that this essence could be extracted by alchemy.

From the late 16th century, *quintessence* has also meant the most perfect or typical example of a quality or class, as in the title of George Bernard Shaw's *The Quintessence of Ibsenism* (1891).

The word comes (in late Middle English) via French from medieval Latin *quinta essentia* 'fifth essence'.

quintuplet each of five children born to the same mother at one birth; the first documented such set known to have survived birth were the ➤ DIONNE *Quintuplets*, born in Canada in the 1934.

quip a witty remark; in archaic use, a verbal equivocation. The word is recorded from the mid 16th century, and may come from Latin *quippe* 'perhaps, forsooth'.

Quirinal one of the Seven Hills on which the ancient city of Rome was built. From the 17th century, *Quirinal* has also been the name of the summer palace of the popes on the Quirinal Hill in Rome, which later became the palace first of the monarchs and then of the presidents of Italy; later, the name denoted the Italian court, monarchy, or government, especially as distinguished from that of the Vatican.

quisling a traitor who collaborates with an enemy force occupying their country, from the name of Major Vidkun *Quisling* (1887–1945), the Norwegian army officer and diplomat who ruled Norway on behalf of the German occupying forces (1940–45), and who was executed for treason.

an arrow in the quiver one of a number of resources or strategies that can be drawn on or followed.

Don Quixote the hero of a romance (1605–15) by Cervantes, a satirical account of chivalric beliefs and conduct. The character of Don Quixote, the poor gentlemen devoted to the ideal of chivalry, who christens his peasant lady-love ➤ DULCINEA, and seeks adventures wearing rusty armour and riding his old horse ➤ ROSINANTE, is typified by a romantic vision and naive, unworldly idealism.

Qumran a region on the western shore of the Dead Sea; the ➤ DEAD *Sea Scrolls* were found (1947–56) in caves at nearby *Khirbet Qumran*, the site of an ancient Jewish settlement. *Qumran* also denotes the religious community located in Khirbet Qumran during the beginning of the Christian era, which preserved the scrolls.

quo vadis Latin for, 'where are you going?'; according to a legend first found in the apocryphal Acts of St Peter, the apostle Peter, fleeing the persecutions in Rome, met Christ on the Appian Way and asked him '*Domine, quo vadis* [Lord, where are you going]'. Receiving the reply that Christ was going to be crucified again, Peter understood that this would be in his place; he accordingly turned back, and was martyred.

quod erat demonstrandum used to convey that a fact or situation demonstrates the truth of one's theory or claim, especially to mark the conclusion of a formal proof; the Latin phrase, meaning literally 'which was to be demonstrated', is a translation of the Greek phrase used in a number of ➤ EUCLID's propositions. It is frequently abbreviated to *QED*.

quondam that once was; former; according to Malory's *Le Morte d'Arthur*, used in the Latin inscription on the tomb of ➤ ARTHUR, 'And many men say that there is written upon his tomb this verse: *Hic iacet Arthurus, rex quondam rexque futurus* [Here lies Arthur, the once and future king].'

quorum originally, a select body of justices of the peace, every member of which had to be present to constitute a deciding body. Later, the minimum number of members of an assembly or society that must be present at any of its meetings to make the proceedings of that meeting valid.

Recorded from late Middle English, the word comes from the text of commissions for committee members designated by the Latin words *quorum vos…unum esse volumus* 'of whom we wish that you…be one'.

quote—unquote to begin quoting—to end quoting. Used parenthetically in spoken English to indicate that one is repeating a statement or passage, especially to emphasize one's detachment from or disagreement with the original.

qwerty denoting the standard layout on English-language typewriters and keyboards, having *q, w, e, r, t,* and *y* as the first keys from the left on the top row of letters.

Rr

R the eighteenth letter of the modern English alphabet and the seventeenth of the ancient Roman one, derived through early Greek ρ from Phoenician, representing the twentieth letter of the early Semitic alphabet. See also ➤ the THREE R's.

Ra in Egyptian mythology, the sun god, the supreme Egyptian deity, worshipped as the creator of all life and typically portrayed with a falcon's head bearing the solar disc. He appears travelling in his ship with other gods, crossing the sky by day and journeying through the underworld of the dead at night. From earliest times he was associated with the pharaoh.

rabbi a Jewish scholar or teacher, especially one who studies or teaches Jewish law. Recorded from late Old English, the word comes via ecclesiastical Latin and Greek from Hebrew *rabbī* 'my master'.

rabbit the *rabbit* is often taken to typify timidity and the word is used for someone who is a poor performer in a sport; the animal is also noted for its prolific breeding.

In North American usage, *rabbit* may be used as a term for hare, and be taken as a type of speed in running (John Updike's character Harry 'Rabbit' Angstrom derives his nickname from this).

Brer Rabbit is the hero of many of the ➤ *Uncle* REMUS stories by Joel Chandler Harris, which typically centre on the unavailing efforts of Brer Fox to outwit and catch the cunning *Brer Rabbit*.

To **pull a rabbit out of a hat** is to achieve an action that is fortuitous, and may involve sleight of hand or deception; the reference is to a stage conjuror making a rabbit appear (or disappear).

A **rabbit's foot** has traditionally been taken as a good-luck charm, and the word *rabbits* spoken on the first day of the month, was supposed to bring good luck. *Rabbits* are also alluded to as typically made to appear or disappear by a conjuror.

Rabelaisian characterized by an earthy humour typical of the writings of the French satirist François *Rabelais* (c.1494–1553).

race to the bottom a struggle for commercial success gained by lowering standards more swiftly than ones competitors.

Rachel in the Bible, the younger daughter of ➤ LABAN, loved by ➤ JACOB, who serves his uncle Laban for seven years for the right to marry her. Tricked into marrying her elder sister Leah, Jacob served another seven years for Rachel, who afterwards became the mother of ➤ JOSEPH and ➤ BENJAMIN.

According to tradition, Rachel's tomb was in Rama, and in connection with this she is a figure of the mother mourning for Israel.

rack an instrument of torture consisting of a frame on which the victim was stretched by turning rollers to which the wrists and ankles were tied; it is first recorded in English in Caxton's translation of *Reynard the Fox* (1481), and is sometimes found in the expression **come rack, come rope**.

To **rack one's brains** is to make a great effort to think of or remember something.

go to rack and ruin gradually deteriorate in condition because of neglect: fall into disrepair; *rack* here is a variant (recorded from the late 16th century) of *wrack* 'damage, disaster'.

rack-rent an extortionate or very high rent; in legal usage, a rent equal to or close to the annual value of the property. Recorded from the early 17th century, the expression was particularly associated with the ➤ PROTESTANT *Ascendancy* in Ireland by the publication in 1800 of Maria Edgeworth's novel *Castle Rackrent*.

St Radegund (518–87), queen of the Franks and wife of Clotaire, son of Clovis; born a princess of Thuringia, she had been captured at the age of twelve and later married to Clotaire. Leaving the court after six years of marriage, she took the veil, and later founded a monastery at Poitiers. Soon after her death, miracles were reported at her tomb; she became one of the first ➤ MEROVINGIAN saints, and her feast was celebrated in France from the 9th century. Her feast day is 13 August.

Radha in Hinduism, the favourite mistress of the god ➤ KRISHNA, and an incarnation of ➤ LAKSHMI. In devotional religion she represents the longing of the human soul for God.

radical advocating thorough or complete political or social reform; representing or supporting an extreme or progressive section of a political party; the word in this sense is first recorded in Shelley's *Oedipus Tyrannus* (1820), 'Kings and laurelled Emperors, Radical butchers'. In a letter of 1832, John Stuart Mill refers to, 'Several friends of mine, radical-utilitarians of a better than the ordinary sort.'

Radical is recorded from late Middle English (in the senses 'forming the root' and 'inherent'), and comes ultimately from Latin *radix, radic-* 'root'.

The term **radical chic**, coined by the American writer Tom Wolfe (1931–), means a fashionable affectation of radical left-wing views or an associated style of dress or life.

Rafferty's rules in Australia and New Zealand, informal expression meaning no rules at all; *Rafferty* is probably an English dialect alteration of *refractory*.

A. J. Raffles a debonair cricket-loving gentleman burglar, hero of *The Amateur Cracksman* (1899) and other books by E. W. Hornung (1866–1921); his name is used allusively for a man of good birth who engages in crime, especially burglary.

ragamuffin a person, typically a child, in ragged, dirty clothes. The term is recorded from Middle English as the name of a demon; and is probably based on *rag* as a piece of old and torn cloth, with a fanciful suffix.

ragged school in the 19th century, informal term for a free school for poor children.

ragged staff a depiction of a staff with projecting knobs (usually in reference to the ➤ BEAR *and ragged staff* crest of the Earls of Warwick).

Ragman roll a set of rolls (formerly preserved in the Tower of London, now in the Public Record Office), in which are recorded the instruments of homage made to Edward I by the Scottish king and nobles in 1296; *ragman*, was originally a legal document recording (alleged) offences. (See also ➤ RIGMAROLE.)

Ragnarök in Scandinavian mythology, the destruction or twilight of the gods; the final

battle between the gods and the powers of evil, in which gods and men will be defeated by monsters and the sky will grow dark, the Scandinavian equivalent of the *Götterdämmerung*. The original Old Norse form is *ragna rök*, from *ragna* 'of the gods' + *rök* 'destined end', but the variant *Ragna rökr* (*rökr* 'twilight'), which occurs in the prose ➤ EDDA, has influenced understanding of the name.

part brass rags with cease friendship or quarrel with; *brass rags* were sailors' cleaning cloths, which friends might keep together or share.

ragtime music characterized by a syncopated melodic line and regularly accented accompaniment, evolved by black American musicians in the 1890s and played especially on the piano; it is now seen as the immediate precursor of jazz.

Ragusa the Italian name of Dubrovnik on the Adriatic coast, in the 16th and 17th centuries a flourishing city-state; origin of the word *argosy*.

rain cats and dogs rain very heavily; the phrase is first recorded in 1738, used by Jonathan Swift, but the variant **rain dogs and polecats** was used earlier in Richard Brome's *The City Witt* (1653). The origin is not known, although explanations adduced include a connection with the supernatural (cats were associated with witches, believed to be able to raise storms), as well as the suggestion that in earlier times heavy rain would have resulted in the bodies of drowned dogs and cats floating in the streets and gutters. Cats and dogs are also proverbial for the enmity between them.

take a rain check said when politely refusing an offer, with the implication that one may take it up at a later date (a **rain check** is a ticket given for later use when a sporting fixture or other outdoor event is interrupted or postponed by rain).

rainbow often taken as a symbol of hope or a promise for peace, traditionally with allusion to Genesis 9:13–16, referring to God's setting a rainbow in the sky as a sign of his covenant with his chosen people (see also ➤ *bow of* PROMISE). It may also more generally be a sign of something distant and (perhaps) unattainable, as in the song 'Over the Rainbow' (1939) by E. Y. ('Yip') Harburg.

The phrase **at the end of the rainbow** is used to refer to something much sought after but impossible to attain, with allusion to the story of a crock of gold supposedly to be found by anyone reaching the end of a rainbow.

Rainbow Bridge is a bridge of natural rock, the world's largest natural bridge, situated in southern Utah, just north of the border with Arizona. Its span is 86 m (278 ft).

A **rainbow coalition** is a political alliance of differing groups, typically one comprising minority peoples and other disadvantaged groups; a phrase originally coined by the American minister and Democratic politician Jesse Jackson in a speech of 1988, 'When I look out at this convention, I see the face of America, red, yellow, brown, black, and white. We are all precious in God's sight—the real rainbow coalition.'

The **rainbow serpent** is a widely venerated spirit of Australian Aboriginal mythology, a large snake associated with water.

Rainbow Warrior was the name of a ship belonging to ➤ GREENPEACE which in 1985 was sunk in Auckland harbour after two bomb explosions; it had been about to sail for Mororua Atoll to protest against French nuclear testing there, and it was subsequently revealed that French intelligence agents had planted the bombs. The French Minister of Defence resigned as a result, and the head of the intelligence service was dismissed.

rainmaker a person who attempts to cause rain to fall, either by rituals or by a scientific technique such as seeding clouds with crystals; in figurative use, a person who is highly successful, especially in business.

it never rains but it pours misfortunes or difficult situations tend to follow each other in rapid succession or to arrive all at the same time; proverbial saying, early 18th century

a rainy day used in reference to a possible time in the future when something, especially money, will be needed.

raise the wind procure money for a purpose; the *wind* is considered here as motive power. In medieval times spirits or witches were commonly thought to be capable of causing winds to blow to help or hinder shipping; the figurative use of this phrase is much later (late 18th century).

the Raj British sovereignty in India before 1947 (also called, **the British Raj**). The word is from Hindi *rāj* 'reign'.

Rajput a member of a Hindu military caste claiming ➤ KSHATRIYA descent.

Rajputana an ancient region of India consisting of a collection of princely states ruled by dynasties. Following independence from Britain in 1947, they united to form the state of Rajasthan, parts also being incorporated into Gujarat and Madhya Pradesh.

rake's progress a progressive deterioration, especially through self-indulgence, from the title of a series of engravings by William Hogarth (1735), showing the rake's life progressing from its wealthy and privileged origins to debt, despair, and death on the gallows.

ram often taken as a type of virility; **the Ram** is the name of the zodiacal sign or the constellation Aries. The word is recorded from Old English, and is of Germanic origin.

Rama the hero of the ➤ RAMAYANA, husband of ➤ SITA. He is the Hindu model of the ideal man, the seventh incarnation of Vishnu, and is widely venerated, by some sects as the supreme god.

Ramadan the ninth month of the Muslim year, during which strict fasting is observed from sunrise to sunset. The name comes from Arabic *ramaḍān*, from *ramaḍa* 'be hot'. The lunar reckoning of the Muslim calendar brings the fast eleven days earlier each year, eventually causing Ramadan to occur in any season; originally it was supposed to be in one of the hot months.

Ramapithecus a fossil anthropoid ape of the Miocene epoch, known from remains found in SW Asia and East Africa, and probably ancestral to the orang-utan; it is named from ➤ RAMA + Greek *pithēkos* 'ape'.

Ramayana one of the two great Sanskrit epics of the Hindus, composed *c.*300 BC. It describes how ➤ RAMA, aided by his brother and the monkey Hanuman, rescued his wife Sita from Ravana, the ten-headed demon king of Lanka.

Rambo an exceptionally tough, aggressive man, from the name of the hero of David Morrell's novel *First Blood* (1972), and subsequent films, a Vietnam war veteran represented as macho, self-sufficient, and bent on violent retribution.

Battle of Ramillies a battle in the ➤ *War of the* SPANISH *Succession* which took place in 1706 near the village of Ramillies, north of

Namur, in Belgium, when the British army under Marlborough defeated the French.

rampant in heraldry, (of an animal) represented standing on one hind foot with its forefeet in the air (typically in profile, facing the dexter (left) side, with right hind foot and tail raised, unless otherwise specified).

Ramses the Great name given to Ramses II (died *c.*1225 BC), Egyptian pharaoh, reigned *c.*1292–*c.*1225 BC. The third pharaoh of the 19th dynasty, he built vast monuments and statues, including the two rock temples at ➤ ABU *Simbel*. (See also ➤ OZYMANDIAS.)

rank and file the ordinary members of an organization as opposed to its leaders (referring to the 'ranks' and 'files' into which privates and non-commissioned officers form on parade).

close ranks unite in order to defend common interests; the idea is of a body of soldiers coming closer together in a line when under attack.

the Rape of the Sabine Women in Roman mythology, the forcible carrying off of the ➤ SABINE women by ➤ ROMULUS, to provide wives for his men of the new settlement of Rome, at a spectacle to which the Sabines had been invited.

Raphael in the Bible, one of the seven archangels in the apocryphal Book of Enoch. He is said to have 'healed' the earth when it was defiled by the sins of the fallen angels.

raptor a dromaeosaurid dinosaur, especially velociraptor or utahraptor. The word *raptor* (from Latin, meaning 'bird of prey') is recorded in English from the 19th century, but in this sense comes directly from a shortened form of *velociraptor*, used originally by palaeontologists and popularized by Michael Crichton's thriller *Jurassic Park* and the Spielberg film (1993) based on it.

rara avis Latin phrase meaning literally a 'rare bird'; a phenomenon, a prodigy. The expression comes from the Roman satirist Juvenal (AD *c.*60–*c.*130), '*Rara avis in terris nigroque simillima cycno* [A rare bird on this earth, like nothing so much as a black swan].'

Rasputin a person exercising an insidious or corrupting influence, especially over a ruler or governor; from the acquired name (lit. 'debauchee') of the Russian monk Grigory Yefimovich Novykh (*c.*1865–1916), mystic and influential favourite at the court of Tsar Nicholas II of Russia. This influence, combined with his reputation for debauchery, steadily discredited the imperial family, and he was assassinated by a group loyal to the tsar; the murder was first attempted by poison, to which he proved impervious, and he was finally shot.

Rastafarian a member of a religious movement of Jamaican origin holding that blacks are the chosen people. *Rastafarians* believe that Emperor Haile Selassie of Ethiopia (who from 1916–30 was known as *Ras Tafari*) was the Messiah, and that black people will eventually return to their African homeland. They have distinctive codes of behaviour and dress, including the wearing of dreadlocks.

rat the rat has traditionally been taken as the type of a cunning and vicious animal, especially (as in the saying that ➤ RATS *desert a sinking ship*) one ready to betray a cause, or **to rat**.

rathe poetic and literary term for prompt and eager; (of flowers or fruit) blooming or ripening early in the year.

rats desert a sinking ship people hurry to get away from a failing enterprise or organization; the idea is that as a ship sank rats would be seen emerging from it to try to seek safety.

rattle someone's cage make someone feel angry or annoyed; the person concerned is being humorously compared with a dangerous caged animal.

raven the raven is traditionally regarded as a bird of ill-omen, and one that as a carrion-bird feeds on corpses, especially of those who have been killed in battle or hanged. Danish vikings had the symbol of a raven on their flag. In Scandinavian mythology, Odin has two ravens, Hugin and Munin, who are his messengers.

A raven is the emblem of ➤ *St* BENEDICT and ➤ *St* OSWALD; ravens are also said to have brought bread to the prophet Elijah when he was living east of the Jordan (1 Kings 17:6), and during the ➤ FLOOD a raven was sent out of the ark by Noah.

Ravenna a city near the Adriatic coast in NE central Italy, which became the capital of the Western Roman Empire in 402 and then of the Ostrogothic kingdom of Italy, afterwards serving as capital of Byzantine Italy. It is noted for its ancient mosaics dating from the early Christian period.

Ravi a river in the north of the Indian subcontinent, one of the headwaters of the Indus, which rises in the Himalayas and is one of the five rivers that gave ➤ PUNJAB its name.

rawhead and bloody bones proverbial type of something terrifying, recorded from the mid 16th century, perhaps associated with the idea that the apparition of a murdered man is traditionally supposed to haunt the scene of his murder.

rayonnant relating to or denoting a French style of Gothic architecture prevalent from c.1230 to c.1350, characterized by distinctive rose windows. The word is French and means literally 'radiating', from the pattern of radiating lights in the windows.

read my lips in US politics, a catch-phrase promoted during the Republican presidential campaign of George Bush (1924–) to emphasize commitment to lower taxes; accepting the Republican nomination in August 1988, Bush said, 'Read my lips: no new taxes'.

the real McCoy the real thing, the genuine article; it is suggested that this originated from the phrase *the real Mackay*, an advertising slogan used by G. Mackay and Co, whisky distillers in Edinburgh in 1870. The form *McCoy* appears to be of US origin.

real presence in Christian theology, the actual presence of Christ's body and blood in the Eucharistic elements.

realpolitik a system of politics or principles based on practical rather than moral or ideological considerations. The word is German, and is recorded in English from the early 20th century.

you reap what you sow you eventually have to face up to the consequences of your actions. A proverbial saying existing in several forms, with allusion to Galatians 6:7.

theirs not to reason why it is not someone's place to question a situation, order, or system. With allusion to Tennyson's poem *The Charge of the Light Brigade* (1854), which describes the notorious incident in the Crimean War when British cavalry unhesitatingly obeyed a suicidal order to ride straight at the Russian guns.

Reb informal name for a Confederate soldier in the American Civil War, recorded from 1862. Also *Johnny Reb*.

Rebecca in the Bible, the wife of ➤ ISAAC and mother of ➤ ESAU and ➤ JACOB.

According to the story in Genesis 24:60, when she left her parents' home for her marriage her family blessed her, saying, 'let thy seed possess the gate of those which hate them.' From this, the name *Rebecca* was given to the leader, dressed as a woman, of a group of rioters who demolished toll-gates in South Wales in 1843–4.

rebel yell a shout or battle cry used by the Confederates during the American Civil War.

rebus a puzzle in which words are represented by combinations of pictures and individual letters; for instance, *apex* might be represented by a picture of an ape followed by a letter *X*.

received pronunciation the standard form of British English pronunciation, based on educated speech in southern England, widely accepted as a standard elsewhere.

recessional a hymn sung while the clergy and choir process out of church at the end of a service.

recherche du temps perdu an evocation of one's early life; a French phrase, literally 'in search of the lost time', title of Proust's novel sequence of 1913–27 (in English translation of 1922–31, 'Remembrance of things past').

Reconstruction the period 1865–77 following the American Civil War, during which the Southern states of the Confederacy were controlled by federal government and social legislation, including the granting of new rights to black people, was introduced. There was strong white opposition to the new measures, and when a new Republican government returned power to white Southern leaders a policy of racial segregation was introduced.

recording angel an angel that is believed to register each person's good and bad actions; the term is recorded from the late 16th century.

recusant a person, especially a Roman Catholic, who refused to attend the services of the Church of England at a time when this was legally required.

The Act of Uniformity of 1558 first imposed fines on all non-attenders of a parish church, but Roman Catholics were the specific target of the Act against Popish Recusants of 1592; subsequent acts through the 17th century imposed heavy penalties on Catholic recusants, the exaction of which persisted up to the Second Relief Act of 1791. Particular pressure was put on Roman Catholics after 1570, when the papal bull 'Regnans in Excelsis' excommunicated Elizabeth I.

red a colour at the end of of the spectrum next to orange and opposite violet, as the colour of blood, fire, or rubies. As a ➤ LITUR-GICAL *colour*, *red* is used for Passion Sunday and Pentecost, and for the feasts of martyrs; figuratively it is associated with the emotions of anger and embarrassment, and in political terms is the colour of radicalism.

Recorded from Old English (as *rēad*), the word is of Germanic origin, from an Indo-European root shared by Latin *rufus*, Greek *eruthros*, and Sanskrit *rudhira* 'red'.

The **Red Army** was originally, the army of the Bolsheviks, the Workers' and Peasants' Red Army; later, the army of the Soviet Union, formed after the Revolution of 1917. The name was officially dropped in 1946. *Red Army* has also been used for the army of China or some other Communist countries. The **Red Army Faction** was a left-wing terrorist group in former West Germany, active from 1968 onwards. It was originally led by Andreas Baader (1943–77) and Ulrike Meinhof (1934–76), and was also called the ➤ BAADER-*Meinhof Group*.

In the UK, the **Red Arrows** are the aerobatic display team of the Royal Air Force.

The **Red Baron** was a nickname for the German fighter pilot Manfred, Freiherr von Richthofen (1882–1918), who flew a distinctive bright red aircraft.

In the UK, a **red box** is a box, typically covered with red leather, used by a Minister of State to hold official documents.

In Irish epic tradition, the **Red Branch** is the name (translating Gaelic *Craebh Ruaid*) of the most famous of the royal houses of Ulster; the **House of the Red Branch** at the capital of ➤ EMAIN *Macha* was the place where the arms of defeated enemies were stored.

The **Red Brigades** were an extreme left-wing terrorist organization based in Italy, which from the early 1970s was responsible for carrying out kidnappings, murders, and acts of sabotage.

In soccer and some other games, a **red card** is shown by the referee to a player who is being sent off the field.

A **red carpet** is a long, narrow red carpet laid on the ground for a distinguished visitor to walk along when arriving.

A **red cent** is the smallest amount of money (the US one-cent coin was formerly made of copper).

The **Red Crescent** is a national branch in Muslim countries of the International Movement of the Red Cross and the Red Crescent. The name was adopted in 1906.

A **red cross** is an upright red cross on a white ground; the symbol of ➤ St GEORGE, especially as the national emblem of England, and as the badge and emblem of Christian forces in the Crusades. In the 17th century, the sign of a *red cross* was placed on the door of a house to indicate the presence within the house of plague; in the mid 19th century, it was taken as the internationally agreed badge of a nursing and ambulance service, when the *Red Cross* was set up in 1864 at the instigation of the Swiss philanthropist Henri Dunant (1828–1910).

In heraldry, the **red dragon** is the badge of Wales, also known as the **red dragon of Cadwallader**.

The **red ensign** is a red flag with the Union Jack in the top corner next to the flagstaff, flown by British-registered ships. It is informally known as the **red duster**.

A **red-eye flight** is a flight (chiefly in North America) on which a passenger cannot expect to get much sleep on account of the time of departure or arrival, especially when a time zone is crossed. In the late 1980s, with transatlantic commuting a reality, it became a fashionable term among British business executives for the overnight flight from New York to London.

The **red flag** is the symbol of socialist revolution or a warning of danger; the anthem of Britain's Labour Party, a socialist song with words written in 1889 by the Irish socialist James M. Connell (1852–1929) and sung to the tune of the German song 'O Tannenbaum'. In Britain, the song is still sung at the conclusion of the annual Labour Party Conference.

The **red hand** is the arms or badge of Ulster, a red left hand (also called *bloody hand*) cut off squarely at the wrist, originally a badge of the O'Neill family.

A **red hat** is a cardinal's hat, especially as the symbol of a cardinal's office; in Christian art, a red hat is often shown in depictions of ➤ St JEROME as a ➤ DOCTOR *of the Church*.

A **red herring** is something, especially a clue, which is or is intended to be misleading or distracting (so named from the practice of using the scent of a dried smoked herring in training hounds).

A **Red Indian** is an old-fashioned term for an American Indian. First recorded in the early 19th century, it has largely fallen out of use, being associated with an earlier period and the corresponding stereotypes of cowboys and Indians and the ➤ WILD *West*.

A **red-letter day** is a day that is pleasantly noteworthy or memorable, from the practice of highlighting a saint's day or other festival in red on an ecclesiastical calendar. The term is recorded from the early 18th century.

A **red-light district** is an area of a town or city containing many brothels, strip clubs, and other sex businesses, from the use of a red light as the sign of a brothel.

Red Power is a movement in support of rights and political power for American Indians.

The **Red Queen** is a main character in Lewis Carroll's *Through the Looking Glass* (1871), who tells Alice that 'it takes all the running you can do to stay in the same place'. The **Red Queen hypothesis** is the hypothesis that organisms are constantly struggling to keep up with one another in an evolutionary race between predator and prey species, named from Lewis Carroll's *Red Queen*.

A **red rag to a bull** is an object, utterance, or act which is certain to provoke someone, from the traditional belief (recorded from the late 16th century) that this colour is particularly irritating to the animal.

A **red rose** is tradionally the emblem of the ➤ House of LANCASTER (as opposed to the ➤ WHITE *rose* of the Yorkists. In the late 20th century, a *red rose* has also been used as a symbol of the British Labour Party.

A **red route** denotes a scheme intended to facilitate the smooth flow of urban traffic by the imposition of severe penalties for stopping and parking along roads marked with a red line, introduced in Britain in the 1990s.

The **Red Sea** is a long, narrow landlocked sea separating Africa from the Arabian peninsula, and now linked to the Indian Ocean in the south by the Gulf of Aden and to the Mediterranean in the north by the Suez Canal. In the biblical account, the Israelites led by Moses escaped from Egypt when the waters of the *Red Sea* were miraculously parted; the army and chariots of the pursuing Egyptians were drowned when the waters once more closed over them. The name here should properly be translated 'Sea, or Lake, of Reeds'; it may in fact refer to the marshes of Lake Timsah, now part of the Suez Canal.

In astronomy, a **red shift** is the displacement of spectral lines towards longer wavelengths (the red end of the spectrum) in radiation from distant galaxies and celestial objects.

Red Square is a large square in Moscow next to the Kremlin. In existence since the late 15th century, under Communism the square was the scene of great parades celebrating May Day and the October Revolution.

Red tape is a term for excessive bureaucracy or adherence to rules and formalities, especially in public business; the expression refers to the reddish-pink tape which is commonly used for securing legal and official documents.

redbreast an informal name for the robin, recorded from late Middle English; in the mid 19th century, *Redbreast* was used as a nickname for ➤ BOW *Street Runners*, who habitually wore bright scarlet waistcoats.

redbrick (designating) a British university founded in the late 19th or early 20th century, usually in a large industrial city, and especially as contrasted with Oxford and Cambridge.

redcoat a traditional name for a British soldier (so named because of the colour of the uniform). In the Civil War the term was commonly applied to the Parliamentary forces, although there were red-uniformed soldiers on both sides.

In the UK from the 1950s, *redcoat* has been used for an organizer and entertainer at a Butlin's holiday camp, who on duty wore a scarlet blazer.

the Redeemer Christ, who has saved humankind from the effects of sin.

a reed shaken by the wind the type of something easily moved and insubstantial, with biblical allusion as to Matthew 11:7, 'What went ye out into the wilderness to see? A reed shaken by the wind?'

Reform Act an act framed to amend the system of parliamentary representation, especially those introduced in Britain during the 19th century.

The first Reform Act (1832) disenfranchised various rotten boroughs and lowered the property qualification, widening the electorate by about 50 per cent to include most of the male members of the upper middle class. The second (1867) doubled the electorate to about 2 million men by again lowering the property qualification, and the third (1884) increased it to about 5 million.

Reform Judaism a form of Judaism, initiated in Germany by the philosopher Moses

Mendelssohn (1729–86), which has reformed or abandoned aspects of Orthodox Jewish worship and ritual in an attempt to adapt to modern changes in social, political, and cultural life.

the Reformation a 16th-century movement for the reform of abuses in the Roman Church ending in the establishment of the Reformed and Protestant Churches. The roots of the Reformation go back to the 14th-century attacks on the wealth and hierarchy of the Church made by groups such as the Lollards and the Hussites. But the *Reformation* is usually thought of as beginning in 1517 in Wittenberg, when the German Protestant theologian Martin Luther (1483–1546) issued ninety-five theses criticizing Church doctrine and practice.

Regency in the UK, the period from 1811–20 when, during the incapacity of George III, the country was ruled by his eldest son as Regent; in particular, relating to or denoting British architecture, clothing, and furniture of the period (1811–20) or, more widely, of the late 18th and early 19th centuries. *Regency* style is generally neoclassical, with a generous borrowing of Greek and Egyptian motifs.

regicide any of those who took part in the trial and execution of Charles I; after the ➤ RESTORATION, several of the *regicides* were tried and executed, and the bodies of Oliver Cromwell and others were dug up, drawn on a hurdle to Tyburn, displayed in their coffins on the scaffold, and finally buried under the gallows.

regimental colour (in the UK) a regimental standard in the form of a silk flag, carried by a particular regiment along with its Queen's colour.

Regina the reigning queen (used following a name or in the titles of lawsuits, e.g. *Regina v. Jones*, the Crown versus Jones).
   Regina Coeli is a Latin epithet ('Queen of Heaven') of the Virgin Mary.

Regius professor (in the UK) the holder of a university chair founded by a sovereign (especially one at Oxford or Cambridge instituted by Henry VIII) or filled by Crown appointment.

Rehoboam son of Solomon, king of ancient Israel *c.*930–*c.*915 BC. His reign witnessed the secession of the northern tribes and their establishment of a new kingdom under Jeroboam, leaving Rehoboam as the first king of Judah (1 Kings 11–14).
   From the late 19th century, the word *rehoboam* has been used for a wine bottle of about six times the standard size.

Reich the former German state, most often used to refer to the Third Reich, the Nazi regime from 1933 to 1945. The **First Reich** was considered to be the Holy Roman Empire, 962–1806, and the **Second Reich** the German Empire, 1871–1918, but neither of these terms are part of normal historical terminology.

Reichenbach Falls in Switzerland, one of the highest falls in the Alps, and scene of the final struggle between ➤ *Sherlock* HOLMES and his arch-enemy Professor ➤ MORIARTY. Conan Doyle was persuaded by popular demand to allow the detective to emerge from the *Reichenbach Falls* alive.

Reichstag the main legislature of the German state under the Second and Third Reichs; the building in Berlin in which this met, which was badly damaged by fire on the Nazi accession to power in 1933, an event believed by many to have been contrived by the Nazis to justify suppression of opposition and the assumption of emergency powers.
   In April 1999, the renovated Reichstag building, parliament of reunited Germany, was formally opened, its new interior having been created by the British architect Norman Foster.

Reims a city of northern France, which was the traditional coronation place of most French kings and is noted for its fine 13th-century Gothic cathedral.

reinvent the wheel be forced by necessity to construct a basic requirement again from the beginning; the *wheel* taken as an essential requirement of modern civilization.

relativism the doctrine that knowledge, truth, and morality exist in relation to culture, society, or historical context, and are not absolute.

relic in religious use, especially in the Greek and Roman Catholic Churches, a part of a deceased holy person's body or belongings kept as an object of reverence. Recorded from Middle English, the word (like ➤ RELIQUARY) comes ultimately from Latin *reliquus* 'remaining'.

Religious Society of Friends official name for the ➤ QUAKERS.

reliquary a container, as a box or shrine, for holy ➤ RELICS; *reliquaries* are often richly ornamented.

Remembrance Sunday (in the UK) the Sunday nearest 11 November, when those who were killed in the First and Second World Wars and later conflicts are commemorated. Also called ➤ REMEMBRANCE *Day*.

St Remigius (d. 533), bishop, of Gaulish parentage, who became known as the *Apostle of the Franks*; he baptized ➤ CLOVIS, king of the Franks, whose queen Clotild was a Christian.

Remigius, who died at Reims on 13 January, was later said to have had the power of touching for the ➤ KING's *evil*; this ability supposedly passed from him to Clovis, and was later claimed by ➤ EDWARD *the Confessor* and the Norman kings of England. It was also said that a miraculous dove had brought the chrism for the baptism of Clovis; until the Revolution, what was left of this, known as the ➤ *la* SAINTE *ampoule*, was kept in Reims Cathedral. His feast day is 13 January; his translation is celebrated on 1 October.

remittance man an emigrant supported or assisted by payments of money from home; typically a disgraced man of good position or family who has been sent abroad by his family and whose payments depend on his remaining there.

Remus in Roman mythology, the twin brother of ➤ ROMULUS; he is said to have quarrelled with his brother over the building of the walls of Rome, and to have been killed by him.

Renaissance the revival of art and literature under the influence of classical models in the 14th–16th centuries; the culture and style of art and architecture developed during this era.

The Renaissance is generally regarded as beginning in Florence, where there was a revival of interest in classical antiquity. Important early figures are the writers Petrarch, Dante, and Boccaccio and the painter Giotto. Classical techniques and styles were studied in Rome by the sculptor Donatello as well as by the architects Bramante and Brunelleschi, who worked on the theory of perspective, which was developed in the innovative frescoes and paintings of Masaccio.

The period from the end of the 15th century has become known as the **High Renaissance**, when Venice and Rome began to share Florence's importance and Botticelli,

Cellini, Raphael, Leonardo da Vinci, and Michelangelo were active. Renaissance thinking spread to the rest of Europe from the early 16th century, and was influential for the next hundred years.

The term **Renaissance man** is used of a person with many talents or interests, especially in the humanities, supposedly exhibiting the virtues of an idealized man of the *Renaissance*.

Rennes originally established as the capital of a Celtic tribe, the *Redones*, from whom it derives its name, later becoming the capital of the ancient kingdom and duchy of Brittany.

Reno a city in western Nevada noted as a gambling resort and for its liberal laws enabling quick marriages and divorces.

republic a state in which supreme power is held by the people and their elected representatives, and which has an elected or nominated president rather than a monarch. **The Republic** is the English title of Plato's most famous work.

Republic Day is the day on which the foundation of a republic is commemorated, in particular (in India) 26 January.

requiem (especially in the Roman Catholic Church) a Mass for the repose of the souls of the dead. Recorded from Middle English, the word comes from Latin (the first word of the Mass), accusative of *requies* 'rest'.

reredos an ornamental screen covering the wall at the back of an altar. The word comes (in late Middle English) via Anglo-Norman French from Old French *areredos*, from *arere* 'behind' + *dos* 'back'.

the Resistance the underground movement formed in France during the Second World War to fight the German occupying forces and the Vichy government. The Resistance was composed of various groups which were coordinated into the *Forces Françaises de l'Intérieur* in 1944, which joined with Free French forces in the liberation of Paris and northern France.

the line of least resistance an option avoiding difficulty or unpleasantness; the easiest course of action.

respond in architectural use, a half-pillar or half-pier attached to a wall to support an arch, especially at the end of an arcade.

the Restoration the re-establishment of Charles II as King of England in 1660. After the death of Oliver Cromwell in 1658, his son

Richard (1626–1712) proved incapable of maintaining the Protectorate, and General Monck organized the king's return from exile. The term itself is first recorded in the early 18th century.

Restoration comedy is a style of drama which flourished in London after the Restoration in 1660, typically having a complicated plot marked by wit, cynicism, and licentiousness.

the Resurrection in Christian belief, Christ's rising from the dead; the rising of the dead at the Last Judgement.

resurrection man in the 18th and 19th centuries, a person who illicitly retrieved corpses to be sold for dissection from rivers, scenes of disaster, or burial grounds.

Reuben in the Bible, a Hebrew patriarch, eldest son of ➤ JACOB and Leah; in the story of ➤ JOSEPH, it is Reuben who persuades his brothers not to kill the boy by prophesying that if they do his blood will be required of them. Later, Reuben loses his birthright as the eldest son because he has slept with his father's concubine; Jacob on his deathbed (Genesis 49:4) says to him, 'Unstable as water, thou shalt not excel.'

From the early 19th century in North America, the name *Reuben* has been used to suggest the conventionally conceived figure of a farmer or rustic, a country bumpkin (there is no evident link with the biblical figure).

Reuters an international news agency founded in London in 1851 by Paul Julius Reuter (1816–99). The agency pioneered the use of telegraphy, building up a worldwide network of correspondents to produce a service used today by newspapers and radio and television stations in most countries.

reveille a signal sounded especially on a bugle or drum to wake personnel in the armed forces. The word comes, in the mid 17th century, from French *réveillez!* 'wake up', ultimately based on Latin *vigilare* 'keep watch'.

the Revelation of St John the Divine the last book of the New Testament, recounting a divine revelation of the future to ➤ St JOHN. Also known as **Revelations**.

revenge tragedy a style of drama, popular in England during the late 16th and 17th centuries, in which the basic plot was a quest for vengeance and which typically featured scenes of carnage and mutilation, real or feigned insanity, and the appearance of ghosts. Examples of the genre include Thomas Kyd's *The Spanish Tragedy* (1592) and John Webster's *The Duchess Of Malfi* (1623).

Revised Version an English translation of the Bible published in 1881–95 and based on the Authorized Version.

revival of learning the ➤ RENAISSANCE in its literary aspect; also called *revival of letters*.

Revolutionary Tribunal a court established in Paris in October 1793 to try political opponents of the French Revolution. There was no right of appeal and from June 1794 the only penalty was death. A principal instrument of the Terror, it existed until May 1795 and was responsible for ordering more than 2,600 executions.

Revolutions of 1848 a series of revolts against monarchical rule in Europe during 1848, springing from a shared background of autocratic government, lack of representation for the middle classes, economic grievances, and growing nationalism. Revolution occurred first in France, where socialists and supporters of universal suffrage caused the overthrow of King Louis Philippe, and in the German and Italian states there were uprisings and demonstrations; in Austria rioting caused the flight of the emperor and of Prince Metternich, and peoples subject to the Habsburg empire, notably the Hungarians, demanded autonomy. All the revolutions ended in failure and repression, but some of the liberal reforms gained as a result (such as universal male suffrage in France) survived, and nationalist aims in Germany and Italy were achieved.

Rex the reigning king (used following a name or in the titles of lawsuits, e.g. *Rex v. Jones*: the Crown versus Jones).

Reynard a name for a fox, especially as a proper name in the *Roman de Renart*, a series of popular satirical fables written in France *c.*1175–1250, and in other stories.

Rhadamanthus in Greek mythology, the son of ➤ ZEUS and Europa, and brother of ➤ MINOS, who, as a ruler and judge in the underworld, was renowned for his justice. In poetic and literary usage, **Rhadamanthine** means showing stern and inflexible judgement.

Rhea in Greek mythology, one of the Titans, wife of ➤ CRONUS and mother of ➤ ZEUS,

Demeter, Poseidon, Hera, and Hades. Frightened of betrayal by their children, Cronus ate them; Rhea rescued Zeus from this fate by hiding him and giving Cronus a stone wrapped in blankets instead.

Rhea Silvia in Roman mythology, princess of Alba Longa, mother of ➤ ROMULUS and Remus by the god Mars.

Rhemish Bible an English translation of the New Testament by Roman Catholics of the English college at Reims, published in 1582.

Rhesus a mythical king of Thrace, son of the muse Terpsichore, whose name was arbitrarily used to name the *rhesus monkey*; he is said in the *Iliad* to have brought his army to support the Trojans, but to have been murdered by a trick by Odysseus and Diomedes.

rhesus factor an antigen occurring on the red blood cells of many humans (around 85 per cent) and some other primates. It is particularly important as a cause of haemolytic disease of the newborn and of incompatibility in blood transfusions. It was named in the 1940s for the *rhesus monkey* in which the antigen was first observed.

rhetoric the art of effective or persuasive speaking or writing, especially the exploitation of figures of speech and other compositional techniques; language designed to have a persuasive or impressive effect on its audience, but which is now often regarded as lacking in sincerity or meaningful content.

In the Middle Ages, *rhetoric* was counted as one of the ➤ SEVEN liberal arts; the word comes via Old French and Latin from Greek.

A **rhetorical question** is a question asked not for information but to produce an effect, e.g. *who cares?* for *nobody cares.*

Rhiannon in Celtic mythology, the Welsh equivalent of the Gaulish horse goddess Epona and the Irish goddess Macha; she is also associated with the underworld, and has power over the dead. In the *Mabinogion*, she is the wife of Pwyll.

Rhine maidens the three water maidens in Wagner's opera *Der Ring des Nibelungen* who are guardians of the golden treasure (the 'Rheingold') of the river Rhine.

Rhodes the largest of the Dodecanese Islands in the SE Aegean, which in the late Bronze Age became a significant trading nation and dominant power; its capital, *Rhodes*, a port on the northernmost tip of the island,

founded *c.*408 BC, was the site of the ➤ COLOSSUS *of Rhodes*.

From 1309 to 1522 it was the headquarters of the order of the ➤ KNIGHTS *Hospitallers*.

Rhodes Scholarship any of several scholarships awarded annually and tenable at Oxford University by students from certain Commonwealth countries, South Africa, the United States, and Germany. They are named after the British-born South African statesman Cecil *Rhodes* (1853–1902), who founded the scholarships in 1902. **Rhodesia**, the large territory in central southern Africa which was divided into Northern Rhodesia (now Zambia) and Southern Rhodesia (now Zimbabwe) was named after him.

rhubarb informal term for the noise made by a group of actors to give the impression of indistinct background conversation or to represent the noise of a crowd, especially by the random repetition of the word 'rhubarb' with different intonations. The word in this sense is recorded from the 1930s.

rhyme correspondence of sound between words or the endings of words, especially when these are used at the ends of lines of poetry. The word was recorded in Middle English in the form *rime*; the current spelling was introduced in the early 17th century under the influence of *rhythm*, and both forms come ultimately via Latin *rhythmus* from Greek *rhuthmos*, related to *rhein* 'to flow'.

Rhyme or reason means, good sense or logic; the phrase (which is found chiefly in negative contexts) is recorded from the mid 17th century.

rhyming slang a type of slang that replaces words with rhyming words or phrases, typically with the rhyming element omitted. For example *butcher's*, short for *butcher's hook*, means 'look' in Cockney rhyming slang.

rhyton a type of drinking container used in ancient Greece, typically having the form of an animal's head or a horn, with the hole for drinking from located at the lower or pointed end. The word comes from Greek *rhuton*, related to *rhein* 'to flow'.

Rialto an island in Venice, containing the old mercantile quarter of medieval Venice; the **Rialto Bridge**, completed in 1591, crosses the Grand Canal between Rialto and San Marco islands.

Richmond¹ earldom (from *Richmond* in Yorkshire) held by Henry VII (1457–1509) before becoming king. **Richmond Park** in Greater London was formerly the site of **Richmond Palace**, built by Henry VII on the site of the earlier *Shene Palace*, and named by him.

Richmond² the state capital of Virginia, a port on the James River, which during the American Civil War was the Confederate capital from July 1861 until its capture in 1865.

Richter scale a numerical scale for expressing the magnitude of an earthquake on the basis of seismograph oscillations. The more destructive earthquakes typically have magnitudes between about 5.5 and 8.9; it is a logarithmic scale and a difference of one represents an approximate thirtyfold difference in magnitude. It is named after Charles F. *Richter* (1900–85), American geologist.

riddle a question or statement intentionally phrased so as to require ingenuity in ascertaining its answer or meaning, typically presented as a game. The word is recorded from Old English (in form *rædels(e)*) 'opinion, conjecture, riddle'.

ride a-cock-horse ride (as) on a child's hobby-horse; recorded from the mid 16th century, and apparently a nursery term applied to anything that a child rides astride upon. It is not clear whether *cock-horse* was originally the name of the plaything, as it appears to have become by the late 16th century.

Riding each of three former administrative divisions of Yorkshire, usually known as the East, North, and West Ridings; the word is recorded in Old English in the form *trithing*, from Old Norse *þriðjungr* 'third part'. The initial *th-* was lost due to assimilation with the preceding *-t* of *East*, *West*, or with the *-th* of *North*.

be riding for a fall be acting in a reckless or arrogant way that invites defeat or failure. A horse-riding expression of the late 19th century, meaning to ride a horse, especially in the hunting field, in such a way as to make an accident likely.

rift within the lute an apparently minor piece of damage likely to have fatal consequences; the phrase comes originally from a poem by Tennyson in *Idylls of the King* (1859), 'It is the little rift within the lute, That by and by will make the music mute.'

Rig Veda in Hinduism, the oldest and principal of the Vedas, composed in the 2nd millennium BC and containing a collection of hymns in early Sanskrit.

Right Bank a district of the city of Paris, situated on the right bank of the River Seine, to the north of the river. The area contains the Champs Élysées and the Louvre.

somewhere to the right of Genghis Khan holding right-wing views of the most extreme kind; *Genghis Khan* taken as the type of a repressive and tyrannical ruler.

right of way the legal right, established by usage or grant, to pass along a specific route through grounds or property belonging to another. It was often locally believed that a funeral procession taking a direct route to a graveyard could cross private ground, and in so doing establish a permanent right of way.

rights of man rights held to be justifiably belonging to any person; human rights. The phrase is associated with the Declaration of the Rights of Man and of the Citizen, adopted by the French National Assembly in 1789 and used as a preface to the French Constitution of 1791.

Rijksmuseum the national art gallery of the Netherlands, in Amsterdam. Established in the late 19th century and developed from the collection of the House of Orange, it contains the most representative collection of Dutch art in the world.

the life of Riley a comfortable pleasant carefree existence; the phrase is said to originate in a late 19th-century song, but this has not so far been traced. To date the earliest version is found in H. Pease's song *My Name is Kelly* (1919), 'my name is Kelly Michael Kelly, But I'm living the life of Reilly.'

Rimmon (in the Bible) a deity worshipped in ancient Damascus. (See also ➤ BOW *down in the house of Rimmon*.)

before the rinderpest in South Africa, a long time ago; referring to the 1896 epidemic of the cattle disease, treated as a landmark.

ring a circle or circular space, especially a circular band worn on a finger as a token of marriage, engagement, or authority, a ring can also be seen as a particularly personal possession, as in the story of ➤ POLYCRATES and his attempt to avert ill-fortune. In traditional legends such as that of the ➤ NIBELUNGENLIED a ring may be an object of power. A *ring* is the emblem of ➤ St CATHERINE *of*

Alexandria, ➤ *St* CATHERINE *of Siena*, and ➤ *St* EDWARD *the Confessor*.

To **hold the ring** is to monitor a dispute or conflict without becoming involved in it; the idea here is of being a spectator at a boxing match.

ring-a-ring o'roses is a singing game played by children, in which the players hold hands and dance in a circle, falling down at the end of the song. It is said to refer to the inflamed ('rose-coloured') ring of buboes, symptomatic of the plague; the final part of the game is symbolic of death.

The **Ring Cycle** is an informal name for Wagner's cycle of operas based on the ➤ NIBELUNGENLIED.

The **ring finger** is the finger next to the little finger, especially of the left hand, on which the wedding ring is worn.

A **ring fort** is a prehistoric earthwork, especially an Iron Age hill fort, defended by circular ramparts and ditches.

The **ring of iron** was the defensive cordon created around Bilbao by the Basques in the Spanish Civil War; the term is a translation of Spanish *cinturón de hierro*.

A **ring of steel** is a security cordon built around (part of) a city, typically as an anti-terrorist measure, employing roadblocks and surveillance procedures; in the UK, the possibility was raised of establishing a *ring of steel* round the City of London after the IRA's bombing of the Baltic Exchange in 1992.

Ringerike a style of late Viking decorative art, characterized by abundant use of foliage patterns, named after a district centred on Honefoss, north of Oslo in Norway.

Riot Act an Act passed by the British government in 1715 (in the wake of the Jacobite rebellion of that year) and repealed in 1967, designed to prevent civil disorder. The Act made it a felony for an assembly of more than twelve people to refuse to disperse after being ordered to do so and having been read a specified portion of the Act by lawful authority.

To **read the Riot Act** is to formally read the specified portion of the act as a notification to an assembly to disperse.

RIP abbreviation of Latin *requiescat in pace*, 'may he (or she) rest in peace' or *requiescant in pace*, 'may they rest in peace', used in memorial notices and inscriptions.

Rip van Winkle the hero of a story in Washington Irving's *Sketch Book* (1819–20), a good-for-nothing who fell asleep in the Catskill Mountains and awoke after twenty years to find the world completely changed.

ripper a murderer who mutilates victims' bodies; the term was first used in the late 19th century in connection with ➤ JACK *the Ripper*, and in the late 1970s began to be used of the **Yorkshire Ripper**, the name given to Peter Sutcliffe (1946–), who murdered 13 women in northern England and the Midlands before being captured in January 1981.

rise from the ashes be renewed after destruction, perhaps alluding to the legend of the ➤ PHOENIX, fabled to burn itself to ashes on a funeral pyre ignited by the sun and fanned by its own wings, only to emerge from the ashes with renewed youth.

Risorgimento a movement for the unification and independence of Italy, which was achieved in 1870. With French aid, the Austrians were driven out of northern Italy by 1859, and the south was won over by Garibaldi. Voting resulted in the acceptance of Victor Emmanuel II as the first king of a united Italy in 1861. The name is Italian, and means literally, 'resurrection'.

rite of passage a ceremony or event marking an important stage in someone's life, especially birth, initiation, marriage, and death. The term is a translation of French *rite de passage*, coined by Arnold van Gennep as the title of a book, *Les rites de passage*, in 1909.

put on the ritz make a show of luxury or extravagance; the hotels in Paris, London, and New York founded by the Swiss-born hotelier César *Ritz* (1850–1918) became synonomous with luxury.

the Riviera part of the Mediterranean coastal region of southern France and northern Italy, extending from Cannes to La Spezia, famous for its beauty, mild climate, and fashionable resorts. The name is Italian, and means literally 'seashore'.

road rage violent anger caused by the stress and frustration of driving a motor vehicle; especially (an act of) violence committed by one motorist against another which is provoked by the supposedly objectionable driving of the victim.

Roanoke Island an island in eastern North Carolina, in the late 16th century site of the *Lost Colony* (see ➤ LOST).

roaring forties stormy ocean tracts between latitudes 40° and 50° south; the name is recorded from the late 19th century.

rob Peter to pay Paul traditional saying, late Middle English; meaning to take away from one person or cause in order to give to another. In early examples, the use of *Peter* and *Paul* apparently represents no more than a conjunction of alliterative names, but in later use the phrase seems to have been influenced by the association of the apostles Peter and Paul as leaders of the early Church and fellow martyrs.

Rob Roy (1671–1734), Scottish outlaw and member of the proscribed Macgregor family, whose reputation as a Scottish ➤ ROBIN *Hood* was coloured by Sir Walter Scott's novel *Rob Roy* (1817).

Robben Island a small island off the coast of South Africa, near Cape Town, the site of a prison which was formerly used for the detention of political prisoners, including Nelson Mandela.

Robespierrist a follower or supporter of the French revolutionary Maximilien *Robespierre* (1758–94), described by Thomas Carlyle as ➤ *the* SEA-*green Incorruptible.*

robin a small brown bird with a red breast, which legendarily was coloured by the blood of Christ. The robin is traditionally taken as a harbinger of death; there was also a tradition that robins would cover the bodies of the unburied dead with leaves. The name comes (in late Middle English, as **robin redbreast**) from Old French, pet form of the given name *Robert.*

Robin Goodfellow a mischievous sprite or goblin believed, especially in the 16th and 17th centuries, to haunt the English countryside; he is also called ➤ PUCK.

Robin Hood a semi-legendary English medieval outlaw, reputed to have robbed the rich and helped the poor. Although he is generally associated with Sherwood Forest in Nottinghamshire, it seems likely that the real Robin Hood operated in Yorkshire in the early 13th century.

Robin Hood, with his lover ➤ MAID *Marian,* is traditionally also a leading figure in the ➤ MORRIS *dance.*

Round Robin Hood's barn means by a circuitous route; *Robin Hood's barn* here represents the type of an out-of-the-way place.

robot (especially in science fiction) a machine resembling a human being and able to replicate certain human movements and functions automatically. The term (from Czech *robota* 'forced labour') was coined in K.

Čapek's play *R.U.R.* 'Rossum's Universal Robots' (1920).

roc a mythical bird of Eastern legend, supposed to be of great size and strength; it is first referred to in ➤ *Marco* POLO's account of Madagascar, but in English use it is known chiefly from the ➤ ARABIAN *Nights*; in the story of ➤ SINBAD it is said to be able to lift elephants in its claws.

In the story of ➤ SINBAD, the **roc's egg** is said to be so large that it is fifty paces round; in extended usage, it may be taken as the type of something rare and fabulous.

St Roch (*c.*1350–*c.*80), hermit, much invoked against the plague; he is said to have caught the plague himself and to have recovered while alone in the woods in Piacenza, where he was brought food by a dog. He is often shown with a plague sore on his leg, or accompanied by a dog with a loaf of bread in its mouth. He is patron saint of invalids and prisoners, and his feast day is 16 August.

Mr Rochester in Charlotte Brontë's *Jane Eyre* (1847), the dark and Byronic owner of Thornfield Hall by whom Jane is employed as a governess and with whom she falls in love; their marriage is at first frustrated by the revelation that Mr Rochester's first wife, a madwoman, is still alive, kept under restraint in an attic room.

rock in figurative usage, *rock* may be taken as the type of something providing a sure foundation and support, as in the words of Jesus Christ to Peter in Matthew 16:18, 'Thou art Peter, and upon this rock I will build my church.' In the parable in Matthew 7 of the two houses, it is the house built on sand which falls, and the house built on rock which stands.

A *rock* in biblical contexts may also be a source of sustenance (with allusion to Numbers 20:11, in which water issued from the rock struck by the staff of Moses), and a shelter, as in Isaiah 32:2, 'the shadow of a great rock in a weary land'.

A *rock* (especially with the notion of one on which a ship may be wrecked) can also be taken as a sign of danger, as in **rocks ahead**.

To be **between a rock and a hard place** is to be in a situation where one is faced with two equally difficult alternatives.

Rock of Ages symbolizes the foundation of Christian belief; the phrase is now probably best-known from the hymn 'Rock of Ages, cleft for me' (1773), by the English clergyman Augustus Toplady (1740–78).

rock and roll a type of popular dance music originating in the 1950s, characterized by a heavy beat and simple melodies. Rock and roll was an amalgam of black rhythm and blues and white country music, usually based around a twelve-bar structure and an instrumentation of guitar, double bass, and drums.

Rockefeller name used allusively as the type of a very rich person, from the American industrialist and philanthropist John D. *Rockefeller* (1839–1937), founder of the Standard Oil Company.

rocket often used as an image of speed; *Rocket* was the name of the steam locomotive (1829) built by George Stephenson (1781–1848) and his son Robert, the prototype for all future steam locomotives.

Up like a rocket and down like the stick means to rise suddenly and dramatically and subsequently fall in a similar manner like the firework; originally with reference to a gibe by Tom Paine about Edmund Burke's oratory in a 1792 debate on the French Revolution.

rococo (of furniture or architecture) of or characterized by an elaborately ornamental late baroque style of decoration prevalent in 18th-century Continental Europe, with asymmetrical patterns involving motifs and scrollwork; extravagantly or excessively ornate. Recorded from the mid 19th century, the word comes from French, as a humorous alteration of *rocaille*, an 18th-century artistic or architectural style of decoration characterized by elaborate ornamentation with pebbles and shells. The word (which is French) comes from *roc* 'rock'.

rod a thin straight bar, especially of wood or metal. In former British usage, a *rod* was a unit of measurement, the equivalent of a ➤ PERCH.

To **make a rod for one's own back** is to do something likely to cause difficulties for oneself later.

The saying **spare the rod and spoil the child** means that if children are not physically punished when they do wrong their personal development will suffer. It is proverbial, from the early 11th century, and often with biblical allusion to Proverbs 13:24.

Roderick (d. 711), the last Visigothic king of Spain, killed in the Moorish invasion. According to legend, Roderick had dishonoured the daughter of one of his nobles, who in revenge brought the Moors into Spain.

rodomontade boastful or inflated talk or behaviour; the word comes (in the early 17th century) via French from the Italian form of *Rodomont*, the the boastful Saracen leader in ➤ ORLANDO *Innamorato* and ➤ ORLANDO *Furioso*. From the late 16th century, *rodomont* came to be used to mean a braggart or boaster.

rogation in the Christian Church, a solemn supplication consisting of the litany of the saints chanted on the three days before Ascension Day. The name comes (in late Middle English) from Latin *rogatio(n-)*, from *rogare* 'ask'.

In the Western Christian Church, the **Rogation Days** are the three days before Ascension Day, traditionally marked by fasting and prayer, particularly for the blessing of the harvest (after the pattern of pre-Christian rituals).

Rogation Sunday is the Sunday preceding the *Rogation Days*. **Rogation week** is the week in which Ascension Day falls.

Roget's Thesaurus common name for the *Thesaurus of English Words and Phrases*, a catalogue of synonyms first published in 1852, and compiled by the English scholar and physician Peter Roget (1779–1869).

rogues' gallery a collection of photographs of known criminals, used by police to identify suspects.

roi fainéant any of the later ➤ MEROVINGIAN kings of France, whose power was merely nominal; the phrase is French, and means literally 'sluggard king'.

roi soleil a title ('sun king') commonly used to designate Louis XIV of France, derived from a heraldic device used by him, and intended to convey his pre-eminence as a ruler.

Roland the most famous of ➤ CHARLEMAGNE's paladins, hero of the *Chanson de Roland* (12th century) and other medieval romances. He is said to have become a friend of Oliver, another paladin, after engaging him in single combat in which neither won. Roland was killed in a rearguard action at the Battle of ➤ RONCESVALLES, refusing until too late to blow the horn ➤ OLIVANT to summon Charlemagne to his aid.

A **Roland for an Oliver** is an effective or adequate retort or response, taking *Roland* and his comrade ➤ OLIVER as the type of a match in skill and courage; the phrase is recorded from the early 17th century.

roll with the punches adapt oneself to adverse circumstances; the idea is of a boxer moving their body away from an opponent's blows so as to lessen the impact.

a rolling stone a person who does not settle in one place will not accumulate wealth or status, or responsibilities or commitments; from the mid 14th-century proverb *a rolling stone gathers no moss*.

Rollo name of the Viking leader (*Hrolf*) said to be ancestor of the Dukes of Normandy; he established himself in Normandy in the early 10th century.

strike someone off the rolls debar a solicitor from practising as a penalty for dishonesty or other misconduct; *rolls* here are the official lists or records, so called from the time when such records were literally kept on parchment or paper rolls.

Roman of, pertaining to, or characteristic of (ancient) Rome.

The **Roman alphabet** is the alphabet used for writing Latin, English, and most European languages, developed in ancient Rome.

Roman Britain was Britain during the period AD 43–410, when most of Britain was part of the Roman Empire. The frontier of the Roman province of Britain was eventually established at Hadrian's Wall; the more northerly Antonine Wall was breached and abandoned (*c.*181).

The **Roman Catholic Church** is the part of the Christian Church which acknowledges the Pope as its head, especially as it has developed since the Reformation, and which is the largest Christian Church, dominant particularly in South America and southern Europe. Roman Catholicism differs from Protestantism in the importance it grants to tradition, ritual, and the authority of the Pope as successor to the Apostle St Peter, and especially in its doctrines of papal infallibility (formally defined in 1870) and of the Eucharist (➤ TRANSUBSTANTIATION), its celibate male priesthood, its emphasis on confession, and the veneration of the Virgin Mary and other saints.

The **Roman Empire** was the empire established by Augustus in 27 BC, which was divided after the death of Theodosius I (AD 395) into the Western Empire and the Eastern or Byzantine Empire (centred on Constantinople). At its greatest extent Roman rule or influence extended from Armenia and Mesopotamia in the east to the Iberian peninsula in the west, and from the Rhine and Danube in the north to Egypt and provinces on the Mediterranean coast of North Africa. Eventually, the sheer extent of the territories led to the collapse of the Western Empire: Rome was sacked by the Visigoths under Alaric in 410, and the last emperor of the West, Romulus Augustulus, was deposed in 476. The Eastern Empire, which was stronger, lasted until 1453.

A **Roman holiday** is an occasion on which entertainment or profit is derived from injury or death; originally a holiday for a gladiatorial combat, as in Byron's *Childe Harold's Pilgrimage* (1812–18), 'Butchered to make a Roman holiday.'

Roman law is the law code of the ancient Romans forming the basis of civil law in many countries today.

A **Roman numeral** is any of the letters representing numbers in the Roman numerical system: I = 1, V = 5, X = 10, L = 50, C = 100, D = 500, M = 1,000. In this system a letter placed after another of greater value adds (thus XVI or xvi is 16), whereas a letter placed before another of greater value subtracts (thus XC is 90).

The **Roman republic** was the ancient Roman state from the expulsion of the Etruscan monarchs in 509 BC until the assumption of power by Augustus (Octavian) in 27 BC. The republic was dominated by a landed aristocracy, the ➤ PATRICIANS, who ruled through the advisory Senate and two annually elected chief magistrates or consuls; the ➤ PLEBEIANS or common people had their own representatives, the tribunes, who in time gained the power of veto over the other magistrates. Dissatisfaction with the Senate's control of government led to civil wars, which culminated in ➤ JULIUS *Caesar*'s brief dictatorship. This established the principle of personal autocracy, and after Caesar's assassination another round of civil war ended with Octavian's assumption of authority.

A **Roman road** follows the line of one made under the Roman empire; typically of military origin, and where possible following the straight route of marching legions.

Roman type is a plain upright kind of type used in ordinary print, especially as distinguished from ➤ ITALIC and ➤ GOTHIC.

Roman de la Rose an extremely influential French poem of the 13th century, an allegorical romance embodying the aristocratic ethic of courtly love. It was composed by two different authors some forty years apart.

Romance the group of Indo-European languages descended from Latin, principally

French, Spanish, Portuguese, Italian, Catalan, Occitan, and Romanian. In Middle English, *Romance* denoted the vernacular language of France as opposed to Latin; the word comes via Old French from Latin *Romanicus* 'Roman'.

Romanesque a style of architecture which prevailed in Europe *c.*1000–1200, although sometimes dated back to the end of the Roman Empire (5th century). *Romanesque* architecture is characterized by round arches and massive vaulting, and by heavy piers, columns, and walls with small windows. Although disseminated throughout western Europe, the style reached its fullest development in France and Germany; the equivalent style in England is often called *Norman*.

Romanov a dynasty that ruled in Russia from the accession of Michael Romanov (1596–1645) in 1613 until the overthrow of the last tsar, Nicholas II, in 1917.

Epistle to the Romans a book of the New Testament, an epistle of St Paul to the Church at Rome.

Romanticism a movement in the arts and literature which originated in the late 18th century, emphasizing inspiration, subjectivity, and the primacy of the individual. Romanticism was a reaction against the order and restraint of classicism and neoclassicism, and a rejection of the rationalism which characterized the ➤ ENLIGHTENMENT. Writers exemplifying the movement include Wordsworth, Coleridge, Byron, Shelley, and Keats.

Romany the language of the gypsies, which is an Indo-European language related to Hindi. It is spoken by a dispersed group of about 1 million people, and has many dialects. The name comes (in the early 19th century) from Romany *Romani*, feminine and plural of the adjective *Romano*, from *Rom* 'man, husband'.

A **Romany rye** is a man who is not a gypsy by birth, but who lives with gypsies; the phrase is first recorded in George Borrow's *Lavengro* (1851), an account of a wandering life apparently based on Borrow's own; the sequel, published in 1857, was called *The Romany Rye*. (*Rye* here represents Romany *rai* 'gentleman'.)

Rome according to tradition the ancient city was founded by Romulus (after whom it is named) in 753 BC on the Palatine Hill; as it

grew it spread to the other six hills of Rome (Aventine, Caelian, Capitoline, Esquiline, Viminal, and Quirinal). Rome was ruled by kings until the expulsion of Tarquinius Superbus in 510 BC led to the establishment of the Roman Republic and the beginning of the Roman Empire.

By the time of the empire's fall the city was overshadowed politically by Constantinople, but emerged as the seat of the papacy and as the spiritual capital of Western Christianity. In the 14th and 15th centuries Rome became a centre of the Renaissance. It remained under papal control, forming part of the Papal States, until 1871, when it was made the capital of a unified Italy.

In allusive use, *Rome* is traditionally seen as standing for the Roman Empire or the Roman Catholic Church: the heart and emblem of a major power.

Rome was not built in a day means that a complex task is bound to take a long time and should not be rushed; proverbial saying, mid 16th century.

The **Treaty of Rome** is a treaty setting up and defining the aims of the European Economic Community. It was signed at Rome on 25 March 1957 by France, West Germany, Italy, Belgium, the Netherlands, and Luxembourg.

When in Rome (do as the Romans do) means that when abroad or in an unfamiliar environment you should adopt the customs or behaviour of those around you; proverbial saying, late 15th century.

Romulus the legendary founder of Rome, one of the twin sons of Mars by the Vestal Virgin ➤ RHEA *Silvia*; he and his brother Remus were exposed at birth in a basket on the River Tiber but were found and suckled by a she-wolf and later brought up by a shepherd family.

Grown to manhood, the twins founded a new settlement on the spot at which they had been washed ashore from the Tiber. An augury in the form of a flight of birds indicated that Romulus should be king, but during the building of the walls of Rome the brothers quarrelled, and Remus was killed.

The new city was settled by Romulus. To find wives for his followers, Romulus is said to have invited the neighbouring ➤ SABINES to witness a spectacle; in the course of this, the Sabine women were carried off (the *Rape of the Sabines*). The fighting which followed was eventually settled without the women returning to their own people.

Battle of Roncesvalles a battle which took place in 778 at a mountain pass in the Pyrenees, near the village of Roncesvalles in northern Spain. The rearguard of ➤ CHARLEMAGNE's army was attacked by the Basques and massacred; one of the paladins, ➤ ROLAND, was killed, an event celebrated in the *Chanson de Roland* (in which the attackers are wrongly identified as the Moors).

rood a crucifix, especially one positioned above the rood screen of a church or on a beam over the entrance to the chancel. Recorded from Old English (in the form *rōd*), the word is related to German *Rute* 'rod'.

shout something from the rooftops talk about something openly and jubilantly, especially something that is personal or has previously been kept secret; adapted from Luke 12:3.

rook[1] in traditional belief, this black crow is associated with death. From the mid 16th century, *rook* also denoted a cheat or swindler, especially in gaming.

The term **rookery**, literally meaning a breeding colony of rooks, typically seen as a collection of nests high in a clump of trees, is used for a dense collection of housing, especially in a slum area.

rook[2] a chess piece, typically with its top in the shape of a battlement, that can move in any direction along a rank or file on which it stands; a *castle*.

The word is recorded from Middle English and comes from Old French *rock*, based on an Arabic word of which the sense remains uncertain.

room at the top opportunity to join an elite or the top ranks of a profession; attributed to the American politician Daniel Webster (1782–1852), when cautioned against entering the legal profession.

have no room to swing a cat very little room; the *cat* originally referred to may be a ➤ CAT-o'-*nine-tails*.

strike at the root affect in a vital area with potentially destructive results. A similar biblical metaphor for imminent destruction is found at Matthew 3:10.

root and branch used to express the thorough or radical nature of a process or operation; originally with biblical allusion to Malachi 4:1 'the day cometh that shall burn them up…that it shall leave them neither root nor branch'.

the root of the matter the essential part of something; the expression comes originally from Job 19:28.

give a man enough rope and he will hang himself given enough freedom of action a person will bring about their own downfall; proverbial saying, mid 17th century.

a rope of sand used in allusion to something providing only illusory security or coherence.

on the ropes in state of near collapse or defeat; the allusion is to a boxer forced against the ropes by the opponent's attack.

Rorschach test a type of projective test used in psychoanalysis, in which a standard set of symmetrical ink blots of different shapes and colours is presented one by one to the subject, who is asked to describe what they suggest or resemble. Also called *ink-blot test*. It is named after Hermann *Rorschach* (1884–1922), Swiss psychiatrist.

rosary (in the Roman Catholic Church) a form of devotion in which five (or fifteen) decades of Hail Marys are repeated (a *decade* is a set of ten), each decade preceded by an Our Father and followed by a Glory Be; a string of beads for keeping count in such a devotion or in the devotions of some other religions, in Roman Catholic use 55 or 165 in number.

The word comes (in late Middle English, in the sense 'rose garden') from Latin *rosarium* rose-garden, from *rosa* 'rose'. In the 16th century (from which this meaning dates) the word was also used as the title of a book of devotion.

Roscius (d. 62 BC), a phenomenally successful comic actor, he later became identified with all that was considered best in acting. A number of famous English actors from the 16th century onwards, notably David Garrick, were nicknamed *Roscius* in reference to his great skill.

In 1761, the English poet Charles Churchill (1732–64) published the satirical poem *The Rosciad*, describing the attempt to find a worthy successor to Roscius.

rose in allusive or emblematic use, the *rose* typifies surpassing qualities of beauty, fragrance, and colour; it may also be referred to in contrast or relation to its thorns.

Roses are the emblem of ➤ St TERESA *of Lisieux*, ➤ St ELIZABETH *of Hungary*, and the Peruvian St Rose of Lima (1586–1617).

The **Rose Bowl** is a football stadium at Pasadena, California, used to designate a football match played between rival college teams annually on New Year's Day at the conclusion of the local Tournament of Roses. The ➤ Super *Bowl* is named after this.

not the rose but near it means not ideal but approaching or near this; the earliest version in English is found in an early 19th century translation of the *Gulistan* by the Persian poet Sadi (*c.*1213–*c.*1291).

A **rose by any other name** is an allusive reference to Shakespeare's *Romeo and Juliet* (1597), 'That which we call a Rose, By any other name would smell as sweet.'

To say that someone is wearing **rose-coloured spectacles** indicates that a person's view of something is unduly favourable, optimistic, or idealistic; recorded from the mid 19th century.

A **rose noble** is a gold coin current in the fifteenth and sixteenth centuries, being a variety of the noble with the figure of a rose stamped upon it, and of varying value at different times and places.

The **rose of Sharon** is an unidentified flower, translating a Hebrew phrase in the Song of Solomon 2:1, 'I am the rose of Sharon, and the lily of the valleys.' (The translators of the Revised Version explain the flower as 'the autumn crocus'.)

The **rose-red city** is the ancient city of ➤ Petra, from a poem by the English clergyman John William Burgon (1813–88).

The **Rose Theatre** was a theatre in Southwark, London, built in 1587. Many of Shakespeare's plays were performed there, some for the first time. Remains of the theatre, which was demolished *c.*1605, were uncovered in 1989.

A **rose window** is a circular window with mullions or tracery radiating in a form suggestive of a rose.

There is no rose without a thorn means that every apparently desirable situation has its share of trouble or difficulty; proverbial saying, late Middle English.

Rosebud in *Citizen Kane*, the enigmatic dying utterance of Charles Foster Kane, symbolizing his secret heart's desire.

rosemary the aromatic leaves of rosemary are an emblem of remembrance, and are particulary associated with the words of ➤ Ophelia in Shakespeare's *Hamlet*, 'There's rosemary for remembrance'.

In traditional belief, rosemary grows best in the garden of a woman who dominates her husband; it is also associated with the Virgin Mary on the Flight into Egypt (as in the story that on the way, having washed her clothes, she hung her blue robe on a rosemary bush to dry).

The name is recorded from Middle English (in form *rosmarine*), and is based on Latin *ros marinus* 'dew of the sea'; it was later understood as primarily associated with *rose* and *Mary* (for the Virgin).

roses, roses, all the way very successful or pleasant; quoting the first line of Robert Browning's *Patriot* (1855), describing the literal throwing of roses at a popular hero as he passed through the streets.

Rosetta Stone an inscribed stone found near Rosetta on the western mouth of the Nile in 1799. Its text, a decree commemorating the accession of Ptolemy V (reigned 205–180 BC), is written in three scripts: hieroglyphic, demotic, and Greek; the deciphering of the hieroglyphs by Jean-François Champollion in 1822 led to the interpretation of many other early records of Egyptian civilization. The *Rosetta Stone* is sometimes taken as the type of a mysterious cryptogram which, when decoded, will unlock other mysteries.

Rosh Hashana the Jewish New Year festival, held on the first (and sometimes the second) day of Tishri (in September). It is marked by the blowing of the shofar, and begins the ten days of penitence culminating in ➤ Yom *Kippur*. The literal meaning in Hebrew is 'head (i.e. beginning) of the year'.

Rosicrucian a member of a secretive 17th- and 18th-century society devoted to the study of metaphysical, mystical, and alchemical lore, especially that concerning the transmutation of metals, prolongation of life, and power over the elements. An anonymous pamphlet of 1614 about a mythical 15th-century knight called Christian *Rosenkreuz* is said to have launched the movement, the emblem of which was an equal-armed cross with a rose at its centre.

Rosinante the name of Don Quixote's horse, taken as the type of a poor, worn-out, and elderly horse.

Roskilde a port in Denmark, on the island of Zealand, which was the seat of Danish kings from *c.*1020 and the capital of Denmark until 1443; it is also the site of a museum of Viking ships, which had been sunk in the harbour.

Roswell a town in New Mexico, the scene of a mysterious crash in July 1947. Controversy has surrounded claims (apparently supported by photographic evidence) by some investigators that the crashed object was a UFO.

the rot set in a rapid succession of (usually unaccountable) failures began; *rot* in cricket, a rapid fall of wickets during an innings. The term is recorded from the mid 19th century.

Rothschild a famous Jewish banking house established in Frankfurt at the end of the 18th century by Meyer *Rothschild* (1744–1812) and spreading its operations all over western Europe; *Rothschild* (like ➤ ROCKEFELLER and ➤ VANDERBILT) is often used as the type of someone who is exceptionally wealthy, a millionaire.

rotten borough a borough that was able to elect an MP though having very few voters. Before the ➤ REFORM *Act* of 1832, in which such boroughs were largely disenfranchised, elections in rotten boroughs were rarely contested and the choice of MP was often in the hands of one person or family. The term derives from the borough's being found to have 'decayed' to the point of no longer having a constituency.

something is rotten in the state of Denmark an expression of moral, social, or political corruption, originally as spoken by the ghost in Shakespeare's *Hamlet*, revealing to his son the story of his brother Claudius's fratricide and usurpation.

Rotten Row a road in Hyde Park, extending from Apsley Gate to Kensington Gardens, much used as a fashionable resort for horse or carriage exercise; the name was formerly applied to a number of streets in different towns, although the reason for this is not clear. Now usually called *the Row*.

Rouen a port on the River Seine in NW France, chief town of Haute-Normandie. Rouen was in English possession from the time of the Norman Conquest until captured by the French in 1204, and again 1419–49; in 1431 ➤ JOAN *of Arc* was tried and burnt at the stake there.

rouge French word for red. In heraldry, two of the four pursuivants of the English College of Arms are **Rouge Croix**, so named from the red cross design on the badge worn by the pursuivant, and **Rouge Dragon**, so named from the red dragon design on the pursuivant's badge.

rough music noisy uproar as intended to display public outrage or discontent at the behaviour of others; *rough music* was traditionally produced by banging together pots, pans, and other domestic utensils; it was likely to accompany the ➤ SKIMMINGTON procession.

Rough Rider an irregular cavalryman; in particular, a member of a volunteer cavalry force during the Spanish-American War, the *Rough Riders*, raised and commanded by Theodore Roosevelt.

round robin a petition, especially one with signatures written in a circle to conceal the order of writing; the term was originally (in the mid 18th century) used by sailors, and was frequently referred to as a nautical term.

Round Table the table at which King Arthur and his knights sat so that none should have precedence, and which came to represent their chivalric fellowship. It was first mentioned in Wace's *Roman de Brut* (1155); from the 15th century, the name has been given to a large circular table preserved at Winchester, bearing the names of Arthur and his most famous knights.

Round Table was also subsequently used for something regarded as resembling Arthur's Round Table as an institution, such as an assembly of knights for the purpose of holding a tournament and festival, especially that instituted by King Edward III in 1345. The name has also been applied to various natural or artificial antiquities seen as having associations with King Arthur.

Since 1927, *Round Table* has also been the name of an organization for professional people between the ages of 18 and 40, intended to promote community service and international understanding.

round tower a high tower of circular plan tapering from the base to a conical roofed top, typically found in Ireland; the purpose of such *round towers* has been debated, but it seems likely that they were intended as the sign of dominance of an area rather than having strategic importance in themselves.

Roundhead a member or supporter of the Parliamentary party in the English Civil War, so called from their custom of wearing the hair close cut. The name is recorded from 1641.

Route One in soccer, the use of a long kick upfield as an attacking tactic. The term comes from a phrase used in the 1960s television quiz show *Quizball*, in which questions (graded in difficulty) led to scoring a goal, *Route One* being the direct path.

routier a member of a band of mercenaries in France in the late medieval period; the word comes from French *route* 'road' From the mid 20th century, *routier* has also denoted a long-distance lorry-driver.

rowan this tree is traditionally a protection against witchcraft. The name (which is recorded from the late 15th century, originally Scots and northern English) is of Scandinavian origin.

royal having the status of or under the patronage of a king or queen. *Royal* is also a name for a paper size, 636 x 480 mm (in full **metric royal**), and a book size, 234 x 156 mm (also **royal octavo**) or 312 x 237 mm (in full **royal quarto**).

The **Royal Academy of Arts** is an institution established in London in 1768, whose purpose was to cultivate painting, sculpture, and architecture in Britain. Sir Joshua Reynolds was its first president and he instituted a highly influential series of annual lectures.

The **Royal and Ancient** is St Andrews Golf Club, formed at St Andrews in Fife, Scotland, in 1754 as the *Society of St Andrews Golfers*; originally for 'noblemen and gentlemen'. The name **The Royal and Ancient Golf Club of St Andrews** was adopted in 1834 by permission of William IV, and in the 19th century the Club became the recognized authority on the rules of golf.

The **Royal Arms** are those used by the sovereign of a country, and generally including dynastic emblems and other traditional badges; the present *Royal Arms* of the United Kingdom, for example, show the leopards of England and lion rampant of Scotland with a harp for Ireland; the supporters, a lion and a unicorn, represent England and Scotland respectively, and the ground beneath the shield and its supporters has the rose of England, the thistle of Scotland, the Irish shamrock, and the Welsh leek. At earlier periods, they have included the lilies of France and the white horse of Hanover.

Royal Ascot is a four-day race meeting held at Ascot in June, traditionally attended by the sovereign; it was initiated in 1711 by Queen Anne.

The **royal assent** is the assent of the sovereign to a Bill which has been passed by Parliament, and which thus becomes an Act of Parliament. *Royal assent* by the sovereign (in person or through commissioners of the Crown) is required before a Bill (or a Measure passed by the General Synod of the Church of England) can come into force as law, but it has not been withheld since 1707.

The **Royal Exchange** was originally founded by Thomas Gresham (1518–79); 'Burse' or Exchange was built in 1566, and received the name *Royal Exchange* from Queen Elizabeth; a name which was retained by the newer building which later housed it. In the 17th century, the two were sometimes respectively referred to as the **Old Exchange** and the **New Exchange**; the older building was burnt in the Great Fire of London. The second *Royal Exchange*, which was opened in 1669, was also destroyed by fire (in 1838); it was finally closed as an institution in 1939.

A **royal flush** is a straight flush including ace, king, queen, jack, and ten all in the same suit, which is the hand of the highest possible value in poker when wild cards are not in use; the term is recorded from the mid 19th century.

The **Royal Greenwich Observatory** is the official astronomical institution of Great Britain. It was founded at Greenwich in London in 1675 by Charles II, and the old buildings now form part of the National Maritime Museum. The Observatory headquarters were moved to Herstmonceux Castle in East Sussex in 1948 and to Cambridge in 1990.

Royal Highness is the title of a prince or princess regarded as being of royal rank; up to the 17th century, ➤ HIGHNESS was the title of English kings and queens. In current British usage, *Royal Highness* is limited to the children, and grandchildren through the male line, of the sovereign.

The **Royal Institution** is a British society founded in 1799 for the diffusion of scientific knowledge. It organizes educational events, promotes research, and maintains a museum, library, and information service.

Royal jelly is a substance secreted by honeybee workers and fed by them to larvae which are being raised as potential queen bees; in figurative use, the quality which means that someone can succeed in a preeminent role.

The **Royal Mint** is the establishment responsible for the manufacture of British coins. Set up in 1810 in London, it moved in 1968 to Llantrisant in South Wales.

The **royal road to** is a way of attaining or reaching something without trouble (usually in negative contexts). With allusion to the riposte by the Alexandrian Greek mathematician Euclid to the Egyptian ruler Ptolemy I, who had asked whether geometry could not be made easier, 'There is no royal road to geometry.'

The **Royal Society** is the oldest and most prestigious scientific society in Britain. It was formed by followers of Francis Bacon (including Robert Boyle, John Evelyn, and Christopher Wren) to promote scientific discussion especially in the physical sciences, and received its charter from Charles II in 1662. Its *Philosophical Transactions*, founded in 1665, is the oldest scientific journal.

The **royal 'we'** is the use of 'we' instead of 'I' by a single person, as traditionally used by a sovereign.

Royalist a supporter of the King against Parliament in the English Civil War; the term is first used in the Puritan pamphleteer William Prynne's *The Sovereign Power of Parliaments and Kingdoms* (1643).

there's the rub there's the difficulty, originally from Shakespeare's *Hamlet*; a *rub* here is literally an impediment in bowls by which a bowl is hindered in or diverted from its proper course.

rub of the green good fortune, especially as determining events in a sporting match, luck; literally, the lie of the green in golf as determining the way a ball will run.

the rubber chicken circuit the circuit followed by professional speakers; referring to what is regarded as the customary menu for the lunch or dinner preceding the speech.

Rube Goldberg designating a device that is unnecessarily complicated, impracticable, or ingenious, from the name of Reuben ('*Rube*') Lucius *Goldberg* (1883–1970), US humorous artist, whose illustrations often depicted such devices.

Rubicon a stream in NE Italy which marked the ancient boundary between Italy and Cisalpine Gaul. ➤ JULIUS *Caesar* led his army across it into Italy in 49 BC, breaking the law forbidding a general to lead an army out of his province, and so committing himself to war against the Senate and Pompey; the ensuing civil war resulted in victory for Caesar after three years.

In general use, *rubicon* came in the 17th century to mean a boundary or limit, and from the late 19th century, in the card-game of piquet, to denote an act of winning a game against an opponent whose total score is less than 100, in which case the loser's score is added to rather than subtracted from the winner's.

To **cross the Rubicon** is to pass a point of no return, as Caesar led his army across the river forming the ancient boundary between Italy and Cisalpine Gaul; the expression has been current since the 17th century.

Rubik's cube a puzzle in the form of a plastic cube covered with multicoloured squares, which the player attempts to twist and turn so that all the squares on each face are of the same colour. It is named after Erno *Rubik* (1944–), its Hungarian inventor, and had a great vogue when first introduced in the 1980s.

rubric a heading on a document; in particular, a direction in a liturgical book as to how a church service should be conducted. The word (in late Middle English in form *rubrish*) originally refers to a heading or section of text written in red for distinctiveness (see also ➤ RED *letter day*); it comes via Old French from Latin *rubrica (terra)* 'red (earth or ochre as writing material)', from the base of *rubeus* 'red'.

From the mid 19th century, the word was used for a descriptive heading or designation, and then for a set of instructions on an examination paper.

ruby a precious stone consisting of corundum in colour varieties varying from deep crimson or purple to pale rose (the term ➤ PIGEON's *blood* is sometimes used of ruby of a particularly deep shade); the name may also be used for the less valuable **spinel ruby**, a deep red variety of the mineral spinel. The *ruby* may also be taken as the type of something exceedingly precious, as in the biblical passage.

A **ruby wedding** is the fortieth (or occasionally, the forty-fifth) anniversary of a wedding; the name is recorded from the early 20th century.

Rudra in the ➤ RIG *Veda*, a Vedic minor god, associated with the storm. In Hinduism, *Rudra* is also one of the names of ➤ SHIVA.

rue a symbol of grief and repentance. The name of his plant, with its bitter strong-scented lobed leaves used in herbal medicine, has often been used with punning allusion to *rue* meaning 'sorrow, regret'. This may have given rise to the alternative name ➤ HERB *of grace*.

Ruggiero the legendary ancestor of the house of Este (also called *Rogero*), son of a Christian knight and a Saracen; he accepts baptism, and fights for Charlemagne. His deeds are celebrated in *Orlando Furioso*.

St Rule (?4th century), a Scottish saint who supposedly brought the relics of St Andrew to Scotland; he is said to have been a native of Patras in the Peloponnese, who was instructed in a dream to set out with the relics; when he reached Fife, he was similarly told to stop, and there he built a church. This was said to be the origin of the name *St Andrews*. His feast day is 17 October (and also, through confusion with St Regulus of Senlis, 30 March).

Rule, Britannia name given to the song from *Alfred: A Masque* (1740), attributed to the Scottish poet James Thomson (1700–48); the name comes from the concluding lines of the verse.

By the end of the 19th century, the singing of *Rule Britannia* was associated with a particularly assertive patriotism.

rule of the road a custom or law regulating the direction in which two vehicles (or riders or ships) should move to pass one another on meeting, or which should give way to the other, so as to avoid collision; the expression is recorded from the late 19th century.

rule of three a method of finding a number in the same ratio to a given number as exists between two other given numbers; recorded from the late 16th century, it is also called the *golden rule*.

rule of thumb a broadly accurate guide or principle, based on experience or practice rather than theory; the expression dates from the late 17th century.

rule the roast be in charge, have full authority; the expression is found frequently from the mid 16th century on, but the precise origin is unclear. The (now more common) form **rule the roost** is recorded from the mid 18th century.

ruling passion an interest or concern that occupies a large part of someone's time and effort; initially perhaps as a quotation from Alexander Pope (1688–1744), in Epistles to Several Persons (1733), 'The ruling passion conquers reason still.'

rum in the British navy, rum was formerly regulation issue for sailors; in Australia during the early days of New South Wales it was also an important medium of exchange.

In North America, from the early 19th century, *rum* has been used generically for intoxicating liquor, particularly by those advocating temperance.

The **Rum Hospital** was a hospital in Sydney, Australia, the building of which was undertaken in return for the granting of a monopoly on the import of spirits from 1810 to 1814.

The **Rum Rebellion** was the rebellion against William Bligh, Governor of New South Wales, by officers of the New South Wales Corps (the **Rum (Puncheon) Corps**) in 1808, when Bligh had attempted to limit the importation of spirits into the Colony.

Rump Parliament the part of the Long Parliament which continued to sit after Pride's Purge in 1648, and voted for the trial which resulted in the execution of Charles I. Dissolved by Oliver Cromwell in 1653, the Rump Parliament was briefly reconvened in 1659 but voted its own dissolution early in 1660.

The origin of the name is uncertain; it is said to derive from *The Bloody Rump*, the name of a paper written before the trial, the word being popularized after a speech by Major General Brown, given at a public assembly; it is alternatively said to have been coined by Clem Walker in his *History of Independency* (1648), as a term for those strenuously opposing the king.

Rumpelstiltskin the name of a vindictive dwarf in one of Grimm's fairy tales; he initially appears beneficent, helping a miller's daughter to fulfil her father's boast to the king that she can spin straw into gold, but as a price on three successive nights he takes her necklace, her ring, and finally the promise of her first child. After she has married the king and born a son, *Rumpelstiltskin* returns for his forfeit; the only way in which she can save the child is to discover the dwarf's name. Over the next three days she sends out messengers to discover names; it is only on the final day that one of the messengers overhears the dwarf gloating that the queen will never discover that 'Rumpelstiltskin is my name'. When the dwarf appears for his prize, the queen is able to name him; Rumpelstiltskin tears himself in two in his frustrated rage.

a run for one's money a satisfactory period of success in return for one's exertions or expenditure; originally from racing, and recorded from the late 19th century.

run the gauntlet undergo the military punishment of receiving blows while running between two rows of men with sticks; alteration (in the mid 17th century) of *gantlope* (from Swedish *gatlopp*, from *gata* 'lane' + *lopp* 'course') by association with *gauntlet*.

runcible a nonsense word used by Edward Lear in formations such as **runcible cat** and (especially) **runcible spoon**; this term was later applied to a fork curved like a spoon, with three broad prongs, one of which has a sharpened outer edge for cutting, although Lear's own illustrations for his books of verse give no warrant for this. The word was perhaps suggested by late 16th-century *rouncival*, denoting a large variety of pea.

rune a letter of an ancient Germanic alphabet, related to the Roman alphabet; the original runic alphabet dates from at least the 2nd or 3rd century, and was formed by modifying the letters of the Roman or Greek alphabet so as to facilitate cutting them upon wood or stone.

In Scandinavian mythology, *runes* (supposedly won for humankind by ➤ ODIN) were also seen as having magical powers; in current British usage, the phrase **read the runes** means to try to forecast the outcome of a situation by analysing all the significant factors involved.

The word comes from Old English *rūn* 'a secret, a mystery', not recorded between Middle English and the late 17th century, when it was reintroduced under the influence of Old Norse *rúnir*, *rúnar* 'magic signs, hidden lore'.

Runnymede a meadow on the south bank of the Thames near Windsor. It is famous for its association with Magna Carta, which was signed by King John in 1215 there or nearby.

Rupert Bear cartoon character created by the illustrator Mary Tourtel, a white bear with a red jacket and black and yellow checked scarf; under the title 'Rupert, the Adventures of a Little Lost Teddy Bear', the cartoon appeared in the *Daily Express* in 1920, and was the first comic strip for children to appear in an adult newspaper.

Rupert of the Rhine popular name for Prince *Rupert* (1619–82), English Royalist general, son of Frederick V (elector of the Palatinate) and Elizabeth Stuart, the ➤ WINTER *Queen*, and nephew of Charles I. The Royalist leader of cavalry, he initially won a series of victories, but was defeated by Parliamentarian forces at Marston Moor (1644) and Naseby (1645). After the Restoration he settled in England; he was one of the founders of the ➤ HUDSON's *Bay Company* and (reflecting his interest in science) of the ➤ ROYAL *Society*.

Prince Rupert's drop is a pear-shaped bubble of glass with a long tail, made by dropping melted glass into water. *Prince Rupert's drops* have the property, due to internal strain, of disintegrating explosively when the tail is broken off or the surface scratched.

Rupert's Land is a historical region of northern and western Canada, roughly corresponding to what is now Manitoba, Saskatchewan, Yukon, Alberta, and the southern part of the Northwest Territories. It was originally granted in 1670 by Charles II to the Hudson's Bay Company and named after Prince Rupert. Also called *Prince Rupert's Land*.

Rurik a member of a dynasty that ruled Muscovy and much of Russia from the 9th century until the death of Fyodor, son of Ivan the Terrible, in 1598. It was reputedly founded by a Varangian chief who settled in Novgorod in 862.

Ruritania an imaginary kingdom in SE Europe used as a fictional background for the adventure novels of courtly intrigue and romance written by Anthony Hope (1863–1933), notably *The Prisoner of Zenda* (1894) and *Rupert of Hentzau* (1898).

rus in urbe an illusion of countryside created by a building or garden within a city. The phrase, which is Latin and means literally 'country in the city', was coined originally by the Spanish-born Latin epigrammatist Martial (AD *c.*40–*c.*104).

Mount Rushmore a mountain in the Black Hills of South Dakota, noted for its giant busts of four US Presidents—George Washington, Thomas Jefferson, Abraham Lincoln, and Theodore Roosevelt—carved (1927–41) under the direction of the sculptor Gutzon Borglum (1867–1941).

russet a coarse homespun reddish-brown or grey cloth traditionally used for simple clothing; *russet* clothing may be taken as a symbol of simplicity and honesty, as in a letter of 1643 written by Oliver Cromwell.

Russian of, pertaining to, or characteristic of Russia.

A **Russian doll** is each of a set of brightly painted hollow wooden dolls of varying sizes, designed to fit inside each other.

The **Russian Orthodox Church** is the national Church of Russia, a branch of the Eastern ➤ ORTHODOX *Church*.

The **Russian Revolution** is the revolution in the Russian empire in 1917, in which the tsarist regime was overthrown and replaced by Bolshevik rule under Lenin. The **Russian Revolution of 1905** is the name given to a demonstration in St Petersburg of that year, which was fired on by troops. The crew of the battleship *Potemkin* mutinied and a soviet was formed in St Petersburg, prompting Tsar Nicholas II to make a number of short-lived concessions including the formation of an elected legislative body or Duma.

Russian roulette is the practice of loading a bullet into one chamber of a revolver, spinning the cylinder, and then pulling the trigger while pointing the gun at one's own head, said to have originated among Russian officers in the early 20th century.

Rust Belt a part of a country considered to be characterized by declining industry, ageing factories, and a falling population, especially the American Midwest and NE states. Coinage of the term is often attributed to the US Democratic politician Walter Mondale, who opposed Ronald Reagan in the presidential election of 1984.

rusticate suspend a student from a university as a punishment (used chiefly at Oxford and Cambridge). Recorded from the late 15th century (in the sense 'countrify' the word comes from Latin *rusticat-* '(having) lived in the country'.

Ruth a book of the Bible telling the story of *Ruth*, a Moabite woman, who when her husband died resolved to accompany her mother-in-law Naomi back to Judah, with the words, 'Intreat me not to leave thee, or to return from following after thee: for whither thou goes, I will go; and where thou lodgest, I will lodge: thy people shall be my people, and thy God my God.'

The two women returned to Judah, and through Naomi's agency Ruth married her deceased husband's kinsman Boaz and bore a son who became grandfather to King David. *Ruth* together with Naomi may be taken as a type of devotion; the image of Ruth herself, in her early days in Judah, may also be that of a lonely stranger.

Ruy Lopez in chess, an opening in which White moves the king's bishop to the fifth rank, usually on the third move, named after *Ruy López* de Segura (fl. 1560), Spanish priest and chess expert, who developed this opening.

Rye House Plot a conspiracy in 1683 to murder Charles II and his heir, his brother James, duke of York as they passed the Rye House, near Hoddesdon in Hertfordshire, on their way back from Newmarket to London. The plan was not in fact put into action, and one of the conspirators revealed its existence to the government in June 1683. Several of those involved, including Algernon Sidney and William Russell, were executed.

Ss

S The nineteenth letter of the modern English alphabet and the eighteenth of the ancient Roman one, derived from a Semitic (Phoenician) character.

Saba an ancient kingdom in SW Arabia, famous for its trade in gold and spices; the biblical ► SHEBA, which Greek and Roman writers believed to be the name of the capital city of the kingdom.

Sabaean a member of an ancient Semitic people who ruled ► SABA in SW Arabia until overrun by Persians and Arabs in the 6th century AD.

Sabaism the worship of stars or of spirits in them, especially as practised in ancient Arabia and Mesopotamia; the term comes (in the early 18th century) via French from Hebrew *ṣābā* 'hosts (of heaven)', after the presumed etymology of ► SABIAN.

Sabaoth the hosts of heaven, in the biblical title **Lord (God) of Sabaoth**; a Hebrew word, literally 'armies, hosts', retained untranslated in the English New Testament (as in the original Greek and in the Vulgate) and in the *Te Deum*. English versions of Old Testament passages in which the word occurs have the rendering 'The Lord of Hosts'.

the Sabbath a day of religious observance and abstinence from work, kept by Jews from Friday evening to Saturday evening, and by most Christians on Sunday; the idea that the ► LORD's Day is a 'Christian Sabbath' or a substitute for the Sabbath occurs in theologicial writings from the 4th century onwards, but was not popularly current before the Reformation. In English, *Sabbath* as a synonym for 'Sunday' did not become common until the 17th century.

Recorded from Old English, the name comes via Latin and Greek from Hebrew *šabbāt*, from *šābaṭ* 'to rest'. 'Remember the sabbath day, to keep it holy' is the fourth (or in medieval reckoning, the third) of the ► TEN *Commandments*.

A **Sabbath day's journey** is the distance (equivalent to 1225 yards) which (according to Rabbinical prescription in the time of Christ) was the utmost limit of permitted travel on the Sabbath.

Sabian of or relating to a non-Muslim sect classed in the Koran with Jews, Christians, and Zoroastrians as having a faith revealed by the true God. It is not known who the original Sabians were, but the name was adopted by some groups in order to escape religious persecution by Muslims; it is said by some Arabic writers that the Sabians were professedly Christian, but secretly worshippers of the stars, the etymology of *Sabian* being presumed to be Hebrew *ṣābā* 'hosts (of heaven)' (see ► SABAISM).

Sabine of, relating to, or denoting an ancient Oscan-speaking people of the central Apennines in Italy, north-east of Rome, who feature in early Roman legends and were incorporated into the Roman state in 290 BC. The Sabines were renowned in antiquity for their frugal and hardy character and their superstitious practices.

The (unhistorical) legend of the ► RAPE *of the Sabine Women* reflects the early intermingling of Romans and Sabines; some Roman religious institutions were said to have a Sabine origin.

sable the heraldic term for black, recorded from Middle English. The word comes from Old French, and is generally taken to be identical with *sable* as the name for a marten with a short tail and dark brown fur, native to Japan and Siberia and valued for its fur.

sabra a Jew born in Israel (or before 1948 in Palestine). The word comes from modern Hebrew *ṣabbār* 'opuntia fruit' (opuntias being common in coastal regions of Israel).

Sabrina a poetic name for the river Severn; in Geoffrey of Monmouth's *History*, from the name of king Locrine's daughter, who was put to death by drowning in the Severn. In Milton's *Comus*, Sabrina is the nymph of the River Severn.

Sacco and Vanzetti the Italian-born political radicals Nicola *Sacco* and Bartolomeo *Vanzetti* were accused and convicted of murder in the US in 1921 in a sensational, controversial trial. In 1927, both men were executed; fifty years later, their names were cleared of any crimes.

sackcloth and ashes used with biblical allusion to the wearing of sackcloth and having ashes sprinkled on the head as a sign of penitence or mourning, as in Matthew 11:21.

sacrament a religious ceremony or act of the Christian Church which is regarded as an outward and visible sign of inward and spiritual divine grace, in particular (in the Roman Catholic and many Orthodox Churches) the seven rites of *baptism*, *confirmation*, the *Eucharist*, *penance*, *anointing of the sick*, *ordination*, and *matrimony*, and among Protestants, the two rites of *baptism* and the *Eucharist*. In Catholic usage, *sacrament* (or the **Holy Sacrament** or the **Blessed Sacrament**) also denotes the consecrated elements of the Eucharist, especially the bread or Host.

The word comes (in Middle English) via Old French from Latin *sacramentum* 'solemn oath' (ultimately from *sacer* 'sacred'), used in Christian Latin as a translation of Greek *mustērion* 'mystery'.

sacred connected with God or a gods; deserving veneration.

A **sacred cow** is an idea, custom or institution held, especially unreasonably, to be above criticism (with reference to the Hindus' respect for the cow as a holy animal). The term is recorded in English in its literal sense from the late 19th century, and in figurative use from the early 20th.

In ancient Rome, the **sacred geese** were kept as guardians of the Capitol; they gave warning of attack by the Gauls in 390 BC, and saved the Capitol when the rest of the city fell.

The **Sacred Heart** is an image representing the heart of Christ, used as an object of devotion among Roman Catholics. In the Roman Catholic Church, the **Feast of the Sacred Heart** is observed on the Friday in the week following ➤ CORPUS *Christi*.

The **Sacred Way** is a route used traditionally for religious processions or pilgrimages; in particular, in ancient Rome, the *Via Sacra*, a street leading to the Forum and passing a number of sacred buildings, including the temple of ➤ VESTA, from which it took its name.

sacrifice an act of slaughtering an animal or person or surrendering a possession as an offering to God or to a divine or supernatural figure; also, the offering itself. In its primary use, a *sacrifice* implies an altar on which the victim is placed, an association often retained in figurative and metaphorical use.

In the Christian Church, the term is used for Christ's offering of himself in the Crucifixion, or for the Eucharist regarded either (in Catholic terms) as a propitiatory offering of the body and blood of Christ or (in Protestant terms) as an act of thanksgiving. The word is recorded from Middle English, and comes ultimately from Latin *sacer* 'holy'.

Sadducee a member of a Jewish sect or party of the time of Christ that denied the resurrection of the dead, the existence of spirits, and the obligation of oral tradition, emphasizing acceptance of the written Law alone. The name is occasionally used allusively for someone of a sceptical and materialist temperament.

Recorded from Old English, the word comes via late Latin and Greek from Hebrew *ṣĕḏōqī* in the sense 'descendant of Zadok' (2 Samuel 8:17). The prevailing modern view is that the Zadok referred to is the high-priest of ➤ DAVID's time, from whom the priesthood of the Captivity and later periods claimed to be descended, and the late Jewish notion of a post-exilian Zadok as the founder of the sect is regarded as baseless.

Sadie Hawkins day a day early in November on which, according to a 'tradition' in the cartoon strip *Li'l Abner* by the US cartoonist Alfred Gerald Caplin (1909–79), a woman may propose marriage to or demand a date from a man; *Sadie Hawkins* herself is a character in the series.

sadism the tendency to derive pleasure, especially sexual gratification, from inflicting pain, suffering, or humiliation on others. The term comes from the name of the French writer and soldier the Marquis de *Sade* (1740–1814), whose career as a cavalry officer was interrupted by periods of imprisonment for cruelty and debauchery, and who while in prison wrote a number of sexually explicit works.

Sadler's Wells a London theatre opened by Lilian Baylis in 1931, known for its ballet and opera companies. Although the Sadler's Wells Ballet moved to the Covent Garden Theatre in 1946, a second company, the Sadler's Wells Theatre Company, and a ballet school were set up at the theatre, the three merging as the Royal Ballet in 1956; in 1968 the opera company moved to the Coliseum in London as the English National Opera.

Sadler's Wells was named after Thomas *Sadler*, who discovered a medicinal spring at the original site in 1683.

Safavid a member of a dynasty which ruled Persia 1502–1736 and installed Shia rather than Sunni Islam as the state religion. The name comes from Arabic *ṣafawī* 'descended from the ruler Sophy'.

there's safety in numbers being in a group of people makes you feel more confident and secure; proverbial, probably originally adapting Proverbs 11:14.

saga a long story of heroic achievement, especially a medieval prose narrative in Old Norse or Old Icelandic, embodying the traditional histories of the Norse families who first settled Iceland or of the kings of Norway. The word is recorded in English from the early 18th century, and comes from Old Norse, literally 'narrative'.

From the mid 19th century, the use of the term has widened to cover stories regarded as resembling traditional sagas, in particular (as with Galsworthy's *The Forsyte Saga*) dealing with the history of a family through several generations. *Saga* may also be used loosely for a long, involved story, account, or series of incidents.

sage¹ in traditional belief, this plant grows best either under the care of the dominant partner of a marriage, or when the wife is dominant.

Sage was formerly regarded as having medicinal properties, and the name comes (in Middle English via Old French) from Latin *salvia* 'healing plant', from *salvus* 'safe'.

sage² a profoundly wise man, especially one who features in ancient history or legend; the word comes (in Middle English, as an adjective, via Old French) from Latin *sapere* 'be wise'.

Sagebrush State informal name for the state of Nevada.

Sagittarius a large constellation (the Archer), said to represent a ➤ CENTAUR carrying a bow and arrow. In astrology, the ninth sign of the zodiac, which the sun enters about 22 November; a person born between 22 November and 21 December is in astrological belief thought to be under its influence.

The name is Latin, from *sagitta* 'arrow'.

Sahara a vast desert in North Africa, extending from the Atlantic in the west to the Red Sea in the east, and from the Mediterranean and the Atlas Mountains in the north to the Sahel in the south, the largest desert in the world. Often used figuratively.

sail under false colours disguise one's true nature or intentions; the *colours* are the flag which signals a ship's nationality.

saint a person acknowledged as holy or virtuous and typically regarded as being in heaven after death; (in the Catholic and Orthodox Churches) a person formally recognized or canonized by the Church after death, who may be the object of veneration and prayers for intercession. In pictorial representations, a saint is typically shown with a ➤ HALO, and often with a symbol particularly associated with them.

The word comes (in Middle English, via Old French) from Latin *sanctus* 'holy'.

The Saint is the nickname of Simon Templar, a fictional character created by the thriller writer Leslie Charteris (1907–93). The *Saint*, a debonair criminal whose lawbreaking excludes such areas as treason and drugrunning, signifies his intervention in a case by leaving the sketch of a stick figure surmounted by a halo.

St Helena a solitary island in the South Atlantic, a British dependency, which from 1659 until 1834 was administered by the East India Company. It is famous as the place of ➤ NAPOLEON's exile (1815–21) and death.

St Leger an annual flat horse race at Doncaster for three-year-olds, held in September, and named after Colonel Barry *St Leger* (1737–89), who instituted the race in 1776.

St Sophia the key monument of Byzantine architecture, originally a church, at Istanbul. Built by order of ➤ JUSTINIAN and inaugurated in 537, its enormous dome is supported by piers, arches, and pendentives and pierced by forty windows. In 1453, when the Turks invaded, orders were given for St Sophia's conversion into a mosque and minarets were added. In 1935 Atatürk declared it a museum. It is also known as *Hagia Sophia* and *Santa Sophia*.

St Trinian's a fictional girls' school invented by the English cartoonist Ronald Searle (1920–) in 1941, whose pupils are characterized by unruly behaviour, ungainly appearance, and unattractive school uniform; *St Trinian's* later also became known through associated books and films.

saint's day a day on which a saint is particularly commemorated in the Christian Church; the term is recorded from late Middle English.

la sainte ampoule the 'holy ampoule' or vessel containing the oil with which kings of France were anointed at their coronation; it was said to have been brought from heaven by a dove at the coronation of ➤ CLOVIS. The English diarist John Evelyn recorded in 1660 being shown it, but it was destroyed during the French Revolution.

Sainte Chapelle a royal chapel in Paris, noted for its stained glass, built in 1248 in high Gothic style by ➤ St LOUIS to house Christ's Crown of Thorns and other relics of the Passion.

Land of Saints and Scholars a name for Ireland, alluding to the holiness and learning associated with the early Celtic Church.

All Saints' Day a Christian festival in honour of all the saints in heaven, held (in the Western Church) on 1 November (see also ➤ HALLOWEEN).

Saiva a member of one of the main branches of modern Hinduism, devoted to the worship of the god ➤ SHIVA as the supreme being.

salad days the period when one is young and inexperienced, one's time of youth; originally as a quotation from Shakespeare's *Antony and Cleopatra* in the words of Cleopatra.

Saladin (1137–93), sultan of Egypt and Syria 1174–93. Saladin invaded the Holy Land and reconquered Jerusalem from the Christians in 1187, but he was defeated by Richard I at Arsuf (1191) and withdrew to Damascus, where he died. He earned a reputation not only for military skill but also for honesty and chivalry.

salamander a mythical lizard-like creature said to live in fire or to be able to stand its effects. The word is recorded from Middle English; from the early 17th century, *salamander* has been used for a newt-like amphibian that typically has bright markings, once thought able to endure fire. The *salamander* may be taken as the type of something able to endure great heat unscathed; it is also found in heraldry as an emblem, for example that of Francis I of France.

salami tactics piecemeal attack on or elimination of (especially political) opposition, in which an opponent's strengths are systematically sliced away.

Salamis an island in the Saronic Gulf in Greece, to the west of Athens. The strait between the island and the mainland was the scene in 480 BC of a crushing defeat of the Persian fleet under ➤ XERXES I by the Greeks under ➤ THEMISTOCLES.

Salem a city and port in NE Massachusetts, north of Boston, which in 1692 was the scene of a notorious series of witchcraft trials. Initially three women were accused by a number of children of having bewitched them; ultimately 19 people were hanged, and many others imprisoned. Arthur Miller's play *The Crucible* (1952) uses the story of the mass hysteria which developed as an illustration of the phenomenon of ➤ MCCARTHYISM.

In the Bible (Genesis 14:18) *Salem* is a place-name understood to be another name for Jerusalem and to mean 'peace'. It was later (chiefly in the nineteenth century) adopted by Methodists, Baptists, and others as the name of a particular chapel or meeting-house, and thus was sometimes used as a synonym for a nonconformist chapel.

Salerno a port on the west coast of Italy, which was formerly the site of a famous medical school.

Salian a member of the *Salii*, a 4th-century Frankish people living near the River Ijssel, from whom the ➤ MEROVINGIANS were descended. Also called *Salic*.

Salic law a law excluding females from dynastic succession, especially as the alleged fundamental law of the French monarchy. Such a law was used in the 14th century by the French to deny Edward III's claim to the French throne (based on descent from his Capetian mother Isabella), so initiating the ➤ HUNDRED *Years War*.

The ancient text which under the name of the *Salic law* was adduced in favour of the succession of Philip V in 1316, and afterwards used to combat the claims of Edward III of England (and his successors) to the French crown, was really a quotation from the *Lex Salica*, a Frankish law-book, written in Latin, and extant in five successively enlarged recensions of Merovingian and Carolingian date. The words however have no reference to succession to the crown, but merely state that a woman can have no portion of the inheritance of 'Salic land' (*terra Salica*); the precise meaning of this term is disputed, and in the earliest form of the code the word 'Salic' is omitted.

Sallust (86–35 BC), Roman historian and politician. As a historian he was concerned with the political and moral decline of Rome after the fall of Carthage in 146 BC. His chief surviving works deal with the ➤ CATILINE conspiracy and the Jugurthine War.

salmon a salmon with a ring is the emblem of ➤ St KENTIGERN.

Salome (in the New Testament) the daughter of Herodias, who danced before her stepfather Herod Antipas. Given a choice of reward for her dancing, she asked for the head of ➤ St JOHN *the Baptist* and thus caused him to be beheaded. Her name is given by Josephus; she is mentioned but not named in the Gospels.

the Salon an annual exhibition of the work of living artists held by the Royal Academy of Painting and Sculpture in Paris, originally in the Salon d'Apollon in the Louvre in 1667.

The **Salon des Refusés** was an exhibition in Paris ordered by Napoleon III in 1863 to display pictures rejected by the Salon. The artists represented included Manet, Cézanne, Pissarro, and Whistler.

salt in proverbial use, *salt* is taken as the type of a necessary adjunct to food, and hence as a symbol of hospitality (as in the expression, **to eat a person's salt**).

With **a grain of salt** means sceptically; a translation of the modern Latin phrase *cum grano salis*, recorded from the mid 17th century.

To **salt a mine** is to introduce extraneous ore or other material into a mineral sample to make the source seem rich.

Salt Lake City is the capital of Utah, situated near the south-eastern shores of the Great Salt Lake, founded in 1847 by Brigham Young. The city is the world headquarters of the Church of Latter-Day Saints (Mormons).

The **salt of the earth** denotes a person or group of people of great kindness, reliability, or honesty; originally with biblical allusion to Matthew 5:13.

the salutation the angel Gabriel's greeting to the Virgin Mary (cf. Luke 1:28–9), which forms the first part of the ➤ AVE *Maria*; it is also called **the angelic salutation**. In art, the virgin is often shown sitting reading; her posture in response to Gabriel may be startled or quiescent. A branch or pot of lilies, for purity, often appears.

Salvation Army a worldwide Christian evangelical organization on quasi-military lines, established by ➤ *William* BOOTH (1829–1912).

The name was adopted in 1878 (the body until then was styled 'the Christian Mission'). The officers bear military titles ('general', 'captain', etc.). In its early years, open-air evangelistic services, featuring its famous brass bands, were the most prominent feature of the *Salvation Army*'s work.

Sama Veda one of the four ➤ VEDAS, a collection of liturgical Hindu chants chanted aloud at the sacrifice. Its material is drawn largely from the ➤ RIG *Veda*.

Samaritan a member of a people inhabiting Samaria in biblical times, or of the modern community claiming descent from them, adhering to a form of Judaism accepting only its own ancient version of the Pentateuch as Scripture.

In the New Testament, the enmity between the Jews and the Samaritans gave especial point to the story (in John ch. 4) of Jesus's asking for water from the woman of Samaria, and to the parable of the **good Samaritan** (see below).

In the UK, **the Samaritans** (taking their name from the parable) are an organization which counsels the suicidal and others in distress, mainly through a telephone service.

A **good Samaritan** is a charitable or helpful person, with reference to the parable told by Jesus in Luke ch. 10 about a man who 'fell among thieves' when travelling from Jerusalem to Jericho. He was left lying by the side of the road, and the first two people who saw him, a priest and a Levite, 'passed by on the other side'. It was the third traveller, a Samaritan, who took pity on him and succoured him.

Samarkand a city in eastern Uzbekistan, one of the oldest cities of Asia, founded in the 3rd or 4th millennium BC. It grew to prominence as a prosperous centre of the silk trade, situated on the Silk Road, and in the 14th century became the capital of ➤ TAMERLANE's Mongol empire; it may be taken as the object of an arduous but worthwhile journey, as in Flecker's poem *The Golden Journey to Samarkand* (1913).

Samarra a city in Iraq, on the River Tigris north of Baghdad; its 17th-century mosque is a place of Shiite pilgrimage.

An **appointment in Samarra** is an unavoidable meeting with death or fate, from a story by Somerset Maugham in the play *Sheppey* (1933), in which a man sees Death in Baghdad and flees to distant Samarra to escape, not realizing that Death had always intended to meet him that night in Samarra.

Samhain the first day of November, celebrated by the ancient Celts as a festival marking the beginning of winter and the Celtic new year. The name is Irish, from Old Irish *samain*.

samite a rich silk fabric interwoven with gold and silver threads, used for dressmaking and decoration in the Middle Ages. In literary use, it is particularly associated with the story of King Arthur; when the sword ➤ EXCALIBUR is finally thrown back into the lake, the arm that reaches out of the water to catch and grasp it is clothed in white samite.

The word comes (in Middle English) via Old French and medieval Latin from medieval Greek, and ultimately from Greek *hexa* 'six' + *mitos* 'thread'; this may mean that the original *samite* was woven of thread consisting of six strands of silk.

samizdat the clandestine copying and distribution of literature banned by the state, especially formerly in the communist countries of eastern Europe. Recorded from the 1960s, the word is Russian and means literally 'self-publishing house'.

Samnite a member of an Oscan-speaking people of southern Italy in ancient times, who spent long periods at war with republican Rome in the 4th to 1st centuries BC.

Samson an Israelite leader (probably 11th century BC) famous for his strength (Judges 13–16). He fell in love with Delilah and confided to her that his strength lay in his uncut hair. She betrayed him to the Philistines who cut off his hair and blinded him, but his hair grew again, and he pulled down the pillars of a house, destroying himself and a large gathering of Philistines.

The name *Samson* is used allusively with reference to his enormous strength, his having been blinded, or his final destruction of his enemies at the price of his own life.

Samuel in the Bible, a Hebrew prophet who rallied the Israelites after their defeat by the Philistines and became their ruler; either of two books of the Bible covering the history of ancient Israel from Samuel's birth to the end of the reign of David. It was Samuel who anointed ➤ SAUL as king of Israel.

San Andreas fault a fault line extending through the length of coastal California. Seismic activity is common along its course and is due to two crustal plates sliding past each other along the line of the fault. The city of San Francisco lies close to the fault, and such movement caused the devastating earthquake of 1906 and a further convulsion in 1989.

sanbenito under the Spanish Inquisition, a penitential garment of yellow cloth, resembling a scapular in shape, ornamented with a red St Andrew's cross before and behind, worn by a confessed and penitent heretic; also, a similar garment of a black colour ornamented with flames, devils, and other devices (sometimes called a *samarra*) worn by an impenitent confessed heretic at an auto-da-fé.

Sanchi the site in Madhya Pradesh of several well-preserved ancient Buddhist stupas. The largest of these was probably begun by the Emperor Asoka in the 3rd century BC.

Sancho Panza the squire of Don Quixote, who accompanies the latter on his adventures. He is an uneducated peasant but has a store of proverbial wisdom, and is thus a foil to his master.

sanctuary a place of refuge or safety; originally, a church or other sacred place where a fugitive was immune, by the law of the medieval Church, from arrest. By English common law, a fugitive charged with any offence but sacrilege and treason might escape punishment by taking refuge in a sanctuary, and within forty days confessing his crime and taking an oath which subjected him to perpetual banishment.

The word is recorded from Middle English in the sense a holy place, a temple, or the inmost recess or holiest part of such a place; it comes ultimately from Latin *sanctus* 'holy'.

A **sanctuary lamp** is a candle or small light left lit in the sanctuary of a church, especially (in Catholic churches) a red lamp indicating the presence of the reserved Sacrament.

sanctum sanctorum the ➤ HOLY *of holies* in the Jewish temple.

Sanctus in the Christian Church, a hymn beginning *Sanctus, sanctus, sanctus* (Holy, holy, holy) forming a set part of the Mass.

sand often taken as a type of unstable or impermanent material. **Built on sand** means lacking a firm foundation, ephemeral; often with biblical allusion to the parable in Matthew 7, in which of two houses it is the house built on rock which withstands the floods, and the house *built on sand* which falls. (See also *plough the sands* at ➤ PLOUGH, ➤ ROPE *of sand*.)

Sandhurst a training college at Camberley, Surrey, for officers for the British army. It was formed in 1946 from an amalgamation of the Royal Military College at Sandhurst in Berkshire and the Royal Military Academy at Woolwich, London.

Sandow a phenomenally strong man, from the name of Eugen *Sandow* (1867–1925), Russo-German exponent of physical culture.

Sandringham House a country residence of the British royal family, north-east of King's Lynn in Norfolk. The estate was acquired in 1861 by Edward VII, then Prince of Wales.

the sands (of time) are running out the allotted time is nearly at an end; the expression, recorded from the mid 16th century, refers to the sand in an hourglass running from one chamber to the other.

sangrail another term for the ➤ GRAIL; recorded from late Middle English, the word comes from Old French *sant graal* 'Holy Grail', although later spurious etymologies suggested that the original form was *sang roial* 'royal blood' or *Sangreal*, referring to the actual blood of Christ.

sangre azul the purity of blood claimed by certain ancient Castilian families, which professed to be free from Moorish or Jewish ancestry (the phrase is Spanish, and means literally 'blue blood').

sanguine (in medieval science and medicine) of or having the constitution associated with the predominance of blood among the bodily humours, supposedly marked by a ruddy complexion and an optimistic disposition; the modern use of *sanguine* to mean cheerfully optimistic derives from this.

In heraldry, *sanguine* is the name for a blood-red stain used in blazoning.

Sanhedrin the highest court of justice and the supreme council in ancient Jerusalem, with seventy-one members. The word comes via late Hebrew from Greek *sunedrion* 'council', from *sun-* 'with' + *hedra* 'seat'.

The title *Sanhedrin* was used by Napoleon as a designation for an assembly of representatives of Jewish rabbis and laymen convened in 1807 to report on certain points of Jewish law.

sannyasi a Hindu religious mendicant, especially, a Brahmin in the fourth stage of his life. The word comes from Sanskrit *saṃnyāsin* 'laying aside, ascetic'.

sans peur et sans reproche without fear and without reproach; the description '*Chevalier sans peur et sans reproche* [Fearless, blameless knight]' was used in contemporary chronicles of Pierre Bayard (1476–1524).

Sans Souci name of the French rococo palace (in French, literally 'Carefree') built near Berlin by Frederick the Great of Prussia (1740–86).

sansculotte a lower-class Parisian republican in the French Revolution; the name, meaning literally 'without knee-breeches', is usually explained as someone wearing trousers as opposed to knee-breeches. The term is first recorded in English in the *Annual Register* for 1790.

sansei an American or Canadian whose grandparents were immigrants from Japan; a third-generation Japanese American, born of ➤ NISEI parents.

Sanskrit an ancient Indo-European language of India, in which the Hindu scriptures and classical Indian epic poems are written and from which many northern Indian (Indic) languages are derived.

Sanskrit was spoken in India roughly 1200–400 BC, and continues in use as a language of religion and scholarship. It is written from left to right in the Devanagari script.

Santa Claus another name for ➤ FATHER *Christmas*; originally, a US usage, recorded from the late 18th century, an alteration of Dutch dialect *Sante Klaas* 'St Nicholas'.

Santa Fe Trail a famous wagon trail from Independence, Missouri, to Santa Fe, New Mexico; an important commercial route in the 19th century.

Santiago de Compostela a city in NW Spain, capital in Galicia, named after ➤ St JAMES *the Great* (Spanish *Sant Iago*), whose remains, according to Spanish tradition, were brought there after his death. According to later accounts, the relics were rediscovered in 813, when a hermit named Pelayo noticed a star hovering above the previously hidden tomb. The story gave rise to a popular folk etymology, in which *Compostela* was seen to mean *campus stellae* 'field of the star', rather than being related to *compostum* 'burial place'.

From the 9th century, when the relics were discovered, the city became the centre of a national and Christian movement against the Moors and an important place of pilgrimage.

Sapphira in the Bible, the wife of ➤ ANANIAS; in Acts 5:1–11, the pair attempted to deceive Peter by keeping back the price of something they had sold, and died of shock when the truth was revealed; the name of either may be used allusively for a liar.

sapphire a transparent precious stone, typically blue, which was the second jewel in the walls of the New Jerusalem, as described in Revelations 21:19.

The word comes (in Middle English, via Old French and Latin) from Greek *sappheiros*, probably denoting lapis lazuli.

A **sapphire wedding** is a forty-fifth wedding anniversary.

Sappho (early 7th century BC), Greek lyric poet who lived on Lesbos. The centre of a circle of women on her native island of Lesbos, she mainly wrote love poems in her local dialect (the term *sapphics* is used for verse in a metre associated with her). Many of her poems express her affection and love for women, and have given rise to her association with female homosexuality, from which the words *lesbian* and *sapphic* in this sense derive.

Saqqara a vast necropolis at the ancient Egyptian city of Memphis, with monuments dating from the 3rd millennium BC to the Graeco-Roman age, notably a step pyramid which is the first known building made entirely of stone (*c.*2650 BC).

Sara in one legend of the arrival of ➤ St MARTHA with Lazarus and Mary in Provence, *Sara* is said to have been Martha's black maidservant who settled at Les Saintes, and became patroness of gypsies.

Saracen an Arab or Muslim, especially at the time of the Crusades; originally, among the later Greeks and Romans, a name for the nomadic peoples of the Syro-Arabian desert which harassed the Syrian confines of the Empire.

The name comes (in Middle English, via Old French and late Latin) from late Greek *Sarakēnos*, perhaps from Arabic *šarḳī* 'eastern'. In medieval times the name was often associated with ➤ SARAH, the wife of Abraham.

A **Saracen's head** is a conventionalized depiction of the head of a Saracen as a heraldic charge or inn sign; recorded from the early 16th century.

Saragossa a city in northern Spain, capital of Aragon; the name is an alteration of *Caesaraugusta*, the name given to the ancient settlement on the site, taken by the Romans in the 1st century BC.

Sarah in the Bible, the wife of ➤ ABRAHAM and mother (in her old age) of ➤ ISAAC. When she herself had a son, she forced Abraham to drive away the maidservant ➤ HAGAR with their child ➤ ISHMAEL.

Sarajevo the capital of Bosnia–Herzegovina, which was taken by the Austro-Hungarians in 1878, and which became a centre of Slav opposition to Austrian rule. It was the scene in June 1914 of the assassination by a Bosnian Serb named Gavrilo Princip of Archduke Franz Ferdinand (1863–1914), the heir to the Austrian throne, an event which triggered the outbreak of the First World War.

Battle of Saratoga either of two battles fought in 1777 during the War of American Independence, near the modern city of Saratoga Springs in New York State. The British defeats are conventionally regarded as the turning point in the war in favour of the American side.

sarcophagus a stone coffin, typically adorned with a sculpture or inscription and associated with the ancient civilizations of Egypt, Rome, and Greece. Recorded from late Middle English, the word comes via Latin from Greek *sarkophagos* 'flesh-consuming'; the stone of which these coffins was made was originally believed to be able to consume the flesh of the dead bodies deposited in it.

Sardanapalus the name given by ancient Greek historians to the last king of Assyria (died before 600 BC), portrayed as being notorious for his wealth and sensuality. It may not represent a specific historical person.

Sardis an ancient city of Asia Minor, the capital of Lydia, whose ruins lie near the west coast of modern Turkey, to the north-east of Izmir; in the Bible, its Church was one of the

➤ SEVEN *Churches of Asia* referred to in Revelations. It was destroyed by ➤ TAMERLANE in the 14th century.

sardius a red precious stone mentioned in the Bible (e.g. Exodus 28:17, as adorning the breastpiece of the high priest, and Revelations 21:20, as set in the wall of the New Jerusalem) and in classical writings, probably ruby or carnelian.

sardonic grimly mocking or cynical, from French via Latin, and ultimately from Greek *sardonios* 'of Sardinia', alteration of *sardanios*, used by Homer to describe bitter or scornful laughter. The usage derives from the idea that eating a 'Sardinian plant' (Latin *herba Sardonia*) would produce facial convulsions resembling horrible laughter, usually followed by death.

sardonyx in Revelations 21:20, said to be the fifth of the precious stones adorning the walls of the New Jerusalem.

Sargasso Sea a region of the western Atlantic Ocean between the Azores and the Caribbean, so called because of the prevalence in it of floating sargasso seaweed; known for its usually calm conditions, its name is often used allusively for a congested and stagnant situation.

Sargon (2334–2279 BC), the semi-legendary founder of the ancient kingdom of Akkad.

sarsen a silicified sandstone boulder of a kind which occurs on the chalk downs of southern England. Such stones were used in constructing ➤ STONEHENGE and other prehistoric monuments. They consist of a form of quartzite, and were probably formed as a duricrust in the Pliocene period. The word is recorded from the late 17th century, and is apparently a variant of ➤ SARACEN.

Sarum an old name for the southern cathedral city of Salisbury, still used as the name of its diocese; in particular, denoting the order of divine service used before the Reformation in the diocese of Salisbury and, by the 15th century, in most of England, Wales, and Ireland. *Sarum* comes from medieval Latin, perhaps from an abbreviated form of Latin *Sarisburia* 'Salisbury'. (See also ➤ OLD *Sarum*.)

Sasquatch another term (a Salish name) for ➤ BIGFOOT.

Sassanian of or relating to a dynasty that ruled Persia from the early 3rd century AD until the Arab Muslim conquest of 651; also

called *Sassanid*. The name comes from *Sasan*, name of the father or grandfather of Ardashir, the first Sassanian.

Sassenach Scottish term for an English person. Recorded from the early 18th century, the word comes from Scottish Gaelic *Sasunnoch*, Irish *Sasanach*, from Latin *Saxones* 'Saxons'.

Satan the Devil, Lucifer. Recorded from Old English, the name comes via late Latin and Greek from Hebrew *śāṭān*, literally 'adversary', from *śāṭan* 'plot against'.

In the Old Testament, the Hebrew word usually denotes a human enemy, but in some of the later books is found as the designation of an angelic being hostile to humankind.

Get thee behind me, Satan is a rejection of temptation; originally, with biblical allusion to the words of Jesus in Matthew 16:23 in which he rebuked Peter for denying the prophecy that Jesus would be put to death in Jerusalem.

Satan rebuking sin is a proverbial expression; recorded from the early 17th century in the form, 'when vice rebuketh sin'; the meaning is that when this happens, the worst possible stage has been reached. In later use, the emphasis is an ironic comment on the nature of the person delivering the rebuke.

Sati in Hinduism, the wife of ➤ SHIVA, reborn as Parvati. According to some accounts, she died by throwing herself into the sacred fire, giving rise to the custom of ➤ SUTTEE.

satire the use of humour, irony, exaggeration, or ridicule to expose and criticize people's stupidity or vices, particularly in the context of contemporary politics and other topical issues. The word comes (in the early 16th century) from French, or from Latin *satira*, later form of *satura* 'poetic medley'.

Saturday the day of the week before Sunday and following Friday, and (together with Sunday) forming part of the weekend. Recorded from Old English (in form *Sætern(es)dæg*) the name is a translation of Latin *Saturni dies* 'day of Saturn'.

In North America, a **Saturday night special** is an informal term for a cheap low-calibre pistol or revolver, easily obtained and concealed.

Saturn in Roman mythology, an ancient god (Latin *Saturnus* may come from Etruscan), originally regarded as a god of agriculture, but in classical times identified with the

Greek ➤ CRONUS, deposed by his son Zeus (Jupiter). His festival in December, ➤ SATURNALIA, eventually became one of the elements in the traditional celebrations of Christmas.

Saturn was the name given to the most remote of the seven planets known to ancient astronomy (now known to be the sixth planet from the sun in the solar system). In astrology, on account of its remoteness and slowness of motion, Saturn was supposed to cause coldness, sluggishness, and gloominess of temperament in those born under its influence, and in general to have a baleful effect on human affairs.

Saturn is also the name of a series of American space rockets, of which the very large **Saturn V** was used as the launch vehicle for the Apollo missions of 1969–72.

Saturnalia the ancient Roman festival of ➤ SATURN in December, which was a period of general merrymaking and was the predecessor of Christmas; the unrestrained revelry of the original festival extended even to slaves.

saturnine (of a person or their manner) slow and gloomy; (of a person or their features) dark in colouring and moody or mysterious. The word is recorded from late Middle English (as a term in astrology) and comes via Old French from Latin *Saturninus* 'of Saturn' (identified with lead by the alchemists and associated with slowness and gloom by astrologers).

satyr in Greek mythology, one of a class of lustful, drunken woodland gods. In Greek art they were represented as a man with a horse's ears and tail, but in Roman representations as a man with a goat's ears, tail, legs, and horns.

In English translations of the Bible the word is applied to the hairy demons or monsters of Semitic superstition, supposed to inhabit deserts, as in Isaiah 13:21.

what's sauce for the goose is sauce for the gander what is appropriate to one case in question is also appropriate to the other. Proverbial, and still often used as a statement that what is right (or wrong) for one sex is right (or wrong) for the other.

Saul (in the Bible) the first king of Israel (11th century BC); chosen as king and anointed by the prophet ➤ SAMUEL. In later life Saul lost God's favour; he became violently jealous of his former favourite ➤ DAVID, who was to succeed him as God's

chosen king after the death of Saul and his son Jonathan in battle against the Philistines.

Saul of Tarsus in the Bible, the original name of ➤ St PAUL[1].

saved by the bell preserved from danger narrowly or by an unexpected intervention. In boxing matches, a floored contestant can be saved from being counted out by the ringing of the bell to mark the end of a round.

Savile Row a street in London which has traditionally been the centre of fashionable and expensive tailoring.

saving grace in Christian belief, the redeeming grace of God; generally, a redeeming quality or characteristic.

the Saviour a name for Jesus Christ, as the rescuer of humankind from sin and its consequences; recorded from Middle English.

Savoy Opera any of Gilbert and Sullivan's operas, originally presented at the *Savoy Theatre*, London, by the D'Oyly Carte company.

Saxe-Coburg-Gotha the name of the British royal house 1901–17. The name dates from the accession of Edward VII, whose father Prince Albert, consort of Queen Victoria, was a prince of the German duchy of Saxe-Coburg and Gotha. During the First World War, with anti-German feeling running high, George V changed the family name to Windsor.

Saxo Grammaticus a 13th century Danish historian, author of the *Gesta Danorum*, a partly mythical Latin history of the Danes (which contains the *Hamlet* story).

Saxon a member of a people that inhabited parts of central and northern Germany from Roman times, many of whom conquered and settled in much of southern England in the 5th–6th centuries. The name comes ultimately from late Latin and Greek *Saxones* (plural), of West Germanic origin; related to Old English *Seaxan*, *Seaxe* (plural), perhaps from the base of *seax* 'knife'.

In modern English usage (primarily as a term used by Celtic speakers), *Saxon* means an English person as distinct from someone of Welsh, Irish, or Scots origin, a ➤ SASSENACH.

The **Saxon Shore** is the coast of Britain, from Norfolk to Hampshire, as fortified by the Romans.

sayyid a Muslim claiming descent from ➤ MUHAMMAD through Husayn, the prophet's younger grandson. The word is Arabic, and means literally 'lord, prince'.

Scaevola ('left-handed'), traditionally the name given to the legendary Roman hero Gaius Mucius, who is said to have saved Rome from the Etruscan king ➤ LARS *Porsena*, *c.*509 BC, during the attempt to restore the Tarquins to rule in Rome. Captured in the Etruscan camp while planning to kill Lars Porsena, and threatened with torture, Gaius Mucius showed his lack of fear by thrusting his right hand into the fire. The king, impressed by such fortitude, ordered his release.

scales an instrument for weighing, originally a simple balance (**a pair of scales**); the notion of a soul's good and evil deeds being weighed after death is present in number of early religions. In ancient Egypt, the heart of a dead person was weighed by the god ➤ ANUBIS; in Zoroastrianism, a person's good and bad deeds were thought to be weighed against each other.

The Scales is the name given to the zodiacal sign or constellation Libra.

Scales (in which souls are weighed) are the emblem of the ➤ *Virgin* MARY and ➤ *St* MICHAEL. Justice personified is shown blindfolded and with a pair of scales.

the scales fall from someone's eyes someone is no longer deceived; originally with biblical reference to Acts 9:18, in which Saul of Tarsus (see ➤ *St* PAUL¹), blinded by his vision on the road to Damascus, received back his sight at the hand of God, 'And immediately there fell from his eyes as it had been scales.'

scallop shell a scallop shell is the emblem of ➤ *St* JAMES *the Great*, and from this association with the shrine at ➤ SANTIAGO, was often used as a pilgrim's badge.

scallywag a disreputable person; in the US, a derogatory term for a white Southerner who collaborated with northern Republicans during the post-Civil War reconstruction period.

Scapa Flow a strait in the Orkney Islands, Scotland, which was an important British naval base, especially in the First World War. The German High Seas Fleet was interned there after its surrender, and was scuttled in 1919 as an act of defiance against the terms of the Versailles peace settlement.

scapegoat in the Bible, a goat sent into the wilderness after the Jewish chief priest had symbolically laid the sins of the people upon it, as in Leviticus 16:22. In the Mosaic ritual of the Day of Atonement, this was the one of two goats that was chosen to be sent alive into the wilderness, while the other was sacrificed.

The English term *scapegoat* appears to have been coined by Tyndale from archaic *scape* 'escape' + *goat*; that is, the goat which was not to be sacrificed.

In the early 19th century, the word acquired the more general meaning of a person who is blamed for the wrongdoings, mistakes, or faults of others, especially for reasons of expediency.

scapular a short monastic cloak covering the shoulders; a symbol of affiliation to an ecclesiastical order, consisting of two strips of cloth hanging down the breast and back and joined across the shoulders. The word comes (in the late 15th century) from late Latin *scapulare*, from *scapula* 'shoulder'.

scarab a large dung beetle of the eastern Mediterranean area, regarded as sacred in ancient Egypt; also called *sacred scarab*. The term is also used for an ancient Egyptian gem cut in the form of this beetle, sometimes depicted with the wings spread, and engraved with hieroglyphs on the flat underside.

Scaramouch a stock character in Italian *commedia dell' arte*, a cowardly and foolish boaster usually represented as a Spanish don, wearing a black costume; the name is an adaptation of Italian *scaramuccia* 'skirmish'.

scarlet a brilliant red colour. The word comes (in Middle English, originally denoting any brightly coloured cloth) via Old French from medieval Latin *scarlata*, which in turn comes via Arabic and medieval Greek from late Latin *sigillatus* 'decorated with small images', from *sigillum* 'small image'.

The **scarlet letter** is a representation of the letter *A* in scarlet cloth which persons convicted of adultery were condemned to wear, as described in the novel (1850) by Nathaniel Hawthorne, in which Hester Prynne, convicted of adultery in 17th-century New England, is sentenced to wear the *scarlet letter* on the breast of her gown for the rest of her life.

The **Scarlet Pimpernel** is the name assumed by Sir Percy Blakeney, the hero of a series of novels by Baroness Orczy (1865–1947), a dashing but elusive Englishman, hiding his true nature beneath a lazy and foppish exterior, who rescued potential victims of the French Reign of Terror; the scarlet pimpernel is the emblem which he often leaves behind to infuriate his baffled enemies.

The **scarlet woman** is an abusive epithet applied to the Roman Catholic Church, in allusion to Revelation 17:3–4, 'And I saw a woman sit upon a scarlet coloured beast…And the woman was arrayed in purple and scarlet colour.'

Miss Scarlett one of the six stock characters constituting the murderer and suspects in the game of ➤ CLUEDO.

sceptic an ancient or modern philosopher who denies the possibility of knowledge, or even rational belief, in some sphere. The leading ancient sceptic was Pyrrho, whose followers at the Academy vigorously opposed Stoicism. Modern sceptics have held diverse views: the most extreme have doubted whether any knowledge at all of the external world is possible, while others have questioned the existence of objects beyond our experience of them.

The term comes (in the late 16th century) via French or Latin from Greek *skeptikos*, from *skepsis* 'inquiry, doubt'.

sceptre an ornamented staff carried by rulers on ceremonial occasions as a symbol of sovereignty; in England, the traditional way of signifying the royal assent to a bill was by the sovereign's touching it with the sceptre. The word comes (in Middle English) via Old French and Latin from Greek *skēptron*, from *skēptein* 'lean on'.

Scheherazade in the *Arabian Nights*, the daughter of the vizier of King Shahriyar, who married the king and escaped the death that was the usual fate of his wives by telling him the tales which compose that work, interrupting each one at an interesting point, and postponing the continuation till the next night.

schism the formal separation of a Church into two Churches or the secession of a group owing to doctrinal and other differences. The word comes ultimately from Greek *skhizein* 'to split'.

Schleswig-Holstein a state of NW Germany, occupying the southern part of the Jutland peninsula, comprising the former duchies of Schleswig and Holstein, annexed by Prussia in 1866. The complexity of the Schleswig-Holstein question was proverbial in 19th-century politics.

Schlieffen plan a plan or model for the invasion and defeat of France formulated by the German general Alfred, Graf von *Schlieffen* (1833–1913) before 1905 and applied, with modifications, in 1914.

scholasticism the system of theology and philosophy taught in medieval European universities, based on Aristotelian logic and the writings of the early Christian Fathers and having a strong emphasis on tradition and dogma.

school of hard knocks the experience of a life of hardship, considered as a means of instruction; the term is originally US, and is recorded from the early 20th century.

schoolman any of a number of writers, from between the 9th and the 14th centuries, who deal with logic, metaphysics, and theology as taught in the medieval universities of Italy, France, Germany, and England; a scholastic theologian.

Schrödinger's cat a paradox suggested in 1935 by the Austrian theoretical physicist Erwin Schrödinger (1887–1961), to illustrate the conceptual difficulties of quantum mechanics. Schrödinger described an experiment in which a cat is put into a sealed box containing a lethal device triggered by radioactive decay; an outside observer cannot know whether the device has been set off and the cat killed. According to quantum mechanics the cat is in an indeterminate state, some combination of alive and dead, until the box is opened, at which point it will be found to be one or the other.

schwa in phonetics, the unstressed central vowel (as in a moment ago), represented by the symbol ə in the International Phonetic Alphabet (from Hebrew *šĕwā'*).

sciapod a monster having the form of a man with a single large foot, in medieval iconography frequently represented with the foot raised as a sunshade, and believed to be from a race found in Libya. The name comes ultimately from Greek *skia* shadow + *pod-, pous* foot.

Scientology trademark name for a religious system based on the seeking of self-knowledge and spiritual fulfilment through graded courses of study and training. It was founded by American science-fiction writer L. Ron Hubbard (1911–86) in 1955.

Sciron in Greek mythology, a brigand on the cliff road from Athens to Megara; he forced travellers to wash his feet, and then kicked them into the sea. He was killed by ➤ THESEUS who threw him over the cliff.

scold's bridle an instrument of punishment for a scolding woman, consisting of an iron framework for the head and a sharp metal gag for restraining the tongue.

Scone an ancient Scottish settlement to the north of Perth, believed to be on the site of the capital of the Picts, where the kings of medieval Scotland were crowned on the ➤ STONE *of Scone*.

scorched earth policy a military strategy of burning or destroying crops or other resources that might be of use to an invading enemy force; the term is first used in English in 1937 in a report of the Sino-Japanese conflict, and is apparently a translation of Chinese *jiāotŭ (zhèngcè)* 'scorched earth (policy)'.

score a group or set of twenty or about twenty. The word comes in late Old English from Old Norse *skor* 'notch, tally, twenty', of Germanic origin.

Scorpio the eighth sign of the zodiac (the Scorpion), which the sun enters about 23 October; a person born under this sign.

scorpion the intense pain caused by the sting of the *scorpion* is proverbial. In traditional belief, its flesh was thought to be a cure for its own sting; it is also said by ancient writers that when surrounded by fire, a scorpion will commit suicide by stinging itself.

The phrase **a whip (or lash) of scorpions** was originally a biblical allusion, as to 1 Kings 12:11; *scorpion* here is taken to denote a kind of whip made of knotted cords, or armed with pieces of lead or steel spikes. The allusive force was subsequently reinforced by Milton in *Paradise Lost* (1667).

Scot a member of a Gaelic people that migrated from Ireland to Scotland around the late 5th century. The name is recorded in Old English (as *Scottas*, plural) and comes from late Latin *Scottus*, of unknown ultimate origin.

Down to the reign of Alfred, *Scottas* was the ordinary word for Irishmen (as *Scotland* for Hibernia). In the next reign there were relations between the Anglo-Saxon kingdom and the kingdom of the Scots in North Britain, and from that time onward the name was no longer associated with Ireland except in historical statements.

scot archaic term for a payment corresponding to a modern tax, rate, or other assessed contribution; the word comes (in late Old English) from Old Norse *skot* 'a shot', reinforced by Old French *escot*, of Germanic origin.

scotch decisively put an end to; render (something regarded as dangerous) temporarily harmless. The sense 'render temporarily harmless' is based on an emendation of Shakespeare's *Macbeth* as 'We have scotch'd the snake, not kill'd it', originally understood as a use of the homonym *scotch* with the meaning 'cut or score the skin of'.

the Scottish play Shakespeare's *Macbeth*; in theatrical tradition, it is unlucky to mention this play by name.

scourge a whip used as an instrument of punishment; a scourge is the emblem of ➤ St GUTHLAC.

The **Scourge of God** is a translation of Latin *flagellum Dei*, the title given by historians to Attila, the leader of the Huns in the 5th century; the term is recorded in English from the 14th century.

Scouse the dialect or accent of people from Liverpool; a native or inhabitant of Liverpool. Recorded in this sense from the mid 20th century, the word is a shortening of *lobscouse*.

Scrabble trademark name for a game in which players build up words on a board from small lettered squares or tiles.

a scrap of paper a document containing a treaty or pledge which one does not intend to honour. The phrase (a translation of German *ein Fetzen Papier*) is attributed to the German Chancellor, Theobald von Bethmann Hollweg (1856–1921), in connection with German violation of Belgian neutrality in August 1914.

scratch a—and find a— an investigation of someone or something soon reveals their true nature. First in English in the early 19th century as **scratch the Russian and you will find the Tartar**, translating French and attributed to Napoleon.

you scratch my back and I'll scratch yours if you do me a favour, I will return it. Proverbial; mutual back-scratching as a metaphor for reciprocity has been current since the early 18th century.

Scribe in biblical contexts, an ancient Jewish record keeper; a member of a class of professional interpreters of the Jewish Law after the return from the Captivity; in the Gospels, often coupled with the ➤ PHARISEES as upholders of ceremonial tradition.

Scripture the sacred writings of Christianity contained in the Bible; also, the sacred writings of another religion. Recorded from Middle English, the word comes from Latin *scriptura* 'writings'.

Ebenezer Scrooge a miserly curmudgeon in Charles Dickens's novel *A Christmas Carol* (1843); his initially grudging and scornful attitude is changed in the course of the book after the warning he receives from the ghost of his late partner ➤ *Jacob* MARLEY.

Scutari a former name for Üsküdar near Istanbul, site of a British army hospital in which Florence Nightingale worked during the Crimean War (see ➤ LADY *of the Lamp*).

Scylla in Greek mythology, a female sea monster who devoured sailors when they tried to navigate the narrow channel between her cave and the whirlpool ➤ CHARYBDIS. In later legend *Scylla* was a dangerous rock, located on the Italian side of the Strait of Messina. To be **between Scylla and Charybdis** is to be between two dangers or pitfalls, as between the cave of the sea-monster and the whirlpool.

Scylla was also the name of the daughter of king Nisus of Megara, who betrayed her father and his city to ➤ MINOS of Crete, and who was drowned in punishment.

scythe a *scythe* is often shown as a symbolic attribute of Time or Death.

A scythe is also the emblem of St Juthwara and St Sidwell, sisters, and reputed British virgin martyrs with cults in the south west of England, St Walstan, an English saint with a local cult in Norfolk among farmers and farm labourers of the Middle Ages, and ➤ *St* ISIDORE *the Farmer*.

Scythian of or pertaining to an ancient region of SE Europe and Asia. The Scythian empire, which existed between the 8th and 2nd centuries BC, was centred on the northern shores of the Black Sea and extended from southern Russia to the borders of Persia.

sea change a profound or notable transformation; originally with allusion to the song in Shakespeare's *Tempest* (1611) which envisages the physical changes that will come to Ferdinand's supposedly drowned father.

the sea-green Incorruptible Thomas Carlyle's name in his *History of the French Revolution* (1837), for the French revolutionary Maximilien Robespierre (1758–94), leader of the radical Jacobins in the National Assembly. Robespierre initiated the ➤ TERROR, but the following year he fell from power and was guillotined.

Sea Peoples any or all of the groups of invaders, of uncertain identity, who encroached on Egypt and the eastern Mediterranean by land and sea in the late 13th century BC. The Egyptians were successful in driving them away, but some, including the Philistines, settled in Palestine. Also called *Peoples of the Sea*.

seal[1] in folklore, seals (as in the legend of the ➤ SELKIE) were believed able to take human form. The name is recorded from Old English, and is of Germanic origin.

seal[2] a piece of wax, lead, or other material with an individual design stamped into it, attached to a document to show that it has come from the person who claims to have issued it. Recorded from Middle English, the word comes via Old French from Latin *sigillum* 'small picture', diminutive of *signum* 'a sign'.

In the Catholic Church, the **seal of the confessional** is the obligation on a priest not to disclose any part of a person's confession.

In the UK, **seals of state** are engraved seals held during tenure of an official position, especially that of Lord Chancellor or Secretary of State, and symbolizing the office held.

Sears Tower a skyscraper in Chicago, the tallest building in the world when it was completed in 1973. It is 443 m (1,454 ft) high and has 110 floors.

by the seat of one's pants by instinct rather than logic or knowledge. Earliest in mid 20th-century aviation slang, meaning 'relying on human judgement rather than navigational instruments'.

St Sebastian (late 3rd century), Roman martyr. According to legend he was a soldier who was shot by archers on the orders of Diocletian, but who recovered, confronted the emperor, and was then clubbed to death.

Sebastian is the patron saint of archers and is often (like ➤ *St* ROCH) invoked against plague. His emblem is an arrow (symbolizing plague), and his feast day is 20 January.

Sebastopol a fortress and naval base in Ukraine, near the southern tip of the Crimea. The focal point of military operations during the Crimean War, it fell to Anglo-French forces in September 1855 after a year-long siege.

Secession the withdrawal of eleven Southern states from the US Union in 1860, leading to the Civil War; the term **War of Secession** is sometimes used for the American Civil War.

second the ordinal number constituting number two in a sequence, coming after the first in time or order. The word comes (in Middle English, via Old French) from Latin *secundus* 'following, second', from the base of *sequi* 'follow'.

In Christian thought, the **second Adam** is Jesus Christ, with reference to 1 Corinthians 15:45; the actual phrase *second Adam* is first recorded in a marginal gloss on this passage from the Geneva Bible (1587).

A **second bite at the cherry** is another attempt or opportunity to do something; a *cherry* as the type of something to be consumed in a single bite (in original proverbial use, to **take two bites at the cherry** indicated a person's behaving with affected nicety).

The **Second Coming** (also known as the **Second Advent**) is the prophesied return of Christ to Earth at the Last Judgement; the term itself is recorded from the late 16th century.

The **Second Empire** was the imperial government in France of Napoleon III, 1852–70. The **Second Republic** was the republican regime in France from the deposition of King Louis Philippe (1848) to the beginning of the Second Empire (1852).

Second sight is the supposed ability to perceive future or distant events; clairvoyance. Reports of the faculty (recorded from the early 17th century) have traditionally been much associated with those of Scottish ancestry.

The **Second World** is the former communist block consisting of the Soviet Union and some countries in eastern Europe.

The **Second World War** was a war (1939–45) in which the ➤ Axis Powers (Germany, Italy, and Japan) were defeated by an alliance eventually including the United Kingdom and its dominions, the Soviet Union, and the United States.

secretary hand a style of handwriting used chiefly in legal documents from the 15th to the 17th centuries.

Section 28 in the UK, a clause in the Local Government Act (1988) prohibiting local authorities from the promotion of homosexuality or the teaching in maintained schools of the acceptability of homosexuality as a family relationship.

the secular arm the legal authority of the civil power as invoked by the Church to punish offenders; the phrase is a translation of medieval Latin *brachium seculare*, and is recorded from late Middle English.

Security Council a permanent body of the United Nations seeking to maintain peace and security. It consists of fifteen members, of which five (China, France, the UK, the US, and Russia) are permanent and have the power of veto. The other members are elected for two-year terms.

Battle of Sedan a battle fought in 1870 near the town of Sedan in NE France, in which the Prussian army defeated a smaller French army under Napoleon III, opening the way for a Prussian advance on Paris and marking the end of the French Second Empire.

Seder a Jewish ritual service and ceremonial dinner for the first night or first two nights of Passover. The name comes from Hebrew *sēḏer* 'order, procedure'.

Battle of Sedgemoor a battle fought in 1685 on the plain of Sedgemoor in Somerset, in which the forces of the rebel ➤ *Duke of* MONMOUTH, who had landed in Dorset as champion of the Protestant cause and pretender to the throne, were decisively defeated by James II's troops.

sedilia a group of stone seats for clergy in the south chancel wall of a church, usually three in number and often canopied and decorated. The word is recorded from the late 18th century, and comes from Latin, meaning 'seat'.

see the place in which a cathedral church stands, identified as the seat of authority of a bishop or archbishop. The word comes (in Middle English, via Anglo-Norman French) from Latin *sedes* 'seat'.

Sefer a book of Hebrew religious literature; a scroll containing the Torah or Pentateuch (usually **Sefer Torah**). The name comes from Hebrew *sēper tōrāh* 'book of (the) Law'.

Seikan Tunnel the world's longest underwater tunnel, linking the Japanese islands of Hokkaido and Honshu under the Tsungaru Strait. Completed in 1988, the tunnel is 51.7 km (32.3 miles) in length.

seisin possession, especially of land; a grant of freehold possession; what is so held. In popular usage, *seisin* has sometimes been understood to mean an actual object, such as a turf, a key, or a staff, handed over as a token of possession. The word comes (in Middle English) from Old French, ultimately from *saisir* 'seize'.

seize the day make the most of the present moment; translating Latin *carpe diem* in the *Odes* of Horace.

Sekhmet in Egyptian mythology, a ferocious lioness-goddess, counterpart of the gentle cat-goddess ➤ BASTET and wife of ➤ PTAH at Memphis. Her messengers were fearsome creatures who could inflict disease and other scourges upon humankind.

selah in the Bible, occurring frequently at the end of a verse in Psalms and Habakkuk, probably as a musical direction.

Selene in Greek mythology, the goddess of the moon, identified with ➤ ARTEMIS. She fell in love with ➤ ENDYMION and asked Zeus to grant him a wish. Endymion chose immortality and eternal youth, which Zeus granted, but only on condition that Endymion remain forever asleep. In another story, Selene visited Endymion nightly as he lay asleep, and bore him fifty daughters.

Seleucid a member of a dynasty ruling over Syria and a great part of western Asia from 311 to 65 BC. Its capital was at Antioch. The name comes from *Seleucus* Nicator (the founder, one of Alexander the Great's generals).

self-denying ordinance a resolution (1645) of the ➤ LONG *Parliament* depriving members of parliament of civil and military office.

the selfish gene hypothesized as the unit of heredity whose preservation is the ultimate explanation of and rationale for human existence; from the title of a book (1976) by Richard Dawkins, which did much to popularize the theory of sociobiology.

Seljuk a member of any of the Turkish dynasties which ruled Asia Minor in the 11th to 13th centuries, successfully invading the Byzantine Empire and defending the Holy Land against the Crusaders. The name comes from Turkish *seljūq*, the name of the reputed ancestor of the dynasty.

selkie an imaginary sea creature resembling a seal in the water but able to assume human form on land; it was traditionally believed unlucky to kill a seal in case it might in fact be at least partially human.

sell one's soul (to the devil) do or be willing to do anything, no matter how wrong, in order to achieve one's objective. With allusion to the contract with the devil that certain people (most famously the German scholar Faust) were formerly believed to have made: the devil would grant them all their desires in this life, and would receive in return their souls for eternity.

Sellafield the site of a nuclear power station and reprocessing plant on the coast of Cumbria in NW England. It was the scene in 1957 of a fire which caused a serious escape of radioactive material. It was formerly (1947–81) called *Windscale*.

Semana Santa in Spain and Spanish-speaking countries, Holy Week.

Semele in Greek mythology, the mother, by ➤ ZEUS, of ➤ DIONYSUS. The fire of Zeus's thunderbolts killed her but made her child immortal.

Semiramis in Greek mythology, the daughter of an Assyrian goddess who married an Assyrian king. After his death she ruled for many years and became one of the founders of Babylon. She is thought to have been based on the historical queen Sammuramat (*c.*800 BC).

Semite a member of any of the peoples who speak or spoke a Semitic language, including in particular the Jews and Arabs. The name comes via Latin from Greek *Sēm* 'Shem', son of Noah in the Bible, from whom these people were traditionally supposed to be descended.

Semitic relating to or denoting a family of languages that includes Hebrew, Arabic, and Aramaic and certain ancient languages such as Phoenician and Akkadian, constituting the main subgroup of the Afro-Asiatic family.

Senate the state council of the ancient Roman republic and empire, which shared legislative power with the popular assemblies, administration with the magistrates, and judicial power with the knights. In modern usage, *Senate* is the title of various legislative or governing bodies, in particular the smaller upper assembly in the US, US states, France, and other countries; the governing body of a university or college.

The name comes (in Middle English, via Old French) from Latin *senatus*, from *senex* 'old man'.

Sennacherib (d. 681 BC), king of Assyria 705–681, son of Sargon II. He devoted much of his reign to suppressing revolts in various parts of his empire, including Babylon (689). In 701 he put down a Jewish rebellion, laying siege to Jerusalem but sparing it from destruction (according to 2 Kings 19:35). He also rebuilt the city of ➤ NINEVEH and made it his capital.

Sennacherib is the Assyrian described in Byron's poem 'The Destruction of Sennacherib' (1815); he was forced to break off his campaign when his army was devastated by divine intervention (2 Kings 35). On his return to Nineveh he was assassinated by his sons.

Sephardi a Jew of Spanish or Portuguese descent. They retain their own distinctive dialect of Spanish (Ladino), customs, and rituals, preserving Babylonian Jewish traditions rather than the Palestinian ones of the ➤ ASHKENAZIM. The name is modern Hebrew, from *sĕpāraḏ*, a country mentioned in Obadiah 20 ('the captivity of Jerusalem, which is in Sepharad') and taken to be Spain.

sepoy former term for an Indian soldier serving under European orders. The word comes from Urdu and Persian *sipāhī* 'soldier', from *sipāh* 'army'.

The **Sepoy Mutiny** is another term for the ➤ INDIAN *Mutiny*; the name is recorded from the mid 19th century.

seppuku another term for ➤ HARA-*kiri*; the word is Japanese, and comes from *setsu* 'cut' + *fuku* 'abdomen'.

sept a clan, originally one in Ireland; the term is recorded from the early 16th century, and is probably a variant of *sect*.

September the ninth month of the year, in the northern hemisphere usually considered the first month of autumn. The name comes (in late Old English) from Latin, from *septem* 'seven' (being originally the seventh month of the Roman year). The native Old English name was *hærfestmōnaþ* ➤ HARVEST *month*.

The **September massacres** were a mass killing of political prisoners in Paris on 2–6 September 1792, an event which initiated the ➤ TERROR.

Septuagesima Sunday the Sunday before Sexagesima. The name comes (in late Middle English) from Latin 'seventieth (day)', probably named by analogy with ➤ QUIN-QUAGESIMA, although it has also been suggested that it refers to 'the seventieth day' before the octave of Easter. Both conjectures were recorded by Alcuin in the 8th century.

Septuagint a Greek version of the Hebrew Bible (or Old Testament), including the Apocrypha, made for Greek-speaking Jews in Egypt in the 3rd and 2nd centuries BC and adopted by the early Christian Churches.

The name is recorded from the mid 16th century (originally denoting the translators themselves), from Latin *septuaginta* 'seventy', because of the tradition that it was produced, under divine inspiration, by seventy-two translators working independently.

sepulchre a small room or monument, cut in rock or built of stone, in which a dead person is laid or buried; the word comes (in Middle English) from Latin *sepulcrum* 'burial place'.

Sequoia National Park a national park in the Sierra Nevada of California, east of Fresno. It was established in 1890 to protect groves of giant sequoia trees, of which the largest, the General Sherman Tree, is thought to be between 3,000 and 4,000 years old.

Sequoya the name of the Cherokee Indian (*c.*1770–1843) who invented the Cherokee syllabary; the sequoia (redwood) tree is named after him.

seraglio the women's apartments (harem) in a Muslim palace. **The Seraglio** was also formerly the term for a Turkish palace, especially the Sultan's court and government offices at Constantinople. The word comes (in the late 16th century) via Italian and Turkish from Persian *sarāy* 'palace'.

seraph an angelic being, regarded in traditional Christian angelology as belonging to the highest order of the ninefold celestial hierarchy, associated with light, ardour, and purity. Also, a conventional representation of such a being, typically as a human face or figure with six wings, as described in Isaiah 6:2.

The word is recorded from Old English, and comes ultimately from the Hebrew (plural) *śěrāpīm*; before the mid 17th century, the singular *seraph* is rare.

Serapis in Egyptian mythology, a god whose cult was developed by Ptolemy I at Memphis as a combination of ➤ Apis and ➤ Osiris, to unite Greeks and Egyptians in a common worship.

serendipity the occurrence and development of events by chance in a happy or beneficial way. The word was coined (in 1754) by Horace Walpole, and was suggested by *The Three Princes of Serendip*, the title of a fairy tale in which the heroes 'were always making discoveries, by accidents and sagacity, of things they were not in quest of'. (*Serendip* is a former name for Sri Lanka.)

Serengeti a vast plain in Tanzania, to the west of the Great Rift Valley. In 1951 the Serengeti National Park was created to protect the area's large numbers of wildebeest, zebra, and Thomson's gazelle.

Serenissima a historic title for Venice or the former Venetian republic; Italian for 'the most serene (city)'.

serial killer a murderer who repeatedly commits the same offence, typically following a characteristic, predictable behaviour pattern. The term was originally a technical one used by the Federal Bureau of Investigation in America; it came to public notice in the 1980s in the wake of a number of notorious cases, notably the crimes eventually traced to Theodore Bundy and John Wayne Gacy.

Sermon on the Mount the discourse of Christ recorded in Matthew 5–7, including the Beatitudes and the Lord's Prayer. The title *Sermon on the Mount* is first recorded in a marginal gloss of the ➤ *Rhemish Bible* (1582).

serpent a large snake; a dragon or other mythical snake-like reptile. The word is recorded from Middle English, and comes via Old French from Latin *serpent-* 'creeping'.

In proverbial and allusive reference, a *serpent* is taken as the type of cunning, treachery, and malignancy. The figure of a serpent with its tail in its mouth is a symbol of eternity.

In the Bible, **the Serpent** is a special designation of Satan, as in Genesis 3:1.

A **brazen serpent** is the figure of a brass serpent on a pole; with reference to the story in Numbers ch. 21, in which, when the people of Israel were punished by 'fiery serpents', Moses was told by God to mount a serpent of brass on a pole. If anyone who had been bitten by a snake looked at this, they would be healed.

the Serpentine a winding lake in Hyde Park, London, constructed in 1730, as part of the laying out of the gardens by the royal gardener Charles Bridgman (d. 1738).

Is thy servant a dog? a biblical saying, with reference to 2 Kings 8:13, in which the Syrian Hazael protests against Elisha's prophecy that he will do harm to Israel.

servant of the servants of God a translation of Latin *servus servorum Dei*, is a title of the Pope, first assumed by ➤ GREGORY *the Great*.

serve two masters take orders from two superiors or follow two conflicting or opposing principles or policies at the same time. With allusion to the biblical warning against trying to serve God and Mammon (Matthew 6:24).

Servian wall a wall encircling the ancient city of Rome, said to have been built by Servius Tullius, the semi-legendary sixth king of ancient Rome (fl. 6th century BC).

make a dead set at make a determined attempt to win the liking of; originally (early 19th century) a sporting idiom, referring to the manner in which a dog such as a setter or pointer stands stock still with its muzzle pointing in the direction of its prey.

set out one's stall display or show off one's abilities, attributes, or experience in order to convince someone of one's suitability for something. From a street trader's setting up a stall to display goods for sale.

Setebos in Shakespeare's *Tempest*, the god worshipped by ➤ CALIBAN's mother Sycorax; *Setebos* was a Patagonian deity, and his name appears in accounts of Magellan's voyages.

Seth¹ in Egyptian mythology, an evil god who murdered his brother ➤ Osiris and wounded Osiris's son ➤ HORUS. Seth is represented as having the head of an animal with a long pointed snout.

Seth² in the Bible, the son of ➤ ADAM who according to Genesis was the father of

➤ NOAH and thus of the existing race of humankind.

Act of Settlement a statute of 1701 that vested the British Crown in Sophia of Hanover (granddaughter of James I of England and VI of Scotland) and her Protestant heirs, so excluding Roman Catholics, including the Stuarts, from the succession. Sophia's son became George I.

seven the number *seven* is often used symbolically, denoting completion or perfection, especially in echoes of biblical phraseology.

In Greek legend, the **Seven against Thebes** is the name given to the expedition against Thebes led by Polynices, son of ➤ OEDIPUS, against his brother Eteocles. When both young men were killed, their uncle Creon decreed that ➤ POLYNICES was not to be buried because he had attacked his own city; his niece ➤ ANTIGONE defied the order.

The **Seven Churches of Asia** were the seven churches addressed by John in Revelation, the Churches of Ephesus, Smyrna, Pergamos, Thyatira, Sardis, Philadelphia, and Laodicea.

The **seven corporal works of mercy**, as enumerated in medieval theology, are taken from Matthew 25:35–37 and Tobit 12:12; they are feeding the hungry, giving the thirsty to drink, sheltering the stranger, clothing the naked, visiting the sick, comforting the prisoner, and (from Tobit) burying the dead.

In Christian tradition, the **seven deadly sins** are the sins of pride, covetousness, lust, anger, gluttony, envy, and sloth. They are listed (with minor variation) by the monk John Cassian (d.435), St Gregory the Great, and St Thomas Aquinas.

In the story of ➤ SNOW *White*, the **Seven Dwarfs** who live in a hut in the forest shelter the fugitive princess from her stepmother; in the Walt Disney cartoon film (1937), they are named Happy, Sleepy, Doc, Bashful, Sneezy, Grumpy, and Dopey.

The **seven gifts of the Holy Spirit** are wisdom, understanding, counsel, fortitude, knowledge, piety, and fear of the Lord. The list is taken from Isaiah 11:2; six as in the AV 'And the spirit of the Lord shall rest upon him, the spirit of wisdom and understanding, the spirit of counsel and might, the spirit of knowledge and of the fear of the Lord,' with piety (*pietas*) added from the Vulgate text.

There are **seven heavens** recognized in later Jewish and in Muslim belief; the highest being the abode of God and the most exalted angels. The division may have been of Babylonian origin, and founded on astronomical theories.

The **Seven Hills of Rome** are the seven hills on which the ancient city of Rome was built: Aventine, Caelian, Capitoline, Esquiline, Quirinal, Viminal, and Palatine. Rome is informally known as the **City of the Seven Hills**.

The **Seven Joys of Mary** are special occasions for joy on the part of the Virgin Mary, as traditionally enumerated; the Annunciation, Visitation, Nativity, Epiphany, Finding in the Temple, Resurrection, and Ascension. The medieval church reckoned five (although lists differ); an early 14th century poem gives the Annunciation, Nativity, Epiphany, Resurrection, and the Assumption of the Virgin, with later Roman Catholic writers adding the Visitation and the Finding as the second and fifth respectively, and making the seventh the Ascension.

The **Seven Last Words** are the last seven utterances of Christ on the Cross: 'Father, forgive them, for they know not what they do' (Luke 23:34); 'Woman, behold thy son!' (John 19:26); 'Behold thy mother!' (John 19:27); 'Eli, Eli, lama sabachthani? [My God, my God, why has thou forsaken me?]' (Matthew 27:46); 'I thirst' (John 19:28); 'It is finished' (John 19:30); 'Father, into thy hands I commend my spirit' (Luke 23:46, a quotation from Psalm 31:5). Also known as the **Seven Words**.

The **seven-league boots** are the boots which in the fairy story of ➤ HOP *o' my Thumb* enabled their wearer to cover seven leagues at each step.

In the Middle Ages, the **seven liberal arts** were the ➤ QUADRIVIUM and the ➤ TRIVIUM, a course of seven subjects of study introduced in the 6th century and regarded as essential grounding for more advanced studies: they are arithmetic, geometry, astronomy, music, grammar, rhetoric, and logic. Also known as the *seven sciences*.

The **seven sacraments** are the sacraments as enumerated in Christian belief, a list thought to have been formulated first by Peter Lombard in the 12th century: Baptism, Confirmation, the Eucharist, Penance, Extreme Unction, Holy Orders, and Matrimony. Since the Reformation, Protestant usage has generally recognized two sacraments, Baptism and the Eucharist or Lord's Supper.

The **Seven Sages** were seven wise Greeks of the 6th century BC, to each of whom a moral saying is attributed. The seven, named in a traditional list found in Plato, are Bias,

Chilon, Cleobulus, Periander, Pittacus, Solon, and Thales.

The **seven samurai** were the eponymous heroes of a Japanese film (1954), depicting a group of warriors who come together to protect a village against marauding bandits (it was remade in 1960 as an American film, *The Magnificent Seven*). In extended usage, the term may be used for a number of individuals who decide to act together when conventional systems, and protection, have failed.

The **seven seas** are all the oceans of the world (conventionally listed as the Arctic, Antarctic, North Pacific, South Pacific, North Atlantic, South Atlantic, and Indian Oceans).

The **Seven Sisters** are the star cluster of the ➤ PLEIADES, traditionally believed to represent the seven daughters of the Titan Atlas and the Oceanid Pleione. In the late 20th century, the seven international oil companies noted for their dominant influence on the production and marketing of petroleum, Exxon, Mobil, Gulf, Standard Oil of California, Texaco, British Petroleum, and Royal Dutch Shell, became known as the *Seven Sisters*.

The **Seven Sleepers**, in early Christian legend, were seven noble Christian youths of Ephesus who fell asleep in a cave while fleeing from the Decian persecution and awoke 187 years later. The legend was translated from the Syriac by Gregory of Tours (6th century) and is mentioned in other sources, including the Koran.

The **Seven Sorrows of Mary** are seven particular griefs of the Virgin Mary, as enumerated in medieval theology: the prophecy of Simeon; the flight into Egypt; the three-day loss of the child Jesus in Jerusalem; the meeting with Jesus on the way to Calvary; the Crucifixion; the taking down from the Cross; and the entombment of Jesus. The Servite order, founded in the 13th century, was devoted to meditation on the sorrows of the Virgin, and the enumeration developed from this.

The **seven spiritual works of mercy** as enumerated in Christian belief are: conversion of the sinner, instruction of the ignorant, counselling the doubtful, comforting the sorrowful, patient endurance of wrong, forgiveness of injuries, and prayer for the living and the dead.

The **seven stars** is a former name for the ➤ PLEIADES and the ➤ GREAT *Bear*.

The **Seven Wonders of the World** are the seven most spectacular man-made structures of the ancient world. Traditionally they comprise (1) the pyramids of Egypt, especially those at Giza; (2) the Hanging Gardens of Babylon; (3) the Mausoleum of Halicarnassus; (4) the temple of Artemis at Ephesus in Asia Minor, rebuilt in 356 BC; (5) the Colossus of Rhodes; (6) the huge ivory and gold statue of Zeus at Olympia in the Peloponnese, made by Phidias *c*.430 BC; (7) the Pharos of Alexandria (or in some lists, the walls of Babylon). The earliest extant list of these dates from the 2nd century BC.

The **seven year itch** originally (in literal use, recorded from the late 19th century) is a condition lasting for or recurring after seven years; now, a supposed tendency to infidelity after seven years of marriage; in modern usage, the term was reinforced by Billy Wilder's film *The Seven Year Itch* (1955), starring Marilyn Monroe.

The **Seven Years War** was a war (1756–63) which ranged Britain, Prussia, and Hanover against Austria, France, Russia, Saxony, Sweden, and Spain. Its main issues were the struggle between Britain and France for supremacy overseas, and that between Prussia and Austria for the domination of Germany. The war was ended by the Treaties of Paris and Hubertusburg in 1763, leaving Britain the supreme European naval and colonial power and Prussia in an appreciably stronger position than before in central Europe.

seventh constituting number seven in a sequence.

To be **in seventh heaven** is to be in a state of ecstasy; the term relates to the concept of ➤ SEVEN *heavens* in late Jewish and Muslim theology.

A **Seventh-Day Adventist** is a member of a strict Protestant sect which preaches the imminent return of Christ to Earth (originally expecting the Second Coming in 1844) and observes Saturday as the sabbath.

seventy traditionally regarded as the natural span of human life (see ➤ THREESCORE *years and ten*).

The Seventy is the name given to the 70 disciples whose mission is recorded in Luke 10:1. It is also used for the interpreters of the ➤ SEPTUAGINT.

Sexagesima Sunday the Sunday before ➤ QUINQUAGESIMA, and (like ➤ SEPTUAGESIMA) probably named on analogy with it.

sexton a person who looks after a church and churchyard, typically acting as bellringer and gravedigger; in early use, often the sacristan in a religious house or cathedral, having charge of the vestments, sacred vessels, and relics. The word comes via Anglo-Norman French from medieval Latin *sacristanus* 'sacristan'.

Sexton Blake name of a fictional detective first introduced in a magazine story of 1898, and subsequently appearing in a number of stories and books by various authors; he is distinguished by his powers of deduction as well as his physical prowess.

sgraffito a form of decoration made by scratching through a surface to reveal a lower layer of a contrasting colour, typically done in plaster or stucco on walls, or in slip on ceramics before firing. The word comes (in the mid 18th century) from Italian, literally 'scratched away'.

shabti each of a set of wooden, stone, or faience figurines, in the form of mummies, placed in an ancient Egyptian tomb to do any work that the dead person might be called upon to do in the afterlife. They were often 365 in number, one for each day of the year.

Shaddai one of the names given to God in the Hebrew Bible. The name is translated as 'Almighty' in English versions of the Bible, but is of uncertain meaning.

the Shades in poetic and literary usage, the underworld, Hades; the realm of disembodied spirits (*shade* here meaning the visible but impalpable form of a dead person, a ghost).

shadow Cabinet the opposition counterpart of government ministers; the term is first recorded in a letter of 1906 from the Conservative statesman Arthur James Balfour (1848–1930).

the shadow of death a place or period of intense gloom or peril; often with reference to Psalm 23:4. The term in biblical usage represents a Hebrew expression which is a poetic word for intense darkness; in English, however, it is likely to be used in a context denoting the sorrow and fear associated with approaching death.

shaggy-dog story a long, rambling story or joke, typically one that is amusing only because it is absurdly inconsequential or pointless. The expression comes from an anecdote of this type, about a shaggy-haired dog (1945).

shah a title of the former monarch of Iran; *shah* is a Persian title equivalent to 'king', and is recorded in English from the mid 16th century in reference to the ruler of Persia.

Shaitan (in Muslim countries) the Devil, Satan, or an evil spirit.

shaken, not stirred popular summary of the directions for making the perfect martini given by ➤ *James* BOND in Ian Fleming's *Dr No* (1958).

Shaker a member of an American religious sect, the United Society of Believers in Christ's Second Coming, established in England *c*.1750 and living simply in celibate mixed communities, so named from the wild, ecstatic movements engaged in during worship. The first of the American communities was founded by Ann Lee (1736–84), who emigrated from England in 1774.

no great shakes not very good or significant. Recorded from the early 19th century, and perhaps referring to the shaking of a dice.

Shakti in Hinduism, the female principle of divine energy, especially when personified as the supreme deity. The name comes from Sanskrit *śakti* 'power, divine energy'.

shalom used as salutation by Jews at meeting or parting, meaning 'peace'.

shaman a person regarded as having access to, and influence in, the world of good and evil spirits, especially among some peoples of northern Asia and North America. Typically such people enter a trance state during a ritual, and practise divination and healing.

shamrock the national emblem of Ireland, and traditionally said to have been employed by ➤ *St* PATRICK to explain the nature of the Trinity. The *shamrock* of legend has been identified with a number of different related plants with three-lobed leaves.

The word is recorded in England from the late 16th century, and comes from Irish *seamróg* 'trefoil', diminutive of *seamar* 'clover'.

Shan Van Vocht one of the names of Ireland conceived as a feminine entity ('the little old woman'), and used as the title of a nationalist song of 1798. Also called *Sean Bhean Bhocht*.

Shang a dynasty which ruled China during part of the 2nd millennium BC, probably the 16th–11th centuries. The period encompassed the invention of Chinese ideographic script and the discovery and development of bronze casting.

shanghai force (someone) to join a ship lacking a full crew by drugging them or using other underhand means; more widely, coerce or trick (someone) into a place or position or into doing something. The term is recorded from the late 19th century, and is taken from the name of *Shanghai*, a port on the estuary of the Yangtze on the east coast of China, which was opened for trade with the west in 1842.

Shangri-La a Tibetan utopia in James Hilton's novel *Lost Horizon* (1933); the term is now used for a place regarded as an earthly paradise, especially when involving a retreat from the pressures of modern civilization.

Shanks's pony used humorously to refer to one's own legs and the action of walking as a means of conveyance; recorded from the late 18th century.

shanti in the Indian subcontinent, peace; the word is repeated three times at the end of an ➤ UPANISHAD as a prayer for the peace of the soul, and was incorporated by T. S. Eliot into *The Waste Land* (1923).

sharia Islamic canonical law based on the teachings of the Koran and the traditions of the Prophet (Hadith and Sunna), prescribing both religious and secular duties and sometimes retributive penalties for lawbreaking. It has generally been supplemented by legislation adapted to the conditions of the day, though the manner in which it should be applied in modern states is a subject of dispute between Islamic fundamentalists and modernists.

sharif a descendant of ➤ MUHAMMAD through his daughter ➤ FATIMA, entitled to wear a green turban or veil. The word comes from Arabic *šarīf* 'noble', from *šarafa* 'be exalted'.

shark the *shark* has become a type for predatory ruthless behaviour, as in ➤ FEEDING *frenzy*; the image of the great white shark typifying particular ferocity was established in the public mind by the film *Jaws* (1975) and its sequels. The word is recorded from late Middle English, although the origin is unknown.

Sharon a fertile coastal plain in Israel, lying between the Mediterranean Sea and the hills of Samaria, mentioned in Chronicles for its

pasturage and the Song of Solomon for its flowers.

Sharpeville massacre the killing of sixty-seven anti-apartheid demonstrators by security forces at Sharpeville, a black township south of Johannesburg, on 21 March 1960. Following the massacre, the South African government banned the African National Congress and the Pan-Africanist Congress.

shastra (in Hinduism and some forms of Buddhism) a work of sacred scripture.

Shavuoth a major Jewish festival held on the 6th (and usually the 7th) of Sivan, fifty days after the second day of Passover. It was originally a harvest festival, but now also commemorates the giving of the Law (the ➤ TORAH). The name comes from Hebrew *šābū'ōt* 'weeks', with reference to the weeks between Passover and Pentecost.

Shazam the magic word (originally the name of a wizard) with which the orphan Billy Batson is transformed into the superhero ➤ *Captain* MARVEL; the letters stood for the wisdom of Solomon, the strength of Hercules, the stamina of Atlas, the power of Zeus, the courage of Achilles, and the speed of Mercury.

She Bible the second of two issues of the Bible printed in 1611, in which the last words of Ruth 3:15 are, 'and she went into the city', where the ➤ HE *Bible* has, 'and he went into the city'.

Sheba the biblical name of ➤ SABA in SW Arabia, whose queen, having heard of the wisdom of Solomon, 'came to prove him with hard questions' (1 Kings 10:1); her verdict was, 'behold, the half was not told me' (1 Kings 10:7).

In Matthew 12:42, Jesus referred to the journey she had made to Jerusalem, as a model for the scribes and Pharisees of his own day.

The **Queen of Sheba** is sometimes taken as a type of beauty and splendour.

Sheela-na-gig a medieval stone figure of a naked female with the legs wide apart and the hands emphasizing the genitals, found in churches in Britain and Ireland. The name comes from Irish *Síle na gcíoch* 'Julia of the breasts'.

sheep the sheep is proverbial for its tendency to follow others in the flock, and for its timidity and inoffensiveness.

In biblical allusions, the people of Israel are likened to *sheep* without a shepherd (Matthew 9:6); in Acts 8:32, the words 'He was led as a sheep to the slaughter' describe the death of Jesus.

To **count sheep** is to count imaginary sheep jumping over a fence one by one in an attempt to send oneself to sleep. The idea of imagining sheep jumping seems to have been known as a soporific from at least the mid 19th century.

To **separate the sheep from the goats** is to divide the good from the bad, with biblical allusion to the parable of the Last Judgement in Matthew 25:32–3.

Sheer Thursday another name for
➤ MAUNDY *Thursday*; *Sheer* (meaning 'blameless, clear') is an allusion to the purification of the soul by confession on that day, in preparation for ➤ GOOD *Friday*, and perhaps also to the traditional washing of the altars.

in a white sheet dressed for formally doing penance, originally for fornication.

sheikh an Arab leader, in particular the chief or head of an Arab tribe, family, or village; the word, which is recorded from the late 16th century, is based on Arabic *šayḵ* 'old man, sheikh'.

In the 1920s the word (chiefly with the spelling *sheik*) came to mean a strong, romantic lover; this derived from the novel *The Sheik* (1919) by E. M. Hull, filmed in 1921 as *The Sheikh*, starring Rudolph Valentino as the desert hero who kidnaps the English girl whose lover he becomes.

shekel silver coin and unit of weight used in ancient Israel and the Middle East; informally, **shekels** is used to mean money, wealth, perhaps originally as a quotation from Byron's *The Age of Bronze* (1823).

shell a (scallop) shell is the emblem of ➤ *St JAMES the Great*.

Shelta an ancient secret language used by Irish and Welsh tinkers and gypsies, and based largely on altered Irish or Gaelic words. The name is recorded from the late 19th century, but is of unknown origin.

Shem (in the Bible) a son of ➤ NOAH (Genesis 10:21), traditional ancestor of the Semites.

Shema a Hebrew text consisting of three passages from the Pentateuch (Deuteronomy 6:4, 11:13–21; Numbers 15:37–41) and beginning 'Hear O Israel, the Lord our God is one

Lord'. It forms an important part of Jewish evening and morning prayer and is used as a Jewish confession of faith. The word is Hebrew, and means literally 'hear'.

Sheol the Hebrew underworld, abode of the dead, envisaged as a subterranean region clothed in thick darkness, return from which was impossible. In the Authorized Version, it was translated variously as 'hell', 'grave', or 'pit'.

shepherd in biblical usage, the image of the shepherd caring for his flock is a strong one; God is seen as the shepherd of his people, and in Luke 2:8 the shepherds to whom the announcement of the Nativity is made are described as 'abiding in the field, keeping watch over their flock by night'.

In pastoral poetry, *shepherd* is a designation of one of the rustic characters; from this, in 16th-century poetry adopting the pastoral convention, the name is often used for the writer and his friends and fellow poets.

sheriff (in England and Wales) the chief executive officer of the Crown in a county, also known as the **high sheriff**, having various administrative and judicial functions; originally (in Anglo-Saxon England) the *shire-reeve* (Old English *scīrgerēfa*) was the representative of royal authority in a shire, and was responsible for the administration of the royal demesne and the execution of the law.

In the US, the *sheriff* is an elected officer in a county, responsible for keeping the peace; in films and books set in towns of the ➤ WILD *West*, the sheriff is often a key figure.

Sherlock informal term for a person who investigates mysteries or shows great perceptiveness; the term comes (in the early 20th century) from the name of Conan Doyle's fictional detective ➤ *Sherlock* HOLMES.

Sherpa a member of a Himalayan people living on the borders of Nepal and Tibet, renowned for their skill in mountaineering; the name is used figuratively of a civil servant or diplomat who undertakes preparatory political work prior to a summit conference.

shewbread twelve loaves of unleavened bread placed every Sabbath in the Jewish Temple and eaten by the priests at the end of the week. David, when in flight from Saul (1 Samuel 21:4–6) once ate the *shewbread* himself; in Matthew 12:3–4, Jesus cites this to the Pharisees to justify his disciples picking and eating ears of corn on the Sabbath.

Recorded in English from the mid 16th century, the term, suggested by German *Schaubrot*, represents Hebrew *lehem pānīm*, literally 'bread of the face (of God)'.

Shia one of the two main branches of Islam, followed especially in Iran, that rejects the first three Sunni caliphs and regards Ali, the fourth caliph, as ➤ MUHAMMAD's first true successor. Adherents are known as **Shiites**. The name comes from Arabic *šī'a* 'party of Ali'.

shibboleth a custom, principle, or belief distinguishing a particular class or group of people, especially a long-standing one regarded as outmoded or no longer important. Of biblical origin, the word comes from the Hebrew word meaning 'ear of corn', used as a test of nationality by its difficult pronunciation, as recounted in Judges 12:14.

shield in the Middle Ages the armorial bearings of a knight were depicted on his shield; decorated shields, made for display rather than use, were often hung on walls in churches or other buildings as a memorial of a knight or noble. The word is recorded from Old English (in form *scild*) and is of Germanic origin; it comes ultimately from a base meaning 'divide, separate'.

shilling a former British coin and monetary unit equal to one twentieth of a pound or twelve pence; the word is recorded from Old English (in form *scilling*), and was traditionally used in emphatic or rhetorical statements when the speaker wished to be understood as reckoning or accounting for the cost of every item.

shilly-shally fail to act resolutely or decisively; originally from a reduplication, *shill I, shall I*, as used in Congreve's *Way of the World* (1700).

hang out one's shingle begin to practise one's profession (in North American usage, a *shingle* is a signboard or nameplate of a lawyer, doctor, or other professional person).

knight in shining armour an idealized or chivalrous man who comes to the rescue of a woman in a difficult situation; the term is recorded (in informal or ironic use) from the mid 20th century.

improve the shining hour make good use of time, make the most of one's time; originally with allusion to Isaac Watts's *Divine Songs for Children* (1715).

Shinto a Japanese religion dating from the early 8th century and incorporating the worship of ancestors and nature spirits and a belief in sacred power (*kami*) in both animate and inanimate things. It was the state religion of Japan until 1945. The word is Japanese, and comes from Chinese *shen dao* 'way of the gods'.

ship in figurative and allusive phrases, a *ship* traditionally typifies the fortunes or affairs of a person, or the person themselves in regard to them. A ship is also the emblem of ➤ St ANSELM, ➤ St NICHOLAS *of Myra*, and ➤ St URSULA, and the 7th-century French abbot St Bertin, whose monastery of Sithiu (Saint-Bertin) in northern France was originally accessible only by water.

   When one's ship comes home is a traditional saying, mid 19th century; referring to a future state of prosperity which will exist when a cargo arrives.

   Ship money was a tax raised in England in medieval times to provide ships for the navy; originally levied on ports and maritime towns and counties. It was revived by Charles I in 1634 without parliamentary consent and abolished by statute in 1640; the actual term is first recorded in William Prynne's *Remonstrance against Shipmoney* of 1636.

   A **ship of fools** is a ship whose passengers represent various types of vice or folly; the expression comes from the title of Sebastian Brant's satirical work *Das Narrenschiff* (1494), translated into English by Alexander Barclay as ship *The shyp of folys of the worlde* (1509). In the 20th century, the American writer Katherine Anne Porter (1890–1980) used *The Ship of Fools* as the title of a novel (1962) depicting a group of passengers (mostly German) on a long voyage in which the ship is a microcosm of contemporary life.

   The **ship of state** is the state and its affairs, especially when regarded as being subject to adverse or changing circumstances; a *ship* is taken here as the type of something subject to adverse or changing weather. The phrase (as **ship of the state**) is first recorded in English in a 1675 translation of Machiavelli's *The Prince*.

   The **ship of the desert** is a camel; in his *Relation of a Journey* (1615), recounting his travels in Turkey and Egypt, the English poet George Sandys wrote, 'Camels. These are the ships of Arabia, their seas are the deserts.'

   A **ship of the line** is a sailing warship of the largest size, used in the ➤ LINE *of battle*; the term is recorded from the early 18th century.

Ships that pass in the night are people whose acquaintance is necessarily transitory; the phrase comes originally from a poem by Longfellow, 'The Theologian's Tale: Elizabeth' (1874).

shire an administrative district in medieval times, consisting of a number of smaller districts (*hundreds* or *wapentakes*); the name comes from Old English *scīr* 'care, official charge, county'.

Since the late 18th century, **the Shires** has been used in reference to parts of England regarded as strongholds of traditional rural culture, especially the rural Midlands.

A **shire horse** is a heavy powerful horse of a draught breed, originally from the English Midlands; the name is recorded from the late 19th century.

Shiva (in Indian religion) a god associated with the powers of reproduction and dissolution. Perhaps a later development of the Vedic god Rudra, Shiva is regarded by some as the supreme being and by others as forming a triad with ➤ BRAHMA and ➤ VISHNU. He is worshipped in many aspects: as destroyer, ascetic, lord of the cosmic dance, and lord of beasts, and through the symbolic lingam. His wife is ➤ PARVATI, and their two sons, Ganesha and Skanda. His mount is the bull Nandi. Typically, Shiva is depicted with a third eye in the middle of his forehead, wearing a crescent moon in his matted hair and a necklace of skulls at his throat, entwined with live snakes, and carrying a trident.

shiva in Judaism, a period of seven days' formal mourning for the dead, beginning immediately after the funeral. The word comes from Hebrew *šib'āh* 'seven'.

the Shoah another term for the Holocaust; the word is modern Hebrew, and means literally 'catastrophe'.

shoe shoes are the emblems of ➤ *St* CRISPIN and ➤ *St* CRISPINIAN.

shofar a ram's-horn trumpet used by Jews in religious ceremonies and as an ancient battle signal.

shogun a hereditary commander-in-chief in feudal Japan. Because of the military power concentrated in his hands and the consequent weakness of the nominal head of state (the mikado or emperor), the shogun was generally the real ruler of the country until feudalism was abolished in 1867.

shoot something down in flames forcefully destroy an argument or proposal. From the literal sense of shooting at an aircraft to cause it to burst into flames and crash.

shooting star a small, rapidly moving meteor burning up on entering the earth's atmosphere; in literary use, sometimes an image for a glorious position that cannot be sustained.

Short Parliament the first of two parliaments summoned by Charles I in 1640 (the other being the ➤ LONG *Parliament*). Due to its insistence on seeking a general redress of grievances against him before granting the money he required, Charles dismissed it after only three weeks.

short, sharp shock a brief but harsh custodial sentence handed down to an offender in an attempt to discourage them from committing further offences. The term attained a high profile in the UK in the early 1980s, following a recommendation to the 1979 Conservative Party Conference of the introduction of a regime of this kind to be applied to young offenders.

Shorter Catechism a form of catechism issued by the Westminster Assembly of Divines and used by the Presbyterian churches.

a shot in the locker a thing in reserve but ready for use; in literal use, the *locker* here is the compartment in which ammunition is kept.

Show Me State informal name for Missouri; 'Show Me' here refers to what was regarded as the characteristically sceptical approach of the people of Missouri.

shower a shower of rain is the emblem of ➤ *St* SWITHIN.

king of shreds and patches used allusively after Shakespeare's *Hamlet*, in which Hamlet describes his usurping uncle as 'a king of shreds and patches'; later reinforced by Gilbert's lines in *The Mikado*.

shrew the shrew was popularly believed to be dangerous, and especially venomous. The name is recorded in Old English (in form *scrēawa*, *scrǣwa*, of Germanic origin); related words in Germanic languages have senses such as 'dwarf', 'devil', or 'fox'.

From the Middle English period, *shrew*, with regard to the animal's reputation, was used to designate a malignant or vexatious person, and from this developed the particular sense of a bad-tempered or aggressively assertive woman.

short shrift rapid and unsympathetic dismissal; curt treatment; the phrase originally meant little time for a criminal to make his confession and be *shriven* (confessed and absolved) between condemnation and execution or punishment.

Shrove Tuesday the day before ➤ ASH *Wednesday*, on which people would be *shriven* (confessed and absolved) in preparation for Lent. Though named for its former religious significance, it is chiefly marked by feasting and celebration, which traditionally preceded the observance of the Lenten fast. **Shrovetide** means *Shrove Tuesday* and the two days preceding it, when it was formerly customary to attend confession.

shuttle diplomacy negotiations conducted by a mediator who travels between two or more parties that are reluctant to hold direct discussions; the concept was particularly associated with Henry Kissinger (1923–), when US Secretary of State in the 1970s.

Shylock a Jewish moneylender in Shakespeare's *Merchant of Venice*, who lends money to Antonio but demands in return a pound of Antonio's own flesh should the debt not be repaid on time; when the debt falls due, and Shylock enforces the penalty, Antonio is saved by ➤ PORTIA, who pleads successfully that if the flesh is taken it must be done without shedding blood, which is not mentioned in the deed.

Siamese twins twins that are physically joined at birth, sometimes sharing organs, and sometimes separable by surgery (depending on the degree of fusion). The term originated with the *Siamese* men Chang and Eng (1811–74), who, despite being joined at the waist, led an active life.

Siberia a vast region of Russia, extending from the Urals to the Pacific and from the Arctic coast to the northern borders of Kazakhstan, Mongolia, and China. Noted for the severity of its winters, it was traditionally used as a place of exile.

sibyl a woman in ancient times supposed to utter the oracles and prophecies of a god; in later times the number of sibyls was usually given as ten, living at different times and places in Asia, Africa, Greece, and Italy. Among them were the **Erythraean Sibyl**,

who ➤ was said to have prophesied to ➤ HECUBA, and the **Cumaean Sibyl**, said in Virgil's *Aeneid* to have been visited by ➤ AENEAS.

It was the *Cumaean Sibyl* who was said to have offered nine books of oracles to Tarquin the Proud (see ➤ TARQUINIUS), the last king of Rome; when he repeatedly refused to pay the price she asked, she burned six of the nine ➤ SIBYLLINE *books* before his eyes.

She was also said to have asked the god Apollo for longevity, which was granted, but to have forgotten at the same time to ask for eternal youth; a character in Petronius's *Satyricon* says that he has seen her in her extreme old age.

The **Sibylline books** were books containing the prophecies of the *Cumaean Sibyl*, three of which she supposedly sold to Tarquinus Superbus, king of ancient Rome, at the price of the original nine.

sic transit gloria mundi thus passes the glory of the world; a Latin sentence spoken during the coronation of a new Pope, while flax is burned to represent the transitoriness of earthly glory. It was first used at the coronation of Alexander V in Pisa, 7 July 1409, but is earlier in origin; it may ultimately derive from '*O quam cito transit gloria mundi* [Oh how quickly the glory of the world passes away]' in the *De Imitatione Christi* of ➤ THOMAS à Kempis.

Sicilian Vespers a massacre of French inhabitants of Sicily, which began near Palermo at the time of vespers on Easter Monday in 1282. The ensuing war resulted in the replacement of the unpopular French Angevin dynasty by the Spanish House of Aragon.

Sick Man of Europe a nickname for Ottoman Turkey deriving from a reported conversation between Tsar Nicholas I of Russia and Sir George Seymour at St Petersburg on 21 February 1853.

Siddhartha Gautama name of the Indian prince who was given the title of ➤ BUDDHA.

Sidhe the fairy people of Irish folklore, said to live beneath the hills and often identified as the remnant of the ancient ➤ TUATHA *Dé Danann*. The name is Irish, and comes from *aos sidhe* 'people of the fairy mound'.

Siege of Sidney Street in January 1911, a gun battle centring on 100 Sidney Street, in which members of an anarchist group suspected of murder and robbery were besieged by the police supported by the army; the then Home Secretary, Winston Churchill, visited the site in person. The house itself was burnt to the ground (two bodies were found in the wreckage) and other gang members arrested, although the supposed leader, 'Peter the Painter', was never found or positively identified.

Sidon a city in Lebanon, on the Mediterranean coast south of Beirut, which was founded in the 3rd millennium BC, it was a Phoenician seaport and city state; in New Testament times it was known for its luxury and wealth.

Sieg Heil a victory salute used originally by Nazis at political rallies; the words are German, and mean literally 'Hail victory'.

Siege of Troy in Greek mythology, the 10-year siege of the city of Troy by ➤ AGAMEMNON and his forces, after Paris, son of Priam king of Troy, had abducted ➤ HELEN, wife of Menelaus of Sparta, brother of Agamemnon; the ➤ TROJAN *War* finally resulted in the fall and destruction of Troy.

Siege Perilous the vacant seat at King Arthur's ➤ ROUND *Table* which could be occupied without peril only by the knight destined to achieve the ➤ GRAIL.

Siegfried the hero of the first part of the *Nibelungenlied*. A prince of the Netherlands, Siegfried obtains a hoard of treasure by killing the dragon Fafner; he marries the Burgundian Kriemhild, and helps her brother Gunther to win Brunhild before being killed by Hagen. His Norse equivalent is ➤ SIGURD.

The **Siegfried line**, named after *Siegfried*, was the line of defence constructed by the Germans along the western frontier of Germany before the Second World War.

Siena a city in west central Italy, in Tuscany, which in the 13th and 14th centuries was the centre of a flourishing school of art. Its central square is the venue for the noted ➤ PALIO horse race.

out of sight, out of mind one soon forgets people or things that are no longer visible or present. Proverbial; current in this form since the mid 16th century.

sign on the dotted line agree formally; the space on a document for a signature is often indicated by a line of small dashes.

doctrine of signatures the belief (common in medieval times and originally advocated by Pliny) that the form or colouring of a medicinal plant in some way resembled the organ or disease it was used to treat.

signed, sealed, and delivered formally and officially agreed and in effect. With allusion to the processing of official documents: the parties put their signatures to them, seal them with their official seals, and finally have them proclaimed or delivered.

the Signet the royal seal formerly used for special purposes in England and Scotland, and in Scotland later as the seal of the Court of Session. The word comes (in late Middle English, meaning a small seal used instead of or with a signature to give authentication to an official document) from Old French or medieval Latin diminutive of *signum* 'token, seal'.

Sigurd in Norse legend the equivalent of the Germanic ➤ SIEGFRIED, the last of the ➤ VOLSUNGS who kills the dragon Fafnir and takes his treasure; betrothed to the Valkyrie Brynhild, he is tricked into forgetting her and marrying the Nibelung princess ➤ GUDRUN. He wins Brynhild for Gudrun's brother Gunnar, but when Brynhild discovers the part he has played, she incites Gunnar and his brother Hogni into killing Sigurd.

The stories of Sigurd are told in a number of poems in the ➤ *Poetic* EDDA. William Morris made him the subject of his long narrative poem, *The Story of Sigurd the Volsung and the Fall of the Niblungs* (1876).

Bill Sikes the violent burglar in Dickens's *Oliver Twist*, an associate of ➤ FAGIN who in the end murders his mistress Nancy and hangs himself while attempting to escape from the mob across the rooftops.

Sikhism a monotheistic religion founded in Punjab in the 15th century by Guru Nanak. Sikh teaching centres on spiritual liberation and social justice and harmony, though the community took on a militant aspect during early conflicts. The last guru, Gobind Singh (1666–1708), passed his authority to the scripture, the ➤ ADI *Granth*, and to the ➤ KHALSA, the body of initiated Sikhs.

Silbury Hill a Neolithic monument near Avebury in Wiltshire, a flat-topped conical mound more than 40 m (130 ft) high, which is the largest man-made prehistoric mound in Europe.

Silchester a modern village in Hampshire, situated to the south-west of Reading, near which is the site of an important town of pre-Roman and Roman Britain, known to the

Romans as Calleva Atrebatum. The site was abandoned at the end of the Roman period, and recent excavations suggest it may have been ritually cursed.

silence is golden it's often wise to say nothing. The fuller form of the saying, recorded from the mid 19th century, is *speech is silver, but silence is golden*.

Silenus in Greek mythology, an aged woodland deity, one of the *sileni*, who was entrusted with the education of Dionysus. He is depicted either as dignified and musical, or as an old drunkard. In general use, a *silenus* denotes a woodland spirit, usually depicted in art as old and having ears like those of a horse, similar to the satyrs.

Silicon Valley a name given to an area between San Jose and Palo Alto in Santa Clara County, California, USA, noted for its computing and electronics industries.

silk the type of something soft, rich, and luxurious. Recorded in Old English (in form *sioloc, seolec*) the word comes via Latin from Greek *Sēres*, the name given to the inhabitants of the Far Eastern countries from which silk first came overland to Europe.

To **take silk** is to become a Queen's (or King's) Counsel; a barrister of this rank has the right to wear a silk gown.

The **Silk Road** was an ancient caravan route linking Xian in central China with the eastern Mediterranean. Skirting the northern edge of the Taklimakan Desert and passing through Turkestan, it covered a distance of some 6,400 km (4,000 miles). It was established during the period of Roman rule in Europe, and took its name from the silk which was brought to the west from China.

the silly season summer regarded as the season when newspapers often publish trivial material because of a lack of important news; the term is first recorded in the *Saturday Review* of 13 July 1861.

Siloam (in the New Testament) a spring and pool of water near Jerusalem, where a man born blind was told by Jesus to wash, thereby gaining sight (John 9:7).

Silurian of or belonging to the ancient British tribe of the Silures, or the south-eastern part of Wales inhabited by them.

In the mid 19th century, *Silurian* was used to denote the third period of the Palaeozoic era, between the Ordovician and Devonian periods, which lasted from about 439 to 409 million years ago. The first true fish and land plants appeared, and the end of the period is marked by the climax of the Caledonian mountain-forming.

Silvanus in Roman mythology, an Italian woodland deity identified with ➤ PAN.

silver a precious metal, in general use ranking next to gold, and valued for use in jewellery and other ornaments as well as formerly in coins. *Silver* is also a tincture in heraldry, but is more usually called ➤ ARGENT. The word is recorded in Old English (in form *seolfor*), and is ultimately of Germanic origin.

In classical Greek and Roman literature, the **silver age** was the second age of the world, inferior to the simplicity and happiness of the first or ➤ GOLDEN *age*; in general use, a period regarded as notable but inferior to a golden age, such as that of so-called silver Latin literature.

A **silver bullet** is a simple and seemingly magical solution to a complicated problem, from the traditional belief that only a bullet made of silver could kill a werewolf.

The phrase **silver cord** is used in biblical allusion to Ecclesiastes 12:6 to indicate the dissolution of life.

Silver-fork designates a school of novelists of about 1830 distinguished by an affectation of gentility.

Silver Latin is literary Latin from the death of Augustus (AD 14) to the mid second century.

The **silver screen** is the cinema; originally, a cinematographic projection screen covered with metallic paint to produce a highly reflective silver-coloured surface; the term is recorded from the 1920s.

The **Silver Star** is a decoration for gallantry awarded to members of the US Army and Navy.

The **Silver State** is an informal name for Nevada, referring to its silver mines.

In the UK, **Silver Stick** is (the bearer of) a silver-tipped rod borne on State occasions by a particular officer of the Life Guards or their successors the Household Cavalry Regiment.

A **silver wedding** is the twenty-fifth anniversary of a wedding.

Silverstone a motor-racing circuit near Towcester in Northamptonshire, built on a disused airfield after the Second World War.

Simeon in the Bible, a Hebrew patriarch, son of Jacob and Leah (Genesis 29:33); also, the tribe of Israel traditionally descended from him.

In the New Testament, *Simeon* is the name of the singer of the ➤ NUNC *Dimittis*, who recognized the child Jesus in the Temple and gave thanks that he had seen the ➤ MESSIAH; he also prophesied to Mary that a sword would pierce her heart (one of the ➤ SEVEN *Sorrows of Mary*).

St Simeon Stylites (*c*.390–459), Syrian monk. After living in a monastic community he became the first to practise an extreme form of asceticism which involved living on top of a pillar; this became a site of pilgrimage.

Simla a city in NE India, situated in the foothills of the Himalayas, which served from 1865 to 1939 as the summer capital of British India, and is now a popular hill resort.

simnel cake a rich fruit cake, now typically with a marzipan covering and decoration, usually eaten at Easter or on the middle or fourth Sunday in Lent, on which the severities of the Lenten fast are traditionally relaxed.

Simnel was originally (in Middle English) a kind of bread or bun made of fine flour; the word comes via Old French from Latin *simila* or Greek *semidalis* 'fine flour'.

Simon personal forename; *Simon* was the original name of the Apostle ➤ St PETER.

St Simon another Apostle, is also known as **Simon the Zealot**. According to one tradition he preached and was martyred in Persia along with St Jude. His feast day (with St Jude) is 28 October.

Simon Magus was a magician, who in Acts 8 was baptized by Philip, and who tried to buy the power of the Holy Spirit from Peter and Paul, and was rejected by them (see also ➤ SIMONY). According to legend, *Simon Magus* was killed attempting to fly to demonstrate his superior magic powers.

In the Bible, **Simon of Cyrene** was a man from Cyrene who in Mark 15:21 was made by the Roman soldiers to carry the Cross on the way to Calvary; Simon helping Jesus with his burden is one of the ➤ STATIONS *of the Cross*.

Simon-pure means completely genuine, authentic, or honest, from *(the real) Simon Pure*, a character in Centlivre's *Bold Stroke for a Wife* (1717), who for part of the play is impersonated by another character.

simony the buying or selling of ecclesiastical privileges, for example pardons or benefices, from the name of ➤ SIMON *Magus*, in reference to his attempt to buy the power of the Holy Spirit from Peter and Paul.

Simple Simon a foolish or gullible person, probably from the name of a character who features in various nursery rhymes; the first known is recorded in a chapbook of the mid 18th century, but it is suggested that the name may be earlier by several centuries.

Simplon a pass in the Alps in southern Switzerland, consisting of a road built by Napoleon in 1801–5 and a railway tunnel (built in 1922) which links Switzerland and Italy.

The Simpsons the dysfunctional family in the American cartoon series *The Simpsons* (1990–, created by Matt Groening). The family includes the patriarch **Homer J. Simpson**, the beer-loving and often frustrated safety inspector of the Springfield Nuclear Power Plant, and his mischievous and sometimes aggressive 10-year-old son **Bart Simpson**.

simurg in Persian mythology, a large mythical bird of great age, believed to have the power of reasoning and speech; the name comes ultimately from Pahlavi *sēn* 'eagle' + *murg* 'bird'.

sin an immoral act considered to be a transgression against divine law; an act regarded as a serious or regrettable fault, offence, or omission. The word is recorded from Old English (in form *synn*), and is probably related to Latin *sons*, *sont-* 'guilty'.

In theological debate, the **sin against the Holy Ghost** is the only sin which may be beyond forgiveness, as indicated in the words of Jesus in Matthew 13:32. In extended modern usage, the phrase may be used for the one thing in a particular context which is seen as beyond toleration.

A **sin-eater** was someone traditionally hired to take upon themselves the sins of a deceased person by means of food eaten beside the dead body; the term is recorded from the mid 17th century, in *Remains of Gentilism and Judaism* by the antiquary John Aubrey (1626–97).

Mount Sinai a mountain in the south of the Sinai peninsula in NE Egypt, the place, according to the Bible, where Moses received the Ten Commandments (Exodus 19–34).

Sinanthropus a former genus name applied to some fossil hominids found in China in 1926 (see ➤ PEKING *man*).

Sinbad the Sailor the hero of one of the tales in the *Arabian Nights*, who relates the fantastic adventures he meets with in his voyages; in one of them, he is abandoned on an island where he finds a roc's egg, 'fifty

good paces' round, and in another he unwisely offers to carry on his back the sheikh
who turns out to be the ➤ OLD *Man of the Sea*,
and who is only dislodged by a trick.

the sinews of war the money and equipment needed to wage a war; the phrase is
first used in English in the mid 16th century,
and refers to the *Fifth Philippic* of the Roman
orator and statesman Cicero (106–43 BC).

sing from the same hymn sheet present
a united front in public by not disagreeing
with one another, especially when referring
to a general policy.

Sing Sing a New York State prison, built in
1825–8 at *Ossining* village on the Hudson River
and formerly notorious for its severe discipline.

singeing of the king of Spain's beard
the attack by ➤ *Francis* DRAKE on the Spanish
fleet in Cadiz harbour in 1587, during which
he sank or burnt 33 Spanish ships; the
phrase is recorded by Francis Bacon in *Considerations touching a War with Spain* (1629).

single currency a currency used by all the
members of an economic federation, specifically, the single European currency proposed for use by the member states of the
European Union, originally having a planned
implementation date of 1999 (when the
➤ EURO was in fact introduced).

Sinis in Greek mythology, a brigand killed
by Theseus; it was *Sinis*'s custom to murder
those he robbed by fastening them to two
pine trees bent down to the ground; when
the branches were released, the trees sprang
upright, and the victim was torn in two.

sinister originally (in late Middle English)
sinister meant 'malicious, underhand'; in the
late 16th century, the sense of 'inauspicious,
unfavourable' developed, especially as denoting omens seen on the left hand, which
was regarded as the unlucky side. From this
in turn developed the current sense, giving
the impression that something harmful or
evil is happening or will happen.
  In heraldry, of, on, or towards the left-
hand side (in a coat of arms, from the
bearer's point of view, i.e. the right as it is
depicted); the opposite of ➤ DEXTER.

siren in Greek mythology, each of a number
of women or winged creatures whose singing lured unwary sailors on to rocks; when
Odysseus sailed past their rock, he made his
men block their ears with wax, and had himself lashed to the mast.
  In the early 19th century, *siren* was the
name given to an acoustical instrument (invented by Cagniard de la Tour in 1819) for
producing musical tones and used in numbering the vibrations in any note; the term
was then extended to an instrument, made
on a similar principle but of a larger size,
used on steamships for giving fog-signals and
warnings. The word thus came to be used
more generally for a device which produces a
piercing note (frequently of varying tone),
used as an air-raid warning, or to signify the
approach of a police car.
  The name comes from Greek and is recorded from Middle English; in earliest use,
it designates an imaginary type of snake,
from glossarial explanations of Latin *sirenes*
in the Vulgate text of Isaiah 13:22.
  A **siren suit** is a one-piece garment for the
whole body which is easily put on or taken
off, originally designed for use in air-raid
shelters, when warning had been given by
the piercing whistle or *siren*.

Sirius the brightest star in the sky, south of
the celestial equator in the constellation
Canis Major. It is a binary star with a dim
companion, which is a white dwarf. Sirius is
conspicuous in the winter sky of the northern hemisphere, apparently following on the
heels of the hunter Orion, and is also known
as the ➤ DOG *Star*. It was important to the ancient Egyptians, as its heliacal rising coincided with the season of flooding of the Nile.

Sistine Chapel a chapel in the Vatican,
built in the late 15th century by Pope *Sixtus
IV*, for whom it is named, containing a
painted ceiling and fresco of the Last Judgement by Michelangelo and also frescoes by
Botticelli and other painters. It is used for the
principal papal ceremonies and also by the
cardinals when meeting for the election of a
new pope.

Sisyphus in Greek mythology, the son of
Aeolus, punished in Hades for his misdeeds
in life by being condemned to the eternal
task of rolling a large stone to the top of a
hill, from which it always rolled down again.

Sita in the Ramayana, the wife of ➤ RAMA;
she is the Hindu model of the ideal woman,
an incarnation of Lakshmi.

six the number equal to one more than five.
  The **Six Counties** are the counties of North-
ern Ireland, Antrim, Down, Londonderry,
Tyrone, and Fermanagh, which by the Treaty

of 1920 were constituted as a separate province.

The **Six Day War** was a war, 5–10 June 1967, in which Israel occupied Sinai, the Old City of Jerusalem, the West Bank, and the Golan Heights and defeated an Egyptian, Jordanian, and Syrian alliance. Arab name ➤ JUNE *War*.

Six of one and half a dozen of the other is a traditional saying, mid 19th century; meaning that there is little or nothing to choose between two sides.

at sixes and sevens a state of confusion or disorder; originally denoting the hazard of one's whole fortune, or carelessness as to the consequences of one's actions; in later use, meaning the creation or existence of, or neglect to remove, confusion, disorder, or disagreement.

The original form of the phrase, *to set on six and seven* (from Chaucer's *Troylus and Criseyde*), is based on the language of dicing, and is probably a fanciful alteration of *to set on cinque and sice*, these being the two highest numbers.

sixty-four thousand dollar question something that is not known and on which a great deal depends; originally (1940s) *sixty-four dollar question*, from a question posed for the top prize in a broadcast US quiz show.

Sizewell a village on the Suffolk coast, the site of two nuclear power stations including a pressurized-water reactor.

skald in ancient Scandinavia, a composer and reciter of poems honouring heroes and their deeds; the complex syllabic and rhyme structure of most **skaldic** verses make it likely that the majority of them have come down from oral tradition uncorrupted. Typically, skalds of the 10th and 11th centuries were court poets, providing praise-poems for the Norse rulers of Norway, Denmark, the Orkneys, and the Viking kingdoms of York and Dublin.

Skanda the Hindu war god, first son of ➤ SHIVA and ➤ PARVATI and brother of Ganesha. He is depicted as a boy or youth, sometimes with six heads and often with his mount, a peacock.

Skara Brae a late Neolithic (3rd millennium BC) settlement on Mainland in the Orkney Islands, overwhelmed by a sand dune and first uncovered by a storm in the mid 19th century. The settlement consists of a group of one-room stone dwellings with built-in stone shelves, chests, and hearths

skeleton in figurative usage.

A **skeleton at the feast** is a reminder of serious or saddening things in the midst of enjoyment, originally in allusion to an ancient Egyptian custom recorded in Herodotus's *Histories*, which tells of a carved and painted wooden corpse in a coffin being carried round the room at parties, and shown to guests with the words, 'Look on this, for this will be your lot when you are dead.'

A **skeleton in the cupboard** is a discreditable or embarrassing fact that someone wishes to keep secret (brought into literary use by Thackeray but probably already an existing expression).

skid row a run-down part of a town frequented by vagrants and alcoholics. The term comes from an alteration of *skid road*, originally a part of a town frequented by loggers.

Skidbladnir in Scandinavian mythology, the magic ship made by the dwarfs for ➤ FREY; it was large enough to carry all the Aesir, but when not at sea it could be taken to pieces and folded up like a cloth to be put into one's pocket.

skimmington a procession made through a village intended to bring ridicule on and make an example of a nagging wife or an unfaithful husband. Recorded from the early 17th century, the term may come from *skimming-ladle*, used as a thrashing instrument during the procession.

Skraeling an Inuit or other indigenous inhabitant of Greenland or ➤ VINLAND (on the NE coast of North America) at the time of early Norse settlement.

skull and crossbones a representation of a skull with two thigh bones crossed below it as an emblem of piracy or death.

skunkworks an experimental laboratory or department of a company or institution, typically smaller than and independent of its main research division; *Skunk Works* was originally the trademark name of an engineering and design technical consultancy service provided by the Lockheed Advanced Development Company.

The term is said to derive from the fact that the original operation was located next to a plastics factory which reminded workers there of the outdoor still called the 'Skonk Works' in the 'L'il Abner' comic strip by the cartoonist, Al Capp. To avoid infringement of copyright, the first vowel was changed when the name was registered.

sky-blue pink a non-existent colour; recorded from the mid 20th century.

Skylon a spire resembling a spindle in shape, especially that originally designed for the South Bank exhibition in London at the Festival of Britain in 1951.

slang a type of language that consists of words and phrases that are regarded as very informal, are more common in speech than writing, and are typically restricted to a particular context or group of people. The word is recorded from the mid 18th century, but the ultimate origin is unknown.

slapstick comedy based on deliberately clumsy actions and humorously embarrassing events; a device consisting of two flexible pieces of wood joined together at one end, used by clowns and in pantomime to produce a loud slapping noise.

slash a genre of science fiction, chiefly published in fanzines, in which any of various male pairings from popular films or books is portrayed as having a homosexual relationship. The term, which refers to an oblique printed stroke / used between the adjoining names or initials of the characters concerned, seems to have originated among fans of the 1960s science-fiction series ➤ STAR *Trek*, in stories centring on the relationship between *Captain Kirk* and *Mr Spock* (*K/S* is an alternative name for the genre).

Slav a member of a group of peoples in central and eastern Europe speaking Slavic languages. The name comes from medieval Greek and late Latin, and is also the base of ➤ SLAVE.

slave a person who is the legal property of another and is forced to obey them. The word comes in Middle English from a shortening of Old French *esclave*, equivalent of medieval Latin *sclava* 'Slavonic (captive)': the Slavonic peoples had been reduced to a servile state by conquest in the 9th century.

The **Slave Coast** is part of the west coast of Africa, between the Volta River and Mount Cameroon, from which slaves were exported in the 16th–19th centuries.

The **Slave Kings** were a dynasty founded by a former slave, Qutb uddin Aibak, which ruled the Delhi Sultanate from 1206 to 1290.

The **Slave of the Lamp**, in the story of ➤ ALADDIN, is a genie summoned by rubbing a magic lamp and bound to perform the wishes of the lamp's possessor.

A **Slave State** was any of the Southern states of the US in which slavery was legal before the Civil War.

the Slayer in the cult TV Series ➤ BUFFY *the Vampire Slayer*, the chosen girl who in each generation is born with special powers to combat vampires and other forces of darkness; in the series, a Californian high-school girl Buffy Summers has become the latest 'Chosen One'.

sleaze factor the sleazy or sordid aspect of a situation as applied to political scandals and alleged corruption involving officials of an administration. The term was applied initially, in US politics, to scandals and alleged corruption involving officials of the Reagan administration; in the UK in the 1980s and 1990s it was applied to a number of political scandals, resignations, and instances of alleged malpractice, such as the ➤ CASH *for questions* affair.

take a sledgehammer to crack a nut use disproportionately forceful means to achieve a simple objective. A *sledge* or *sledgehammer* is a large heavy hammer wielded by blacksmiths. *Sledgehammer* has been used figuratively in the context of heavy-handed or brutal criticism since the late 18th century.

Sleeping Beauty the heroine of a fairytale, Charles Perrault's *La belle au bois dormant*, who is put under a curse by a resentful fairy who has not been invited to her christening; as a result, the princess pricks her finger on a spindle and falls into a sleep which last for a hundred years, while a hedge of briars grows up around the sleeping palace. Finally a young prince finds his way into the castle and wakes the princess with a kiss.

let sleeping dogs lie avoid interfering in a situation that is currently causing no problems but may well do so as a result of such interference. Proverbial; in its present form recorded from the early 19th century.

Sleepy Hollow in Washington Irving's *Sketch Book* (1820), a name given to a place with a soporific atmosphere or characterized by torpidity (from the name of a valley near Tarrytown (Irving's home) in Westchester county, New York State).

Sleipnir in Scandinavian mythology, the name of Odin's eight-legged horse, son of

➤ SVADILFARI and the god ➤ LOKI in the shape of a mare.

the best thing since sliced bread a particularly notable invention or discovery.

slings and arrows used with reference to adverse factors or circumstances; originally from Shakespeare's *Hamlet*.

there's many a slip ('twixt cup and lip) many things can go wrong between the start of a project and its completion; nothing is certain until it has happened. Proverbial; in this form recorded from the 18th century.

slippery slope an idea or course of action which will lead to something unacceptable, wrong, or disastrous.

Sloane Ranger a fashionable upper-class young person (typically a woman) of independent means, especially one living in London. The term was coined in the 1970s, from *Sloane* Square, London + Lone *Ranger*, the name of a fictitious cowboy hero.

Slough of Despond a deep boggy place in John Bunyan's *The Pilgrim's Progress* (1678) between the City of Destruction and the gate at the beginning of ➤ CHRISTIAN's journey; in extended use, the term is used for any general condition of hopelessness and gloom.

slow but sure not quick but achieving the required result eventually. The saying *slow and steady wins the race*, perhaps quoting from R. Lloyd Poems (1762), provides the variant **slow and steady**.

slughorn a trumpet; from a misunderstanding by Thomas Chatterton (1752–70) of an earlier variant of *slogan* 'a war-cry', from Scottish Gaelic *sluagh-ghairm*, from *sluagh* 'army' + *gairm* 'shout'.

slype a covered way or passage between a cathedral transept and the chapter house or deanery. Recorded from the mid 19th century, the word may be a variant of dialect *slipe* 'long narrow piece of ground'.

small not large; in figurative use, trivial, unimportant.

Small beer is a thing that is considered unimportant, from an archaic term for weak beer. The figurative use may originally have referred to Shakespeare's *Othello* (1602–4).

The **small hours** are the early hours of the morning after midnight, denoted by the low numbers one, two, and so on; the term is first recorded in Dickens's *Sketches by Boz* (2nd series, 1836).

Small is beautiful is used, especially in environmentalism, to express the belief that something small-scale is better than a large-scale equivalent. From the the title of a book by E. F. Schumacher (1973).

Small print is printed matter in small type; inconspicuous details or conditions printed in an agreement or contract, especially ones that may prove unfavourable.

smart quick-witted, clever.

A **smart alec** is a person considered irritating because they know a great deal or always have a clever answer to a question; the term is recorded from the mid 19th century, and is originally US.

A **smart bomb** is a radio-controlled or laser-guided bomb, often with inbuilt computer. The concept of such missiles which could home in on a target with very high levels of accuracy dates from the early 1970s, but enjoyed considerable exposure during the Gulf War of 1991.

Originally (in the late 17th century), **smart money** was money paid to sailors, soldiers, and others as compensation for disablement or injuries received while on duty or at work; *smart* here meant 'physical pain'. In the modern usage of *smart money*, money bet or invested by people with expert knowledge, recorded from the 1920s, *smart* is the adjective meaning 'quick-witted'.

smell of the lamp show signs of laborious study and effort; the reference is to an oil-lamp, and according to Plutarch the criticism was once made of the work of ➤ DEMOSTHENES, 'His impromptus smell of the lamp', meaning that his speeches were written rather than spoken orations.

Smersh the popular name for the Russian counter-espionage organization, originating during the Second World War, responsible for maintaining security within the Soviet armed and intelligence services.

smiley a symbol which, when viewed sideways, represents a smiling face, formed by the characters :-), an ➤ EMOTICON used in electronic communications to indicate that the writer is pleased or joking.

Smith Square a square in Westminster, London, the location since 1958 of the headquarters of the British Conservative Party and (between 1928 and 1980) of the Labour Party (see ➤ TRANSPORT *House*). *Smith Square* has thus been used for the leadership of the Conservative Party (and occasionally, for the leadership of both parties).

Smithfield a locality in London, long the site of a cattle and horse market and then a meat-market; the name was originally *Smethefield*, from *smethe* 'smooth'. In the 16th century, it was also the place where heretics were executed at the stake.

Smithsonian Institution a US foundation for education and scientific research in Washington DC, opened in 1846 and now responsible for administering many museums, art galleries, and other establishments. It originated in a £100,000 bequest in the will of the English chemist and mineralogist James Smithson (1765–1829).

smog fog or haze intensified by smoke or other atmospheric pollutants; the word is recorded from the early 20th century, and is a blend of *smoke* and *fog*.

smoke in a number of figurative phrases.

No smoke without fire means that there's always some reason for a rumour. It comes from the proverb *there's no smoke without fire*, in this form in English since the late 16th century.

Smoke and mirrors (originally, with reference to the illusion created by conjuring tricks) are deception, dissimulation, bluff; especially, an obscuring or embellishment of the truth with misleading or irrelevant information.

A **smoke-filled room** is regarded as the characteristic venue of those in control of a party meeting to arrange a political decision, from a news report, filed 12 June 1920 of how Warren Harding of Ohio was chosen as the Republican presidential candidate.

Watch someone's smoke means, observe another person's activity. The fanciful implication is that the activity will be so fast and furious that it will cause smoke, which will be the only thing visible.

Smokey Bear the name of an animal character used in US fire-prevention advertising and characteristically wearing a wide-brimmed hat; *Smokey Bear* was then used in the US as a name for a state policeman, since the hats worn by state troopers resembled those in the cartoon.

a smoking pistol a piece of incontrovertible incriminating evidence; on the assumption that a person found with a smoking pistol or gun must be the guilty party; particularly associated with Barber B. Conable's comment on a Watergate tape revealing President Nixon's wish to limit FBI involvement in the investigation.

snail mail the ordinary postal system as opposed to electronic mail; the term is recorded from the first half of the 1980s.

snake proverbial allusions to the snake focus on its venomous bite as representing a lurking danger; it is a type of deceit and treachery, as with reference to the fable by Aesop, in which the man who had warmed a chilled snake in his own bosom was bitten for his pains. The word is recorded from Old English (in form *snaka*) and is of Germanic origin.

Snakes are the emblems of ➤ St PATRICK, who was said to have banished them from Ireland.

A **snake charmer** is an entertainer who appears to make snakes move by playing music, although the snake is in fact following the movement of the player's instrument rather than the sound of the music. The image is of longstanding, as in the biblical reference in Psalm 58:4–5.

A **snake in the grass** is a treacherous or deceitful person. The expression comes originally from Virgil's *Eclogues*.

Snake-oil is a term for a substance with no real medicinal value sold as a remedy for all diseases.

snakepit a pit containing poisonous snakes; in early legends, used as a means of execution, as in the story of ➤ GUNNAR, who is said to have been put to death in this way by Atli.

In the 20th century, the term has been used for a scene of vicious behaviour or ruthless competition, and specifically (after the title of a novel (1947) by M. J. Ward), a mental hospital.

snakes and ladders a children's game in which players move counters along a board, gaining an advantage by moving up pictures of ladders or a disadvantage by moving down pictures of snakes; the game was put on the market in the early part of the 20th century.

snakes in Iceland an allusive phrase referring to something posited only to be dismissed as non-existent; the reference is to Dr Johnson's comment on Horrebow's *Natural History of Iceland* (1758), to the effect that 'he could repeat a complete chapter...the whole of which was exactly thus:—"Chap. lxxii. *Concerning Snakes*. There are no snakes to be met with throughout the whole island".'

snapdragon a game (typically played at Christmas) which consisted of snatching raisins out of a bowl or dish of burning brandy and eating them while still alight. The term is recorded from the early 18th century.

snark an imaginary animal (used to refer to someone or something that is difficult to track down); the name is a nonsense word coined by Lewis Carroll in *The Hunting of the Snark* (1876).

cock a snook openly show contempt or disrespect for someone, literally by placing one hand so that the thumb touches one's nose and the fingers are spread out, in order to express contempt. The expression, recorded from the late 18th century, is of obscure origin. Suggestions as to the origin of the gesture include a mimicry of the erect comb of a fighting cock or the making of a grotesque nose in reference to the long-nosed effigies that are part of folk tradition in many cultures.

Snoopy cartoon character, a frustrated beagle given to fantasies, from Charles M. Schulz's comic strip ➤ PEANUTS.

Snorri Sturluson (1178–1241), Icelandic historian and poet. A leading figure of medieval Icelandic literature, he wrote the *Younger Edda* or *Prose Edda* and the *Heimskringla*, a history of the kings of Norway from mythical times to the year 1177.

snow often taken as a type of whiteness and brightness.

A **Snow Queen** is a cold-hearted woman, from the chief character in a Hans Christian Andersen fairy tale with this title; the cruel but beautiful queen who carries off Kay to her frozen kingdom, from which he is ultimately rescued by his playmate Gerda.

Snow White, in the traditional fairy story, is the princess whose wicked stepmother attempts to murder her, and who finds refuge with the ➤ SEVEN *Dwarfs*. The queen seeks out the dwarfs' cottage in the guise of a pedlar and tries to kill her stepdaughter, with a poisoned lace, a poisoned comb, and finally a poisoned apple, one bite of which apparently kills her. The Dwarfs, who cannot revive her, place her in a coffin of glass; she is found there by a prince who raises her so that the piece of apple falls from her lips and she regains consciousness.

Snowdon a mountain in NW Wales, the highest mountain in Wales, the Welsh name of which is *Yr Wyddfa*.

snuff movie a pornographic film or video recording of an actual murder (the name refers to the *snuffing out* of life which such a film or video portrays). Privately circulated *snuff videos* were allegedly known to the police in the 1970s, and figured briefly in the news in 1990 in reports of a paedophile ring involved in the production of such films.

soapbox a box or crate, originally one in which soap had been packed, used as a makeshift stand by a public speaker.

soap opera a television or radio drama serial dealing typically with daily events in the lives of the same group of characters, so named (in the 1930s) because such serials were originally sponsored in the US by soap manufacturers.

socage a feudal tenure of land involving payment of rent or other non-military service to a superior. Recorded from Middle English, the word comes from Anglo-Norman French *soc*, a variant of ➤ SOKE.

social chapter the section of the ➤ MAAS-TRICHT *Treaty* dealing with social policy, and in particular workers' rights and welfare. It originated in the *social charter* of December 1989, signed by eleven European member states, and dealing in particular with workers' rights and welfares. The *social chapter*, which developed from this, recommended among other things the adoption of a minimum wage.

socialism a political and economic theory of social organization which advocates that the means of production, distribution, and exchange should be owned or regulated by the community as a whole. The first use of French *socialisme* appears to have been in the Globe of 13 February 1832, where it was used in contrast to *personnalité*; in its modern sense it has been variously attributed to Leroux or Reybaud, writing a few years after this. An alternative theory is that the word was coined in 1835 in the discussions of a society founded by the Welsh social reformer Robert Owen (1771–1858).

socialist realism the theory of art, literature, and music officially sanctioned by the state in some Communist countries (especially in the Soviet Union under Stalin), by which artistic work was supposed to reflect and promote the ideals of a socialist society.

Society of Jesus official name for the ➤ JESUITS.

sock a light shoe worn by comic actors on the ancient Greek and Roman stage; hence used allusively to denote comedy or the comic muse.

The phrase **sock and buskin** means comedy and tragedy, the drama or theatrical profession as a whole.

Socrates (469–399 BC), ancient Athenian philosopher. As represented in the writings of his disciple Plato, he engaged in dialogue with others in an attempt to reach understanding and ethical concepts by exposing and dispelling error (the **Socratic method**). Charged with introducing strange gods and corrupting the young, Socrates was sentenced to death and died by drinking hemlock.

from soda to hock from beginning to end; in the game of faro, *soda* is the exposed top card at the beginning of a deal, and *hock* is the last card remaining in the box after all the others have been dealt.

Sodom a town in ancient Palestine, probably south of the Dead Sea, which according to Genesis 19:24 was destroyed by fire from heaven, together with Gomorrah, the other of the two ➤ CITIES *of the Plain*, for the wickedness of its inhabitants.

The term *sodomy* derives from the late Latin *peccatum Sodomiticum* 'sin of Sodom', since it is implied in Genesis 19:5 that the men of Sodom practised homosexual rape.

Sol in Roman mythology, the sun, especially when personified as a god; recorded in English from late Middle English.

solar an upper chamber in a medieval house; the word comes (in Middle English, via Anglo-Norman French) from Latin *solarium* 'gallery, terrace'.

soldier of fortune a person who works as a soldier for any country or group that will pay them; a mercenary; the term is first recorded in 1661.

solecism a grammatical mistake in speech or writing; a breach of good manners, or piece of incorrect behaviour. The word is recorded from the mid 16th century, and

comes ultimately from Greek *soloikismos*, from *soloikos* 'speaking incorrectly'.

Solemn League and Covenant an agreement made in 1643 between the English Parliament and the Scottish ➤ COVENANTERS during the English Civil War, by which the Scots would provide military aid in return for the establishment of a Presbyterian system in England, Scotland, and Ireland.

solid South the politically united Southern states of America, traditionally regarded as giving unwavering electoral support to the Democratic Party. The phrase was used in 1876 in a letter by the former Confederate general John Singleton Mosby (1833–1916).

Solidarity an independent trade union movement in Poland which developed into a mass campaign for political change and inspired popular opposition to Communist regimes across eastern Europe. Formed in 1980 under the leadership of Lech Wałęsa, it was banned in 1981 following the imposition of martial law. Legalized again in 1989, it won a majority in the elections of that year. The name is a translation of Polish *Solidarność*.

solitaire in the early 18th century, a person living in seclusion, a recluse; also, a precious stone, usually a diamond, set by itself.

From the mid 18th century, the term was also given to a game for one player, as a form of patience, or a game played by removing pegs one at a time from a board by jumping others over them from adjacent holes, the object being to be left with only one peg.

The word comes from Latin *solitarius* 'solitary'.

Solnhofen a village in Bavaria, Germany, near which there are extensive, thinly stratified beds of lithographic limestone dating from the Upper Jurassic period. These beds are noted as the chief source of ➤ ARCHAEOPTERYX fossils.

Solomon son of David, king of ancient Israel *c.*970–*c.*930 BC, builder of the first Jewish ➤ TEMPLE in Jerusalem. In the Bible Solomon is traditionally associated with the Song of Solomon, Ecclesiastes, and Proverbs, while his wisdom is illustrated by the ➤ JUDGEMENT *of Solomon*. Discontent with his rule, however, led to the secession of the northern tribes in the reign of his son Rehoboam.

James I and VI of England and Scotland was known as **the English Solomon**.

Solomon's ring was a magic ring belonging to Solomon, which according to the

➤ HAGGADA was thrown into the river and retrieved from a fish that had swallowed it.

Solomon's seal is a figure like the Star of David. It is also the name for a plant of the lily family, with arching stems that bear a double row of broad leaves with drooping green and white flowers in their axils; the name has been variously explained as referring to markings seen on a transverse section of the rootstock, to the round scars left by the decay of stems, or to the use of the root 'to seal and close up green wounds'.

Solon (*c.*630–*c.*560 BC), Athenian statesman and lawgiver. One of the ➤ SEVEN *Sages*, he revised the code of laws established by ➤ DRACO), making it less severe. His division of the citizens into four classes based on wealth rather than birth laid the foundations of Athenian democracy.

solstice either of the two times in the year, the ➤ SUMMER *solstice* and the ➤ WINTER *solstice*, when the sun reaches its highest or lowest point in the sky at noon, marked by the longest and shortest days. Recorded from Middle English, the word comes via Old French from Latin *solstitium*, from *sol* 'sun' + *stit-* 'stopped, stationary'.

soma an intoxicating drink prepared from a plant and used in Vedic ritual, believed to be the drink of the gods.

Somerset House in London, on the site of the house built by the Duke of *Somerset*, Lord Protector for Edward VI; the current neoclassical building dates from the late 18th century, and was built by the Scottish architect Sir William Chambers (1723–96); since 1990 it has housed the Courtauld Institute Galleries. Between its establishment in 1837 and 1990, the national registry for births, marriages, and deaths was at *Somerset House*.

Somme a river of northern France, the upper valley of which was the scene of heavy fighting in the First World War. The **Battle of the Somme** was a major battle of the First World War between the British and the Germans, on the Western Front in northern France July–November 1916.

son a male child of someone. (See also ➤ SONS.)

A **horny-handed son of toil** is a labourer. The phrase was originally coined by the Conservative statesman Lord Salisbury in 1873. The expression was popularized in the US by Denis Kearney (1847–1907).

Son of a gun is a jocular or affectionate way of addressing or referring to someone (with reference to the guns carried aboard ships: the epithet is said to have been applied originally to babies born at sea to women allowed to accompany their husbands).

Son of Heaven was a title given to the Emperor of China, translating Chinese *tiānzǐ*.

Son of Man is a title of Jesus Christ, as in Matthew 8:20.

song often taken as the type of something very cheap and inexpensive, as in **for a song**; perhaps originally a reference to old ballads being sold cheaply at fairs.

A **song in one's heart** is a feeling of joy or pleasure; originally with allusion to Lorenz Hart 'With a Song in my Heart', 1930 song.

The **Song of Roland** is the medieval chanson which tells of the death of the paladin ➤ ROLAND at ➤ RONCESVALLES.

The **Song of Songs** is a book of the Bible containing an anthology of Hebrew love poems traditionally ascribed to ➤ SOLOMON but in fact dating from a much later period. Jewish and Christian writers have interpreted the book allegorically as representing God's relationship with his people, or with the soul.

The **Song of the Three Holy Children** is a book of the Apocrypha, an addition to the book of Daniel, telling of three Hebrew exiles, Ananias, Azarias, and Misael, thrown (with Daniel) into a furnace by Nebuchadnezzar; protected by God from the flames, they sang the words which in the Anglican service of matins is the canticle of the ➤ BENEDICITE. (See also ➤ BURNING *fiery furnace*.)

sons the male children of someone.

Sons of Belial are evildoers. The original reference is biblical (from 1 Samuel 2:12), and was reinforced in the 17th century both by a reference in the 1663 *Book of Common Prayer* to the execution of Charles I, and then by Milton in *Paradise Lost* (1667)

The **sons of thunder** is an epithet of the apostles James and John, the sons of Zebedee, given as the translation of ➤ BOANERGES.

In the Ulster cycle of early Irish literature, the **sons of Uisneach** are Naoise, husband of ➤ DEIRDRE, and his brothers, all killed by Conchobar in punishment for Naoise's elopement with Deirdre, Conchobar's promised wife.

Sooner State informal name for Oklahoma. *Sooner* here is in the sense 'one who acts prematurely', i.e. a person who tried to get into the frontier territory of Oklahoma before the US government opened it to settlers in 1889.

give a sop to Cerberus in allusion to the story in the *Aeneid* of the descent of Aeneas into the underworld; he was able to pass safely by the monstrous watchdog ➤ CER-BERUS by drugging him with a specially prepared cake.

St Sophia legendary mother of three virgin martyrs, Faith, Hope, and Charity; she supposedly died three days after their death, while praying at their tomb. The legend originated in the Eastern Church, and can be understood as an allegory of Divine Wisdom (*Haga Sophia*) from whom proceed the virtues of faith, hope, and charity. Her feast day is 30 September.

sophist a paid teacher of philosophy and rhetoric in Greece in the Classical and Hellenistic periods, associated in popular thought with moral scepticism and specious reasoning. Recorded from the mid 16th century, the word comes ultimately via Latin from Greek *sophizesthai* 'devise, become wise', from *sophos* 'wise'.

Sophocles (*c.*496–406 BC), Greek dramatist. His seven surviving plays are notable for their complexity of plot and depth of characterization, and for their examination of the relationship between mortals and the divine order.

sophomore in North America, a second-year university or high-school student. The word is recorded from the mid 17th century (originally, as a second-year student at Cambridge University), and comes from *sophum*, *sophom*, obsolete variants of *sophism* 'a fallacious argument, especially one used deliberately to deceive and serving as a University exercise'.

Sorbonne the seat of the faculties of science and literature of the University of Paris. It was originally a theological college founded by Robert de *Sorbon*, chaplain to Louis IX, *c.*1257.

sorcerer a person who claims or is believed to have magic powers; a wizard. Recorded from late Middle English, the word comes ultimately, via Old French, from Latin *sors*, *sort-* 'lot, fortune'.

A **sorcerer's apprentice** is a person who instigates a process or project which they are then unable to control without assistance. The phrase is a translation of French

l'apprentit sorcier, the title of a symphonic poem by Paul Dukas (1897), after *der Zauberlehrling*, a ballad by Goethe (1797), in which the apprentice through the use of spells instigates processes which he cannot control.

Soroptimist a member of an international association of clubs for professional and business women founded in California in 1921. The name comes from Latin *soror* 'sister' + *optimist*.

sortes divination, or the seeking of guidance, by chance selection of a passage in the Bible (**sortes Biblicae**) or another text regarded as authoritative (**sortes Virgilianae**). Recorded from the late 16th century, the word is Latin, and means 'chance selections (of the Bible or other chosen work)'.

SOS an international code signal of extreme distress, used especially by ships at sea. The letters were chosen as being easily transmitted and recognized in Morse code; by folk etymology they are taken as an abbreviation of *save our souls*. The earlier and original distress call for shipping (as used by the ➤ TI-TANIC) was *CQD*.

Sothic of or relating to ➤ SIRIUS (the Dog Star), especially with reference to the ancient Egyptian year fixed by its heliacal rising. The word comes (in the early 19th century), from Greek *Sōthis*, from an Egyptian name of the Dog Star.

soul the spiritual or immaterial part of a human being or animal, regarded as immortal. The word is recorded from Old English (in form *sāwol*, *sāw(e)l*), and is of Germanic origin.

Soul music is a kind of music incorporating elements of rhythm and blues and gospel music, popularized by American blacks. Characterized by an emphasis on vocals and an impassioned improvisatory delivery, it is associated with performers such as Marvin Gaye, Aretha Franklin, James Brown, and Otis Redding.

the Souls a late 19th-century aristocratic circle with predominantly cultural and intellectual interests; the name was said to have been given by Lord Charles Beresford in 1888. Members of the group included Curzon, Arthur Balfour, and Margot Tennant (later Margot Asquith).

sound bite a short extract from a recorded interview, chosen for its pungency or aptness, or a one-liner deliberately produced to be used in this way. Use of the technique and the term, first recorded in the 1980s, has steadily increased, with the US presidential campaigns of 1988 and 1992 making great use of the *sound bite* to carry their messages to the public.

sour grapes an expression or attitude of deliberate disparagement of a desired but unattainable object, alluding to Aesop's fable of 'The Fox and the Grapes', in which a fox, unable to reach a tempting bunch of grapes, comforted himself with the reflection that the fruit was probably sour and was therefore no loss.

souterrain an underground chamber or passage. The word comes (in the mid 18th century) from French, from *sous* 'under' + *terre* 'earth'.

south the direction towards the point of the horizon 90° clockwise from east, or the point on the horizon itself. In literary contexts, it is often contrasted as a region with the more temperate *north*. From the late 20th century, *south* has been used as a collective term for the industrially and economically less advanced countries of the world, typically situated to the south of the industrialized nations.

To **go south** (chiefly in US usage) is to deteriorate, fail, or fall in value.

The **South Bank** is the southern bank of the Thames, noted for the cultural complexes and public gardens developed between Westminster and Blackfriars bridges for and since the ➤ FESTIVAL *of Britain* in 1951. *South Bank* is also used with reference to the policy of the Anglican diocese of Southwark to re-express traditional beliefs and practices in ways that would make them better suited to contemporary life.

South Park is an American cartoon series (1998–), featuring the (often scatological humour) of a group of third-grade boys, Waspy Stan, Kenny, Eric, and Kyle. Despite compulsory late-night showing for its strong language, the series became a popular hit with young viewers.

The **South Sea Bubble** was a speculative boom in the shares of the **South Sea Company** in 1720 which ended with the failure of the company and a general financial collapse.

See also ➤ *the* SOLID *South*.

Joanna Southcott's box a locked and sealed box said to contain the prophecies of Joanna Southcott, (1750–1814), a former Wesleyan Methodist who announced herself as the woman spoken of in Revelation 12, who is seen 'clothed with the sun, and the moon under her feet'. The box was supposed to be opened in a time of national emergency and in the presence of the Anglican bishops. It was finally opened in 1927; a woman's nightcap and a lottery ticket were among its contents.

Southern blot a procedure for identifying specific sequences of DNA, in which fragments separated on a gel are transferred directly to a second medium on which assay by hybridization may be carried out. It is named after the British biochemist Edwin M. *Southern* (1938–).

Southern Cross the constellation *Crux Australis*, four stars of which form a cross; the name **land of the Southern Cross** has been used for Australia since the late 19th century. *Southern Cross* is also a name for the ➤ EUREKA *flag*.

Southern Lights another name for the *aurora australis*.

sovereign a supreme ruler, especially a monarch; in early use, applied to God in relation to created things.

From the early 16th century, *sovereign* also denoted a gold coin, originally, one minted in England from the time of Henry VII to Charles I and at first of the value of 22s. 6d.; later, a British coin worth one pound sterling, now only minted for commemorative purposes.

The word is recorded from Middle English and comes from Old French *soverain*, based on Latin *super* 'above'; the change in ending was due to association with *reign*.

The sovereign good is the greatest good, especially that of a state or its people; the phrase is recorded from Middle English.

have the right sow by the ear have the correct understanding of the situation; recorded from the mid 16th century, the phrase has been attributed to Henry VIII, when in 1529 ➤ *Thomas* CRANMER suggested that in the question of the projected divorce from Catherine of Aragon, the king should consult divines at the universities.

sow one's wild oats go through a period of wild or promiscuous behaviour while young, late 16th century; *wild oat*, a wild grass related to the cultivated oat which was traditionally a weed of cornfields, is recorded from the mid 16th to the early 17th century as a name for a dissolute young man.

parable of the sower in the Bible (Matthew 13:3–8), the story told by Jesus of how 'a sower went forth to sow', to illustrate the varying readiness of those he taught to receive Jesus's message.

Soweto a large urban area, consisting of several townships, in South Africa southwest of Johannesburg. In 1976 demonstrations against the compulsory use of Afrikaans in schools resulted in violent police activity and the deaths of hundreds of people.

watch this space further developments are expected and more information will be given later; *space* here is an area of a newspaper available for a specific purpose, especially for advertising.

spade[1] a long-handled tool for digging and cutting earth and turf; a *spade* is the emblem of ➤ St FIACRE and ➤ St PHOCAS. Recorded from Old English (in form *spadu*, *spada*), the word is of Germanic origin and is ultimately (like ➤ SPADE[2]) related to Greek *spathē* 'blade, paddle'.

The expression **call a spade a spade** means speak plainly without avoiding unpleasant or embarrassing issues. The expression is recorded in English from the mid 16th century, and derives ultimately from Plutarch's *Apophthegmata*, which uses Greek *skaphē* 'basin'. Erasmus, perhaps confusing this with derivatives of *skaptein* 'dig', rendered this as Latin *ligo* 'mattock', and Nicholas Udall, translating Erasmus in 1542, used the word *spade*.

spade[2] one of the four suits in a conventional pack of playing cards, denoted by a black inverted heart-shaped figure with a small stalk. The word is recorded from the late 16th century, and comes from Italian *spade*, plural of *spada* 'sword', ultimately from Greek *spathē* (cf. ➤ SPADE[1]).

Spades are the highest-ranking suit in Bridge, and from this comes the informal **in spades**, very much, extremely.

spaghetti junction a complex multi-level road junction, especially one on a motorway, and originally applied to a major interchange on the M6 near Birmingham in the UK.

spaghetti western informal term for a western film made cheaply in Europe by an Italian director.

spaghettification in physics, the process by which (in some theories) an object would be stretched and ripped apart by gravitational forces on falling into a black hole.

spam to send irrelevant or inappropriate messages on the Internet to a large number of newsgroups or users, often for the purpose of advertising. The term is recorded from the first half of the 1990s and derives from *Spam*, trademark name for a type of tinned meat, apparently in allusion to a sketch by the British *Monty Python* comedy group, set in a café in which every item on the menu includes Spam.

Spanish of, pertaining to, or associated with Spain.

Spanish flu is influenza caused by an influenza virus of type A, in particular that of the pandemic which began in 1918.

The **Spanish Inquisition** was an ecclesiastical court established in 1478 and directed originally against converts from Judaism and Islam but later also against Protestants. It operated with great severity, especially under its first inquisitor, Torquemada, and was not suppressed until the early 19th century. **Nobody expects the Spanish Inquisition** is a catchphrase from a *Monty Python* script, in which the Inquisitors consistently fail to make a successful announcement of their arrival and identity.

The **Spanish Main** was the former name for the NW coast of South America between the Orinoco River and Panama, and adjoining parts of the Caribbean Sea.

Spanish practice is another term for ➤ OLD *Spanish custom.*

The **War of the Spanish Succession** was a European war (1701–14), provoked by the death of the Spanish king Charles II without issue. The Grand Alliance of Britain, the Netherlands, and the Holy Roman emperor threw back a French invasion of the Low Countries, and, although the Peace of Utrecht confirmed the accession of a Bourbon king in Spain, prevented Spain and France from being united under one crown.

Spartacus (died *c.*71 BC), Thracian slave and gladiator. He led a revolt against Rome in 73, increasing his army from some seventy gladiators at the outset to several thousand rebels, but was eventually defeated by Crassus in 71 and crucified.

The **Spartacus League** was a German revolutionary socialist group (the **Spartacists**) founded in 1916 by Rosa Luxemburg and Karl Liebknecht (1871–1919) with the aims of overthrowing the government and ending the First World War; they took their name from the Thracian slave and revolutionary *Spartacus*. At the end of 1918 the group became the German Communist Party, which in 1919 organized an uprising in Berlin that was brutally crushed.

Spartan a citizen of Sparta, a powerful city state in the 5th century BC, which defeated its rival Athens in the Peloponnesian War to become the leading city of Greece until challenged by Thebes in 371 BC. The ancient Spartans were renowned for the military organization of their state and for their rigorous discipline, courage, and austerity.

Speaker the presiding officer in a legislative assembly, especially the House of Commons; the first person mentioned as formally holding the office in the English Parliament is Sir Thomas de Hungerford (d. 1398), although Sir Peter de la Mare had preceded him in the post in the Parliament of 1376, but without the title.

spear a *spear* is the emblem of ➤ St THOMAS *the Apostle*.
   A **spear-carrier** is an actor with a walk-on part; an unimportant participant in something.
   The **spear side** is the male side or members of a family, the opposite of the *distaff side*.

Special Operations Executive a secret British military service during the Second World War, set up in 1940 to carry out clandestine operations and coordinate with resistance movements in Europe and later the Far East. Abbreviation, **SOE**.

special pleading argument in which the speaker deliberately ignores aspects that are unfavourable to their point of view; the term was originally (in the late 17th century) used for a legal pleading drawn with particular references to the circumstances of a case, as opposed to general pleading.

the special relationship the relationship between Britain and the US, regarded as particularly close in terms of common origin and language. The expression is associated with Winston Churchill, as in the House of Commons 7 November 1945.

Speenhamland system a system of poor relief first adopted in the late 18th century and established throughout rural England in succeeding years, named after the village of *Speenhamland* near Newbury, Berkshire, where the system was adopted by the magistrates in 1795.

Speewah an imaginary Australian cattle station or place used as a setting for tall stories of the outback; recorded from the late 19th century.

spell a form of words used as a magical charm or incantation. Recorded from Old English, the word originally meant 'narration', and is of Germanic origin; the current sense is found first in late Middle English, in **night-spell**, a spell intended as a protection against harm at night.

Spenglerism the philosophy of the German philosopher Oswald *Spengler* (1880–1936), who in his book *The Decline of the West* (1918–22) argues that civilizations undergo a seasonal cycle of a thousand years and are subject to growth and decay analogous to biological species.

Sphinx in Greek mythology, a winged monster of Thebes, having a woman's head and a lion's body. It propounded a riddle about the three ages of man, killing those who failed to solve it, until Oedipus was successful, whereupon the Sphinx committed suicide.
   The name *sphinx* was later used for the sculptured or carved figure of an imaginary creature with a human head and breast and the body of a lion, in particular, an ancient Egyptian stone figure having a lion's body and a human or animal head, especially the huge statue near the Pyramids at Giza.
   The word is recorded from late Middle English (and comes via Latin from Greek, apparently from *sphingein* 'draw tight'); from the early 17th century, the name is used for a person held to resemble the sphinx, in posing difficult questions, or in being of a mysterious or inscrutable nature.

Spice Islands former name for the Molucca Islands, from which spices were traditionally imported to the west; the name is recorded from the early 18th century.

spider in proverbial and traditional allusion, references are made to the cunning, skill, and industry of the spider, as well as its power of secreting or emitting poison; in a traditional story of ➤ *Robert the* BRUCE watching a spider in a cave attempting to spin a thread long enough to reach another piece of rock, it becomes a type of perseverance.
   A spider is also said to have helped ➤ MUHAMMAD. According to the story, the Prophet and his friend Abu-Bakr were in flight from

the men of Mecca and took shelter in a cave; to protect them, pigeons built their nests and a spider spun its web across the mouth of the cave, so that the pursuers assumed that it was undisturbed.

In Greek mythology, the weaver ➤ ARACHNE who challenged Athene to a contest of skill was changed into a spider by the angry goddess.

Spiderman name of an American comic-strip hero first appearing in 1952; *Spiderman* is the alter ego of a shy bookish teenager called Peter Parker, who develops arachnid powers after being bitten by a radio-active spider.

spike someone's guns thwart someone's plans. Recorded from the late 17th century, the expression then referred literally to the practice of hammering a metal spike into the touch-hole of an enemy cannon to render it unusable.

spikenard a costly perfumed ointment much valued in ancient times; in John 12:3, Mary 'took…a pound of ointment of spikenard, very costly, and anointed the feet of Jesus'.

spin a yarn tell a long far-fetched story; the expression is a nautical one, and is recorded from the early 19th century.

spin doctor a spokesperson employed to give a favourable interpretation of events to the media, especially on behalf of a political party. The term comes from US politics, and originated in a sporting metaphor, with the idea of the *spin* put on the ball, for example by a pitcher in baseball.

spinster in current usage, the term carries overtones of a stereotypical woman in this situation who is regarded as prissy and repressed.

Spinster is first recorded in late Middle English in the sense of 'a woman who spins', and in early use it was appended to the names of women to denote their occupation. From the 17th century the word was appended to names as the official legal description of an unmarried woman (as in, **spinster of this parish**); the current sense dates from the early 18th century.

spirit the non-physical part of a person which is the seat of emotions and character; the soul; such a part regarded as a person's true self and as capable of surviving physical death or separation, or manifested as an apparition after their death; a ghost. The word is recorded in Middle English, and comes via Anglo-Norman French from Latin *spiritus* 'breath, spirit'.

The spirit is willing (but the flesh is weak) means that someone has good intentions but fails to live up to them; with biblical allusion to Matthew 26:41.

The spirit moves me, meaning 'I am inclined to do something', is a phrase originally in Quaker use with reference to the ➤ HOLY *Spirit*.

The **Spirit of St Louis** was the name of the single-engined monoplane in which Charles Lindbergh made the first solo transatlantic flight in 1927.

Spiritualism is a system of belief or religious practice based on supposed communication with the spirits of the dead, especially through mediums; the word in this sense is recorded from the mid 19th century.

spit and polish extreme neatness or smartness, originally with allusion to the cleaning and polishing duties of a serviceman.

spitting image the exact double of (another person or thing); the term is recorded from the early 20th century, and is an alteration of *spitten image*, which itself is an alteration of *split and image*.

In Britain in the 1980s and 1990s, *Spitting Image* was the title of a satirical television programme, featuring puppets of British politicians and the British royal family.

spleen an abdominal organ involved in the production and removal of blood cells in most vertebrates and forming part of the immune system, which in earlier belief was held to be the seat of such emotions as bad temper and spite; *spleen* thus came to be used in these senses.

splice join or connect (a rope or ropes) by interweaving the strands at the ends; the word is recorded from the early 16th century, and by the mid 18th century the slang sense 'to join in matrimony, to marry' had developed.

In naval use, to **splice the mainbrace** was to serve an extra ration of rum (the *mainbrace* was the brace attached to the main yard).

split infinitive a construction consisting of an infinitive with an adverb or other word inserted between *to* and the verb, e.g. *she seems to really like it*. Although it is still widely held that such a construction is wrong, the dislike of it is not well-founded, being based on an analogy with Latin, where infinitives consist of only one word.

In English, the placing of an adverb may be extremely important in giving a particular emphasis; in some cases, splitting an infinitive can only be avoided at the cost of losing such emphasis.

Dr Spock popular name for the American paediatrician and writer Benjamin Maclane Spock (1903–98). His influential manual *The Common Sense Book of Baby and Child Care* (1946) challenged traditional ideas of discipline and rigid routine in child-rearing in favour of a psychological approach.

Mr Spock a character in the science fiction series ➤ STAR *Trek*; a ➤ VULCAN who is characterized by his use of logic, lack of emotions, and pointed ears.

put a spoke in someone's wheel prevent someone from carrying out a plan; the expression is recorded from the late 16th century in the form 'I will sett a spoke to your cogge'; the current form became established in the early 17th century. *Spoke* here is probably a mistranslation of Dutch *spaak* meaning 'bar, stave'.

spontaneous combustion the ignition of organic matter (e.g. hay or coal) without apparent cause, typically through heat generated internally by rapid oxidation. Alleged reports of human death caused by such a phenomenon have long been the subject of controversy.

spontaneous generation the supposed production of living organisms from non-living matter, as inferred from the apparent appearance of life in some infusions. Also called *abiogenesis*.

make a spoon or spoil a horn make a determined effort to achieve something, whatever the cost. With reference to the practice of making spoons out of the horns of cattle or sheep.

spoonerism a verbal error in which a speaker accidentally transposes the initial sounds or letters of two or more words. The word comes (in the early 20th century) from the Revd William Archibald *Spooner* (1844–1930), Warden of New College, an English scholar who reputedly made such errors in speaking, although many of those now attributed to him are probably apocryphal.

the sport of kings proverbial phrase for hunting and (now, most usually) horse-racing, although the earliest uses of the expression related to war, as in Dryden's *King Arthur* (1691).

SPQR *Senatus Populusque Romanus*, the Senate and People of Rome, used in documents and inscriptions (as on standards) in ancient Rome.

a sprat to catch a mackerel a small expenditure made, or a small risk taken, in the hope of a large or significant gain, recorded from the mid 19th century.

spread eagle a representation of an eagle with body, legs, and both wings displayed, especially as the emblem of various states or rulers, as of imperial Russia or Germany, or as an inn sign.

spree killer a person who kills in a sudden, random, and apparently unpremeditated manner, especially one killing a number of people at a single location in such an attack. Since the early 1980s, criminologists have identified two kinds of multiple murderer, the ➤ SERIAL *killer* and the spree killer.

spring the season after winter and before summer, in which vegetation begins to appear, in the northern hemisphere from March to May and in the southern hemisphere from September to November; in figurative usage, a time of youth and strength, associated with fresh growth. The word is recorded in Middle English in the obsolete sense of 'the first sign of day, the beginning of a season'; as a name for the season, it dates from late Middle English.
  A **spring tide** is a tide just after a new or full moon, when there is the greatest difference between high and low water.

Spy Wednesday the Wednesday before Easter, as the anniversary of the day on which ➤ JUDAS secretly visited the Jewish authorities to betray Jesus.

squander-bug a symbol of reckless extravagance; a person who recklessly squanders money. The *squander-bug*, introduced in 1943 by the National Savings Committee, appeared in Ministry of Information posters as a devilish insect inciting to reckless spending.

square a plane figure with four equal straight sides and four right angles; in astrology, an aspect of 90° (one quarter of a circle).
  From the late 16th century, *square* was the term for a body of infantry drawn up in rectangular formation, as on a battlefield or parade ground.
  From the late 17th century, *square* has been used (often as part of a place-name) for an

open space or area in a town or city, especially one of approximately quadrilateral and rectangular shape enclosed by houses.

The **Square Mile** is an informal name for the City of London.

Back to square one means back to the starting-point, with no progress made (*square one* may be a reference to a board-game such as Snakes and Ladders, or derive from the notional division of a football pitch into eight numbered sections for the purpose of early radio commentaries).

To **square the circle** is to construct a square equal in area to a given circle (a problem incapable of a purely geometrical solution); thus, do something that is considered to be impossible.

squarson former term for an Anglican clergyman who also held the position of squire in his parish. The word, coinage of which has been attributed to Bishop Samuel Wilberforce (1805–73), Sydney Smith, and others, is formed from a blend of *squire* and *parson*, and is recorded from the late 19th century.

squint an oblique opening through a wall in a church permitting a view of the altar from an aisle or side chapel.

squire in feudal times, a young nobleman acting as an attendant to a knight before becoming a knight himself; from the late 16th century, a young man attending or escorting a lady, a gallant or lover.

From the 17th century, *squire* came to denote a man of high social standing who owns and lives on an estate in a rural area, especially the chief landowner in such an area.

The word is recorded from Middle English, and is originally a shortening of Old French *esquier* 'esquire'.

SS the Nazi special police force, the *Schutzstaffel* 'defence squadron'. Founded in 1925 by Hitler as a personal bodyguard, the SS provided security forces (including the Gestapo) and administered the concentration camps. It was headed by Heinrich Himmler 1929–45.

Stabat Mater a medieval Latin hymn on the suffering of the Virgin Mary at the Crucifixion, named from the opening words *Stabat mater dolorosa* 'Stood the mother, full of grief'.

staff a staff (with the child Jesus) is the emblem of ➤ *St* CHRISTOPHER.

The **staff of life** is bread; the usage probably derives from the biblical translation of a Hebrew phrase meaning 'cut off the supply of food', as in Leviticus 26:26. The use of *staff of life* to mean bread is recorded from the mid 17th century.

stag a *stag* is the emblem of ➤ *St* EUSTACE, ➤ *St* GILES, ➤ *St* HUBERT, and St Osyth (d. *c.*700), supposedly protected from the unwanted attentions of her husband by a white stag. The word is recorded from Middle English, and is related to Old Norse *steggr* 'male bird' and Icelandic *steggi* 'tomcat'.

From the mid 19th century, stag has been used in Stock Exchange jargon for a person who applies for shares in a new issue with a view to selling at once for a profit.

A **stag night** is a celebration held for a man shortly before his wedding, attended by his male friends only.

stake a wooden post to which a person was tied before being burned alive as a punishment; **the stake** was thus used for the punishment of death by burning, especially in times of religious persecution.

stake a claim assert one's right to something; with allusion to the practice of putting stakes around the perimeter of a piece of land to which one is laying claim. The expression *stake (out) a claim* was originally US, dating from the California gold rush of 1849.

Stakhanovite a worker in the former USSR who was exceptionally hard-working and productive; an exceptionally hard-working or zealous person. From the name of Aleksei Grigorevich *Stakhanov* (1906–1977), Russian coal miner.

Stalag (in the Second World War) a German prison camp, especially for non-commissioned officers and privates. The word is German, a contraction of *Stammlager*, from *Stamm* 'base, main stock' + *Lager* 'camp'.

stalemate in chess, a position counting as a draw, in which a player is not in check but cannot move except into check. The word comes (in the mid 18th century) from obsolete *stale* (from Anglo-Norman French *estale* 'position', from *estaler* 'be placed'), + *mate*.

Battle of Stalingrad a long and bitterly fought battle of the Second World War, in which the German advance into the Soviet Union was turned back at Stalingrad (now Volgograd, until 1925 Tsaritsyn) in SW Russia in 1942–3. The Germans surrendered after suffering more than 300,000 casualties.

The **Sword of Stalingrad** was given by Britain to the Soviet people in 1943 in recognition of the defence of Stalingrad; the sword, presented by Winston Churchill at the Tehran Conference, had engraved on its blade, 'To the steelhearted citizens of Stalingrad, a gift from King George VI as a token of the homage of the British people.'

stalking horse a screen traditionally made in the shape of a horse behind which a hunter may stay concealed when stalking prey. Later, a false pretext concealing someone's real intentions; a candidate in an election for the leadership of a political party who stands only in order to provoke the election and thus allow a stronger candidate to come forward.

Stalky nickname of Lionel Corkran, the leader of three schoolboys in Kipling's *Stalky & Co* (1899); the name implies the character's high degree of stealth and cunning, and had originally belonged to Kipling's schoolfriend Lionel 'Stalky' Dunsterville.

Stamp Act an act regulating stamp duty, especially that imposing the duty on the American colonies in 1765 and repealed in 1766.

stand and deliver! a highwayman's traditional order to travellers to halt and hand over their money and valuables; the expression is recorded from the early 18th century.

standard-bearer a soldier whose duty is to carry a standard, especially in battle; in extended usage, a conspicuous advocate of a cause, one who is in the forefront of a political or religious party.

standard time a uniform time for places in approximately the same longitude, established in a country or region by law or custom, and given a particular name, as *Eastern Standard Time*, *Greenwich Mean Time*.

St Stanislaus (1030–79), patron saint of Poland, known as **St Stanislaus of Cracow**. As bishop of Cracow (1072–79) he excommunicated King Boleslaus II. According to tradition Stanislaus was murdered by Boleslaus while taking Mass. His feast day is 11 April (formerly 7 May).

the Stannaries the districts comprising the tin mines and smelting works of Cornwall and Devon, formerly under the jurisdiction of stannary courts. The name is recorded from late Middle English, and comes ultimately from late Latin *stannum* 'tin'.

The **Stannary Court** was a legal body for the regulation of tin miners in the Stannaries. The phrase *Stannaria curia* is found in a charter of 1337; by the Stannaries Courts Abolition Act of 1896 the jurisdiction of these courts was transferred to the County Court.

staple former term for a centre of trade, especially in a specified commodity, such as wool; originally, a town or place, appointed by royal authority, in which was a body of merchants with exclusive right of purchase for certain classes of goods destined for export. An ordinance of Edward III in 1353, the **Statute of the Staple**, established *staples* in a number of English towns as well as at Carmarthen, Dublin, Waterford, Cork, and Drogheda.

At various times the chief staple was overseas; from about 1390 to 1558 it was at Calais, which was sometimes called **the Staple**.

star in allusive or proverbial use, a type of brightness and remoteness, or as representing an innumerable host or multitude.

A *star* is the emblem of ➤ St DOMINIC, ➤ St THOMAS *Aquinas*, ➤ St VINCENT *Ferrer*, and ➤ St NICHOLAS *of Tolentino*.

In astrology, the *stars* denote the planets and zodiacal constellations which are supposed to influence human affairs or (from their position at the time of a person's birth) affect their destiny.

The **Star Chamber** was an English court of civil and criminal jurisdiction that developed in the late 15th century, trying especially those cases affecting the interests of the Crown. It was noted for its arbitrary and oppressive judgements and was abolished in 1641. The name may have come from decorative stars on the ceiling of the room in which the court was originally held.

To be **star-crossed** is to be thwarted by bad luck; often with allusion to Shakespeare's *Romeo and Juliet* 'a pair of star-crossed lovers'.

Star Dust was the name of a British Lancastrian civil aircraft which in 1947 disappeared mysteriously in a flight from Buenos Aires to Santiago in Chile. Despite many searches nothing more was heard of the plane until January 2000, when wreckage was found in the Andes. It is now thought that the plane crashed into a glacier, from which its remains have finally begun to emerge. (See also ➤ STENDEC.)

A **Star of Bethlehem** is a plant of the lily family with star-shaped flowers which typically have green stripes on the outer surface, found in temperate regions of the Old World.

The **Star of David** is a six-pointed figure consisting of two interlaced equilateral triangles, used as a Jewish and Israeli symbol; the ➤ MAGEN *David*.

Star of the Sea is a title of the Virgin Mary, an English translation of ➤ STELLA *Maris*.

The **Star-spangled Banner** is a song written in 1814 with words composed by Francis Scott Key (1779–1843) and a tune adapted from that of a popular English drinking song, *To Anacreon in Heaven*. It was officially adopted as the US national anthem in 1931.

Star Trek is the title of a cult science-fiction drama series created by Gene Roddenberry (1921–91); the series chronicled 'the voyages of the starship *Enterprise*', whose five-year mission was 'to boldly go where no man has gone before', and which was commanded by Captain James Kirk.

Star Wars is the title of the first (1977) of a trio of films by George Lucas; the films told the story of the young Luke Skywalker who with the training of ➤ OBI-*Wan Kenobi*, last of the Jedi knights, plays the key role in resisting the Imperial forces under the command of ➤ DARTH *Vader*. *Star Wars* was also the popular name for *Strategic Defense Initiative*, a projected US system of defence against nuclear weapons, proposed by President Reagan in 1983, using satellites armed with lasers to intercept and destroy intercontinental ballistic missiles.

starboard the side of a ship or aircraft that is on the right when one is facing forward, opposite to *port*. The word comes from Old English *stēorbord* 'rudder side', because early Teutonic sailing vessels were steered with a paddle over the right side.

Stars and Bars the flag of the Confederate States, which had two horizontal red bars separated by a narrow white bar, and in the top left-hand corner, a circle of eleven white stars on a blue background for the eleven states of the Confederacy.

Stars and Stripes the national flag of the US. When first adopted by Congress (14th June 1777) it contained 13 stripes and 13 stars, representing the 13 states of the Union; it now has 13 stripes and 50 stars. An informal name for the flag is ➤ OLD *Glory*.

under starter's orders waiting to start; referring to horses, runners, or other competitors ready to start a race and just waiting for the signal.

State of the Union message a yearly address delivered in January by the President of the US to Congress, giving the administration's view of the state of the nation and plans for legislation. The expression itself is recorded only from 1945, but the requirement for such an address is enshrined in the Constitution of 1787. Also called **State of the Union address**.

Stationers' Hall the hall of the Stationers' Company in London, formerly used for the registration of books for purposes of copyright.

Stations of the Cross fourteen pictures or carvings representing successive incidents during Jesus' progress from Pilate's house to his crucifixion at Calvary, before which devotions are performed in some Churches. They are, in order: Jesus before Pilate, Jesus carrying the Cross, Jesus falling for the first time, Jesus meeting the Virgin Mary, Jesus with Simon of Cyrene helping to carry the Cross, St Veronica wiping the face of Jesus, Jesus falling for the second time, Jesus and the weeping Women of Jerusalem, Jesus falling for the third time, Jesus stripped of his clothing, Jesus nailed to the Cross, Jesus's death on the Cross, the taking down of Jesus's body, and the entombment of Jesus.

statute originally, a law or decree made by a monarch or a legislative authority, a divine law. Later, a decree or enactment passed by a legislative body, and expressed in a formal document, an Act of Parliament. The word is recorded from Middle English and comes ultimately (via Old French and late Latin) from Latin *statuere* 'set up' from *status* 'standing'.

The **statute book** is the book containing the statutes of a nation or state; a nation's laws regarded collectively.

stave church a church of a type built in Norway from the 11th to the 13th century, the walls of which were constructed of upright planks or staves.

steady as she goes keep on with the same careful progress; in nautical parlance, *steady* is the instruction to the helmsman to keep the ship on the same course.

steady state an unvarying condition in a physical process, especially as in the theory that the universe is eternal and maintained by constant creation of matter. The steady state theory postulates that the universe maintains a constant average density, with more matter continuously created to fill the void left by galaxies that are receding from one another. The theory has now largely been abandoned in favour of the ➤ BIG *bang* theory and an evolving universe.

steeple-house a building with a steeple, especially (as a derogatory term) in early Quaker usage; the English founder of the Society of Friends, George Fox (1624–91), uses the term in describing the effect on him of seeing the spires of Lichfield.

steeplechase a horse race run on a race-course having ditches and hedges as jumps, originally so called because a *steeple* marked the finishing point across country; the term is first recorded in the *Sporting Magazine* of April 1793 of a race of this kind run near Galloway.

stela an upright stone slab or column typically bearing a commemorative inscription or relief design, often serving as a gravestone.

Stella Maris a female protector or guiding spirit at sea (a title sometimes given to the Virgin Mary); the phrase is Latin, and means 'Star of the Sea', and is first attested as an epithet of the Virgin in St Jerome.

Stellenbosch transfer to a post of minimal responsibility as a response to incompetence or lack of success, from the name of a town in Cape Province, South Africa, traditionally the place selected for command by unsuccessful military personnel.

Stendec mysterious word in the final transmission from the lost plane ➤ STAR *Dust*; its meaning has never been resolved.

Stentor name of a Greek herald in the Trojan War, 'whose voice was as powerful as fifty voices of other men'; in extended use, a person with a powerful voice.

step- denoting a relationship resulting from a remarriage. This combining form comes (in Old English) from a Germanic base meaning 'bereaved, orphaned'.

The **wicked stepmother** is a traditional fairy-tale figure of evil, as in the story of ➤ SNOW *White*.

Stephen male forename; name of two saints.

St Stephen (died *c.*35), was one of the original seven deacons in Jerusalem appointed by the Apostles. He was charged with blasphemy and stoned, thus becoming the first Christian martyr. Saul of Tarsus (see ➤ St PAUL[1]) was present at his execution. He is patron of deacons, bricklayers, and those suffering from headaches, and his emblem is a stone, as a sign of his martyrdom. His feast day is (in the Western Church) 26 December; (in the Eastern Church) 27 December.

St Stephen's was an occasional former name for Parliament, from the chapel of *St Stephen* in which the Commons used to sit.

St Stephen of Hungary (*c.*977–1038), was king and patron saint of Hungary, reigned 1000–38. The first king of Hungary, he united Pannonia and Dacia as one kingdom and took steps to Christianize the country. His feast day is 2 September or (in Hungary) 20 August.

Steptoe and Son British television comedy series (1964–73) about a rag-and-bone man father and son, in which Harold Steptoe's social aspirations are constantly frustrated by his father's contentment with their current lifestyle; the name *Steptoe* may be used allusively for a dealer in second-hand goods.

sterling British money. Recorded from Middle English, the word probably comes from *steorra* 'star' + *-ling* (because some early Norman pennies bore a small star). Until recently one popular theory was that the coin was originally made by *Easterling* moneyers (from the 'eastern' Hanse towns), but the stressed first syllable would not have been dropped.

Stern Gang the British name for a militant Zionist group that campaigned in Palestine during the 1940s for the creation of a Jewish state. Founded by Avraham Stern (1907–42) as an offshoot of Irgun, the group assassinated the British Minister for the Middle East, Lord Moyne, and Count Bernadotte, the UN mediator for Palestine.

be made of sterner stuff be more resolute, be less inclined to yield; originally with reference to Shakespeare's *Julius Caesar* (1599).

stet let it stand (Latin word used as an instruction on a printed proof to indicate that a correction or alteration should be ignored).

steward a person employed to manage another person's property, especially a large house or estate; in the UK, an officer of the royal household, especially an administrator of Crown estates. Recorded from Old English (in form *stīweard*), the word comes from *stig* (probably in the sense 'house, hall') + *weard* 'ward'.

The **unjust steward**, in a parable from Luke 16, is a rich man's steward who, accused by his master of being thriftless and fearing destitution from being dismissed, arranges with his master's debtors to reduce the apparent amount of the debts they owe.

Stewart an alternative spelling of the name ➤ STUART.

stick-and-carrot a method of persuasion combining the threat of punishment with the promise of reward; a *carrot* dangled in front of a donkey was a proverbial method of tempting the animal to move.

sticking-place a place in which something stops and holds fast; in allusion to Shakespeare's *Macbeth* (1606), where the reference seems to be to the screwing-up of the peg of a musical instrument until it becomes tightly fixed in the hole.

sticky wicket a cricket pitch that has been drying after rain and is difficult to bat on; a tricky or awkward situation. The term is recorded in its literal sense from 1882, in a reference to the Australians finding themselves on a sticky wicket; the first figurative example is found in the 1950s.

stiff upper lip a quality of uncomplaining stoicism; the phrase is now regarded as characteristically British, although it is first recorded in US usage.

stigma originally (in the late 16th century) a mark made on the skin by pricking or branding, as punishment for a criminal or a mark of subjection, a brand; in extended usage, a mark of disgrace associated with a particular circumstance, quality, or person. The word comes via Latin from Greek *stigma* 'a mark made by a pointed instrument, a dot'; its plural form gives ➤ STIGMATA.

stigmata (in Christian tradition) marks corresponding to those left on Christ's body by the Crucifixion, said to have been impressed by divine favour on the bodies of ➤ *St FRANCIS of Assisi* and others; the word (plural of ➤ STIGMA) is recorded in this sense from the early 17th century.

still life a painting or drawing of an arrangement of objects, typically including fruit and flowers and objects contrasting with these in texture, such as bowls and glassware. The term is recorded from the late 17th century, in John Dryden's translation of Du Fresnoy's *De Arte Graphica* (1695), and was influenced by Dutch *stilleven* in the same sense.

still waters run deep a quiet or placid manner may conceal a passionate nature; proverbial, from late Middle English.

Stir-up Sunday the Sunday next before Advent, so called from the opening words of the collect for the day, 'Stir up, we beseech thee, O Lord, the wills of thy faithful people.' The name also became associated with the stirring of the Christmas mincemeat, which it was customary to begin making that week.

stirrup the device probably originated in the Asian steppes around the 2nd century BC, and was of great military value. The word comes (in Old English) from the Germanic base of obsolete *sty* 'climb' + *rope*, indicating that the original stirrup must have been a looped rope.

The expression **hold the stirrup**, as in helping a person to mount, indicates an expression of homage or reverence.

A **stirrup cup** is a cup of wine or other alcoholic drink offered to a person on horseback who is about to depart on a journey.

a stitch in time saves nine if you sort out a problem immediately it may save a lot of extra work later; proverbial, from the mid 18th century.

the Stoa the great hall in Athens in which the ancient Greek philosopher ➤ ZENO *of Citium* gave the founding lectures of the philosophic school of ➤ STOICISM. Also known as *the Porch*.

Stock Exchange a market in which securities are bought and sold; the level of prices in such a market. The term is first used (in the late 18th century) of the London *Stock Exchange* in Threadneedle Street, which replaced Jonathan's coffee house in Exchange Alley, the former mart for *stockjobbers*, the archaic term for a principal or wholesaler who dealt only on the Stock Exchange with brokers (now called ➤ JOBBERS).

stockbroker a broker who buys and sells securities on a stock exchange on behalf of clients; the term is recorded from the early 18th century.

A **stockbroker belt** is an affluent residential area outside a large city, supposedly typical of the lifestyle of a successful stockbroker. **Stockbroker's Tudor** is an associated style of mock-Tudor architecture.

Stockholm syndrome feelings of trust or affection felt in many cases of kidnapping or hostage-taking by a victim towards a captor, with reference to the aftermath of a bank robbery in Stockholm.

hang up one's stocking on Christmas Eve, put an empty stocking ready as a receptacle for small gifts, supposedly to be filled by Santa Claus.

Stoicism an ancient Greek school of philosophy founded at Athens by ➤ ZENO of Citium, and named for ➤ *the* STOA in which he taught. The school taught that virtue, the highest good, is based on knowledge; the wise live in harmony with the divine Reason (also identified with Fate and Providence) that governs nature, and are indifferent to the vicissitudes of fortune and to pleasure and pain.

stole a priest's silk vestment worn over the shoulders and hanging down to the knee or below. Recorded from Old English (in the senses 'long robe' and 'priest's vestment'), the word comes via Latin from Greek *stolē* 'clothing'.

an army marches on its stomach a group of soldiers or workers can only fight or function effectively if they have been well fed. Proverbial, translating French *c'est la soupe qui fait le soldat*, a maxim of Napoleon.

stone a *stone* may be the type of motionlessness or fixity, or of hardness, and thus insensibility (as in **stone-blind**) or stupidity.

A stone is the emblem of ➤ St STEPHEN and ➤ St JEROME.

The phrase **set in stone** is used to emphasize that something is fixed and unchangeable (often in negative contexts). The allusion is to the Ten Commandments handed down to Moses on tablets of stone (Exodus 31:18).

The **Stone Age** was a prehistoric period when weapons and tools were made of stone or of organic materials such as bone, wood, or horn; it covers a period of about 2.5 million years, from the first use of tools by the ancestors of man (*Australopithecus*) to the introduction of agriculture and the first towns.

The **Stone of Scone** was the stone on which medieval Scottish kings were crowned at ➤ SCONE. It was brought to England by Edward I and preserved in the coronation chair in Westminster Abbey, and returned to Scotland in 1996. Also called *Coronation stone*, *Stone of Destiny*.

Stonehenge a megalithic monument on Salisbury Plain in Wiltshire. Completed in several constructional phases from *c.*2950 BC, it is composed of a circle of sarsen stones surrounded by a bank and ditch and enclosing a circle of smaller bluestones. Within this inner circle is a horseshoe arrangement of five trilithons with the axis aligned on the midsummer sunrise, an orientation that was probably for ritual purposes.

Stonehenge is popularly associated with the Druids, although this connection is now generally rejected by scholars; the monument has also been attributed to the Phoenicians, Romans, Vikings, and visitors from other worlds. Geoffrey of Monmouth says that the main stones were brought from Ireland by the magic of ➤ MERLIN.

The second element of the name may have meant something 'hanging or supported in the air'. A spurious form *Stanhengest* is found in some (*a.* 1500) Latin chronicles, with a story associating Stonehenge with a massacre of British nobles by the Saxon leader ➤ HENGIST (see also ➤ NIGHT *of the long knives*).

throw stones cast aspersions; often with reference to the proverbial saying, those who live in glass houses should not throw stones, the earliest variant of which is recorded in the mid 17th century. (See also ➤ CAST *the first stone*.)

Stonewall[1] nickname of Thomas Jonathan Jackson (1824–63), Confederate general during the American Civil War.

Stonewall[2] a gay bar in Greenwich Village where in 1969 those present responded violently to a police raid; the riot has subsequently been commemorated annually during Gay Pride week in June.

stool of repentance traditionally in the Presbyterian Church, on which a person sat to do formal penance before the rest of the congregation.

stool pigeon a police informer, a person acting as a decoy, so named from the original use in wildfowling of a pigeon fixed to a stool as a decoy.

fall between two stools fail to be or take one of two satisfactory alternatives; with allusion to the proverb *between two stools one falls to the ground*.

pull out all the stops make a very great effort to achieve something; with reference to the stops of an organ.

stork the white stork is traditionally known as the bringer of children, and other legends associate the bird as a bringer of luck to houses where it nests.

In Aesop's fable of Jupiter and the frogs who asked for a king, **King Stork** is the harsh ruler who replaces the inert ➤ *King* LOG.

Stormont Castle a castle in Belfast which was, until 1972, the seat of the Parliament of Northern Ireland and in 1999 became the headquarters of the Northern Ireland Assembly.

stormy petrel a small seabird formerly believed to be a harbinger of bad weather; a person who causes or presages unrest.

stoup a basin for holy water, especially on the wall near the door of a Roman Catholic church for worshippers to dip their fingers in before crossing themselves. Recorded from Middle English, the word originally denoted 'pail, small cask'.

collapse of stout party standard dénouement in Victorian humour; the phrase is supposed to come from *Punch*, as the characteristic finishing line of a joke, but no actual example has been traced, although the character *Stout Party* appeared in a cartoon of 1855.

Strabo (*c*.63 BC–*c*.23 AD), historian and geographer of Greek descent. His only extant work, *Geographica*, in seventeen volumes, provides a detailed physical and historical geography of the ancient world during the reign of Augustus.

Stradivarius a violin or other stringed instrument made by the Italian violin-maker Antonio *Stradivari* (*c*.1644–1737), who devised the proportions of the modern violin, or his followers; sometimes informally shortened to **Strad**.

strafe attack repeatedly with bombs or machine-gun fire from low-flying aircraft; humorous adaptation of the German First World War catchphrase *Gott strafe England* 'may God punish England', coined by the German writer Alfred Funke (b. 1869).

the straight and narrow the honest and morally acceptable way of living; a misunderstanding of Matthew 7:14, 'Strait is the gate, and narrow is the way.'

straight from the horse's mouth expression for the original, authentic source of information; recorded from the 1920s, and probably referring to the ideal source for a racing tip.

strain at a gnat make a difficulty about accepting something trivial; with allusion to Matthew 23:24 'Ye…strain at a gnat, and swallow a camel.'

Dr Strangelove a person who ruthlessly considers or plans nuclear warfare, from the character in the film of that name (1963).

Strasbourg a city in NE France, in Alsace, close to the border with Germany, annexed by Germany in 1870, and returned to France after the First World War. It is the headquarters of the Council of Europe and of the European Parliament.

A **Strasbourg goose** is a goose fattened in such a way as to enlarge the liver for use in pâté de foie gras.

Stratford-upon-Avon a town in Warwickshire, on the River Avon, famous as the birth and burial place of William Shakespeare, which is also the site of the Royal Shakespeare Theatre.

straw in proverbial or allusive use, something of small value, lack of substance or value, or inflammability. (See also ➤ STRAWS.)

To **draw the short straw** is to be the unluckiest of a group of people, especially in being chosen to perform an unpleasant task; with reference to a method drawing lots that involves holding several straws of varying lengths with one end concealed in the hand, and inviting other members of the group to take one each.

The **final straw** is a further difficulty or annoyance, typically minor in itself but coming on top of a whole series of difficulties, that makes a situation unbearable; with allusion to the proverb, *the last straw breaks the (laden) camel's back.*

A **man of straw** was originally, a dummy or image made of straw; from this, a person compared to a straw image, a sham; a sham argument set up to be defeated.

A **straw poll** is an unofficial ballot conducted as a test of opinion. The term is recorded from the mid 20th century; the earlier **straw vote** dates (in the US) from 1866.

Strawberry Hill a house in Twickenham rebuilt after the Gothic style between 1750 and 1770 by Horace Walpole, which gave its name to an early phase of the Gothic revival inspired and epitomized by this house.

strawberry leaves the row of conventional figures of the leaf on the coronet of a duke, marquis, or earl.

straws in figurative phrases.

To **grasp at straws** is to be in such a desperate situation as to resort to even the most unlikely means of salvation. From the proverb, *a drowning man will clutch at a straw.*

The phrase **straws in one's hair** denotes a state of insanity, from the supposed characteristic practice of a deranged person; the first explicit reference to the expression is found in Lewis Carroll's description of the illustration by Tenniel of the ➤ MARCH *Hare* in *Alice in Wonderland.*

stream of consciousness a person's thoughts and conscious reactions to events, perceived as a continuous flow; a literary style in which a character's thoughts, feelings, and reactions are depicted in a continuous flow uninterrupted by objective description or conventional dialogue. The term was introduced by William James in his *Principles of Psychology* (1890)

streets paved with gold proverbial view of a city in which opportunities for advancement are easy; as in George Colman the Younger's *The Heir at Law* (1797).

strength through joy the promotion of physical and cultural recreational activities among working people, from the name of *Kraft durch Freude*, a movement founded in Germany by the National Socialist Party in 1933.

strike while the iron is hot make use of an opportunity immediately; proverbial, with reference to the process of working iron in a blacksmith's forge, when the metal can only be hammered into shape when it is hot.

Strine the English language as spoken by Australians; the Australian accent, especially when considered pronounced and uneducated. The name represents an alleged Australian pronunciation of *Australian*, coined by A. A. Morrison (1911–) in 1964.

string and sealing-wax (the type of) simple or unpretentious scientific equipment, with which great scientific discoveries may yet be made.

have a second string to one's bow have an alternative resource or course of action in case another one fails; a metaphor from shooting with a bow and arrow.

different strokes for different folks different things appeal to different people. Used as a slogan in the early 1970s in a Texan drug project.

strong meat something acceptable only to strong or instructed minds; often with biblical allusion to Hebrews 5:12.

strong verb a verb (of Germanic origin) forming the past tense and past participle by means of a change of vowel in the stem rather than by the addition of a suffix (e.g. *swim*, *swam*, *swum*).

strophe the first section of an ancient Greek choral ode or of one division of it; a turn in dancing made by an ancient Greek chorus. Recorded from the early 17th century, the word comes from Greek *strophē*, literally 'turning', from *strephein* 'to turn'. The term originally denoted a movement from right to left made by a Greek chorus, or lines of choral song recited during this.

Struldbrug in Swift's *Gulliver's Travels* (1726), given as the native appellation of 'the immortals' in the kingdom of Luggnagg, who were incapable of dying, but after the age of eighty continued to exist in a state of miserable decrepitude, regarded as legally dead, and receiving a small pittance from the state.

strut one's stuff dance or behave in a confident and expressive way, display one's ability.

Struwwelpeter a character in a collection of children's stories of the same name by Heinrich Hoffmann (1809–94), with long thick unkempt hair standing out from his head and extremely long fingernails; also known as *shock-headed Peter.*

Stuart the royal family (also called *Stewart*) ruling Scotland 1371–1714 and Britain 1603–1649 and 1660–1714. The name of the royal house comes ultimately from ➤ STEWARD, and the accession in 1371 to the throne of Scotland as Robert II of Robert the Steward, grandson of Robert the Bruce by Bruce's daughter Marjory and her husband Walter, Steward of Scotland.

in a brown study absorbed in one's thoughts; apparently originally from *brown* in the sense 'gloomy'.

stuffed owl referring to poetry which treats trivial or inconsequential subjects in a grandiose manner. The phrase comes from the title of Wyndham Lewis's *The Stuffed Owl: an anthology of bad verse* (1930), and ultimately alludes to Wordsworth's lines 'The presence even of a stuffed owl for her Can cheat the time.'

stumbling block a circumstance that causes difficulty or hesitation; especially with biblical allusion to Romans 14:13.

on the stump engaged in political campaigning; in rural America, the *stump* of a felled tree was used as an impromptu platform for an orator.

Stupor mundi Latin phrase meaning the marvel of the world, an object of admiring bewilderment and wonder; it was originally used by the 13th-century chronicler Matthew Paris to describe the Emperor Frederick II of Germany (1194–1250).

Sturm und Drang a literary and artistic movement in Germany in the late 18th century, influenced by ➤ *Jean-Jacques* ROUSSEAU and characterized by the expression of emotional unrest and a rejection of neoclassical literary norms. The phrase is German, and means literally 'Storm and Stress'.

Stygian of or relating to the River ➤ STYX or to the underworld of classical mythology; in extended usage, dark and gloomy.

stylite an ascetic living on top of a pillar, especially in ancient or medieval Syria, Turkey, and Greece in the 5th century AD. Recorded from the mid 17th century, the word comes ultimately from ecclesiastical Greek *stulos* 'pillar'.

Stymphalian birds in Greek mythology, harmful birds which infested *Stymphalus*, a district in Arcadia, and were destroyed by Hercules as the fifth of his twelve labours.

Styx in Greek mythology, one of the nine rivers in the underworld, over which ➤ CHARON ferried the souls of the dead, and by which the gods swore their most solemn oaths. It was into the Styx that his mother Thetis dipped the child ➤ ACHILLES to make his body invulnerable. The name comes from Greek *Stux*, from *stugnos* 'hateful, gloomy'.

sub rosa happening or done in secret; the phrase (recorded from the mid 17th century) is Latin, and means literally 'under the rose', taken as an emblem of secrecy.

be subdued to what one works in become reduced in capacity or ability to the standard of one's material, in allusion to Shakespeare's Sonnet 111.

subfusc the formal clothing worn for examinations and formal occasions at some universities; in poetic and literary use, *subfusc* as an adjective means 'dull, gloomy'. The

term, recorded from the early 18th century, comes from Latin *subfuscus*, from *sub-* 'somewhat' + *fuscus* 'dark brown'.

submerged tenth the supposed fraction of the population permanently living in poverty, implicitly contrasted with the ➤ UPPER *ten thousand*: the term was used by the Salvationist William Booth (1829–1912) in *In Darkest England* (1890).

subpoena a writ ordering a person to attend a court; originally, a writ issued by chancery ordering a person to answer a matter alleged against them. The word is recorded from late Middle English and comes from Latin *sub poena* ('under penalty'), the first words of the writ.

Act of Succession (in English history) each of three Acts of Parliament passed during the reign of Henry VIII regarding the succession of his children.

The first (1534) declared Henry's marriage to Catherine of Aragon to be invalid and disqualified their daughter Mary from succeeding to the throne, fixing the succession on any child born to Henry's new wife Anne Boleyn. The second (1536) cancelled this, asserting the rights of Jane Seymour and her issue, while the third (1544) determined the order of succession of Henry's three children, the future Edward VI, Mary I, and Elizabeth I.

Succoth a major Jewish festival held in the autumn (beginning on the 15th day of Tishri) to commemorate the sheltering of the Israelites in the wilderness. It is marked by the erection of small booths covered in natural materials. Also called *Feast of Tabernacles*.

succubus a female demon believed to have sexual intercourse with sleeping men; recorded from late Middle English, the word comes from medieval Latin *succubus* 'prostitute'.

sudarium in the Roman Catholic Church, a cloth supposedly impressed with an image of Christ's face, with which ➤ *St* VERONICA is said to have wiped his face on the way to Calvary. Recorded from the early 17th century, the word comes from Latin, literally 'napkin', from *sudor* 'sweat'.

Sudetenland an area in the north-west part of the Czech Republic, on the border with Germany. Allocated to Czechoslovakia after the First World War, it became an object of Nazi expansionist policies and was ceded to Germany as a result of the Munich Agreement of September 1938.

Sudra a member of the worker caste, lowest of the four Hindu castes.

Suetonius (*c*.69–*c*.150 AD) Roman biographer and historian. His surviving works include *Lives of the Caesars*, covering Julius Caesar and the Roman emperors who followed him, up to Domitian.

Suez Canal a shipping canal connecting the Mediterranean at Port Said with the Red Sea. It was constructed between 1859 and 1869 by Ferdinand de Lesseps. In 1875 it came under British control.

Its nationalization by Egypt in 1956 prompted the **Suez Crisis**, a short conflict in which Britain and France made a military alliance with Israel to regain control of the canal, but international criticism forced the withdrawal of forces.

suffragan an assistant or subsidiary bishop peforming episcopal functions in a certain diocese but having no jurisdiction; in the Church of England, a bishop appointed to help a diocesan bishop. The word is recorded from late Middle English, and comes ultimately from medieval Latin *suffraganeus* 'assistant bishop'.

suffragette a woman seeking the right to vote through organized protest; the term is recorded from 1906, in an account in the *Daily Mail* of 10 January of a meeting between 'Mr Balfour and the Suffragettes'.

The *suffragettes* were more formally members of the Women's Suffrage Movement, an organization which initiated a campaign of demonstrations and militant action, under the leadership of the Pankhursts, after the repeated defeat of women's suffrage bills in Parliament.

Sufi a Muslim ascetic and mystic. The word is recorded from the mid 17th century and comes from Arabic, perhaps ultimately from ṣūf 'wool', referring the the woollen garment worn by such a person.

Sufism the mystical system of the Sufis, the esoteric dimension of the Islamic faith, the spiritual path to mystical union with God. It is influenced by other faiths, such as Buddhism, and reached its peak in the 13th century. There are many Sufi orders, the best-known being the dervishes.

Sui a dynasty which ruled in China AD 581–618 and reunified the country, preparing the ground for the cultural flowering of the succeeding Tang dynasty.

suicide the action of killing oneself intentionally; a person who does this. The term is recorded from the mid 17th century, and comes ultimately from Latin *sui* 'of oneself' and *caedere* 'kill'.

In Christian theology, suicide is regarded as a sin; it was also formerly a criminal act in the UK (see ➤ FELO *de se*). A person who had killed themselves was regarded as someone whose ghost might walk; there was a traditional belief that this could be averted by a stake through the heart, or by the body's being buried at a crossroads. Suicides were also buried at the north side of a churchyard.

suit informal term for a high-ranking executive in a business or organization, typically one regarded as exercising influence in an impersonal way.

suit the action to the word carry out one's stated intentions. With allusion to Hamlet's instructions to the actors in Shakespeare's *Hamlet*.

Suleiman the Magnificent name given to Suleiman I (*c*.1494–1566), sultan of the Ottoman Empire 1520–66; also known as **Suleiman the Lawgiver**. The Ottoman Empire reached its fullest extent under his rule; his conquests included Belgrade (1521), Rhodes (1522), and Tripoli (1551), in addition to those in Iraq (1534) and Hungary (1562). He was also a noted administrator and patron of the arts.

sultan a Muslim sovereign; **the Sultan** was the title given to the sultan of Turkey. The word is recorded in English from the mid 16th century, and comes (via French or medieval Latin) from Arabic sulṭān 'power, ruler'.

Sumer an ancient region of SW Asia in present-day Iraq, comprising the southern part of Mesopotamia. From the 4th millennium BC it was the site of city states which became part of ancient Babylonia.

The **Sumerians**, an indigenous non-Semitic people of the region, had the oldest known written language, whose relationship to any other language is unclear. Theirs is the first historically attested civilization and they invented cuneiform writing, and the sexagesimal system of mathematics, and the socio-political institution of the city state with bureaucracies, legal codes, division of labour, and a form of currency.

summer the warmest season of the year, in the northern hemisphere from June to August and in the southern hemisphere from December to February. Recorded from Old

English (in form *sumor*), the word is of Germanic origin, and is ultimately related to Sanskrit *samā* 'year'.

The **Summer Palace** was a palace (now in ruins) of the former Chinese emperors near Beijing.

The **summer solstice** is the occasion of the longest day in the year, when the sun reaches its greatest altitude north of the equator, on approximately 21 June (or in the southern hemisphere, south of the equator, on approximately 21 December).

Summer time is time as adjusted to achieve longer evening daylight in summer by setting clocks an hour ahead of the standard time; originally introduced in the UK in 1916, from 21 May to 30 September, and subsequently adopted for ➤ DAYLIGHT *saving* from March to October. The principle of adjusting clocks in this way was suggested first by Benjamin Franklin in an essay of 1784; the notion of daylight saving was the originator of the English builder William Willett (1856–1915).

sumpsimus a correct expression taking the place of an incorrect but popular one. The word comes from Latin, and means 'we have taken' (see ➤ MUMPSIMUS).

sumptuary relating to or denoting laws that limit private expenditure on food and personal items. The word is recorded from the early 17th century, and comes ultimately from Latin *sumptus* 'cost, expenditure' from *sumere* 'take'.

sun the star round which the earth orbits and from which it receives light and warmth; it is the central body of the solar system and provides the light and energy that sustains life on earth, and its changing position relative to the earth's axis determines the terrestrial seasons.

In the ancient and medieval world, it was believed (in accordance with the ➤ PTOLEMAIC *system*) that the earth is the stationary centre of the universe. The heliocentric theory was proposed by the Polish astronomer ➤ COPERNICUS (1473–1543) in *De Revolutionibus Orbium Coelestium* (1543), and later supported by ➤ GALILEO (1564–1642); although he was forced to recant by the Inquisition, the theory continued to gain ground.

The sun has been an object of worship in a number of religions, and has thus been personified as a male being, sometimes identified with a particular god, especially ➤ APOLLO, who in classical mythology was believed to drive his chariot across the sky.

Proverbially the sun is a type of brightness and clearness, and in literary and poetic usage often stands for a person or thing regarded as a source of glory, inspiration, or understanding; the word may also be used with reference to someone's success or prosperity.

Recorded from Old English (in form *sunne*), the word is of Germanic origin, and comes ultimately from an Indo-European root shared by Greek *hēlios* and Latin *sol*.

In heraldry, a **sun in splendour** is the sun as heraldically blazoned, depicted with rays and often a human face; it was an emblem of the ➤ *House of* YORK.

The **Sun King** is a designation of Louis XIV of France, a translation of French ➤ ROI *soleil*.

The **Sun of Righteousness** is an epithet of Jesus Christ, after Malachi 4:2.

Originally in nautical usage, **when the sun is over the yardarm** meant the time of day (noon) when it is permissible to begin drinking; the earlier variant **when the sun is over the foreyard** dates from the mid, and this from the late, 19th century.

sunbelt a strip of territory receiving a high amount of sunshine, especially the southern US from California to Florida.

Sunday the day of the week before Monday and following Saturday, observed by Christians as a day of rest and religious worship and (together with Saturday) forming part of the weekend. Recorded in Old English as *Sunnandæg* 'day of the sun', the name is a translation of Latin *dies solis*.

A **Sunday school** is a class held on Sundays to teach children about Christianity; such schools are now intended only for religious instruction, but originally also taught some secular subjects.

Sunday's child is a child born on Sunday, traditionally greatly blessed or favoured; the belief is the culmination of the traditional rhyme *Monday's child is fair of face*.

Sunflower State informal name for Kansas.

Sung a dynasty that ruled in China AD 960–1279. The period was marked by the first use of paper money and by advances in printing, firearms, shipbuilding, clockmaking, and medicine. Also **Song**.

Sunna the traditional portion of Muslim law based on Muhammad's words or acts, accepted (together with the Koran) as authoritative by Muslims and followed particularly by ➤ Sunni Muslims. The word is Arabic, and means literally 'form, way, course, rule'.

Sunni one of the two main branches of Islam, commonly described as orthodox, and differing from ➤ Shia in its understanding of the ➤ Sunna and in its acceptance of the first three caliphs. The word is Arabic, and means literally, 'custom, normative rule'.

Sunningdale agreement an agreement negotiated on 9 December 1973 by the British and Irish governments and representatives of Northern Irish political parties following the suspension of the Stormont parliament in 1972. The initiative foundered in the strike subsequently called by the Ulster Workers' Council, and the agreement was never ratified.

Sunset Boulevard a road which links the centre of Los Angeles with the Pacific Ocean 48 km (30 miles) to the west. The eastern section of the road between Fairfax Avenue and Beverly Hills is known as **Sunset Strip**.

Sunshine State any of the states of New Mexico, South Dakota, California, and Florida.

sunyata in Buddhism, the doctrine that phenomena are devoid of an immutable or determinate intrinsic nature. It is often regarded as a means of gaining an intuition of ultimate reality. The word comes from Sanskrit śūnyatā 'emptiness'.

Super Bowl (in the US) the National Football League championship game played annually between the champions of the National and the American Football Conferences; the title is after ➤ Rose *Bowl*.

Super Tuesday in the US, a day on which several states hold primary elections for the presidential nominations.

Superman a US cartoon character having great strength, the ability to fly, and other extraordinary powers, who conceals his true nature behind the identity of mild-mannered reporter Clark Kent. Superman was created in 1938 in a comic strip by writer Jerry Siegel (1914–96) and artist Joe Shuster (1914–92).

superman in philosophy, the ideal superior man of the future; the term in English originally a translation of German *Übermensch* in the philosophy of Nietzsche (1844–1900).

Act of Supremacy (in English history) either of two Acts of Parliament of 1534 and 1559 (particularly the former), which established Henry VIII and Elizabeth I as supreme heads of the Church of England and excluded the authority of the Pope. The term is used particularly with reference to the Act of 1534.

supreme sacrifice the laying down of one's life for one's country; the term is particularly associated with the First World War.

sura a chapter or section of the Koran.

surf the net move from site to site on the ➤ Internet, an expression recorded from the first half of the 1990s. The usage probably comes from *channel-surfing*, the activity of switching between channels on a television set to see what is available.

surgical instruments the emblem of ➤ St Luke, and of St Cosmas and St Damian, martyrs of the early Church said in a late legend to have been twin brothers who were doctors.

surplice a loose white linen vestment varying from hip-length to calf-length, worn over a cassock by clergy and choristers at Christian church services. The word is recorded from Middle English, and comes via Old French from medieval Latin *superpellicium*, from *super-* 'above' + *pellicia* 'fur garment'.

surrealism a 20th-century avant-garde movement in art and literature which sought to release the creative potential of the unconscious mind, for example by the irrational juxtaposition of images. Launched in 1924 by a manifesto of André Breton and having a strong political content, the movement grew out of symbolism and Dada and was strongly influenced by Sigmund Freud.

Sursum corda in Latin Eucharistic liturgies, the words addressed by the celebrant to the congregation at the beginning of the Eucharistic Prayer; in English rites, the corresponding versicle, 'Lift up your hearts'.

Surtsey a small island to the south of Iceland, formed by a volcanic eruption in 1963, and named for the fire-giant *Surtr* of Scandinavian mythology, who at ➤ Ragnarök will lead the forces of evil from the east to do battle with the gods.

survival of the fittest the continued existence of organisms which are best adapted to their environment, with the extinction of others, as a concept in the Darwinian theory of evolution. The phrase was coined by the

English philosopher and sociologist Herbert Spencer (1820–1903), in *Principles of Biology* (1865).

Surya the sun god of later Hindu mythology, originally one of several solar deities in the Vedic religion. The name comes from Sanskrit *sūrya* 'sun'.

Susanna in the Apocrypha, a woman of Babylon falsely accused of adultery by two Elders but saved by the sagacity of ➤ DANIEL, who questioned the accusers and demonstrated that their accounts were contradictory, in particular in the name of the tree under which she was alleged to have met her lover. The story of Susanna is told in the Apocryphal book of this name.

Sutlej a river of northern India and Pakistan which rises in the Himalayas in SW Tibet. It is one of the five rivers that gave ➤ PUNJAB its name.

sutra a rule or aphorism in Sanskrit literature, or a set of these on grammar or Hindu law or philosophy; also, a Buddhist or Jainist scripture. The word comes from Sanskrit *sūtra* 'thread, rule', from *siv* 'sew'.

suttee the former Hindu practice of a widow immolating herself on her husband's funeral pyre; a widow who committed such an act. The word, which is Hindi, comes from Sanskrit *satī* 'faithful wife', from *sat* 'good'.

Sutton Hoo the site in Suffolk of a Saxon ship burial of the 7th century AD, containing magnificent grave goods including jewellery, decorated weapons, and gold coins, which are now in the British Museum.

Svadilfari in Scandinavian mythology, the horse belonging to a giant who agreed to build a wall around ➤ ASGARD for the gods; if he completed his work within the stated time, the goddess Freya, and the sun and moon, would be his reward. When it appeared he would succeed, ➤ LOKI delayed the work by changing himself into a mare and decoying *Svadilfari* away. Odin's magic horse ➤ SLEIPNIR was born of their union.

Svengali a person who exercises a controlling or mesmeric influence on another, especially for a sinister purpose, from the name of a musician in George du Maurier's novel *Trilby* (1894) who trains ➤ TRILBY's voice and controls her stage singing hypnotically; his influence over her is such that when he dies her voice collapses and she loses her eminence.

swallow popularly regarded as a harbinger of summer, and taken as a type of swift movement.

In classical mythology, a *swallow* was one of the birds (the other was a nightingale) into which Procne and her sister Philomel were turned.

One swallow does not make a summer means that what follows will also be good; proverbial saying, mid 16th century, earlier in Greek as 'one swallow does not make a spring'.

swan swans have numerous legendary associations, including the story in Irish mythology that the ➤ *Children of* LIR were changed into swans by enchantment, and the Finnish belief that the swan sings once before it dies. In classical mythology the swan was sacred to Apollo and to Venus (occasionally, as by Shakespeare, also ascribed to Juno).

In reference to its pure white plumage and graceful appearance, the *swan* is often taken as a type of faultlessness or excellence.

A swan is the emblem of ➤ St HUGH *of Lincoln*.

In Norse and Germanic folk tales, a **swan maiden** is a girl who has the power of transforming herself into a swan by means of a dress of swan's feathers or of a magic ring or chain.

The **Swan of Avon** is a name for Shakespeare, deriving from Ben Jonson's 'Sweet Swan of Avon!' in his poem 'To the Memory of My Beloved, the Author, Mr William Shakespeare' (1623).

Swan-upping is the action or practice of 'upping' or taking up swans and marking them with nicks on the beak in token of being owned by the crown or some corporation.

swansong a song fabled to be sung by a dying swan, originally as translating German *Schwangen(ge)sang*; in extended usage, a person's final public performance or professional activity.

swashbuckle engage in daring and romantic adventures with ostentatious bravado or flamboyance; a **swashbuckler** was originally a person who made a noise by striking his own or his opponent's shield with his sword.

swastika an ancient symbol in the form of an equal-armed cross with each arm continued at a right angle, used (in clockwise form) as the emblem of the German Nazi party. The word is recorded in English from the late 19th century, and comes ultimately from Sanskrit *svasti* 'well-being'.

swear like a trooper swear a great deal. A *trooper* was originally (mid 17th century) a private soldier in a cavalry unit, and from the mid 18th century was proverbial for coarse behaviour and bad language.

by the sweat of one's brow by one's own hard work, typically manual labour; often with allusion to God's sentence on Adam after the Fall, 'In the sweat of thy face shalt thou eat bread' (Genesis 3:19).

Swedenborgian an adherent or follower of Emanuel *Swedenborg* (1688–1772), Swedish scientist, philosopher, and mystic. The spiritual beliefs which he expounded after a series of mystical experiences blended Christianity with pantheism and theosophy. His followers founded the New Jerusalem Church in 1787.

Sweeney Todd legendary barber who murdered his customers, the central character of a play by George Dibdin Pitt (1799–1855) and of later plays; from the mid 1930s, *Sweeney* was used by rhyming slang as a name for the Flying Squad. The original *Sweeney Todd* was said to kill his victims by cutting their throats while they sat waiting to be shaved; the bodies were then disposed of through a trapdoor and made into sausages.

sweepstake a form of gambling, especially on horse races, in which all the stakes are divided among the winners; the word originally (from the late 14th century) meant someone who 'sweeps', or takes the whole of, stakes in a game; in figurative usage, someone who took or appropriated everything. From the 15th to the 17th century, *Sweepstake* was often used as a ship's name.

From the late 18th century, the word meant a prize won in a race or contest in which the whole of the stakes contributed by the competitors were taken by the winner or a limited number of them; the current meaning developed from this.

sweetness and light social or political harmony; a phrase taken from originally Swift in his preface to *The Battle of the Books* (1704). The term was taken up and used with aesthetic or moral reference, initially by Matthew Arnold in *Culture and Anarchy* (1869).

swing a style of jazz or dance music with an easy flowing but vigorous rhythm; the term is recorded from the end of the 19th century.

Captain Swing the fictitious instigator of a system of intimidation practised in agricultural districts of the South of England in 1830–1, consisting in sending to farmers and landowners threatening letters over the signature of 'Captain Swing', followed by the incendiary destruction of their ricks and other property.

swing the lead malinger, shirk one's duty; originally, with nautical allusion to the lump of lead suspended by a string, slowly lowered to ascertain the depth of water.

Swiss guard Swiss mercenaries employed as a special guard, formerly by sovereigns of France, now only at the Vatican. They have been the pope's personal guard since 1506 (many of them were killed during the sack of Rome in 1527 by Spanish troops).

St Swithin (d. 862), English ecclesiastic. He was bishop of Winchester from 852. The tradition that if it rains on St Swithin's Day it will do so for the next forty days may have its origin in the heavy rain said to have occurred when his relics were to be transferred to a shrine in Winchester cathedral. His feast day is 15 July.

sword taken as a symbol of warfare and massacre, as in Matthew 10:34.

A *sword* is also the emblem of ➤ St Paul[1] and many other saints executed by a sword.

He who lives by the sword dies by the sword means that the weapon on which your success is based will in the end be the means of your downfall. Proverbial saying, ultimately with biblical allusion to Matthew 26:52 'All they that take the sword shall perish with the sword.'

Sword-and-sorcery is a genre of fiction characterized by heroic adventures and elements of fantasy; the related term *sword-and-sandal*, centring on this form of fiction set in the ancient world, is also recorded.

In classical mythology, the **sword of Damocles** was the sword suspended over the head of ➤ Damocles.

The **Sword of State** is a sword borne before the sovereign on State occasions.

In the Bible, **the sword of the Lord and of Gideon** was the battle-cry of ➤ GIDEON in his attack on the Midianites and Amalekites (Judges 7:20).

See also *Sword of Stalingrad* at ➤ *Battle of* STALINGRAD.

beat swords into ploughshares devote resources to peaceful rather than warlike ends; with biblical allusion to Isaiah 2:4 and Micah 4:3.

sybarite a person who is self-indulgent in their fondness for sensuous luxury. Originally (in the mid 16th century) the word denoted an inhabitant of *Sybaris*, an ancient Greek city in southern Italy, noted for luxury.

sycophant a person who acts obsequiously towards someone in order to gain advantage; a servile flatterer. The term is recorded from the mid 16th century, as denoting an informer, especially in ancient Athens; Plutarch suggests that the Greek word *sukophantēs* 'informer' derives from *sukon* 'fig', and refers to the practice of informing against the illegal exportation of figs, but this is not substantiated. The current sense is recorded from the late 16th century.

Sydney Opera House a striking building at Sydney harbour the roof of which is composed of huge white shapes resembling sails or shells. Designed by the Danish architect Jōrn Utzon (1918–), it was opened in 1973.

Sydney or the bush Australian expression meaning all or nothing; originally, it was used in the context of someone who gambled on the prospect of making a fortune which would bring with it an easy urban life; failure meant that work would have to be sought in the outback.

syllogism an instance of a form of reasoning in which a conclusion is drawn (whether validly or not) from two given or assumed propositions (premises) that each share a term with the conclusion, and that share a common or middle term not present in the conclusion (e.g. *all dogs are animals; all animals have four legs; therefore all dogs have four legs*).

sylph a member of a race of beings or spirits supposed to inhabit the air (originally in the system of ➤ PARACELSUS); the word is recorded from the mid 17th century, coming from modern Latin *sylphes, sylphi*, and the German plural *Sylphen*, and may ultimately be based on Latin *sylvestris* 'of the woods' + *nympha* 'nymph'. From the mid 19th century,

the term has been applied to a slender and graceful woman or girl.

sylvan in classical mythology, an imaginary being believed to haunt woods or groves; a spirit of the woods.

Sylvester Eve New Year's Eve, from St *Sylvester* (d. 335), Pope from 314 to 335; his feast-day is 31 December.

symbol originally (in late Middle English), *symbol* denoted a formal authoritative statement or summary of the religious belief of the Christian Church, in particular, the ➤ APOSTLES' *Creed*. This use is first found in the writing of Cyprian, bishop of Carthage (*c*.250), who used Latin *symbolum* for the baptismal Creed, this Creed being the mark or sign of a Christian as distinguished from a heathen.

The current meaning, a thing that represents or stands for something else, especially a material object representing something abstract, is recorded from the late 16th century.

The word comes via Latin *symbolum* 'symbol, Creed' from Greek *sumbolon* 'mark, token'.

Symbolism an artistic and poetic movement or style using symbolic images and indirect suggestion to express mystical ideas, emotions, and states of mind. It originated in late 19th century France and Belgium, with important figures including Mallarmé, Maeterlinck, Verlaine, Rimbaud, and Redon.

symposium originally (in the late 16th century) a drinking party or convivial discussion, especially as held in ancient Greece after a banquet (and notable as the title of a work by Plato); the word comes ultimately from Greek *sumpotēs* 'fellow drinker'.

From the late 18th century, the word has been used to denote a conference or meeting to discuss a particular subject, and from the mid 20th century, a publication consisting of essays or papers on a given subject by a number of contributors.

synagogue the regular assembly of Jews for religious observance and instruction; a building or place of worship for this purpose. The word is recorded from Middle English and comes via Old French and late Latin from Greek *sunagōgē* 'meeting'.

In religious controversy from the Middle Ages, the word was given derogatory use as a term for an assembly of the wicked or heretical; in medieval iconography, *Synagogue* may be shown as a blindfolded figure contrasted with the sighted *Church*.

synod an assembly of the clergy of a particular Church, nation, province, or diocese, sometimes with representatives of the laity, duly convened for discussing and deciding ecclesiastical affairs. The term is recorded from late Middle English, and comes via late Latin from Greek *sunodos* 'meeting'.

synonym a word or phrase that means exactly or nearly the same as another word or phrase in the same language, for example *shut* is a synonym of *close*.

Synoptic Gospels the Gospels of Matthew, Mark, and Luke, which give an account of the events from a similar point of view, as contrasted with that of John.

The **Synoptic problem** is the question of the relationship between these Gospels. The general view is that Mark is the earlier text and that Matthew and Luke draw on it; it is widely thought that they also had access to a hypothetical source (▸ Q), from which comes the material which is not in Mark. An alternative explanation is that Luke's Gospel was written from a knowledge of both Mark and Matthew.

syntax the arrangement of words and phrases to create well-formed sentences in a language. Recorded from the late 16th century, the word comes via French or late Latin from Greek *suntaxis*, from *sun-* 'together' + *tassein* 'arrange'.

syphilis a chronic bacterial disease that is contracted chiefly by infection during sexual intercourse, but also congenitally by infection of a developing fetus. The word is recorded in English from the early 18th century, and is modern Latin, originally from the title of a poem, *Syphilis, sive Morbus Gallicus*, published 1530 by Girolamo Frastoro or Hieronymus Fracastorius (1483–1553), a physician, astronomer, and poet of Verona; it was translated by Nahum Tate in 1686 with the title 'Syphilis: or, a Poetical History of the French Disease'. The illness was known from the early 16th century as the *great pox*, to distinguish it from *smallpox*.

Syphilis was used as the name of the disease in the poem itself; the subject is the shepherd 'Syphilus', the first sufferer from the illness. (The ultimate origin of his name is disputed; it has been suggested that it is a corrupt medieval form of *Sipylus*, a son of ▸ NIOBE.)

Syrinx in Greek mythology, the name of a nymph loved by Pan, who was changed into a reed in order to escape him; the set of pan pipes created by him were named *syrinx* for her.

all systems go everything functioning properly, so ready to proceed; originally used especially of the systems on a spacecraft.

Tt

T the twentieth letter of the modern English alphabet and the nineteenth of the ancient Roman one, corresponding to Greek *tau*, Hebrew *taw*.

To a T means exactly, to perfection. Recorded from the late 17th century, this idiom may reflect the idea of completing the letter T by putting in the cross-stroke. However, an earlier expression in the same sense was *to a title*, so T may be an abbreviation. Attempts to link it with a golfer's tee or a builder's T-square are unconvincing.

pick up the tab pay for something (chiefly North American); used literally in the sense of picking up a bill or account that has been presented to one, as after a restaurant meal, with the intention of paying it, but also used figuratively of taking financial responsibility for something.

tabard a coarse sleeveless jerkin consisting only of front and back pieces with a hole for the head as the outer dress of medieval peasants and clerics, or worn as a surcoat over armour; a herald's official coat emblazoned with the arms of the sovereign.

The **Tabard Inn** in Chaucer's *Canterbury Tales* is the inn in Southwark at which the pilgrims meet before setting out for Canterbury.

tabernacle in biblical use, a fixed or movable habitation, typically of light construction; a tent used as a sanctuary for the Ark of the Covenant by the Israelites during the Exodus and until the building of the Temple. The word is recorded from Middle English, and comes via French from Latin *tabernaculum* 'tent', diminutive of *taberna* 'hut, tavern'.

From the late 15th century, the term has also been used to denote an ornamented receptacle or cabinet in which a pyx containing the reserved sacrament may be placed in Catholic churches, usually on or above an altar.

The **Feast of Tabernacles** is another name for ➤ SUCCOTH.

Tabitha in the Bible (Acts 9:36:42), name of the charitable woman at Joppa who was raised from the dead by Peter. *Tabitha* is the Aramaic form of the Greek *Dorcas*, and means 'gazelle'.

turn the tables reverse one's position relative to someone else, especially by turning a position of disadvantage into one of advantage. Until the mid 18th century, *tables* was the usual name for the boardgame backgammon, and early (mid 17th-century) uses of the phrase make it clear that it comes from the turning of the board so that a player has to play the opponent's position.

taboo a social or religious custom prohibiting or restricting a particular practice or forbidding association with a particular person, place, or thing. The word comes (in the late 18th century) from Tongan *tabu* 'set apart, forbidden', and was introduced into English by Captain Cook in *A Voyage to the Pacific Ocean* (1784).

Tacitus (*c.*56–*c.*120 AD), Roman historian. His *Annals* (covering the years 14–68) and *Histories* (69–96) are major works on the history of the Roman Empire.

Taegu a city in SE South Korea, nearby to which is the Haeinsa temple, established in AD 802, which contains 80,000 Buddhist printing blocks dating from the 13th century, engraved with compilations of Buddhist scriptures.

Taffy a mid-17th century term (informal, and often offensive) for a Welshman, representing a supposed Welsh pronunciation of the given name *Davy* or *David* (Welsh *Dafydd*).

tag a brief and usually familiar quotation added for special effect; a much used quotation or stock phrase. The word in this sense is recorded from the early 18th century.

Tages name of an Etruscan god, a boy with the face of a wise old man who sprang originally from the ploughed fields and who is said to have taught the Etruscans how to predict the future.

the tail wags the dog the less important or subsidiary factor or thing dominates a situation; the usual or expectable roles are reversed.

Tain-Bo-Cuailgne the 'Cattle Raid of Cooley', the chief epic of the Ulster cycle of Irish mythology, the story of the raid of Queen Maeve of Connaught to secure the Brown Bull of Cuailgne (pronounced 'Cooley'), and her defeat by ➤ CUCHULAIN.

Taiping Rebellion a sustained uprising against the Qing dynasty in China 1850–64. The rebellion was led by Hong Xinquan (1814–64), who had founded a religious group inspired by elements of Christian theology and proposing egalitarian social policies. His large army captured Nanjing in 1853 but was eventually defeated at Shanghai at the hands of an army trained by the British general Charles Gordon. The rebellion was finally defeated after the recapture of Nanjing, some 20 million people having been killed, but the Qing dynasty was severely weakened as a result. The name comes from Chinese *T'ai-p'ing-wang* 'Prince of great peace', a title given to Hong Xinquan.

Taj Mahal a mausoleum at Agra built by the Mogul emperor Shah Jahan (1592–1666) in memory of his favourite wife, completed *c.*1649. Set in formal gardens, the domed building in white marble is reflected in a pool flanked by cypresses.

a tale of a tub an apocryphal story; mid 16th century. The phrase was used as the title of a comedy (1633) by Ben Jonson, and then in 1696 (published 1704) as the title of a prose satire by Swift; the allusion was to Hobbes's *Leviathan* and its criticism of contemporary religion and government.

talent originally (in Old English, in the form *talente, talentan*) this denoted an ancient unit of weight, especially one used by the Athenians and Romans, equivalent to nearly 57 lb (26 kg), or such a weight of silver or (occasionally) gold used to represent a sum of money.

The **parable of the talents** (Matthew 25:14–30) tells the story of a wealthy man who, before going on a journey, gave each of his servants a certain number of talents. According to the story, the man who had received five talents and the man who had received two doubled them by trading, but the man who had been given one talent buried it for safety. When their master returned he commended those who had increased their talents as good and faithful, but the man who buried his was condemned as wicked and slothful, and ordered to hand over his one talent to the man who had ten.

From this parable, *talent* in late Middle English came to mean a person's mental ability or particular faculty regarded as something divinely entrusted to them for their use and improvement; this developed (in the early 17th century) to the current sense of natural aptitude or skill.

The **Administration of All the Talents** was an ironical name for the ministry of Lord Grenville (1806–7), implying that it combined all possible talents in its members; the term is recorded from 1807.

Taliban a fundamentalist Muslim movement which in 1996 set up an Islamic state in Afghanistan. The Taliban were overthrown in 2001 by US-led forces and Afghan groups following the terrorist attacks of 11 September. The name comes from Pashto or Dari, from Persian, literally 'students, seekers of knowledge'.

Taliesin a British bard of the 6th century, perhaps a mythic personage, first mentioned in the *Saxon Genealogies* appended to the *Historia Britonum* (*c.*690).

talisman an object, typically an inscribed ring or stone, that is thought to have magic powers and to bring good luck. The word is recorded from the mid 17th century, and is based on Arabic *tilsam*, apparently from an alteration of late Greek *telesma* 'completion, religious rite'.

tall poppy syndrome a perceived tendency to discredit or disparage those who have achieved notable wealth or prominence in public life; with allusion to the idea of the ➤ POPPY as a flower whose showy appearance does not represent real worth.

tally a current score or amount; the original meaning (in late Middle English) was a stick or rod of wood scored across with notches for the items of an account; it was customary for the debtor and creditor to split the piece of wood in half lengthways through the notches, each party keeping one piece. The word comes via Anglo-Norman French from Latin *talea* 'twig, cutting'.

tally-ho a huntsman's cry to the hounds on sighting a fox. The term is recorded from the late 18th century; it is apparently an alteration of French *taïaut*, of unknown origin.

Talmud the body of Jewish civil and ceremonial law and legend comprising the Mishnah and the Gemara. There are two versions of the Talmud: the Babylonian Talmud (which dates from the 5th century AD but includes earlier material) and the earlier Palestinian or Jerusalem Talmud.

The **Talmud Torah** is the field of study that deals with the Jewish law.

Tam o' Shanter the hero of Robert Burns's poem of that name, a Scottish farmer who on his way home from an alehouse comes across witches dancing, and is chased by them; the name *tam o'shanter* is used for a round woollen or cloth cap of Scottish origin, with a bobble in the centre, of a kind formerly worn by Scottish ploughmen.

Tamerlane (1336–1405), Mongol ruler of Samarkand 1369–1405; Tartar name *Timur Lenk* ('lame Timur'). Leading a force of Mongols and Turks, he conquered Persia, northern India, and Syria and established his capital at Samarkand; he was the ancestor of the Mogul dynasty in India. He is also known as *Tamburlaine*, the spelling used by Marlowe in *Tamburlaine the Great* (1590).

From the late 16th century, *Tamerlane* has been referred to as the type of a savage conqueror or despot.

Tammany Hall in the US, a powerful organization within the Democratic Party that was widely associated with corruption. Founded as a fraternal and benevolent society in 1789, it came to dominate political life in New York City in the 19th and early 20th centuries, before being reduced in power by Franklin D. Roosevelt in the early 1930s.

Tammuz a Mesopotamian god, lover of Ishtar and similar in some respects to the Greek Adonis. He became the personification of the seasonal death and rebirth of crops.

Tanagra an ancient Greek city in Boeotia, site of a battle in 457 BC during the Peloponnesian War. It has given its name to a type of terracotta figurine, often of a young woman, made there and elsewhere mainly in the 4th and 3rd centuries BC.

Tang a dynasty ruling China 618–c.906, a period noted for territorial conquest and great wealth and regarded as the golden age of Chinese poetry and art.

a tangled web a complex, difficult, or confusing situation or thing. Originaly as a quotation from Sir Walter Scott's *Marmion* (1808).

it takes two to tango both parties involved in a situation or argument are equally responsible for it. *Takes Two to Tango* was the

title of a song by Hoffman and Manning (1952), and the expression is now proverbial.

tanist the heir apparent to a Celtic chief, typically the most vigorous adult of his kin, elected during the chief's lifetime. The word comes (in the mid 16th century) from Irish, Scottish Gaelic *tánaiste*, literally 'second in excellence'.

A **tanist stone** is any of a number of large monoliths in Scotland, popularly supposed to mark the spot where tanists were elected.

tanner former informal name for a silver sixpence; recorded from the early 19th century, but of unknown origin.

Tannhäuser (*c.*1200–*c.*1270), German poet. In reality a Minnesinger whose works included lyrics and love poetry, he became a legendary figure as a knight who visited Venus's grotto (see ➤ VENUSBERG) and spent seven years in debauchery, then repented and sought absolution from the Pope.

Tantalus in Greek mythology, a Lydian king, son of Zeus and father of Pelops. For his crimes (which included killing Pelops) he was punished by being provided with fruit and water which receded when he reached for them. His name is the origin of the word *tantalize*.

tantony pig the smallest pig of a litter; a pig here is the emblem of ➤ St ANTHONY *of Egypt*, who is represented as the patron of swineherds, and often shown accompanied by a pig. *Tantony* is from an alteration of the saint's name.

tantra a Hindu or Buddhist mystical or magical text, dating from the 7th century or earlier. The word is Sanskrit, and means literally 'loom, groundwork, doctrine', from *tan* 'stretch'.

Tao in Chinese philosophy, the absolute principle underlying the universe, combining within itself the principles of yin and yang and signifying the way, or code of behaviour, that is in harmony with the natural order. The interpretation of Tao in the Tao-te-Ching developed into the philosophical religion of Taoism.

The **Tao-te-Ching** is the central Taoist text, ascribed to Lao-tzu, the traditional founder of Taoism. Apparently written as a guide for rulers, it defined the Tao, or way, and established the philosophical basis of Taoism.

Taoism a Chinese philosophy based on the writings of Lao-tzu, advocating humility and religious piety. The central concept and goal is the Tao, and its most important text is the Tao-te-Ching. Taoism has both a philosophical and a religious aspect. Philosophical Taoism emphasizes inner contemplation and mystical union with nature; wisdom, learning, and purposive action should be abandoned in favour of simplicity and *wu-wei* (non-action, or letting things take their natural course). The religious aspect of Taoism developed later, *c.*3rd century AD, incorporating certain Buddhist features and developing a monastic system.

have something taped understand a person or situation fully. Recorded from the early 20th century, and perhaps referring either to the idea of measuring or 'sizing up' a person with a measuring tape, or tying someone up with tape, and thus getting them under control.

tar and feather smear with tar and then cover with feathers as a punishment, a practice originally imposed by an ordinance of Richard I in 1189 as a punishment in the navy for theft. In 18th-century America in particular, the punishment was sometimes inflicted by the mob on an unpopular or scandalous character.

tar baby a difficult problem which is only aggravated by attempts to solve it, with allusion to the doll smeared with tar as a trap for ➤ *Brer* RABBIT, in J. C. Harris's *Uncle Remus* (1880).

Tar Heel State informal name for North Carolina, with allusion to tar as a principal product of that state.

Tara a hill in County Meath in the Republic of Ireland, site in early times of the residence of the high kings of Ireland and still marked by ancient earthworks.

tarantella a rapid whirling dance originating in southern Italy. The word comes (in the late 18th century) from Italian, from the name of the seaport *Taranto*; so named because it was thought to be a cure for ➤ TARANTISM, the victim dancing the tarantella until exhausted.

tarantism a psychological illness characterized by an extreme impulse to dance, prevalent in southern Italy from the 15th to the 17th century, and widely believed at the time to have been caused by the bite of a *tarantula*, a large black wolf spider of southern Europe.

Tardis the time machine, resembling a police box, of the science fiction hero ➤ *Doctor* WHO.

Targum an ancient Aramaic paraphrase or interpretation of the Hebrew Bible, of a type made from about the 1st century AD when Hebrew was ceasing to be a spoken language.

the Tarot playing cards, traditionally a pack of 78 with five suits, used for fortune telling and (especially in Europe) in certain games. The suits are typically swords, cups, coins (or pentacles), batons (or wands), and a permanent suit of trumps. The name is recorded from the late 16th century, and comes via French from Italian *tarocchi*; the ultimate origin is unknown.

Tarpeia in Roman mythology, one of the Vestal Virgins, the daughter of a commander of the Capitol in ancient Rome. According to legend she betrayed the citadel to the Sabines in return for whatever they wore on their arms, hoping to receive their golden bracelets; however, the Sabines killed her by throwing their shields on to her.

The **Tarpeian Rock** was a cliff in ancient Rome, at the south-western corner of the Capitoline Hill, named for *Tarpeia*, over which murderers and traitors were hurled.

Tarquinius the name of the semi-legendary Etruscan kings of ancient Rome; anglicized name *Tarquin*. **Tarquinius Superbus**, 'Tarquin the Proud', reigned *c.*534–510 BC. Noted for his cruelty, he was expelled from the city after his son's rape of ➤ LUCRETIA, and the Republic was founded. He repeatedly, but unsuccessfully, attacked Rome, assisted by ➤ *Lars* PORSENA.

Tarsus an ancient city in southern Turkey, the capital of Cilicia and the birthplace of ➤ *St* PAUL[1], originally known as **Saul of Tarsus**.

tartan a woollen cloth woven in one of several patterns of coloured checks and intersecting lines, especially of a design associated with a particular Scottish clan. (The attribution of particular designs is comparatively modern, dating from around 1800.)

Recorded from the late 15th century, the word may come from Old French *tertaine*, denoting a kind of cloth; compare with *tartarin*, a rich fabric formerly imported from the east through Tartary.

Tartar a member of the combined forces of central Asian peoples, including Mongols

and Turks, who under the leadership of
➤ GENGHIS *Khan* conquered much of Asia
and eastern Europe in the early 13th century,
and under Tamerlane (14th century) established an empire with its capital at Samarkand.

Tartarus a part of the underworld where
the wicked suffered punishment for their
misdeeds, especially those such as ➤ IXION
and ➤ TANTALUS who had committed some
outrage against the gods.

Tartary a historical region of Asia and eastern Europe, especially the high plateau of
central Asia and its NW slopes, which
formed part of the Tartar empire in the Middle Ages.

Tartuffe a religious hypocrite, or a hypocritical pretender to excellence of any kind,
from the name of the principal character (a
religious hypocrite) in Molière's *Tartuffe*
(1664).

Tarzan a fictitious character created by
Edgar Rice Burroughs. Tarzan (Lord
Greystoke by birth) is orphaned in West Africa in his infancy and reared by apes in the
jungle; he is noted for his agility and powerful physique (typified by the image of his
swinging himself through the trees, or at the
end of a liana stem), and for his yodelling
call.

In the late 1980s and 1990s, *Tarzan* was
used by the popular press as a nickname for
the Conservative politician Michael
Heseltine (1933–).

Abel Tasman (1603–*c*.1659), Dutch navigator. Sent in 1642 by the Governor General of
the Dutch East Indies, Anthony van Diemen
(1593–1645), to explore Australian waters, he
reached Tasmania (which he named Van
Diemen's Land) and New Zealand, and in
1643 arrived at Tonga and Fiji.

Tass the official news agency of the former
Soviet Union, renamed ITAR-Tass in 1992.

Tate Gallery a national museum of art at
Millbank, London, founded in 1897 by the
sugar manufacturer Sir Henry *Tate* (1819–99)
to house his collection of modern British
paintings, as a nucleus for a permanent national collection of modern art. In the 20th
century modern foreign paintings and sculpture (both British and foreign) were added.

Tattersalls an English firm of horse auc-
tioneers founded in 1776 by the horseman
Richard *Tattersall* (1724–95), originally sited at
Hyde Park Corner.

tau the nineteenth letter of the Greek alphabet. It was sometimes used in the sense 'last
letter', as *tau* was originally in Greek.
The word is also used for the ➤ ANKH of ancient Egyptian symbolism.

A **tau cross** is a T-shaped cross, both as a
sacred symbol and in heraldry; it is the emblem of ➤ St ANTHONY *of Egypt*.

Taurus in astronomy, a constellation (the
Bull), said to represent a bull with brazen
feet that was tamed by Jason. In astrology,
Taurus is the second sign of the zodiac,
which the sun enters on about 21 April.

tautology the saying of the same thing
twice over in different words, generally considered to be a fault of style (e.g. *they arrived
one after the other in succession*).

tawdry showy but cheap and of poor quality. Recorded from the early 17th century, the
word is short for *tawdry lace*, a fine silk lace or
ribbon worn as a necklace in the 16th–17th
cents, contraction of *St Audrey's lace: Audrey*
was a later form of ➤ St ETHELDREDA (died
679), patron saint of Ely where tawdry laces,
along with cheap imitations and other cheap
finery, were traditionally sold at a fair.

Te Deum a Latin hymn beginning *Te Deum
laudamus*, 'We praise Thee, O God', sung at
matins or on special occasions such as a
thanksgiving.

tea and sympathy kind and attentive behaviour towards someone who is upset or in
trouble; the phrase was used as a film title in
1956.

not for all the tea in China there is nothing at all that could induce one to do something; an emphatic expression recorded
from the mid 20th century.

Teapot Dome the name of a naval oil reserve in Wyoming, irregularly leased by the
US government in 1922, and referred to allusively in connection with the resulting political scandal.

teddy bear a soft toy bear; the *teddy bear*
came into vogue about 1907, and was so
called in humorous allusion to ➤ *Theodore*
ROOSEVELT (US President 1901–9), whose
bear-hunting expeditions occasioned a celebrated comic poem, accompanied by cartoons, in the *New York Times* of 7 January 1906,
concerning the adventures of two bears
named 'Teddy B' and 'Teddy G'. These names
were transferred to two bears (also known as
the 'Roosevelt bears') presented to Bronx Zoo
in the same year; finally the fame of these

bears was turned to advantage by toy dealers, whose toy 'Roosevelt bears', imported from Germany, became an instant fashion in the US.

A **teddy bears' picnic** is an occasion of innocent enjoyment; from the title of a song (*c.*1932) by Jimmy Kennedy and J. W. Bratton.

Teddy boy (in the 1950s) a young man of a subculture characterized by a style of dress based on Edwardian fashion (typically with drainpipe trousers, bootlace tie, and hair slicked up in a quiff) and a liking for rock-and-roll music.

teetotum a small spinning top spun with the fingers, especially one with four sides lettered to determine whether the spinner has won or lost.

telamon a male figure used as a pillar to support an entablature or other structure, from the name of *Telamon*, a hero of Greek mythology, king of Salamis and father of ➤ AJAX and ➤ TEUCER.

Telemachus in Greek mythology, the son of ➤ ODYSSEUS and ➤ PENELOPE, who grows up while his father is away, and is guided and advised by Athena in the guise of ➤ MENTOR. When Odysseus returns, Telemachus assists him in defending their house against Penelope's suitors.

telepathy the supposed communication of thoughts or ideas by means other than the known senses; the term was coined in the late 19th century by the poet and essayist Frederic William Henry Myers (1843–1901), who in 1882 became one of the founding members of the Society for Psychical Research.

televangelist chiefly in the US, an evangelical preacher who appears regularly on television to promote beliefs and appeal for funds.

temenos a piece of ground surrounding or adjacent to a temple; a sacred enclosure or precinct. The word is recorded from the early 19th century, and comes from Greek, from the stem of *temnein* 'cut off'.

Téméraire an English battleship, named after a captured French ship (the word in French means 'bold' or 'rash'), which was built in 1798. She took part in the battle of Trafalgar (1805), where she was the second ship of the line, closely following the Victory; her share in the action was considered notable. The *Téméraire* was broken up in 1838; her final journey was the subject of one of Turner's most famous paintings, *The Fighting Téméraire* (1838), and of a poem by Newbolt.

tempera a method of painting with pigments dispersed in an emulsion miscible with water, typically egg yolk. The method was used in Europe for fine painting, mainly on wood panels, from the 12th or early 13th century until the 15th, when it began to give way to oils.

tempest-tossed thrown violently about (as) by a tempest; originally used with allusion to Shakespeare's *Romeo and Juliet* and *Macbeth*. In the 19th century, the phrase was used by the American poet Emma Lazarus in the lines inscribed on the ➤ Statue of LIBERTY.

Templar a member of the ➤ KNIGHTS *Templars*.

temple a building devoted to the worship, or regarded as the dwelling place, of a god or gods or other objects of religious reverence. The word is recorded from Old English (in form *temp(e)l*), and was reinforced in Middle English by Old French *temple*; both come from Latin *templum* 'open or consecrated ground'.

The Temple is the name given to either of two successive religious buildings of the Jews in Jerusalem. The first (957–586 BC) was built by Solomon and destroyed by Nebuchadnezzar; it contained the Ark of the Covenant. The second (515 BC–AD 70) was enlarged by Herod the Great from 20 BC and destroyed by the Romans during a Jewish revolt; all that remains is the Wailing Wall. Also called **Temple of Solomon**.

A group of buildings in Fleet Street, London, which stand on land formerly occupied by the headquarters of the Knights Templars is also known as **the Temple**; the Inner Temple and the Outer Temple, two of the ➤ INNS *of Court*, are located there.

Temple Bar is the name of the barrier or gateway closing the entrance into the City of London from the Strand; removed in 1878. Heads of those executed for treason were traditionally exposed there.

temporal power the power of a bishop or cleric, especially the Pope, in secular matters.

the Temptation the tempting of Jesus by the Devil, as told in Matthew 4, when Jesus was challenged to demonstrate his miraculous powers, firstly in the wilderness by turning stones into bread, and then in the holy city, by flinging himself from a pinnacle of the temple. Lastly he was taken up into a high mountain and shown the kingdoms of the world, all of which he was promised if he would worship the Devil.

The expression is also used to refer to the tempting of certain medieval saints, as in the **Temptation of St Anthony**, in which demons in the form of beautiful women tried to tempt the hermit ➤ St ANTHONY *of Egypt*; this was a favourite subject of early paintings.

ten a cardinal number equivalent to the product of five and two; one more than nine. Recorded from Old English (in form *tēn*, *tīen*) and of Germanic origin, the word comes ultimately from an Indo-European root shared by Latin *decem*.

In the Bible, the **Ten Commandments** were the divine rules of conduct given by God to Moses on Mount Sinai, according to Exodus 20:1–17. The commandments are generally enumerated as: have no other gods; do not make or worship idols; do not take the name of the Lord in vain; keep the sabbath holy; honour one's father and mother; do not kill; do not commit adultery; do not steal; do not give false evidence; do not covet another's property or wife.

The **ten-minute rule** is a rule of the House of Commons allowing brief discussion of a motion to introduce a bill, each speech being limited to ten minutes; the standing order imposing this limitation was passed in 1888.

The **ten persecutions** were persecutions of the early Church, as enumerated by 5th-century writers; ➤ OROSIUS popularized the idea of ten Roman emperors as persecutors, namely Nero, Domitian, Trajan, Marcus Aurelius, Septimius Severus, Maximinus Thrax, Decius, Valerian, Aurelian, and Diocletian, although in fact treatment of Christians in the different reigns varied widely.

tender passion romantic love; the term dates from the late 18th century and is first recorded in Sheridan's *Duenna* (1775).

tenderloin in the US, informal name for a district of a city where vice and corruption are prominent. Recorded from the late 19th century, the name was originally a term applied to a district of New York, seen as a 'choice' assignment by police because of the bribes offered to them to turn a blind eye to criminal activity.

La Tène the second cultural phase of the European Iron Age, following the Halstatt period (*c.*480 BC) and lasting until the coming of the Romans. This culture represents the height of Celtic power, being characterized by hill forts, rich and elaborate burials, and distinctively crafted artefacts.

The name is recorded from the late 19th century, and comes from the name of a district in Switzerland, where remains of the culture were first identified.

Tenebrae in the Roman Catholic Church, matins and lauds for the last three days of Holy Week, at which candles are successively extinguished, in memory of the darkness at the Crucifixion. Several composers have set parts of the office to music. The word is Latin, and means literally 'darkness'.

Tenochtitlán the ancient capital of the Aztec empire, founded *c.*1320. In 1521 the Spanish conquistador Cortés, having deposed the Aztec emperor Montezuma and overthrown his empire, destroyed it and established Mexico City on its site.

on tenterhooks in a state of suspense or agitation because of uncertainty about a future event; a *tenterhook* was originally a hook used to fasten cloth on a drying frame or *tenter*.

the tenth Muse a person or thing considered to be a source of inspiration comparable to one of the mythological Muses, especially in a particular field; the term is recorded from the early 17th century, in one of Shakespeare's *Sonnets*, and was used in 1650 by the poet Anne Bradstreet (1612–72) in the title of her collection of poems.

Teotihuacán the largest city of pre-Columbian America, situated about 40 km (25 miles) north-east of Mexico City. Built *c.*300 BC, it reached its zenith *c.*300–600 AD, when it was the centre of an influential culture which spread throughout Meso-America.

teratology mythology relating to fantastic creatures and monsters. The term is recorded from the late 17th century, and comes from Greek *teras*, *terat-* 'monster'.

terce a service forming part of the Divine Office of the Western Christian Church, traditionally said (or chanted) at the third hour of the day (i.e. 9 a.m.). The word is recorded from late Middle English, and comes via Old French from Latin *tertia*, feminine of *tertius* 'third'.

Terence (*c.*190–159 BC), Roman comic dramatist. His six surviving comedies are based on the Greek New Comedy; they use the same stock characters as are found in Plautus, but are marked by more realism and a greater consistency of plot.

Teresa female forename, name of two saints.

St Teresa of Ávila (1515–82) was a Spanish Carmelite nun and mystic, who combined vigorous activity as a reformer with mysticism and religious contemplation. She instituted the 'discalced' reform movement with St John of the Cross, establishing the first of a number of convents in 1562. In 1970 she became the first woman to be declared a ➤ DOCTOR *of the Church*. Her emblems are a fiery arrow or a dove above her head, and her feast day is 15 October.

St Teresa of Lisieux (1873–97), was a French Carmelite nun. Her cult grew through the publication of her autobiography *L'Histoire d'une âme* (1898) in which she taught that sanctity can be attained through continual renunciation in small matters, and not only through extreme self-mortification. She is represented in her Carmelite habit and holding roses, as a sign of her promise to 'let fall a shower of roses' of miracles and other favours. Her feast day is 3 October.

termagant a harsh-tempered or overbearing woman; originally (in the early 13th century) the name of an imaginary deity held in medieval Christendom to be worshipped by Muslims: in the mystery plays represented as a violent overbearing personage. In ➤ LAYAMON's *Brut*, the name is used for the gods of the Romans and the heathen Saxons.

the Terminator the deadly robot who in the film *Terminator* (1984) and its sequel is sent back from the future to find and kill the humans who are destined to provide the leadership for human resistance to the 21st-century computer Skynet.

terminator gene in a genetically modified crop, a gene which ensures that nothing can be grown from the seeds of a plant; the commercial development of such a gene has been one of the points of dispute in this debate.

terminological inexactitude a humorous euphemism for a lie, first used by Winston Churchill in a Commons speech in 1906.

terminus in ancient Rome, a boundary marker consisting of a figure of a human bust or an animal ending in a square pillar from which it appears to spring. *Terminus* was

originally the name of the deity who presided over boundaries and landmarks.

Terpsichore in Roman mythology, the Muse of lyric poetry and dance.

terra firma dry land; the ground as distinct from the sea or air. Recorded from the early 17th century, the phrase denoted originally the territories on the Italian mainland which were subject to the state of Venice.

terra incognita unknown or unexplored territory; the term is first recorded in John Smith's *Description of New England* (1616), in a reference to the supposed southern continent (➤ AUSTRALIA).

Terrapin State an informal name for Maryland.

the Terror the period of the French Revolution between mid 1793 and July 1794 when the ruling Jacobin faction, dominated by Maximilien Robespierre (1758–94), ruthlessly executed anyone considered a threat to their regime; it ended with the fall and execution of Robespierre.

tertiary a lay associate of certain Christian monastic organizations, as of the Franciscan ➤ THIRD *Order*.

Tertullian (*c*.160–*c*.240), early Christian theologian. His writings include Christian apologetics and attacks on pagan idolatry and Gnosticism. He later joined the Montanists, urging asceticism and venerating martyrs.

Test Act in the UK, an act in force between 1673 and 1828 that made an oath of allegiance to the Church of England and the supremacy of the monarch as its head and repudiation of the doctrine of transubstantiation a condition of eligibility for public office.

Test Act also designates an act of 1871 relaxing restrictions on university entrance for candidates who were not members of the Church of England.

Test-Ban Treaty an international agreement not to test nuclear weapons in the atmosphere, in space, or under water, signed in 1963 by the US, the UK, and the USSR, and later by more than 100 governments.

test match an international cricket or rugby match, typically one of a series, played between teams representing two different countries; the term is first recorded in an account of five cricket *test matches* played between England and Australia in the season of 1861–2.

testudo in ancient Rome, a screen on wheels and with an arched roof, used to protect besieging troops; a protective screen formed by a body of troops holding their shields above their heads in such a way that the shields overlap. Recorded from late Middle English, the word is Latin, and means literally 'tortoise', from *testa* 'tile, shell'.

Tet the Vietnamese lunar New Year. In the Vietnam War, the **Tet offensive** was launched in January–February 1968 by the Vietcong and the North Vietnamese army. Timed to coincide with the first day of the Tet, it was a surprise attack on South Vietnamese cities, notably Saigon. Although repulsed after initial successes, the attack shook US confidence and hastened the withdrawal of its forces.

Tethys in Greek mythology, a goddess of the sea, daughter of ➤ URANUS (Heaven) and ➤ GAIA (Earth), and consort of ➤ OCEANUS.
In astronomy, *Tethys* was the name given to a satellite of Saturn, the ninth closest to the planet and probably composed mainly of ice, discovered by Cassini in 1684. In geology, it is the name of an ocean formerly separating the supercontinents of Gondwana and Laurasia, the forerunner of the present-day Mediterranean.

Tetragrammaton the Hebrew name of God transliterated in four letters as *YHWH* or *JHVH* and articulated as *Yahweh* or *Jehovah*. The word is Greek, the neuter of *tetragrammatos* 'having four letters'.

tetramorph in painting or sculpture, the representation of the iconographical symbols of the four evangelists.

tetrarch in the Roman Empire, the governor of one of four divisions of a country or province; later, more generally, a subordinate ruler.

Teucer in Greek mythology, the legendary ancestor of the Trojan kings through his daughter, the wife of Dardanus.
Teucer is also the name of the son of Telamon and half-brother of Ajax, who fought as an archer with the Greeks at the siege of Troy.

Teuton a member of a people who lived in Jutland in the 4th century BC and fought the Romans in France in the 2nd century BC; from the mid 19th century, the term was used generally to denote Germanic-speaking races and peoples.

Teutonic Knights a military and religious order of German knights, priests, and lay brothers, originally enrolled *c.*1191 as the **Teutonic Knights of St Mary of Jerusalem**. They took part in the Crusades from a base in Palestine until expelled from the Holy Land in 1225. Abolished by Napoleon in 1809, the order was re-established in Vienna as an honorary ecclesiastical institution in 1834 and maintains a titular existence.

Texas Ranger a member of the Texas State police force (formerly, of certain locally mustered regiments in the federal service during the Mexican War).

Thaddaeus an apostle named in Matthew 10:3 who is traditionally identified with ➤ *St* JUDE.

Thais Athenian courtesan who is said to have caused Alexander the Great to set fire to ➤ PERSEPOLIS.

thalassa in Greek, the sea. In ➤ XENOPHON's account of the war between Artaxerxes II of Persia and his younger brother Cyrus, he relates how retreating Greek soldiers of the defeated Cyrus fought their way through the Armenian mountains and finally reached the Black Sea; when they first saw the sea, they cried out, '*thalassa, thalassa!*'

Thales (*c.*624–*c.*545 BC), Greek philosopher, mathematician, and astronomer, living at Miletus. One of the ➤ SEVEN *Sages* listed by Plato and judged by Aristotle to be the founder of physical science, he is also credited with founding geometry. He proposed that water was the primary substance from which all things were derived.

Thalestris name of a legendary queen of the Amazons, who is said to have met Alexander the Great on the border of India.

Thalia in Greek mythology, the Muse of comedy and idyllic poetry; in classical mythology, she is also one of the three Graces. The name is Greek, and means literally 'rich, plentiful'.

thalidomide a drug formerly used as a sedative, but withdrawn in the UK in the early 1960s after it was found to cause congenital malformation or absence of limbs in children whose mothers took the drug during early pregnancy.

Father Thames in literary use, the personification of the *Thames*, a river of southern England, flowing eastwards from Gloucestershire through London to the North Sea (see also *set the Thames on fire* at ➤ FIRE).

Thammuz (in the Jewish calendar) the tenth month of the civil and fourth of the religious year, usually coinciding with parts of June and July. Also called *Tammuz*.

Thanatos in Greek mythology, the god of Death, brother of Hypnos (Sleep); in Freudian theory, *Thanatos* is used for the death instinct (often contrasted with ➤ EROS).

thane in Anglo-Saxon England, a man who held land granted by the king or by a military nobleman, ranking between an ordinary freeman and a hereditary noble (see also ➤ THEGN); in Scotland, a man, often the chief of a clan, who held land from a Scottish king and ranked with an earl's son.

General Thanksgiving a form of thanksgiving in the *Book of Common Prayer*.

Thanksgiving Day (in North America) an annual national holiday marked by religious observances and a traditional meal including turkey. The holiday commemorates a harvest festival celebrated by the ➤ PILGRIM *Fathers* in 1621, and is held in the US on the fourth Thursday in November. A similar holiday is held in Canada, usually on the second Monday in October.

Thebes¹ the Greek name for an ancient city of Upper Egypt, whose ruins are situated on the Nile about 675 km (420 miles) south of Cairo. It was the capital of ancient Egypt under the 18th dynasty (*c*.1550–1290 BC) and is the site of the major temples of Luxor and Karnak. Its monuments (on both banks of the Nile) were the richest in the land, with the town on the east bank and the necropolis, with tombs of royalty and nobles, on the west bank. It was already a tourist attraction in the 2nd century AD.

The **Theban Legion** was a Roman legion recruited near Thebes in Egypt and composed solely of Christians; with their leader, the soldier saint ➤ St MAURICE, they are said to have been massacred *c*.287 when during an expedition against the Gauls, the emperor Maximian commanded his army to sacrifice to the gods for success. When the Theban Legion refused to obey, they were first decimated, and then massacred.

Thebes² a city in Greece, in Boeotia, northwest of Athens, traditionally founded by ➤ CADMUS and the seat of the legendary king ➤ OEDIPUS. Thebes became a major military power in Greece following the defeat of the Spartans at the battle of Leuctra in 371 BC. It was destroyed by Alexander the Great in 336 BC.

The Greek poet ➤ PINDAR (*c*.518–*c*.438 BC) was born in Thebes, and from this is known as the **Theban bard** and the **Theban eagle**.

thegn an English thane. The word is a modern representation of Old English *theg(e)n*, adopted to distinguish the Old English use of ➤ THANE from the Scots use made familiar by Shakespeare in *Macbeth*.

theism belief in the existence of a god or gods, especially belief in one god as creator of the universe, intervening in it and sustaining a personal relation to his creatures. The word is recorded from the late 17th century, and comes from Greek *theos* 'god'.

Themis in Greek mythology, a goddess, daughter of ➤ URANUS (Heaven) and ➤ GAIA (Earth). In Homer she was the personification of order and justice, who convened the assembly of the gods.

Themistocles (*c*.528–462 BC), Athenian statesman, who helped build up the Athenian fleet (see ➤ WOODEN *walls*), and defeated the Persian fleet at Salamis in 480. He was ostracized in 470, and eventually fled to the Persians in Asia Minor.

Theodora (*c*.500–48), Byzantine empress, wife of ➤ JUSTINIAN, said to have been an actress, and the daughter of a bearkeeper. As Justinian's closest adviser, she exercised a considerable influence on political affairs and the theological questions of the time. She is depicted in the mosaics of the church of San Vitale at Ravenna.

Theodoric (*c*.454–526), king of the Ostrogoths 471–526; known as **Theodoric the Great**. At its greatest extent his empire included Italy, which he invaded in 488 and conquered by 493, Sicily, Dalmatia, and parts of Germany. He established his capital at Ravenna.

Theodosius I (*c*.346–95), Roman emperor 379–95, known as **Theodosius the Great**. Proclaimed co-emperor by the Emperor Gratian in 379, he took control of the Eastern Empire and ended the war with the Visigoths. A pious Christian, in 391 he banned all forms of pagan worship.

theological virtues the three virtues of faith, hope, and charity, as enumerated in 1 Corinthians 13:13. They were traditionally distinguished from the cardinal virtues of Plato and classical philosophers (see ➤ CARDINAL²), and were particularly studied by ➤ St THOMAS *Aquinas* and the schoolmen.

theosophy any of a number of philosophies maintaining that a knowledge of God may be achieved through spiritual ecstasy, direct intuition, or special individual relations, especially the movement founded in 1875 as the Theosophical Society by Helena Blavatsky (1831–91) and Henry Steel Olcott (1832–1907), following Hindu and Buddhist teachings and seeking universal brotherhood.

Theotokos Mother of God (used in the Eastern Orthodox Church as a title of the Virgin Mary); the word is ecclesiastical Greek, and comes from *theos* 'god' + *-tokos* 'bringing forth'.

Theravada the more conservative of the two major traditions of Buddhism (the other being Mahayana), which developed from Hinayana Buddhism. It is practised mainly in Sri Lanka, Burma (Myanmar), Thailand, Cambodia, and Laos.

theriac archaic name for an ointment or other medicinal compound used as an antidote to snake venom or other poison. The word is recorded from late Middle English, and comes from Latin *theriaca*, from the Greek base of ➤ TREACLE.

It was traditionally believed that the flesh of a viper was a necessary ingredient of the antidote to its venom, as recorded in Topsell's *History of Serpents* (1608).

Thermidor the eleventh month of the French Republican calendar (1793–1805), originally running from 19 July to 17 August. Also, a reaction of moderates following a revolution, such as that which occurred in Paris on 9 Thermidor (27 July 1794) and resulted in the fall of Robespierre. The name is French, and comes from Greek *thermē* 'heat' + *dōron* 'gift'.

laws of thermodynamics laws describing the general direction of physical change in the universe; the **first law of thermodynamics** states the equivalence of heat and

work and reaffirms the principle of conservation of energy; the **second law of thermodynamics** states that heat does not of itself pass from a cooler to a hotter body (another, equivalent formulation of the second law is that the entropy of a closed system can only increase); the **third law of thermodynamics** states that it is impossible to reduce the temperature of a system to absolute zero in a finite number of operations.

Thermopylae a pass between the mountains and the sea in Greece, about 200 km (120 miles) north-west of Athens, originally narrow but now much widened by the recession of the sea. In 480 BC it was the scene of the defence against the Persian army of Xerxes I by 6,000 Greeks; among them were 300 Spartans, all of whom, including their king ➤ LEONIDAS, were killed.

The pass was the traditional invasion route from northern Greece and was subsequently used by the Gauls in 279 BC and by Cato the Elder in 191 BC.

Thersites a member of the Greek forces at the siege of Troy, noted for his scurrilous and backbiting tongue; he was killed by ➤ ACHILLES after Thersites had jeered at him for mourning the death of the Amazon queen ➤ PENTHESILEA.

thesaurus originally, a dictionary or encyclopedia; after the publication of ➤ ROGET's *Thesaurus*, the meaning narrowed to its current sense of a book that lists words in groups of synonyms and related concepts. Recorded in English from the late 16th century, the word comes via Latin from Greek *thēsauros* 'storehouse, treasure'.

Theseus in Greek mythology, the legendary hero of Athens, son of Poseidon (or, in another account, of Aegeus, king of Athens) and husband of ➤ PHAEDRA.

Aegeus had left the child Theseus and his mother at her father's court in Troezen, with the instruction that when the boy was old enough to lift a certain rock, he was to come to Athens with the sword and sandals he would find beneath it; it was on this journey that he encountered and killed such bandits as ➤ PROCRUSTES and ➤ SINIS.

At Athens, he became one of the boys and girls sent as tribute to Crete; there he slew the Cretan ➤ MINOTAUR with the help of ➤ ARIADNE, and returned to Athens. Forgetting an earlier agreement with his father, he did not change his ship's sails from black to white in token of success, and Aegeus is said to have killed himself in despair on seeing the black-sailed ship. Theseus became king of Athens; his many subsequent adventures (often in the company of ➤ HERCULES) included the capture of the Amazon queen ➤ HIPPOLYTA.

Thespis (6th century BC), Greek dramatic poet, regarded as the founder of Greek tragedy; Aristotle named him the originator of the role of the actor in addition to the traditional chorus. His name gives rise to the word *thespian*.

Epistle to the Thessalonians either of two books of the New Testament, the earliest letters of St Paul, written from Corinth to the new Church at Thessalonica.

theta the eighth letter of the Greek alphabet (Θ, θ), transliterated as 'th'. In ancient Greece, on the ballots used in voting upon a sentence of life or death, this character stood for *thanatos* 'death', which gave rise to allusive uses.

Thetis in Greek mythology, a sea nymph, mother of ➤ ACHILLES.

Thetis was also the name of the Royal Navy submarine lost in Liverpool Bay, 1 June 1939, on her first dive; only four of her crew escaped. The cause of the accident has never been fully explained.

Good Thief a traditional name for the penitent thief, ➤ St DISMAS.

the thin red line the British army (in reference to the traditional scarlet uniform); the phrase first occurs in the war correspondent William Howard Russell's book *The British Expedition to the Crimea* (1877) of the Russians charging the British at Balaclava. Russell's original dispatch to *The Times*, 14 November 1854, had read 'That thin red streak topped with a line of steel'. In an alteration of the phrase, the police are sometimes referred to as **the thin blue line**.

Thing in Scandinavian countries or settlements: a public meeting or assembly, especially, a legislative council, a parliament, a court of law.

things that go bump in the night supernatural beings, ghosts. A humorous way of referring to the supernatural, originally as a quotation from *The Cornish or West-Country Litany*, recorded from the early 20th century.

third constituting number three in a sequence.

The **third estate** is the common people as part of a country's political system. The first two estates were formerly represented by the clergy, and the barons and knights; later the Lords spiritual and the Lords temporal.

In Hinduism and Buddhism, the **third eye** is the 'eye of insight' in the forehead of an image of a deity, especially the god Shiva.

The **third man** is an unidentified third participant in a crime; the phrase in this sense derives from the screenplay (1949) by Graham Greene, later filmed by Carol Reed, in which the plot centres on the doings of this shadowy figure. After the flight in 1951 of the Soviet agents Guy Burgess and Donald Maclean to Moscow, the phrase was used in connection with the third party (later demonstrated to be Kim Philby) who was thought to have warned them.

The 3rd of May is an informal name for Goya's picture 'The 3rd of May 1808: The Execution of the Defenders of Madrid', painted to commemorate the execution by the French of Spanish insurgents against the invading Napoleonic forces; it later influenced Manet's depiction of the execution of the Emperor Maximilian of Mexico (1832–67).

The **Third Order** is an order for lay members retaining the secular life and not subject to the strict rule of the regular orders, originated by St Francis of Assisi and now established among Franciscans, Dominicans, and others.

In the US, a **third rail** is a subject, especially Social Security, considered by politicians too dangerous to modify or discuss; literally, an additional rail supplying electric current as used in some electric railway systems.

The **Third Reich** was the Nazi regime, 1933–45, considered as succeeding the Holy Roman Empire (962–1806) and the German Empire (1871–1918) as the previous periods of empire (see ➤ REICH). The name, which is a translation of German *drittes Reich*, is recorded in English from 1930, in an interview in *The Times* of 26 September 1930 with Hitler.

In politics, a **third way** is a middle way between conventional right- and left-wing ideologies or policies; an ideology founded on political centrism or neutrality. In the 1990s the *third way* became identified with the political programmes of centre-left parties in Western Europe and North America, characterized by both market-driven economic policy and a concern for social justice; in this context it is conceived of as an alternative to, rather than a compromise between, conventional right- and left-wing ideologies, and in the UK has been particularly associated with the premiership of Tony Blair.

The **Third World** is the developing countries of Asia, Africa, and Latin America. The phrase was first applied in the 1950s by French commentators who used *tiers monde* to distinguish the developing countries from the capitalist and Communist blocs.

thirteen one more than twelve. The number *thirteen* has been widely regarded as unlucky; there is a traditional belief that if thirteen people sit down to table, the first to get up will die. This may go back to the ➤ LAST *Supper*, at which Jesus, sitting at table with the twelve disciples, told them that one of them (Judas) would betray him.

The **Thirteen Colonies** were the British colonies that ratified the Declaration of Independence in 1776 and thereby became founding states of the US. They were Connecticut, Delaware, Georgia, Maryland, Massachusetts, New Hampshire, New Jersey, New York, North Carolina, Pennsylvania, Rhode Island, South Carolina, and Virginia.

thirty the number equivalent to the product of three and ten, ten less than forty.

The **Thirty-nine Articles** are a series of points of doctrine historically accepted as representing the teaching of the Church of England. Adopted in 1571, the Articles often allow a wide variety of interpretation.

Thirty pieces of silver was the price for which ➤ JUDAS betrayed Jesus to the Jewish authorities, as told in Matthew 26:15; Judas is subsequently said to have repented, and to have thrown down the money in the temple before killing himself. Because it was regarded as blood money it could not be returned to the treasury; it was therefore used to purchase the ➤ POTTER's *field*.

Thirty-something is an unspecified age between thirty and forty; the term was widely publicized by the successful US television series *Thirtysomething* which from 1987 recounted the ups and downs and family lives of a group who had reached their thirties in the 1980s.

The **Thirty Tyrants** were the magistrates imposed by Sparta on Athens at the end of the Peloponnesian War; their repressive rule was ended when Critias, leader of the oligarchy, was killed, and democracy restored.

The **Thirty Years War** was a European war of 1618–48 which broke out between the Catholic Holy Roman emperor and some of his German Protestant states and developed into a struggle for continental hegemony with France, Sweden, Spain, and the Holy Roman Empire as the major protagonists. It was ended by the Treaty of Westphalia.

Thisbe in Roman mythology, a Babylonian girl, lover of ➤ PYRAMUS.

thistle the Scottish national emblem; the **Order of the Thistle** is the highest order of Scottish knighthood, instituted by James II in 1687 and revived by Queen Anne in 1703.

In biblical use, *thistle* is also generally used as the type of an unrewarding crop, as in God's words to Adam (Genesis 3:17–18).

Thomas male forename, and name of several saints.

St Thomas was an an Apostle, known as **Doubting Thomas**. He earned his nickname by saying that he would not believe that Christ had risen again until he had seen and touched his wounds (John 20:24–9). According to tradition he preached in SW India. A non-canonical gospel of Thomas, found in a Coptic text, is apparently a Gnostic work. His feast day is 21 December.

Thomas à Kempis (*c.*1380–1471), was a German theologian. An Augustinian canon in Holland, he is the probable author of *On the Imitation of Christ* (*c.*1415–24), a manual of spiritual devotion.

St Thomas Aquinas (1225–74), was an Italian philosopher, theologian, and Dominican friar; known as *the Angelic Doctor*. He is regarded as the greatest figure of scholasticism; one of his most important achievements was the introduction of the work of Aristotle to Christian western Europe. His works include commentaries on Aristotle as well as the *Summa Contra Gentiles*, intended as a manual for missionaries, and *Summa Theologiae*, the greatest achievement of medieval systematic theology. He also devised the official Roman Catholic tenets as declared by Pope Leo XIII. His feast day is 28 January. **Thomism** is the theology of ➤ St THOMAS *Aquinas* or of his followers.

See also ➤ *St Thomas à* BECKET.

Thor in Scandinavian mythology, the god of thunder, the weather, agriculture, and the home, the son of Odin and Freya (Frigga). He is represented as armed with a hammer. Thursday is named after him.

thorn an Old English and Icelandic runic letter, þ or Þ. It was eventually superseded by the digraph *th*, but has been used as a phonetic symbol for the voiceless dental fricative.

thorn in the flesh a constant affliction, a source of continual trouble and annoyance; often with biblical allusion to 2 Corinthians

12:7. The phrase **thorn in the side** is also frequently used.

Thoth in Egyptian mythology, a moon god, the god of wisdom, justice, and writing, patron of the sciences, and messenger of Ra, identified by the Greeks with Hermes. He is most often represented in human form with the head of an ibis surmounted by the moon's disc and crescent.

Thousand and One Nights another name for the ➤ ARABIAN *Nights*.

Thousand-Year Reich the German ➤ THIRD *Reich* (1933–45), as a regime envisaged by the Nazis as established for an indefinite period.

thread of life in classical mythology, the extent of a person's life, as spun, measured, and cut off by the ➤ FATES.

Threadneedle Street a street in the City of London containing the premises of the Bank of England, which is also known as the ➤ OLD *Lady of Threadneedle Street*. *Threadneedle* here comes from *three-needle*, possibly from a tavern with the arms of the city of London Guild of Needlemakers.

three equivalent to the sum of one and two; one more than two.

Three acres and a cow were regarded as the requirement for self-sufficiency; as a political slogan associated with the radical politician Jesse Collings (1831–1920) and his land reform campaign begun in 1885. Collings used the phrase in the House of Commons, 26 January 1886; it had also been used earlier by Joseph Chamberlain.

In Greek mythology, the **Three Graces** were three beautiful goddesses (Aglaia, Thalia, and Euphrosyne), daughters of Zeus. They were believed to personify and bestow charm, grace, and beauty.

The **Three Kings** are the ➤ MAGI, who came from the East to worship the new-born Christ. They are also known as **The Three Kings of Cologne**, from a prevalent belief that their bodies were preserved at that city, having been removed thither in 1164 from Milan, where they were alleged to have been discovered in 1158.

Three Mile Island is an island in the Susquehanna River near Harrisburg, Pennsylvania, site of a nuclear power station. In 1979 an accident caused damage to the reactor core, provoking strong reactions against the nuclear industry in the US.

The **three-mile limit** is the limit of territorial waters for Britain, America, and other states.

In Dumas' novel *Les Trois Mousquetaires* (1844), Athos, Porthos, and Aramis, are the **Three Musketeers** who befriend the young ➤ D'ARTAGNAN, and assist him in defeating the scheming agent of Cardinal Richelieu; in extended use, the phrase means three close associates.

The **three R's** are reading, writing, and (a)rithmetic; a phrase said to have originated in a toast by Sir William Curtis (1752–1829).

Three sheets in the wind means, very drunk; a *sheet* is a rope or chain attached to the lower corner of a sail for securing the sail or altering its direction relative to the wind.

Three strikes (and you're out) describes legislation which provides that an offender's third felony is punishable by life imprisonment or other severe sentence, a phrase which developed in the US in the 1980s, and which comes from the terminology of baseball, in which a batter who has had three strikes, or three fair opportunities of hitting the ball, is out.

The **Three Wise Men** is another name for the ➤ MAGI.

threescore years and ten the age of seventy as one's allotted span, with biblical allusion to Psalm 90.

Throgmorton Street the name of the street in the City of London where the Stock Exchange is located, used allusively for the Stock Exchange or its members.

throne a ceremonial chair for a sovereign, bishop, or similar figure. Recorded from Middle English, the word comes via Old French and Latin from Greek *thronos* 'elevated seat'.

The **Great White Throne** is the throne of God, with allusion to Revelation 20:11.

The **Throne of Grace** is the place where God is conceived as sitting to answer prayer, as in Hebrews 4:16.

In traditional Christian angelology, **thrones** are the third-highest order of the ninefold celestial hierarchy.

throw someone to the wolves sacrifice another person in order to avert danger or difficulties for oneself; probably in allusion to stories of wolves in a pack pursuing travellers in a horse-drawn sleigh.

throw up the sponge abandon a contest or struggle, submit, give in; in boxing, throw up the sponge used to wipe a contestant's face as a sign that a fight has been abandoned.

Thucydides (*c*.455–*c*.400 BC), Greek historian. He is remembered for his *History of the Peloponnesian War*, which analyses the origins and course of the war, and includes the reconstruction of political speeches of figures such as Pericles; he fought in the conflict on the Athenian side, but having failed successfully to defend a valuable colony, was condemned in his absence and exiled.

Thug a member of a religious organization of robbers and assassins in India. Devotees of the goddess ➤ KALI, the Thugs waylaid and strangled their victims, usually travellers, in a ritually prescribed manner. They were suppressed by the British in the 1830s. The name is recorded from the early 19th century and comes from Hindi *thag* 'swindler, thief', based on Sanskrit *sthagati* 'he covers or conceals'.

Thule a country described by the ancient Greek explorer Pytheas (*c*.310 BC) as being six days' sail north of Britain, variously identified with Iceland, the Shetland Islands, and most plausibly, Norway. It was regarded by the ancients as the northernmost part of the world. (See also ➤ ULTIMA *Thule*.)

thumb the breadth of the thumb, taken as equal to an inch, was formerly used as a measure; in the cloth trade, it was customary to allow a *thumb* in addition to each yard of cloth measured. The word is recorded from Old English (in form *thūma*), of West Germanic origin; it comes ultimately from an Indo-European root shared by Latin *tumere* 'swell'.

Thumbs up (or **thumbs down**) is an indication of satisfaction or approval (or of rejection or failure), with reference to the signal of approval or disapproval, used by spectators at a Roman amphitheatre; the sense has been reversed, as the Romans used 'thumbs down' to signify that a beaten gladiator had performed well and should be spared, and 'thumbs up' to call for his death.

thunder traditionally regarded as the destructive agent producing the effects usually attributed to lightning. In biblical phrases, *thunder* denotes great force and energy, as in Job 39:19.

To **steal someone's thunder** is to win praise for oneself by pre-empting someone else's attempt to impress. The phrase comes from an exclamation from the English

dramatist John Dennis (1657–1734), on hearing his new thunder effects used at a performance of *Macbeth*, following the withdrawal of one of his own plays after only a short run.

thunderbolt a supposed bolt or shaft believed to be the destructive agent in a lightning flash, especially as an attribute of a god such as Jupiter or Thor.

the Thunderer epithet of a deity regarded as causing thunder, such as Jupiter or Thor; recorded from late Middle English.

From the mid 19th century, the *Thunderer* became the nickname of the *Times* newspaper, initially with reference to the writing of the journalist Edward Sterling (1773–1847).

Thundering Legion a name for the 12th Roman Legion, said to come from their having saved themselves and the whole army in an expedition under Marcus Aurelius against the Germanic tribes. Parched with thirst, the Christians among them successfully prayed for rain; their prayers also caused lightning and thunderbolts to fall on the enemy.

Thursday the day of the week before Friday and following Wednesday. The name comes from Old English *Thu(n)resdæg* 'day of thunder', translation of late Latin *Jovis dies* 'day of Jupiter' (god associated with thunder).

Thyestes in Greek mythology, the brother of ➤ ATREUS and father of ➤ AEGISTHUS, whose brother tricked him into eating the flesh of his own children at a feast; part of the curse on the house of Atreus.

thyrsus in ancient Greece and Rome, a staff or spear tipped with an ornament like a pine cone and sometimes wreathed with ivy or vine branches, carried by ➤ BACCHUS and his followers.

Tiamat in Babylonian mythology, a monstrous she-dragon who was the mother of the first gods. She was slain by Marduk.

Tiananmen Square a square in the centre of Beijing adjacent to the Forbidden City, the largest public open space in the world. In spring 1989 it was occupied by hundreds of thousands of student-led protesters of the emerging pro-democracy movement. Government troops opened fire there on unarmed protesters, killing over 2,000.

Tiber a river of central Italy, upon which Rome stands. It figures in the doom-laden prophecy of Virgil's *Aeneid*, book 6, 'I see…the Tiber foaming with much blood', a

line referred to by the Conservative politician Enoch Powell (1912–98) in April 1968
when he predicted disastrous results for
Britain's immigration policy.

Tiberius (42 BC–AD 37), Roman emperor AD
14–37. The adopted successor of his stepfather and father-in-law Augustus, he became increasingly tyrannical and his reign
was marked by a growing number of treason
trials and executions. In 26 he retired to
Capri, never returning to Rome.

Tichborne claimant name given to Arthur
Orton (1834–98), English butcher, who in
1866 returned to England from Australia
claiming to be Sir Roger Tichborne (lost at
sea in 1854) and thus heir to the valuable
Tichborne estate in Hampshire. When the
case finally came to court, Orton lost his
claim and was tried and imprisoned for perjury.

tide a particular time, season, or festival of
the Christian Church; *tide* meaning 'time,
period, era' is recorded from Old English (in
form *tīd*) and is of German origin, ultimately
related to German *Zeit*.

From late Middle English, the word has
also meant (now the current meaning) the alternate rising and falling of the sea, usually
twice in each lunar day at a particular place,
due to the attraction of the moon and sun.

tiger the *tiger* is proverbial for its ferocity
and cunning.

To **have a tiger by the tail** is to have embarked on a course of action which proves
unexpectedly difficult but which cannot easily or safely be abandoned. Recorded from
the late 20th century; an alternative way of
referring to the same predicament is **ride a
tiger**, with allusion to the Chinese saying *he
who rides a tiger cannot dismount* (recorded in
English from the late 19th century). (See also
have a wolf by the ears at ➤ WOLF.)

The term **tiger economy** was in the 1980s
used for the dynamic economy of one of the
smaller East Asian countries, especially that
of Singapore, Taiwan, or South Korea, or of
Hong Kong; these original **Four Tigers** of the
early 1980s were later joined by Malaysia,
Thailand, and the Philippines, before economic problems in the 1990s sharply reduced the strength and dominance of the
region. The successful Irish economy of the
last years has frequently been designated as
the **Celtic Tiger**.

Tiger Tim is a cartoon character, leader of a
group of animals known as the Bruin Boys,
who first appeared in the *Daily Mirror* in 1904,

and subsequently in the *Children's Encyclopae-
dia* monthly reissue from 1910 and *Rainbow*
(1914–56). He has also figured in a number of
annuals.

Tigger the irrepressible and bouncy tiger
character created by A. A. Milne as one of
➤ WINNIE-*the-Pooh*'s companions; he makes
his first appearance in *The House at Pooh Corner* (1928).

Tikal an ancient Mayan city in the tropical
Petén region of northern Guatemala, with
great plazas, pyramids, and palaces. It flourished AD 300–800, reaching its peak towards
the end of that period.

Tilbury in 1588, the point on the north
bank of the River Thames at which troops for
the defence of England against the Armada
were assembled, and the site of Elizabeth I's
speech to her forces.

tilt at windmills attack imaginary obstacles, in the manner of ➤ *Don* QUIXOTE, who
mistook a group of windmills in the distance
for giants.

Timbuctoo a distant or remote place, from
the name of *Timbuktu*, a town in northern
Mali which was founded by the Tuareg in the
11th century, and which became a Muslim
centre of learning, and a major trading centre for gold and salt on the trans-Saharan
trade routes.

time traditionally personified as **Father
Time**, an old man with a scythe and hourglass, and sometimes also bald but with a
forelock.

Time and tide wait for no man means that
if you do not make use of a favourable opportunity, you may never get the same chance
again. *Time and tide* was an alliterative reduplication in Middle English, as *tide* simply
meant 'time, occasion'; from the 16th century, however, it has often been understood
as 'the tide of the sea'.

From **time immemorial** means from so
long ago that people have no knowledge or
memory of it. Legally in Britain, the time up
to the beginning of the reign of Richard I in
1189.

Time is money is often used to mean that
time spent fruitlessly on something represents a real loss of money which could
have been earned in that time; proverbial
saying, late 16th century. In classical Greek,
the saying 'the most costly outlay is time' is
attributed to the Athenian orator and politician Antiphon of the 5th century BC.

Time's arrow is the direction of travel from past to future in time considered as a physical dimension. The phrase comes from Arthur Eddington (1882–1944) *The Nature of the Physical World* (1928).

timeo Danaos et dona ferentes Latin quotation from Virgil's *Aeneid* meaning, 'I fear the Greeks even when they bring gifts'; the warning given to the Trojans that they should not trust the ➤ TROJAN *Horse*.

Times Square a square in Manhattan, New York City, at the intersection of Broadway, 42nd Street, and Seventh Avenue; it is named after the building formerly occupied by the *New York Times*, which still transmits news flashes in lights on its façade. It is often taken as the type of an area of the entertainment industry in a major city.

Timon of Athens semi-legendary Athenian misanthrope, who according to a story in Plutarch became a recluse because of the ingratitude of his friends, refusing to see anyone but Alcibiades. Shakespeare's play (*c*.1607) is based on Plutarch.

Epistle to Timothy either of two books of the New Testament, epistles of St Paul addressed to St Timothy.

St Timothy (1st century AD), convert and disciple of St Paul. Traditionally he was the first bishop of Ephesus and was martyred in the reign of the Roman emperor Nerva. His feast day is January 22 or 26.

Timur Tartar name of ➤ TAMERLANE. A **Timurid** is one of his descendants; a member of the Turkic dynasty founded by him, which ruled in central Asia until the 16th century.

tin in figurative use, the name of this metal can indicate something of little value.
A **little tin god** is a person, especially a minor official, who is pompous and self-important; an object of unjustified veneration or respect.
In North America, **tin lizzie** is a dated informal expression for a motor car, in particular a very early Ford.
In the story of the ➤ WIZARD *of Oz*, the **Tin Man** is one of Dorothy's companions in the search for the magician.
Tin Pan Alley is the name given to a district in New York (28th Street, between 5th Avenue and Broadway) where many songwriters, arrangers, and music publishers were formerly based. The phrase is now used for the world of composers and publishers of

popular music, particularly with reference to the works of such composers as Irving Berlin, Jerome Kern, George Gershwin, Cole Porter, and Richard Rodgers.
In the US, a **tin wedding** is a 10th wedding anniversary.

Tinseltown Hollywood, or the superficially glamorous world it represents.

Tintagel a village on the coast of northern Cornwall. Nearby are the ruins of Tintagel Castle, the legendary birthplace of King Arthur and a stronghold of the Earls of Cornwall from the 12th to the 15th centuries.

Tintin boy reporter and detective, cartoon character created by the Belgian artist Hergé (1907–83); *Tintin* and his dog Snowy first appeared in 1929 in the Belgian newspaper *Le Vingtième Siècle*.

tip-and-run an informal way of playing cricket in which the batsman must run after every hit; from 1918, the term is also recorded as an expression for a short, sudden wartime attack.

tip of the iceberg the small perceptible part of a much larger situation or problem that remains hidden, as the larger part of an iceberg remains submerged.

Tipperary a county in the province of Munster, made famous by the song (1912) by Jack Judge and Harry Williams, popular as a British soldiers' song in the First World War, 'It's a Long Way to Tipperary'.

tipstaff a sheriff's officer; a bailiff. Originally (in the mid 16th century) the word denoted a metal-tipped staff: contraction of *tipped staff* (carried by a bailiff).

Tir-nan-Og a land of perpetual youth, the Irish equivalent of Elysium; the name means literally in Irish, 'land of the young'.

tired and emotional humorous phrase, associated particularly with the British satirical magazine *Private Eye*, used euphemistically to indicate that someone is drunk; an earlier variant was **tired and overwrought**.

Tiresias a blind Theban prophet, so wise that even his ghost had its wits and was not a mere phantom. According to some legends, he spent seven years as a woman. He was said to have been asked by Zeus and Hera whether a man or a woman derived more pleasure from the act of love; when he answered that a man did, Hera blinded him, but Zeus gave him in recompense a gift for unfailing prophecy.

Tisiphone one of the ➤ Furies; the name is Greek, and means literally 'avenger of blood'.

Titan in Greek mythology, any of the older gods who preceded the Olympians and were the children of ➤ Uranus (Heaven) and ➤ Gaia (Earth). Led by ➤ Cronus, they overthrew Uranus; Cronus' son, ➤ Zeus, then rebelled against his father and eventually defeated the Titans.

In early poetry, *Titan* is used as a name for the sun-god, or for the sun personified, or for the elder brother of Cronus as the first-born of the race. From the early 19th century, *titan* has denoted a person or thing of very great strength, intellect, or importance.

Titania the name of the queen of the fairies in Shakespeare's *A Midsummer Night's Dream*; in the play she has quarrelled with her husband Oberon, and in revenge he causes her by enchantment to fall in love with ➤ Bottom *the Weaver*. The name is used by Ovid in *Metamorphoses* to designate Diana, Circe, and others as descended from the Titans.

Titanic a British passenger liner, the largest ship in the world when she was built and supposedly unsinkable, that struck an iceberg in the North Atlantic on her maiden voyage in April 1912 and sank with the loss of 1,490 lives.

tithe one tenth of annual produce or earnings, formerly taken as a tax for the support of the Church and clergy. The practice derived from Jewish custom, as recorded in Jacob's vow at Bethel, Genesis 28:22.

Tithonus a Trojan prince with whom the goddess Aurora fell in love. She asked Zeus to make him immortal but omitted to ask for eternal youth, and he became very old and decrepit although he talked perpetually. Tithonus prayed her to remove him from this world and she changed him into a grasshopper, which chirps eeaselessly.

tittle a tiny amount or part of something; a small written or printed stroke or dot. Recorded from late Middle English, the word comes from Latin *titulus* 'title', in medieval Latin 'small stroke, accent'; the phrase ➤ *not one* JOT *or tittle* is from Matthew 5:18.

Titus (AD 39–81), Roman emperor, son of ➤ Vespasian. In 70 he ended a revolt in Judaea with the conquest of Jerusalem; he fell in love with the Jewish Queen Berenice, daughter of Herod Agrippa, who accompanied him back to Rome, although he was forced by the disapproval of his own people to send her away.

The **Arch of Titus** is a triumphal arch, commemorating the capture of Jerusalem by ➤ Titus, erected in the Forum at Rome by Titus's brother and successor ➤ Domitian.

Epistle to Titus a book of the New Testament, an epistle of St Paul addressed to St Titus.

St Titus (1st century AD), Greek churchman. A convert and helper of St Paul, he was traditionally the first bishop of Crete. His feast day is (in the Eastern Church) 23 August; (in the Western Church) 6 February.

Tityrus in Virgil's first Eclogue, the name of a shepherd. The word (said to represent 'satyr' in Doric) is also used for a fictitious monster supposed to be bred between a sheep and a goat.

A **tityre-tu** was any of a group of well-to-do ruffians on the streets of London in the 17th century. The name comes from Latin *Tityre tu* 'you Tityrus', the first two words of Virgil's first eclogue, addressed to a man lying at ease beneath a tree.

toad traditionally taken as the type of something unpleasant (and formerly believed to be venomous).

In Kenneth Grahame's *The Wind in the Willows* (1908), the wealthy, boastful, spoiled, but ultimately good-hearted *Toad* needs to be rescued and redeemed from his self-indulgent ways by Ratty, Mole, and Badger.

toadstone a gem, fossil tooth, or other stone formerly supposed to have been formed in the body of a toad, and credited with therapeutic or protective properties.

toady a person who behaves obsequiously to someone important. Recorded from the early 19th century, the word is said to be a contraction of *toad-eater*, a charlatan's assistant who ate toads; toads were regarded as poisonous, and the assistant's survival was thought to be due to the efficacy of the charlatan's remedy.

toast sliced bread browned on both sides by exposure to heat; the practice of drinking a toast in honour of a person or thing goes back to the late 17th century, and originated in naming a lady whose health the company was requested to drink, the idea being that the lady's name flavoured the drink like the pieces of spiced *toast* that were formerly placed in drinks such as wine.

Be toast means be or be likely to become finished, defunct, or dead.

To have someone **on toast** is to be in a position to deal with someone as one wishes; with reference to a food item served up on a slice of toast.

Tobit a pious Israelite living during the Babylonian Captivity, described in the Apocrypha; the book of the Apocrypha telling the story of Tobit and his son Tobias, from whom Tobias night is named.

Tobruk a port on the Mediterranean coast of NE Libya, which was the scene of fierce fighting during the North African campaign in the Second World War.

Toby the name of the trained dog introduced (in the first half of the 19th century) into the ➤ PUNCH *and Judy* show, which wears a frill round its neck.

toby jug a jug or mug in the form of a stout old man wearing a long and full-skirted coat and a three-cornered hat. The term comes from the mid 19th century (as a pet form of the given name *Tobias*), and is said to come from an 18th-century poem about *Toby Philpot* (with a pun on *fill pot*), a soldier who liked to drink.

Toc H in the UK, a society, originally of ex-service personnel, founded after the First World War by the Australian-born British clergyman Philip 'Tubby' Clayton (1885–1972) for promoting Christian fellowship and social service.

The name comes from *toc* (former telegraphy code for *T*) and *H*, from the initials of *Talbot House*, a soldier's club established in Belgium in 1915.

Tocharian either of two extinct languages (**Tocharian A** and **Tocharian B**) spoken by this people, the most easterly of known ancient Indo-European languages, surviving in a few documents and inscriptions and showing curious affinities to Celtic and Italic languages.

toe the line accept the authority, principles, or policies of a particular group, especially under pressure; from the literal sense

'stand with the tips of the toes exactly touching a line', as competitors lined up at the beginning of a race.

toga a loose flowing outer garment worn by the citizens of ancient Rome, made of a single piece of cloth and covering the whole body apart from the right arm. The word is Latin, and is related to *tegere* 'to cover'.

token a characteristic or distinctive sign or mark, especially a badge or favour worn to indicate allegiance to a particular person or party. In early biblical translations, *token* is used to denote an act which demonstrates divine power or authority.

The word is recorded from Old English (in form *tā(e)n*) and is of Germanic origin, related to *teach*.

Tokenism is the practice of making only a perfunctory or symbolic effort to do a particular thing, especially by recruiting a small number of people from under-represented groups in order to give the appearance of sexual or racial equality within a workforce.

Tokyo Rose the name given by American servicemen in the Second World War to a woman broadcaster of Japanese propaganda; the name in fact covered a number of women broadcasting Japanese propaganda, although one Japanese-American, Iva Toguri, was tried and convicted of treason after the war. Later evidence suggested that she and others had in fact tried to subvert the propaganda effort, and in 1977 she was pardoned by President Ford.

Toledo a city in central Spain on the River Tagus, which from the first century was famous for its steel and sword blades; from the late 16th century, *Toledo* was used for a sword made there, or for one of that kind.

Toleration Act an act of 1689 granting freedom of worship to dissenters (excluding Roman Catholics and Unitarians) on certain conditions. Its real purpose was to unite all Protestants under William III against the deposed Roman Catholic James II.

Tollund Man the well-preserved corpse of an Iron Age man (c.500 BC–AD 400) found in 1950 in a peat bog in central Jutland, Denmark. Around the neck was a plaited leather noose, indicating that Tollund Man had met his death by hanging, a victim of murder or sacrifice.

Tolpuddle martyrs six farm labourers from the village of Tolpuddle in Dorset who attempted to form a trade union and were sentenced in 1834 to seven years' transportation on a charge of administering unlawful oaths. Their harsh sentences caused widespread protests, and two years later they were pardoned and repatriated from Australia.

Tom male personal forename.

Tom and Jerry were names of the two chief characters in Egan's *Life in London*, 1821, and its continuation, 1828; whence in various allusive and attributive uses, especially as name of a compound alcoholic drink, a kind of highly-spiced punch.

Tom and Jerry are also the names of the cat and mouse cartoon characters (created by William Hanna and Joseph Barbera) who first appeared in *Puss Gets the Boot* (1939); in their constant and violent battles, the large black-and-white cat is in the end outwitted by the adroit mouse.

Tom, Dick, and Harry collectively refer to ordinary people in general; the phrase in this form is recorded from the mid 18th century, but Shakespeare in *1 Henry IV* (1597) has 'Tom, Dick, and Francis' in a similar sense.

A **Tom o'Bedlam** was a madman, a deranged person discharged from Bedlam and licensed to beg; in Shakespeare's *King Lear* (1605–6), the banished Edgar disguises himself as the mad 'Poor Tom'.

Tom Thumb was the hero of an old children's story, the son of a ploughman in the time of King Arthur who was only as tall as his father's thumb; the story of his life was popular as a chapbook publication, and was the subject of Fielding's mock-heroic *Tom Thumb, a Tragedy* (1730).

Tom Tiddler's ground is the name of a children's game. One of the players is *Tom Tiddler*, his territory being marked by a line drawn on the ground; over this the other players run, crying 'We're on Tom Tiddler's ground, picking up gold and silver'. They are chased by Tom Tiddler, the first, or sometimes the last, caught taking his place.

Tommy Atkins a name for the typical private soldier in the British army; deriving from the casual use of *Thomas Atkins* in the specimen forms given in official regulations from 1815 onwards; although other names were also used, *Thomas Atkins* became best known as used in all forms for privates in the cavalry and infantry.

tomorrow is another day used after a bad experience to express one's belief that the future will be better; proverbial saying, early 16th century; more recently, particularly associated with Scarlett O'Hara, Southern heroine of Margaret Mitchell's *Gone With the Wind* (1936).

Mount Tongarira a mountain in North Island, New Zealand, which is held sacred by the Maoris.

tongs tongs are the emblem of ➤ St DUN-STAN and ➤ St ELOI.

with tongue in cheek without really meaning what one is saying or writing; putting one's tongue in one's cheek is a traditional gesture of sly humour.

the gift of tongues in the Christian Church, the ability to speak in a language unknown to the speaker, or to vocalize freely, usually in the context of religious (especially pentecostal or charismatic) worship, identified as a gift of the Holy Spirit.

tonic sol-fa a system of naming the notes of the scale (usually *doh, ray, me, fah, soh, lah, te*) used especially to teach singing, with doh as the keynote of all major keys and lah as the keynote of all minor keys.

Gulf of Tonkin an arm of the South China Sea, bounded by the coasts of southern China and northern Vietnam. An incident there in 1964 led to increased US military involvement in the area prior to the Vietnam War.

tonsure a part of a monk's or priest's head left bare on top by shaving off the hair. In the Eastern church the whole head is shaven (the **tonsure of St Paul**), in the Roman Catholic Church, the tonsure consists of either a circular patch on the crown, or the whole upper part of the head so as to leave only a fringe or circle of hair (the **tonsure of St Peter**), and in the ancient Celtic Church, the head was shaved in the front of a line drawn from ear to ear (the **tonsure of St John**).

Recorded from late Middle English, the word comes from Old French or from Latin *tonsura*, from *tondere* 'shear, clip'.

tontine an annuity shared by subscribers to a loan or common fund, the shares increasing as subscribers die until the last survivor enjoys the whole income. The word comes (in the mid 18th century) from French, and is named after Lorenzo *Tonti* (1630–95), a Neapolitan banker who started such a scheme to raise government loans in France (c.1653).

Tonton Macoute a member of a notoriously brutal militia formed by President François Duvalier of Haiti, active from 1961–86. The name is Haitian French, apparently with reference to an ogre of folk tales.

Tony (in the US) any of a number of awards given annually for outstanding achievement in the theatre in various categories. The name comes from the nickname of Antoinette Perry (1888–1946), American actress and director.

Tophet a term for hell, from the name of a place in the Valley of Hinnom near Jerusalem used for idolatrous worship, including the sacrifice of children, and later for burning refuse.

Topkapi Palace the former seraglio or residence in Istanbul of the sultans of the Ottoman Empire, last occupied by Mahmut II (1808–39) and now a museum.

Topsy name of the young slave girl in Harriet Beecher Stowe's *Uncle Tom's Cabin* (1852), who says of herself 'I s'pect I growed. Don't think nobody never made me.' From this, *Topsy* is taken as the type of something which seems to have grown of itself without anyone's intention or direction.

Torah in Judaism, the law of God as revealed to Moses and recorded in the first five books of the Hebrew scriptures (the ➤ PENTATEUCH).

torch figuratively, *the* valuable quality, principle, or cause, which needs to be protected and maintained.
Torch was the codename for the Allied landings on the western coast of North Africa in 1942.

Toronto blessing a manifestation of religious ecstasy, typically involving mass fainting, with speaking in tongues, laughter, or weeping, associated with a charismatic revival among evangelical Christians which originated in a fellowship meeting at *Toronto* airport chapel in 1994.

Torquemada a ruthless inquisitor; from the name of the Spanish cleric and Grand Inquisitor Tomás de *Torquemada* (c.1420–98). A Dominican monk, he became confessor to Ferdinand and Isabella, whom he persuaded to institute the Inquisition in 1478, and was

also the prime mover behind the expulsion of the Jews from Spain in and after 1492.

Torrey Canyon name of the oil-tanker which in March 1967 struck the rocks off the Isles of Scilly; the resulting pollution devastated the Cornish coastline, and the ship itself, which continued to lose oil, was finally bombed to destroy the cargo and prevent further damage to the environment.

torso the trunk of a statue, without or considered independently of the head and limbs; the trunk of the human body. The word is recorded from the late 18th century and comes from Italian, literally 'stalk, stump', from the Latin base of ➤ THYRSUS.

tortoise the *tortoise* is taken (as in the story of ➤ *the* HARE *and the tortoise*) as the type of something which moves slowly and laboriously, but with determination.
According to an anecdote, the Greek dramatist ➤ AESCHYLUS was killed when an eagle dropped a tortoise on to his bald head.

Tory now (in the UK) a member or supporter of the Conservative Party; originally, a member of the English political party opposing the exclusion of James II from the succession. It remained the name for members of the English, later British, parliamentary party supporting the established religious and political order until the emergence of the Conservative Party in the 1830s.
The name comes (in the mid 17th century, denoting Irish peasants dispossessed by English settlers and living as robbers) from Irish *toraidhe* 'outlaw, highwayman', from *tóir* 'pursue'; it was then extended to other marauders especially in the Scottish Highlands. It was then adopted *c.*1679 as an abusive nickname for supporters of the Catholic James, Duke of York, later James II.

totem a natural object or animal that is believed by a particular society to have spiritual significance and that is adopted by it as an emblem. The word is recorded from the mid 18th century, and comes from Ojibwa *nindoodem* 'my totem'.
A **totem pole** is a pole on which totems are hung or on which the images of totems are carved.

touchstone a piece of fine-grained dark schist or jasper formerly used for testing alloys of gold by observing the colour of the mark which they made on it; in figurative usage, something which acts as a test of genuineness, a criterion.

Touchstone is also the name of the fool in Shakespeare's *As You Like It*, who loyally accompanies Rosalind and Celia into exile.

touchy-feely openly expressing affection or other emotions, especially through physical contact. In its literal senses, *touchy-feely* is associated with the development in the 1960s and 1970s of encounter groups in which participants sought psychological benefit through close contact with one another. By the 1990s, the figurative use of the term was strongly established; it is often used to sum up the attitude implicit in the 'caring nineties' and the values of a ➤ NEW *Age* society.

tough love promotion of a person's welfare, especially that of an addict, child, or criminal, by enforcing certain constraints on them, or requiring them to take responsibility for their actions. The concept developed in America in the early 1980s as an appropriate way for family members in co-operation with professional carers to deal with children and young adults affected by drug abuse.

Tour de France a French race for professional cyclists held annually since 1903, covering approximately 4,800 km (3,000 miles) of roads in about three weeks, renowned for its mountain stages. The overall leader after each stage wears the famous yellow leader's jersey.

Tourist Trophy a motorcycle-racing competition, often abbreviated to **TT**, held annually on roads in the Isle of Man since 1907.

Tournai a town in Belgium, on the River Scheldt near the French frontier, which became the Merovingian capital in the 5th century and was the birthplace of the Frankish king ➤ CLOVIS.

tournament in the Middle Ages, a sporting event in which two knights (or two groups of knights) jousted on horseback with blunted weapons, each trying to knock the other off, the winner receiving a prize.

tower a *tower* is the emblem of ➤ St BARBARA.

Tower Bridge is a bridge across the Thames in London, famous for its twin towers and for the two bascules of which the roadway consists, able to be lifted to allow the passage of large ships. It was completed in 1894.

The **Tower of London** is a fortress by the Thames just east of the City of London. The oldest part, the White Tower, was begun in 1078. It was later used as a state prison, and is now open to the public as a repository of ancient armour and weapons, and of the Crown jewels (which have been kept there since the time of Henry III).

A **tower of silence** is a tall open-topped structure on which Parsees traditionally place and leave exposed the body of someone who has died.

A **tower of strength** is a source of strong and reliable support; perhaps originally alluding to the *Book of Common Prayer* 'O Lord...be unto them a tower of strength.'

A **Tower pound** is a pound weight of 5400 grains (= 11¼ Troy ounces), which was the legal mint pound of England prior to the adoption of the Troy pound of 5760 grains in 1526.

town and gown the permanent residents of a university town and the members of the university, especially as seen in opposition to one another.

Toytown setting for the children's stories of S. G. Hulme Beatman (1886–1932), first published in 1925 and in 1929 adapted for Children's Hour on radio; *Toytown*, inhabited by ➤ LARRY *the Lamb* and his friends, is referred to allusively as a type of small or insignficant town.

kick over the traces become insubordinate or reckless; the *traces* here are each of the two side straps, chains, or ropes by which a horse is attached to a vehicle that it is pulling.

the wrong side of the tracks a poor or less prestigious part of town; with reference to the railway tracks of American towns, once serving as a line of demarcation between rich and poor quarters.

Tractarianism another name for ➤ OXFORD *Movement*; from the title *Tracts for the Times*.

Tracts for the Times the title of a series of pamphlets on theological topics started by John Henry Newman and published in Oxford 1833–41, which set out the doctrines on which the ➤ OXFORD *Movement* or *Tractarianism* was based.

Dick Tracy American plainclothes detective with a jutting jaw whose slogan (like the FBI's) is 'Crime doesn't pay', and who is ready to use violence in the service of right, in the cartoon strip created in 1931 by the American cartoonist Chester Gould (1900–85).

trade wind a wind blowing steadily towards the equator from the north-east in the northern hemisphere (the **north-east trade wind**) or the south-east in the southern hemisphere (the **south-east trade wind**), especially at sea. Two belts of trade winds encircle the earth, blowing from the tropical high-pressure belts to the low-pressure zone at the equator; the system is seasonally displaced respectively to the north and south of the equator in the northern and southern summers.

trademark a symbol, word, or words, legally registered or established by use as representing a company or product.

Battle of Trafalgar a decisive naval battle fought on 21 October 1805 off the cape of Trafalgar on the south coast of Spain during the Napoleonic Wars. The British fleet under Horatio Nelson (who was killed in the action) defeated the combined fleets of France and Spain.
  Trafalgar Day is 21 October, the anniversary of the Battle of Trafalgar.
  Trafalgar Square is a square in central London, planned by John Nash and built between the 1820s and 1840s. It is dominated by Nelson's Column, a memorial to Lord Nelson.

tragedy in classical and Renaissance drama, a serious verse play (originally a Greek lyric song), written in an elevated style, in which the protagonist (usually a political leader or royal personage) is drawn to disaster or death by an error or fatal flaw. Later, a drama of a similarly serious nature and unhappy ending but typically dealing with an ordinary person or people. Recorded from late Middle English, the word comes ultimately via Old French and Latin from Greek *tragōidia*, apparently from *tragos* 'goat' + *ōidē* 'song'.

trahison des clercs a betrayal of intellectual, artistic, or moral standards by writers, academics, or artists. The (French) phrase, literally 'treason of the scholars', is the title of a book by Julien Benda (1927).

Trail of Tears the forced removal, in 1838–9, of the Cherokee people from their homeland and sent on a march from Georgia to Oklahoma; many died on the journey.

trail one's coat deliberately provoke a quarrel or fight; the idea is of making it

likely that someone will step on the trailing coat, providing reason for a quarrel.

trainspotter a person who obsessively studies the minutiae of any minority interest or specialized hobby; the interest and knowledge brought by the *trainspotter* to their chosen hobby are seen as negated by the trivial nature of the selected subject area (as, collecting train or locomotive numbers).

Traitors' Gate the gate to the ► Tower *of London* by which state prisoners brought by river entered.

Trajan (*c*.53–117 AD), Roman emperor 98–117. His reign is noted for the many public works undertaken and for the Dacian wars (101–6), which ended in the annexation of Dacia as a province, and which are illustrated on ► Trajan's *Column* in Rome.
  The **Arch of Trajan** is a monumental arch at Benevento, decreed or dedicated *c.* 115 AD, and showing Trajan's achievements at home and abroad.
  Trajan's Column is a monument erected 106–113 AD in Rome, commemorating his successful Dacian campaign; his ashes were deposited at its base.

Trans-Siberian Railway a railway running from Moscow east around Lake Baikal to Vladivostok on the Sea of Japan. Begun in 1891 and virtually completed by 1904, it opened up Siberia and advanced Russian interest in eastern Asia.

transept in a cross-shaped church, either of the two parts forming the arms of the cross shape, projecting at right angles from the nave.

the Transfiguration Christ's appearance in radiant glory to three of his disciples, Peter, James, and John; they are said to have seen with him Moses and Elijah (Matthew 17:2 and Mark 9:2–3).

Transport House a building in ► Smith *Square*, Westminster, London, between 1928 and 1980 the headquarters of the British Labour Party until the move to ► Millbank.

transubstantiation the conversion of the substance of the Eucharistic elements into the body and blood of Christ at consecration, only the appearances of bread and wine still remaining. The belief was defined at the Lateran Council of 1215, based on Aristotelian theories on the nature of 'substance', and is the official doctrine of the Roman Catholic

Church; the word itself has been used from the mid 16th century. It was rejected by Luther, Zwingli, and other Protestant reformers.

Trappist a member of a branch of the Cistercian order of monks founded in 1664 at *La Trappe* in Normandy and noted for an austere rule including a vow of silence.

Traveller name of the grey horse ridden during the American Civil War by Robert E. Lee. His bones are now buried near the grave of General Lee.

treacle originally (in Middle English) any of various medicinal salves formerly used as antidotes to poisons or venomous bites; the word comes via Old French and Latin from Greek *thēriakē* 'antidote against venom', ultimately from *thērion* 'wild beast'. The current sense of uncrystallized syrup dates from the late 17th century.

The **Treacle Bible** is another name for the ➤ BISHOPS' *Bible*, in which *Jeremiah* 8:22 reads 'Is there no tryacle in Gilead?' where the Authorized Version has 'balm'.

treason the crime of betraying one's country, especially by attempting to kill or overthrow the sovereign or government. Formerly, there were two types of crime to which the term *treason* was applied: **petty treason**, the crime of murdering one's master, and **high treason**, the crime of betraying one's country. The crime of **petty treason** was abolished in 1828 and in modern use the term **high treason** is now often simply called *treason*.

The word is recorded from Middle English and comes via Anglo-Norman French from Latin *traditio(n-)* 'handing over'.

Treason of the clerks is another term for ➤ TRAHISON *des clercs*.

treasure originally, wealth or riches stored or accumulated, especially in the form of precious metals; later, a quantity of precious metals, gems, or other valuable objects. The word is recorded from Middle English, and comes ultimately from the Greek base of ➤ THESAURUS.

In biblical allusions, *treasure* often denotes something valued by a person above all else, as in Matthew 6:21, 'Where your treasure is, there will your heart be also.'

The **Treasure State** is an informal name for Montana, noted for its gold, silver, copper, and coal mines.

Treasure trove is valuables of unknown ownership that are found hidden (as opposed to lost or abandoned) and declared the property of the Crown; the British law of *treasure trove* was abolished in 1996. Recorded from late Middle English, the term comes from Anglo-Norman French *tresor trové*, literally 'found treasure'.

Treasury originally, a room or building in which precious or valuable objects are kept, the funds or revenue of a state; later (in some countries), the government department responsible for budgeting for and controlling public expenditure, management of the national debt, and the overall management of the economy.

In the UK, the **First Lord of the Treasury** is the Prime Minister. The **Treasury Bench** is the front bench in the House of Commons occupied by the Prime Minister, the Chancellor of the Exchequer, and other members of the government.

Treaty Stone the stone on which the Treaty of Limerick (3 October 1691) was reputedly signed by representatives of the Jacobite and Williamite forces in Ireland; it became a symbol of English failure to honour the terms of the treaty.

Trebizond former name of *Trabzon*, a port on the Black Sea in northern Turkey, which was founded by Greek colonists in 756 BC. Its ancient name was *Trapezus*. In 1204, after the sack of Constantinople by the Crusaders, an offshoot of the Byzantine Empire was founded with Trebizond as its capital, which was annexed to the Ottoman Empire in 1461.

Treblinka a Nazi concentration camp in Poland in the Second World War, where a great many of the Jews of the Warsaw ghetto were murdered.

tree a *tree* is sometimes taken as the type of height and strength. In poetic use, the word may refer to the cross on which Christ was crucified; the word may also be used for the gallows.

From Middle English, the word has also been used for a genealogical table or **family tree**, in which the original ancestor is seen as the root, and the various lines of descent as the branches.

The word is recorded from Old English (in form *trēow, trēo*), and comes from a Germanic variant of an Indo-European root shared by Greek *doru* 'wood, spear', *drus* 'oak'.

Tree-hugger is a (derogatory) term for an environmental campaigner, used in reference to the practice of embracing a tree in an attempt to prevent it from being felled.

In the Bible, the **tree of knowledge** is the 'tree of the knowledge of good and evil' (Genesis 2:9) in the Garden of Eden, the fruit of which was forbidden to Adam and Eve, but which they ate as a result of the serpent's temptation of Eve. The **tree of life** is a tree in the Garden of Eden whose fruit imparts eternal life; in Genesis 3:24, God judges that disobedient man must be expelled from Eden 'lest he put forth his hand, and take also of the tree of life, and eat, and live for ever'.

The phrase *tree of life* is also used for an imaginary branching, tree-like structure representing the evolutionary divergence of all living creatures; in the Kabbalah, it is a diagram in the form of a tree bearing spheres, each of which represents a ➤ SEPHIRA.

trefoil an ornamental design of three rounded lobes like a clover leaf, used typically in architectural tracery.

Trekkie informal term for a fan of the cult US science-fiction television programme ➤ STAR *Trek*.

trench a ditch dug by troops to provide a place of shelter from enemy fire, often as part of a connected system of such ditches forming an army's line; **the trenches** is the term used for the battlefields of northern France and Belgium in the First World War.

Trench fever was a highly contagious rickettsial disease transmitted by lice, that infested soldiers in the trenches in the First World War.

Trench foot was a painful condition of the feet caused by long immersion in cold water or mud and marked by blackening and death of surface tissue, often suffered by soldiers in the trenches in the First World War.

Council of Trent an ecumenical council of the Roman Catholic Church, held in three sessions between 1545 and 1563 in Trento. Prompted by the opposition of the Reformation, the council clarified and redefined the Church's doctrine, abolished many ecclesiastical abuses, and strengthened the authority of the papacy. These measures provided the Church with a solid foundation for the Counter-Reformation.

Trent affair during the American Civil War, an incident in which two Confederate commissioners were seized by the Union navy from the *Trent*, a neutral British ship; the British govenment demanded an apology, and to avert war the Secretary of State William Seward acknowledged that the matter should have been brought to adjudication.

Tretyakov Gallery an art gallery in Moscow, one of the largest in the world. It houses exhibits ranging from early Russian art to contemporary work, and has a huge collection of icons. It is named after P. M. Tretyakov (1832–98), who founded it in 1856.

triad a group or set of three connected people or things, as, a Welsh form of literary composition with an arrangement of subjects or statements in groups of three.

The name *Triad* is used for a secret society originating in China, typically involved in organized crime; it comes from Chinese *San Ho Hui*, literally 'triple union society', which was said to mean 'the union of Heaven, Earth, and Man'. The original society was formed in the early 18th century, with the alleged purpose of ousting the ➤ MANCHU dynasty.

Trianon either of two small palaces in the great park at Versailles in France. The larger was built by Louis XIV in 1687; the smaller, the **Petit Trianon**, built by Louis XV 1762–8, was used first by his mistress Madame du Barry (1743–93) and afterwards by ➤ MARIE *Antoinette*. Both *Trianon* and *Petit Trianon* may be used allusively to refer to the imitation of peasant life practised there by Marie Antoinette and her court.

Tribes of Israel the twelve divisions of ancient Israel, each traditionally descended from one of the twelve sons of Jacob. Ten of the tribes (Asher, Dan, Gad, Issachar, Levi, Manasseh, Naphtali, Reuben, Simeon, and Zebulun, known as the **Lost Tribes**) were deported to captivity in Assyria *c.*720 BC, leaving only the tribes of Judah and Benjamin. Also called ➤ TWELVE *Tribes of Israel*.

tribune an official in ancient Rome (also known as the **tribune of the people**) chosen by the plebeians to protect their interests; in extended and figurative usage, a popular leader, a champion of the people. The word is recorded from late Middle English, and comes from Latin *tribunus*, literally 'head of a tribe'.

The **Tribune Group** is a left-wing group within the British Labour Party consisting of supporters of the views put forward in the weekly journal *Tribune*.

in a trice in a moment; very quickly. *Trice* as a noun, meaning 'a single pull or attempt', is obsolete except in this phrase.

trick or treat a children's custom of calling at houses at Halloween with the threat of pranks if they are not given a small gift (often used as a greeting by children doing this); the practice is first recorded in the US in the mid 20th century.

trickle-down of an economic system, in which the poorest gradually benefit as a result of the increasing wealth of the richest.

tricolour a flag with three bands or blocks of different colours, especially the French national flag (adopted at the Revolution) with equal upright bands of blue, white, and red.

tricoteuse a woman who sits and knits, used in particular in reference to a number of women who did this, during the French Revolution, while attending meetings of the Convention or watching public executions.

trident a three-pronged spear, especially as an attribute of ➤ POSEIDON (Neptune) or ➤ BRITANNIA.

Tridentine of or relating to the ➤ *Council of* TRENT (1545–63), especially as the basis of Roman Catholic doctrine; the name comes from *Tridentum*, Latin name of the city of Trent in the Tyrol.

The **Tridentine mass** is the Latin Eucharistic liturgy used by the Roman Catholic Church from 1570 until the changes instituted by the ➤ *Second* VATICAN *Council* (1962–5) came into effect.

triffid in the science fiction novel *The Day of the Triffids* (1951) by John Wyndham, the *triffids* are a race of predatory plants which are capable of growing to a gigantic size and are possessed of locomotor ability and a poisonous sting. The name is used allusively of plants showing vigorous growth, or more widely to denote invasive and rapid development.

The name is probably an alteration of *trifid* 'divided into three', as the original plants were supported on 'three bluntly-tapered projections'.

triforium a gallery or arcade above the arches of the nave, choir, and transepts of a church. The Anglo-Latin term is found first in the chronicle of Gervase of Canterbury, *c.*1185, and originally referred only to Canterbury Cathedral; it was mentioned by Viollet-le-Duc in his *Dictionnaire d'Architecture* (1868)

as having been introduced into architectural nomenclature by the English archaeologists, and from the 19th century was extended as a general term. The origin of the word is unknown.

Trilby name of the heroine of George du Maurier's eponymous novel (1894), a beautiful artist's model who becomes a successful singer under the tutelage of ➤ SVENGALI. The *trilby* hat, a soft felt hat with a narrow brim and indented crown, is named for her, as such a hat was worn in the stage version, and in the first part of the 20th century feet were informally known as *trilbies*, as du Maurier's heroine was admired for her feet.

Trimurti in Hinduism, the trinity of ➤ BRAHMA, ➤ VISHNU, and ➤ SHIVA; the word comes from Sanskrit *tri* 'three' + *mūrti* 'form'.

the Trinity the three persons of the Christian Godhead; Father, Son, and Holy Spirit. The term is recorded from Middle English, and comes ultimately from Latin *trinus* 'threefold'.

Trinity House is a guild or fraternity originally established at Deptford, incorporated in the reign of Henry VIII, formerly having the official regulation of British shipping, and now chiefly concerned with the licensing of pilots and the erection and maintenance of lighthouses, buoys, and other aids to navigation, on the coasts of England and Wales.

Trinity Sunday is the next Sunday after Pentecost, observed in the Western Christian Church as a feast in honour of the Holy Trinity.

Trinity term is a session of the High Court beginning after Easter; (in some universities) the term beginning after Easter.

the Tripitaka the sacred canon of ➤ THERAVADA Buddhism, written in the Pali language. The name comes from Sanskrit, meaning literally 'the three baskets or collections'.

triple consisting of or involving three things, parts, or people.

A **Triple Alliance** is a union or association between three powers or states, in particular that made in 1668 between England, the Netherlands, and Sweden against France, and that in 1882 between Germany, Austria-Hungary, and Italy against France and Russia.

The **triple crown** is a name for the ➤ PAPAL *tiara*, recorded from the mid 16th century, and referred to in Shakespeare's *2 Henry VI* (1592). In horse-racing, the *triple crown* is the winning of the Two Thousand Guineas, the Derby, and the St Leger by the same horse.

In the US, the **triple-witching hour** is an informal name for the unpredictable final hour of trading on the US Stock Exchange before the simultaneous expiry of three different kinds of options; the term is a development of ➤ WITCHING *hour.*

trippant in heraldry, (of a stag or deer) represented as walking.

triptych a picture or relief carving on three panels, typically hinged together vertically and used as an altarpiece. The word is recorded from the mid 18th century, and denoted originally a set of three writing tablets, hinged or tied together; it is formed from *tri-* 'three' on the pattern of *diptych.*

Trisagion a hymn, especially in the Orthodox Church, with a triple invocation of God as holy. The word is recorded from late Middle English and comes from Greek, from *tris* 'three times' + *hagios* 'holy'.

triskelion a Celtic symbol consisting of three legs or lines radiating from a centre, as in the emblem of the Isle of Man.

Trismegistus an epithet, meaning 'thrice-greatest', of the Egyptian god Hermes (see ➤ HERMES *Trismegistus*).

Tristram in medieval legend, a knight (also called *Tristan*) who was the lover of ➤ ISEULT and nephew of her husband king Mark of Cornwall; sent by the king to Ireland to bring the princess to Cornwall, Tristram falls in love with her, a love which is reinforced by the love potion which they accidentally drink, and which binds them to one another.

Despite their fated love, Tristram leaves Cornwall, and later marries Iseult of Brittany; in some versions of the story, he returns to Cornwall and is killed by the jealous Mark, in others (used by Wagner) he falls ill, and asks that Iseult of Ireland be sent for. The ship bringing her is to fly a white sail if she is on board; his jealous wife tells him that it is black, and Tristram dies before Iseult of Ireland can reach him.

The story of Tristram is now seen as one of the Arthurian romances, but it was incorporated at a late stage.

Tristram Shandy paradox a paradox of infinity, named after the eponymous hero of Sterne's novel *Tristram Shandy* (1759–67), who concluded that it was hopeless to attempt writing his autobiography since at the end of two years he had recorded the events of only the first two days of his life.

Triton in Greek mythology, a minor sea god usually represented as a man with a fish's tail and carrying a trident and shell-trumpet.

A **Triton of the minnows** is the type of something large or great contrasted with something small and insignificant, often with reference to Shakespeare's *Coriolanus* (1608).

triumph the processional entry of a victorious general with his army and spoils of the campaign into ancient Rome, permission for which was granted by the senate in honour of an important achievement in war. Recorded from late Middle English, the word comes via Old French from Latin *triump(h)us*, probably from Greek *thriambos* 'hymn to Bacchus'.

right as a trivet perfectly all right, in good health; with reference to a trivet's always standing firm and steady on its three legs.

Trivia name by which John Gay invoked a 'goddess of the highways' in his poem *Trivia, or the Art of Walking the Streets of London* (1716), from Latin *trivium* 'place where three roads meet'.

The modern word *trivia* 'details, considerations, or pieces of information of little importance or value' dates from the early 20th century.

Trivial Pursuit trademark name for a board game in which players advance by answering general knowledge questions in various subject areas.

trivium an introductory course at a medieval university involving the study of grammar, rhetoric, and logic; with the ➤ QUADRIVIUM, forming the ➤ SEVEN *liberal arts*. The word comes from Latin, and means literally 'place where three roads meet'.

Troilus a Trojan prince, the son of ➤ PRIAM and Hecuba, killed by ➤ ACHILLES. In medieval legends of the Trojan war he is portrayed as the forsaken lover of Cressida.

To be as **true as Troilus** is to be completely devoted; with allusion to Troilus's speech to Cressida in Shakespeare's *Troilus and Cressida* (1602).

Trojan of or pertaining to ancient Troy.

In Greek mythology, the **Trojan Horse** was a hollow wooden statue of a horse in which the Greeks are said to have concealed themselves in order to enter and capture Troy; despite the warning of ➤ LAOCOON, the Trojans breached the city walls to draw the horse inside, so that the Greeks were able the following night to overrun and sack the city.

Trojan Horse in figurative use denotes a person or thing intended secretly to undermine or bring about the downfall of an enemy or opponent; in computing, it is a program designed to breach the security of a computer system while ostensibly performing some innocuous function.

The **Trojan War** was the legendary ten-year siege of Troy by a coalition of Greeks led by ► AGAMEMNON, described in Homer's *Iliad*. The Greeks were attempting to recover ► HELEN, wife of Menelaus, who had been abducted by the Trojan prince Paris. The war ended with the capture of the city by a trick: the Greeks ostensibly ended the siege but left behind a group of men concealed in a hollow wooden horse (the *Trojan Horse*).

troll¹ a mythical, cave-dwelling being depicted in folklore as either a giant or a dwarf, typically having a very ugly appearance. The word was adopted in English from Scandinavian in the middle of the 19th century, but in Shetland and Orkney, where the form is now *trow*, it has survived from the Norse dialect formerly spoken there.

troll² send (an e-mail message or posting on the Internet) intended to provoke a response from the reader by containing errors. The word is a figurative use of the verb *troll* 'fish by trailing a baited line along behind a boat'.

trompe l'œil visual illusion in art, especially as used to trick the eye into perceiving a painted detail as a three-dimensional object. The term is French, and means literally 'deceive the eye'.

troop the colour perform the ceremony of parading a regiment's flag along ranks of soldiers as part of the ceremonial of the mounting of the guard; the first standing order on the subject (although it does not contain the word) is dated May 1755, but the name may date back to the time of Marlborough.

In Britain a ceremony of **trooping the colour** is carried out on the monarch's official birthday.

trooper a soldier in a troop of cavalry; the term was used in connexion with the Covenanting Army which invaded England in 1640, and was used in the English Army in 1660.

The expression **swear like a trooper** meaning 'swear profusely' is recorded from the mid 18th century.

trophy in ancient Greece or Rome, the weapons of a defeated army set up as a memorial of victory, originally on the field of battle, later in any public place. The term was then extended to mean a spoil or prize won in war or hunting, especially one kept or displayed as a memorial, and finally a cup or other object serving as a prize or memento of victory or success.

The word is recorded from the late 15th century, and comes via French and Latin from Greek *tropaion*, from *tropē* 'a rout', from *trepein* 'to turn'.

A **trophy wife** is a young, attractive wife regarded as a status symbol for an older man; the term is recorded from the late 1980s.

tropic the parallel of latitude 23°26' north (**tropic of Cancer**) or south (**tropic of Capricorn**) of the equator; **the tropics** is the name given to the region between the tropics of Cancer and Capricorn. The word is recorded from late Middle English, denoting the point on the ecliptic reached by the sun at the solstice.

Trotskyism the political or economic principles of the Russian revolutionary Leon *Trotsky* (1879–1940), especially the theory that socialism should be established throughout the world by continuing revolution.

troubador a French medieval lyric poet composing and singing in Provençal in the 11th to 13th centuries, especially on the theme of courtly love. The word is French, and comes from Provençal *trobador*, from *trobar* 'find, invent, compose in verse'.

the Troubles any of various periods of civil war or unrest in Ireland, especially in 1919–23 and (in Northern Ireland) since 1968; the expression is first recorded in the 19th century as referring to the Irish rebellion of 1641.

Troy in Homeric legend, the city of King ► PRIAM, besieged for ten years by the Greeks during the ► TROJAN *War*. It was regarded as having been a purely legendary city until the German archaeologist Heinrich Schliemann (1822–90) identified the mound of Hissarlik on the NE Aegean coast of Turkey as the site of Troy. Excavations showed the mound to be composed of nine main strata, dating from the early Bronze Age to the Roman era. The stratum known as Troy VIIa is believed to be that of the Homeric city; the city was apparently sacked and destroyed by fire in the mid 13th century BC, a period co-inciding with the Mycenaean civilization of Greece.

troy weight a system of weights used mainly for precious metals and gems, with a pound of 12 ounces or 5,760 grains. The expression comes (in late Middle English) from a weight used at the fair of *Troyes* in northern France.

truce of God a suspension of hostilities between armies, or of private feuds, ordered by the Church during certain days and seasons in medieval times.

true-blue in early use (from the mid 17th century), applied to the Scottish Presbyterian or Whig party, the Covenanters having adopted *blue* as their colour in contradistinction to the royal *red*. Later (in the current sense), staunchly loyal to the Tory, or Conservative, Party; in the US, extremely loyal or orthodox.

true-love knot a kind of knot with interlacing bows on each side, symbolizing the bonds of love.

Truman doctrine the principle that the US should give support to countries or peoples threatened by Soviet forces or Communist insurrection. First expressed in 1947 by US President Harry S. Truman (1884–1972), the doctrine was seen by the Communists as an open declaration of the cold war.

trump in bridge, whist, and similar card games, a playing card of the suit chosen to rank above the others, which can win a trick where a card of a different suit has been led; (in a tarot pack) any of a special suit of 22 cards depicting symbolic and typical figures and scenes. The word is an alteration of *triumph*, once used in card games in the same sense.

what is truth? in biblical allusion, often with reference to the account in John 18:38 of the examination of Jesus by Pilate, when 'Pilate saith unto him, What is truth?'

Truth and Reconciliation Commission a commission set up by a South African Parliamentary Act on 26 July 1995 to investigate claims of abuses during the Apartheid era.

the truth, the whole truth, and nothing but the truth the absolute truth, without concealment or addition; part of the formula of the oath taken by witnesses in court.

tsar an emperor of Russia before 1917. The Russian word *tsar* reprents Latin *Caesar*; it is first recorded in English in the mid 16th century. In Russia itself it was partially used by the Grand Duke Ivan III (1462–1505) and his son, but was formally assumed by Ivan IV in 1547. The title *tsar* was also used by Serbian rulers of the 14th century.

Tsarevich was the title of the eldest son of an emperor of Russia.

Tuatha Dé Danann in Irish mythology, the members of an ancient race said to have inhabited Ireland before the historical Irish. Formerly believed to have been a real people, they are credited with the possession of magical powers and great wisdom. The name is Irish, literally 'people of the goddess Danann'.

tub a tub is the emblem of ➤ *St* NICHOLAS *of Myra*.

Friar Tuck a member of ➤ ROBIN *Hood*'s company, a fat and jovial friar who despite his order is noted for his pugnacity.

Tudor name of the English royal dynasty which held the throne from the accession of Henry VII in 1485 until the death of Elizabeth I in 1603; they were descended from the Welsh Owen Tudor, who married Catherine, widowed queen of Henry V.

A **Tudor rose** is a conventionalized, typically five-lobed figure of a rose used in architectural and other decoration in the Tudor period, in particular a combination of the red and white roses of Lancaster or York adopted as a badge by Henry VII.

Tuesday the day of the week before Wednesday and following Monday. In Old English the form of the word was *Tíwesdæg* named after the Germanic god *Tiw* (associated with Mars); translation of Latin *dies Marti* 'day of Mars'.

Tuileries formal gardens next to the Louvre in Paris, laid out by André Le Nôtre in the mid 17th century. The gardens are all that remain of the Tuileries Palace, a royal residence begun in 1564 by Catherine de' Medici and burnt down in 1871 during the Commune of Paris. The name is French and means literally 'tile-works', as the palace was built on the site of an ancient tile-works.

Tula the ancient capital city of the Toltecs, generally identified with a site near the town of Tula in Hidalgo State, central Mexico.

Tulipomania the excessive enthusiasm for tulips current in Holland in the 17th century, during which tulip bulbs became the subject of much financial investment and speculation, resulting in the crash of 1637.

tumbril an open cart that tilted backwards to empty out its load, in particular one used to convey condemned prisoners to the guillotine during the French Revolution.

tumulus an ancient burial mound; a barrow. Recorded from late Middle English, the word is from Latin, and is related to *tumere* 'to swell'.

Disgusted of Tunbridge Wells a reactionary middle-class person, supposedly a typical resident of the spa town in Kent, probably deriving from a 1978 BBC radio program called *Disgusted, Tunbridge Wells*.

there's many a good tune played on an old fiddle someone's abilities do not depend on their being young; proverbial saying, early 20th century.

the turf horse racing or racecourses, from the grassy track or course over which a race takes place; the term is recorded from the mid 18th century.

turf war an acrimonious dispute between rival groups over territory or a particular sphere of influence. The phrase comes (in the 1970s) from the notion of a *war* over *turf* in the informal sense 'area regarded as personal territory' (originally the area controlled by, for example, a street gang or criminal).

Turin Shroud a relic, preserved at Turin in NW Italy since 1578, venerated as the winding-sheet in which Christ's body was wrapped for burial. It bears the imprint of the front and back of a human body as well as markings that correspond to the traditional stigmata. Scientific tests carried out in 1988 dated the shroud to the 13th–14th centuries.

Turing machine a mathematical model of a hypothetical computing machine which can use a predefined set of rules to determine a result from a set of input variables. It is named for the English mathematician Alan Mathison *Turing* (1912–54), who developed the concept of a theoretical computing machine, a key step in the development of the first computer, and carried out important code-breaking work in the Second World War.

Turk archaic term for a member of the ruling Muslim population of the Ottoman Empire, or for a member of any of the ancient central Asian peoples who spoke Turkic languages, including the Seljuks and Ottomans; in extended usage, the name was applied to anyone regarded as showing the harshness or cruelty associated with the Turks by Western Europeans.

turkey as food it is especially associated with festive occasions such as Christmas and (in the US) Thanksgiving. The name (recorded from the mid 16th century) is short for *turkeycock* or *turkeyhen*, originally applied to the guineafowl (which was imported through Turkey), and then erroneously to the American bird.

To **talk turkey** is to talk frankly and informally; a US expression recorded from the early 19th century, which originally could also mean talk agreeably or affably. The origin is not clear, but *turkey* appears to stand for something of substance (the 'meat') needing to be said.

one good turn deserves another if someone does you a favour, you should take the chance to repay it; proverbial saying, early 15th century.

a turn-up for the book a completely unexpected (especially welcome) result or happening; *turn-up* the turning up of a particular card or die in a game; *book* as kept by a bookie on a race-course.

turncoat a person who deserts one party or cause in order to join an opposing one; the term dates from the mid 16th century, and reflects the idea that the person's outer clothing carries the badge of their allegiance.

Turpin in a number of chansons de geste, archbishop of Rheims and friend and companion of ➤ CHARLEMAGNE, killed at ➤ RONCESVALLES.

Dick Turpin (1706–39), English highwayman who was hanged at York for horse-stealing. His escapades (including a dramatic ride from London to York on his horse Black Bess) were romanticized by Harrison Ainsworth in his novel *Rookwood* (1834).

turtle¹ archaic name for a ➤ TURTLE *dove*, as in the Song of Solomon 2:12.

turtle² the name *turtle* is an alteration (originally by English sailors) of *tortoise*. The flesh of various species of the turtle is used as food, and it was traditionally regarded as a feature of civic banquets; in the late 19th century the term **turtledom** was coined for aldermen as consumers of turtle-dinners.

In Terry Pratchett's ➤ DISCWORLD series, the world is said to be supported by four elephants carried on the back of a giant turtle; the idea of the universe supported on a turtle's back is derived from Hindu mythology.

To **turn turtle** is chiefly (of a boat) to turn upside down. From turtle-hunters' flipping over turtles on to their backs to render them helpless. Used figuratively from the early 19th century for turning upside down something held to resemble a turtle in shape.

turtle dove a small Old World dove with a soft purring call, noted for the apparent affection shown for its mate. The name comes ultimately from Latin *turtur*, of imitative origin.

Tuscan order a classical order of architecture resembling the Doric but lacking all ornamentation.

Madame Tussaud (1761–1850), French founder of Madame Tussaud's waxworks, resident in Britain from 1802. She took death masks in wax of prominent victims of the French Revolution and later toured Britain with her wax models. In 1835 she founded a permanent waxworks exhibition in Baker Street, London.

Tutankhamen (died *c.*1352 BC), Egyptian pharaoh of the 18th dynasty, reigned *c.*1361–*c.*1352 BC. He abandoned the worship of the sun god instituted by ➤ AKHENATEN, reinstating the worship of Amun and making Thebes the capital city once again.

His tomb, containing a wealth of rich and varied contents, was discovered virtually intact by the English archaeologist Howard Carter in 1922. Lord Carnarvon, who had sponsored the excavation, died the following year of blood-poisoning following a mosquito bite in the Valley of the Kings; this gave rise to the belief that to open the tomb had been unlucky.

never the twain shall meet used to suggest that two things are too different to exist alongside each other; from Rudyard Kipling's 'Oh, East is East, and West is West, and never the twain shall meet'. (*Barrack-room Ballads*, 1892).

Tweed Ring the political group which under 'Boss' *Tweed* (1823–78) controlled the municipal government of New York, *c.*1870.

Tweedledum and Tweedledee originally names applied to the composers Bononcini (1670–1747) and Handel, in a 1725 satire by John Byrom (1692–1763), 'Strange all this difference should be, 'Twixt Tweedledum and Tweedle-dee.'

The nursery rhyme featuring Tweedledum and Tweedledee, and their agreement to 'have a battle', is recorded from the early 19th century, and they were later developed as two identical characters in Lewis Carroll's *Through the Looking Glass* (1872).

twelfth constituting number twelve in a sequence. The phrase **The Twelfth** denotes both 12 July, celebrated by upholders of Protestant supremacy in Ireland as the anniversary of William III's victory over James II at the Battle of the Boyne, and (in the UK) 12 August, the day on which the grouse-shooting season begins.

In cricket, a **twelfth man** is a player nominated to act as a reserve in a game, typically carrying out duties such as fielding as a substitute and taking out drinks.

Twelfth Night is 6 January, the feast of the Epiphany. Strictly, this denotes the evening of 5 January, the eve of the ➤ EPIPHANY and formerly the twelfth and last day of Christmas festivities.

twelve one more than eleven, the number of certain well known sets or groups, as the twelve Apostles, the twelve Labours of Hercules, and the twelve signs of the zodiac.

Recorded from Old English (in form *twelf(e)*, the word is of Germanic origin and comes from the base of *two* + a second element probably expressing the sense 'left over'.

The **twelve days of Christmas** are the traditional period of Christmas festivities, from Christmas Day to the feast of the Epiphany.

Twelve good men and true are the twelve members of a jury; the expression is recorded from the mid 17th century.

The **Twelve Tribes of Israel** were the twelve divisions of ancient Israel, each traditionally descended from one of the twelve sons of Jacob. Ten of the tribes (Asher, Dan, Gad, Issachar, Levi, Manasseh, Naphtali, Reuben, Simeon, and Zebulun, known as the *Lost Tribes*) were deported to captivity in Assyria *c.*720 BC, leaving only the tribes of Judah and Benjamin.

twenty the cardinal number equivalent to the product of two and ten; ten less than thirty; 20. Recorded from Old English (in form *twentig*) the word comes from the base of *two* + *-ty*.

Twenty questions is a parlour game in which a participant has twenty questions (answered by either 'yes' or 'no') to identify a chosen object. The first recorded reference is in a letter from Hannah More of 1786. In the 20th century, *Twenty Questions* became the name of a popular radio panel game.

The **Twenty-four seven** (usually written 24/7) means twenty-four hours a day, seven days a week.

The **Twenty-six Counties** are the counties constituting the Republic of Ireland, separated from the ➤ SIX *Counties* of Northern Ireland by the peace agreement of 1921–22.

Twenty-twenty is the Snellen fraction for normal visual acuity, expressed in feet; used informally to denote good eyesight.

Twickenham originally a village in Middlesex, site of Horace Walpole's ➤ STRAWBERRY *Hill*, and from 1718 home of the poet Alexander Pope (1688–1744). It is now known primarily as the site of the English Rugby Football Union's ground, acquired in 1907.

twilight of the gods in Scandinavian and Germanic mythology, the destruction of the gods and the world in a final conflict with the powers of evil, ➤ RAGNARÖK, ➤ GÖTTER-DAMMERUNG; the phrase is first recorded in English in Thomas Gray's note to his *Descent of Odin* (1768).

Twinkie defence a legal defence of diminished responsibility in which irregular behaviour is attributed to an unbalanced diet of convenience food, from a proprietary name for a brand of cupcake with a creamy filling.

The *Twinkie defence* was first employed in 1979 in a San Francisco Supreme Court murder trial. It was disallowed as a legal defence by the US Congress in 1981.

in the twinkling of an eye in an instant, very quickly; recorded from Middle English, but often with biblical allusion to Corinthians 15:51.

the Twins the zodiacal sign or constellation ➤ GEMINI; the name is recorded from late Middle English.

twist the lion's tail provoke the resentment of the British (taking a *lion* as the symbol of the British Empire); the expression is first recorded in the late 19th-century US.

two recorded from Old English (in form *twā*) and of Germanic origin, the word comes ultimately from an Indo-European root shared by Latin and Greek *duo*.

The **two cultures** are literature and science as disciplines that tend to be mutually incompatible or hostile; the term was coined by the novelist and scientist C. P. Snow (1905–80) in 'The two cultures and the scientific revolution', title of The Rede Lecture given at Cambridge in 1959.

A **two-minute silence** is observed on the anniversary of Armistice Day (11 November 1918), or on Remembrance Sunday; the *Times* of 12 November 1919 recorded that 'At 11 o'clock yesterday morning the nation, in response to the King's invitation, paid homage to the Glorious Dead by keeping a two minutes' silence.' (Later sources refer to a silence of two minutes' duration having been observed by Canadian railways and churches in memory of those Canadians who drowned in the *Titanic* disaster of 1912, but contemporary use of the phrase is not recorded.)

The **two nations** are the rich and poor members of a society seen as effectively divided into separate nations by the presence or absence of wealth; the phrase comes from Disraeli's novel *Sybil* (1845), and has given rise to the expression ➤ ONE *Nation*.

The **Two Sicilies** are the former kingdom of Naples and Sicily. Originally a single state uniting the southern peninsula of Italy with Sicily, it was divided in the 13th century between the Angevin dynasty on the mainland territory and the Aragonese dynasty on the island; both claimed title to the kingdom of Sicily. In the mid 15th century the state was reunited under Alfonso V of Aragon, who took the title '*rex Utriusque Siciliae* [king of the Two Sicilies]'.

Tyburn a place in London, near Marble Arch, where public hangings were held *c.*1300–1783. It is named after a tributary of the Thames, which flows in an underground culvert nearby.

tycoon a title applied by foreigners to the shogun of Japan in power between 1857 and 1868; the word comes from Japanese *taikun* 'great lord'.

In the US, *Tycoon* was used as a nickname of Abraham Lincoln (1809–65); it subsequently developed the current general meaning of a wealthy and powerful person in business or industry.

Tyndale's Bible the translation of the New Testament from Greek to English made by the English translator and Protestant martyr William *Tyndale* (*c.*1494–1536), and printed at Worms 1525–6; in 1530 his translations from Hebrew of the Pentateuch and the Book of Jonah were printed at Marburg.

Typhoid Mary the nickname of *Mary* Mallon (died 1938), an Irish-born cook who as an unwitting carrier of the disease transmitted typhoid fever in the US.

Tyr in Scandinavian mythology, the god of battle, identified with Mars, after whom ➤ TUESDAY is named; he is one-handed, the other hand having been bitten off by the wolf ➤ FENRIR when it was shackled by the gods.

tyrannosaur a very large bipedal carnivorous dinosaur of the late Cretaceous period, with powerful jaws and small claw-like front legs; **Tyrannosaurus rex** is the best-known species. The name is modern Latin, and is formed from Greek *turannos* 'tyrant' + *sauros* 'lizard', on the pattern of *dinosaur*.

Tyre a port on the Mediterranean in southern Lebanon, founded in the 2nd millennium BC as a colony of Sidon, it was for centuries a Phoenician port and trading centre. Its prosperity did not decline until the 14th century.

Tyrian purple was ➤ PURPLE or crimson dye traditionally made at ancient Tyre.

Uu

U the twenty-first letter of the modern English alphabet and the twentieth of the ancient Roman one, a differentiated form of the letter V. Latin manuscripts written in capitals have V only, but other Latin manuscripts also have a modified form of this, resembling u. Both forms occur in OE manuscripts: capital V represents either V or U, and the modified form usually represents the vowel u. In ME the symbols u and v both occur, but without formal distinction of use.

During the 16th century continental printers began to distinguish lower case u as the vowel symbol and v as the consonant symbol, and by the mid 17th century this was also the case in English. Capital V continued to be used for both V and U into the 17th century, but in the course of that century it was replaced, for the vowel, by capital U. From about 1700 the regular forms have been U u for the vowel, and V v for the consonant. However, many dictionaries continued into the 19th century to give items beginning with u or v in a single alphabetic sequence.

U is used (of language or social behaviour) to mean characteristic of or appropriate to the upper social classes. The expression is an abbreviation of upper class, and was coined in 1954 by Alan S. C. Ross, professor of linguistics, the term was popularized by its use in Nancy Mitford's *Noblesse Oblige* (1956).

Übermensch the ideal superior man of the future who could rise above conventional Christian morality to create and impose his own values, originally described by Nietzsche in *Thus Spake Zarathustra* (1883–5). Nietzsche thought that such a being could arise when any man of superior potential shook off the conventional Christian morality of the masses to create and impose his own values.

Uffizi an art gallery and museum in Florence, housing one of Europe's finest art collections. Italian Renaissance painting is particularly well represented, although the collection also contains sculptures, drawings, and Flemish, French, and Dutch paintings. The building, the Uffizi palace, was designed by Giorgio Vasari *c*.1560 as offices for the Medici family.

UFO a mysterious object seen in the sky (an *Unidentified Flying Object*) for which it is claimed no orthodox scientific explanation can be found. UFO incidents range from sightings of unidentified lights in the sky to accounts of supposed abductions by alien beings.

Ugarit an ancient port and Bronze Age trading city in northern Syria, founded in Neolithic times and destroyed by the Sea Peoples in about the 12th century BC. Late Bronze Age remains include a palace, temples, and private residences containing legal, religious, and administrative cuneiform texts in Sumerian, Akkadian, Hurrian, Hittite, and Ugaritic languages. Its people spoke a Semitic language written in a distinctive cuneiform alphabet.

ugly American an American who behaves offensively when abroad; the phrase was originally used as the title of a book in 1954.

ugly duckling a person who turns out to be beautiful or talented against all expectations. The term comes from the title of one of Hans Christian Andersen's fairy tales, in which the 'ugly duckling' is in fact a cygnet which becomes a swan.

ulema a body of Muslim scholars who are recognized as having specialist knowledge of Islamic sacred law and theology. The word comes from the plural of Arabic '*ulamā*' 'learned', from '*alima* 'know'.

Ulfilas (*c*.311–*c*.381), bishop and translator. Believed to be of Cappadocian descent, he became bishop of the Visigoths in 341. His translation of the Bible from Greek into Gothic (of which fragments survive) is the earliest known translation of the Bible into a Germanic language. Ulfilas is traditionally held to have invented the Gothic alphabet, based on Latin and Greek characters. Also called **Wulfila**.

Ulpian (died *c*.228), Roman jurist, born in Phoenicia. His numerous legal writings provided one of the chief sources for
➤ JUSTINIAN's *Digest* of 533.

Ulster a former province of Ireland, in the north of the island; with Leinster, Munster, and Connaught one of the original four provinces, the 'four green fields' of Ireland. The nine counties of Ulster are now divided between Northern Ireland (Antrim, Down, Armagh, Londonderry, Tyrone, and Fermanagh) and the Republic of Ireland (Cavan, Donegal, and Monaghan). The name is also used generally for Northern Ireland, particularly in a political context.

Ulster King of Arms was formerly the chief heraldic officer for Ireland; since 1943, the office has been united with that of *Norroy King of Arms*.

ultima Thule a distant unknown region; the extreme limit of travel and discovery; the Latin phrase means 'furthest Thule' (see ➤ THULE).

Ultra in the Second World War, codename given to the project at ➤ BLETCHLEY *Park* in which British crytographers broke the German Enigma code.

ultramarine a brilliant deep blue pigment originally obtained from lapis lazuli. The word comes (in the late 16th century) from medieval Latin *ultramarinus* 'beyond the sea'; the name of the pigment is from obsolete Italian *(azzurro) oltramarino*, literally '(azure) from overseas'.

ultramontane advocating supreme papal authority in matters of faith and discipline. Recorded from the late 16th century, the name originally denoted a representative of the Roman Catholic Church north of the Alps.

Ulysses the Roman name for ➤ ODYSSEUS; he is referred to as the type of a traveller or adventurer, and also of a crafty and clever schemer.

Ulysses' bow was able to be bent by ➤ ULYSSES alone; on his return to Ithaca, he finds that his wife Penelope has agreed that she will marry whichever of her suitors can bend and string the bow, and only Ulysses can achieve this.

Umayyad a member of a Muslim dynasty that ruled the Islamic world from AD 660 (or 661) to 750 and Moorish Spain 756–1031. The dynasty claimed descent from *Umayya*, a distant relative of Muhammad.

The **Ummayad Mosque** is a mosque in Damascus, Syria, built AD 705–15 on the site of a church dedicated to St John the Baptist.

Within the mosque is a shrine believed to contain the relic of the saint's head.

Umbrian School a Renaissance school of Italian painting developed in Umbria in central Italy in the 15th century, to which Raphael and Perugino belonged.

umlaut the process in Germanic languages by which the quality of a vowel was altered in certain phonetic contexts, resulting for example in the differences between modern German *Mann* and *Männer* or (after loss of the inflection) English *man* and *men*.

umma the whole community of Muslims bound together by ties of religion. The word is Arabic and means literally, 'people, community'.

House Un-American Activities Committee a committee of the US House of Representatives (HUAC) established in 1938 to investigate subversives. It became notorious for its zealous investigations of alleged communists, particularly in the late 1940s, although it was originally intended to pursue Fascists also.

Una in Spenser's *Faerie Queene*, the personification of single-minded adherence to true religion, and the antithesis of the falsity of ➤ DUESSA.

Unabomber the media nickname for a terrorist who carried out a series of bomb attacks in the US between 1978 and 1995 as part of an anarchist, anti-technology personal crusade; because the attacks were made on academic institutions (and particularly scientists), the name *Unabomber*, a blend of *university* and *bomber*, was coined. Theodore Kaczynski was finally tried and convicted in 1998.

uncial of or written in a majuscule script with rounded unjoined letters which is found in European manuscripts of the 4th–8th centuries and from which modern capital letters are derived. The term is recorded from the late 17th century and comes from late Latin *unciales littera* 'uncial letters', the original application of which is unclear. (One explanation has been that the phrase stands for 'letters of an inch long' from Latin *uncia* 'inch'; the emendations *initiales* 'initial' and *uncinales* 'hooked, bent' have also been suggested.)

uncle the brother of one's father or mother or the husband of one's aunt; the word comes (in Middle English, via Old French) from a late Latin alteration of Latin *avunculus* 'maternal uncle'.

From the mid 18th century, *uncle* has been used as an informal name for a pawnbroker, perhaps as a humorous reference to the relationship implied by the pawnbroker's taking charge of a person's possessions.

Uncle Joe was the British wartime nickname for Joseph Stalin (1879–1953) as the personification of Soviet Russia; the name is first recorded in a comment made by Winston Churchill to Franklin Roosevelt in 1943.

Uncle Remus is the elderly slave who is the narrator of Joel Chandler Harris's ➤ *Brer* RABBIT stories; the first book in the series (published 1880) was entitled *Uncle Remus, his songs and his sayings; the folk-lore of the old plantation*.

Uncle Sam is a personification of the federal government or citizens of the US. Recorded from the early 19th century, it is said (from the time of the first recorded instances) to have arisen as a facetious expansion of the letters US.

An **Uncle Tom** is a black man considered to be excessively obedient or servile, from the name of the hero of Harriet Beecher Stowe's *Uncle Tom's Cabin* (1852). The book was seen at the time as dramatizing the question of abolition.

the unco guid Scottish term for those who are professedly strict in matters of morals and religion; *unco* (an alteration of *uncouth*) means 'extremely, remarkably', and the expression comes from the title of Robert Burns's 'Address to the Unco Guid, or the Rigidly Righteous' (1786).

St Uncumber another name for ➤ *St* WILGEFORTIS, said by St Thomas More to refer to the belief that if an offering of oats were made at her shrine by an unhappy wife, the saint would relieve her of her troubles. Her feast day is 20 July.

Underground Railroad in the US, a secret network for helping slaves escape from the South to the North and Canada in the years before the American Civil War. Escaped slaves were given safe houses, transport, and other assistance, often by members of the free black community.

underworld the mythical abode of the dead, imagined as being under the earth; in classical mythology, various heroes such as ➤ ODYSSEUS and ➤ AENEAS were said to have visited the underworld and to have returned.

undine a female spirit or nymph imagined as inhabiting water, a water-nymph; recorded from the early 19th century, the word comes from modern Latin *Undina* (in Paracelsus *De Nymphis*), from Latin *unda* 'wave'.

Unfinished Symphony informal name for Schubert's *Symphony in B Minor* (1822).

Uniate denoting or relating to any community of Christians in eastern Europe or the Near East that acknowledges papal supremacy but retains its own liturgy. The name comes via Russian from Latin *unio(n-)* 'unity'.

unicorn a mythical animal typically represented as a horse with a single straight horn projecting from its forehead; a heraldic representation of such an animal, with a twisted horn, a deer's feet, a goat's beard, and a lion's tail.

The unicorn has at various times been identified or confused with the rhinoceros, with various species of antelope, or with other animals having a horn (or horns) or horn-like projection from the head. According to Pliny it had a body resembling that of a horse, the head of a deer, the feet of an elephant, and the tail of a lion, with one black horn projecting from the middle of the forehead. In biblical translation, *unicorn* may be used for a kind of wild ox.

The horn of this animal was reputed to possess medicinal or magical properties, especially as an antidote to or preventive of poison. It was also said that it could only be captured by a virgin.

In heraldry, the unicorn is a supporter of the ➤ ROYAL *Arms* of the United Kingdom.

A **unicorn's horn** was a horn regarded as or alleged to be obtained from the legendary unicorn, but in reality that of the rhinoceros, narwhal, or other animal, frequently mounted or made into a drinking cup and employed as a preventive of or charm against poison.

Unification Church an evangelistic religious and political organization founded in 1954 in Korea by Sun Myung Moon.

Act of Uniformity in British history, any of four acts (especially that of 1662) establishing the foundations of the English Protestant Church and securing uniformity in public worship and use of a particular Book of Common Prayer. The first two Acts were passed in the reign of Edward VI but repealed under his Catholic successor Mary I; a third was passed in the reign of Elizabeth I, and a final Act in 1662 after the Restoration.

Unilateral Declaration of Independence the declaration of independence from the United Kingdom made by Rhodesia under Ian Smith in 1965. Abbreviation, **UDI**.

Act of Union in British history, either of the parliamentary acts by which the countries of the United Kingdom were brought together as a political whole. By the first Act of Union (1707) Scotland was joined with England to form Great Britain. The second Act of Union (1801) established the United Kingdom of Great Britain and Ireland. Wales had been incorporated with England in 1536.

Union flag the national flag of the United Kingdom, consisting of red and white crosses on a blue background and formed by combining the flags of St George, St Andrew, and St Patrick; the name ➤ UNION *Jack* is now frequently used.

Union Jack originally and properly a small ➤ UNION *flag* flown as the *jack* of a ship (a small version of a national flag flown at the bow of a vessel in harbour to indicate its nationality); more generally, the ➤ UNION *flag* in any size or adaptation, regarded as the national ensign.

Unitarian a person, especially a Christian, who asserts the unity of God and rejects the doctrine of the Trinity; a member of a Church or religious body maintaining this belief and typically rejecting formal dogma in favour of a rationalist and inclusivist approach to belief.

United Irishman a member of the Society of United Irishmen, a political association, originally formed to promote union between Protestants and Catholics, which became a separatist secret society and took part in organizing the rebellion of 1798.

United Kingdom a country of western Europe consisting of England, Wales, Scotland, and Northern Ireland. England (which had incorporated Wales in the 16th century) and Scotland have had the same monarch since 1603, when James VI of Scotland succeeded to the English crown as James I; the kingdoms were formally united by the Act of Union in 1707. An Act of Parliament joined Great Britain and Ireland in 1801, but the Irish Free State (later the Republic of Ireland) broke away in 1921.

United Nations an international organization of countries set up in 1945, in succession to the ➤ LEAGUE *of Nations*, to promote international peace, security, and cooperation. Its members, originally the countries that fought against the Axis Powers in the Second World War, now number more than 150 and include most sovereign states of the world, the chief exceptions being Switzerland and North and South Korea.

United Reformed Church a Church formed in 1972 by the union of the Congregational Church in England and Wales with the Presbyterian Church in England.

United States the US originated in the ➤ *War of* AMERICAN *Independence*, the successful rebellion of the British colonies on the east coast in 1775–83; The original thirteen states (see ➤ THIRTEEN *Colonies*) which formed the Union drew up a federal constitution in 1787, and George Washington was elected the first President in 1789.

Universal Declaration of Human Rights declaration adopted by the United Nations in 1948, the first article of which states, 'All human beings are born free and equal in dignity and rights.'

University of the Third Age an organization providing courses of education for retired or elderly people, founded in 1981.

the unkindest cut of all the most hurtful thing that could be done or said; originally as a quotation from Shakespeare's *Julius Caesar* (1598), 'Through this the well-beloved Brutus stabb'd…This was the most unkindest cut of all.'

unknown god an unidentified god, especially one to whom an altar has been set up so no god would feel overlooked; in Acts 17:23, St Paul sees an altar in Athens with the inscription 'to the Unknown God', and proclaims to the Athenians that this God is in fact Jesus Christ.

Unknown Soldier an unidentified representative member of a country's armed forces killed in war, given burial with special honours in a national memorial; also called the *Unknown Warrior*. In Britain the tomb of the *Unknown Soldier* is in Westminster Abbey.

unparliamentary language contrary to the rules or procedures of parliament; the term is used more generally to cover what is regarded as an offensive form of speech.

unruly member the tongue; with biblical allusion to James 3:8.

untouchable a member of the lowest-caste Hindu group or a person outside the caste system. Contact with untouchables is traditionally held to defile members of higher castes. The term *untouchable* and the social restrictions accompanying it were declared illegal in the constitution of India in 1949 and of Pakistan in 1953.

Up-Helly-Aa an annual festival held at Lerwick in the Shetland Islands, celebrated as the revival of a traditional midwinter fire festival. The name comes from a variant of Scots *Uphaliday*, denoting Epiphany as the end of the Christmas holiday, and the current festival dates from the late 19th century.

up to a point, Lord Copper quotation from Evelyn Waugh's *Scoop* (1938) used to indicate limited agreement with a policy or proposition; Lord Copper in the novel is the overbearing proprietor of the popular newspaper *The Beast*.

Upanishad each of a series of Hindu sacred treatises written in Sanskrit *c.*800–200 BC, expounding the ➤ VEDAS. The *Upanishads* mark the transition from ritual sacrifice to a mystical concern with the nature of reality; polytheism is superseded by a pantheistic monism derived from the basic concepts of atman and Brahman.

upas tree in folklore, a Javanese tree alleged to poison its surroundings and said to be fatal to approach. An account of the tree was given in the *London Magazine* of 1783, and was said to be translated from one written in Dutch. The physician Erasmus Darwin (1731–1802) adopted and gave currency to the fiction, but it was in fact invented by the writer and critic George Steevens (1736–1800).

upper room in the Bible, the room in which the ➤ *Last Supper* was celebrated, and in which the Holy Spirit descended to the disciples at ➤ PENTECOST.

upper ten thousand the aristocracy; the term is first recorded in the US in 1844.

Ur an ancient Sumerian city formerly on the Euphrates, in southern Iraq. It was one of the oldest cities of Mesopotamia, dating from the 4th millennium BC, and reached its zenith in the late 3rd millennium BC.
In the Bible (Genesis 12:31), **Ur of the Chaldees** is named as the original home of Abraham (the connection with the Chaldeans may be of later date). *Ur of the Chaldees* is sometimes referred to as the type of a place from the infinitely distant past.

uraeus a representation of a sacred serpent as an emblem of supreme power, worn on the headdresses of ancient Egyptian deities and sovereigns. The word comes (in the mid 19th century, via modern Latin) from Greek *ouraios*, representing the Egyptian word for 'cobra'.

Urania in classical mythology, the Muse of astronomy; the name is Greek, and means literally, 'heavenly female'.

Uranus in Greek mythology, a personification of heaven or the sky, the most ancient of the Greek gods and first ruler of the universe. He was overthrown and castrated by his son ➤ CRONUS.

urban myth an entertaining story or piece of information circulated as though true, especially one purporting to involve someone vaguely related or known to the teller. *Urban myths* or **urban legends** have been recognized as a form since the early 1980s, but the kind of story covered by the term is likely to be of very long standing.

urbi et orbi Latin phrase meaning, 'to the city (of Rome) and to the world', as used in papal proclamations and blessings.

Urdu an Indic language closely related to Hindi but written in the Persian script and having many loanwords from Persian and Arabic. It is the official language of Pakistan, and is also widely used in India and elsewhere, with about 50 million speakers worldwide.

Uriah in the Bible, a Hittite officer in David's army, whom David, desiring his wife Bathsheba, caused to be killed in battle.

Urim and Thummim two objects of a now unknown nature, possibly used for divination, worn on the breastplate of a Jewish high priest. They are first mentioned in the Bible at Exodus 28:30, and the role of Urim is hinted at in Numbers 27:21 and I Samuel 28:6.

Urnes a style of late Viking decorative art, characterized by the use of animal motifs and complex interlacing. The term comes from the town of *Urnes* in western Norway, site of an 11th-century stave church decorated in this style.

uroboros a circular symbol depicting a snake, or less commonly a dragon, swallowing its tail, as an emblem of wholeness or infinity. The word comes from Greek *(drakōn) ouroboros* '(snake) devouring its tail'.

Ursa Major one of the largest and most prominent northern constellations (the *Great Bear*). The seven brightest stars form a familiar formation variously called the Plough, Big Dipper, or Charles's Wain, and include the Pointers.

Boswell's father, Lord Auchinleck (1706–82) gave the name *Ursa Major* to Dr Johnson.

Ursa Minor a northern constellation (the *Little Bear*), which contains the north celestial pole and the pole star Polaris. The brightest stars form a shape that is also known as the Little Dipper.

St Ursula a legendary British saint and martyr, said to have been put to death with 11,000 virgins after being captured by Huns near Cologne while on a pilgrimage. The legend probably developed from an incident of the 4th century or earlier. Her feast day is 21 October.

Ursuline a nun of an order founded by St Angela Merici (1470–1540) at Brescia in 1535 for nursing the sick and teaching girls. It is the oldest teaching order of women in the Roman Catholic Church.

Uruk an ancient city in southern Mesopotamia, to the north-west of Ur. One of the greatest cities of Sumer, it was built in the 5th millennium BC and is associated with the legendary hero Gilgamesh. Excavations begun in 1928 revealed great ziggurats and temples dedicated to the sky god Anu.

Usonian of or relating to the United States, in particular, relating to or denoting the style of buildings designed in the 1930s by Frank Lloyd Wright, characterized by inexpensive construction and flat roofs. The word is recorded from 1915, and is a partial acronym, from the initial letters of *United States of North America + -ian*.

Utgard in Scandinavian mythology, the home of the giants.

Uther Pendragon in Arthurian legend, king of the Britons and father of ➤ *King* AR-THUR.

utilitarianism the doctrine that actions are right if they are useful or for the benefit of a majority; the doctrine that an action is right in so far as it promotes happiness, and that the greatest happiness of the greatest number should be the guiding principle of conduct.

Utnapishtim in Babylonian mythology, a figure equivalent to ➤ NOAH who survives a devastating flood.

Utopia an imagined place or state of things in which everything is perfect. The word was first used as the name of an imaginary island, governed on a perfect political and social system, in the book *Utopia* (1516) by Sir Thomas More. The name in modern Latin is literally 'no-place', from Greek *ou* 'not' + *topos* 'place'.

Peace of Utrecht a series of treaties (1713–14) ending the War of the Spanish Succession. The disputed throne of Spain was given to the French Philip V, but the union of the French and Spanish thrones was forbidden. The House of Hanover succeeded to the British throne and the former Spanish territories in Italy were ceded to the Habsburgs.

Vv

V the twenty-second letter of the modern English alphabet and the twentieth of the ancient Roman one, of which U is a differentiated form.

The **V-1** was a small flying bomb powered by a simple jet engine, used by the Germans in the Second World War. Also called *doodlebug*.

The **V-2** was a rocket-powered flying bomb, which was the first ballistic missile, used by the Germans in the Second World War.

A **V-sign** is a sign resembling the letter V made with the first two fingers pointing up and the palm of the hand facing outwards, used as a symbol or gesture of victory; a similar sign made with the back of the hand facing outwards, used as a gesture of abuse or contempt.

vade mecum a handbook or guide that is kept constantly at hand for consultation. The phrase is Latin and means 'go with me'; it is first used (in the early 17th century) as the title of a book.

Vaisya a member of the third of the four Hindu castes, comprising the merchants and farmers.

vajra in Buddhism and Hinduism, a thunderbolt or mythical weapon, especially one wielded by the god Indra. Being struck by such a weapon is said to bring spiritual illumination.

Valdez Principles a set of guidelines drawn up in 1989, designed to regulate and monitor the conduct of corporations in matters relating to the environment. They are named after the Exxon *Valdez*, an oil tanker which ran aground off the Alaskan coast in 1989, causing considerable environmental damage.

vale of tears the world as a place of sorrow and difficulty; the expression dates from the mid 16th century, and earlier variants are *vale of woe* and *vale of weeping*.

valentine originally (in late Middle English), a person chosen (sometimes by lot) to be one's sweetheart. Later, a card sent, often anonymously, on ➤ St VALENTINE's Day, 14 February, to a person one loves or is attracted to; a person to whom one sends such a card or whom one asks to be one's sweetheart.

St Valentine either of two early Italian saints (who may have been the same person) traditionally commemorated on 14 February—a Roman priest martyred *c*.269 and a bishop of Terni martyred at Rome. St Valentine was regarded as the patron of lovers, a tradition which may be connected with the old belief that birds pair on 14 February or with the pagan fertility festival of ➤ LUPERCALIA (15 February). His feast day is 14 February.

The **St Valentine's Day Massacre** was the shooting on 14th February 1929 in Chicago by some of Al Capone's men, disguised as policemen, of seven members of the rival gang of 'Bugsy' Moran.

Valerian (d.260), Roman emperor 253–60, who renewed the persecution of the Christians initiated by Decius. He died after being captured while campaigning against the Persians of the Sassanian dynasty.

Valhalla in Scandinavian mythology, a palace in which heroes killed in battle were believed to feast with Odin for eternity. The name is from modern Latin, and comes from Old Norse *Valhǫll*, from *valr* 'the slain' + *hǫll* 'hall'.

Valkyrie in Scandinavian mythology, each of Odin's twelve handmaids who conducted the slain warriors of their choice from the battlefield to Valhalla. The name comes from Old Norse *Valkyrja*, literally 'chooser of the slain'.

valley a low area of land between hills or mountains.

Valley Forge was the site on the Schuylkill River in Pennsylvania, about 32 km (20 miles) to the north-west of Philadelphia, where George Washington's Continental Army spent the winter of 1777–8, during the War of American Independence, in conditions of extreme hardship.

Valley Girl is an informal term for a fashionable and affluent teenage girl, often using ➤ VALSPEAK, from the San Fernando valley in southern California.

The **Valley of the Kings** is a valley near ancient Thebes in Egypt where the pharaohs of the New Kingdom (c.1550–1070 BC) were buried. Most of the tombs, typically consisting of a richly decorated chamber at the end of a long series of descending corridors, were robbed in antiquity; the exception was the tomb of ➤ TUTANKHAMEN, almost untouched until discovered in 1922.

The **Valley of the Queens** is a valley near ancient Thebes in Egypt where the wives and daughters of pharaohs of the 20th dynasty were buried.

Valois the French royal house from the accession of Philip VI, successor to the last Capetian king, in 1328 to the death of Henry III (1589), when the throne passed to the Bourbons.

Valspeak a variety of slang originating among teenage girls (➤ VALLEY *Girls*) in the San Fernando Valley of southern California and characterized by the use of filler words such as *like* and *totally* and a limited group of adjectives expressing approval or disapproval.

vampire in European folklore, a corpse supposed to leave its grave at night to drink the blood of the living by biting their necks with long pointed canine teeth. The word comes (in the mid 18th century) via French from Hungarian *vampir*, perhaps from Turkish *uber* 'witch'.

The 20th-century *vamp* for a woman who uses sexual attraction to exploit men is an abbreviation of this word.

Van Diemen's land former name (until 1855) for Tasmania (see ➤ *Abel* TASMAN).

Vandal a member of a Germanic people that ravaged Gaul, Spain, Rome (455), and North Africa in the 4th–5th centuries, destroying many books and works of art. They were eventually defeated by the Byzantine general Belisarius (c.505–65), after which their North African kingdom fell prey to Muslim invaders.

The name is recorded in English from the mid 16th century; from the mid 17th century, the word *vandal* is used for a person who deliberately destroys or damages public or private property.

Vanderbilt name used allusively as the type of a very wealthy person, from the American businessman and philanthropist Cornelius *Vanderbilt* (1794–1877). He amassed a fortune from shipping and railroads, and subsequent generations of his family increased the family wealth.

vanilla having no special or extra features; ordinary. The term is a figurative use of *vanilla* as the default or standard flavour of ice-cream; it was used first with reference to sexual activity, and then from the early 1980s was applied particularly to computing equipment in the form supplied as standard by the manufacturer, without any optional additions or extra equipment.

Vanir in Scandinavian mythology, a race of gods responsible for commerce and fertility while the ➤ AESIR were responsible for war; ➤ NJORD and ➤ FREY were two of the Vanir.

vanitas vanitatum vanity of vanities, futility (frequently as an exclamation of disillusionment or pessimism). The phrase is late Latin and comes from the Vulgate translation of Ecclesiastes 1:2.

Vanity Fair the world regarded as a place of frivolity and idle amusement, originally with reference to Bunyan's *Pilgrim's Progress* (1678), and the fair set up by Apollyon and named *Vanity Fair*. Thackeray later used the title for his satirical novel (1847–8) of 19th-century society life.

Varanasi a city on the Ganges, in Uttar Pradesh, northern India, which is a holy city and a place of pilgrimage for Hindus, who undergo ritual purification in the Ganges.

Varangian any of the Scandinavian voyagers who travelled by land and up rivers into Russia in the 9th and 10th centuries AD, establishing the Rurik dynasty and gaining great influence in the Byzantine Empire. The name comes from medieval Latin *Varangus*, ultimately from Old Norse, and probably based on *vár* 'pledge'.

The **Varangian guard** was the bodyguard of the later Byzantine emperors, comprising Varangians and later also Anglo-Saxons.

variorum an edition of an author's works having notes by various editors or commentators, and often including variant readings from manuscripts or earlier editions. The word is Latin, and comes (in the early 18th century) from *editio cum notis variorum* 'edition with notes by various (commentators)'.

varna each of the four Hindu castes, Brahman, Kshatriya, Vaisya, and Sudra. In the Vedic religion of the ancient Aryans, the first three classes of society were Brahman, Kshatriya, and Vaisya. The fourth class, Sudra, was probably added later after contact with the indigenous people of the subcontinent. Each class was considered equally necessary to the social order, the separate functions being complementary.

Varuna in Hinduism, one of the gods in the Rig Veda. Originally the sovereign lord of the universe and guardian of cosmic law, he is known in later Hinduism as god of the waters.

Vasa name of a Swedish dynasty, descended from an Uppland family, ruling Sweden between 1523 and 1818.

vassal a holder of land by feudal tenure on conditions of homage and allegiance; the word comes (in late Middle English, via Old French) from medieval Latin *vassalius* 'retainer', of Celtic origin.

the Vatican the palace and official residence of the Pope in Rome, built on and named for the Vatican Hill; the administrative centre of the Roman Catholic Church. The name is recorded in English from the mid 16th century.

Vatican City is an independent papal state in the city of Rome, the seat of government of the Roman Catholic Church. It covers an area of 44 hectares (109 acres) around St Peter's Basilica and the palace of the Vatican. Having been suspended after the incorporation of the former Papal States into Italy in 1870, the temporal power of the Pope was restored by the Lateran Treaty of 1929.

Vatican Council is each of two general councils of the Roman Catholic Church, held in 1869–70 and 1962–5. The first (**Vatican I**) proclaimed the infallibility of the Pope when speaking *ex cathedra*; the second (**Vatican II**) made numerous reforms, abandoning the universal Latin liturgy and acknowledging ecumenism.

VE day the day (8 May) marking the Allied victory in Europe in 1945.

Veda the most ancient Hindu scriptures, written in early Sanskrit and containing hymns, philosophy, and guidance on ritual for the priests of Vedic religion. Believed to have been directly revealed to seers among the early Aryans in India, and preserved by oral tradition, the four chief collections are the Rig Veda, Sama Veda, Yajur Veda, and Atharva Veda. In its wider sense, the term also includes the Brahmanas and the mystical Aranyakas and Upanishads.

Vedanta a Hindu philosophy based on the doctrine of the Upanishads, especially in its monistic form.

Vedic religion the ancient religion of the Aryan peoples who entered NW India from Persia *c.*2000–1200 BC. It was the precursor of Hinduism, and its beliefs and practices are contained in the Vedas.

Its characteristics included ritual sacrifice to many gods, especially Indra, Varuna, and Agni; social classes (varnas) that formed the basis of the caste system; and the emergence of the priesthood which dominated orthodox Brahmanism from *c.*900 BC. Transition to classical Hinduism began in about the 5th century BC.

vegan a person who does not eat or use animal products. The word was coined in 1944 as the existing terms *vegetarian* and *fruitarian* were already associated with the permitted consumption of dairy produce.

velociraptor a small dromaeosaurid dinosaur of the late Cretaceous period, given great prominence in the novel and film *Jurassic Park*; the current general use of ➤ RAPTOR for this kind of dinosaur comes from a shortening of this word.

velvet revolution a non-violent political revolution, especially the relatively smooth change from Communism to a Western-style democracy in Czechoslovakia at the end of 1989.

Vendean an inhabitant of the Vendée (*La Vendée*) in western France, who took part in the insurrection of 1793 against the Republic.

Vendemiaire the first month of the French Republican calendar (1793–1805), originally running from 22 September to 21 October. The name is French, and comes from Latin *vindemia* 'vintage'.

vendetta a blood feud in which the family of a murdered person seeks vengeance on the murderer or the murderer's family, especially as traditionally prevalent in Corsica and Sicily. Recorded from the mid 19th century, the word is Italian, and comes from Latin *vindicta* 'vengeance'.

venerable accorded a great deal of respect, especially because of age, wisdom, or character; (in the Anglican Church) a title given to an archdeacon; (in the Roman Catholic Church) a title given to a deceased person who has attained a certain degree of sanctity but has not been fully beatified or canonized. The **Venerable Bede** is the traditional name for ➤ St BEDE.

veni, vidi, vici Latin for 'I came, I saw, I conquered', an inscription displayed in Julius Caesar's Pontic triumph (according to Suetonius) or (according to Plutarch), written in a letter by Caesar, announcing the victory of Zela (47 BC) which concluded the Pontic campaign.

venial in Christian theology, denoting a sin that is not regarded as depriving the soul of divine grace. The word comes ultimately (in Middle English, via Old French) from late Latin *venia* 'forgiveness'.

Venice a city in NE Italy, situated on a lagoon of the Adriatic and built on numerous islands that are separated by canals and linked by bridges. It was a powerful republic in the Middle Ages and from the 13th to the 16th centuries a leading sea power, controlling trade to the Levant and ruling parts of the eastern Mediterranean.

Venite Psalm 95 used as a canticle in Christian liturgy, chiefly at matins; *venite* is Latin for 'come ye', and is the first word of the psalm.

Ventose the sixth month of the French Republican calendar (1793–1805), originally running from 19 February to 20 March. The word is French and comes from Latin *ventosus* 'windy'.

Venus in Roman mythology, a goddess, worshipped as the goddess of love in classical Rome though apparently a spirit of kitchen gardens in earlier times. She is the mother of ➤ CUPID and (though wife of Hephaestus), lover of ➤ MARS. Her Greek equivalent is ➤ APHRODITE.

Venus Anadyomene is Venus portrayed rising from the sea, according to Pliny's *Natural History* in a picture by the Greek artist ➤ APELLES, and represented in Botticelli's The Birth of Venus.

The **Venus de Medici** is a classical sculpture in the Uffizi Gallery at Florence.

The **Venus de Milo** is a classical sculpture of Aphrodite dated to *c.*100 BC. It was discovered on the Greek island of Melos in 1820 and is now in the Louvre in Paris, having formed part of the war loot acquired by Napoleon on his campaigns.

Venusberg in German legend, the court of Venus, said to have been visited by the poet

➤ TANNHÄUSER; in transferred use, any environment whose primary environment is sensual pleasure.

verbatim in exactly the same words as were used originally; the word is recorded from the late 15th century, and comes ultimately from Latin *verbum* 'word'.

Vercingetorix Gallic leader of a revolt against Rome; defeated by Julius Caesar in the ➤ GALLIC *Wars*, he was put to death in 46 BC.

Battle of Verdun a long and severe battle in 1916, during the First World War, at the fortified town of Verdun in NE France, in which the French, initially unprepared, eventually repelled a prolonged German offensive but suffered heavy losses.

verger an official in a church who carries a rod before a bishop or dean as a symbol of office; an officer who carries a rod before a bishop or dean as a symbol of office. The word is recorded from Middle English, and comes ultimately from Latin *virga* 'rod'.

vermilion a brilliant red pigment made from mercury sulphide (cinnabar). Recorded from Middle English, the word comes via Old French and ultimately from Latin *vermiculus*, diminutive of *vermis* 'worm'.

Verner's law the observation that voiceless fricatives in Germanic predicted by Grimm's Law became voiced if the preceding syllable in the corresponding Indo-European word was unstressed. It is named after Karl A. *Verner* (1846–96), Danish philologist.

vernicle a vernicle, or cloth supposedly impressed with Christ's face, is the emblem of ➤ St VERONICA.

St Veronica according to tradition, a woman of Jerusalem who offered her headcloth to Christ on the way to Calvary, to wipe the blood and sweat from his face. The cloth is said to have retained the image of his features, and is called a *vernicle* or *veronica* in her honour.

The term veronica also denotes the movement of a matador's cape away from a charging bull; this is said to be by association of the attitude of the matador with the depiction of St Veronica holding out a cloth to Christ.

Versailles a palace built for Louis XIV near the town of Versailles, south-west of Paris. It was built around a château belonging to

Louis XIII, which was transformed by additions in the grand French classical style.

The **Treaty of Versailles** is the name given to both a treaty which terminated the War of American Independence in 1783, and to a treaty signed in 1919 which brought a formal end to the First World War.

versicle a short sentence said or sung by the minister in a church service, to which the congregation gives a response.

verso a left-hand page of an open book, or the back of a loose document. The word is Latin, and comes from the phrase *verso (folio)* 'on the turned (leaf)'.

vert green, as a heraldic tincture. The word is recorded from Middle English (as an adjective), and comes via Old French from Latin *viridis* 'green'.

Vesak the most important Buddhist festival, taking place at the full moon when the sun is in the zodiacal sign of Taurus, and commemorating the birth, enlightenment, and death of the Buddha. Also, the month in which this festival occurs.

Vesalian of or pertaining to Andreas *Vesalius* (1514–64), Flemish anatomist, the founder of modern anatomy. His major work, *De Humani Corporis Fabrica* (1543), contained accurate descriptions of human anatomy, but owed much of its great historical impact to the woodcuts of his dissections.

vesica piscis a pointed oval figure (also called *mandorla*) used as an architectural feature and as an aureole enclosing figures such as Christ or the Virgin Mary in medieval art. The term is Latin, and means literally 'fish's bladder'; the reason for the name is not clear, although it may refer to the shape.

Vespasian (AD 9–79), Roman emperor 69–79 and founder of the Flavian dynasty, father of ➤ TITUS. He was acclaimed emperor by the legions in Egypt during the civil wars following the death of Nero and gained control of Italy after the defeat of Vitellius.

Vesper in poetic and literary use, Venus as the evening star; Hesper, Hesperus.

vespers a service of evening prayer in the Divine Office of the Western Christian Church (sometimes said earlier in the day). In modern Roman Catholic use, the services for Sundays and solemn feasts begin on the preceding evening with first vespers and end with second vespers.

Amerigo Vespucci (1451–1512), Italian merchant and explorer. He travelled to the New World, reaching the coast of Venezuela on his first voyage (1499–1500) and exploring the Brazilian coastline in 1501–2. The Latin form of his first name is believed to have given rise to the name of *America*.

Vesta in Roman mythology, the goddess of the hearth and household. She was worshipped in a round building in the Forum at Rome, probably an imitation in stone of an ancient round hut. Her temple in Rome contained no image but a fire which was kept constantly burning and was tended by the Vestal Virgins.

The **Vestal Virgins** were virgins consecrated to Vesta and vowed to chastity, sharing the charge of maintaining the sacred fire burning on the goddess's altar; there were originally four, and later six, of these priestesses.

vestry a room or building attached to a church, used as an office and for changing into ceremonial vestments; a meeting of parishioners, originally in a vestry, for the conduct of parochial business; a body of parishioners meeting in such a way.

Vesuvius an active volcano near Naples, in southern Italy, 1,277 m (4,190 ft) high. A violent eruption in AD 79 buried the towns of ➤ POMPEII and Herculaneum.

veteran a person who has had long experience in a particular field, especially military service. Recorded from the early 16th century, the word comes ultimately from Latin *vetus* 'old'. In the US, **Veterans Day** is a public holiday held on the anniversary of the end of the First World War (11 November) to honour US veterans and victims of all wars. It replaced ➤ ARMISTICE *Day* in 1954.

In the UK, a **veteran car** is an old style or model of car, specifically one made before 1916, or (strictly) before 1905.

via a road or highway; in particular, one of the great Roman roads (in Latin *via* means 'road' or 'way').

The preposition *via*, travelling through (a place) en route to a destination, comes (in the late 18th century) from Latin, ablative of *via* 'way, road'.

Via Crucis is the Latin name for the ➤ WAY *of the Cross*.

The **via dolorosa** is the route believed to have been taken by Christ through Jerusalem to Calvary. The name is Latin, and means literally 'painful path'.

In theology, **via negativa** is a way of describing something by saying what it is not, especially denying that any finite concept of attribute can be identified with or used of God or ultimate reality.

vials of wrath stored-up anger, originally with allusion to Revelation 15:7, 'seven golden vials full of the wrath of God'.

viatical settlement an arrangement whereby a person with a terminal illness sells their life insurance policy to a third party for less than its mature value, in order to benefit from the proceeds while alive; the system (referred to informally as *death futures*) developed with the spread of Aids and the heightened awareness of the possibility of long-drawn-out terminal illness requiring nursing care for previous healthy young people.

The term is recorded from the 1990s, and comes from Latin *viaticus* 'relating to a journey or departing'.

viaticum the Eucharist as given to a person near or in danger of death; the word comes (in the mid 16th century) from Latin, ultimately from *via* 'road'.

vicar (in the Church of England) an incumbent of a parish where tithes formerly passed to a chapter or religious house or layman; (in other Anglican Churches) a member of the clergy deputizing for another; (in the Roman Catholic Church) a representative or deputy of a bishop; (in the US Episcopal Church) a clergyman in charge of a chapel. The word is recorded from Middle English, and comes ultimately from Latin *vicarius* 'substitute'.

A **vicar apostolic** is a Roman Catholic missionary; a titular bishop.

A **vicar general** is an Anglican official serving as a deputy or assistant to a bishop or archbishop; (in the Roman Catholic Church) a bishop's representative in matters of jurisdiction or administration.

In the Roman Catholic Church, **Vicar of Christ** is a title of the Pope, as Christ's representative on earth, dating from the 8th century.

vice immoral or wicked behaviour; often personified, especially as a character in a morality play.

vice versa with the main items in the preceding statement the other way round. The phrase is Latin, recorded in English from the early 17th century, and means literally 'inturned position'.

Vichy a town in south central France which during the Second World War was the headquarters of the regime (1940–4) that was set up under Marshal Pétain after the German occupation of northern France, to administer unoccupied France and the colonies. Never recognized by the Allies, the regime functioned as a puppet government for the Nazis.

vicious circle a sequence of reciprocal cause and effect in which two or more elements intensify and aggravate each other, leading inexorably to a worsening of the situation.

Vicksburg a city on the Mississippi River, in western Mississippi. In 1863, during the American Civil War, it was successfully besieged by Union forces under General Grant. It was the last Confederate-held outpost on the river and its loss effectively split the secessionist states in half.

Victoria name of Queen Victoria (1819–1901), Queen of the United Kingdom from 1837. The phrase **Victorian values**, embodying aspirations for what were seen as the 19th-century virtues of self-reliance and morality, was associated with Margaret Thatcher's Conservative government of the 1980s.

The **Victoria and Albert Museum** is a national museum of fine and applied art in South Kensington, London, having collections principally of pictures, textiles, ceramics, and furniture. Created in 1852 out of the surplus funds of the Great Exhibition, the museum moved to its present site in 1857.

The **Victoria Cross** is a decoration awarded for conspicuous bravery in the Commonwealth armed services, instituted by Queen Victoria in 1856. The medals were originally struck from the metal of Russian guns captured at Sebastopol during the Crimean War.

The **Victoria Falls** are a spectacular waterfall 109 m (355 ft) high, on the River Zambezi, on the Zimbabwe–Zambia border, discovered in 1855 by David Livingstone. Its native name is *Mosi-oa-tunya* 'the smoke that thunders'.

victory success over an opponent; *Victory* was the name of the flagship of Lord Nelson at the Battle of Trafalgar, launched in 1765. It has been restored, and is now on display in dry dock at Portsmouth.

A **victory sign** is a signal of triumph or celebration made by holding up the hand with the palm outwards and the first two fingers spread apart to represent the letter V; also known as the ➤ V-sign.

See also ➤ PYRRHIC *victory*, ➤ WINGED *Victory*.

Vidar in Scandinavian mythology, the son of ➤ ODIN who will avenge his father at Ragnarök by killing the wolf ➤ FENRIR.

Congress of Vienna an international conference held 1814–15 to agree the settlement of Europe after the Napoleonic Wars. Attended by all the major European powers, it was dominated by Prussia, Russia, Britain, Austria, and France. The guiding principle of the settlement was the restoration and strengthening of hereditary and sometimes despotic rulers; the result was a political stability that lasted for three or four decades.

Vietnam War a war between Communist North Vietnam and US-backed South Vietnam.

Since the partition of Vietnam in 1954 the Communist North had attempted to unite the country as a Communist state, fuelling US concern over the possible spread of Communism in SE Asia. After two US destroyers were reportedly fired on in the Gulf of Tonkin in 1964, a US army was sent to Vietnam, supported by contingents from South Korea, Australia, New Zealand, and Thailand, while American aircraft bombed North Vietnamese forces and areas of Cambodia.

The Tet Offensive of 1968 damaged US confidence in its ability to win the war, which was arousing immense controversy and resentment at home, and US forces began to be withdrawn, finally leaving in 1973.

vigilante a member of a self-appointed group of citizens who undertake law enforcement in their community without legal authority, typically because the legal agencies are thought to be inadequate. The word comes (in the mid 19th century) from Spanish, and means literally 'vigilant'.

Viking any of the Scandinavian seafaring pirates and traders who raided and settled in many parts of NW Europe in the 8th–11th centuries. The name comes from Old Norse *vík* 'creek' or Old English *wīc* 'camp, dwelling place'.

The name *Viking* was also given to either of two American space probes sent to Mars in 1975, each of which consisted of a lander that conducted experiments on the surface and an orbiter.

villain originally (in Middle English) a rustic, a boor; later, a person with ignoble ideas or instincts, a scoundrel; a person guilty or capable of a crime or wickedness. The word comes via Old French from Latin *villa* a country residence, the same base as ➤ VILLEIN.

The **villain of the piece** is the main culprit; the character in a play or novel whose evil motives or actions are important to the plot. The first recorded use of *villain* in this sense is from Charles Lamb's *Elia* (1822); *villain of the piece* is recorded from the mid 19th century.

villein in medieval England, a feudal tenant entirely subject to a lord or manor to whom he paid dues and services in return for land. The word is recorded from Middle English, and is a variant of ➤ VILLAIN.

Battle of Vimy Ridge an Allied attack on the German position of Vimy Ridge, near Arras, during the First World War. One of the key points on the Western Front, it had long resisted assaults, but on 9 April 1917 it was taken by Canadian troops in fifteen minutes, at the cost of heavy casualties.

Vincent personal forename of two saints.

St Vincent de Paul (1581–1660) was a French priest. He devoted his life to work among the poor and the sick and established institutions to continue his work, including the Congregation of the Mission (1625) and the Daughters of Charity (Sisters of Charity of St Vincent de Paul) (1633). His feast day is 19 July.

St Vincent of Saragossa (d. 304), Spanish deacon and martyr, is said to have been tortured on a gridiron, and who was the centre of a widespread early cult; he is typically shown either with a palm as a sign of being a deacon, or with a gridiron. His feast day is 22 January, and his emblems are a vine, a palm, and a gridiron.

vine in Christian iconography, the *vine* sometimes stands for Jesus Christ, in allusion to John 15:1 and 15:5. A *vine* is also the emblem of ➤ St VINCENT *of Saragossa*.

The word is recorded from Middle English and comes via Old French from Latin *vinea* 'vineyard, vine' from *vinum* 'wine'.

vinegar the type of something sour and acrid-tasting, as in Proverbs 10:26. *Vinegar* was offered to Christ on the Cross in response to his words 'I thirst'; this was later sometimes understood as an infliction of further suffering.

According to Livy, Hannibal cleared a way over the Alps by felling trees, burning logs on the rocks to heat them, and then pouring *vinegar* over them to make them crumble.

In figurative use, *vinegar* denotes sourness or peevishness of behaviour, character, or speech.

The **Vinegar Bible** is an edition of 1717 by John Baskett, in which one of the running-heads for *Luke* reads 'The parable of the vinegar' instead of 'The parable of the vineyard'.

Vinegar Hill, in the Irish insurrection of 1798, was the main rebel encampment, successfully stormed on 21 June, and remembered as the Wexford rebel forces' decisive defeat.

vineyard in figurative usage, a sphere of action or labour, as in biblical allusion to Matthew 20:1 and 21:28.

In the **parable of the vineyard** in Luke's gospel, which gave its name to the ➤ VINEGAR *Bible*, the vineyard stands for the world created by God. The parable tells the story of a man who planted a vineyard and let it out to husbandmen while he was away. On his return, he sent his servants (the prophets) for the fruit, but they were beaten and driven away; when he sent his son (Jesus Christ), the husbandmen planned to kill him.

Vinland the region of the NE coast of North America which was visited in the 11th century by Norsemen led by Leif Ericsson. It was so named from the report that grapevines were found growing there. The exact location is uncertain: sites from the northernmost tip of Newfoundland, where Viking remains have been found, to Cape Cod and even Virginia have been proposed.

The **Vinland Map** is supposedly a 15th century map, first published in 1965, showing the northeastern coastline of the North American continent as an island named Vinland, with an inscription describing its discovery by Leif Ericsson; the authenticiy of the map is debated.

vintage the harvesting of grapes for winemaking; the grapes or wine produced in a particular season.

vintage car an old style or model of car, specifically one made between 1917 and 1930.

violet traditionally regarded as a flower of spring, the *violet* is also sometimes taken as emblematic of modesty and shyness.

viper a venomous snake, taken as the type of malignancy and treachery, but whose flesh was formerly believed to have great nutritive or restorative properties, and was used medicinally. Early allusive references include some to the statement in Pliny's *Natural History* that the female viper was killed by her young eating their way out at birth.

Recorded from the early 16th century, the word comes ultimately from Latin *vivus* 'alive' + *parere* 'bring forth'.

A **viper in one's bosom** is a person who betrays those who have helped them; from the fable (found in Aesop) of the viper which was reared or warmed in a person's bosom, and which ended by biting its nurturer.

virago a domineering, violent, or bad-tempered woman; formerly, a woman of masculine strength or spirit; a female warrior. The word is recorded in Old English (used only as the name given by Adam to Eve, following the Vulgate), from Latin 'heroic woman, female warrior', from *vir* 'man'. The current sense dates from late Middle English.

Virgil (70–19 BC), Roman poet. He wrote three major works: the *Eclogues*, ten pastoral poems, blending traditional themes of Greek bucolic poetry with contemporary political and literary themes; the *Georgics*, a didactic poem on farming, treats the relationship of human beings to nature, and the *Aeneid* is an epic poem about the Trojan Aeneas.

Virgil was highly regarded in the Middle Ages (see ➤ MARO, *Prophet of the Gentiles*). In Dante's poem Virgil guides the poet through Hell and Purgatory.

Virgilian lots were a method of divination by selecting a passage of Virgil at random in the *sortes Virgilianae* (see ➤ SORTES).

virgin originally (in ecclesiastical usage) an unmarried woman esteemed for her chastity and piety within the Christian Church; a woman (especially a young woman) who remains in a state of inviolate chastity (in early use chiefly of **the Virgin** or the ➤ *Virgin* MARY as the mother of Jesus).

Virgin was then used of a girl or young woman, as one likely to be chaste; it is used in this sense in the parable of the **wise and foolish virgins** (Matthew 25:1–13), in which ten young women taken their lamps and go out in a bridal party to meet the bridegroom. Five of them are wise and take extra oil for their lamps; the five who are foolish do not, and when the bridegroom is delayed their lamps run dry. Going to buy more oil, they miss their opportunity to join the wedding feast.

The **Virgin Birth** is the doctrine of Christ's birth from a mother, Mary, who was a virgin.

The **Virgin Queen** is a name for Queen Elizabeth I of England, who died unmarried; the state of ➤ VIRGINIA takes its name from this epithet.

Virgo a large constellation (the Virgin), said to represent a maiden or goddess associated with the harvest. It contains several bright stars, the brightest of which is Spica, and a dense cluster of galaxies.

In astrology, Virgo is the sixth sign of the zodiac, which the sun enters about 23 August.

virtue a quality considered morally good or desirable in a person; the important virtues are traditionally the four *cardinal virtues* (see ➤ CARDINAL²), justice, prudence, temperance, and fortitude, valued by the classical philosophers and adopted by the scholastic philosophers, and the three ➤ THEOLOGICAL *virtues* of faith, hope, and charity, enumerated by St Paul.

Vishnu a god, originally a minor Vedic god, now regarded by his worshippers as the supreme deity and saviour, by others as the preserver of the cosmos in a triad with ➤ BRAHMA and ➤ SHIVA. His consort is Lakshmi, his mount the eagle Garuda. Vishnu is considered by Hindus to have had nine earthly incarnations or avatars, including Rama, Krishna, and the historical Buddha; the tenth avatar will herald the end of the world.

Visigoth a member of the branch of the Goths who invaded the Roman Empire between the 3rd and 5th centuries AD and ruled much of Spain until overthrown by the Moors in 711. The name comes from Latin *Visigothus*, and the first element may mean 'west' (as the ➤ OSTROGOTHS were members of the eastern branch of Goths).

the vision splendid the dream of some glorious imagined time; the phrase is originally a quotation from Wordsworth from 'Ode. Intimations of Immortality' (1807).

vision thing a political view encompassing the longer term as distinct from short-term campaign objectives. The expression comes from the response of the American Republican statesman George Bush (1924–) to the suggestion that he turn his attention from short-term campaign objectives and look to the longer term.

the Visitation the visit of the Virgin Mary to her cousin Elizabeth related in Luke 1:39–56, during which, on being greeted by Elizabeth, Mary responded with the words which form the ➤ MAGNIFICAT.

The **Order of the Visitation** is an order of nuns founded in 1610 by St Jane Frances de Chantal under the direction of St Francis de Sales; they are known as *Visitandines*.

visiting fireman in the US, a visitor to an organization given especially cordial treatment on account of his or her importance. The usage is recorded from the 1920s, but there is a much earlier literal example on record, in an 1855 Baltimore paper.

vita nuova a fresh start or new direction in life, especially after some powerful emotional experience. The phrase is Italian, literally 'new life', the title of a work by Dante describing his love for Beatrice.

Vitoria a city in NE Spain, site of a battle in 1813 in which Wellington defeated a French force and thus freed Spain from French domination.

Vitruvius (fl. 1st century BC), Roman architect and military engineer. He wrote a comprehensive ten-volume treatise on architecture which includes matters such as acoustics and water supply as well as the more obvious aspects of architectural design, decoration, and building.

St Vitus (d. *c.*300), Christian martyr, who is said to have been martyred during the reign of Diocletian. He was invoked against rabies and as the patron of those who suffered from epilepsy and certain nervous disorders, including St Vitus's dance. He is traditionally regarded as one of the ➤ FOURTEEN *Holy Helpers*. His feast day is 15 June.

St Vitus's dance is an old-fashioned term for Sydenham's chorea, a neurological disorder in children characterized by jerky involuntary movements; it is so named because appealing to *St Vitus* was believed to alleviate the disease.

Vivien in the Arthurian legend, an enchantress (otherwise Nimue or Niniane) who entrapped ➤ MERLIN and imprisoned him in a tower of air in the forest of Broceliande.

viz. namely; in other words (used especially to introduce a gloss or explanation). The expression (dating from the mid 16th century) is an abbreviation of Latin *videlicet* 'it is permissible'; the *z* represents the ordinary medieval Latin symbol of contraction for *et*.

vizier a high official in some Muslim countries, especially in Turkey under Ottoman rule. The word is recorded from the mid 16th century and comes via Turkish from Arabic *wazīr* 'caliph's chief counsellor'.

VJ day the day (15 August) in 1945 on which Japan ceased fighting in the Second World War, or the day (2 September) when Japan formally surrendered.

Voice of America an official US radio station founded in 1942, operated by the Board for International Broadcasting, that broadcasts around the world in English and other languages.

volcano a mountain or hill, typically conical, having a crater or vent through which lava, rock fragments, hot vapour, and gas are or have been erupted from the earth's crust; in figurative usage, an intense suppressed emotion; a situation liable to burst out suddenly. Recorded from the early 17th century, the word comes from Italian, from Latin *Volcanus* ➤ VULCAN.

Volscian a member of an ancient Italic people who fought the Romans in Latium in the 5th and 4th centuries BC until absorbed into Rome after their final defeat in 304 BC.

Volstead Act a law which enforced alcohol prohibition in the US from 1920–33. It is named after Andrew J. *Volstead* (1860–1947), American legislator.

Volsung in Scandinavian mythology, a dynasty of heroes (including ➤ SIGURD) whose deeds are the subject of *Volsunga Saga* and a number of Eddic poems.

Volund in Norse mythology, a Lappish prince and skilled worker in metal who is the equivalent of the Anglo-Saxon ➤ WAYLAND. Bereft of his swan-maiden wife, he is captured by the king of Sweden and held prisoner to work with the king's gold. He escapes, after killing the king's sons and leaving his daughter pregnant.

Volunteer State informal name for Tennessee, given in allusion to the large number of volunteers contributed by Tennessee to the Mexican War of 1847.

voodoo a black religious cult practised in the Caribbean and the southern US, combining elements of Roman Catholic ritual with traditional African magical and religious rites, and characterized by sorcery and spirit possession. The word comes (in the early

19th century) from Louisiana French, from Kwa *vodũ*.

Voortrekker a member of one of the groups of Dutch-speaking people who migrated by wagon from the Cape Colony into the interior from 1836 onwards, in order to live beyond the borders of British rule. The word is Afrikaans and comes from Dutch *voor* 'fore' + *trekken* 'travel'.

Vorticist a member of a British artistic movement of 1914–15 influenced by cubism and futurism and favouring machine-like forms. The name comes from Latin *vortex*, *vortic-* 'eddy'; the origin was explained by Ezra Pound in *Fortnightly Review* September 1914.

Vortigern a legendary 5th-century British king traditionally said to have invited the Saxons under ➤ HENGIST and Horsa into Britain and to have married Hengist's daughter Rowena; according to Geoffrey of Monmouth's chronicle he was defeated and killed by ➤ AMBROSIUS *Aurelianus*, leader of Romano-British resistance to the Saxon invasion.
   Vortigern and Rowena was the title of an alleged Shakespeare play which the forger William Henry Ireland (1777–1835) pretended to have discovered; it was produced by Kemble in 1796, but was derided by the public.

vox populi the opinions or beliefs of the majority; the Latin phrase is recorded in English from the mid 16th century.
   The abbreviation **vox pop** means popular opinion as represented by informal comments from members of the public, especially when broadcast or published; the term is recorded from the 1960s.

Voyager either of two American space probes launched in 1977 to investigate the outer planets. Voyager 1 encountered Jupiter and Saturn, while Voyager 2 reached Jupiter, Saturn, Uranus, and finally Neptune (1989).

Vulcan¹ in Roman mythology, the god of fire; equivalent of the Greek ➤ HEPHAESTUS. His lameness, and his betrayal by his wife ➤ VENUS for ➤ MARS, are both subjects for literary allusion; he is also taken as the type of a blacksmith or metalworker.
   A **Vulcanist** is a supporter of the theory (now accepted) that rocks such as granite were formed by solidification from the molten state, as proposed by the Scottish geologist James Hutton and others, rather than by precipitation from the sea.

Vulcan² in the ➤ STAR *Trek* science fiction series, a member of the race to which ➤ *Mr* SPOCK belongs, characterized by their logic, lack of emotion, and mental prowess, as well as by their pointed ears and green-tinged skin.

vulgar Latin informal Latin of classical times; vulgar in this sense means 'in ordinary use, used by the people', and comes ultimately from *vulgus* 'common people'.

Vulgate the principal Latin version of the Bible, prepared mainly by St Jerome in the late 4th century, and (as revised in 1592) adopted as the official text for the Roman Catholic Church. The name comes from Latin *vulgata (editio)* '(edition) prepared for the public'.

vulpine foxy; crafty, cunning. The word comes from Latin *vulpes* 'fox', the base of Italian *Volpone*, the crafty schemer in Jonson's play (1607).

vulture a large bird of prey, feeding chiefly on carrion and reputed to gather with others in anticipation of the death of a sick or injured animal or person; a contemptible person who preys on or exploits others.

Vulture may also be used allusively for something that preys on one's mind, such as a consuming or torturing passion, especially with reference to the punishment inflicted on ➤ TITYUS.

Ww

W The twenty-third letter of the modern English alphabet, originating from a ligature of the Roman letter represented by *U* and *V* of modern alphabets.

Wade–Giles a system of romanized spelling for transliterating Chinese, devised by the British diplomat Sir Thomas Francis *Wade* (1818–95), professor of Chinese at Cambridge, and modified by his successor Herbert Allen *Giles* (1845–1935). It has been largely superseded by Pinyin. It produces spellings such as *Peking*, *Mao Tse-tung* rather than *Beijing*, *Mao Zedong*.

wafer a thin disc of unleavened bread used in the Eucharist; the term is recorded first in an injunction of Elizabeth I in 1559.

Waffen SS the combat units of the ➤ SS in Nazi Germany during the Second World War; *Waffen* is German and means 'armed'.

Wagnerian having the enormous dramatic scale and intensity of an opera by the German composer Richard *Wagner* (1813–83). He developed an operatic genre which he called music drama, synthesizing music, drama, verse, legend, and spectacle.

Wagner was forced into exile after supporting the German nationalist uprising in Dresden in 1848; in the same year he began writing the text of *Der Ring des Nibelungen* (*The Ring of the Nibelungs*), a cycle of four operas (*Das Rheingold*, *Die Walküre*, *Siegfried*, and *Götterdämmerung*) based loosely on ancient Germanic sagas.

Wahhabi a member of a strictly orthodox Sunni Muslim sect founded by Muhammad ibn Abd al-Wahhab (1703–92). It advocates a return to the early Islam of the Koran and Sunna, rejecting later innovations; the sect is still the predominant religious force in Saudi Arabia.

Wailing Wall a high wall in Jerusalem said to stand on the site of the Jewish Temple, where Jews traditionally pray and lament on Fridays.

Treaty of Waitangi a treaty signed in 1840 at the settlement of Waitangi in New Zealand, which formed the basis of the British annexation of New Zealand. The Maori chiefs of North Island accepted British sovereignty in exchange for protection, and direct purchase of land from the Maoris was forbidden. Subsequent contraventions of the treaty by the British led to the Maori Wars.

Waitangi Day is the anniversary of the signing of the Treaty of Waitangi, celebrated as a public holiday in New Zealand on 6 February since 1960.

wake a watch or vigil held beside the body of someone who has died, sometimes accompanied by ritual observances including eating and drinking.

wake up and smell the coffee become aware of the realities of a situation, however unpleasant; usually in imperative.

wakes in some parts of the UK, a festival and holiday held annually in a rural parish, originally on the feast day (originally the *wake* or vigil before the festival) of the patron saint of the church.

In northern England, **Wakes Week** is an annual holiday in towns such as Leeds, traditionally when mills closed for a stated period.

waldo a remote-controlled device for handling objects, named after *Waldo* F. Jones, a fictional inventor described by Robert Heinlein in a science-fiction story.

walk the walk and talk the talk suit one's actions to one's words.

Walkyrie in Anglo-Saxon England, any of a group of supernatural female warriors supposed to ride through the air over battlefields and decide who should die, the equivalent of the Scandinavian ➤ VALKYRIE; the word in Old English is found as rendering the name of the Roman war-goddess ➤ BELLONA, or designating the ➤ FURIES or ➤ GORGONS of classical mythology.

Wall Street a street at the south end of Manhattan, where the New York Stock Exchange and other leading American financial institutions are located, used allusively to refer to the American money market or financial interests. It is named after a wooden stockade which was built in 1653 around the original Dutch settlement of New Amsterdam.

The **Wall Street Crash** was the collapse of prices on the New York Stock Exchange in October 1929, a major factor in the early stages of the ➤ DEPRESSION; many investors became bankrupt, and there were a number of suicides from high-rise Wall Street buildings.

Wallace name of the cheese-loving inventor, owner of the dog ➤ GROMIT, in Nick Park's claymation films of his two plasticine figures.

Wallace Collection a museum in Manchester Square, London, containing French 18th-century paintings and furniture, English 18th-century portraits, and medieval armour. The collection was built up by the fourth marquis of Hertford and Richard Wallace (1819–90), his illegitimate son or half-brother; Richard Wallace's widow gave it to the nation in 1897.

Wallace's line a hypothetical line, proposed by Alfred Russel Wallace, marking the boundary between the Oriental and Australian zoogeographical regions. Wallace's line is now placed along the continental shelf of SE Asia. To the west of the line Asian mammals such as monkeys predominate, while to the east of it the fauna is dominated by marsupials.

walls have ears be careful what you say as people may be eavesdropping; proverbial saying, late 16th century.

Walpurgis Night (in German folklore) the night of April 30 (May Day's eve), when witches meet on the ➤ BROCKEN mountain and hold revels with the Devil. It is named after St *Walburga*, an English nun who in the 8th century helped to convert the Germans to Christianity; her feast day coincided with an ancient pagan festival whose rites were intended to give protection from witchcraft.

Walsingham a village in Kent which is the site of the shrine of *Our Lady of Walsingham*, a popular place of pilgrimage in the Middle Ages.

The **Walsingham way** was the ➤ MILKY *Way*, as fancifully supposed to have been used as a guide by pilgrims travelling to the shrine of Our Lady of Walsingham.

wandering Jew a legendary person said to have been condemned by Christ to wander the earth until the second advent; according to a popular belief recorded from the 13th century and current at least until the 16th, he was said to have insulted Jesus on his way to the Cross. In the earliest versions of the story he is called Cartaphilus, but in the best-known modern version it is given as Ahasuerus.

wannabe a person who tries to be like someone else or to fit in with a particular group of people. Coined in the 1980s, the word represents a pronunciation of *want to be*.

Wansdyke an ancient east-west fortification system running from near Portishead to near Marlborough, and probably constructed as a defence against Saxon invasion.

wapentake in the UK, a subdivision of certain northern and midland English counties, corresponding to a hundred in other counties. Recorded from late Old English, the word comes from Old Norse *vápnatak*, from *vápn* 'weapon' + *taka* 'take', perhaps with reference to voting in an assembly by a show of weapons.

war game a military exercise carried out to test or improve tactical expertise; a simulated military conflict carried out as a game, leisure activity, or exercise in personal development. The term is recorded from the early 19th century, and is the equivalent of the German ➤ KRIEGSPIEL.

war to end wars a war which is intended to make subsequent wars impossible; in particular, applied to the First World War. *The War That Will End War* (1920) was the title of a book by H. G. Wells.

Warburg Institute founded to house a library dedicated to preserving the classical heritage of Western culture, built up in Hamburg from 1905 by the German art historian Aby *Warburg* (1866–1929). In 1933 it was transferred to England and housed in the *Warburg Institute* (part of the University of London).

Wardour Street originally used as a modifier denoting the pseudo-archaic diction affected by some modern writers of historical novels, and later used allusively to refer to the British film industry. It is the name of a street in central London, formerly mainly occupied by dealers in antique furniture, now the site of the central offices of the British film industry.

warlock a man who practises witchcraft; a sorcerer. In Old English *wǣrloga* meant 'traitor, scoundrel, monster', and also 'the Devil', from *wǣr* 'covenant' + an element related to *lēogan* 'belie, deny'. From its application to the Devil, the word was transferred in Middle English to a person in league with the devil, and hence a sorcerer. It was chiefly Scots until given wider currency by Sir Walter Scott.

warming pan a wide, flat brass pan on a long handle, filled with hot coals and used for warming a bed, formerly used in allusion to the story that James II's son, afterwards called the ➤ OLD *Pretender*, was a supposititious child introduced into the Queen's bed in a warming pan.

warn someone off tell someone forcefully or threateningly to go or keep away from somewhere; originally *warn someone off the course*, in horse-racing, prohibit someone who has broken the laws of the Jockey Club from riding or running horses at meetings under the Jockey Club's jurisdiction.

Wars of the Roses the 15th-century English civil wars between the Houses of York and Lancaster, represented by white and red roses respectively, during the reigns of Henry VI, Edward IV, and Richard III. The struggle was largely ended in 1485 by the defeat and death of the Yorkist king Richard III at the Battle of Bosworth and the accession of the Lancastrian Henry Tudor (Henry VII), who united the two houses by marrying Elizabeth, daughter of Edward IV.

Warsaw Pact a treaty of mutual defence and military aid signed at Warsaw on 14 May 1955 by Communist states of Europe under Soviet influence, in response to the admission of West Germany to NATO.

warts and all including features or qualities that are not appealing or attractive; the term derives from a request supposedly made by Oliver Cromwell as ➤ PROTECTOR to the portraitist Peter Lely; it is in fact a popular summary of Cromwell's words as reported by Horace Walpole.

wash one's hands of disclaim responsibility for; the original allusion is to the biblical story of ➤ *Pontius* PILATE who, when he was forced to condemn Jesus, sent for a bowl of water and ritually washed his hands as a sign that he was innoceant of 'this just person' (Matthew 27:24). In proverbial usage, the attempt at avoiding guilt is often seen as futile.

Wasp an upper- or middle-class American white Protestant, considered to be a member of the most powerful group in society. The word is an acronym from *white Anglo-Saxon Protestant*.

wassail spiced ale or mulled wine drunk during celebrations for Twelfth Night and Christmas Eve; lively and noisy festivities involving the drinking of plentiful amounts of alcohol; revelry. The word comes from Middle English *wæs hæil* 'be in (good) health', from Old Norse *ves heill*. The drinking formula *wassail* (and the reply *drinkhail* 'drink good health') were probably introduced by Danish-speaking inhabitants of England, and then spread, so that by the 12th century the usage was considered by the Normans to be characteristic of Englishmen.

waste not, want not if you use a commodity or resource carefully and without extravagance you will never be in need; proverbial saying, late 18th century.

the watch a watchman or group of watchmen who patrolled and guarded the streets of a town before the introduction of the police force.

watch and ward the performance of the duty of a watchman or sentinel, especially as a feudal obligation. It has traditionally been suggested that *watch* referred to service by night and *ward* to service by day, but there is no evidence for this as an original meaning.

The Watch on the Rhine a German patriotic song, *Die Wacht am Rhein* (1840), written by Max Schneckenburger, which was set to music by Karl Wilhelm in 1854, and became a popular Prussian soldiers' song in the ➤ FRANCO-*Prussian War*.

the watches of the night the night-time; *watch* originally each of the three or four periods of time, during which a watch or guard was kept, into which the night was divided by the Jews and Romans.

watchful waiting phrase used by Woodrow Wilson to describe American policy towards Mexico during Mexico's revolutionary period, in a State of the Union address, December 1913.

Watchnight originally a religious service extending over midnight held monthly by Wesleyan Methodists; in later use a service held (by Methodists and others) on New Year's eve, lasting until midnight; also, the night upon which the service is held.

water one of the four elements in ancient and medieval philosophy and in astrology (considered essential to the nature of the signs Cancer, Scorpio, and Pisces).

The word is recorded from Old English (in form *wæter*) and is of Germanic origin; it comes from an Indo-European root shared by Lain *unda* 'wave' and Greek *hudōr* 'water'.

Of the first water refers to the highest grade of diamond. The three highest grades of diamond were formerly known as first, second, and third water, and the phrase *of the first water* is used generally to indicate the finest possible quaility. The usage may come ultimately from Arabic, where this sense of water is a particular application of 'lustre, splendour' (e.g., of a sword).

The **Water Bearer** is the zodiacal sign or constellation ➤ AQUARIUS, also called the **Water Carrier**.

The phrase **water under the bridge** is used to refer to events or situations that are in the past and consequently no longer to be regarded as important or as a source of concern.

Watergate a US political scandal in which an attempt to bug the national headquarters of the Democratic Party (in the Watergate building in Washington DC) led to the resignation of President Nixon (1974).

Five men hired by the Republican organization campaigning to re-elect Richard Nixon President were caught with electronic bugging equipment at the offices. The attempted cover-up and subsequent inquiry gravely weakened the prestige of the government and finally led to the resignation of the President in August 1974.

Battle of Waterloo a battle fought on 18 June 1815 near the village of Waterloo (in what is now Belgium), in which Napoleon's army was conclusively defeated by the British (under the Duke of Wellington) and Prussians. *Waterloo* is often used as a word for a decisive defeat or failure.

A **Waterloo ball** is a frivolous entertainment preceding a serious occurrence (with reference to a ball given in Brussels by the Duchess of Richmond on the eve of the Battle of Waterloo).

Watford a town in Hertfordshire, SE England, used with allusion to the view attributed to Londoners that north of the metropolis there is nothing of any significance to English national or cultural life.

Watling Street a Roman road (now largely underlying modern roads) running north-westwards across England, from Richborough in Kent through London and St Albans to Wroxeter in Shropshire. The predominant form of the name in Old English is *Wæclinga stræt*; the first element may represent a (real or imaginary) family or clan.

Dr Watson a doctor who is the companion and assistant of ➤ Sherlock HOLMES in detective stories by Arthur Conan Doyle; his good nature and lack of perspicacity make him a foil to the more difficult but brilliant Holmes. (See also ➤ ELEMENTARY, *my dear Watson*.)

Wattle Day in Australia, an annual celebration, the date of which varies locally, of the blossoming of the wattle, the floral emblem of Australia.

Waverley Novels the novels of Sir Walter Scott; *Waverley* was the title of his first novel (1814), set in the Jacobite rising of 1745.

waxen image an effigy in wax representing a person whom it is desired to injure by witchcraft; it was believed that the victim would waste away as the wax melted in the fire, and feel pain if the figure was pricked or pierced.

the Way in the Acts of the Apostles, the Christian religion; with allusion to John 24:6.

way of all flesh death; go the way of all flesh, meaning 'die', is an early variant of the biblical 'go the way of all the earth', as in 1 Kings 2:2. The *way of all flesh* is also sometimes used to mean the experience common to humankind in its passage through life.

Wayland the Smith in Anglo-Saxon mythology, a smith with supernatural powers, in English legend supposed to have his forge in a Neolithic chambered tomb (**Wayland's Smithy**) on the downs in SW Oxfordshire. His Norse equivalent is ➤ VOLUND.

wayzgoose an annual summer dinner or outing held by a printing house for its employees. The term is recorded from the mid 18th century, as an alteration of the earlier *waygoose*; there is no evidence as to its etymology (there is, for instance, nothing to suggest that *goose* was eaten at the dinner).

we plural pronoun, especially as used in formal contexts by a sovereign or ruler of a country, or by a writer or editor (as supported by an editorial staff collectively), to refer to himself or herself.

We are not amused is a comment attributed to Queen Victoria; recorded in Caroline Holland *Notebooks of a Spinster Lady* (1919), and popularly regarded as typifying the repression associated with the Victorian age.

We name the guilty men is a cliché of investigative journalism; *Guilty Men* (1940) was the title of a tract by Michael Foot, Frank Owen, and Peter Howard, published under the pseudonym of 'Cato', which attacked the supporters of Munich and the appeasement policy of Neville Chamberlain.

We shall not be moved is the title of a labour and civil rights song (1931), adapted from an earlier gospel hymn.

We shall overcome is the title of a song, originating from before the American Civil War, adapted as a Baptist hymn ('I'll Overcome Some Day', 1901) by C. Albert Tindley; revived in 1946 as a protest song by black tobacco workers, and in 1963 during the black Civil Rights Campaign.

the weak link the point at which a system, sequence, or organization is most vulnerable; the least dependable element or member. Often with allusion to the proverbial saying, *a chain is only as strong as its weakest link*, and most recently used in intensive form in reference to the television game show *The Weakest Link*.

the weaker vessel a wife, a female partner; originally in allusion to 1 Peter.

the weakest go to the wall proverbial saying, early 16th century; usually said to derive from the installation of seating around the walls in churches of the later Middle Ages. *Go to the wall* in figurative use means, succumb in a conflict or struggle.

the Weald a formerly wooded district including parts of Kent, Surrey, and East Sussex.

Wealden denotes a style of timber house built in the Weald in the late medieval and Tudor periods.

wear one's heart on one's sleeve make one's feelings apparent; perhaps originally with reference to Shakespeare's *Othello*, 'For I will wear my heart upon my sleeve, For daws to peck at'.

Wearing of the Green Irish nationalist song, dating from the end of the 18th century; ➤ GREEN had been recognized as the national colour of Ireland since the 17th century, and was adopted particularly by the United Irishmen at the time of the insurrection of 1798.

weasel the *weasel* as a small and agile carnivore is taken as a type of cunning; a deceitful or treacherous person.

Weasel words are words or statements that are intentionally ambiguous or misleading; the expression was popularized by the American Republican statesman Theodore Roosevelt (1858–1919) in a speech of May 1915.

weathercock a weathervane in the form of a cockerel, which turns with its head to the wind; traditionally taken as a symbol of mutability or fickleness.

Weatherman a member of a violent revolutionary group in the US, founded *c.*1970, and apparently named from a line in a song by Bob Dylan, 'You don't need a weatherman to know which way the wind blows'.

Penelope's web in the Greek legend, woven every day by ➤ PENELOPE, wife of Odysseus, and unravelled every night; she had told the many suitors who had gathered in Odysseus's absence that she would not marry again until the work was finished.

wedding-finger another name for the ➤ RING-*finger*; it was traditionally believed that a particular nerve runs from the fourth finger of the left hand to the heart. The use of the ring-finger is directed in the ➤ SARUM rite for this reason.

wedge issue in the US, a divisive political issue, especially one that is raised by a candidate for public office in the hope of attracting or alienating an opponent's supporters.

Wednesday the day of the week before Thursday and following Tuesday. Recorded from Old English (in the form *Wōdnesdæg*) it is named after the Germanic god *Odin*, and is the equivalent of late Latin *Mercurii dies*.

Wee Free a member of the minority group nicknamed the **Wee Free Kirk** which stood apart from the Free Church of Scotland when the majority amalgamated with the United Presbyterian Church to form the United Free Church in 1900. The group continued to call itself the Free Church of Scotland after this date.

Feast of Weeks another term for the Jewish festival of ➤ SHAVUOTH.

weeper a hired mourner at a funeral (recorded from late Middle English); also, a figure in the niche of a funeral monument, typically one of a number representing mourners.

weeping willow a Eurasian willow with trailing branches and foliage reaching down to the ground, regarded as symbolical of mourning.

Wei the name of several dynasties which ruled in China, especially that of AD 386–535.

weighed in the balance and found wanting biblical saying, from Daniel 5:27; part of the message of the ➤ WRITING *on the wall* which prophesied imminent destruction to the king of Babylon.

Weimar Republic the German republic of 1919–33, so called because its constitution was drawn up at Weimar, a city in Thuringia, central Germany, which was famous in the late 18th and early 19th century for its intellectual and cultural life. It was eventually overthrown by the Nazi Party of Adolf Hitler.

weird a person's fate or destiny (now chiefly in Scottish use); the word is recorded from Old English (in form *wyrd*), and is of Germanic origin; it was used in plural form to mean ➤ *the* FATES.

the weird sisters originally (in late Middle English) ➤ *the* FATES; from the early 17th century, used for the three witches in Shakespeare's *Macbeth* (1606), with the meaning that they had the power to control destiny; this in turn gave rise (in the early 19th century) to *weird* as meaning 'unearthly'.

welkin the sky, heaven, especially in the phrase **make the welkin ring**, make a very loud sound. The word is recorded from Old English (in form *wolcen*, meaning 'cloud, sky') and is of Germanic origin.

well a well is the emblem of St Juthwara and St Sidwell, sisters, and reputed British virgin martyrs with a cult in the south west of England. *Wells*, representing springs of natural water, are often associated with holy sites, as that of the shrine of ➤ *St* WINEFRIDE in Wales.

Well-dressing is the decoration of wells with flowers, an ancient custom at Whitsuntide especially in Derbyshire.

Wellerism a form of humorous comparison in which a familiar saying or proverb is identified with something said by a person in a specified but inapposite situation, from the name of Samuel *Weller* or his father, characters in Dickens's *Pickwick Papers*.

Wells, Fargo, & Co. a US transportation company founded in 1852 by the businessmen Henry Wells (1805–78) and William Fargo (1818–81) and others. It carried mail to and from the newly developed West, founded a San Francisco bank, and later ran a stagecoach service (having bought the *Pony Express* system) until the development of a transcontinental railway service.

Welsh of or relating to Wales, its people, or their Celtic language. Old English *Welisc*, *Wælisc* comes from a Germanic word meaning 'foreigner', from Latin *Volcae*, the name of a Celtic people; the Welsh name for Wales is *Cymru* and for its people, *Cymry*.

A **Welsh dragon** is a red heraldic dragon as the emblem of Wales.

Welsh harp is another name for the triple harp, a large harp without pedals and with three rows of strings, the middle row providing sharps and flats; the name is recorded from the mid 17th century.

Welsh rarebit is a dish of melted and seasoned cheese on toast, sometimes with other ingredients; the term is a late 18th century alteration of the earlier *Welsh rabbit* (early 18th century), but the reason for the use of *rabbit* is unknown.

The **Welsh Wizard** was a nickname for the Welsh politician and British Prime Minister David Lloyd George (1863–1945).

welterweight a weight in boxing and other sports intermediate between lightweight and middleweight, which in the amateur boxing scale ranges from 63.5–67 kg. It is recorded from the early 19th century, but the origin of *welter* is unknown.

Wembley Stadium a sports stadium in Wembley, NW London, where the FA Cup Final and the England football team's home matches are played; it was the venue for the 1966 World Cup Final.

wen a runic letter, used in Old and Middle English, later replaced by *w*.

St Wenceslas (*c*.907–29), Duke of Bohemia and patron saint of the Czech Republic; also known as **Good King Wenceslas**. He worked to Christianize the people of Bohemia but was murdered by his brother; he later became venerated as a martyr and hero of Bohemia. The story told in the Christmas carol 'Good King Wenceslas' appears to have no basis in fact. His feast day is 28 September.

Wendy house a toy house large enough for children to play in, named after the house built around *Wendy* by the Lost Boys and ➤ PETER *Pan*.

werewolf in myth or fiction, a person who changes for periods of time into a wolf, typically when there is a full moon. Recorded from late Old English, in form *werewulf*; the first element has usually been identified with Old English *wer* 'man'. In modern use the word has been revived through folklore studies.

wergeld in Germanic and Anglo-Saxon law, the price put on a man according to his rank, payable as a fine or compensation by a person guilty of homicide or certain other crimes.

Wertherism morbid sentimentality, regarded as characteristic of *Werther*, the hero of Goethe's romance 'Die Leiden des jungen Werther' (1774), a sensitive artist who is at odds with the world and unhappily in love, and who commits suicide.

Wesleyan of, relating to, or denoting the teachings of the English preacher John *Wesley* (1703–91), or the main branch of the Methodist Church which was founded by him. Wesley was a committed Christian evangelist who won many working-class converts, often through open-air preaching. The opposition they encountered from the Church establishment led to the Methodists forming a separate denomination in 1791. His brother Charles (1707–88) was also a founding Methodist, and both wrote many hymns.

Wessex the kingdom of the West Saxons, established in Hampshire in the early 6th century and gradually extended by conquest to include much of southern England. Under Alfred the Great and his successors it formed the nucleus of the Anglo-Saxon kingdom of England. Athelstan, Alfred's grandson, became king of England. The name was revived in the 19th century by Thomas Hardy to designate the south-western counties of England (especially Dorset) in which his novels are set.

Wessi a term used in Germany (especially since reunification) to denote a citizen of the former Federal Republic of Germany; a West German as opposed to an East German or ➤ OSSI.

west the direction towards the point of the horizon where the sun sets at the equinoxes, on the left-hand side of a person facing north, or the part of the horizon lying in this direction. The word is recorded from Old English and is of Germanic origin; it comes from an Indo-European root shared by Greek *hesperos*, Latin *vesper* 'evening'.

From the Middle Ages **the West** has designated Europe (and later America) as seen in contrast to other civilizations; in the 20th century, the term also denoted the non-Communist states of Europe and America contrasted with the former Communist states of eastern Europe. **The West** was also traditionally used for the western part of the United States, especially the states west of the Mississippi.

The *west* is also referred to allusively as the place of the sun's setting.

The **West Bank** is a region west of the River Jordan and north-west of the Dead Sea. It contains Jericho, Hebron, Nablus, Bethlehem, and other settlements. It became part of Jordan in 1948 and was occupied by Israel following the Six Day War of 1967. In 1993 an agreement was signed which granted limited autonomy to the Palestinians; withdrawal of Israeli troops began in 1994.

The **West End** is the entertainment and shopping area of London to the west of the City; the name is recorded from the late 18th century.

The **West Lothian question** is a rhetorical question that identifies the constitutional anomaly that MPs for Scottish and Welsh constituencies are unable to vote on Scottish or Welsh matters that have been devolved to those assemblies, but are able to vote on equivalent matters concerning England, whilst MPs for English constituencies have no reciprocal influence on Scottish or Welsh policy. It is named for *West Lothian*, a former parlimentary constituency in Central Scotland, whose MP, Tam Dalyell, persistently raised this question in Parliament.

West Point is the US Military Academy, founded in 1802, located on the site of a former strategic fort on the west bank of the Hudson River in New York State.

The **West Side** is the western part of any of several North American cities or boroughs, especially the island borough of Manhattan, New York.

The **West Wing** is the part of the White House housing the executive offices of the President, including the ➤ OVAL *Office*.

Western Church the part of the Christian Church historically originating in the Latin Church of the Western Roman Empire, including the Roman Catholic Church and the Anglican, Lutheran, and Reformed Churches, especially as distinct from the Eastern Orthodox Church.

Western Empire the western part of the Roman Empire, after its division in AD 395.

Western Front the zone of fighting in western Europe in the First World War, in which the German army engaged the armies to its west, i.e. France, the UK (and its dominions), and, from 1917, the US. For most of the war the front line stretched from the Vosges mountains in eastern France through Amiens to Ostend in Belgium.

Westminster an inner London borough which contains the Houses of Parliament and many government offices; often used in reference to the British Parliament.

The **Palace of Westminster** is the building in Westminster in which the British Parliament meets; the Houses of Parliament. The present building, designed by Sir Charles Barry, was formally opened in 1852. The original palace, a royal residence supposed to date from the 11th century until it was damaged by fire in 1512, was destroyed by a fire in 1834.

The **Statute of Westminster** is a statute of 1931 recognizing the equality of status of the dominions as autonomous communities within the British Empire, and giving their legislatures independence from British control.

Westminster Abbey is the collegiate church of St Peter in Westminster, originally the abbey church of a Benedictine monastery. The present building, begun by Henry III in 1245 and altered and added to by successive rulers, replaced an earlier church built by Edward the Confessor. Nearly all the kings and queens of England have been crowned in Westminster Abbey; it is also the burial place of many of England's monarchs and of some of the nation's leading figures.

The **Westminster Confession** is a Calvinist doctrinal statement which was issued by the synod appointed to reform the English and Scottish Churches in 1643, and became widely accepted among Presbyterian Churches.

Treaty of Westphalia the peace accord (1648) which ended the ➤ THIRTY *Years War*, signed simultaneously in Osnabrück and Münster.

wetback a Mexican living in the US, especially one who is an illegal immigrant, so named from the practice of swimming the Rio Grande to reach the US.

wetware chiefly in science fiction, computer technology in which the brain is linked to artificial systems, or used as a model for artificial systems based on biochemical processes.

whale in early translations of the Bible, a *whale* is given as the 'great fish' which swallowed Jonah. A whale is the emblem of ➤ *St* BRENDAN and the 6th–7th bishop St Malo, who is regarded as the apostle of Brittany.

wheel a wheel is the emblem of ➤ *St* CATHERINE *of Alexandria*.

The **wheel of Fortune** is the wheel which ➤ FORTUNE is fabled to turn, as an emblem of mutability. Also called *Fortune's wheel*.

wheelbarrow a *wheelbarrow* is the emblem of the 8th-century Anglo-Saxon hermit St Cuthman, who is said to have made a wheeled bed for his invalid mother out of a wheelbarrow.

wheels within wheels used to indicate that a situation is complicated and affected by secret or indirect influences; perhaps originally after the description of the vision of four creatures in Ezekiel 1:16.

where's the beef advertising slogan for Wendy's Hamburgers in campaign launched 9 January 1984, and subsequently taken up by Walter Mondale in a televised debate with Gary Hart from Atlanta, 11 March 1984.

Whig originally, an adherent of the Presbyterian cause in Scotland in the 17th century; the name is probably a shortening of Scots ➤ WHIGGAMORE. At the end of the 17th century, *Whig* designated a person who opposed the succession of the Catholic James II to the crown; an exclusioner.

From the early 18th century, *Whig* was used for a member of the British reforming and constitutional party that after 1688 sought the supremacy of Parliament and was eventually succeeded in the 19th century by the Liberal Party. The name was further applied, again in the early 18th century, to an American colonist who supported the American Revolution.

A **Whig historian** is a historian who interprets history as the continuing and inevitable victory of progress over reaction; the term is first recorded in George Bernard Shaw's preface to *St Joan* (1924).

Whiggamore a member of a body of rebels from the western part of Scotland who in 1648 marched on Edinburgh in opposition to Charles I. The name comes from *whig* 'to drive' + *mare* 'female horse', and is probably the origin of ➤ WHIG.

whip an official of a political party appointed to maintain parliamentary discipline among its members, especially so as to ensure attendance and voting in debates. The term is recorded from the mid 19th century, and is a shortening of *whipper-in*, literally a huntsman's assistant who keeps the hounds from straying by driving them back with the whip into the main body of the pack.

whipping boy a person who is blamed or punished for the faults or incompetence of others; an extended use of the original term (mid 17th century) denoting a boy educated with a young prince or other royal person and punished instead of him.

whirling dervish a member of an order of ➤ DERVISHES known for their dancing ritual.

reap the whirlwind suffer serious consequences as a result of one's actions; from the proverbial *sow the wind and reap the whirlwind*, often with biblical allusion to Hosea 8:7.

whispering campaign a systematic circulation of a rumour, typically in order to damage someone's reputation; the term originated in US politics of the early 20th century.

whispering gallery a typically circular or elliptical gallery situated under a dome, whose acoustic properties are such that a whisper may be heard round its entire circumference; there is a famous example in the dome of St Paul's Cathedral in London.

whistle down the wind let something go; abandon something, originally meaning to turn a trained hawk loose by casting it off with the wind, instead of against the wind in pursuit of prey.

whistle for a wind traditional practice among sailors; it was believed that whistling would bring a wind during a calm spell, and that refraining from whistling could calm a gale.

Whit Sunday the seventh Sunday after Easter, a Christian festival commemorating the descent of the Holy Spirit at ➤ PENTECOST (Acts 2). The name is recorded from Old English, in form *Hwīta Sunnandæg*, literally 'white Sunday', probably with reference to the white robes of those newly baptized at Pentecost.

Synod of Whitby a conference held in Whitby in 664 that resolved the differences between the Celtic and Roman forms of Christian worship in England, in particular the method of calculating the date of Easter. The Northumbrian Christians had followed the Celtic method of fixing the date while those of the south had adopted the Roman system. King Oswy (612–70) of Northumbria decided in favour of Rome, and England as a result effectively severed the connection with the Celtic Church.

white a colour or pigment of the colour of milk or fresh snow, due to the reflection of all visible rays of light; the opposite of black, traditionally taken as the colour of innocence and purity.

From the 17th century, white was specially associated with royalist and legitimist causes, as in the *white cockade* of the Jacobites and the *white flag* of the Bourbons.

Mrs White is one of the six stock characters constituting the murderer and suspects in the game of ➤ CLUEDO.

The **White Army** was any of the armies which opposed the Bolsheviks during the Russian Civil War of 1918–21.

The **White Boar** was the personal badge of Richard III (1452–85), alluded to in the political rhyme beginning ➤ *the* CAT, *the rat, and Lovell the dog.*

White-bread means of, belonging to, or representative of the white middle classes; not progressive, radical, or innovative; the term (which is recorded from the late 1970s, originally in North America) refers to the colour and perceived blandness of white bread as a commodity, and may also be a pun on 'white bred'.

A **white Christmas** is Christmas with snow on the ground, a term first recorded in Charles Kingsley *Two Years Ago* (1857), 'We shall have a white Christmas, I expect. Snow's coming.', and popularized by Irving Berlin's song 'White Christmas' (1942).

The **white cliffs of Dover** are the chalk cliffs on the Kent coast near Dover, taken as a national and patriotic symbol, and popularized as such in the patriotic wartime song by Nat Burton 'The White Cliffs of Dover' (1941).

The **white cockade** was a Jacobite badge, worn by the supporters of Charles Edward Stuart; according to a note in Boswell's *Life of Samuel Johnson*, in 1745 Boswell himself 'wore a white cockade, and prayed for King James'.

White-collar means of or relating to the work done or those who work in an office or other professional environment; denoting non-violent crime committed by white-collar workers, especially fraud. References to a *white collar* as the sign of a clerical or non-manual worker are found from the 1920s.

The **White Company** was the name of a mercenary company led by John Hawkwood (d. 1394), who were active in Italy in the mid 14th century; it is suggested that the name reflected the splendour of their equipment.

In John Webster's eponymous play (1612), the **White Devil** is the name given to the central character, Vittoria Corombona, who connives at the murder of her husband and her lover's wife, and who is finally herself murdered; the play is based on the historical character Vittoria Accoramboni (1557–85).

A **white dwarf** is a small very dense star that is typically the size of a planet. A white dwarf is formed when a low-mass star has exhausted all its central nuclear fuel and lost its outer layers as a planetary nebula.

A **white elephant** is a possession that is useless or troublesome, especially one that is expensive to maintain or difficult to dispose of, from the story that the kings of Siam gave such animals as a gift to courtiers considered obnoxious, in order to ruin the recipient by the great expense incurred in maintaining the animal.

The **white ensign** is a white flag carrying a St George's cross with the Union Jack in the top corner next to the flagstaff, flown by the Royal and most Commonwealth navies (other than that of Canada) and the Royal Yacht Squadron.

A **White Father** is a member of the Society of Missionaries of Africa, a Roman Catholic order founded in Algiers in 1868; the term is a translation of the French *Père Blanc*, for the white habits worn by the order.

A **white flag** is a white flag or cloth used as a symbol of surrender, truce, or a desire to parley; Livy's *Roman Histories* refer to a Carthaginian ship displaying white flags as a sign of peace. The *white flag* was also the flag of the house of Bourbon, and thus the national flag of pre-Revolutionary France.

A **White Friar** is a ➤ CARMELITE monk, so named because of the white habits worn by the monks.

The **White Goddess** in the poetic thought of Robert Graves (1895–1985) is the triple mother goddess as the source of poetic inspiration.

The **White Hart** was the personal badge of Richard II (1306–1400), shown wearing a golden collar; his mother's personal badge had been a white hind.

White heat is the temperature or state of something that is so hot that it emits white

light; a state of intense passion or activity. Since the 1960s the term has been associated with the phrase 'the white heat of technology', a popular misquotation of a passage from a speech by Harold Wilson in 1963.

The **White Highlands** are an area in western Kenya formerly (1909–59) reserved for Europeans.

A **White Horse** is the figure of a white horse, reputed (by later writers) as the ensign of the Saxons when they invaded Britain, and the heraldic ensign of Brunswick, Hanover, and Kent; also, the figure of a horse cut on the face of chalk downs in England, and popularly supposed to represent the 'white horse' of the Saxons; notably that near Uffington in Berkshire.

White horses are white-crested waves at sea; the term is recorded from the mid 19th century, and in poetry is often used in an extended metaphor.

The **White House** is the official residence of the US president in Washington DC. The White House was built 1792–9 of greyish-white limestone from designs of the Irish-born architect James Hoban (*c.*1762–1831). The building was restored in 1814 after being burnt by British troops during the War of 1812, the smoke-stained walls being painted white. It was first formally designated the *White House* in 1902.

White information is positive information about a person's creditworthiness held by a bank or similar institution; the term is recorded from the late 1980s, and is the opposite of the kind of *black information* which might cause a person to be blacklisted.

A **white knight** is a hero or champion; in allusion to the amiable and confused White Knight in Lewis Carroll's *Through the Looking-Glass* (1872), a term for an amiable but ineffectual person. Later, the phrase was used without irony in Stock Exchange slang to mean a company which comes to the aid of another which is facing an unwelcome takeover bid.

The **White Knight** is one of three hereditary Irish titles (the others being the *Knight of Glin* and the *Knight of Kerry*). The title of the *White Knight* (which is currently in abeyance) was granted to the Fitzgibbon family in the 14th century when Maurice Fitzgibbon was reputedly knighted by Edward III after distinguishing himself at the battle of Halidon Hill in Scotland in 1333.

A **white lie** is a harmless or trivial lie, especially one told to avoid hurting someone's feelings; the term is first recorded in the *Gentleman's Magazine* of 1741.

White-livered means feeble-spirited, cowardly; reflecting the traditional belief that a light-coloured liver indicated a deficiency of bile or ➤ CHOLER, and thus of vigour, spirit, or courage.

White magic is magic used only for good purposes, the opposite of ➤ BLACK *magic*.

The **white man's burden** is the supposed task of whites to spread the benefits of civilization. The term derives from a poem by Kipling, 'The White Man's Burden' (1899), written with particular reference to the colonial role of the US in the Philippines:

The **white man's grave** is equatorial West Africa considered as being particularly unhealthy for whites; recorded from the mid 19th century.

A **White Monk** is a ➤ CISTERCIAN monk, so named (in late Middle English) because of the habits of undyed wool worn by the monks. ·

The **White Nile** is the name for the main, western branch of the ➤ NILE between the Ugandan–Sudanese border and its confluence with the Blue Nile at Khartoum.

In the UK, a **White Paper** is a government report giving information or proposals on an issue; (prior to 1940), an Order Paper of the House of Commons which was a corrected and revised version of one (a *Blue Paper*) issued earlier the same day.

The **white plague** is an archaic term for tuberculosis, reflecting the perception of it as a widespread and often fatal disease.

The **White Rabbit** is a character in Lewis Carroll's *Alice's Adventures in Wonderland* (1865), who was always running from fear of being late; his typical ejaculation is 'Oh my ears and whiskers!'

The **White Raja** is the name given to any of the three Rajas belonging to the English family of Brooke who ruled Sarawak from 1841 to 1941.

The **white rose** is the emblem of the House of York in the ➤ WARS *of the Roses* or (later) of Yorkshire, directly opposed to the ➤ RED *rose* of Lancaster. In the 18th century, the *white rose* was adopted as an emblem by the Jacobites.

A **White Russian** is a Belorussian; an opponent of the Bolsheviks during the Russian Civil War.

The **White Sands** are an area of white gypsum salt flats in central New Mexico, designated a national monument in 1933. It is surrounded by a large missile-testing range, which, in 1945, as part of the ➤ MANHATTAN *Project*, was the site of the detonation of the first nuclear weapon.

The **White Ship** is the name of the ship which in November 1120 foundered in the channel with the loss of nearly all on board, including Henry I's only legitimate son.

A **White Sister** is a member of the Congregation of the Missionary Sisters of Our Lady of Africa, founded in 1869 to assist the White Fathers, or of the Congregation of the Daughters of the Holy Ghost, founded in 1706 in Brittany.

A **white slave** is a white person treated like a slave, especially a woman tricked or forced into prostitution, typically one taken to a foreign country for this purpose; the term is first recorded in the debates of the US Congress, 13 May 1789.

A **white stone** was traditionally used as a memorial of a happy day; to **mark with a white stone**, meaning to regard as specially fortunate or happy, derives from this.

White Surrey was the name of Richard III's horse, which he rode at the battle of ➤ BOSWORTH.

The **White Tower** is the keep which is the oldest part of the ➤ TOWER *of London*.

A **white van man** is an aggressive male driver of a delivery or workman's van (typically white in colour).

A **white wedding** is a wedding at which the bride wears a formal white dress, traditionally as a sign of virginity.

White Wednesday is a Eurosceptic name for ➤ BLACK *Wednesday*.

A **white witch** is a person, typically a woman, who practises magic for altruistic purposes, one who practises *white magic*.

See also ➤ *show the white* FEATHER.

Whitechapel a district in the East End of London, scene of the ➤ JACK *the Ripper* murders in 1888.

whited sepulchre a hypocrite, an ostensibly virtuous or pleasant person who is inwardly corrupt; originally as a biblical reference to Matthew 23:27.

Whitehall a street in Westminster, London, in which many government offices are located, used as an allusive reference to the British Civil Service. The name is taken from the former royal palace of *White Hall*, originally a residence of Cardinal Wolsey.

Whitsuntide the weekend or week including ➤ WHIT *Sunday*.

Dick Whittington (d. 1423), English merchant and Lord Mayor of London; full name Sir Richard Whittington. Whittington was a mercer who became Lord Mayor three times (1397–8; 1406–7; 1419–20) and left legacies for rebuilding Newgate Prison and establishing a city library.

The legend of his early life as a poor orphan was first recorded in 1605. According to the popular story, he was a kitchen boy who was so badly treated that he was about to run away, when he heard the bells of London ringing as though saying, 'Turn again Whittington, Lord Mayor of London.'

Doctor Who central character of a long-running British television science fiction series beginning in 1963, played first by William Hartnell and later by others including Tom Baker; the time-travelling *Doctor Who* is a Time Lord whose survival includes regular changes of physical appearance. He travels in the *Tardis* (Time And Relative Dimensions In Space) which resembles an old-fashioned London police telephone box.

Who's Who an annual biographical dictionary of contemporary men and women. It was first issued in 1849 but took its present form in 1897, when it incorporated material from another biographical work, *Men and Women of the Time*; earlier editions of *Who's Who* had consisted merely of professional lists, etc. The entries are compiled with the assistance of the subjects themselves, and contain some agreeable eccentricities particularly in the section labelled 'Recreations'.

whodunnit informal term for a story or play about a murder in which the identity of the murderer is not revealed until the end; the term is recorded from 1930.

the whole nine yards everything possible or available.

Whore of Babylon derogatory name for the Roman Catholic Church, first recorded in Tyndale's *The Practyse of Prelates* (1530), where it is applied to the Pope; originally with biblical allusion to Revelation 17:1 and 17:5–6.

Wicca the religious cult of modern witchcraft, especially an initiatory tradition founded in England in the mid 20th century and claiming its origins in pre-Christian pagan religions. *Wicca* as a modern term is recorded from the late 1950s; it represents Old English *wicca* 'witch'.

no peace for the wicked no rest or tranquillity for the speaker, incessant activity, responsibility, or work; originally with reference to Isaiah 48:22 and 57:21.

widdershins in a direction contrary to the sun's course, considered as unlucky; anticlockwise. The term is recorded from the early 16th century, chiefly in Scottish sources, and comes ultimately from Middle High German *widersinnes*, from *wider* 'against' + *sin* 'direction'; the second element was associated with Scots *sin* 'sun'.

widow a woman who has lost her husband by death and has not married again. The word comes (in Old English) from an Indo-European root meaning 'be empty', and may be compared with Sanskrit *vidh* 'be destitute', Latin *viduus* 'bereft, widowed', and Greek *ēitheos* 'unmarried man'.

The **widow** is an informal term for champagne, from a translation of French *la Veuve* Clicquot, a firm of wine merchants.

The **Widow at Windsor** was Queen Victoria after the death of the Prince Consort, in reference to her prolonged withdrawal from public life; the phrase was used as the title of a poem by Rudyard Kipling (1890).

Widow Twankey is the name given to Aladdin's mother in in H. J. Byron's dramatization of the story of ► ALADDIN as a pantomime. She was so named in reference to a kind of green tea which was then popular (Byron's play had a number of jokes about China tea). *Widow Twankey* is now one of the stock characters for this pantomime.

A **widow's cruse** is an apparently small supply that proves inexhaustible, with biblical allusion to 1 Kings 17:10–16, in the story of the widow to whom Elijah was sent for sustenance. When he asked her for bread, she replied that all she had for herself and her son was 'an handful of meal…and a little oil in a cruse'; Elijah told her to make a cake of it for him first, and then to make food for herself and her son, since by God's decree neither meal nor oil should be exhausted.

A **widow's mite** is a small monetary contribution from someone who is poor, with biblical allusion to Mark 12:42–44 which tells the story of a poor widow who gave to the Temple treasury 'two mites, which make a farthing'; Jesus, who saw her, told his disciples that she had given more than the richest contributor, because she had given all that she had.

A **widow's peak** is a V-shaped growth of hair towards the centre of the forehead, especially one left by a receding hairline in a man; held to resemble the peak of a cap traditionally worn by a widow.

Widow's weeds are black clothes worn by a widow in mourning, traditionally including a crape veil and broad white cuffs or 'weepers'.

Wiesenthal Centre an institution to trace and track down Nazi criminals, founded by the Austrian Jewish investigator of Nazi war crimes Simon *Wiesenthal* (1908–). After spending three years in concentration camps he began a campaign to bring Nazi war criminals to justice, tracing some 1,000 unprosecuted criminals including Adolf Eichmann.

the Wife of Bath a character in Chaucer's *Canterbury Tales*, notable for her sexual appetites and outspoken tongue.

wigs on the green violent or unpleasant developments, ructions; the term is recorded from the mid 19th century, and suggests literally a physical fight in which wigs may be dislodged or pulled off.

wild untamed, savage.
  The **wild blue yonder** is the far distance, a remote place; from R. Crawford *Army Air Corps* (song, 1939).
  Wild Children is a term used to describe children who in different places and at different periods have been discovered apparently living independently in the wild, and perhaps reared or nurtured by animals; ➤ PETER *the Wild Boy* is one historical example. Although there are a number of well-documented cases of such discoveries, how the children concerned reached the state in which they were found remains a matter of conjecture; it has been suggested that in a number of cases the child had in fact been abandoned comparatively recently by its parents.
  Children reared in the wild by animals (especially wolves) have a long fictional history, from ➤ ROMULUS and Remus of Roman mythology, to ➤ MOWGLI and ➤ TARZAN in the 19th and 20th centuries.
  The **wild geese** is a name for the Irish Jacobites who emigrated to the Continent after the defeat of James II, especially after the Treaty of Limerick in 1691 (see ➤ TREATY *Stone*). The name is first found in a verse by Michael Joseph Barry (1817–89).
  A **wild goose chase** is a foolish and hopeless search for or pursuit of something unattainable; originally, a kind of horse-race or sport in which all competitors had to follow accurately the course of the leader (at a definite interval), like a flight of wild geese.
  The **Wild Huntsman** is a phantom huntsman of Teutonic legend, fabled to ride at night through the fields and woods with shouts and baying of hounds.

The **Wild West** was the western US in a time of lawlessness in its early history. The Wild West was the last of a succession of frontiers formed as settlers moved gradually further west. The frontier was officially declared closed in 1890, and the *Wild West* disappeared.

wildcat taken as a type of savagery and hot temper, especially in a woman.
  From the early 19th century *wildcat* has been used to designate a person engaging in a risky or unsafe enterprise, or an unsound business undertaking. It was applied specifically to banks in the western US which, before the passing of the National Bank Act of 1863, fraudulently issued notes supported by little or no capital; the use of the name is said to derive from the fact that the notes of a bank in Michigan carried the device of a panther or 'wild cat'.

Battle of the Wilderness in the American Civil War (5–7 May, 1864), a battle between the Union army under Grant and the Confederates under Robert E. Lee. Fighting took place in a wooded area, known as the Wilderness, and many of the wounded died in the burning undergrowth. After two days, Grant moved his troops on to Spotsylvania.

in the wilderness of a politician or political party, out of office, removed from influence; originally with allusion to Numbers 14:33
  A **voice in the wilderness** is an unheeded advocate of reform, originally in allusion to the words of John the Baptist in John 1:23.

St Wilfrid (*c.*633–709), Northumbrian-born bishop of York and afterwards of Hexham, who at the ➤ *Synod of* WHITBY in 664 was a chief proponent of the case for calculating the date of Easter by the Roman rather than the Celtic method. His feast day is 12 October.

St Wilgefortis virgin and martyr, legendary daughter of a pagan king of Portugal, who grew a beard to discourage an unwanted suitor. Also known as ➤ *St* UNCUMBER. Her feast day is 20 July.

Wilhelmstrasse the name of a street in Berlin, the site of the German foreign office until 1945; hence used for the pre-war German foreign office and its policies.

wili in Slavonic and eastern German legends, a spirit of a betrothed girl who has died from grief at being jilted by her lover (used especially with reference to the ballet *Giselle*).

will-o'-the-wisp a phosphorescent light seen hovering or floating at night on marshy ground, thought to result from the combustion of natural gases. Recorded from the early 17th century, the expression was originally *Will with the wisp*, the sense of *wisp* being 'handful of (lighted) hay'.

will the real—please stand up? catchphrase from an American TV game show (1955–66) in which a panel was asked to identify the 'real' one of three candidates all claiming to be a particular person; after the guesses were made, the compère would request the 'real' candidate to stand up.

William male forename.

St William of Norwich was said to have been murdered in 1144, supposedly by Jews for ritual purposes; his anti-Semitic cult, resembling that of ➤ *Little St* HUGH, had a local popularity, and images of him survive in screen paintings in East Anglia.

William of Occam (*c.*1285–1349), was an English philosopher and Franciscan friar. A defender of nominalism, he is known for the maxim called *Occam's razor*, that in explaining a thing no more assumptions should be made than are necessary.

Williamsburg a city in SE Virginia, between the James and York Rivers. First settled as Middle Plantation in 1633, it was the state capital of Virginia from 1699, when it was renamed in honour of William III, until 1799, when Richmond became the capital. A large part of the town has been restored and reconstructed so that it appears as it was during the colonial era.

willow traditionally a symbol of unrequited love, or of mourning or loss, as in **wear the willow** and **the willow garland**.

Willow pattern is a conventional design representing a Chinese scene in blue on white pottery, typically showing three figures on a bridge, with a willow tree and two birds above. It was introduced by the English potter Thomas Turner (1749–1809).

Wimbledon an annual international tennis championship on grass for individual players and pairs, held at the headquarters of the All England Lawn Tennis and Croquet Club in the London suburb of Wimbledon. Now one of the world's major tennis championships, it has been played since 1877;

women were first admitted in 1884, and professionals in 1968.

wimmin non-standard spelling of 'women' adopted by some feminists to avoid the word ending -*men*. The first examples date from the 1970s, and by the mid 1980s, it had come to be associated particularly with militant feminism.

Lord Peter Wimsey aristocratic fictional amateur detective created by Dorothy L. Sayers (1893–1957); Wimsey is a duke's son who is a keen bibliophile and expert on wine; he also suffers from a degree of war-induced nervous insomnia.

win one's spurs gain a knighthood by an act of bravery; Froissart's *Chronicle*, referring to the Black Prince at the battle of Crécy in 1346, refers to the instruction given by his father Edward III that those with the prince should 'suffre hym this day to wynne his spurres', often quoted as 'Let the boy win his spurs.'

you can't win them all said to express consolation or resignation after failure in a contest (also, **win some, lose some**).

Winchester school a style of manuscript illumination of the 10th and 11th centuries originating at Winchester, a city in southern England which became capital of the West Saxon kingdom of Wessex in 519.

wind the perceptible natural movement of the air, especially in the form of a current of air blowing from a particular direction, especially (in **the four winds**) blowing from each of the points of the compass, and often personified as such. The wind is traditionally taken as a type of swift light movement; it can also stand for mutability, and as a force that cannot be predicted or controlled.

In classical mythology, the winds were counted as gods; in Greece, ➤ BOREAS (the North Wind) and ➤ ZEPHYR (the West Wind) were of particular importance. Virgil in the *Aeneid* describes the winds as being under the control of ➤ AEOLUS, who had been given charge of them by Zeus and who kept them confined in a cave.

It's an ill wind that blows nobody any good means that few things are so bad that no one profits from them; proverbial saying, mid 16th century.

A **wind of change** is an influence or tendency to change that cannot be resisted; the phrase in this sense derives from a speech in February 1960 by the Conservative politician

Harold Macmillan (1894–1986) about the current of unstoppable change he was seeing in Africa.

See also ➤ GOD *tempers the wind to the shorn lamb*.

windfall an apple or other fruit blown down from a tree or bush by the wind; a piece of unexpected good fortune, typically one that involves receiving a large amount of money.

windigo (in the folklore of the northern Algonquian Indians) a cannibalistic giant; a person who has been transformed into a monster by the consumption of human flesh. The name comes from Ojibwa *wintiko*.

Windmill Theatre popular variety theatre of the 1930s and 1940s near Piccadilly Circus in London, which between 1932 and 1964 presented its *Revudeville* (named from a blend of *revue* and *vaudeville*), a continuous variety performance. The Windmill Theatre's wartime motto was, 'We Never Closed'.

a window of opportunity a free or suitable interval or period of time for a particular event or action; the expression was first used in connection with the US–Soviet arms race in the early 1980s.

window of vulnerability an opportunity to attack something that is at risk (especially as a cold war claim that America's land-based missiles were easy targets for a Soviet first strike).

window tax a tax on windows or similar openings that was imposed in the UK in 1695 and abolished in 1851; while it was in force, a number of windows in larger houses were bricked up to escape the tax.

Windrush a former troopship, the 'Empire Windrush', which in 1948 brought the first organized party of Caribbean immigrants, many of whom were former British servicemen, to Britain; the term **Windrush generation** is now used allusively to refer to this group and the period of their arrival.

Windscale former name (1947–81) for ➤ SELLAFIELD; associated particularly with the fire which occurred there in 1957.

Windsor name (from the royal residence of ➤ WINDSOR *Castle*) of the British royal house from 1917, changed as a result of anti-German feeling; the previous name was ➤ SAXE-*Coburg-Gotha*. The title conferred on Edward VIII on his abdication in 1936 was **Duke of Windsor**.

Windsor Castle is a royal residence at Windsor, founded by William the Conqueror on the site of an earlier fortress and extended by his successors, particularly Edward III. The castle was severely damaged by fire in 1992.

Windy City informal name for Chicago, recorded from the late 19th century.

good wine needs no bush a proverbial saying, early 15th century, meaning that there is no need to advertise or boast about something of good quality as people will always discover its merits; the expression refers to the fact that a bunch of ivy was formerly the sign of a vintner's shop.

new wine in old bottles something new or innovatory added to an existing or established system or organization. With allusion to the proverb *you can't put new wine in old bottles*, referring to the warning in Matthew 9:17 that the result of so doing is that the bottles break and the wine is lost.

St Winefride (7th century), Welsh virgin, supposedly killed by a rejected suitor and then raised from the dead to become a nun. The chapel and well at Holywell, where she is said to have been abbess, became an important pilgrimage centre. Her feast day is 3 November, and her translation is celebrated on 2 June.

In 1138 her relics were translated to the abbey of Shrewsbury, one account of which is given in the first of the popular ➤ *Brother* CADFAEL mysteries by Ellis Peters.

a wing and a prayer reliance on hope or the slightest chance in a desperate situation; the phrase comes from a song by the American songwriter Harold Adamson (1906–80), derived from the contemporary comment of a wartime pilot, speaking from a disabled plane to ground control.

Winged Victory a winged statue of ➤ NIKE, the Greek goddess of victory, especially the Nike of Samothrace (*c*.200 BC) preserved in the Louvre in Paris.

winged words highly apposite or significant words (travelling swiftly as arrows to the mark); the phrase comes originally from Homer's *Iliad*.

Winnie-the-Pooh Christopher Robin's bear in the stories by A. A. Milne; *Winnie-the-Pooh* (1926) is the first of the books, and Pooh, the 'bear of very little brain' with his liking for honey, is the central character of the nursery animals.

Winnie was originally the name of a black bear which was the mascot of a Canadian regiment, and which was brought to London zoo (where it remained) while the regiment was fighting in France in the First World War; *Pooh* was borrowed from the name first given by Christopher Robin to a swan.

winter the coldest season of the year, in the northern hemisphere from December to February and in the southern hemisphere from June to August. In figurative and allusive usage, *winter* can stand for old age, or a time or state of affliction or distress. The word is recorded from Old English, and is of Germanic origin.

The **Winter Olympics** are an international contest of winter sports held every four years at a two year interval from the summer games. They have been held separately from the main games since 1924.

The **Winter Palace** is the former Russian imperial residence in St Petersburg, stormed in the Revolution of 1917 and later used as a museum and art gallery.

The **Winter Queen** was the name given to Elizabeth Stuart (1596–1662), princess of Great Britain, married to Frederick, Elector Palatine of the Rhine; he was elected king of Bohemia in 1619 but driven out the following year, and they spent the rest of their lives in exile.

The **winter solstice** is the solstice at midwinter, at the time of the shortest day, about 22 December in the northern hemisphere and 21 June in the southern hemisphere.

The **Winter War** was the war between the USSR and Finland in 1939–40. Heavily outnumbered by invading Soviet troops, the Finns were defeated and forced to cede western Karelia to the Soviet Union.

wipe the slate clean forgive or forget past faults or offences, make a fresh start. Shopkeepers and landlords used formerly to keep a record of what was owing to them by writing on a tablet or slate; a *clean slate* was one on which no debts were recorded.

Wisden short name for *Wisden's Cricketers' Almanack*, an annual publication which first appeared in 1864, published by the English cricketer John *Wisden* (1826–84).

wisdom literature the biblical books of Job, Proverbs, Ecclesiastes, Song of Songs, Wisdom of Solomon, and Ecclesiasticus collectively; similar works, especially from the ancient Near East, containing proverbial sayings and practical maxims.

Wisdom of Solomon a book of the Apocrypha ascribed to Solomon and containing a meditation on wisdom. The book is thought actually to date from about 1st century BC to the 1st century AD.

wisdom tooth each of the four hindmost molars in humans which usually appear at about the age of twenty; the phrase (in plural) represents Latin *dentes sapientiae*, as the teeth were said by the ancient Greek physician ➤ HIPPOCRATES not to appear until years of discretion were reached.

be wise after the event understand and assess an event or situation only after its implications have become obvious.

Wise Men of Gotham fools (➤ GOTHAM was proverbial for the folly of its inhabitants).

wise use environmental policy which favours stricter controls on existing methods of exploiting natural resources, as opposed to policies which seek either to find alternative resources or to prevent such exploitation altogether.

wise woman a woman considered to be knowledgeable in matters such as herbal healing, magic charms, or other traditional lore.

the wish is father to the thought we believe a thing because we wish it to be true; with allusion to Shakespeare's *2 Henry IV*.

if wishes were horses, beggars would ride if you could achieve your aims simply by wishing for them, life would be very easy; proverbial saying, early 17th century.

wishing well a well into which one drops a coin and makes a wish.

witan another term for ➤ WITENAGEMOT; the name represents the Old English plural of *wita* 'wise man'.

witch a person, typically a woman, who practises magic or sorcery and was traditionally thought to have evil magic powers; such witches are popularly depicted as wearing a black cloak and pointed hat, and flying on a broomstick, and are associated with ➤ HALLOWEEN.

In the Middle Ages and the 16th and 17th centuries, ➤ WITCHCRAFT was a capital offence and there were numerous trials and executions of suspected witches; sometimes a whole community became involved, as in ➤ SALEM, Massachusetts, in 1692.

In the 20th century, the term *witch* is now used also for a follower or practitioner of modern witchcraft; a Wiccan priest or priestess.

A **witch ball** is a ball of decorated, typically coloured or silvered blown glass, originally used as a charm against witchcraft.

A **witch doctor**, among tribal peoples, is a magician credited with powers of healing, divination, and protection against the magic of others.

A **witch-hunt** is a search for and subsequent persecution of a supposed witch; a campaign directed against a person or group holding unorthodox or unpopular views.

In the Bible, the **Witch of Endor** is the woman who with the help of her familiar spirit conjured up the spirit of the dead prophet Samuel for Saul. She is taken as a type of this kind of divination.

witches' sabbath a supposed annual midnight meeting of witches with the Devil; belief in the occurrence of such meetings fuelled the persecution of witchcraft in the 16th and 17th centuries.

the witching hour midnight; the time when witches are proverbially active; after Shakespeare's *Hamlet*. (See also ➤ TRIPLE-*witching hour*.)

witenagemot an Anglo-Saxon national council or parliament. The name is Old English, and comes from *witena*, genitive plural of *wita* 'wise man' + *gemōt* 'meeting'. The name ➤ WITAN is also used.

withdrawal symptoms the feeling of being depressed by the absence of something; literally, the unpleasant physical reaction that accompanies the process of ceasing to take an addictive drug.

wither on the vine fail to be implemented or dealt with because of neglect or inaction; with allusion to an abortive crop on a grapevine, probably originally with reference to the biblical image of a withered vine as a metaphor for physical or spiritual impoverishment.

the five wits the five (bodily) senses of hearing, sight, smell, taste, and touch; the term is recorded from Middle English.

Wittenberg a town in eastern Germany, on the River Elbe north-east of Leipzig, which was the scene in 1517 of Martin Luther's campaign against the Roman Catholic Church, a major factor in the rise of the Reformation.

wizard a man who has magical powers, especially in legends and fairy tales. Recorded from late Middle English, the word originally meant 'philosopher, sage', and comes from *wise*; the sense of a person skilled in the occult arts dates from the mid 16th century.

In *The Wonderful Wizard of Oz* (1900) by L. Frank Baum, the orphaned Dorothy, who has been carried by a cyclone to the land of Oz, joins the Cowardly Lion, the Scarecrow, and the Tin Man in their search for the magician (the **Wizard of Oz**) who can give them their heart's desire, although the wizard's power is in the end illusory.

woad a yellow-flowered European plant, formerly widely grown in Britain as a source of blue dye. It is often referred to allusively as typifying an early and uncivilized era in which the skin was patterned with woad.

Woden another name for ➤ ODIN.

wolf in figurative and allusive use, the *wolf* is often taken as the type of savagery and rapacity, explicitly or implicitly contrasted with the meek and vulnerable sheep. From the mid 19th century, the term has also been used as an informal designation of a sexually aggressive male.

A *wolf* is the emblem of ➤ St EDMUND *the Martyr*, ➤ St FRANCIS *of Assisi*, and (as a play on his name) the 10th-century Swabian bishop St Wolfgang.

To **cry wolf** is to call for help when it is not needed, with the effect that one is not believed when one really does need help, with allusion to the fable of the shepherd boy who deluded people with false cries of 'Wolf!'; when he was actually attacked and killed, his genuine appeals for help were ignored.

To **have a wolf by the ears** is to be in a precarious position; the expression is of classical origin, and means that the present situation can neither be maintained nor safely ended.

To **keep the wolf from the door** is to have enough money to avert hunger or starvation; the *wolf* here is a type of something that will devour and destroy, as hunger or famine.

A **wolf in sheep's clothing** is a person or thing that appears friendly or harmless but is really hostile; often with biblical allusion to Matthew 7:15, 'Beware of false prophets, which come to you in sheep's clothing, but inwardly they are ravening wolves.'

A **wolf's head** is an archaic term for an out-law, from *cry wolf's head*, in Anglo-Saxon England uttering a cry for the pursuit of an outlaw as one to be hunted down like a wolf.

Wolfenden Report a study produced in 1957 by the Committee on Homosexual Offences and Prostitution in Britain which recommended the legalization of homosexual relations between consenting adults.

Wolverine State informal name for Michigan, where wolverines are found.

women beneath a cloak a group of women beneath a cloak is the emblem of ➤ St URSULA, who was said to have been put to death with 11,000 virgins.

women's liberation the liberation of women from inequalities and subservient status in relation to men, and from attitudes causing these (now generally replaced by the term *feminism*).

eighth wonder of the world a particularly impressive person or thing, regarded as an addition to the ➤ SEVEN *Wonders of the World*.

wonderland a land or place full of wonderful things, a fairyland; the term is recorded from the late 18th century, but is most frequently used with reference to the country which Alice found down a rabbit-hole in Lewis Carroll's *Alice's Adventures in Wonderland* (1866).

not see the wood for the trees fail to grasp the main issue or gain a general view among a mass of details; the term is recorded from the mid 16th century.

wooden made of wood.
   The **wooden horse** is an alternative name for the ➤ TROJAN *Horse*. *The Wooden Horse* (1949) was the account by the writer Eric Williams of how he and two companions, when prisoners of war in Germany, successfully used a wooden vaulting horse to disguise the escape tunnel which they constructed over four and a half months.
   In the 17th and 18th centuries, *wooden horse* also denoted an instrument of military punishment, a structure with a sharply ridged back on which offenders were made to sit astride, sometimes with their hands bound and weights on their feet (**riding the wooden horse**).
   A **wooden spoon** is a real or imaginary prize given in fun to the person who is last in a race or competition; originally a spoon

given to the candidate coming last in the Cambridge mathematical tripos, a custom recorded from the early 19th century.
   The **wooden walls** were the wooden ships of the Royal Navy, considered as Britain's defences. The term derives from a story in Herodotus of how the Athenian statesman ➤ THEMISTOCLES (*c*.528–*c*.462 BC) interpreted the words of the Delphic oracle before the battle of ➤ SALAMIS, that 'the wooden wall' would help them. Themistocles is said to have told the Athenians, 'The wooden wall is your ships.'
   In the US, a **wooden wedding** is a 5th wedding anniversary, on which it is appropriate to give presents made of wood.

Woodhenge a prehistoric henge, near Stonehenge, in the form of a circular bank and ditch believed to have contained a circular timber structure; the first of its kind to be discovered.

Woodstock a small town in New York State, situated in the south-east near Albany. It gave its name in the summer of 1969 to a huge rock festival held some 96 km (60 miles) to the south-west.

woodwose a wild man of the woods; a savage; a satyr, a faun; the representation of such a being, as a decoration or as a heraldic bearing or supporter. The term is recorded from late Old English, and the first element *wood* means 'mad'.

Woolsack in the UK, the Lord Chancellor's wool-stuffed seat in the House of Lords. It is said to have been adopted in Edward III's reign as a reminder to the Lords of the importance to England of the wool trade.

Woolwich the old dockyard and the Royal Arsenal in Woolwich, an area of Greater London (formerly in Kent).

Woolworth Building on Broadway in New York, built in 1913; it was for a time the tallest building in the world.

Woomera a town in central South Australia, the site of a vast military testing ground used in the 1950s for nuclear tests and since the 1960s for tracking space satellites. The name (which comes from Dharuk *wamara*) means 'an Aboriginal stick used to throw a dart or spear more forcibly'.

Bertie Wooster fictional character created by P. G. Wodehouse, a pleasant, affluent, and idle young man about town who is much persecuted by his aunts, but who is usually protected by his valet ➤ JEEVES.

Worcester a cathedral city in western England, where in 1651 during the English Civil War, Oliver Cromwell defeated a Scottish army under Charles II.

the Word From the mid 16th century, *the Word* or **the Word of God** has been a term used for the Bible, as embodying divine revelation, often with allusion to John 1:1.

the word on the street a rumour or piece of information currently being circulated.

workers of the world, unite the usual rendering of the closing words of Marx and Engels's *The Communist Manifesto* (1848), 'the proletarians have nothing to lose but their chains. They have a world to win. WORKING MEN OF ALL COUNTRIES, UNITE!'

a bad workman always blames his tools a person who has done something badly will seek to lay the blame on their equipment rather than admit their own lack of skill; proverbial saying, early 17th century.

works of supererogation in the Roman Catholic Church, the performance of good works beyond what God commands or requires, which are held to constitute a store of merit which the Church may dispense to others to make up for their deficiencies.

Workshop of the World informal term for England in the 19th century; the expression was used by Disraeli in the House of Commons in 1838, in reference to the British manufacturing and industrial capacity.

world the earth; all the people on the earth.
All the world and his wife means everyone; the term is first recorded in Swift's Polite Conversation (1738).
The **World Bank** is an international banking organization established to control the distribution of economic aid between member nations, and to make loans to them in times of financial crisis.
The **World Council of Churches** is an association established in 1948 to promote unity among the many different Christian Churches. Its member Churches number over 300, and include virtually all Christian traditions except Roman Catholicism and Unitarianism. Its headquarters are in Geneva.
World English is the English language including all of its regional varieties, such as

North American, Australian, New Zealand, and South African English.
A **World Heritage Site** is a natural or manmade site, area, or structure recognized as being of outstanding international importance and therefore as deserving special protection. Sites are nominated to and designated by the World Heritage Convention (an organization of UNESCO).
The world is one's oyster means that the world is one's prize; the whole world is available to one; perhaps originally with allusion to Shakespeare's *Merry Wives of Windsor* (1597).
The world, the flesh, and the devil are all forms of temptation to sin; the phrase comes from the ➤ LITANY, 'From all the deceits of the world, the flesh, and the devil, Good Lord, deliver us.'
The **World Trade Center** was a complex of buildings in New York featuring twin skyscrapers 110 storeys high, designed by Minoru Yamasaki and completed in 1972. It was destroyed, with great loss of life, when terrorists flew hijacked passenger planes into its twin towers on 11 September, 2001.
World War I is another term for ➤ FIRST *World War*, and **World War 2** is another term for the ➤ SECOND *World War*.
The **World Wide Fund for Nature** is an international organization established (as the World Wildlife Fund) in 1961 to raise funds for projects including the conservation of endangered species or of valuable habitats. Its symbol is a panda, typifying endangered species.
The **World Wide Web** is a widely used information system on the Internet, which provides facilities for documents to be connected to other documents by hypertext links, enabling the user to search for information by moving from one document to another.
World without end means for ever, eternally; a translation of Late Latin *in saecula saeculorum* to the ages of ages, as used in *Morning Prayer* and other services.

the best of both worlds the benefits of widely differing situations, enjoyed at the same time; the variant all possible worlds is an allusion to the ever-optimistic Dr Pangloss in Voltaire's *Candide* (1759), usually quoted in English as, 'Everything is for the best in the best of all possible worlds.'

worm in archaic use, a serpent, snake, or dragon. Recorded from Old English (in form *wyrm*) the word originally also meant any animal which creeps or crawls, a reptile or insect.

The current meaning of an earthworm or similar invertebrate animal with a long slender soft body also dates from Old English, and gives rise to the allusive uses of worm as the type of weakness, humility, or nakedness.

Worm has also been used from Old English for a maggot, or in popular belief, an earthworm, supposed to eat dead bodies in the grave; in biblical allusion, this becomes one of the pains of hell, as in Mark 9:48.

Worms an industrial town in western Germany, on the Rhine north-west of Mannheim, which was the scene in 1521 of the condemnation of Martin Luther's teaching, at the ➤ DIET *of Worms*.

wormwood a woody shrub with a bitter aromatic taste, used as an ingredient of vermouth and in absinthe and in medicine; in figurative use, a state or source of bitterness or grief, originally with biblical allusion, as to Deuteronomy 29:18.

The word is recorded from Old English, in form *wermōd*; the change in spelling in late Middle English was due to association with *worm* and *wood*.

Wotan another name for ➤ ODIN.

wound a wound in the head is the emblem of St Peter the Martyr, a 13th-century Dominican friar and priest born in Verona, who was attacked and killed while travelling from Como to Milan; he was wounded in the head with an axe, while the friar who was with him was stabbed.

Battle of Wounded Knee the last major confrontation (1890) between the US Army and American Indians, at the village of Wounded Knee on a reservation in South Dakota. More than 300 largely unarmed Sioux men, women, and children were massacred. A civil rights protest at the site in 1973 led to clashes with the authorities.

Five Wounds the wounds in the hands, feet, and side of the crucified Jesus; devotion to the *Five Wounds* developed during the Middle Ages, and they are symbolized by five signs of the cross made over the host during a Mass, five grains of incense in a Paschal candle, and five crosses inscribed on an altar.

wrecker a person on the shore who tried to bring about a shipwreck in order to plunder or profit from the wreckage; the term is first recorded in Washington Irving's *Sketch Book*

(1820) in a reference to a crowd watching a shipwreck.

wren the *wren* is proverbial for its small size. It was traditionally regarded as a sacred bird, and Pliny notes that there was antipathy between the wren and the eagle because the wren had been given the title of the 'king of the birds'; this relates to the fable in which the wren concealed itself on the eagle's back, and could thus claim that it had flown higher than the eagle.

In the UK, *Wren* (as a partial acronym) is a name for a member of the former *Women's Royal Naval Service*.

wring the withers stir the emotions or sensibilities; after Shakespeare's *Hamlet* 'let the galled jade wince, our withers are unwrung.' The *withers* are the highest part of a horse's back, lying at the base of the neck above the shoulders, and the word is apparently a reduced form of *widersome*, from obsolete *wither-* 'against, contrary' (as the part that resists the strain of the collar).

writer to the Signet in Scotland, a senior solicitor conducting cases in the Court of Session; originally a clerk in the Secretary of State's office who prepared writs for ➤ *the* SIGNET.

the writing on the wall a warning of impending disaster; the phrase is biblical, and comes from the story in Daniel 5 of writing that appeared on the palace wall at a feast given by Belshazzar, last king of Babylon, foretelling that he would be killed and the city sacked.

The words written were said to be *Mene, Mene, Tekel, Upharsin*; Daniel interpreted this as *Mene* 'God hath numbered thy kingdom, and finished it', *Tekel* 'Thou are weighed in the balances, and art found wanting', and *Peres* 'Thy kingdom is divided and given to the Medes and Persians.'

Wulfstan (d. 1023), archbishop of York, author of *Sermo Lupi ad Anglos* 'Address of Wulf to the English', which depicts the destruction brought about by the Danish raids of the early 11th century.

St Wulfstan (*c.*1008–95), Benedictine monk, bishop of Worcester; he was instrumental in ending the trade in slaves to Ireland, and was one of the Anglo-Saxon clergy who continued to hold office after the Conquest. His cult was early and popular. His feast day is 19 January.

John Wyclif (*c.*1330–84), English religious reformer. He criticized the wealth and power of the Church and upheld the Bible as the sole guide for doctrine; his teachings were disseminated by itinerant preachers and are regarded as precursors of the Reformation. Wyclif instituted the first English translation of the complete Bible. His followers were known as ➤ LOLLARDS.

Wykehamist a past or present member of Winchester College. Recorded from the mid 18th century, the name derives from modern Latin *Wykehamista*, from the name of William of *Wykeham* (1324–1404), bishop of Winchester and founder of the college.

WYSIWYG denoting the representation of text on-screen in a form exactly corresponding to its appearance on a printout; acronym (dating from the 1980s) from *what you see is what you get*.

wyvern a winged two-legged dragon with a barbed tail. Recorded from late Middle English (denoting a viper) the word comes via Old French from Latin *vipera* ➤ VIPER.

X The twenty-fourth letter of the modern English alphabet and the twenty-first of the ancient Roman one, in the latter an adoption of Greek *khi*.

X is traditionally used to signify an unknown person or thing, or to note the location of a particular place, as in **X marks the spot**.

The **X chromosome**, in humans and other mammals, is a sex chromosome, two of which are normally present in female cells (designated XX) and only one in male cells (designated XY).

The **X files** is a cult American television series (1993–, created by Chris Carter) in which two special agents, *Fox Mulder* and the more sceptical *Dana Scully*, repeatedly investigate cases which appear to involve the paranormal; final proof of extra-terrestrial activity, however, is always lacking, although it is indicated that this may be deliberately suppressed by government agency. The slogan of the series, 'The truth is out there', has become a catchphrase.

Xanadu the name of (*Shang-tu*) of an ancient city in SE Mongolia, as portrayed in Coleridge's poem *Kubla Khan* (1816). *Xanadu* is used to convey an impression of a place as almost unattainably luxurious or beautiful; in Orson Welles's film *Citizen Kane*, in which the protagonist is explicitly modelled on the newspaper publisher William Randolph Hearst, the name of the luxurious residence modelled on Hearst's castle at San Simeon, California, is *Xanadu*.

Xanthian Marbles sculptures found in 1838 at the site of the ancient Lycian town of *Xanthus* (now in Turkey), which are now in the British Museum. The figures are Assyrian in character and are believed to have been executed before 500 BC; the subjects include processions, athletic activity, sieges, and tomb scenes.

Xanthippe (5th century BC), wife of the philosopher Socrates. Her allegedly bad-tempered behaviour towards her husband has made her proverbial as a shrew.

St Francis Xavier (1506–52), Spanish Catholic missionary; known as **the Apostle of the Indies**. One of the original seven Jesuits, from 1540 he travelled to southern India, Sri Lanka, Malacca, the Moluccas, and Japan, making thousands of converts. His feast day is 3 December.

Xenophon (*c*.435–*c*.354 BC), Greek historian, writer, and military leader. From 401 he fought with Cyrus the Younger against Artaxerxes II, and led an army of 10,000 Greek mercenaries in their retreat of about 1,500 km (900 miles) after Cyrus was killed; the campaign and retreat are recorded in the *Anabasis*. Other notable writings include the *Hellenica*, a history of Greece.

Xerxes I (*c*.519–465 BC), son of Darius I, king of Persia 486–465. He continued his father's attack on the Greeks for their support of the Ionian cities that had revolted against Persian rule. His invasion of Greece achieved victories in 480 at Artemisium and ►THERMOPYLAE, but defeats at ►SALAMIS (480) and Plataea (479) forced him to withdraw.

Ximenes variant spelling in English of Spanish *Jiménez* in the name of the Spanish cardinal and statesman ►Francisco JIMÉNEZ *de Cisneros* ((1436–1517), Grand Inquisitor for Castile and Léon from 1507 to 1517.

Xmas an informal term for Christmas, in which the X represents the initial *chi* of Greek *Khristos* 'Christ'.

XYZ Affair a diplomatic incident of the late 18th century in which American ministers in Paris to negotiate a trade agreement to protect US shipping were approached by three French agents, referred to as X, Y, and Z in diplomatic correspondence, who suggested the payment of bribes to facilitate negotiations. The occurrence became publicly known in the US, and there was an outcry which nearly led to war.

Yy

Y the twenty-fifth letter of the modern English alphabet and the twenty-second of the ancient Roman one, representing Greek *upsilon*, a differentiated form of the early Greek vowel-symbol, now also represented by U and V.

The **Y chromosome**, in humans and other mammals, is a sex chromosome which is normally present only in male cells, which are designated XY.

yahoo a rude, noisy, or violent person, from the name of an imaginary race of brutish creatures in Swift's *Gulliver's Travels* (1726).

From the mid 19th century *yahoo* (perhaps a different word in origin) has also been used in Australia for a mythical creature resembling a big hairy man, said to haunt eastern Australia.

Yahweh a form of the Hebrew name of God used in the Bible. The name came to be regarded by Jews (*c.*300 BC) as too sacred to be spoken, and the vowel sounds are uncertain. Compare with ➤ JEHOVAH.

Yahwist the postulated author or authors of parts of the first six books of the Bible, in which God is regularly named *Yahweh*. Compare with ➤ ELOHIST.

Yajur Veda in Hinduism, one of the four Vedas, based on a collection of sacrificial formulae used in early Sanskrit in the Vedic religion by the priest in charge of sacrificial ritual.

Yalta Conference a meeting between the Allied leaders Churchill, Roosevelt, and Stalin in February 1945 at Yalta, a Crimean port on the Black Sea. The leaders planned the final stages of the Second World War and agreed the subsequent territorial division of Europe.

Yama in Hindu mythology, the first man to die. He became the guardian, judge, and ruler of the dead, and is represented as carrying a noose and riding a buffalo.

yang in Chinese philosophy, the active male principle of the universe, characterized as male and creative and associated with

heaven, heat, and light. Contrasted with ➤ YIN.

Yangshao a Neolithic civilization of northern China, dated to *c.*5000–2700 BC and preceding the Longshan period. It is marked by pottery painted with naturalistic designs of fish and human faces and abstract patterns of triangles, spirals, arcs, and dots. It is named after *Yang Shao Cun*, the first settlement of this period to be excavated (1921).

Yankee an often derogatory term for a person who lives in, or is from, the US, especially, an inhabitant of New England or one of the northern states, or a Federal soldier in the Civil War. The term is recorded from the mid 18th century but the origin is uncertain; it may come (as a nickname) from Dutch *Janke*, diminutive of *Jan* 'John'.

Yankee Doodle Dandy is a song popular during the War of American Independence, now regarded as a national song; the tune is said to have been composed in 1755 by Dr Richard Shuckburgh, a British surgeon in Lord Amherst's army, in derision of provincial troops.

The **Yankee State** is an informal name for Ohio.

yashmak a veil concealing all of the face except the eyes, worn by some Muslim women in public; the word comes (in the mid 19th century) via Arabic from Turkish.

Yayoi a Japanese culture following the Jomon period and dated to *c.*300 BC–AD 300. It was marked by the introduction of rice cultivation, and the appearance of large burial mounds has suggested the emergence of an increasingly powerful ruling class. It is named after a street in Tokyo where its characteristic pottery (chiefly wheel-made) was first discovered.

yclept archaic adjective meaning 'by the name of'; the word represents Old English *gecleopod*, past participle of *cleopian* 'call'.

ye pseudo-archaic term for *the*. In origin this is a graphic variant; in late Middle English the letter þ (see ➤ THORN) came to be written identically with y, so that *the* could be written *ye*. This spelling (usually yᵉ) was kept as a convenient abbreviation in handwriting down to the 19th century, and in printers' types during the 15th and 16th centuries, but it was never pronounced as 'ye'.

year the time taken by the earth to make one revolution around the sun. The length of the year depends on the manner of calculation. For ordinary purposes the important period is the **tropical year** (also called **astronomical year**, **equinoctial year**, or **solar year**) which is the time between successive spring or autumn equinoxes, or winter or summer solstices, roughly 365 days, 5 hours, 48 minutes, and 46 seconds in length. This period thus marks the regular cycle of the seasons.

The **calendar year** or **civil year** is the period of 365 days (or 366 days in leap years) starting from the first of January, used for reckoning time in ordinary affairs.

The word is recorded from Old English (in form *gē(a)r*) and is of Germanic origin; it comes from an Indo-European root shared by Greek *hōra* 'season'.

A **year and a day** is a legal period constituting a term for certain purposes, in order to ensure the completion of a full year.

Year of grace is year—AD, suggested by medieval Latin *anno gratiae*, used by chroniclers to indicate the year as reckoned from the birth of Christ. **Year of Our Lord** is year—AD, as reckoned from the birth of Christ; ➤ ANNO *domini*.

The **Year 2000 problem** (also called **Y2K**) is another name for the ➤ MILLENNIUM *bug*.

A **year's mind** is the anniversary of a person's death or burial, as an occasion for special prayers; a Requiem Mass held on such an anniversary; the term is recorded from the 11th century.

yeast in figurative usage, ➤ LEAVEN.

Yekaterinburg an industrial city in central Russia, in the eastern foothills of the Urals, where the last tsar, Nicholas II, and his family were shot in 1918.

yellow of the colour between green and orange in the spectrum, a primary subtractive colour complementary to blue; coloured like ripe lemons or egg yolks. *Yellow* is traditionally the colour associated with jealousy and cowardice.

Recorded from Old English (in form *geolu*, *geolu*) the word is of West Germanic origin, and is related to ➤ GOLD.

A **yellow alert** is the preliminary stage of an alert, when danger is thought to be near but not actually imminent; a warning of such a situation.

The **Yellow Book** was an illustrated literary periodical published quarterly in the UK between 1894 and 1897, associated with the Aesthetic Movement. Often controversial, it contained contributions from writers including Max Beerbohm, Henry James, Edmund Gosse, Arnold Bennett, and H. G. Wells. The art editor was Aubrey Beardsley. It was so named because of its distinctive yellow binding.

A **yellow card**, in soccer and some other games, is a yellow card shown by the referee to a player being cautioned.

In the US, a **yellow-dog contract** is an agreement by which an employee undertakes not to join a union, as a condition of employment; *yellow dog* here implies something regarded as of little account. Contracts of this kind were common in the 1920s; they were prohibited in 1932.

In the US, a **yellow-dog Democrat** is a diehard Democrat, who will vote for a Democratic candidate, regardless of their personal qualities; the term implies someone who would vote for even a *yellow dog* if it were on the party ticket.

Yellow fever is a tropical virus disease affecting the liver and kidneys, causing fever and jaundice and often fatal, which is transmitted by mosquitoes. It was also known informally as *yellow jack*.

A **yellow flag** is a ship's yellow or quarantine flag (denoting the letter Q), indicating a request for customs clearance when flown alone.

Yellow jack is an archaic term for yellow fever, or for a ship's yellow quarantine flag.

The **yellow jersey** in a cycling race involving stages, is a yellow jersey worn each day by the rider who is ahead on time over the whole race to that point, and presented to the rider with the shortest overall time at the finish of the race.

In the UK, the **Yellow Pages** are a telephone directory, or a section of one, printed on yellow paper and listing businesses and other organizations according to the goods or services they offer. Its advertising slogan of the 1960s, 'Let your fingers do the walking', has become well-known.

Yellow peril is a dated and derogatory term for the supposed danger posed by Asiatic peoples to the rest of the world; the expression is recorded from 1900.

The **yellow press** are newspapers of an unscrupulously sensational character; journalists working on such papers. The use of *yellow* in this sense derives from the appearance in 1895 of a number of the *New York World* in which a child in a yellow dress ('The Yellow Kid') was the central figure of the cartoon, an experiment in colour-printing designed to attract purchasers.

The **Yellow River** is the second-largest river in China, which rises in the mountains of west central China and flows over 4,830 km (3,000 miles) in a huge semicircle before entering the gulf of Bo Hai.

A **yellow star** was a piece of yellow cloth bearing the Star of David, which the Nazis required Jews to wear.

yellowback a cheap novel in a yellow board binding, sold in late 19th-century railway bookstalls.

Yellowhammer State an informal name for Alabama.

Yellowstone National Park a national park in NW Wyoming and Montana. Named after the Yellowstone River, a tributary of the Missouri which runs through it, the park was established in 1872 and was the first national park in the US. It is noted for its many geysers, hot springs, and mud volcanoes, especially Old Faithful, a geyser which erupts every 45 to 80 minutes to a height of about one hundred feet.

yeoman a man holding and cultivating a small landed estate; a freeholder; a person qualified for certain duties and rights, such as to serve on juries and vote for the knight of the shire, by virtue of possessing free land of an annual value of 40 shillings. The term is recorded from Middle English, and probably comes from *young* + *man*.

A **Yeoman of the Guard** is a member of the British sovereign's bodyguard, first established by Henry VII, now having only ceremonial duties and wearing Tudor dress as uniform. Also called *Beefeater*.

Yeoman Usher in the UK, the deputy of ➤ BLACK *Rod*.

Yeoman Warder a warder at the Tower of London.

yeti a large hairy creature resembling a human or bear, said to live in the highest part of the Himalayas; it is informally known as the ➤ ABOMINABLE *Snowman*. The term is recorded in English from the 1930s, and comes from Tibetan *yeh-teh* 'little manlike animal'.

yew the poisonous *yew* is linked with folklore and superstition and can live to a great age; they are often planted in churchyards, and from this are regarded as symbolizing

loss and grief. The timber was traditionally used to make longbows.

Yggdrasil a huge ash tree located at the centre of the earth, with three roots, one extending to ➤ NIFLHEIM (the underworld), one to *Jotunheim* (land of the giants), and one to ➤ ASGARD (land of the gods). Although threatened by a malevolent serpent that gnaws at its roots and by deer eating its foliage, the tree survives because it is watered by the Norns from the well of fate.

The name is Old Norse, and apparently comes from *Yggr* 'Odin' + *drasill* 'horse'; Odin hanged himself on the tree for nine nights and days to win the runes for humankind.

Yiddish a language used by Jews in central and eastern Europe before the ➤ HOLOCAUST. It was originally a German dialect with words from Hebrew and several modern languages, and still has some 200,000 speakers, mainly in the US, Israel, and Russia. The name is recorded from the late 19th century, and comes from Yiddish *yidish (daytsh)* 'Jewish German'.

yin in Chinese philosophy, the passive female principle of the universe, characterized as female and sustaining and associated with earth, dark, and cold. Contrasted with ➤ YANG.

ylem in the ➤ BIG *bang* theory the primordial matter of the universe, originally conceived as composed of neutrons at high temperature and density. The word comes (in the 1940s) from late Latin *hylem* (accusative) 'matter'.

Ymir in Scandinavian mythology, the primeval giant killed by ➤ ODIN and the other gods, from whose body they created the world; his blood formed the seas, and his bones the rocks.

Yoda in the second film of the ➤ STAR *Wars*, the last surviving master of ➤ JEDI skills who trains *Luke Skywalker*.

yoga a Hindu spiritual and ascetic discipline, a part of which, including breath control, simple meditation, and the adoption of specific bodily postures, is widely practised for health and relaxation; the name comes from Sanskrit, and means literally 'union'.

The yoga widely known in the West is based on **hatha yoga**, which forms one aspect of the ancient Hindu system of religious and ascetic observance and meditation, the highest form of which is **raja yoga** and the ultimate aim of which is spiritual purification and self-understanding leading to *samadhi* or union with the divine.

yogh a Middle English letter (ȝ) used mainly where modern English has *gh* and *y*. The name is recorded from Middle English, but the origin is unknown.

Yogi Bear a cartoon bear, the central character of a series set in *Jellystone Park* and created by William Hanna (1910–) and Joseph Barbera (1911–); *Yogi Bear*, with his companion *Boo-Boo*, spends his time trying to circumvent the *Ranger* and steal or beg food from tourists.

Yom Kippur the most solemn religious fast of the Jewish year, the last of the ten days of penitence that begin with ➤ Rosh *Hashana* (the Jewish New Year). It is also called the ➤ Day *of Atonement*.

  The **Yom Kippur War** is the Israeli name for the Arab–Israeli conflict in 1973. The war lasted for less than three weeks; it started on the festival of *Yom Kippur* (in that year, 6 October) when Egypt and Syria simultaneously attacked Israeli forces from the south and north respectively. The Syrians were repulsed and the Egyptians were surrounded. A ceasefire followed and disengagement agreements over the Suez area were signed in 1974 and 1975.

yoni in Hinduism, the vulva, especially as a symbol of divine procreative energy conventionally represented by a circular stone. The word is Sanskrit, and means literally 'source, womb, female genitals'.

House of York the English royal house which ruled England from 1461 (Edward IV) until the defeat and death of Richard III in 1485, with a short break in 1470–1 (the restoration of Henry VI).

  Descended from Edmund of Langley (1341–1402), 1st Duke of *York* and 5th son of Edward III, the House of York fought the ➤ Wars *of the Roses* with the ➤ House *of* Lancaster, both houses being branches of the Plantagenet line. Lancaster eventually prevailed, through their descendants, the Tudors, but the houses were united when the victorious Henry VII married Elizabeth, the eldest daughter of Edward IV (1486).

  The Yorkist emblem was a ➤ White *rose*.

yorker in cricket, a ball bowled so that it pitches immediately under the bat, perhaps originally introduced by Yorkshire players.

Yorkist an adherent or a supporter of the ➤ *House of* York, especially in the Wars of the Roses. The term is recorded from the early 17th century.

Yosemite National Park a national park in the Sierra Nevada in central California. It includes Yosemite Valley, with its sheer granite cliffs and Yosemite Falls, the highest waterfall in the US.

Young Pretender a name for ➤ *Charles Edward Stuart* (1720–80), as son of the ➤ Old *Pretender*; the name is first recorded from 1745 (the year of the second Jacobite Rising).

Young Turk a member of a revolutionary party in the Ottoman Empire who carried out the revolution of 1908 and deposed the sultan Abdul Hamid II; in extended usage, a young person eager for radical change to the established order.

Ypres a town in NW Belgium, near the border with France, in the province of West Flanders, the scene of some of the bitterest fighting of the First World War, and now site of the ➤ Menin *Gate*.

  The **Battle of Ypres** is the name given to each of three battles on the Western Front near Ypres during the First World War in 1914, 1915, and 1917. In the first battle (October–November 1914) Allied forces prevented the Germans breaking through to the Channel ports; the second battle (April–May 1915) was an inconclusive trench conflict in which poison gas was used for the first time, while the third battle (1917) was the slaughter of ➤ Passchendaele.

yuga in Hindu belief, any of the four ages of the life of the world.

Yule archaic term for *Christmas*. The name comes from Old English *gēol(a)* 'Christmas Day'; compare with Old Norse *jól*, originally applied to a heathen festival lasting twelve days, later to Christmas.

  A **yule log** is a large log traditionally burnt in the hearth on Christmas Eve.

  Yuletide is the time of Yule, Christmas.

yuppie informal and derogatory term for a well-paid young middle-class professional who works in a city job and has a luxurious lifestyle. The term is recorded from the 1980s, seen as the period at which such people flourished, and is an elaboration of the acronym from *young urban professional*. It has generated a number of similar terms.

Zz

Z the last letter of the modern English alphabet and of the ancient Roman one, corresponding to Greek ζ and Hebrew *zayin*.

Zacchaeus in the Bible (Luke 19:1–10) a tax collector who climbed a tree for a better view of Jesus. He was called down by Jesus, who visited his house.

Zacharias in the Bible, the father of ➤ JOHN *the Baptist*, to whom the archangel Gabriel foretold his son's birth; Zacharias from that moment was unable to speak until the moment when the child was to be named, and he wrote the words 'His name is John' (Luke 1:63).

Zadok in the Bible, name of the priest who supported Solomon's accession to the throne of David and anointed him as king (1 Kings 1:39); *Zadok the Priest* is the title of one of the coronation anthems composed by Handel for the coronation of George II.

Zapata moustache a type of moustache in which the two ends extend downwards to the chin, as worn by Marlon Brando in the film *Viva Zapata!* in 1952, about the Mexican revolutionary Emiliano *Zapata* (1879–1919).

Zarathustra the Avestan name for the Persian prophet ➤ ZOROASTER, used in the title of Nietzsche's *Also Sprach Zarathustra* [Thus Spake Zarathustra] (1883).

Zealot a member of an ancient Jewish sect aiming at a world Jewish theocracy and resisting the Romans until AD 70. The name is recorded from the mid 16th century, and comes via ecclesiastical Latin from Greek *zēlōtēs*, from *zēloun* 'be jealous', from *zēlos* 'zeal'.

The extended sense of *zealot* as a person who is fanatical and uncompromising in pursuit of their religious, political, or other ideals is recorded from the mid 17th century.

Zebulun in the Bible, a Hebrew patriarch, son of Jacob and Leah (Genesis 30:20); also, the tribe of Israel traditionally descended from him.

Zechariah a Hebrew minor prophet of the 6th century BC. Also, a book of the Bible including his prophecies, urging the restoration of the Temple, and some later material.

Zedekiah in the Bible, the last king of Judaea, who rebelled against Nebuchadnezzar and was carried off to Babylon into captivity (2 Kings 24–5, 2 Chronicles 36).

zeitgeist the defining spirit or mood of a particular period of history as shown by the ideas and beliefs of the time. Recorded from the mid 19th century, the word is German, and comes from *Zeit* 'time' + *Geist* 'spirit'.

Zem Zem name of a sacred well near Mecca, said to have been revealed to Hagar when she and her son ➤ ISHMAEL were dying of thirst in the desert.

Zen a Japanese school of Mahayana Buddhism emphasizing the value of meditation and intuition rather than ritual worship or study of scriptures. Zen Buddhism was introduced to Japan from China in the 12th century, and has had a profound cultural influence. The aim of Zen is to achieve sudden enlightenment (satori) through meditation in a seated posture (zazen), usually under the guidance of a teacher and often using paradoxical statements (koans) to transcend rational thought.

Zend an interpretation of the Avesta, each Zend being part of the ➤ ZEND-*Avesta*; the word comes from Persian *zand* 'interpretation'.

Zend-Avesta the Zoroastrian sacred writings, comprising the ➤ AVESTA (the text) and ➤ ZEND (the commentary).

zenith the highest point reached by a celestial or other object; the point in the sky or celestial sphere directly above an observer; in figurative usage, the time at which something is most powerful or successful. Recorded from late Middle English, the word comes via Old French from medieval Latin *cenit*, based on Arabic *samt (ar-ra's)* 'path (over the head)'.

Zeno (fl. 5th century BC), Greek philosopher. A member of the Eleatic school, he defended Parmenides' theories by formulating paradoxes which appeared to demonstrate the impossibility of motion, one of which shows that once Achilles has given a tortoise a start he can never overtake it, since each time he arrives where it was, it has already moved on.

Zeno of Citium (*c.*335–*c.*263 BC), Greek philosopher, founder of Stoicism. He founded the school of Stoic philosophy, but all that remains of his treatises are fragments of quotations.

Zenobia (3rd century AD), queen of Palmyra *c.*267–272. She conquered Egypt and much of Asia Minor. When she proclaimed her son emperor, the Roman emperor Aurelian attacked, defeated, and captured her. She was later given a pension and a villa in Italy.

Zephaniah a Hebrew minor prophet of the 7th century BC; a book of the Bible containing his prophecies.

Zephyr in classical mythology, the god of the west wind; from the late 17th century, *zephyr* has also been a literary term for a soft gentle breeze.

Zeppelin a large German dirigible airship of the early 20th century, long and cylindrical in shape and with a rigid framework, named for its inventor, the German aviation pioneer Ferdinand *Zeppelin* (1838–1917).

Zeppelins were used during the First World War for reconnaissance and bombing, and after the war as passenger transports until the 1930s; their popularity decreased sharply after the *Hindenburg* disaster of 1937, when the dirigible, which had completed its first transatlantic crossing, burst into flames while landing at Lakehurst, New Jersey, with considerable loss of life.

Zermatt an Alpine ski resort and mountaineering centre near the Matterhorn, in southern Switzerland.

zero no quantity or number; nought; the figure 0. The word is recorded from the early 17th century, and comes via French or Italian from Old Spanish and ultimately from Arabic *ṣifr* 'cypher'.

Zero hour is the time at which a planned operation, typically a military one, is set to begin.

Zeus in Greek mythology, the supreme god, the son of ➤ CRONUS (whom he dethroned)

and Rhea, and husband of Hera, traditionally said to have his court on ➤ OLYMPUS. Zeus was the protector and ruler of humankind, the dispenser of good and evil, and the god of weather and atmospheric phenomena (such as rain and thunder). His Roman equivalent is *Jupiter.*

ziggurat in ancient Mesopotamia, a rectangular stepped tower, sometimes surmounted by a temple. Ziggurats are first attested in the late 3rd millennium BC and probably inspired the biblical story of the ➤ *Tower of* BABEL (Genesis 11:1–9).

Zimri in the Bible, (1 Kings) *Zimri* is a captain who kills the king of Israel and makes himself king; he himself in turn is defeated and killed. In Dryden's ➤ ABSALOM *and Achitophel,* the name is given to Buckingham.

Zingaro a gypsy; the name probably comes from the Italian equivalent of Greek *Athigganoi,* name of an oriental people. It is recorded in English from the early 17th century; **I Zingari** (or **The Zingari**) is the name of an amateur cricket club founded in 1845.

Zinoviev letter a letter published in the press in 1924 as having been sent by the Soviet politician Grigori *Zinoviev* (1883–1936) to British Communists, inciting them to subversion; it was later discovered to be a forgery.

Zion the hill of Jerusalem on which the city of David was built; the citadel of ancient Jerusalem; (in Christian thought) the heavenly city or kingdom of heaven. Also, the Jewish people or religion.

Zionism a movement for (originally) the re-establishment and (now) the development and protection of a Jewish nation in what is now Israel. It was established as a political organization in 1897 under Theodor Herzl, and was later led by Chaim Weizmann.

zodiac a belt of the heavens within about 8° either side of the ecliptic, including all apparent positions of the sun, moon, and most familiar planets, which is divided into twelve equal divisions or signs (Aries, Taurus, Gemini, Cancer, Leo, Virgo, Libra, Scorpio, Sagittarius, Capricorn, Aquarius, Pisces). The supposed significance of the movements of the sun, moon, and planets within the zodiacal band forms the basis of astrology. However, the modern constellations do not represent equal divisions of the zodiac, and the ecliptic now passes through a thirteenth (Ophiuchus).

Owing to precession, the signs of the zodiac now roughly correspond to the constellations that bear the names of the *preceding* signs.

The word is recorded from late Middle English and comes via Old French and Latin from Greek *zōidiakos*, from *zōidion* 'sculptured animal figure', diminutive of *zōion* 'animal'.

zombie a corpse said to be revived by witchcraft, especially in certain African and Caribbean religions. Recorded from the early 19th century, the word is of West African origin.

Zoroaster (*c*.628–*c*.551 BC), Persian prophet and founder of Zoroastrianism; Avestan name *Zarathustra*. Little is known of his life, but traditionally he was born in Persia and began to preach the tenets of what was later called Zoroastrianism after receiving a vision from ➤ AHURA *Mazda*.

Zoroastrianism a monotheistic pre-Islamic religion of ancient Persia founded by Zoroaster in the 6th century BC. According to the teachings of Zoroaster the supreme god, ➤ AHURA *Mazda*, created twin spirits, one of

which chose truth and light, the other untruth and darkness. Later writings present a more dualistic cosmology in which the struggle is between Ahura Mazda (Ormazd) and the evil spirit ➤ AHRIMAN. The scriptures of Zoroastrianism are the Zend-Avesta. It survives today in isolated areas of Iran and in India, where followers are known as Parsees.

Zorro fictional character ('The Fox') created by Johnston McCulley in a 1919 magazine story; *Zorro* is the pseudonym of Diego de la Vida, the apparently weak son of a landowning Spanish family in California who seeks to protect the weak against tyranny, and whose swashbuckling habits include the cutting of a Z (the **mark of Zorro**) with his sword as a signature.

Zwinglian an adherent or supporter of the Swiss Protestant reformer Ulrich *Zwingli* (1484–1531), the principal figure of the Swiss Reformation. He was minister of Zurich from 1518, where he sought to carry through his political and religious reforms. He rejected papal authority and many orthodox doctrines, and although he had strong local support in Zurich, his ideas met with fierce resistance in some regions. Zwingli was killed in the civil war that resulted from his reforms.

AskOxford**.**com

Oxford Dictionaries Passionate about language

For more information about the background to Oxford Quotations and Language Reference Dictionaries, and much more about Oxford's commitment to language exploration, why not visit the world's largest language learning site, www.AskOxford.com

Passionate about English?

What were the original 'brass monkeys'? **Ask**Oxford**.**com

How do new words enter the dictionary? **Ask**Oxford**.**com

How is 'whom' used? **Ask**Oxford**.**com

Who said, 'For also knowledge itself is power?' **Ask**Oxford**.**com

How can I improve my writing? **Ask**Oxford**.**com

If you have a query about the English language, want to look up a word, need some help with your writing skills, are curious about how dictionaries are made, or simply have some time to learn about the language, bypass the rest and ask the experts at www.AskOxford.com.

Passionate about language?

If you want to find out about writing in French, German, Spanish, or Italian, improve your listening and speaking skills, learn about other cultures, access resources for language students, or gain insider travel tips from those **Ask**Oxford**.**com in the know, ask the experts at

OXFORD

Oxford Paperback Reference

The Concise Oxford Dictionary of English Etymology
T. F. Hoad

A wealth of information about our language and its history, this
reference source provides over 17,000 entries on word origins.

'A model of its kind'

Daily Telegraph

A Dictionary of Euphemisms
R. W. Holder

This hugely entertaining collection draws together euphemisms from all
aspects of life: work, sexuality, age, money, and politics.

Review of the previous edition
'This ingenious collection is not only very funny but extremely
instructive too'

Iris Murdoch

The Oxford Dictionary of Slang
John Ayto

Containing over 10,000 words and phrases, this is the ideal reference for
those interested in the more quirky and unofficial words used in the
English language.

'hours of happy browsing for language lovers'

Observer

OXFORD